Published in association with A.H. & A.W. REED PTY LTD
First published 1981

© Agricultural Protection Board of Western Australia 1981

ISBN 0 7153 8180 6

Printed in Hong Kong

CONTENTS

Key to Maps   5

Foreword   6

Preface   7

Acknowledgements   9

Introduction   10

Systematic List of Introduced Birds   21

Bibliography   495

List of Alternative Geographic Names   519

Index to Scientific Names   520

Index to Common Names   525

Dedication

To Melinda Leisl and Timothy Latham

KEY TO MAPS

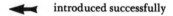 introduced successfully

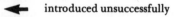 introduced unsuccessfully

native range

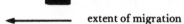 extent of migration

native range on small islands or groups of islands

 indicates groups of islands where native or introduced (depending on arrow)

?   (a) appearing before introduced arrow indicates location of introduction not known

      (b) appearing after introduced arrow indicates species probably successful or probably unsuccessful

      (c) appearing near native range indicates boundaries not well defined

introduced range

FOREWORD

IN 1960, the Agriculture Protection Board of Western Australia and the State's Department of Fisheries and Wildlife were warned that some introduced aviary birds being offered for sale were potential pests. Some of these species were known to be pests elsewhere in the world. Little was known about the pest potential of many other species which were just as readily available in Western Australia. In fact, our general lack of knowledge on the possible dangers to our resources and environment posed by exotic birds became apparent.

It was decided that the most reasonable policy would be to allow only those birds which were known to be harmless to be introduced to Western Australia, or kept here. To this end Mr J.L. Long, an officer of the Agriculture Protection Board, collated information on birds exotic to Western Australia and other parts of the world, irrespective of whether they were thought to be harmful or harmless. The result of his work is this book which has been published because of its interest to many engaged in the study of ornithology, aviculture and environmental conservation.

Very little of the information presented in this book was readily available and Mr Long is to be admired for his dedication and tenacity on researching the material. There is undoubtedly other information which he did not unearth: a publication such as this can probably never be considered really complete. However, this book is an authoritative reference which will be an invaluable source of information and a guide for all interested in the subject of birds.

I thank Mr Long for his work and the Agriculture Protection Board of Western Australia for their support for the project.

A.R. Tomlinson
Chief Executive Officer
Agriculture Protection Board of Western Australia

PREFACE

Scope and Arrangement

THE OBJECT OF this volume is to provide a single reference book on introduced birds throughout the world — a subject which has been previously covered by only a few general accounts and some older, more thorough ones, of a regional nature.

The book has been arranged so that the reader can obtain a quick summary of the description, range and habits of each species in its native country, where it has been introduced and its success or failure to become established. A more detailed history of the introduction of each species is then given, together with information on the damage it causes both in its country of origin and where it has been introduced.

The terms 'naturalisation' and 'acclimatisation' have both been applied to introductions of animals in different parts of the world. In some respects the two terms are used synonymously, thus a bird can be both naturalised and acclimatised in an area. Naturalisation refers to the introduction into another country or region and acclimatisation to the habituation to a new climate or surrounding. It would seem better to apply the term naturalisation to birds which have been introduced either accidentally or deliberately into the wild in an area outside their native range, as acclimatisation does not necessarily mean that this is so. However, it must be noted that when used in this context naturalisation implies success. For the purposes of this book they are loosely termed introductions although of course the emphasis here is on those which have been introduced primarily for naturalisation in the wild rather than for aviculture and other purposes. However, it will become obvious later that many species became somewhat acclimatised as avicultural, zoo and domestic species before becoming naturalised in the wild. In many cases it is now difficult to determine whether or not some species were actually released from the captive state.

Introductions are either successful (the species becomes established) or unsuccessful (the species fails to become established) and can occur either accidentally or deliberately. Deliberate introductions occur by the deliberate release of birds by man and include such terms as re-introductions (introduction into former range), transplants (introduction within the present range, country or region) and restocking (introduction into inhabited range to increase numbers). Accidental introductions occur when birds escape from cages and enclosures (escapees), escape from domestication (feral species) or are introduced indirectly by man's activities (e.g. by ship or other means).

Natural colonisations by birds are not generally included in detail in this volume, whether or not such colonisation was perhaps assisted directly or indirectly by man. However, known details of any colonisation have been included where the species has been introduced. Other brief notes on colonisation may be found in the main text under the family headings.

Classification Followed

The classification followed has been: down to familial level, that by R.W. Storer in D.S. Farner and J.R. King (eds) *Avian Biology*, London and New York, Academic Press, 1971, pp.7-15; that for the order of the genera and species, the works of J.L. Peters (1931-) *Checklist of the Birds of the World*, Heffernan Press, Cambridge, Massachusetts, volumes 1-15. Departures from these works have been noted in the text.

Common names used generally follow those listed in the various regional works of the country of origin of the species. Where these vary it has been, in most cases, the personal choice of the author.

General Characteristics, General Distribution, Introduced Distribution and General Habits

As far as practicable for each species these sections have been kept to a minimum of material. Further details are available in a host of regional books and field guides. References to assist the reader to obtain further and more detailed information are located after each description and general habits section. These vary in their ability to enhance the 7 information given and generally only the few most recent articles or books are referred to, although there may be others which may be of equal relevance. The selection of the references has to some extent reflected availability and the personal knowledge of the author.

References to coloured plates or photographs of each species are included as part of one or more of the references given. Such plates and photographs vary in quality and the merit of some is arguable. However, the attempt has been to provide reference to a coloured plate for every species.

Range Maps
Range maps are notorious for their inaccuracies in minor detail and those given will be found to be no exception. They are composites drawn from the sometimes-limited material available and are designed only as a quick reference to the general range of the species. Each map shows the breeding range, extent of migration, if any, where they have been introduced and their success.

Notes on Introductions
The history of the introduction of each species forms the main part of the book. The notes are arranged by country of introduction and the text is referenced. Each reference is contained in full in the bibliography.

The histories of the introduction for each species represent all the information that could be assembled for that country. Because of the fragmentary nature of much of the data on introduced birds and the scope of the book, undoubtedly more information than that given will come to light in time. After all, apart from a few early accounts, only in the last decade or so have introduced species gained much mention in the many handbooks and field guides on birds.

Damage
Many of the species included in this work have not been adequately studied and the assessment of their impact in a new environment can, to some extent, only be subjective. This situation appears to be rapidly changing in the 1970s with more and more people studying exotic species. Already there are a number of lessons to be learned from the indiscriminate introduction of birds. However, for many species there is still little information and it is hoped that the inclusion of material in this section, whether the species was successfully established or not, will assist those who may wish to pass judgement on some of them.

Line Drawings
Every effort has been made to depict those birds illustrated as accurately as possible. Primarily, the species illustrated are those which have been introduced with some success, but in certain cases the availability of material has played a part in the final selection. Generally, the males of the species have been drawn, but where both are shown and in those cases where only the female is shown, these have been noted accordingly.

Predominantly the drawings are of a typical representative of the species, rather than a particular subspecies unless otherwise indicated.

Finally, although every effort has been made to present the text in as accurate a manner as possible, errors will doubtless be found with time and use. I would be glad to correspond with anyone who wishes to point out such errors or omissions.

ACKNOWLEDGEMENTS

I AM INDEBTED to a large number of people for their generosity in answering my correspondence, supplying articles and information, drawing my attention to information, and helping in other ways. Without their help the task of compiling such a book would have been considerably more difficult. I would like to make mention of the following:

Dr H. Abdulali (India), Mr A. Angus (N. Rhodesia), Mrs R. Balmford (Australia), Mr E. J. H. Berwick (Borneo), Mr C. H. Blake (USA), Mr L. H. Brown (Kenya), Mr J. Bull (USA), Dr G. Bump (USA), Mr P. Council (Australia), Dr S. J. J. F. Davies (Australia), Mrs A. S. de Dod (Dominican Republic), Sn V. de la Cruz (Philippines), Professor R. Escalante (Uruguay), Professor B. N. Falkenstein (USSR), Mr J. Forshaw (Australia), Mr J. W. Good (Nigeria), Mr H. R. Goode (S. Rhodesia), Mr D. G. Gooding (Australia), Dr M. Gorman (Scotland), Dr W. E. Howard (USA), Mr Hamid Sir el Khatim (Sudan), Mr M. Keffer (USA), Dr G. S. Keith (USA), Dr D. King (Australia), Mr H. R. Leach (USA), Dr H. J. Lavery (Australia), Sir Christopher Lever (England), Mr G. C. Long (Australia), Mrs J. P. Long (Australia), Mr D. C. Lourens (South Africa), Professor A. R. Main (Australia), Dr L. Medway (Malaya), Mr A. J. Oliver (Australia), Dr O. T. Owre (USA), Sn M. A. Plenge (Peru), Sn C. Ponce del Prado (Peru), Dr C. J. Ralph (Hawaii), Dr J. T. R. Sharrock (England), Dr D. L. Serventy (Australia), Mrs P. Short (Australia), Mr H. B. Shugg (Australia), Dr H. Sick (Brazil), Dr T. Spence (Australia), Mr T. Saunders (Japan), Mr B. N. Smallman (Canada), Mr and Mrs A. Tingay (Australia), Mr A. R. Tomlinson (Australia), Mr D. A. Turner (Kenya), Mr W. Vader (Norway), Mr J. A. Whellan (Southern Rhodesia), Mr D. H. Woodside (Hawaii), Mr D. B. Wingate (Bermuda), Dr J. G. Williams (Kenya) and Mr C. F. Zeillemaker (Hawaii).

For their encouragement in the initial stages of the project I am grateful to Mr H. B. Shugg (formerly Chief Fauna Warden, Department of Fisheries and Wildlife, Western Australia), Dr D. L. Serventy (formerly Officer in Charge, CSIRO Wildlife Division, Western Australia), Professor A. R. Main (Zoology Department, University of Western Australia) and Mr A. R. Tomlinson (Chief Executive Officer, Agriculture Protection Board, Western Australia). Mr Tomlinson has supported the project from its inception and, in fact, initiated the Agriculture Protection Board's investigations on introduced birds which led to the idea of the production of such a book. During the latter stages of writing I am particularly grateful to both he and Dr Stephen Davies (Officer in Charge, CSIRO Wildlife Division, Western Australia) for their enthusiasm and support when it was most needed.

Dr Dennis King and Dr Stephen Davies read a draft of the manuscript at one stage or another and Dr T. Spence a part thereof. My thanks go to them for allowing me to encroach on their time in this way and for their suggestions and help in improving the manuscript.

To the Librarians and staff who have assisted me at various times over a number of years I am truly grateful. These include the State Reference Library of Western Australia, Murdoch University Library, Zoology Department Library of the University of Western Australia, CSIRO Division of Wildlife Research Libraries at Helena Valley and Canberra, Royal Australasian Ornithological Union Library at Melbourne and particularly the Western Australian Department of Agriculture Library at South Perth which has borne the brunt of my requests over the years.

My sincere thanks go to Susan Tingay who completed the line drawings, a somewhat difficult task at times, whilst heavily involved in her own studies.

During two visits to the United States I (and my family on the second visit) could not have managed without the generous help of Barbara and Howard Leach and family.

A special thanks must go to Mrs Jean Hitchcock and Mrs Helen Hicks of the Agriculture Protection Board staff who typed the drafts and final copy.

Finally, I would like to thank the Agriculture Protection Board which made funds available, for travel to and time spent in the eastern states of Australia, the line drawings, typing, and the time for me to complete the manuscript.

INTRODUCTION

S INCE THE EARLY peoples roamed the earth animals have been domesticated, caged and bred. Man in his primitive state probably had little idea of their use except as food. At an early stage, however, it must have been customary to tame or attempt to tame and keep them. Domestication itself probably began in the Mesolithic Period and the caging and keeping of animals in captivity would have assisted the process.

The acclimation of birds under human management was certainly an early practice. Birds such as geese and pigeons were kept in captivity from Neolithic times (7000 years ago) and the fowl was probably domesticated before 3200 BC. Pelicans were kept in enclosures by the ancient Egyptians (1420–1411 BC) and other species such as guineafowl, peafowl and pheasants from about the first century BC. The Romans in early times (800 BC–AD 450) kept quail and many other species in cages.

The early Norsemen (before AD 800) carried cages of live birds on their long sea voyages for release at sea to determine the nearness of land. If the birds failed to return it was taken that land was close at hand. Generally, a variety of animals were carried by the early Indian, Dutch, Portuguese, Spanish and English traders, whalers and explorers for food and trade in the sixteenth, seventeenth and eighteenth centuries.

Intentionally, and in some cases unintentionally, animals were transported with man as he colonised new areas of the world. These species became acclimatised in new climates or environments.

Although the transportation of birds from one place to another can be traced back to the early civilisations, little seems to be known of when it became a practice to attempt the deliberate establishment of such species in the wild. Certainly, from the time that birds were first caged they have probably been escaping from captivity. Doubtless some became established for periods in suitable areas in early times.

There are fairly early records of feral species of birds such as the fowl, guineafowl, pigeon and some waterfowl which probably escaped from domestic flocks. However, widespread deliberate attempts at naturalisation in the wild rather than simply acclimatisation in cages, do not appear to have become an important facet of life until the colonisation of the New World by western Europeans in the last century.

Naturalisation may have been a natural progression from the keeping and breeding of animals on estates and the release of them at hunts, a practice which appears to have been prevalent in the Middle Ages. Those released for hunting generally failed to prosper because of the hunting pressure and the haphazard manner in which the liberations were carried out. They were designed, however, only to last the period or season of the hunt. Some of those species kept on estates in Europe survived there for considerable periods, but only with the help of their owners, whilst others have successfully spread.

Few introductions were documented until the era of the 'acclimatisation societies' in the nineteenth and early part of the twentieth centuries. These societies liberated hundreds of species in various countries of the world for such reasons as food, hunting and sport, and for other more aesthetic motives. In many cases the reason may only have been because the species was readily available and easily caught and transported. A longing for the sights and sounds of home by many western European emigrants was apparently justification enough for some attempts at naturalisation of a number of birds.

Although domesticated animals of use to the early emigrants were the first imports, once the settlers and their animals were established, they began to look at ways of filling the so-called 'vacuums' that they thought were there or which they had created through agriculture and the destruction of forests. Generally their first thoughts appear to have been to increase their own enjoyment of life and landscape.

The transplanting of species within countries or regions, re-introductions and restocking have become common practices in the twentieth century, primarily due to overshooting and depletion of the species' natural habitats. They are terms which are generally and popularly applied, mainly to game birds, in both Europe and North America and have probably assisted in the maintenance of some populations which would not otherwise be viable.

Re-introductions of birds, where they have become extinct or rare for one reason or another, appear to be of fairly recent origin and to have become prominent only in the last decade or two. Some re-introductions occurred before the second World War in both Europe and America when it appeared popular to transplant birds, often many hundreds of one species, from place to place, in the same general region to increase populations for hunting.

Escape from captivity, both from domestication and aviculture has been occurring for centuries. However, consequent with a boom in aviculture, escapees from this source have become increasingly important, probably from about the 1950s on.

The Reasons for Introducing Birds

Aesthetics

Certainly many of the early deliberate introductions of songbirds in the nineteenth and twentieth centuries were made for aesthetic reasons by people emigrating from the western world. In North America, Australia, South Africa and New Zealand in particular, many species were released because the settlers longed for the sights and sounds of the countries they had left. There is good evidence to indicate that some birds of European origin were considered by early North American and Australian settlers to be superior songsters to the native species.

Not all of the species introduced in the New World during this early period were, however, aesthetically beautiful to everyone, nor are they in retrospect. Often the introduction of particular species was opposed, but such opposition was generally too late to prevent the attempt.

A number of purely ornamental birds have been introduced into Europe. Golden Pheasants *(C. pictus)*, Silver Pheasants *(L. nycthemera)* and many waterfowl have been introduced for aesthetic reasons. The mere presence of species such as these on an estate, park or other area, gave status to those responsible for their establishment.

The general sameness of the species which have been introduced to the different regions of the world suggests that many of the early introductions were of birds which were either popular cage birds or those which could be easily caught in numbers and transported.

Food, Hunting and Sport

A number of species have been introduced where the predominant thought or reason behind such liberations may have been to provide birds for food. It has been suggested that this was the case for many of the early introductions of foreign animals and plants into New Zealand, but the reference may have been directed at the mammals and plants rather than the birds. Some members of the Galliformes (pheasants, partridges, quails, etc.) have almost certainly been introduced for this reason.

The release of birds for hunting and sport probably has its origin somewhere in antiquity. It was, as previously mentioned, a common practice in the Middle Ages. However, not until the nineteenth and more particularly in the twentieth century, have real efforts been made to establish species for these reasons. In this period, in both Europe and North America, the introduction of game birds reached gigantic proportions with attempts to naturalise dozens of species and transplant many others.

In the United States at least fifty species of game birds were released prior to 1900 and a further thirty at least have been released since that time. Of seventy-five species of game birds liberated in the Hawaiian Islands at least seventeen are still surviving there.

Controlling Pests

Many of the early introductions of such species as sparrows, starlings, mynas and bulbuls were made with the intention of controlling insect pests. Thus, the House Sparrow *(P. domesticus)* was introduced to control a moth in Argentina, combat a mosquito problem in Brazil and to control dropworm in the United States. The Myna *(A. tristis)* was released in Queensland, Australia, to control locusts, and to several of the Mascarene Islands for the same reason. More recently, the Cattle Egret *(A. ibis)* was deliberately introduced to the Seychelles and the Hawaiian Islands to control flies.

All of these species, with the exception of the Cattle Egret in the Hawaiian Islands, have themselves become pests. In the Hawaiian Islands the Cattle Egret is still spreading and one can only wonder what effects on other birds' populations it may have in the future.

The control of one pest species by another seems to have been a biological principle with little factual basis which appeals to many people, and which has prompted a number of introductions. Possibly the introduction of predatory insects, which appears to have been somewhat successful, has added to its appeal. However, biological control does not seem to have been applied successfully over a wide area with either mammal or bird introductions. Generally, the introduced species have made little difference to the populations they were intended to destroy and have become pests themselves.

Escapees and Aviculture
Many of the birds now established in the world owe their success as introduced species to the fact that they are domesticated, favourite cage birds, or are avicultural subjects. They are easily acclimatised and thus are generally more easily naturalised, although mere acclimatisation does not mean that they will automatically become naturalised.

Five orders of birds stand out as subjects for enclosures, cages and aviculture, and from the same orders come most of the birds which have been successfully introduced. These are the Anseriformes (ducks and geese), Galliformes (pheasants, quail, etc.), Psittaciformes (parrots and cockatoos), Columbiformes (pigeons and doves) and the Passeriformes (perching birds). They represent about three-quarters of the living birds in the world today and although those kept under aviculture and those which are introduced are often the same species this is not of course always the case.

Species from all these groups are well represented by established populations which originated from escapees and intentional and unintentional liberations from captivity. Escapees from domestication have been the basis of important introductions in the past, as such species as the fowl transported by the early colonising Polynesians and the pigeon transported widely by western Europeans attest. Cage bird escapees such as the red-whiskered bulbul, red-vented bulbul, some mynas and the Chinese thrush owe their success in some areas to their ability to escape and become established. Many estrildine and ploceine finches and weavers such as the Common Waxbill *(E. astrild)*, Red Avadavat *(A. amandava)* and Spotted-backed Weaver *(P. cucullatus)* have successfully established themselves from groups which escaped or were released from aviaries.

The keeping of birds in cages and for avicultural purposes, reached what appears to have been a world-wide boom in the twentieth century, with most people seeming to keep birds at some period in their lives. In the 1960s the practice reached tremendous heights in some countries, the importation of live birds becoming so vast that an international convention was held in the United States in 1973 to examine the biological impact of the international trade.

In North America more than half a million cage birds passed through the Miami Port of Entry in a single year. Between 1968 and 1970 some 123 721 birds of one species (Canary-winged Parakeets) were imported into the United States among some 300 000 parrots. From 1968 to 1972, 3 706 500 birds were imported into that country, although this figure was said to be several hundred thousand on the low side, as both canaries and some parrots were exempt from records at the time.

A similar situation existed in Europe in the same period. Some 1540 species of birds were held in captivity and imported from 1970 to 1975 into Great Britain alone.

How many of these birds escape, or are accidentally or intentionally liberated may never be known. However, it is certain that many do obtain their freedom from one cause or another. The evidence that they do escape or are released is obvious when one examines the ornithological literature from areas where importations were common.

Accidental Introductions
Accidental introductions have become a problem in many countries of the world. Some have occurred by birds accompanying ships and some have occurred as a result of the transport of large numbers of birds by aircraft.

The House Crow *(C. splendens)* arrived fairly regularly in Australia between 1950 and 1967 and probably owes its successful establishment in some South-East Asian and African ports to ships.

The House Sparrow arrived in the Falkland Islands by boat from Montevideo, Uruguay. It may also have been introduced to some of the Mascarene Islands by early Indian traders.

In 1963 an aircraft carrying a large consignment of birds from Cuba to Europe made an emergency landing at Nassau, New Providence. Many of these birds died during the subsequent delay, but many others were released. The Cuban Grassquit *(T. canora)* and probably the Yellow-faced Grassquit *(T. olivacea)* are now successfully established there as a result of this release.

Introduced Species in Various Regions of the World

Before examining what benefits and harm introduced birds may have caused let us examine the situation for different countries or areas of the world. Although most bird introductions have failed, there have been considerable successes. Generally, those which have been successful have been better documented than those which have failed. But, probably through lack of documentation, poor identification in earlier times and a wish to remain anonymous in more recent years, the exact numbers of attempts will never be known. Certainly many birds were introduced in North America, Great Britain, Australia and probably into New Zealand before the time of the 'acclimatisation societies' and this is probably the case for most areas of the world.

It has been claimed that the formation of the acclimatisation societies commencing with the first 'La Societe Imperiale d'Acclimatation' formed in France in 1854 resulted in increased interest in attempts at naturalisation and increased interest in the formation of other societies in other countries. More than likely though, the societies resulted from the increased interest in exotic animal forms. However, there followed such institutions as the 'Society for the Acclimatisation of Animals, Birds, Fishes, Insects and Vegetables within the United Kingdom' in 1860, a number of societies in Australia and New Zealand commencing with the 'Zoological and Acclimatisation Society of Victoria' in 1861, the many acclimatisation societies in New Zealand in the 1860s and also a number of American acclimatisation societies in the 1870s.

The earliest known societies to attempt naturalisation of birds and other animals appears to have been the Zoological Society of London formed in 1826 and which had as one of its primary objectives, the introduction of new and useful animals to the United Kingdom, and the Natural History Society in America in 1846.

The advent of the acclimatisation societies did however result in a better, though fragmentary, documentation of events.

Table I over page outlines the species of birds which have been introduced to various land masses and islands. As already mentioned, the totals given for numbers introduced are based on the details documented in this work. The totals for numbers established have relied on the most recent information available and can at best be only an approximation. Some effort has been made to distinguish between those that are well established and those that are not, but the division is arbitrary and based on the latest reports of the species.

The inclusion of transplanted and re-introduced species in the table is irksome for those who wish to consider exotics only, but to separate them is sometimes difficult. One needs to define 'transplanted' in relation to a faunal region, country or part thereof. Often it is not reliably known if a species was introduced or arrived unaided by man in any way. Table II lists, for seven regions, the number of species which have been transplanted or re-introduced. In this context a transplanted species has been defined as one which has been transferred within the region mentioned.

At least 119 species have been introduced into North America. The total may have exceeded 100 as early as 1948 and there is a record which suggests that more than eighty species were released before 1934.

One group of persons in Cincinatti liberated 3000 birds of twenty species between 1872 and 1874 without success. However, as early as 1846 the Natural History Society in America

TABLE I
NUMBERS OF BIRDS KNOWN TO HAVE BEEN INTRODUCED
(Including Transplants, Reintroductions, etc.)

Region	Total Introduced	Established Definite	Established Probable	Failed or Probably Failed
North America	119	39	17	63
South America	24	12	3	9
Hawaiian Islands	162	45	25	92
New Zealand	133	38	2	93
Australia	96	32	12	52
Tahiti	56	8	2	46
Fiji	25	10	1	14
Tonga	5	2	1	2
Samoa	3	3	—	—
Norfolk Island	4	4	—	—
Lord Howe Island	5	2	—	3
Guam	3	—	3	—
Pitcairn Island	1	—	—	1
Solomon Islands	4	1	3	—
New Hebrides	4	—	4	—
New Caledonia	6	4	2	—
New Britain, Bismarck Archipelago	1	1	—	—
Washington Island (Pacific Ocean)	1	1	—	—
Fanning Island	1	1	—	—
Christmas Island (Pacific Ocean)	1	1	—	—
Cook Island	1	—	1	—
Nauru	1	1	—	—
New Guinea	1	—	—	1
Marianas	2	1	1	—
Palau Archipelago	4	1	3	—
Japan	14	4	2	8
Hong Kong	11	4	4	3
Taiwan	3	—	1	2
P'enghu Liehtao	1	1	—	—
Philippines	9	6	3	—
Borneo	7	4	2	1
Indonesia	18	6	11	1
Singapore	14	5	3	6
Pinang	2	1	1	—
South-East Asian mainland	15	7	6	2
Andaman Islands	7	—	3	4
Nicobar Islands	5	2	1	2
Sri Lanka	3	1	—	2
Laccadive Islands	1	—	1	—
Cocos-Keeling Islands	6	3	—	3
Christmas Island (Indian Ocean)	3	1	2	—
Chagos Archipelago	33	16	1	16
Réunion	23	9	8	6
Rodrigues Island	9	5	3	1
Malagasy	5	2	—	3
Seychelles	14	10	—	4
Amirante Islands	8	5	2	1
Archipel des Comores	10	5	2	3
Ascension	5	4	—	1
Isles Glorieuses	4	1	1	2
Assumption	1	—	1	—
Aldabra Island	1	—	1	—
Cosmoledo Island	1	—	1	—
Farquhar Island	1	—	1	—
Cargados Garajos	1	—	—	—
Agalega Island	1	—	1	—
St Paul Island (Indian Ocean)	1	1	—	—
Amsterdam Island	1	1	—	—

TABLE I—*continued*

Region	Total Introduced	Established Definite	Probable	Failed or Probably Failed
Kerguelen Island	1	—	—	1
Africa-Arabia	31	14	6	7
Falkland Islands	3	1	—	2
Tristan de Cunha	1	1	—	—
South Georgia	3	1	—	2
St Helena	35	8	4	23
Cape Verde Islands	8	4	1	3
Canary Islands	3	1	2	—
Açores	5	4	—	1
Madeira	4	1	—	3
Porto Santo	4	—	1	3
Principé	3	2	—	1
Annobon	2	1	1	—
São Tomé Island	5	1	4	—
Fernando Poo	1	—	1	—
Greenland	1	—	—	1
Europe	69	27	11	31
Cuba	10	3	5	2
Jamaica	10	4	1	5
Grand Cayman	1	—	—	1
Haiti, West Indies	8	4	—	4
Dominican Republic	8	4	—	4
Puerto Rico	15	7	5	3
St Thomas Island, Virgin Islands	3	3	—	—
St Croix Island, Virgin Islands	1	—	—	1
Lesser Antilles				
Barbuda	2	2	—	—
St Kitts	2	—	1	1
Nevis	1	—	—	1
Antigua	3	1	—	2
Guadeloupe	2	1	—	1
Dominica	1	—	—	1
Martinique	3	1	—	2
St Lucia	1	—	1	—
St Vincent	1	1	—	—
Grenadines	3	2	—	1
Barbados	6	1	1	4
Grenada	1	—	—	1
Trinidad and Tobago	8	1	1	6
Curaçao	1	—	1	—
Bahamas	9	4	2	3
St John, Virgin Islands	3	—	2	1
Bermuda	14	6	1	7

TABLE II

NUMBERS OF TRANSPLANTED SPECIES IN SEVEN AREAS OF THE WORLD

Region	Transplanted and Re-introduced Species		Definitely Established		Possibly or Probably Established	
New Zealand	7	(126)	6	(32)	—	(2)
Hawaiian Islands	3	(159)	2	(43)	—	(25)
Australia	25	(71)	7	(25)	10	(2)
North America	21	(98)	14	(25)	5	(12)
Europe	27	(42)	15	(12)	5	(6)
South America	9	(15)	5	(7)	2	(1)
Africa-Arabia	12	(19)	6	(8)	3	(6)

(Exotics in parenthesis)

15

imported many birds of which a number were seen in the wild in following years near Brooklyn, New York. Many others were imported by the Brooklyn Institute between 1850 and 1853 including the ubiquitous House Sparrow. The Trustees of the Green-Wood Cemetery, Long Island, imported and released a number of species towards the end of 1852. Acclimatisation societies such as the American Acclimatisation Society, Cincinatti Acclimatisation Society, Portland-Oregon Song Bird Club and other organisations and private individuals released many in the period from the 1870s to 1900.

That the emphasis in North America has been on the introduction of game birds which were thought to be suitable for hunting is borne out by the following figures. Some fifty species of game birds had been introduced before 1900, of which five became naturalised, and thirty species after this date of which four became established.

From about the 1920s and 1930s the introduction of birds in North America has largely been in the hands of the various Fish and Game Departments. Thousands have been released to increase the ranges of already established species, new races and species have been constantly tried and many native species have been transplanted and re-introduced. Not until the 1960s do we find non-game species escaping or being released in any numbers as a result of an increased trade in live birds.

The Hawaiian Islands have gained more exotic species than any other island group in the world. The introduction of animals and plants to these islands has been so great that it has been recently claimed that 98% of the fauna and flora is now exotic. At least 162 species of birds now appear to have been introduced there and as many as seventy of them may be established at present. Some may not continue to survive their present tenuous existence forever, but others will adapt to the changing landscape, become numerous and probably become pests.

In the 1920s when the then-current status of introduced species in New Zealand was examined, it was found that about 132 different species of birds had probably been released in that country. However, some difficulties were experienced in distinguishing between those which were liberated and those which were imported merely as cage birds.

By 1933 the numbers of species introduced had risen above 140, of which about thirty-two were said to be established. Now, some thirty-six deliberately introduced or escaped birds are to be found in New Zealand.

The number of exotic species which have been released in Australia is difficult to assess. At least seventy-one and probably more, perhaps eighty or ninety, are known to have been liberated, but many more may have been released before the time of the acclimatisation societies and the somewhat-better documentation of events.

Twenty-seven species are now established. Some such as the ring-necked pheasant, California quail and jungle fowl are established only on small islands off the mainland coast.

Small islands in the Indian, Pacific and Atlantic Oceans have been the target of many attempted introductions of birds. Notably, the Mascarene Islands, Tahiti, Fiji, St Helena and the West Indies now have many exotic birds as part of their avifauna. In the late 1930s E. Guild liberated about fifty different species on Tahiti 'because there was practically no bird life'. H. Bruins-Lich, an agricultural officer, released at least sixteen species on St Helena in 1929, for unknown reasons, but probably because there were few land birds other than those already introduced.

The Menace of Naturalised Birds
The successful introduction of birds in areas where they do not occur naturally has caused and is still causing problems in many areas of the world. Such problems as the exotic species ousting the native ones by competition for food and habitat, the introduction of diseases and parasites, and damage to agricultural crops can occur as a consequence of introducing alien birds. Not only can such problems arise from deliberately or accidentally introduced species, but also from escapees from aviaries and cages.

Competition with Native Species
There are many examples in which an introduced bird species appears to be directly or indirectly affecting a population of native ones. Generally speaking, however, there is little

direct and much indirect evidence of the effects introduced forms may be having on the native populations. Much of this evidence comes from islands, thus in the Hawaiian Islands, New Zealand and the West Indies exotics are believed to have played a part in the extinction of some endemics.

On continents, the effects that exotics may have or have had on native species are less evident, and although it may be obvious that they do compete, the results of such competition are somewhat less apparent. For example, in Australia the introduced Starling *(S. vulgaris)* and Myna *(A. tristis)* have been recorded to utilise the nests of some parrot species, but their effects on the numbers of any one parrot are largely unknown.

Direct competition with native forms seems likely, especially when an aggressive species which is able to compete with others for food or nesting sites is introduced. They would have more chance of survival where the native one(s) is specialised in some way, or where there is a niche not occupied by native species. Many of the successfully introduced European forms in Australia, New Zealand, South Africa and North America, fall into this latter category as they have been introduced into and largely occupy disturbed habitats. An example of a less specialised species being better equipped than more specialised native forms is provided by the introduction of the Spice Finch *(L. punctulata)* into Australia. This species can live in a greater variety of habitats, is adapted to more methods of obtaining its food, and can outbreed the native finches.

The fact that introduced species of birds are capable of, and likely to, compete with native forms illustrates the potential danger of introducing them.

Effects of Disease and Parasites
There appear to be few definite examples of the transfer of diseases or parasites with introduced birds. The subject is still not well studied and the consequences not well known. However, there are sufficient circumstantial and more or less proven examples to point out the inherent dangers of such transfers. More recently, in some countries and in particular in Australia, interest has been shown in the reservoir that introduced populations may provide for exotic disease outbreaks.

The possible introduction of bird malaria into the Hawaiian Islands with birds of Asian origin has often been quoted as an example of how a disease introduced with liberated birds may affect indigenous species. In these islands, following the early introductions of birds, many of the honeycreepers became extinct. This focused attention on the possible importance of disease as a factor in their extermination. More recently it has been suggested that following the introduction of the night mosquito *(Culex pipiens fatigans)*, epizootics of bird pox and other debilitating diseases subsequently spread through the native bird populations causing their widespread disappearance. Although the evidence is not conclusive it does appear that exotic diseases may have been responsible for the extinction and decline of some species and that these diseases may have come from imported birds.

Positive Newcastle disease isolations from 'pet trade' birds have recently come from some species of birds including parrots, and influenza Type A virus from cage birds imported from South-East Asia into North America.

Not only the indigenous fauna may be affected by diseases, but the human population as well. Feral pigeons and others are known to carry a number of diseases which may affect man, and there is reasonable evidence that they can provide a reservoir for such diseases as ornithosis and play some part in the transmission of encephalitis and histoplasmosis. In Brazil, the House Sparrow has been implicated in the spread of Chagas' disease, an infection which is sometimes fatal to man.

The House Sparrow and Starling have long been accused of spreading the cestodes and nematodes of poultry. Both Senegal and Spotted Turtledoves have been accused of assisting in the spread of stickfast fleas in Western Australia.

A leucocytozoon infestation of pigeons and introduced species of doves has been diagnosed in the Hawaiian Islands. Here also, an examination of a number of introduced game birds on the island of Hawaii revealed thirteen new host records of worm parasites and four species of parasites were recorded for the first time on the island. What effects these may have on the birds is unknown.

There are probably many more examples of diseases and parasites carried by exotics, but until the subject has been further studied and the implications become better known, we should guard against or at least be aware of the consequences they may have.

Hybridisation

The introduction of one form of an introduced species into the existing range of another form of the same species could result in the production of a mixed race. The complications of such hybridisation could be serious, especially if the introduced species is in some way less desirable than the native one.

The dangers from hybridisation are not limited to exotic species imported from overseas, but also from native species transplanted from one area or region to another on the same continent.

There are examples of such hybridisation occurring, but few where the results are obviously deleterious. The Scarlet Ibis *(E. ruber)* which was introduced into Florida, USA, has bred with the White Ibis *(E. albus)* resulting in the loss of the red-plumaged birds. In this case the red plumage was the aesthetic reason for the introduction.

In Australia, the Mallard *(A. platyrhynchos)* breeds with the native Black Duck *(A. superciliosa)* and it is thought by hunters that the hybrid produced is a less desirable game bird. This species also hybridises with the Black Duck in New Zealand and there the cross has become so numerous in some places that it threatens to replace it altogether.

In North America, the Bobwhite *(C. virginianus)* has been transplanted, introduced and re-introduced in many areas. The results of such efforts have not always been welcomed. The lighter southern variety has been introduced into northern areas where it crossed with the heavier and sturdier stock. The resulting offspring were neither as large nor as strong as the northern bird and not as well equipped to cope with the prevailing conditions.

These examples serve as a warning of the more drastic effects that, perhaps, could manifest themselves through hybridisation.

Genetic Changes

Genetic changes that may occur after the introduction of a species into a new habitat, due possibly to the limited genetic material available from relatively few individuals which are initially released, are certainly likely. The rapidity with which these changes can take place has now been amply demonstrated with the House Sparrow in North America. Here, in a relatively few generations the sparrow has assumed the genetic variation comparable with its ancestors in Europe.

Among introduced birds there appear to be no examples of genetic changes which have been harmful to a particular species, but such changes have probably assisted in their establishment and spread in new environments. They are the most likely reason for the sudden explosive nature of some introduced bird populations. For example, the Spotted-backed Weaver *(P. cucullatus)* which was introduced into the West Indies remained an innocuous species on Hispaniola for at least seventy and perhaps for almost two hundred years. In about 1961 a population explosion caused it to become so abundant that it became a serious pest to rice crops.

Agricultural Damage

Numerous examples of agricultural damage by introduced species can be provided. The classical examples are illustrated by the introduction of such species as sparrows and starlings and these serve to point out the associated dangers of exotics. Certainly a point worthy of mention is that those species which cause damage, however minor, to agricultural crops in their native habitats will cause similar or worse damage in those into which they have been introduced.

Agricultural practices themselves change and a species which was not previously a pest could become one, merely by the growing of different crops. The reverse has certainly happened in the Hawaiian Islands where rice was once grown extensively. This has now changed to the growing of pineapples and sugar cane, but whilst the rice was grown the introduced Spice Finch was a pest of that crop. Since rice culture has ceased, the species has been described as 'an interesting wayside bird' of little economic significance.

Changing agronomic practices have probably led to the Skylark *(A. arvensis)* becoming a more significant pest in Great Britain at present. Although damage by this species to germinating cereals has been reported for over 100 years, only recently, since the increased tendency to remove hedges and trees and to have long-term leys, has the population in Great Britain increased and so consequently has the damage to such seedlings as sugar beet, lettuce, cauliflowers and cereals.

That an introduced bird can become a worse pest in a new environment is exemplified by the introduction of the Yellow-fronted Canary *(S. mozambicus)* in the Mascarene Islands and by the Spotted-backed Weaver in Hispaniola. Both appear to be regarded as no more than minor pests in Africa, but where introduced they have become so numerous as to constitute more serious pests.

Some so-called harmless species to agriculture can in some situations become pests. Thus the Grey Francolin *(F. pondicerianus)*, which is generally regarded as a most desirable game bird of little agricultural significance, became a pest of maize crops on Rodrigues Island following its introduction there.

Despite claims to the contrary, introduced game birds do sometimes become pests of agricultural crops. The Ring-necked Pheasant in North America does in some situations, where populations are high, cause damage to such crops as tomatoes and other high-value produce.

Generally, those introduced species which have become abundant and widespread have become pests. This always leads to a demand for control measures and investigations that are both time consuming and expensive. Additionally, the fact that no well-established exotic has yet been completely eliminated by existing control methods tends to emphasise the arguments against introducing them.

Continued Spread of Introduced Birds

Successfully introduced birds only rarely stay in the specific areas where they have been introduced. The Starling *(S. vulgaris)* and House Sparrow *(P. domesticus)* were introduced into the eastern United States and have now colonised most of North America. The latter species has now reached Guatemala in Central America and is also rapidly completing colonisation of the South American continent from introductions in Chile, Argentina and Brazil. Both species threaten to colonise the remaining suitable areas in Australia.

Many of the Passerines introduced to New Zealand and Australia have subsequently colonised the smaller offshore and outlying islands, from Macquarie Island in the south to Norfolk Island and the Kermadecs in the north. The Starling has reached Ono-i-lau in the Fijian Group, probably from the Kermadecs.

The Benefits to be gained from Naturalisation

Recreation

Although the arguments against the naturalisation of birds are many, not all introductions are bad. There are some benefits to be gained under some circumstances. Undoubtedly many have accrued from the introduction, restocking and transplanting of game birds in particular. That some people and groups of people derive satisfaction from recreations such as the hunting for sport, and eating game birds, is undeniable. Whether the aesthetics derived from these practices and the various related wildlife values are necessary to humans or could be obtained in other ways is not debated here. It is sufficient to assume by the popularity of these activities that some people do enjoy and gain satisfaction from them. Many, however, may argue that the expenditure in establishing exotics may have been better spent on the management and conservation of native species, even for the same purposes.

That some bird species themselves have benefited from naturalisation is at least apparent, and indeed some owe their present widespread existence to the practice. Certainly, the introductions of ring-necked pheasants and various partridges provide industry for many persons in Europe and North America. Large numbers are constantly being released, and these are often new strains and subspecies used for restocking, re-introduction and for increasing both their numbers and ranges in these countries.

Control of Pests

Once exotic species have become widely established few studies have been made of them with the object of deciding what benefits rather than what damage they may do. Few people would at this time consider introducing the Starling to New Zealand, Australia or North America if they were not already there, yet recent studies have shown that in some cases locally large populations of them can inflict considerable mortality on certain stages in the life cycle of some insects.

Preservation and Conservation

In more recent years a number of re-introductions have been made to re-establish some species which are in danger of extinction. Such introductions are praiseworthy indeed.

The Wildfowl Trust in England, together with the Hawaiian Department of Lands and Natural Resources, has done much to re-establish the Nene or Hawaiian Goose *(B. sandvicensis)* in the Hawaiian Islands. The Pheasant Trust in England has bred a number of Swinhoe Pheasants *(L. swinhoei)* which have been returned to the Taiwan authorities to enable them to re-establish the bird on that island. Before this effort there were probably only approximately 120 of them left in the wild.

Successful efforts have been made in New Zealand to establish and re-establish the Saddleback *(C. curunculatus)* on a number of offshore islands. The population was as low as about 1200 birds and their range had been considerably reduced prior to these attempts.

The more recent introductions of this species were made more necessary by the accidental introduction of the ship rat in 1963, and the subsequent extinction of the Saddleback, on three of the southern islands.

More recently, Cheer Pheasants *(C. wallichii)* which are becoming rare in the wild were bred in England and returned to a reserve in Pakistan. This was the first step in a programme which may save the species from extinction. There are probably many other similar examples of which the merits are obvious.

The Future

Man has made tremendous ecological changes in nearly every part of the world and the desire and capability are there to continue these changes at an ever-increasing rate. As the fauna in various regions and areas are extirpated or become rare as a consequence of destruction of forests and the development of agriculture and cities, there will be an increasing need for conservation and management of animal populations. Although the introduction of exotics has at times been another form of man's pollution of the environment, perhaps in the future, if not already, it will be an integral part of both conservation and management. If this is to occur, let us examine past introductions and not repeat the chaos nor create the associated problems which have so often arisen.

Systematic List of
INTRODUCED BIRDS

ORDER: TINAMIFORMES

Family: *Tinamidae* Tinamous

42 species in 9 genera, 4 introduced, 1 successfully
The only species to have had any success when introduced appears to have been the Chilean Tinamou on Easter Island, where it is still precariously established.

In 1968, some eight species for trial introduction into the United States were recommended, including the Crested Tinamou, Canyon Tinamou, Large Brushland Tinamou, Spotted Tinamou, Pale-spotted Tinamou, Red-winged Tinamou, Blue Tinamou and Chilean Brushland Tinamou (Bump). Whether any of these species have yet been released into the wild appears undocumented.

It seems likely that a number of tinamous, other than the Rufous Tinamou, may have been introduced into Great Britain, but these attempts appear to be poorly documented.

INTRODUCTIONS OF TINAMIDAE

Species	Date introduced	Region	Manner introduced	Reason
(a) Successful introductions				
Chilean Tinamou	1885	Easter Island	deliberate	game ?
(b) Unsuccessful introductions				
Great Tinamou	1923	Sapelo Island, USA	deliberate	?
Rufous Tinamou	before 1956 ?	Great Britain	deliberate	game ?
	after 1900?	Texas, USA	deliberate	game ?
Chilean Tinamou	1966	Hawaiian Islands	deliberate	game
Martineta Tinamou	early ?	France (?)	deliberate	game ?

GREAT TINAMOU
Tinamus major (Gmelin)

DISTINGUISHING CHARACTERISTICS
37-45 cm (14.5-17.7 in)
Crown and sides of head rufous or blackish; back light or dark brown, with fine black markings; throat white or greyish; underparts olive-brown or greyish brown, paler on abdomen and more or less vermiculated or speckled fuscous; flanks barred with brown and blackish brown; under tail-coverts cinnamon; tail short; bill slightly decurved, upper mandible greyish-brown, lower yellowish. Female: larger.
Blake, vol.1, 1977, pp.19-23 and pl.1.

GENERAL DISTRIBUTION
Central and South America: south-eastern Mexico to Ecuador, eastern Peru, northern Bolivia and central Brazil.

INTRODUCED DISTRIBUTION
Introduced unsuccessfully to Sapelo Island, Georgia, USA.

GENERAL HABITS
Status: common. *Habitat:* forest and woodland with dense canopy and open floor. *Gregariousness:* singly, pairs or small parties. *Movements:* sedentary. *Foods:* fruits, seeds and a few insects. *Breeding:* no information. *Nest:* on the ground. *Eggs:* no information, probably 5-7.

NOTES ON INTRODUCTIONS
USA. In 1923 some fifteen Great Tinamou *(T.m. robustus)* from Guatemala were released on Sapelo Island, off the coast of Georgia, but they failed to become permanently established there (Phillips, 1928; Gottschalk, 1967). Phillips records that only one bird remained alive on the island by 1926.

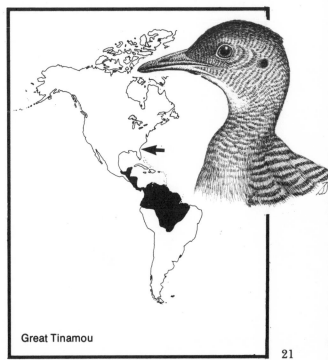

Great Tinamou

RUFOUS TINAMOU
(Rufous-winged or Red-winged Tinamou, Argentine Tinamou)
Rynchotus rufescens (Temminck)

DISTINGUISHING CHARACTERISTICS
35-42.5 cm (13.7-16.7 in). 1kg (2.2 lb)
Crown and back barred black and brown or buff;
crest black streaked tawny-brown; throat white; neck
and upper breast cinnamon (neck occasionally
streaked and breast barred black); underparts buff
or greyish, barred with black on sides of body,
abdomen and flanks; edge of wing, primaries and
outer secondaries cinnamon-rufous; tail greyish
brown to whitish; long decurved bill greyish.
Blake, vol.1, 1977, pp.54-55 and fig.6. pl.1.

GENERAL DISTRIBUTION
South America: central and eastern Brazil, southern
Bolivia, Paraguay, Uruguay and northern and
central Argentina.

INTRODUCED DISTRIBUTION
Introduced unsuccessfully to Great Britain and the
USA.

GENERAL HABITS
Status: range reduced, but fairly common (?).
Habitat: open country and grasslands (pampas).
Gregariousness: solitary, pairs and trios. *Movements:*
sedentary. *Foods:* seeds, fruits, berries, tubers, roots,
spiders, earthworms and insects. *Breeding:* Sept-Jan.
Nest: slight depression on the ground, sometimes with
a few leaves. *Eggs:* 5, 7-9, 12 (more than one female
lays in a nest).
Grzmek, pt.1, vol.7, 1972, pp.81-87.
Weeks, *Zoologica*, vol.58, no.1, 1973, pp.13-40.

NOTES ON INTRODUCTIONS
Great Britain. Attempted introductions of Rufous
Tinamous in Britain failed, and the species did not
become established (Koch, 1956; Sick in Thomson,
1964).

Rufous Tinamou, *Rynchotus rufescens*

USA. Rufous Tinamous were released on the King
Ranch, in Texas, some time after 1900 but failed to
become established (Lehmann, 1948).

CHILEAN TINAMOU
Northoprocta perdicaria (Kittlitz)

DISTINGUISHING CHARACTERISTICS
25-32 cm (9.8-12.5 in)
Upper parts greyish brown or olive-brown, spotted
black and finely lined cinnamon and spotted white;
throat and centre of abdomen whitish; lower neck,
breast and sides greyish; flanks barred; wing
primaries greyish and secondaries brown; upper tail-
coverts barred black and white or buff; bill, upper
mandible black, lower mandible grey.
Blake, vol.1, 1977, pp.58-59.

GENERAL DISTRIBUTION
Northern and central Chile from Atacama to
Llanquihue.

Rufous Tinamou

Chilean Tinamou

INTRODUCED DISTRIBUTION
Introduced successfully to Easter Island, and unsuccessfully to the Hawaiian Islands.

GENERAL HABITS
Status: fairly common but considerably decreased in numbers. *Habitat:* semi-arid grasslands and cultivated fields. *Gregariousness:* singly, pairs or small coveys. *Movements:* sedentary. *Foods:* plant parts, seeds, fruits and possibly insects and small animals. *Breeding:* Dec-Feb. *Nest:* loosely-built grass structure, amongst weeds or long grass. *Eggs:* 5-8, 12. Johnson, vol.1, 1965, pp.49-51.

NOTES ON INTRODUCTIONS
Easter Island. The Chilean Tinamou was introduced to this island in 1885 and is still established there, but has not spread much (Johnson, Millie and Moffett, 1970). The race introduced is *N.p. perdicaria* (Hellmayr, 1932).
Hawaiian Islands. Two races, *N.p. perdicaria* and *N.p. sanborni* from Chile, were introduced to these islands in 1966 (Walker, 1967). Berger (1972) indicates that they were introduced as potential game birds to the islands of Hawaii *(perdicaria)* and Kauai *(sanborni)*, but are not now known to be established on either.

MARTINETA TINAMOU
(Elegant Tinamou, Elegant Crested-Tinamou)
Eudromia elegans d'Orbigny and Geoffroy

DISTINGUISHING CHARACTERISTICS
36-41 cm (14-16 in)
Generally greyish-brown, spotted white or buff; long slender crest black; streak behind eye and on throat buff; throat white; back finely spotted black and buff; breast finely barred black; wing primaries black, secondaries brown, both barred whitish; remainder of underparts barred black and buff; bill blackish.
Grzmek, pt.1, vol.7, 1972, pl.p.87.
Blake, vol.1, 1977, pp.71-75.

GENERAL DISTRIBUTION
South America: southern Argentina from northern Chebut to the Santa Cruz River, and in Aysen, Chile.

INTRODUCED DISTRIBUTION
Probably introduced, unsuccessfully, to France.

GENERAL HABITS
Status: fairly common. *Habitat:* pampas on open tablelands, grasslands, scrub and thorny thickets, open woodlands, arid hills and barren flats. *Gregariousness:* coveys or flocks of 6-20, 30 and

Martineta Tinamou

sometimes up to 100 birds in the non-breeding season. *Movements:* sedentary. *Foods:* leaves, seeds, fruits (?) and insects. *Breeding:* in Oct, but little information. *Nest:* on the ground. *Eggs:* 5-7 and up to 12 or 16 (? more than one female).
Johnson, vol.1, 1965, p.56.
Grzmek, pt.1, vol.7, 1972, pp.81-87.

NOTES ON INTRODUCTIONS
France. The Martineta Tinamou was probably introduced in the wild in France at Vaux-de-Cernay and in Aisne, but failed to become permanently established (Etchécopar, 1955).

ORDER: RHEIFORMES
Family: *Rheidae* Rheas

2 species in 2 genera; 2 introduced, 1 successfully
Although both species have been introduced only the Lesser Rhea, on Tierra del Fuego, appears to have become established. The specific identity of the bird introduced into the Ukraine is not known and it seems doubtful that it is still established there.

INTRODUCTIONS OF RHEIDAE

Species	Date introduced	Region	Manner introduced	Reason
(a) Successful introductions				
Lesser Rhea	prior 1936 ?	Tierra del Fuego	not known	?
(b) Unsuccessful introductions				
Greater Rhea	late 19th Century (1880?)	France	deliberate ?	game ?
(c) Possibly successful introductions (status uncertain)				
(?) Lesser Rhea	before 1939	Ukraine	?	?

Greater Rhea, *Rhea americana*

GREATER RHEA
(Common Rhea)
Rhea americana (Linnaeus)

DISTINGUISHING CHARACTERISTICS
127-150 cm (50-59 in). 20-25 kg and up to 40 kg (44-55 lb, up to 88 lb)
Generally grey with black or pale areas on neck and back (white individuals not uncommon); crown, nape, back of neck and patch at base of neck dark brown or blackish; front of neck sometimes whitish; bill yellowish brown.
Grzmek, pt.1, vol.7, 1972, pl.p.88.
Blake, vol.1, 1977, pp.8-9.

GENERAL DISTRIBUTION
South America: eastern and central Brazil, Paraguay, Uruguay, Bolivian Chaco and northern and central Argentina.

INTRODUCED DISTRIBUTION
Possibly introduced, unsuccessfully, to France.

GENERAL HABITS
Status: fairly common, but greatly reduced in numbers with the advance in agriculture. *Habitat:* open pampas grassland and brush country. *Gregariousness:* solitary, small groups 3-5 and up to 15, or flocks of 20-30, and up to 100 birds in non-breeding winter season. *Movements:* sedentary. *Foods:* grass, leaves, grain, roots, seeds, insects (including grasshoppers) and also small invertebrates. *Breeding:* Sept-Dec; polygamous with successive polyandry. *Nest:* hollow scraped in the ground, lined and edged with grass, sticks and stems, often in thick grass. *Eggs:* 10-50 but sometimes 60 or more found in a nest where as many as 10-15 females may lay.
Raikow, *Wilson Bulletin*, vol.80, 1968, pp.312-319.
Raikow, *Wilson Bulletin*, vol.81, no.2, 1969, pp.196-206.
Bruning, *Living Bird*, vol.13, 1974, pp.251-294.

NOTES ON INTRODUCTIONS
France. An attempt may have been made to establish the Greater Rhea in France in the late nineteenth century. M. Beauger kept six young birds at liberty in a park in 1881 (Etchecopar, 1955) and it seems probable that the attempt was made to naturalise the species.

LESSER RHEA
(Darwin's Rhea)
Pterocnemia pennata d'Orbigny

DISTINGUISHING CHARACTERISTICS
90-100 cm (35-39 in)
Smaller than the preceding species and has the feathers of the underparts tipped white; otherwise plumage generally brownish; head, neck and upper parts greyish brown to yellowish brown; feathers of back and wings often white tipped; abdomen whitish; bill brownish.
Blake, vol.1, 1977, pp.9-11 and fig.3, p.10.

Greater Rhea

Lesser Rhea

GENERAL DISTRIBUTION
South America: from southern Peru, Bolivia, north-western Argentina, and northern Chile to the Straits of Magellan.

INTRODUCED DISTRIBUTION
Introduced successfully on Tierra del Fuego, Chile, and possibly in the Ukraine (status uncertain).

GENERAL HABITS
Status: fairly common, but reduced in numbers. *Habitat and Gregariousness:* generally similar to *P. americana* as far as is known. *Movements:* sedentary. *Foods:* grass and herbs. *Breeding:* Sept-Dec (July in north Chile). *Nest and Eggs:* similar to *P. americana* as far as is known.

Johnson, vol.1, 1965, pp.46-48.

NOTES ON INTRODUCTIONS
Tierra del Fuego. Johnson (1965) records that there are about fifty descendants of introduced Lesser Rheas living on Tierra del Fuego at the present time. According to Humphrey *et al* (1970), they are a breeding resident of the northern, non-forested part. Some were noted in February 1936 on one of the farms on the island, and some near Manantiales in 1950 by Philippi, who was told that they had been introduced some years before and that a group of fifty maintains itself in the wild.

Ukraine. A flock of Rheas (species uncertain) was acclimatised in Askania Nova, Ukraine, before the second World War. Only six out of some thirty or forty birds survived the war, but by 1951 there were again some thirty birds present there. The population was said to be declining in the late 1950s (Salganskii and Salganskaya, 1959).

ORDER: STRUTHIONIFORMES

Family: *Struthionidae* Ostrich

1 species; introduced successfully

The Ostrich became feral in Australia following the collapse of a feather industry in earlier times and is still present in numbers in a few areas of South Australia. The birds have not been recorded as causing any problems recently. They appear to be increasing in numbers and range.

ORDER: CASUARIIFORMES

Family: *Dromaiidae* Emu

1 species; introduced successfully

The Emu appears to have been established successfully on Kangaroo Island, off the coast of South Australia, where it still exists in small numbers.

Family: *Casuariidae* Cassowaries

3 species in 1 genus; 1 species possibly introduced successfully

It seems doubtful from the information available that the Double Wattled Cassowary has been introduced to Seram. More than likely the species is native to the island.

Although this Cassowary becomes feral in parts of New Guinea there appear to be no records of it maintaining feral populations by breeding.

Bennett's Cassowary *(Casuarius bennetti)* was imported to New Zealand in 1868, but it is not known if any were released in the wild.

Note: In more recent classifications the tendency is to unite the above orders as the Struthioniformes. They are dealt with together here for that reason.

OSTRICH

Struthio camelus (Linnaeus)

DISTINGUISHING CHARACTERISTICS
175-275 cm (68-108 in). 63-136 kg (139-300 lb)
Body black; bare skin of head (absent in some races), neck and thighs lead-grey to whitish grey, but varies to pinkish or red in some races; wings and tail white; bill horn coloured, edge and base of upper mandible reddish. Female: pale brown or grey.

Mackworth-Praed and Grant, 1952-73, ser.1, vol.1, pp.1-3; ser.2, vol.1, pp.1-2; ser.3, vol.1, pp.1-2.

GENERAL DISTRIBUTION
Africa and formerly Arabia and Syria.

INTRODUCED DISTRIBUTION
Introduced and established locally in south-eastern Australia.

GENERAL HABITS
Status: locally common some parts, very rare or extinct in others; range considerably reduced and possibly now found only truly wild in reserves or in the Kalahari Desert. *Habitat:* open savannah. *Gregariousness:* solitary or flocks of 5-15, but larger flocks

INTRODUCTIONS OF STRUTHIONIDAE, DROMAIIDAE AND CASUARIIDAE

Species	Date introduced	Region	Manner introduced	Reason
(a) Successful introductions				
Ostrich	1869	South Australia	deliberate	feather industry
Emu	1926-29	Kangaroo Island, Australia	deliberate	?
Double Wattled Cassowary	?	Seram (?)	(may be native)	?
	often ?	New Guinea	feral	pet bird
(b) Unsuccessful introductions				
Ostrich	before 1912	Western Australia	deliberate	?
Emu	?	Heron Island, Australia	deliberate	tourist attraction
	1864-71	New Zealand	deliberate	?

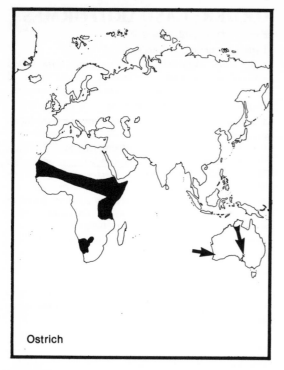

Ostrich

Australia. The Ostrich was first introduced to Australia for a feather industry in 1869, but by 1882 the South Australian Government began to encourage Ostrich farming and large flocks were developed near Port Augusta and Coorong (Frith, 1973). Farm birds were released prior to 1933 at Point Sturt (Lake Alexandrina) and Mundoo Island, near the River Murray mouth. At the latter place, they had increased to such an extent at this time that they were said to have become a nuisance (Condon, 1968). A liberation of some birds may have occurred at Port Augusta as early as 1913. When the industry collapsed after the first World War, many birds were set free; feral populations exist at Redcliffe, near Maryan, South Australia; certainly near Port Augusta; small numbers also in the upper Coorong district (Younghusband Peninsula) up until the late 1950s (Condon, 1975). There are now hundreds, perhaps even thousands, of birds around the Flinders Ranges (Davies, pers. comm., 1978). The race established in South Australia may be *australis* or a mixture with *camelus* (Condon). Ostriches were also released in Western Australia before 1912 (Long, 1972). Some may have been liberated at Gingin and some were released at Mount Morgan (east of Leonora) in the goldfields, but they failed to become established in that State.

DAMAGE

None known.

sometimes in non-breeding season. *Movements:* sedentary and nomadic. *Foods:* fruits, seeds, leaves, creepers, shrubs, cactoid plants and small animals. *Breeding:* season variable depending on rains (July-Jan in north and east Africa); polygamous but sometimes monogamous, hens sharing nests. *Nest:* a slight hollow on the ground. *Eggs:* 6-8 per female, but often 10-30 or more found in one nest.

Sauer and Sauer, *Living Bird* vol.5, 1966, pp.45-75.
Sauer and Sauer, *Ostrich* suppl. no.6, 1966, pp.183-191.
Leuthold, *Ibis* vol.119, no.4, 1977, pp.541-544.

Ostrich, *Struthio camelus*

EMU

Dromaius novaehollandiae (Latham)

DISTINGUISHING CHARACTERISTICS

180-200 cm (70.8-78.7 in). 23-53 kg (50.8-117 lb)

Generally dark to light grey-brown; body feathers long and double; whitish ruff at base of neck; face

Emu

Emu, *Dromaius novaehollandiae*

and throat bare, pale grey-blue; wings vestigial; bill blackish.
Reader's Digest, 1977, p.25 and pls. p.24 and 25.

GENERAL DISTRIBUTION
Australia, except the dense tropical forests; formerly widespread but not now in many settled areas or considerably reduced in numbers. Extinct in Tasmania.

INTRODUCED DISTRIBUTION
Introduced successfully on Kangaroo Island, South Australia. Introduced unsuccessfully on Heron Island, Queensland, and possibly to New Zealand.

GENERAL HABITS
Status: common, but reduced numbers in settled areas. *Habitat:* open plains to sclerophyll forests. *Gregariousness:* pairs, scattered parties and sometimes large flocks of 100 birds. *Movements:* sedentary and nomadic. *Foods:* green vegetable material, seeds, fruits, insects, including grasshoppers and caterpillars. *Breeding:* Apr-Nov. *Nest:* on the ground usually with some grass, bark and leaves in a shallow depression often circled with stones or sticks. *Eggs:* 5-11, 20.

Davies, *Proc. Ecol. Soc. Aust.* vol.3, 1968, pp.160-166.
Eastman, 1969.

NOTES ON INTRODUCTIONS
Kangaroo Island. Eight emus were introduced to Kangaroo Island between 1926 and 1929 (Anon, 1948) and a few birds are still present on the island (Wheeler, 1960; Condon, 1968; Abbott, 1974).
Heron Island. A single emu was at one time introduced to a tourist resort on Heron Island, but is no longer present there (Kikkawa and Boles, 1976).
New Zealand. Emus were imported in 1864, 1868 and in 1871, but there is no record of any being released. Sir George Grey introduced a number to Kawau Island in 1868, but they all died (Thomson, 1922).

DAMAGE
Emus are known to cause damage to crops in Western Australia, mainly on the edges of arable agricultural land but also in some areas of the south-west where farms are surrounded by forest country. Such damage has been reduced by the construction and maintenance of 'Emu-proof fences' which prevent large-scale movements of birds from pastoral areas in the north and east of the State into the agricultural areas in the south.
In recent years a management plan has been implemented so that the bird is protected as much as possible and control is only carried out in areas where this is absolutely necessary (Riggert, 1975).

DOUBLE WATTLED CASSOWARY
(Australian Cassowary)
Casuarius casuarius (Linnaeus)
DISTINGUISHING CHARACTERISTICS
150-200 cm (59-78.7 in). 29.2-58.5 kg (64.5-129 lb)

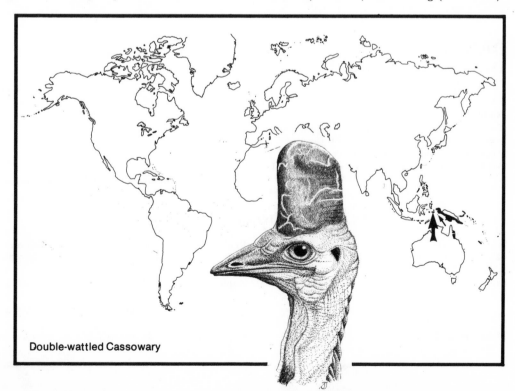

Double-wattled Cassowary

Plumage black; wattles vary from a long pendant, forked at tip on front of neck to a pair of wattles, one on each side of neck; bare neck blue and red or pink, sometimes with some yellow; bill dark brown. Female: larger and more brightly-coloured; helmet taller.

Reader's Digest, 1977, p.27 and pl.p.26.

GENERAL DISTRIBUTION
New Guinea-Australia: Seram (?), western and southern New Guinea lowlands, Aru Islands and north Australia (Cape York to near Townsville).

INTRODUCED DISTRIBUTION
Possibly introduced successfully to Seram and probably feral in parts of New Guinea.

GENERAL HABITS
Status: fairly common (common — Australia); commonly kept as pets whilst young in New Guinea. *Habitat:* forest and woodlands. *Gregariousness:* solitary for most of the year, or small family groups. *Movements:* sedentary. *Foods:* fallen fruits, berries, fungi, snails and insects. *Breeding:* June-Oct (Australia). *Nest:* in a depression on the ground, occasionally with some leaves, grass and other material added. *Eggs:* 3-8.

NOTES ON INTRODUCTIONS
Seram. Rand and Gilliard (1967) indicate that the Double Wattled Cassowary may have been introduced into Seram. There appears no other indication that the species has been introduced.
New Guinea. The cassowary is carried about as a pet in New Guinea and sometimes traded long distances by natives. They make fine pets when young, but become aggressive with age and are often allowed to become feral in woodlands near villages (Rand and Gilliard, 1967).

DAMAGE
It is known that in times of food shortages cassowaries will enter gardens and orchards to eat cultivated fruits such as bananas and mulberries, but there appear to be no records of them becoming agricultural pests.

ORDER: DINORNITHIFORMES

Family: *Apterygidae* Kiwis

3 species in 1 genus; 2 species introduced, both successfully

Both the Brown Kiwi and Little Spotted Kiwi have been introduced to Kapiti Island, off the west coast of the North Island, and the former species to Little Barrier Island, off the east coast of the North Island of New Zealand.

Although little data is here recorded on these introductions, they were more than likely made to preserve these rare birds.

BROWN KIWI
Apteryx australis (Shaw)

DISTINGUISHING CHARACTERISTICS
45-55cm (17.7-21.6 in). 1-3.3 kg (2.2-7.2 lb)
Generally dark grey streaked reddish brown and black; head greyish; no tail and remnant wings hidden in plumage; bill white to pinkish. Female: larger size and longer bill.
Buller, 1872-73, pl.33.
Oliver, 1955, pp.47-48, 51.

GENERAL DISTRIBUTION
New Zealand and some offshore islands. Parts of North and South Island and Stewart Island.

INTRODUCED DISTRIBUTION
Introduced successfully on Kapiti and Little Barrier Islands, New Zealand.

GENERAL HABITS
Status: rare and considerably reduced in range by settlement, but still common some areas of the North Island. *Habitat:* formerly only forested areas, now in

Brown Kiwi

INTRODUCTIONS OF APTERYGIDAE

Species	Date introduced	Region	Manner introduced	Reason
(a) Successful introductions				
Brown Kiwi	?	Kapiti Island, N.Z.	deliberate ?	preservation ?
	?	Little Barrier Island, N.Z.	deliberate ?	preservation ?
Little Spotted Kiwi	early 1900	Kapiti Island, N.Z.	deliberate ?	preservation ?

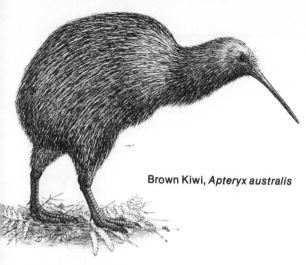

Brown Kiwi, *Apteryx australis*

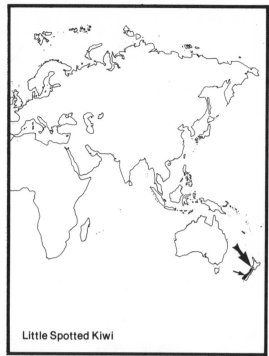

Little Spotted Kiwi

forest edges and partly-cleared scrub. *Gregariousness*: pairs. *Movements*: sedentary. *Foods*: ground animals such as worms, insects and their larvae, also fallen fruits. *Breeding*: July-Feb. *Nest*: in holes amongst dense vegetation, in hollow logs and between roots of trees, sometimes partly excavated by birds. *Eggs*: 1-2.

Oliver, 1955, pp.49-50, 51-52.

NOTES ON INTRODUCTIONS
New Zealand. The North Island race (*A.a. mantelli*) and South Island race (*A.a. australis*) have been introduced to Kapiti Island and the latter race also to Little Barrier Island (Falla *et al*, 1966). Both introductions appear successful, but little information was available.

DAMAGE
None known.

LITTLE SPOTTED KIWI
Apteryx oweni (Gould)

DISTINGUISHING CHARACTERISTICS
35-45 cm (13.7-17.7 in)
Body irregularly banded and mottled with brownish black on buffy pale grey background; head grey; bill pale.

Buller, 1872-73, pl.36.
Oliver, 1955, pp.53-54.

GENERAL DISTRIBUTION
In the western districts of the South Island of New Zealand.

INTRODUCED DISTRIBUTION
Introduced successfully on Kapiti Island, New Zealand.

GENERAL HABITS
Status: probably reduced in range and uncommon. *Habitat*: forested areas. *Movements*: sedentary. *Gregariousness*: singly or pairs. *Foods*: worms, insects and berries. *Breeding*: no information, probably

similar to Brown Kiwi. *Nest*: similar to Brown Kiwi. *Eggs*: 1-2.

Oliver, 1955, p.54.

NOTES ON INTRODUCTIONS
New Zealand. The Little Spotted Kiwi has been introduced on Kapiti Island where it is well established (Falla *et al*, 1966). Five birds were released on the island at the beginning of the century and the population now numbers at least 200 birds (Mills and Williams, 1979).

DAMAGE
None known.

ORDER: SPHENISCIFORMES
Family: *Spheniscidae* Penguins

17 species in 6 genera; 1 or more introduced, none successfully

The King Penguin, and perhaps some other species, have been introduced in northern Norway. It seems likely that some penguins existed there for a period of about ten years before they finally disappeared.

It is said that whalers operating from Europe occasionally brought penguins back following their operations in southern seas. Some of these birds were probably released or escaped in northern waters, but there appear to be no documented records of events and certainly none have become established there.

INTRODUCTIONS OF SPHENISCIDAE

Species	Date introduced	Region	Manner introduced	Reason
(a) Unsuccessful introductions				
King Penguin	1936	Norway	deliberate	?
'Golden' and 'Spectacled' Penguins	1938	Norway	deliberate	?

KING PENGUIN

Aptenodytes patagonica Miller

DISTINGUISHING CHARACTERISTICS

90-110 cm (35-43 in). 10-18.1 kg (22-40 lb)

Generally black and white with a small orange-yellow neck patch which continues around neck as a border to black of head; upper parts black; underparts white; bill black with orange at base of lower mandible.

Watson, 1975, pp.66-67, and pl.1.

GENERAL DISTRIBUTION

Antarctica, Staten Island, South Georgia, Heard, Kerguelen, Prince Edward and Macquarie Islands. Reaches the tip of South America occasionally and Cape Horn.

INTRODUCED DISTRIBUTION

Introduced unsuccessfully in northern Norway.

GENERAL HABITS

Status: fairly common and numbers increasing, although extirpated in some areas. *Habitat*: low latitude Antarctic and sub-Antarctic islands and waters. *Gregariousness*: highly gregarious. *Movements*: generally found near breeding sites. *Foods*: fish, and cephalopods. *Breeding*: Oct-Mar; breed twice per season; colonial. *Nest*: on low-lying stony areas devoid of vegetation. *Eggs*: 1.

Watson, 1975, pp.66-70.

NOTES ON INTRODUCTIONS

Norway. Penguins, King Penguins and other species, were first liberated in northern Norway by the Nature Protection Society in 1936, at Rost in Lofoten and at Gjesvaer in Finmark (Lund, 1955). Lund indicates that according to the scientific journal *Naturfredning i Norge*, nine King Penguins were given to the Society by consul Lars Christensen, and the release was made by the author, Carl Schoyen, in August 1936. He reports the following records of them: A single bird was later (October 1936) killed by people at Moskenes; those released at Finmark were noted at various places in the following autumn and the one killed was on a farm at Gamvik. In the summer of 1938 the National Federation for the Protection of Nature again released some penguins at Rost. These were believed to have been both 'Golden' and 'Spectacled' species. Several years elapsed without any being seen, then in 1944 two (apparently King Penguins) were found at Sandholmen. From 1944 to 1947 no further penguins were seen, although two or three may have been shot at Kåfjord. In 1948 some six or seven penguins visited Sakrisoy, near Reine in Lofoten, and three visited Eggum, in Borge. In February 1949 it was reported in the press (*Vest finnmark Arbeiderblad*) that a pair were at Komagfjorden near Gåshopen. In Nordland some were reported (*Vesteralens Avis*) at Dverberg, on Andoya, and these were thought to have been some of those released at Rost. The last record of penguins in Norway appears to have been a report in the press (*Lofotposten*) that a single bird had been seen at Selsoyodden, outside Kyllingmark in Hamaröy.

ORDER: PELECANIFORMES

Family: *Phalacrocoracidae* Cormorants

30 species in 3 genera; 2 species introduced, probably unsuccessfully

Of the two species introduced, only the Guanay appears to have had some success. This species was introduced to San Geronimo Island, Baja California, Mexico, before 1953, where it became established and was reported to be doing well at that date. As there appear to be no further records it has been assumed it has now died out there.

Family: *Pelecanidae* Pelicans

8 species in 1 genus. 1 introduction known

The Brown Pelican (*Pelecanus occidentalis*) has been

Species	Date introduced	Region	Manner introduced	Reason
(a) Unsuccessful introductions				
Common Cormorant	?	Hawaiian Islands, (Kauai and Lanai)	deliberate	?
(b) Probably unsuccessful introductions				
Guanay	before 1953 ?	San Geronimo Islands, Mexico	deliberate ?	guano ?
Brown Pelican	1968-73	Louisiana, USA	deliberate	re-introduction

successfully re-introduced to Louisiana from Florida. The original introductions occurred between 1968 and 1973 and the population built up from 465 to about 500 birds, but was severely reduced by the use of pesticides. A further 100 birds were transplanted from Florida in about 1975 to the Barataria Bay system in Louisiana to bolster the sagging population (Blus *et al*, 1975; USDI, 1976).

Phalacrocoracidae

COMMON CORMORANT
(Black Cormorant, Great Cormorant, White-breasted Cormorant)
Phalacrocorax carbo (Linnaeus)

DISTINGUISHING CHARACTERISTICS
75-100 cm (29.5-39.3 in). 1.5-2.9 kg and up to 4.9 kg (3.3-6.4 lb, up to 10.8 lb)
Generally black, with bluish or greenish sheen; cheeks white or yellow; white patch on flanks in breeding season; throat and neck white or yellowish (races vary: *sinensis* has white cheeks and throat); underparts whitish (or black in some races); bill grey, skin at base yellow.
Palmer, 1962, vol.1, pp.316-319.
Reader's Digest, 1976, p.71 and pl.p.71.

GENERAL DISTRIBUTION
Coastal and inland waterways of Europe, Asia, Africa, Iceland, Greenland, eastern North America, Philippines, Indonesia, Australia and New Zealand. Migrant in Malaysia and Hong Kong.

INTRODUCED DISTRIBUTION
Introduced unsuccessfully to the Hawaiian Islands.

GENERAL HABITS
Status: fairly common. *Habitat*: coastal areas, lagoons and bays, inland lakes and larger waterways including large rivers and marshes. *Gregariousness*: solitary and in flocks, sometimes large. *Movements*: sedentary and migratory. *Foods*: fish and small crustaceans (shrimps). *Breeding*: Apr-Feb (Africa); Mar-July (Europe); Mainly Mar-Nov but throughout the year (Australia); colonial. *Nest*: roughly built, large stick and branch nest, or seaweed nest, in tree or

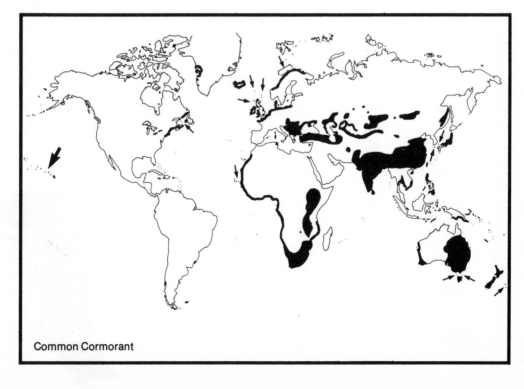

Common Cormorant

on cliff ledges, rocks or sandbars. *Eggs*: 2-6 (Britain 3-5; Australia 3-5; USA 3-4).

Palmer, vol.1, 1962, pp.319-325.

NOTES ON INTRODUCTIONS

Hawaiian Islands. A single Chinese fishing cormorant (*P.c. sinensis*) was released by the Gay and Robinson families at Makaweli, on Kauai (Munro, 1960). Munro gives no date for this release but says that the bird was not seen again. Caum (1933) indicates that there was another introduction on Lanai, but this liberation also failed to become established.

DAMAGE

In many places of the world there has been much dispute as to the influence this species has on fishing interests. From the information available, their consumption of small fish doubtfully affects commercial fisheries to any extent.

GUANAY
(Peruvian Cormorant, Guanay Cormorant)
Phalacrocorax bougainvillei (Lesson)

DISTINGUISHING CHARACTERISTICS

50-76 cm (19.6-30 in). 1.9 kg (4.2 lb)

Black with underparts from neck white; head crested; orbital skin green; patch of white feathers above eye; facial patch red; under tail-coverts dark; long hook-ended bill whitish, upper mandible is blackish along edge, lower mandible is yellowish green at base, both are black tipped. In winter lacks nuchal crest and facial patch.

Blake, vol.1, 1977, pp.147-148 and pl.2.

GENERAL DISTRIBUTION

South America: breeds on islands off the west coast from Lobos de Tierra, Peru, south to Mocha Island, Chile. Occasionally occurs northwards to Ecuador and southwards to the Straits of Magellan.

INTRODUCED DISTRIBUTION

Possibly introduced on San Geronimo Island, Baja California (now failed ?).

GENERAL HABITS

Status: very common. *Habitat*: coastal islands, rocks, etc. *Gregariousness*: huge flocks. *Movements*: some movements north and south from breeding areas. *Foods*: surface fish (anchovies). *Breeding*: most of the year, peak in Nov and Dec; possibly 2 broods; in dense colonies. *Nest*: on the ground. *Eggs*: 2-4.

Johnson, vol.1, 1965, pp.124-128.

NOTES ON INTRODUCTIONS

San Geronimo Island. The Guanay was introduced to this island and was reported to have become established and to be nesting there in April 1953 (A.O.U., 1957). However, Blake (1977) says that the reputed successful introduction on this island appears to be unfounded.

DAMAGE

None known.

ORDER: ANSERIFORMES

Family: *Anatidae* Ducks, Swans and Geese

150 species in 45 genera; 29 species introduced, probably 18 established

At least some twenty-nine species of the *Anatidae* have been introduced. Eighteen of them have had some success in establishing populations as feral, deliberately introduced or re-introduced species. About nineteen species are known to have had some success as self-introductions or colonists, but details for these species have only been included in the text where the species has been deliberately introduced somewhere.

The most successful introductions in this family have been of the Mallard, which has been successful in a number of areas, the Mute Swan which has had considerable success in eastern North America and the Canada Goose which has been successful in Europe, particularly in England and Sweden.

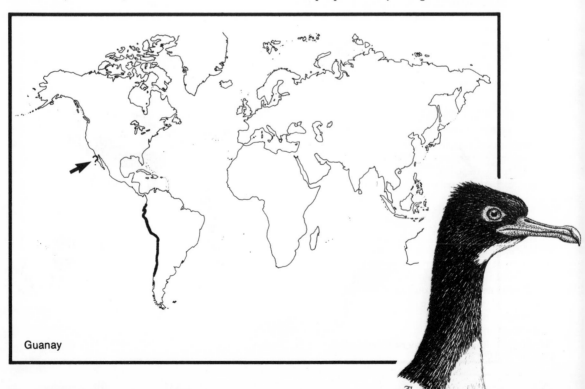

Guanay

Although the introductions of ducks, swans and geese have caused little agricultural damage anywhere, few of them have yet become very widespread. Concern has been expressed at the increasing numbers of Mallards in Australia and New Zealand, because of possible competition with native species and the effects of hybridisation. Similarly some biologists in North America are concerned that the Mute Swan, because of its possibly deleterious habits and probable competition with native species, may cause problems in the future.

The Canada Goose has already caused problems in England by grazing agricultural lands. The damage may not yet be classed as of economic importance, but large numbers of this species in Europe may, in time, have a devastating effect on the populations of native geese and ducks. A number of ducks and geese not mentioned in the following text, some of which are not specifically known, have been introduced and in some cases released into the wild in various countries. Thus the Whitefronted Goose (*Anser albifrons*), Swan Goose (*A. cygnoides*), Canvasback (*Anas vallisneria*), Teal (*A. crecca*), American Black Duck (*A. obscura*), Korean Duck (*Eunetta falcata*) and Black Brant (*Branta nigricans*) were imported into New Zealand between 1871 and 1905, but it is not known if they were released in the wild. In Australia, 'China geese', 'Indian ducks', 'East India ducks', 'English wild ducks', 'Toulouse geese' and geese ? were released in Victoria and South Australia between 1866 and 1880, but all failed to become established there. Similarly in the British Isles, where considerable efforts have been made to naturalise many waterfowl species, such species as the Swan Goose, Muscovy Duck (*Cairina moschata*) and Redbreasted Pochard (*Netta rufina*) occasionally breed as feral species.

In New Zealand efforts are being made to reintroduce and re-establish the Brown Teal (*Anas aucklandica chlorotis*) in areas where they were formerly common. A single wild bird and nine captive-reared birds were released on Kapiti Island in 1968. Since captive-rearing began in earnest in 1975 some twenty to twenty-five birds have been released annually. Private persons have released 143 birds, mainly in an area north of Wellington.

TRUMPETER SWAN
Olor buccinator (Richardson)

DISTINGUISHING CHARACTERISTICS
147-183 cm (57.8-72 in). 7.3-12.5 and up to 17.2 kg (16-27.5 lb, up to 38 lb)
Large white swan; bare skin in front of eye black; bill pinkish, black at base.
Godfrey, 1966, p.47 and pl.p.47.
Palmer, vol.2, 1976, pp.55-57.

GENERAL DISTRIBUTION
North America: from south to south-eastern Alaska, western and south-eastern Alberta, south-western Saskatchewan, Queen Charlotte Islands, Vancouver Island, to eastern Idaho, south-western Montana and Wyoming. Formerly more widespread. Winters in southern parts of range.

INTRODUCED DISTRIBUTION
Introduced and re-introduced successfully in some areas of the USA and Canada.

Trumpeter Swan   ---former range

GENERAL HABITS
Status: range and numbers considerably reduced. *Habitat:* lakes, ponds, large rivers, bays and sometimes grain fields. *Gregariousness:* parties and small flocks. *Movements:* sedentary and partly migratory. *Foods:* leaves and stems of aquatic plants, seeds, grain, tubers, insects, snails, small reptiles and fish, molluscs and crustaceans occasionally. *Breeding:* Apr-May. *Nest:* large bulky platform of aquatic vegetation, lined with down, on a beaver house, island, or margin of a lake. *Eggs:* 2, 4-6, 10. Palmer, vol.2, 1976, pp.59-71.

Trumpeter Swan, *Olor buccinator*

INTRODUCTIONS OF ANATIDAE

Species	Date introduced	Region	Manner introduced	Reason
(a) Successful introductions				
Trumpeter Swan	from 1940s on	USA	re-introduction and transplants	preservation
Mute Swan	A.D. 1186 on	Europe	feral	preservation ?
	1910-12 ? or earlier	USA	semi-feral escapee	ornamental
	1866-71	New Zealand	semi-feral escapee	ornamental
	1886, 1897-1912 ?	Australia	semi-feral escapee	ornamental
	about 1920s	South Africa	escaped captives	?
Black Swan	1864-70	New Zealand	deliberate	ornamental
	1955-60	Japan	semi-feral	?
Cape Barren Goose	1972	King Island, Australia	re-introduction	?
Greylag Goose	1930, 1933, 1942	Scotland	re-introduction	conservation and hunting ?
	since 1961	England and Ireland	re-introductions and escapees	conservation
Canada Goose	probably 1731 on	Great Britain	semi-feral escapee	?
	1936, 1958 on	Norway	deliberate	?
	1933	Sweden	semi-feral escapee	hunting ?
	1964	Finland	deliberate	?
	1876-1915, 1920, 1950	New Zealand	deliberate	hunting ?
	1930s on	USA	re-introductions and transplants	conservation
	1931 and recently	Canada	transplanted	?
Hawaiian Goose	1960 on	Hawaiian Islands	re-introduction	preservation
Black-bellied Tree-Duck	?	Cuba	deliberate ?	?
Paradise Shelduck	1915-17, 1920-21, 1959-69	New Zealand	transplanted	conservation and hunting
Egyptian Goose	late 1800s	France	semi-feral	?
	1795 on	England	semi-feral escapee	
Mallard	?	(eastern) USA	transplanted	hunting and restocking
	about 1960	Bermuda	semi-feral escapee	?
	1860s-1912 ?	Australia	deliberate ?	
	1867-1918, 1939-50s	New Zealand	deliberate	hunting
	1960s on	Hawaiian Islands	re-introduction and transplants	preservation of subspecies
Meller's Duck	about 1850	Mauritius (?)	deliberate ?	?
Common Pintail	prior 1954	St Paul and Amsterdam Islands	?	?
	since 1964	Great Britain	deliberate and colonisation	
Gadwall	about 1850, 1930s and later	England	deliberate, feral and colonisation	
	1957-1965	USA	transplanted	hunting ?
American Wood Duck	1873, 1960s	England	feral	ornamental ?
	1884 on	USA	transplanted	hunting ?
Mandarin Duck	1866, 1904 on	England	semi-feral escapee	conservation ?
Redhead	1952-63	USA	transplanted	hunting, conservation
Ruddy Duck	1952-53, 1956 on	England	captive escapee	
(b) Unsuccessful introductions				
Mute Swan	1920	Hawaiian Islands	deliberate	ornamental ?
Black Swan	1938	Tahiti	deliberate	
	occasional	Europe	escapees	
	occasional	North America	escapees	
Spur-winged Goose	1912-20	Australia	deliberate	
Snow Goose	1877	New Zealand	deliberate	

Species	Date introduced	Region	Manner introduced	Reason
Greylag Goose	? 1769, 1867, 1892	New Zealand	deliberate	
Canada Goose	prior 1920 ?	Australia	deliberate ?	
	mid-1930s	Denmark	deliberate	
Magellan Goose	1910 or 1911, 1959	South Georgia Island	deliberate	?
Australian Wood Duck	1922	Hawaiian Islands	possibly not released ?	
Black-bellied Tree-Duck	?	Jamaica		
Egyptian Goose	1860 ?, 1869	New Zealand	semi-feral escapee	ornamental ?
	late 1800s or early 1900s	Australia	deliberate	?
	prior 1928	USA	escapees	captive bird
Muscovy Duck	1885	Auckland Island N.Z.	deliberate	
Mallard	1938	Tahiti	deliberate	hunting ?
Meller's Duck	?	Réunion (?)	deliberate ?	?
Blue-winged Teal	1922	Hawaiian Islands	?	re-establishment
	1961-64	USA	transplanted	
	1960 on	Great Britain	escapees and vagrants	
European Wigeon	1868-97, 1904	New Zealand	deliberate	hunting ?
American Wood Duck	1867-1906	New Zealand	deliberate	hunting ?
	1938	Tahiti	deliberate	
Mandarin Duck	1860s	Australia	deliberate	
	1938	Tahiti	deliberate	
Pochard	1894-98	New Zealand	deliberate	hunting ?
Tufted Duck	1870	New Zealand	deliberate	hunting ?
	before 1976	USA	escapees	captive bird

(c) Introductions of which the results are uncertain
(including species (?) which it is not certain were introduced)

Species	Date introduced	Region	Manner introduced	Reason
Trumpeter Swan	prior 1966	Canada	re-introductions	preservation
Cape Barren Goose	prior 1869, 1871, 1912	New Zealand	deliberate	?
Bean Goose	1960s	Finland	deliberate	experimental
Canada Goose	prior 1967	Hawaiian Islands	deliberate	insect pest control
Black-bellied Tree-Duck	1967-75	Trinidad and Tobago	deliberate	conservation
White-faced Whistling Duck	prior 1912	Mauritius (?)	?	?
Muscovy Duck	late 1960s ?	USA	feral or deliberate	?
Mallard	1930s	Falkland Islands	deliberate ?	hunting ?
	about 1949	Macquarie Island, Australia	?	?
	1959, and later	Kerguelen Island	deliberate	?
Mandarin Duck	?	New Zealand (?)	uncertain if released	
Pochard	after 1936	Great Britain	feral	ornamental ?

NOTES ON INTRODUCTIONS

USA. In 1935 an integrated programme was initiated in the United States to avert the extinction of the Trumpeter Swan (Johns and Erickson, 1970). Colonies were re-introduced prior to 1957 in wildlife refuges at Malheur, Oregon and at Ruby Lakes, Nevada (A.O.U, 1957). Twenty birds were transplanted from Red Rock Lakes, Montana, to Malheur in 1944, and another twenty birds in 1945; some were taken from here to Ruby Lakes refuge in 1946 (Delacour, 1954). Fifty-seven Trumpeters were transplanted from Red Rock Lakes to the South Dakota Wildlife Refuge in 1960, and were nesting there in 1963 (Monnie, 1966).

Some four pairs nested on Malheur National Wildlife Refuge, Oregon, in 1963 and young were seen on Ruby Lakes National Wildlife Refuge, Nevada; they successfully nested at Lacreek National Wildlife Refuge in South Dakota and this represented the first hatching of Trumpeters on the Great Plains in nearly eighty years (Udall, 1963). Breeding populations are now successfully established in Oregon, Nevada and South Dakota (Scott, 1972) and another colony in north-western Wyoming (Peterson, 1961).

Birds transferred from Red Rock Lakes to Jackson, Wyoming, established a small breeding colony in the National Elk Refuge (Gabrielson *et al*, 1956).

Pinioned Trumpeters were also transplanted from Red Rock Lakes in 1963, and free-flying birds in 1964 (eleven birds) and 1966 (twenty) to the Turnbull Refuge in north-eastern Washington where they nested in 1967, 1968 and 1969 (Johns and Erickson, 1970).

Canada. Trumpeter Swans were being re-introduced at Swan Lake near Vernon in British Columbia (Godfrey, 1966) and a single bird was bred there in 1968, but more recent details for this venture appear to be undocumented. Some five cygnets were released at Delta, Manitoba, in 1972 (Palmer, 1976) but details of any success there are also lacking.

DAMAGE
None known.

MUTE SWAN
(White Swan)
Cygnus olor (Gmelin)

DISTINGUISHING CHARACTERISTICS
130-160 cm (51-63 in). 5.5-15 kg, up to 22.5 kg occasionally (12-33 lb, up to 49.6 lb)
Plumage white; bill orange or pinkish with black base; knob on forehead black.
Delacour, vol.1, 1954, p.63 and pl.p.64.

GENERAL DISTRIBUTION
Eurasia: from Denmark, central and southern Sweden, northern Germany, Poland, Romania, central USSR, Asia Minor, central Asia and east to Mongolia and Dauria. Possibly native in Britain in the past. Migrant to south-eastern Europe, northern Africa and southern Asia.

INTRODUCED DISTRIBUTION
Introduced, re-introduced and/or semi-domesticated in western Europe and England; introduced successfully in North America, New Zealand (semi-feral), Australia (semi-feral) and South Africa (feral). Introduction to the Hawaiian Islands failed.

GENERAL HABITS
Status: range and numbers considerably reduced, but numbers increasing in recent years. *Habitat:* fresh water pools, lakes, slow flowing rivers and estuaries with fresh or brackish water, usually with lush shore vegetation. *Gregariousness:* often singly, but occasionally large flocks of more than 100 in winter.

Movements: mainly sedentary, sometimes migratory. *Foods:* stems and leaves of water and marsh plants, algae, grass, aquatic animals (frogs, fish, etc.) including molluscs and crustaceans occasionally. *Breeding:* Apr-June (Britain), Sept-Jan (New Zealand); generally solitary but colonial at times. *Nest:* broad mass of reeds, grass, etc., with down lining to cup; near water's edge on a reedy bank or island. *Eggs:* 3-7, 12 (Britain, 1-11; New Zealand 5-7; Rhode Island, 3-9).
Scott, 1972.

NOTES ON INTRODUCTIONS
Europe. White Swans were introduced long ago and semi-domesticated in many parts of western Europe (Delacour, 1954). Some had been introduced and naturalised on rivers around Paris, France, by the end of the seventeenth century (Mayaud, 1962 in Palmer, 1976). According to Voous (1960) the species is now markedly dependent on man and human cultivation. Evidence for the former theory that Mute Swans were introduced to England in early times appears incorrect and more than likely they were indigenous, at least to some areas. The species is very common in a feral state in England where they are likely to have been natives of Lincolnshire, Cambridgeshire, Huntingdonshire, Norfolk, Suffolk and probably to the Thames and perhaps other areas. The original wild stock was more than likely brought by capture and pinioning into semi-domestication, commencing prior to A.D. 1186, and ceased to exist as a wild race (Witherby *et al*, 1938; Delacour, 1954).

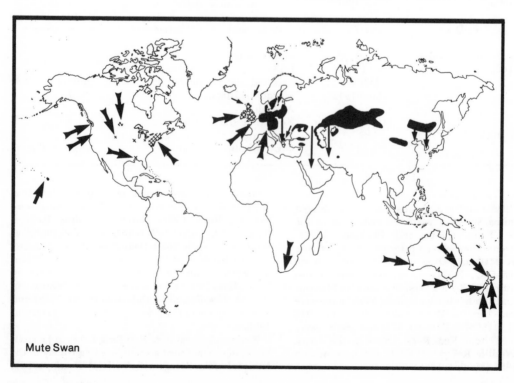

Mute Swan

Mute Swan, *Cygnus olor*

During the eighteenth and nineteenth centuries many colonies in Europe died out until few remained. However, in the twentieth century following the decline in numbers, the species has due to introductions and natural spread from what are probably feral or semi-domestic stock, increased its range considerably. Introductions such as those in the Faeroes (c. 1940), Åland Islands Finland (c. 1934), northern Italy, Greece (c.1967), Switzerland (c. mid-nineteenth century) and possibly elsewhere have probably contributed. Natural spreads, through greater protection for the species, have occurred in the Netherlands, Sweden, Denmark, Norway, Poland, Czechoslovakia, Yugoslavia, Bulgaria and the USSR (Scott, 1972; Cramp and Simmons, 1977).

North America. The Mute Swan has been introduced in New York and wanders to eastern Massachusetts, Rhode Island, New Jersey, Ohio, Pennsylvania, West Virginia (A.O.U., 1957), Kentucky (Kleen, 1976), Alabama (Imhof, 1962) and other areas of the United States. They have been established on the Oregon coast (Wing, 1956) and in Michigan and New England (Reese, 1975).

The original introductions probably occurred as semi-domestic birds in eastern North America (Delacour, 1954), but there appears to be no record of when the species was first imported. Some were imported in 1910 (216 birds) and in 1912 (328), but earlier specimens are apparently known there. According to Bump (1941) they were released by private individuals in New York State prior to 1900.

They were established on the Lower Hudson and on Long Island, New York, in a semi-wild state before 1928 (Phillips, 1928). Here, they were reported to have been accidentally liberated and in 1920 numbered some twenty-six birds (Cook and Knappen, 1941). Unpinioned White Swans kept on estates at Newport, Rhode Island, are believed to have been responsible for a population which increased and spread rapidly from the 1950s. Some were released at Oakdale, Long Island (Cooke and Knappen), and the population there by 1967 numbered about 700 birds (Palmer, 1976). In New Jersey, a number of feral birds were established by 1940 and they nested there in the 1950s. These had built up to a population of some 118 birds by 1957.

A captive flock was wing clipped annually, from 1911 until 1934, near Akron, Ohio, and then allowed to migrate (Cooke and Knappen). A single bird was noted on Lake Erie, Ohio, in January 1936 (Skaggs, 1936).

These releases and probably many others have contributed to the present population of Mute Swans in the United States.

In Canada they have appeared occasionally (e.g. 1934), and were recently reported to be nesting and wintering in Regina, Saskatchewan, probably after wandering from the New York region (Godfrey, 1966).

The Mute Swan now appears to be fairly well established in eastern North America. Scott (1972) indicates that they are established from Massachusetts south to New Jersey, and in north-west Michigan. The United States Fish and Wildlife Service reported in 1976 that they are now locally abundant along the east, west and gulf coasts and in the Great Lakes areas.

Reese (1975) records recent substantial increases in the population at Travers City, Michigan, where they have built up from one pair to about 500 birds since 1948. They were released or escaped from captivity into Chesapeake Bay on the east coast in 1962, when one or two pairs were present. In the last decade these have bred up to a population which now numbers some 500 birds.

Hawaiian Islands. In about 1920, Mr W. A. Wise brought some Mute Swans to Hilo and released them near the town, where they appeared to become established (Munro, 1960). There appear to be no further records of the species for these islands; presumably they failed to become established there.

New Zealand. Six Mute Swans were introduced at Canterbury in 1866, nine at Otago in 1968-69, fourteen at Auckland in 1869-71, and several birds were introduced by private individuals and dealers at about that time (Thomson, 1922). Other early introductions include some which were made at Christchurch in 1866, Auckland in 1867 and Dunedin in 1868, when two or more birds were released at a time (Oliver, 1955).

Thomson reports that the species was nowhere common in the 1920s, but Oliver records that there were a few present at such places as Pupuke Lake, Foxton, Ashley Mouth, Kaituna, Akaroa, Tomahawk, Lake Waihala and some other areas in the 1950s. A Whaleford farmer was fined for killing two birds on his farm dam in June 1946 (Anon., 1946).

According to Wodzicki (1965) the Mute Swan is established locally in both the North and South Islands. Falla *et al* (1966) report that the species was introduced from Great Britain as an ornamental bird and still exists in a semi-feral state except on Lake Ellesmere where there is a considerable breeding population (200 birds). Small populations (twelve to twenty birds) breed on Lake Poukawa, Wanstead Lagoon and other lakes in central and southern Hawke's Bay.

Australia. One of the first introductions of Mute Swans to Australia may have been made when Mr T. H. Dardel, of Paradise Vineyards, Batesford, brought two white swans out from Paris on the steamer *Kaikoura* in 1886; they were reported to be there in 1887 on a river near the property, but one bird apparently disappeared later in the same year (Tarr, 1950). However, a pair of white swans were released on Phillip Island, Victoria, in 1866 (Jenkins, 1977; Balmford, 1978) and four white swans arrived in Melbourne on the *Medway* in 1853 and were presented to the Botanical Gardens (Balmford, 1978). Both imports were probably Mute Swans. Balmford also records that a single white swan may have been noted in the wild before 1859.

Condon (1975) reports that the Mute Swan has been introduced in northern Tasmania and south-western Western Australia. He records that one bird has been sighted near Booligal, on the Lachlan River in New South Wales. Tarr says that the species is probably feral on some waters near Sydney, but that there are no records of them breeding there. Six birds were released in Launceston, Tasmania, in the 1920s and progeny from these were released in other areas (Jenkins, 1977).

In Western Australia the Mute Swan was introduced some time between 1897 and 1912 (Long, 1972). They are sometimes found on ornamental waters around Perth and a small colony is still established on the Avon River at Northam, 80 km (50 miles) east of Perth. Some have been liberated in other areas of the south-west of Western Australia, but the species has shown little inclination to extend its range or increase markedly in numbers (Serventy and Whittell, 1962). In 1978 the Avon River colony only numbered some thirty-one birds.

South Africa. The origin of the Mute Swan in the eastern Cape is still uncertain, but they appear to have escaped from captivity (Winterbottom, 1966) and are probably descendants of birds introduced from Europe fifty years ago (Siegfried, 1970).

Winterbottom reports that the species is established in a feral state on the Kromme River and one or two neighbouring estuaries in the vicinity of Humansdorp. Siegfried indicates that the population in Cape Province is about 120 birds.

DAMAGE

In England, Mute Swans graze riverside meadows and cause problems from time to time, but their depredations are not often economically important (Seubert, 1964). Kear (1964) records that they feed on winter wheat and grass occasionally and cause some damage. She says that, along with other species, they may cause a reduction in yield of wheat and retarded growth of grass at times, particularly when they graze heavily after growth commences in spring.

An intensive survey was recently undertaken in Sweden to assess the effect on commercial fisheries of large concentrations of Mute Swans (Scott, 1972). The results were entirely in the swans' favour as they did not take either spawn or fry, nor were they spoiling the spawning grounds by uprooting the bottom vegetation.

In the USA, where rapid increases in swan populations have occurred, Reese (1975) says that the species has presented biologists with management problems. He indicates that the influence of large populations on native waterfowl is unknown, but that they are known to occasionally attack children and native waterfowl, to collide with and break power lines and to compete with native species for food.

BLACK SWAN
Cygnus atratus (Latham)

DISTINGUISHING CHARACTERISTICS

90-105 cm (35-41 in). 3.7-8.7 kg (8-19 lb)

Generally black with white wing tips; bill reddish orange with white bar near tip.

Frith, 1967, pp.90-91.

Reader's Digest, 1977, pl.p.97.

GENERAL DISTRIBUTION

Australia, except the north-central part; Tasmania. Wanders to inland waters and recorded north to Darwin.

INTRODUCED DISTRIBUTION

Introduced successfully to New Zealand. Acclimatised in Europe, America and Japan, but probably not in a feral state. Introduced unsuccessfully to Tahiti.

GENERAL HABITS

Status: fairly common. *Habitat:* swamps, lakes, estuaries and rivers. *Gregariousness:* small to large flocks; both solitary and colonial at breeding. *Movements:* sedentary and nomadic. *Foods:* leaves and stems of water vegetation, algae and also seeds and grass. *Breeding:* variable, determined largely by rains. *Nest:* rough bulky platform of sticks and vegetation, on the ground (islands) or in water vegetation. *Eggs:* 4-10, 14 (New Zealand 1-14).

Frith, 1967, pp.91-105.

NOTES ON INTRODUCTIONS

New Zealand. The Black Swan was first introduced to New Zealand in 1864 by the Nelson Acclimatisation Society which imported seven birds (Thomson, 1922) from Australia. Thomson records that they were also released by the Canterbury Society in the same year, when four were liberated on the Avon River to control watercress. In 1866 this society imported five more birds, but their subsequent fate is unknown. Other introductions include those by the Otago Society which liberated sixty-one birds between 1866 and 1870 and those of the Southland Society which liberated six birds in 1869.

Shortly after their introduction Black Swans began appearing in areas hundreds of kilometres away from the release points. A colony of several thousand was established at the mouth of the Opawa River, near Marlborough, in 1895 (Scott, 1972).

They are said to have quickly established themselves in New Zealand and spread to a number of

Black Swan, *Cygnus atratus*

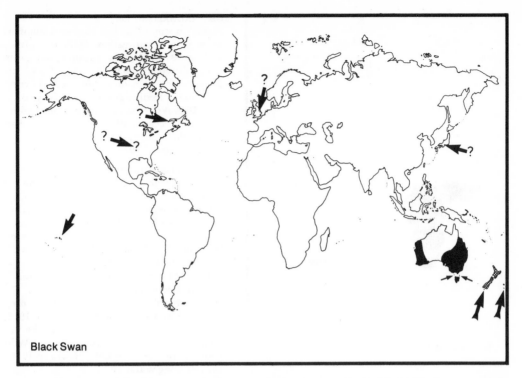

Black Swan

offshore islands. They were plentiful in the Kapara district around 1912 and on the Chatham Islands shortly before 1922 (Thomson). By the 1930s they were well spread, especially on lakes and lagoons near the coast, in the North and South Islands (Stidolph 1933; Oliver, 1930).

According to Falla *et al* (1966) the Black Swan was introduced to New Zealand from Australia as an ornamental bird. It increased phenomenally in some districts, and is now the predominating species of waterfowl on Lake Whangape in Lower Waikato, Lake Ellesmere and on the Chatham Islands, and occurs in most other districts in varying numbers. Cutten (1966) indicates that some 5000 pairs bred at Lake Ellesmere in 1963-64. Wodzicki (1965) records that they are now widespread and common in the North and South Islands and on Stewart Island. Scott (1972) says that the evidence available indicates that there are now some 200 000 Black Swans in New Zealand.

Europe, America and Japan. The Black Swan is well acclimatised in Europe and America, where they breed freely, but has never been established in a feral state (Delacour, 1954). Odd pairs appear to escape from time to time but no one seems to have released large numbers of them (Scott, 1972). Some have been introduced to eastern Quebec (Blake, 1975), but it is not known whether they are established as wild birds.

In England they were introduced as early as 1851 at Carshalton, Surrey, and apparently bred there.

Black Swans were established in some parks and zoos in Japan following the second World War. Pairs were introduced in the Kyoto, Tokyo and Osaka areas between 1955 and 1960, and have bred there in a captive and semi-captive state (Kikkawa and Yamashina, 1966).

Tahiti. Evidently Black Swans were introduced to

Tahiti in about 1938 (Guild, 1938), but apparently have not survived there in the wild.

DAMAGE

In New Zealand it has been reported (Oliver, 1955) that Black Swans compete for food with native ducks and the pukeko, causing them to leave their feeding grounds. However, there appears to have been little research on the subject. The population in New Zealand is now apparently managed on a massive scale (Scott, 1972), many birds are shot on organised drives and many eggs are collected under permit and sold.

SPUR-WINGED GOOSE

Plectropterus gambensis (Linnaeus)

DISTINGUISHING CHARACTERISTICS

Males 5.4-6.8 and up to 10 kg (12-15, and up to 22 lb); females 4-5.4 kg (9-12 lb)

Large black and white bird; iridescent bronze and green on upper parts; abdomen white; bare skin around eyes and sides of face and neck grey; frontal knob dull purplish red; pinkish patch from bill and around eye; bill dusky, but pinkish at base.

Delacour, vol.3, 1959, pp.136-7 and pl.p.128.

GENERAL DISTRIBUTION

Africa south of the Sahara Desert.

INTRODUCED DISTRIBUTION

Introduced unsuccessfully to Western Australia.

GENERAL HABITS

Status: common. *Habitat:* swamps, marshes, lakes and rivers, open grasslands and cultivation. *Gregariousness:* generally flocks up to 50, sometimes enormous flocks. *Movements:* sedentary. *Foods:* young grass, seeds, crops, fallen figs and some small animals. *Breeding:* irregular, throughout year. *Nest:* cup of reeds and roots in grass, reed beds, ant hills, trees or hills amongst rocks. *Eggs:* 7-15, or more.

Spur-winged Goose

Mackworth-Praed and Grant, 1952-73, ser.1, vol.1, p.114; ser.2, vol.1, p.113; ser.3, vol.1, p.91.

NOTES ON INTRODUCTIONS

Western Australia. The Spur-winged Goose was probably liberated in Western Australia some time after 1912, and some may have been released up until about 1920 (Long, 1972). During this period releases may have been made at such places as Moora, Wagin, Coolup and Pinjarra in the south-west. The species did not become established and there are no further records of the birds which were released.

DAMAGE

In Africa the Spur-winged Goose can cause damage to crops (Mackworth-Praed and Grant, 1962). According to Rutgers and Norris (1970) they visit cultivated fields and sometimes cause great damage to crops of young grain, sweet potatoes and groundnuts.

CAPE BARREN GOOSE
Cereopsis novaehollandiae Latham

DISTINGUISHING CHARACTERISTICS

75-100 cm (29.5-39 in). 3.6-5.9 kg (8-13 lb)
Generally ash-grey with whitish crown; wings black spotted; upper tail-coverts and tail black; bill black with a large greenish yellow cere.
Frith, 1967, pp.126-7.
Reader's Digest, 1977, pl.p.99.

GENERAL DISTRIBUTION

Southern Australia: islands off the coast of southern Australia from the Recherche Archipelago (Western Australia) to the Furneaux Group (northern Tasmania). Visits mainland coastal swamps in Victoria, South Australia and south-west Western Australia.

INTRODUCED DISTRIBUTION

Introduced successfully to New Zealand but has probably now failed; probably re-introduced on King Island (Bass Strait), Australia.

GENERAL HABITS

Status: uncommon, but increased numbers in some areas due to cultivation. *Habitat:* offshore islands with grass and scrub, pastures and swamp edges. *Gregariousness:* small to large flocks up to 250. *Movements:* sedentary, but local movements from breeding to feeding grounds. *Foods:* grass. *Breeding:* May-Dec. *Nest:* on the ground, lined with grass and down, but occasionally in a bush or tree. *Eggs:* 4-6.
Frith, 1967, pp.127-137.
Reader's Digest, 1977, p.99.

NOTES ON INTRODUCTIONS

New Zealand. Before 1869, the Auckland Acclimatisation Society liberated two Cape Barren Geese at River Head; in 1871 the Canterbury Society received two birds (Thomson, 1922). Both these introductions apparently failed (Thomson, 1922; Williams, 1968) but a third introduction may have been temporarily successful.

In 1912, the Otago Society received two Cape Barren Geese and bred them at the Government Poultry Farm at Milton. Four of the progeny were liberated at Lake Hawea in 1914 or 1915, and the remaining birds were sent to a hatchery at Clinton (Thomson; Williams). According to Williams, five young were reared on Lake Hawea in 1916 and more the following year.

A pair of birds from Clinton was liberated at Minarets Station, Lake Wanaka in 1917.

Although Thomson records that the geese were 'doing well' by 1920, Williams has indicated that in the Annual Report of the Otago Society for 1923 it is mentioned that only a few were at the head of Lake Hawea and in the Lake Wanaka district. Some twenty-seven birds were there in 1927 and some were reported from Lake Hawea and Lake Thomson in 1936. Williams says that the birds noted in 1927 were subjected to illegal hunting and that the last was seen

Cape Barren Goose

in 1946 in the Hunter Valley. He gives further records of their occurrence in New Zealand but claims that they were probably birds blown there by winds from Australia. Two were seen at Lake Thomson, west of Middle Fiord of Lake Te Anau in 1934, two on Lake Maree in south-west Fiordland in 1947, two on Lake Hankinson also in 1947, some on the Ahuriri River in 1966 and one at Sutherland Sound, Fiordland, in 1967.

Wodzicki (1965) records that the species is still established locally in the South Island of New Zealand, but Falla *et al* (1966) indicate that there are no subsequent records after 1947. It is doubtful that the species is at present established in New Zealand.

King Island. The Cape Barren Goose reaches King Island naturally. McGarvie and Templeton (1974) report six birds at Reekara in August 1972. They state that thirty-eight half-grown goslings were introduced in December 1972 and are now dispersed over the island in small groups.

DAMAGE

On Flinders and other islands in Bass Strait, Cape Barren Geese have substantially increased in numbers, probably due to the clearing of Atriplex scrub and subsequent conversion to pastures (Guiler, 1974). Guiler reports that these increases have led to the appearance of certain sensitive areas where goose pressure upon agriculture has become intolerable. Farmers complain that the geese eat and trample young crops, foul crops and water holes and damage clover pastures. Guiler suggested management to reduce the damage and preserve the status of the birds.

Oliver (1955) says that in New Zealand sheep will not graze on pastures that have been browsed by Cape Barren Geese, but there appear to be no records of this actually happening and it is doubtful if they were ever in sufficient numbers in New Zealand for this to have occurred.

SNOW GOOSE
(Blue Goose, Lesser Snow Goose, Greater Snow Goose)
Anser caerulescens (Linnaeus)

DISTINGUISHING CHARACTERISTICS

63-79 cm (25-31 in). 1.8-4.7 kg (4-10.3 lb)

All white, but often rust stained on head, with black wing tips; bill pink, black on edges. Also an all blue phase: ashy blue-grey, with head, neck, rump, tail-coverts, vent and parts or whole of the abdomen and breast white.

Delacour, vol.1, 1954, p.125 and pl.7, p.128.

Palmer, vol.2, 1976, pp.122-129.

GENERAL DISTRIBUTION

North America, Greenland and eastern Asia: Arctic coast of north-eastern Siberia, northern Alaska, Arctic Canada and northern Greenland. In winter south to Korea (rare), Japan, California and along the Gulf Coast to Mexico, Texas to western Florida, and from New Jersey to South Carolina and the West Indies (rare).

INTRODUCED DISTRIBUTION

Introduced unsuccessfully in New Zealand.

GENERAL HABITS

Status: common. *Habitat:* tundra (summer), fresh and saltwater marshes, ponds, bays, lakes, streams and grain fields. *Gregariousness:* huge flocks up to hundreds of thousands on migration, at other times small flocks. *Movements:* migratory. *Foods:* grass and other vegetation, berries and insects. *Breeding:* May-July; in loose colonies or solitary. *Nest:* down lined hollow in tundra. *Eggs:* 2-5, 8.

Palmer, vol.2, 1976, pp.130-153.

NOTES ON INTRODUCTIONS

New Zealand. In 1877, the Auckland Acclimatisation Society received ten birds from a Mr T. Russell and ultimately liberated them at Matamata, but they

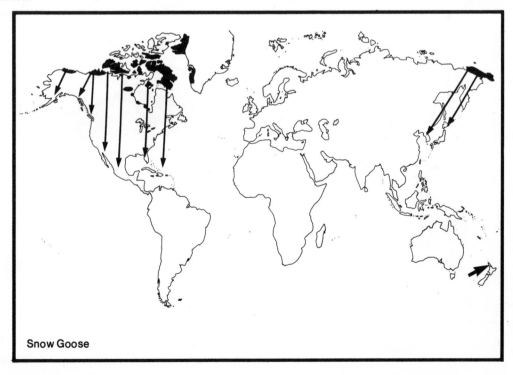

Snow Goose

failed to become established (Thomson, 1922). The race introduced appears to have been that of the Lesser Snow Goose *(A.c. hyperborea)*.

DAMAGE

None known.

GREYLAG GOOSE

Anser anser (Linnaeus)

DISTINGUISHING CHARACTERISTICS

75-90 cm (29.5-35.4 in). 2-4.5 kg (4.4-10 lb)

Head, neck and upper parts grey-brown; lower breast and abdomen dull white; upper parts marked with darker transverse lines; rump and wing-coverts blue-grey; bill orange to pinkish white, with white tip.

Delacour, vol.1, 1954, pp.98, 100-101 and pl.5, p.104.

GENERAL DISTRIBUTION

Eurasia: Iceland, Scotland, discontinuous distribution in Europe, across Asia to Manchuria and south-eastern Siberia. (Disintegration of the breeding range probably resulted from direct persecution by man and the species originally extended over the whole of Europe.)

Winters in south of breeding range, south to the Mediterranean, North Africa, Iraq, Iran, and parts of southern Asia including northern India and Indochina.

INTRODUCED DISTRIBUTION

Re-introduced successfully in Great Britain; introduced unsuccessfully in New Zealand.

GENERAL HABITS

Status: range reduced, but fairly common. *Habitat:* rivers, lakes, grain fields and grasslands. *Gregariousness:* flocks of six to hundreds or even thousands, but family groups or small flocks while breeding. *Movements:* migratory. *Foods:* grass, water plants, grain and crops (including potatoes, turnips and other tubers). *Breeding:* Mar-June.

Nest: scraped hollow on ground amongst reeds near water, often made of heather, reeds or twigs and lined with down. *Eggs:* 4-7, 12 (Britain 3-9, 15).

Delacour, vol.1, 1954, pp.99, 101-102.

NOTES ON INTRODUCTIONS

Great Britain. The Greylag has been exterminated as a breeding species over most of Britain with the exception of parts of north-west Scotland and the Hebrides.

Re-introductions occurred in south-west Scotland, around 1930, when Lord William Percy brought eggs and later goslings from the native colony on South Uist to Lochinch near Stranraer in Wigtownshire (Young, 1972).

According to Young, birds from various sources were also introduced between 1933 and 1942 by G. Maxwell to Monreith, Wigtownshire, and spread to nearby lochs at Mochrum. Some were placed on Barfad Loch around 1960 and some on Logan House Loch, from Lochinch stock, possibly at about the same date. Birds hatched from Lochinch eggs were introduced to Earlstoun Loch, Kirkcudbrightshire in 1967. Other colonies, now between Dumfries and Stranraer in south-west Scotland, have resulted from colonisation mainly from the original population at Lochinch.

Young indicates that from three colonies established in the early 1940s (first record of breeding in 1939) there was little extension in range until about 1951 when a pair bred at Loch Ochiltree, some thirty-two kilometres (twenty miles) from Lochinch. They became established at Loch Dornal in 1957, continued to increase in numbers and range, and reached many places in Galloway. They now breed in four counties (Wigtownshire, Kirkcudbrightshire, Dumfriesshire and Ayrshire) at some thirty or more sites. An estimate in 1971 of the total population was 1160 birds, numbers appearing to increase at the rate of 4.6 per cent per annum.

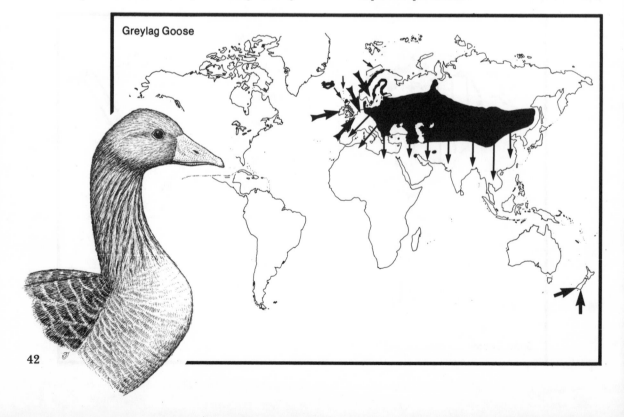

Greylag Goose

Since 1961, eggs have been donated to the Wildfowlers Association of Great Britain and Ireland and these have been used to found colonies elsewhere in Britain. By 1970 this Association had released 938 hand-reared Greylags at thirty-three sites in thirteen English and Welsh counties (Ellwood, 1971). A feral population in east Norfolk probably descended from two birds brought from Scotland before the second World War. A semi-feral colony at Castlecoole is believed to date from about 1700 (Fitter, 1959). A number of other birds have escaped from ornamental ponds where waterfowl collections are kept. Some thirty-nine birds imported from Belgium were released in Kent in 1973 and there is now an expanding population there (Sharrock, 1976). Feral groups are now widely scattered through a large part of England and Scotland and there are probably in the vicinity of 700-800 breeding pairs in Britain and Ireland of which about seventy-five per cent are derived from introduced stock.

Europe. Greylag geese have been introduced locally in Belgium, Sweden and to the Netherlands with some success (Cramp and Simmons, 1977).

New Zealand. In about 1769, Captain Cook is said to have liberated five geese from the Cape of Good Hope at Dusky Sound on the east coast of the South Island, New Zealand. It is thought that those released may have been of this species.

In 1867, the Southland Acclimatisation Society liberated seven geese (probably *A.a. cinereus*) at Mataura River, but these birds apparently disappeared. The Otago Society placed goose eggs in swans' nests on Lake Onslow (Upper Taieri) in 1892. Apparently the eggs hatched and young were raised. These birds were allowed to breed and increase in numbers, but were reported to have been nearly shot out by 1905 (Thomson, 1922). Thomson also reports the sighting of a flock of twenty geese on the east lagoon on Ruapuke in Foveaux Straits in 1887, and

another flock some years later at Bench Island (perhaps Greylag geese?).

DAMAGE

In England the Greylag occasionally feeds on agricultural crops such as grass, winter wheat, spring cereals, grain, potatoes, swedes, kale and bean crops (Kear, 1964). Kear says that some damage can be caused to grass and other crops but that the main damage appears to be to potato and swede turnip crops. The birds may feed on unharvested potatoes and make harvesting difficult by trampling. In some areas they have increased in numbers in recent years and damage amounting to up to ten per cent of the swede turnip crop has been recorded.

BEAN GOOSE
(Pink-footed Goose)
Anser fabalis (Latham)

DISTINGUISHING CHARACTERISTICS

60-90 cm (23.6-35.4 in). 1.5-4.3 kg (3.3-9.4 lb)
Generally grey-brown, head and neck darker brown; breast and back lighter; pale edges to feathers of mantle, wings and sides; upper and under tail-coverts white; tail ash-brown, edges and tips white; bill black with yellow (or pink) patch near tip.

Delacour, vol.1, 1954, pp.114, 116, 118-9, 122, 123 and pl.6, p.120.

GENERAL DISTRIBUTION

Eurasia: Iceland, Greenland, Spitzbergen, northern Norway, Sweden, Finland, USSR, northern Mongolia and the Altai. In winter south to southern Europe and southern Asia as far as the Mediterranean, the Black and Caspian seas, Asia Minor, Iran, Turkestan, China and Japan.

INTRODUCED DISTRIBUTION

Introduced in Finland, but its present status is not known.

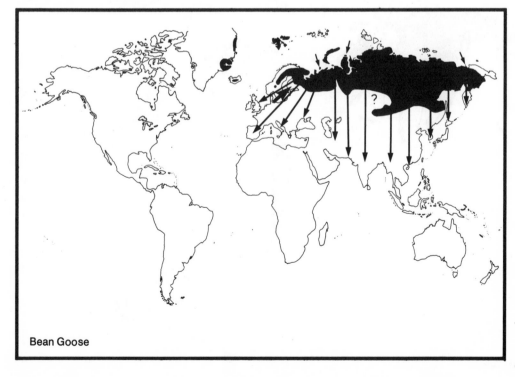

Bean Goose

GENERAL HABITS

Status: fairly common. *Habitat:* muddy seashores, marshes, lakes, slow flowing rivers, grass steppes, meadows, rice fields, tundra, coniferous forest and taiga. *Gregariousness:* small groups or flocks, but in winter several hundred to thousands on migration. *Movements:* migratory. *Foods:* mainly vegetable material (i.e., buds, stalks, grass, leaves and seeds), occasionally grain, insects and crustaceans. *Breeding:* May-July; partly colonial. *Nest:* depression, lined with grass, moss, etc., and down, on islands, under trees or bushes, in open country or on rocky slopes. *Eggs:* 3-8.

Delacour, vol.1, 1954, pp.114-125.

NOTES ON INTRODUCTIONS

Finland. The Bean Goose was experimentally introduced in the western parts of central Finland (Sainio, 1966) in the 1960s, but the results of the attempt are not known.

DAMAGE

In Scotland the Pink-footed Goose sometimes feeds on agricultural crops such as corn, but the chief conflict with agriculture occurs in spring when they graze young grass (Newton and Campbell, 1970, in Palmer, 1976) which would be available to stock.

CANADA GOOSE
(Honker)
Branta canadensis (Linnaeus)

DISTINGUISHING CHARACTERISTICS

55-100 cm (21.6-39.3 in). Three forms differ markedly in size, largest from 3.6-6.4 kg (8-14 lb) and smallest 1-1.6 kg (2.2-3.5 lb)

Generally grey-brown with large white chin strap from cheek patches; remainder of head and neck black; underparts brownish grey, pale tipped; tail black; bill black.

Delacour, vol.1, 1954, p.160, pl.8.
Palmer, vol.2, 1976, pp.183-188.

GENERAL DISTRIBUTION

North America: Komandorskiye Islands, western Alaska, eastwards across the Arctic mainland, Southampton and southern Baffin Islands to Labrador and Newfoundland. South to north-eastern California, Utah, Kansas and Massachusetts. In winter south to Japan (Honshū), northern Baja California, mainland Mexico and the Gulf States. Accidental to Asia on Komandorskiye and Kurile Islands, western Greenland (breeds occasionally), Hawaiian Islands and the West Indies.

INTRODUCED DISTRIBUTION

Introduced successfully in Europe and New Zealand. Re-introduced in some areas of the USA and Canada. Introduced unsuccessfully to the Hawaiian Islands (? failed), and to Western Australia.

GENERAL HABITS

Status: range reduced, but common. *Habitat:* lakes, bays, marshes, coastal plains, prairies, grain fields and tundra. *Gregariousness:* flocks, sometimes made up of family parties, from a few to hundreds of birds; flocks on migration may reach 50 000 birds. *Movements:* sedentary (some areas) and migratory. *Foods:* grass and other vegetation including seeds, berries and grain and also worms, insects and snails. *Breeding:* Mar-June (Britain Mar-June; New Zealand Oct-Jan). *Nest:* platform, lined with sticks

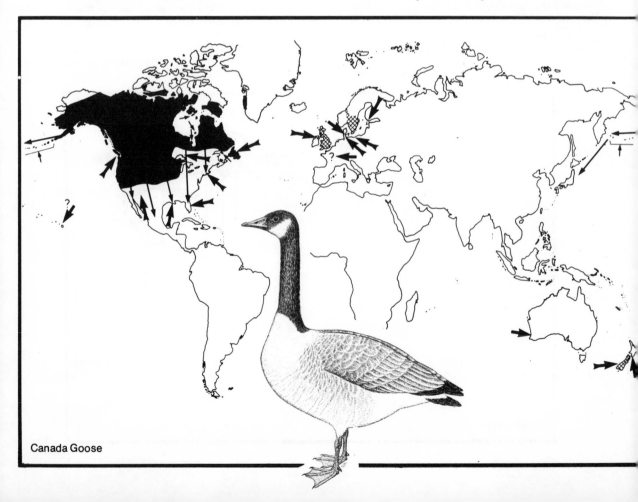

Canada Goose

and down, on the ground, or on a muskrat house, islet, in marshes, old trees or on cliffs. *Eggs:* 2-6, 11 (Britain 3-7; New Zealand 4-6).

Van Wormer, 1968.

Palmer, vol.2, 1976, pp.188-234.

NOTES ON INTRODUCTIONS

Europe. The Atlantic Canada Goose *(B.c. canadensis)* was brought to Europe probably before 1676 as some were present in St James Park, London, at this time. They had been breeding in large numbers in the park at Versailles, France, since early times (Delacour, 1954). Lever (1977) records that they were kept from about 1665 onwards on many· estates in England.

The species has become well established and breeds in a feral state in Great Britain and Sweden, and has occurred in Ireland, The Faeroes, Norway, Denmark, Holland and France (Peterson *et al,* 1963).

Lever reports that the first record of escaped birds in England appears to be that of a single bird which was shot at Brentford in Middlesex in 1731. The species was often found at large during the nineteenth century and twentieth century introductions include: at Leighton, Montgomeryshire in 1908; at Radipole Lake, near Weymouth, Dorset, before 1932; at West Wycombe Park, Buckinghamshire, in 1933-34; in Kent by the Wildfowlers Association of Great Britain and Ireland in the 1950s; at Frampton, Gloucestershire, by the Wildfowl Trust in 1953; and at Anglesey, Pembrokeshire, Staffordshire and at Hyde Park, London, from Leicestershire and Yorkshire in 1955.

Between 1953 and 1957 the Wildfowl Trust (and in the late 1950s the Wildfowlers Association) caught and transferred some 1400 or more birds. These transfers resulted in an enormous increase in the population of the Canada Goose in Britain between 1953 and 1969.

The species was fairly widespread prior to 1938, but scarce in the south-west, most of the northern counties, and also in Wales. Their numbers had decreased in Scotland, although they were still well established in several parts of the Tay and Forth areas but scarce elsewhere. They had been recorded breeding at Antrim, Down and at Dublin, Northern Ireland, and noted in some other areas (Witherby *et al,* 1938).

By 1953 between 2000 and 4000 birds were present, distributed in isolated groups, but there was little attempt to colonise new waters (Blurton-Jones, 1956); however, during the 1950s and 1960s many birds were caught and released in new waters and the population in 1967-68 numbered about 10 500 (Ogilvie, 1969). There were 200 birds in Ireland in 1970 (Merne, 1970).

Although the transplanting of birds has virtually ceased, the geese have now established themselves in many new areas. A census in 1976 revealed that the population had increased to some 19 400 birds, an annual growth rate of eight per cent (Ogilvie, 1977).

The Canada Goose now has a wide range in Great Britain from the south coast of England almost to the Scottish border in the north, in Dumfriesshire, Perthshire and East Lothian in Scotland, and on the east coast of Northern Ireland. The population continued to increase in the 1970s and at the present rate is expected to be in the vicinity of 40 000 birds by 1985 (Ogilvie, 1977).

Canada Geese were first introduced into the wild in Sweden in 1933, spread rapidly and are now widely distributed (Fabricius, 1970). Fabricius says they breed there in evident harmony with other native geese, and are migratory, wintering in Denmark, Germany, Holland and 'Belgium.

The first Canada Geese probably were imported by Bengt Berg from North America and Holland, and the first Swedish brood was hatched at Varnanes in the Kalmar area in 1930. Berg apparently released some geese at Blekinge and these were likely to have been the source of stock for numerous other releases (Tangen, 1974). In 1960 there existed in Sweden some 150 nesting pairs, which had built up to about 2000 by about 1970, with a total population of almost 10 000 geese.

An increasing number of Canada Geese shelter in Denmark during the winter, and they are observed along the North Sea coast for longer periods. Numbers apparently fluctuate from month to month and from year to year. In January 1969 over 630 were counted (Fog, 1972). In the mid-1930s attempts were made to establish Canada Geese in Denmark, but those released gradually decreased in numbers and eventually disappeared and the species remains only as a park bird.

Canada Geese were imported into Finland from Sweden in the summer of 1964, and established themselves locally in the environs of Porvoo (east of Helsinki). Prior to 1971 two pairs had produced some twenty-nine young (Korhonen, 1973) but the species does not seem to have spread much.

According to Lund (1963), the first Canada Geese were imported to Norway in 1936 by T. Røer and eleven were released at Nesodden, Oslo. No further releases were documented until efforts to establish the species recommenced in 1958.

From 1958 until at least 1972 a number of introductions occurred in Norway. Canada Geese were released in Orkdal, South-Trøndelag in 1958-60 (nine birds), and between 1963 and 1966 at Meraker in North-Trøndelag (twenty-seven); in 1965-66 at inner Bjugn, off Ørlandet, Trondheimsfjorden (six), and also at Østensjøv, Oslo (four); in 1970 at Steinkjer, North-Trøndelag (twenty-five); and in 1972 at Storelval (eight), Bømlo (ten) and at Frognerdam (eight) and Ekeberg (fifteen), near Oslo (Tangen, 1974).

The species now appears to be fairly well established around Trondheim and Oslo and is regularly observed between these areas. Tangen indicates that Norway can now expect a significant population of Canada Geese during the next fifteen to twenty years if suitable biotopes are utilised and there is a willingness to make the introduction of the species a success.

The race or races at present in Europe have not been definitely established. Palmer (1976) suggests that those in the British Isles are *moffitti* and those in Norway and Sweden are either this race or *interior.*

New Zealand. The Wellington Acclimatisation Society liberated Canada Geese in 1876 (three birds) and in 1879 (fifteen), but these disappeared after a few months (Thomson, 1922).

In 1905 the New Zealand Government imported fifty birds and distributed them widely (Delacour, 1954). Delacour records that the North Canterbury Society received eight birds, of which six were liberated on a lagoon at Glenmark and a pair were kept in the gardens of Hagley Park in Christchurch. Each year progeny from this pair were released elsewhere but the only other colony established was in the Cold Lakes district of Otago.

Thomson reports that the Canterbury Society liberated six birds at Glenmark in 1907 and some at Lake Sumner and Mt. White in 1912. The Southland Society liberated some at Lake Manapouri in 1905 (eleven) and in 1909 (three). The Otago Society liberated some at Telfords Lagoon, Waiwera, in 1912, and at Lake Hawea in 1915 (twelve).

Although Thomson says that the species was doing well in several parts of New Zealand in 1915, the North Canterbury Society imported ten birds (Delacour) from Dr A. R. Baker, Chairman of the Game Conservation Board, Vancouver, in 1920. By 1930 the Canada Goose had disappeared from the North Island, but was well established in several localities in Otago and Canterbury in the South Island (Oliver, 1930). The situation did not seem to change much to the 1950s, although they had become plentiful in those districts in the South Island (Oliver, 1955). In the North Canterbury and Otago districts a brief shooting season was opened in 1925 (Imber and Williams, 1968). Later, protection was removed and the species could be shot throughout the year (Delacour).

The Canada Goose is now widespread and common in the South Island (Wodzicki, 1965) and according to Falla et al (1966) they are abundant at Canterbury and Otago, but do not breed in the North Island of New Zealand.

The 1920 introductions were probably made with the race B.c. taverneri, but in 1950 B.c. canadensis was introduced to the North Canterbury region and so the present population may be a mixed one (Delacour). Palmer (1976) suggests that the birds are possibly of the race moffitti although Yokum (1970) and Imber (1971) considered them to be maxima.

Hawaiian Islands. According to Scheffer (1967), Canada Geese were introduced to these islands for the control of pasture insect pests. Their present status is not known, but it would appear that they did not become established there.

Western Australia. The Canada Goose was introduced in the south-west of Western Australia between 1912 and 1920 (Long, 1972), and again at a later date, but they failed to become established.

USA. Since the 1930s several races of the Canada Goose have been involved in numerous transplantings and releases of wild and semi-domesticated birds (A.O.U., 1957). The first successful re-establishment of the species appears to have been in 1927, when the bird was restored as a nesting species, at the Kellogg Bird Sanctuary, Wintergreen, Lake Michigan (Pirnie, 1938). Since then a number of programmes have been successfully initiated to establish them in areas where they were extirpated or have not formerly nested (Nelson, 1963; Dill and Lee, 1970). The race B.c. canadensis has been introduced into several parts of the former range of the Giant Canada Goose (maxima) which at the time appeared to be extinct (Delacour, 1954). Introductions and transplants of the race interior have been numerous and breeding flocks have been established in New York and perhaps other places. Some were released at Sherburne Game Farm (two to forty birds per year) in New York State as early as 1919, where they bred locally, and in two other localities in 1934 with the same results (Bump, 1941). In the early 1970s some were transplanted from New Jersey to Maine and northern and central Florida. The race moffitti has also been introduced and transplanted widely, particularly in the prairie regions (Palmer, 1976). Forty-three geese transplanted in 1939 from Bear R. Refuge in northern Utah east to Necedah Refuge in central Wisconsin apparently migrate as far as Montana and southern Illinois (Samson, 1971, in Palmer). Canada Geese introduced to the White Mountain area of Arizona from 1966 had raised young there in 1972.

According to Hankla (1968), in the south-east of the United States a transplant programme involving some 20 734 geese has resulted in the doubtful establishment of only one new migratory population. However, some success appears to have been achieved in south-western Louisiana where twenty-seven birds obtained from Wisconsin were placed in the Rockefeller Wildlife Refuge in October 1960 (Chalbreck et al, 1974). In February 1961 a further thirty-four birds were added; mostly crippled birds picked up from public shooting areas, as were those of the first release. A pair nested in 1961 and five pairs nested in 1962, so the project appeared to establish a resident flock which is increasing.

Canada. About a dozen birds of the race B.c. canadensis were transferred from Okanagan Valley to Elk Lake near Victoria, Vancouver Island, in 1931, and established a population there; 200 birds existed around Elk Lake in 1957-58 but now appear to have dispersed in smaller flocks in a number of localities on the Saanich Peninsula (Carl and Guiguet, 1972).

In more recent years other transfers and introductions have been made by private individuals to the lower mainland and on Vancouver Island (Halliday, 1971, in Carl and Guiguet).

In Newfoundland nesting colonies of the race canadensis may have begun with escaped captive stock augmented by birds from the wild. Breeding flocks of the race interior have also been established in Ontario (Palmer, 1976).

One of the most successful re-introductions of Canada Geese (race maxima) in North America occurred when seventy birds were released at Marshy Point in Manitoba (Cooper, 1978) between 1951 and 1957. Establishment was effected by holding the birds in captivity until they had nested, reducing hunter mortality and by feeding them even after release. Numbers in the area rose from 100 in 1957 to some 10 000 birds by 1969 and 1970.

DAMAGE

Canada Geese became a problem in New Zealand because they almost exclusively inhabit privately farmed areas in predominantly agricultural country (Imber and Williams, 1968). They graze pastures and cattle and sheep will not feed there after this happens (Oliver, 1955).

Imber and Williams say that complaints from farmers about these geese increased until in 1931 legal protection was removed. They continued to cause concern until 1963, but had been able to increase their numbers despite the lack of protection. Between 1950-51 some 3000 were killed and in 1951-52 about 1700 were killed by the Wildlife Service in the North Canterbury area.

Where Canada Geese have been introduced in England they have been reported to feed on a number of agricultural crops, e.g. grass, winter wheat, spring cereals, grain and bean crops; the damage is generally small (Kear, 1964). Various control measures have been resorted to, including the destruction of eggs, shooting and the rounding up of birds and transporting them to other sites. This latter measure which appeared to be successful in earlier years was probably largely responsible for the increase in population and range during the 1950s and early 1960s.

HAWAIIAN GOOSE
(Nene, Sandwich Island Goose)
Branta sandvicensis (Vigors)

DISTINGUISHING CHARACTERISTICS
55-75 cm (21.6-29.5 in). 1.8-2.3 kg (4-5 lb)
Heavily barred, grey-brown goose; crown, face and throat black; cheeks yellow-buff; neck buff with dark ribbing; breast brown; rump, retrices and primaries black; tail-coverts white with grey bases; bill black.
Berger, 1972, p.73 and pl.23, p.58.

GENERAL DISTRIBUTION
Hawaiian Islands: confined to the island of Hawaii, but formerly on Maui.

INTRODUCED DISTRIBUTION
Re-introduced successfully on Hawaii and Maui in the Hawaiian Islands. Possibly introduced, unsuccessfully, in New Zealand.

GENERAL HABITS
Status: very rare. *Habitat:* sparsely vegetated areas on old lava flows. *Gregariousness:* pairs, or small groups or flocks. *Movements:* sedentary. *Foods:* vegetation, leaves and berries. *Breeding:* Oct-Mar; 2-3 clutches per year. *Nest:* down lined hollow in sparsely vegetated area on lava flow. *Eggs:* 2-8.
Berger, 1972, pp.73-75.

NOTES ON INTRODUCTIONS
Hawaii and Maui. Prior to the re-introductions the species had become very rare (Peterson, 1961) and probably numbered less than one hundred wild live birds (Gaselee, 1963).

Restoration of the species began in about 1949 (Berger, 1972) and has continued since then, with some success, until the present time.

Until 1957 only thirty-six birds were bred in captivity; two of them were sent to the Wildfowl Trust in England in 1950, two in 1960, and two in 1967 (Berger). Since 1957 they have continued to be bred at Puhakuloa on Hawaii and at the Wildfowl Trust in England (Hawaiian Audubon Society, 1975). From the few birds sent to England the Trust succeeded in raising over 200 birds between 1952 and 1967. At Puhakuloa some 800 were raised between 1950 and 1970 (Berger).

The first releases of Hawaiian Geese were made into the wild in 1960, and by 1969 some 498 birds had been released at three different sites in Hawaii (Walker, 1970). By June 1975 some 1061 had been released on the island of Hawaii and 391 on Maui, all reared at Puhakuloa with the exception of five in 1963 and two in 1965 which were reared in Connecticut, USA, and released on Maui (Department of Lands and Natural Resources, 1976).

In 1962 birds bred in England were returned to the Hawaiian Islands. They were to be established in a

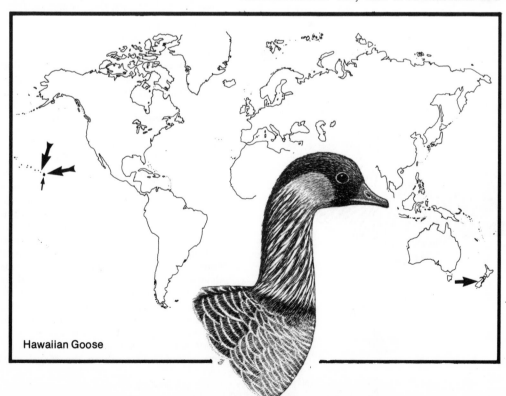

Hawaiian Goose

National Park in the crater of Haleakala on the island of Maui, where the original stock had been exterminated. According to Summer-Smith (1964), thirty-two were returned to Maui and some 210 to the wild in Hawaii. However, Berger later indicates that in efforts to extend the range to Maui, thirty-five were released in the Pakiku area of the Haleakala Crater in 1962 and a total of 242 birds were released there between 1962 and 1969. Of those released 142 were raised in England, ninety-three at Pohakuloa and seven at Connecticut in the USA. Until June 1975 some 197 birds raised in England were released on the island of Maui (Department of Lands and Natural Resources, 1976).

The Hawaiian Audubon Society reports that both the Wildfowl Trust and Pohakuloa bred stock has been provided for re-introduction to Haleakala and their former range on Hawaii. A breeding programme has now begun to re-establish them in former lower elevation habitat in Hawaiian Volcanoes National Park, but any success is not yet known.

New Zealand. Some Hawaiian Geese were imported to New Zealand in 1871, but it is not known if any were released in the wild (Thomson, 1922).

DAMAGE
None known.

MAGELLAN GOOSE
(Greater or Lesser Magellan Goose, Falkland Upland Goose)
Chloephaga picta (Gmelin)

DISTINGUISHING CHARACTERISTICS
57-72.5 cm (22.4-28.3 in)
Variable species, white with black or black and white tail; black bars on mantle and flanks (entirely or part); wings white and dark grey; speculum metallic green; bill black. Female: smaller, deep reddish

Magellan Goose

Magellan Goose, *Chloephaga picta*

cinnamon, barred with black on mantle and lower parts.
Delacour, vol.1, 1954, pp.216, 218-19, 220 and pl.12, p.224.

GENERAL DISTRIBUTION
South America: southern Argentina, Chile and Tierra del Fuego, and also the Falkland Islands. Partial winter migrant to Colchagua, Chile, and Buenos Aires Province, Argentina.

INTRODUCED DISTRIBUTION
Introduced but now extirpated on South Georgia Island (South Atlantic Ocean) and Great Britain.

GENERAL HABITS
Status: fairly common. *Habitat:* lagoons, rivers and sea coasts, also semi-arid grasslands away from water. *Gregariousness:* small parties, but large flocks to 100 birds outside breeding season. *Movements:* partially migratory (in extreme north and extreme south of range) and sedentary. *Foods:* grass and other vegetation. *Breeding:* Aug-Nov (or later ?). *Nest:* a grass or twig nest lined with down in dry situations amongst bushes and grass. *Eggs:* 5-8.
Delacour, vol.1, 1954, pp.217-221.

NOTES ON INTRODUCTIONS
South Georgia. The race *C.p. leucoptera* from the Falkland Islands has been established on South Georgia Island (Delacour 1954; Scott, 1965). The species was introduced in about 1910 or 1911 (Bennett, 1926) to provide fresh meat for whale and seal hunters (Watson, 1975). Bennett says that they were increasing in numbers there in the 1920s. Delacour indicates that they were scarce there around 1954 and Watson, who reports that they were never abundant, says that they were extirpated by 1950. Watson also records that a second introduction in 1959 was extirpated shortly afterwards.

Great Britain. An attempt was made (T. Spence, pers. comm.) to establish the Magellan Goose in

Great Britain and although the population reached the hundreds they did not become permanently established.

DAMAGE

In South America the Magellan Goose is regarded locally as a pest because they assemble in large flocks on grasslands. These are grazed until they are bare, and covered with droppings so that the ground is unfit for sheep (Rutgers and Norris, 1970). A bounty was placed on their heads because it was estimated that eight geese ate as much grass as one sheep (Johnson, 1965). Johnson relates how as many as 50 000 eggs were destroyed on one farm alone. Although the birds have declined in numbers they are still abundant in some areas.

WOOD DUCK
(Maned Goose)
Chenonetta jubata (Latham)

DISTINGUISHING CHARACTERISTICS

44-50 cm (17.3-19.6 in). 662-955 g (1.4-2 lb)
Head and neck brown with mane of black feathers; lower back and tail black; general body colour and wings grey; speculum green edged black; abdomen and under tail black; bill dark brown. Female: head brown-grey with white stripe above and below eye; quills black; flanks white.

Frith, 1967, pp.256-257.
Reader's Digest, 1977, pl.p.109.

GENERAL DISTRIBUTION

Australia, but most numerous in the eastern portion.

INTRODUCED DISTRIBUTION

Possibly introduced, unsuccessfully, to the Hawaiian Islands and New Zealand.

GENERAL HABITS

Status: common. *Habitat:* lightly timbered and grassy areas, swamps, lakes and rivers. *Gregariousness:* solitary in breeding season, at other times in large flocks. *Movements:* sedentary and nomadic. *Foods:* green vegetation, mainly grasses. *Breeding:* variable, after rains, mainly Aug-Nov (south), Jan-Mar (north); solitary breeder. *Nest:* hole in a tree, lined with down. *Eggs:* 9-12.
Frith, 1967, pp.257-268.
Reader's Digest, 1977, p.109.

NOTES ON INTRODUCTIONS

Hawaiian Islands. A few Maned Geese were imported to Oahu in 1922, but did not survive (Munro, 1960). Apparently they were not actually released in the wild.
New Zealand. Maned Geese were imported to New Zealand in 1867, but it is not known if any were released in the wild (Thomson, 1922).

DAMAGE

In Australia the species occasionally visits grain fields and causes some damage. At times, when open waters are scarce, they may settle with other species in large flocks on man-made dams where they are accused of fouling the water. The species' successful establishment in the Hawaiian Islands would not have been welcomed in the light of present restoration of some native ducks.

BLACK-BELLIED TREE-DUCK
(Red-billed Whistling Duck, Black-bellied Whistling Duck)
Dendrocygna autumnalis (Linnaeus)

DISTINGUISHING CHARACTERISTICS

38-56 cm (15-22 in). 478-1020 g (1-2.2 lb)
Mostly rusty red-brown; belly black; breast chestnut; greyish facial patch from bill around eye and around chin and throat; white eye-ring; broad white patch on forewing; remainder black; tail black; bill bright coral pink, with bluish nail.
Delacour, vol.1, 1954, pp.46,48-49 and pl.1, p.40.
Palmer, vol.2, 1976, pp.28-30.

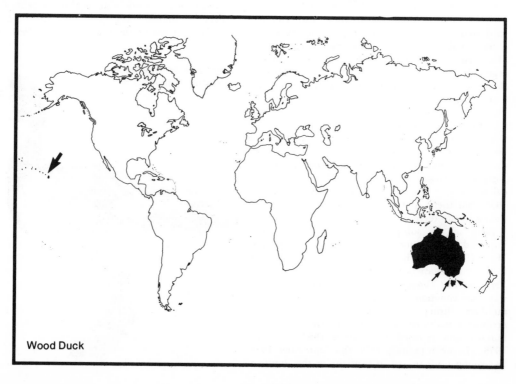

Wood Duck

Black-bellied Tree-Duck

Pierre Wildfowl Trust have been released. Some eleven other birds were also released in Tobago at Speyside.

DAMAGE

In the United States the Black-bellied Tree-Duck is known to attack maize crops.

In Trinidad, before the population was decimated through shooting, flocks of these birds caused damage to rice fields north-west of the Nariva Swamps (Ffrench, 1976). Apparently the need to conserve the species outweighs the damage that they may cause, at least as far as the aviculturists are concerned.

WHITE-FACED TREE-DUCK
(White-faced Whistling Duck)
Dendrocygna viduata (Linnaeus)

DISTINGUISHING CHARACTERISTICS

35-47 cm (13.7-18.5 in). 700 g (1.5 lb)
Face and foreneck white; back of head, neck, band across throat, lower breast, centre of abdomen, lower back, rump and tail black; upper back, breast and shoulders chestnut; mantle brown with buff edged feathers; sides finely barred black and white; bill slate grey with pale band.

Delacour, vol.1, 1954, p.45 and pl.1, p.40.

GENERAL DISTRIBUTION

South America and Africa: From southern Costa Rica south over tropical South America, Trinidad, to northern Argentina, Paraguay and Uruguay; Africa, south of the Sahara Desert to southern Angola, Transvaal and Natal; Malagasy and the Archipel des Comores.

INTRODUCED DISTRIBUTION

Probably introduced to Mauritius, but now extinct.

GENERAL HABITS

Status: very common. *Habitat:* swamps, salt-water lagoons, estuaries, pools and rivers. *Gregariousness:* flocks, and occasionally congregate in huge flocks. *Movements:* considerable local movements (Africa). *Foods:* mainly vegetable material. *Breeding:* variable, most of the year (Africa). *Nest:* of grass

GENERAL DISTRIBUTION

North, Central and South America: from southern Texas to southern Brazil, Paraguay and north-western Argentina, and generally east of the Andes. Vagrant to Lesser Antilles, Virgin Islands and Puerto Rico.

INTRODUCED DISTRIBUTION

Introduced unsuccessfully to Cuba and Jamaica, Greater Antilles; re-introduced on Trinidad and Tobago (re-stocking).

GENERAL HABITS

Status: common. *Habitat:* shallow ponds, lagoons, marshes, rivers, tidal flats; they also frequent cultivated areas feeding on crops. *Gregariousness:* pairs, small groups or sometimes large flocks. *Movements:* sedentary and migratory. *Foods:* vegetable matter and small aquatic animals. *Breeding:* May-Oct. *Nest:* in a tree cavity or in a marsh. *Eggs:* 8-12, 16.

Palmer, vol.2, 1976, pp.31-37.

NOTES ON INTRODUCTIONS

Greater Antilles. The Black-bellied Tree-Duck has been introduced to Cuba and Jamaica on several occasions from Central America (Delacour, 1954). They were released in 1931 in the Province of Pinar del Rio and in the Zapata Swamp in Cuba (Bond, 1956) but there appear to be few recent records of their presence there.

Birds of the subspecies *D.a. autumnalis* were imported to Kingston, Jamaica, from the Spanish Main (Delacour). Bond (1960) indicates that the introductions have been without success.

Trinidad and Tobago. The Black-bellied Tree-Duck was once common on these islands but declined in numbers through shooting. As a conservation measure aviculturists at Pointe-a-Pierre have bred a number and released them since 1967 (Ffrench, 1976). Between January 1967 and September 1975, 243 young birds reared in captivity at the Pointe-a-

White-faced Tree-Duck,
Dendrocygna viduata

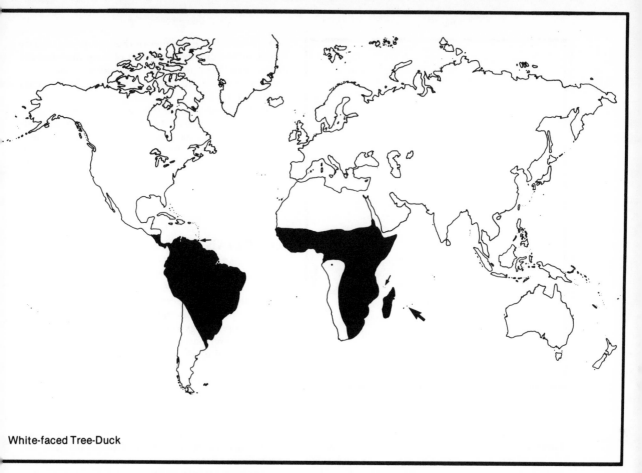

White-faced Tree-Duck

and reeds, down-lined, in a hollow tree, but mainly in reed beds and grass on the ground. *Eggs:* 8-12 (South America); 6-12 (Africa).

Delacour, vol.1, 1954, p.46.

Mackworth-Praed and Grant, 1952-73, ser.1, vol.1, p.108; ser.2, vol.1, p.109; ser.3, vol.1, p.87.

NOTES ON INTRODUCTIONS

Mauritius. The White-faced Tree-Duck is believed to have been introduced to Mauritius probably from Malagasy; however, it may have reached there as a migrant (Rountree *et al*, 1952). Meinertzhagen (1912) reports that it had been introduced from Malagasy recently. The species appears to have become established there as Rountree *et al* say that it is confined to marshy tracts on the coastal plain. However, more recently Staub (1976) says that the species has become extinct due to persistent hunting.

DAMAGE
None known.

PARADISE DUCK
(Paradise Shelduck)
Tadorna variegata (Gmelin)

DISTINGUISHING CHARACTERISTICS
62.5 cm (24.4 in)
Predominantly black, back barred with fine white lines; abdomen reddish-brown; head black with metallic sheen; speculum green; bill black. Female: head white; body bright chestnut.
Delacour, vol.1, 1954, pp.245-246 and pl.13, p.240.

GENERAL DISTRIBUTION
New Zealand: In the South Island and southern part of the North Island.

INTRODUCED DISTRIBUTION
Successfully introduced in the North Island of New Zealand.

GENERAL HABITS
Status: range probably reduced, but still common in most areas. *Habitat:* lakes, estuaries, rivers, mostly in mountains and foothills. *Gregariousness:* pairs and family groups, non-breeding flocks to 150 birds. *Movements:* sedentary, but local movements in winter. *Foods:* vegetable material (grass and herbs) and insects and crustaceans. *Breeding:* Aug-Jan; often double brooded. *Nest:* of grass and down, well hidden on ground or in hollow trees. *Eggs:* 5-11.
Delacour, vol.1, 1954, p.246.

Paradise Duck, *Tadorna variegata*
(male on right, female on left)

Paradise Duck

were released at eight sites in that district in January 1965, although only forty-eight of them may actually have been liberated. The only other introduction known involved at least twelve birds at Te Paki Station in 1961.

Williams concluded that at least 506 Paradise Ducks had been released in Northland but that many releases may not have been recorded. Nevertheless, the species has now become increasingly common in Northland and is now found throughout the North Island.

DAMAGE

None known.

EGYPTIAN GOOSE
Alopochen aegyptiacus (Linnaeus)

DISTINGUISHING CHARACTERISTICS

63-73 cm (25-29 in). 1.5-2.5 kg (3.3-5.5 lb)
Generally buff, but varies from pale to brown; chestnut patch from bill around eye and also on breast; upper wings white, lower with iridescent green sheen on lower parts and chestnut above; primaries, rump and tail black; bill mottled pale pink, dusky at base.

Delacour, vol.1, 1954, pp.235-236 and pl.13, p.240.
Cramp and Simmons, vol.1, 1977, pp.447, 450 and pls.57 and 61.

GENERAL DISTRIBUTION

Africa: except the desert and deep forest areas, extending to Palestine, Syria and further north.
Sporadic in Europe.

INTRODUCED DISTRIBUTION

Occurs in a feral state in Europe. Introduced unsuccessfully in New Zealand, Australia and the USA.

GENERAL HABITS

Status: common; common in captivity in some parts of the world. *Habitat:* streams, dams, ponds, rivers and marshes. *Gregariousness:* pairs, small parties, or large flocks after breeding. *Movements:* sedentary (and possibly somewhat nomadic). *Foods:* grass, leaves, seeds and animal food. *Breeding:* July-Jan, and later, Mar-Apr (Britain). *Nest:* grass and reeds lined with grey down, on the ground or in holes in trees or cliffs. *Eggs:* 5-9, 12.

Delacour, vol.1, 1954, pp.237-238.

NOTES ON INTRODUCTIONS

Europe. The Egyptian Goose is probably better established than many waterfowl as a captive and feral bird in various parts of the world (Delacour, 1954). Although they occur sporadically in Europe the majority recorded are feral birds. Free-living populations have been established in England, France and probably other countries, although they are never found in large numbers.

During the nineteenth century when efforts were made to introduce a number of new plants and animals into France, Egyptian Geese were propagated on a large scale and a large breed was selected. There are not, however, many of these birds left today (Delacour).

Egyptian Geese are still established in a feral state in England, but present stocks are small (Scott, 1965) although the species maintains its numbers by breeding in the wild (Sharrock, 1972).

NOTES ON INTRODUCTIONS

New Zealand. The Paradise Duck originally occurred only in the southern section of the North Island. There have been a number of liberations in the centre of that island and the species was in the mid-1960s well established and breeding south of a line approximately from Tailhope to East Cape and was extending its range further northwards (Falla *et al,* 1966).

Liberation of Paradise Ducks in the centre of the North Island occurred in 1915 and 1917 when eight birds were released at Mahuia Prison Camp (Williams, 1971). Williams records that shortly after this release they became established on Rotoaira, and fifteen more birds were added in 1920-21.

Many were liberated in Northland from the National Park (Waimarino District) but the records are incomplete and inconsistent with the numbers of birds supplied. Some time prior to 1936 they were released on Lake Rotomahana, where Oliver (1955) says that they were shot out in a very short time. However, Williams reports that they became locally abundant in the area. Oliver mentions that the species was transferred to Kapiti in about 1931 and to Kawau by Sir George Grey.

A number of introductions of the Paradise Duck occurred between 1959 and 1969. Williams reports that forty to fifty were released in the Whangarei district in 1959, and in 1961 or 1962 some twenty-four pairs from Gisborne and Waimarino were also released. Further birds were forwarded to the area in 1963 (probably 182), but there is no record of their liberation and about 100 may have been released into the area in 1969.

The Bay of Plenty Islands Acclimatisation Society liberated ten birds onto Lake Owhareiti in January 1964 and approval for one hundred more was given, but no release was documented. The Hobson Acclimatisation Society reported that eighty birds

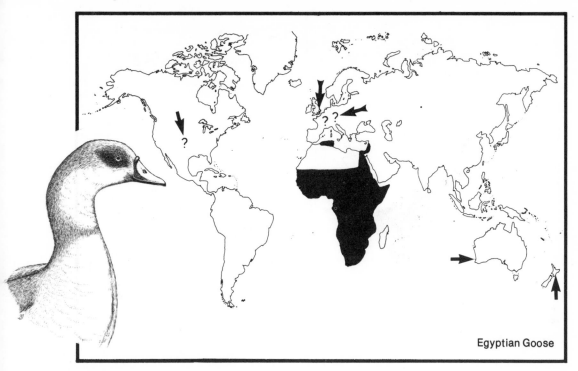

Egyptian Goose

Lever (1977) records that a bird was shot in 1795 at Thatcham, Berkshire, and that some were killed near Buscot, Berkshire, in 1803-04. A great many were either recorded or shot during the period 1808-49, and considerable numbers of free-flying and breeding colonies were established on estates in southern and eastern England as well as other parts of Britain during the mid-nineteenth century.

In the early part of the twentieth century a pair bred near London for several years; other pairs or small groups were recorded in Hertfordshire in 1934-35, Berkshire in 1935 and 1941-42, and in the Royal Botanic Gardens at Kew in 1957. Between 1954 and 1956 some bred in Norfolk, near Norwich.

The Egyptian Goose is now found principally in northern Norfolk in the Holkham-Beeston area and in the valley of the river Bure. Between 1971 and 1975 a large number of colonies or individuals have been recorded in this area and there has been some spread into the Breckland area of Suffolk. It is estimated that there are some 300-400 free-flying birds in Norfolk and there appears to be some expansion of range into East Suffolk where they were breeding in 1976 (Gooders, 1969; Sharrock, 1976; Lever, 1977).

New Zealand. Thomson (1922) reports that Sir George Grey brought eight to ten Egyptian Geese from Cape Province, South Africa, to New Zealand in 1860. These were said to have bred freely in captivity on Kawau and some apparently crossed to the mainland where Thomson reported them established in the vicinity of Hawke's Bay. Apparently these were destroyed at some later date. In 1869 the Auckland Acclimatisation Society imported further birds which were kept in aviaries and were not, as far as it is known, liberated (Thomson). The Egyptian Goose did not become established in New Zealand.

Australia. The Egyptian Goose appears to have been a fairly early introduction to Rottnest Island, off the coast of Western Australia, as they are reported to

have disappeared before 1956 (Long, 1972). Details of their release do not appear to have been documented.

USA. Before 1928 at least, the Egyptian Goose was commonly kept in the United States where it frequently escaped and was sometimes shot in the wild (Phillips, 1928). It did not, however, become permanently established as a wild bird in that country.

DAMAGE

According to Mackworth-Praed and Grant (1962), Egyptian Geese can do great damage to native cultivation when in large flocks in Africa. Where they are established in England no damage appears to have been reported, but the species has not yet become very numerous or widespread.

MUSCOVY DUCK
Cairina moschata (Linnaeus)

DISTINGUISHING CHARACTERISTICS

Males 65-89 cm (25.5-35 in). Females 58-71 cm (23-28 in). 2.5-5 kg — in captivity 3.6-6.6 kg (5.5-11 lb — 8-14.5 lb)

Large blackish green duck; face bare with red warty protuberances; large white patch on wing; bill black with bluish band. Female: lacks warty protuberances, crest of plumes on head and weighs less. Domesticated birds may be white, black or patched.

Delacour, vol.3, 1959, pp.127 and pl.10, p.132.

GENERAL DISTRIBUTION

Central and South America: from Mexico southwards to Colombia, Ecuador, Peru and northern Argentina; also Trinidad (casual).

INTRODUCED DISTRIBUTION

The Muscovy Duck at times becomes feral, probably in many parts of the world. In many areas of South America feral stock have probably mixed with the

53

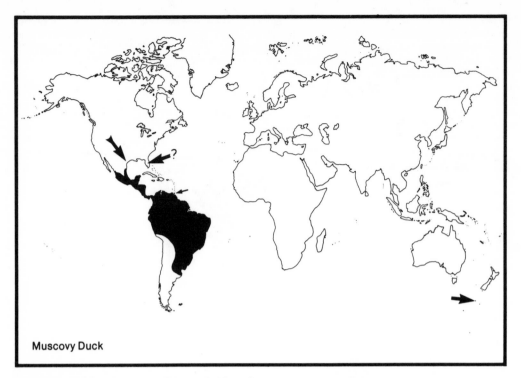

Muscovy Duck

true wild stock; in the USA they probably exist in some south-eastern States. An introduction to Adams Island, New Zealand, was unsuccessful.

GENERAL HABITS

Status: common but numbers reduced, less common in Peru due to persecution; common as domestic species. *Habitat:* forest, wooded streams, marshes, ponds, swamps and lagoons. *Gregariousness:* pairs and small groups of separate sexes, flocks to 50 outside breeding season. *Movements:* sedentary. *Foods:* mainly vegetation, but also small fish, crabs, insects and worms. *Breeding:* Mar-Apr (Surinam); male polygamous. *Nest:* hole in tree, lined with down. *Eggs:* 8-15, 20.

Delacour, vol.3, 1959, pp.126-130.

NOTES ON INTRODUCTIONS

USA. Muscovy Ducks occur as a feral bird in Live Oak and San Patricio Counties of Texas (Bolen, 1971). Palmer (1976) says that they probably occur in other areas in the Gulf of Mexico coastal region. He records that they have been introduced into the Florida region but that it is not known whether they are established there. Four birds from Paraguay and ninety-seven from Venezuela were liberated in various localities of Florida, and plans were made to import further birds. Those released in this region are said to have been exterminated by raccoons or other predators, but some may still exist there.

New Zealand. In 1885 Captain Norman liberated six Muscovy Ducks on Adams Island (Auckland Islands), south of New Zealand, but they failed to establish themselves there (Thomson, 1922).

DAMAGE

No agricultural damage is known. The Muscovy will cross with the Mallard and other species, producing infertile crosses, and is also aggressive towards other waterfowl (Bolen, 1971). Some concern has been expressed at the attempts to introduce the species into the United States for these reasons.

54

MALLARD
(Common Mallard, Green-headed Mallard)
Anas platyrhynchos (Linnaeus)

DISTINGUISHING CHARACTERISTICS

50-71 cm (19.6-28 in) . 0.8-1.8 kg (1.7-4 lb)

Head and neck iridescent green; white collar at base of neck; breast purplish chestnut; underparts whitish lined with dark bars; rump black; wings brownish grey with purplish blue speculum and bordered at sides with black and white bars; bill yellowish or greenish. Female: head and neck buff, streaked brown; body mottled and streaked chestnut-brown.

Delacour, vol.2, 1956, pp.40-53 and pl.2, p.46.

Palmer, vol.2, 1976, pp.275-285.

GENERAL DISTRIBUTION

Eurasia to North America. Iceland, The Faeroes, across Europe and Asia from south of the Arctic Circle to the Mediterranean, Turkestan, Mongolia and Japan; the Aleutian and Pribilof Islands and North America from north-western Alaska, north-western and south-eastern Canada to northern Baja California, southern Texas, Illinois, Ohio and Virginia. Winters in Eurasia south to the Canary Islands, Ethiopia, Gambia, Kenya, Arabia, India, Malaysia and China; in North America south to Florida, Mexico, Panama and West Indies (rare). In the Pacific they reach the Hawaiian Islands and the Marianas.

INTRODUCED DISTRIBUTION

Introduced successfully in the eastern USA, Bermuda, Australia and New Zealand; introductions on the Falkland Islands (failed), Macquarie Island (status uncertain) and Kerguelen (status uncertain) may be successful; re-introduction of the Hawaiian Islands race appears to have been successful. An introduction to Tahiti has failed.

GENERAL HABITS

Status: common and abundant. *Habitat:* fresh or

brackish water, preferably shallow and still, but also found on salty coastal lagoons and in grain fields and cultivation. *Gregariousness:* pairs, small flocks and with other species, large flocks in the non-breeding season; migrating flocks of 10-15 to 200 birds. *Movements:* sedentary and migratory (irregular movements not well studied). *Foods:* aquatic vegetation and animals including water and marsh plants, seeds, roots, insects, snails, worms, fish fry, seaweed, molluscs and grain. *Breeding:* Mar-Oct (Europe); Apr-July (North America); Dec-May (Hawaiian Islands); Aug-Oct (New Zealand); may have two broods per year in some areas. *Nest:* of grasses, reeds and leaves lined with down, usually on ground, trees rarely. *Eggs:* 5-15, 18 (New Zealand 10-15).

Palmer, vol.2, 1976, pp.286-308.

NOTES ON INTRODUCTIONS

USA. According to Palmer (1976) the range of the Mallard in North America has increased, over many decades, especially in the east and then to the north. He says that the situation is complicated by domestic birds reverting to the wild and transplants and/or liberations of pen-reared stock within and beyond their natural breeding range.

Foley *et al* (1961, in Palmer) have recorded that no wild stock was definitely known to breed in New York in 1934 and that the present stock is believed to be derived from released birds. Delacour (1954) states that the species does not occur in much of the eastern United States, but has been introduced in many places. George and Wingard (1967) indicate that Mallards are raised on marshes and ponds and established locally in areas not generally occupied by native wildfowl.

Over 30 000 Mallards were reared and released in New York State in the period 1934 to 1952 inclusive (Palmer). However, from 1912 to 1940 New York State authorities released between 7000 and 22 500 birds and private individuals and clubs are estimated to have released somewhere between 280 000 and 420 000 birds (Bump, 1941). The total number released in States on and near the Atlantic coast in the last thirty years was probably in the vicinity of 50 000 birds annually. Some 223 hand-reared birds were released in two localities of Sackville, New Brunswick, in 1953-55 (Boyer, 1966, in Palmer). Many thousands have been released in the Great Lakes region and probably elsewhere for stocking purposes.

The Mallard is now established over a large area of eastern USA, probably through increased agriculture, stocking, transplants and introductions.

Bermuda. The establishment of a wild Mallard population from domestic stock took place in about 1960 and since that time the species has increased rapidly (Wingate, 1973). Wingate reports that they breed at Spittal Pond and various waterfront homes where they are fed by the nearby inhabitants.

Falkland Islands. Some Mallards were released in the East Falklands in the 1930s and were said to be breeding there in very small numbers in the 1960s (Cawkell and Hamilton, 1961). No mention of them is made by Wood (1975) in the mid 1970s.

Australia. English Mallards were liberated on Botanical Gardens Lake in Melbourne, Victoria, in 1871 and a further eighty were released in 1872

(Ryan, 1906). Ryan indicates that these had almost disappeared in the early 1900s. Some may have been released on Phillip Island in 1864 as Hardy (1928) refers to English wild duck being released there at this date.

In 1950 they were reported to be present on some lakes around Sydney and Melbourne (Tarr, 1950).

In Western Australia Mallards were breeding on a number of ornamental waters around Perth prior to 1912 (Long, 1972). They have remained established there to the present day but do not show much inclination to spread or increase in numbers greatly (Serventy and Whittell, 1967). They are, however, occasionally found in the south-west of the State.

The Mallard is now common in city parks and gardens in most of the larger cities in Australia and also some country towns. They are occasionally found in the wild (away from human habitation) e.g. in the interior of New South Wales, in south-eastern South Australia, and the south-west of Western Australia.

New Zealand. Attempts were made to naturalise the Mallard in New Zealand from 1867, when birds were initially imported from Australia (Thomson, 1922).

Between 1867 and 1881 the Otago Acclimatisation Society introduced twenty-three birds; apart from the initial pair from Melbourne in 1867 the remaining birds came from London. In 1870 (two birds), 1886 (four) and 1897 the Auckland Society imported birds for breeding. In 1893 (nineteen) and 1904 (four) the Wellington Society also imported birds for breeding, and later distributed several hundred of their progeny into the wild. According to Balham (1952) this society, between 1896 and 1916, released birds at the rate of twenty to 170 per year at Manawatu, Rangitikei and in the Wairarapa districts. In 1898 the Taranaki Society imported Mallards and apparently liberated some of them.

The early introductions in the Otago area were unsuccessful and this Society imported more birds in 1896 (twenty-one) and 1897. Between 1910 and 1918, the Southland Society liberated 1350 birds in their district. Some were liberated on Lake Okareka by a Mr McBean, some time before 1906.

Although Thomson records that the Mallard was established in the southern parts of the South Island before the 1920s, Oliver (1930) reported that in

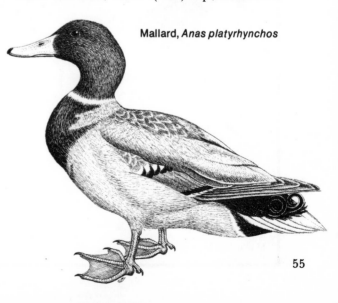

Mallard, *Anas platyrhynchos*

nearly all cases the species had failed but was still present in some districts.

In 1939 interest in establishing the Mallard in the Wellington district was revived and the Society was presented with 500 eggs from American stock (Balham, 1952). For several years approximately 300 birds per year were liberated, mainly in the Manawatu and Rangitikei districts. Balham estimated that in 1931 the annual take of Mallards by shooters was five per cent of the total harvest, and this increased until in the 1947-49 period they made up fifty-two per cent of the ducks taken.

Possibly many more introductions of Mallards occurred in New Zealand. Oliver (1955) indicates that they were still being imported, reared on game farms and constantly liberated. They are now widespread and common in the North and South Islands and on Stewart Island (Wodzicki, 1965; Falla *et al*, 1966).

Falla *et al* say that as American and English stock were introduced the present New Zealand birds are probably of mixed race.

Macquarie Island. The Mallard was first recorded on Macquarie Island in August 1949 (Gwynn, 1953) and has been sighted a number of times since then. It may now be established there as a breeding bird (Watson, 1975).

Kerguelen. Some four pairs of Mallards were introduced to Kerguelen in January 1959 but within five years all had disappeared. Others have been subsequently introduced, but the species' current status there is not known (Prévost and Mougin, 1970).

Tahiti. Mallards are reported by Guild (1938) to have been released, by him, on Tahiti in 1938. He records that they were breeding there shortly after their introduction. However, there appear to be no further reports of them.

Hawaiian Islands. The Hawaiian Duck *(A.p. wyvilliana)*, a subspecies of the Mallard, is a resident mainly on the islands of Kauai and Oahu, but is casual on the other islands of the group. This subspecies has recently been transplanted onto the island of Hawaii (Peterson, 1961) and pen-reared birds have been released on Hawaii and Oahu to re-establish them in former habitats (Swedberg, 1969). Released captive-bred birds have been noted on Oahu and Hawaii (Hawaiian Audubon Society, 1975) and are probably the results of the recent introductions.

The Wildfowl Trust, in England, are breeding this subspecies in an attempt to save it from possible extinction (Summers-Smith, 1964).

DAMAGE

In at least parts of its native range the Mallard is a pest of agricultural crops. In western Canada, in company with other species, they cause damage in grain fields (Smallman, 1964, pers. comm.). Sugden (1976) reports that waterfowl, of which the Mallard is a chief offender, cause damage to crops in Alberta, Saskatchewan and Manitoba. He says that damage to crops first became severe in the 1940s when agricultural changes such as new practices of allowing grain to ripen in swathes before threshing, and cultivation of increased acreages occurred. The Mallard damages primarily barley and wheat and losses are most severe in wet autumns that delay harvesting. Damage tends to be chronic near large wetlands that harbour ducks in autumn. From all species, losses average one per cent of the crop value, and currently exceed US$10 million annually.

In England, Mallards feed on such agricultural crops as grain, potatoes and cabbages (Kear, 1964). With other species they can make the harvesting of potatoes more difficult because of trampling.

In the areas where the Mallard has been introduced it does not appear to have become an agricultural

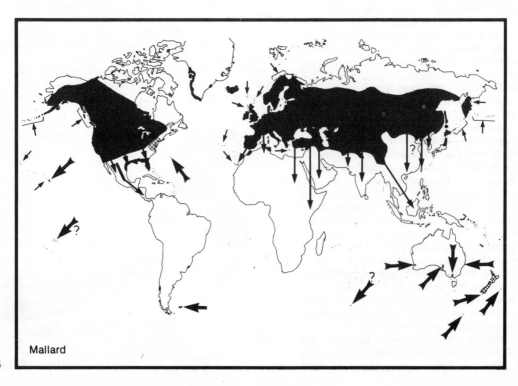

Mallard

pest. However, its ability to breed with closely related species has caused anxiety amongst some biologists.

In New Zealand, Mallards have been hybridising with the Grey Duck *(A. superciliosa)* since about 1917 (Thomson, 1922) and in some areas the hybrids are becoming numerous (Oliver, 1955; Sage, 1958). The species has been reported to compete with native ducks for food and in many areas appears to be replacing the native species. The Mallard may pose a greater threat in New Zealand in the future. Australian hunters have claimed that Mallard x Black Duck progeny are producing inferior game birds in that country. Recently, attempts were made in Victoria and northern Australia to remove the Mallard, presumably to prevent hybridisation.

MELLER'S DUCK
Anas melleri Sclater

DISTINGUISHING CHARACTERISTICS
55 cm (21.6 in)
Generally dark reddish brown with elongated dark spots; head and neck have narrow dusky streaks; speculum green and black with narrow white border; bill greyish green, with black on nail and at base. Both sexes resemble the female of the Mallard *(A. platyrhynchos)* but with the speculum green.
Delacour, vol.2, 1956, p.67 and pl.4, p.62.
Milon *et al,* pt.35: Birds, 1973, pp.71-72 and pl.11, Fig.5.

GENERAL DISTRIBUTION
Malagasy.

INTRODUCED DISTRIBUTION
Probably introduced, successfully on Mauritius, and unsuccessfully on Réunion where now extirpated.

GENERAL HABITS
Status: common, but becoming scarcer through intense hunting. *Habitat:* open ponds, lakes, bays, streams, marshy areas and rice fields. *Gregariousness:* pairs or small groups. *Movements:* sedentary. *Foods:* probably similar to Mallard. *Breeding:* most months of year (Oct-Nov Mauritius). *Nest:* pile of straw, lined with down, under a bush on dry ground or on a raised tuft of grass on the edge or middle of a swamp. *Eggs:* 5, 8-10.
Delacour, vol.2, 1956, pp.67-68.
Milon *et al,* pt.35: Birds, 1973, pp.71-72.

NOTES ON INTRODUCTIONS
Mauritius. Meller's Duck has been introduced to Mauritius from Malagasy (Peters, 1930; Delacour, 1954). There appears to be some doubt as to whether the species is a resident or has been introduced. Carie (1916, in Rountree *et al,* 1952) lists the species as a resident, and Meinertzhagen (1912) says that they were introduced from Malagasy in about 1850. Rountree *et al,* appear to favour the view that the species is a native one.

Whether resident or introduced, Meinertzhagen indicates that they had increased in numbers only slowly. Carie, in 1916, says that they were confined to remote marshy tracts in the forest zone of the central plateau on the island. Benedict (1957) reports that they are now extremely rare there. The species is still apparently present on Pinton du Milieu and Valetta Lakes, where they are protected, but now only number about fifty birds (Staub, 1976).
Réunion. Meller's Duck also may have been

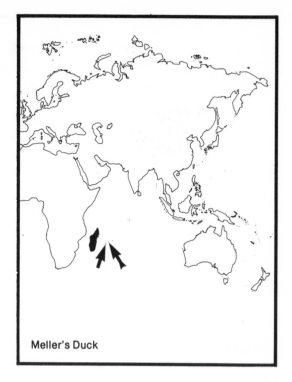

Meller's Duck

introduced to Réunion but has now disappeared, possibly due to over-hunting (Staub, 1976).

DAMAGE
In Malagasy, Meller's Duck has been reported to visit rice fields where they are said to do considerable damage (Rand, 1936; Rutgers and Norris, 1970).

BLUE-WINGED TEAL
Anas discors Linnaeus

DISTINGUISHING CHARACTERISTICS
33-42.5 cm (13-16.5 in). 290-590 g (.63-1.3 lb).
Head and neck lead grey with purplish tinge; white crescent patch in front of eye; chin blackish; breast, abdomen and sides brown, crossed and spotted with black; back, rump and tail dark brown; forewing chalk blue; speculum bright green; bill bluish grey; eclipse plumage duller than female. Female: chin and throat whitish.
Delacour, vol.2, 1956, pp.167-170 and pl.18, p.174.
Palmer, vol.2, 1976, pp.463-471.

GENERAL DISTRIBUTION
North America: from British Columbia, northern Saskatchewan, southern Quebec and Nova Scotia, south to southern California, southern Mexico, central Texas, Louisiana, Tennessee and North Carolina. Winters south to Central America, West Indies, Peru and Uruguay.

INTRODUCED DISTRIBUTION
Extended breeding range naturally in North America where transplants have failed; possibly introduced to the Hawaiian Islands but failed; stragglers and/or escaped captives have failed to establish in Great Britain and Europe.

GENERAL HABITS
Status: range reduced, but abundant. *Habitat:* freshwater ponds, marshes, lakes and weedy river margins; usually avoids salt water. *Gregariousness:* small flocks and large flocks of up to 500 or more on

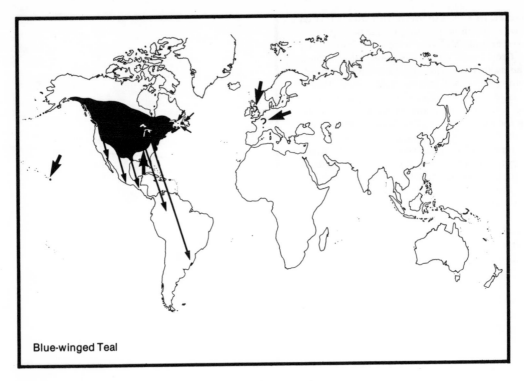

Blue-winged Teal

migration or at feeding places. *Movements:* migratory. *Foods:* grain, vegetable material and aquatic insects, molluscs and crustacea. *Breeding:* May-July. *Nest:* down-lined hollow of grass, in grass near water. *Eggs:* 6-13, 15.

Palmer, vol.2, 1976, pp.472-482.

NOTES ON INTRODUCTIONS

North America. The Blue-winged Teal has extended its breeding range in North America, particularly in coastal areas, and has increased in numbers in California, Oregon, Washington and British Columbia and also down the Atlantic coast (Palmer, 1976). These increases have probably been due to the extension of agricultural areas since the beginning of the twentieth century.

During a three-year period, prior to 1964, 377 locally bred flightless young and fourteen adult birds were transplanted from Minnesota to Missouri in an attempt to re-establish nesting populations (Vaught, 1964). By 1964 the attempt was thought to have been unsuccessful.

Hawaiian Islands. In 1922 Teal reported as *A. discors* were imported to Honolulu from Australia (?). The species is not a native of that country. However, Munro (1960) says it is more likely that an Australian Teal species was imported. Whatever the true identity of the species, it failed to become established in the Hawaiian Islands.

Great Britain and Europe. The Blue-winged Teal now breeds in a number of waterfowl collections in Europe and Great Britain. Since the 1960s reports of birds in the wild have increased in these areas, but it has been impossible to distinguish between those that are presumed to be natural occurrences and those which are escaped captive birds. By 1972 about two dozen records of this Teal had been recorded (Palmer).

DAMAGE
None known.

COMMON PINTAIL
(Pintail, Northern Pintail)
Anas acuta Linnaeus

DISTINGUISHING CHARACTERISTICS
50-72.5 cm (19.6-28 in). 710 g - 1.4 kg (1.5-3 lb)
Head and upper neck brown; hindneck blackish; lower neck, line extending up sides of neck and underparts white; back finely lined black and white; wing-coverts grey; speculum bronze-green; tail long and pointed, black; bill blue-grey. Female: head and neck fawn; back greyish brown; tail dark brown, barred white. (In the sub-Antarctic race nuptial plumage of males is similar to eclipse plumage of northern race males; birds generally smaller.)
Delacour, vol.2, 1956, pp.129-136 and pl.14, p.134.
Palmer, vol.2, 1976, pp.437-445.

GENERAL DISTRIBUTION
Eurasia-North America: Northern Europe, northern Asia, Komandorskiye and Aleutian Islands, northern North America and Iceland. (Also Kerguelen and Crozet islands in the southern Indian Ocean.) Winters south to central Africa, southern Asia, some Pacific islands (Hawaiian), West Indies and northern South America.

INTRODUCED DISTRIBUTION
Established in Great Britain mainly through natural colonisation, but also assisted by introductions. Introduced successfully on St Paul and Amsterdam islands in the southern Indian Ocean. Possibly introduced, unsuccessfully, in New Zealand.
(Note: the sub-Antarctic population of the Pintail is regarded as having originated from direct colonisation by northern birds (Voous, 1960)).

GENERAL HABITS
Status: common. *Habitat:* lagoons, ponds, marshes

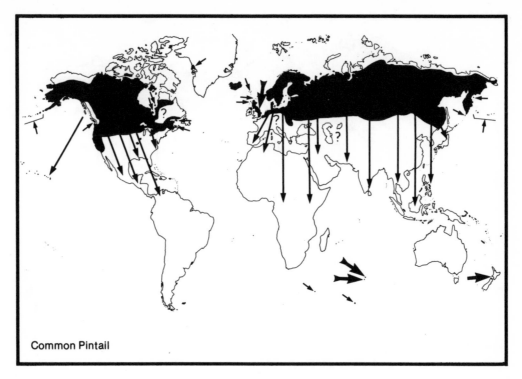

Common Pintail

and swamps, usually shallow and fresh and surrounded by open level areas. *Gregariousness:* usually small parties or flocks, sometimes flocks of over 1000 on migration. *Movements:* migratory. *Foods:* mainly aquatic vegetation and animals such as beetles, insects, worms and larvae. *Breeding:* Apr-June (Europe), Apr-Jly (North America), Nov-Feb (Kerguelen Island). *Nest:* of dry material, lined with down, amongst grass, heather or other low vegetation, near water. *Eggs:* 5, 6-9, 12.
Palmer, vol.2, 1976, pp.446-460.

NOTES ON INTRODUCTIONS
St Paul and Amsterdam. The subspecies *A.a. eatoni* has been introduced to St Paul and Amsterdam islands (Delacour, 1954; Scott, 1965), where it is still established (Watson, 1975).
Britain. The Common Pintail colonised Britain in the nineteenth century and now breeds over a fairly wide area. They were first found breeding in Scotland in 1869, in England in 1910, and in Ireland in 1917, and have slowly increased their range until recently (Sharrock, 1976).
Since 1964 pinioned birds have been kept at Millorn in Cumberland and the young have been released (Swift, 1974). Some have bred around this reserve and possibly elsewhere.
New Zealand. Pintails of this species were imported into New Zealand in 1885, 1896 and in 1905, but it is not known if any were released in the wild (Thomson, 1922).

DAMAGE
The Common Pintail causes damage to agricultural crops in England and Canada. According to Kear (1964) they occasionally feed on grain crops in England. In company with other ducks, principally Mallards, they cause some damage to grain crops in Alberta, Saskatchewan and Manitoba (Sugden, 1976).

EUROPEAN WIGEON
(Wigeon)
Anas penelope Linnaeus

DISTINGUISHING CHARACTERISTICS
45-51 cm (17.7-20 in). 400-1090 g (.8-2.4 lb)
Forehead and crown whitish; chin, neck and throat chestnut; cheeks and neck minutely spotted dark green; breast white and remainder of underparts grey; shoulders white with terminal black bar; speculum green tipped black below; wing and tail dark brown; bill dull blue, tip black. *Female:* upper parts mottled greyish brown; speculum greyish green; underparts buffy white.
Delacour, vol.2, 1956, p.114 and pl.12, p.118.

GENERAL DISTRIBUTION
Eurasia: Iceland, The Faeroes, British Isles, Scandinavia, northern Finland and Russia to Kamchatka and Komandorskiye islands south to the Netherlands (rare), Denmark (rare), northern Poland, across Asia to Sakhalin. Winters south to the Canary Islands, southern Europe, Ethiopia, Kenya, Arabia, Asia Minor, Iraq, Iran, southern India, Indochina, Sulawesi and the Philippines.

INTRODUCED DISTRIBUTION
Established in Great Britain mainly through natural colonisation, but assisted (in southern areas) by escapees. Introduction in New Zealand failed.

GENERAL HABITS
Status: very common. *Habitat:* freshwater pools, lakes and marshes, moors and tundra. *Gregariousness:* family groups or small to large flocks, thousands on migration. *Movements:* migratory. *Foods:* vegetable material including grass and seaweed, insects, worms and shellfish. *Breeding:* Apr-June. *Nest:* slight hollow on ground, down lined, amongst grass or reeds or other plants. *Eggs:* 6, 8-9, 12.
Delacour, vol.2, 1956, pp.114-115.

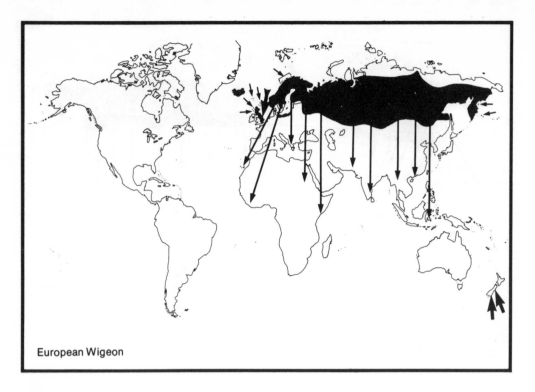

European Wigeon

NOTES ON INTRODUCTIONS

Britain. The European Wigeon apparently colonised Britain in the nineteenth century. The first breeding record appears to have been that in Sutherland in 1834 and they bred at Yorkshire, England, by 1897. Some of the records of birds further south may have involved escapees from waterfowl collections (Sharrock, 1976). At present the species breeds on many waters in Britain but does not appear to be expanding further.

New Zealand. The Canterbury Acclimatisation Society imported Wigeons in 1868 (eight birds) and 1885, and the Otago Society in 1896 (eight), but there are no further records of them. In 1897 some were liberated on private ponds by W. Telford at Clifton, and the government imported a number in 1904, some of which were liberated at Lake Kaniere by the Westland Society (Thomson, 1922). The Wigeon failed to become established in New Zealand.

DAMAGE

The Wigeon feeds on grain crops in England and with other species may cause some damage if harvesting is late (Kear, 1964).

GADWALL

Anas strepera Linnaeus

DISTINGUISHING CHARACTERISTICS

45-57 cm (17.7-22.4 in). 0.7-1.3 kg (1.5-2.8 lb)

Head and neck grey speckled black; back dark grey, barred white, some scapulars edged brownish; wing greyish at bend, then chestnut, then black; speculum white; breast brown-black with white crescent marks; sides grey with wavy white lines; upper and under tail-coverts black; tail brownish grey; bill dark grey. Female: brownish; back, scapulars, rump, upper tail-coverts, breast and sides dusky with buffy edges and markings; bill dull orange with greyish culmen and spots.

Delacour, vol.2, 1956, pp.108, 111-112, and pl.10, p.102.

Palmer, vol.2, 1976, pp.380-386.

GENERAL DISTRIBUTION

Eurasia and North America: western North America from southern British Columbia, central Alberta, Saskatchewan, central-western Manitoba and southern Ontario (locally) south to California and Colorado; eastern Europe from Denmark, Germany, Rumania and eastern Bulgaria, across central Asia to the Okhotsk Sea and North Korea. Winters south to north-west Africa, Egypt, Iran, India, Burma, north-western Thailand, China and Japan: Mexico, Cuba, Jamaica and other parts of the West Indies (rare).

INTRODUCED DISTRIBUTION

Expanded range in North America naturally, but established in some southern areas as a result of introduction; established in Iceland, England and Scotland as a result of natural colonisation. Possibly introduced, unsuccessfully, in New Zealand.

GENERAL HABITS

Status: fairly common. *Habitat:* sloughs, shallow margins of lakes bordered by good cover, occasionally grain fields; not often near salt water. *Gregariousness:* flocks up to 6, and on migration flocks to 25, occasionally up to 50 or more. *Movements:* migratory. *Foods:* aquatic vegetation and animals, including grass, seeds, buds, leaves, molluscs and insects. *Breeding:* Apr-July (Europe); May-July (North America). *Nest:* of grass, weed stalks, reeds and other vegetation, lined with down, on the ground near water. *Eggs:* 5-15.

Palmer, vol.2, 1976, pp.387-401.

NOTES ON INTRODUCTIONS

North America. The Gadwall has expanded its range northwards in recent times in Canada and Alaska, and also southwards into the United States (Palmer, 1976). It has become established as a breeding bird from releases in 1957 and 1965, at Great Meadows

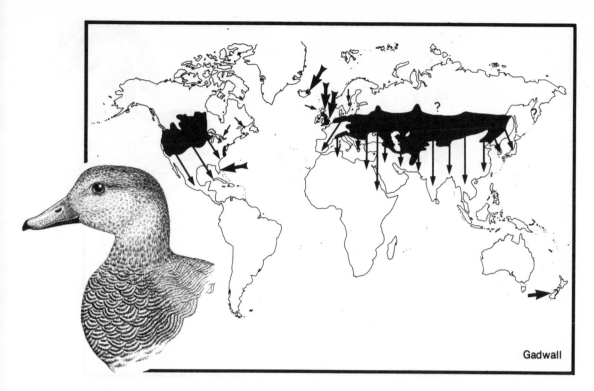

Gadwall

Ponds near Concord, Massachusetts (Borden and Hochbaum, 1966). Young birds from Delta, Manitoba, were released in the Chassahowitzka Refuge in Florida in August 1968 (Cornwell, 1969, in Palmer) and may have become established there. *Iceland.* The Gadwall established itself in Iceland in about 1862, and now exists in considerable numbers as a breeding population at Lake Myvatn (Voous, 1960).
England and Scotland. The Gadwall became naturalised in two small areas in south-eastern England at the same time as an apparently natural colonisation from the continent took place in Scotland (Thomson, 1964). Populations breeding in Suffolk and Norfolk appear to have been established artificially (Delacour, 1954). Most of the Gadwalls now breeding in East Anglia are believed to be descended from a pair released in the Breckland district of south-west Norfolk in about 1850 (Lever, 1977) and where a substantial population had built up by 1875. However, they are more than likely reinforced, from time to time, by migrants from continental Europe. The present population has probably been derived from artificial and natural means, the presence of feral stock inducing migratory birds to stay and breed. Other known releases include birds which escaped from St James Park, London, in the 1930s when sixty young flew away, and a feral population which was established in the London area possibly as a result of introductions prior to 1965 by the Wildfowlers Association of Great Britain and Ireland. Some were released in the Isles of Scilly in the 1930s and some have escaped from the Wildfowl Trust at Slimbridge (Sharrock, 1976).
New Zealand. Gadwall were imported to New Zealand in 1894-95, but it is not known if any were released into the wild (Thomson, 1922).
DAMAGE
None known.

AMERICAN WOOD DUCK
(North American Wood Duck, Carolina Duck)
Aix sponsa (Linnaeus)

DISTINGUISHING CHARACTERISTICS
43-52.5 cm (17-20.5 in). 589-900 g (1.3-1.98 lb)
Head crested; iridescent green and blue to purplish black below eye; chin, throat and foreneck white; a white line above eye to back of neck and another from eye to back of neck; upper breast reddish chestnut; back, rump and upper tail bronze-green; speculum bluish green with white line behind; bill ridge, edges and tip black, sides pinkish and base red with narrow yellow border. *Female:* dark brown, lighter flanks, white belly and white patch around eye.
Delacour, vol.3, 1959, pp.100-105 and pl.7, p.96.
Palmer, vol.3, 1976, pp.252-260.

GENERAL DISTRIBUTION
North America: in the western portion from south-western British Columbia, southern Alberta (rare) and eastern Saskatchewan (rare) south to central California, Arizona (rare) and New Mexico: in the eastern portion from southern Canada south to Florida and south-east Texas, and west to about Dakota and eastern Nebraska, Kansas and Oklahoma. Winter south to southern California, central Mexico, Jamaica and the Bahamas.

INTRODUCED DISTRIBUTION
Extended breeding range naturally in North America, but in some areas extensions due to or assisted by introductions. Introduced successfully in Great Britain. Introductions in New Zealand and Tahiti have failed.

GENERAL HABITS
Status: uncommon to common; range and numbers reduced. *Habitat:* wooded swamps, rivers and ponds; seldom on salt water. *Gregariousness:* singly, pairs or

61

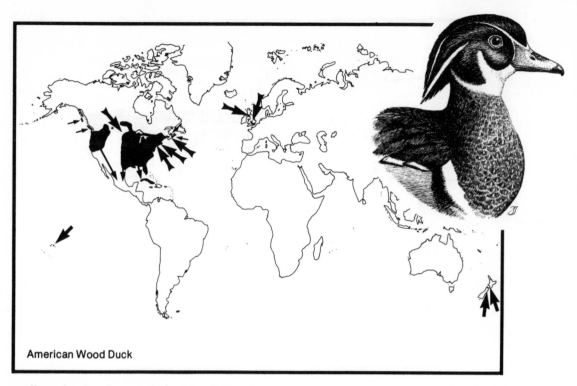

American Wood Duck

small parties, but large groups up to thousands in autumn and winter. *Movements:* migratory. *Foods:* seeds, berries, crustaceans, small fish, snails, acorns, nuts, aquatic insects and other aquatic animals. *Breeding:* Apr-July; some have 2 broods per season. *Nest:* in a tree cavity, lined with down. *Eggs:* 6-15, 31.

Hester and Dermid, 1973.

Palmer, vol.3, 1976, pp.260-277.

NOTES ON INTRODUCTIONS

North America. The Wood Duck has extended its main breeding range northwards, locally westwards, and possibly in the south. Some of the extensions may have been due to, or assisted by, liberations of pen-reared stock. Some were released as early as 1884-85 in New Jersey (Phillips, 1928) and between 1913 and 1940, two to 150 birds per year were released in New York State (Bump, 1941). At the Arrowhead National Wildlife Refuge in eastern central North Dakota, captive-reared young were released and artificial nest boxes installed in 1968 (Doty and Kruse, 1972). With the help of these artificial means the breeding range was extended to this locality in 1969. Several hundred pen-reared stock were annually reared in Connecticut from 1925 to 1939 and released at various places (Ripley, 1951, in Palmer, 1976). Palmer (1976) indicates that captive reared birds have also been released near Truro, Nova Scotia, probably over a number of years. Some ninety-seven pen-reared birds were transferred and released in Madison, Wisconsin — 320 kilometres (200 miles) from the hatch site — in August 1944 and a similar release was made in Indiana in the same year to test the birds' homing instinct (McCabe, 1947).

Great Britain. According to Lever (pers. comm., 1976) the Wood Duck is now established in Great Britain from introductions in the 1960s. However, these populations may or may not be self-supporting (Sharrock, 1972). Lever (1977) reports that a small

flock of fourteen birds was noted near Plymouth in 1873. Since the late 1960s small colonies have been recorded in Surrey, on Virginia Waters in 1969 and in Windsor Great Park and other areas; between 1964-70 on Vann Lakes between Dorking and Horsham; in 1970 near Guildford; in 1972 at Rode, Somerset (fifty birds) and at East Deneham, Norfolk; in 1973 at Broughton, Cumberland, and from 1972 to 1975 near Eccles Hall in Staffordshire. Lever says that breeding by feral birds, between 1968 and 1971, has been recorded at six sites in Surrey and one in Norfolk.

New Zealand. Wood Ducks were introduced to New Zealand between 1867 and 1906 by the Auckland, Canterbury, Wellington and Otago Acclimatisation Societies. A total of ten birds were imported during this period (Thomson, 1922). Thomson reports that only the Wellington Society appears to have released Wood Ducks — four were liberated in 1899. So-called Canadian Wood Ducks were reported to have been released on Lake Okareka and were said to have been present there for some years. Although the species was reported to be thriving at Christchurch in 1908, there appear to be no further records of them and the Wood Duck did not become permanently established in New Zealand.

Tahiti. Wood Ducks were reported to have been liberated in Tahiti by C. B. Nordhoff (Guild, 1938). Evidently they failed to become established there because there appears to be no further mention of them.

DAMAGE

None known.

MANDARIN DUCK
(Mandarin)

Aix galericulata (Linnaeus)

DISTINGUISHING CHARACTERISTICS

40-49 cm (15.7-19.3 in). 444-672 g (.97-1.48 lb)

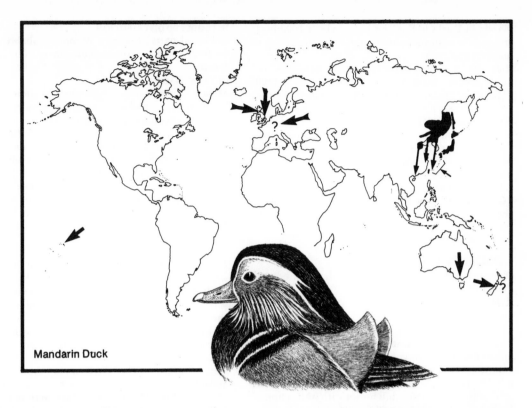

Mandarin Duck

Crown and crest glossy green and purple; face buff; upper parts brown glossed bronze-green; long chestnut hackles on throat; upper breast purple with black and white stripes on sides; flanks yellow or dull brown with bright orange raised wing fans; side whiskers orange; white eye-stripe from bill to nape; bill orange or dark red (eclipse). Eclipse plumage similar to female, but bill reddish. *Female:* brownish grey, mottled whitish below; chin white; bill greyish brown.

Delacour, vol.3, 1959, pp.105-106 and pl.7, p.96.

Cheng, 1963, pp.161-162 and pl.5, no.17.

GENERAL DISTRIBUTION

Eastern Asia: eastern China, Japan, Sakhalin and Manchuria. Winters south to Ryūkyū Islands, Taiwan and in China from Kwang Toung west to Nanking. Rare resident in Korea and rare migrant to central Burma.

INTRODUCED DISTRIBUTION

Established as a feral bird in England and possibly in other areas of Europe. Introductions in Australia, New Zealand and Tahiti failed.

GENERAL HABITS

Status: reduced in numbers and range, possibly uncommon. *Habitat:* wooded inland waters, ponds, parks, shrines and gardens, and also marshes and rice fields. *Gregariousness:* pairs, small flocks of about twelve or so, large flocks in winter of up to 100 birds. *Movements:* partly migratory. *Foods:* seeds, acorns, nuts, insects, snails, worms, and fish-spawn and other small animals. *Breeding:* Apr-July (China); Apr-May (England). *Nest:* in a hollow tree, lined with grass and down; rarely on the ground. *Eggs:* 7, 9-12. Delacour, vol.3, 1959, pp.106-109.

Cheng, 1963, pp.173-175.

NOTES ON INTRODUCTIONS

Europe. Mandarin Ducks have been acclimatised in a number of places in England (Delacour, 1954) and may be established and breeding in other areas of Europe (Peterson *et al*, 1963). The species is still established in limited areas of England, mainly in a semi-wild state (Thomson, 1964; Scott, 1965; Rutgers and Norris, 1970), and maintains its numbers by breeding in the wild (Sharrock, 1972). Hundreds of these ducks were feral near Woburn Abbey where the Duke of Bedford released them in about 1904, and in Surrey and Berkshire where they were well established around Windsor and Virginia Waters from birds reared at liberty by A. Ezra at Cobham, Surrey. Other early colonies were established at various times but generally they did not thrive. A few still remain in Shropshire, descendants of birds reared by R. and N. Stevens at Walcot Hall before 1939. Some were released at the Wildfowl Trust, Gloucestershire, and at Leckford, Hampshire. There were a number at Cleres in 1940 but these were destroyed during the second World War. According to Lever (1977) the first escaped bird was shot near the Thames at Cookham, Berkshire, in 1866. Lever indicates that those bred by A. Ezra soon spread into the surrounding areas of Surrey, Buckinghamshire and Middlesex. Ezra, with the help of others, in 1930 attempted to establish the Mandarin as a free-flying duck in many of the parks in London by releasing some ninety-nine birds. The venture largely failed but those at Virginia Waters succeeded and now form one of the two largest colonies in the country.

In recent years there has been an expansion of the populations living in Windsor Park and at Virginia Waters. They have penetrated into other parts of Surrey and Berkshire as well as into Buckinghamshire and Middlesex. In 1972-73 a small colony of feral birds established themselves near Horsham, West Sussex, where they now breed. The population of

Mandarin Ducks in England is now about 1000 birds and present indications are that they are increasing in numbers and range.

Australia. A pair of Mandarin Ducks were liberated at Macedon Reservoir, Victoria, in the 1860s (McCance, 1962), but there appear to be no further records of these birds.

New Zealand. Mandarin Ducks were apparently imported a number of times to New Zealand before the 1920s, but there are no records of them having been released in the wild (Thomson, 1922).

Tahiti. Mandarin Ducks were reported to have been released on Tahiti in about 1938 by C. B. Nordhoff (Guild, 1938), but there are no further records of them.

DAMAGE
None known.

COMMON POCHARD
(Pochard, White-backed Pochard, Red-headed Pochard)
Aythya ferina (Linnaeus)

DISTINGUISHING CHARACTERISTICS
42-49 cm (16.5-19.3 in). 0.6-1.1 kg (1.3-2.42 lb)
Head and neck chestnut; breast and upper back black; underparts greyish white; speculum grey; tail-coverts black; bill black with a blue band across middle. In eclipse plumage like female, but head golden brown. *Female:* dull brown with white chin.
Delacour, vol.3, 1964, pp.60-61 and pl.4, p.64.

GENERAL DISTRIBUTION
Eurasia: from the British Isles, north-eastern and eastern Europe, across central Asia to Lake Baikal and possibly parts of eastern Asia; also Crete and coastal Tunisia in North Africa. Winters south to southern Europe, Pakistan, northern India and Indochina. Eastern and western boundaries of breeding range are extremely fluid (Voous, 1960).

INTRODUCED DISTRIBUTION
Colonised parts of western Europe, probably assisted by feral colonies. An introduction to New Zealand failed.

GENERAL HABITS
Status: fairly common. *Habitat:* shallow fresh or brackish waters and salt water lakes usually with rich bottom vegetation and surrounded by reeds, etc. *Gregariousness:* pairs or flocks. *Movements:* migratory. *Foods:* aquatic vegetation and animals including leaves, roots, seeds, buds, shellfish and insects. *Breeding:* Apr-July (Europe); some individuals parasitic, laying in other nests including those of other species. *Nest:* on ground or slightly raised in tall floating vegetation or reeds, lined with grass and down. *Eggs:* 6-10, 12.
Delacour, vol.3, 1964, pp.61-62.

NOTES ON INTRODUCTIONS
Great Britain: The Common Pochard has spread westwards in Europe as a breeding bird since about 1850. It has bred in Great Britain for many years but it is possible that they were rare there before 1840. In the past thirty to forty years the species has extended its range somewhat. It is thought that a number of colonies may perhaps have started with feral birds (Sharrock, 1976).

New Zealand. The Wellington Acclimatisation Society imported Common Pochards in 1894 (six birds) and in 1895 (three). More were imported in 1897 in conjunction with the Canterbury, Nelson, Taranaki and other societies and some were brought in by private persons and dealers. In 1902 the Taranaki Society reported that nothing had been seen of the pochards liberated in 1898 (Thomson, 1922). The species failed to become established in New Zealand.

DAMAGE
None known.

Common Pochard

Redhead

REDHEAD
Aythya americana (Eyton)
DISTINGUISHING CHARACTERISTICS
19-23 cm (7.5-9 in)
Head and upper neck brownish red; breast, lower neck, fore-back, rump and under tail black; back, sides and underparts greyish and finely barred black; belly white; bill bluish, grading to white subterminally and with a black hooked tip. In winter almost uniformly brownish with white belly. *Female:* lacks brown head and neck, and black breast of male; head, neck, breast and sides greyish brown with mantle finely barred.
Delacour, vol.3, 1964, pp.62-63 and pl.4, p.64.
Palmer, vol.3, 1976, pp.162-169.
GENERAL DISTRIBUTION
North America: western and western central North America from the southern part of western Canada, south to California, central Arizona, north-western New Mexico, western Nebraska, northern Iowa and southern Wisconsin in the United States. Also breeds in some localities of south-eastern Canada and north-eastern USA, and in Alaska. Winters from southern California and the Lakes Region, and south to Florida, Cuba, Central America and southern Mexico.
INTRODUCED DISTRIBUTION
Extended breeding range naturally and established through introductions in some areas in North America.
GENERAL HABITS
Status: fairly common but declined in numbers in recent years due to the decrease in habitat. *Habitat:* marshy areas, shallow lakes, slow moving rivers, lagoons and bays. *Gregariousness:* pairs, small flocks and large flocks of 5000-20 000 or more birds in winter (winter flocks almost entirely segregated, sex

and age). *Movements:* migratory. *Foods:* aquatic animals, insects and larvae including molluscs, amphipods, gastropods, etc.; also aquatic weeds, seeds, tubers and algae. *Breeding:* Apr-July; most semi-parasitic, some parasitic, laying in other water birds' nests. *Nest:* dried vegetation, cupped and lined with down, over shallow water and occasionally on dry ground, or in other water birds' nests. *Eggs:* 8-16, larger communal nests up to 30-90.
Palmer, vol.3, 1976, pp.169-181.
NOTES ON INTRODUCTIONS
North America. The Redhead has increased its breeding range in Alaska and north-western Canada since about the 1950s. Attempts to establish the species by release of pen-reared and hand-reared birds outside the natural breeding range have resulted in local breeding at widely separate localities in New York (Benson, 1969; Palmer, 1976). Palmer indicates that those found breeding at Lake St Francis and Quebec are derived from one of those introductions. Only one such introduction appears to have been well documented. Some fifty young birds were released in 1952, and 1972 young and 1911 adults between 1957 and 1963 in New York (Benson and Browne, 1969; Benson, 1969).

TUFTED DUCK
Aythya fuligula (Linnaeus)
DISTINGUISHING CHARACTERISTICS
40-47 cm (15.7-18.5 in). 400-1028 g (.88-2.26 lb)
Head and neck iridescent violet and purple; long crest on head; chest, upper parts, wing-coverts, tail, upper and under tail-coverts black; underparts white; white bar on wing; bill slate blue. *Female:* black of male replaced by dusky or sooty brown; crest smaller.
Delacour, vol.3, 1964, pp.76-77 and pl.6, p.80.
GENERAL DISTRIBUTION
Eurasia: from the British Isles and Sweden across northern Asia to Kamchatka, south to northern Hokkaido (Japan) and eastwards to European Russia. Winters south to Africa, Arabia, southern India and Indochina.
INTRODUCED DISTRIBUTION
Colonised Iceland and western Europe naturally: occurs in North America occasionally as an escapee. Introduced unsuccessfully to New Zealand.
GENERAL HABITS
Status: fairly common. *Habitat:* freshwater lakes and ponds, slow flowing rivers with shore and bottom vegetation. *Gregariousness:* large flocks in winter. *Movements:* migratory. *Foods:* small aquatic animals (molluscs, fish, insects) and water plants. *Breeding:* May-Aug (Europe); somewhat colonial and some females lay in other birds' nests and sometimes in communal nests. *Nest:* down-lined, on the ground, amongst herbage and under low bushes and also on islets. *Eggs:* 7-10, 14 or more.
Delacour, vol.3, 1964, pp.77-78.
NOTES ON INTRODUCTIONS
Iceland and Western Europe. Voous (1960) says it is unlikely that the Tufted Duck settled for the first time in western and north-western Europe only from about the end of the nineteenth century. It has, however, increased its breeding range in western Europe in the course of this century. The Tufted Duck was recorded 65

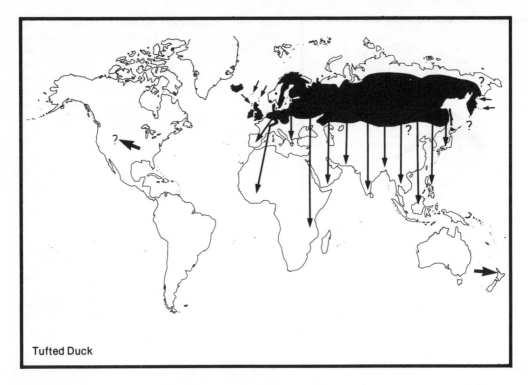

Tufted Duck

breeding in Iceland between 1890 and 1895, Holland in 1835, eastern Germany in 1906, southern Germany since 1930 and Switzerland since 1940. More recently they were recorded breeding in The Faeroes and are now widespread in Iceland. They were not known to breed in Great Britain until about 1849, but by the 1930s were widespread throughout (Sharrock, 1976). Voous interprets this expansion of range as a distribution fluctuation possibly brought about by the contraction of many south-west Asiatic inland lakes districts.

North America. The Tufted Duck is a favourite of aviculturists, at least in North America, and occasionally birds escape into the wild. According to Palmer (1976) a number of them have been found in North America, but there have been no records of any breeding.

New Zealand. Tufted Ducks *(Fuligula cristatus = A. fuligula)* were introduced to New Zealand in 1870 by the Auckland Acclimatisation Society which received five birds from Victoria, Australia. They were released with Canadian Wood Ducks at Lake Okareka but apparently did not increase or survive for long (Thomson, 1922).

DAMAGE
None known.

RUDDY DUCK

Oxyura jamaicensis (Gmelin)

DISTINGUISHING CHARACTERISTICS
35-48 cm (13.7-19 in). 312-816 g (.68-1.79 lb).
Upper parts reddish brown or chestnut; cheeks, chin and sides of head below eye white; crown and nape black; abdomen whitish mixed dusky brown; rump and tail brown, tail fan-shaped; under tail-coverts white; bill blue. *Female:* dark greyish brown, whitish below; bill blue. In eclipse plumage male resembles
female, apart from crown and cheek patch.

Delacour, vol.3, 1959, pp.226, 228, 231, 234 and pl.17, p.232.
Palmer, vol.3, 1976, pp.501-508.

GENERAL DISTRIBUTION
North to South America: from the southern part of western Canada to northern Central America (Costa Rica), the West Indies and western South America (Andean Highlands) from Colombia, Ecuador, Peru, Chile and south to Tierra del Fuego. Northern birds winter south to Florida and as far as Costa Rica.

INTRODUCED DISTRIBUTION
Established as a feral bird in Great Britain.

GENERAL HABITS
Status: common. *Habitat:* primarily freshwater lakes, ponds and reed beds. *Gregariousness:* solitary or small flocks of 5-10, and occasionally flocks of 30-500. *Movements:* sedentary and migratory. *Foods:* seeds and parts of water plants, molluscs, insects and their larvae. *Breeding:* Sept-May; Apr-July (Great Britain); singly or colonially and occasionally double brooded. *Nest:* bulky floating structure of woven marsh vegetation amongst and anchored to rushes or in mangroves. *Eggs:* 4-12, 20.
Palmer, vol.3, 1976, pp.508-518.

NOTES ON INTRODUCTIONS
Great Britain. The Ruddy Duck became established in England from introductions in 1952-53 (Lever, pers. comm., 1976), although it was reported to have failed (Scott, 1967). The species now maintains its numbers by feral breeding populations (Sharrock, 1972) and has been placed on the official British Trust for Ornithology list in England (Lever). According to Hudson (1976) and Lever (1977) the ducks now breeding in the wild in several south-western and west Midland counties are descendants of birds which escaped from the Wildfowl Trust's reserve at Slimbridge, Gloucestershire, where breeding of the species began in 1949. Two birds escaped in 1952-53

Ruddy Duck

and from 1956 a number have escaped from open breeding ponds. Up until 1973 it was estimated that some seventy had flown away from these ponds. Reports of wild birds date from about 1954 at Higham, Norfolk, and some were found to be breeding in the wild at the Chew Valley Reservoir, northern Somerset, in 1960. Lever says that the spread of the Ruddy Duck has been more spectacular and rapid than for any other feral duck in Britain. By 1975, fifty to sixty nesting pairs and between 300 and 350 birds — of which about 120 were at Somerset, 190 at Staffordshire, ten to fifteen in Shropshire, Cheshire and Leicestershire — existed in England.

DAMAGE
None known.

ORDER: PHOENICOPTERIFORMES

Family: *Phoenicopteridae* Flamingos
6 species in 3 genera; 1 introduced successfully (?)

The Common Flamingo now appears to be established, probably as a semi-domestic species, in the Florida area of the United States.

COMMON FLAMINGO
(Flamingo, Greater Flamingo)
Phoenicopterus ruber (Linnaeus)

DISTINGUISHING CHARACTERISTICS
120-124 cm (47.24-49 in). 2.9-3.6 kg (6.39-8 lb)
Large pink or vermilion bird, with black flight feathers; bill, tip black, middle orange and grading to buffy yellow at the base.
Palmer, vol.1, 1962, pp.542-544.

GENERAL DISTRIBUTION
Eurasia, Africa and Central and South America: southern Europe, the warmer parts of Asia, Africa, Galápagos Islands and the Bahamas to South America. Wanders in the non-breeding season to areas outside the breeding range.

INTRODUCED DISTRIBUTION
Introduced successfully in the USA (semi-domestic in Florida) and unsuccessfully in the Hawaiian Islands.

GENERAL HABITS
Status: colonies and numbers reduced, probably by man's activities. *Habitat:* shallow lagoons, mudflats and lakes. *Gregariousness:* large flocks which may number thousands. *Movements:* periodically migratory? *Foods:* aquatic animals and algae including molluscs, crustaceans, insects, fish, seeds

INTRODUCTIONS OF PHOENICOPTERIDAE

Species	Date introduced	Region	Manner introduced	Reason
(a) Successful introductions				
Common Flamingo	Since 1930	Florida, USA	escapee	captive bird
(b) Unsuccessful introductions				
Common Flamingo	1929	Kauai, Hawaiian Islands	deliberate	?

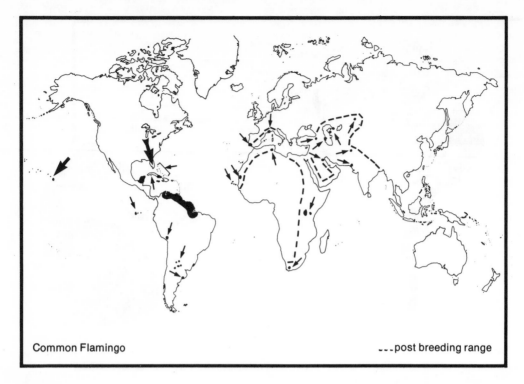

Common Flamingo   - - -post breeding range

and other material. *Breeding:* Feb-June; colonial. *Nest:* mud platform on mud-flat island, or in shallow water. *Eggs:* 1-2.

Allen, National Audubon Society: New York, Res. Rep. no.5, 1956, pp.1-285.

Palmer, vol.1, 1962, pp.544-550.

Kear and Duplaix-Hall, 1975, pp.1-246.

NOTES ON INTRODUCTIONS

USA. There are many records since 1930 of the Flamingo in Florida. Most of these records are probably due to escaped birds from the many captive flocks in the area. At least one colony of semi-domestic birds appears to exist at present. A free-flying colony lives in semi-domestication at Hialeah, Miami, in Florida (Blake, 1977).

Hawaiian Islands. Mr H. D. Sloggett introduced three Flamingos from Cuba to Kauai in 1929 where they lived for about a year (Munro, 1960). The species was unsuccessful in becoming permanently established (Berger, 1972).

ORDER: CICONIIFORMES

(Note: often called **ARDEIFORMES**)

Family: *Ardeidae* Herons, Bitterns, Boatbill

66 species in 32 genera; 3 species introduced, 2 successfully

The Cattle Egret has had tremendous success as a colonist throughout the world, particularly in the New World and in Australia. Its success as a deliberately introduced species is not as well known, and in this respect it has had some notable success on small islands. As a colonist the species is generally said to have been a beneficial acquisition, or at least neutral, to most areas because of its insect eating capabilities. However, on some of the smaller Mascarene Islands they may be affecting colonies of seabirds, some of which are rare.

The White-faced Heron *(Ardea novaehollandiae)*, an occasional visitor to New Zealand from Australia since pre-European times and possibly a restricted resident since 1886, has from about 1940 on become established as a breeding bird (Carrol, 1970). The details of its colonisation are not documented here, but it now occurs commonly throughout the North and South Islands of New Zealand.

The Black-crowned Night-Heron now appears to be fairly well established in Scotland as a feral species and may well increase and spread there.

Family: *Threskiornithidae* Ibises, spoonbills

32 species in 20 genera; 1 introduced successfully (?)

The Scarlet Ibis is probably established in Florida in the United States where it has been indicated that hybridisation with the White Ibis *(E. albus)* may be undesirable.

The Royal Spoonbill *(Platalea regia)*, largely an Australian species but prone to wandering, was first recorded in New Zealand in 1861 and since 1950 has established itself as a breeding bird in the Westland area of the South Island (Wodzicki, 1965; Falla *et al,* 1966; Williams, 1973). As the species appears to have been a colonist, details are not documented here.

Ardeidae

CATTLE EGRET

(Buff-backed Heron)

Ardeola ibis (Linnaeus)

DISTINGUISHING CHARACTERISTICS

42-54 (16.5-21.25 in). 300-413 g (10.58-14.57 oz)

All-white plumage, but in the breeding season has some buff on crown, breast and back; facial skin greenish yellow; bill yellow, in breeding season orange-pink.

Palmer, vol.1, 1962, pp.438-440.

Cramp and Simmons, vol.1, 1977, pp.279, 285-286 and pl.37.
Reader's Digest, 1977, p.79, pl.p.79.

GENERAL DISTRIBUTION

Sporadic distribution with erratic migratory movements from southern Spain and Portugal to Japan, and south to Java, Lesser Sunda Islands, Sri Lanka, Malagasy and most of Africa. Occurs on a number of Indian Ocean islands (including Amirantes, Aldabra, Assumption) and has expanded its range widely in the past 60 or 70 years, especially in Africa.

INTRODUCED DISTRIBUTION

Colonised eastern and western North America, the West Indies, Central America, northern South America, Galápagos Islands, New Guinea, Australia and New Zealand: deliberately introduced, successfully in the Hawaiian Islands, Chagos

Cattle Egret, *Areola ibis*

Archipelago, Seychelles, possibly to Rodrigues and unsuccessfully to Australia and Mauritius. Recently found breeding in Korea.

GENERAL HABITS

Status: common and increasing in numbers and range. *Habitat:* grasslands, marshes, swamps, meadows, rice fields, river banks and other open or cultivated areas; frequently in association with cattle. *Gregariousness:* small flocks of 2-30 birds, but sometimes large flocks. *Movements:* sedentary and nomadic, with erratic migratory irruptions. *Foods:* insects disturbed by grazing cattle; probably small fish. *Breeding:* throughout the year (Australia), most of the year (Africa); often colonially in rookeries on small islands; in some areas breeds twice a year. *Nest:* platform of twigs, grass and leaves in shrubbery or low tree, often near or over water. *Eggs:* 3-4, 9.

Palmer, vol.1, 1962, pp.440-448.

NOTES ON INTRODUCTIONS

America. Cattle Egrets were first noted in the New World between 1877 and 1882 in Surinam, and later in 1911-12 in Guyana (A.O.U., 1957). Crosby (1972) says that the first birds were found on the Courantyne River which forms the boundary between Surinam and Guyana. He indicates that some Cattle Egrets may have been present in the lower Rio Magdalena, Colombia, in 1916 or 1917 (Graham, 1921, in Crosby), but that the sightings cannot now be authenticated. According to Voous (1960), the colonisation of northern South America reported after 1910 resulted from independent, erratic, transoceanic flights from Africa. From about 1930 they extended their range explosively to the north and south. Crosby, after studying the prevailing winds between Africa and South America, concluded that the species probably came from North Africa or southern Europe.

The explosive nature of the spread in the Americas can be gauged from the following records: they are recorded in Guyana in 1930 and 1937; Florida, USA, in 1941-42; Guarico, Venezuela, in 1943; Aruba in 1944; Surinam and Florida in 1946; Puerto Rico in 1948 and in Florida again in 1949; the lower Rio San Juan, Colombia, in 1951; off (Grand Banks)

INTRODUCTIONS OF ARDEIDAE AND THRESKIORNITHIDAE

Species	Date introduced	Region	Manner introduced	Reason
(a) Successful introductions				
Cattle Egret	1959-61	Hawaiian Islands	deliberate	insect control
	1960	Frigate and Praslin islands, Seychelles	deliberate	insect control
	1953-55	Chagos Archipelago	deliberate	insect control
Black-crowned Night-heron	1950	Scotland	escapee and deliberate (from zoo)	zoo bird
Scarlet Ibis	1954 on	Florida, USA	escapees and egg transplantation	aesthetic
(b) Unsuccessful introductions				
Cattle Egret	1933	Western Australia	deliberate	insect control
Nankeen Night-heron	1852	New Zealand	deliberate	?

Newfoundland, in Trinidad and in Florida and Massachusetts, USA, in 1952; Bolivia and Bermuda in 1953; Panama (Canal Zone), western Colombia (Cauca Valley), Costa Rica (Guanacaste) and again in Florida in 1954; St Croix (Virgin Islands), West Indies in 1955; Panama, Barbados, Jamaica, Haiti, north-eastern Peru (Rio Itaya), Canada (Ontario) and many areas of the United States (North and South Carolina, Louisiana, Maine, New Hampshire, Massachusetts, Florida and Texas) in 1956; Cuba, Canada, Alabama (USA) in 1957; Guatemala, Ecuador and southern Mexico in 1958; Mississippi (USA) in 1960 and Canada (Ontario) and Oklahoma (USA) in 1962. They reached the west coast of the United States at San Diego, California, in 1964 and were reported from southern Peru and northern Chile in 1970 (Voous, 1960; Land, 1970; Leveque, 1964; Koepcke and Koepcke, 1964-71; Crosby, 1972; et al).

Crosby indicates that the first specimen of a Cattle Egret was actually collected in South America at Buxton, Guyana, in 1937. They were common in Surinam in 1947-48 and by 1950 were well established throughout Surinam and Guyana (Haverschmidt, 1951, in Crosby). Following the collection of a specimen in Colombia in 1951, the species spread through that country and was well established there as a year-round resident by 1957 (Lehmann, 1959, in Crosby). Lehmann apparently indicates that they had penetrated the interior of Colombia by 1959.

During the 1950s the Cattle Egret colonised much of Central America and they were found to be breeding at Veracruz, Mexico, in 1963. They had by this time become widespread in the Gulf coastal lowlands in southern Mexico (Crosby) and probably were well established throughout Mexico (Wolfe, 1961, in Crosby). Power and Rising record that the species is well established in northern and western Mexico and has recently been sighted on the peninsula in central Baja California.

Although Cattle Egrets were sighted as early as 1941-42 in North America, no real proof appears to have existed until photographs were taken and a specimen collected in 1952. By 1953 they are recorded nesting near Okeechobee, Florida, by Crosby who also reports that the species was well established in North America before being reported from the West Indies. By 1956 Cattle Egrets were reported breeding in North and South Carolina and in Louisiana (Sprunt, 1956). Specimens had been obtained in a number of areas and the birds had been sighted in many places in the eastern half of the USA. Voous reports that at this time some 6000 pairs were breeding there. They had by then colonised most of the eastern half of the United States from Texas and Florida to the New York region and had bred as far north as Rhode Island (Mayr, 1965). In 1964 one was collected for the first time in the western USA in San Diego County, California (McCaskie, 1965). They have now been found over a wide area of California from just north of San Francisco south to San Diego. In Canada, Cattle Egrets were noted in Ontario as early as 1956 or 1957, and the first breeding was recorded there in 1962 (Crosby, 1972; Godfrey, 1966). The species has now been recorded over much of south-eastern Canada in Ontario, Quebec, Nova Scotia and Manitoba provinces (Godfrey, 1966).

Galápagos Islands. According to Leveque *et al* (1966,

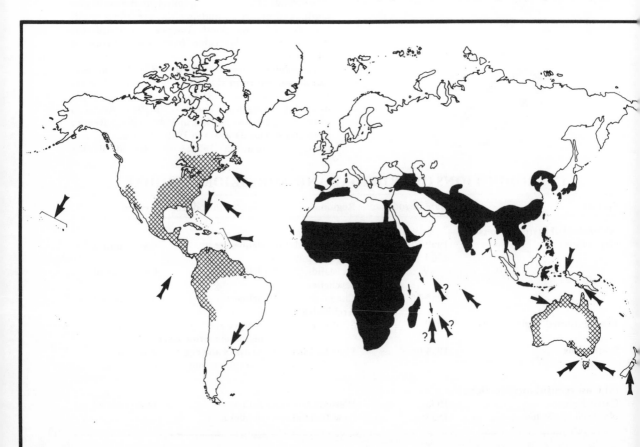

Cattle Egret

in Crosby, 1972) the Cattle Egret reached the Galápagos Islands from South America. Harris (1974) records that some arrived there in 1964 and that at present it is a regular visitor between July and April each year.

New Guinea. Rand and Gilliard (1967) list the Cattle Egret as a rare straggler in New Guinea and indicate that prior to this date there are only two records of its presence. However, it appears the Cattle Egret may have commenced colonising New Guinea in about 1960. Hoogerwerf (1971) records them at Marokwari, north-western New Guinea, in 1963 and reports that they are present there between December and April each year.

Australia. Twenty Cattle Egrets were imported from Calcutta, India, in 1933, and eighteen were subsequently liberated along the Lennard River at Kimberley Downs Station, near Derby, in the north of Western Australia. These birds apparently disappeared. Colonisation of Australia by the Cattle Egret appears to have begun in the 1940s. They were first noted in the Oenpelli area, Arnhem Land, (Chalmers, 1972) in the Northern Territory in 1948 (Morgan and Morgan, 1965), and subsequently in many parts of the eastern States and Western Australia. Accounts of their spread in Australia are given by Hewitt (1960), Jenkins and Ford (1960), Wheeler (1962) and others.

In eastern and southern Australia Cattle Egrets have been recorded from Cororook, near Lake Colac, Victoria, in 1949; Mt Isa in 1952; Clarence River, New South Wales, 1954; Innisfail and Grafton, Queensland, in 1961; Atherton Shire in 1962-66 and the Brisbane area of Queensland in 1963-65; in South Australia in 1964, Tasmania and King Island in 1965; and Flinders Island, off Eyre Peninsula, South Australia, in 1970. In Western Australia they are recorded from Millstream Station on the Fortescue River in 1949, Three Springs in 1952, Norseman 1952-53, Bunbury, Kellerberrin and Perth in 1954, at Many Peaks and Ravensthorpe on the south coast in 1958 and throughout most of the south-west of the State in 1959. Cattle Egrets have been recorded breeding in New South Wales, Queensland and the Northern Territory. The species appears to be spreading in Australia, particularly in the eastern States (Chalmers, 1972). Condon (1975) indicates that it is the race *A.i. coromanda* which has colonised Australia.

New Zealand. The Cattle Egret appears to have reached New Zealand in 1963 (Turbott *et al,* 1963) and more recently strong circumstantial evidence suggests that they are now breeding there (Westerskov, 1974). The species was first reported at Christchurch in 1963 and in the following year was reported from widely separated areas in the North and South Islands (Falla *et al,* 1966).

Korea. Cattle Egrets have only relatively recently been found breeding at Haenam, Cholla-namdo province and Chongwon, Chunchongpukdo province in South Korea. Previously the species was considered to be a straggler in South Korea (Gore and Won, 1971).

Hawaiian Islands. The Cattle Egret was deliberately introduced to the Hawaiian Islands from Florida in 1959 to control insect pests such as houseflies, hornflies and others which cause damage to hides (Breese, 1959). Apparently, funds for the import were provided by ranchers on the islands. Peterson (1961) had earlier suggested that their appearance on the Hawaiian Islands may have been due to colonisation. Some 105 Cattle Egrets were released on five islands between July and August of 1959. They were released at one site on Kauai, Molokai and Maui and at two on Oahu and Hawaii. Another twenty-two were released on Oahu in July 1961, and by that time a further twenty-six had been released from the Honolulu Zoo where a number had been kept from the 1959 introduction (Berger, 1972). By July 1962 the population of Cattle Egrets on Oahu exceeded 150 (Thistle, 1962). Active rookeries were found on Oahu in 1960 and in 1963. The species is now common on Oahu and a few exist on the other main islands (Hawaiian Audubon Society, 1975). More recently they have been recorded on Laysan Island and Tern Island (French Frigate Shoals) (Pyle, 1978).

Chagos Archipelago. Twelve Cattle Egrets were deliberately introduced in 1955, from the Seychelles by Captain G. Lanier, in an attempt to control flies (Loustau-Lalanne, 1962). Hutson (1975) says that according to the Seychellois in 1971, some nine Cattle Egrets were released in 1953. Loustau-Lalanne says that they were well established in the early 1960s, and adds that local opinion is that they serve the purpose for which they were introduced. However, it is feared that they may spread and become a serious pest to the breeding colonies of seabirds on some of the islands. In 1960 there was an established colony of twenty-seven nests at Point Est; they were still breeding there in 1965 and the colony was flourishing in 1967 (Bourne, 1971). Hutson (1975) recorded that they were common around the island. Both Bourne and Hutson have indicated that the Cattle Egret reaches Diego Garcia as a rare visitor and that the present population may be from hybridisation of birds of Asiatic and Ethiopian origin.

Seychelles. Penny (1974) reports that the Seychellois say the Cattle Egret was introduced to the island near the beginning of the twentieth century. Penny says that one cannot rely on such evidence, but their occurrence there at this time appears to fit the time of colonisation of the species elsewhere. Penny indicates that they were deliberately introduced to Frigate and Praslin islands in 1960 to control flies and have become well established on both of these islands. The present stock, which is little different to *B.i.ibis,* may be a hybrid between an old endemic race and introduced birds, as early specimens of *B.i. seychellarum* show evidence of Asiatic rather than African origin. The species is now widely distributed in the Seychelles.

Mauritius. Cattle Egrets reach Mauritius as winter visitors. Rountree *et al* (1952) say that a few are introduced from Malagasy occasionally, but are invariably exterminated.

DAMAGE

Cattle Egrets are generally said to be beneficial in areas which they have colonised and been introduced to deliberately. Their association with cattle gains them a twofold advantage of obtaining as much as one-and-a-half times as much food by expending two-thirds as much energy per unit time compared with non-association (Heatwole, 1965). Cattle Egrets have been recorded to prey on small birds. Cunningham (1965) reports one eating an adult Blackpoll Warbler *(Dendroica striata)* in Florida, USA, and says that one has also been seen eating a Myrtle Warbler *(D. coronata)*. On some Mascarene Islands they may be having some effects on other bird species, some of which appear to be rare. Cattle Egrets are predators of eggs and chicks on seabird islands, such as Bird Island in the central group and Desnoeufs Island in the Amirantes, and raid breeding Fairy Terns on Frigate Island in the Seychelles (Penny, 1974). Penny reports that their expansion on Frigate Island should be examined carefully. Loustau-Lalanne (1962) expresses similar sentiments for the species on the Chagos Archipelago where he indicates that they may become a serious pest to the breeding colonies of seabirds.

NANKEEN NIGHT-HERON
Nycticorax caledonicus (Gmelin)

DISTINGUISHING CHARACTERISTICS
54-63 cm (21.25-24.8 in). 670-822 g (1.47-1.8 lb)
Forehead to nape black, nape with three long white plumes; remainder of upper parts chestnut; white streak above eye to forehead; underparts creamy white; face yellow-green; bill black and/or olive-green.
Reader's Digest, 1977, p.83, pl.p.82.

GENERAL DISTRIBUTION
Philippines, Bonin (extinct) and Lesser Sunda Islands, Sulawesi to New Guinea, New Caledonia, Solomon Islands, Australia and Tasmania.

INTRODUCED DISTRIBUTION
Introduced unsuccessfully in New Zealand and Western Australia (extirpated).

GENERAL HABITS
Status: fairly common. *Habitat:* margins of rivers, swamps and sheltered sea inlets. *Gregariousness:*

Nankeen Night-heron

solitary and in flocks. *Movements:* sedentary, but occasionally wanders long distances. *Foods:* small aquatic animals and insects. *Breeding:* most months of year, mainly Oct-Mar; colonial with other water birds. *Nest:* roughly made of sticks, on horizontal branches of trees, in or near water, but also on the ground. *Eggs:* 2-3, 5 (Australia).
Reader's Digest, 1977, p.83.

NOTES ON INTRODUCTIONS
New Zealand. Some Nankeen Night-herons were liberated unsuccessfully near Wellington in 1852. The species is a rare straggler to New Zealand but there are few records during the twentieth century. They possibly bred at Blenheim in 1957-59, and one bird was observed at Kaitaia in 1961 (Falla *et al,* 1966).
Western Australia. In 1900 a colony of 200 night-herons bred on Bird Island, off mainland Western Australia. This colony disappeared but from a group of seven birds introduced from there to the Zoological Gardens, South Perth, in 1914, a large nesting colony was built up numbering several thousand birds. Between 1939 and 1941, on the grounds that the birds were killing fish in goldfish ponds, the nests and young were destroyed and the colony dispersed. The Nankeen Night-heron does have colonies elsewhere in the south-west of Western Australia where it occurs naturally (Serventy and Whittell, 1967).

DAMAGE
None known.

BLACK-CROWNED NIGHT-HERON
(Night Heron)
Nycticorax nycticorax (Linnaeus)

DISTINGUISHING CHARACTERISTICS
50-70 cm (19.7-27.5 in). 525-1014 g (1.15-2.23 lb)
Crown and back black, with greenish gloss; forehead white; 2-4 long white nuptial plumes on hindneck; neck, wings, rump and tail white or grey; underparts white tinged grey, except on throat; bill blackish.
Palmer, vol.1, 1962, pp.472-475.
Blake, vol.1, 1977, pp.166-167 and pl.3.

GENERAL DISTRIBUTION
America, Africa and Eurasia: in America from eastern Washington, southern Idaho and southern Canada, south to Mexico, Central America and South America, the West Indies, Falkland Islands and the Hawaiian Islands. In Eurasia sporadically in western Europe to southern Japan and south to the Philippines and Indonesia. In Africa throughout, and breeds in parts of northern Africa, southern Africa, Zanzibar, Malagasy and St Helena. European birds migrate as far south as South Africa.

INTRODUCED DISTRIBUTION
A feral colony of the North American race is established in Scotland. In some areas of central and western Europe it has become established, through recolonisation.

GENERAL HABITS
Status: common, but decreasing in some areas of Europe. *Habitat:* salt and freshwater swamps and marshes, tidal estuaries, mud-flats, edges of lakes, ponds, sluggish rivers and ricefields. *Gregariousness:* pairs, small parties and flocks to 50 or 60 birds. *Movements:* sedentary and migratory. *Foods:* largely fish, but also frogs, crayfish, crustacea and other aquatic animals, also small rodents and downy Tern

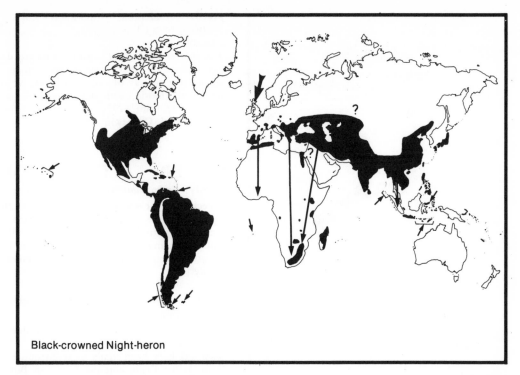

Black-crowned Night-heron

chicks. *Breeding:* most of year (Africa), May-July (Europe and Hawaii); colonial. *Nest:* loose platform of sticks, lined with rushes, in a tree or bush, rarely on the ground and sometimes in reeds above water. *Eggs:* 1, 2-6, 8 (America), 3 (Africa), 2-4 (Hawaii), 2-5, 8 (Europe).

Palmer, vol. 1, 1962, pp.476-484.

NOTES ON INTRODUCTIONS

Great Britain. A feral colony, of the race *N.n. hoactli* from North America, became established in about 1950 in the grounds of Edinburgh Zoo, Scotland (Dorward, 1957; Lever, 1976, pers. comm.). Lever (1977) records that initially some birds escaped, but that later the whole colony of eighteen birds were allowed their freedom. The colony was the progeny of birds imported from North America, in 1936 and 1946, by the Royal Zoological Society of Scotland, Edinburgh. The population has now built up to forty to fifty birds, which have been recorded over a wide area of up to thirteen kilometres (eight miles) from the zoo, and possibly now breeds outside the zoo grounds.

Europe. In many places in Europe this night-heron has disappeared as a breeding bird as a result of persecution by man and reclamation of habitat,

especially in western and central Europe and to a lesser extent in North America. The species re-established itself in the Netherlands as a breeding bird in about 1940 after several unsuccessful attempts (Voous, 1960) in about 1908-09 (Lever, 1977).

Note: See further details in Cramp and Simmons, 1977.

DAMAGE

None known.

Threskiornithidae

SCARLET IBIS

Eudocimus ruber Linnaeus.

DISTINGUISHING CHARACTERISTICS

53.7-68.7 cm (21-26.8 in). 505-935 g (1.13-2.06 lb)
Entirely scarlet with black primaries; bare skin on face duller red; bill variable, from blackish to buffy brown.

Thomson, no.4, 1964, pl.18, p.304.

Blake, vol. 1, 1977, pp.199-200.

GENERAL DISTRIBUTION

South America: northern and eastern South America from Venezuela to eastern Brazil, Colombia, and Trinidad and Margarita Island. Wanders to West Indies outside the breeding season.

INTRODUCED DISTRIBUTION

Introduced, probably successfully, in Florida, USA; possibly introduced (escapees?) unsuccessfully in Canada.

GENERAL HABITS

Status: common in parts of range, but species not well known. *Habitat:* coastal swamps, mangroves, estuaries, tidal flats and rivers. *Gregariousness:* flocks, sometimes large flocks up to 200 birds. *Movements:* sedentary with wide seasonal dispersal, occasionally over considerable distances. *Foods:* small fish, molluscs, crustaceans, worms, insects and vegetable material. *Breeding:* Apr-Oct; colonial.

Black-crowned Night-heron,
Nycticorax nycticorax

Scarlet Ibis

Nest: loose platform of sticks in mangroves. *Eggs:* 2-4.

Palmer, vol.1, 1962, pp.529-532.

NOTES ON INTRODUCTIONS

Canada. Scarlet Ibis were first observed in Canada in 1937 (Godfrey, 1966). Those noted since may have been birds which have escaped from captivity and the species is not established in Canada.

USA. Some Scarlet Ibis escaped from a zoo in Lee County in October 1954 but their fate appears to be unknown. According to Reilly (1968) the species became established in 1960 in Florida by egg transplantation. Eggs were placed in the nests of the White Ibis *(E. albus);* however, as a result of this practice considerable hybridisation occurred between the two species (Blake, 1977).

DAMAGE

The Scarlet Ibis is not known to cause any damage to agriculture. However, there is some danger that the scarlet species may hybridise with the White Ibis, a native of Florida, with deleterious effects on that species. Heilbrun (1976) reports two hybrids were noted in Dade County in 1975.

ORDER: FALCONIFORMES

Family: *Cathartidae* American Vultures or Condors

7 species in 5 genera; 1 introduced successfully

Apart from the Turkey Vulture — which has been successfully introduced into Puerto Rico, Hispaniola, and to Bahama Island — there appear to have been no other attempts at introducing members of this family.

Family: *Accipitridae* Kites, Hawks, Eagles and Old World Vultures

217 species in 64 genera; 2 species introduced (status uncertain)

Attempts have been made to re-introduce both the White-tailed Eagle and the Common Buzzard, the former in Scotland and the latter in Northern Ireland. More recent attempts have been made to re-introduce the Bearded Vulture *(Gypaetus barbatus)* in the Alps of Europe (Geroudet, 1977), to transplant Golden Eagles *(Aquila chrysaetos)* in Montana, and to transplant the eggs and young of Bald Eagles *(Haliaeetus leucocephalus)* in New York and Maine in the United States (USDI, 1976). Also, radio-tagged Bald Eagles have recently been released in western Washington during investigations of rehabilitation techniques (Servheen and English, 1976). It is not clear how much success these species have had, but they may all have been re-established to some extent.

INTRODUCTIONS OF CATHARTIDAE, ACCIPITRIDAE AND FALCONIDAE

Species	Date introduced	Region	Manner introduced	Reason
(a) Successful introductions				
Turkey Vulture	about 1880 or between 1874 and 1899	Puerto Rico	deliberate	?
	after 1931 ?	Dominican Republic	deliberate?	?
	after 1931 ?	Haiti, West Indies	deliberate?	?
	recent	Bahama Island, Bahamas	?	?
Marsh Harrier	about 1885	Society Islands	deliberate	rat control
Chimango Caracara	1928	Easter Island	deliberate?	?
(b) Possibly successful introductions				
White-tailed Eagle	1959 and (?) more recently	Scotland and Inner Hebrides	deliberate	preservation?
Peregrine Falcon	1975 and 1977	USA	deliberate	conservation
Bearded Vulture	mid-1970s	Europe	deliberate	re-introduction
Common Buzzard	mid-1970s	Europe	deliberate	conservation?

The Swamp Harrier has been deliberately introduced into the Society Islands with much success.

Family: *Falconidae* Falcons and allies

61 species in 10 genera; 2 introduced, 1 successfully
The Chimango Caracara has been successfully introduced on Easter Island (Pacific Ocean) off the coast of Chile, where it is now apparently well established. Although this species is occasionally a nuisance to stock in South America, nothing appears to have been documented on its status in this regard on Easter Island.

Releases of Peregrine Falcons in the United States as yet appear to be experimental rather than anything else. However, the decline of this and other Falconiformes in North America and Europe will probably generate more introductions amongst this group.

A species of Falcon (*Falco* sp.) was introduced to the Hawaiian Islands in Hilo Harbour when two birds from Vancouver, British Columbia, escaped from a ship on its way to Japan. One bird was apparently killed and the other disappeared (Munro, 1960).

Cathartidae
TURKEY VULTURE
(Carrion Crow, Crow)
Cathartes aura (Linnaeus)

DISTINGUISHING CHARACTERISTICS
63.5-80 cm (25-31.5 in). 0.8-2.4 kg (1.76-5.29 lb)
Generally brownish black with bare crimson or purplish red head and upper neck (some races have whitish or yellow bands on hindneck); two-tone blackish wings; feathers of back and wings edged brown; underside black and greyish; tail, long and slender, black; bill, hooked, whitish, and red basally.
Brown and Amadon, vol.1, 1968, pp.175-177 and pl.1, nos. 4-6, p.179.
Blake, vol.1, 1977, pp.266-268.

GENERAL DISTRIBUTION
North, Central and South America and the West Indies: from southern British Columbia, central Alberta, southern Saskatchewan, southern Manitoba and western and southern Ontario in southern Canada, south to the Straits of Magellan, South America and the Falkland Islands; also Trinidad, Margarita Island, Ile of Pines, Jamaica, Cuba and

Turkey Vulture, *Cathartes aura*

Turkey Vulture

coastal cays, and north-western Bahamas (Grand Bahama, Abaco and Andros). Northern populations winter in central California, south-western Arizona, southern Texas and south to Panama.

INTRODUCED DISTRIBUTION
Introduced successfully to Puerto Rico and Hispaniola in the West Indies, and possibly to the Bahamas.

GENERAL HABITS
Status: very common. *Habitat:* open country, large towns, wilderness areas, farms, woods and orchards. *Gregariousness:* singly, pairs or small groups, but larger flocks gather at food sources and on migration (several hundred). *Movements:* sedentary, and migratory in north of range. *Foods:* carrion and occasionally live animals including birds and small domestic animals. *Breeding:* Aug-Oct (South America); Feb-June (North America) and Nov-Mar (Trinidad). *Nest:* among rocks in sides of cliffs, caves, hollow logs or stumps, or on bare ground in a thicket. *Eggs:* 1-2, 3.
Brown and Amadon, vol.1, 1968, pp.175-177.

NOTES ON INTRODUCTIONS
West Indies. The Turkey Vulture was introduced to Puerto Rico from Cuba in about 1880, and only fairly recently became established in Hispaniola where they are found in the north-eastern portion of the Dominican Republic (Bond, 1960). Dod (1977, pers. comm.) says the species was introduced into the Dominican Republic and Haiti from Cuba some time after 1931. She indicates they are now well established in the north-eastern portion of the island and have extended their range to the north-central part, as far west as the Sierra de Oca. The race introduced in Puerto Rico appears to have been that of *C. aura aura* (A.O.U., 1957). Wetmore (1927) reports that the species is said to have been brought there from Cuba many years ago by Spanish government agencies and 75

to have established itself in the south-west corner of the island where it is increasing slowly if at all. He says that Gundlach was emphatic that it did not occur there in 1874 and they appear to have been recorded by a naturalist for the first time in 1899. In May 1912 he estimated that there were about twenty-five birds there and by 1922 the population had increased to about fifty. Blake (1975) indicates that the Turkey Vulture has also been introduced to Bahama Island, but less successfully than on Puerto Rico.

Accipitridae

WHITE-TAILED EAGLE
(Grey Sea Eagle)
Haliaeetus albicilla (Linnaeus)

DISTINGUISHING CHARACTERISTICS

67.5-92.5 cm (26.39-36.24 in). Females 3.6-6.5 kg (8-14.3 lb); males 3-4.9 kg (6.6-10.8 lb)
Generally dark brownish; crown, nape and sides of neck brown, with tips of feathers paler; remainder of upper parts dark brown with some whitish mottling; chin, throat and upper breast as for crown and nape; remainder of underparts as for upper parts; tail white, the feathers having brown bases, and some white mottling; wings brown; bill and cere pale yellow.
Brown and Amadon, vol.1, 1968, pp.291-292 and pl.26, nos. 3-4, p.293.

GENERAL DISTRIBUTION

Coastal south-western Greenland, western Iceland and Eurasia: in Eurasia from coastal Scandinavia, northern USSR, south to the Kurile Islands, Sakhalin, Manchuria and north-east China, southern USSR, extreme northern Iran, northern Iraq, Turkey and south-eastern Europe. In winter south to Korea, China and India, and probably other areas south of breeding range. Formerly more widespread in western Europe.

INTRODUCED DISTRIBUTION

Re-introduced in Scotland (status uncertain).

GENERAL HABITS

Status: fairly common, but declined in western Europe. *Habitat:* rivers, lakes, pools, estuaries, sea coasts and open country. *Gregariousness:* pairs. *Movements:* sedentary and partially migratory. *Foods:* fish, water birds, ptarmigan, snow hares, lambs, seals and carrion. *Breeding:* Feb-mid-May. *Nest:* large nest of sticks and branches in an isolated tall tree or forest, or rocks on sea coasts. *Eggs:* 1-3.
Brown and Amadon, vol.1, 1968, pp.292-296.

NOTES ON INTRODUCTIONS

Scotland. The White-Tailed Eagle formerly inhabited the whole of Europe and last bred in the British Isles in the Shetlands in 1908 (Voous, 1960). Until the eighteenth century the species bred in the Isle of Man and in the Isle of Wight at least up until 1780, and was widely distributed in Ireland and Scotland. They were still present in fair numbers up until the mid-nineteenth century in northern Scotland and islands, and in parts of Ireland. Towards the end of the nineteenth century they had been reduced to a few pairs in some of the islands off the north and west coast of Scotland, became extinct in Ireland about 1911 and in the Shetlands were reduced to one pair which bred until 1908 (Witherby *et al,* 1938-41).

An attempt was made to re-introduce the species to Scotland in the Fair Isle (south of the Shetlands) in the late 1950s. Sandeman (1965) records that one adult and two young were imported from Norway and released in Scotland. In July 1959 these birds were released at Glen Etive where they had been kept tethered for about fourteen days. The adult bird was caught about one month later and eventually placed in the Edinburgh Zoo. One young bird was found in a fox trap in January 1960 and the other bird was perhaps still there in 1963. Sharrock (1976) indicates that attempts are currently under way to re-introduce

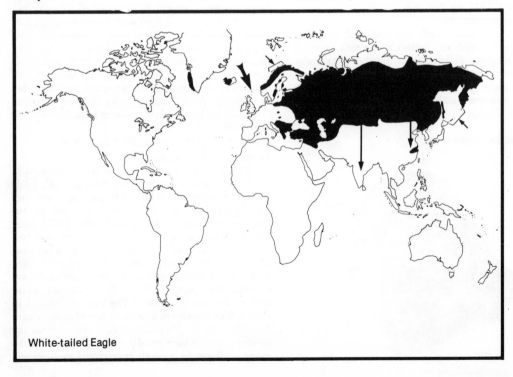

White-tailed Eagle

this species in the Inner Hebrides. A second attempt appears to have been made to establish them on the Fair Isle in 1967 when four juveniles from Norway were released, but this introduction also failed after a short period.

COMMON BUZZARD
(Buzzard, Steppe Buzzard)
Buteo buteo (Linnaeus)

DISTINGUISHING CHARACTERISTICS

50-55 cm (19.7-21.65 in)

Variable species, varying from white with brown spots and bars to dark chocolate-brown. Generally, back dark brown, sometimes with buff edging; breast variably brown; tail buff, with broad brown subterminal band and with narrow darker bands above (white phase); bill and cere yellow. Female larger.

Brown and Amadon, vol.2, 1968, pp.609-612, pl.104, nos.1-4, p.611.

GENERAL DISTRIBUTION

Eurasia-Africa. From the Cape Verde Islands, British Isles and Scandinavia east across central Asia to Sakhalin and Japan. Also East and South Africa and Malagasy. Northern birds winter south to South Africa, India, northern Thailand, China and South Korea.

INTRODUCED DISTRIBUTION

Re-introduced in Northern Ireland (re-established?) and on the European mainland (status not known).

GENERAL HABITS

Status: becoming uncommon, at least in western Europe. *Habitat:* woody and rocky regions, forests bordering grasslands and moors. *Gregariousness:* large flocks in mass migrations. *Movements:* sedentary and migratory. *Foods:* small mammals (e.g. rabbits, hares, voles, mice and other rodents), birds, snakes, carrion, large insects, worms and snails.

Breeding: Mar-June. *Nest:* large, untidy bowl-shaped structure of branches, sticks and roots, lined with grass, wool, lichen and twigs, on a rocky ledge, in a tree or on the ground. *Eggs:* 2-3, 6.

Brown and Amadon, vol.2, 1968, pp.612-616.

NOTES ON INTRODUCTIONS

Europe. The Common Buzzard has been re-established as a breeding bird in northern Ireland (Peterson *et al,* 1963) where it has not bred for many years. More recently Toso (1977) gives an account of the release in the wild of two Common Buzzards reared in captivity in Europe.

MARSH HARRIER
(Swamp Harrier, Swamp Hawk)
Circus aeruginosus (Linnaeus)

DISTINGUISHING CHARACTERISTICS

Male 47.5-58 cm (18.5-22.8 in), female to 60 cm (23.6 in); male 427-580 g (.94-1.27 lb), female 600-1100 g (1.32-2.42 lb)

Generally brown to black upper parts with buff or whitish and black streaks; crown and nape paler and yellower (in some races at least); underparts whitish to buff or chestnut, streaked dark brown; tail and wings greyish; wing primaries black; tail with faint barring (noticeably so in *ranivorus*); upper tail-coverts with white band; cere green-yellow; bill blue-black, brown at base. (Races variable and there is a sooty black and sooty brown phase.) Female: browner, yellowish head and shoulders and more heavily streaked underparts.

Brown and Amadon, vol. 1, 1968, pp.380-382 and pl.49, nos.1-2, p.381.

Reader's Digest, 1977, p.131 and pl. p.131.

GENERAL DISTRIBUTION

Eurasia-Africa and Australasia: In Eurasia from the Iberian Peninsula, south-eastern England and south-eastern Sweden to Sakhalin Island: in north-west

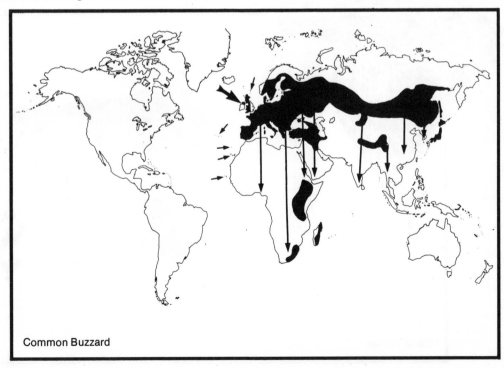

Common Buzzard

Africa and southern Africa from north-eastern Congo, Zaire, Uganda and Kenya southwards; also Malagasy: in south-eastern New Guinea, south-western and eastern Australia including Tasmania, New Zealand, Norfolk and Lord Howe islands, New Caledonia and Fiji. Northern population winters south to South Africa, Arabia, Pakistan, India, Sri Lanka, Bangladesh, Burma, Malay Peninsula, Thailand, Vietnam, China, Hainan, Borneo, Taiwan, the Philippines, South Korea and Japan.

INTRODUCED DISTRIBUTION

Introduced successfully to Tahiti and has spread to other islands in the Society Group.

GENERAL HABITS

Status: not uncommon; as a result of cultivation of breeding grounds and direct persecution totally exterminated in Ireland and most of Great Britain. *Habitat:* reed beds, marshes, swamps, grasslands near water and open low-lying country. *Gregariousness:* solitary or pairs, sometimes groups gather at a food source. *Movements:* migratory and sedentary. *Foods:* small birds (coots, waders, etc.), small mammals (rats, voles, etc.), small reptiles, frogs and fish, eggs of swamp birds, large insects and probably carrion. *Breeding:* Feb-Dec (in Africa); Sept-Jan (in Australia). *Nest:* stalks and sticks, lined with grass, on the ground in swamp vegetation or low bush or reeds, etc. *Eggs:* 3-6, 8 (Africa 3-4).

Brown and Amadon, vol.1, 1968, pp.382-386.

NOTES ON INTRODUCTIONS

Society Islands. The Marsh Harrier was introduced to Tahiti in about 1885 by the German Consul, who desired to exterminate rats (Holyoak, 1974). They reached other islands in the Society Group by themselves but were probably aided by the presence of man. In 1900 they were apparently rare, as few were collected, but by 1920 they were somewhat common. The Whitney Expedition collected specimens on Tahiti, Raiatea, and Moorea, and two birds were found on Bora Bora in 1922, and many on Tetiaroa (Holyoak). Thibault (1976) indicates that they probably colonised Tetiaroa from Tahiti, but the present population does not exceed a couple of pairs. Holyoak found the Marsh Harrier on Tahiti, Moorea, Raiatea and Bora Bora in 1972, and indicates that they probably exist on Huahine and possibly some other islands (Maupiti ?). In Tahiti the species was common everywhere. On the other islands it was widespread except perhaps for the towns and villages, which it avoids.

DAMAGE

It is thought by Thibault (1976) that the Marsh Harriers' predation on colonies of *Gygis alba* on Tetiaroa may be important, but the numbers of harrier on the atoll are small so the effects may also be small. Holyoak (1974) agrees that the harrier may be responsible to some extent for the rarity of this species throughout the Society Islands. Holyoak also maintains that there is at least some circumstantial evidence that the harrier may have played a part in the extinction of the parrot *Vini peruviana* on some islands. He says that two Marsh Harriers were noted on Bora Bora in 1922 and at a time when *Vini* was abundant there. In 1972 there were at least a score of pairs of the hawk but the parrot had completely disappeared. Holyoak indicates that many Tahitians claim that the harrier became abundant in about 1930 and that the parrots disappeared at about this time. Also with the increase of the harrier, the pigeon *Ptilinopus purpuratus* has become rare in the Society Islands. The harrier is known to prey on the pigeon and may also have assisted towards its present rarity.

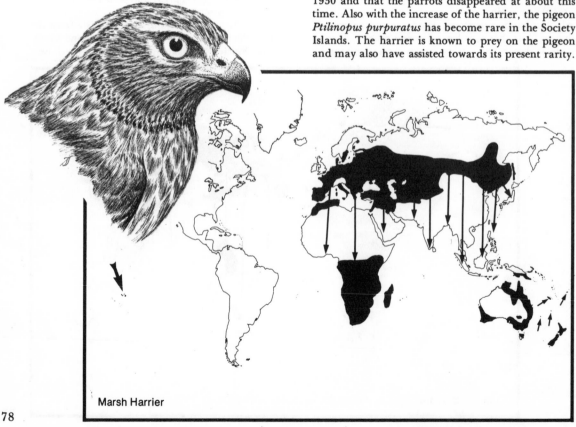

Marsh Harrier

78

Although some people (*vide* Bruner, 1972) have pleaded in favour of conserving the Marsh Harrier, others (*vide* Holyoak) feel that it is more realistic to recommend its extermination in the Society Islands.

Falconidae
PEREGRINE FALCON
Falco peregrinus Tunstall

DISTINGUISHING CHARACTERISTICS
36-55 cm (14.17-21.65 in). 330-1222.5 g (.73-2.7 lb) Crown, hindneck, face and moustachial stripe, blackish; back, upper wings and rump ashy blue barred with dark slate; tail barred and tipped whitish; underparts buffy whitish to pinkish (chestnut in some races) with blackish brown bars on sides of thighs; black spots on abdomen; cere greenish yellow; bill slaty blue, blackish at tip. Female: larger.
Brown and Amadon, vol.2, 1968, pp.850-852 and pl.162, p.837; pl.163, p.841; pl.164, p.845; pl.165, p.849.
Reader's Digest, 1977, p.132 and pl.p.132.

GENERAL DISTRIBUTION
Eurasia, Africa, America and Australasia: in Eurasia breeds spasmodically over most except parts of south-central Asia, Indochina and Arabia. Breeds in parts of South, East and West Africa, coastal north-eastern Africa and in Egypt, the Canary Islands and Malagasy. In North America breeds from Alaska and Canada south to the southern US and northern Mexico. Breeds on Sumatra, Borneo, Sulawesi to New Guinea, Australia, Tasmania, New Caledonia and the New Hebrides. In the non-breeding season migrates south in Eurasia to West and South Africa, Arabia, India and Malaysia; in North America south through Central America and the West Indies to northern Chile and northern Argentina. (A southerly breeding population in southern Patagonia and Tierra del Fuego migrates north at least as far as northern Chile.) In Australia appears to be nomadic.

INTRODUCED DISTRIBUTION
Re-introduced in some parts of the USA (status?).

GENERAL HABITS
Status: has declined in numbers sharply in many regions of the world in recent years; has become rare in many places. *Habitat:* lightly wooded regions, mountainous and rocky regions in deserts, savannahs and arctic scrub and tundra; open country, marshes and shores. *Gregariousness:* solitary or pairs. *Movements:* sedentary, migratory and nomadic. *Foods:* mainly birds but exceptionally small mammals. *Breeding:* June-Nov (Africa), Aug-Dec (Australia) and Apr-May (Great Britain). *Nest:* scrape on edge of cliffs, tall buildings, hollow in tree and occasionally on the ground. *Eggs:* 2-4, 7 (2-3 Australia).
Brown and Amadon, vol.2, 1968, pp.853-856.

NOTES ON INTRODUCTIONS
USA. In 1975, three hand-reared birds were fitted with radio transmitters and released at Barnegat, New Jersey, in an experimental effort at re-introduction of the species. They were seen later some distance south at Brigantine (National Wildlife Refuge), New Jersey (Paxton *et al,* 1976). The Cornell University, New York, has released a number of captive-bred peregrines in areas east of the Mississippi River. In 1975 some sixteen were liberated at five locations and at least twelve birds were thought to have been successfully re-established. The United States Fish and Wildlife Service reported in 1976 that during 1975, thirty-seven captive-bred young peregrines had been released at eight sites by seven different States. At least twenty-two of these birds had survived to the winter of 1976. More recently, about 1977, some forty-two pen-reared birds were released by the Cornell University.

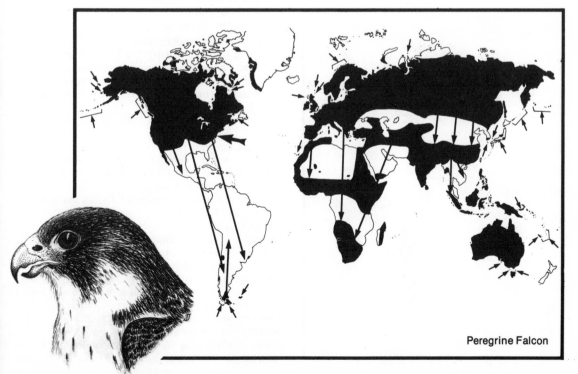

Peregrine Falcon

CHIMANGO CARACARA
(Chimango Carrion-hawk, Chimango)
Milvago chimango (Vieillot)

DISTINGUISHING CHARACTERISTICS
37.5-42.5 cm (14.58-16.55 in)
Cinnamon or rufous-brown, streaked dark brown on the crown and nape; feathers of the upper parts pale edged and vaguely barred reddish brown; upper tail-coverts white; tail buffy white, mottled and barred greyish, subterminal band greyish, and a pale tip; wing-coverts brown, pale near ends and with a dark tip; bill horn.
Brown and Amadon, vol.2, 1968, pp.739-740 and pl.133, no.3, p.737.

GENERAL DISTRIBUTION
South America: From north-central Chile, Argentina and extending into Bolivia, Paraguay, Uruguay and south-western Brazil south to southern Chile, Tierra del Fuego and southern Argentina. Southern populations migrate north in winter to northern Argentina.

INTRODUCED DISTRIBUTION
Introduced successfully on Easter Island, Pacific Ocean.

GENERAL HABITS
Status: very common. *Habitat:* plains, savannah and pampas, cultivated areas, often near water and cattle; forest areas locally and wooded areas. *Gregariousness:* small groups, hundreds in cultivated areas. *Movements:* sedentary and partly migratory. *Food:* insects and carrion (grubs, larvae, caterpillars, frogs, crabs, small fish, etc.). *Breeding:* Sept-Jan; two broods per year. *Nest:* bulky structure of thorny sticks with deep cup, lined with soft vegetable fibres, wool, etc., in a tree, or on the ground in treeless country. *Eggs:* 2-4.
Brown and Amadon, vol.2, 1968, pp.740-741.

Chimango Caracara

NOTES ON INTRODUCTIONS
Easter Island. Introduced in 1928, the Chimango Caracara became established and has now overrun the island (Johnson, Millie and Moffett, 1970). No other details of this species' introduction to Easter Island were found.

DAMAGE
This species may occasionally become a nuisance as they have the habit of sitting on the backs of cattle while removing ticks and sometimes tend to open up sores on cattle. No information on any effects the species may have had on the fauna of Easter Island appear to be documented.

ORDER: GALLIFORMES

Family: *Cracidae* Curassows, guans, chachalacas.

44 species in 11 genera; 6 species introduced, 1 successful and 1 possibly successful
Attempts to introduce members of the *Cracidae,* probably as game birds, have been largely unsuccessful. The Plain Chachalaca has had some success on Sapelo and Blackbeard islands in Georgia in the United States; the Rufous-tailed Chachalaca may have been introduced to some small islands in the Lesser Antilles, but may also have arrived there as a colonist; the Great Curassow may yet be successfully re-established on Barro-Colorado Island in Panama.

The introduction of six 'Powi Birds' at Royal Park, Melbourne, in Victoria, Australia, in about 1866 is thought to refer to a curassow of the genus *Pauxi* or *Pipile,* but the true identity of those released does not appear to have been established beyond doubt. A species known as Paui or Paoui (the White-crested Curassow *Pipile pipile*) is endemic to Trinidad.

BLACK CURASSOW
(Crested Curassow)
Crax alector Linnaeus

DISTINGUISHING CHARACTERISTICS
85-96 cm (33.46-37.79 in). 2.4-3.7 kg (5.29-8.15 lb)
Generally glossy black; belly, flanks and under tail-coverts white; head with prominent crest; tail black; bill blackish, base yellow to red. Female similar but crest barred white.
Delacour and Amadon, 1973, p.221 and pl.30, pp.234-235.

GENERAL DISTRIBUTION
South America: Guyana, southern Venezuela and northern Brazil west to the Rio Negro.

INTRODUCED DISTRIBUTION
Possibly introduced, unsuccessfully, to Haiti (West Indies) and New Zealand.

GENERAL HABITS
Status: fairly common. *Habitat:* forest. *Gregariousness and movements:* no information. *Foods:* animal and vegetable material such as fruits, nuts, birds, insects and frogs. *Breeding:* Dec-Apr (Surinam). *Nest:* platform of sticks lined with leaves and bark, in a tree. *Eggs:* 2-3.
Delacour and Amadon, 1973, pp.221-222.

NOTES ON INTRODUCTIONS
Haiti. According to Wetmore and Swales (1931) the Crested Curassow was introduced into Haiti from

INTRODUCTIONS OF CRACIDAE

Species	Date introduced	Region	Manner introduced	Reason
(a) Successful introductions				
Plain Chachalaca	1923	Sapelo and Black-beard Islands, USA	deliberate	game ?
(b) Possibly successful introductions				
Rufous-tailed Chachalaca	before late 17th century ?	Lesser Antilles (Grenadines, Bequia, Union and St Vincent)	deliberate or colonisation ?	?
Great Curassow	recent ?	Barro-Colorado Island, Panama	deliberate	re-establishment
(c) Unsuccessful introductions				
Chestnut-winged Chachalaca	1928	Hawaii, Hawaiian Islands	presumed released ?	game ?
Plain Chachalaca	1929-68	San Diego Zoo, USA	at freedom	?
Black Curassow	before 1931 ?	Haiti ?	deliberate ?	?
Great Curassow	1928	Hawaiian Islands	presumed released ?	game
	1923	USA	deliberate	game ?
	before 1931 ?	Haiti	deliberate ?	?
	1888-92	France	kept at liberty	game ?
Crested Guan	1928	Hawaiian Islands	deliberate ?	game

Mexico. However, the species now known as Crested does not occur in Mexico, and there may have been some confusion with the Great Curassow which is crested and very similar in appearance. Bond (1960) and Delacour and Amadon (1973) make no mention of the species in the West Indies so the introduction was evidently unsuccessful.

New Zealand. Black Curassows were imported to New Zealand in 1873 and 1874, but it is not known if any were liberated (Thomson, 1922).

DAMAGE
None known.

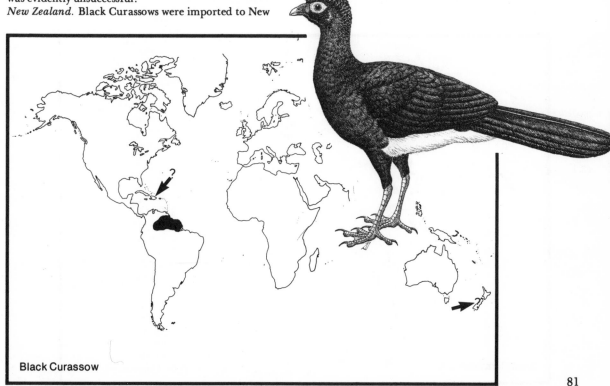

Black Curassow

GREAT CURASSOW

Crax rubra Linnaeus

DISTINGUISHING CHARACTERISTICS
75-97 cm (29.52-38.18 in). 4.6-4.8 kg (10.14-10.58 lb)

Generally glossy black; frilly rounded crest black; abdomen, flanks and under tail-coverts white; tail sometimes tipped white; bill black, with bulbous yellow knob at base of upper mandible, and base of lower mandible yellow. Female: head and neck black, spotted with white; crest barred white; remainder chestnut, paler on belly; tail black and buff; lacks knob on bill. Plumage is variable in this species, both a red and barred black phase are known. Delacour and Amadon, 1973, p.211, and pls.27, p.219, and 28, p.225.

GENERAL DISTRIBUTION
Central and South America: from northern Mexico south to Colombia and western Ecuador.

INTRODUCED DISTRIBUTION
Introduced unsuccessfully to the Hawaiian Islands USA (?), Haiti, France and Panama.

GENERAL HABITS
Status: fairly common, but numbers being reduced by settlement. *Habitat:* dense rain forest. *Gregariousness:* singly, pairs, small groups of up to six birds. *Movements:* sedentary. *Foods:* fruits, nuts, acorns, buds, insects, leaves, shoots, flowers and snails. *Breeding:* no information — apparently unrecorded. *Nest:* loosely woven structure of twigs, lined with green leaves, in a tree. *Eggs:* 2-3. Delacour and Amadon, 1973, pp.211-215.

NOTES ON INTRODUCTIONS
Hawaiian Islands. The race *C.r. rubra* was imported to these islands from Panama in 1928 as a potential game bird (Munro, 1960). There appear no records of its release, but apparently it was unsuccessful.

USA. H. E. Coffin and the Bureau of Biological Survey imported nine birds from Mexico in 1923 and released them on Blackbeard Island, off Georgia (Phillips, 1928). Phillips records that only two birds were left by 1926.

Haiti. Possibly introduced to Haiti (see Black Curassow) some time prior to 1931, the Great Curassow apparently failed to become established as there is no subsequent mention of it in the West Indies.

France. The Great Curassow was introduced and kept at liberty in France, at least in one area, from 1888 to 1892 (Etchécopar, 1955). Etchecopar records that they bred in the wild there at this time. The fate of those birds which became established is not recorded, but the colony evidently failed or was shot out.

Panama. A pair of Great Curassows have been introduced to Barro-Colorado Island, Panama, in an attempt to re-establish the species there (Delacour and Amadon, 1973), but recent information is lacking.

DAMAGE
None known.

CRESTED GUAN
(Purple Penelope, Purplish Guan)

Penelope purpurascens Wagler

DISTINGUISHING CHARACTERISTICS
76-92 cm (30-36 in). 1.7-1.9 kg (3.74-4.18 lb)

Head, hindneck, upper back and wings bronze-olive; head with short, bushy crest; chest and breast dark brown streaked white; lower back, belly, rump and under tail-coverts chestnut; tail coppery olive, lateral edges white; bare skin around eye blue; bare skin on neck red; bill blackish brown. Delacour and Amadon, 1973, p.136 and pl.13, p.137.

GENERAL DISTRIBUTION
Central and South America: eastern and western

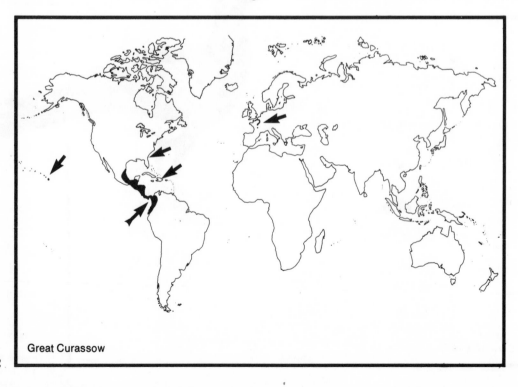

Great Curassow

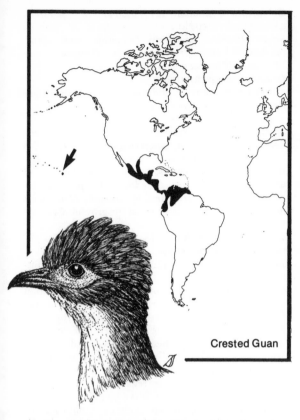

Crested Guan

Plain Chachalaca

Mexico south to Colombia, Venezuela and western Ecuador.

INTRODUCED DISTRIBUTION

Introduced unsuccessfully to the Hawaiian Islands.

GENERAL HABITS

Status: fairly common. *Habitat:* humid lowland rain forest and secondary growth, and some drier areas. *Gregariousness:* small groups and large flocks (up to 800 birds ?). *Movements:* sedentary. *Foods:* fruits, berries, seeds, acorns, flowers, leaves, buds and other vegetable material, and insects. *Breeding:* Mar-June (Venezuela); monogamous. *Nest:* bulky structure of leafy twigs, lined with leaves, in a tree or on a stump. *Eggs:* 3.

Delacour and Amadon, 1973, pp.136-140.

NOTES ON INTRODUCTIONS

Hawaiian Islands. Purple Guans *(P.p. aequitorialis)* were imported from Panama as a potential game bird in 1928, but did not succeed in establishing themselves in the Hawaiian Islands (Munro, 1960).

PLAIN CHACHALACA
(Common Chachalaca, Eastern Chachalaca)
Ortalis vetula (Wagler)

DISTINGUISHING CHARACTERISTICS

48-64 cm (18.89-25.2 in). 300-794 g (.66-1.75 lb) Generally grey-brown; upper parts brownish olive; crown and throat stripe dull blackish brown; face and throat bare, with blue facial skin and red throat; breast olive-brown or greyish brown; remainder of underparts vary from whitish to brownish; tail long, rounded, dusky, glossed bluish and white tipped; bill light hornish bluish. (Races vary from dark to pale birds.)

Delacour and Amadon, 1973, p.88 and pl.5, p.88.

GENERAL DISTRIBUTION

Central and North America: the lower Rio Grande Valley, Texas, south through eastern and southern Mexico to western Nicaragua, Honduras and north-western Costa Rica.

INTRODUCED DISTRIBUTION

Introduced successfully on Sapelo and Blackbeard (?) islands, Georgia, USA.

GENERAL HABITS

Status: common. *Habitat:* dense thickets, open woodland, clearings, tall brush and forest edges. *Gregariousness:* small (family ?) flocks, and loose feeding flocks in autumn and winter. *Movements:* sedentary (?). *Foods:* fruits, seeds, leaves, buds, shoots, twigs, berries, flowers and small animals (i.e. snails, worms, caterpillars and bugs). *Breeding:* Mar-May (Yucatan). *Nest:* small frail construction of sticks, twigs, grass and leaves in a bush or tree or, rarely, on the ground. *Eggs:* 2, 3-4 (a nest of 9 recorded).

Delacour and Amadon, 1973, pp.88-95.

Plain Chachalaca, *Ortalis velula*

USA. The subspecies *O.v. mccalli* has been introduced and established on Sapelo and Blackbeard islands, Georgia. The forty-two birds introduced came from Tamaulipas State, Mexico, and were released by H. E. Coffin in 1923 (Phillips, 1928). Phillips reports that they were breeding there in 1924, and by 1926 their numbers had increased considerably. Recent reports indicate that they are still established, at least on Sapelo Island, and possibly on Blackbeard Island (Heilbrun, 1976; Blake, 1975). Some were also established at freedom in the San Diego Zoo, California, from 1929 until 1968 where they bred regularly but were never numerous (twelve in 1947) (Delacour and Amadon, 1973).

DAMAGE

When natural foods are scarce the Plain Chachalaca occasionally damages crops in south Texas, in fields near its natural habitat (Marion, 1976). Crops reported eaten include cantaloupes, melons, citrus, lettuce, sorghum and tomatoes, but damage is negligible and farmers are not greatly concerned about it. No damage appears to have been recorded from Georgia.

RUFOUS-TAILED CHACHALACA
(Rufous-vented Chachalaca)
Ortalis ruficauda Jardine

DISTINGUISHING CHARACTERISTICS

45-61 cm (17.71-24 in). 455-800 g (1-1.76 lb)
Forehead and malar regions black; crown and sides of head grey; bare skin around eye dark blue; bare sides of throat red; upper parts and chest olive-green; lower back browner; lower breast and belly greyish brown; flanks and under tail-coverts rufous; tail bronze-green, tipped white or chestnut; bill dusky horn.

Rufous-tailed Chachalaca

Delacour and Amadon, 1973, p.98 and pl.6, p.99.

GENERAL DISTRIBUTION

South America: northern Colombia, west across northern Venezuela, south to Orinoco; also Margarita Island and Tobago.

INTRODUCED DISTRIBUTION

Colonised or were introduced to the Grenadines, Bequia, Union and St Vincent in the Lesser Antilles.

GENERAL HABITS

Status: common. *Habitat*: forest edges and thorny deciduous brushlands. *Gregariousness*: flocks of 6-8 birds, and up to 50 may occur together. *Movements*: sedentary. *Foods*: berries, fruits, leaves, flowers and other vegetable matter. *Breeding*: May-June; partly polygamous and form nesting colonies. *Nest*: stick nest, well hidden in a tree or on the ground. *Eggs*: 2-3, 4.

Delacour and Amadon, 1973, p.98.

NOTES ON INTRODUCTIONS

Lesser Antilles. Peters (1934) records that Rufous-tailed Chachalacas were introduced from Tobago and established on the islands of Bequia and Union. Bond (1960) reports that they were possibly taken to the Grenadines from Tobago or Venezuela by early European settlers or by the Caribs. He indicates that the species was established on the Grenadines, and apparently also on St Vincent, as early as the late seventeenth century. Delacour and Amadon (1973) say that although they are regarded as having been introduced to these islands, it is a fact that the species has colonised Margarita and Tobago without human assistance and that this suggests their presence on the Grenadines and St Vincent was due to colonisation. Delacour and Amadon indicate that the history of the island and the Ola people insist that the birds are native to the islands.

DAMAGE

According to Ffrench (1976), farmers on Trinidad and Tobago say, without adequate evidence, that the species attacks certain crops.

CHESTNUT-WINGED CHACHALACA
(Grey-headed Chachalaca)
Ortalis garrula (Humboldt)

DISTINGUISHING CHARACTERISTICS

45-60 cm (17.71-23.62 in). 630-755 g (1.38-1.66 lb)
Head and neck rufous-brown or grey; facial skin red or blackish *(cinereiceps)*; throat and breast brownish olive or chestnut-brown; remainder of underparts whitish or buffy brown; wings rufous-chestnut; tail bronze-green, central feathers tipped white or buff; bill pale bluish horn, darker basally.

Delacour and Amadon, 1973, p.95 and pl.6, p.99.

GENERAL DISTRIBUTION

South and Central America: Nicaragua south to northern Colombia from the vicinity of the Sinu River east to south-western, western and north-western foothills of the Santa Marta Mountains and the Lower Magdalena Valley.

INTRODUCED DISTRIBUTION

Probably introduced, unsuccessfully, to the Hawaiian Islands.

GENERAL HABITS

Status: fairly common (?). *Habitat*: thickets, scrub and open woodland. *Gregariousness*: small flocks of 6-12 and up to 20 birds throughout the year.

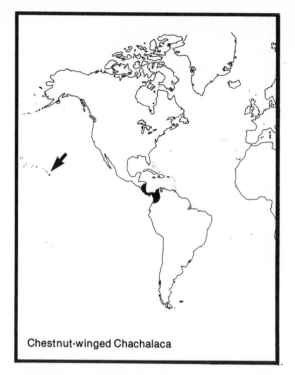

Chestnut-winged Chachalaca

Both the Malleefowl and Brush-Turkey have been introduced to Kangaroo Island, South Australia, where the latter species may still be established. The Brush-Turkey may also be established on Dunk Island, off northern Queensland.

MALLEEFOWL
Leipoa ocellata Gould
DISTINGUISHING CHARACTERISTICS
55-60 cm (21.65-23.62 in). Female 1.6 kg (3.52 lb) Head, neck and breast lead grey; black bar down centre of breast; crest brown; wings, tail and back dark brown, with black spots on white backgrounds; underside light brown; tail with irregular black bars; bill dark grey.
Frith, 1962.
Reader's Digest, 1977, pl.pp.136-7.
GENERAL DISTRIBUTION
Australia: semi-arid and arid inland southern Australia, from Griffith, New South Wales, to the west coast of Western Australia.
INTRODUCED DISTRIBUTION
Introduced unsuccessfully to Kangaroo and Rottnest islands, Australia.
GENERAL HABITS
Status: fairly common. *Habitat:* mainly in mallee scrubs and heaths. *Gregariousness:* solitary. *Movements:* sedentary, but with some local movements. *Foods:* seeds, fruits, flowers, buds and insects. *Breeding:* Sept-Apr. *Nest:* mound of earth and vegetable material up to 1.5 m (5 ft) high and may measure 4.5 m (15 ft) at the base. *Eggs:* 5, 15-24, 35.
Frith, 1962.
Reader's Digest, 1977, pp.136-137.
NOTES ON INTRODUCTIONS
Kangaroo Island. Seventeen Malleefowl were introduced to this island by the Royal Australian Ornithological Union in 1911. At this time it was said that the species would be safe, on Kangaroo Island, from the introduced fox which was apparently exterminating ground-living species on the mainland (Mellor, 1911). There were several subsequent introductions up until 1936. Several pairs were liberated in 1912, one pair in 1923, one pair in 1924

Movements: sedentary (?). *Foods:* fruits, berries, drupes and vegetable matter such as leaves. *Breeding:* Feb-May (Costa Rica). *Nest:* broad shallow saucer of vines, sticks and green leaves, in a bush or small tree, or a small amount of decayed matter in a stump. *Eggs:* 2-3.
Skutch, *Wilson Bulletin,* vol.75, no.3, 1968, p.262.
Delacour and Amadon, 1973, pp.95-97.
NOTES ON INTRODUCTIONS
Hawaiian Islands. According to Munro (1960) the race *cinereiceps* was brought to the island of Hawaii from Panama in 1928. Presumably some were released, but failed to become established.
DAMAGE
None known.

Family: *Megapodiidae* Moundbuilders
18 species in 7 genera, 2 species introduced, possibly 1 established

INTRODUCTIONS OF MEGAPODIIDAE

Species	Date introduced	Region	Manner introduced	Reason
(a) Possibly established introductions				
Brush-Turkey	1936 and later ?	Kangaroo Island, Australia	deliberate	conservation ?
	about 1935	Dunk Island, Australia	deliberate	?
(b) Unsuccessful introductions				
Malleefowl	1911, 1912, 1923, 1924 and 1936	Kangaroo Island, Australia	deliberate	conservation ?
	1928	Rottnest Island, Australia	died before release	?
Brush-Turkey	1869	New Zealand	deliberate	?
	1870-71 and about 1888-90	France	deliberate	?

Malleefowl

BRUSH-TURKEY
(Scrub Turkey)
Alectura lathami Gray

DISTINGUISHING CHARACTERISTICS
65-75 cm (25.6-29.52 in).
Skin of head and neck bright red, with some black hair-like feathers; base of neck and wattles yellow or purplish white; upper parts black; underparts brownish black, mottled buffy white; bill black.
Reader's Digest, 1977, p.139 and pl.p.139.

GENERAL DISTRIBUTION
Australia: eastern Australia from Cape York, Queensland, to the Hawkesbury River, New South Wales.

INTRODUCED DISTRIBUTION
Introduced and possibly still established on Kangaroo Island, South Australia, and Dunk Island, Queensland; introduced unsuccessfully in New Zealand and France.

GENERAL HABITS
Status: fairly common, but numbers reduced in many areas. *Habitat:* rain forests, dense vegetation along creeks and inland scrubs. *Gregariousness:* solitary. *Movements:* unknown, probably sedentary. *Foods:* insects and other small animals, fruits, berries and seeds. *Breeding:* Aug-Dec, or longer. *Nest:* mound of vegetable material measuring about 1 m (3 ft) high by 4 m (13 ft) across. *Eggs:* 18-24 to 30 or more.
Reader's Digest, 1977, p.139.

NOTES ON INTRODUCTIONS
Kangaroo Island. A pair of Brush-Turkeys were introduced to Flinders Chase on Kangaroo Island in 1936 and perhaps others were released at a later date. The race introduced was *A.l. lathami* (Condon, 1975). Brush-Turkeys were present on the island in 1948 (Anon, 1948), three were seen in 1969 (Lendon, 1971) and Lees (1972, in Abbott, 1974) saw one bird and two mounds in about 1972. It is

and six birds in 1936 (Anon, 1948; Condon, 1948; Condon, 1968). According to Abbott (1974) there have been no subsequent records of the Malleefowl on Kangaroo Island, and Condon (1975) indicates that the species is probably now extinct there.

Rottnest Island. Malleefowl were taken to Rottnest, off the coast of Western Australia, in 1928 but died before they could be released (Storr, 1965).

DAMAGE
None known.

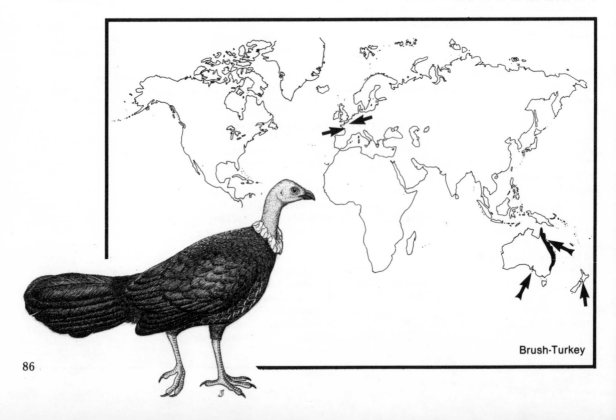

Brush-Turkey

possible that the species is still established there.

Dunk Island. The race *A.l. lathami* was introduced on Dunk Island, off northern Queensland, in about 1935 (Condon, 1975) and is apparently still established there?

New Zealand. In 1869 Sir George Bowen sent two birds from Australia to the Auckland Acclimatisation Society in New Zealand. These were liberated at Kaipara but failed to become established (Thomson, 1922).

France. The Brush-Turkey was kept in a park at Touraine by M. Cornely from 1870-1871, where they bred, and by the Marquis d'Hervy of St Denis at Bréan-sous-Nappe in Seine-et-Oise, who kept them in semi-captivity (?), but they disappeared after the harsh winters of 1888-90 (Etchécopar, 1955).

DAMAGE

None known.

Family: *Numididae* Guineafowl

7 species in 5 genera; 1 species introduced successfully Guineafowl have been widely introduced throughout the world with some success. Most of the successes appear to have been reduced, largely by overhunting, at some period or other. Nevertheless, they exist in many areas in a feral or semi-feral state.

The species was probably domesticated by natives of the Guinea Coast of Africa and probably introduced into the civilised world by the Greeks and Romans, but certainly before the fifteenth century (Wing, 1956).

They are said to have reached Greece hardly before the fifth century B.C. (Zeuner, 1963).

HELMETED GUINEAFOWL
(Tufted Guineafowl, Guinea Fowl)
Numida meleagris Linnaeus

DISTINGUISHING CHARACTERISTICS

60 cm (23.62 in). 775-2000 g (1.7-4.4 lb)

Generally blackish, or greyish, thickly spotted with white; variably shaped bony red-brown crest; penduline wattles blue, tipped red; some fine barring on chest and wing; bare skin on face and sides of neck blue; bill reddish with yellow tip.

Mackworth-Praed and Grant, 1952-1973, ser.1, vol.1, pp.271-274 and pl.21; ser.2, vol.1, pp.230-232 and pl.15; ser.3, vol.1, pp.198-200 and pl.16.

Bannerman and Bannerman, vol.4, 1963-68, pp.292-296 and pl.43, opp. p.292.

GENERAL DISTRIBUTION

Africa: most of Africa except the northern parts (now confined to a small portion of central Morocco), and south-western Africa.

INTRODUCED DISTRIBUTION

Introduced successfully in South and East Africa, Hispaniola, Cuba and the Isle of Pines; probably introduced successfully in Arabia, Malagasy, Archipel des Comores, Mauritius, Agalega Islands, Annobon Island, Cape Verde Islands and Barbuda (feral); introduced but now extirpated on Rodrigues Island; introduced but now extinct on Ascension Island, Chagos Archipelago (?), St Helena (?), Jamaica and Puerto Rico; introduced and occasionally becomes, or is, feral locally in France (?), New Zealand, Australia and the Hawaiian Islands. Introduced unsuccessfully to Trinidad, Gonave Island (West Indies), (?) Madeira and/or Porto Santo and the USA.

GENERAL HABITS

Status: fairly common, but range and numbers reduced. *Habitat:* forest edges, grassland, scrubland and clearings, acacia forest, thorn or open bush country, savannah and old cultivation. *Gregariousness:* pairs in the breeding season, at other times flocks of 20 or more, and larger flocks of up to hundreds in some areas. *Movements:* sedentary. *Foods:* insects (incl. beetles and grasshoppers), worms, molluscs, seeds, roots, tubers, bulbs and crops of all kinds. *Breeding:* Oct-June (Dec-Feb on Agalega); 2 birds often lay in same nest. *Nest:* scrape on the ground, well hidden. *Eggs:* 6-10, 20.

Mackworth-Praed and Grant, 1952-73, ser.1, vol.1, pp.271-275; ser.2, vol.1, pp.231-232; ser.3, vol.1, pp.198-201.

Bannerman and Bannerman, vol.4, 1963-68, pp.292-296.

NOTES ON INTRODUCTIONS

Africa. Guineafowl have been shot out over much of their former range in Africa, but have been re-introduced in some areas, such as around Cape Town. They were introduced to Stellenbosch and neighbouring areas of south-western Cape Province many years ago, probably at about the end of the nineteenth century, and to Likome Island, Lake Nyasa, in 1912 (Mackworth-Praed and Grant, 1952-73). The race introduced in Cape Province and in East Africa is *N.m. mitrata.*

Arabia. Meinertzhagen (1954) says that Guineafowl were probably introduced to Arabia. They are resident only from the northern parts of the Peoples Democratic Republic of Yemen and throughout Yemen to Asir Tihama where the northern limits appear to be Wadi Itwad. The race in Arabia does not differ from that on mainland Africa in the Sudan.

Malagasy and Archipel des Comores. According to Thomson (1964), Guineafowl are represented on these islands by what are probably introduced birds. However, they are generally listed as a native species on both and if they were introduced it must have been many years ago. Neither Rand (1936) nor Milon *et al* (1973) make any mention of any introduction to Malagasy, but report that the species is common in the east and west of the island and less common in the central regions.

Benson (1960) reports that *N.m. mitrata* occurs on Grande Comore, Anjouan and Mayotte. He states that they were probably introduced over a century ago because specimens were obtained there in 1843 and the species was plentiful in 1876.

Mauritius. The race *N.m. mitrata* was probably introduced in the eighteenth century from Malagasy to Mauritius but is now rare in a wild state, although several domesticated races still exist there (Rountree *et al*, 1952; Benedict, 1957). Staub (1976) records that mention of Guineafowls on Mauritius was made by Bernardin de Saint Pierre in 1769. Staub says that the species was reported to be present around 1970 in the Black River Gorges on the island.

Ascension Island. Guineafowl were presumably introduced and flourished on this island during the 1830s. At about this time 1500 were reported to have been shot in one day (Stonehouse, 1962). By 1864, they were still plentiful but could be shot only under licence. According to Stonehouse the reason for their extinction towards the end of the century is unknown. However, it may have been due to hunting pressure. The race appears to have been *N. m. galeata*.

Rodrigues Island. Guineafowl were possibly introduced to Rodrigues Island (Gill, 1967). Staub (1976) records that P. Marragon, Civil Agent for Rodrigues, wrote to the Council governing the Mascarenes in August 1803, saying that he was doing his best to introduce the species to the island. It would

INTRODUCTIONS OF NUMIDIDAE: NUMIDA MELEAGRIS

	Date introduced	Region	Manner introduced	Reason
(a) Successful introductions	Various times	Africa	deliberate re-introductions	hunting and re-stocking
	end nineteenth century	Cape Province, South Africa	deliberate re-introduction	hunting ?
	1912	Malawi, South Africa	deliberate	?
	1508 ?	Antilles	deliberate	domestic species — food
	before 1733	Hispaniola, West Indies	feral ?	food ?
	before 1889	Barbuda, Lesser Antilles	feral ?	food ?
	?	Cuba and Isle of Pines	feral ?	food ?
(b) Probably introduced successfully	early ?	Yemen ?	(	
	early ?	Malagasy ?	(	
	prior 1843 ?	Archipel des Comores	(May have been deliberately	
	before 1769	Mauritius ?	introduced or may	
	about 1860 ?	Annobon Island ?	have become feral,	
	?	Agalega Islands	but possibly native	
	before 1683 ?	Cape Verde Islands ?	at least to some islands.	
(c) Introduced and established locally at times	1864, 1867 and later	New Zealand	deliberate, feral, escapee	captive bird ?
	1870-73, prior 1912 and later	Australia	deliberate, feral, escapee	captive bird ?
	1960-70	Heron Island, Australia	deliberate ?	?
	1874, 1914 and later	Hawaiian Islands	deliberate, feral, escapee	captive bird ?
	early and recent ?	France	?	?
(d) Probably introduced unsuccessfully	prior 1830s ?	Ascension Island?	(	
	1803	Rodrigues Island ?	May have been	
	prior 1907 ?	Chagos Archipelago ?	deliberately intro- duced or become	
	before 1588 ?	St Helena ?	feral, but possibly	
	?	Madeira and Porto Santo ?	native to some islands, now extirpated on all.	
(e) Introduced unsuccessfully	1890, 1903, 1929-30 and 1942	Oregon and California, USA	deliberate	?
	1700	Trinidad	deliberate	food ?
	before 1836 ?	Puerto Rico	domestic bird ?	food ?
	before 1889 ?	Barbados	domestic bird ?	food ?
	early eighteenth century	Jamaica	?	?
	?	Gonave Island, Haiti	deliberate	game
	?	Rottnest Island, Australia	deliberate	?

appear that it did not occur there previously. Gill indicates that they were numerous there in 1864 and were still present until a few years ago. Staub says the species was deliberately exterminated because it became a pest to crops.

Chagos Archipelago. Loustau-Lalanne (1962) indicates that Gadow and Gardiner (in 1907) found a few wild Guineafowl on Takamaka, Fouquet and Anglaise islands in the Chagos Group. He found no signs of them on his visit just prior to 1962. Bourne (1971) records that they have been reported from Salomon Island. It seems doubtful that Guineafowl would be found naturally in the Chagos Group and it is assumed that they were introduced there. It seems doubtful that they still exist but they may well be on some of the less regularly visited islands as Bourne's observation indicates.

Agalega Islands. (South of Seychelles 10°20′S and 56°04′E) Watson *et al* (1963) record that Guineafowl have been introduced to Agalega and occur there in grassy areas.

Annobon Island. Guineafowl are resident and have probably been introduced on Annobon Island, although there is no evidence of them being domesticated (Fry, 1961). Fry says they are common in cultivated country in the north of the island where they have maintained their numbers for over one hundred years.

St Helena. According to Peters (1934) the race *N.m. galeata* has been introduced to the island of St Helena. Melliss (1870) indicates that they may have been present there in 1588. In 1870 they were apparently present as domesticated and wild birds.

Haydock (1954) does not record their presence on the island in 1952.

Cape Verde Islands. N.m. galeata were probably introduced to the Cape Verdes by the early Portuguese settlers. They may have been sighted at Sal by Dampier in 1683, were certainly abundant in 1709 in Maio, and Darwin found them on São Tiago in 1832 (Bannerman and Bannerman, 1968). Bannerman says they were found by Bolle on the islands of São Nicolau, São Vincente, Fogo, Mayo and Santiago, in about 1856. Bolle apparently mentions that the species had died out on Brava, but had been recently re-introduced there.

They were recorded on São Tiago, Brava, São Nicolau, São Vincente, Santo Antão and Boa Vista Islands (Barboza du Bocage, 1898) and much later were recorded from Fogo again (Murphy, 1924). Bannerman reports that the species has now disappeared from Brava and São Vincente islands, but is apparently present on most of the other islands mentioned.

Madeira and Porto Santo. Guineafowl are reported to have been introduced to Madeira and/or Porto Santo, but do not now occur there in a wild state (Bannerman, 1965).

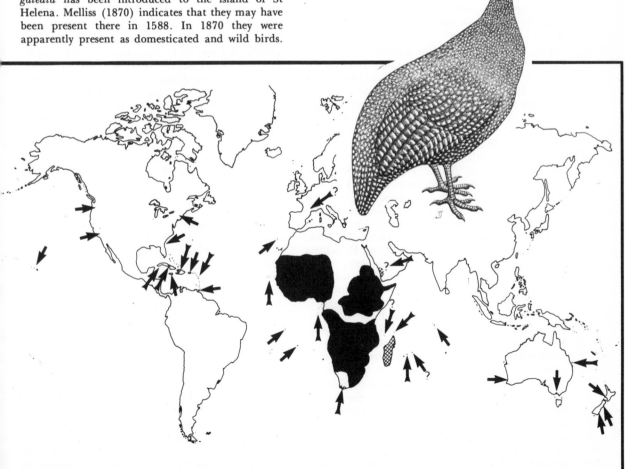

Helmeted Guineafowl

West Indies. Introduced into Hispaniola many years ago, Guineafowl were well established and widespread in the eighteenth century (Wetmore and Swales, 1931). Wetmore and Swales say they are reported to have been brought to the Antilles in about 1500, but that this date can not now be substantiated. Wetmore (1927) and Bond (1960) indicate that they arrived in 1508. They were common in a domesticated state on Barbados and Barbuda in 1889 and had apparently run wild in at least some areas of Barbuda (Feilden, 1889). In 1700 a pair were freed on the island of Trinidad (Murphy, 1915).

Guineafowl were present in Hispaniola in 1733, 1797 and 1798 and were apparently common there in 1799. In 1810 they were slaughtered in large numbers on the plains of Neiba and sold as cheap food (Wetmore and Swales). They were common as domesticated and wild birds in 1897 (Christy, 1897) and were still present in many localities, mostly in Haiti in 1930 (Wetmore and Swales). Danforth (1929) found them common in woods by the Yaqui River near Monte Cristi and a few at La Vega, San Juan, L'Archahaie, St Marc and Les Salines.

In Puerto Rico, Wetmore (1927) records that Moritz (in 1836) found them in the mountains on the island; they were reported by Sundevall in 1869 as not rare there, and Gundlach found them present in 1878. In 1911-12 Wetmore says that they were reported to still range in areas of natural forest, on Cerro Gordo and Monte del Estado above Maricao, in Caguana near Barros, and on El Yunque de Luquillo. By 1927, he doubted their existence on Puerto Rico.

Elsewhere in the West Indies Guineafowl have been introduced to Gonave Island (Wetmore and Swales), Jamaica, Cuba (Peters, 1934) and on the Isle of Pines (Bond, 1960). Attempts to establish them as a game bird appear to have failed on Gonave Island, but they may be established in many other areas. They apparently flourished on Jamaica in the eighteenth century and the first part of the nineteenth century, and there were still a few present at the end of the nineteenth century (Lack, 1976). However, the species is now extinct there. Bond reports that they are domesticated throughout the West Indies and that they would have been feral in many places had it not been for predation by the mongoose. He indicates that they are still feral in Cuba (from Las Villas Province eastwards), on the Isle of Pines, Hispaniola and on Barbuda. More recently, Blake (pers. comm. 1977) says they still survive quite well in the West Indies but do not spread much, due probably to hunting pressure.

In the Dominican Republic, Dod (pers. comm. 1977) says that although they are well established there, numbers are decreasing rapidly due to overhunting and predation by the introduced mongoose.

New Zealand. Guineafowl were first introduced to New Zealand by early missionaries on the Bay of Islands (Thomson, 1922). Thomson indicates that in 1864 a shipment of these birds arrived from India and were probably liberated by the Canterbury Acclimatisation Society. A further shipment was received by the Otago society in 1867 but they apparently did not become established. Both Thomson and Oliver (1930-55) mention that

Guineafowl were liberated at various places by private individuals or were abandoned when homesteads were vacated. In the 1920s Guineafowl were common in the Aberfeldy district of Wanganui and were reported from the Waikato district at later dates. They were introduced to Raoul Island by T. Bell in 1906 and were last reported there in 1909. The Guineafowl is probably not now established in New Zealand (Wodzicki, 1965). Some may possibly exist locally but little is known of them (Falla *et al*, 1966).

Australia. Apparently Guineafowl were released in Australia in large numbers (about 170) in about 1870-71 at Gembrook Reserve, Cape Liptrap, Lillydale and other areas in Victoria but failed to become established there (Ryan, 1906). Some may have been released in Victoria in 1872 and in 1873. They were liberated in Western Australia from importations made prior to 1912 (Long, 1972). Most were kept in captivity and the young allowed to roam in the hope that they would become established in the wild. Although they were reported to be thriving in some coastal districts in the 1920s, they did not become permanently established in Western Australia. Guineafowl were introduced to Rottnest Island, off the coast of Western Australia, but failed there also (Storr, 1965). Between 1960 and 1970 they were liberated on Heron Island, Queensland, are now localised on the Capricorn Island Group (Lavery, 1974) and have been reported breeding there (Kikkawa and Boles, 1976).

Hawaiian Islands. As early as 1874 Guineafowl (domestic escapees) were introduced to the Hawaiian Islands (Walker, 1967). Some were released on Lanai in 1914 but apparently died out (Munro, 1960). Munro says large numbers were released on several islands but did not appear to be doing very well up until about 1944. The species may still be established in the Hawaiian Islands but it is not open to hunting (Walker), and probably exists only on private lands (Berger, 1972). The Hawaiian Audubon Society (1975) reports that some appear to exist on the island of Hawaii, but that their present status is poorly known.

USA. Long domesticated in the United States, the Guineafowl has been the subject of a number of attempts to establish them in the wild. Some forty or fifty birds were released on Jekyl Island, Georgia, in about 1890 (*Forest and Stream* 54: 209, 1900) without any permanent success (Phillips, 1928). Phillips also reports that in about 1903 temporary success was achieved with a release in California. In 1886-90 some were liberated in Tuxedo Park in the State of New York by the Tuxedo Park Club, but these birds soon disappeared (Bump, 1941). Some 278 were released in the southern Willamette Valley, Oregon, in 1929-30, but there are no subsequent records of these birds (Gullion, 1951) and they presumably failed to become established. Some were liberated in Georgia and California in 1942 but had only temporary success and failed to become permanently established at either place (Gottschalk, 1967).

France. Apparently the Guineafowl was an early introduction into France for hunting but proved an inferior game bird and the efforts to establish them were not pursued (Etchécopar, 1955). However,

Heinzel et al (1976) record that they are still found in southern France, but those established are possibly the results of more recent introductions.

DAMAGE

There are few records of Guineafowl becoming a pest to crops. An early record of damage by them is that quoted by Wetmore (1927) who says: 'that Gundlach in 1878 remarked that the Guineafowl on Puerto Rico sometimes cause damage to bananas by destroying the fruit'. Staub (1976) indicates that they were deliberately exterminated on Rodrigues as they proved a pest to the staple maize crops.

Family: *Tetraonidae* Grouse

18 species in 11 genera; 11 introduced, 4 established, another 4 possibly but doubtfully established
Only two species of the family, the Ruffed and Blue Grouse, appear to have had much success as introduced species. The Capercaillie and Willow Grouse have succeeded where they were introduced into their former range. The Black, Hazel and Sage Grouse have failed and the remaining species are still doubtfully established.

None of them has been sufficiently well established to have become pests, although a number of them are

INTRODUCTIONS OF TETRAONIDAE

Species	Date introduced	Region	Manner introduced	Reason
(a) Successful introductions				
Capercaillie	1837, 1862, 1865 and 1870	Scotland	deliberate re-introduction	game ?
	1900	Bulgaria	deliberate re-establishment	?
	1933-39	Estonia, Latvia, Lithuania	deliberate re-establishment	?
Black Grouse	1933-39	Poland	deliberate	?
Willow Grouse	1820s and 1915-16	England	deliberate	?
Ruffed Grouse	1911, 1940-41 1944, 1948-49 and 1956-57	Michigan, USA	deliberate transplants	?
	1959-63	Missouri, USA	deliberate re-introduction	?
	recent	Nevada, USA	deliberate	?
	?	Anticosti Island, Canada	?	?
	1956-66	Newfoundland, Canada	deliberate	?
(b) Possibly established introductions				
Capercaillie	prior 1930s ?	Denmark	deliberate re-establishment	?
	1955-65	USSR	deliberate re-establishment and re-stocking	?
Black Grouse	1969, 1971	England	deliberate	?
	1955-65	USSR	deliberate re-establishment and re-stocking	?
Blue Grouse	1970	Gulf Islands, Canada	deliberate ?	?
Willow Grouse	early 1890s	Belgium	deliberate	?
	early 1890s	Germany	deliberate	?
	1933-39	Poland	deliberate	?
	1955-65	USSR	deliberate	re-stocking
Spruce Grouse	1964	Newfoundland, Canada	deliberate	?
	1957, 1959	Kodiak and Woody Islands, Alaska	deliberate	?
Ruffed Grouse	1970 ?	Gulf Islands, Canada	deliberate transplant	?
Hazel Grouse	1933-39	Poland	deliberate	?
Sharp-tailed Grouse	1938-52	Michigan, USA	deliberate	?

91

continued

INTRODUCTIONS OF TETRAONIDAE

Species	Date introduced	Region	Manner introduced	Reason
Greater Prairie Chicken	various times ?	USA (various areas)	deliberate transplants	conservation ?

(c) Unsuccessful introductions

Species	Date introduced	Region	Manner introduced	Reason
Capercaillie	1823 and 1967-71	England	deliberate	?
	1827-31	Scotland	deliberate	?
	1842	Ireland	deliberate	?
	1741-1938	Europe (mainland)	deliberate re-establishments	?
	1936-48	Poland	deliberate	
	1903, 1906-07	Canada	deliberate	game ?
	1893, 1895, 1900, 1903, 1904-05, 1906, 1907 and 1949-50	USA	deliberate	game ?
Black Grouse	1921 and later ?	Great Britain	deliberate	
	eighteenth and nineteenth century	Ireland	deliberate	
	1886, 1895, 1900, 1903, 1904-05, 1906-07 and 1949-50	USA	deliberate	game ?
	1886, 1903, 1906	Canada	deliberate	?
	1873, 1879, 1900	New Zealand	deliberate	?
Blue Grouse	1963, 1964	Kodiak and Woody Islands, Alaska	deliberate	?
Willow Grouse	?	Shetland Islands, Scotland	?	?
	early ? and 1971-73	Ireland	deliberate re-stocking	population increase
	?	Outer Hebrides	?	?
	1912, 1939	France	deliberate	?
	1955-65	USSR	deliberate re-introductions and re-stocking	hunting
	1870, 1872, 1873	New Zealand	deliberate	?
	1905, 1948-49	USA	deliberate and transplants	? game ?
	several prior 1926	Fiji	deliberate	?
Ptarmigan	1960	Japan	deliberate transplant	?
Hazel Grouse	1905-06	USA	deliberate	?
Ruffed Grouse	1880s, 1900-01, 1923-24 and prior 1948	Wisconsin, Mississippi, New York, and other States, USA	deliberate transplants and re-introductions	?
Sage Grouse	1958	Vancouver, Canada	deliberate transplant	
	1942	Montana, USA	deliberate re-establishment	game ?
Sharp-tailed Grouse	1932	Hawaiian Islands	deliberate	game ?
	1880s-1904, 1924-25	USA (various areas)	deliberate	game ?
	1876	New Zealand	deliberate	?
Greater Prairie Chicken	1895, 1934	Hawaiian Islands	deliberate	?
	1879, 1881-82	New Zealand	deliberate	?
	1860-93	USA	deliberate	game ?
Lesser Prairie Chicken	unknown ?	Hawaiian Islands	deliberate	?
Greater and/or Lesser Prairie Chicken	1861, 1874-75	Europe	?	game ?

capable of causing damage in forestry areas where the replanting of trees is undertaken.

CAPERCAILLIE

Tetrao urogallus Linnaeus

DISTINGUISHING CHARACTERISTICS

Male 60-90 cm (23.62-35.43 in), female 57-66 cm (22.44-26 in)

Head and neck greyish; bare skin above eye red; below eye a white spot; elongated black throat feathers; breast metallic green, belly black with white spots; wings brown, speckled black; rump and flanks with wavy black and greyish lines; bill whitish. *Female:* barred and spotted with tawny red, black and white.

Witherby *et al,* vol.5, 1938-41, pp.210, 213-16 and pls. 144 opp. p.204, 146 opp. p.228.

Gilliard, 1958, p.83, pl.39.

GENERAL DISTRIBUTION

Eurasia: northern Spain, central and eastern Europe, Scandinavia and east to central Siberia. Formerly more widespread.

INTRODUCED DISTRIBUTION

Re-introduced successfully in Scotland and possibly successfully in mainland Europe and western Asia, but unsuccessful in most areas. Introductions to North America have failed.

GENERAL HABITS

Status: range and numbers reduced. *Habitat:* mixed broadleaf and coniferous forests, woodlands with undergrowth, and taiga and bogs. *Gregariousness:* solitary in summer, family parties and large parties of males in winter. *Movements:* sedentary. *Foods:* leaves, twigs, shoots, pine needles, seeds, nuts, conifer buds, heather, grass, beetles, grubs and other insects and their larvae. *Breeding:* Apr-June (Great Britain); polygamous. *Nest:* shallow depression, with a little lining of pine needles, moss and grass, on the ground under cover. *Eggs:* 4-8, 18.

Witherby *et al,* vol.5, 1938-41, pp.209-213.

Voous, 1960, p.80

Borset and Krafft, *Oikos* vol.24, 1973, pp.1-7.

NOTES ON INTRODUCTIONS

Great Britain. Capercaillie formerly occurred in the original pine forests covering the British Isles and the northern portions of Europe and Asia (Gilliard, 1958). They became extinct in Scotland about 1785 (Pennie, 1950-51; Gilliard, 1958) or even earlier between 1745 and 1760 (Bump, 1963), in Ireland about 1760 and in England possibly a century earlier (Witherby *et al,* 1941). Large-scale clearing of the forests in about 1760 is said to have led to the extermination of the species in these areas.

A number of early attempts were made to re-introduce the Capercaillie in Scotland, Ireland and England (Lever, 1977). In 1823 T. F. Buxton unsuccessfully introduced a pair in Norfolk. Between 1827 and 1831 attempts were made by the Earl of Fife to re-introduce birds from Sweden at Braemar, Aberdeenshire. Other unsuccessful introductions included those in Perthshire in the late 1830s; to Buckinghamshire and Lancashire in 1842; at Stronvar, Perthshire, in 1845; at Eslington, Northumberland, between 1872 and 1877; at Glengariff with birds from Sweden in 1879; at Inverenam, Strathdon, in Aberdeenshire, between 1870 and 1873; at Lochnabo, near Elgin, Morayshire, in about 1852; and further unsuccessful attempts in 1860, 1878 and 1883. Attempts by Lord Bantley were made to introduce them in Ireland in 1842.

Capercaillie of Scandinavian stock (from Sweden) were successfully re-introduced in 1837 at Taymouth, Perthshire (Pennie). Some twenty-eight birds were released at this date and a further sixteen females,

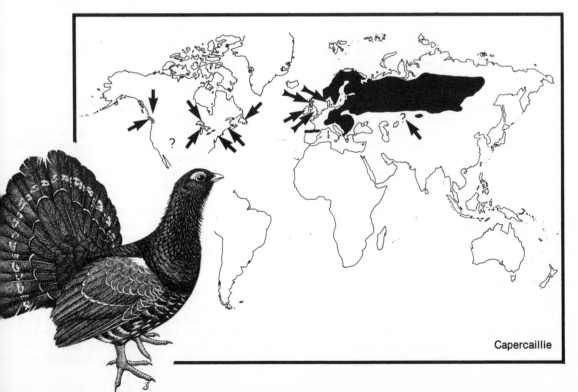

Capercaillie

also from Sweden, were released in the following year (Lever). By 1839 it was estimated that between sixty and seventy birds were present at Perthshire. This had risen to about 1000 in 1862 and the Capercaillie had spread over all the wooded parts of the highlands as far as Aberdeen.

Further releases occurred in Perthshire in 1862 and in 1865 and at Drumtochty, Kincordineshire, in 1870, and in both these areas they spread rapidly. Other introductions of eggs or birds include those at Gordon Castle in 1897; Beauly, Inverness-shire, in 1843; at Abernethy and Kinreachy about 1860; Guisachan in 1868; Abernethy and Guisachan in 1895; the Black Isle in 1888 and in 1910-11; at Coulin, Kinlochewe, in 1930; Bonar Bridge, Sutherland, in 1870; Tulliallan, Fife, in 1864; Lathirsk, near Falkland, in 1874; to Blackmount Forest prior to 1867; Broderick Castle, Isle of Arran, in 1843 and 1846; Isle of Bute in 1922 and Islay in the 1920s; between 1860 and 1870 to Douglas, Lanarkshire; Broughton, in 1902-04 and Stobo, Peeblesshire, in 1929-31; Glenapp in 1841-42; at Sanquhar, Dumfriesshire, in 1865 (Lever, 1977).

By 1914 Capercaillie had spread as far as Sutherland in the north and Argyll in the west. According to Pennie (1950-51) the spread was halted between the two World Wars and in some areas a decrease in numbers resulted, consistent with decreases in forest areas due to human agency. In the late 1930s they were spread from Tay, Dee and Moray areas as far north as Dornoch Firth, west in southern Argyll, also south to the Firth of Forth and Stirling, Dumberton, Lanark and sporadically to other places (Witherby et al).

The Capercaillie is now established throughout northern and central Scotland, but does not occur south of the Forth and Clyde (Johnstone, 1967). According to Lever (1977) the maximum spread of the bird in Scotland was reached before the first World War, and he indicates that there has been little advance in the past sixty years.

In England, more recent introductions from 1967 to 1971 at Grizedale, Lancashire, do not appear to have been very successful. Some thirty-five birds were released in 1971 and nesting was reported to have occurred in 1973 (Grant and Cubby, 1973).

Mainland Europe. Capercaillie were exterminated in Denmark but were re-introduced from Sweden to East Jutland and Bornholm prior to the 1930s (Witherby et al). However, their present status there is not known. Lindemann (1956) records that there were many attempts to re-establish Capercaillie in Europe between 1741 and 1938. He says that they failed to become established because they were unable to survive in the intensively cultivated areas into which they were transplanted. He reports similar results for introductions into unsuitable range at Warthegan (formerly western Poland) in 1936-48. Lindemann records successful introductions to Scotland and Bulgaria in 1900, and Poland, Estonia, Latvia and Lithuania in 1933-39. Lever (1977) records that introductions in Europe between about 1870 and 1924 and later failed.

USSR. Yanushevich (1966) points out that Capercaillie were introduced in the RSFSR in the 1960s, but as Sumina (1963) indicates these instances may only have been re-acclimatisations within the former range of the species. The success or failure of these introductions is not known. However, it is known that between 1955 and 1965 more than one hundred birds were released in the European part of the Soviet Union for re-stocking purposes (Osmolovskaya, 1969).

Canada. In 1906 some fourteen Capercaillie were released near Cowichan Lake on Vancouver Island, and eight were liberated near Lake Bunsen on the mainland of British Columbia (Carl and Guiguet, 1972). Carl and Guiguet say the stock was obtained from Denmark and was released by Messrs Chaldecott and Musgrove in those localities. However, they failed to become established in either area. Prior to these introductions, birds imported from Denmark or Sweden were released at Algonquin Park, Ontario, by the provincial authorities (Phillips, 1928). Phillips reports that about sixty-five (or fifty-two ?) Capercaillie were released in 1903. He also records that in 1907 twenty-three birds were shipped from Copenhagen to Newfoundland and subsequently released without success between Whitbourne and Colinet on the peninsula of Avalon.

USA. Capercaillie have been liberated in various areas of North America but have failed to become established anywhere (Gottschalk, 1967). Bump (1963) records that the following releases were made: in 1893 (two birds), 1895 (four), 1900 (?), 1903 (fifty-seven), 1904-05 (eight), 1906 (?), 1907 (?) and in 1949-50 birds from Sweden were introduced. According to Bump they all disappeared after release, but sometimes after a year or two. Phillips (1928) reports that four birds were liberated at New Sweden in northern Maine in 1895; 143 on Grand Island, Michigan, by the Cleveland Cliffs Iron Co. in 1904, followed by fifty-eight more in 1905; a few were placed in Litchfield Park near Big Tupper Lake in the Adirondacks from a large number imported in 1906. Bump (1941) indicates that twelve were released by E. H. Litchfield at Litchfield Park and that William Rockefeller also released twelve at Bay Pond Reserve in New York State in 1906. In both areas the birds soon disappeared.

DAMAGE

Capercaillie in Europe are reported to peck the buds of young trees, making them stag-headed and thus causing considerable damage in forests (Thompson, 1953). Bjor (1959) found serious damage to Norway Spruce *(Picea abies)* after repeated browsing by Capercaillie in Norway.

In Great Britain, damage by Capercaillie has been recorded as early as in the nineteenth century (in Harvie-Brown, 1879), when they supposedly often damaged forest plantations by feeding on young trees. Fisher (1907) stated that they peck off buds and young shoots of pine in winter and spring. Severe damage by the species to forest nurseries in the Black Isle, Rossshire, has been reported by Bannerman (1963).

Johnstone (1967) records that Capercaillies may take individual buds, remove whole clusters of terminal buds, and also take part of the shoot. They also tend to peck off the ends of needles, or strip them right off the twig. Johnson found that mainly Scots Pine, Lodgepole Pine, Sitka Spruce and larch were browsed by Capercaillie throughout the year. The browsing occurred mostly in late winter when damage was done to young conifers before the leading shoots grew above the critical grazing height. Damage by this and other species was known to be as high as eighty per cent of the trees having their leaders removed, but was usually around thirty to fifty per cent where the birds were common. The effects of the damage were the loss of growth and a change in tree form; repeated browsing for several seasons led to trees taking on a bush-like form with little increase in height. Both types of damage caused increased expense for foresters in prolonged maintenance costs and late returns on investments. In Great Britain, at least, the recovery of trees from Capercaillie attacks depends on the vigour of such trees and in an actively growing stand there may be little trace of damage after five or six years (Palmar, 1965).

BLACK GROUSE
Tetrao tetrix (Linnaeus)

DISTINGUISHING CHARACTERISTICS

40-60 cm (15.74-23.62 in). Males 1.2-1.5 kg (2.64-3.3 lb), females 0.9-1.05 kg (1.98-2.31 lb)

Generally black with a violet sheen; broad white band on wings, secondaries tipped white; lower tail-coverts white; naked eyebrows vermilion; a white spot beneath eye; bill black-brown. *Female:* generally rust-red and brown; head, neck and tail barred black; belly brown with red and whitish bars.

Witherby *et al,* vol.5, 1938-41, pp.216-217, 219-221 and pls. 144 opp. p.204, 146 opp. p.228.

GENERAL DISTRIBUTION

Eurasia: from England and Scotland, Scandinavia and eastern Europe, east to central and western Asia.

INTRODUCED DISTRIBUTION

Re-introduced and possibly established, and introduced successfully in some areas of Great Britain

and the USSR (?); re-introduced in Poland (?). Introductions in Ireland, North America and New Zealand have failed.

GENERAL HABITS

Status: reduced in range and numbers but still inhabits forest edges of central European mountains: increased in Great Britain possibly due to re-stocking and introductions. *Habitat:* forest surrounded by open areas, conifer plantations, upland meadows, swampy heathlands, moorlands, bogs and agricultural lands near other habitats. *Gregariousness:* singly, or in small mixed sex flocks prior to breeding; formerly in larger flocks. *Movements:* sedentary, but some local movements with season. *Foods:* shoots, buds, catkins, leaves of heather, grass, herbs and conifers; also berries, flowers, seeds and other herbage; insects occasionally. *Breeding:* Apr-June (Great Britain); polygamous. *Nest:* hollow with sparse lining of grass, leaves, etc., on the ground under heath or a bush. *Eggs:* 5-10, 13.

Witherby *et al,* vol.5, 1938-41, pp.216-217, 219-221.

Voous, 1960, p.79.

Borset and Krafft, *Oikos* vol.24, 1973, pp.1-7.

Great Britain. Black Grouse were formerly more widespread in both England and Scotland. They disappeared from many localities in the late nineteenth and early twentieth centuries. An upsurge in numbers in the 1940s and 1950s resulted in them being found in many areas from which they were believed to be absent. Some of the increase in populations has possibly been due to afforestation since the mid 1940s, but re-stocking and introductions may have helped. Black Grouse were introduced in some localities in Great Britain some time prior to 1921, but did not thrive and failed to become established (Hudson, 1921). Witherby *et al* (1941) indicate that Black Grouse have been introduced to Sussex, Surrey, Berkshire, Buckinghamshire, Norfolk, Suffolk, the Orkney Islands and northern

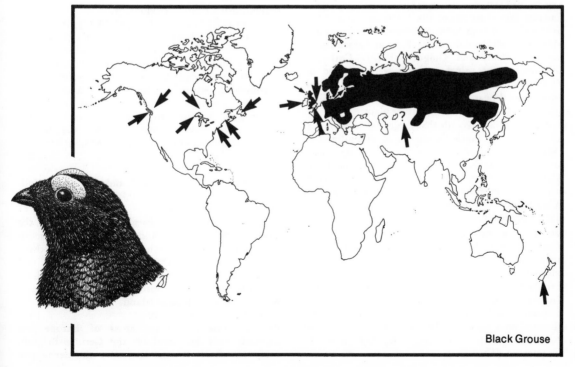

Black Grouse

Wales, but generally unsuccessfully. Hand-reared birds were apparently released on Exmoor (in Somerset and Devon) in 1969 and 1971 and a small population still exists in that locality (Sharrock, 1976).

Ireland. Hudson (1921) indicates that Black Grouse are not indigenous to Ireland but that perhaps they had been established there, or attempts had been made to establish them. Barrett-Hamilton (1899) records that repeated introductions in the eighteenth and nineteenth centuries always failed. Johnstone (1967) says that none now occur in Ireland.

Poland. Lindemann (1956) indicates that Black Grouse *(L.t. tetrix)* were successfully introduced into Poland in 1933-39.

USA. Black Grouse have been introduced into Northern America but did not succeed in becoming established (Bump, 1963). Bump records that birds from Scotland were liberated there in 1886, 1895, in about 1900, 1903, 1904-05 and 1906-07 from Denmark. In 1949-50 birds from Norway and Finland were also released. Amongst these introductions some birds survived for a year or more, but all finally disappeared. Of the early attempts in the United States, the 1895 introduction was made at New Sweden, Maine (Phillips, 1928), and those in 1904-05 at Lake Superior and the Adirondacks regions (Gottschalk, 1967). They were also released, fifty-eight at a time, at Grand Island, Michigan, in Lake Superior by the Cleveland Cliffs Iron Co. at this latter time (Phillips). Phillips records that a few were released on an estate near Big Tupper Lake, in the Adirondacks, in about 1900, where they were sighted for about a year before vanishing entirely. This liberation was made by E. H. Litchfield at Litchfield Park in New York State (Bump, 1941) where six birds were released. A further introduction occurred in this State in 1906 when William Rockefeller released eighteen birds in Franklin County and where a single bird was seen as late as 1912.

Canada. Introductions of Black Grouse occurred in British Columbia in 1906, by Messrs Chaldecott and Musgrove, who obtained stock from Copenhagen, Denmark (Carl and Guiguet, 1972). Carl and Guiguet say that nineteen birds were released on Vancouver Island and adjacent islands, and sixteen were released near Nicomen on the mainland. They did not become established at either place.

Phillips (1928) records that large-scale attempts at introduction of Black Grouse in Newfoundland in 1886 through the efforts of R. Langrishe-Mare were unsuccessful, as was one by Ontario authorities at Algonquin Park, Ontario, in about 1903. Further attempts, when fifty or more birds were released at Whitbourne, Newfoundland, in 1906 or 1907, were also unsuccessful.

New Zealand. An attempt to import Black Grouse to New Zealand in 1873 ended in failure. The Otago Acclimatisation Society imported ten birds and released them in 1879 (Thomson, 1922). From this introduction three birds were reported in 1879, one at Tuapeka Mouth and two at Waitahuna, but they were not recorded again. In 1900 a further three were liberated on a reserve at the junction of Leithan and Pomahaka runs, near Dunedin, but they all disappeared (Thomson).

USSR. Black Grouse were apparently introduced in the RSFSR in the 1960s (Yanushevich, 1966), but the results of the attempt(s) are not known. Between 1955 and 1965 more than five hundred were released in the European part of the Soviet Union for re-stocking purposes (Osmolovskaya, 1969).

DAMAGE

In Europe, Black Grouse can cause quite severe damage to young plantations of *Pinus sylvestris* and *Pinus nigra* (Nef, 1959, in Armour, 1963) by pecking the buds and causing the trees to become stag-headed (Thompson, 1953). In southern Finland they are known to eat the terminal shoots of *P. sylvestris* in nurseries, when snowfall removes much of their other sources of food (Loyttyniemi, 1968).

Damage by Black Grouse to forest plantations in England was reported as early as in the nineteenth century (Harvie-Brown, 1879). Fisher (1907) considered that they caused less damage than the Capercaillie. Gordon (1915) reported severe damage mainly to Scots Pine *(Pinus sylvestris)* and to larch, so much so that some plantings were abandoned. Gladstone (1923) records them damaging young European Larch *(Larix decidua)* in January, and to this species and also Japanese Larch *(Larix leptolepis)* in February.

Black Grouse remove the buds from the ends of shoots and occasionally take the needles of such species as Scots Pine, Lodgepole Pine and, less often, Sitka Spruce *(Picea sitchensis)* (Johnstone, 1967). Most of the damage occurs in late winter and early spring to young conifers before they grow too high for the birds to reach. The damage caused is similar to that of the Capercaillie and only locally reaches a level where economic losses result.

WILLOW GROUSE
(Willow Ptarmigan, Red Grouse)
Lagopus lagopus (Linnaeus)

DISTINGUISHING CHARACTERISTICS

33-43 cm (13-17 in). 525-804 g (1.15-1.77 lb)

Generally rufous-brown, with black bars (summer), or white (winter); wings, abdomen and under tail-coverts white; bare patch above eye red; tail white, black on outer edge; bill black. Distinguished from Ptarmigan *L. mutus* by more red on neck and breast. *Female:* brown above; lacks red eyebrows; underparts barred and spotted with black; distinguished from Ptarmigan by larger size, heavier and broader bill and by presence of red loral bar.

Witherby *et al,* vol.5, 1938-41, pp.222, 225-227, 228 and pl.145 opp. p.222.

Johnsgard, 1973, pp.209-212 and pls. 44-46, foll. p.236.

GENERAL DISTRIBUTION

Arctic regions of the Northern Hemisphere: from the Aleutian Islands, Alaska and northern Canada, south to British Columbia, North-west Territories, northern Manitoba, northern Ontario, central Quebec and Newfoundland; Ireland, Scotland, northern England, Scandinavia, northern Europe and Asia to Kamchatka and Sakhalin Island.

INTRODUCED DISTRIBUTION

Re-introduced in several areas of Europe but probably only successful on the German-Belgium border, in Great Britain (Exmoor) and perhaps in

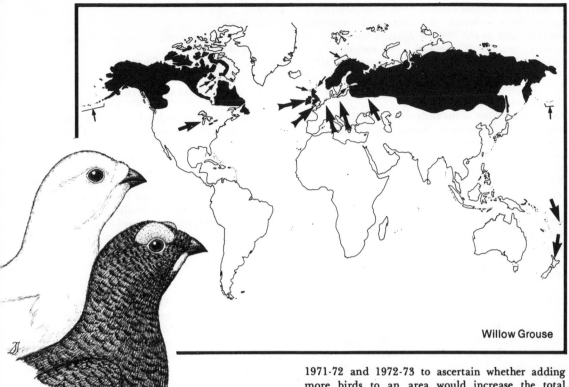

Willow Grouse

Poland; re-introductions in the USSR appear to have failed. Introductions to New Zealand, Fiji and the USA have failed.

GENERAL HABITS
Status: somewhat reduced in numbers and range. *Habitat:* birch and willow forest, willow scrubs, tundra, marshy heathlands (moors) and stubble fields. *Gregariousness:* solitary, pairs, small flocks (unisexual), or family groups, but occasionally as many as 5000 birds are known to mass for migration. *Movements:* mainly sedentary; northern populations sometimes undergo extensive southerly mass migrations. *Foods:* seeds, leaves, buds, shoots, berries, catkins and insects. *Breeding:* Apr-June (Britain); monogamous. *Nest:* hollow on the ground sparsely lined with grass, feathers and leaves. *Eggs:* 5-10, 17.
Witherby *et al*, vol.5, 1938-41, pp.222, 225-227, 228.
Johnsgard, 1973, pp. 212-224.
Savory, *J. Anim. Ecol.* vol.47, 1978, pp. 259-282.

NOTES ON INTRODUCTIONS
Europe. Introductions of Willow Grouse prior to the 1940s occurred in Great Britain in Surrey, Norfolk, Suffolk, Devon and Somerset and the race *L.l. scoticus* had at this time been well established in the Exmoor area (Witherby *et al*, 1941). Attempts to introduce *scoticus* to Exmoor in the early 1820s failed, though further introductions there and on Dartmoor in 1915-16 were successful (Sharrock, 1976). Unsuccessful early attempts were also made to introduce them to the Shetland Islands, various parts of Ireland and in the Outer Hebrides.

Releases were made in Ireland in the winters of 1971-72 and 1972-73 to ascertain whether adding more birds to an area would increase the total population, but these appear to have been unsuccessful (Lance, 1974). Captive hatched birds *(L.l. scoticus* var. *hibernicus)*, ranging in age from seven months to three years, were released near Glenamoy in north-west Mayo County and near Bray in Wicklow County. The method was said to be poor because the birds were unable to discriminate between good and bad habitat and better results were achieved by habitat improvement.

In western Europe prior to the 1940s Willow Grouse had been acclimatised in Belgium at Hautes Fagnes, Ardennes, and in western Germany at Hoch Venn, Eifel (Witherby).

A number of attempts have been made to establish the race *scoticus* in France, the first by the Prince of Monaco in about 1912 (Etchécopar, 1955). Etchécopar indicates that attempts were made in Bretagne in 1939 but were interrupted by the second World War; and at Dauphine, Larzac, Lannemezan and at Spa in the Ardennes, but all have been unsuccessful though initially promising.

According to Peterson *et al* (1963), *L.l. scoticus* has been introduced and is established in eastern Belgium. Some seventy pairs were released on the German-Belgium border by Scheibler, a textile manufacturer, at Hoch Venn in the early 1890s (Grzmek, 1972). The introduction was successful but the population has now declined and it is said that only a few now remain near Botrange.

Lindemann (1956) has indicated that *L.l. rossicus* was successfully introduced into Poland in 1933-39.
USSR. Introductions of Willow Grouse were made in the RSFSR in the 1960s (Yanushevich, 1966; Safronov, 1963), and a release of birds near Moscow in 1956 failed to become established (Yanushevich). Attempts have also been made to re-acclimatise them in the Central Zone (Sergeeva and Sumina, 1963). 97

Sergeeva and Sumina say that birds from Arkhangel district were released in Leningrad, Kalinin, Yaroslavl and in the Moscow districts but failed to become established because of environmental differences. Between 1955 and 1965 more than 6000 Willow Grouse were released in the European part of the Soviet Union for re-stocking purposes (Osmolovskaya, 1969).

New Zealand. Most of the early attempts to introduce grouse to New Zealand failed because of the difficulties experienced in getting the birds to that country alive (Thomson, 1922). In 1870 a shipment for the Auckland Acclimatisation Society failed. In 1872 some thirty-three birds were shipped, two pairs were landed in New Zealand, one died and the other was released at Matamata. In 1873 only one pair survived shipping and these were also released at Matamata. The Otago society attempted to import some in 1871 but these also died on the ship. Thomson indicates that most of the birds released were of the race *L.l. scoticus*. The Willow Grouse failed to become established in New Zealand.

USA. As with most of the European grouse introductions to the United States, Willow Grouse did not succeed (Bump, 1963). Phillips (1928) records that some were introduced in 1905-06, when thirty-five wild trapped birds from Norway were released unsuccessfully on Grand Island, Michigan. Birds of the North American race were trapped in northern Saskatchewan in the winter of 1948-49 and subsequently eighty-three were transplanted to the upper peninsula of Michigan (Dalrymple, 1950). There appear to be no further records of these birds, but they more than likely failed to become established.

Fiji. Grouse *L. lagopus scoticus* were probably released without success in the Fijian group (Wood and Wetmore, 1926). Wood and Wetmore say they heard of several attempts to establish the species there some time before 1926.

DAMAGE
None known.

PTARMIGAN
(Rock Ptarmigan, Snow Grouse)
Lagopus mutus (Montin)

DISTINGUISHING CHARACTERISTICS

32-39.4 cm (12.6-15.37 in). 427-575 g (.94-1.26 lb).
In winter: white with black loral bar (not always present) through eye; outer tail-feathers black; a red fringe above eye; beak black. *In summer:* wings, under tail-coverts and central tail-feathers white; outer tail-feathers black, some tipped white; remainder ashy brown, marked with black lines and dusky spots. *Female:* without black loral bar; more heavily barred. Female is similar to female Willow Grouse *L. lagopus* which has a red loral bar.

Godfrey, 1966, pp.111-112 and pl.22, no.5, opp. p.129.

Johnsgard, 1973, pp.225-228 and pls. 47-49, foll. p.236.

GENERAL DISTRIBUTION

Circumpolar: Arctic Ocean islands and coasts of Eurasia to Iceland and southern Greenland and locally in mountains of Scotland, France, Spain, Austria, central Asia and northern Japan; in North America south to southern Alaska, central British Columbia, southern Mackenzie, northern Quebec and Newfoundland.

INTRODUCED DISTRIBUTION

A single transplant in Japan appears to have failed after a few years. Possibly introduced, unsuccessfully, to New Zealand.

GENERAL HABITS

Status: common. *Habitat:* arctic and alpine highlands; generally north of Arctic above tree line, in shrub, moss, lichen, tundra and barren, rugged mountain regions near snow and ice. *Gregariousness:* solitary, pairs in summer and unisexual flocks up to

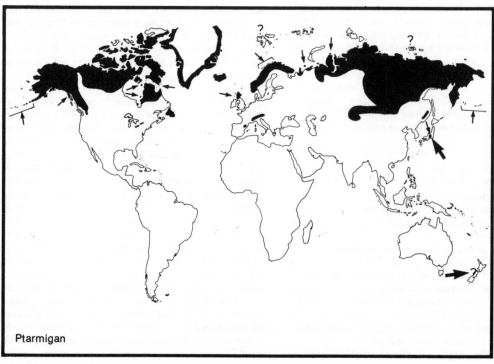

Ptarmigan

fifty or more in early winter. *Movements:* mainly sedentary. *Foods:* leaves, flowers, seeds and berries. *Breeding:* May-June; monogamous. *Nest:* depression in the ground, lined with vegetable material and feathers, often sheltered by a rock or low vegetation. *Eggs:* 3, 6-9, 13.

Voous, 1960, p.79.

Johnsgard, 1973, pp.228-239.

Andreev, *Zoologicheskii zhurnal,* vol.54, 1965, pp.727-733.

NOTES ON INTRODUCTIONS
Japan. The race *japonica* was released on Mt Fuji in 1960 and bred there. In 1970 its survival at this location was not confirmed (Ornithological Society of Japan, 1974).

New Zealand. Ptarmigan were imported to New Zealand in 1897 but it is not known if they were released into the wild (Thomson, 1922).

DAMAGE
None known.

Blue Grouse

BLUE GROUSE
(Dusky Grouse, Sooty Grouse)
Dendragapus obscurus (Say)

DISTINGUISHING CHARACTERISTICS
38.7 - 56 cm (15-22 in). 800-1600 g (1.76-3.52 lb. Generally dusky grey or black; whitish line from be. to eye and beyond; yellow or orange comb above eyes; under chin and to sides of throat white, with a black patch and much barring; breast slaty coloured; tail rounded or squarish, black, sometimes lightly banded at tip. *Female:* grey-brown, barred black; distinguished from Spruce Grouse by slaty centre of breast which is not barred.

Johnsgard, 1973, pp.175-178 and pls. 36-39, foll. p.236.

GENERAL DISTRIBUTION
North America: from southern Alaska, western USA (mountains) south to southern California, northern and eastern Arizona, and west central New Mexico.

INTRODUCED DISTRIBUTION
Introduced on Kodiak and Woody islands (failed ?) in the Gulf of Alaska and to several Gulf islands in British Columbia, Canada.

GENERAL HABITS
Status: common. *Habitat:* coniferous forest, open slash and burns. *Gregariousness:* family groups (broods), sometimes solitary ? *Movements:* local movements according to season, males move to higher elevations. *Foods:* berries, seeds, conifer needles, buds and insects; in winter mainly conifer buds and needles. *Breeding:* Mar-Aug; polygamous. *Nest:* depression lined with fern, moss, leaves and feathers, on the ground near a log or tree. *Eggs:* 5-10, 16.

Zwickel and Bendell, 1972, pp.150-169.

Johnsgard, 1973, pp.178-192.

NOTES ON INTRODUCTIONS
Alaska. According to Burris (1965) Blue Grouse were liberated on Kodiak Island in 1963 (one bird released) and 1964 (twenty birds) and on Woody Island in 1964 (one bird). The results of these introductions are not known, but presumably they have failed.

Canada. In recent years, under the supervision of the Fish and Wildlife Branch, Blue Grouse have been transferred from Vancouver Island to several undisclosed Gulf islands. These transfers were made as part of a study of the species by the universities of Victoria, British Columbia and Alberta (Mundy, 1971, in Carl and Guiguet, 1972).

In 1970 some 120 Blue Grouse from three localities on Vancouver Island were introduced to Moresby Island, forty birds to Portland Island from Copper Canyon (Vancouver Island), forty birds to Sidney Island from Comox Burn and forty birds to Stuart Island from Middle Quinsam (Bergerud and Hemus, 1975). These introductions were made by Bergerud and Hemus for population studies and the species was still surviving in 1972-73, apparently on all the islands.

DAMAGE
Weatherby (1947, in Thompson, 1953) reports that Blue Grouse can cause high seed and seedling losses in coniferous trees in British Columbia, Canada.

SPRUCE GROUSE
(Spruce Partridge, Franklin's Grouse, Black Partridge)
Dendragapus canadensis (Linnaeus)

DISTINGUISHING CHARACTERISTICS
37.5-43 cm (14.58-17 in). 450-700 g (1-1.54 lb) Generally a dusky colour, back and wings barred black and grey; throat and sides of head below eye black, bordered with a broken white line; breast black, white spotted on sides; red bare skin comb above eye; tail short, with chestnut band at tip, or with a row of white spots; bill black. *Female:* rusty brown, thickly barred; tail blackish; lacks red above eye; resembles female Ruffed Grouse but back is barred, has a shorter tail with no subterminal band and no ruff.

99

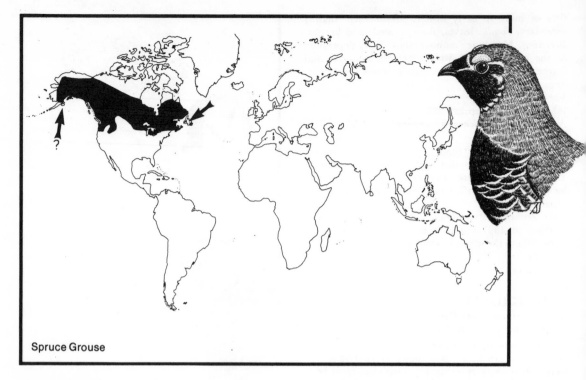

Spruce Grouse

Johnsgard, 1973, pp.193-195 and pls. 40-43, foll. p.236.

GENERAL DISTRIBUTION

North America: from western and northern Alaska, throughout most of Canada except for the far north, and parts of the northern United States south to north-eastern Oregon, central Idaho, north-western Wyoming, northern Wisconsin, northern Michigan, northern Vermont, New Hampshire and Maine.

INTRODUCED DISTRIBUTION

Introduced on Newfoundland and to Kodiak and Woody islands in the Gulf of Alaska, and may perhaps be established in both areas.

GENERAL HABITS

Status: common, but rare in some areas. *Habitat:* forest, mainly spruce but also in jack and lodgepole pines. *Gregariousness:* solitary, or in mixed sex flocks. *Movements:* sedentary. *Foods:* mainly buds and needles of conifers, but also berries and insects. *Breeding:* polygamous. *Nest:* depression lined with leaves and grass, on the ground under a conifer. *Eggs:* 4, 8-12, 16.

Ellison, *Condor* vol.75, no.4, 1973, pp.375-385.
Johnsgard, 1973, pp.196-208.
Ellison, *Journal of Wildlife Management,* vol.40, no.2, 1976, pp.205-213.

NOTES ON INTRODUCTIONS

Newfoundland. The race *D.c. canadensis* was introduced to Newfoundland from Northwest River, Labrador, in 1964 (Tuck, 1968). Tuck records that at this time forty-eight were released at Butterpot Park, thirty-nine at Grand Lake and thirty-nine at Little Gander Lake. The species may still be established in these regions.

Alaska. Spruce Grouse were released on Kodiak Island in 1957 (six birds) and 1959 (ten), and also on Woody Island in 1957 (fourteen). One bird was also released on Wood Island, off Kodiak, in 1959. It is

not known whether the species is still established there.

DAMAGE

None known.

HAZEL GROUSE
(Hazel Hen)
Tetrastes bonasia (Linnaeus)

DISTINGUISHING CHARACTERISTICS

31.5-35 cm (12.22-13.77 in) . 340-400 g (.75-.88 lb)
Upper parts grey-brown, spotted and barred dark brown; underparts whitish, mottled brown; broad black band from beak down throat, followed by a white band on sides of neck; head slightly crested; tail grey, with a black border fringed with white. *Female:* throat band buffish white.

Cheng, 1963, pp.246-248.

GENERAL DISTRIBUTION

Eurasia: from central Europe to Scandinavia, east across Asia to Siberia and Sakhalin, and south to North Korea and northern Japan (Hokkaido).

INTRODUCED DISTRIBUTION

Introduced in the USA (failed) and in Poland (?).

GENERAL HABITS

Status: locally common. *Habitat:* mixed broad-leaf and coniferous forests, woods along river banks, swampy areas and lake shores with trees. *Gregariousness:* solitary, pairs, and highly territorial. *Movements:* sedentary. *Foods:* buds, leaves, catkins, twigs, flowers, fruits, seeds, berries and insects. *Breeding:* Apr-July and Sept; monogamous. *Nest:* on the ground under the protection of trees and shrubs. *Eggs:* 6-10, 14.

Voous, 1960, pp.80-81.
Cheng, 1963, pp.248-251.

NOTES ON INTRODUCTIONS

USA. Hazel Grouse were introduced to Lake Superior in the early 1900s, but failed to become established

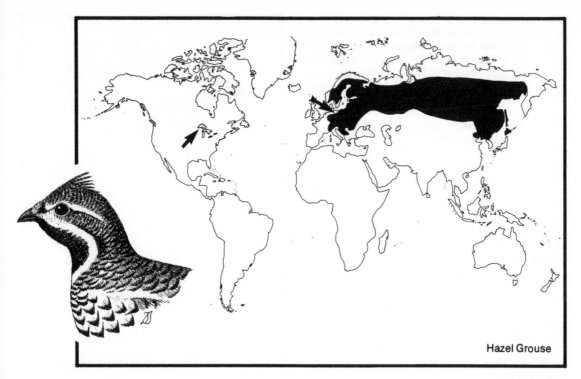

Hazel Grouse

(Gottschalk, 1967). Bump (1963) says they were introduced in 1905-06 to Grand Island, Michigan, from an unknown source but soon disappeared. Phillips (1928) reports that the birds came from Europe and that two introductions were made by the Cleveland Cliffs Iron Co. to Grand Island; twelve birds in 1905 and nineteen in 1906.

Poland. Lindemann (1956) indicates that Hazel Grouse were successfully introduced in Poland in 1933-39.

DAMAGE
None known.

RUFFED GROUSE
*Bonasia umbellus (*Linnaeus)

DISTINGUISHING CHARACTERISTICS
40-49 cm (15.74-19.29 in). 500-770 g (1.10-1.69 lb)
Generally red-brown or grey-brown and spotted; head crested; blackish patch on side of lower neck; chest and abdomen yellowish white, barred brown; back feathers with broad yellowish white centre stripe, mottled brown-black; rump mottled yellowish white; tail rufous or grey, fan-shaped, with black band near tip. *Female:* smaller; shorter ruff and incomplete tail band.
Johnsgard, 1973, pp.253-256 and pls. 52-54, foll. p.236.

GENERAL DISTRIBUTION
North America: from western Alaska and most of southern Canada, south to the northern United States; occurs as far south as northern California in the coastal belt, north-eastern Oregon, central Utah, Wyoming, western South Dakota, Minnesota, Michigan and northern Georgia.

INTRODUCED DISTRIBUTION
Successfully introduced in the USA in Michigan, Missouri and Nevada, unsuccessfully elsewhere in that country; introduced successfully on Anticosti Island

and in Newfoundland in Canada; possibly established in Saskatchewan and several Gulf Islands in British Columbia, Canada.

GENERAL HABITS
Status: fairly common. *Habitat:* mixed or deciduous woodlands and forest, and forest clearings. *Gregariousness:* solitary, family parties and unisexual flocks. *Movements:* sedentary. *Foods:* insects, seeds, buds, berries, twigs and leaves. *Breeding:* May-July; polygamous. *Nest:* sheltered depression on forest floor near a log or bush. *Eggs:* 6, 8-14, 23.
Johnsgard, 1973, pp.257-273.
Doerr *et al,* 1974, *Journal of Wildlife Management,* vol.38, pp.601-615.

NOTES ON INTRODUCTIONS
USA. Phillips (1928) lists a number of early unsuccessful introductions of Ruffed Grouse; in 1884-85 some were said to have been released on P. Lorillard's game preserve at Jobstown, New Jersey; a small shipment of birds from northern New Hampshire were probably liberated at Wareham, Massachusetts, in the late 1880s; in 1900 W. Barnhart released (fifty-six ?) birds at Green Bay on Washington Island, Wisconsin; in 1923 a shipment from Alberta, Canada, were placed on an island in Puget Sound, Washington, where they remained for at least two years; eight birds were liberated in Connecticut in 1923 and 115 in 1924.

Ruffed Grouse have been successfully introduced on five of Michigan's Great Lakes Islands where they are not found naturally (Moran and Palmer, 1963). Moran and Palmer say that wild trapped birds were established on High Island in 1956 and on Garden Island in 1957. They were established on Beaver, Bois Blanc and Drummond islands in 1948-49 with stock from Wisconsin. Two earlier releases on Drummond Island, made by the Michigan Department of Conservation in 1944, with birds obtained from

Alberta, Canada, disappeared after a few years. Not until 200 birds (fifty on Bois Blanc, sixty-eight on Beaver and eighty-two on Drummond) were released in 1948-49 did they become permanently established (Ammann and Palmer 1958). Following their introduction to these islands Ruffed Grouse dispersed rapidly and an irruptive build-up in numbers caused the populations to reach saturation levels in only four breeding seasons. Two seasons after release the species was open to hunting on the three islands.

An early successful introduction of Ruffed Grouse occurred in Wisconsin. In about 1900, a Mr W. Barnhart of Sturgeon Bay released several birds on the south side of Washington Island, near Detroit Harbour (Palmer, 1913). The following year two more males and a female were released in the same area. Palmer records that they were reported to be on the island in 1913 and to be breeding and increasing their numbers.

Private attempts were made to establish the species on North Manitou Island in 1911, when a hen and twenty-six chicks were released by T. Grosvenor, and in 1940 and 1941 by the North Manitou Island Association which released approximately fifty birds of north Michigan stock (Ammann and Palmer). The earlier release failed, but after 1941 occasional reports of birds on the island were received up until at least the 1950s.

There were some early introductions of Ruffed Grouse in the New York area (Studholme, 1948), but evidently these were unsuccessful. Bump (1941) records that from 1931 to 1939 at least 346 were released by clubs, private individuals and State authorities in Franklin, Dutchess, Delaware and West counties where some survived and bred.

Ruffed Grouse were almost extirpated in Missouri in the 1900s and re-introductions in the 1940s failed (Lewis, McGowan and Baskett, 1968). Liberations of wild trapped birds from Ohio and Indiana were made in 1959 at Ashland (thirty-nine birds) and Boone Forest (eighteen). Subsequent releases up until 1963 brought the total of birds released to 119 at Ashland and 143 at Boone and successfully established them in these areas. In 1966 they were still established in both areas but densities were low and the occupation of habitat beyond the release points was limited.

The Ruffed Grouse has, more recently, been successfully introduced in the Ruby Mountain Range

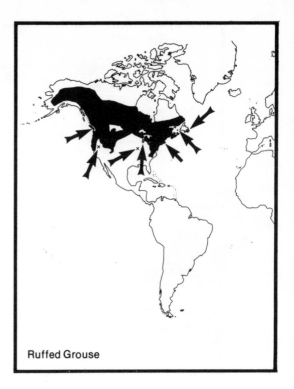

Ruffed Grouse

Ruffed Grouse,
Bonasia umbellus

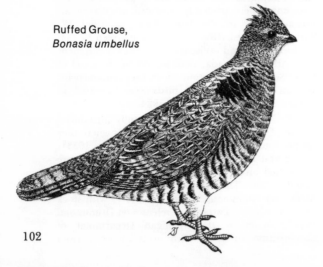

of north-eastern Nevada (McColm, 1970, in Johnsgard, 1973).

Canada. Ruffed Grouse have been introduced and established on Anticosti Island in the Gulf of St Lawrence (Godfrey, 1966).

From introductions in 1956 Ruffed Grouse have become so well established in Newfoundland that open hunting seasons were being contemplated in about 1967 (Tuck, 1968). Here wild trapped birds were released, became established in three to four years, and then spread (Bergerud, 1963). Tuck records a number of introductions in Newfoundland from 1956 to 1966: forty birds were taken from Wisconsin to Cormack and thirty-eight to Badger in 1956; twenty-eight to Clarenville and twenty-nine to South Branch in 1958; thirty-four to Badger in 1959; thirty to Salmonier from Nova Scotia in 1961; forty-two to Salmonier in 1962 and thirty-nine to Butterpot Park; also in 1962, eighteen birds were taken from Maine to Barrachois Park; forty-two to Salmonier and twenty-nine to Mollyguajeck in 1963; eleven to Mollyguajeck, thirty-nine to Milltown and fifty to Gander Lake in 1964; twenty-seven to Corner Brook in 1965; twenty-eight to Hawkes Bay and fifteen more to Corner Brook in 1966.

The species has recently been transferred in British Columbia to several Gulf Islands, from Vancouver Island. under the supervision of the Fisheries and Wildlife Branch (Mundy, 1971, in Carl and Guiguet, 1972).

The only early introduction of Ruffed Grouse recorded appears to have been a release some time before 1925. This was made in the Cypress Hills in Saskatchewan where the species did not occur naturally with stock from the Qu' Appelle Valley, Regina (Phillips, 1928).

DAMAGE
None known.

SAGE GROUSE

(Sage Hen, Sage Chicken)

Centrocercus urophasianus (Bonaparte)

DISTINGUISHING CHARACTERISTICS

Male 65-76 cm (25.6-30 in), female 47-59 cm (18.5-23.2 in). Male and female 1.1-2.9 and up to 3.6 kg (2.4-6.4, up to 8 lb)

Generally greyish brown on upper parts with marbled appearance; belly black; chest whitish; chin and throat black with a white collar; yellow air sacs on sides of neck, and also a patch of stiff black feathers; bare skin above eye yellow; tail long and pointed. *Female:* lacks black throat and tuft of stiff feathers.

Johnsgard, 1973, pp.155-157 and pls. 32-35, foll. p.236.

GENERAL DISTRIBUTION

North America: from extreme south-western Canada (south-east Alberta and southern Saskatchewan), south to eastern California, western Colorado, south-eastern Wyoming, Nevada and Utah.

INTRODUCED DISTRIBUTION

Introductions in Montana, USA, and British Columbia, Canada, have failed. Re-established in New Mexico, USA.

GENERAL HABITS

Status: common, but range and numbers considerably reduced. *Habitat:* sage brush plains. *Gregariousness:* unisexual flocks, flocks of a few hundred males congregate prior to breeding. *Movements:* some movement to lower elevations in winter; may travel 160 kilometres (100 miles) to wintering grounds. *Foods:* buds, leaves, shoots, berries, seeds, flowers and insects including ants. *Breeding:* May; polygamous. *Nest:* on the ground under sagebrush. *Eggs:* 7-13, 17.

Wiley, *Animal Behaviour Monograph* no.6, pt.2, 1973, pp.87-169.

Johnsgard, 1973, pp.157-174.

Sage Grouse

NOTES ON INTRODUCTIONS

USA. Trapping and transplanting of Sage Grouse was carried out in Montana in 1942 in an attempt to re-establish them in formerly inhabited areas and in several locations outside their natural range (Martin and Pyrah, 1971). A total of 242 birds were released at eight locations in seven counties, but the attempts were unsuccessful. Sage Grouse have been successfully re-established in New Mexico (Johnsgard, 1973).

Canada. Fifty-seven Sage Grouse from Oregon were introduced to the Richter Pass area in 1958 by the Canadian Fisheries and Wildlife Branch (Guiguet, 1961; Carl and Guiguet, 1972). No birds have been reported from there since 1960, indicating the failure of the attempt.

DAMAGE

None known.

SHARP-TAILED GROUSE

(Brush Grouse, Pin-tailed Grouse, White-breasted Grouse)

Pedioecetes phasianellus (Linnaeus)

DISTINGUISHING CHARACTERISTICS

37.5-50 cm (14.58-19.7 in). 800-1000 g (1.76-2.2 lb)

Generally yellowish brown, speckled dark brown; abdomen and under tail whitish; head slightly crested; dull whitish stripe behind eye, and dull whitish patch on either side of neck; breast and neck with numerous U- and V-shaped spots of brown; tail short, pointed, white with central feathers barred; bill dark horn, with paler lower mandible.

Johnsgard, 1973, pp.300-302 and pls. 59-60, foll. p.236.

GENERAL DISTRIBUTION

North America: from north and central Alaska, north-western and southern Canada (east to central Quebec) and the northern United States east to northern Michigan and south to northern Wisconsin, northern Minnesota, Nebraska, Colorado, Utah and eastern Oregon. Formerly inhabited north-eastern California, western Kansas and northern Illinois.

INTRODUCED DISTRIBUTION

Introductions and transplants in the USA have failed, with the probable exception of those in Michigan; introductions in the Hawaiian Islands and New Zealand have failed.

GENERAL HABITS

Status: fairly common, but range considerably curtailed, numbers reduced. *Habitat:* forest edges, open woodlands and thickets, bushland, prairies, clearing and brushy parklands. *Gregariousness:* family groups and winter mixed sex flocks; formerly flocks of several hundred. *Movements:* sedentary, but with some irregular local movements. *Foods:* insects, seeds, buds, catkins, tender shoots and berries. *Breeding:* Mar-July; polygamous. *Nest:* grass-lined depression on the ground in grass or bush. *Eggs:* 5, 7-13, 16.

Johnsgard, 1973, pp.302-319.

Rippin and Boag, *Journal of Wildlife Management,* vol.38, 1974, pp.616-621.

NOTES ON INTRODUCTIONS

USA. Although Sharp-tailed Grouse spread into Michigan from Minnesota and Wisconsin, the spread was helped by the transplanting of several thousand trapped birds which were released in unoccupied

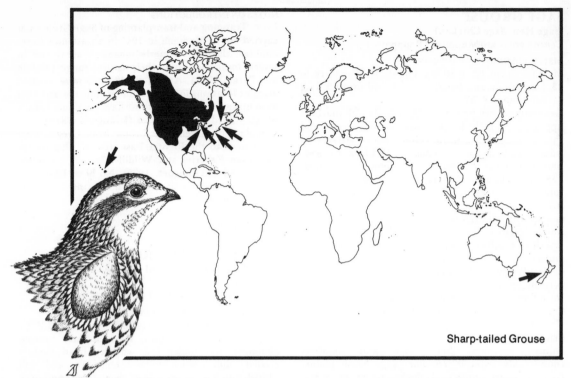

Sharp-tailed Grouse

areas (Ruhl, 1941). They were introduced to Michigan between 1938 and 1952 (Bump, 1963) and of twenty-three releases totalling some 1491 birds four were successful, three partially or probably successful, fifteen were failures and one is of uncertain status. More than likely Sharp-tailed Grouse are still established in Michigan but more recent details are lacking. Studholme (1948) indicates that some success has been achieved with releases in mid-west States, but generally widespread introductions have failed.

Phillips (1928) records that in the late 1880s and early 1890s at least 146 birds were released in Massachusetts, together with other grouse and quail; also in the 1890s some were liberated near St Johnsbury in northern Vermont, but both introductions were unsuccessful. In 1904, seventy-two were released on Grand Island in Lake Superior, Michigan, and in 1924-25 some were released in Maryland, also unsuccessfully. There were also two introductions in 1939 in Albany and Tompkins counties in New York State when thirty-two birds were released (Bump, 1941). The latter liberation persisted for a while but both were eventually unsuccessful.

Hawaiian Islands. Thirty birds of the race *P.p. columbianus* were taken to the island of Hawaii from the United States in 1932 (Munro, 1960). According to Walker (1967) they were liberated there, but are not now known to be established on the island.

New Zealand. P.p. columbianus from Utah, USA, were liberated at Piako in New Zealand in 1876 (twenty-two birds) (Thomson, 1922). According to Thomson there are no further records of them and so the species evidently failed to become established in New Zealand.

DAMAGE
None known.

GREATER PRAIRIE CHICKEN
(Prairie Chicken, Pinnated Grouse)
Tympanuchus cupido (Linnaeus)

DISTINGUISHING CHARACTERISTICS
40-47 cm (15.74-18.5 in). 0.7-1.3 kg (1.54-2.86 lb)
Upper parts yellowish brown, heavily barred or spotted with brownish black; lower parts whitish, barred dusky brown; crown mottled with black and brown spots; air sacs orange; tuft of long black feathers on neck; head slightly crested; tail short, rounded, black; stripe from gape to nape beneath eye brownish black. *Female:* tail barred, neck tuft smaller and less conspicuous.
Johnsgard, 1973, pp.274-277 and pls. 55-57, foll. p.236.

GENERAL DISTRIBUTION
North America: from southern Canada (prairies) south through the Dakotas, eastern Colorado, Kansas to coastal Texas east of the Rocky Mountains, and to the Mexican border. Formerly more widespread. (More recent surveys indicate that species is less widespread than that shown on the map; see Johnsgard, 1973.)

INTRODUCED DISTRIBUTION
Probably introduced successfully in some areas of the USA; introductions in the Hawaiian Islands, New Zealand and Europe were unsuccessful.

GENERAL HABITS
Status: locally common, range and numbers reduced. *Habitat:* tall grass prairies, meadows and plains. *Gregariousness:* mixed and unisexual flocks. *Movements:* sedentary; possibly some slight migratory movement in autumn. *Foods:* insects, seeds, fruits, buds, leaves and berries. *Breeding:* polygamous. *Nest:* grass-lined hollow on the ground, amongst tall grass. *Eggs:* 5, 7-17, 21.
Johnsgard, 1973, pp.277-299.

USA. According to Wing (1956) Greater Prairie Chickens have been moved in some areas of the United States and are therefore considered by him to be exotics in some areas. Early historical records show that the species extended its range westwards and northwards, keeping pace with the early settlers' grainfields (Phillips, 1928; Roberts, 1960). Roberts reports that in these areas the species increased in numbers rapidly and became abundant. In many of these areas they have now declined in numbers.

Although some birds were taken to New Jersey as early as 1852, the first attempt to establish the species in the wild may have been in California in about 1860. Phillips (1928) records that there were probably many early attempts to establish and re-establish this species in the United States between 1869 and 1893, particularly in the eastern States; early introductions are known in Maine, Vermont, New York, Massachusetts, New Jersey, Pennsylvania and Maryland. Other efforts were apparently made in Washington and in Saginaw, Michigan, the latter with some success. Both *cupido* and *pallidicinctus* were probably introduced but mainly (?) the former species.

In New York State, W. E. Newton liberated about sixty birds in 1872 at Pine Barrens on Long Island, and in 1916 the State released about twenty-one from a game farm on the island (Bump, 1941).

Hawaiian Islands. Caum (1933) and Munro (1960) say that the race *T.c. americanus* was introduced by Mr A. S. Wilcox on Oahu in 1895 when up to twelve birds may have been released. According to Walker (1967) *T.c. pinnatus* was introduced to the Hawaiian Islands from an unknown source and at an unknown date. Greater Prairie Chickens were released in the central part of Niihau in about 1934, but were reported to be scarce there by the 1950s (Fisher, 1951). Munro records that they may also have been liberated on Kauai, but are not present there, or on Oahu, now.

New Zealand. Seventeen 'prairie hens' were imported by the Canterbury Acclimatisation Society in 1879, from Topeka, Kansas, USA, and released at Mt Thomas (Thomson, 1922). Thomson says they were reported to be present there in 1880 and in 1885, but that this is the last record of them. In 1881-82 the Auckland society imported sixty birds from San Francisco, some of which were sent to Otago, but there are no records of their liberation. The Prairie Chicken did not become established in New Zealand.

Europe. Large numbers of Prairie Chickens (*cupido* or *pallidicinctus* or both ?) were exported from the United States to England in the nineteenth century. Phillips (1928) says that large shipments were made in 1874 and were subsequently released on English game preserves. He reports that one dealer of birds is said to have sent some 2000 to England in a single year, and an equal number to the European mainland in the same year. Some were taken to Germany as long ago as 1861 (*Prairie Farmer* no.23, 1861, p.56). A few clutches of eggs were also sent to England in 1874-75 but successful hatching from these was limited and the project was soon abandoned. The Prairie Chicken did not become established in Europe.

DAMAGE
None known.

LESSER PRAIRIE CHICKEN
(Typanuchus pallidicinctus (Ridgway)

DISTINGUISHING CHARACTERISTICS
37.5-40 cm (14.58-15.74 in). 600-893 g (1.32-2 lb)
Generally brown, paler on underparts, but heavily barred as is the Greater Prairie Chicken; tail black;

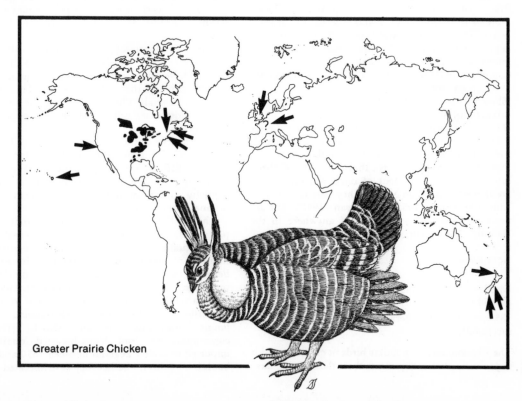

Greater Prairie Chicken

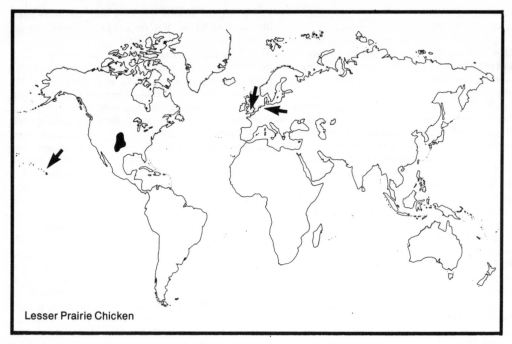

Lesser Prairie Chicken

head crested; air sacs red; black tuft of feathers on neck. Generally smaller than the Greater species. (Note: now treated by many as a subspecies of the Greater Prairie Chicken.)

Johnsgard, 1973, pp.274-277 and pl.58, foll. p.236.

GENERAL DISTRIBUTION

North America: within the same range as *cupido*.

INTRODUCED DISTRIBUTION

Introduced in the Hawaiian Islands but have probably failed to become established.

GENERAL HABITS

Status: uncommon; range much reduced. *Habitat:* short grass prairie and probably similar to the Greater Prairie Chicken. *Gregariousness:* mixed sex flocks. *Movements:* sedentary. *Foods:* seeds of grasses, leaves, acorns, flowers and insects. *Nest:* grass lined depression on the ground under a bush. *Breeding:* no information; polygamous. *Eggs:* 6, 11-13.

Campbell, *Journal of Wildlife Management,* vol.36, 1972, pp.689-699.

Johnsgard, 1973, pp.277-279.

NOTES ON INTRODUCTIONS

Hawaiian Islands. Walker (1967) says that Lesser Prairie Chickens were introduced to these islands from unknown sources and at unknown dates. Peterson (1961) records that they have been introduced, are at present of uncertain status, but possibly established on Nihoa. They were reported on Niihau by Fisher (1951) and Bryan (1958), but are not now known to be established anywhere in the Hawaiian Islands (Berger, 1972).

DAMAGE

None known.

Family: *Phasianidae* Pheasants, francolins, partridges, quails

185 species in 58 genera; 50 species introduced, 23 successfully

The *Phasianidae* are popular birds in captivity and it is probable that many more than those listed have been the subject of attempts at naturalisation in the wild. As game birds they have been introduced and are still being introduced widely throughout the world. More recently a few introductions have been made for conservation purposes and even preservation of some species.

The notably successful species are the Ring-necked Pheasant, Chukar Partridge and European Partridge, particularly in North America but also in other areas of the world. Apart from the House Sparrow, Starling and related species, they have the widest introduced distribution amongst exotic birds. However, in many areas they are re-stocked regularly and it is sometimes difficult to ascertain where the populations are truly self-maintaining, or would be so for any length of time.

The value of introducing game birds is still debated and may never be satisfactorily resolved. That they can and have caused agricultural and other damage is certain, although their role in this regard may be, and generally is, small. The pressure for game for hunting has in most cases eclipsed those who oppose their introduction.

Some species of the *Phasianidae* are now becoming rare in a wild state through destruction of their habitat. Efforts are being made, notably by the Pheasant Trust in England, to breed many species in captivity and if possible to return them to their original haunts or to reserves set aside for the purpose.

The specific identity of many early introductions of partridges, pheasants and quails and whether they were actually released is difficult to determine. A number of partridges were released in Australia between 1866 and 1907, among them the Mexican partridges, Ceylon partridges, Chinese partridges and just partridges ?, all of which failed to become established. Elliot's Pheasant *(Syrmaticus ellioti),* jungle pheasants, Indian Quail *(Coturnix coramandelica),* and black-breasted quail were imported into New Zealand between 1870 and 1909, but it is not known whether they were liberated.

INTRODUCTIONS OF PHASIANIDAE

Species	Date introduced	Region	Manner introduced	Reason
(a) Successful introductions				
Mountain Quail	1860-61	Vancouver Island, Canada	deliberate	game
	1860s on	USA	deliberate introduction and re-introduction	game and re-stocking
Scaled Quail	about 1913 and 1960s	Washington and Nevada, USA	deliberate	game ?
California Quail	1862-1945	New Zealand	deliberate	game ?
	prior 1855 and later	Hawaiian Islands	deliberate	game ?
	about 1864, 1870 and later	Chile	deliberate	game ?
	about 1870	Argentina	deliberate	game ?
	1912-13	Juan Fernandez Island	deliberate	?
	1860-1912	British Columbia, Canada	deliberate	game
	1857 on, and recently	USA	deliberate and re-introductions	game and re-stocking
	1930	King Island, Australia	deliberate	game
	1895	Norfolk Island	deliberate	?
Gambel's Quail	1928, 1958 and 1960-61	Hawaiian Islands	deliberate	game
Bobwhite Quail	end eighteenth century	Haiti	deliberate ?	game ?
	1889-90 or about 1925	Dominican Republic	deliberate ?	game ?
	about 1956 and 1965	Suffolk and Tresco, Great Britain	deliberate	game
	1898-99 and 1947	New Zealand	deliberate	game ?
	about 1840 on, 1930-68	USA	deliberate and re-introductions	game and re-stocking
	before 1880	Bahamas	deliberate	?
Crested Quail	before 1860	St Thomas, Virgin Islands	deliberate ?	?
	?	Mustique Island, Grenadines	?	?
Chukar Partridge	1893 on	USA	deliberate	game
	1940 and 1950-56	Canada	deliberate	game
	?	Baja California, Mexico	deliberate ?	game ?
	1923 and 1959	Hawaiian Islands	deliberate	game
	1926-36 and 1949-50	New Zealand	deliberate	game
	1953 and 1960-63	Crimea and Transcarpathia, USSR	deliberate	game ?
	1964	South Africa	deliberate	?
Red-legged Partridge	sixteenth century on ?	Europe (various mainland areas)	deliberate and re-introductions	game and re-stocking
	sixteenth century on	British Isles	deliberate	game
	eighteenth century ?	Açores	?	?
	prior 1450 and recently ?	Madeira	deliberate	game
Barbary Partridge	?	Gibraltar	?	?
	prior 1913	Canary Islands	deliberate ?	?

continued

INTRODUCTIONS OF PHASIANIDAE

Species	Date introduced	Region	Manner introduced	Reason
Black Francolin	1959, 1960-61 and later	Hawaiian Islands	deliberate	game
Chinese Francolin	about 1750	Mauritius	deliberate ?	
	prior 1934 ?	Luzon, Philippines	?	?
Grey Francolin	prior 1934 ?	Amirante Islands	?	?
	about 1750	Mauritius	deliberate ?	?
	?	Seychelles	feral and deliberate ?	sporting bird
	?	Reunion	?	?
	prior 1934 ?	Rodrigues Island	deliberate ?	food and sport
	prior 1907 or before 1960	Diego Garcia, Chagos Archipelago	?	?
	1958, 1960-66	Hawaiian Islands	deliberate	game
Erkel's Francolin	1957-61	Hawaiian Islands	deliberate	game
Red-throated Francolin	?	Ascension Island	?	?
European Partridge	early (1750 on) and recently	Europe (numerous areas)	deliberate and re-introductions	game and re-stocking
	prior 1879 on	USA	deliberate	game
	1904, 1924-25	Canada	deliberate and colonisation from USA	game
Bearded Partridge	?	Luzon, Philippines	?	?
	1956-65	USSR	deliberate and re-introductions	game and re-stocking
Madagascar Partridge	eighteenth century	Réunion	deliberate ?	?
Common Quail	1921 and 1944	Hawaiian Islands	deliberate	game
Brown Quail	1866-1912	New Zealand	deliberate	game ?
Bamboo Partridge	1919, 1920 and 1930-31	Japan	deliberate	?
	1959 and 1961	Hawaiian Islands	deliberate	game
Kalij Pheasant	1962	Hawaiian Islands	deliberate	game
Red Jungle Fowl	sixteenth century or earlier	Indonesia ?	feral	food ?
	very early ?	Philippines ?	feral	food ?
	prior sixteenth century	Micronesia, Melanesia and Polynesia	feral	food ?
	recently ?	Réunion	deliberate ?	?
Cheer Pheasant	1971-73	India	deliberate re-introduction	preservation
	1880 and early 1900s	Capricorn Group, Australia	deliberate ?	game ?
Ring-necked Pheasant	prior Romans on ?	Europe	deliberate ?	game ? or food ?
	1890s on	Asian region, USSR	deliberate and re-introduction	game ?
	1882 on	USA	deliberate	game
	1882-1954	Canada	deliberate	game
	late 1950s	Newfoundland	deliberate	?
	prior 1957	Baja California, Mexico	?	?
	1865 on	Hawaiian Islands	deliberate	game
	1910	King Island, Australia	deliberate	?
	prior 1950	Tasmania, Australia	deliberate	?
	1928	Rottnest Island, Australia	deliberate	?
	1842-98, 1912 on	New Zealand	deliberate	game ?

INTRODUCTIONS OF PHASIANIDAE

Species	Date introduced	Region	Manner introduced	Reason
	1924 and later	Japan	re-introduction of other races	?
	1886, 1914	Chile	deliberate	?
	1513 or 1588 ?	St Helena	?	?
Amherst Pheasant	1890s on	Great Britain	deliberate	?
Common Peafowl	prior 1973 ?	California, USA	?	?
	1912	Rottnest Island, Australia	deliberate	?

(b) Probably successful introductions

Species	Date introduced	Region	Manner introduced	Reason
Mountain Quail	1929	Hawaiian Islands	deliberate	game
Gambel's Quail	1885 on	Idaho and New Mexico, USA	deliberate	game ?
Bobwhite Quail	prior 1934 ?	St Kitts, West Indies, Andros Island, New Providence, Bahamas Eleuthera Island, Bahamas Cuba (?)	?	?
Chukar Partridge	prior 1588	St Helena (?)	?	?
	?	Eleuthera Island, Bahamas	?	?
Red-legged Partridge	prior 1866	Canary Islands (?)	?	?
	about 1850 and 1925	Porto Santo	deliberate	?
Barbary Partridge	?	Sardegna (?)	?	?
Black Francolin	prior 1954 ?	Kutch, Bombay, India	?	?
	1932	southern USSR	deliberate	?
	1957-64	Florida and Louisiana, USA	deliberate	game ?
	prior 1968	Guam	deliberate	game
Red-billed Francolin	1963-64	Hawaiian Islands	deliberate	game
Common Quail	?	Andaman Islands	deliberate	?
	?	Réunion	?	?
Brown Quail	?	Fiji	deliberate ?	?
Blue-breasted Quail	1864, 1872 and later	southern Australia	deliberate	?
	prior 1934 ?	Réunion	?	?
	1984	Guam	deliberate ?	?
Silver Pheasant	late 1960s	Western Australia	feral	cage bird
Swinhoe Pheasant	1967	Taiwan	re-introduction	preservation
Crested Fireback Pheasant	?	Isle of Bangka, Borneo (?)	?	?
Red Jungle Fowl	prior 1870	St Helena	feral ?	food ?
Reeves Pheasant	various since 1870	Europe	deliberate	aesthetic and game ?
Golden Pheasant	various since 1845	Great Britain	deliberate	?
Common Peafowl	before 1878 ?	Sind, India	feral	?
	1860s and 1890s	Hawaiian Islands	deliberate ?	?
	1843, 1867, 1862	New Zealand	deliberate and/or feral	?

(c) Probably unsuccessful introductions

Species	Date introduced	Region	Manner introduced	Reason
Bobwhite Quail	1877, 1882-1922, 1967-71	British Columbia, Canada	deliberate	game ?
	1906, 1954-61	Hawaiian Islands	deliberate	game
	recent ?	Natal and Zimbabwe	deliberate ?	?

109

continued

INTRODUCTIONS OF PHASIANIDAE

Species	Date introduced	Region	Manner introduced	Reason
Gambel's Quail	1885 on	USA (various places)	deliberate	game ?
Seesee Partridge	1963-64	Nevada and Texas, USA	deliberate	game
	1959	Hawaiian Islands	deliberate	game
Snow Partridge	1962-65 ?	Nevada, USA	deliberate	game
	1959-64	Hawaiian Islands	deliberate	game
Chukar Partridge	1950	southern France	deliberate	game ?
	late 1920s, early 1930s and recently	Great Britain	deliberate	game
	prior 1966	Ukraine	deliberate	game ?
Red-legged Partridge	?	Hawaiian Islands	?	game ?
Barbary Partridge	1958-61	Hawaiian Islands	deliberate	game
Arabian Chukar	about 1890	Eritrea, Ethiopia	deliberate ?	?
Chinese Francolin	?	Malagasy	?	?
	about 1750	Réunion	?	?
	prior 1867	Seychelles	?	?
	prior 1954	Arabia	escapee ?	cage bird ?
	1961-62	Hawaiian Islands	deliberate	game
Grey Francolin	1959-67 ?	USA	deliberate	game
Erkel's Francolin	1959-61	USA	deliberate	game
Bare-throated Francolin	1958, 1960-61	Hawaiian Islands	deliberate	game
European Partridge	about 1962	New Zealand	deliberate	game ?
Swamp Quail	1866, 1869	New Zealand	deliberate	?
Blue-breasted Quail	first half 18th century	Mauritius	?	?
	1910 and later	Hawaiian Islands	deliberate	game
Swinhoe Pheasant	late 1930s ?	Japan	?	?
Red Jungle Fowl	?	Chagos Archipelago	?	?
	1930 and 1954	France	deliberate ?	game ?
Green Jungle Fowl	between 1880-90	Cocos-Keeling Islands	deliberate ?	?
Ring-necked Pheasant	1934-42	Alaska	deliberate	game
	about 1959 and later	Flinders Island, Australia	deliberate	?
	1970-74 ?	Peru	deliberate	hunting
	1950s	Dominican Republic	deliberate	sport
	prior 1959 ?	Eleuthera Island, Bahamas	?	?
Reeves Pheasant	1880 and later, 1947-68	USA	deliberate	game ?
	1957, 1960-61	Hawaiian Islands	deliberate	game ?
(d) Unsuccessful introductions				
Mountain Quail	1860-61	Canada (mainland)	deliberate	game
	1876-1882	New Zealand	deliberate	game ?
Scaled Quail	1961	Hawaiian Islands	deliberate	game ?
California Quail	1908-10	Queen Charlotte Islands, Canada	deliberate	?
	about 1906 ?	Natal, South Africa (?)	not known if released	?
	1852-69 ?	France	?	?
	1863-76 and 1930s	Australia (various mainland areas)	deliberate	?
	1917	Fiji	deliberate ?	?
	1938	Tonga	deliberate ?	?
	prior 1935, and 1938	Tahiti	deliberate	?

INTRODUCTIONS OF PHASIANIDAE

Species	Date introduced	Region	Manner introduced	Reason
Bobwhite Quail	before 1800 and in 1856	Bermuda	deliberate	game
	1886-87	Antigua, Lesser Antilles	deliberate	?
	1886-87	Guadeloupe, Lesser Antilles	deliberate	?
	1886-87	Barbados	deliberate	?
	?	Martinique	deliberate	?
	1809 ?	St Croix, Virgin Islands	deliberate	?
	1860	Puerto Rico	deliberate	?
	1747 or 1800 and 1953	Jamaica	deliberate	?
	about 1891	China	deliberate	?
	1975 and later	Peru	deliberate	game
	1854-1900	France	deliberate	game
	1813-98 and later	British Isles	deliberate	game ?
Harlequin Quail	1961	Hawaiian Islands	deliberate	game ?
Chukar Partridge	1938	Alaska	deliberate	game ?
	1864-65, 1872 and recently	Australia	deliberate	game
Red-legged Partridge	1896, 1955-61	USA (various areas)	deliberate	game
	1860s, 1873	Australia	deliberate	?
	prior 1897, 1899	New Zealand	deliberate	game ?
Barbary Partridge	early 19th century	Porto Santo, Madeira	?	?
	?	Great Britain	?	?
	about 1929-30	France	deliberate	?
	1868 ?, 1892, 1894	New Zealand	deliberate	game ?
	1960-63	USA	deliberate	game
Black Francolin	1880s	USSR	deliberate	?
	prior 1954	Arabia	escapee ?	captive bird
	1891, and prior 1957	USA	deliberate	game
Grey Francolin	1890	Andaman Islands	?	?
Heuglin's Francolin	1961	Hawaiian Islands	deliberate	game
Clapperton's Francolin	1958-62	Hawaiian Islands	deliberate	game
European Partridge	1895 and later	Hawaiian Islands	deliberate	game
	1867-1912	New Zealand	deliberate	game
	prior 1926	Fiji	not known if liberated	?
	1871-72, 1897-1912 ?, 1936	Australia	deliberate	game ?
	before 1932	Chile	deliberate	?
Bearded Partridge	1923	Japan	deliberate	?
Madagascar Partridge	about 1750 and prior 1912	Mauritius	deliberate	?
Comon Quail	1870s-1925, 1955-60s	USA (various areas)	deliberate	game
	1862	Australia (?)	?	?
	early ? and in 1914	New Zealand	deliberate and escapee	?
	about 1867	Seychelles	?	?
	several in 18th century	Mauritius	?	?
	about 1920	Tahiti	deliberate ?	?
	1935	France	deliberate	increased stock for hunting

continued

INTRODUCTIONS OF PHASIANIDAE

Species	Date introduced	Region	Manner introduced	Reason
Stubble Quail	about 1870s	New Zealand	deliberate	?
	1922 and later	Hawaiian Islands	deliberate	game ?
Blue-breasted Quail	prior 1922	New Zealand	not known if released	cage bird ?
	?	USA	?	?
Jungle Bush-Quail	prior 1812 or 1905	Mauritius	?	?
	?	Réunion	?	?
Formosan Hill Partridge	1924	Japan	deliberate	?
Red-crested Wood Partridge	1924	Hawaiian Islands	deliberate	?
Bamboo Partridge	1904 on, and 1960s	USA	deliberate	game
	1956-60s	USSR	deliberate	game ?
Impejan Pheasant	1871	Australia	deliberate	game ?
	prior 1955	France	deliberate	hunting ?
Brown-eared Pheasant	1940	Alaska	deliberate	game
Silver Pheasant	1868-71	New Zealand	deliberate	?
	1865-67, 1870 and later	Hawaiian Islands	deliberate	game ?
	1884 and various times since	USA	deliberate	game ?
	1920s	USSR	deliberate ?	hunting ?
	prior 1955	France	?	hunting
	1880s, 1905, 1928-29	Great Britain	deliberate	?
	prior 1968	Colombia	deliberate	hunting ?
	prior 1925	Canada	deliberate	?
Kalij Pheasant	1941	Alaska	deliberate	game
	before 1926, 1958-66	USA	deliberate	game
Crested Fireback Pheasant	1871	Australia	deliberate	?
Red Jungle Fowl	1860s and 1880s	Australia	deliberate	?
	1773, 1778 and 1814	New Zealand	deliberate	?
	1840	Auckland Island, New Zealand	deliberate	?
	1865	Campbell Island	deliberate	?
	1960-68	USA	deliberate	game
	1493	Hispaniola, West Indies	feral ?	food ?
	?	Grenadines, Lesser Antilles	?	?
	1839	Trinidad	deliberate	game ?
	1882-93	Isles Glorieuses	deliberate ?	?
Grey Jungle Fowl	1962	Hawaiian Islands	deliberate	game
Cheer Pheasant	1940	Alaska	deliberate	game ?
Ring-necked Pheasant	?	Madeira and/or Porto Santo	?	?
	1733, 1790, 1870 and 1880s	USA	deliberate	game
	19th century	Bermuda	deliberate	?
	1864-73, 1944, 1961	Australia (mainland)	deliberate	game ?
	1882	Tasmania, Australia	deliberate	?
	about 1880	Mauritius	deliberate ?	?
	1938 and later	Tahiti	deliberate	?
	about 1935	Pitcairn Island	deliberate	food ?
	1940, 1947	Alaska	deliberate	game ?
	1959	Panama	deliberate	?
	1929	Taiwan	deliberate	?

Species	Date introduced	Region	Manner introduced	Reason
Reeves Pheasant	after 1899 ?	New Zealand	deliberate	?
Copper Pheasant	1885 and later ?	USA	deliberate	?
	1907-14	Hawaiian Islands	deliberate	?
Golden Pheasant	1786 on, 1930	USA and Canada	deliberate	?
	1865 and recently	Hawaiian Islands	deliberate	?
	early ?	New Zealand	not known if released	?
	prior 1968 ?	Colombia	deliberate ?	hunting ?
	1938	Tahiti	deliberate	?
Amherst Pheasant	1931-33	Hawaiian Islands	deliberate	game ?
	prior 1922 ?	New Zealand	not known if released	?
	prior 1968	Colombia	deliberate	hunting ?
Common Peafowl	about 1798, 1810	Dominican Republic	feral ?	?
	prior 1912	Western Australia (mainland)	deliberate	?
	?	Madeira and/or Porto Santo	?	?
	about 1920	Society Islands	?	?
	prior 1870	St Helena	?	?
Tragopan (sp. unknown)	early 1880s	Protection Island, USA	deliberate	?

MOUNTAIN QUAIL
(Mountain Partridge, Painted Quail)
Oreortyx pictus (Douglas)

DISTINGUISHING CHARACTERISTICS
26-29 cm (10.23-11.41 in). 230-292 g (8.1-10.3 oz)
Generally bluish grey on head, chest and neck and brown on the remainder; head plume black; chin and throat chestnut with white border to sides of throat; lores whitish; chest greyish brown; centre and lower abdomen pale chestnut, white and chestnut bars on sides; back, wings and tail olive-brown; bill blackish, with pale base. *Female:* duller and with shorter plume.
Johnsgard, 1973, pp.343-345 and pl.91, foll. p.364.

GENERAL DISTRIBUTION
North America: west coast of the United States from Washington and south-western Idaho to northern Baja California, and formerly New Mexico.

INTRODUCED DISTRIBUTION
Introduced successfully on Vancouver Island, Canada, and in some areas of the USA; possibly introduced successfully in the Hawaiian Islands. Introduced unsuccessfully to New Zealand.

GENERAL HABITS
Status: fairly common. *Habitat:* brushy forest and brushy mountain slopes. *Gregariousness:* parties or coveys of 10-30 birds, occasionally large flocks. *Movements:* sedentary, but some altitudinal migration to higher altitudes in autumn. *Foods:* seeds, insects, buds, flowers, plant shoots, tubers, roots, leaves and fruits. *Breeding:* Apr-July; possibly 2 broods per year. *Nest:* hollow under vegetation lined with grass, leaves, needles and feathers. *Eggs:* 6, 10-12, 22.
Johnsgard, 1973, pp.345-355.

NOTES ON INTRODUCTIONS
Canada. Mountain Quail were introduced to British Columbia at Fraser Valley on the mainland, and to Vancouver Island in the 1860s (Guiguet, 1961). They were liberated by C. Wylde at Victoria, Vancouver Island, in 1860 or 1861, and are said to have been released in the Fraser Valley at about the same time (Carl and Guiguet, 1972). In the Fraser Valley there is a record of the species at Vedder Mountain in 1921, but no subsequent authenticated reports since that time. On Vancouver Island the initial introductions failed, but later ones were successful and the species became established there. They appear to have been fairly common in 1928 (Alford, 1928). According to Carl and Guiguet they are largely confined to the south end of the island and have become abundant in some areas. In the late 1950s they were not numerous but some were present in the Sooke Hills, Highland district and north sporadically as far as Duncan. More recently, in the 1970s Carl and Guiguet report them in small numbers in the Highland district (Durrance Lake, Wark Mt and Todd Inlet) near Victoria, and near Duncan. *O.p. palmeri* is apparently the race established in Canada (A.O.U., 1957).

USA. Mountain Quail have been introduced in a number of areas of the United States. The race *O.p. palmeri* was introduced to Washington State in the late 1800s (Johnsgard 1973). Some were introduced to San Juan and Whidbey islands, Washington, in the 1860s (Carl and Guiguet, 1972). They may have been introduced in Mesa County, western Colorado, in 1965 and have possibly become established there; they may or may not be a native species in western Idaho, and their occurrence in northern and western Nevada may be due to introduced stock (Johnsgard). According to Reilly (1968) they have been 113

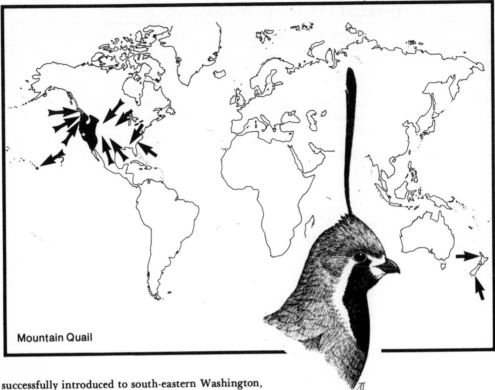

Mountain Quail

successfully introduced to south-eastern Washington, eastern Oregon, western Idaho and to central Nevada.

In Washington State they have been repeatedly introduced to various areas, although they are indigenous to the western part (Jewett *et al*, 1953). A few may have been introduced to the Willamette Valley in the 1860s; several shipments were obtained from California between 1880 and 1890 and were probably released, and fifty birds were liberated in Benton County in 1915. The species is now permanently established in areas east and west of the Cascades.

There were probably many introductions of Mountain Quail into eastern and north-eastern States in the 1870s and 1880s when stocking there with this species was being recommended (Phillips, 1928). Phillips indicates that most of these introductions were on a small scale and that all were failures. Trial introductions were also apparently conducted in Alabama, Nebraska and North Carolina without success, and in western Idaho prior to 1920, where they were successful.

Hawaiian Islands. The race *palmeri* was imported from California in 1929 (Caum, 1933; Walker, 1967) and apparently released on the islands of Hawaii and Kauai (Munro, 1960). The species may not be established there (Walker), but according to Lewin (1971) they may still be breeding on the island of Hawaii where Californian game farm stock were released in 1960 (fifty-two birds), 1961 and in 1963 (thirty-six).

New Zealand. A number of introductions of Mountain Quail were made in New Zealand between 1876 and 1882 but all were unsuccessful. In 1876 the Auckland Acclimatisation Society introduced six birds, and in 1877 another nine. The latter were released at Matamata. A large number were imported in 1881, of which forty were liberated near Lake Omapere and forty in the Upper Thames district. Also in 1881, the Otago society introduced 122 birds, liberating half of them at Gladbrook, Strath-Taieri, and half at Mataura Bridge, Ventlaw Station. Further introductions were made by the Auckland and Otago societies. In 1882 some sixty-four birds were imported and liberated at Rock and Pillar Range (Thomson, 1922).

DAMAGE
None known.

SCALED QUAIL
(Blue Quail, Scaly Colon, Mexican Quail)
Callipepla squamata (Vigors)

DISTINGUISHING CHARACTERISTICS
25-30 cm (9.84-11.8 in). 170-234 g (6-8.2 oz)
Generally greyish blue, more so on the neck and throat; upper breast to back feathers edged black, giving a scaly appearance; bushy brownish white crest on head; wings tinged brown; sides of abdomen greyish, streaked with white stripes; bill horn.
Johnsgard, 1973, pp.356-358 and pl.95, foll. p.364.

GENERAL DISTRIBUTION
North America: in south-western USA from southern Arizona, northern New Mexico, eastern Colorado, south-western Kansas and western Oklahoma south to Jalisco and Guanajuato States in central Mexico.

INTRODUCED DISTRIBUTION
Introduced successfully in some areas of the USA and probably unsuccessfully to the Hawaiian Islands.

GENERAL HABITS
Status: fairly common. *Habitat:* desert, cultivated areas, grassland and brush in arid and semi-arid

114

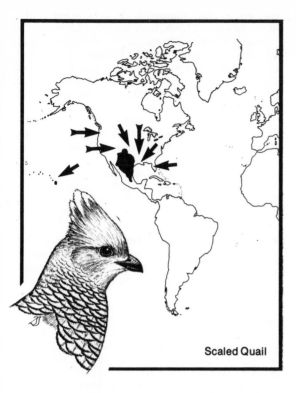

Scaled Quail

areas. *Gregariousness:* small flocks and coveys of 10-23 birds, but in late summer and winter large flocks of up to 200. *Movements:* sedentary. *Foods:* insects, seeds, buds, berries, leaves and other vegetable material. *Breeding:* May-Aug; 2-3 broods per season. *Nest:* slight hollow, lined with leaves and grass, under or near a clump of grass or weeds. *Eggs:* 5, 10-12, 22.

Johnsgard, 1973, pp.358-369

NOTES ON INTRODUCTIONS

USA. the race of *C.s. pallida* has been successfully introduced into Yakima (A.O.U., 1957) and Grant counties, Washington (Johnsgard, 1973). They were experimentally introduced into Nevada in the early 1960s (Christensen, 1963) and are now well established in several localities in eastern Nevada (Johnsgard). In Washington a few may have been introduced prior to 1913 as they may have been established in Yakima County as early as 1915; however, at least 471 were released there between 1914 and 1917, and 118 by the Grays Harbour County Bird Committee in 1919, the latter unsuccessfully (Jewett *et al,* 1953).

Phillips (1928) indicates that because of the confusion with early names applied to this quail it is now difficult to distinguish between extensions in range and those brought about by introductions. He records that the species was introduced unsuccessfully around Denver, Colorado, by W. C. Bradbury in about 1898; other introductions at Colorado Springs and perhaps at Canyon City, Colorado, may have had some success, but he suggests that it is doubtful whether they had much effect on the birds' range. Further introductions occurred on two occasions in southern Louisiana and once in Florida, some time prior to 1928, but all were unsuccessful.

Hawaiian Islands. Introductions of the race *C.s. castanogastris* from the United States occurred in these islands in 1961, but the species is not now known to be established there (Walker, 1967). According to Lewin (1971) the birds came from a Texas game farm and fourteen were released on the Puu Waawaa Ranch on the island of Hawaii.

DAMAGE

None known.

CALIFORNIA QUAIL
(Valley Quail, 'Californian' Quail)
Lophortyx californicus (Shaw and Nodder)

DISTINGUISHING CHARACTERISTICS

23.7-27.5 cm (9-10.64 in). 130-207 g (4.58-7.3 oz) Upper parts greyish brown; forward curved 'teardrop'-shaped head plume black; chin and throat black, with a white border; white line from across top of crown over eye to neck, with a black line behind this across brow of crown; forehead whitish, with black lines; sides and flanks with longitudinal white stripes; upper abdomen scaly; bill black. *Female:* lighter coloured throat, no head markings and shorter crest. Johnsgard, 1973, pp.391-393 and pl.98, foll. p.364.

GENERAL DISTRIBUTION

North America: in the United States from southern Oregon and western Nevada south to the cape region of Baja California.

INTRODUCED DISTRIBUTION

Introduced successfully in New Zealand, the Hawaiian Islands, Chile, Juan Fernandez, Argentina, some areas of Canada and the USA, King and Norfolk Islands (Australia). Introduced unsuccessfully in Australia (including Tasmania), Europe (France), Tahiti and probably Fiji, Tonga and South Africa.

GENERAL HABITS

Status: common, though decreased in numbers and range since the early 1900s. *Habitat:* chaparral, woodland edges, coastal scrub, parks, heaths and grasslands. *Gregariousness:* pairs and small coveys of 25-60 birds; larger flocks in non-breeding season up to 500-600. *Movements:* sedentary. *Foods:* seeds, fruits, leaves, berries, grain, insects and vegetable material. *Breeding:* Apr-Sept (N.Z. Aug-Feb; King Isl. Sept-Jan); two broods recorded. *Nest:* shallow depression of dry grass on the ground, generally under the cover of a bush, etc. *Eggs:* 9, 10-18, 28 (Hawaiian Isls. 6-12; N.Z. 8-22).

Johnsgard, 1973, pp.393-407.

Leopold, 1978.

NOTES ON INTRODUCTIONS

New Zealand. California Quail appear to have been introduced to New Zealand for the first time when two pairs were released by M. W. Hay at Papakura, near Auckland, in 1862 (Williams, 1952). Some were introduced by the Nelson Acclimatisation Society in 1865 and there were many subsequent releases by other acclimatisation societies: Auckland society in 1867 (113 birds), and in 1868 (forty-two); Canterbury society in 1867 (?), 1868 (four) and in 1871 (520 ?); Otago society in 1868 (eighteen) and in 1871 (120); Southland society in 1873 (two) and in 1874 (twenty-nine); Wellington society in 1874 (266) and in 1875 (eighteen). The species was also liberated by Sir George Grey on Kawau Island in 1867 (Thomson, 1922).

Williams records many introductions, in the North Island between 1862 and 1917, and in the South Island from 1865 to 1887 and from 1914 to 1945. He says that credit for the establishment of the California Quail is due to the various acclimatisation societies in New Zealand, but to trace the records of liberations is extremely difficult because inadequate records were kept.

After the initial liberations between 1860 and 1870 the spread of this quail in New Zealand was brought about by trapping and re-liberating locally bred stock and the natural spread from many liberation points (Williams). The success the species has had can be gauged by the fact that between 1878 and 1880 a large export trade was built up (Oliver, 1930; Hjersman, 1948). Thousands of quail were canned and frozen and sent to England and the European mainland.

According to Hjersman, California Quail were abundant in New Zealand until about 1880. They became plentiful again in about 1900 and then gradually declined until they were scarce in the 1930s. Williams (1963) says that in New Zealand there appears to be a regular population cycle of about four years, which is not apparent amongst these quail within their native range.

Probably *L.c. californicus* and *L.c. brunnescens* were released in New Zealand, thus the present population may be a mixed one. California Quail are now widespread and common in the North and South Islands, and on the Chatham Islands (Wodzicki, 1965) where they were introduced in about 1900 (Williams, 1952).

Hawaiian Islands. Two races of the California Quail,

californicus and *brunnescens*, have been introduced to the Hawaiian Islands, both with some success.

Munro (1960) indicates that the California Quail was established on the islands of Molokai and Hawaii in the 1890s. Walker (1967) says that *californicus* and *brunnescens* were introduced from California prior to 1855. Fisher (1951) says the species was established on the island of Niihau in about 1900, but that several subsequent imports were made from the United States and Kauai. They were common on Kauai in 1936 and on Niihau in 1939 (Munro).

Twelve pairs were liberated on Lanai in 1937-38, and there was a small population there in 1946-47 (Schwartz and Schwartz, 1950). Schwartz and Schwartz indicate that by 1946-47 the California Quail occupied an area of some 4662 square kilometres (2897 square miles) and ranged from sea-level to 3300 metres (3610 feet). They estimate that the total population was probably some 78 000 quail.

Further releases were made on the island of Hawaii from 1959 to 1961, when eight liberations totalling 412 birds from Wisconsin and Californian game farms were made at the Puu Waawaa Ranch, where the species is now abundant (Lewin, 1971).

Both *californicus* and *brunnescens* (Berger, 1972) are still established on all the main islands, being common in the drier parts of Hawaii, Maui and Molokai (Hawaiian Audubon Society, 1975), and the species is open to hunting there (Walker).

South America. Both *L.c. brunnescens* (Peters, 1934) and *L.c. californicus* (A.O.U., 1957) may

California Quail

have been introduced into South America. The race *californicus* appears to be that established in Chile (A.O.U.), although more recently Blake (1977) indicates that *brunnescens* is established there. They were introduced from California in about 1870, when attempts were made to naturalise them in the Southern Lake area of Chile, but these attempts were unsuccessful (Johnson, 1965). Escalante (pers. comm., 1976) indicates that they were introduced to Chile and Argentina in 1870; however, it is not known definitely whether they spread into Argentina from Chile or were the result of a separate introduction.

Information collected by Swarth (1927) indicates some birds escaped at Limache, near Valparaiso, Chile, in about 1864 and shortly after. He also indicates that C. J. Lambert released many birds from San Francisco (USA) at La Compania, Province of Coquimbo, in 1881 or 1882, where they increased and spread into the surrounding country. Phillips (1928) records that from the original nucleus established in 1870 they were introduced at other points such as in the valley of Nilahue, Curico Province, in 1914 and were said by Barros (*Rev. Chilena Hist. Nat.* 23: 1919, 15-16) to be increasing there in about 1919.

Attempts to establish the species in Chile in and after 1870 were certainly successful, and in 1965 Johnson recorded that they were established from Atacama to Concepción. More recently Sick (1968) says they are spread from Coquimbo and as far south as Port Montt. He noted them at Los Angeles in central Chile.

Olrog (1959) records that the California Quail (*L.c. brunnescens*) is established in San Juan and Mendoza, Argentina. The species now occurs along the Andes in the provinces of Cordoba and San Juan, and south as far as Neuquen and Rio Negro, and also near San Carlos de Bariloche (Sick).

The species was released on Juan Fernandez, off the coast of Chile, in 1912 or 1913 (Skottsberg, 1920; Hellmayr, 1932) by Captain Wahlbom (or Wakelborn ?). The population at first increased and the species was very common on Masafuera but not on Masatierra in the 1930s. It later declined due to the pressure of predation by rats which are abundant there. They are, however, still established on the island (Sick; Johnson).

Canada. Introductions of California Quail between 1860 and 1912 in British Columbia, Canada, have been quite successful. The species was first introduced in 1860-61 by C. Wylde, who released them near Victoria on Vancouver Island (Carl and Guiguet, 1972). Brown (1868) refers to some which had been set free in Metchosin, to add to the game bird species on the island.

Carl and Guiguet outline numerous introductions which occurred in this part of Canada: birds from the San Juan Islands were released by H. M. Peers in 1860-61 and in the 1870s by S. Tolmie, Colonel Pendercast, Major Gillingham and others; in the 1890s some were introduced to Vancouver Island and the lower mainland; in 1908-1910 to Nicola in the southern interior and on the Queen Charlotte Islands; in 1907-09 some thirty birds were released on South Pender Island by A. R. Spalding and H. R. Pooley.

Lewin (1965) maintains that California Quail were liberated in the Okanagan Valley in 1912, but Munro and Cowan (1947) say the Okanagan Valley may have been populated by birds moving northward from Washington, USA.

According to Guiguet (1961), introductions of California Quail in the Fraser Valley were only partly successful, but in the southern interior of British Columbia they became abundant in some areas. They were plentiful around Osoyoos in 1950. On Vancouver Island the population built up tremendously and for a number of years they were abundant from Sooke north to Comox, but thereafter declined. They were common there in 1928 (Alford, 1928). In the Okanagan and Similkameen valleys in 1963 (Lewin) they were established over an area of approximately 1000 square kilometres (621 square miles) and the population was estimated to be in the vicinity of 50 000 quail.

California Quail are now well established on Vancouver Island, mainly in the Saanich Peninsula and Sooke areas, but occur sporadically north at least to Comox. Numbers vary but the present population is low. A few birds still exist on Pender Island, but the lower mainland introductions have been largely unsuccessful. Small numbers may still exist around Tsawwassen, Centennial Beach and Beach Cove. They are still well established in the southern interior where they appear to be maintaining their numbers, but have failed to become established on the Queen Charlotte Islands as did transferred stock in the Vanderhoof area (Carl and Guiguet). The race *L.c. brunnescens* was introduced to Vancouver Island and the mainland, but other introductions were probably of mixed races (A.O.U., 1957).

USA. At least four and probably more races of the California Quail appear to have been introduced, or re-introduced, in areas within the United States.

According to Peters (1934) *L.c. brunnescens* has been introduced in several areas in western North America. *L.c. plumbeus* has been introduced in southern California, *L.c. californicus* has been established in eastern Washington, western Idaho, eastern Oregon, Nevada, central and northern Utah (A.O.U., 1957) and Colorado (Johnsgard, 1973). The race *L.c. catalinensis* has been established on Santa Cruz and Santa Rosa islands off the coast of southern California (Miller, 1951). Other introductions have apparently been made in Washington (Pearson, 1936) with mixed stock and in northern Oregon and Colorado (Peterson, 1961).

Two early introductions were made near Olympia, Washington, in about 1857, and other early records refer to some made in the vicinity of Fort Townsend (Phillips, 1928; Jewett *et al*, 1953). Some 468 birds were released between 1914 and 1918 by the game committees of Garfield, Walla Walla and Yakima counties (Phillips). The California Quail is now established in small numbers west of the Cascades in Washington.

During the 1880s many California Quail were liberated along the Columbia River, Oregon, but the first successful liberation was made in 1914 when the State Game Committee released eighteen birds at Reed College. They remained there for some years before disappearing (Jewett and Gabrielson, 1929). 117

In 1914 about 1200 birds were trapped in Jackson and Josephine counties and released in sixteen other counties in Oregon (Phillips). Further introductions were made in 1933 (thirty-four birds) and in 1948 (Gullion, 1951).

Huey (1932) mentions that Grinnell (1897) caught six birds on San Clemente Island, California, in 1897 and reported that 144 had been released there about twelve years previously (1885). However, Phillips indicates that they were released successfully on the island prior to 1875. In 1946 twelve pairs of artificially bred birds were liberated near Shandon in San Luis Obispo County. These are said to have survived and by January 1947 had increased to forty-nine birds, but their subsequent fate is not known.

In Utah the first introduction probably occurred over a century ago (Johnsgard, 1973). They may have been released near Salt Lake City in about 1870 or earlier, and further introductions in about 1900 (Phillips). The species is now found in scattered areas in the State but is primarily limited to the semi-arid foothills and valleys (Johnsgard). Attempts were made to establish the California Quail in Massachusetts in 1890 and probably before; some were released by W. D. Blaisdell in Macon, Illinois, in 1896; some were released before the Civil War by General Cadwallader in Maryland and some probably in Delaware around the same period; some in Missouri in 1879 and some in Idaho (Phillips) at the same time. All these introductions were apparently unsuccessful, however the species is now established in the Boise Valley of Idaho (Johnsgard).

In 1852 thirty birds were released on Long Island, and in 1874 and 1892 some were released on Gardiners Island in New York, but these also failed to become established (Phillips). In the 1870s several dozen birds were released by W. Dorman near Virginia City, Nevada, and became successfully established. Prior to 1895 some were liberated at Paradise Valley, Nevada, and in 1902 some were taken to Lovelock (Phillips). Other introductions occurred in the Carson City and Reno regions of Nevada. More recently Johnsgard has indicated that an introduced population occurred for a while in north-central Colorado but has now been extirpated. Fairly recently attempts have been made to establish the species in Arizona and these may have been successful in the vicinity of Little Colorado River near Springerville. The project began with the release of 356 hand-reared offspring of wild birds captured in Sonora in 1968. An introduction near Austwell, on the central Texas coast of 252 birds in 1933-35, was apparently unsuccessful (Halloran and Howard, 1956).

Australia. New Zealand bred California Quail were taken to Victoria and Tasmania between 1863 and 1874 (Ryan, 1906), and there were unsuccessful liberations at Gembrook and elsewhere in Victoria in 1863, 1872 and 1874 (Hutton, 1905). Ryan records that six were liberated in Victoria in 1863, a large number at Gembrook in 1872 and forty more in 1874. He reports that for a time these introductions appeared to be successful, but later they all disappeared. Altogether more than 260 California Quail may have been liberated unsuccessfully in Victoria in 1873-74 (Jenkins, 1977). One pair were liberated at Pewsey Vale by the South Australian Acclimatisation Society in about 1879-80 and some were released at Liverpool Plains, Bathurst, Blue Mountains, etc., in New South Wales in 1880 (Jenkins). According to McCance (1962) some were seen at Sandhurst, Gembrook and Lilydale, but the species was declining at Gembrook in 1886. Further liberations may have occurred in the 1930s because birds were sighted in 1938 (Chisholm, 1950) and some may have been present at Wonthaggi. Other releases of California Quail occurred in the Prospect district, near Sydney, New South Wales, in 1944 (Tarr, 1950; Condon, 1975). They were reported to be breeding there at about this time (Tarr).

California Quail are established on King Island in Bass Strait where they were introduced in 1930 to produce a game bird to replace the declining native brown quail (Frith, 1973). Coveys of up to thirty birds were reported on the island in the early 1970s (McCarvie and Templeton, 1974). Some California Quail were shot near Bridgewater, Tasmania, before 1950 (Tarr, 1950; Sharland, 1958), but there appear no further records of the species in this State. They were reported to have been plentiful at one time on Huon Island, off Tasmania (Tarr). On Phillip Island, Victoria, some time after 1860, eggs of the species were placed in the nests of native quail in an attempt to establish them on that island. American quail (possibly some California Quail ?) were introduced to Rottnest Island, Western Australia, by Governor Ord in 1876 but they failed to become established (Storr, 1965). California Quail were also introduced to Queensland before 1919 but apparently they did not survive for any length of time (Chisholm, 1919).

Norfolk Island. Williams (1952) records that there were introductions of California Quail to Norfolk Island in 1895 from New Zealand. The species became established there (Oliver, 1955) and is now common in the more open habitats on the island (Smithers and Disney, 1969).

Fiji and Tonga. New Zealand bred California Quail were exported to Fiji in 1917 and to Tonga in 1938 (Williams, 1952). Whether they were released and their subsequent fate does not appear to be recorded, but the species is not now established in either country.

Tahiti. According to Holyoak (1974) California Quail were introduced to the district of Papeari where they were established in 1935 (Curtiss, 1938), but have not been observed since that date. However, E. Guild (1938) released some in 1938 and reported that they had nested and reared young. He also records that some were also liberated at about this time by C. B. Nordhoff.

South Africa. According to Phillips (1928) the Government of Natal, South Africa, was considering (*Forest and Stream* no.56, 1906, p.455) the introduction of this quail in 1906, but it was not known whether any birds were exported to that country and released.

Europe. In France, California Quail were experimented with as long ago as 1852 (Phillips, 1928). Phillips gives a list of references which may be of interest:

Bohm, R., *Deut Acclim* (organ Deut ver

Vogelzucht und Acclim), no.5, 1879, p.17.

Bull. Soc. Natn. Acclim. Fr. no.1, 1864, p.402; no.2, series 2, 1865, p.637; no.6, series 2, 1869, p.509.

Thus, whether many birds were actually released has not been ascertained, but Phillips mentions that temporary success, at least, was achieved near Canflans sur Aines, France.

DAMAGE
In New Zealand by 1910-15, California Quail had become so numerous in some districts that farmers were complaining of the damage caused by them (Thomson, 1922). In some cases poisoned grain was sown with seeds in the hope of reducing the numbers of birds. Oliver (1955) reports that although they are useful birds, consuming weed seeds and many insects, complaints of grape and strawberry crops being ruined by them had been received. The main complaint was their habit of eating clover seed, especially when it was germinating (Oliver; Hjersman, 1948).

There appear to be few records of the California Quail becoming a pest in North America. Some of the earlier records prior to about 1936 indicate that the species may have been considered a pest of grain crops and it had certainly earned a bad reputation in vineyards. Boudreau (1972) indicates that they are still perhaps a problem in California by eating grapes in some vineyards.

GAMBEL'S QUAIL
(Desert Quail)
Lophortyx gambelii (Gambel)

DISTINGUISHING CHARACTERISTICS
23.7-30.2 cm (9-11.8 in). 156-207 g (5.5-7.3 oz)
Similar appearance to the California Quail, but with a black patch on the whitish abdomen; forehead black streaked white; sides chestnut, with white

Gambel's Quail

stripes; bill black. *Female:* has greyish brown head, smaller brown crest, no head markings and a whitish throat.

Johnsgard, 1973, pp.376-378 and pls. 94, 96, foll. p.364.

GENERAL DISTRIBUTION
North America. South-western USA from southern Nevada, southern Utah, western Colorado and western Texas, south to north-western Mexico from north-eastern Baja California, central Sonora and north-western Chihuahua.

INTRODUCED DISTRIBUTION
Introduced with some success in the USA (some areas) and successfully in the Hawaiian Islands.

GENERAL HABITS
Status: fairly common. *Habitat:* desert thickets usually near water. *Gregariousness:* small flocks or coveys of 20-50 birds, but larger flocks in the non-breeding season. *Movements:* sedentary. *Foods:* seeds, flowers, grain, berries, leaves, plant shoots and insects. *Breeding:* Apr-Aug; monogamous; occasionally 2 broods per year. *Nest:* hollow on ground, sparsely lined with grass and leaves, beneath a bush or grass tuft. *Eggs:* 6, 10-12, 19.

Johnsgard, 1973, pp.378-390.

NOTES ON INTRODUCTIONS
USA. Introductions of Gambel's Quail were made to Montrose, Colorado, between 1885 and 1889, but the species now appears to have died out there (A.O.U., 1957). Almost 1000 birds were released during this period and the species became well established in the mid-western part of that State (Phillips, 1928). Attempts in eastern Colorado failed completely. Other introductions have been made to north-central Idaho and to San Clemente Island, California; these may also have died out (A.O.U.) although it is possible that an isolated population is still present in Idaho (Johnsgard, 1973). They appear to have been introduced successfully in eastern New Mexico (Reilly, 1968) but there is little recent information. There have been many attempts to establish them in northern California; in 1912 about 700 birds were liberated in Los Angeles, Orange, Ventura and San Benito counties without success (Phillips). The San Clemente Island introduction occurred in about 1912 when M. Howland released birds from California; some 240 were taken to the island but half died before liberation (Huey, 1932).

Early attempts were made to establish Gambel's Quail in Massachusetts in 1890, 1891 and 1893, when at least 320 were released mainly on Marthas Vineyard Island, where they survived for a few years. Other introductions may have occurred at Winchendon and in Berkshire and Bristol counties of Massachusetts in 1893. Some attempts were made in 1919-20 in Pennsylvania, when 180 birds were released, and a few were possibly liberated at Bardstown, Kentucky, in 1921. A few attempts at introducing them have been made in Arizona and New Mexico north of the species' native range, but most of these appear to have failed. Large-scale releases in Washington by the Chalan County Game Commission (some time prior to 1928) also appear to have failed (Phillips).

Hawaiian Islands. Gambel's Quails were established on the island of Kahoolawe from an introduction by

Mr H. A. Baldwin in 1928. They have apparently remained established there since that date. Further introductions were made to the Hawaiian Islands in 1958 (Walker, 1967), initially to Hawaii (Peterson, 1961) and probably later to other islands. Some sixty-five birds were released on Hawaii, 114 on Lanai, and some on Maui in about 1960. The quail became established on Lanai but failed on the other two islands (Western States Exotic Game Bird Committee, 1961).

Lewin (1971) records that between 1959 and 1963 248 California and Oklahoma game farm birds were liberated on Hawaii by State Division of Fish and Game personnel, and that 294 were released between 1958 and 1961 at Puako. He also indicates that none have been seen on the island since 1963. Gambel's Quails are now well established in the Hawaiian Islands and are open to hunting on Lanai and Hawaii (Walker; Hawaiian Audubon Society, 1975).

DAMAGE
Boudreau (1972) indicates that this species may sometimes be a nuisance in vineyards in California by eating the grapes.

BOBWHITE QUAIL
(Virginia Quail or Colon, Bob-White Quail, Common Bobwhite)
Colinus virginianus (Linnaeus)

DISTINGUISHING CHARACTERISTICS
20-26.5 cm (7.87-10.25 in). 148.6-256 g (5.24-9 oz)
Generally red-brown, with black and tawny markings; forehead, lores, chin and throat white (plumage extremely variable in southern parts of range and chin and throat varies from white to black); stripe from bill, over eye and down neck white; black stripe from gape, under eye and around white of throat; abdomen white, barred black and with several V-shaped black markings on sides centrally coloured red-brown; feathers of crown erectile; bill blackish horn. *Female:* chin buff (black in some Mexican races); pale yellow present at base of lower mandible.
Johnsgard, 1973, pp.408-412 and pl.99, foll. p.364.

GENERAL DISTRIBUTION
North and Central America: from southern Ontario in south-eastern Canada, central and eastern USA to eastern Mexico, Guatemala, Cuba and the Isle of Pines.

INTRODUCED DISTRIBUTION
Introduced and re-introduced successfully in parts of the USA; introduced successfully in Haiti, Dominican Republic, Andros, New Providence, Eleuthera, England and New Zealand; introduced successfully but now extirpated on Jamaica, Puerto Rico, Antigua, Guadeloupe, Martinique, Barbados, St Croix, St Kitts and Bermuda.

Introduced unsuccessfully in Peru, Canada, the Hawaiian Islands, France, Ireland, Scotland and China; introduced probably without success in South Africa.

GENERAL HABITS
Status: locally common but numbers and range

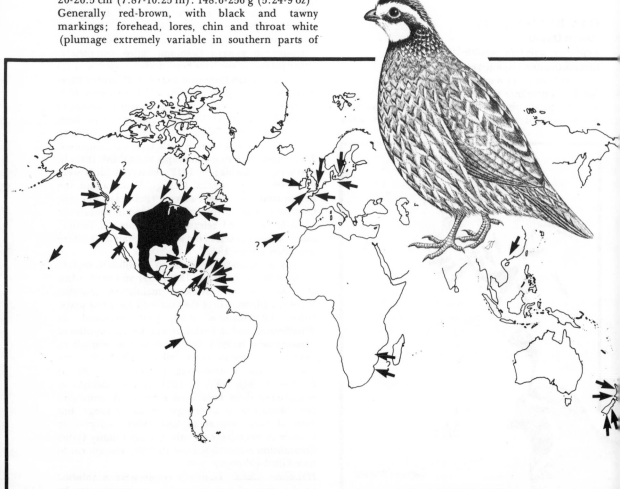

reduced by agriculture. *Habitat:* woodlands, open country with brush and weeds, grasslands, croplands and roadsides. *Gregariousness:* flocks or coveys from 10-15 in winter, at other times up to 30 birds. *Movements:* sedentary. *Foods:* seeds, fruits, grasses, grains, corn, acorns and insects. *Breeding:* Apr-June. *Nest:* scrape on the ground, lined with dry grass, leaves or weed stalks. *Eggs:* 7, 12-18, 28.

Rosene, 1969.

Johnsgard, 1973, pp.412-430.

NOTES ON INTRODUCTIONS

West Indies. Rosene (1969) reports that there have been more attempts to introduce the Bobwhite into the West Indies than anywhere else. Bobwhite Quail *C.v. virginianus* (A.O.U., 1957) were introduced to Haiti during the French colonial period at the close of the eighteenth century. They were apparently common there in 1881 and were established fairly widely by the 1930s (Wetmore and Swales, 1931).

The Cuban Bobwhite *C.v. cubanensis* is said to have been introduced in about 1925 to the Dominican Republic, at San Domingo, by an American sugar planter by the name of Bass. (Note: Phillips, 1928, gives the date as 1889-90 for the Dominican introduction by Bass and the reference as *Field Columb. Mus. Pub. 10, Ornith. series* 1 (1), 1896.) The introduction was apparently successful and they were said to be increasing rapidly in numbers in the early 1930s (Wetmore and Swales). They are now common and widespread in the Republic. (Dod, pers. comm., 1977.)

According to Peters (1934) the race *C.v. virginianus* has been introduced to the islands of Jamaica, St Croix and St Kitts. Bond (1960) reports that continental forms are also established on Andros, New Providence, Eleuthera and other islands with varied success. Some may also have been originally introduced to Cuba, although this appears doubtful because the Cuban race is well characterised. The race *C.v. floridanus* has possibly been introduced to the Bahamas (Peters). Brudenell-Bruce (1975) says they are well established on the Bahamas (and quotes Cory, 1880, as saying that they were introduced many years ago). Rosene (1969) records that attempts to establish the species have also been made on Antigua, Guadeloupe and Martinique, but that they have now been extirpated. According to Phillips (1928) they were taken to Antigua, Guadeloupe and Barbados in 1886-87.

Blake (pers. comm., 1977) says most of the Bobwhite introductions to the West Indies came from North America, but due to unfavourable environment and shooting the species has now been largely eliminated. He indicates that the Cuban race has been to some extent distributed artificially in Cuba. On St Croix, in the Virgin Islands, *C.v. virginianus* may have been an early introduction, but Wetmore (1927) considers that it is more likely to have been the Cuban subspecies. He records that the Newtons (*Ibis,* 1, 1859, p.254) state that 'Bobwhite had been introduced to St Croix about fifty years ago by one of the Governors and had become very numerous there'. Until 1927 at least, there were no other records for the species on the island. The Cuban race was introduced and established on Puerto Rico at an early date, but had probably disappeared prior to

1927. Wetmore quotes Gundlach as saying in 1878 (*J. Ornith,* no. 26, 1878. p.161) that Cuban quail were brought to Puerto Rico by Don Ramón Soler, who established them in the Hacienda Santa Ines near Vega Baja in 1860. Wetmore further indicates that Sundervall collected specimens there in 1869, and Stahl collected two in 1883, but later reported (in 1900) that they had been exterminated.

According to Phillips (1928) Bobwhite were taken to Jamaica at least fifty years before Gosse's time (Gosse, P. H. and Hill, R. *A Naturalist's Sojourn in Jamaica,* 1851), perhaps in 1800. They suffered greatly when the mongoose was introduced but later increased again. Lack (1976) indicates that the introduction occurred on Jamaica in about 1747 and the species flourished there in the eighteenth and the first part of the nineteenth century, but only few remained by the end of the century. Although another unsuccessful attempt was made to introduce them in 1953, the Bobwhite is now extinct there.

Bermuda. Bobwhite Quail (race *virginianus*) were introduced to Bermuda before 1800, but had died out there by 1840. Some were introduced again in 1856. The species became common, but was rare in the eastern end of the group in 1940 and some were still established near the centre of the island in 1941, but thereafter the population declined (Bourne, 1957). Wingate (1973) records that the Bobwhite had only temporary success in Bermuda and indicates that the species is now not established there.

Peru. Some Bobwhites were released in a marsh south of the city of Lima in about 1975, but none have been seen there since this date so they evidently have failed to become established (Plenge, pers. comm., 1977). Plenge says the species is raised in captivity in Peru for food, and so it is possible that there have been other attempts at introduction.

Canada. Either pure (*C.v. virginianus*) or mixed stock have been introduced in the Fraser Valley of British Columbia (A.O.U., 1957). Some 156 birds were released on the lower mainland at an early date (Carl and Guiguet, 1972). Some were also released at Winnipeg in Manitoba (at an early date ?), but failed to become established, and some went to Nova Scotia and Ontario in 1877 (Phillips, 1928). Carl and Guiguet record that 132 were released near Ashcroft, British Columbia, in 1900; thirty-two near Shuswap in 1905; thirty-five at Coldstream Ranch, near Vernon, in 1907; and that additional birds were released near Victoria, on Vancouver Island, in 1922. Some Bobwhite are said to have been present on Pender Island in 1882 and to have disappeared from there in about 1900, but there are no official records of this introduction.

Munro and Cowan (1947) report that the Bobwhite became well established in the southern interior of British Columbia, around Vernon, Ashcroft and Osoyoos Lake, and for many years were present in these areas. The last authentic record of them appears to have been in 1912. Several flocks also survived near Huntingdon on the United States border, but they were exterminated in the severe winter of 1947-48 (Carl and Guiguet). More recently further introductions have occurred in British Columbia. In 1967-68 Mr N. Milani of Ladner released some on his property where they were noted in 1969 (Gates in Carl and Guiguet). Some twenty birds were released at the Reifel Waterfowl Refuge, near Vancouver, in 1971 but apparently died out the following winter (Campbell in Carl and Guiguet).

Hawaiian Islands. Bobwhite Quail *C.v. virginianus* were introduced to the Hawaiian Islands as early as 1906 (Walker, 1967). This introduction appears to have had little success although Munro (1960) records that efforts to establish the species on Hawaii appear to be succeeding. Lewin (1971) records that they have been liberated on various islands since 1954 by field trial clubs. He says that 108 birds from Californian, New Mexico and Texas game farms were released on the Puu Waawaa Ranch, Hawaii, between 1959 and 1961, but the species has not become permanently established there. Some efforts were being made in 1960 and 1961 to establish them on Maui and perhaps other islands; ninety birds were apparently released in early 1961 (Western States Exotic Game Bird Committee, 1961). Walker reports that *C.v. ridgwayi* was released in 1960 and *C.v. virginianus* in 1961, but that neither race appears to have become established. More recently, Berger (1972) says the Bobwhite has not become established in the Hawaiian Islands.

Europe. Unsuccessful attempts have been made to establish Bobwhite Quail in the southern part of Europe (Rutgers and Norris, 1970). Early attempts occurred in France in 1858, 1861, 1865, 1898, 1899 and in 1900, but none was successful (Etchécopar, 1955). Some were taken from the United States to France as early as 1854 (Phillips, 1928). Phillips also records that about forty were released in Hannover, Germany, in 1872, and that attempts may have been made to introduce them in Sweden. Some were apparently taken there in about 1887 (?) and 5000 were sent to Count Lewenhaupt at Fosslorjo in 1901. Rosene (1969) has recorded that attempts in Germany and Sweden were without success.

In England, however, the Bobwhite appears to be established in the Minsmere area of Suffolk and on Tresco in the Scilly Isles where they have been reported to breed (B.O.U., 1974). They appear to have become established from introductions in about 1956 (Lever, pers. comm., 1976) and were breeding there between 1968 and 1971 (Sharrock, 1972). Lever (1977) records that the Bobwhite was released more than a dozen times in the nineteenth century, mainly in England, but also in Scotland, Ireland and Wales. Although they were released in Norfolk shortly after 1813, Windsor Park in 1840, Norfolk in 1867, Hampshire in 1860, Northamptonshire in 1870-71 and in Staffordshire in 1898, only the Northamptonshire birds survived for any length (ten years) of time. Phillips (1928) indicates that efforts were made to establish them as early as 1831, and earlier, and in 1885 at Norfolk. Newton and Newton (1859) record the failure of the species to become established in the eastern counties of England and Europe up until 1859.

In 1956 some sixty Bobwhite Quail were liberated on the coast of Suffolk where they succeeded for some years. A further release occurred at Stowmarket in 1957. Some were noted at a number of places between 1961 and 1966. In 1964 (six) and in 1965 (six) Bobwhites were released at Tresco where they became established and began to breed. Many other releases were made in England during the 1970s (in Gloucestershire, Herefordshire, Wiltshire and elsewhere) but most have probably failed. The species continues to breed at Minsmere and on Tresco (Lever, 1977). Just prior to 1970 small numbers were liberated in counties Kildare and Cork in Ireland (O'Gorman, 1970) but any success here is not known.

Southern Africa. Winterbottom (1966) reports that the Bobwhite has recently been introduced in Zimbabwe and Natal. He indicates that it is too early to gauge the species' success, but says that it is doubtful that they will remain there without man's help.

New Zealand. In 1898 the Wellington Acclimatisation Society introduced about four hundred Bobwhite and in the following year about 750 more (Thomson, 1922). Thomson reports that these birds were distributed throughout the country from Auckland to Southland for release by various societies. The following societies received birds: Otago (eighty), Canterbury (forty), Stratford (twenty), New Plymouth (twenty) and Wellington (240) in 1898; Southland (twenty-two), Otago (forty-six), Canterbury (ninety), Blenheim (seventy), Wellington (100), Wanganui (sixty), Stratford (forty-four), New Plymouth (thirty-two), Napier (thirty), Waikaremoana (fifty-six), Gisborne (six) and Auckland (200). Bobwhite appeared to become established in at least some of these areas, but had disappeared in many by 1909. In 1922 a number were caught south of Auckland, proving that they were still established there (Oliver, 1930). In 1952 some were found at Wairoa, Hawke's Bay, and shortly after at Waingaro, Waikaremoana, and again at Wairoa (Oliver, 1955).

The Otago society obtained a permit to import 1000 eggs from the United States in 1947 (Gurr, 1953). Two separate consignments of 200 eggs were forwarded from Oakland, California, arriving in Dunedin in June and July 1947. These eggs were incubated at the society's game farm at Waitati, but of sixty-four chicks hatched only forty survived the first two weeks and all later died.

The Bobwhite Quail is now established in New Zealand and is locally common in the North Island (Wodzicki, 1965), but is confined to the Wairoa district of Hawke's Bay (Falla *et al*, 1966). Westerskov (1957) lists the race introduced as *C.v. taylori*.

Madeira. According to Bannerman (1965), Bobwhite have recently been introduced to Madeira. Any success for the species there is not known.

USA. Bobwhite Quail have been introduced and/or re-introduced successfully and unsuccessfully to many States including Montana, Idaho, Oklahoma, Colorado, Oregon, Washington, Arizona, California, Massachusetts, Texas, Virginia, Wyoming, Arizona. Large numbers of quail *(L.c. texanus)* were imported from Mexico from 1910 onwards. Peak importation was probably reached in 1937 when the Mexican government issued permits for 250 000 to be shipped to the United States for propagation purposes (Rosene, 1969). Importation of Mexican birds continued until at least 1948.

According to Goodrum (1949), twenty-three States

were re-stocking with Bobwhite Quail in 1939, but this had been reduced to seventeen by 1948. However, during this period at least thirty States participated in some form of re-stocking, mainly with pen-raised birds. Only five States tried with trapped wild birds. Goodrum estimated that about 1 483 373 pen-raised Bobwhite Quail had been re-stocked between 1920 and 1947, but that there may have been many introductions which were not recorded.

Bobwhite Quail have been successfully introduced, either as pure *(C.v. virginianus)* or mixed stock, in Montana, Idaho, Colorado and Washington. The Mexican race *C.v. texanus* has been widely introduced, mainly from Mexico, in many parts of the United States beyond the ranges of other races, but has not become established. The race *C.v. taylori* has been successfully introduced into Washington, Oregon and Idaho, where they are now established locally in a relatively pure form. Re-introductions of *C. v. ridgwayi* into Arizona have not been successful (A.O.U., 1957).

The race *virginianus* was liberated in various parts of the Willamette Valley, adjacent to Portland, Oregon, between 1899 and 1929 and some birds persisted there between 1920 and 1926 (Jewett and Gabrielson, 1929). Fairly recently, the race *taylori* was introduced and became established in the Columbia and Snake River basins of Washington, Oregon and Nevada and has also had some success in the Bighorn and Shoshone river valleys of north-western Wyoming. The race *taylori* has been repeatedly introduced into Washington and early introductions include some on Whidbey Island in 1871 (twenty-four) (Phillips, 1928); Puyullup Valley in about 1877 (eighteen birds); a large shipment from Alabama in 1906 and 1907; some 5037 liberated by various county game committees between 1913 and 1918; and 1200 birds from Mexico released in Spokane County in 1920 (Jewett *et al*, 1953).

The earliest Bobwhite Quail introductions in the United States appear to have been those at Fort Snelling, near St Paul, Minnesota, in about 1840, and at Walla Walla, Washington, in about 1865 (?). In the 1870s there were many releases, including some in Idaho where a few pairs were released at Boise in 1875, but there may have been some before 1871. Others in the 1870s include: California, where introductions began in 1872 when several dozen were liberated in Sonoma County; in Utah from about 1872 or earlier; and in Bent County, eastern Colorado, as long ago as 1870. Some were introduced in Massachusetts about fifteen to twenty years before the Civil War and between 1890 and 1895 there were probably many in the eastern and north-eastern parts of the United States. They were released in Mesa County, Colorado, in about 1891, and occurred there until 1908. Some were also released at Montrose, Colorado, in 1895. In 1892 they were common in Utah, probably as a result of earlier liberations. They were stocked in the Willamette Valley, Oregon, at least from 1893, and were distributed to other areas including islands in Puget Sound (Phillips).

After 1904-05, during which time severe winters had decimated the populations in eastern areas, tremendous efforts were made to introduce the Bobwhite. Pennsylvania, one of the largest importers

of the species, brought in some 47 000 between 1916 and 1925. Another large importer, Kentucky, imported at least 13 000 birds in 1922 and 1923. There were many other introductions at the time, and in more western regions Oklahoma liberated 1000 birds at a point from which some of the largest shipments had formerly been made. Prior to 1928 liberations occurred in Arizona, New Mexico, Wyoming and South Dakota (Phillips). Although prior to 1930 there had been a number of releases of Bobwhite in New York State by private individuals and clubs, little success was achieved. However, from 1930 to 1939 the State released 67 736 Bobwhites and these became established in a number of localities including Long Island and southern New York, and in forty-four counties of the State (Bump, 1941).

Records show that from 1930 to 1945 almost 98 000 quail of three species (including Bobwhite Quail) have been released in California, but the Bobwhite has been unsuccessful there. Introductions in western Texas (El Paso) have had some success (Peterson, 1961) as have some in Massachusetts. Some seventeen birds from Cape Cod were liberated on Great Island, West Yarmouth, Massachusetts, in 1954, and the species still survived there in 1964 (Cookingham and Ripley, 1964). Johnsgard (1973) records that between 1938 and 1968 some 110 663 Bobwhites have been released in the United States as a result of the Pittman-Robertson (P-R) programmes.

In 1946-47 200 birds were released on the King Ranch, Texas, and these were said to have helped the increase in numbers of the local population (Lehmann, 1948). The race *texanus*, and others, have been re-stocked in Kentucky, but according to Mengel (1965) it has not been demonstrated that this has assisted in any lasting beneficial effects.

China. A large-scale attempt to establish the Bobwhite was made in Kashing, in eastern China, in about 1891 or earlier (?) *(Forest and Stream*, no.37, 1891, p.325) with birds from Kansas, USA (Phillips, 1928). The attempt apparently failed.

DAMAGE
None known.

CRESTED BOBWHITE
(Crested Quail, Crested Colon)
Colinus cristatus Linnaeus

DISTINGUISHING CHARACTERISTICS
17.8-23.7 cm (6.72-9 in). 131-153 g (4.62-5.39 oz)
Lance-shaped crest buff or white; forehead, line above eye, ear-coverts and chin white; cheeks chestnut; throat white, buff or brownish; hindneck and upper back black, spotted white; remainder of upper parts brown, barred and spotted black; breast and sides reddish brown, with yellowish markings outlined with black; abdomen yellowish patterned with cinnamon and black; bill black. Female: similar, but crest barred brown; throat spotted black; back brown; hindneck and sides mottled white, black and buff.
Blake, vol.1, 1977, pp.447-451 and pl.10.
Meyer de Schauensee and Phelps, 1978, p.57 and pl.1.

GENERAL DISTRIBUTION
Central and South America: Guatemala south to Columbia and Venezuela, and east to Guyane, north-

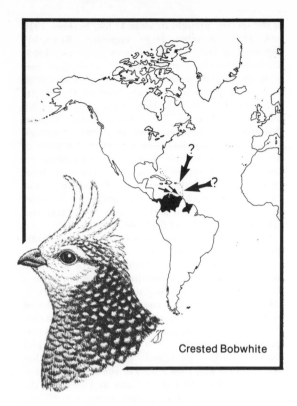

Crested Bobwhite

eastern Brazil, Aruba, Curaçao and Margarita Island.

INTRODUCED DISTRIBUTION

Introduced successfully on Mustique Island in the Grenadines and to St Thomas in the Virgin Islands.

GENERAL HABITS

Status: common. *Habitat:* semi-arid areas, grasslands, scrub, wooded open country and forest edges. *Gregariousness:* in coveys up to about 12 birds. *Movements:* sedentary. *Foods:* berries, fruits, seeds and insects. *Breeding:* nearly all year. *Nest:* on the ground. *Eggs:* 8-16.

Meyer de Schauensee and Phelps, 1978, p.57.

NOTES ON INTRODUCTIONS

St. Thomas. Crested Bobwhites *(C.c. sonnini)* have been introduced to St Thomas where they were formerly common (Wetmore, 1927). Wetmore indicates that in 1860 Cassin recorded that a specimen was collected by Robert Swift who was told they had been introduced to the island some years before from Venezuela. Swift apparently found them to be well established there and breeding freely. Wetmore says that in 1852 Knox reported that 'quail' were very rare, and that Todd (in 1920) examined skins of specimens from St Thomas and identified them as Crested Bobwhites. He reports in 1927 that there have been no recent records of the Crested Bobwhite on the island and that it is doubtful that they are still established there. In 1977 Blake (1977) records that Crested Bobwhites have been introduced to St Thomas, and indicates that the species is still present there.

Mustique Island. Blake (1977) records that the Crested Bobwhite has been introduced to Mustique Island in the Grenadines and indicates that the species is still established there.

DAMAGE

None known.

HARLEQUIN QUAIL
(Mearn's Quail, Montezuma Quail, Painted Quail)
Cyrtonyx montezumae (Vigors)

DISTINGUISHING CHARACTERISTICS

17-24 cm (6.7-9.5 in). 156-224 g (5.5-7.9 oz)

Generally grey, spotted and streaked with black, reddish and brown on the upper parts, and red and grey below. Pale bushy crest; forehead, throat and chin black; a black streak on cheeks and below and over eye, continuous with one on the lower side of the head, remainder white; band across chest from nape black; wings black spotted; sides and flanks white, or buff spotted (southern race has purplish brown spots on lower sides); middle line of breast and abdomen chestnut; bill blackish. Female: brown, with less obvious facial markings.

Johnsgard, 1973, pp.461-463 and pls.104-106, foll. p.364.

GENERAL DISTRIBUTION

North America: locally from southern and eastern central Arizona, central New Mexico and western Texas, south to southern Mexico.

INTRODUCED DISTRIBUTION

Introduced unsuccessfully to the Hawaiian Islands.

GENERAL HABITS

Status: uncommon, but locally common in remote areas. *Habitat:* grassy oak canyons and wooded mountain slopes with grass. *Gregariousness:* singly or pairs, and coveys of 3-25 birds in non-breeding season. *Movements:* sedentary, but perhaps some altitudinal movements in autumn and winter. *Foods:* acorns, nuts, bulbs, tubers, seeds, grasses, leaves and some insects and other arthropods. *Breeding:* May-Sept. *Nest:* hollow, lined with grass and leaves, on ground in grass, sometimes arched. *Eggs:* 6, 8-14, 16.

Leopold and McCabe, *Condor* vol.59, no.1, 1957, pp.3-26.

Johnsgard, 1973, pp.463-474.

Harlequin Quail

Hawaiian Islands. Introduced from the United States and liberated on these islands in 1961, the Harlequin Quail is not known to be established there (Walker, 1967; Berger, 1972). Apparently a single release of eight birds *(C.m. mearnsi)* was made at the Lowell Sanctuary on the Puu Waawaa Ranch on the island of Hawaii (Lewin, 1971).

DAMAGE

None known.

SEESEE PARTRIDGE
(Sand Partridge)
Ammoperdix griseogularis (Brandt)

DISTINGUISHING CHARACTERISTICS

24-26 cm (9.44-10.23 in). 198-240 g (6.98-8.46 oz)
Generally sandy grey-brown, with conspicuous facial markings of a white stripe through eye, flanked by a black stripe above and a narrower one below; chin and neck greyish; pinkish buff on chest; flanks barred chestnut and black; back brown, vermiculated; lower abdomen whitish; outer tail-feathers chestnut; bill yellowish or orange. Female: brown vermiculated; white patch behind eye; ear-coverts brown; belly and under tail-coverts greyish.
Ali and Ripley, vol. 2, 1968-74, pp.8-9 and fig.3, pl.19, opp. p.16.

GENERAL DISTRIBUTION

Asia: in south-western Asia from Iran to Afghanistan, Pakistan and extreme north-western India, and north to Bukhara in the southern USSR.

INTRODUCED DISTRIBUTION

Introduced unsuccessfully in the USA and the Hawaiian Islands.

GENERAL HABITS

Status: fairly common locally, but abundant in remote areas. *Habitat:* barren, rocky, stony hills and plains, and eroded areas in desert situations. *Gregariousness:* pairs, or coveys of 20 or more birds. *Movements:* no information. *Foods:* seeds, green plant material and possibly insects. *Breeding:* Apr-Sept (Mar-June India). *Nest:* scrape on the ground, occasionally sparsely lined with grass and feathers, under shelter of a rock or in the open. *Eggs:* 5-8 and up to 16.
Ali and Ripley, 1968-74, vol.2, pp.9-10.

NOTES ON INTRODUCTIONS

USA. According to Christensen (1963) the Seesee Partridge has been experimentally introduced into Nevada. Presumably it has failed to become established as there appear to be no recent records of any success. Some 263 birds were introduced in Armstrong County in northern Texas in 1956-57, but disappeared soon after their release (Jackson, 1957 and 1964).

Hawaiian Islands. Seesee Partridges from the United States were introduced to these islands in 1959 but the species is not known to be established there (Walker, 1967; Berger, 1972). In 1959 twenty birds from a Californian game farm were released on the Puu Waawaa Ranch, Hawaii; young were seen in the spring following their release, but no further birds have been sighted (Lewin, 1971).

DAMAGE

None known.

HEY'S SEESEE PARTRIDGE
(Hey's Sand Partridge, Sand Partridge, Seesee Partridge)
Ammoperdix heyi (Temminck)

DISTINGUISHING CHARACTERISTICS

Upper parts pinkish brown, finely vermiculated on coverts, rump and tail; lores whitish; crown brownish mixed with blue-grey; chin cinnamon; throat pinkish

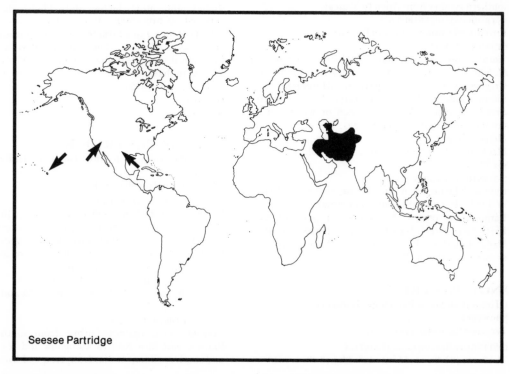

Seesee Partridge

Hey's Seesee Partridge

grey-brown; breast sandy brown to dark brown; abdomen whitish buff; flanks white with chestnut and black bars; bill yellow. Female: sandy brown, darker on upper parts; head barred brown; upper parts speckled brown; breast and flanks vermiculated dark sandy.

Meinertzhagen, 1954, pp.566-567.
Mackworth-Praed and Grant, ser.1, vol.1, 1955-73, pp.226-227 and pl.20, opp. p.263.

GENERAL DISTRIBUTION
Middle East: lower Egypt and from Berber, on the Nile, to the Red Sea, Jordan Valley and the Dead Sea region in Palestine south to the Sinai Peninsula, and southern Arabia from Aden to Muscat.

INTRODUCED DISTRIBUTION
Introduced unsuccessfully in Cyprus.

GENERAL HABITS
Status: no information, probably uncommon. *Habitat:* barren, stony, desert mountains. *Gregariousness:* small parties. *Movements:* no information, probably sedentary. *Foods:* berries. *Breeding:* Apr-? *Nest:* depression or scrape on the ground, under a desert bush. *Eggs:* 5-7.

Meinertzhagen, 1954, pp.566-567.
Mackworth-Praed and Grant, ser.1, vol.1, 1955-73, pp.226-227.

NOTES ON INTRODUCTIONS
Cyprus. The race *A.h. nicolli* was released on Cyprus in 1937 (Bannerman and Bannerman, 1971). The Bannermans record that some ten pairs of Sand Partridges were released at Ayios Napa and Pyroi Napa, but these disappeared after having bred and spread somewhat at Pyroi.

SNOW PARTRIDGE
(Himalayan Snow Partridge, Himalayan Snowcock)
Tetraogallus himalayensis Gray

DISTINGUISHING CHARACTERISTICS
54-72 cm (21.25-28.34 in). 1.3-3 kg (2.86-6.6 lb)

Generally whitish grey; crown and ear-coverts greyish; chin and throat band white, with a dark brown collar on lower chin and neck; bands of white and brown on neck continue up sides of neck and to eyes; upper breast barred dark brown; breast and mantle brownish white; wings greyish, brown tipped; bill brown.

Ali and Ripley, vol.2, 1968-74, pp.13-16 and Fig.11, pl.21, opp. p.64.
Etchécopar and Hüe, 1978, pp.214-215.

GENERAL DISTRIBUTION
Asia: central Asia from Turkestan east to Ching Hai (China) and south to the northern Himalayas and Nepal.

INTRODUCED DISTRIBUTION
Introduced unsuccessfully to the Hawaiian Islands and probably to the USA.

GENERAL HABITS
Status: fairly common. *Habitat:* open country in hills. *Gregariousness:* pairs or family parties of 3-5 birds, and coveys of up to 20 or more birds. *Movements:* sedentary, but some altitudinal migration. *Foods:* roots, tubers, leaves, berries, grass-heads and other plant material and insects (?). *Breeding:* Apr-June; male monogamous. *Nest:* shallow depression on the ground. *Eggs:* 3, 5-7, 9.

Ali and Ripley, vol.2, 1968-74, pp.14-16.

NOTES ON INTRODUCTIONS
USA. Snow Partridges were experimentally introduced into Nevada prior to 1963 (Christensen, 1963). Numbers have been bred in captivity in the United States for some years (Bump and Bohl, 1964) and it is possible that there have been a number of releases made. In Nevada in 1962 some nineteen birds were released at Robinson Lake, Elko County, where they became established near the release site (Christensen, 1967). This release was the result of birds imported from Hunza, Pakistan, between 1961 and 1964 when some 197 were shipped, but due to disease and other factors only about eighty-nine survived (Christensen, 1965). Those not released were kept on a game farm for breeding purposes.

Hawaiian Islands. The Snow Partridge was introduced in the Hawaiian Islands in 1959 but is not known to have become established there (Walker, 1967; Berger, 1972).

DAMAGE
None known.

CHUKAR PARTRIDGE
(Rock Partridge, Chukar, Chukor, Indian Hill Partridge)
Alectoris graeca (Meisner)

DISTINGUISHING CHARACTERISTICS
31-38 cm (12.2-15 in). 300-1090 g (.66-2.4 lb)
Generally grey-brown with a light throat, bordered by a black necklace; sides of body barred in grey, white, black and brown; abdomen pale brown or ashy; tail rufous; white line above eye; bill red.

Cheng, 1963, pp.256-259 and pl.34, no.29.
Ali and Ripley, vol.2, 1968-74, pp.17-20 and Fig.11, pl.19, opp. p.16.

GENERAL DISTRIBUTION
Eurasia: south-eastern Europe from south-eastern France, east into Asia to Mongolia and Manchuria and south to China, India, Iran, Iraq and Syria.

126

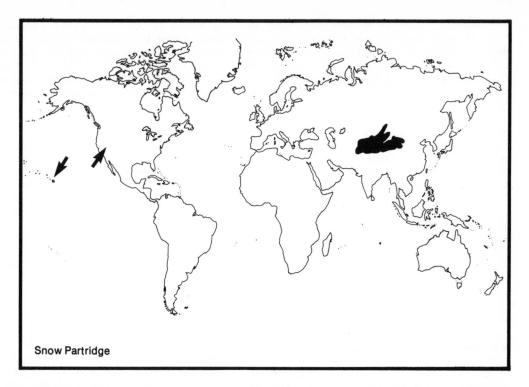

Snow Partridge

INTRODUCED DISTRIBUTION
Introduced successfully in the USSR, England, USA, Canada, Mexico, the Hawaiian Islands, New Zealand and on St Helena. Doubtfully introduced successfully in Australia (New South Wales), Eleuthera (Bahamas) and South Africa. Introduced unsuccessfully to France, Ukraine and Alaska.

GENERAL HABITS
Status: common. *Habitat:* rocky arid regions with light scrub and low grass cover from lowlands and semi-deserts to alpine regions. *Gregariousness:* small coveys of 12-20 birds which break up in breeding season; occasionally larger coveys up to 100 birds. *Movements:* sedentary (some altitudinal migration in North America). *Foods:* grass seeds and other herbage including leaves, stems, buds, roots, shoots, fruits, berries; also insects (termites) and spiders. *Breeding:* Apr-Aug (Apr-Sept in USA); monogamous; female may lay two clutches simultaneously, but incubates only one. *Nest:* hollow on the ground, under a bush or amongst rocks. *Eggs:* 5, 8-14, 16 (Hawaiian Islands 10-14; North America 8-20).

Voous, 1960, p.81.
Ali and Ripley, vol.2, 1968-74, pp.17-20.
Menzdorf. *Vogelwelt* vol.96, 1975, pp.135-139.

NOTES ON INTRODUCTIONS
Europe. Efforts have been made to establish a subspecies of the Chukar *(A.g. chukar)* in southern France in areas not inhabited by the indigenous race *(A.g. saxatilis)* (Etchécopar, 1955). In 1950, 250 pairs were purchased from the United States and distributed as follows: to the mouth of the Rhône (fifty pairs), Hérault (fifty), Lot (fifty-five), Lower Pyrénées (twenty-five) and the Upper Garonne (ten). Some sixty pairs were kept for introductions at Chambord and Pierrefitte-sur-Sauldre, and for trials at Maroc (Rabat). The results of these introductions were apparently not encouraging but were to be continued.

The Chukar was introduced into the Crimea in 1953 when fifty birds were released, followed by another 130 in 1961 (Dourdine, 1975). The species has now spread along the Crimean coast from Alushta to Feodosya and also from Bakhchisaay as far as Sevastopol, and the population now numbers some 8000 birds. Some were also introduced in the Ultra-Carpathian region, Transcarpathia, in the period 1960-63. Releases were made of some 180 birds near Beregovo, Vinogradov and Svaliany, but the introduction is said by Dourdine to have been somewhat unsatisfactory, although a census in 1970 revealed about 1000 Chukars were in the area.

Lever (1977) reports that there have been several attempts to introduce *A.g. chukar* and *A.g. graeca* into Great Britain. In the late 1920s or early 1930s F. R. S. Balfour introduced the species near Stobo, Peeblesshire, but they did not become properly established in the wild. In more recent years many have been bred and released, resulting in small local populations on South Downs, Sussex, and in parts of Aberdeenshire.

Attempts have been made to establish the Chukar Partridge in the Ukraine (Yanushevich, 1966), but presumably these have been unsuccessful.

USA. Bump (1968) reports that Chukars have probably been introduced into every State in the United States but have become established only in areas west of the Rocky Mountains. Early introductions of the species include some in 1893 and some after 1928 (Gottschalk 1967). Whitney (1971) records that since 1893 they have been introduced in at least forty-two States and that huntable populations now exist in Washington, Idaho, Colorado, Wyoming, Nevada, California, Arizona, Oregon, Utah and Montana.

127

Considerable efforts to establish the Chukar in California were made between 1932 and 1961. E. Booth imported them into San Francisco in 1925 from India (Bade, 1937). The Californian Department of Fish and Game obtained five pairs of these in 1928 and in the following year five pairs from Calcutta, India, for breeding purposes. Some from Calcutta, together with many game farm reared birds, which originated from the same area, were released in 1932. By 1936 4600 birds had been released in twenty-six counties (True, 1937), in eighty different sections of the State (Bade) and a breeding stock of at least 600 birds were available to implement further releases.

The Californian Department of Fish and Game raised some 22 000 birds for release between 1942 and 1943 and nearly 7000 were liberated between 1947 and 1949. Harper et al (1958) estimated that from 1932 until December 1955 some 52 184 game farm reared Chukars (race A.g. chukar) were liberated. However, the total released in the State may have been nearer 85 500 birds. These were released in nearly every county in California, in nearly every conceivable type of terrain including dense stands of timber and brush in coastal ranges, mountains, and to the arid desert lands receiving from less than 127 to 1270 mm (5 to 50 in) of rainfall. The most successful of them were in the semi-arid areas where rainfall seldom exceeds 254 mm (10 in) per year, and where only a small proportion of the land was under cultivation. Trapping and transplanting of wild birds began in 1953, to unstocked areas similar to those where some success had been achieved. From 1953 to 1955, 2899 were released in seven counties during this project. In 1958, 200 game farm reared Turkish Chukars (A.g. cypriotes) were obtained from New Mexico and stock from this nucleus of breeders was liberated by State authorities in 1960: in Shasta Valley (423 birds), San Ardro (444), Kennedy Tables (440), Little Rock Canyon (440), Camp Pendleton (440). A further 500 were released in 1961. The first hunting season for Chukar opened in California in 1954 and in the first few seasons the average yearly bag of birds was about 4000. By 1959 this figure had risen to an annual take of some 50 000 birds.

Chukars were introduced into Nevada as early as November 1934, when fifty birds were liberated on the R. L. Douglass Ranch near Fallon in Churchill County (Alcorn and Richardson, 1951). In 1935, 289 were released in central and western Nevada (Dorian, 1965). Alcorn and Richardson indicate that local hunting clubs probably released them prior to these dates, but that no accurate records were kept. However, by 1941 nearly all counties in Nevada had received Chukars.

Between 1947 and 1949 many were trapped and released at new locations in Nevada. The total number of birds liberated will probably never be known, but Alcorn and Richardson say that their records showed that between 5000 and 10 000 individuals were released. Dorian estimated that 6400 had been released by 1953 at which time the species occupied an area of some sixty-five square kilometres (forty square miles), mainly in western and central Nevada. Many more releases occurred in the period 1956-58 when they became established in the Virgin

Mountains in southern Nevada (Western States Exotic Game Bird Committee, 1961). Hunting of Chukars has been enjoyed in Nevada since 1947; the annual harvest in 1959 was 19 600 birds. The Nevada Fish and Game Commission (1963) have estimated that from 1947 until 1963 some 525 000 were taken by hunters in Nevada.

Prior to 1950 fewer than 3000 Chukars had been released in Idaho. Between 1950 and 1962 nearly 25 000 more were liberated and by 1958 the annual harvest by hunters had reached 69 000 birds (Bizeau, 1963). Early plantings of the species between 1938 and 1942 in some eighteen or twenty counties resulted in the successful establishment of the species in Idaho and open hunting seasons by 1949 (Moreland, 1950; Salter, 1953).

Probably less spectacular but nonetheless good results for the introduction of Chukars have been achieved in other parts of the United States. Nearly 76 000 of them were released in Oregon from 1951 to 1961. Here, the annual harvest of birds rose from a mere 4000 in 1956 to nearly 38 000 in 1960 and the total estimated hunter kill through 1967 was 1 235 000 Chukars.

In Wyoming, over 37 000 Chukars have been released since 1938, and more were being liberated in the 1960s. The first release in Wyoming occurred in 1934 when Judge W. S. Owens of Cody liberated some and probably up until 1941 released about 400 birds. The State bird farm inaugurated its programme in 1938 when it released fifty-five Chukars in Natrona County, and between 1939 and 1955 it averaged nearly 1000 birds released each year (Bossenmaier, 1957). All of the early releases, some of which became established in limited areas (Wells, 1953), were made with pen-reared birds and not until 1954-55 were the first wild-trapped Chukars liberated in the southern part of the State.

Chukars were imported into Missouri by the Windsor Game Farm from California in 1934 (Nagel, 1945). Initially there were two small introductions with game farm reared birds prior to 1937 when stocking began in earnest (Nagel, 1939). In 1937 556 birds were released in twelve counties, in 1938 some 450 birds in nine counties and another 350 in five counties, and in 1939 482 birds in seven counties. Although these releases appeared to become well established initially, Nagel stated that the species was generally not well adapted to conditions in Missouri.

Oregon authorities began liberating game farm reared Chukars in the early 1950s and in five consecutive years 50 000 were released (Bohl, 1968). Hunting began in the sixth year and has continued since then.

The first successful release of Chukars in Washington occurred in 1938 and between this date and 1942 some 3962 game farm reared birds from California and Colorado were liberated (Barnett, 1953). During this time Barnett records that forty-six liberations were made in twenty counties of the State and in 1951 a further 1879 birds were released in ten counties in eastern Washington. Open seasons were declared for the first time in 1949 and until 1951 it was estimated that 69 080 Chukars were taken by hunters.

The first of eighty-nine recorded releases of

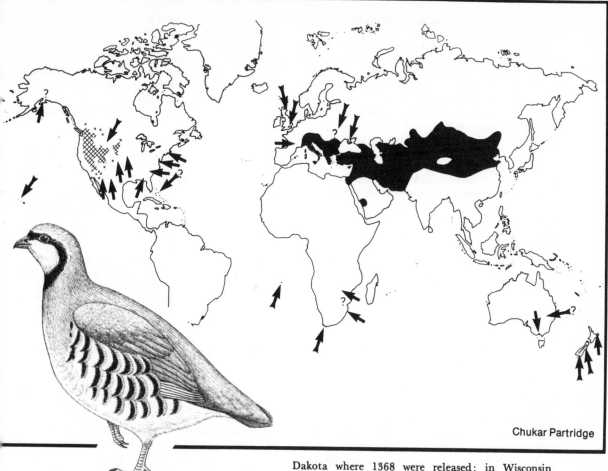

Chukar Partridge

Chukars was made in Montana in 1933 (Whitney, 1971). From this date until 1940, 365 were introduced to sixteen counties. However, the greater number were released after 1950 when under a stocking programme 5000 were liberated. By 1958 they were established in a few small areas, the most successful of which was the Fromberg-Red Lodge-Bighorn Canyon area, south of Bilings. Since 1959 there has been some hunting of Chukars in Montana.

Nearly 50 000 Chukars were liberated in Minnesota from 1937 to 1941 (Blair, 1942) and the total had reached 84 414 by 1953 (Barnett, 1953). Although the species appeared to be becoming established it was still ranked a failure in the early 1950s.

Attempts were made to establish them in Pennsylvania in 1936 and 1939 and altogether some 2021 were released. All the birds released were said to vanish within a few weeks and the attempts were discontinued (Gerstell, 1941).

Some were released in New York State between 1936 and 1939 by R. L. Gerry on the Aknusti Estate in Delaware County, where they were liberated at the rate of twenty-five to 150 per year but few remained after they were hunted (Bump, 1941). Releases in Utah at Salt Lake City in 1947, 1951 and 1952 appeared to become established and they were spreading there in the early 1950s (Greenhalgh and Nielson, 1953).

Campaigns to establish the Chukar in South Dakota where 1368 were released; in Wisconsin where 17 550 were released prior to 1953 (Barnett); in Michigan by private individuals before 1940 (Ruhl, 1941); in Kansas before 1934; in Tennessee in about 1939; in Nebraska where an extensive campaign was launched and where they were planted in some twenty-seven areas (Johnsgard, 1973); and in Alabama (Imhof, 1962) were largely unsuccessful.

Between 1957 and 1958 the Chukar was liberated in Arizona at Jerome (333 wild trapped birds) and at Snake Gulch (800 farm reared birds). In 1961 1000 birds were released in western Colorado and some 7700 birds of two subspecies were released in New Mexico. At least 8000 had previously been liberated in Colorado. The species may now be established in New Mexico as they were noted at Santa Fe in 1964 (Bump 1968).

A number of different races of the Chukar Partridge have been tried in the United States. The Indian race *(A.g. chukar)* has been released in Wyoming, Oregon, New Mexico, Nevada, Idaho, Colorado, California and Arizona, but appears to have become established only in Wyoming, Nevada, Colorado and California. The Turkish race *(cypriotes)* has been released in New Mexico and California, and the Greek race probably only in California. Most of the early United States introductions were of the Indian race and possibly with some of the Persian race *(koroviakovi)*.

In the United States the Chukar now ranges over much of the western States, from Washington and Oregon south to Baja California and east to western Colorado, Wyoming and Montana. Small 129 populations may also exist in Arizona, New Mexico and western South Dakota.

Canada. The first introduction of the Chukar Partridge to Canada appears to have been that by A. D. Hitch in 1940, at Dog Creek in British Columbia (Guiguet, 1961). Although this introduction was unsuccessful further attempts were made in 1950 when seventeen birds were released by the Fish and Wildlife Branch at Harper Ranch, near Kamloops, and in 1951 when fifty-two were released in the same area, eighty near Savona and 139 near Oliver (Guiguet). Introductions were continued annually until 1956 with stock obtained at Mr Hitch's game farm at Whonock (Carl and Guiguet, 1972).

Carl and Guiguet say the population in British Columbia increased greatly, spread widely in the release areas, and also along the Thompson and Fraser Rivers. They spread to such an extent that open seasons were initiated in 1955 and have been maintained since. The species suffered a population decline in the winter of 1964-65, but coveys are still present in many areas (Ritcey and Spalding, 1970, in Carl and Guiguet). Chukars have also been established locally in south-east Alberta (Peterson, 1961), probably from independent introductions, or have spread across the border from the United States. They have also been introduced in Saskatchewan but any success there is not known (Godfrey, 1966).

Mexico. The Chukar Partridge has been successfully introduced into the mountains of northern Baja California (Peterson and Chalif, 1973).

Alaska. Chukar Partridges from Wisconsin, USA, were introduced in the Matanuska Valley of Alaska in 1938, when seventeen adult birds were released (Gabrielson and Lincoln, 1959; Burris, 1965). Some were apparently still present there in 1943 but there appears to be no more recent information and the species has probably failed to become established.

Hawaiian Islands. The race *A.g. chukar* was introduced to the Hawaiian Islands in 1923 (Walker, 1967), being released on the islands of Oahu, Molokai and Kahoolawe, but apparently only became established on the latter island (Munro, 1960). Birds of the Turkish race *(A.g. cypriotes)* were introduced from the United States in 1959 and were reported to have become established on Kauai. In 1961 seventy-six birds from a Californian game farm were released on the Puu Waawaa Ranch, Hawaii, but these failed to become established (Lewin, 1971). According to Walker (1967) and Bump (1968) both the above-mentioned races are now open to hunting in the Hawaiian Islands. However, Berger (1972) indicates that only *A.g. chukar* is now present there. The Chukar Partridge is now established on all the main islands in the group and is particularly plentiful on Hawaii, Lanai and Maui. On Oahu, small numbers occur on the leeward slopes of the Waianae Mountains (Hawaiian Audubon Society, 1975).

Bahamas. Brudenell-Bruce (1975) records that the Chukar has been introduced near Rock Sound on Eleuthera, but gives no further details.

New Zealand. Early attempts to establish the Chukar Partridge in the North Island of New Zealand failed (Thomson, 1922). In 1920 the Otago Acclimatisation Society imported twenty-four birds but they all died before release. The Waimarino society landed sixty-two from a consignment of eighty-two birds in 1925, but these died in a zoo some time before 1927 (Williams, 1950). The first successful liberations of Chukars in New Zealand occurred when fifteen pairs arrived from Calcutta for the Ashburton society in 1926. These were set free at Barossa in the Lake Heron district. In the same year the Otago society released twenty-five birds (also from a consignment from Calcutta) at the head of Lake Hawea (Williams, 1950; Oliver, 1955).

From 1926 on a number of Chukars were imported to New Zealand and released in mainly South Island localities. One of the early difficulties associated with these introductions appears to have been that of importing large numbers of them. Many appear to have died on the way to New Zealand. In 1927 four birds were imported for the Ashburton society, the Otago society received one bird from another consignment and forty-two arrived from a consignment of 500 from Calcutta. At this time twenty-four were released at Hunter Valley. Twenty-eight birds from a consignment of forty-six from Calcutta were released on the property of S. Middleton near Lowburn Ferry, central Otago, in 1928. These were reported to have successfully established themselves. In 1929 the Auckland society released twenty-four at Taringamotu Valley, near Taumarunui in the North Island, but these eventually disappeared. In 1932 the North Canterbury Society made six liberations when 192 out of 200 birds *(A.g. koroviakovi)* were landed from Quetta, Baluchistan. Thirty-five pairs were liberated at Lake Lyndon; ten at Lake Taylor; five at Purau and Teddington and two at Waipara. It is generally thought that the birds now in North Canterbury and Marlborough owe their origin to these releases.

In 1932 some 700 birds left India for Auckland but only sixty-six reached New Zealand alive and most are believed to have died before any releases were made. The Auckland society received eighty-three birds in 1933 from 122 landed from Horbol, Baluchistan. After quarantine only six remained, but all had died by 1935. Six liberations were made in North Canterbury in 1933. Some twenty-five birds were released at Rutherfords, Medip Hills; fifty at the Upper Hurunui River; twenty-five at St. Helens Estate, Hamer; twenty-five at McAlpines, Craigieburn; twenty-five at Eskhead on the Hurunui River; and twenty-six at Clarence River, Marlborough. The North Canterbury society apparently released all their remaining birds in 1936, half of them on Mt Herbert and half on Castle Hill. In the North Island two further introductions were made, one in 1949, when eight birds from Alexandra, central Otago, were liberated at Manaia on Coromandel Peninsula, and in late 1950 when thirteen birds captured in central Otago and Marlborough were also set free at Manaia (Williams, 1950; Marples and Burr, 1953).

According to Williams (1950 and 1951) there were in New Zealand some eighteen liberations in the South Island and three in the North Island. Up until 1950 in the South Island, the species had spread some eighty to ninety-six kilometres (49.7 to 59.6 miles) in the twenty-two years it had been established. At this time they occupied a broad belt of country in the centre of the island extending from Marlborough (Wairau River) south to Kingston in central Otago. They flourished in the high country east of the Southern Alps where rainfall is less than 635 millimetres (25 in) per year. The area inhabited is closely allied, as far as rainfall and winter temperature are concerned, to the species' native haunts in India. The density in New Zealand has reached ten birds per sixty-one hectares (150 acres) in areas where they are common.

The Chukar Partridge is now widespread in hilly country of the South Island east of the Southern Alps from Nelson to Otago (Falla et al, 1966), but failed to become established in the North Island.

Australia. The race *A.g. chukar* was liberated in Australia in 1864 when twenty-three birds were released in Victoria (Ryan, 1906). Further liberations occurred in 1865 when thirteen more were released, and in 1872 when eight were released. Other liberations may have occurred in about 1874. These releases were all unsuccessful and the species did not become established in Australia. A more recent attempt to establish the Chukar was reported by a private individual in Victoria (Harvey, 1975), but investigations revealed that no such attempt had been made. However, they have recently been reported to be thriving in an area of the Gulgong district, New South Wales, in forested hilly country with rocky outcrops (Anon, 1977).

Southern Africa. Winterbottom (1966) records that Chukar Partridges have recently been introduced in Zimbabwe and Natal (South Africa), but little appears to be known of the attempt. Three coveys were seen by Siegfried (1971) on Robben Island off Cape Town, South Africa. He was informed that they were first liberated on this island in 1964, when six birds were confiscated by Customs officers at Cape Town and sent to the island. The population at this time (1971) was said to be about 500 birds.

St Helena. Benson (1950) says that Chukar Partridges were possibly introduced to St Helena from the Persian Gulf, as Gosse (1938) has indicated. Some were there in 1936 and the total population in 1949 was said to be in the hundreds. More recently they have become scarce and would appear to be decreasing in numbers (Haydock, 1954). Melliss (1870) indicates they may have been there as early as 1588, but that there is no record of their introduction. He suggested the birds may have come from northern India and reports that they were abundant there in about 1870.

DAMAGE

Little damage of economic significance caused by Chukars appears to have been recorded in North America. Alcorn and Richardson (1951) record that the species will eat corn and wheat, especially during the winter and spring. They dig out the shoots and serious damage has been reported to recently sprouted fields of corn when Chukars have dug out the kernels. Several tonnes of potatoes were destroyed by Chukars in one locality in Nevada.

Although the Chukar is not a great fruit eater it has been recorded to eat raspberries, currants, strawberries, apples and Russian olives in Nevada. Generally, however, the species feeds mainly on seeds, grasses and insects and is considered a valuable game bird and not a pest of agriculture.

In California, Harper et al (1958) record damage to apples, pears, peaches, apricots, grapes, potatoes, beans, watermelons, tomatoes, corn, wheat, oats, alfalfa and clover in summer and autumn. They say agricultural damage has occasionally been reported from the Inyo-Mono area and Lucerne Valley regions of the Mojave Desert, but in all cases such damage was considered light and of little economic importance. Crops were generally affected in years of drought, when the birds moved down from the higher slopes of mountain ranges to feed on green vegetation around small ranches and farms.

The only known record of damage within the species' native range is given by Cheng (1963), who reports that they are considered a menace to any reafforestation projects during the seed-planting time in China.

RED-LEGGED PARTRIDGE
(French Partridge)
Alectoris rufa (Linnaeus)

DISTINGUISHING CHARACTERISTICS
32-35 cm (12.6-13.77 in)

Upper parts chestnut-brown, shading to grey on crown; cheeks and throat white, bordered by a black band; white stripe above eyes; skin around eye red; breast blue-grey; flanks barred white, black and chestnut; belly and under tail rufous; bill red.

Witherby et al, vol.5, 1938-41, pp.246-247, 248-250 and pls.146 opp. p.228, 147 opp. p.234.

Bannerman and Bannerman, vol.1, 1963-68, pp.68-72 and pl.7, opp. p.68.

GENERAL DISTRIBUTION

Europe: western Europe from south and south-western France to the north-western tip of Italy; also Mallorca and Corse. In historic times had a wider distribution in Western Europe than at present (Voous, 1960).

INTRODUCED DISTRIBUTION

Introduced successfully in Great Britain, the Açores, Madeira, France, Holland, Belgium and Germany; possibly introduced successfully on the Balearic Islands (Mediterranean), Canary Islands, Porto Santo and in northern Spain and Portugal. Introduced unsuccessfully in the USA, the Hawaiian Islands and New Zealand.

GENERAL HABITS

Status: common. *Habitat:* scrub in lowlands and hills, vineyards, dry meadows, heathlands and cultivated areas. *Gregariousness:* in coveys. *Movements:* sedentary. *Foods:* grass seeds, grain, buds, fruits, berries, leaves and green plant material, insects and spiders. *Breeding:* Apr-Sept; some birds lay two clutches simultaneously. *Nest:* hollow on the ground, scantily lined with grass and leaves. *Eggs:* 9-12, 16 and occasionally up to 20.

Voous, 1960. pp.81-82.

Witherby et al, vol.5, 1938-41, pp.246-248.

Menzdorf, *Vogelwelt,* vol.96, 1975, pp.135-139.

NOTES ON INTRODUCTIONS

Europe. Instances of the occurrence of Red-legged Partridges *(A.r. rufa)* in northern France, Holland, Belgium and western Germany, are thought to be due to the introduction of birds (Peters, 1934) as may those found in northern and north-western Spain and in northern Portugal. Peters also indicates that the

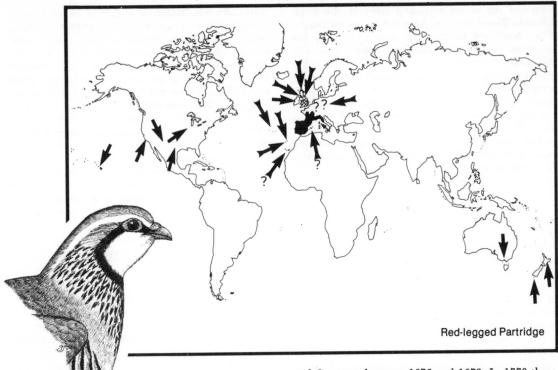

Red-legged Partridge

species may have been introduced to the Balearic Islands, in the Mediterranean, but others (Voous, 1960, etc.) list them as a resident there.

The Red-legged Partridge disappeared from Switzerland in the nineteenth century the last of them probably being killed in about 1918. There seems little doubt that they once inhabited Switzerland as a breeding bird (Lueps, 1975). Lueps records that they were successfully released there in the eighteenth century, and with little or no success in the twentieth century.

Early attempts to establish Red-legged Partridges in south-western Germany were successful and up to the sixteenth century they lived in the middle Rhine area near Bacharach (Grzmek, 1968-72). More recently, just prior to 1971, some 640 adults and 890 young Red-legged Partridges were released in the Hautes-Alpes Department, France, to ascertain the success of farm raised birds in the wild (Birkan, 1971).

The present occurrence of Red-legged Partridges in England and Wales is not a natural one and the species was introduced by human agency in the eighteenth century (Voous, 1960). Lever (pers. comm., 1976) says they were established from introductions in about 1770. Witherby *et al* (1941) record that there were many introductions of the species into England. The exact number may never be known, but Fitter (1959) traced more than forty attempts since 1830 in twenty-six counties in England; twelve in Wales in seven different counties; and in Scotland some eight attempts in six counties. Early introductions include some birds which were probably introduced in Leicestershire in 1682, and at Wimbledon, Surrey, between 1712 and 1729. There may have been feral Red-legged Partridges on Jersey

and Guernsey between 1676 and 1678. In 1770 there were probably several introductions in East Suffolk, Northumberland, and in Essex. Those released in Suffolk apparently became established (Lever, 1977).

In the early 1940s the Red-legged Partridge was abundant in Yorkshire, the Midlands and southwards, west to Somerset and sparingly in north Wales and other parts (Witherby *et al*). They now appear to be established over most of the south-east part of Great Britain, as far west as western Wales and eastern Devon, and north to northern Yorkshire.

Although there were early introductions to Scotland (1840) and Ireland (prior to 1844), none appears to have been successful. In the 1970s further introductions occurred in Scotland and the species may be established in Sutherland, Banffshire, Kirkcudbrightshire, Dumfriesshire and Perthshire. Some 100 birds were released at Caithness in about 1974.

Açores. Voous (1960) records that Red-legged Partridges were introduced to the Açores in the eighteenth century. Bannerman and Bannerman (1966) say the species was apparently abundant on the island of Santa Maria in 1865, were rare on São Miguel and Terceira, but are not mentioned as being present on Pico. In 1903, the species was numerous on Pico, rare on São Miguel and restricted in range on Terceira (Ogilvie-Grant, 1905, in Bannerman). They are recorded again on Pico in 1922, and in 1932 were relatively common on both Santa Maria and Pico, but had become extinct on São Miguel and Terceira. Marler and Boatman (1951) found them to be present in small numbers on Pico. By the mid-1960s the Bannermans say they were rare on Santa Maria but still present in small numbers on Pico.

Madeira. Red-legged Partridges were probably introduced to Madeira before 1450 from northern Portugal (Bernstrom, 1951, in Bannerman, 1965).

They were scarce on the island in 1851 and 1871 and apparently remained scarce until more recently when birds were regularly bred and released there (Bannerman, 1965). The race introduced to Madeira is *A.r. hispanica* (Peters, 1934).

Canary Islands. The race *A.r. australis* was thought by Bannerman (1963) to have been introduced on Gran Canaria. He admits being unable to find any evidence for their introduction and later says that they are natural residents on the island. He reports them as present on Gran Canaria as early as 1866, and says they still have a restricted distribution on the island.

Porto Santo. An early introduction in about 1850 apparently died out on Porto Santo (Sarmento, 1936, in Bannerman, 1965). A further introduction of two pairs of Red-legged Partridges, in 1925 from Algarve, were successfully established and the species is possibly still established there (Bannerman).

USA. Red-legged Partridges were first introduced to the United States in 1896, but failed to become established (Gottschalk, 1967). Phillips (1928) indicates that W. O. Blaisdell released some at Macomb, Illinois, in about 1896, but that these birds vanished soon after.

Spanish *(A.r. hispanica)* and French *(A.r. rufa)* races were imported from Spain and France by Californian authorities in 1959 (Californian Department of Fish and Game, 1961). Some success was achieved in breeding the French race on game farms in California and some were released into the wild. These were liberated (341 birds) in San Mateo County, south of San Francisco in 1963 (Harper, 1963) and it was planned to release birds of the Spanish race in the following year.

In 1961 twenty-eight birds of the Spanish race were liberated in Larimer County, Colorado, but this and some previous releases were unsuccessful (Western States Exotic Game Bird Committee, 1961). The first release in Colorado occurred in 1952 when 119 birds from Spain were released, forty in Cottonwood Canyon, twenty-seven in Skull Canyon and twenty-eight in Whitby Canyon in the south-east of Colorado (Kleinschnitz, 1957). In 1954 a further 118 birds were released at Cottonwood Canyon. Further releases were made in other areas including the foothills near Masonville, south-west of Fort Collins, in 1955 (eighty-two birds) and 1956 (149), and at Little Thompson Canyon, north-west of Longmont, in 1957 (eighty). Some birds from these introductions were seen around the release sites for some months subsequently, but the species apparently failed to become permanently established.

During 1955-57 332 birds of the Spanish race were released in northern Texas. Some were released in Cottle County (248 birds) and some in Lipscomb County, at opposite ends of the Texas Panhandle (Jackson, 1957). These birds persisted for a few months and then disappeared (Jackson, 1964).

There have probably been many more introductions in the United States but the Red-legged Partridge does not appear to have been successful anywhere.

Hawaiian Islands. Blake (1975) lists the Red-legged Partridge as introduced to these islands, but there appear to be no records of any releases or of any success there.

Australia. Red-legged Partridges were released at Colac in Victoria (McCance, 1962) probably in the 1860s or 1870s, with other partridge species but failed to become established. Nine birds may have been liberated in the bush near Melbourne in 1873.

New Zealand. According to Thomson (1922) Red-legged Partridges were introduced to New Zealand at various times before 1897. They were reported to be increasing in the Rangitikei district at this date. The Canterbury Acclimatisation Society imported two birds in 1867, and in 1899 eighteen birds from London were liberated on Stewart Island. Thomson indicates that the species was probably established in several parts of New Zealand in about 1915. The Red-legged Partridge is not now established in New Zealand (Williams, 1950).

DAMAGE

In Great Britain the Red-legged Partridge is regarded, along with the pheasant and the partridge, as a major pest of sugar beet by the British Sugar Corporation (Dunning, 1974). They apparently peck at the leaves of seedling beet, thus reducing crop yields.

BARBARY PARTRIDGE
Alectoris barbara (Bonnaterre)

DISTINGUISHING CHARACTERISTICS

32.5 cm (12.61 in)

Upper parts sandy brown; crown and nape chestnut; collar chestnut with white spots; face, eye-stripe, throat and upper breast blue-grey; ear-coverts yellowish brown; shoulder feathers blue-grey with reddish tips; flanks barred black and white; skin around eye orange; bill red.

Bannerman and Bannerman, vol.1, 1963-1968, pp.72-78 and pl.7, opp. p.68.

Gooders, vol.3, 1969, pp.675-676.

GENERAL DISTRIBUTION

North Africa: from Morocco to Libya.

INTRODUCED DISTRIBUTION

Introduced successfully in the Canary Islands and on Porto Santo (died out); possibly introduced successfully to Sardegna and Gibraltar. Introduced unsuccessfully to Great Britain, New Zealand, Australia, the USA, and the Hawaiian Islands (?).

GENERAL HABITS

Status: no information. *Habitat:* rocky ground with scrub, thorny margins, grass steppe and alpine meadows, stream borders, lowland deserts and semi-cultivated areas. *Gregariousness:* coveys. *Movements:* sedentary. *Foods:* seeds, berries, grain, shoots, buds, fruits, other herbage and insects. *Breeding:* Mar-May. *Nest:* depression on the ground, lined with grass and other vegetation, under a rock or bush. *Eggs:* 8, 10-16, 18.

Bannerman and Bannerman, vol.1, 1963-68, pp.72-78.

Gooders, vol.3, 1969, pp.675-676.

NOTES ON INTRODUCTIONS

Sardegna. Voous (1960) reports that he is uncertain whether the Barbary Partridge was introduced by man or occurs naturally on the island of Sardegna.

Gibraltar. According to Voous (1960) and Gooders (1969) the Barbary Partridge was introduced to Gibraltar by man. The species still occurs on the island.

Canary Islands. Barbary Partridges were introduced by man to the islands of Gran Canaria, Hierro and La Palma in the Canary Islands (Voous, 1960). According to Bannerman (1963) repeated attempts to introduce them to the island of Palma were unsuccessful. Bannerman indicates that Barbary Partridges now occur on Tenerife and Gomera, but are rare or extinct on the island of Lanzarote. They have apparently been established on Fuerteventura since 1913 and were still there in 1957. The species has from time to time been introduced to other islands in the group but from one cause or another did not survive for long.

Porto Santo. Also introduced to this island (Voous, 1960) the Barbary Partridge has since died out (Bannerman, 1965). Bannerman records that the race *A. b. barbara* was introduced at the beginning of the nineteenth century but has now been replaced by the Red-legged Partridge from southern Portugal.

Great Britain. The Barbary Partridge may have been introduced at some time to Great Britain as Koch (1956) claims. No details of any introduction could be found.

France. According to Clegg (1941) two liberations have occurred in France, one in about 1929, and the other in 1930, at La Capelliere, Ile de la Camargue in the south of France. The introductions appear to have been unsuccessful.

New Zealand. Thomson (1922) records that two Barbary Partridges were imported by the Auckland Acclimatisation Society in 1868, but that there is no further record of them. In 1892 the Wellington society imported nineteen birds from Tenerife; six died but the remaining birds were released on Kapiti Island. Some nine birds are said to have been seen in 1894, but there are no further records of them. Williams (1950) says the Barbary Partridge *(A. b. koenigi)* failed to become established in New Zealand.

Australia. Some Barbary Partridges were introduced in Victoria in 1873, but were all said to have soon disappeared (Ryan, 1906) and the species did not become permanently established.

USA. The Californian Department of Fish and Game reported in 1961 that to June 1960 there had been 475 plantings of Barbary Partridges in Tulare County and 316 in Fresno County. Although some birds had been sighted in the release areas in 1961, there was no evidence of a successful establishment. Harper (1963) indicates that some 3000 were released in eight areas of California without a single success.

In the early 1960s 150 birds were liberated in Nevada, but the species did not spread there (Nevada Fish and Game Commission, 1963).

There may have been many other introductions of the Barbary Partridge in the United States, but the species has failed to gain a permanent foothold.

Hawaiian Islands. The race *A. b. barbara* from the United States was introduced to these islands without success in 1958 (Walker, 1967). In 1959 104 birds from a Californian game farm were released on the Puu Waawaa Ranch, Hawaii (Lewin, 1971). Lewin records that the Division of Fish and Game also made releases in the Kohala Mountains in 1959. In 1961 further releases were made on Lanai (sixty-three birds), Molokai (sixty-five) and on Maui (139), but the birds soon disappeared (Western States Exotic Game Bird Committee, 1961). According to the Hawaiian Audubon Society (1975) and Berger (1972), the species may still be established but their current status is poorly known.

DAMAGE

None known

ARABIAN CHUKAR
Alectoris melanocephalus (Rüppell)

DISTINGUISHING CHARACTERISTICS
32-37 cm (12.6-14.6 in)

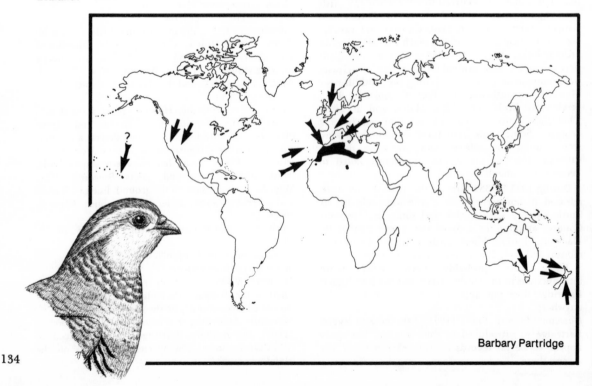

Barbary Partridge

134

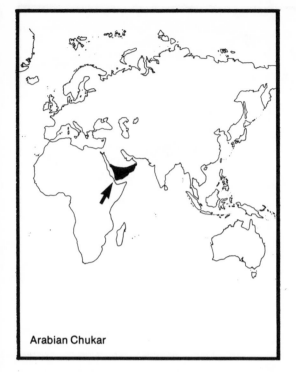

Arabian Chukar

Forehead to nape, streak under eye, patch behind ear-coverts and V-shaped collar on sides of neck and meeting at the front, black; stripe over eye, cheeks, chin and throat white; ear-coverts streaked black and white; sides of neck pale brown; chest, flanks and tail pale grey; bill red. Female: lacks spurs.

Meinertzhagen, 1954, pp.562-564 and pl.18.

Mackworth-Praed and Grant, ser.1, vol.1, 1955-73, p.226.

GENERAL DISTRIBUTION

Arabia: from Jiddah in Saudi Arabia to Muscat in Oman.

INTRODUCED DISTRIBUTION

Possibly introduced, unsuccessfully, to Eritrea in northern Ethiopia.

GENERAL HABITS

Status: uncommon. *Habitat:* rocky hillsides amongst grass and bush. *Gregariousness:* coveys of 3 or 4 and up to 8 birds. *Movements:* sedentary. *Foods:* seeds, corn, grass and weeds. *Breeding:* Mar (Arabia), July-Aug (Eritrea); polygamous (?). *Nest:* scrape under a bush. *Eggs:* up to 12.

Meinertzhagen, 1954, pp.562-564.

Mackworth-Praed and Grant, ser.1, vol.1, 1955-73, p.226.

NOTES ON INTRODUCTIONS

Eritrea. The Arabian Chukar has been recorded from the Assab area in southern Eritrea, but not since about 1890. According to Smith (1957) they were probably imported and released birds, but proof is lacking.

DAMAGE

None known.

BLACK FRANCOLIN
(Black Partridge, Indian Black Francolin)
Francolinus francolinus (Linnaeus)

DISTINGUISHING CHARACTERISTICS

31-34 cm (12.2-13.4 in). 227.2-570 g (.5-1.25 lb)

Underparts black, spotted white down sides of breast and flanks; lower abdomen and thighs pale chestnut; head black; cheek patch white; collar chestnut; scaled markings on upper parts; wings dark brown, pale edges to coverts; bill blackish. Female: generally brown and chestnut; mottled and speckled black and white; nape patch chestnut; bill dusky brown. Ali and Ripley, vol.2, 1968-74, pp.21-25 and fig.1, pl.19, opp. p.16.

GENERAL DISTRIBUTION

Asia and formerly Europe (Spain and Sicily): southwestern Asia from Cyprus, the Middle East and Transcaucasia to northern India, Nepal, Bangladesh and Assam.

INTRODUCED DISTRIBUTION

Introduced successfully in India (Kutch), USSR, USA (Florida and Louisiana), the Hawaiian Islands and Guam (Pacific Ocean). Possibly introduced, unsuccessfully, to Saudi Arabia.

GENERAL HABITS

Status: fairly common. *Habitat:* tall grass jungle, grasslands, tamarisk and cultivated lands including millet and cane fields. *Gregariousness:* singly, pairs or trios, or scattered flocks of 3-5 birds in non-breeding season. *Movements:* sedentary. *Foods:* plant material including leaves, rhizomes, tubers, inflorescences, berries, fruits, seeds, waste grain, and small animals including ants, beetles, spiders and other insects and their larvae. *Breeding:* Mar-Oct; monogamous; possibly double brooded. *Nest:* shallow depression on the ground, lined with grass, in a crop or grassy field. *Eggs:* 4, 6-8, 10 (India), (Transcaucasia 8-12; southern USSR up to 15 and 18).

Ali and Ripley vol.2, 1968-74, pp.21-25.

NOTES ON INTRODUCTIONS

India. According to Ali (1954, in Ripley, 1961), Black Francolins occur in the Kutch district of Bombay where they have been introduced. This area is just south of the species' natural range.

USSR. The Black Francolin was introduced, in the 1880s, to a number of areas of the USSR where it does not occur naturally (Yanushevich, 1966), but failed to become established anywhere. In 1932 three male and two female Black Francolins were released in the Agri-Tschai Valley in the Nukha area of Kachetia (Caucasus) in southern USSR. By 1947 they had spread throughout the valley and had reached the Alazan river valley, over one hundred kilometres (sixty-two miles) away. This area appears to be slightly north of the species' usual range.

Saudi Arabia. A single specimen found at Al Húfúf was probably an escapee, as the Black Francolin is frequently kept in captivity there (Meinertzhagen, 1954).

USA. The first introductions of Black Francolins in the United States occurred in 1891, but these failed and not until the late 1950s or early 1960s were further attempts made (Gottschalk, 1967). Releases of wild trapped and game farm reared birds were made in the States of Alabama, Arkansas, Florida, Kentucky, Louisiana, Oklahoma and Virginia between 1960 and 1962 (Murray, 1963). During this three-year period 3251 wild trapped and ninety-eight game farm reared birds were released in these States. The best results were obtained in Avon Park, Florida,

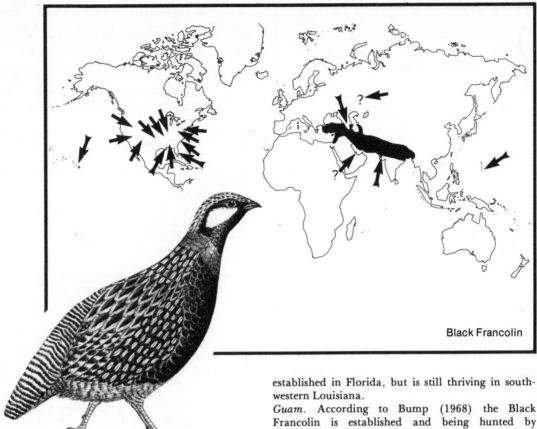

Black Francolin

at Oak Ridge and Gum Cove, Louisiana, and in the York Prison area in South Carolina. Also at this time, efforts to establish the species were being made in Nevada and New Mexico.

Beginning in 1960 (Robinson, 1969), some 5000 Black Francolins were liberated in some twelve States, chiefly in the south-east of the United States. Between 1957 and 1966 some 2000 Black Francolins were liberated in Virginia (Hart, 1967), apparently without success.

In South Carolina, where 421 birds (F.f. asiae) were released in four different areas and breeding was reported, all had disappeared some three years later (Robinson, 1969). The race F.f. asiae was experimentally introduced in Nevada in 1959-61 (Christensen, 1963) when 285 birds were released in the Moapa Valley (Western States Exotic Game Bird Committee, 1961) and a total of 609 were released in Nevada (Nevada Fish and Game Commission, 1963). According to Bump and Bohl (1964), in these and probably other initial introductions the Black Francolin demonstrated an ability to survive, reproduce and increase substantially in the release areas.

In 1964 Black Francolins were being hunted in Louisiana and Florida (Bump, 1968), but had failed to become established in Kentucky (Nelson, 1962). Bump (1970) announced that he felt it was too early to evaluate the success of the species in the United States. More recently it would appear from reports (Edscorn, 1977 *et al*) that the species is not well

established in Florida, but is still thriving in south-western Louisiana.

Guam. According to Bump (1968) the Black Francolin is established and being hunted by sportsmen on Guam. Bohl (1968) indicates that the birds are expanding their range on the island.

Hawaiian Islands. Black Francolins were probably first introduced to these islands from India in 1959 (Walker, 1967). The initial introductions failed to become established but showed sufficient promise for further efforts to be made in 1960-61. Between 1959 and 1961 some 116 Californian and Texan game farm reared birds were liberated in two localities of the Puu Waawaa Ranch, Hawaii (Lewin, 1971). Lewin also records that the Division of Fish and Game liberated forty-four birds in 1960 at Kipuka Ainahou and sixty-six more at Kohala Mountains in 1962. He says the birds are now found established along the perimeters of sugar-cane fields, irrigation ditches and drier pasture areas of the latter regions.

Evidently the releases in the Hawaiian Islands were successful because the species was being hunted there in 1964-68 (Bump, 1968; Bohl, 1968). Black Francolins now frequent the lowlands on all the main islands with the exception of Lanai and Oahu (Hawaiian Audubon Society, 1975).

DAMAGE

Black Francolins are reported (Faruqi, Bump *et al*, 1960) to cause little or no damage to farm crops in India and to be a most desirable game bird.

CHINESE FRANCOLIN
Francolinus pintadeanus (Scopoli)

DISTINGUISHING CHARACTERISTICS
28-35 cm (11-13.78 in) . 284-397g (10-14 oz)
Forehead and sides of head chestnut; centre of crown and nape black; cheeks and throat white with a black line between them; mantle, neck, breast and upper

belly black with white spots; rump, upper tail-coverts and tail black, narrowly barred white or buff; shoulders and scapulars chestnut, marked with black and white; wings brown, spotted and barred buff; bill black. Female: cheek patch buff; mantle and hindneck barred buff; rump, upper tail-coverts and tail broadly barred black and brown, and narrowly with buff; underparts buff, barred black; bill, upper mandible horn, lower pale yellowish.

Ali and Ripley, vol.2, 1968-1974, pp.28-29 and pls.23, fig.4, opp. p.112 and 19, fig.4, opp. p.16.

Etchécopar and Hüe, 1978, p.221 and pl.7, p.224.

GENERAL DISTRIBUTION

Asia: south-eastern Asia from Manipur (Assam) east through Indochina to south-eastern China and Hainan.

INTRODUCED DISTRIBUTION

Introduced successfully in Mauritius and the Philippines (Luzon); probably introduced successfully in Malagasy and possibly introduced in the Seychelles (no evidence of occurrence); introduced successfully but now extinct on Réunion. Introduced unsuccessfully in Oman and the Hawaiian Islands.

GENERAL HABITS

Status: very common; commonly kept as pets. *Habitat:* dry lowland scrub, brushlands and forest. *Gregariousness:* singly or small scattered groups of 3-5 birds. *Movements:* sedentary (possibly some seasonal movements ?). *Foods:* insects, nuts, seeds and shoots. *Breeding:* Apr. (China); Mar-Sept (Burma); Mar. (Muscat); in some areas may lay twice a year. *Nest:* scrape on the ground under a bush, lined with grass. *Eggs:* 3-6, 7 (Muscat, 4-18).

Cheng, 1963, pp.260-263.

Ali and Ripley, vol.2, 1968-74, pp.28-29.

NOTES ON INTRODUCTIONS

Malagasy. Chinese Francolins *F.p. pintadeanus* have been introduced into Malagasy (Peters, 1934).

Mauritius. Rountree *et al* (1952) report that the Chinese Francolin was introduced from Indochina, probably about the middle of the eighteenth century, to Mauritius but has never become abundant there and is at present rare. Meinertzhagen (1912) records that the species was introduced by the French in about 1750. In the 1950s the species was confined to areas of cultivated land near rivers on the higher parts of the central plateau. According to Staub (1976) it is still established on the island.

Réunion. The race *F.p. pintadeanus* is reported to have been introduced to Réunion (Peters, 1934). Watson *et al* (1963) record that the species is not common there and Staub (1976) says it is now extinct. Staub indicates it may have been introduced as early as about 1750.

Seychelles. Newton (1867) records the presence of a francolin (possibly this species) in the Seychelles in early times. According to Gaymer *et al* (1969) there is no clear evidence of their previous success or distribution on these islands. However, Penny (1974) says they are reared for the table on some estates.

Oman. Chinese Francolins are resident around Muscat where they may have been introduced because they are a common cage bird in southern Iran (Meinertzhagen, 1954).

Philippines. The race *F.p. pintadeanus* has been introduced to the island of Luzon in the Philippines (Peters, 1934) from China, and still occurs around the city of Manila (du Pont, 1971).

Hawaiian Islands. Chinese Francolins were introduced from the United States in 1961, but the species is not known to be established in these islands (Walker, 1967; Berger, 1972). In 1962 ten birds from Hong Kong were released on the Puu Waawaa Ranch, Hawaii, but they were not sighted again (Lewin, 1971).

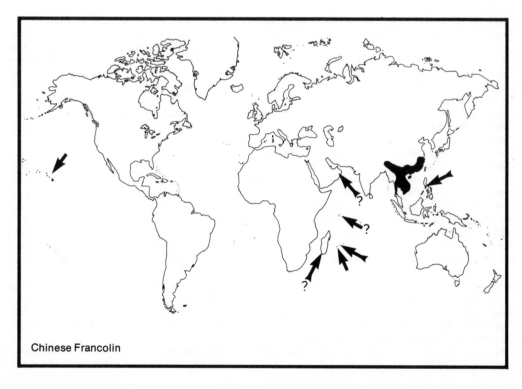

Chinese Francolin

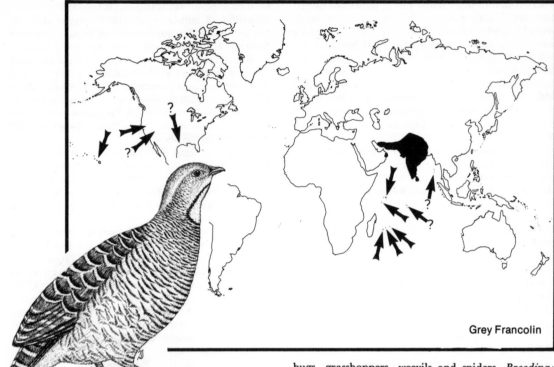

Grey Francolin

GREY FRANCOLIN
(Grey Partridge, Gray Francolin, Brown Partridge)
Francolinus pondicerianus (Gmelin)

DISTINGUISHING CHARACTERISTICS

30-33 cm (11.8-13 in). 200-340.8 g (7-12 oz)
Generally brownish with greyish breast and
prominent black barring; back chestnut and brown,
barred buff; upper parts greyish brown and chestnut,
each feather crossed with a whitish band bordered by
dark brown; outer tail-feathers chestnut; bill dusky
red-brown.

Ali and Ripley, vol.2, 1968-74, pp.29-33 and fig.2,
pl.19, opp. p.16.

GENERAL DISTRIBUTION

Asia: southern Asia from southern Iran and Pakistan
to India (north to Himalayas) and Sri Lanka; also in
Oman on the Arabian Peninsula.

INTRODUCED DISTRIBUTION

Introduced successfully to the Amirante Islands,
Mauritius (rare), Réunion (rare), Seychelles (feral),
Rodrigues and the Hawaiian Islands; possibly
introduced successfully in the USA (California, Texas
and Nevada); introduced successfully but now
extinct on Diego Garcia (Chagos Group), and in the
Andaman Islands.

GENERAL HABITS

Status: common; common cage bird and also kept as
a fighting bird. *Habitat:* tropical thorn forest, light
dry jungle, dry scrub, dry open grassland and desert
areas adjacent to cultivation. *Gregariousness:* pairs,
and family parties or coveys of 4-8 birds when not
breeding. *Movements:* sedentary. *Foods:* plant
material including seeds, grain, buds, flowers, leaves,
rhizomes, shoots, fruits and drupes, and insects
including termites, ants, beetles and their larvae,

bugs, grasshoppers, weevils and spiders. *Breeding:*
irregular, almost throughout the year, but mainly
Feb-June (India). *Nest:* shallow depression, lined
with grass and leaves, on the ground in scrub, crop,
grassland or ploughed field, near a tuft of grass or
bush. *Eggs:* 4-8, 10 (India).

Ali and Ripley, vol.2, 1968-74, pp.29-33.

NOTES ON INTRODUCTIONS

Andaman Islands. The race *F.p. pondicerianus* was
introduced to the Andamans (Peters, 1934) at Port
Blair in 1890 (Ali and Ripley, 1968-1974) and was
possibly still established there (Ripley, 1961) in the
1960s. Abdulali (1967) says he heard them at Haddo,
Port Blair, in 1963 and 1964, but indicates that they
do not appear to be present there now. However, Ali
and Ripley (vide vol.2, 1969, p.31) record that the
species is still established in the Port Blair
neighbourhood.

Amirante Islands. Peters (1934) records that *F.p.
pondicerianus* has been introduced to the Amirante
Islands and Penny (1974) indicates that the species
still occurs there.

Mauritius. Meinertzhagen (1912) and Rountree *et al*
(1952) report that the Grey Francolin was introduced
from India to Mauritius in about 1750 and became
common and abundant on the island. Rountree *et al*
record that in 1952 the species was established locally
and was confined to the rocky plains of the coastal
belt. It was suggested by them that they had been
considerably reduced in numbers by depredations of
the mongoose. Benedict (1957) indicates later in the
1950s that the species was only precariously
established on the island, and Loustau-Lalanne
(1962) found that they still occurred there on his visit
in 1962. More recently Staub (1976) has reported
that they maintain a precarious existence in the drier
parts of Mauritius.

Réunion Watson *et al* (1963) record that the species
has been introduced to Réunion, where it is reported

to breed in December on the plain of St Paul. Staub (1976) reports that recent droughts and cyclones have greatly reduced their numbers and that they are now rare there.

Seychelles. The Grey Francolin was introduced on some islands in the Seychelles as a sporting bird and evidently became at one time widespread. They have failed to survive except on Desroches, where they are feral (Penny, 1974). Penny records that they are still reared for the table on some estates in the Seychelles. In November 1971 two birds were found on African Island (north of Desroches), but they had disappeared some two weeks later.

Rodrigues. The race *F.p. pondicerianus* has been introduced to Rodrigues (Peters, 1934) where they are still common and hunted for food and sport (Gill, 1967).

Diego Garcia. According to Loustau-Lalanne (1962) the Grey Francolin occurs on Diego Garcia where they may have been introduced from Mauritius or possibly one of the other Mascarene Islands. Bourne (1971) records that they were possibly introduced before 1907 (see Gadow and Gardiner, 1907), otherwise, they were first recorded there in 1960. A species of francolin was apparently still present on the island in 1964, but none was noted in 1971. Hutson (1975) reports that the species is probably now extinct there.

USA. The northern race of the Grey Francolin *F.p. interpositus* from northern India was introduced in Nevada from 1959-61 onwards (Christensen, 1963). Up until 1963 some 2300 birds were released in Nevada (Nevada Fish and Game Commission, 1963), at least 600 birds in 1960 and over 300 in 1961 in the southern part of Nevada (Western States Exotic Game Bird Committee, 1961).

In 1959 some were released in Texas (270 birds) and these birds and also those in Nevada appeared to be surviving at least at the release sites (Bump and Bohl, 1964). Some were surviving and breeding in the Imperial Valley, California, in 1966 and 1967 (Bohl, 1968), indicating that they had also been released in that State.

In April 1954 161 Grey Francolins, presented to the United States by the Government of Pakistan, were released near the Gila River south-west of Buckeye, Arizona (Webb, 1957). Further birds were released in May 1955 (103) and in August 1956 (thirteen). Although breeding near the release sites was observed, no birds were seen after August 1956.

It is indicated that releases of Grey Francolins continued in the United States at least until 1964 (Bump and Bump, 1964) and possibly until 1967 (Gottschalk, 1967). However, it was stated in 1970 (Bump, 1970) that it was still too early to evaluate their success.

Hawaiian Islands. Grey Francolins (*F.p. interpositus ?*) from India were released in 1958 and the species is now open to hunting in the Hawaiian Islands (Walker, 1967). They are found in dry open and grassy and shrubby country, on all the islands except Oahu, and are most common on Lanai (Hawaiian Audubon Society, 1975).

Besides those released in 1958, further birds were introduced in 1960-61 when ninety-six were liberated on Maui and sixty-five on Lanai (Western States Exotic Game Bird Commission, 1961). In 1959-61

and 1965-66 a total of 214 Californian game farm reared birds were released on the Puu Waawaa Ranch, Hawaii (Lewin, 1971). Lewin reports that these were most successful, and that the species has become common on the ranch and is still spreading there. He also indicates that the Division of Fish and Game liberated one hundred birds on the slopes of Mauna Kea at Pohakuloa in 1961; a second group of 166 birds at Ahumoa, also on Mauna Kea; and that a third group were released at Keomuka between Mauna Kea and Puu Hualalai, on Hawaii. There may have been other introductions because the species appeared to become established rapidly, and hunting was in progress as early as 1964 (Bump, 1968).

DAMAGE

In India Grey Francolins are said to do little if any damage to farm crops and are considered a most desirable game bird (Faruqi, Bump *et al*, 1960). However, where introduced on the island of Rodrigues they are considered to be pests because of the damage they do to young maize plants (Gill, 1967).

RED-BILLED FRANCOLIN
Close-barred Francolin
Francolinus adspersus Waterhouse

DISTINGUISHING CHARACTERISTICS

30-38 cm (11.8-15 in)

Head, mantle, scapulars, wing-coverts and rump earth brown, finely barred lighter and darker; nape and upper mantle finely barred brown and white; lores black; underparts finely barred black and white; lower flanks and under tail-coverts barred brown and buff; bare skin around eye yellow; bill red. Female: lacks spurs.

Mackworth-Praed and Grant, ser.2, vol.1, 1962, p.213 and pl.14.

GENERAL DISTRIBUTION

Africa: southern Africa from southern Angola to south-west Zambia, South-West Africa (Nambia) and Botswana.

INTRODUCED DISTRIBUTION

Probably introduced successfully to Hawaii in the Hawaiian Islands.

GENERAL HABITS

Status: locally common. *Habitat:* bush country, flood plains, and old watercourses. *Gregariousness:* coveys of 10-12 birds and up to 20. *Movements:* sedentary. *Foods:* seeds, plant shoots and insects. *Breeding:* all year, but generally Dec-Apr. *Nest:* depression on the ground lined with leaves and grass, in thick cover. *Eggs:* 4-10.

Mackworth-Praed and Grant, ser.2, vol.1, 1962, p.214.

NOTES ON INTRODUCTIONS

Hawaiian Islands. Red-billed Francolins were introduced from the United States in 1963, but are not known to be established in the Hawaiian Islands (Walker, 1967; Berger, 1972). Some were introduced on the Puu Waawaa Ranch, Hawaii, when four birds were released in 1964 (Lewin, 1971). These were present in 1965 but were said to have disappeared after that time, and the species does not appear to have been established anywhere at the time of Lewin's paper. More recently, however, the Hawaiian Audubon Society (1975) reports that the

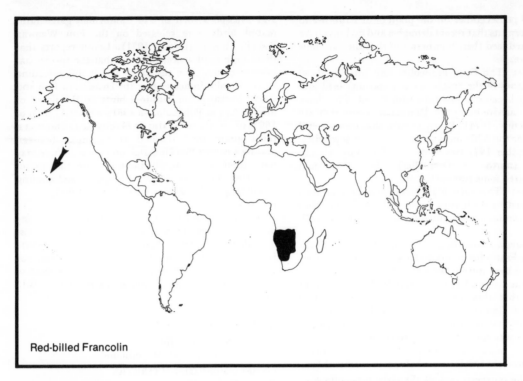

Red-billed Francolin

species is probably well established and breeding on Hawaii at present.

DAMAGE

None known.

HEUGLIN'S FRANCOLIN
Francolinus icterorhynchus Heuglin

DISTINGUISHING CHARACTERISTICS

Upper parts greyish brown, speckled and barred darker; neck and mantle with crescentic white markings; eye-stripe and throat white; underparts whitish with black blobs and crescentic markings; bill orange-yellow. Female: lacks spurs.

Mackworth-Praed and Grant, 1952-73, ser.1, vol.1, pp.244-245 and pl.18; ser.3, vol.1, pp.184-185 and pl.15.

GENERAL DISTRIBUTION

Africa: central Africa from the Central African Republic and north-eastern Congo to south-western Sudan and Uganda.

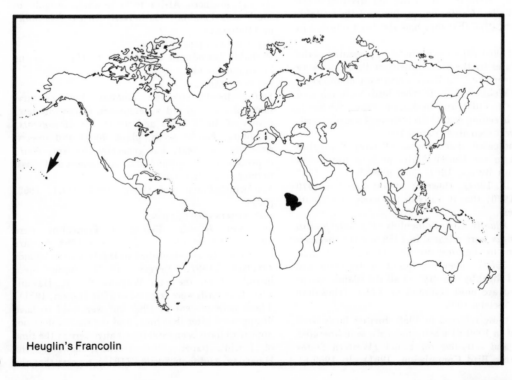

Heuglin's Francolin

Introduced unsuccessfully in the Hawaiian Islands.

GENERAL HABITS

Status: fairly common (?). *Habitat:* open grassy country, grass amongst scrub and in or near cultivation. *Gregariousness:* pairs, or small coveys of 3-5 birds. *Movements:* sedentary. *Foods:* seeds, berries and insects. *Breeding:* most of the year. *Nest:* depression on the ground, under a bush or other cover. *Eggs:* 6-8.

Mackworth-Praed and Grant, 1952-73, ser.1, vol.1, pp.245-246; ser.3, vol.1, p.185.

NOTES ON INTRODUCTIONS

Hawaiian Islands. Heuglin's Francolins were introduced from the United States in 1961 but are not known to be established in the Hawaiian Islands (Walker, 1967; Berger, 1972). Nine birds from a Texas game farm were released on the Puu Waawaa Ranch in Hawaii in 1961 but these were said to have disappeared soon after their release (Lewin, 1971).

DAMAGE

In some areas of Africa Heuglin's Francolins cause some damage to native crops of potatoes and ground nuts. They are said to make up for this by consuming many insects (Mackworth-Praed and Grant, 1957).

CLAPPERTON'S FRANCOLIN
(Sharpes Francolin)
Francolinus clappertoni Children

DISTINGUISHING CHARACTERISTICS

Upper parts greyish brown with white edges to feathers; nape black and white; a variable black moustachial streak; patch around eyes vermilion-red; eye-stripe and throat white; underparts whitish blobbed with black; bill black, base of lower mandible red. Female; lacks spurs.

Mackworth-Praed and Grant, 1952-73, ser.1, vol.1,

pp.246-248 and pl.18; ser.3, vol.1, pp.185-186 and pl.15.

GENERAL DISTRIBUTION

Africa. The Sudan, Eritrea and north and central Ethiopia.

INTRODUCED DISTRIBUTION

Introduced unsuccessfully in the Hawaiian Islands.

GENERAL HABITS

Status: common. *Habitat:* rocky hillsides, open plains with scrub or grass, savannah and cultivated areas. *Gregariousness:* coveys. *Movements:* sedentary. *Foods:* insects, seeds, berries and small molluscs. *Breeding:* Mar-Dec. *Nest:* scrape on the ground. *Eggs:* no information.

Mackworth-Praed and Grant, 1952-73, ser.1, vol.1, pp.246-248; ser.3, vol.1, p.186.

NOTES ON INTRODUCTIONS

Hawaiian Islands. Clapperton's Francolins were introduced from the United States in 1958 but they are not known to be established in the Hawaiian Islands (Walker, 1967; Berger, 1972). Ten birds from a Californian game farm were released in 1959 and 1962 on the Puu Waawaa Ranch on Hawaii but disappeared after their release (Lewin, 1971). The race introduced was probably *F.c. sharpii.*

DAMAGE

None known.

ERKEL'S FRANCOLIN
Francolinus erkelii (Rüppell)

DISTINGUISHING CHARACTERISTICS

40 cm (15.75 in). 1.1-1.6 kg (2.42-3.52 lb)

Upper parts olive-grey, with a chestnut crown and chestnut stripes on the neck; mantle, wing-coverts, eye-stripe and forehead black; throat white; breast grey; abdomen white with chestnut streaks; bill black. Female: lacks spurs.

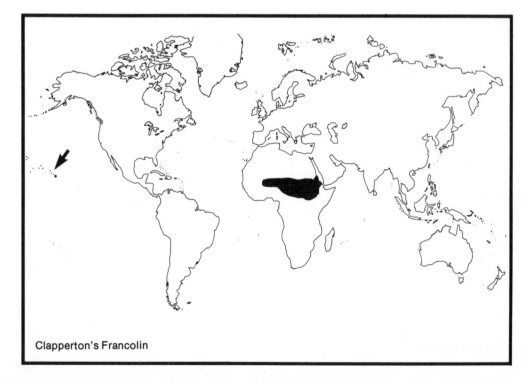

Clapperton's Francolin

Mackworth-Praed and Grant, ser.1, vol.1, 1957, pp.255-256 and pl.18.

GENERAL DISTRIBUTION

Africa: north-eastern Africa from the Sudan to northern and central Ethiopia.

INTRODUCED DISTRIBUTION

Introduced successfully to the Hawaiian Islands and unsuccessfully in the USA.

GENERAL HABITS

Status: fairly common. *Habitat:* woodlands and upland scrub. *Gregariousness:* coveys. *Movements:* sedentary. *Foods:* grass, shoots, seeds and insects. *Breeding:* Apr-May, and Oct. *Nest:* scrape on the ground lined with grass. *Eggs:* no information.

Mackworth-Praed and Grant, ser.1, vol.1, 1957, p.256.

NOTES ON INTRODUCTIONS

Hawaiian Islands. The nominate race of Erkel's Francolin (game farm reared birds) was first introduced to the Hawaiian Islands from the United States in 1957 (Walker, 1967). By 1960 they had been released on Hawaii, Maui and Lanai — and were surviving around the release sites — and on Kauai and Molokai, where they had disappeared.

According to Lewin (1971) thirty-four birds were released at Pohakuloa, Hawaii, in 1958 and the following year a further 117; the Division of Fish and Game released thirty-eight birds at Puako in 1957 and 107 Californian and Oklahoma game farm reared birds were released in 1959 and 1960 on the Puu Waawaa Ranch on Hawaii. By 1970 the species was well established in these three areas. Further releases were made in the period 1960-61 on Hawaii (forty-seven birds), Oahu (sixty-one), Kauai (thirty-seven), Molokai (ninety-four) and on Lanai (forty), to supplement previous introductions (Western States Exotic Game Bird Commission, 1961). The Hawaiian Audubon Society (1975) reports that Erkel's

Francolins are now common on the islands of Hawaii, Lanai, Oahu and Kauai. Some were recorded at Waimea Canyon on Kauai in late 1977 (Pyle, 1978).

USA. Some 244 Erkel's Francolins were released in three areas of California in 1959-60 (Western States Exotic Game Bird Commission, 1961). The fate of these birds and possibly of other introductions is not known, but the species does not appear to be established anywhere in the United States.

DAMAGE

None known.

RED-THROATED FRANCOLIN
(Spurfowl, Red-necked Francolin)
Pternistes afer (Müller) = *P. cranchii* (Leach)

DISTINGUISHING CHARACTERISTICS

30-40 cm (11.8-15.75 in). 600-700 g (1.32-1.54 lb)
(Variable species, nominate race described.) Top of head brown; nape mottled black or brown and white; forehead, superciliary stripe and moustachial stripe white; remainder of upper parts brown with blackish centres to feathers; wings and tail brown; skin around eye, chin and throat reddish; underparts streaked black and white; bill red. Female: lacks spurs; broader blackish centres to feathers of upper parts.

Mackworth-Praed and Grant, 1952-73, ser.1, vol.1, pp.256-261 and pl.19; ser.2, vol.1, pp.221-226 and pl.14; ser.3, vol.1, pp.190-191 and pl.14.

GENERAL DISTRIBUTION

Africa: Angola, Zaire, Uganda and Kenya, south to Cape Province in South Africa except South-West Africa (Namibia) and eastern South Africa.

INTRODUCED DISTRIBUTION

Introduced successfully to Ascension Island.

GENERAL HABITS

Status: common. *Habitat:* forest in low country, clearings, cultivation and roadsides. *Gregariousness:*

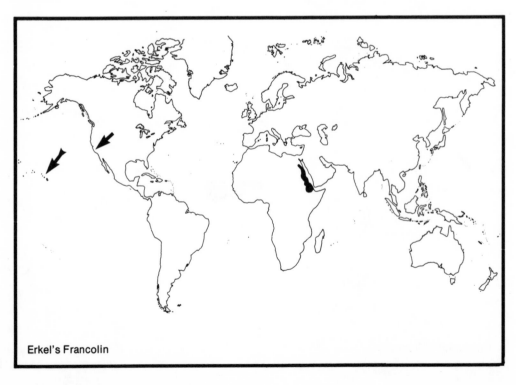

Erkel's Francolin

142

Red-throated Francolin

established on Ascension Island and is still present there in small numbers.

DAMAGE

The Red-throated Francolin is recorded to cause damage to mealie (maize) crops locally in Moçambique (Mackworth-Praed and Grant, 1957).

BARE-THROATED FRANCOLIN
(Bare-necked Francolin, Yellow-throated Francolin)
Pternistes leucoscepus (Gray)

DISTINGUISHING CHARACTERISTICS
Upper parts pale olive-brown with cream stripes; underparts mottled greyish brown and cream with chestnut on the flanks and abdomen; throat yellow; patch around eye yellow; bill black. Female: lacks spurs.

Mackworth-Praed and Grant, ser.1, vol.1, 1957, pp.262-264 and pl.19.

GENERAL DISTRIBUTION
Africa: eastern Africa from Ethiopia and Somali to the Sudan, Uganda and north-eastern Tanzania.

INTRODUCED DISTRIBUTION
Introduced, probably unsuccessfully, to the Hawaiian Islands.

GENERAL HABITS
Status: no information, probably fairly common. *Habitat:* cultivated ground, dry river beds, grass glades, and scrub near swamps. *Gregariousness:* coveys or small parties. *Movements:* no information, probably sedentary. *Foods:* grain, seeds, bulbs, roots and insects. *Breeding:* most months of year except September, dependent on rains. *Nest:* scrape on the ground lined with grass. *Eggs:* 3-7.

Mackworth-Praed and Grant, ser.1, vol.1, 1957, pp.262-264.

NOTES ON INTRODUCTIONS
Hawaiian Islands. Bare-throated Francolins were

singly, pairs, or more usually small parties or coveys. *Movements:* sedentary. *Foods:* bulbs, roots, insects and seeds. *Breeding:* irregular, recorded most months of year. *Nest:* hollow lined with grass and well concealed. *Eggs:* 5-9 or more.

Mackworth-Praed and Grant, 1952-73, ser.1, vol.1, pp.257-261; ser.2, vol.1, pp.222-225; ser.3, vol.1, pp.191-192.

NOTES ON INTRODUCTIONS
Ascension Island. According to Stonehouse (1962), the Red-throated Francolin has been introduced and

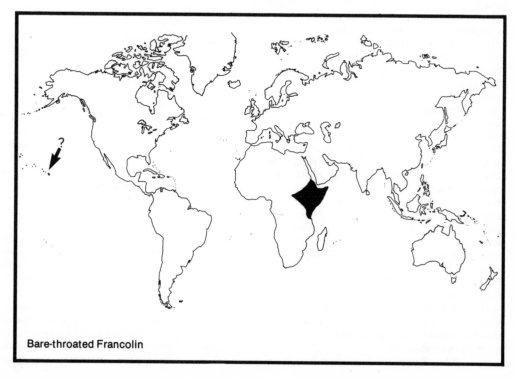

Bare-throated Francolin

introduced to the Hawaiian Islands from the United States in 1958, but are not known to be established anywhere (Walker, 1967; Berger, 1972). Efforts to establish the species were made privately on the Dillingham Ranch in 1960-61, but they appeared to be unsuccessful (Western States Exotic Game Bird Commission, 1961). Limited success at reproduction in the wild has been achieved (Lewin, 1971) on the Puu Waawaa Ranch. Liberations totalling some twenty-seven birds of Californian and Texan game farm origin were made in 1959 and 1961 on Puu Waawaa Ranch. These birds were said to be reproducing but not spreading much, and some were noted there as late as 1967.

DAMAGE

None known.

EUROPEAN PARTRIDGE
(Common Partridge, Grey or Gray Partridge, Hungarian Partridge)
Perdix perdix (Linnaeus)

DISTINGUISHING CHARACTERISTICS

30-35 cm (11.8-13.78). 361-480 g (.80-1 lb)
Generally a dull brown bird; upper parts greyish brown; face, throat and chin rusty or reddish brown; chest greyish; breast with a U-shaped dark chestnut patch; belly whitish with chestnut bars on sides of flanks; tail rufous; bill grey.
Witherby *et al*, vol.5, 1938-41, pp.240-241, 243-246 and pls.146, opp. p.228, and 147, opp. p.234.

GENERAL DISTRIBUTION

Eurasia: from northern Spain and Portugal, Great Britain and central France to Iran, southern USSR and Mongolia. Distribution difficult to survey in Europe because the species has been introduced on a large scale for game (Voous, 1960).

INTRODUCED DISTRIBUTION

Introduced and re-introduced in many areas of Europe including the USSR, Finland, Great Britain, France, Italy and probably elsewhere; introduced successfully in the USA and Canada.

Introduced unsuccessfully in the Inner Hebrides, Orkney Islands, Outer Hebrides, Norway, the Hawaiian Islands, Fiji, Australia (including Tasmania), New Zealand and Chile.

GENERAL HABITS

Status: declining, but still fairly common. *Habitat:* cultivated land, cornfields, weedy fallows, arable fields and undergrowth arising from clearing (formerly forest edges, natural meadows, steppes and moorland). *Gregariousness:* family parties, coveys of 10-30 birds and sometimes larger flocks. *Movements:* sedentary. *Foods:* seeds, fruits, berries, waste grain, grass and vegetable material, green shoots, insects, spiders and worms. *Breeding:* Apr-June (Apr-Aug North America). *Nest:* hollow or depression, lined with grass and leaves, on the ground amongst dense grass, bush or forests. *Eggs:* 7, 10-20, 22 (North America 6-20).
Witherby *et al*, vol.5, 1938-41, pp.240-243.
Voous, 1960, p.82.
Southwood, *Journal of Animal Ecology*, vol.36, 1967, pp.549-556; Southwood *et al*, vol.36, 1967-69, pp.557-562 and vol.38, pp.497-509.

NOTES ON INTRODUCTIONS

Europe. The European Partridge has been re-introduced in many areas to supplement waning stocks, and introduced in some areas where it may not have occurred formerly. Efforts have been made to reacclimatise them in at least some areas of the Ukraine (Yanushevich, 1966), but the results of these attempts are not known. Between 1955 and 1965 more than 28 000 *P. perdix* and *P. barbata* were released in the European part of the Soviet Union for re-stocking purposes (Osmolovskaya, 1969).

The species' appearance in Finland was probably as a result of colonisation and introduction by man. The first birds may have been successfully introduced as early as 1750, however. The partridge appeared in many places in Finland between 1895 and 1898 (Merikallio, 1958). Various efforts to establish them have been made in parts of Norway, other than in the extreme south-east where they occur naturally (Vader, pers. comm., 1977). As far as it is known the introductions in Norway have been unsuccessful.

European Partridges were introduced, not very successfully, to Raasay in the Inner Hebrides just prior to 1904 (Collier, 1904). Birds introduced there were said to disappear gradually. Introductions to the Outer Hebrides and on the Orkney Islands were also unsuccessful (Witherby *et al,* 1941). Both pheasants and the partridge were introduced to Shapinsay in the Orkneys in 1905, but the Partridge apparently died out (Lack, 1943). Birds from Hungary have been introduced to Great Britain (Thomson, 1964) and many cultivated areas of France (Witherby) to increase hunting for sportsmen. Some 360 adults and 1000 young were released in the Yonne Department, and 260 adults and 950 young in the Hautes-Alpes Department, France, just prior to 1971 to ascertain the success of farm-raised birds released in the wild (Birkan, 1971). Both imported and local races, at least some 10 697, have been released in every month of the year in Italy (Toschi, 1962) to ascertain movements and survival of the birds. From 1950-58 some 13 200 were marked and released in Denmark (Paludan, 1963).

USA. The European Partridge was first introduced to the USA by the same son-in-law of Benjamin Franklin who introduced the pheasant (Roberts, 1960). This and other introductions into the Atlantic Coast States failed and have continued to fail in areas east of the Allegheny Mountains in spite of the fact that many thousands have been liberated. Guiguet (1961) reports that they were introduced to North America in the latter part of the nineteenth century, prior to 1879. They were liberated in California in 1877 (California Department Fish and Game, 1950) and other attempts were probably made in Virginia and New Jersey some time prior to 1900.

Further introductions occurred in California in 1908, when thirty-five birds were released, and in 1909, when some 2000 were liberated in some ninety localities. Attempts continued in California at least into the 1950s and beyond, yet they have only become established in the north-east of California.

Many more introductions probably occurred elsewhere in the United States in the period from 1905 to 1914. Some were released in Nevada at least as early as 1923 (Gullion and Christensen, 1957) and some in Oregon from 1925 to 1932 (Gullion, 1951). Other introductions in about the same period occurred in eastern Washington, Iowa, Utah, Idaho and New York.

Apparently over the years attempts were made to introduce the European Partridge to most of the United States (A.O.U., 1957), but not until after the 1930s did they become successful in the north and central portions (Gottschalk, 1967).

In the western United States in 1960, 1700 birds were released (bred from eggs obtained from Denmark), and the total released in various States since 1950 and up until 1960 has totalled some 6000 birds in at least some ten different sites (Western States Exotic Game Bird Commission, 1961).

Early releases in New York in 1916 and 1921 failed, but between 1927 and 1932 some 27 750 Partridge were released (Brown, 1954). Most of these birds disappeared but the species persisted in a few areas. Along the St Lawrence River, in northern New York, they gradually increased in numbers until in 1952 an open hunting season was declared.

The first release of European Partridges in Michigan occurred in about 1910 when 200 birds were released near Saginaw Bay (Dale, 1943). This was followed by further liberations in 1918 (100 birds), some by H. Jewett in 1927 by allowing young birds to escape, and about 600 which were introduced in the vicinity of Oxford between 1926 and 1930. Dale indicates that probably 1000 Partridges were released in southern Michigan over a fairly wide area from 1910 to 1930. The Michigan Department of Conservation began propagation in 1925 with 108 Partridges imported from Europe, and between 1930 and 1940 3297 were released in forty areas of that State. Most of the liberations were failures. However, the European Partridge did become established on the southern border of Michigan.

From 1912 to 1948 over 650 European Partridges were released in Utah, in widely separate localities, without success (Porter, 1955). Idaho authorities, between 1939 and 1942, transplanted 924 birds from northern Idaho into the south-east portion of the State. These were successful, and by 1948 they were spreading into Utah.

European Partridges were first introduced to Iowa in 1910, but have never extended their range beyond the north-central part of the State (Green and Hendrichson, 1938, in Johnsgard, 1973). Between 1909 and 1940, a total of 17 420 were imported from Europe and liberated in Iowa (Westerskov, 1956). Their numbers increased until about 1937-40, but thereafter the population declined (Westerskov, 1949).

Of 401 European Partridges liberated in Oregon between 1925 and 1932, the last were sighted in 1942. Previous attempts in the Willamette Valley in 1900 (ninety-seven birds), in various areas in 1913 (218), and at Portland in 1914 (sixty-four) with birds imported directly from Europe to Oregon, largely failed to become established (Jewett and Gabrielson, 1929). According to Schneider (1957), two shipments totalling 1314 Partridges arrived from Europe in 1913-14 and these were sent to various counties for release. He says the result of introductions from 1901 to 1934 was the successful establishment of the species over much of eastern Oregon, but failure in the remainder of the State except for a few remnant populations. Some 1255 birds, the progeny from 850 eggs flown out from Denmark in 1949-50, were

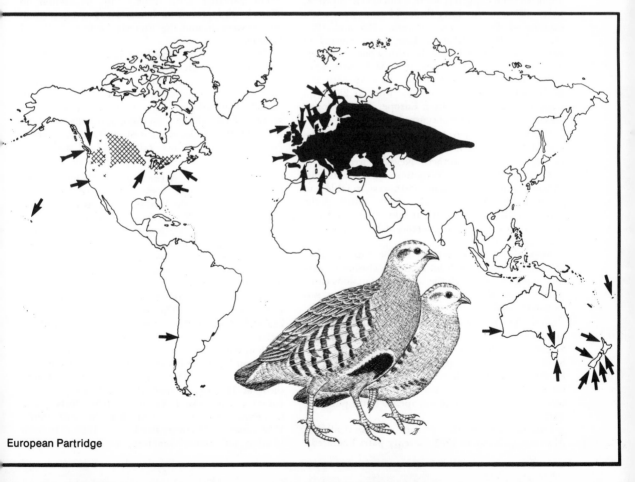

European Partridge

released in the Willamette Valley in western Oregon in 1956-57.

Initially, introductions occurred in Washington in 1906 when 250 pairs of European Partridges were released in Spokane County where they became firmly established (Jewett *et al*, 1953). From 1906 onwards they were released fairly generally throughout Washington State: in 1908, twenty-five pairs in Columbia County; in 1909, 200 birds in Lincoln County; in 1913, one hundred pairs in Columbia County, and about 1000 birds in Chelan County, followed by more in succeeding years. From 1913 to 1915 some 4794 Partridges were liberated, by which time they were established throughout the State and an open hunting season in two counties occurred in 1915.

Before 1915, European Partridges were introduced into Montana by private individuals, but not until the period 1922-26 when the Montana Fish and Game Commission purchased 6000 of them from Europe, (Trueblood and Weigand, 1971) did they become widely established in that State. The Montana Commission distributed the birds throughout the State, and the species has become a leading game bird there.

Wisconsin had considerable success with the European Partridge following its introduction in 1908, and the species extended its range northwards at a rate of 6.5 kilometres (four miles) per year. The species was released in Nebraska as early as 1907, but did not become established there (Johnsgard, 1973).

At least 9806 European Partridges, mainly imported from Hungary, Austria and Czechoslovakia, were liberated in forty-three of the sixty-seven counties of Pennsylvania between 1926 and 1930 (Gerstell, 1941). Although these were reported to have become established in thirty-one counties, introductions were continued in 1931-32 with 1572 birds; in 1933 with 1194 birds; in 1935 with 200 birds; and from 1935 to 1939 with 21 287 wild trapped birds imported from Europe. The first open season, in three counties, occurred in 1939.

The European Partridge is now established in the United States from the Canadian border to north-eastern California, northern Nevada, western and northern Utah, northern Wyoming, northern Illinois, Indiana, southern Michigan, north-western Ohio and northern New York (A.O.U., 1957). Much of the success of the species in the northern United States may have been due to the spread of birds across the Canadian border.

Most of the stock released in the United States appears to have come from England, Czechoslovakia and Hungary, although the later introductions came mainly from Czechoslovakia because this race was said to be hardier.

Canada. The first liberations of European Partridges in Canada occurred on the coast near Vancouver, British Columbia, in March 1904 when fifty-seven birds were released (Carl and Guiguet, 1972). Further birds were liberated in 1905 (thirty-two birds), 1907-08 (sixty-seven), 1909 (167) and in succeeding years. Hunting was opened to the public in 1915.

Introductions on the western plains (Calgary, Alberta) occurred in 1908 (seventy pairs liberated) and 1909 (207 pairs). These met with considerable success and a further 230 birds were liberated near Edmonton at a later date. The species flourished in this area and had spread some ninety-seven kilometres in five years. The Calgary introduction had meanwhile spread across the prairies into Saskatchewan (Guiguet, 1961). Some were noted there at Piapot in 1921 (Dexter, 1922). In 1924-25 further introductions in Manitoba (eighty-five pairs) were successful and the Partridge became established there.

Early introductions in British Columbia include those of J. L. and A. E. Todd who released 500 Partridges on Vancouver Island in 1908-09, seventy-two birds on James Island and thirty-two on Sidney Island (Gulf Islands). A. R. Spalding and H. R. Pooley released ten birds on South Pender Island in 1909 (Carl and Guiguet).

Releases of European Partridges in Washington, USA, are thought to have spread across the border into British Columbia as early as 1917 and extended their range north to the Kamloops (Guiguet). They were abundant in the Okanagan Valley in 1925-26, but abruptly declined in numbers after 1927 and have since only remained at a low level (Munro, 1947). Some are still present at Osoyoos and small flocks were noted on Sea and Lulu Islands in the lower Fraser Valley in 1958, but there are no recent records of them there. Some were sighted at Boston Bar in 1966 and a few along the Fraser Canyon from Lillooet north to Empire Valley in 1968-69 (Gates, 1970, in Carl and Guiguet). On Vancouver Island two small flocks persisted until 1968. The population in Victoria disappeared in the early 1960s, but a small one survives around the Victoria airport (Carl and Guiguet).

There appear no records of introductions of this Partridge in eastern Canada. Bendell (1957) suggests that birds in southern Ontario may have originated from established populations in Michigan, USA. In Canada, the European Partridge is now established in southern Saskatchewan, southern Manitoba, southern and central Ontario, south-western Quebec, southern New Brunswick, Prince Edward Island and Nova Scotia (Godfrey, 1966).

Hawaiian Islands. According to Caum (1933) European Partridges were introduced from an unknown source to the Hawaiian Islands in 1895 and later. Munro (1960) records that *P.p. perdix* has been introduced a number of times. However, they are not known to be established anywhere in these islands (Munro, 1960; Berger, 1972).

New Zealand. The Nelson Acclimatisation Society first imported European Partridges in 1864 (four birds), but there are no further records of them (Thomson, 1922). The first liberations in New Zealand appear to have been those of the Auckland society in 1867, when seventeen birds were set free.

Thomson details the many introductions of the European Partridge between 1867 and 1909 and their subsequent fate: The Auckland society liberated them at Howick in 1868 (twenty birds), in 1871 (nine) and at Lake Takapuna in 1875 (forty). The Canterbury society imported them in 1867 (ten), 1868 (one), 1871 (thirty-two brace), 1880 (240 from London of which nineteen arrived and were liberated), 1875 (?) and in 1879 (twenty-five brace, of which few survived for release). Some of these were liberated on the Hororata. In 1869 the Otago society liberated thirty-one birds, and in 1871 some 130 in country south and west of Dunedin. These survived and were not an uncommon sight from Oamaru to Invercargill in 1877, but had completely disappeared by 1892. Further attempts by this society were made in 1896 (twenty), 1897 (nine) on Taieri Plains, 1897 (fourteen) at Otanomomo, 1900 (forty-four) and in 1909 (?) at Milton, but these had disappeared by 1912-13. Between 1899 and 1900 the Southland society imported and liberated forty-eight birds on Stewart Island, but they failed to become established. In 1899 private attempts were made to introduce the species in the Wellington area, but these were also unsuccessful. The Wellington society obtained birds in 1890 (three), and in 1891 (fifteen). Seven of those obtained in 1891 were liberated at Upper Hutt, but were not sighted again. Another release of birds occurred at Masterton in 1897. The Taranaki society obtained and released four pairs in 1894, and although some were later reported from the Koru district in 1904 they failed to become established in this area also. Finally, in 1912, the Auckland society imported thirty-nine birds of which fifteen were liberated at Kaipara and four at Waikata, the remainder died.

Thomson records that by 1922 the European Partridge had not survived anywhere in New Zealand. Recently (in about 1962), further introductions were made (Wodzicki, 1965) and birds were released in the North and South Islands, but their success has not yet been proven (Falla *et al*, 1966).

Fiji. According to Wood and Wetmore (1926) the European Partridge may have been introduced to Fiji, but certainly unsuccessfully.

Australia. The Royal Society of Victoria liberated partridges from India, Sri Lanka and China on Phillip Island and at Gembrook in 1871-72 (McCance, 1962), but they failed to become established. Some partridges (probably this species ?) were introduced in Western Australia, some time between 1897 and 1912, but were later reported to have been unsuccessful (Long, 1972). Littler (1902) indicates that they were an early introduction to Tasmania, but were also unsuccessful there. In 1936 the Tasmanian Game Protection and Acclimatisation Society, assisted by the Animals and Birds Protection Board, imported 110 partridges from England (Sharland, 1958). These were liberated at Marrawah, Garden Island (in Norfolk Bay) and at Whiteford and Colebrook. They survived at Marrawah and bred there but later disappeared. Tarr (1950) records that those liberated some years ago in different districts in Tasmania had now disappeared. The European Partridge is not established at present anywhere in Australia.

Chile. Hellmayr (1932) records that European Partridges were introduced to Chile, but failed to become established.

DAMAGE
In North America no damage appears to have been recorded for this species. Although they show a liking for cultivated fields, cornfields and open farmlands, their main food is waste grain, weed seeds, and a variety of animal and vegetable matter and they do not appear to have affected man's crops in any way. Westerskov (1965 and 1966), who studied the ecology of the species on the Canadian prairies, considered the bird to be morphologically well adapted to survive the cold winters with limited snow which are found in the area. He suggests that the main factor in the species' successful survival in this region has been the change in choice of food, coupled with the abundance of preferred food in the prairies.

In Europe the bird feeds mainly on green leaf material during the cold winters whilst on the Canadian prairies they feed almost exclusively on waste grain and weed seeds. However, in Great Britain they are regarded by the British Sugar Corporation as a major pest of sugar beet (Dunning, 1974) because they peck at the leaves of the seedlings.

A study of the food habits and agricultural importance of this species in Hungary (Vertse *et al*, 1955) indicates that they feed mainly on grass and weed seeds and insects. Although they are sometimes accused of damage to cereal crops these did not appear prominent in the diet and were taken from stubble. Various cultivated plants such as flax, broom, millet and corn are occasionally eaten in small quantities.

BEARDED PARTRIDGE
(Mongolian Partridge, Chinese Partridge, Daurian Partridge)
Perdix barbata Verreaux and Des Murs
= *P. dauuricae* (Pallas)

DISTINGUISHING CHARACTERISTICS
26.2-30 cm (10.24-11.8 in). 230-290 g (8.11-10.23 oz)
Resembles European Partridge; lanceolate feathers under the chin form a beard; remainder similar but paler than the European Partridge. Female: more

Bearded Partridge

spotted and striped on crown; heavier barring on underparts, and lacks black patch on abdomen.

Cheng, 1963, pp.263-264 and pl. (b and w) 37, no.30.

Etchécopar and Hüe, 1978, p.223

GENERAL DISTRIBUTION

Asia: Transbaykalia, Mongolia, northern China (Shensi, Shansi and Chihli), Middle Amur and Ussuriland, eastern Turkestan, north and east to Minusinsk, north-western Mongolia and eastern Tian Shans; also Tsaidam, eastern Nan Shan, region of Ching Hai, Tatung Mountains and northern Kansu.

INTRODUCED DISTRIBUTION

Introduced successfully to Manila in the Philippines. Re-introduced in some parts of the USSR (?). Introduced unsuccessfully to Japan

GENERAL HABITS

Status: fairly common. *Habitat:* steppe. *Gregariousness:* pairs and small groups, and large coveys outside breeding season. *Movements:* sedentary, but move somewhat in harsh winters. *Foods:* seeds, spores and insects. *Breeding:* Apr-July. *Nest:* similar to European Partridge. *Eggs:* 10, 13-18, 22.

Cheng, 1963, pp.264-265.

Etchécopar and Hüe, 1978, pp.223 and 226.

NOTES ON INTRODUCTIONS

Philippines. The race *P.b. barbata* has been introduced from China and established around Manila in the Philippines (du Pont, 1971).

USSR. Attempts have been made to acclimatise the Bearded Partridge in the central zone (Sergeeva and Sumina, 1963). Sergeeva and Sumina indicate that the species was released in the Moscow area to replace the Willow Grouse which has almost vanished in this area. They record that from 1956 to 1961 some 9500 were released in the Tuvinian district, but that the birds dispersed in all directions up to two hundred kilometres (124 miles) from the release point. They were said to have failed to become permanently established because of environmental differences between the area of origin and the release area.

Between 1955 and 1965 more than 28 000 *P. perdix* and *P. barbata* were released in the European part of the Soviet Union for re-stocking purposes (Osmolovskaya, 1969).

Japan. The Bearded Partridge was imported and released in Japan, from southern Manchuria in 1923, but failed to become established (Kuroda, 1937).

DAMAGE

In China the Bearded Partridge is reported to destroy some agricultural crops such as sorghum, maize, oats, etc, but is apparently not considered of much economic importance except as a frozen meat export (Cheng, 1963).

MADAGASCAR PARTRIDGE

Margaroperdix madagascariensis (Scopoli)

DISTINGUISHING CHARACTERISTICS

31 cm (12.2 in)

Black face stripe and throat; eyebrow, temple stripe and cheek band white; crown reddish brown spotted black and white; sides of head, neck and breast grey; underparts black spotted white; flanks reddish brown with black shaft stripe; remainder of upper parts reddish brown striped white; bill bluish at base, with

Madagascar Partridge

a black tip. Female: paler; chin and abdomen whitish.

Milon *et al*, pt.35: Bds., 1973, pp.91-92 and pl.7, figs.16 and 17.

GENERAL DISTRIBUTION

Malagasy.

INTRODUCED DISTRIBUTION

Introduced successfully but now extinct on Mauritius, and to Réunion.

GENERAL HABITS

Status: common but numbers diminishing in some areas. *Habitat:* heath areas of mountainous country, secondary brush, grasslands, weedy cultivated fields and rice fields. *Gregariousness:* solitary, pairs, trios, and small coveys of 6-12 birds in non-breeding season. *Movements:* sedentary. *Foods:* seeds and insects (?). *Breeding:* Jan-June. *Nest:* well hidden in a tuft of grass on the ground. *Eggs:* 15-20.

Milon *et al*, pt.35: Bds., 1973, pp.91-92.

NOTES ON INTRODUCTIONS

Mauritius. The Madagascar Partridge was introduced to Mauritius from Malagasy, probably by the Dutch in the seventeenth century and perhaps on several later occasions (Rountree *et al*, 1952). According to Rountree *et al*, the species did not prosper in Mauritius and the last birds disappeared as a result of a cyclone in April 1892.

Meinertzhagen (1912) records the date of introduction as about 1750, and says the species became extinct at this time, but that there have been several recent attempts to again introduce them. These must have failed because the Madagascar Partridge does not at present occur on Mauritius.

Réunion. According to Watson *et al* (1963) this species has been introduced to Réunion but was said to be becoming scarce in the 1940s and 1950s. Staub (1976) records that it was introduced several times during the eighteenth century and is still established between 400 and 2000 metres (1311 and 6557 feet), at the fringe of the forests.

DAMAGE

None known.

COMMON QUAIL
(European Quail, Coturnix Quail, Japanese Quail, Migratory Quail)
Coturnix coturnix (Linnaeus)

DISTINGUISHING CHARACTERISTICS

12.3-20 cm (4.73-7.87 in). 64.8-127.5 g (.14-.28 lb) Upper parts brown with black and buff streaks; whitish streak from eye and down neck; underparts brown to buff-brown; flanks with broad whitish streaks; throat white with central dark stripe; bill brown, tipped black, and a pale base to lower mandible. Female: blackish edges to chest patches, and no throat stripe (variable species in size and colour).

Bannerman and Bannerman, 1963-68, vol.1, pp.78-83 and pl.7; vol.2, pp.36-38; vol.3, pp.102-104; vol.4, pp.297-300 and pl.43.

Ali and Ripley, vol.2, 1968-74, pp.37-41, and fig.3, pl.21, opp. p.64.

GENERAL DISTRIBUTION

Eurasia: British Isles and Portugal to Sakhalin and Japan and south to northern India, Iran, northern Africa, Açores, Cape Verde, Madeira and Canary Islands; also southern and eastern Africa, Malagasy and other islands. Winters south to Thailand, central India, central and north-western Africa.

INTRODUCED DISTRIBUTION

Introduced successfully in the Hawaiian Islands and on Réunion. Introduced unsuccessfully to the USA and Tahiti; possibly introduced, unsuccessfully, to Australia, New Zealand, Seychelles and Mauritius; re-introduced unsuccessfully (?) in France.

GENERAL HABITS

Status: common; kept as fighting birds and for eating in parts of southern Asia. *Habitat:* woodlands, grasslands, croplands and cultivation, riversides, seashores with grass, alpine meadows and grass steppes. *Gregariousness:* usually pairs, large flocks congregate at food sources, and large flocks up to thousands on migration. *Movements:* sedentary and migratory; autumn mass migrations observed in eastern Mediterranean countries. *Foods:* seeds, grain, shoots, termites and other insects. *Breeding:* most of the year (Great Britain May-June; India Mar-July). *Nest:* shallow depression on the ground, sparsely lined with grass. *Eggs:* 3, 6-10, 15.

Bannerman and Bannerman, 1963-68, vol.1, pp.78-83; vol.2, pp.36-38; vol.3, pp.102-104; vol.4, pp.297-300.

Ali and Ripley, vol.2, 1968-74, pp.37-41.

NOTES ON INTRODUCTIONS

Hawaiian Islands. The Japanese race of the Common Quail *(C.c. japonica)* was released on Maui and Lanai in 1921 and quickly became established (Munro, 1960). Some were released on Kauai in 1944 (Munro) and by the 1960s they were reported to be well established on Kauai, Molokai, Lanai, Maui, and Hawaii (Peterson, 1961) and open to hunting there (Walker, 1967).

The Common Quail is still said to be well established and breeding on all the above mentioned islands and including Oahu (Hawaiian Audubon Society, 1975). Woodside (1977 pers. comm.) believes that in recent years current populations of the quail have interbred with domestic strains released for the purpose of training bird dogs.

USA. Both the European *(C.c. coturnix)* and Asiatic races *(C.c. japonica)* of the Common Quail were released in the United States from the 1870s to about 1925. The European race was released in some

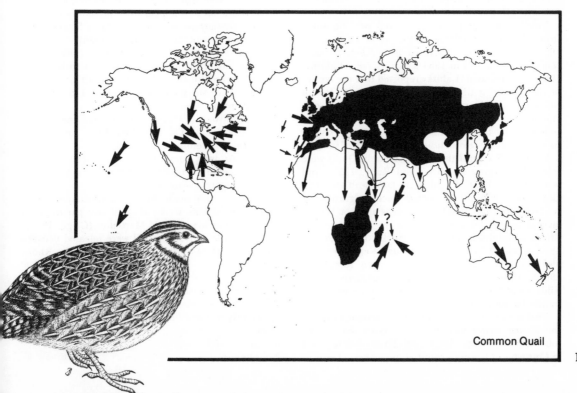

Common Quail

eastern States and the Asiatic race in the Pacific coastal regions, but in no areas did they appear to establish themselves (Job, 1923; Stanford, 1957; Cottam and Stanford, 1958; Kirkpatrick, 1959).

Early unsuccessful attempts were made to establish them in south-eastern Canada and the eastern United States, during the period 1875 to 1880, and many birds were imported from Italy for this purpose (Phillips, 1928). McAtee (1944) records that there were releases in Maine prior to 1882; Vermont and Pennsylvania prior to 1880-81; Connecticut prior to 1879-80 and in 1913; New York prior to 1881; and Vermont prior to 1878-79. He reports that they were seen in some areas for two or three years after release and that in some areas, e.g. Connecticut and Vermont, were breeding two years later. Phillips, who summarised the early introductions, makes mention of only a few notable liberations: the first introduction of the Common Quail appears to have been near Ayer, Massachusetts, shortly after 1875 when 189 birds were released; 200 were released at Rutland, Vermont in 1877; in 1880 some 5100 quail arrived in the United States and were placed in some sixteen different localities. The race *japonica* was introduced to Washington State prior to 1904, and again in 1923 (500 birds), and also in California in the period 1900-1904 with birds imported from northern China (Phillips, 1928; Taylor, 1923). These efforts were also unsuccessful.

More recent Common Quail propagation in the United States began in 1955 in Missouri with aviary bred birds *(japonica)* from California (original birds from Japan in 1953) (Stanford, 1957). Progeny from these birds was made available to other States including Florida, Illinois, Indiana, Kentucky, Missouri, Nebraska, New Hampshire, North Carolina, Ohio, Oklahoma, Tennessee and Texas. By 1958, they had been liberated by some nineteen States, one United States territory, and one Canadian province (Cottam and Stanford, 1958).

Progeny of game farm reared stock were obtained from Missouri for release in Illinois in 1957-58. In 1957 998 quail were liberated near Sibley in east-central Illinois, and in 1958 a further 500 (Labisky, 1961) were released. Labisky reported that the failure of the species in Illinois was possibly due to loss of wildness and vigour, loss of reproductiveness, wrong climatic conditions and migration. However, he indicates that the lack of data on the species' ecology precluded accurate conclusions for the lack of success.

In 1956-57 several thousand Common Quail were released in Tennessee (Due and Ruhr, 1957) and some of these banded birds were later seen over 644 kilometres (400 miles) away. Such migration of released birds has often been given as a reason for the lack of success for the species in the United States. Efforts to establish them in Kentucky, from 1957 to 1959, when 24 147 pen-reared quail were liberated, also failed in part for the same reason (Stephens, 1962). Although some reproduction occurred in the wild, some birds migrated south, but generally all finally disappeared.

That the attempt to establish the Common Quail in the United States was massive is born out by the following comments. Some 1000 birds were released in Cottle and Lipscomb counties in northern Texas in

1955-57 (Jackson, 1964). Cottam and Stanford (1958) found that some 363 000 of these quail had been released by State Game Departments during 1956 to mid-1958. Four States gave 19 000 eggs and over 60 000 young birds to sportsmen for propagation. An unknown number of eggs, young and adults were purchased from private game farms by sportsmen for release in nearly two-thirds of the then forty-eight US States.

In 1960 Kirkpatrick (1959) reported that the Common Quail stocking programme had not been impressive, and that most people had become discouraged with the poor results of their efforts. He felt at this time that if a suitable ecological niche were available the species may become established. Further attempts in Alabama (Imhoff, 1962), probably in the early 1960s, were also unsuccessful. The Common Quail has failed to become established in North America (Gottschalk, 1967).

Australia. In 1862, twelve 'Madagascar Quail' were imported into Victoria (McCance, 1962). The subsequent fate and true identity of these birds does not appear to be known.

New Zealand. 'Egyptian Quail' were released by the Canterbury Acclimatisation Society on Kinlock Estate, but apparently did not become established there (Thomson, 1922). Thomson also records that in 1914 some quail escaped but were not recorded again. The identity of these birds is not known but it is thought that they may have been Common Quail.

Seychelles. Newton (1867) records the presence of a quail (possibly this species ?) in the Seychelles, but Common Quail do not occur there at present and there is no clear evidence of their previous success or distribution (Gaymer *et al,* 1969).

Mauritius. Rountree *et al* (1952) say the Common Quail (race *africana)* was introduced from Africa on several occasions in the eighteenth century, although some may have reached the island as migrants. The species does not now appear to be present in the wild. Apparently they are still raised in cages for food, but are rarely found in the wild (Staub, 1976).

Réunion. According to Watson *et al* (1963), *C.c. africana* has probably been introduced to Réunion, where it breeds in December. Staub (1976) says it is the most successful game bird introduced to the island and is plentiful there.

Tahiti. Holyoak (1974) reports that Common Quail were introduced to Tahiti in about 1920, but were not successful in becoming established.

France. At least some efforts have been made to increase the numbers of Common Quail available for hunting in parts of southern France.

An attempt was made, by Le Comité National de la Chasse, to increase stocks of quail and partridges in the Camargue area west of Marseilles (Clegg, 1941). Clegg records that 1000 quail were released between the 15 and 31 May 1935 in the valleys of the Rhône and the Durance, Department of Vaucluse, and 1000 in the Department of Bouches du Rhône. Some 589 of them were liberated at Vaucluse in 1936, and 583 in Bouches du Rhône. Many of those released were apparently recovered during hunting shortly after the release.

DAMAGE

None known.

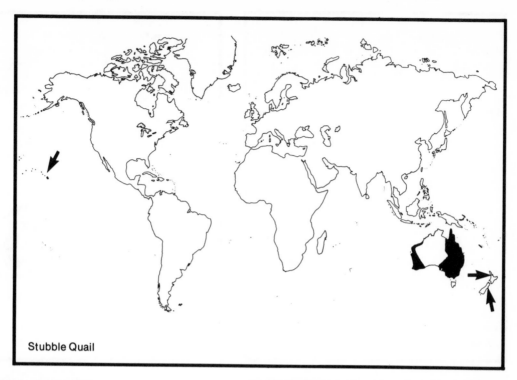

Stubble Quail

STUBBLE QUAIL
(Pectoral Quail, Grey Quail)
Coturnix pectoralis Gould
= *C. novaezelandiae* Quoy and Gaimard (See *Emu* 78 (2) : 84)

DISTINGUISHING CHARACTERISTICS
15-19.3 cm (6-7.5 in). 99-128 g (3.49-4.51 oz)
Upper parts brownish grey, streaked buffy white; crown and nape brownish black; buff-white streak above eye; throat cinnamon; upper breast black, mottled white, and lower breast and belly white, streaked black; sides mottled brown and black, streaked white; bill brownish black. Female: throat white, lacks black on upper parts and brown on underparts.
Reader's Digest, 1977, p.141 and pl. p.141.

GENERAL DISTRIBUTION
Australia generally, but rare in Tasmania.

INTRODUCED DISTRIBUTION
Introduced unsuccessfully to New Zealand and the Hawaiian Islands.

GENERAL HABITS
Status: fairly common. *Habitat:* grassland, stubble and crops, saltbush and swamp fringes. *Gregariousness:* pairs or small flocks. *Movements:* nomadic or migratory. *Foods:* seeds, grains, buds, leaves, flowers, insects and their larvae. *Breeding:* mainly Oct-Feb. *Nest:* scrape on the ground in grass, roughly lined with grass. *Eggs:* 7, 8-14.
Reader's Digest, 1977, p.141.
Frith *et al, CSIRO* Technical Paper no.32, 1977, pp.1-70.

NOTES ON INTRODUCTIONS
New Zealand. Stubble Quail were introduced into Auckland and Canterbury before 1871 (Thomson, 1922). They were liberated in the Hokianga district in the 1870s but failed to become established there. Further interest in introducing this species was apparently shown by several acclimatisation societies in New Zealand but it is not known whether any other liberations were made.
Hawaiian Islands. Stubble Quail were imported from Australia by the Maui County in 1922 and released on the islands of Maui and Lanai (Munro, 1960). Munro records that they did not persist on Lanai and that there appear to be no further records of those released on Maui. Fisher (1951) says this quail was released on the island of Niihau within the past fifteen years, and Peterson (1961) records that they have been reported to have become established there. There are no further records of the Stubble Quail in the Hawaiian Islands and according to Berger (1972) the last record was that by Fisher in 1947.

DAMAGE
None known.

SWAMP QUAIL
(Brown Quail)
Cotornix ypsilophorus (Bosc.)

DISTINGUISHING CHARACTERISTICS
17.5-21 cm (6.7-8.26 in). 85-106 g (3-3.74 oz)
Crown and nape blackish brown, with whitish central streak; remainder of upper parts greyish brown, mottled thinly with black and white; underparts brownish, barred with blackish double crescentic markings; bill dark grey above, blue-grey below. Female: upper parts thinly blotched with black.
Macdonald, 1973, p.124 and pl.5, after p.288.

GENERAL DISTRIBUTION
Australia: south-eastern Australia including Tasmania.

INTRODUCED DISTRIBUTION
Introduced to New Zealand (probably failed).

GENERAL HABITS
Status: fairly common. *Habitat:* grassy areas, especially near swamps. *Gregariousness:* loose flocks 151

Swamp Quail

Brown Quail

or parties. *Movements:* sedentary and nomadic. *Foods:* seeds, grains, buds and insects and their larvae. *Breeding:* throughout the year. *Nest:* shallow depression on the ground, in grass lined with grass and leaves; often the grass is formed into a canopy over nest. *Eggs:* 7-11, 20.

Macdonald, 1973, p.124.

NOTES ON INTRODUCTIONS

New Zealand. Swamp Quail may have been introduced into New Zealand in 1866 (Condon, 1975). Some were introduced to Auckland in the North Island in 1869 (Oliver, 1930 and 1955). Until 1930 Swamp Quail had been reported on only three occasions, and Oliver reported that they may now be extinct or to have become swamped by crossing with the more commonly found introduced quail *C. australis.*

DAMAGE

None known.

BROWN QUAIL
(Swamp Quail)
Coturnix australis (Latham)

DISTINGUISHING CHARACTERISTICS

15-20.3 cm (6-7.88 in)

Similar to the preceding species *C. ypsilophorus* (and perhaps a subspecies), but generally smaller in size.

Reader's Digest, 1977, p.142 and pl. p.142.

GENERAL DISTRIBUTION

Australia-Indonesia: Australia, New Guinea, and the Lesser Sunda Islands, Indonesia. (May have occurred naturally in New Zealand.)

INTRODUCED DISTRIBUTION

Introduced successfully to New Zealand and Fiji.

GENERAL HABITS

Status: common. *Habitat:* open grassland and scrub in the vicinity of swamps. *Gregariousness:* singly, pairs, or coveys up to 6 and occasionally 15 or more.

Movements: nomadic. *Foods:* seeds, buds, insects and their larvae. *Breeding:* throughout the year (?). *Nest:* similar to preceding species. *Eggs:* 4-6 recorded, but probably as for preceding species.

Reader's Digest, 1977, p.142.

NOTES ON INTRODUCTIONS

New Zealand. Brown Quail (and more than likely some Swamp Quail) were imported to New Zealand for release between 1866 and 1912 (Thomson, 1922). The Canterbury Acclimatisation Society introduced them in 1866 (one pair), 1868 (five birds) and in 1871 (?). The Auckland society imported them in 1864 (four) and in 1871 (510), and the Otago society released some in 1868 (three) and in 1870 (nine) on Green Island off Dunedin. The Southland society liberated four at Wallacetown in 1872, twenty-five at Awarua Plains in 1911 and some at Mason Bay on Stewart Island in 1912.

Brown Quail, *Coturnix australis*

By 1877 Brown Quail had become common in parts of the North Island but were almost unknown in the South Island. In 1885 the species was reported to be rapidly increasing in numbers along the west coast between Waikanae and Manawatu, and on the east coast at Wairarapa. They were common in the Bay of Plenty in 1913 and have remained so since that date. In 1915-17 they were said to be increasing at Waimarino and were very common in the Auckland district. Oliver (1955) records that Brown Quail are plentiful around the Bay of Plenty, and northwards, and also on Three Kings and Mayor islands. They had been recorded on Mokohinau and Little Barrier islands before 1955 but were apparently scarce in Taranaki, Hawke's Bay and Wellington provinces on the mainland.

Brown Quail are now established, but are restricted in distribution and only locally common in the North Island, and also occur on Three Kings, Poor Knights, Alderman, Mayor, Great and Little Barrier islands. (Wodzicki, 1965). According to Falla *et al* (1966) the species may have reached New Zealand unaided as they appear to occur naturally on many of the offshore islands. The race introduced to New Zealand was *C.a. australis* (Condon, 1975).

Fiji. According to Condon (1975) the Brown Quail has been introduced successfully in Fiji. Mercer (1966) and Blackburn (1971) report that they are established on Viti Levu and Vanua Levu.

DAMAGE
None known.

BLUE-BREASTED QUAIL
(King Quail, Painted Quail, Chinese Quail, Pigmy Quail)
Coturnix chinensis (Linnaeus)

DISTINGUISHING CHARACTERISTICS
10.8-15 cm (3.96-5.9 in). 42.7-57 g (1.51-2.01 oz)

Upper parts dark brown with black, and streaked white; face below eye and throat black, bordered white; cheeks white; face above eye, sides of neck, breast and flanks blue-grey; abdomen and under tail-coverts chestnut; bill black. Female: throat white; underparts densely barred black.
Ali and Ripley, vol.2, 1968-74, pp.42-44 and pl.23, fig.7, opp. p.112.
Reader's Digest, 1977, p.143 and pl. p.143.

GENERAL DISTRIBUTION
Asia-Australia: from India, Sri Lanka and Bangladesh to south-eastern China, the Philippines, Indonesia, New Guinea and northern and eastern Australia.

INTRODUCED DISTRIBUTION
Introduced successfully to Guam Island, and in south-eastern Australia; introduced successfully but now extinct on Mauritius, Réunion (?) and the Hawaiian Islands. Possibly introduced, unsuccessfully, in New Zealand.

GENERAL HABITS
Status: common; common aviary bird. *Habitat:* open country, grasslands, crops and swampy heaths. *Gregariousness:* solitary, pairs, or small flocks (family parties) of 5-6 and up to 40 birds. *Movements:* sedentary and nomadic. *Foods:* seeds, green vegetable material, buds, leaves, insects and small invertebrates. *Breeding:* most months of the year; Mar-Aug (India); Jan-Aug (Malaysia). *Nest:* depression on the ground, lined with grass and roofed with a canopy of bent grass. *Eggs:* 4, 5-10.
Robinson and Chasen, vol.3, 1936, pp.13-14.
Ali and Ripley, vol.2, 1968-74, pp.42-44.
Reader's Digest, 1977, p.143.

NOTES ON INTRODUCTIONS
Australia. Six Blue-breasted Quail may have been introduced into Victoria in 1862 (McCance, 1962). Ryan (1906) indicates that the species was introduced

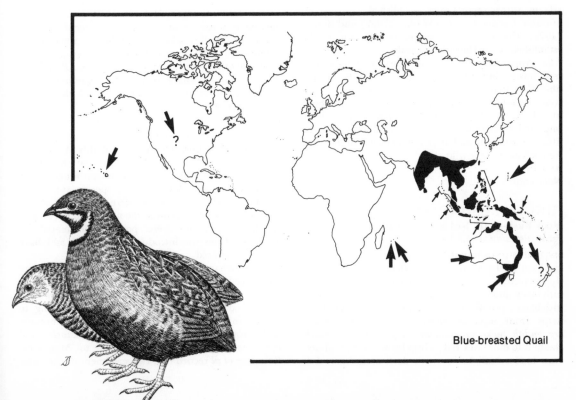

Blue-breasted Quail

in 1864 when eighty were liberated near Melbourne and seventy on Phillip Island, and sixty more in 1872. There may have been some released at later dates at Melbourne and on Phillip Island (Condon, 1975) but details appear to be lacking. A pair are said to have been found in the wild east of Perth in the early 1970s, and two males were captured at Kelmscott in Western Australia in 1976, but these are thought to have been aviary escapees.

Mauritius. The race *C.c. chinensis* has been introduced and established on Mauritius (Peters, 1934). They were introduced in the first half of the eighteenth century but were practically exterminated by the introduced Indian mongoose (Rountree *et al*, 1952; Benedict, 1957).

The species was apparently common there in the early 1900s (Meinertzhagen, 1912) and may still have occurred there in the late 1960s (Rutgers and Norris, 1970). However, Staub (1976) indicates that it is now extinct on Mauritius.

Réunion. The race *chinensis* has been introduced and established (Peters, 1934) on Réunion and was apparently there in the late 1960s (Rutgers and Norris, 1970). Staub (1976) records that it has never done well on Réunion and that it may well be extinct at this time.

Guam. Birds from the Philippines *(C.c. lineata)* were introduced from Manila to Guam in 1894 (Wetmore, 1919 in Peters, 1931). They are apparently still established there (Mayr, 1945), but are confined to the grasslands in the southern part of the island (Stophlet, 1946).

Hawaiian Islands. Blue-breasted Quail were brought from the Orient to Kauai in the Hawaiian Islands in 1910, and became established there. They were later taken to other islands but were unsuccessful (Munro, 1960). Lewin (1971) records that eight birds of unknown origin were liberated on the Puu Waawaa Ranch, Hawaii, in 1961 but disappeared after their release. Munro reports them established on the island of Oahu, but according to Walker (1967) and Berger (1972) the race *chinensis* is not known to be established in the Hawaiian Islands.

USA. Apparently Blue-breasted Quail may have been introduced, but there appear no records of any liberations in the United States.

New Zealand. Blue-breasted Quail may have been introduced to New Zealand in 1897 when some were imported (Thomson, 1922), but there appears to be little information and it is not known whether any were released in the wild.

DAMAGE
None known.

JUNGLE BUSH-QUAIL
(Rock Bush-quail, Red Bush-quail)
Perdicula asiatica (Latham)

DISTINGUISHING CHARACTERISTICS
15-17 cm (5.9-6.69 in). 78 g (2.75 oz)
Upper parts fulvous-brown, streaked and mottled with black and buff; underparts white, closely barred with black; prominent buff and chestnut superciliary stripe from forehead down sides of neck (race *argoondah* lacks superciliary stripe); throat patch chestnut to dull brick red; wings brown, vermiculated dark brown; tail brown with dark cross bars; bill

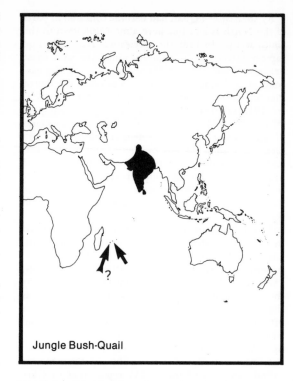

Jungle Bush-Quail

blackish with blue-grey base. Female: lower parts pale pinkish rufous; throat patch paler or lacking.
Ali and Ripley, vol.2, 1968-74, pp.45-51 and figs. 1 and 2, pl.21, opp. p.64.

GENERAL DISTRIBUTION
Asia: India from Kashmir and the outer Himalayas, south to Sri Lanka.

INTRODUCED DISTRIBUTION
Introduced to Mauritius, probably successfully but now extinct, and to Réunion where it may still occur.

GENERAL HABITS
Status: fairly common. *Habitat:* scrub country, open deciduous forest, stony grasslands. *Gregariousness:* coveys or small flocks of 5-20 birds. *Movements:* sedentary. *Foods:* grass and weed seeds, grain, tender shoots, lentils, termites and other insects. *Breeding:* Aug-Apr, but possibly longer; monogamous. *Nest:* slight depression at base of grass tussock, lined with grass. *Eggs:* 4-8.
Ali and Ripley, vol.2, 1968-74, pp.45-51.

NOTES ON INTRODUCTIONS
Mauritius. The Bush-Quail was probably at one time an exotic resident of the island of Mauritius (Rountree *et al*, 1952). Some were introduced from India at an early date and the species apparently became established. They were reported to be confined to the dry plains of the north and north-west of the island, but were possibly decimated by predation from the introduced mongoose and have since disappeared.

Meinertzhagen (1912) indicates that they were introduced prior to 1812 by the French, but Staub (1976) gives the date as 1905. They were still established there but scarce in 1912 according to Meinertzhagen, but Staub says they never became acclimatised. Evidently two races, *P.a. asiatica* and *P.a. argoondah,* were introduced to Mauritius. Rountree *et al* record that two specimens of the latter race, collected in Mauritius, are present in the Natural History Museum in Paris.

Réunion. Staub (1976) indicates that the Bush-Quail could still occur on Réunion. Presumably, it was introduced at about the same time as it was on Mauritius.

DAMAGE
None known.

FORMOSAN HILL PARTRIDGE
Arborophila crudigularis (Swinhoe)

DISTINGUISHING CHARACTERISTICS
27 cm (10.62 in)

Upper parts olive-brown, each feather barred black; fore-crown ashy; nape mixed chestnut, black and white, forming an indistinct ring; wings blackish brown with chestnut and green tinge; lores, ears, cheeks, chin, upper throat and centre of abdomen white; behind eye and lower throat black; breast and flanks greyish; under tail-coverts black, barred yellowish white; bill black. Female: similar but spurless.

Hachisuka and Udagawa, *Q. J. Taiwan Mus.,* vol.4, pts.1 and 2, 1951, 180 pp.

Etchécopar and Hüe, 1978, p.233 and pl.7, p.224.

GENERAL DISTRIBUTION
Taiwan.

INTRODUCED DISTRIBUTION
Introduced unsuccessfully in Japan.

GENERAL HABITS
Status: fairly common? *Habitat:* forest and thick undergrowth in mountains. *Gregariousness:* small flocks. *Movements:* sedentary. *Foods:* insects and vegetable material. *Breeding:* May-June. *Nest:* depression on the ground with leaves, near the root of a tree. *Eggs:* little information, possibly 2 or more.

Hachisuka and Udagawa, *Q. J. Taiwan Mus.,* vol.4, pts.1-2, 1951, 180 pp.

Formosan Hill Partridge

NOTES ON INTRODUCTIONS
Japan. The Formosan Hill Partridge was introduced from Taiwan to Japan in 1924 but failed to become established (Kuroda, 1937).

RED-CRESTED WOOD PARTRIDGE
(Roulroul, Crested Green Wood Partridge)
Rollulus roulroul (Scopoli)

DISTINGUISHING CHARACTERISTICS
23-27.5 cm (9-10.64 in)

Generally dark glossy green-blue; crest light red to

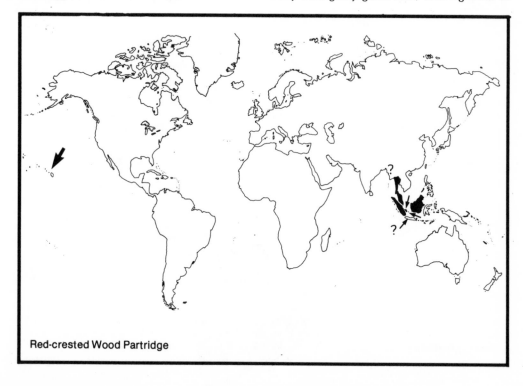
Red-crested Wood Partridge

maroon; orbital skin and patch on bill red; crown patch white; face black; wings dark brown; back green, remainder blackish blue; bill black. *Female:* Generally green; scapulars chestnut; head dark grey; lacks red crest.

Robinson and Chasen, vol. 3, 1936, pp.10-11 and pl.3, opp. p.10.

King *et al*, 1976, pl.9, no.173, opp. p.96.

GENERAL DISTRIBUTION

Asia: peninsular Burma, Malaysia, southern Thailand, Sumatra, Bangka, Belitung, Borneo and Java (?).

INTRODUCED DISTRIBUTION

Introduced unsuccessfully in the Hawaiian Islands.

GENERAL HABITS

Status: common. *Habitat:* dense forest, secondary forest, bamboo groves and old clearings. *Gregariousness:* singly, pairs or family groups of 4-5 and up to 15. *Movements:* sedentary. *Foods:* worms, berries, seeds, fruits, plant parts, insects and other small invertebrates. *Breeding:* probably all year. *Nest:* domed structure on the ground of dead leaves and stems, with a side entrance. *Eggs:* 4, 5-6, 10.

Robinson and Chasen, vol.3, 1936, pp.10-11.

Gooders, vol.3, 1969, p.689.

NOTES ON INTRODUCTIONS

Hawaiian Islands. Introduced from Singapore to the island of Oahu in 1924, the Red-crested Wood Partridge failed to become established in the Hawaiian Islands (Munro, 1960; Walker, 1967).

DAMAGE

None known.

BAMBOO PARTRIDGE
(Chinese Partridge, Chinese Bamboo Partridge)
Bambusicola thoracica (Temminck)

DISTINGUISHING CHARACTERISTICS
28-30 cm (11-11.81 in)

Face, sides of neck, throat and lower breast red-brown; stripe above eye greyish; throat grey; underparts yellowish; red-brown spots on flanks; upper parts brown; back olive-brown marked chestnut, mottled buff, white and black; bill brownish. *Female:* lacks spurs, and is paler and smaller.

Cheng, 1963, pp.269-270 and pl.10, no.34.

Etchécopar and Hüe, 1978, p.236 and pl.7, p.224.

GENERAL DISTRIBUTION

Asia: southern China from southern Shensi and Szechwan to Fukien and Kwangsi; extreme northern Burma; also on the island of Taiwan.

INTRODUCED DISTRIBUTION

Introduced successfully in Japan and the Hawaiian Islands.

Introduced unsuccessfully in the USA and the USSR.

GENERAL HABITS

Status: uncommon, often kept in captivity by Chinese. *Habitat:* forest, bamboo groves, bushy weedy thickets usually adjacent to cultivation. *Gregariousness:* coveys. *Movements:* sedentary. *Foods:* fruits, leaves, seeds, peas, grain, locusts, termites and ants. *Breeding:* May-July (Burma). *Nest:* on the ground. *Eggs:* 3-7 or more (?).

Smythies, 1953, p.445.

Cheng, 1963, pp.270-271.

NOTES ON INTRODUCTIONS

Japan. Bamboo Partridges *(B.t. thoracica)* were imported from south China in 1919 and *B.t. sonorivox* from Taiwan in 1924 (Kuroda, 1937). They were probably liberated at these dates. Some may have been released in 1920 (Kaburaki, 1934) and some in about 1930 (Sakane, 1960). Sakane indicates that mainland Chinese birds were released in about 1930 and became established and thrived, and that Taiwan birds were also introduced.

Kaburaki (1940) reported that Bamboo Partridges were widespread in Japan proper around 1940, but

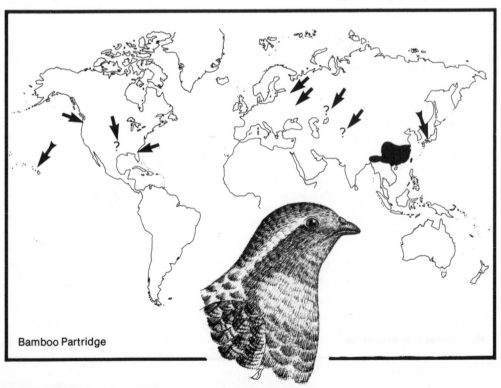

Bamboo Partridge

Sakane in 1960 could only find a small group of twenty birds in a limited area near the site of the original 1930 introductions in the Hyogo area. However, Yamashina (1961) says they are breeding on Honshū, Seven Islands of Izu, Shikoku and Kyushū. More recently the Ornithological Society of Japan (1974) records that *B.t. thoracica* has spread widely in Honshū and southwards since 1919 from Tokyo's Kanagawa area. *B.t. sonorivox*, which was released at Kōbe on Honshū in 1931 and probably also at Koshigaya in the Saitama Prefecture, is still established in the Kōbe area.

Hawaiian Islands. Birds of the Chinese race *B.t. thoracica* were introduced in 1959 to the island of Maui from Japan (Walker, 1967). They were establishing and breeding on this island in the early 1960s (Western States Exotic Game Bird Committee, 1961) and were being hunted there in 1967 (Bump, 1968).

At present the species is still well established on Maui (Hawaiian Audubon Society, 1975). Introductions to the island of Hawaii in 1961 and 1965, when twelve birds from Californian and Texan game farms were released, were unsuccessful in becoming established (Lewin, 1971).

USA. According to Gottschalk (1967) Bamboo Partridges have been released at various times in the United States from 1904 on, but to date have been unsuccessful in becoming established. The species was introduced on a large scale in Stevens, Spokane, Yakima and Garfield counties of Washington (Phillips, 1928) some time between 1904 and 1928. Many Bamboo Partridges were being kept on game farms in Oregon in the 1960s for eventual release into the wild (Western States Exotic Game Bird Committee, 1961). Bump (1968) indicates that some were liberated recently, but he felt (1967) it was too early to ascertain their success. In 1968 (Bohl, 1968) it was indicated that experimental introduction of this species in the south-eastern United States had been discontinued through lack of success.

USSR. Introductions of Bamboo Partridges in the Ukraine, the RSFSR in the 1960s, western Siberia, Bashkivia in 1961, and in Moscow from 1956 on, have all been unsuccessful to date (Yanushevich, 1966).

DAMAGE
None known.

TRAGOPAN

Tragopan sp.

NOTES ON INTRODUCTIONS
USA. Two females of a species of Tragopan were reported to have been liberated on Protection Island, Washington, in the early 1880s together with golden pheasants (Merriam, C. H., Report of Ornithology and Mammalogy for 1888, 1889, p.487), but the species did not become established there (Phillips, 1928). Phillips records that Cabot's, Temminck's and the Satyra Tragopan were imported to the United States from 1900 on, but that no releases of them were known up until 1928.

New Zealand. Temminck's Tragopans *(Tragopan temmincki)* were imported to New Zealand in 1871, but it is not known if any were released into the wild (Thomson, 1922).

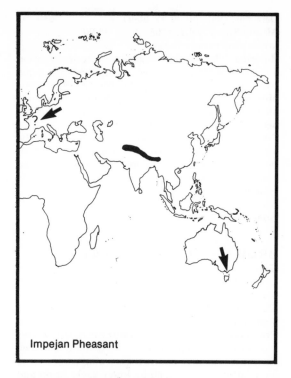

Impejan Pheasant

IMPEJAN PHEASANT
(Monal Pheasant, Himalayan Monal, Impeyan)
Lophophorus impejanus (Latham)

DISTINGUISHING CHARACTERISTICS
55-72 cm (21.65-28.34 in). 1.8-2.3 kg (3.96-5 lb)
Head, throat and crest iridescent metallic green; bare skin around eye bluish; nape and sides of neck reddish copper; mantle green; wings purple and blue; lower back white; underparts black; tail rufous-chestnut; bill blackish, with a white band.
Female: generally dark brown, upper parts marked pale buff; lower back barred buff and brown; throat and collar white; tail brown barred rufous.
Delacour, 1965, pp.95-97 and pl. opp. p.98.
Ali and Ripley, vol. 1, 1968-74, pp.88-90 and fig. 9, pl.21, opp. p.64.

GENERAL DISTRIBUTION
Asia: south-central Asia in the Himalayas from Afghanistan east to Bhutan and south-east Tibet; also probably in extreme south-west China.

INTRODUCED DISTRIBUTION
Introduced unsuccessfully in Australia and probably in France.

GENERAL HABITS
Status: common and abundant in some areas.
Habitat: rocky mountain forest, open forest on slopes, mainly between 2000 and 3700 metres (6 500 and 12 000 feet). *Gregariousness:* singly, parties of 3-4 birds, and small flocks to 30 birds (sexes separate in winter); small flocks of males in breeding season.
Movements: sedentary, but move to higher altitudes in spring. *Foods:* buds, berries, fruits, shoots, seeds, roots, tubers and insects and their larvae. *Breeding:* Apr-July. *Nest:* depression on the ground, with vegetative cover, among rocks or against tree stumps, and lined with leaves, moss and debris. *Eggs:* 2, 4-6, 8.

Delacour, 1965, pp.90-95, 96-97.
Ali and Ripley, vol.2, 1968-74, pp.88-90.

NOTES ON INTRODUCTIONS

Australia. The Royal Zoological and Acclimatisation Society of Victoria liberated this species in a game park (Gembrook) near Melbourne in 1871. Four birds were also released on Phillip Island, probably at about the same date. The Impejan Pheasant failed to become established in Australia.

France. The Impejan was probably introduced in the wild in France. Etchécopar (1955) indicates that they were introduced with only limited success and the species is not known to have become permanently established there.

DAMAGE

None known.

BROWN-EARED PHEASANT
(Hoki)

Crossoptilon mantchuricum Swinhoe

DISTINGUISHING CHARACTERISTICS

88.5-100 cm (34.66-39.37 in), tail 55 cm (21.65 in); about 1.7 kg (3.74 lb)

Crown black; chin, throat and stiff ear-coverts white; face wattles crimson; neck black, shading to brown on lower mantle and wings; wing-coverts and secondaries glossed purplish; lower back, rump and upper tail-coverts white; underparts and flanks dark brown; tail dull white with brownish black terminal portion; bill reddish brown. *Female:* lacks spurs.

Delacour, 1965, p.196 and pl.19 opp. p.198.
Etchécopar and Hüe, 1978, p.246 and pl.9, p.256.

GENERAL DISTRIBUTION

China: in the mountains of northern China (southern Charhar in Inner Mongolia, northern and north-west Hopeh and Shansi, south to the region of Taiyuan). Said to be practically extinct now in Hopeh (Cheng, 1963).

INTRODUCED DISTRIBUTION

Introduced unsuccessfully in Alaska.

GENERAL HABITS

Status: range considerably reduced, numbers reduced and the species is considered to be in some danger of extinction in the wild. *Habitat:* mountain regions with rocky terrain and covered with grass. *Gregariousness:* pairs and small flocks of 10-30. *Movements:* sedentary. *Foods:* tubers, bulbs, acorns, roots, seeds, leaves, stems, shoots, insects and earthworms. *Breeding:* little information, probably Apr-May; monogamous. *Nest:* depression on the ground between rocks and grass, sometimes (?) lined with grass and leaves. *Eggs:* 5, 9-14 (in captivity 12-16).

Cheng, 1963, pp.285-286.
Delacour, 1965, pp.187-188, 196-197.

NOTES ON INTRODUCTIONS

Alaska. Twelve adult Brown-eared Pheasant from Wisconsin, USA, were released at Petersburg on Mitkof Island in 1940 but they failed to become established there (Gabrielson and Lincoln, 1959; Burris, 1965).

DAMAGE

None known.

SILVER PHEASANT
Lophura nycthemera (Linnaeus)

DISTINGUISHING CHARACTERISTICS

50-125 cm (19.68-49.21 in), tail of males 51.8-67.5 cm (20.11-26.39 in); females about 1.6 kg (3.52 lb)

Crest, chin, throat and underparts black (crest often white); face wattles bright red, upper parts white with thin wavy black lines; curved tail white; bill white. *Female:* olive-brown finely mottled with dusky lines; central tail feathers olive-brown, outer feathers black with brown and white lines; crest brownish

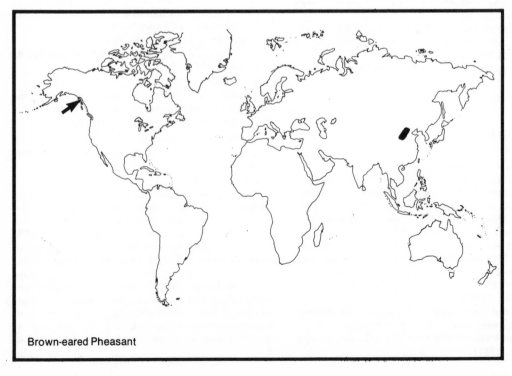

Brown-eared Pheasant

158

black; throat brownish white; belly brown, sometimes streaked grey.

Delacour, 1965, pp.139, 141-143, 145-147, 149-151, 153-155 and pl.7, opp. p.128.

Etchecopar and Hüe, 1978, pp.252-253 and pl.10, p.257.

GENERAL DISTRIBUTION

Asia: in mountains of southern China (Yunnan and Tonkin), Burma (Shan States), northern Laos, south-west Kampuchea, North Vietnam, central South Vietnam, Thailand and Hainan.

INTRODUCED DISTRIBUTION

Introduced unsuccessfully in New Zealand, Hawaiian Islands, USA, Canada, France, Great Britain and Colombia. Introduced successfully in the USSR and became feral in Western Australia, but now extirpated.

GENERAL HABITS

Status: uncommon to rare; range probably now greatly reduced and the species appears to exist chiefly as an aviary bird. *Habitat:* mountain forest and hills, bamboo thickets and bush mainly between 600 and 200 metres (2000 and 6500 feet).

Gregariousness: pairs or small groups. *Movements:* sedentary. *Foods:* berries, fruits, seeds, buds, shoots, flower petals, leaves, roots, tubers, bulbs, insects including termites, and grubs and worms. *Breeding:* Apr-May; polygamous. *Nest:* scrape on the ground under cover of vegetation. *Eggs:* 4-6, 8 (in captivity 4-6 and in zoos 6-14 known).

Cheng, 1963, pp.287-290.

Delacour, 1965, pp.141-143, 145-147, 149-151, 154-155.

NOTES ON INTRODUCTIONS

New Zealand. Silver Pheasants were introduced and liberated in New Zealand by the Hon. H. Walton, near Whangerei in 1868. Further birds were imported by the Auckland Acclimatisation Society in 1870 and by the Otago society in 1871, but it is not known

Silver Pheasant, *Lophura nycthemera*

whether any further liberations occurred (Thomson, 1922). The species did not become established in the wild in New Zealand.

Hawaiian Islands. The Silver Pheasant was introduced in 1865 (Walker, 1967) and/or in 1870 (Berger, 1972) and possibly at some later dates in the Hawaiian Islands (Munro, 1960). Some may have been introduced in 1867, and again after 1932 when some were apparently raised at a game farm and liberated on Oahu (Schwartz and Schwartz, 1951). The species has failed to become established in the Hawaiian Islands.

USA. Some Silver Pheasants were introduced in Washington State (Gottschalk, 1967) and there were probably many more liberations in other parts of the United States at various times. The Silver Pheasant has not become established anywhere in North America. In about 1884 a shipment containing Silver and other pheasants was made to Washington by Judge O. N. Denny (Jewett *et al,* 1953). Some of these birds were released on Protection Island but failed to become established there. Some were placed on Goat Island in San Francisco Bay, California, many years

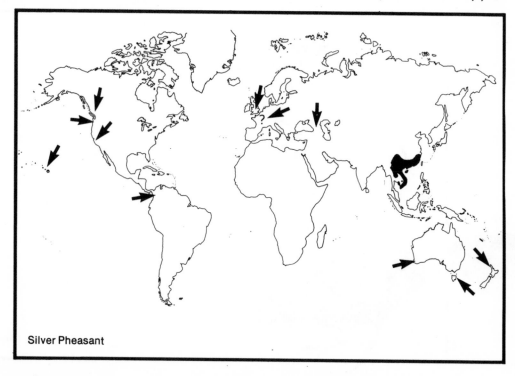

Silver Pheasant

ago, but also failed to become established (Phillips, 1928).

Canada. The Silver Pheasant was introduced into British Columbia some time prior to 1925 but failed to become established (Phillips, 1928).

USSR. Apparently the Silver Pheasant became established in Transcaucasia in the 1920s but some time later failed (Yanushevich, 1966). It is not known whether the species died out or succumbed to shooting pressure.

France. Silver Pheasants have been kept in parks and for hunting in France, but there seem to have been no attempts to acclimatise them in the wild (Etchécopar, 1955).

Great Britain. According to Lever (1977), Silver Pheasants were released at Rutland in the 1880s, in the following ten years at Woburn (Bedfordshire), at Cairnsmore (Galloway), at Mount Stewart (died out by the 1920s) and at Richmond Park (Surrey) in 1928-29, but they did not survive. Some may have been released in a park north-east of Ayr in about 1905, but the Silver Pheasant has not become established anywhere in the wild in Great Britain.

Colombia. Attempts by hunt clubs and the Ministry of Agriculture to introduce Silver Pheasants and other pheasants into Colombia, South America, have been unsuccessful (Sick, 1968).

Australia. Silver Pheasants were kept in semi-captivity by a roadhouse proprietor in the Porongorups area of Western Australia for many years. When the roadhouse closed down the birds were allowed to wander off and some became established in one or two areas of the Porongorup ranges. In 1976 there may have been fifteen to twenty birds present in the ranges, which are one of Western Australia's National Parks. The colonies are now believed to have been extirpated. Some were released in Tasmania (Sharland, 1958), possibly at an early date, but failed to become established there. They were imported into

Victoria in 1858 (Balmford, 1978) but there is no record of any being liberated at this time.

DAMAGE
None known.

KALIJ PHEASANT
(Nepal Kalij, White-crested Kalij, Nepal Pheasant, Kaleej)
Lophura leucomelana (Latham)

DISTINGUISHING CHARACTERISTICS
50-73 cm (20-29 in). 0.5-1.7 kg (1-3.7 lb)
Crest black; head and neck purplish black; mantle bluish black; lower back and rump black with white terminal fringe; tail black, tipped brown; wings, chin and throat blackish brown; breast and flanks grey to whitish; face wattles scarlet; bill greenish white, dusky at tip (races vary considerably and the above description is nearer the nominate). *Female:* crest brown; upper parts brown, finely spotted black and edged grey; wing-coverts and underparts edged white.
Delacour, 1965, pp.126-127, 129-131, 133-138 and pl.7, opp. p.128.
Ali and Ripley, vol.2, 1968-74, pp.94-102 and figs. 2 and 8, pl.23, opp. p.112.

GENERAL DISTRIBUTION
Asia: southern Asia from northern Pakistan east through Burma, Thailand, Indochina, to southern China and Hainan.

INTRODUCED DISTRIBUTION
Introduced successfully in the Hawaiian Islands. Introductions in the USA and Alaska appear to have been unsuccessful.

GENERAL HABITS
Status: still fairly common in some areas. *Habitat:* forest with thick undergrowth, ravines, bamboo thickets and dense scrub. *Gregariousness:* pairs or family parties. *Movements:* sedentary, but move to

Kalij Pheasant

higher altitudes in summer. *Foods:* tubers, roots, stems, pods, seeds, berries, fruits, grain, young shoots, worms, insects and their larvae, and small reptiles. *Breeding:* Feb-Oct; male polygamous. *Nest:* collection of leaves, grass and rubbish, in a scrape on the ground, near a rock or grass tuft. *Eggs:* 4, 6-9, 15. Delacour, 1965, pp.127-128, 130-131, 133-138. Ali and Ripley, vol.2, 1968-74, pp.94-102.

NOTES ON INTRODUCTIONS

Hawaiian Islands. Kalij Pheasants were introduced from the United States in 1962 by the leaseholders of the State-owned Puu Waawaa Ranch (Mull, 1978) on Hawaii. At this time sixty-seven birds from Michigan and Texan game farms were released on the ranch (Lewin, 1971). Both Walker (1967) and Berger (1972) say they are not known to be established in the Hawaiian Islands, but the Hawaiian Audubon Society (1975) indicates that they may now be established and breeding on the island of Hawaii. More recent information indicates that the species has now spread from the original site of introduction on Hawaii to other North Kona areas. In 1977 it was added to the official bird list and can now be hunted on the island (Mull).

Alaska. Twelve adult Kalij Pheasants originating from Wisconsin, USA, were released at Petersburg, Mitkof Island, in 1941 but failed to become established there (Gabrielson and Lincoln, 1959; Burris, 1965).

USA. The only known early introduction of Kalij Pheasants into the United States, occurred when the game commission of Connecticut purchased five pairs from W. J. MacKenson, and released them somewhere in that State before 1926 (Phillips, 1928).

In Virginia, 1068 Kalij Pheasants *(L.l. hamiltonii)* were released, between 1958 and 1966 (Hart, 1967) and were said to be exhibiting 'good survival' in woodland mountains (Bohl, 1968). Tuttle (1963) records that 138 were released in April 1963 in the Jefferson National Forest in Giles County. Bump (1968) says that it is too early to ascertain the success of the species in the United States, and Gottschalk (1967) indicates that further attempts were being considered in the late 1960s. There appears to be no recent information on the species' success in North America and more than likely it has failed to become established. Blake (1975) says it has been stated that the species is 'free' in a park in Vancouver, British Columbia, Canada.

DAMAGE
None known.

SWINHOE PHEASANT
(Swinhoe's Pheasant, Swinhoe's Kalij)
Lophura swinhoei (Gould)

DISTINGUISHING CHARACTERISTICS
Male 80 cm (31.49 in), female 52.5 cm (20.5 in)
Crest white with some blue-black feathers; head, neck and underparts dark blue; upper back with large white patch; lower back, rump and upper tail-coverts metallic blue; scapulars maroon; wing-coverts black with metallic green border; central tail long and curved, white, remainder blue; face wattles red; bill greyish, black at base. *Female:* lacks crest; crown chestnut-brown, barred black; face and throat grey; breast buff with V-shaped black markings; upper

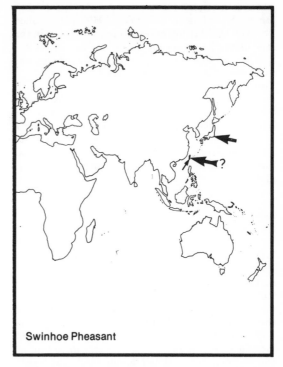

Swinhoe Pheasant

back, scapulars and wing-coverts chestnut with black borders and buff central markings; lower back, rump and tail-coverts mottled black and brown.
Delacour, 1965, pp.161-162 and pl.7, opp. p.128.
Etchécopar and Hüe, 1978, pp.253-254 and pl. 10, p. 257.

GENERAL DISTRIBUTION
Taiwan.

INTRODUCED DISTRIBUTION
Successfully (?) re-introduced to Taiwan. Introduced unsuccessfully to Japan.

GENERAL HABITS
Status: extremely rare; in some danger of extinction, and now exists chiefly as an aviary bird. *Habitat:* mountain forests. *Gregariousness:* no information. *Movements:* sedentary. *Foods:* seeds, buds, shoots, and insects. *Breeding:* no information (early spring?). *Nest:* scrape on the ground, under cover of vegetation. *Eggs:* 6-10, 12.
Delacour, 1965, p.163.

Swinhoe Pheasant,
Lophura swinhoei

NOTES ON INTRODUCTIONS

Japan. According to Kaburaki (1940) the Swinhoe Pheasant was thriving in certain parts of Tokyo in the late 1930s. There appear no further records of the species in that country and doubtless it was unsuccessful in becoming established.

Taiwan. The Taiwan authorities were presented with thirty Swinhoe Pheasants by the Ornamental Pheasant Trust at Great Wichingham, England, for release at Mount Alishan in the spring of 1967 (Wayre, 1966). Six pairs were released in the central mountain range, near Hsitou, in an experimental forest managed by the Taiwan National University, and another nine pairs were kept by the Taiwan authorities for their own breeding scheme (Wayre, 1969).

DAMAGE
None known.

CRESTED FIREBACK PHEASANT
Lophura ignita (Shaw and Nodder)
DISTINGUISHING CHARACTERISTICS
55-70 cm (19.68-27.55 in)

Face wattles blue; neck, upper back, crest and upper wings dark purplish blue; lower back, rump flanks and belly bronze-red; upper tail-coverts fringed metallic blue; central tail-feathers cinnamon-buff or whitish, remainder of tail bluish black; abdomen black; bill whitish. *Female:* head, crest and upper parts chestnut; wing and tail-coverts finely spotted black; tail black; chin and throat white; breast, flanks and thighs chestnut to dark brown with white borders.

Delacour, 1965, pp.169, 171-172, 175 and pl.18, opp. p.178.

GENERAL DISTRIBUTION
Asia. from Thailand (Isthmus of Kra south) throughout the Malay Peninsula, Sumatra and Borneo.

Crested Fireback Pheasant

162

INTRODUCED DISTRIBUTION
Possibly or probably introduced to the Isle of Bangka (Sumatra). Introduced unsuccessfully in Australia.

GENERAL HABITS
Status: little information, probably still fairly common. *Habitat:* lowland jungle and forest. *Gregariousness:* pairs and small groups or family parties of 5-6 birds. *Movements:* sedentary. *Foods:* seeds, vegetation, grubs and insects. *Breeding:* little information, Apr (Malacca). *Nest:* scrape on the ground. *Eggs:* 4-8.

Delacour, 1965, pp.168, 171-172, 173-174, 176.

NOTES ON INTRODUCTIONS
Bangka. Rutgers and Norris (1970) record that *L.i. ignita* has been introduced, and Wayre (1969) indicates that the species has probably been introduced to the Isle of Bangka.

Australia. Crested Fireback Pheasants were liberated with Impejan Pheasants in a game park (Gembrook) near Melbourne, Victoria, in 1871, but apparently failed to become established (McCance, 1962).

DAMAGE
None known.

RED JUNGLE FOWL
(Jungle Fowl, Common Fowl, Domestic Fowl)
Gallus gallus Linnaeus
DISTINGUISHING CHARACTERISTICS
37.9-75 cm (15-29.52 in). 0.4-1.3 kg (0.88-2.87 lb)

Serrated comb, wattles, naked throat and face scarlet; crown and neck feathers golden brown to red; mantle and wing-coverts metallic green; scapulars, back and median wing-coverts reddish brown to orange-red on rump; wing primaries blackish brown, secondaries rufous; tail metallic green; underparts black; bill reddish at base, upper mandible brown, lower pale horn. *Female:* duller; crown and nape reddish; neck dull brown and yellowish; upper parts dull brown with black lines; breast reddish brown; remainder of underparts paler; comb small. (The description is of the wild form and feral domestic varieties may differ considerably.)

Delacour, 1965, pp.108-109, 110-111, 113 and pl.5, opp. p.112.

Ali and Ripley, vol.2, 1968-74, pp.102-106 and fig.3, pl.23, opp. p.112.

GENERAL DISTRIBUTION
Asia: from the north-western Himalayas, northern India to southern China (s-e Yunnan and Kwangsi), the Indochinese region generally, Hainan, Sumatra and (?) Java.

INTRODUCED DISTRIBUTION
Probably introduced and became feral in many areas of the Indonesia-Philippines region; introduced and became feral in many parts of Micronesia, Melanesia and Polynesia; introduced successfully in Réunion and the Grenadines (Kick-em-Jenny); feral in Australia (Capricorn Group) and probably in New Zealand and South Africa; became feral or was introduced in Hispaniola, Isles Glorieuses, Chagos Archipelago and on St Helena, but now extinct. Introduced unsuccessfully in the USA, Trinidad (?) and France (?).

GENERAL HABITS
Status: common; very common as a domestic species.

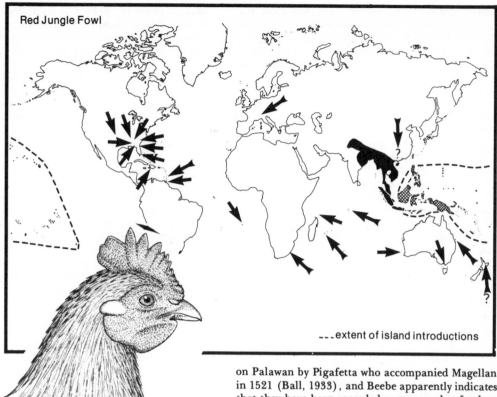

Red Jungle Fowl

---extent of island introductions

Habitat: forest with scrub, near cultivation, secondary forest, woodlands, oil palm estates, banks of rivers and rice stubble. *Gregariousness:* small parties (1 male to 2-5 females) and occasionally larger flocks of 10-20 birds in winter. *Movements;* sedentary. *Foods:* grain, vegetable shoots, buds, nuts, seeds, fruits, berries, worms, spiders, termites. *Breeding:* Mar-May (India), and Dec-May (Malaysia) but possibly most of the year. *Nest:* shallow depression on ground, lined with leaves and undergrowth. *Eggs:* 4, 5-9, 12.

Delacour, 1965, pp.105-107, 109-111, 113.
Ali and Ripley, vol.2, 1968-1974, pp.102-106.

NOTES ON INTRODUCTIONS

Indonesia and the Philippines. There appears to be some doubt as to whether the Jungle Fowl has been introduced or is native to Java. Ball (1933) says that Beebe (*Monograph of the Pheasants,* London, 1921) records that they were native only to Sumatra, and had been recorded as a more or less feral inhabitant of Java. Later authors (Peters, 1934; Mayr, 1945 and Delacour, 1951) record them as a native species. They were certainly domesticated there when Stavorinus visited the island in about 1672 (Ball).

It is also recorded, apparently by Beebe, that Jungle Fowls are absent on Borneo, although they are later recorded to be feral there.

Feral fowl are present on the Lesser Sunda Islands (including Lombok, Timor and Wetar), Palawan, Sulawesi, Borneo and probably many other islands (Peters, 1934; Streseman, 1936; Mayr, 1945; Delacour, 1951). They were noted to be domesticated on Palawan by Pigafetta who accompanied Magellan in 1521 (Ball, 1933), and Beebe apparently indicates that they have been recorded as more or less feral on Timor, Lombok, Balabac and Palawan prior to 1921.

Delacour (1951) suggested that fowl had been introduced to the Philippines at a very early date, but Parkes (1962) indicates it is perhaps an indigenous species. Rabor and Rand (1958) found no hybrid flocks as one would expect if they interbred freely and suggested the birds there may represent different colonisations or introductions. They are, however, feral or 'wild' throughout the area.

The race introduced in this region is *G.g. gallus* (Peters, 1934).

Micronesian, Melanesian and Polynesian Islands. It is probable that early seafaring peoples from southeastern Asia took along the fowl when they colonised these islands. Seafaring Polynesians took chickens on many colonising trips, kept them in semi-domestication and some became wild on nearly all the islands (Mayr, 1945). Certainly they were present on most of the inhabited islands in the sixteenth century, when most of the islands were discovered by Europeans (Ball, 1933).

Ball attempted to reconstruct the status of the fowl when Europeans first arrived in the Pacific by examining the works of the early explorers: fowl appear to have been discovered firstly in the area by Pigafetta (accompanying Magellan in 1521); they were noted in the Marianas at this time and were plentiful in the wild on Tinian (as found by Pascoe in 1742 and by Byron in 1765). They were probably present on Santa Cruz, in the New Hebrides, in 1565, and on the Marquesas were noted by Quiros in 1595. Tasman records them from Namuka in 1642, where they were later noted again by Cook. They were present on Mehetia (Osnaburg Island) in the Society Islands in 1767 when Wallis visited them. He also records them from Niuatoputapu (Keppel Island), 163

Tonga, and on the Tuamotus and Tahiti. Cook also records them from these latter islands and also from Raiatea, Society Islands in 1769, and from Easter Island, Tongatapu and Eua (Tonga) on his visit in 1774. Fowl were earlier mentioned from Easter Island by Roggewein, who discovered Rapanui in 1722, and by Gonzales in 1770. Crozet indicates that they were plentiful on Guam in 1772, and Bligh mentions their presence on Aitutaki (Cook Islands) on his visit in 1789.

With the advent of Europeans in the Pacific it is apparent that European Fowl were introduced in at least some areas. Ball says there is a strong probability that between Cook's discovery of Tahiti in 1767 and the visit of the US Exploring Expedition in 1840, many introductions from Europe had occurred. Certainly, some were stolen by natives, some were given away, and some were left by the Spanish missionaries between 1772 and when they left in 1775. There is some evidence that they were introduced to the Marquesas during this time. Ball concluded that there is little doubt that introductions of European Fowl became more frequent after 1840.

Most of the early references refer to fowl in the possession of the native peoples, but there are a few records of birds in the wild, and they are worthy of mention: Ball records that they were wild in the unfrequented parts of Tahiti, as reported by Peale who accompanied Wilkes in 1840-42. They were wild in the Taioa Valley of Nukuhiva (Marquesas) in 1840, and were said to be descendants of poultry introduced by an English sea captain who visited there not many years before this date.

Many wild fowl existed in the forests around Papeete in the Society Islands when the Whitney South Sea Expedition visited them in 1921. Wild birds were collected, between 1920 and 1926, for the Whitney Collection on six archipelagos in the south Pacific. Specimens were taken on Tahiti, Moorea, Raiatea (Society Islands), Uahuka, Nukuhiva, Hivaoa, Mohotani, Tahuata, Eiao (Marquesas), Tabuai (Austral Islands), Ata (Tonga Islands), Koro, Kio, Makongai, Kambara, Vanua, Mbalavu, Taveuni (Fiji Islands), Efate, Espiritu Santo, and Hiw (New Hebrides).

In more recent times, Mayr (1945) reports the presence of wild fowl on the Marianas, Palau Archipelago, Caroline Island, Samoa, Tonga, Fiji, Tahiti and the Marquesas. Delacour (1954) records them on the Marshall Islands, New Hebrides, and on New Caledonia. Yaldwyn (1952) notes that they are spread through the Samoan Islands, although earlier Armstrong (1932) said they were scarce on Upolu, and are constantly receiving new blood from the domestic birds of the Samoans. Williams (1960) reports them well established on Pitcairn Island and Pearson (1962) from Ocean Island. Lancum and Mougin (1974) record them in the wild on the Gambier Archipelago (Mangareva, Aukena, and Tekava) and in the Tuamotu Archipelago, and Holyoak (1974) found them widespread and common in the mountains far from houses on Tahiti, Moorea, Raiatea, Tahoa and Bora Bora in 1972. Mercer (1966) reports that they are still found on islands which are free of the introduced mongoose such as Bega and Taveuni. Delacour (1966) records that they

still occur on the Isle de Pins, New Caledonia.

Hawaiian Islands. Fowl were undoubtedly introduced to these islands by the early Polynesians. They were certainly present on Kauai when Cook visited the island in 1776.

The species was apparently formerly well known on all the main islands of the Hawaiian group (Ball, 1933; Peterson, 1961), but may have become extinct since about 1900 when a few still existed on Kauai. However, it is said that some were taken to Lanai in 1902, where they were recorded to have existed at least until about the 1940s (Munro, 1960). Fowl were liberated on Niihau some time between about 1940 and 1950 (Fisher, 1951). In 1962 or 1963 *G.g. ferrugineus* from the United States were released in the Hawaiian Islands, but were not known to have become established (Walker, 1967).

The species was common on Kauai in mountain areas and was said to exist on Niihau and on Hawaii in the early 1970s (Berger, 1972). At present the Jungle Fowl appears to be established and breeding on Kauai and Hawaii (Hawaiian Audubon Society, 1975).

Australia. Jungle Fowl were introduced in the Plenty Ranges, Victoria (probably in the 1860s or 80s), and were seen running wild near the railway line at Royal Park as late as 1916 (McCance, 1962). Ryan (1906) records that some were released at Gembrook Reserve, and Jenkins (1977) that eleven were liberated on Phillip Island in 1866. They were liberated on North-West Island (Great Barrier Reef) in about 1880 (Lavery, 1974) and on Heron Island, Capricorn Group in Queensland, in the early 1900s (Tarr, 1950; Storr, 1973). They may still be established locally on that group of islands. Tarr reports that the original birds introduced in this area were gamefowl carried by Japanese guano-traders, but later they interbred with birds taken there from mainland Australia. They are known to have bred on Heron Island and are reported to be increasing in numbers in recent years (Kikkawa and Boles, 1976).

Some fowl were introduced on Rottnest Island, Western Australia, in 1912 (Serventy, 1948), but they are no longer present on that island.

New Zealand. In 1773, Captain Cook liberated fowl in West Bay, Queen Charlotte Sound, but a year later there was no trace of them, although the natives reported that they were seen occasionally.

On his second voyage in 1778 Cook gave some more to the natives to domesticate and liberated further birds. In 1814 a Mr Marsden brought fowl to the Bay of Plenty Islands from Sydney, Australia. According to Thomson (1922), from this date natives acquired them and carried them throughout the country.

The progeny of escaped birds were found in many parts of the North Island from Hawke's Bay to Lake Taupo in the period 1882-1892. In 1840 poultry were landed on Auckland Island during the Ross Expedition, and in 1865 Captain Norman liberated some on Campbell Island, but both introductions were unsuccessful (Thomson).

USA. Some 289 fowl were liberated in western Kentucky between August 1964 and April 1966 (Kays, 1972), but by 1967 only a remnant population remained.

According to Gottschalk (1967) the species was

being studied for release in the United States in the mid 1960s. Bump (1968) indicates that some liberations have occurred but infers that they have been too recent to ascertain their success.

Jungle Fowl *(G.g. murghii)* imported from Dehra Dun, India, were received by the States of Alabama, Oklahoma and Virginia in 1960, and since that time the States of Florida, Kentucky, South Carolina and Tennessee have initiated work with this species (Keeler, 1963). Keeler reports that at least four States have made trial liberations, Alabama has made two small releases and Oklahoma some six. A large scale release occurred in Oklahoma in February 1963 when 165 birds were released, but all the others involved less than fifty birds. Georgia made one release of sixty birds and Texas made two releases of sixty-five birds each. Some birds were released in three areas of South Carolina (Robinson, 1969) in 1965 (172 birds plus twenty-four hybrid fowl x bantam), and in 1968 (148 pure birds plus 102 others).

In 1969 these introductions showed some promise of being successful. Studies of the releases of 261 birds — made from May 1962 to April 1967 in Baldwin County, Alabama, by Smith (1969) — have indicated that pen-reared stock were unsuccessful.

The Jungle Fowl does not appear to have become established anywhere in the United States.

West Indies. Columbus included fowl amongst the animals he took to Hispaniola on his second voyage in 1493. Wetmore and Swales (1931) say the species was reported to be wild near Caracal in 1928. Bond (1960) reports the domestic fowl is thriving on the islet of Kick-em-Jenny in the Grenadines. In 1839 Sir James Clark Ross *(Voyage of Discovery and Research,* 1847) on a voyage from England placed two males and two females on the island of Trinidad, to 'add something useful to the stock of creatures' (Murphy, 1915).

Chagos Archipelago. Bourne (1971) records that fowl are reported to have run wild on Ile Poule, in the Peros Banhos Group, but details are lacking.

Isles Glorieuses. Benson *et al* (1975), quoting Ridgway (1896), say the fowl was plentiful on Grande Glor in 1896. They say the species was presumably introduced by man between 1882 and 1893. Some were present in 1906 and in 1908, but in 1970-71 there was no sign of any and the species must have been extirpated.

Réunion. According to Staub (1976) the Jungle Fowl is a recent introduction to Réunion and now occurs in small numbers along the east coast in thick forest and also in the cirques.

South Africa. According to Burton (1969), fowl have been established in the wild in Natal, South Africa, but little appears to be known of the species in Africa generally. They appear to be a common domestic or semi-domestic bird in many parts of that country.

France. Jungle Fowl were established at Cadarache by Inspector General Muge in about 1930. In 1954 other attempts to establish the species were made at Draguingnan and at Aix (Etchécopar, 1955).

St Helena. The Jungle Fowl *G. gallus bankiva* appears to have been an early introduction on St Helena. Melliss (1870) says they were reared abundantly on the island in 1870 and had become feral in some places. Haydock (1954) in the 1950s makes no mention of the presence of the Jungle Fowl on the island.

Damage

None known.

GREEN JUNGLE FOWL
Gallus varius (Shaw and Nodder)

DISTINGUISHING CHARACTERISTICS

Males 70 cm (27.5 in), females 40 cm (15.74 in). Males and females 454-795.2 g (1-1.75 lb) Rounded comb, green and purplish; wattles red, yellow and blue; nape, neck and upper mantle black, edged greenish bronze; lower mantle green, edged black; lower back and rump black, edged pale yellow; tail glossy green; primaries and underparts black. *Female:* head, neck and mantle sandy brown; remainder of upper parts brownish black, edged buff; tail black with buff and metallic patches; throat white; breast pale brown, edged black; abdomen buff, mottled dark brown or black.
Delacour, 1965, p.118 and pl.5 opp. p.112.

GENERAL DISTRIBUTION

Indonesia: on the islands of Java, Madura, Kangean, Bawean, Bali, Lombok, Sumbawa, Flores, Alor and Sumba.

INTRODUCED DISTRIBUTION

Introduced successfully in the Cocos-Keeling Islands, Indian Ocean; but may now be extinct.

GENERAL HABITS

Status: common. *Habitat:* seashores, coastal valleys, rocky scrubland bordering cultivation and occasionally inland forest. *Gregariousness:* singly, pairs or family parties. *Movements:* sedentary. *Foods:* seeds, grain, shoots, buds, insects and invertebrates. *Breeding:* June-Nov; Mar-July (East Java); monogamous. *Nest:* on the ground, under vegetation. *Eggs:* 6-10.
Delacour, 1965, pp.118-119.

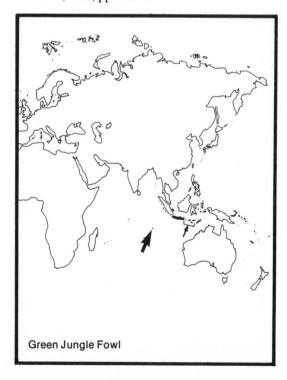

Green Jungle Fowl

Cocos-Keeling Islands. Green Jungle Fowl were introduced to Pulo Panjang, on the main atoll, between 1880 and 1890 (Gibson-Hill, 1949). They were apparently preserved for the benefit of the owners of the island, but despite this only occurred in small numbers and are probably no longer present.

DAMAGE

None known.

GREY JUNGLE FOWL
(Sonnerat's Junglefowl)
Gallus sonneratii Temminck

DISTINGUISHING CHARACTERISTICS

45-80 cm (17.7-31.49). 705-1136 g (1.5-2.5 lb)
Dented comb, lappets, bare face and throat red; neck hackles black, fringed grey with yellowish spots; tail purplish black; wing-coverts black with white shafts and yellowish tips; remainder of wing black; bill horn-brown. Female: crown reddish brown; face pale brown; neck brown, the feathers having buff centres; mantle mottled light brown and black; wings mottled black and brown with black primaries; breast white with brown and black borders; abdomen pale buff; tail black.

Delacour, 1965, p.115 and pl.5 opp. p.112.
Ali and Ripley, vol.2, 1968-74, pp.106-109 and fig.8, pl.22, opp. p.80.

GENERAL DISTRIBUTION

Asia: western and southern India from Mt Abu in the north-west and east to the Godavari River, and also central India and Rajputana.

INTRODUCED DISTRIBUTION

Introduced unsuccessfully in the Hawaiian Islands.

GENERAL HABITS

Status: fairly common. *Habitat:* forest, forest clearings, plains, hills and bamboo groves. *Gregariousness:* singly, pairs, family parties of 5-6

birds, and larger numbers at food sources. *Movements:* probably sedentary. *Foods:* grain, shoots, tubers, bulbs, berries, termites and other insects. *Breeding:* probably throughout year, mainly Feb-May; monogamous ? *Nest:* shallow depression on the ground. *Eggs:* 3, 4-8, 13.

Delacour, 1965, p.117.
Ali and Ripley, 1968-74, vol.2, pp.106-109.

NOTES ON INTRODUCTIONS

Hawaiian Islands. Grey Jungle Fowl were introduced to the Hawaiian Islands in 1962 but are not known to have become established (Walker, 1967). According to Lewin (1971) fourteen birds from a Californian game farm were liberated on the Puu Waawaa Ranch, Hawaii, at this time.

DAMAGE

None known.

CHEER PHEASANT
(Chir Pheasant)
Catreus wallichii (Hardwicke)

DISTINGUISHING CHARACTERISTICS

Males 90-118 cm (35.43-46.45 in), females 61-76 cm (24-30 in). Male and Female 1.2-1.7 kg (2.64-3.74 lb)
Narrow crest, crown and face brown; orbital patch red; upper parts pale buff, barred black with grey fringes; back and rump rusty buff with subterminal black bars; tail-coverts buff; tail buff with wide black bars and irregularly mottled brown and chestnut; chin, throat, neck and upper breast pale grey; middle breast and flanks pale grey with subterminal black bars; abdomen black; vent greyish or buff; bill yellow-brown or bluish horn. Female: crest shorter; crown blackish with buff border; upper parts spotted rusty brown and black, with subterminal black bar; back and rump lack bars; chin and throat greyish buff; neck and upper breast black with white

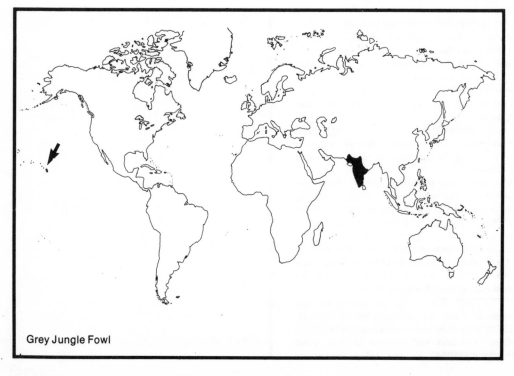

Grey Jungle Fowl

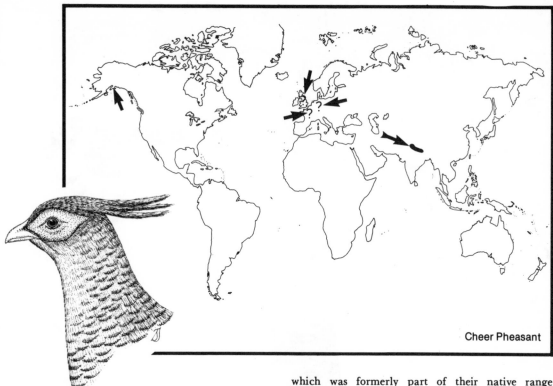

Cheer Pheasant

borders; middle breast and flanks chestnut-buff; abdomen, vent, flanks and under tail-coverts buff, the latter with black barring and spots.

Delacour, 1965, pp.202-203 and pl.5, opp. p.112.
Ali and Ripley, vol.2, 1968-74, pp.116-118 and fig.5, pl.22, opp. p.80.

GENERAL DISTRIBUTION

Asia: the Himalayas from north-east Pakistan to Nepal.

INTRODUCED DISTRIBUTION

Re-introduced successfully in India. Introduced unsuccessfully in Alaska and Europe.

GENERAL HABITS

Status: probably nowhere common, and may be in danger of extinction. *Habitat:* temperate forest in ravines and rocky hillsides, scrub and open meadows, mainly between 1200 and 3000 metres (4000 and 10 000 feet). *Gregariousness:* pairs, family parties, or coveys of 5-6 birds. *Movements:* sedentary. *Foods:* grubs, insects, seeds, roots, tubers, berries, tender shoots and leaves. *Breeding:* Apr-June; monogamous. *Nest:* slight depression on ground with a few leaves and bits of grass, under cover of vegetation. *Eggs:* 7-9, 14.

Delacour, 1965, pp.204-206.
Ali and Ripley, vol.2, 1968-74, pp.116-118.

NOTES ON INTRODUCTIONS

Alaska. Four adult Cheer Pheasants from Wisconsin, U.S.A. were released at Kenai and Cooper Landing in August 1940, but they failed to become established (Gabrielson and Lincoln, 1959; Burris, 1965).

India. Captive Cheer Pheasants were sent from the Pheasant Trust in England to the Government of Himachal Pradesh in 1971 and 1973, in what was reported to be a successful attempt to re-introduce the species. They were released in a reserve near Simla,

which was formerly part of their native range (Wayre, 1975).

Europe. In the nineteenth century Cheer Pheasants were liberated in England, France and Germany, but never successfully (Delacour, 1951).

DAMAGE

None known.

RING-NECKED PHEASANT
(Common Pheasant, Chinese Ringneck, Mongolian Pheasant, Green Pheasant)
Phasianus colchicus Linnaeus

DISTINGUISHING CHARACTERISTICS

Male 75-90 cm (29.5-35.4 in) tail 50 cm (19.68 in). 0.9-3 kg (1.98-6.6 lb). Female 52-65 cm (20.47-25.6 in), tail 20-25 cm (7.87-9.8 in). 0.5-1.1 kg (1.1-2.2 lb)

(Nominate race) crown metallic green, remainder of head dark green; wattles scarlet; ear-tufts green; neck purplish; mantle breast and flanks coppery brown, margined black and with a purplish gloss; lower back, rump and upper tail-coverts reddish brown, glossed purple; wing-coverts pale brown; mid-breast and flanks dark brown, mixed rufous; central tail olive with narrow black bars, fringed rufous and glossed purple. Races vary considerably: (*colchicus* group) purplish plumage with buff upper wing-coverts and absence of white collar; (white-winged group) more reddish upper parts, white or whitish wing-coverts, and some have an incomplete white collar; (Mongolian group) white on wings, more coppery in appearance and with an incomplete white collar; (*torquatus* group) grey on wings, rump and upper tail-coverts, more heavily barred black on the tail and more variegated in plumage pattern, and some races of this group have white 'eyebrows' and a white collar. Female: smaller generally dull or pale

167

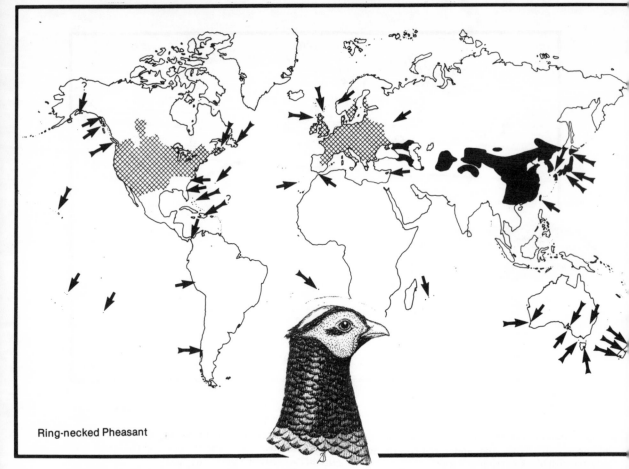

Ring-necked Pheasant

brown, barred black; back and sides of neck pinkish with metallic purple and green margins; mantle, sides of breast and flanks chestnut with black centres and pinkish grey margins to feathers; central tail reddish brown shading to sandy olive with irregular black and buff bars on the outer feathers.

Cheng, 1963, pp.300-301 and pl.12, no.41.

Delacour, 1965, pp.241-265 and pl.24, opp. p.258.

GENERAL DISTRIBUTION

Asia Minor to Japan: native locally from the Black Sea to Manchuria, Japan, Taiwan, south to southern China, Sinkiang, northern Afghanistan and Georgia, and the Caucasus in southern USSR.

INTRODUCED DISTRIBUTION

Introduced successfully in Europe, North America, the Hawaiian Islands, New Zealand, Japan, Chile, St Helena and on King Island, Rottnest Island and Tasmania; introduced possibly successfully on Eleuthera (Bahamas), Flinders Island (Australia) and in South Australia; introduced successfully but now extirpated in the Dominican Republic (?), Panama, Pitcairn Island and Taiwan.

Introduced unsuccessfully in Madeira and/or Porto Santo, Alaska, Bermuda, Peru, Tahiti, Mauritius, Kangaroo Island, and other areas in mainland Australia, and Cyprus.

GENERAL HABITS

Status: common, largely due to introductions and re-introductions; common in captivity. *Habitat:* open forest, brushlands, woodlands, marshes, farmland (particularly irrigated lands), croplands and pastures. *Gregariousness:* solitary, pairs, or mixed groups. *Movements:* sedentary. *Foods:* seeds, grain, grass, berries, acorns, beechmast and other vegetable material; also ants, beetles, grasshoppers, worms, grubs and other insects. *Breeding:* Apr-July (Mar-June Hawaii); polygamous. *Nest:* hollow on the ground, under cover and lined sparsely with grass and leaves. *Eggs:* 6, 8-14, 18 (Great Britain 10-12 common; North America 6-15; Hawaii 6-11).

Cheng, 1963, pp.301-309.

Delacour, 1965, pp.234-241.

NOTES ON INTRODUCTIONS

Europe. According to Voous (1960) the Ring-necked Pheasant is probably not in origin a European breeding bird, but was introduced from Asia Minor and later from China and Japan. Lowe (1933) says it is commonly believed that the English Pheasant was introduced to Britain by the Romans. He indicates that historians at this time felt it was the Argonauts (1300 B.C.), returning from Colchis in search of the Golden Fleece, who introduced them to Greece from where they spread further into Europe. Lowe considers that this spread was probably aided by the influence of the Romans who are said to have acclimatised the pheasant and introduced it into Italy, the south of France and Germany. However, Lever (1977) says there is now documentary evidence that the pheasant existed in Britain before the Romans and was possibly introduced between 1042 and 1066, in the time of Edward the Confessor.

The exact date that the Pheasant became naturalised in Great Britain as a feral breeding bird is not known, but it was well enough established in the late fifteenth century to warrant legal protection from the Crown (Lever). Artificial rearing of pheasants may have occurred in England as early as 1523. They appear to have been well established in England in the sixteenth century (Wayre, 1969), probably reached Ireland in the late sixteenth century (O'Gorman, 1970) and Wales in the seventeenth century or earlier (Matheson, 1963), but did not occupy the whole of Britain until the late eighteenth century and were not a prominent part of the game bag until the nineteenth century.

In the late 1580s birds from Ireland were introduced in St Bride's Bay, Pembrokeshire, Scotland, and there were further introductions in other areas in 1841, 1842 and in about 1860 (Lever). Some were introduced to the island of Raasay in the Inner Hebrides prior to 1904 (Collier, 1904), and to Rousay and Shapinsay in the Orkneys in 1905 (Lack, 1943). They were still present on both the latter islands in about 1943.

The original English race (colchicus) appears to have been decimated in about the eighteenth century (Koch, 1956) by overshooting, which prompted the introduction of a number of others. Wayre records that Chinese Ring-necks (torquatus) were imported in about 1768, Green Pheasants (versicolor) from Japan by Lord Derby in 1840, Mongolians (mongolicus) by Lord Rothschild in 1898 or 1900 and Prince of Wales Pheasants (principalis) by Colonel Sutherland in 1902.

Lever reports that principalis was introduced at the same time as mongolicus and that at least two other races, pallasi before 1930 and satschuensis in 1942, were also introduced.

All have probably bred with the nominate race to form a mixed population in Great Britain.

On mainland Europe, torquatus and colchicus were widely introduced (Peters, 1931) in early times. Later versicolor was introduced, so that the present birds there are a mixture of these and possibly other races (Delacour, 1951). The race versicolor was imported to France from 1850 on, and later both formosanus and mongolicus, the latter being imported to Europe by Carl Hagenbech in about 1900. In 1930 a mutant strain (tenebrosus) was introduced into France and this bird is said to have had much success in that country (Etchecopar, 1955).

The first Ring-necked Pheasants were released in Norway at Baerum (near Oslo) in 1875-76 (Haftorn, 1966) and many more introductions have occurred, mostly in southern Norway but also in a number of other localities (Myrberget, 1976). W. Vader (1977, pers. comm.) indicates that they are probably still being tried in many areas of southern and western Norway, with mixed results. The more important pheasant areas are the cultivated areas in Ostfold, Akershus and Vestfold, where they apparently breed in some years and stock is maintained in reasonable numbers (Myrberget).

In the USSR a number of introductions and reacclimatisations have been attempted, some successfully. They were established locally in Transcaucasia in 1890 and have been reacclimatised in the northern Caucasus since 1930. Attempts in Moldavia from 1949 to 1961 have failed or have become established only locally, as have efforts in the RSFSR between 1960 and 1964, and those in west Siberia and the Ukraine (Yanushevich, 1966). Some

500 birds were released in the Moscow area in 1958-59 (Anon, 1959), but presumably failed to become established. In 1958, a number of Ring-necked Pheasants were imported from Czechoslovakia and released on Biryuchiy Island where they became established and shortly after were reported breeding there (Shlapak, 1959). Other attempts in the same year occurred in the Ukraine when 445 birds were liberated, but the results were said to have been poor (L'vov, 1962). Attempts have also been made to acclimatise them in Odessa and adjacent districts of the USSR in the past ten years (1953-63?) (Nazarenka and Gurskii, 1963), but these also appear to have been without much success. Between 1955 and 1965 more than 9000 were released in the European part of the Soviet Union for re-stocking purposes (Osmolovskaya, 1969). During these introductions the best results were said to have been obtained with the releases of the northern Caucasian race.

In Finland Ring-necked Pheasants were first introduced by an industrialist K. Fazer, near Helsinki in 1901 (Merikallio, 1958). He established a pheasant farm in 1903 from which they were distributed to various parts of the country. Some were introduced at Öja, near Kokkola, and the population in 1955 had built up to forty to sixty pairs. Following the second World War the Finnish population was probably not more than 300 pairs of Ring-necked Pheasants, but by about 1958 it was estimated to be 20 000 birds. However, the population in that country is maintained by continuous introductions and fluctuates greatly.

At present the Ring-necked Pheasant is a universal game bird in Europe, artificially preserved by man in most of its haunts (Voous, 1960). It is established widely from the British Isles, southern Norway and southern Sweden to Spain, France, Corse, Italy, Germany, Hungary, Yugoslavia, Greece and Bulgaria (A.O.U., 1957). Attempts were made to establish them in Cyprus in 1910-11 and again in 1952 at Troödos, Paphos, Aghirda, Athalassa, Kouklia and Lanaca amongst other places, but all ended in failure (Bannerman and Bannerman, 1971).

Ring-necked Pheasant, *Phasianus colchicus* (male on left, female on right)

169

Madeira and/or Porto Santo. According to Bannerman (1965) the Ring-necked Pheasant was introduced to one or both of these islands, but is not now present in a wild state on either.

USA. Silverstein and Silverstein (1974) say that the Governor of New York released six pairs of Ring-necked Pheasants in 1730, but these failed to become established. However, Brown (1959) records that they were first introduced in the United States at New York in 1733. Allen (1962) reports that as early as 1790 Richard Bache attempted unsuccessfully to introduce them into New Jersey. The Californian Department of Fish and Game (1950) indicate that there were some unsuccessful private releases of pheasants in Santa Cruz County in the 1870s or 1880s. Some were sent to George Washington in 1786 by the Marquis de Lafayette, and Judge O. N. Denny sent sixty birds to Oregon in 1881 (Silverstein and Silverstein). Both these introductions apparently failed to become established.

The first successful liberations of Ring-necked Pheasants in the United States appear to have been those in the Willamette Valley, Oregon, in 1882, when several dozen were released from a consignment of birds sent from China by Judge O. N. Denny (Roberts, 1960; Allen, 1962). More from China were released in about 1884. The first successful release in the eastern United States may have been when Rutherford Stuyvesant released English birds in 1887 at Allamuchy, in New Jersey.

Ten years after liberation of the Ring-necked Pheasant in Oregon, hunters took a crop estimated at between a quarter and half a million birds (Allen). Other early introductions of pheasants include those in Colorado in 1885 (Sandfort, 1963), Montana before 1895 (Janson *et al*, 1971), Illinois in the 1890s (Ellis and Anderson, 1963), North Beverley, Massachusetts in 1897-98 (Allen, 1962), New York in 1877, Pennsylvania in 1892-1895, Georgia (Jekyl Island) in 1888, Washington in 1883, Utah since 1900 (Phillips, 1928), New York in 1886-1891 (Bump, 1941), in a number of areas in California in 1889 (California Department of Fish and Game, 1950) and in Ohio, Michigan, Wisconsin and the Lake States at the turn of the present century (Bump, 1963). More than a dozen attempts were made between 1892 and 1900 in Wisconsin (Schorger, 1947).

Following the initial introductions, and probably many subsequent ones, the pheasant in Colorado was first hunted in 1929. There have been annual open seasons since that date, and the harvest from 1957 to 1961 was over 206 000 birds (Sandfort).

In California, numerous introductions followed the initial ones in 1889. A State game farm was established in 1908 and during the next ten years 4000 birds were raised for release, yet the Ring-necked Pheasant showed little sign of becoming established until the early 1920s. From 1926 to 1949 approximately 583 878 Pheasants were liberated in California in an effort to establish them widely.

In 1950 during a ten-day season in California the annual hunter take of cock pheasants was estimated to be upwards of 450 000 (California Department Fish and Game). According to Allen, rice growing in the Sacramento Valley from 1912 on increased the pheasant population during the next twenty years. The Sacramento and San Joquin Valley rice belt is still the best pheasant country in California and most other areas need regular replenishment of stock.

The first releases of Ring-necked Pheasants in Illinois in the 1890s and the many subsequent ones established self maintaining populations in the north-west of Illinois during the 1920s (Ellis and Anderson). They spread westwards and southwards by the 1930s, but did not establish self maintaining populations in either the central western or southern counties, except in a few small areas locally (Greely *et al*, 1962). Large-scale releases began in 1928 and a total of 1 500 000 pheasants were released up until 1953 (Robertson, 1958). Densities of sixty to ninety birds per 1.6 kilometre (one mile) were common in at least some areas of Illinois in the late 1950s (Ellis and Anderson). Efforts to establish them in more southern areas of Illinois began in 1959-61 (Anderson, 1964). On an area some thirty-two kilometres (twenty miles) south of the self maintained populations, some 900 game farm birds from eastern and central Illinois were unsuccessfully released. Further efforts were being made in these areas in 1963-64 (Anderson, 1968).

New England Ring-necked Pheasants were derived from introductions in Massachusetts in 1897-98, and from these they spread to New Hampshire, Maine and Vermont (Allen). From the early introductions in New York they apparently became established in all of the suitable habitats in that State by 1920. Their numbers steadily increased until 1928, but since then they have fluctuated somewhat (Brown).

From 1931 to 1937 the Ring-necked Pheasant was widely planted in Wisconsin and by 1957 it was estimated that 250 000 (Gigstead, 1937) had been liberated. Further introductions occurred here just prior to 1964, when 2386 birds were released on a shooting preserve to assess the numbers remaining after the hunting season (Burger, 1964).

Just prior to 1938 some 30 000 artificially propagated Ring-necked Pheasants and Bobwhite Quail were released in Pennsylvania (Gerstell, 1938). Between 1949 and 1964 about 3000 game farm reared birds were released near Centre Hall, Pennsylvania, but these failed to become established (Myers, 1970). However, between 1964 and 1966 1006 wild trapped birds were released in the same area and these succeeded and the population reached its highest record in 1969.

Ring-necked Pheasants were privately released in Michigan in 1893, but little success was achieved until the State conservation department began liberating them in the period 1917-1925 (Ruhl, 1941). In this period 35 000 birds were released and 222 000 eggs were distributed to clubs and private individuals for breeding purposes. The species was well established in Michigan by 1925 and has enjoyed open seasons since that date.

Early attempts to establish the Ring-necked Pheasant in New York State in 1886-1891 (4120 birds), about 1895 (few ?), 1896-1902 (300-500) and in 1897 (?) by private persons failed and all the birds released were reported to have disappeared. However, State authorities between 1897 and 1939 released 595 056 Pheasants, in most areas of the State, and also distributed 3 519 179 eggs to various organisations and individuals. From these introductions the Pheasant became established and up to 500 000 were shot annually (Bump, 1941).

According to Allen, Ring-necked Pheasants distributed themselves rapidly in mid-continent ranges of the United States in the early part of this century, following the cultivation of the prairies. Numerous early attempts to establish them in South Dakota evidently failed. However, in prairie regions some 35 000 birds in twenty years were transplanted to other ranges and this founded a pheasant dynasty that in South Dakota alone may have aggregated sixty million birds in 1944. At no time since have they been as numerous and it is probable that this area has produced a larger annual crop of pheasants than any other area of comparative size. As early as 1927 some 1.5 to two million birds had been harvested.

Introductions of the Ring-necked Pheasant occurred in Montana before 1895, but from 1909-29 some 7000 birds, most of which came from other States, were released in Montana (Janson et al, 1971). Several thousand eggs were purchased and distributed to private persons so that they could breed and release pheasants. Although they became abundant in some areas by 1926, and hunting commenced in 1928, the Wildlife Restoration Division trapped and transplanted a total of 5677 pheasants during the period 1941-1948.

In North America generally Ring-necked Pheasant populations appear to have been building up in the 1920s and 1930s and probably by 1930 had populated the best ranges, but in the Lakes States particularly they had not penetrated into some parts that would later support some birds (Allen). They were still being released widely in the United States and continued to be during the next two decades. In 1938 some twenty-five States released 782 977 of them for re-stocking purposes, and this had risen in some States to 1 356 902 in 1948 (Wandell, 1949).

The breeding ability of the pheasant in favourable habitat in the United States is illustrated by the following account: On Protection Island in the Straits of Juan de Fuca, Washington, two cock and six hen pheasants (P.c. torquatus) were released on this 980 hectare (1072 acre) island in 1937 by Co-operative Wildlife Research Unit staff from Corvallis, Oregon (Einarsen, 1945). The population expanded to a count of 2000 birds by 1942, an average increase from year to year of 277 per cent.

The release of Ring-necked Pheasants in the United States has continued into the 1970s in their established range and in many new areas. From 1958 to 1966 some 23 151 were released in Virginia (Hart, 1967), and from 1965 to 1969, 84 505 were released in Minnesota (Shields and Neudahl, 1970). Many of the later introductions have been with new strains and varieties to areas where they have previously been least successful. Thus Virginia received thirty green pheasants from Japan in 1959 and the first releases were made in 1960, when 204 were liberated in Accomac County, Chesapeake Bay (Tuttle, 1963). In all, until 1963, some 585 were released in this area, 511 in Northampton County and 600 in Northumberland County and the species showed promise of becoming established.

The original stocks of birds in the United States came from China and England and were of the races *colchicus* and *torquatus*. The Mongolian subspecies *mongolicus* was introduced in California probably around 1894 (California Department of Fish and Game). The Green or Japanese Pheasant *(versicolor)* was introduced as early as 1885 (Gottschalk, 1967). The Afghan White-winged race *bianchii* was first released in Nevada, between 1963 and 1966, when 390 birds were released at Virgin Valley in Clark County, and in 1967, when eighty-eight were released in the Moapa Valley (Christensen 1963 and 1967). This subspecies was being hunted in New Mexico and Nevada in 1964 (Bump, 1968). Korean and Japanese strains were being introduced into New York State in 1968 (Colson, 1968). More than 9000 'green' pheasant were released in northern Idaho from 1963 to 1973, but are not known to have bred there (McNeel, 1973). Bump records that eastern Iranian black-necked pheasants *(P.c. persicus)* have been tried in the eastern United States with little success, and that the South Korean ring-neck has been tried in north and mid-western States. Western Iranian black-necked pheasants *(P.c. talischensis)* were released in five areas of South Carolina from 1961 to 1968 (Robinson, 1969). According to Nelson (1963) altogether some 42 262 pheasants of the black-necked group (including crosses) have been released in south-eastern States in the past six years, with results which have varied from failure to success. He records that since 1960 three States have released 1202 birds *(talischensis)* and that favourable results have been reported in Kentucky and Virginia and perhaps Florida; since 1958, eight States have released 14 462 birds *(talischensis x torquatus)* including Florida, Missouri, Virginia, Alabama, Arkansas, South Carolina and Kentucky; since 1956 six States including Kentucky, Maryland, Missouri and Virginia released 23 941 birds *(persicus);* and in 1959-62 some 500 pure *P.c. persicus* and seventeen crosses *(talischensis x persicus x torquatus)* were released in two areas of Virginia.

The Ring-necked Pheasant is now established in the United States from the Canadian border south through Washington to California, and in the east from at least south-central Maine through New York, Pennsylvania, New Jersey, northern Maryland, Indiana, north-western Missouri, north-western Oklahoma, and to northern Texas, New Mexico and south-east Arizona.

Canada. Ring-necked Pheasants were first brought to Canada by C. W. R. Thompson of Victoria (Vancouver, B.C.) in 1882, when a consignment of twenty birds arrived from England, but all birds subsequently died (Carl and Guiguet, 1974). According to Phillips (1928) there were sporadic attempts to introduce the species into New Brunswick (before 1925 ?), Nova Scotia (1893-1896 ?), on Prince Edward Island (before 1925 ?) and probably to parts of Quebec, all without success. In the warmer parts of southern Ontario the pheasant was established on the Niagara Peninsula for some time at an early date (before 1924 ?). Carl and Guiguet give details of a number of other early introductions into British Columbia. In 1883 Thompson released twenty-five birds from China at Esquimalt and these survived and bred well. In 1886 E. Musgrave released twelve Chinese birds on Saltspring Island, and in 1890 twelve birds of this race were released on Prevost Island. Also in 1890, the Mainland Protection Association released twenty birds at Point Grey, and in 1893 released twenty-three at Ladner. Between 1890 and 1900 some eighty-three were released, some on Pender Island.

In 1910 the Game Commission took over the breeding and release of pheasants in British Columbia and thousands were released annually within the province until 1954 when the practice was discontinued. Raising of pheasants at the government game farm in Saanich was discontinued in 1933 and thereafter supplementing of stocks was done with birds purchased from commercial breeders. Experimental releases were made during this period on the Queen Charlotte Islands and in the Vanderhoof area, but in both areas failed to achieve any success after a short period (Carl and Guiguet, 1974).

According to Guiguet (1961) three races of Ring-necked Pheasants, *colchicus, torquatus* and *mongolicus*, were introduced into Canada and have interbred to form the present mixed populations.

At present the Ring-necked Pheasant is established in Canada only in the very southern parts of British Columbia, southern Alberta, southern Saskatchewan, southern Manitoba, southern Ontario, southern Quebec, New Brunswick, Nova Scotia, and to the United States border (A.O.U., 1957; Godfrey, 1966).

Newfoundland. A few pairs of Ring-necked Pheasants were released at St Johns, Newfoundland, in the late 1950s, and a few still survive, nesting on the fringes of farmland sixteen kilometres (ten miles) from that city (Tuck, 1968).

Alaska. Introductions of Ring-necked Pheasants from Washington, USA, were made to a number of places in Alaska from 1934 to 1942 (Gabrielson and Lincoln, 1959). Gabrielson and Lincoln and Burris (1965) give details of these introductions. In 1934 225 birds were released on Baranof Island at Sitka and Goddard Hot Springs, in 1936 (100) and 1939 (twelve) at Ketchikan, and also in 1936 (?) at Cordova. Some 500 were released at Matanuska in 1938, and at Fairbanks and Wrangell Island in 1936 and in 1952. Wrangell Island also received a further release (thirty-two) in 1940. In 1939 (seventy-five) and 1940 (sixty) they were liberated at Petersburg, and also in this same year at Kenai Lake (eighty-five). They were liberated in 1942 (forty-six) at Haines.

According to Gabrielson and Lincoln all the introductions in Alaska have failed to become established, except for a few which survived in 1952 from a shipment of 500 birds from Minnesota in 1938. The present status of these birds is not known.

Mexico. The Ring-necked Pheasant occurs in Baja California (A.O.U., 1957), northern Mexico. Peterson and Chalif (1973) record that they are still established in the Mexicali Valley in extreme north-eastern Baja California.

Bermuda. Ring-necked Pheasants were introduced to Bermuda in the nineteenth century, but apparently had little success there (Bourne, 1957) and only survived temporarily (Wingate, 1973).

Bahamas. Brudenell-Bruce (1975) says the Ring-necked Pheasant has been introduced at Hatchet Bay, on the island of Eleuthera, where some were seen in 1959.

Hawaiian Islands. In the Hawaiian Islands, the Mongolian race *(P.c. mongolicus)* has been introduced since 1865, the Chinese race *(torquatus)* in about 1875 and the Green Pheasant *(versicolor)* some time prior to 1900 (Caum, 1933; Walker, 1967).

According to Munro (1960) the race *torquatus* became well established on most islands, especially on Lanai where they are numerous and are probably present in a pure form, the race *versicolor* did not appear to have become well established and may have hybridised with the Chinese race, and the Mongolian race which also did not appear to have persisted in a pure form.

In about 1950, Schwartz and Schwartz (1951) estimated that the population of Ring-necked Pheasants in the Hawaiian Islands was 70 000 birds and varied from 3.86 to 38.6 birds per square kilometre (.625 square mile).

Peterson (1961) reported that the race *versicolor* from Japan was established on Kauai, Molokai, Lanai, Maui and Hawaii, and that *colchicus* was established locally on all the major islands. Although the two races often hybridise, pure *versicolor* was still in evidence on the islands mentioned.

Walker records that mutant pheasants *(P. colchicus* mut. *tenebrosus)* were introduced into the Hawaiian Islands in 1960 and English Blacknecks in 1959. These may have hybridised with other races there. Stocks of *torquatus* (forty-four birds), *colchicus* (119), *tenebrosus* (seventy-three) and *versicolor* (eight) from United States game farms were released on the Puu Waawaa Ranch, Hawaii between 1959 and 1966 (Lewin, 1971).

Ring-necked Pheasants are now found in open grasslands on all the main islands, *P.c. versicolor* probably only on the slopes of Mauna Kea and Mauna Loa, Hawaii, in a pure form, and *P.c. colchicus* also on Hawaii, but its present status is poorly known (Hawaiian Audubon Society, 1975).

Australia. The Victoria Zoological and Acclimatisation Society released Ring-necked Pheasants in 1864 (eight at Phillip Island), 1870 (thirty), 1871 (fifteen), 1872 (seventy), and in 1873 (over 100), and many more were liberated by private persons in Victoria (Ryan, 1906; Frith, 1973). Jenkins (1977) records that there were several introductions in or before 1855. He reports that they were spreading at Gembrook at this time and that eleven had been released on Phillip Island and four at Sandstone and Churchill Island. Balmford (1978) indicates that several were imported in 1858, at which time the species was reported to be breeding in the colony, and eleven in one shipment and more in another in 1859. All of these introductions were apparently unsuccessful.

Some were introduced to Tasmania in about 1882, but the species did not become established there at this date (Littler, 1902). Sharland (1958) records that Chinese and mutant pheasants were released in

Tasmania but failed to become established.

The Ring-necked Pheasant has been established, probably since about 1910, on King Island in Bass Strait. They are still present on this island where they are said to be common (Tarr, 1950; Condon, 1975).

Introductions occurred at Sandford, Carlton, Cambridge and other parts of Tasmania (Sharland, 1958) some time before 1950. They were reported to be doing well at Cambridge, certainly before this date (Tarr). Efforts were being made to establish them on Bruny Island and the Tasmanian mainland in the early 1960s. They were introduced to Flinders Island (Bass Strait) in about 1959 and later (Green, 1969, in Condon, 1975). There may have been earlier releases as a bird was found on Flinders Island before this time (Tarr).

Some birds may have been released in the Hawkesbury district of New South Wales in 1944 (Tarr), but apparently none have survived.

In 1961 Ring-necked Pheasants were deliberately released by the Upland Game Association at Echunga, and other places in the Mt. Lofty Ranges in South Australia (Condon, 1968). At this time it was reported (in the press) that some fifty birds had been set free. Although there were many protests about such an introduction and approaches were made to the government for the prohibition of further releases, the Upland Game Association claimed to have liberated over 500 pheasants in various parts of South Australia. According to Olsen (1970, pers. comm.) some 600 were released by this association over a three-year period on Fleurien Peninsula, near Adelaide. A single bird was released on Kangaroo Island off South Australia in 1969 (Vincent, 1971, in Abbott, 1974), but the present status of 'pheasants' on this island is not known.

Off the Western Australian coast the Ring-necked Pheasant was introduced to Rottnest Island from the Zoological Gardens at South Perth in January 1928 (Serventy, 1948), when one male and three females were released. The species is still established on that island where it is described as a moderately common resident (Storr, 1965). Other liberations of pheasants were made on mainland Western Australia before 1912 but they were unsuccessful (Long, 1972).

According to Condon (1975), the Ring-necked Pheasants introduced into Australia are of mixed hybrid stock. They probably exist at present only on Rottnest Island, King Island and in Tasmania.

New Zealand. The first Ring-necked Pheasants were imported into New Zealand in 1842 when six birds arrived (Thomson, 1922). From this shipment only one cock and three hens may have been all that were landed at Wellington (Westerskov, 1962). More birds were imported in 1843. The first liberation and successful establishment appears to have occurred when pheasants were released at Wanganui by Mr W. Brodie in 1845 (Thomson).

Repeated importations, large-scale propagation and releases have led to the successful naturalisation of the Ring-necked Pheasant in suitable areas in the North and South islands of New Zealand (Westerskov).

Following the first successful release and up until 1869, some Ring-necked Pheasants were liberated at Tauranga, Tolago Bay, Raglan, Kawau, Bay of Islands and at Napier. In 1850 some were taken to Banks Peninsula, and in 1853 to the Nelson district. Thomson records a number of early introductions to different parts of New Zealand: between 1865 and 1877 the Otago Acclimatisation Society released 193 birds, and in 1867-68 the Canterbury society imported thirty-four birds which were more than likely liberated. Between 1867 and 1869 the Auckland society released nine birds and some were privately released at Hokonius. By 1871 pheasants were reported to be well established from Oamaru to Invercargill.

All of the early introductions were with the blackneck race *(P.c. colchicus)* from England. Not until 1851 were the first birds from China *(P.c. torquatus)* released. These (seven birds) were liberated at Waitakere in the Auckland district and were followed by a further introduction (six birds) in 1856. Here they slowly increased in numbers until in 1875 they were reported to be a common bird in this district. The Wellington society imported twenty-four birds of the Chinese race in 1874-75, and the Otago society three in 1864 and fifteen in 1877. The Canterbury society obtained three birds in 1867, and between 1869 and 1870 the Southland society liberated a large number of pheasants.

From 1879 on the Nelson Acclimatisation Society made many releases of Ring-necked Pheasants. In 1879 (twenty birds) and 1880 (another eighteen) birds were obtained from the Auckland society and released at Maitai Valley. A further five were released at Atawhai Valley in 1882. In 1898 releases of pheasants were made at Aniseed Valley, Wakapuaka, Hope, Pokororo and at Eares Valley with twenty birds imported from England. Introductions at Pokororo and Wakapuaka were made with twenty birds obtained from Hawke's Bay. More introductions were made from 1912 until 1945, when it was reported that over 400 pheasants had been released, in areas including Golden Downs, Thorpe, Woodstock, Baton, Stanley Brook, Pokororo, Wai-iti Valley, Redwoods Valley, Moutere, Motueka Valley and Waiwhero. Between 1945 and 1956 some were reared and released by private individuals in these same areas (Westerskov).

In other parts of New Zealand, the Otago society released nine birds from Auckland between Lake Waihola and the coast in 1895. They also imported birds from England in 1897 (twenty-two birds) and in 1899 (twenty-one). Releases of pheasants apparently continued in the Otago district until at least 1914-15. The Southland society attempted to stock Stewart Island, from 1869 to 1910, when some 310 birds were released there. The Wellington society released 1351 pheasants between 1897 and 1912 (Thomson).

There appears no doubt that the Ring-necked Pheasant was fairly abundant in a number of areas in the 1870s and 1880s. Thereafter numbers appear to have declined. Thomson indicates that they almost disappeared in the Otago area from 1882 to 1892. They were reported to be decreasing in the Wellington area, in the period 1885 to 1888, and were rare around Christchurch in 1890. At this time they were said to have been exterminated at Invercargill. Possible causes for their decline during these years were given by Thomson as the increase in the use of phosphorus to poison rabbits, the importation of stoats and weasels in 1882 and the decrease in the food supply due to the introduction of other bird species. Oliver (1955) also indicates that fires may have destroyed many pheasant eggs and chicks. Whatever the causes, by 1922 the Ring-necked Pheasant was not common anywhere in the North Island and extremely rare in the South Island.

According to Westerskov since the first introduction of Ring-necked Pheasants, several hundred thousand have been liberated in all the likely habitats in New Zealand. He records that they reached peak density in the 1870s and 1880s, and that this success was associated with bush burns and the weed tangles that followed such burns.

Present populations of Ring-necked Pheasants in New Zealand are assisted largely by the breeding and release of birds annually (Falla et al, 1966), although in many areas they maintain their populations without such help. The species is now widespread and common (Wodzicki, 1965), being established over much of the North Island and with scattered populations in Nelson, Canterbury and Otago in the South Island (Westerskov, 1963). The annual kill of cock pheasants has been as high as 6000 birds in one district and populations of between 2.3 and 13.8 birds per square kilometre are known (Westerskov).

Although the Ring-necked Pheasants introduced to New Zealand have been mainly the races colchicus and torquatus, the Mongolian race (mongolicus) was first imported in 1923 and melanistic mutants in 1938. In spite of the liberation of various subspecies and hybrids the wild population has attained a fairly uniform look, being a dark coloured ring-neck-blackneck cross (Westerskov, 1963).

Japan. The Green Pheasant (P.c. versicolor) is a widely distributed native of Japan, with the exception of Hokkaido (Sakane, 1960). The race karpowi was introduced from Korea to Honshū (Tsushima, near Nagoya) in about 1924 (Kaburaki; 1934 and 1940) and has been introduced on Hokkaido from the same area (Sakane). This race has also been introduced, in 1965 or 1966, to Hachijō Jima and also to Miyake Jima (Ornithological Society of Japan). The Hokkaido introduction occurred in 1930, at Oshamambe and Hidaka, where the birds have increased since then (Ornithological Society of Japan, 1974).

Kuroda (1922) says that the pheasant has been on Tsushima Island, Korea Strait, since its introduction in the Middle Ages, and also on Urishima. They were common on both islands in 1922.

Chile. Ring-necked Pheasants were imported to Chile from England in 1886 or 1887 by C. J. Lambert, who established a bird farm (Hellmayr, 1932; Johnson, 1965). Two pairs were apparently placed in a park at La Compania, sixteen kilometres (ten miles) from the Bay of Coquimbo, and by 1897 had increased in numbers and spread up to twenty-four kilometres (fifteen miles) inland (Hellmayr). These birds finally died out, but a second import from Germany in 1914 became established in restricted areas of Valdivia and Cautin. According to Johnson they probably numbered some 1000 birds in about 1965.

Sick (1968) reports that the Ring-necked Pheasant has probably been introduced in a number of areas of South America but has only survived under the constant care of man in Chile. The present status of the birds in Chile is not well known, but Escalante (1976, pers. comm.) indicates that Goodall et al (1951-57) say they survived only at Pichi Colcuman Island (Ranco Lake) in Valdivia. However, Blake (1977) indicates that those released on a farm at Allipēn, Cautin, and those on Pichi Colcuman Island, still survive.

Peru. A hunt club has released small groups of Ring-necked Pheasants, since 1970, in mountains fifty kilometres (thirty-one miles) east of Lima at an altitude of 1800 metres (5908 feet); many have been hunted, others have disappeared, but no breeding in the wild has been observed (Plenge, 1977, pers. comm.). Plenge states that some pheasants were also released in about 1974, somewhere east of Yauca-Chala in the Department of Arequipa, with much the same results as those experienced on the previous occasion.

Dominican Republic. Ring-necked Pheasants were introduced to the Dominican Republic in the 1950s by Ramfis Trujillo for sport. They became established but have largely been decimated by hunting before they became well naturalised (Dod, 1977, pers. comm.). Dod says a few pairs survive in the hills on the Alcoa Project near Cabo Rojo, but the species is very rare there.

Panama. In September 1959, eighty Ring-necked Pheasants were released on a private property near El Volcán in Chiriquí, Panama. These were successfully established for some years but were eventually all destroyed by hunters before 1965 (Wetmore, 1965).

St Helena. Introduced and established on St Helena, Ring-necked Pheasants were present there in 1936 and the population numbered nearly one hundred birds in 1949 (Benson, 1950). Haydock (1954) found them to be moderately common in the early 1950s and estimated that there were about seventy-five pairs on the island. Melliss (1870) records that pheasants were found there in 1588 and were abundant there in 1870. Gladstone (1923) places the date of introduction to St Helena as 1513, and quotes his source for this information as T. H. Brook, History of the Island of St Helena (1808, pp.37-38).

Mauritius. According to Meinertzhagen (1912) the Ring-necked Pheasant was introduced to Mauritius from St Helena in about 1880 but died out before it became established.

Tahiti. E. Guild (1938) reports that Ring-necked Pheasants (P.c. torquatus) were liberated in Tahiti, in about 1938, and were breeding there shortly after their release. Holyoak (1974) says they were introduced many times but did not seem to breed and have always died out.

Pitcairn Island. Williams (1960) reports that the Ring-necked Pheasant was liberated on this island in about 1935 but was apparently soon eaten into extinction.

Taiwan. According to Hachisuka and Udagawa (1951), a few pairs of P.c. formosanus were introduced into Kashoto (Hwoshaotao) in 1929, where they became established, but have since been exterminated there.

DAMAGE

Generally the Ring-necked Pheasant is prized as a

game bird and any references to damage irritates hunters. However, this pheasant does damage crops in Europe and North America, where it is an introduced species.

In Europe there appear to be few examples to suggest that the introduction of the Ring-necked Pheasant has been detrimental. Seubert (1964) reports that they have caused damage to newly sown grain, low hanging fruit and sprouting bulbs in Holland. In Great Britain the pheasant, with other game birds, is considered by the British Sugar Corporation to be a significant pest of sugar beet (Dunning, 1974). They peck the leaves of seedlings from May to July, and in many cases the pecking results in complete felling of the plants.

Since the Ring-necked Pheasant has become well established in North America there appears to have been an increasing number of records of damage. The species is, however, an important game bird in that area and there is a tendency to disregard the amount of damage which may be nationally small but locally severe at times. Dambach and Leedy (1948 and 1949) record that interest in finding a means of preventing pheasant damage developed in the 1940s concurrent with the peak in overall Ring-necked Pheasant populations in the United States. Prevention of damage, at this time, was considered in Michigan, Nebraska, Ohio, South Dakota, Wisconsin and probably elsewhere. Dambach and Leedy claimed that in all cases examined at this time damage caused was local and heaviest in areas of high pheasant population. Losses usually totalled considerably less than one per cent of the crop and they thought that most was probably attributable to ground squirrels. At about the same time (Jewett et al, 1953) farmers in Washington State were asserting that pheasants were too fond of ranch products and reported that they dug up growing corn, ate potatoes and were destructive in gardens.

According to Janson et al (1971), in periods of abundance Ring-necked Pheasant can cause appreciable damage to farm crops. They say that in 1941-42 complaints of damage to sprouting corn and grain in shocks assumed serious proportions in Yellowstone Valley, but that since then reports of damage have been relatively few.

Undoubtedly some damage is caused by Ring-necked Pheasants in North America to such crops as grains, melons, potatoes, tomatoes, strawberries and corn. In grain crops probably only a small proportion is taken from the standing crop, most being taken as gleanings from the ground (Ferrel et al, 1949). The principal damage to corn is done when the crop is newly planted and green shoots are protruding from the ground, but the total loss is probably not great.

More than likely the greatest damage caused by Ring-necked Pheasants is to small fruits and vegetable crops, especially in areas where the species is abundant. Allen (1962) and Bump (pers. comm., 1970) have recorded that where high populations of pheasants exist they become a crop liability especially to high value produce such as tomatoes, strawberries and maize.

Research work in Idaho has indicated that where populations reach a level of 57.9 to 77.2 birds per square kilometre crop damage becomes important.

Bump (pers. comm.) says that 2.5 birds per hectare (2.47 acres) will reduce crop yields by between one and five per cent. In vegetable growing areas of British Columbia, Canada, where populations of Ring-necked Pheasants have exceeded 154.4 birds per square kilometre, damage to tomatoes has been found to run as high as about fifty dollars (US) per hectare.

In New Zealand and Australia there have been few complaints against the Ring-necked Pheasant. Their depredations are local in New Zealand and confined to market gardens and young maize crops. In Tasmania they have been reported to be a minor nuisance to crops at times. The species is not established well enough in these areas nor are they present in large enough numbers to constitute much of a pest to agriculture.

On St Helena, where the introduced population is relatively small, Haydock (1954) says they are proving a nuisance to farmers by causing damage to potato crops. In the Hawaiian Islands they are locally destructive to some truck crops, principally sweet potatoes, tomatoes and sprouting corn (Schwartz and Schwartz, 1951).

REEVES PHEASANT
(Reeves's Pheasant)
Syrmaticus reevesii Gray

DISTINGUISHING CHARACTERISTICS
Male 210-273 cm (82.67-107 in); tail 155-180 cm (61-70.86 in). 0.9-1.7 kg (1.98-3.74 lb); female 66-75 cm (26-29.5 in)
Crown, neck and patch beneath eye white; forehead, cheeks, ear-coverts, lower abdomen, vent and thighs black; narrow band above and behind eye red; broken blackish ring around lower neck; mantle, back and rump mustard-coloured, each feather with a black border; wing-coverts white margined with black or black and chestnut borders; upper breast with black and chestnut collar; lower breast and flanks chestnut barred with black and white; tail centrally silver, barred black, the outer feathers yellowish; bill blackish. *Female:* smaller; crown reddish, remainder buff; nuchal collar and ear-coverts black; mantle spotted black and chestnut with white markings; remainder mainly greyish brown with various markings of black, whitish and buff.
Delacour, 1965, pp.225, 227 and pl.21, opp. p.224.
Etchécopar and Hüe, 1978, pp.255-258, and pl.10, p.257.

GENERAL DISTRIBUTION
China: hill country of northern and central China from western Chihli, Shansi, south-western Shensi, Hupeh, western Honan, Anhwei and north-western Szechwan.

INTRODUCED DISTRIBUTION
Introduced, probably successfully, in France and Great Britain; introduced, possibly successfully, in the Hawaiian Islands.

Introduced unsuccessfully in Ireland, the USA, Alaska and New Zealand.

GENERAL HABITS
Status: little information, probably common; common aviary bird. *Habitat:* wooded mountainous areas, valleys with steep canyons. *Gregariousness:* pairs, trios, or in winter small family parties or flocks of 10-20 birds. *Movements:* sedentary. *Foods:* seeds, 175

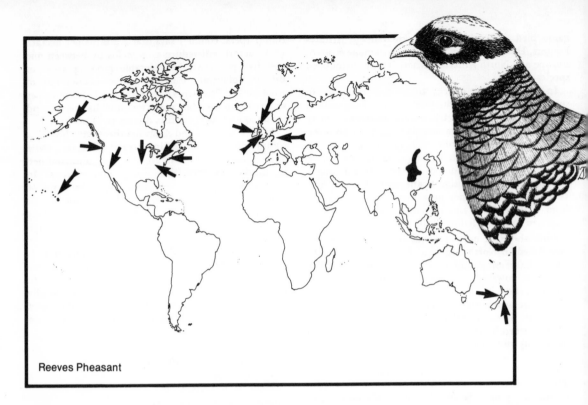

Reeves Pheasant

corn, pine cones, small fruits, grain, acorns, tubers, insects, small invertebrates and green vegetable material. *Breeding*: no information; monogamous. *Nest*: unlined scrape on the ground, in long grass or under a bush. *Eggs*: 6, 7-8, 15.

Cheng, 1963, pp.310-312.

Delacour, 1965, pp.227-228.

NOTES ON INTRODUCTIONS

Europe. According to Hanzak (1974), Reeves Pheasants have been successfully introduced into several parts of Europe. They are reported to have been successfully acclimatised in northern France (Bump, 1964 and 1968) and to have been established in the wild there (Thomson, 1964). Prior to 1955 they appear to have been released only at hunts in France (Etchécopar, 1955).

They are one of a number of pheasants which have been introduced into Great Britain (Koch, 1956), are still possibly to be found in a wild state in England and Scotland, as well as in mainland Europe, following their release as a game bird (Wayre, 1969). Sharrock (1972) indicates that they are not known to maintain feral breeding populations in Great Britain, but Lever (1976, pers. comm.) says some are still established there from introductions in the twentieth century.

A number of introductions are recorded in Great Britain (Gray, 1882; Fitter, 1959; Sharrock, 1976; Lever, 1977). Some became established for a few years from one pair released in 1870 and four males at a later date, in Guisachan, Inverness-shire. Prior to 1882, they appear to have been established in Guisachan, in Tulliallan, Clackmannanshire and at Elvedon in Surrey. Before 1894 introductions were made at Lilford Park in Northamptonshire, Woburn in Bedfordshire, Tortworth in Gloucestershire, and Bedgebury in Kent. Other attempts at about the same time were made in Scotland in Aberdeenshire, at Tulliallan in Fife, on the Isle of Bute and in Kirkcudbrightshire. In Ireland they were unsuccessfully introduced by E. H. Cooper at Markree Castle in County Sligo.

In more recent times a small number were released at Elveden Hall, Suffolk, in 1950, and some may have existed there up until about 1972. In 1970, fifty were released at Kinveachy Forest, Inverness-shire, but these have probably now died out. Other releases occurred in Morayshire and Cumberland in 1969, and feral populations are said to have existed in Ross-shire and Dorset until at least the mid-1950s.

USA. Reeves Pheasants were introduced unsuccessfully in several northern and mid-western States in the United States (Bump, 1968). They were unsuccessfully released in California, when 649 birds in 1947, 106 birds in 1948 and sixty birds in 1949 were liberated (Californian Department of Fish and Game, 1950).

From October 1954 to the end of 1961 some 21 735 Reeves Pheasants were released in Ohio (Seibert, 1965; Seibert and Donohoe, 1965). Although they showed some potential to survive they mostly disappeared. Korschgen and Chambers (1970) evaluated the success of Reeves Pheasant as a game bird in Missouri from 1956 to 1968. Some nineteen wild birds from France and 659 pen-reared progeny of wild birds were released in Missouri during this period but the species failed to become established anywhere. Korschgen and Chambers reported that this pheasant's vulnerability to predation, lack of inherent wildness, monogamous mating habits and poor production and survival of young were the main reasons for their failure.

Investigations of the Reeves Pheasant as a suitable introduction were carried out in Kentucky between 1959 and 1965, but future liberations of the species were not recommended (Stephens, 1966). Pen-reared birds were released at Black Mountain and Kentucky Ridge in 1959, and introductions continued in these areas until 1963 (Stephens, 1967). During this period 7674 birds (6815 juvenile and 859 adults) were liberated in a variety of habitats at seven release sites.

These introductions were generally unsuccessful and Stephens stated that excessive mortality and lack of reproductive success were probably the most important factors influencing their survival. Much the same situation had been found earlier in New York State (Edminster, 1937). Here introductions commenced in 1931 with stock from game breeders. A release of 102 birds at Sherburne and 29 at Connecticut Hill in the autumn of 1931 had almost all disappeared by May 1932. Eggs (thirty-four) from Sherburne Game Farm were placed in grouse nests on Connecticut Hill in 1933, and an additional fourteen young birds were released, but only four birds were found in 1934. Of fifty birds released in a refuge east of the Hudson River in 1933 all had disappeared by 1935. Bump (1941) records that at least 233 birds were released by State authorities in New York (Chenango, Dutchess and Tompkins counties and elsewhere) between 1931 and 1933, but all the birds soon disappeared.

In the early 1960s (Bump and Bohl, 1964) it was thought that some semi-domestic strains of Reeves Pheasant may have been still established in the United States, but later in the same decade (Gottschalk, 1967) they were reported to have been unsuccessful everywhere.

There appear to be few early records of Reeves Pheasant introductions in the United States. Some may have been released on an estate in New Jersey in the late 1880s, and the game commissioners of Yakima County purchased and liberated twenty birds in 1914 (Phillips, 1928). Some may have been present in the latter area at least until 1919.

Hawaiian Islands. Introductions of Reeves Pheasants were made to these islands from the United States in 1957 (Walker, 1967; Berger, 1972). They were released on the islands of Hawaii, Molokai and Oahu in 1960-61 (Western States Exotic Game Bird Committee, 1961). In late 1961 they were still surviving, at least on Hawaii.

A total of 180 birds from California, Michigan and Wisconsin game farms were released on the Puu Waawaa Ranch, Hawaii, in 1959-60, 1964 and 1966. Most of these birds disappeared soon after their release but Lewin (1971) reports that a few of them have remained around the release site.

At present Reeves Pheasants are thought to be established on Kauai, Molokai and Lanai, but their present status on the islands is poorly known (Hawaiian Audubon Society, 1975).

Alaska. In 1940 three adult Reeves Pheasants from Wisconsin were released at Kenai Lake, Alaska, and in 1947, forty-seven more from the same source. These birds survived the first winter there but all were subsequently killed by the extreme winters (Gabrielson and Lincoln, 1959).

New Zealand. Nine Reeves Pheasants were imported by the Wellington Acclimatisation Society in 1897 and several by the Wanganui society in 1899. Two birds, which later died, were kept in captivity by the Wanganui society and some were liberated on the Wanganui River. These disappeared and were not recorded again (Thomson, 1922).

DAMAGE

None known.

COPPER PHEASANT
Syrmaticus soemmerringii (Temminck)

DISTINGUISHING CHARACTERISTICS

Male 125-137.5 cm (49.21-54 in), female 50-75 cm (19.68-29.52 in)

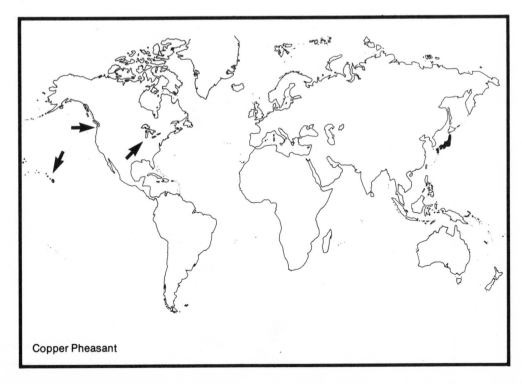

Copper Pheasant

Upper parts chestnut; margins of breast feathers purplish red to gold; ventral plumage reddish chestnut; tail cinnamon with black bars, and broadly bordered chestnut above and buff spotted black below; face wattles red. *Female:* crown brown; throat reddish buff; cheeks, sides of neck, mantle and breast marked blackish brown forming an uneven collar; back and rump tinted grey; tail centrally barred grey and chestnut.

Delacour, 1965, pp.221-223 and pl.21, opp. p.224.

GENERAL DISTRIBUTION
Japan: on the islands of Hondo, Shikoku and Kyūshū.

INTRODUCED DISTRIBUTION
Introduced unsuccessfully in the Hawaiian Islands and the USA.

GENERAL HABITS
Status: reported to be declining rapidly in numbers in the wild. *Habitat:* thickly wooded areas, forest with undergrowth in the vicinity of streams. *Gregariousness:* probably solitary (?), or pairs. *Movements:* sedentary (?). *Foods:* insects, seeds, buds, leaves, roots, acorns, berries, grain, grubs, earthworms and other green plant material. *Breeding:* Mar-July; monogamous or polygamous ? *Nest:* scrape on the ground, often in a tussock of grass, or at the base of a tree. *Eggs:* 6, 7-10, 14.

Delacour, 1965, pp. 219-221, 223, 225.

NOTES ON INTRODUCTIONS
Hawaiian Islands. Copper Pheasants were introduced to the Hawaiian Islands (Walker, 1967). Stock from Japan was released on several islands in the group but failed to become established on any of them (Munro, 1960; Berger, 1972). They have been liberated on the islands of Kauai, Oahu, Maui and Hawaii (Reilly, 1968); on Oahu, Maui and Kauai at various times between 1907 and 1914 (Schwartz and Schwartz, 1951).

USA. In 1885 Copper Pheasants were introduced in the United States but were not successful in establishing themselves (Gottschalk, 1967). Phillips (1928) records that probably about three pairs were released on Protection Island, Washington, in 1885, and some may have been introduced in Illinois in the late 1870s and 1880s, where they were mentioned at this time in the early game laws.

DAMAGE
None known.

GOLDEN PHEASANT
Chrysolophus pictus (Linnaeus)

DISTINGUISHING CHARACTERISTICS
Male 100-110 cm (39.37-43.3 in), tail 80 cm (31.49 in); female 61-67.5 cm (24-26.39 in), tail 35 cm (13.77 in). Male 875 g (1.92 lb)

Crest, back and rump gold coloured; ear-coverts greyish; sides of neck, chin and throat reddish brown, sides of neck barred black; upper back metallic green, each feather bordered black; upper tail-coverts tipped scarlet; wings brown and blue, dark red on the tip; underparts scarlet shading to brownish on abdomen and thighs; under tail-coverts scarlet; tail barred black and buff; naked skin around eye pale yellow; bill greyish yellow. *Female:* crown black; remainder mainly various shades of brown, mottled or barred.

Delacour, 1965, pp.269-271 and pl.24, opp. p.258.
Etchécopar and Hüe, 1978, pp.262-263 and pl.10, p.257.

GENERAL DISTRIBUTION
China: mountains of central China from south-eastern Ching Hai, southern Kansu and Tsinling Shan south to Szechwan and central Hupeh.

INTRODUCED DISTRIBUTION
Introduced successfully in Great Britain. Introduced unsuccessfully in the USA, Canada, Hawaiian Islands, New Zealand, Colombia and to Tahiti.

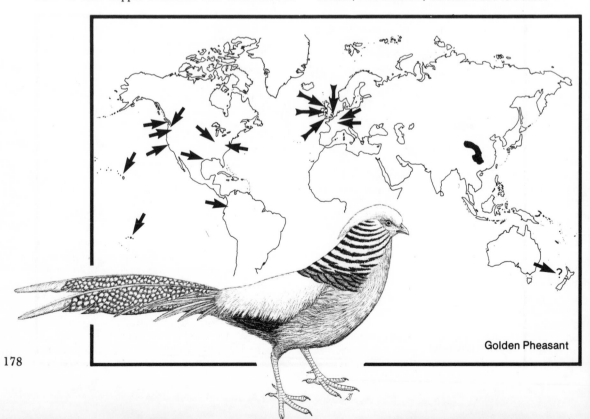

Golden Pheasant

GENERAL HABITS

Status: fairly rare; possibly exists chiefly as an aviary bird (?) *Habitat:* rocky hillsides in low scrub and bamboo thickets. *Gregariousness:* pairs, or small family parties. *Movements:* sedentary, but some altitudinal movements. *Foods:* buds, grass, berries, grain, seeds, insects, worms and green vegetable material such as tender shoots and leaves. *Breeding:* little information, probably May-June. *Nest:* not known (unlined scrape on the ground in captivity). *Eggs:* no information (6-16 in captivity).

Cheng, 1963, pp.318-320.

Delacour, 1965, pp.268-271.

NOTES ON INTRODUCTIONS

Europe. Before the second World War the Golden Pheasant was to be found at liberty at hunts in France, near Compiégne and at Livry, but does not appear to have existed in the wild since that time (Etchécopar, 1955).

Golden Pheasants have been naturalised in limited areas of Great Britain (Thomson, 1964) from introductions in the twentieth century (Lever, 1976, pers. comm.) and in some instances they have maintained their numbers as feral breeding populations (Sharrock, 1972).

Lever (1977) records that the earliest record of a Golden Pheasant in the wild in Britain was in Norfolk in 1845. Introductions occurred in the western Highland, the Gigha Island (off the west coast of Kintyre) before 1892 (Harvie-Brown and Buckley, 1892), and during the 1890s a number were introduced to Tortworth, Gloucestershire, where they remained successfully established for a number of years (Lever). In about 1895 some pheasant hybrids (Golden x Amherst) were released near Newton Stewart in Galloway where they became established and eventually reverted to the pure golden type (Maxwell, 1905).

Some were introduced by Lord Montagu of Beaulieu near Southampton in 1925, where they interbred with Amherst Pheasants released at the same time. Some were found on the Isle of Bute in 1927, at Sevenoaks in Kent in 1942, at Penninghome in Galloway in 1952 and near Bournemouth in Hampshire. They were also introduced to a number of estates in East Anglia, where they continue to breed today.

More recently a few were found breeding in Candrona Forest, Peeblesshire, in 1964, and smaller numbers on Tresco in the Scilly Isles (where two pairs were released and chicks were seen in 1975), on the Isle of Anglesey, and in other areas in Norfolk. Some were also noted in Bedford in 1972, at South Downs in Hampshire in 1968-71, and at Scone in Perthshire in 1974.

The total British and Irish population of Golden Pheasants may number between 500 and 1000 pairs at present (Sharrock, 1976).

USA. According to Gottschalk (1967) Golden Pheasants have been liberated in the United States from 1786 onwards, many times, but have been unsuccessful in establishing themselves. Since 1883 (perhaps as early as 1857) there are records of about one hundred birds that were liberated in Washington State. Some were liberated on Protection Island in that State in about 1885. Early introductions

occurred in California as some were released on Goat Island in San Francisco Bay. The game commissioner of Illinois liberated some on Arsenal Island, near Moline, some time prior to 1909, and some were possibly liberated at Lynn Haven, in Virginia (Phillips, 1928).

In the southern Willamette Valley of Oregon, in 1930, sixteen Golden Pheasants were released, but there are no subsequent records of these birds (Gullion, 1951). Some time between 1900 and 1948 probably one hundred or more birds were released on the King Ranch, Texas, but these disappeared (Lehmann, 1948).

Canada. Phillips (1928) records that some were released at Nanaimo, British Columbia, some time before 1926 but failed to become permanently established.

Hawaiian Islands. Golden Pheasants from an unknown source were introduced to the Hawaiian Islands in 1865 but failed to become established (Walker, 1967; Berger, 1972). Some may have been released in 1867 and 1870, and again after 1932 when these and other pheasants were raised at a game farm and liberated on Oahu (Schwartz and Schwartz, 1951). Munro (1960) records that besides the earlier introductions they were tried again more recently, but with the same results.

New Zealand. Golden Pheasants were imported to New Zealand in early times (1867-91) but it is not known whether any were released in the wild (Thomson, 1922).

Colombia. Attempts by hunt clubs and the Ministry of Agriculture to introduce Golden Pheasants and other pheasant species into Colombia, South America, have ended in failure (Sick, 1968).

Tahiti. The Golden Pheasant was introduced on Tahiti by E. Guild in 1938, and they were reported by him to be breeding there soon after their release (Guild, 1938). There appear no subsequent records of the species on this island.

DAMAGE

In a wild state in China the Golden Pheasant lives mainly deep in the mountains and does not conflict with agriculture, but in winter moves to lower elevations in search of food and will do a certain amount of damage to winter crops such as winter wheat, etc. (Cheng, 1963).

AMHERST PHEASANT
(Lady Amherst's Pheasant)
Chrysolophus amherstiae (Leadbeater)

DISTINGUISHING CHARACTERISTICS

Male 130-170 cm (51.18-67 in), tail 85-115 cm (33.46-45.27 in); female 65-67.5 cm (25.6-26.39 in), tail 30-37.5 cm (11.8-14.58 in). Males 600-691 g (1.32-1.52 lb)

Crown metallic green; small narrow crest scarlet; bare facial skin bluish white; face and throat black with metallic green spots; back of neck white with blue and black borders to feathers; mantle and scapulars metallic bluish green, each feather bordered black; back green, feathers bordered black; wings blue with black borders; breast similar to mantle, the remainder of underparts white; tail-coverts mottled black and white with orange-red tips; tail whitish with black bars; under tail-coverts black

179

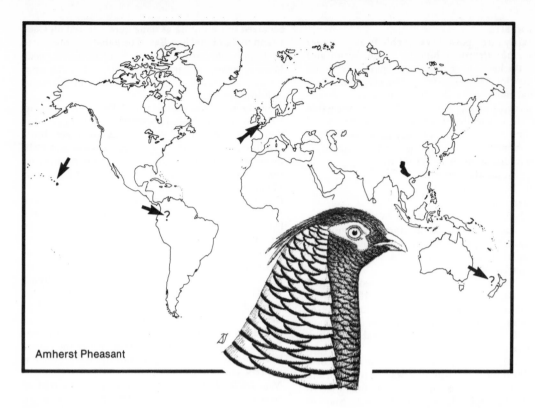

Amherst Pheasant

and dark green and marked with white; bill bluish grey. *Female:* upper parts tinted reddish chestnut; tail barred black, buff and pale grey; facial skin blue-grey.

Delacour, 1965, pp. 271, 273 and pl.24, opp. p.258.

Etchécopar and Hüe, 1978, pp.263-264 and pl.10, p.257.

GENERAL DISTRIBUTION

Asia: south-eastern Tibet, south-western China (Szechwan south to western Kweichow and Yunnan), to upper Burma and the Shan States.

INTRODUCED DISTRIBUTION

Introduced successfully in England. Introduced unsuccessfully in the Hawaiian Islands, (?) New Zealand and Colombia.

GENERAL HABITS

Status: fairly rare in wild; fairly common in captivity. *Habitat:* mountain forests, rocky mountain slopes, woods and scrub. *Gregariousness:* singly, pairs, trios, family parties, and small flocks of 20-30 birds in winter. *Movements:* sedentary, but move to lower elevations in winter. *Foods:* buds, leaves, insects, worms and other invertebrates, spiders, bamboo shoots and fern. *Breeding:* May-June. *Nest:* bare, shallow scrape on the ground, often amongst bamboo. *Eggs:* 6-12, 20.

Cheng, 1963, pp.314-316.

Delacour, 1965, pp.268-269, 274-275.

NOTES ON INTRODUCTIONS

Great Britain. The Amherst Pheasant has been established in England from introductions in the twentieth century and the species is now on the official B.T.O. list in that country (Lever, 1976, pers. comm.). They maintain their numbers by breeding as a feral species (Sharrock, 1972).

Introductions of Amherst Pheasants occurred on the Isle of Bute, Cairnsmore, near Newton Stewart,

and at Woburn in Bedfordshire in the 1890s. They were introduced at Beaulieu Manor Woods in Hampshire in 1925, Richmond Park in Surrey in 1928-29 and 1931-32 (when twenty-four were released), Whipsnade Park in Bedfordshire in the 1930s, and at Elveden in Suffolk in 1950 (Fitter, 1959; Sharrock, 1976; Lever, 1977).

Lever says the Amherst Pheasant was established in an area of thirteen to sixteen kilometres (eight to ten miles) radius of Exbury in the New Forest in the late 1950s, and that eleven birds were still present there in 1973. He reports that the main centre of establishment of the species is in the east Midlands, where limited numbers breed in woods south of Bedfordshire and the neighbouring parts of Buckinghamshire and Hertfordshire. In 1973 some bred at Guist and Quidenham in Suffolk, but feral populations of Amherst Pheasants in Britain are generally small and localised.

Hawaiian Islands. Amherst Pheasants were imported to the Hawaiian Islands in 1931 and 1932 but are not known to have become established anywhere (Munro, 1960). Some were liberated on Oahu in 1932 and on Hawaii in 1933 (Caum, 1933; Schwartz and Schwartz, 1951). According to Walker (1967) all the birds came from the United States.

Berger (1972) reports that the species is not known to be established in the Hawaiian Islands.

New Zealand. The Amherst Pheasant was imported into New Zealand in 1907, but is not known to have been liberated there (Thomson, 1922).

Colombia. Attempts by hunt clubs and the Ministry of Agriculture to introduce Amherst Pheasants into Colombia, South America, were unsuccessful (Sick, 1968).

DAMAGE

None known.

COMMON PEAFOWL
(Peafowl, Indian Peafowl, Blue Peafowl)
Pavo cristatus Linnaeus

DISTINGUISHING CHARACTERISTICS
Male 90-130 cm (35.43-51.18 in), tail 2-2.5 m (78.74-80.70 in); female 86-100 cm (33.85-39.37 in). Male and female 2.7-6 kg (5.95-13.22 lb)
Fan-shaped crest and head metallic blue; a white band from nostril to eye; patch below eye white; neck and upper breast royal blue; back metallic green, each feather bordered black and with V-shaped brown patch; lower breast, abdomen and flanks black and dark green; wings brownish black with blue tinge; tail metallic green with bronze and purple reflections, subterminal ocellus formed by a blue patch surrounded by a bright blue and bronze ring, in turn surrounded by green and another of purple.
Female: crest, lores and upper neck chestnut-brown, each feather bordered bronze-green; eyebrows, sides of head and throat white; lower neck, upper breast and upper back metallic green; remainder of upper parts dull brown; lower breast dark brown; abdomen pale buff; wings blackish brown with spots.
Delacour, 1965, pp.313-316 and pl.31, opp. p.320.
Ali and Ripley, vol.2, 1968-74, pp.123-126 and vol.1, pl.6.

GENERAL DISTRIBUTION
Asia: Pakistan, India north to the Himalayas, Sri Lanka, Nepal and Bangladesh.

INTRODUCED DISTRIBUTION
Introduced successfully in Pakistan, the USA (California), Hawaiian Islands, Andaman Islands, New Zealand, and Rottnest Island, Heron Island and King Island in Australia; introduced successfully but died out in the Dominican Republic, St Helena and on Tahiti.
Introduced unsuccessfully to Madeira and/or Porto Santo.

GENERAL HABITS
Status: common; frequently kept in captivity. *Habitat:* open woods, forest edges, bushland and dense scrub, deciduous jungle and parks. *Gregariousness:* small groups, 1 cock and 4-5 hens, and after breeding segregated parties are common. *Movements:* sedentary. *Foods:* grain, shoots, insects, lizards, small snakes, molluscs, grubs, buds, berries and seeds. *Breeding:* Jan-Oct; male polygamous. *Nest:* shallow depression on the ground, in a dense thicket, and sometimes lined with sticks and leaves; in a semi-feral state often nest in ruins and on flat roofs of homes. *Eggs:* 3-8, 20.
Delacour, 1965, pp.312-315.
Ali and Ripley, vol.2, 1968-1974, pp.123-126.

NOTES ON INTRODUCTIONS
Pakistan. According to Whistler (1923), Peafowl have apparently been introduced in Sind (Pakistan) and neighbouring desert areas. Ticehurst (1924) says that Butler in 1878 quotes Doig as the authority for saying the species was introduced in the east Narra district. Ticehurst adds that they are present at Bobi near Mirpurkhas, at Umarkot, near Sukkur, and semi-wild at Sehwan; probably as a result of independent introductions and have not spread there as the desert prevents any extensions in range. Ali and Ripley (1968-1974) say that they are now established as a semi-feral bird in Sind including Hyderabad, Mirpurkhas, Umarkot and the Sehwan areas.
Andaman Islands. Ali and Ripley (1968-1974) record

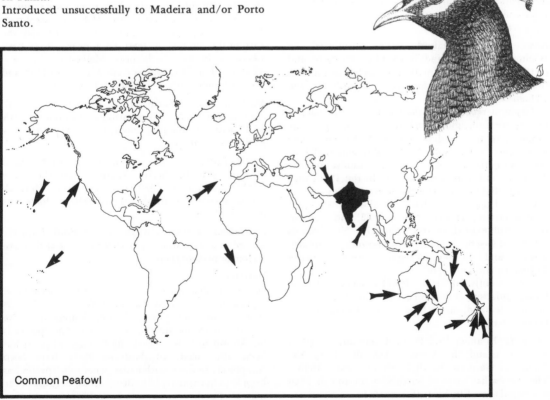

Common Peafowl

that the Peafowl has been introduced successfully in the Port Blair area of the Andamans and also elsewhere there.

USA. Peafowl are established in the vicinity of Palos Verdes Estates, Rolling Hills and Portuguese Bend, in California, where an estimated population of twenty to thirty adults have been breeding for some years (Hardy, 1973). At least fifteen birds were still present in the area in 1975 (Heilbrun, 1976).

Hawaiian Islands. Mrs F. Sinclair is reported to have introduced Peafowl to the Hawaiian Islands in 1860 (Munro, 1960). Fisher (1951) records that they were released on the island of Hawaii in the 1860s, and on Niihau in the 1890s. Two birds were released on the Puu Waawaa Ranch, Hawaii, in 1909 and the species has remained living around the homestead there. From here some birds have been distributed to several other land holders on the island (Lewin, 1971).

Peafowl were apparently plentiful on Niihau in the 1940s (Munro) and well established but confined to the lowlands in 1950 (Fisher). They were also reported to be plentiful on Kauai in 1936, and some were taken by C. Gray to Lanai from Kauai where they remained for some years.

Although in about 1960 they may have been established in small areas of Niihau, Kauai, Oahu, Molokai, Maui and Hawaii (Peterson, 1961), the Peafowl was not open to hunting as a game bird in the mid-1960s (Walker, 1967). According to the Hawaiian Audubon Society (1975) the species is now only well established and breeding probably on Oahu, Maui and Hawaii.

Dominican Republic. Wetmore and Swales (1931) say that Peafowl possibly became wild on the plains of Neyba in the Dominican Republic near the close of the eighteenth century. They were present there in 1798 and in 1810, but there appear no subsequent records of them.

New Zealand. Peafowl were introduced in Wellington, New Zealand, in 1843 by a Mr Petre, and in 1867 the Otago Acclimatisation Society introduced two birds, but there are no further records of them (Thomson, 1922).

Thomson records that the species was introduced by private individuals and dealers, and in some instances escaped and became wild. He says there were several colonies at Hawke's Bay and that they were formerly numerous in the valleys of the Turakina and Wangaehu Rivers. In the 1920s they were reported to be present inland from Wanganui.

Oliver (1955) reports that Peafowl were introduced at Waimarama, Hawke's Bay in 1862, and that this colony still existed in the 1950s. He also records colonies at Gisborne, Mahia, Waimarama, Wairoaiti, Tutira, and on the Wanganui River between Tokomaru and Longacre.

More recently Falla *et al* (1966) report that several feral populations of Peafowl occur in the North Island of New Zealand, from Kaipara to Wanganui and Hawke's Bay.

Australia. In about 1912 Peafowl were introduced to Rottnest Island in Western Australia from the Zoological Gardens, South Perth (Serventy, 1948). The species has survived on this island and in 1960 numbered some fifty birds (Storr, 1965).

On the Western Australian mainland young Peafowl, bred at the Zoological Gardens in South Perth, were released in various areas of the State prior to 1912. Some were liberated at Gingin and Pinjarra near Perth (Long, 1972). By 1959 apparently only a limited number survived at Pinjarra (Jenkins, 1959). Some birds were kept in a semi-captive state near Northam, before the 1950s, and odd colonies have been established for a while in other areas. Some birds were apparently noted (Chisholm, 1950) near Onslow in the north-west of the State.

In other parts of Australia colonies exist or have existed in a number of places. Chisholm (1950) and Tarr (1950) report them from Sister and Prince Seal Island in the Furneaux Group, Tasmania (where they were said to have become feral), on the Snowy River, New South Wales, and in the Blackall and Gladstone districts of Queensland. They were liberated in the Gladstone area in the period 1940-50 but are now uncommon there. They have also been introduced on the Capricorn Island Group (Lavery, 1974) and have been reported to be breeding on Heron Island (Kikkawa and Boles, 1976) in Queensland.

In the 1950s Peafowl were being kept in a semi-feral state by some people in the Finley and Deniliquin districts of New South Wales (Hobbs, 1961), and have more recently been reported from Murrays Lagoon on Kangaroo Island, South Australia (Condon, 1975).

Peafowl have been introduced to King Island in Bass Strait where a flock of twelve, at Pass River, was reported in the 1970s (McGarvie and Templeton, 1974). McGarvie and Templeton say that single birds have been observed at Porky Beach and at Loorana on the island since about 1972.

The Peafowl was also apparently an early introduction into Victoria where some were reported to have been turned out (Ryan, 1906) on Gembrook Reserve with jungle fowl and Guinea fowl before the turn of the century. At least ten appear to have been liberated in the bush near Melbourne in 1870 (Balmford, 1978), four at Cape Liptrap in 1872 and probably more 'in the bush' in 1873 (Jenkins, 1977).

Madeira and/or Porto Santo. Bannerman (1965) records that Peafowl were introduced to one or both of these islands, but that they are not now present in a wild state on either.

Society Islands. Peafowl were introduced to the island of Raiatea in the Society Islands where they were established in about 1920 (Holyoak, 1974). Holyoak says they were also introduced on Tahiti but have died out in both places.

St Helena. Melliss (1870) says Peafowl formerly existed in a feral state on St Helena but that they are no longer present there.

DAMAGE

Generally, Peafowl do not appear to be accused of damaging man's crops. However, Wayre (1969) says that at times they do considerable damage to native cultivation within their native range. The species is not known to have caused any damage where it has been introduced. In Australia there have been complaints to some authorities, where the species has been kept in captivity in built-up areas, because of the noise they make.

Family: *Meleagrididae* Turkey

Note: this family is now placed by some within the *Phasianidae*

2 species in 2 genera; 1 species introduced successfully

The only successful introduction has been that of the Turkey both as a domestic species and a wild bird. As a domestic bird it has been introduced by man throughout much of the world. It is said to have been introduced to Europe probably through Spain (Flatt, 1921), and may have reached there in about 1523 or 1524 (Zeuner, 1963). They may have been domesticated in Mexico from Neolithic times (Wood-Gush, in Thomson, 1964).

The wild birds have been established and re-established in a number of areas in North America.

Introductions in Europe and to some islands have also been successful. Generally these introductions have been made as game birds.

It is known that the other species, the Ocellated Turkey *(Agriocharis ocellata)*, was the subject of an early attempt to naturalise birds on Sapelo Island in Georgia, USA. Five birds were obtained from Guatemala in 1923 but died soon after arrival.

INTRODUCTIONS OF MELEAGRIDIDAE

Species	Date introduced	Region	Manner introduced	Reason
(a) Successful introductions				
Turkey	late 1800s on	USA (many States)	deliberate	re-stocking and hunting
	1961-62	Sidney Island, Canada	deliberate	hunting ?
	1962	Alberta, Canada	deliberate	game
	1815 on	Hawaiian Islands	deliberate	hunting
	1571, before 1939, 1959-66	Germany	deliberate	hunting
	prior 1950	Prince Seal Island, Australia	deliberate	?
	1892, 1922, 1950	New Zealand	feral occasionally	domestic bird
	?	USSR	deliberate ?	hunting ?
(b) Unsuccessful introductions				
Turkey	before 1926	Fiji (?)	deliberate ?	?
	1877	Santa Cruz Island, USA	deliberate	sport
	1910	James Island, Canada	deliberate	hunting
	prior 1954	Sidney and Prevost Islands, Canada	deliberate	hunting
	1931	South Pender Island, Canada	deliberate	hunting
	about 1788	Hispaniola, West Indies	feral	domestic bird
	1954	Andros Island, Bahamas	feral ?	?
	1875, 1888, 1891	France	deliberate	hunting
	1890	Chatham Island	feral ?	?

TURKEY
(Wild Turkey)

Meleagris gallopavo Linnaeus

DISTINGUISHING CHARACTERISTICS

90-125 cm (35.43-49.21 in). Males 4.7-15.8 kg (10.36-34.83 lb), females 2.1-6.3 kg (4.6-13.88 lb) Generally iridescent coppery bronze; head and neck naked, red, more purplish or blue on excrescences; each feather broad, squared, and giving a scaly appearance, abruptly margined black, becoming greenish or purplish where colours meet; lower back and rump blackish; tail dark brown, barred black, and with a subterminal band; bill yellowish white, tinged red. *Female:* naked area pinkish or pale red; without metallic gloss.

Hewitt, 1967, pp.26-44 and pls. 1, 2 and 3.

GENERAL DISTRIBUTION

North America: from southern USA to northern Mexico. Formerly parts of central, north-eastern and eastern USA and the extreme south-eastern part of Canada, and southern Mexico.

INTRODUCED DISTRIBUTION

Introduced, re-introduced and transplanted widely in the USA and Canada with some success; introduced successfully in the Hawaiian Islands, Germany, New Zealand and the Prince Seal Island (Tasmania); feral

183

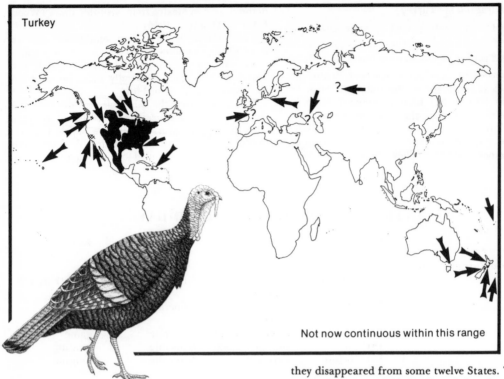

Turkey

Not now continuous within this range

but died out in Hispaniola. Introduced unsuccessfully in Fiji. Introduced throughout the world as a domestic species.

GENERAL HABITS

Status: range and numbers reduced, but increasing under management. *Habitat:* mountain forests, broken woodlands and coastal plains. *Gregariousness:* small groups (1 male and several females), sexes segregate in flocks in the non-breeding season. *Movements:* sedentary, but may wander extensively. *Foods:* berries, acorns, nuts, seeds, insects, shoots, buds, and crustaceans, amphibians and reptiles. *Breeding:* May-Aug; polygamous. *Nest:* concealed leaf-lined depression on the ground. *Eggs:* 8-15, 20.

Hewitt, 1967.

Lewis, 1963.

NOTES ON INTRODUCTIONS

USA. There have been many introductions, re-introductions and transplants of pen-reared and wild turkeys within the United States. It would be difficult indeed to make mention of all of them and the following is but a brief summary. Individual accounts up until 1967 for most areas in the United States are contained in the volume edited by Hewitt (1967), *The Wild Turkey and its Management* by authors including Bailey and Rinell, Shaffer and Gwynn, Powell, Glazener, and MacDonald and Jantzen.

According to Hewitt (1967) and others, following settlement of the continent by Europeans, the wild turkey disappeared from large sections of their original range due to the relentless exploitation to which they were subjected. Much of their original forest habitat was eliminated, and other factors such as disease from domestic poultry may have aided the rapid reduction of numbers. From 1813 to about 1907

they disappeared from some twelve States. Today the species is more widely distributed than it was during the early part of the twentieth century due to improvement of habitat, introductions, re-introductions, re-stocking and transplanting. It now also occurs in some areas which were certainly not its ancestral home within historic times.

Before about 1925 there appear to have been only a few attempted introductions of the Turkey, although many may not have been documented. In the 1870s J. D. Caton bred many birds at Ottawa, Illinois, and these were shipped to many areas for release. Mexican turkeys were liberated on Santa Cruz Island (off California) in 1877, where they survived for some ten years. Some were liberated unsuccessfully in Pennsylvania in 1879, and an attempt was made to re-introduce the species in Wisconsin in 1887. Between 1888 and 1918 about 1240 Mexican turkeys were released in California, but these introductions were largely failures. Some were introduced in New York State at Tuxedo Park by J. L. Breese before 1893 and there were further liberations in 1912-14 in Broome County, in 1932 in Cattaraugus County and by State authorities between 1930 and 1936, all without success (Bump, 1941). About 1771 wild or partly wild birds were released in Pennsylvania between 1915 and 1925. Further unsuccessful introductions were made in the Sequoia National Park, California, after 1910. Other introductions in this period include: some unsuccessfully to Grand Island, Lake Superior before 1925; small unsuccessful releases in Oregon and Washington before 1926; various attempts in Maryland, Virginia, Wisconsin and Minnesota before 1928; and efforts by sportsmen's associations in Arizona to restore birds to their former range. Unsuccessful releases were made in Massachusetts between 1915 and 1918. The first successful liberation in that State occurred on Naushon Island in 1922, where some birds were still present in 1967. A number of introductions probably occurred in Maryland in the early 1920s. Further information on these introductions may be found in Phillips (1928), Schorger (1942), Burger (1954) and Bailey and Rinell (1967), etc.

From 1925 on, Turkey introductions and re-stocking in the United States seems to have gathered momentum, becoming more widespread in the 1950s and 1960s when the use of domestic and hybrid pen-reared birds waned, and wild birds were more extensively introduced and transplanted. Leopold (1944), and later others, found the former to have a poor survival rate as compared with the latter.

In 1949 twelve western States (west of the Mississippi River) reported attempts by government organisations and private individuals and sportsmen to establish the Turkey outside their former range (Walker, 1949). They were successful in Washington, Minnesota, Utah, Montana, Idaho, and Nebraska; with questionable results in Wyoming and Oregon; while in Arizona, California and South Dakota there were some signs of successful establishment. Efforts in Utah, Montana and Idaho were not successful. Walker reports that in seven of these States at least 3752 turkeys were released.

By 1957 parts of the range of the race *silvestris* (Eastern Turkey) had been re-established with turkeys by stocking with domestic and western strains; the race *intermedia* (Rio Grande Turkey) had been re-established by stocking in northern and central Texas and *merriami* (Merriams' Turkey) had been re-introduced to south-western Texas, the coastal ranges of central California, eastern Utah, central Wyoming and south-western South Dakota (A.O.U., 1957).

Anon (1964) records that a summary of turkeys stocked by Fish and Game Departments under Federal Aid schemes shows that thirty-one States liberated 12 030 birds between 1938 and 1963.

From other data available until 1967 it is indicated that at least forty-one continental States have made efforts to either introduce, re-introduce, re-stock or transplant turkeys in the United States. At least twenty-eight of these appear to have had some success and a further eleven may have had limited success. Only two States, Oklahoma and Iowa, appear to have had little or no success.

Most of the introductions have probably been made with the eastern race or hybrids. MacDonald and Jantzen (1967) report that Wyoming, South Dakota, Montana, Nebraska and North Dakota each have thriving populations as a result of wild trapped Merriams' Turkey introductions. Glazener (1967) says the Rio Grande Turkey has failed in Alabama, Georgia, South Carolina and Mississippi, and that releases in California, Iowa, Nebraska, Ohio and South Dakota are too recent to gauge whether they may be successful.

To illustrate the success that has been achieved with some introductions several examples are given.

The release of turkeys in Missouri commenced in 1925 and until 1943 some 14 122 artificially propagated birds were liberated (Leopold, 1944). Some were of domestic and some of mixed stock, but the release of hybrids was discontinued after 1943. Since the restoration project with native wild trapped birds began, eleven areas were stocked of which at least seven were successful and the first hunting season for twenty-three years was held in 1960 (Lewis, 1961).

In 1948 eight turkeys were released near Spearfish in the Black Hills of South Dakota and were said to be increasing there (Walker, 1949). By 1958 the population had reached 5000 birds and numerous transplants from this area to others were made from 1952 to 1960 (MacDonald and Jantzen, 1967).

The wild bird disappeared in Michigan in about 1900 but was re-established in the Allegan Forest area in 1954 when 202 birds were released by the Michigan Department of Conservation. They became well established and by 1958 occupied an area of 600 square kilometres (373 square miles), but were unable to spread further because of unfavourable habitat (Wilson and Lewis, 1959; Lee and Lewis, 1959). Other successful re-introductions occurred in Michigan in 1954 with the release of 782 game farm reared birds, which by 1962 numbered some 2000 in seven areas (Bailey and Rinell, 1967).

The Turkey was probably not a native of Montana but was the subject of many unsuccessful introductions by sporting clubs and private individuals prior to 1954. At this time the Montana Fish and Game Department commenced a series of releases which has resulted in some twenty-five flocks of Merriams' Turkey, with huntable populations, in seven areas of Montana (Greene and Ellis, 1971). The first of these introductions occurred in November 1954 when thirteen stock birds from Colorado were released near Lewistown. From 1954 to 1969, 626 were released, of which fifty-seven were originally released in three areas and 569 of which were transplanted from these and other areas.

Although in 1949 (Walker) it was indicated that the turkey was in a precarious position in the United States its future at present seems assured for at least some time to come. Through introductions, re-introductions and re-stocking it still inhabits many areas within its former range and now exists in some regions not previously inhabited. By 1967 the race *silvestris* had been established in north-central Michigan (Oscoda County), central Wisconsin (Wood County), south-eastern Massachusetts (Naushon Island), south-eastern Ohio, central Michigan, central Wisconsin and north-west of its normal range in central-south North Dakota; a population in south-west Oklahoma (Wichita Mountains) was the result of wild stock from Missouri, and also domestic and mixed stock; the race *intermedia* was established north of its range in central-western North Dakota and also in parts of eastern Texas, Oklahoma and Kansas; the race *merriami* was established in northern Montana, south-west North Dakota, and also south-central California, central-northern Nebraska and western South Dakota; areas in Montana, Wyoming, Utah, and south-eastern Arizona had also been re-stocked with this race.

Canada. Two pairs of wild Turkey were introduced to James Island in 1910 by Sir Richard McBride and a group of associates who purchased the island for hunting purposes. Turkeys were numerous there for some years, but had disappeared by 1929. Some thirty to forty of them were liberated on Sidney and Prevost islands prior to 1954, and some on South Pender Island in 1931, but neither release was successful. They were tried again on Sidney Island in 1961 (ten birds) and 1962 (twelve birds) when released by Mr J. Todd. A small protected population now exists on that island (Carl and Guiguet, 1972), built up from those released in 1962.

Birds wild trapped in South Dakota were released at Cypress Hills in Alberta, Canada, in 1962 and after one season had increased to some fifty birds (MacDonald and Jantzen, 1967).

Godfrey (1966) indicates that there have been a number of attempts to re-introduce the Turkey in Canada but only modest results have been achieved.

Hawaiian Islands. Turkeys were taken to the Hawaiian Islands from Chile and released as early as 1815 (Caum, 1933; Walker, 1967). According to Fisher (1951), thousands were liberated at various times on Niihau. In the 1960s they were still being released in the Hawaiian Islands (Western States Exotic Game Bird Committee, 1961), although some success had already been achieved on Niihau and on the leeward side of Hawaii (Peterson, 1961). Lewin (1971) records that twelve birds from a Californian game farm were released on the Puu Waawaa Ranch, Hawaii, in 1959, 103 *(M.g. silvestris)* from a New York game farm in 1960, and twenty-eight *(M.g. intermedia)* from a Texan game farm and wild birds from the King Ranch, Texas, in 1961. He also reports that the State Division of Game and Fish released 'turlock' turkeys on south-east Mauna Kea in 1958, *M.g. silvestris* from the King Ranch in 1961 and thirty-seven more birds at Omaokoili near Pohakuloa in 1962. Both the Puu Waawaa and State Authority introductions were successful and the species has become well established on Hawaii.

In 1960-61 the introduction of 'turlock' turkeys was discontinued and the Rio Grande subspecies was tried there. Small numbers were released on Hawaii, Kauai, Molokai, Lanai and Maui. They were breeding on Hawaii and Molokai, surviving on Lanai, but not doing well on Maui and Kauai (Western States Exotic Game Bird Committee) in about 1961.

In the late 1960s it was reported that the Turkey was established in the Hawaiian Islands but had not had tremendous success and was still not open to hunting (Walker). In more recent years the Hawaiian Audubon Society (1975) records that they are probably well established and breeding on Kauai, Oahu, Molokai, Lanai, Maui and Hawaii. The Rio Grande race *(intermedia)* is possibly established on Hawaii, but its present status is poorly known.

West Indies. The Turkey was apparently, at one time, feral in Hispaniola (Wetmore and Swales, 1931). Wetmore and Swales record that Baron de Wimpffen in his voyages to Saint Domingo in 1788, 1789 and 1790, said 'turkeys which the Jesuits seem only to have domesticated for themselves, have run wild again'.

Turkeys were introduced to Andros in 1954, but are probably not established as a feral species (Bond, 1960).

Europe. Kauffman (1962) indicates that hundreds of eggs were being shipped to various parts of Germany from the United States in an effort to re-populate forests with wild turkeys. The results of this and apparently earlier efforts are not known. Frank (1970) reports that 127 wild turkeys were introduced in Germany between 1959 and 1966.

Turkeys were reared in flocks in the Lower Rhine as early as 1571 (Zeuner, 1963). According to Lindzey (1967) some small populations were established in Germany prior to the second World War, but little data is available on them and they are reported to have disappeared during the war. Hunting was formerly carried out in the Wein area on the Donau River. Two small populations are still reported to exist in this region, resulting from game farm eggs and adults as a source of planting stock.

They were introduced in France in 1875 and although given much attention failed to become established as a wild bird. Attempts at introducing them in 1888 and in 1891 at Sologne failed, and only limited success was attained in the park at Cadarache (Etchécopar, 1955).

In the USSR, Aliev and Khanmamedov (1963) mention the Turkey as being an excellent game bird bred successfully for a long time in the hunting districts of Pomerania, East Prussia, Hanover, Austria and Latvia. They also claim that 'interesting experiments' with this species have been made in Transcaucasia, but the status of the Turkey in these regions is not known.

Australia. A number of turkeys were introduced to Prince Seal Island in the Furneaux Group, Tasmania, and were reported to be established there in 1950 (Tarr, 1950).

New Zealand. According to Oliver (1955) wild turkeys were present in Hawke's Bay, Canterbury and Nelson provinces, and in the Chatham Islands in 1890. They were mostly in the vicinity of homesteads and did not remain established for long periods. Thomson (1922) records that they were common about Hawke's Bay in 1892, and in some localities inland from Wanganui in 1922.

In the 1950s turkeys were present in some localities in Wellington, Hawke's Bay and the Marlborough Province and appeared to be permanently established (Oliver). They are apparently still established in New Zealand and are locally common in both the North and South Islands (Wodzicki, 1965; Falla *et al,* 1966).

The race introduced in New Zealand is *M.g. mexicana* (Oliver).

Fiji. According to Wood and Wetmore (1926) there may have been introductions of turkeys on Fiji. Evidently the species failed to become established in that country because there appears to be no further mention of them.

DAMAGE

Bailey and Rinell (1967) record that many game species create crop damage problems, but turkeys rarely conflict with man's agricultural pursuits. Occasionally they may damage truck crops and grain but in most instances the owner is more than happy to bear the costs of such damage.

ORDER: GRUIFORMES

Family: *Rallidae* Rails, coots

138 species in 52 genera; 6 species introduced, 3 successfully

The Weka has been established on a number of small islands off New Zealand and probably in one or two areas of the North Island. The early introductions were more than likely made by sealers or whalers as a source of food, but the more recent ones probably for preservation of the species.

Little appears to be documented on the introduction of the Common Gallinule to St Helena or on the Gough Moorhen introduced to Tristan da Cunha. The Purple Gallinule may or may not have been introduced to Mauritius.

Although not documented here the Common Coot *(Fulica atra australis)* has colonised New Zealand, now breeding on both the North and South Islands, after having been first recorded there in 1890 (Wodzicki, 1965; Williams, 1973).

The Land Rail *(Rallus philippensis)* and the Coot *(Fulica atra)* were imported to New Zealand in 1875 and 1869 respectively, but are not known to have been liberated there.

Family: *Turnicidae* Button-quails

14 species in 2 genera; 2 species introduced, 1 successfully (?)

Madagascar Button-quail appear to have been established on Réunion and in the Isles Glorieuses. In the latter place they may have reached the island through colonisation, rather than deliberate introduction, and establishment aided by clearing of the islands' flora. They may have been established on Mauritius for some time, but do not occur there now.

Family: *Gruidae* Cranes

14 species in 4 genera; 2 species introduced, both unsuccessfully

Introduction of the Demoiselle Crane in France and the Brolga in Fiji were both unsuccessful.

INTRODUCTIONS OF RALLIDAE, TURNICIDAE AND GRUIDAE

Species	Date introduced	Region	Manner introduced	Reason
(a) Successful introductions				
Weka	1872	Macquarie Island, Australia	deliberate	food ?
	1863	Kawau Island, New Zealand	deliberate	?
	1905, 1962	Chatham Islands	deliberate	conservation
	early 1900s	Southern Islands off New Zealand	deliberate	food ?
	1958 and 1966-71	North Island, New Zealand	deliberate re-introductions and transplants	preservation ?
Common Gallinule	about 1930	St Helena	deliberate ?	?
Gough Moorhen	early 1950s	Tristan da Cunha	deliberate	preservation ?
Madagascar Button-quail	?	Réunion	?	?
(b) Probably successful introductions				
Weka	?	Kapiti Island, N.Z.	?	?
Purple Gallinule	prior 1812 ?	Mauritius	deliberate or may be native	?
	?	Argentina	?	?
Madagascar Button-quail	recent	Isles Glorieuses	deliberate or colonisation	sport ?
(c) Unsuccessful introductions				
Weka	about 1864	Auckland Islands, N.Z.	deliberate	food ?
Corncrake	1874-77	Ohio, USA	deliberate ?	?
Laysan Rail	1887, 1891, 1913, 1929	Hawaiian Group (small islands in)	deliberate	conservation or preservation
Common Gallinule	?	Hawaiian Islands	deliberate re-introductions	conservation?
Purple Gallinule	1928 and later	Hawaiian Islands	deliberate	?
Painted Button-quail	1922	Hawaiian Islands	deliberate	game ?
	prior 1871	New Zealand	not known if released	cagebird ?
Madagascar Button-quail	prior 1969 ?	Mauritius	deliberate ?	?
Demoiselle Crane	about 1914	France	deliberate ?	?
Brolga	prior 1926 ?	Fiji	deliberate	?

Rallidae

WEKA
(New Zealand Woodhen)
Gallirallus australis (Sparrman)

DISTINGUISHING CHARACTERISTICS

52.5 cm (21 in). Males 532-1117 g (1.2-2.5 lb),
females 382-1010 g (.8-2.2 lb)
Large flightless rail, mottled black and various shades
of brown; subspecies vary, the North Island race
having more grey on the underparts, the South Island
race having the breast streaked red-brown and black,
others are darker; bill blackish or rufous-brown.
Oliver, 1955, pp.360-371 and pl. foll. p.320.
Ripley, 1977, pp.141-146 and pl. 15, p.143.

GENERAL DISTRIBUTION

New Zealand and surrounding islands: parts of both
the North and South Islands, and Stewart Island and
the Chathams.

INTRODUCED DISTRIBUTION

Introduced successfully on Macquarie Island,
Chatham Islands, islands off the south and west coasts
of the South Island of New Zealand (Jacky Lee, Big
Solander and Codfish) and in parts of the North
Island of New Zealand; re-established successfully in
parts of the North Island of New Zealand; probably
introduced successfully on Kapiti Island and to Pitt
Island. Possibly introduced, unsuccessfully, to
Auckland Island and Kawau.

GENERAL HABITS

Status: range reduced, but locally common in some
areas. *Habitat:* forest edges, shrub country and sub-
Antarctic islands. *Gregariousness:* no information.
Movements: sedentary. *Foods:* grass, clover, seeds,
leaves, stalks and other vegetable material, rats, mice,
birds, eggs, beetles, earthworms, snails, slugs,
grasshoppers, myriapods, molluscs and crustaceans.
Breeding: all year, but mainly June-Sept; up to four
broods per year. *Nest:* of grass, sedges and leaves,
well concealed. *Eggs:* 2, 3-4, 6.
Oliver, 1955, pp 360-371.
Ripley, 1977, pp 141-146.

NOTES ON INTRODUCTIONS

Macquarie Island. Peters (1934) records that the
Weka *G.a. australis* has been introduced and
established on Macquarie Island. According to Falla

Weka, *Gallirallus australis*

Weka

et al (1966) the Stewart Island form *(scotti)* which
was introduced on Macquarie was numerous there in
the late 1960s. Watson (1975) indicates that the
species was still numerous there in the mid-1970s.

The Weka may have been introduced to Macquarie
by early sealers as a source of food. Oliver (1955)
records that they were introduced in 1872 by Captain
Printz of the *Sarah Pile* and that some may have been
taken there by Captain Gilroy as early as 1830. Others
were apparently introduced in 1879 by Elder.

Chatham Islands. Peters (1934) records that the race
G.a. australis has been introduced to the Chatham
Islands. According to Atkinson and Bell (1973) the
Buff Weka *(G.a. hectori)* of the eastern South Island
was introduced to both the Chatham and Pitt Islands
in 1905. The successful establishment of the species on
the Chathams enabled sixteen birds to be re-
introduced at Arthur's Pass National Park in the
South Island in February 1962, where they are now
established and doing well (Falla *et al*, 1966).

Southern islands. Wekas were introduced in the early
1900s to Open Bay Islands, off the west coast of the
South Island (Atkinson and Bell, 1973). Atkinson
and Bell record that *G.a. scotti* originally occurred
only on the mainland and on Stewart Island. It was
introduced as an alternative food supply for mutton-
birders and sealers on a number of islands off New
Zealand. They now occur on at least Jacky Lee Island,
Big Solander and Codfish Island off the south coast
(Foveaux Strait).

Kapiti Island. The Wekas on Kapiti are said to be
hybrids of the races *greyi* and *scotti* (Falla *et al*, 1966)
so perhaps one or both have been introduced there.

Kawau. The Buff Weka *(G.a. hectori)* is said to have
been introduced to Kawau by Sir George Grey in 1863
and to have become well established there (Oliver,
1955).

Auckland Island. Oliver (1955) records that it is said

that after the wreck of the *Grafton* (in 1864) Wekas were released on Auckland Island, but if so, they did not become established there.

North Island. In the North Island the Weka is now confined to the Gisborne area. The species disappeared from many districts in 1918, was still plentiful in some in 1936, but difficult to find by 1940. The decline of the Buff Weka in the South Island became apparent prior to the 1920s and the last known bird was recorded in 1924.

In attempts to re-establish them *(greyi)* in some of their old haunts, hundreds have been caught near Gisborne and released in North Island areas where conditions for their survival appeared favourable (Falla *et al,* 1966). Carroll (1963) indicates that many were trapped in this area for transplanting prior to 1963, when complaints of their damage increased. Birds from Poverty Bay (east coast of North Island) have also been released in other areas (Pracy, 1969). Two liberations were made in 1958, on the Pararaki River, Aorangi Range and at the Orongorongo Research Station, Rimutaka Range, but were both unsuccessful, probably due to the small numbers liberated (thirteen birds) and other environmental factors. In December 1966, forty birds were introduced at Whatarangi (Palliser Bay region on south-east tip of North Island), followed by the release of a similar number near the Matakitaki Stream, Cape Palliser in February 1968, with further liberations at later dates in the same areas. By 1969 four releases had been made, with the additional liberation of eight birds at Whatarangi to support the already-established birds in that locality. Both Whatarangi and Matakitaki liberations appeared successful, chicks being found in both areas, although dispersion of birds from the liberation sites was limited.

North Island Wekas *(greyi)* were also successfully established at Rawhiti (Bay of Islands in the North Island) as a result of five liberations in the summers of 1966 to 1971 (Robertson, 1976). Some 149 birds, about thirty-two at a time, were released in this area and the species is now probably established in a sixteen-kilometre strip from Cape Brett to Whangaruru North Head. The present population is reported to number more than ninety-five birds of which some have been recorded breeding. Other attempts to introduce them have been made in the nearby areas of the Russell Forestry Unit (thirty-two kilometres south of Rawhiti) in 1967, when thirty-two birds were liberated, and at South Kaipara Head in 1968 (thirty-two birds) and 1969 (thirty-two) (Robertson). A pair was seen in the latter area in 1974, but these introductions do not appear to have been very successful.

DAMAGE

Carrol (1963) says that in the Gisborne area of New Zealand, Wekas became a nuisance locally to farmers and market gardeners by pecking tomatoes, melons and pumpkins, robbing fowl yards and digging up plants in search of insects. Many were trapped prior to 1963 for release in other areas following complaints of their damage.

Wekas on the Open Bay Islands appear to be adversely affecting other birds by their predatory habits (Atkinson and Bell, 1973). According to Atkinson and Bell they have assisted in the depletion of the fauna on the Southern Islands in Foveaux Strait. On some islands their effects have been likened to those of the feral cat.

On Jacky Lee Island in 1932 many dead diving petrels were found with their stomachs eaten out by Wekas. Wekas have also been observed to dig out young fairy prions and eat them. By 1940 the fairy prions had been greatly reduced in numbers because of this habit.

The scarcity of burrowing petrels on Big Solander Island has been attributed by Falla to depredations by Wekas. Large numbers of mottled petrels were apparently being eaten by Wekas on Codfish Island in 1968, and an extensive Cook's Petrel colony had already gone, presumably as a result of Weka predation.

CORNCRAKE
(Landrail)
Crex crex (Linnaeus)

DISTINGUISHING CHARACTERISTICS
22.5-27.5 cm (9-11 in)
Upper parts pale tawny brown, with blackish centres to feathers; upper and under wing-coverts chestnut; ash grey patches above eyes in breeding season; throat white; breast greyish buff; belly white; flanks barred brown and whitish; bill pale brown, tip darker.
Witherby *et al,* vol.5, 1938-41, pp.174-180 and pl.143, opp. p.186.
Mackworth-Praed and Grant, 1952-73, ser.1, vol.1, p.287; ser.2, vol.1, p.240; ser.3, vol.1, pp.211-212 and pl.17.
Ripley, 1977, pp.211-215 and pl.26, p.213.

GENERAL DISTRIBUTION
Eurasia: from the British Isles, southern Scandinavia and north-eastern Spain, eastern to central Asia. In winter south to the Açores, South Africa, Arabia and (?) India. (Has occurred, apparently accidentally, in a number of regions of the world well away from its normal range, e.g. New Zealand (1865), Australia (1893 and 1944), Greenland, West Indies and the USA.)

INTRODUCED DISTRIBUTION
Introduced unsuccessfully in the USA. Extended breeding range northwards in Eurasia.

GENERAL HABITS
Status: fairly common, but numbers diminished in some areas. *Habitat:* grasslands, hayfields, meadows, grass marshes, grassy clearings in forest and arable lands. *Gregariousness:* singly, rarely more than two together. *Movements:* migratory. *Foods:* small animals (beetles, weevils, slugs, snails, earthworms, millipedes, spiders), seeds and green shoots. *Breeding:* May-June (Great Britain). *Nest:* wad of dry grass and leaves in a hollow on the ground amongst grass and herbage. *Eggs:* 7-10, 14.
Witherby *et al,* vol.5, 1938-41, pp.174-180.
Voous, 1960, p.86.
Ripley, 1977, pp.211-215.

NOTES ON INTRODUCTIONS
USA. The Corncrake was introduced in Cincinnati, Ohio in 1872-74, but failed to become established there (Phillips, 1928). The species is however, occasionally recorded in the United States as a straggler from the Old World.

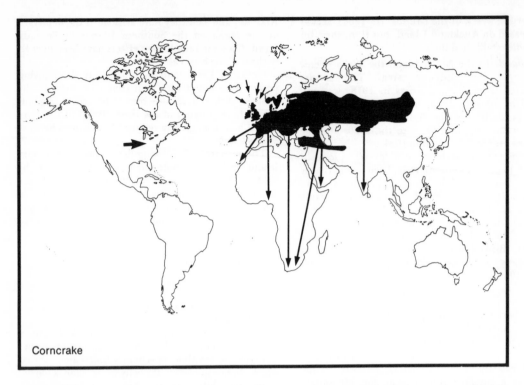

Corncrake

Eurasia. With extensions in cultivation in northern Europe and western Siberia the Corncrake has been able to extend its breeding range northwards in the present century (Voous, 1960).

DAMAGE
None known.

LAYSAN RAIL
(Laysan Island Rail)
Porzanula palmeri Frohawk

DISTINGUISHING CHARACTERISTICS
15 cm (6 in)
Top of head pale brown with dark streaks; sides of head and line over eye slate-grey; back pale brown, with darker shafts; scapulars, flanks and sides sandy brown; breast mouse grey; bill green.
Berger, 1972, pp.86-89 and pl.29, p.78.
Ripley, 1977, pp.235-236 and pl.30, p.245.

GENERAL DISTRIBUTION
Formerly Laysan Island, now extinct (from about 1944).

INTRODUCED DISTRIBUTION
Introduced successfully but now extirpated on Eastern Island (Midway Atoll), Lisianski Island, Pearl and Hermes Reef and Sand Island in the Hawaiian Group.

GENERAL HABITS
Status: extinct. *Habitat:* coastal and other areas of Laysan Island. *Gregariousness:* pairs and family groups. *Movements:* sedentary. *Foods:* omnivorous — insects, carrion, seeds, green plant material and eggs. *Breeding:* Apr-July. *Nest:* on or near the ground in a thicket or tussock, arched, with a side entrance. *Eggs:* 2-3, 4.
Berger, 1972, pp.86-89.
Ripley, 1977, pp.235-236.

NOTES ON INTRODUCTIONS
Hawaiian Islands. Laysan Rails may have been transplanted to Eastern Island (Midway Atoll) as

early as 1887 (Baldwin, 1945), and it is known that a pair were released there in 1891. By 1905 on Eastern Island they were said to be almost as common as they were on Laysan. However, Berger (1972) indicates that more than 100 were liberated on Lisianski and Eastern Island in March 1913. He says that they probably did not survive on Lisianski because of the introduction of rabbits which destroyed the vegetation there.

A Captain Anderson took seven pairs from Midway

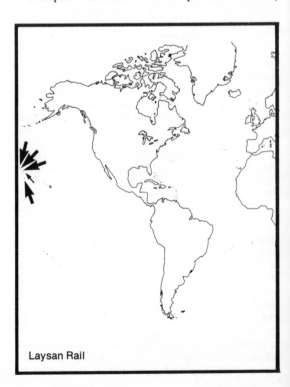

Laysan Rail

and released them on one of the small islands at Pearl and Hermes Reef in 1929 (Fisher and Baldwin, 1945), but they did not survive there. In 1910 employees of the Cable Co. released rails on Sand Island.

An estimate of some 5000 rails was made on the two islands at Midway in 1922 and they were numerous there in 1939 and 1940. Following the introduction of rats in 1943, the last birds were seen on Sand Island in November 1943 and the last on Eastern Island in June 1944 (Berger, 1972).

Evidently, attempts were also made to introduce them to the main islands in the Hawaiian Group. According to Munro (1960) an experiment made to introduce Laysan Rails to cane fields on the main islands 'naturally failed'.

DAMAGE

None known.

COMMON GALLINULE
(Moorhen)
Gallinula chloropus (Linnaeus)

DISTINGUISHING CHARACTERISTICS

30-40 cm (12-16 in). 241-505 g (.53-1.1 lb)

Head and neck black; slate colour on breast and flanks *(G.c. meridionalis* has olive-brown wings, *sandvicensis* has slaty blue underparts with brown wings); flanks streaked white; back brownish; outer and under tail-coverts white, inner black; middle of abdomen whitish (not in *sandvicensis*); frontal shield red; bill red, tipped yellowish.

Witherby *et al,* vol.5, 1938-41, pp.197-204 and pl.144, opp. p.204.

Mackworth-Praed and Grant, 1952-73, ser.1, vol.1, pp.301-302; ser.2, vol.1, pp.253-254 and pl.16; ser.3, vol.1, pp.223-224 and pl.17.

Ripley, 1977, pp.279-288 and pls.35 and 40, pp.283 and 329.

GENERAL DISTRIBUTION

North, Central and South America, Eurasia and Africa: in America from California, the Great Lakes and extreme south-eastern Canada, south through Central America and the West Indies to Uruguay, northern Argentina and northern Chile in South America. In Eurasia from the British Isles, southern Scandinavia and the Mediterranean region, east to Sakhalin, Japan, Marianas, Philippines and western Indonesia. In Africa, most of southern Africa south of the Sahara, north-western and north-eastern Africa. Also Malagasy, Mascarene Islands, Seychelles, Açores, Bermuda, Galápagos and Hawaiian Islands.

INTRODUCED DISTRIBUTION

Introduced successfully to St Helena Island. Efforts at re-establishment on Hawaii and Maui, Hawaiian Islands, have been unsuccessful.

GENERAL HABITS

Status: common. *Habitat:* freshwater swamps, marshes and the waterside edges of lakes, ponds, slow rivers and reservoirs. *Gregariousness:* pairs, family groups or small flocks. *Movements:* sedentary and migratory. *Foods:* worms, slugs, snails, molluscs, waterplants, reeds, marsh and water insects (mosquito larvae), seeds and fruits. *Breeding:* breeds irregularly; June-Apr (Africa), Mar-July (Great Britain), June-Sept (India); may have 2-3 broods per season; somewhat colonial. *Nest:* untidy basket-like platform of grass or marsh vegetation, with central cup often attached to living plants above or at water level, or on the ground amongst aquatic herbage, or less frequently in a bush or low tree. *Eggs:* 4-13.

Mackworth-Praed and Grant, 1952-73, ser.1, vol.1, pp.301-302; ser.2, vol.1, pp.253-254; ser.3, vol.1, pp.223-224.

Fieldsa, 1977.

Ripley, 1977, pp.279-288.

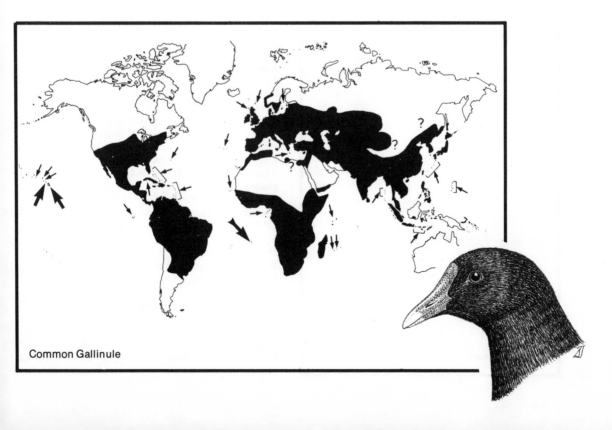

Common Gallinule

Hawaiian Islands. Peterson (1961) reports that the Hawaiian Gallinule *G.c. sandvicensis* has recently been re-introduced to the island of Maui. The species is a resident locally on the islands of Kauai, Oahu and Molokai, but formerly inhabited both Maui and Hawaii. Evidently the introduction to Maui was not successful as the species is not now found on this island (Hawaiian Audubon Society, 1975). Attempts to re-establish them on Hawaii also appear to have been unsuccessful to date (Berger, 1972).

St Helena. The race *G.c. meridionalis* was introduced successfully to St Helena in about 1930 (Mackworth-Praed and Grant, 1962).

DAMAGE

None known.

GOUGH MOORHEN
(Tristan da Cunha Moorhen)
Gallinula nesiotis (Sclater)

DISTINGUISHING CHARACTERISTICS

27 cm (11 in) 400 g (14 oz)

Generally black; head, neck and underparts black and body sooty grey, washed brown on the back and wings; wing primaries edged white; under tail-coverts white; frontal plate red; bill red, basally coral and tip yellow.

Ripley, 1977, pp.273-274 and pl.35, p.283.

GENERAL DISTRIBUTION

Tristan da Cunha (formerly) and Gough Island (South Atlantic Ocean).

INTRODUCED DISTRIBUTION

Re-introduced successfully (?) to Tristan da Cunha.

GENERAL HABITS

Status: extinct on Tristan da Cunha, but still not uncommon on Gough Island. *Habitat:* forest and tree fern zones, along shores, boggy areas, and in grass and undergrowth along streams. *Gregariousness:* no

Gough Moorhen

information. *Food:* grass heads and littoral organisms. *Movements:* sedentary. *Breeding:* Sept-Nov (?). *Nest:* well hidden, scrape on ground lined with dead grass. *Eggs:* 2.

Ripley, 1977, pp.273-274.

NOTES ON INTRODUCTIONS

Tristan da Cunha. Flightless moorhens have been re-discovered on Tristan by Dr M. E. Richardson, possibly they are derived from birds re-introduced from Gough Island in the early 1950s (Wace and Holdgate, 1976). The Tristan race *(nesiotis)* is now extinct (extirpated in late nineteenth century), but the subspecies *G.n. comeri* still occurs on Gough Island (Thomson, 1964).

DAMAGE

None known.

PURPLE GALLINULE
(Swamphen, Pukeko, Purple Moorhen)
Porphyrio porphyrio (Linnaeus)

DISTINGUISHING CHARACTERISTICS

42-56 cm (16.8-22.4 in). 700 g-2 kg (1.5-4.5 lb)

Generally purple bluish or dark bluish; nape and back black (*alba* greenish); breast colour varies (*melanotus* purple, *bellus* sky blue); bill and frontal shield red; large white patch under tail.

Mackworth-Praed and Grant, 1952-73, ser.1, vol.1, p.299; ser.2, vol.1, pp.251-252; ser.3, vol.1, pp.221-222 and pl.17.

Ripley, 1977, pp.297-304 and pls.36 and 40, pp.293 and 329.

Reader's Digest, 1977, p.159 and pl. p.159.

GENERAL DISTRIBUTION

Southern Europe and Asia, southern Africa, the Philippines, New Guinea, Australia, New Zealand and Melanesia.

INTRODUCED DISTRIBUTION

Probably successfully introduced to Mauritius. Introduced unsuccessfully in the Hawaiian Islands and in ? Argentina.

GENERAL HABITS

Status: fairly common (once common in southern Europe). *Habitat:* margins of swamps, lakes, ponds, creeks, rivers, ricefields and plantations. *Gregariousness:* solitary, pairs or small parties. *Movements:* sedentary or nomadic. *Foods:* seeds and fruits of marsh plants, shoots, grain, tubers, rhizomes, worms, snails, marsh and water insects, frogs, fish, molluscs and eggs. *Breeding:* all year (Australia); June-Sept (India). *Nest:* untidy flat platform of swamp vegetation or interwoven reeds in floating debris or reeds. *Eggs:* 2, 3-8.

Mackworth-Praed and Grant, 1952-1973, ser.1, vol.1, p.299; ser.2, vol.1, pp.251-252; ser.3, vol.1, pp.221-222.

Reader's Digest, 1977, p.159.

Ripley, 1977, pp.297-304.

NOTES ON INTRODUCTIONS

Hawaiian Islands. The Indian race *P.p. poliocephalus* was introduced to the Hawaiian Islands via San Francisco in 1928, but as far as it is known it was unsuccessful in becoming established. The Swamphen *P.p. melanotus* was also an early introduction to these islands and apparently was established for a time, then disappeared (Munro,

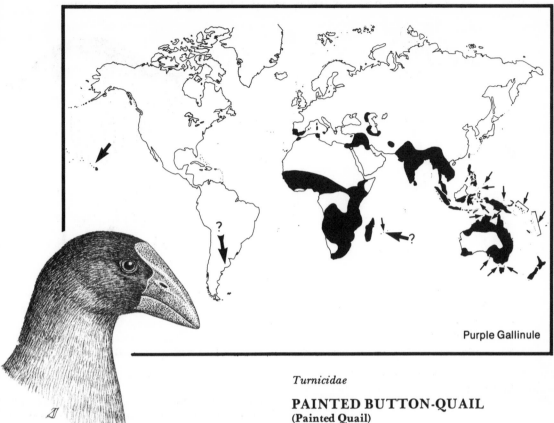

Purple Gallinule

1960; Bryan, 1958). It is not now known to be established in these islands (Berger, 1972).

Mauritius. Newton (1888, in Rountree *et al,* 1952) records the Purple Gallinule *(P. madagascariensis)* as an endemic resident, but according to Rountree *et al* most others indicate that it is an introduced species as it is not mentioned in early manuscripts of the birds on the island. They say that Milbert (1812) states that it was introduced from Malagasy. The species was, however, confined to remote marshy tracts on Mauritius and was always apparently rare there. Staub (1976) records that it has now become extinct there through persistent hunting.

Argentina. Other than a remark by Condon (1975) that the species has been introduced in Argentina, no further details were found.

DAMAGE

The Purple Gallinule is accused of damage to crops in a number of areas of the world. In India they are said to be locally destructive to young padi crops (Ali, 1961). On some Pacific islands such as Samoa they cause extensive damage to the young taro crop (Yaldwyn, 1952), and in Fiji to bananas and root crops on Naiqani Island (Parham, 1954).

In 1949 a project was initiated in the Wageningen district of Surinam to grow rice on a large scale (Burton and Burton, 1969). Purple Gallinules became a pest there when they gathered in non-breeding flocks and broke the rice plants by attempting to perch on them. Many were poisoned with an insecticide for this reason.

Turnicidae

PAINTED BUTTON-QUAIL
(Painted Quail)
Turnix varia (Latham)

DISTINGUISHING CHARACTERISTICS
15.6-20.6 cm (6.2-8.2 in). 78-127 g (3-4.5 oz)
Centre of crown and nape purplish grey; side of crown blackish; remainder of upper parts purplish grey, blotched black with some brown blotches and some white streaks; wing with chestnut patch on shoulder, and blotched white; breast grey spotted white; flanks grey; belly creamy white; bill grey-brown. Female: larger (20 cm; 8 in), and with brighter colouring.
Reader's Digest, 1977, p.147 and pl. p.147.

GENERAL DISTRIBUTION
Australia — New Caledonia: eastern and southern Australia including Tasmania, Kangaroo Island and Abrolhos Islands; also New Caledonia.

INTRODUCED DISTRIBUTION
Introduced unsuccessfully to the Hawaiian Islands and possibly to New Zealand.

GENERAL HABITS
Status: fairly common. *Habitat:* coastal heathland, open forest, and occasionally croplands. *Gregariousness:* solitary or small parties. *Movements:* sedentary and (?) nomadic. *Foods:* insects and seeds. *Breeding:* Sept-Mar and in other months in the north; females polyandrous. *Nest:* slight depression on the ground lined with grass and leaves, at the base of tussock of grass. *Eggs:* 4.
Reader's Digest, 1977, p.147.

NOTES ON INTRODUCTIONS
Hawaiian Islands. The race *T.v. varia* was introduced to Maui in 1922, but apparently did not become established there (Munro, 1960).

193

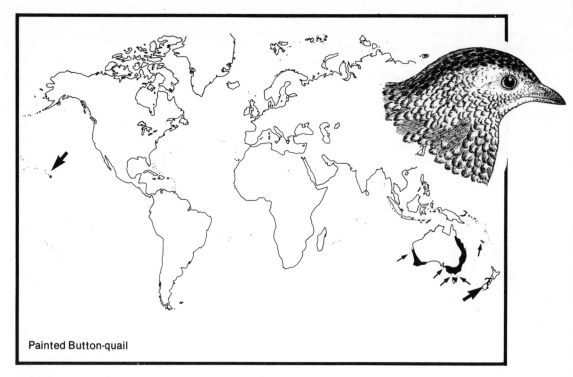

Painted Button-quail

New Zealand. Painted Button-quails were imported to New Zealand prior to 1871, but it is not known whether any were released there (Thomson, 1922).

DAMAGE
None known.

MADAGASCAR BUTTON-QUAIL
(Black-necked Quail)
Turnix nigricollis (Gmelin)

DISTINGUISHING CHARACTERISTICS
16 cm (6.4 in)
Female: upper parts red-speckled dark brown; head speckled white; some back feathers edged laterally white; wings white-spotted; shoulder and flanks red-brown; patch from middle of neck extending to abdomen black. Male: noticeably smaller; lacks black patch on neck and abdomen; bill bluish grey.
Milon *et al,* 1978, p.98 and pl.7, figs.12 and 13.

GENERAL DISTRIBUTION
Malagasy.

INTRODUCED DISTRIBUTION
Introduced or colonised successfully the Isles Glorieuses and Réunion. Introduced successfully on Mauritius but has now died out.

GENERAL HABITS
Status: common. *Habitat:* grasslands, brush areas, plains and cultivated land. *Gregariousness:* singly, twos or threes, or small groups 6-12 females with 1 male. *Movements:* sedentary. *Foods:* seeds, and insects and their larvae. *Breeding:* Sept-Jan. *Nest:* structure of dry grass and leaves, partially domed, on the ground at base of a grass tussock. *Eggs:* 3-5.
Milon *et al,* 1978, p.98.

NOTES ON INTRODUCTIONS
Mauritius. The Madagascar Button-quail is said to have been an exotic resident of Mauritius introduced from Malagasy prior to 1669, but no longer occurs on the island (Rountree *et al,* 1952). Meinertzhagen

(1912) indicates that the species was introduced just prior to 1912 (?).

Réunion. According to Watson *et al* (1963) the Madagascar Button-quail may have been introduced to Réunion where it now occurs and breeds in January. Staub (1976) indicates that it was introduced at an early date and still occurs on the island.

Isles Glorieuses. Benson *et al* (1975) say that Penny is of the opinion that the Madagascar Button-quail was obviously introduced by man (for sport ?), as there

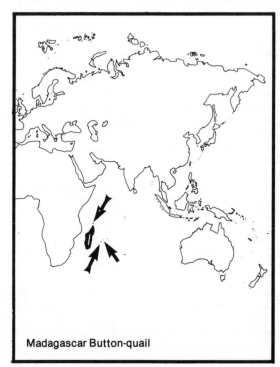

Madagascar Button-quail

194

are no early records of them on the island. They report that recent activities have made the habitat suitable for the button-quail by removing much of the scrub and trees. They do not however, overlook the fact that it may have reached the island of its own accord.

The Madagascar Button-quail is now widespread on the island and as many as 300 pairs may have been present in 1970-71.

DAMAGE

None known.

Gruidae

DEMOISELLE CRANE
Anthropoides virgo (Linnaeus)

DISTINGUISHING CHARACTERISTICS

76-95 cm (30.4-38 in), 2.2-3.0 kg (4.9-6.6 lb)
Generally grey with a black face and neck; feathers of the lower neck black, lanceolate and long, and falling over the breast; white ear-tufts behind eyes; brownish grey secondaries drooping over tail; bill yellow, or greenish grey, black near base.
Gooders, vol.3, 1969, pp.754-755 and pl. p.754.
Ali and Ripley, vol.2, 1968-74, pp.146-151 and fig.2, pl.26, opp. p.176.

GENERAL DISTRIBUTION

Eurasia-North Africa: south-eastern Europe to Mongolia, south to North Africa. Winters in north-eastern Africa, India, Burma, Pakistan and China.

INTRODUCED DISTRIBUTION

Introduced unsuccessfully to France.

GENERAL HABITS

Status: common. *Habitat:* cultivated fields, marshes, sandbanks on rivers and grassy plains. *Gregariousness:* large flocks. *Movements:* migratory. *Foods:* tender shoots, grain, insects, amphibians and small reptiles, grass and seeds. *Breeding:* May-July.

Nest: huge mass of reeds, rush stems and straw, in a flooded field, marsh, or on the ground. *Eggs:* 1-3, normally 2.
Ali and Ripley, vol.2, 1968-74, pp.146-151.
Etchécopar and Hüe, 1978, p.274.

NOTES ON INTRODUCTIONS

France. Attempts were made to acclimatise the Demoiselle Crane in France in about 1914, but these efforts were unsuccessful (Etchécopar, 1955).

DAMAGE

Ali and Ripley (1968-74) report that the large quantity of wheat, grain and paddy found in the stomachs of these birds, although partly obtained from stubble, indicates the magnitude of the damage to cereal crops that flocks of hundreds of thousands must cause annually.

BROLGA
(Native Companion)
Grus rubicundus (Perry)

DISTINGUISHING CHARACTERISTICS

Males 105-125 cm (42-50 in), females 95-115 cm (38-46 in). Males 4.7-7.9 kg (10.4-17.4 lb), females 4.3-7.0 kg (9.5-15.4 lb)
Mainly pale grey, wing primaries darker and rump paler; naked crown, grey-green; ear-coverts grey; naked skin on back of head and around and under chin orange-red to bright red; bill long, straight and grey-green.
Reader's Digest, 1977, p.162 and pl. p.162.

GENERAL DISTRIBUTION

New Guinea-Australia: New Guinea lowlands, and northern, eastern and southern Australia.

INTRODUCED DISTRIBUTION

Introduced unsuccessfully to Fiji.

GENERAL HABITS

Status: common. *Habitat:* coastal tropical areas, swamplands, grassland and cultivation.

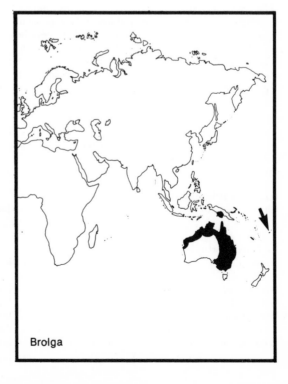

Demoiselle Crane

Brolga

Gregariousness: flocks, sometimes large, and up to 12 000 around drying wetlands. *Movements:* sedentary. *Foods:* sedge tubers, insects, spiders, frogs, molluscs and crustaceans. *Breeding:* Oct-Apr. *Nest:* platform of grass or sedge, with little or no lining and over one metre in diameter. *Eggs:* 2.

Lavery and Blackman, 1969, *Qld Agric. J.,* March 1969, pp.156-162.

Reader's Digest, 1977, p.162.

NOTES ON INTRODUCTIONS

Fiji. Wood and Wetmore (1926) record that a planter introduced several Brolgas to Mango (an island near Taveuni), where they reportedly survived for some time before 1926, but did not become permanently established. Blackburn (1971) also records that the species failed to become permanently established in Fiji.

DAMAGE

In Queensland, Brolgas are known to invade sorghum, maize, improved pastures and other agricultural crops, particularly during the period of grain maturation (Lavery and Blackburn, 1969). This behaviour is also known to occur in other parts of northern Australia. For instance, on the Ord River in Western Australia they have become a pest of ground nuts (Davies, pers. comm., 1979).

Control measures, such as frightening the birds from the crops are sometimes necessary when they are present in large numbers. The species may not have been a welcome addition in Fiji had it become established.

ORDER: CHARADRIIFORMES

Family: *Recurvirostridae* Stilts

6 species in 3 genera; none known to have been introduced

The Red-necked Avocet *(Recurvirostra novae-hollandiae)* was tenuously established in New Zealand as a self-colonist between 1859 and 1878. It became established mainly in the South Island (Condon, 1975), but did not persist as a breeding bird beyond the end of the nineteenth century although it has been sighted there on a few occasions since then (Williams, 1973).

Family: *Charadriidae* Plovers, lapwings

16 species in 8 genera; 3 introduced, all unsuccessfully

The Lapwing, Grey Plover and Golden Plover were all unsuccessfully introduced into New Zealand. However, two other species, the Masked Plover and Black-fronted Dotterel have been successfully established as colonists.

The Masked Plover *(Vanellus miles)* has been breeding in New Zealand since about 1932; numbers have increased there up until the 1960s and the species now has a restricted range in the South Island (Barlow, 1972). In Australia they have fairly recently (since 1950s) colonised the south-west of Western Australia (Serventy and Whittell, 1967).

The Black-fronted Dotterel *(Charadrius melanops)* has also colonised New Zealand from Australia; first recorded in 1954 and breeding there in 1960-61, it now breeds in both the North and South Islands and is still spreading there (Wodzicki, 1965; Williams, 1973).

Family: *Scolopacidae* Woodcocks, snipe, sandpipers, turnstones, phalaropes, etc.

85 species in 23 genera; 2 species introduced

The Eastern Curlew was imported into New Zealand in 1868, but is not known to have been released there (Thomson, 1922). The Chatham Island race of the New Zealand Snipe *(Coenocorypha aucklandica pusilla),* formerly restricted to South East Island where it was extremely rare in the 1950s, has been transferred successfully to Mangere Island also in the Chatham group. In the early 1970s about twenty birds were transferred to the island; these became established and the population has now increased to some 200 birds (Mills and Williams, 1979).

Family: *Laridae* Gulls, terns

85 species in 17 genera; 2 species introduced, both unsuccessfully

Both the Silver and Western Gulls have been introduced to the Hawaiian Islands without success, the latter species several times.

INTRODUCTIONS OF CHARADRIIDAE, SCOLOPACIDAE AND LARIDAE

Species	Date introduced	Region	Manner introduced	Reason
(a) Successful introductions				
Chatham Island Snipe	early 1970s	Mangere Island, Chathams	deliberate	preservation
(b) Unsuccessful introductions				
Lapwing	1872, 1873, 1897, 1900, 1904	New Zealand	deliberate	?
Grey Plover	1867, 1881	New Zealand	deliberate	?
Golden Plover	1875, 1877, 1897	New Zealand	deliberate	?
Silver Gull	1924	Oahu, Hawaiian Islands	escapee	
Western Gull	Several	Hawaiian Islands	deliberate	?

Charadriidae

LAPWING
(Green Plover, Peewit)
Vanellus vanellus (Linnaeus)

DISTINGUISHING CHARACTERISTICS
30-31 cm (12-12.4 in)
Long and narrow black feathered crest; chin, throat and breast white with black chest band; upper parts iridescent green and purple; flight feathers black with whitish tips; upper and under tail-coverts chestnut; tail white with black subterminal band; bill black.
Witherby *et al,* vol.4, 1938-41, pp.395-403 and pl.123, opp. p.396.

GENERAL DISTRIBUTION
Eurasia: breeds from Scandinavia, the British Isles and France across central Asia to Manchuria. Winters in southern parts of breeding range and south as far as northern India, Pakistan, Arabia and (?) Africa, but rarely reaches the Equator.

INTRODUCED DISTRIBUTION
Introduced unsuccessfully to New Zealand.

GENERAL HABITS
Status: common; increasing range northwards in Europe. *Habitat:* grasslands, arable fields, shore meadows, moors, swamps, mud-flats and flat coastal regions. *Gregariousness:* pairs of scattered flocks, frequently in large flocks especially on migration. *Movements:* sedentary and migratory. *Foods:* beetles and caterpillars and many other insects and their larvae, spiders, worms, snails and small weed seeds. *Breeding:* Mar-June. *Nest:* shallow depression on ground amongst grass or low herbage. *Eggs:* 3-5.
Witherby *et al.,* vol.4, 1938-41, pp. 395-403.
Voous, 1960, p.90.

NOTES ON INTRODUCTIONS
New Zealand. The Lapwing was liberated in both the North and South Islands of New Zealand between 1872 and 1904 (Thomson, 1922). In 1872 the Auckland Acclimatisation Society liberated thirty-six birds, and an unknown number were set free in 1904. In 1873 the Canterbury society liberated nine birds. The Otago society liberated five at Clifton in 1897 and eight more at Goodwood estate in 1900. The Wellington society liberated thirty-five in 1904, and in the same year the Westland society liberated thirty at Upper Kohatahi. Most of those liberated disappeared soon after their release. The species did not become established in New Zealand.

DAMAGE
None known.

GREY PLOVER
(Black-bellied Plover)
Pluvialis squatarola (Linnaeus)

DISTINGUISHING CHARACTERISTICS
25-31 cm (10-12.4 in) . 220 g (7.75 oz)
Upper parts greyish brown dappled white; underparts white with black axillaries; wing bar and rump white; faint brown bars on white tail; eyebrow stripe pale grey and a broad white band above eye; bill black.
Godfrey, 1966, pp.135-136 and pl.24, no.3, opp. p.137.
Ali and Ripley, vol.2, 1968-74, pp.220-221 and pl.27, fig.5, opp. p.208.

GENERAL DISTRIBUTION
Eurasia-North America: breeds in northern Alaska, arctic Canada and northern Asia. Winters in North America from British Columbia, Canada and New Jersey, USA, to Chile and southern Brazil; in Eurasia to southern Europe, southern Africa, Malagasy, Mauritius, India, Sri Lanka, Sumatra and Australia.

INTRODUCED DISTRIBUTION
Introduced unsuccessfully to New Zealand.

GENERAL HABITS
Status: common. *Habitat:* beaches, coastal mudflats

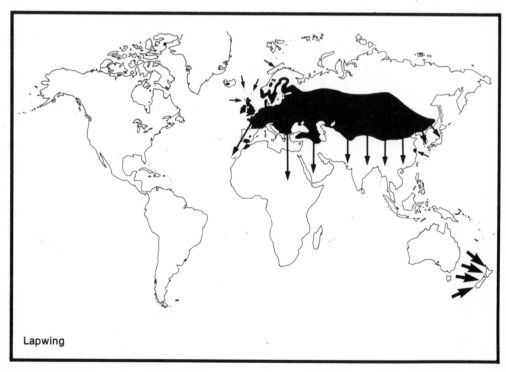

Lapwing

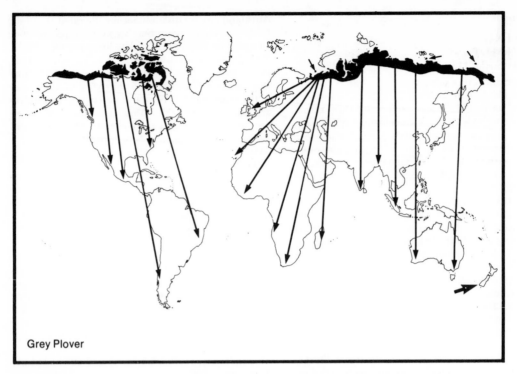

Grey Plover

and marshes, pools, sandbars and occasionally inland lakes and swamps, and cultivated areas. *Gregariousness:* solitary, parties of 5-6, or small flocks of 20-30; large flocks of 1000s on migration. *Movements:* migratory. *Foods:* small invertebrates including worms, molluscs and crustaceans, and occasionally seeds. *Breeding:* May-July. *Nest:* shallow depression on the ground lined with lichen or moss. *Eggs:* 4.

Voous, 1960, p.90.

Ali and Ripley, vol.2, 1968-74, pp.220-221.

NOTES ON INTRODUCTIONS

New Zealand. The Grey Plover was introduced in the South Island of New Zealand in 1867 and 1881 by the Otago Acclimatisation Society (Thomson, 1922). In 1867, two birds were liberated, and in 1881, eight were liberated on Launder Station, Manuherikia. The first birds liberated were not seen again, those from the latter introduction were seen for some time before disappearing. The species did not become established in New Zealand.

DAMAGE

None known.

GOLDEN PLOVER

Pluvialis apricaria (Linnaeus)

DISTINGUISHING CHARACTERISTICS

23-27 cm (9.2-10.8 in). 88-121 g (3.1-4.27 oz)

Upper parts yellowish golden, axillaries white; rump and tail golden brown; underparts entirely black or may be limited on breast, chin and throat; wing bar white; bill black. Plumage duller in non-breeding season and without white wing bar.

Witherby *et al,* vol.4, 1938-41, pp.364-371 and pl.121, opp. p.364.

Ali and Ripley, vol.2, 1968-74, pp.221-222 and pl.27, fig.8, opp. p.208.

GENERAL DISTRIBUTION

Breeds Iceland, the Faeroes and eastwards across northern Europe from northern Scandinavia, northern USSR and western Siberia south to the British Isles, Denmark, northern Germany, Poland and the Baltics. In winter to the Mediterranean region, Pakistan and Assam, India.

INTRODUCED DISTRIBUTION

Introduced unsuccessfully in New Zealand.

GENERAL HABITS

Status: range reduced but still common. *Habitat:* moorland, pastureland, arable fields and mudflats. *Gregariousness:* solitary or small flocks, but large flocks when migrating. *Movements:* partly sedentary, and migratory. *Foods:* animal and vegetable matter including insects, small molluscs and crustaceans, worms, grass and seeds. *Breeding:* Apr-May (Great Britain). *Nest:* hollow on ground sometimes lined with wisps of grass or moss. *Eggs:* 4 (Great Britain).

Voous, 1960, p.90.

Witherby *et al,* vol.4, 1938-41, pp.364-371.

NOTES ON INTRODUCTIONS

New Zealand. The Canterbury Acclimatisation Society imported Golden Plovers in 1875, and the Wellington society introduced four in 1877, but there appear to be no further records of these birds (Thomson, 1922). In 1897 the Otago society liberated two birds at Clifton, near Dunedin, but they were not seen again. The species did not become established in New Zealand.

DAMAGE

None known.

Laridae

SILVER GULL

Larus novaehollandiae Stephens

DISTINGUISHING CHARACTERISTICS

38-44 cm (15.2-17.6 in). 312-340 g (11-12 oz)

Mainly white with grey back (but considerable

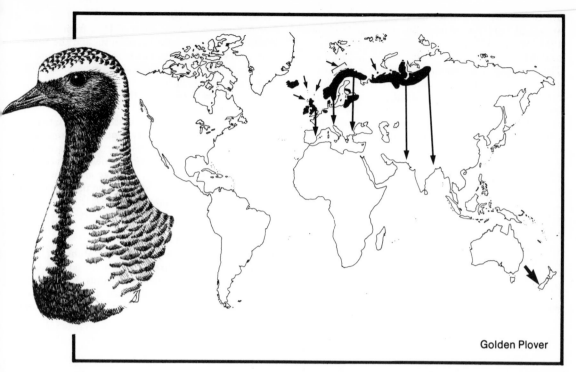

Golden Plover

variation); wing tips black with white patches; bill orange to bright red with dark tip.
Reader's Digest, 1977, p.206 and pl. pp.206 and 207.

GENERAL DISTRIBUTION

Australia, Tasmania, New Caledonia, New Zealand and the Chatham, Snares, Campbell and Auckland Islands, and south-west Africa.

INTRODUCED DISTRIBUTION

Introduced unsuccessfully in the Hawaiian Islands.

GENERAL HABITS

Status: very common. *Habitat:* coastal, and rarely inland waters. *Gregariousness:* flocks. *Movements:* sedentary and/or migratory (sometimes regular seasonal movements). *Foods:* omnivorous. *Breeding:* variable, Sept-Dec and Mar-June; colonial. *Nest:* roughly made platform with inner cup of any material, on the ground (mainly small islands), or on bare ground among rocks, or in a tree. *Eggs:* 2-3, 4.
Reader's Digest, 1977, p.206.

NOTES ON INTRODUCTIONS

Hawaiian Islands. Several Silver Gulls escaped from the Honolulu Zoo on Oahu when a cage was

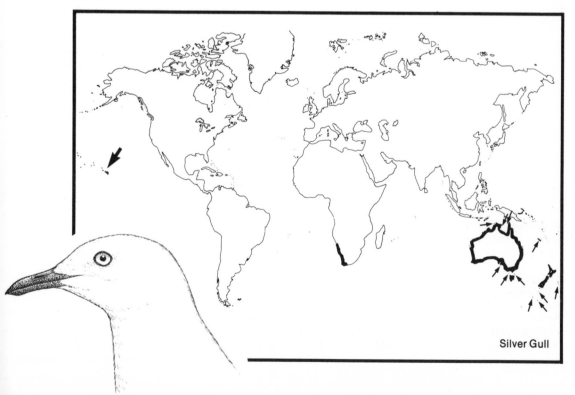

Silver Gull

overturned by the wind in 1924. However, they apparently did not survive on the island (Caum, 1933; Munro, 1960).

DAMAGE
The Silver Gull occasionally becomes a hazard to aircraft in Australia, especially where the dumping of rubbish is carried out in the vicinity of airfields near the coast. Populations of them have also become rather large at times in some cities, necessitating their control because of the risk of the spread of such infections as Salmonella.

WESTERN GULL
Larus occidentalis Audubon

DISTINGUISHING CHARACTERISTICS
61-68 cm (24.4-27.2 in)
Head and tail white; back and wings dark; underparts white; primaries and subterminal band on tail black; bill yellow with red spot.
Godfrey, 1966, p.177 and pl.33, no.6, opp. p.172.
Reilly, 1968, pp.193-194.

Western Gull

GENERAL DISTRIBUTION
North America. Pacific coast of USA from northern Washington south to Baja California and the Sonora coast, Mexico. Winters north to British Columbia, Canada, and south to Nayarit, Mexico.

INTRODUCED DISTRIBUTION
Introduced unsuccessfully to the Hawaiian Islands.

GENERAL HABITS
Status: common. *Habitat:* coastal waters, estuaries, beaches, piers and city waterfronts. *Gregariousness:* small to large flocks. *Movements:* mainly sedentary with some northward winter movements. *Foods:* fish, carrion, molluscs, shellfish, garbage and refuse, etc. *Breeding:* colonial. *Nest:* of grass, on the ground, on offshore islands or mainland cliffs. *Eggs:* 2-4.
Godfrey, 1966, p.177.
Reilly, 1968, pp.193-194.

NOTES ON INTRODUCTIONS
Hawaiian Islands. According to Munro (1960) Western Gulls have been introduced several times from the USA to the Hawaiian Islands, but have not succeeded in becoming established there. Some were apparently liberated on Hawaii at Honolulu and Hilo, but always failed to persist (Caum, 1933).

DAMAGE
None known.

ORDER: COLUMBIFORMES
(Sandgrouse, Pigeons and Doves)
Family: *Pteroclididae* Sandgrouse*

16 species, in 2 genera; 3 introduced; 1 doubtfully established

Although a number of introductions of sandgrouse have been attempted they have not been very successful. The recent status of the Common Sandgrouse in both Hawaii and the USA is not well documented and this species may be established there. In the light of previous failures however, this appears doubtful.

Another species *P. bicinctus* which has not been detailed in the text, was imported to New Zealand in 1892, but it is not known if any were released in the wild (Thompson, 1922).

*Sandgrouse have been left under the Columbiformes, although more recently they have been placed as a sub-order of the Charadriiformes.

INTRODUCTIONS OF PTEROCLIDIDAE

Species	Date introduced	Region	Manner introduced	Reason
(a) Probably unsuccessful introductions				
Common Sandgrouse	1881 on, 1959-61	USA	deliberate	game ?
	1961-62	Hawaiian Islands	deliberate	game ?
(b) Unsuccessful introductions				
Pallas's Sandgrouse	1881, before 1928?	USA	deliberate	game ?
Pintailed Sandgrouse	1882	New Zealand	deliberate	?
Imperial Sandgrouse	early 1960s	USA	deliberate	game ?
Common Sandgrouse	1863, 1864, 1872	Australia	deliberate	?

PALLAS'S SANDGROUSE
Syrrhaptes paradoxus (Pallas)

DISTINGUISHING CHARACTERISTICS
32.5-40.6 cm (13-16.2 in)
Upper parts sandy buff, barred with blackish brown; head and throat orange; conspicuous black patch on belly; remainder of underparts sandy grey; pectoral band dull white, barred black; wings pointed, sandy brown with some black bars and flight feathers greyish; tail elongated; bill horn. *Female:* lacks pectoral band; head and throat yellowish; head spotted and barred black.

Witherby *et al*, vol.4, 1938-41, pp.147-151 and pl.103, opp. p.146.

Cheng, 1963, pp.390-393.

Etchécopar and Hüe, 1978, pp.415, 418 and fig. p.418.

GENERAL DISTRIBUTION
Central Asia: extreme south-eastern USSR and central Asia east to Mongolia and extreme north-eastern China, north to the Kirghiz Steppes, the Altai, north-western Mongolia, southern Transbaykalia, south to Tien Shan, Dzungaria and north-eastern Kansu. Irruptions have reached England (1888), Korea (1908) and China.

INTRODUCED DISTRIBUTION
Introduced unsuccessfully to the USA.

GENERAL HABITS
Status: fairly common. *Habitat:* sandy plains and steppes. *Gregariousness:* parties of 7-8 birds and larger groups. *Movements:* sedentary, but irregularly irruptive to areas well outside range. *Foods:* seeds and shoots. *Breeding:* Apr-July; 2-3 broods. *Nest:* sparsely lined scrape in open. *Eggs:* 2-4.

Witherby *et al*, vol.4, 1938-41, pp.147-151.

Gooders, vol.4, 1969, pp.1099-1100.

NOTES ON INTRODUCTIONS
USA. Pallas's Sandgrouse were liberated in Spokane, Stevens, Yakima and Garfield counties of Washington just prior to 1928, but they disappeared and were not seen again (Phillips, 1928). Phillips records that some may also have been released near Portland and at Clatsop Plains, Oregon in 1881. These birds were imported with pheasants from Shanghai by Judge O. N. Denny, but were not successfully established.

DAMAGE
None known.

PINTAILED SANDGROUSE
(Large Pintailed Sandgrouse, White-bellied Sandgrouse)
Pterocles alchata (Linnaeus)

DISTINGUISHING CHARACTERISTICS
30-38 cm, incl. 10-18 cm tail (12-15.2 in, incl. 4-7.2 in tail). 225-340 g (8-12 oz).
Upper parts greenish yellow with black and yellow bars; lower breast and belly whitish with a chestnut breast band, bordered with a thin black band; some races darker above and below; upper tail-coverts barred black and yellow; chin and throat black; shoulder of wing chestnut, fringed white and black; axillaries blackish; tail long and pointed; bill dark grey or dusky green to dull brown. In winter mottled yellow upper parts. *Female:* upper parts barred black, yellow and grey; throat white; black bar across lower throat, then buff, black, chestnut and black bars; shoulder of wing whitish, fringed black.

Gooders, vol.4, 1969, pp.1094-1096 and pls. p.1095 and 1097.

GENERAL DISTRIBUTION
South-western Europe, North Africa and south-western Asia: from Portugal, southern Spain and France, northern Africa from central Morocco to the Sahara, Asia Minor, Caucasus, Transcaspia, Iran, Afghanistan, Pakistan (Baluchistan) and north-

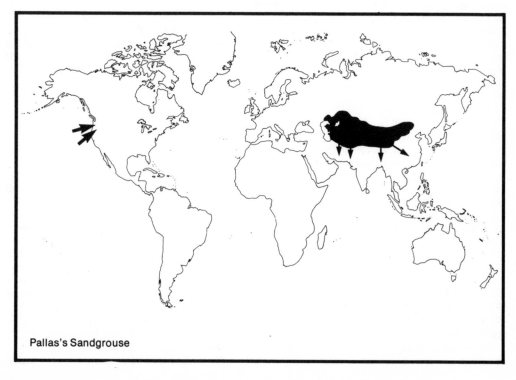

Pallas's Sandgrouse

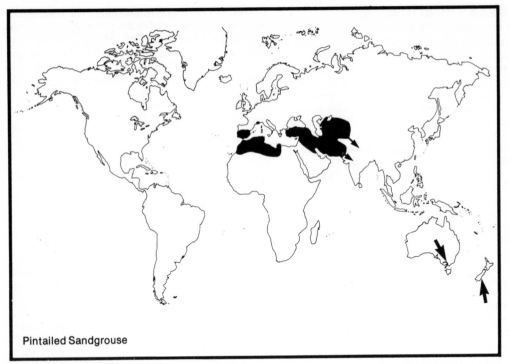

Pintailed Sandgrouse

western India. Winter south to Sind, Rajasthan and east to the Punjab and Delhi, India.

INTRODUCED DISTRIBUTION

Introduced unsuccessfully to New Zealand and probably to Australia.

GENERAL HABITS

Status: common, but numbers decreasing. *Habitat:* steppe, stone deserts, scrub semi-deserts, sandy shores of broad rivers, grasslands and grainfields. *Gregariousness:* frequently occurs in winter flocks of hundreds of thousands. *Movements:* sedentary and migratory. *Foods:* leaves and seeds of desert plants, and grain, shoots and insects. *Breeding:* Apr-Sept (May-July Iraq); 2 broods per season; somewhat colonial. *Nest:* depression on the ground, usually near a tussock. *Eggs:* 2-3 (4 recorded).

Voous, 1960, p.135.

Gooders, vol.4, 1969, pp.1094-1096.

Maclean, 1976, pp.502-516.

NOTES ON INTRODUCTIONS

New Zealand. Pintailed Sandgrouse were liberated in 1882 by the Otago Acclimatisation Society at the foot of the Rock and Pillar Range in New Zealand, but were not recorded again (Thomson, 1922).

Australia. Either this species or possibly the Imperial Sandgrouse may have been introduced in Australia but details appear to be lacking. So-called 'Algerian Sandgrouse' were liberated on Phillip Island (Victoria) in about 1864.

DAMAGE

None known.

IMPERIAL SANDGROUSE
(Black-bellied Sandgrouse)
Pterocles orientalis (Linnaeus)

DISTINGUISHING CHARACTERISTICS

33-39 cm (13.2-15.6 in). 410-650 g (.9-1.4 lb)

202 Forehead, crown and nape grey; upper parts mottled

and marked yellow, blackish and olive-black; throat and cheeks chestnut; belly black; chest with black band extending around shoulder; wing-coverts yellowish; tail grey, barred rufous-brown and white tipped, central feathers elongated; bill whitish to dark reddish brown, tipped black. *Female:* barred and blotched black and yellowish above; lower throat and breast yellowish, spotted black; chin buff.

Gooders, vol.4, 1969, pp.1093-1094 and pl. p.1093.

Etchécopar and Hüe, 1978, pp.414-415 and pl.12, p.321.

GENERAL DISTRIBUTION

South-western Europe, North Africa and south-western Asia: from the Canary Islands, Iberian Peninsula, north-western Africa, Middle East, south-eastern USSR to the Iranian frontier, Afghanistan and Baluchistan. Winter on plains of northern India and deserts of central Arabia.

INTRODUCED DISTRIBUTION

Introduced to Nevada in the USA, probably unsuccessfully.

GENERAL HABITS

Status: fairly common. *Habitat:* open steppe, stone deserts and semi deserts. *Gregariousness:* pairs and small flocks of 15-30 birds, but large flocks of several hundred not uncommon and occasionally up to thousands concentrate at water sources. *Movements:* sedentary and migratory; frequent extensive dispersal movements. *Foods:* plant material and seeds, berries, roots, small bulbs, shoots, insects and grain. *Breeding:* Apr-June (Africa-Asia) (Feb-May Canary Islands); 2 broods common. *Nest:* shallow scrape or depression on the ground, sometimes lined with a few pieces of grass and circled by small stones, in exposed sites but sometimes near a bush. *Eggs:* 2-3.

Bannerman, vol.1, 1963, pp.121-127.

Gooders, vol.4, 1969, pp.1093-1094.

NOTES ON INTRODUCTIONS

USA. Imperial Sandgrouse were experimentally

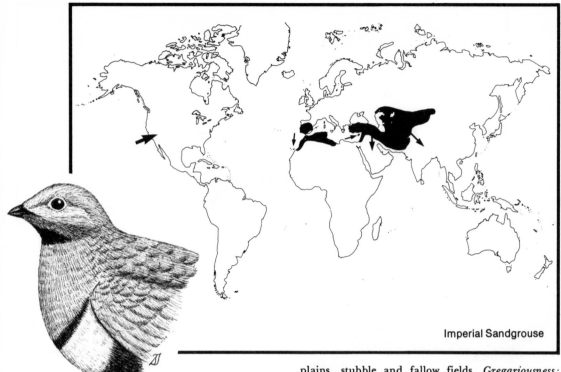

Imperial Sandgrouse

introduced in Nevada in the 1960s (Christensen, 1963), but the results of the attempt are not known. Presumably, they have failed to become established as there appears to be no recent mention of them.

DAMAGE

None known.

COMMON SANDGROUSE
(Indian Sandgrouse, Small Pintailed Sandgrouse, Chestnut-bellied Sandgrouse)
Pterocles exustus (Temminck and Langiers)

DISTINGUISHING CHARACTERISTICS

28-30 cm incl. tail 12 cm (11.2-12 in, incl. tail 4.8 in). 212-284 g (7.48-10.02 oz).

Generally yellowish sandy brown; narrow black band across breast; abdomen brownish black or chestnut; cheeks, chin and throat dull yellow; wings and tail pointed; wing-coverts with chocolate and white spots; bill brownish red. *Female:* generally buff, streaked and spotted and barred with black, except on chin; broken narrow, black breast band.

Gooders, vol.4, 1969, pl. p.1097.

Mackworth-Praed and Grant, 1952-73, ser.1, vol.1, pp.449-450 and pl.28; ser.3, vol.1, p.327 and pl.23.

Ali and Ripley, vol.3, 1968-74.

GENERAL DISTRIBUTION

Northern Africa, Arabia and south-western Asia: northern and north-east Africa from Senegal to the Sudan, Somali Republic, Tanzania and Egypt, Arabia and east to Pakistan (Baluchistan) and India.

INTRODUCED DISTRIBUTION

Introduced unsuccessfully in Australia and probably to the USA and the Hawaiian Islands.

GENERAL HABITS

Status: common. *Habitat:* stony semi-deserts and dry plains, stubble and fallow fields. *Gregariousness:* parties of 3-5 and flocks of 10-30 birds, exceptionally up to 200; larger flocks gather at watering points where they may number in thousands. *Movements:* no information. *Foods:* weed and grass seeds, vegetable shoots, grains and insects. *Breeding:* mainly Jan-May; may have 2-3 broods per year. *Nest:* shallow unlined scrape or depression on the ground, in open or stony country. *Eggs:* 2-3.

Mackworth-Praed and Grant, 1952-73, ser.1, vol.1, pp.449-450; ser.3, vol.1, pp.327-328.

Ali and Ripley, vol.3, 1968-74.

NOTES ON INTRODUCTIONS

USA. Common Sandgrouse of the race *P.e. hindustan* were captured in the Thar Desert (Jodhpur, Rajasthan, India) for eventual release in Nevada, USA (Christensen, 1963). Some 2030 birds were released in southern Nevada from 1959 to 1961. Areas of release included the Moapa Valley, Pahrangat Valley and at Pahrump (Nevada Fish and Game Committee, 1963).

Although they were released in desert regions of Nevada, none were found near the release sites after the first winter. Some were later found in Navajoa, Sonora, in Mexico in 1962, in latitudes similar to those of their native range.

According to Gottschalk (1967) Common Sandgrouse have been introduced into the USA from about 1881 onwards at various times. They have failed to become established anywhere (Gottschalk; Bump and Bohl, 1964), although more recent introductions in the late 1960s have been made (Bump, 1968) and about which little appears to have been documented.

Hawaiian Islands. The race *P.e. hindustan* from India was introduced to the Hawaiian Islands in 1961, but is not known to be established there (Walker, 1967; Berger, 1972). In early 1961 some 118 birds

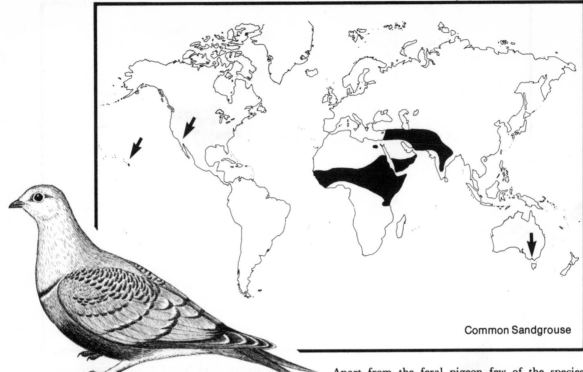

Common Sandgrouse

were released on the island of Kauai, 114 on Molokai and 123 on Hawaii (Western States Exotic Game Bird Committee, 1961). Also in 1961, 104 birds were released at Ahumoa, and in 1962, 266 more on the south side of Puu Hualalai and Hale Laau, Hawaii, but these were said to have all disappeared by 1966 (Lewin, 1971).

The Hawaiian Audubon Society (1975) has recently indicated that the species may still be established on Hawaii, but that their present status is poorly known.

Australia. Ryan (1906) records that Common Sandgrouse (?) were released at Melbourne, Victoria in 1863; ten sandgrouse were liberated on Phillip Island in 1864, and a number in 1872; they were said to have all disappeared soon after their release.

DAMAGE
None known.

Family: *Columbidae* Pigeons and doves

306 species in 59 genera; 32 species introduced, 10 established, 5 doubtfully established or introduced

Of the introduced and established species of pigeons, by far the most widespread is the Rock Dove. As a feral species it now occurs in many regions of the world and has reverted to the wild state in some areas. It is now a nuisance in many cities because of the fouling of buildings, etc. and for epidemiological reasons.

Other widely established species include the Spotted and Senegal Turtledoves and perhaps the Peaceful Dove. Both the Collared Turtledove and Stock Dove *(Columba oenas)* have increased their ranges fairly recently, and rather substantially in Europe.

Apart from the feral pigeon few of the species introduced appear to have become more than minor pests of man or his agriculture. However, many species in the family would appear to have much pest potential in this respect.

Not mentioned in the following text, the Flock Pigeon *(Phaps histrionica)* in 1869, 'Indian pigeons' and 'Indian doves' in 1907 and Solomon Island pigeons in 1870 and 1872 were imported into New Zealand, but it is not known if any were released in the wild.

ISLAND IMPERIAL PIGEON
(Pink-headed Imperial Pigeon, Imperial Pigeon, Christmas Island Imperial Pigeon)
Ducula rosacea (Temminck)

DISTINGUISHING CHARACTERISTICS
43.6-48.8 cm (17.4-19.5 in)

Head and upper throat salmon pink with a mauve tinge; whitish ring around eye; throat and neck pale grey; upper breast pinkish grey, lower breast and belly pale mauve-pink; upper parts iridescent bronze-green and bluish green washed silver-grey; primaries blackish; under tail-coverts chestnut; tail blackish green; white band at base of bill; bill blue-grey or slate grey, with red or purple cere.

Temminck, 1835, pl. col., livr., 98, pl.578.

Goodwin, 1970, pp.406-407.

GENERAL DISTRIBUTION
Indonesia: the Lesser Sunda Islands from Flores to Babar, Duizend Islands, Satonda Island, Tukang Besi Islands, islands in the Flores Sea, Tanimbar, Kai Islands, Sudest Islands, Arends Island, Solombo Besar Island and Christmas Island.

INTRODUCED DISTRIBUTION
Introduced successfully but now extinct on the Cocos-Keeling Islands, Indian Ocean.

Species	Date introduced	Region	Manner introduced	Reason
(a) Successful introductions				
Feral (domestic) Pigeon	from early times	Eurasia	feral	domestication
	1606-07	North America	feral	domestication
	after white colonisation	South America	feral	domestication
	after white colonisation	Central America	feral	domestication
	prior 1917	Masatierra Island, Juan Fernandez	feral	domestication
	?	Easter Islands	?	?
	beginning 19th century	Society Islands	feral	domestication
	?	Bermuda	feral ?	domestication
	?	West Indies	feral ?	?
	after 1796	Hawaiian Islands	feral	domestication
	after white colonisation	Australia	feral	domestication
	about 1850s	New Zealand	feral	domestication
	before 1969	Norfolk Island	feral ?	?
	about 1715	Mauritius	feral	?
	prior 1870 ? and 1914-18	St Helena	feral ?	?
	prior 1961	Fiji	feral	?
	about 1915	Tierra del Fuego	feral ?	?
	early 1970s	Western Samoa	feral ?	?
	?	Eleuthera, Bahamas	feral	?
	about 1968	South Georgia Island	feral ?	?
White-winged Dove	1959 and early 1970s	Southern Florida, USA	deliberate	game ?
Madagascar Turtledove	?	Mauritius	?	?
	prior 1867	Seychelles	deliberate ?	food ?
	after 1907	Diego Garcia, Chagos Archipelago	?	?
	recent ?	Amirantes	?	?
Collared Turtledove	early 16th century or after 1700	south-eastern Europe	?	?
	?	Northern China and Korea	deliberate or range expansion ?	?
	18th or early 19th century	Japan	escapee	cage bird ?
	prior 1921	Florida and California, USA	?	?
	about 1971	New Zealand	feral	cage bird
Red-eyed Dove	1933	Cape Peninsula, South Africa	deliberate or colonisation	?
Spotted Turtledove	1835	Sulawesi, Moluccas and isles in Flores Sea, Indonesia	deliberate ?	?
	prior to 1941	Fiji	escapees	cage bird ?
	?	New Britain	?	?
	1939	New Caledonia	?	?
	early 19th century	New Zealand	escapees ?	cage bird
	prior 1900 (and recently?)	Hawaiian Islands	deliberate	?
	about 1917 or 1918 or earlier	USA	escapees ?	cage bird

205

continued

INTRODUCTIONS OF COLUMBIDAE

Species	Date introduced	Region	Manner introduced	Reason
	1870, 1872, 1874, 1881, 1898, and 1912	Australia	deliberate	aesthetic ?
	1781 or early 19th century	Mauritius	?	?
Senegal Turtledove	about 1905	Principé, Gulf of Guinea	?	?
	1898	Western Australia	deliberate	aesthetic ?
Peaceful Dove	prior 1870	St Helena	deliberate	?
	?	Réunion	?	?
	about 1750 or 1781	Mauritius	deliberate ?	?
	early Indian traders and prior 1867	Seychelles	deliberate ?	food ?
	1764	Rodrigues Island	?	?
	1969	Isles Glorieuses	deliberate	?
	about 1960 ?	Chagos Archipelago	deliberate	?
	after 1914	central and northern Thailand	deliberate	?
	1965	Sabah	deliberate	?
	prior 1893	Philippines	deliberate or escapee	cage bird
	1938 or 1950	Tahiti	deliberate	?
	1922	Hawaiian Islands	deliberate	?
Emerald Dove	?	Hong Kong	?	?

(b) Possibly successful introductions (results uncertain or uncertain if introduced)

Species	Date introduced	Region	Manner introduced	Reason
Feral (domestic) Pigeon	1898	Andaman and Nicobar Islands	deliberate ?	?
Mourning Dove	1929 and/or 1930, 1962-65	Hawaiian Islands	deliberate ?	game ?
White-winged Dove	1961 and 1965	Hawaiian Islands	deliberate ?	game ?
	?	Western Cuba	transplanted	?
Common Turtledove	1960-61	Alma-Ata, USSR	re-acclimatisation	?
Red Turtledove	1933 and 1940s	Malaya	deliberate or vagrants	?
Madagascar Turtledove	?	Réunion	?	?
Javan Turtledove	before 1946	Mariana Islands ?	?	?
	?	Borneo ?	?	?
	before 1947	Sumatra	?	?
	?	Philippines ?	?	?
	?	Palestine, Syria,	?	?
Senegal Turtledove	prior 1926 ?	Lebanon, Turkey, Malta, southern Algeria		
	?	Mafia Island, Africa	?	?
Peaceful Dove	?	Cosmoledo	?	?
	?	Farquhar, (Providence bank)	?	?
	?	southern Borneo	deliberate	?
	prior 1936	Sulawesi and Amboina	?	?
Inca Dove	about 1966 ?	Florida, USA	?	?
Common Ground Dove	prior 1900	Bermuda	?	?
Common Bronzewing	1937	Kangaroo Island, Aust.	deliberate	preservation
Crested Pigeon	1937 and 1940	Kangaroo Island, Aust.	deliberate	?
	1922, 1964	Hawaiian Islands	deliberate	aesthetic ?
White-bellied Dove	after 1920s	New Providence	deliberate re-establishment	re-stocking ?

INTRODUCTIONS OF COLUMBIDAE

Species	Date introduced	Region	Manner introduced	Reason
(c) Unsuccessful introductions				
Island Imperial Pigeon	about 1885	Cocos-Keeling Islands	?	?
Woodpigeon	1910-13	USA	deliberate ?	game ?
Common Turtledove	1872	Australia	deliberate	?
	about 1871	New Zealand	not known if released	cage bird ?
Red Turtledove	1940	Singapore	escapees ?	cage bird
Madagascar Turtledove	prior 1883	Isles Glorieuses ?	deliberate or colonisation	cage bird
Collared Turtledove	prior 1950s	Great Britain	deliberate	?
	1946 and 1975	Australia	escapees	cage bird
	1866-82	New Zealand	deliberate ?	cage bird
	1920, 1928 and 1961	Hawaiian Islands	deliberate	game ?
Javan Turtledove	1867 and 1875	New Zealand	deliberate	?
Peaceful Dove	prior 1879	Malagasy	deliberate ?	?
	1938	Tahiti	deliberate	?
	1937 and 1940	Kangaroo Island, Aust.	deliberate	?
Diamond Dove	prior 1922	New Zealand	not known if released	?
	1922 and 1928	Hawaiian Islands	deliberate	?
	1937	Kangaroo Island, Aust.	deliberate	?
	1974	King Island, Aust.	escapee ?	?
Bar-shouldered Dove	1922 ?	Hawaiian Islands	deliberate ?	?
	1940	Kangaroo Island, Aust.	deliberate	?
Namaqua Dove	1860s	Kawau, N.Z.	deliberate	?
	1960s	Western Australia	escapees ?	cage bird
Emerald Dove	1924	Hawaiian Islands	deliberate	?
	1867	New Zealand	not known if released	cage bird ?
Common Bronzewing	1864-84	New Zealand	deliberate	?
	1922	Hawaiian Islands	deliberate	?
Crested Pigeon	1960s	Europe	deliberate ?	cage bird
	1876-77, 1887	New Zealand	deliberate	?
	1922	Hawaiian Islands	deliberate	?
	before 1925	USA	escapee	cage bird
Partridge Pigeon	1922	Hawaiian Islands	deliberate	?
	1866	New Zealand	not known if released	cage bird ?
Spinifex Pigeon	1922	Hawaiian Islands	deliberate	?
	1940	Kangaroo Island, Aust.	deliberate	?
White-tipped Dove	1933	Hawaiian Islands	deliberate	?
Ruddy Quail Dove	1933	Hawaiian Islands	deliberate	?
Bleeding-heart Pigeon	1924	USA	deliberate	?
	1922 and later	Hawaiian Islands	deliberate	?
Wonga Pigeon	1864-76	New Zealand	deliberate	?
	1922	Hawaiian Islands	deliberate	?
	1946	Kangaroo Island, Aust.	deliberate	?
Blue-headed Quail Dove	18th century and prior 1937	Jamaica	deliberate or escapee	cage bird
	1928	Hawaiian Islands	deliberate	?
Nicobar Pigeon	1922 and 1928	Hawaiian Islands	deliberate	?

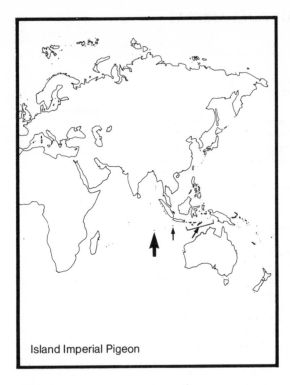

Island Imperial Pigeon

GENERAL HABITS
Little information available or known. *Habitat:* forest on small islands with fruiting trees. *Foods:* fruits and probably seeds.

NOTES ON INTRODUCTIONS
Cocos-Keeling. According to Gibson-Hill (1949) the Island Imperial Pigeon was introduced to these islands in about 1885; was practically extinct there in 1906 and was not present and unknown in 1941. The race introduced was apparently *D.r. whartoni* from Christmas Island.

DAMAGE
None known.

ROCK DOVE
(Common Pigeon, Domestic Pigeon, Feral Pigeon)
Columba livia Gmelin

DISTINGUISHING CHARACTERISTICS
29-36 cm (11.6-14.4 in), 194-398 g (6.84-14.04 oz)
Variable species but generally blue-grey with green and purple sheen on neck; wings with two black bars; rump white; cere whitish; bill black. (The above refers to the wild form; many patterns among feral birds from white, red and black.)
Goodwin, 1970, pp.54-55, 58-59.
Reader's Digest, 1977, pl. p.231.

GENERAL DISTRIBUTION
Eurasia-North Africa. Probably they originally inhabited mainly coastal cliff and rocky areas from the British Isles, the Mediterranean region and North Africa, east to India.

The range of the wild species is now difficult to reconstruct because of extensions in range brought about by crossing with domestic stock. (Note: the accompanying range map shows only the approximate range of this pigeon. The data available from many areas is meagre and incomplete, thus the species undoubtedly occurs in many cities and towns outside the limits illustrated.)

INTRODUCED DISTRIBUTION
Undoubtedly feral in many areas of Eurasia and North Africa. Introduced and became feral in North, Central and South America, the West Indies, the Bahamas, Bermuda, Juan Fernandez, Easter Islands, Society Islands, Samoa, Fiji, Hawaiian Islands, Australia, New Zealand, Norfolk Island, Mauritius, the Andaman and Nicobar Islands, South Georgia, St Helena, Marquesas (Ua Huka) and probably elsewhere.

GENERAL HABITS
Status: considerably reduced in range and numbers in the wild, but very common as a feral species. *Habitat:* cities, towns, villages, farms and cliffs. *Gregariousness:* small groups to extremely large flocks of thousands. *Movements:* sedentary. *Foods:* seeds, grain, green shoots, berries, earthworms, slugs and snails. *Breeding:* most of the year; as many as 5 broods per year. *Nest:* slight nest of twigs, grass and/or seaweed, in buildings, cliffs, caves, under bridges, water tanks and occasionally in tree hollows. *Eggs:* 2.
Goodwin, 1970, pp.55-60.

NOTES ON INTRODUCTIONS
Eurasia. The flocks of pigeons that swarm around the roofs, facades of the large buildings, towers and monuments in many of the large cities in Europe and Asia probably consist exclusively of feral domestic pigeons, or at most, contain a very small proportion of wild Rock Doves (Voous, 1960).

In many areas of Europe their numbers increased following the second World War (Ringleben, 1960; Rakhilin, 1968). In Great Britain (Thomson, 1964) and Siberia particularly, the present widespread distribution is the result of the establishment of feral stock.

The so called Rock Doves of Korea, Manchuria and Japan seem almost exclusively to have sprung from domestic pigeons which have escaped or run wild (Voous). They are thought to have been introduced into Thailand (Peters, 1937), long ago from India, and are now feral near human habitation throughout that country (Deignan, 1963; Lekagul and Cronin, 1974). Populations in Mongolia and northern China are possibly native ones, but they may also be feral birds (Goodwin, 1970; Etchécopar and Hüe, 1978).

Pigeons live in a semi-domestic state in Burma (Smythies, 1960), and in India semi-feral stock exist in most towns (Ali, 1961). A few hundred feral birds are resident in the neighbourhood of the Victoria Theatre in Singapore (Ward, 1968), but they are now found in many other areas of the island also. The only feral populations known from Malaysia are in the Batu Caves in Selangor (Medway and Wells, 1976).

King *et al* (1975) list the pigeon as a common resident in most of south-east Asia, with perhaps the exception of Malaya and Vietnam.

In Africa, Payn (1948) says that pigeons in both Tunisia and Algeria all appear to be domestic or feral birds.

America. Feral pigeons sustain themselves about many cities in the United States and Canada and are established widely in Central and South America, particularly the larger cities, from feral domestic stock (A.O.U., 1957; Peterson, 1961).

They are permanent residents in both cities and farmland in southern Canada from coast to coast (Godfrey, 1966), after having been first brought to Nova Scotia, Canada by Lescarbot in 1606-07 (Saunders, 1935, in Carl and Guiguet, 1972; Schorger, 1952). Undoubtedly many subsequent introductions were made, the first in the United States probably in 1621 (Schorger, 1952) or shortly before.

In parts of central Washington and possibly other States the species has become completely feral living and nesting in areas far from settlements. No colonies of this nature existed in British Columbia until about 1966. At about this time they were found nesting in cliffs along the east side of the Okanagan Valley from Osoyoos to Vaseux Lake (Carl and Guiguet, 1972).

Pigeons have been found as far north as Sitka and Anchorage in Alaska (Heilbrun, 1976), but only in these towns.

In Mexico they sustain themselves in a feral or semi-feral state around many towns and possibly in some canyons and cliffs (Peterson and Chalif, 1973). Further south in Guatemala they are domesticated in most parts of the country and are often seen flying around farms and villages, but are not often truly feral (Land, 1970).

Sick (1968) indicates that pigeons have become feral in most towns in South America. They were certainly present in the cities and environs of Rio de Janeiro, Montevideo, Buenos Aires and Santiago, Chile, when I visited them in 1961. Escalante (pers. comm., 1976) says that they are usually near towns and populated regions mostly in the south of South America. They have been introduced and are probably a breeding resident on Isla Grande, Tierra del Fuego, where a specimen was shot in 1915 at Bahia Buen Suceso and more recently (in 1960) some were noted near Ushuaia (Humphrey *et al,* 1970). In the north they are common in the mountains and coast around towns in Peru, but do not appear to be common in the eastern lowlands (Plenge, 1977, pers. comm.). Plenge informs me that in Peru they are probably the descendants of birds brought by the Spanish expeditions. Olrog (1959) reports that they are established in Argentina in cities and various parts of the country as a semi-feral species.

Rock Dove, *Columba livia*

Juan Fernandez. The pigeon was introduced to Masatierra Island in the Juan Fernandez Archipelago many years ago (Johnson, 1967), probably by the first colonists. Johnson reports that they were found there in 1917, when they were abundant on the high cliffs overlooking Cumberland Bay. They are absent from Masafuera and Santa Clara Islands in the archipelago. Sick records that only on Juan Fernandez has the species become truly wild in the South American region.

Easter Islands. Apparently pigeons have been introduced on these islands, but details appear to be lacking.

Society Islands. Pigeons were apparently introduced to Tahiti at the beginning of the nineteenth century (Lancan and Mougin, 1974). Lancan and Mougin say they are present on the Gambier Archipelago (Mangareva), but are totally absent from the south-east of the Tuamotu Archipelago. In Mangareva they are found principally on the slopes and in the cliffs of Mount Duff, and are seen feeding in the cultivated areas bordering the sea.

Introduced to Tahiti at the beginning of the nineteenth century (Murphy, 1924), they are not mentioned in the wild by Wilson (1907) nor by the Whitney Expedition, but are later mentioned by Curtiss (1938). Holyoak (1974) found semi-wild birds breeding in Tahiti, Moorea, Raiatea and Bora Bora, and indicates that they probably also exist on Huahine and Maupiti. They are apparently found mainly in the coastal zone, but are not very abundant in the towns. Holyoak counted seventy in the environs of Vaitapi (on Bora Bora).

Samoan Islands. A small colony of twenty Pigeons were noted in 1972 at Savaii which du Pont (1972) says were undoubtedly domestic birds gone wild. The species had not previously been recorded from Western Samoa.

Fiji. A large feral pigeon population lives around Suva on the island of Viti Levu and some exist in several villages on Taveuni (Holyoak, 1979). Those in Suva have been present for many years as I observed a few in the vicinity of the wharf in 1961.

Bermuda. Pigeons have been introduced to Bermuda but there appears to be no record of their introduction (Bourne, 1957). Bourne indicates that there are several flocks of parti-coloured feral birds in the cliffs of Harrington Sound, the South Shore and elsewhere. Wingate (1973) says that the species is not common in Bermuda, but colonies still breed at High Point, Southampton and at Abbott's Cliff, Harrington Sound.

Bahamas. The feral pigeon is recorded from Eleuthera in the Bahamas (Heilbrun, 1977).

West Indies. Semi-feral birds are established in and near the towns (Bond, 1960) of most of the larger cities in the West Indies (A.O.U., 1957). They have been recorded from the United States Naval Base in Cuba, at Cabo Rojo in Puerto Rico, on St Croix in the Virgin Islands (Heilbrun, 1976), on Trinidad (Heilbrun, 1977), and on Antigua (Holland and Williams, 1978).

In Jamaica they stay around their dovecotes and apparently are not found in a truly feral state (Lack, 1976).

Hawaiian Islands. The pigeon was introduced to the

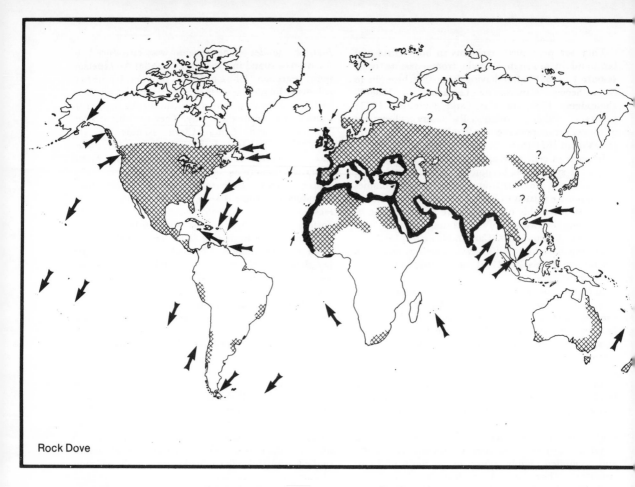

Rock Dove

Hawaiian Islands in 1796 (Walker, 1967) where it probably escaped from domestication (Munro, 1960) to become established. Munro records that there were immense flocks on the island of Hawaii in 1891 and also on Molokai in the early 1900s. They were apparently formerly abundant on all the main islands except Kauai, but in the 1940s had declined in numbers and only 2550 birds were estimated (on Hawaii, Lanai, Oahu, and Molokai) to be there in 1949, mostly on Hawaii (Schwartz and Schwartz, 1949).

The species sustained itself in the wild about towns, farms and cliffs and was locally established on the islands of Midway, Lanai, Oahu, Molokai and Hawaii (Peterson, 1961) in the 1960s. According to the Hawaiian Audubon Society (1975) they are now well established and breeding on these islands, with perhaps the exception of Midway, and are also present on the islands of Kauai and Maui.

Australia. Feral pigeons exist in most of the larger cities and towns in most States of Australia (Serventy and Whittell, 1951; McGill, 1960; Condon, 1962; Long, 1972; Lavery, 1974).

In South Australia they occur about Adelaide and in rural districts in fairly large numbers as a semi-domesticated commensal of man. Abbott (1974) reports that they were recorded on Kangaroo Island in 1967. In New South Wales they are feral in many cities and towns and some have reverted to living and breeding on cliffs. Much the same situation pertains in Queensland (Lavery) where they are common in cities and towns on the east coast and in the south-east interior, having been first introduced in the late nineteenth century. They are present in Townsville in northern Queensland (Lavery and Hopkins, 1963) and in the Atherton Shire (Bravery, 1970).

Pigeons have probably been escaping from captivity in Western Australia since the time of the early settlers. They were present on Rottnest Island before 1890 (Storr, 1965). In the 1950s and 1960s they were reported to be breeding in trees and to be living in some bush areas away from settlement in country areas (Serventy and Whitell, 1951 and 1962). Surveys in 1968-69 showed they were widely distributed in the Perth Metropolitan Area and were in some seventy-seven country centres in the south-west of Western Australia (Long).

New Zealand. According to Oliver (1955) there are no records of the first introductions of pigeons to New Zealand. However, Wodzicki (1965) places the date of introduction at about the 1850s, and Falla *et al* (1966) indicate it was certainly in the early days of settlement of that country.

In the 1920s Thomson (1922) records that they had gone wild in many parts of New Zealand including Strath-Taieri, Middlemarch to Waipiata, central Otago, Duntroon, Dunstan Range and at Napier. By 1955 (Oliver) they were in most cities and country districts throughout New Zealand.

At present the pigeon is restricted but abundant in both the North and South Islands (Wodzicki, 1965) and in some areas, notably the Auckland west coast, Hawke's Bay and Banks Peninsula, they have become truly wild and reverted to the traditional habit of breeding in caves, on sea cliffs and inland cliffs (Falla *et al*).

210

Norfolk Island. Feral pigeons occur around buildings and nest in colonies in caves on the shore cliffs on Norfolk Island (Smithers and Disney, 1969). They are apparently as yet not present in large numbers, but appear to be well established there.

Mauritius. Probably introduced from Europe at the beginning of the French occupation in about 1715 (Rountree *et al,* 1952), domestic varieties of pigeons are now found throughout Mauritius, but more commonly near human habitation. In earlier years the species was confined to the Port Louis and Signal Mountain areas (Meinertzhagen, 1912).

Andaman and Nicobar Islands. Feral pigeons are reported to live around Nancowry in the Nicobars and at Port Blair in the Andamans (Abdulali, 1967). Kloss (1903) refers to an introduction to Car Nicobar in 1898 and to seeing numbers of them there in 1900.

South Georgia. Feral pigeons were reported at the Whaling Station on South Georgia island in January, 1968 (Watson, 1975).

St Helena. Some pigeons were present near Jamestown in 1949 and the species was reported to have been plentiful there in 1938 (Benson, 1950). Melliss (1870) reports that they were abundant both in the wild and as a domestic species around 1870.

Haydock (1954) says that it is quite possible that this species did exist on the island in early times. He indicates that some were released by troops stationed on the island after the first World War and that there are now hundreds living in a wild state and breeding on the ledges of Cat Hole at the Heartshape Waterfall in the north-east of the island.

DAMAGE

Pigeons have become a nuisance in most of the larger cities in the world because of their fouling of buildings, statues, etc. with droppings. They are also generally regarded as potential health hazards to humans in urban environments.

There appears to be reasonable evidence that they provide a reservoir for ornithosis and play some part in the transmission of such diseases as encephalitis and histoplasmosis (Shuyler, 1963; Morris, 1969).

Pigeon droppings deface and accelerate deterioration of buildings, statues and automobiles and are sometimes deposited on unwary pedestrians. They are common contaminators of grain destined for human consumption. Their nests clog drainpipes, their droppings mar window sills, interfere with awnings and render fire escapes hazardous. They irritate people with the noise they make and their manure produces objectionable odours especially when deposited in ceilings and on sills.

Although pigeons are not generally thought of as agricultural pests they do occasionally interfere with man's crops. In India for instance they are sometimes destructive to newly sown maize, pulse and ground nuts (Ali, 1944), and in England damage does occur to cereal crops occasionally (Lancum, 1961). In Queensland, Australia, they have become a significant pest where intensive animal production is based on rations high in grain (Morris, 1969).

WOODPIGEON
(Wood Pigeon, Ring-dove)
Columba palumbus Linnaeus

DISTINGUISHING CHARACTERISTICS

40-45 cm (15.7-17.7 in). 500 g (1.1 lb)

Generally bluish grey, paler on underparts; dusky reddish tinge on breast; mark on neck and wing bar white; purple and green sheen above white neck patch; tail slate grey; bill orange and pink with whitish at base and the remainder shading from yellow to brown at tip.

Witherby *et al,* vol.3, 1938-41, pp.130-134 and pl.102, opp. p.130.

Goodwin, 1970, pp.70-71.

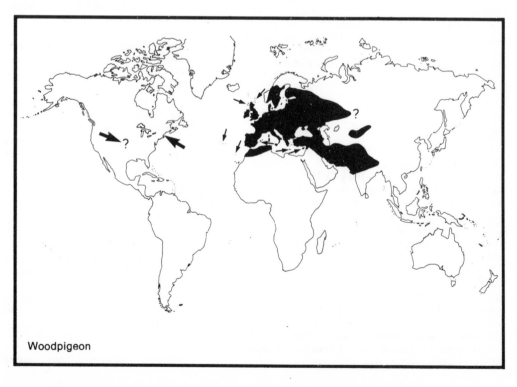

Woodpigeon

GENERAL DISTRIBUTION

Eurasia: all Europe north to 66° N., east to Iran and northern India, south to the Açores, Madeira and north-west Africa. Winters in southern parts of range.

INTRODUCED DISTRIBUTION

Increased breeding range northwards in Europe. Introduced unsuccessfully to the USA.

GENERAL HABITS

Status: very common. *Habitat:* forests, lowlands, parks, villages, towns, roadsides and other cultivated areas. *Gregariousness:* singly or small groups, but large flocks at food sources. *Movements:* sedentary and migratory. *Foods:* seeds, small fruits, buds, leaves, acorns, nuts, berries, grain, green shoots, caterpillars and slugs. *Breeding:* Apr-Oct; 2-3 clutches per season. *Nest:* small flat nest of sticks, in trees, bushes or buildings. *Eggs:* 2.
Goodwin, 1970, pp.71-72.

NOTES ON INTRODUCTIONS

Europe. During the past one hundred years the Woodpigeon has increased its breeding range in north-western Europe towards the north, possibly attributable to the gradual increase of the mean annual temperature in these regions (Voous, 1960). In Great Britain the species appears to be still spreading (Sharrock, 1976).

USA. Woodpigeons were introduced to the United States in the period 1910-13, but failed to establish themselves (Gottschalk, 1967). Phillips (1928) records that of the thirty birds released in Bronx Park, New York, between these dates, not one was seen again after their liberation.

DAMAGE

The Woodpigeon has become a serious pest in Great Britain and at least in parts of Europe, because in areas of high population density they feed on crops planted by man (Murton and Westwood, 1963; Seubert, 1964). They will feed on all kinds of crops including, wheat, oats, barley, rye, beans, peas, cabbages, turnips, rape, swedes, potatoes, clover, flax, currants, cherries, gooseberries and plums, although for the greater part of the year their diet is primarily weed seeds. Probably the most significant damage is caused to brassica, legumes and the clover pastures.

MOURNING DOVE
(Turtle Dove)
Zenaida macroura (Linnaeus)

DISTINGUISHING CHARACTERISTICS

27-33 cm (10.8-13.2 in). 90-130 g (3.17-4.59 oz)
Forehead fawn, back of head grey; black spot on ear-coverts; upper parts greyish brown, glossed bronze-purple on nape; rump slate grey; underparts pinkish; tail long, graduated and pointed, with a black sub-terminal bar and broad white tips; wing-coverts spotted black; bill black.
Godfrey, 1966, pp.207-208 and pl.37, no.4, p.192.
Goodwin, 1970, pp.205-206.

GENERAL DISTRIBUTION

North and Central America: from south-eastern Alaska and southern Canada south to Mexico, the Bahamas, Greater Antilles and to Puerto Rico. Winter south to Panama and Colombia. Wander widely outside breeding range.

Mourning Dove

INTRODUCED DISTRIBUTION

Successfully colonised Bermuda. Introduced, probably successfully to Hawaii in the Hawaiian Islands.

GENERAL HABITS

Status: common. *Habitat:* open country, woods, groves, arid desert areas, alpine areas and tundra, towns and cultivated areas. *Gregariousness:* singly, pairs or family groups, winter flocks of ten or more, and large flocks gather at food sources. *Movements:* partly migratory and nomadic. *Foods:* seeds, small fruits, mast, grain, snails and probably other invertebrates. *Breeding:* all year; usually singly, but occasionally colonies; two broods per year. *Nest:* fragile platform of twigs, in a bush or tree, rarely on the ground. *Eggs:* 2, rarely from 1-3, 4.
Goodwin, 1970, pp.206-207.

NOTES ON INTRODUCTIONS

Hawaiian Islands. Bryan (1958) reports that Mourning Doves were introduced from America to the Hawaiian Islands in about 1929 or 1930. Walker (1967) indicates that the race *Z.m. marginella* from an unknown source was introduced in 1929, but that

Mourning Dove, *Zenaida macroura*

it is not known to have become established in any of the islands. More recently, the Hawaiian Audubon Society (1975) records that the species may be established on the island of Hawaii, but that its present status is poorly known. Lewin (1971) reported breeding at the Puu Waawaa Ranch, Hawaii, following the releases of some 168 birds of Californian game farm origin in 1962, 1964 and 1965. He indicates that in 1966 the species was spreading on the ranch.

Bermuda. The Mourning Dove colonised Bermuda naturally in the mid-1950s and is now one of the commonest land birds breeding on the island (Wingate, 1973).

DAMAGE

In North America the Mourning Dove appears to be rarely implicated in the causing of any agricultural damage. Royal and Neff (1961) report that this species, in company with other small passerines, has been a major cause of the failure of natural and artificial seeding of pines in Louisiana and adjacent States. The damage attributable to the Mourning Dove alone however is not clear.

WHITE-WINGED DOVE
(Mesquite Dove)
Zenaida asiatica (Linnaeus)

DISTINGUISHING CHARACTERISTICS
23-32 cm (9.2-12.8 in). 126-183 g (4.44-6.45 oz)
Generally brownish grey; conspicuous white wing patch; forehead, face, neck and breast buff, shading to greyish around base of bill; lower neck and breast tinged vinous pink; crown and hindneck deep mauve-pink; black mark on side of head behind eye; mantle, scapulars and central tail-feathers reddish; underparts pale bluish grey; lower back and rump bluish grey with brown; outer tail-feathers bluish grey, with black sub-terminal bar and white tip; bill black.
Goodwin, 1970, p.212.
Peterson and Chalif, 1973, p.69 and pl.11.

GENERAL DISTRIBUTION
North, Central, South America, West Indies and the Bahamas: from south-eastern California, southern Nevada, central Arizona, southern New Mexico and western Texas, south to Costa Rica: in western South America from south-western Ecuador, south to Peru and northern Chile: also from the southernmost Bahamas, Cuba, Jamaica, Grand Cayman, Swan Island, Old Providence, St Andrew, Hispaniola, Gonave, Tortue and Mona.

INTRODUCED DISTRIBUTION
Introduced successfully in Florida, USA and probably on Hawaii in the Hawaiian Islands; may have been successfully transplanted in western Cuba.

GENERAL HABITS
Status: fairly common. *Habitat:* open woodlands, wooded hills, river woods, mesquite, mangroves, desert oases, towns, farms and cultivated areas. *Gregariousness:* singly, pairs or small parties, larger numbers gather at food sources. *Movements:* sedentary and migratory. *Foods:* seeds, grain, berries and fruits. *Breeding:* prolonged, Mar-Sept; in colonies. *Nest:* flimsy platform of twigs in a shrub or tree. *Eggs:* 1-3, usually 2.
Goodwin, 1970, pp.212-213.

NOTES ON INTRODUCTIONS
Hawaiian Islands. Some forty birds of the race *Z.a. mearnsi* from a Californian game farm were introduced in 1961 and 1965 on the Puu Waawaa Ranch, Hawaii (Lewin, 1971), but are not known to be established there (Walker, 1967; Berger, 1972). More recently, the Hawaiian Audubon Society (1975) indicate that the species may be established on the island of Hawaii, but that their present status

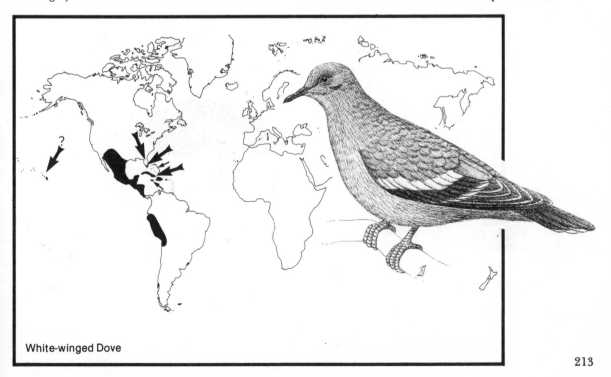

White-winged Dove

there is poorly known. Lewin gives the impression that they are still established around the homestead there.

USA. White-winged Doves are established in Dade County, southern Florida, over an area of some one hundred and four square kilometres (40 square miles) (Owre, 1973).

Twenty-five birds were released near Homestead in 1959 and some 200 were noted there in 1968 (Owre). Some were reported from the Lower Keys in October 1975 (Edscorn, 1976) and one was reported from Naples on the west coast in the same year (Heilbrun, 1976). The species is still spreading in Florida and recently Stevenson (1977) recorded 1140 at Davie in Broward County.

Kale (1977) indicates that the Florida Game and Fresh Water Fish Commission for the past two breeding seasons have been capturing and transporting these doves from the Upper Keys—Homestead population and releasing them in central Florida for game.

Cuba. Blake (1975) indicates that the species has been transplanted (or introduced ?) into western Cuba and apparently (?) established there.

DAMAGE
None known.

COMMON TURTLEDOVE
(Turtle Dove, European Turtledove)
Streptopelia turtur (Linnaeus)

DISTINGUISHING CHARACTERISTICS
26-28 cm (10.4-11.2 in)
Head, flanks and rump light grey; back brown with black markings; underparts pinkish, a few black and white stripes on sides of neck; orbital skin reddish purple; wing-coverts red-brown with black spots in centre of each feather; tail dark grey, white tipped; bill blackish with purplish tinge.

Witherby *et al,* vol.4, 1938-41, pp.141-145 and pl.103, opp. p.146.
Goodwin, 1970, pp.120-121.

GENERAL DISTRIBUTION
Eurasia-North Africa: from the British Isles and Scandinavia to central Asia and south to Madeira, Canary Islands, northern Africa, Kirghiz, Turkestan and Afghanistan: in north Africa not south of the Sahara. Winters in tropical Africa.

INTRODUCED DISTRIBUTION
Possibly re-established in some areas of the USSR. Introduced unsuccessfully in Australia and (?) New Zealand.

GENERAL HABITS
Status: common. *Habitat:* forest, forest edges, open woodland, desert oases, palm groves, parks, gardens and open fields. *Gregariousness:* pairs or small groups, larger flocks gather at food sources and during migration. *Movements:* mainly migratory, southern populations more or less sedentary. *Foods:* small seeds, green shoots, grain, leaves, buds and insects including invertebrates. *Breeding:* Apr-Sept; 2-3 broods per season. *Nest:* thin flimsy nest of twigs in a bush or tree. *Eggs:* 2.
Goodwin, 1970, pp.121-122.

NOTES ON INTRODUCTIONS
Australia. Turtledoves from England (eight birds named *Turtur communis*) were probably introduced to Australia in 1872 (Ryan, 1906), but failed to become established there.
USSR. Eastern Turtledoves were reacclimatised in the Alma-Ata in 1960-61 and were established and spreading (Yanushevich, 1966). It is not certain which species was introduced but it is possible that it was *S. orientalis* and not *S. turtur.*
New Zealand. Common Turtledoves were imported into New Zealand in 1871, but it is not known if any were released there (Thomson, 1922).

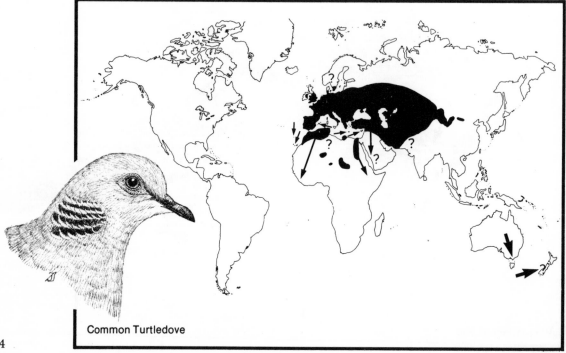

Common Turtledove

Where the seeds of millet are sown in the USSR this bird is said to be a potential pest to newly sown crops (Murton, Isaacson and Westwood, 1965). However, it seems that the Common Turtledove is in no way comparable to either the Woodpigeon or Stock Dove as a pest, and only becomes so when in large numbers. It feeds mainly on fumeria, grass and stellaria seeds but collects grains from the ground.

RED TURTLEDOVE
(Red-Collared Dove)
Streptopelia tranquebarica (Hermann)

DISTINGUISHING CHARACTERISTICS
22-23 cm (8.8-9.2 in). Males 104 g (3.67 oz)
Vinaceous red body and upper wing-coverts; head and throat grey; flight feathers blackish; black ring on hindneck; lower back to tail slaty grey; under tail-coverts white; outer tail-feathers broadly tipped white; bill black. Female: brown with reddish tinge; head and lower back to tail greyish brown.
Goodwin, 1970, pp.138-139.
Etchécopar and Hüe, 1978, p.432 and pl.16, p.417.

GENERAL DISTRIBUTION
Southern Asia: from India, Bangladesh, Pakistan (Baluchistan), Tibet, Burma, Thailand, northern China, Hainan and Taiwan south to Sri Lanka, the Andaman Islands, southern Thailand, the Indochinese region and the northern Philippines.

INTRODUCED DISTRIBUTION
Sporadic appearance in Singapore and Malaysia may be due to escapees or merely vagrants.

GENERAL HABITS
Status: very common. *Habitat:* open country, dry woodland, scrub, secondary growth, gardens, villages and generally around human habitation. *Gregariousness:* singly or pairs, but sometimes in

Red Turtledove

flocks with other dove species. *Movements:* sedentary and locally migratory. *Foods:* seeds, grain, buds and leaves. *Breeding:* undefined, probably throughout the year (June-July ? eastern China). *Nest:* sparse platform of twigs and sometimes grass, in a tree or shrub. *Eggs:* 2 (sometimes 3).
Goodwin, 1970, pp.139-140.
Etchécopar and Hüe, 1978, p.432.

NOTES ON INTRODUCTIONS
Singapore. Two male birds of the race *S.t. humilis* were captured in Singapore in December 1940. Gibson-Hill (1949) suggests that they may have been escaped cage birds.
Malaysia. The Red Turtledove appears to be an occasional visitor to Malaya and it has been recorded in Perak and has been known to breed in the Dindings near the coast (Glenister, 1974). There is some doubt as to whether some of the birds found have been introduced or are genuine visitors, nevertheless, the species may be establishing itself in Perak. According to Medway and Wells (1976) they make limited to sporadic appearances on the Perak coast, where a pair nested in 1933, and Malacca and Singapore.

DAMAGE
None known.

MADAGASCAR TURTLEDOVE
(Red Turtledove)
Streptopelia picturata (Temminck)

DISTINGUISHING CHARACTERISTICS
28 cm (11.2 in). 110-135 g (3.88-4.76 oz)
Generally grey-brown, with more or less reddish head and mantle; sides of neck spotted with black; chest barred dull chestnut; abdomen whitish, greyish or brownish; rump brown; skin around eye purplish; tail grey-brown, outer feathers black with greyish white terminal band; under tail grey-brown to white; bill bluish grey, base purplish. Races vary: *rostrata* with reddish head and chestnut mantle: *coppingeri* vinous purple upper parts: *picturata* with grey head and purplish mantle.
Goodwin, 1970, pp.140-141.
Penny, 1974, pl.3., opp. p.80.

GENERAL DISTRIBUTION
Islands off the African coast: Malagasy, Anjouan Island (Comores Group), Aldabra Island, Assumption Island (now extinct), the Amirante Islands, Seychelles and Diego Garcia (Chagos Archipelago).

INTRODUCED DISTRIBUTION
Introduced successfully to Mauritius (may have been native?), Diego Garcia (may have been endemic race) and Réunion; a race other than that occurring there has been introduced successfully to the Seychelles and Amirantes; either colonised or was possibly introduced successfully, but now extinct on the Isles Glorieuses.

GENERAL HABITS
Status: common. *Habitat:* forest edges, secondary brush, plantations, rice fields, cultivated and open areas. *Gregariousness:* singly, pairs, or flocks of 10-30 birds. *Movements:* sedentary. *Foods:* weed seeds, grain, castor oil seeds, copra and insects including caterpillars and beetles. *Breeding:* July-Nov (July-Apr Mauritius). *Nest:* platform of grass and interlaced sticks in a tree or bush. *Eggs:* 2.

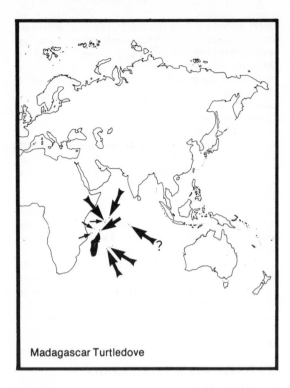

Madagascar Turtledove

Goodwin, 1970, p.141.
Milon *et al,* 1973, pt.35: Bds., p.142.
NOTES ON INTRODUCTIONS
Mauritius. The race *S.p. picturata* has been introduced to this island (Peters, 1937). Rountree *et al* (1952) record that Carié in 1916 suggested that they were indigenous to Mauritius, but that most agree it is probably an exotic there. Meinertzhagen (1912) says that they were once abundant, but became scarce some time prior to 1912. In the 1950s they were said to be still scarce, local and confined to remote wooded areas. However, Staub (1976) reports that they are now widespread there.
Seychelles. The race *picturata* was introduced to the Seychelles from Mauritius (Peters, 1937) or Malagasy (Gaymer *et al,* 1969). According to Newton (1867) they were established but not very common on Mahé

Madagascar Turtledove, *Streptopelia picturata*

in 1867 and were said to have been introduced by an Inspector of Police a few years earlier. Penny (1974) says that they were probably released by one of the early ships which carried the species as a food supply.
Both Benson (1970) and Penny indicate that this race has extensively hybridised with the endemic *rostrata.* In fact, Penny says that *picturata* has now replaced or diluted *rostrata* on all but one or two of the smaller islands.
Réunion. The race *picturata* has also been introduced to this island (Peters, 1937) where it is rather scarce except in the south-east around Saint Philippe (Staub, 1976).
Diego Garcia. The Madagascar Turtledove is believed to have been introduced to Diego Garcia from the Seychelles, but there is no record of any introduction (Loustau-Lalanne, 1962).
Loustau-Lalanne records that there were apparently none there in 1907, but that they were well established over the whole island especially near Pointe Est in the early 1960s. The species was still common there in 1971 (Hutson, 1975).
According to Bourne (1971) the Madagascar Turtledove may not have been introduced, but may be an endemic race *S.p. chuni.* He adds that Ripley (in Bourne, 1971) does not agree with Benson (1970) that the species is a hybrid between the Madagascar and Comore forms *(picturata* x *comorensis).*
Amirantes. The race *S.p. picturata* appears to have been a recent introduction to the Amirantes from the Seychelles (Benson, 1970), which will probably hybridise with the native race *saturata.* Penny (1974) reports that *S.p. aldabrana* still survives in the Amirantes where however it has been mixed with *S.p. picturata.*
Isles Glorieuses (Glorioso Islands). Although a specimen of the Madagascar Turtledove was collected as early as 1883, Ridgeway (1895) thought that the species had probably been introduced to the Isles Glorieuses. Benson (1970) and Penny (1971) suggest that they may have colonised these islands from Aldabra. However, the Madagascar Turtledove may have become extinct there before 1906 as there are no further records of it (Benson *et al,* 1975).
DAMAGE
According to Gaymer *et al* (1969) the race *picturata* has now almost swamped the Seychelles Turtledove, *rostrata,* out of existence on the Seychelles Islands.

COLLARED TURTLEDOVE
(Collared Dove, Barbary Dove, Ring Dove)
Streptopelia decaocto (Frivaldszky)

DISTINGUISHING CHARACTERISTICS
26-33 cm (10.4-13.2 in). 138-156 g (4.87-5.5 oz)
Generally greyish fawn; upper parts pale brown, head and underparts pale grey; conspicuous yellow eye-ring; narrow black collar around back of neck; upper wing-coverts greyish; under tail-coverts grey; bill black.
Smythies, 1953, pl.21, fig.9, p.428.
Goodwin, 1970, pp.128-129.
Note. The Barbary Dove (or domestic form) has not been separated here from the Collared Turtledove, although the weight of evidence supports the fact that it has been derived from the African Collared Turtledove *Streptopelia roseogrisea.* The two species

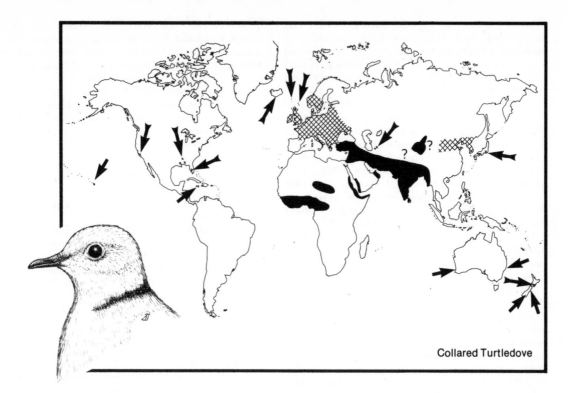

Collared Turtledove

resemble one another in general appearance and I have found some difficulty in establishing which of them has been introduced in some areas.

Mackworth-Praed and Grant, ser.3, vol.1, 1970, p.347 and pl.24 *(S.d. roseogrisea)*.

GENERAL DISTRIBUTION

Europe, southern Asia and North Africa: in Asia from Turkey, Israel, Jordan and Iraq, east to Burma (Arakan) and Sri Lanka; also in western China, North and South Korea: in North Africa in Ethiopia and Somali Republic, the Sudan and from Senegal to the Camerouns and the Central African Republic. (Note: African distribution shown on range map is of *S. roseogrisea*.)

INTRODUCED DISTRIBUTION

Successfully colonised most of mainland Europe, the British Isles and southern Scandinavia; introduced successfully in northern China, Korea, Japan, USA and New Zealand; possibly introduced successfully on Hawaii in the Hawaiian Islands. Introduced unsuccessfully in Australia, England and Jamaica. (Note: African distribution shown on range map is of *S. roseogrisea*.)

GENERAL HABITS

Status: very common. *Habitat:* woods, open arid regions with trees, oases in deserts, palm groves, towns, villages, parks, gardens, farmyards, roadsides and cultivated areas. *Gregariousness:* flocks of up to 100 birds, sometimes larger flocks. *Movements:* sedentary, although sometimes dispersal movements and local movements. *Foods:* small seeds, grain, berries and shoots of grasses. *Breeding:* now found breeding in every month of the year in Europe; may have 4-5 broods per year. *Nest:* small structure of twigs lined with grass and roots, in a tree or rarely on a building. *Eggs:* 1-3.

Goodwin, 1970, pp.128-130.

Rana, *Auk* vol.92, 1975, pp.322-332.

NOTES ON INTRODUCTIONS

Europe. During the twentieth century the Collared Turtledove has extended its range far into Europe (Voous, 1960). Voous suggests that they were introduced into south-eastern Europe by the Turks sometime after 1700, or perhaps as early as the sixteenth century. The species was a common city bird in Constantinople (Istanbul) so a natural immigration from Asia Minor rather than a man-induced one has to be considered.

Vaurie (1961) says that the species' original range is a matter for speculation, but probably consisted of the semi-arid or drier regions of southern and central Asia. Probably, they were introduced at an early date into Iran and from there were introduced or colonised westerly to Iraq, the Near East, Turkey and thence into south-eastern Europe.

They were found well into Europe for the first time in Bulgaria in 1853 and after 1900 the advance into other parts was fairly rapid. They were at Belgrade (Yugoslavia) in 1912, southern Hungary in 1930, Romania in 1933, Czechoslovakia in 1936, Bulgaria in 1937, Bucharest (Romania) and Austria in 1938, Greece in 1939, Vienna in 1943, Venice, north-western Slovakia and Braila (Romania) in 1944, Italy in 1944, Germany in 1946, the Netherlands in 1948-49, Denmark in 1948, Sweden and Switzerland in 1949, Belgium and Norway in 1952, Poland in 1950, Soviet Moldavia in 1952, France in 1950, England in 1955, Luxembourg in 1956, Estonia in 1957 and Scotland in 1958. They were confirmed to be breeding in Norway in 1955, Switzerland in the same year and in France in 1956. In 1953 odd birds were found as far north as Finland and in 1957 in central Sweden. Here, the species was first recorded in 1949 and was breeding at Scania, Sweden in 1951 (Reuterwall, 1956). Stolt and Risberg (1971) record that they arrived in Uppsala, Sweden in 1957 and since 1964 have been increasing markedly in numbers. The species has also colonised Norway and occurs in scattered populations as far north as Tromsö (69° 30′) where they have been present since 1969 (Vader, 1977, pers. comm.).

According to Hudson (1972) the Collared Turtledove was not breeding west of Hungary, Czechoslovakia and Austria in 1940, but was present in all Europe with the exception of Iceland, Finland, Spain and Portugal. They have now nested in southern Finland (Ojala and Sjöberg, 1968), were present in the Faeroe Islands (at Thorshavn) in 1970 (Hudson), one was observed in eastern Iceland (at Lodmundarfjord) in August 1964 (Langseth, 1965) and two pairs nested in southern Iceland in 1971.

In Holland the Collared Turtledove bred in 1949-50 and by 1963 some 5000 were breeding there in an estimated population of twenty to thirty thousand birds (Leys, 1964).

Many attempts were made to deliberately introduce the species to Great Britain but all ended in failure (Koch, 1956), however the Collared Turtledove arrived unaided in 1955. They began breeding at Norfolk in England in 1955, at Morayshire in Scotland in 1957, at Dublin and Galway in Ireland in 1959, at Cardiganshire and Pembrokeshire in Wales in 1961 and on the Isle of Man in 1964. They colonised the Shetland Islands and have bred on the mainland since 1965 and at Unst in 1970 (Hudson). By 1964 they had colonised some seventy-five counties in the British Isles (Hudson, 1965).

They arrived in County Down, Ireland in 1960 and by 1965 had become established in all the counties of Northern Ireland with the exception of Tyrone (Ennis, 1965).

The northward movement of the Collared Turtledove in Europe is said to have been favoured by amelioration of the climate and by the spread of cultivation, the species' favoured habitat (Mayr, 1965).

Northern China and Korea. Goodwin (1970) records that the Collared Turtledove had been introduced to northern China and Korea from India. He agrees with Stresemann and Nowak (1958) who believe that the species was brought to northern China by sea from India and escaped to settle in the region. Vaurie (1961) however, suggests that it would have been easier and more likely that they came from western China and/or Inner Mongolia, by natural expansion or through introductions or both. He points out that birds from northern China are identical to the Chinese or Turkestan subspecies.

There appear to be no details of any introductions to Korea. Gore and Won (1971) report that the Collared Turtledove occurs only on Hong-do Island and a few islands off the south-west coast.

Japan. The Collared Turtledoves living in Japan probably originated exclusively from escaped cage birds (Voous, 1960) brought over from China to Honshū in the eighteenth or early nineteenth century, certainly by 1830 (Fisher, 1953).

According to Fisher they became plentiful in the Kwanto area near Tokyo in 1875, but were reduced in numbers by shooting before 1900. By 1925 they were known only from the Saitama and Chiba areas

(Taka-Tsukasa and Hachisuka, 1925) and were almost extirpated following the second World War (Udagawa, 1949). Only a few score birds existed in Koshigaya in the Saitama Prefecture and Tokyo areas up until the 1960s (Yamashina, 1961).

The Ornithological Society of Japan (1974) reports that the species is now restricted to the Kanto Plain in the Saitama Prefecture, but is at present increasing in numbers from a once-reduced, small population possibly of introduced origin.

USA. The Collared Turtledove has become naturalised in a wild state about Los Angeles, California, around Miami, Florida (A.O.U., 1957), and more recently in a number of areas in Alabama (Imhof, 1978).

Cooke and Knappen (1941) have indicated that the domestic variety of the Collared Turtledove was often liberated by aviculturists in California prior to the 1940s and that the first record of a specimen in the wild was at Buena Park, Los Angeles in 1909. They were reported from Central Park in that city in 1921 and Cooke and Knappen record a flock of twenty-five birds in this park in 1926 and twenty in Pershing Square in 1929, where at least one bird has nested. Grinnel (1929) estimated that there were about twenty pairs there in February 1929.

From the central Los Angeles area they have spread only slowly, but had reached San Bernardino, Redlands and most of the San Fernando Valley areas by the late 1950s. In 1975 they appeared to extend from at least Pasadena to Redlands and the Palos Verdes Peninsula.

In Florida the Collared Turtledove has become established in a limited area in the southern parts of the State (Gottschalk, 1967). Some were recently reported from St Petersburg (Heilbrun, 1976) which indicates that the species is still established at least locally in the area.

The domestic variety of the Collared Turtledove is now rapidly becoming established throughout suburban Alabama where it has been found in Athens, five suburbs of Birmingham, Auburn, Montgomery, Hayneville and in Mobile where it has nested for at least two years at Springhill (Imhof).

Australia. The first record of the Collared Turtledove in the wild in Australia was reported in August 1946 in the suburban area of Sydney, New South Wales (McGill, 1948). This bird was probably an isolated escapee from captivity.

In 1975 a small colony numbering some fifteen birds was found to be established in the Wattle Grove area, near Perth, Western Australia. These birds were destroyed by the Agriculture Protection Board and no further reports of any have been received.

New Zealand. According to Thomson (1922) the Collared Turtledove was commonly imported into New Zealand from about 1862 until 1922. Thomson says that some were liberated at various times by private individuals around homesteads and dwellings.

The first importations were probably made by the Canterbury Acclimatisation Society in 1866, the Nelson society in 1867 and possibly by the Auckland society also in 1867. Apparently some were living in the wild in the Christchurch domain and suburban gardens in Dunedin in the 1920s, but the species apparently did not remain established in New Zealand at that time.

Stidolph (1974) found two Barbary Doves at Masterton in 1971, and in 1972 as many as thirty had turned up. Some were seen again in 1973-74 and the species appears to have become feral in Masterton Park and in the suburban region to the west of the town where there is an abundance of trees and shrubs. Stidolph suggests that these birds were liberated by private individuals.

Hawaiian Islands. The Collared Turtledove was introduced in 1920 to the island of Kauai, to Oahu in 1928, and to the Puu Waawaa Ranch, Hawaii in 1961 (Lewin, 1971) where they may still be established around the homestead there. Other introductions of the Collared Turtledove have failed to become established in the Hawaiian Islands (Walker, 1967; Berger, 1972).

Jamaica. According to Lack (1976), March (in 1863-64) reported that domestic doves *(S. risoria)* were sometimes seen in the company of the wild *Z. asiatica,* but that there are no later records of their occurrence in Jamaica.

DAMAGE

It has been reported that the Collared Turtledove may become a pest in cherry orchards in Europe, but there appears to be little information documented. In England there have been complaints that the species causes damage in gardens to such plants as brassicas and lettuce, but the actual damage may be caused by other species. Hudson (1972) indicates that although they can be a local nuisance in areas where they are numerous, especially in localities where grain is stored or processed, they have not yet become a serious pest of economical significance at a national level. On poultry farms, at granaries, mills, malthouses etc., large feeding flocks can build up and develop 'nuisance value' through their depredations on grain and accumulations of droppings.

RED-EYED DOVE
(Half-collared Dove)

Streptopelia semitorquata (Rüppell)

DISTINGUISHING CHARACTERISTICS

152-220g (5.36-7.76 oz)

Nape, neck and throat to belly brown; crown grey; a black half-collar on sides of neck, almost joining at back; remainder of upper parts umber-brown; bare skin around eye purplish red; vent and under tail grey; bill black.

Mackworth-Praed and Grant, 1952-73, ser.1, vol.1, p.471 and pl.30; ser.2, vol.1, p.385 and pl.22; ser.3, vol.1, p.343 and pl.24.

Goodwin, 1970, p.135.

GENERAL DISTRIBUTION

Africa: southern Africa south of the Sahara, except south-western Africa; also on Zanzibar, Pemba and Mafia Islands.

INTRODUCED DISTRIBUTION

Introduced and/or colonised south-west Cape Peninsula, South Africa.

GENERAL HABITS

Status: common. *Habitat:* woodlands, forest clearings and cultivated areas. *Gregariousness:* singly, pairs or small parties, but large numbers at food sources. *Movements:* no information. *Foods:*

Red-eyed Dove

grain, seeds, berries, peanuts, small tubers, termites and probably other insects. *Breeding:* throughout the year. *Nest:* loosely built of twigs and grass stems, lined with rootlets, at some height from the ground. *Eggs:* 1-2.

Goodwin, 1970, pp.135-136.

NOTES ON INTRODUCTIONS

South Africa. The Red-eyed Dove was introduced to the Cape Peninsula and south-west Cape in 1933 from Beira, Moçambique (Mackworth-Praed and Grant, 1962). Winterbottom (1956) records that they were released at Elgin in September, 1933. Because the species has colonised much of the western Cape it is not known whether any of the birds now present originated from the Elgin introduction. Some of the birds released were also aviary-bred specimens from other regions of the Cape.

Damage

In Africa the Red-eyed Dove is a tame species, often seen on cultivated ground and among domestic stock. It was unprotected in southern Rhodesia (Goode, 1962).

JAVAN TURTLEDOVE
(Javanese or Philippine Collared Dove, Java Ring Dove)

Streptopelia bitorquata (Temminck)

DISTINGUISHING CHARACTERISTICS

30 cm (12 in)

Forehead, crown and nape grey; broad black, white-edged, half collar on hindneck; remainder of neck and upper mantle pinkish, often with rusty tinge; breast mauvish pink; belly and under tail-coverts white or greyish white; flanks greyish; back brown; primaries and secondaries blackish, remainder of wing blue-grey; rump dark grey-brown; central tail-feathers brown, outer feathers pale grey with basal third dark grey, under tail greyish white with basal

third black; bill blackish or dark grey, red at nape.
Smythies, 1960, pl. 11, no. 4, opp. p.240.
Goodwin, 1970, pp.138-139.

GENERAL DISTRIBUTION
Indonesia-Philippines: Java, Bali, Lesser Sunda Islands (Lombok, Sumbawa, Flores, Solor and Timor), Palawan and the Philippines.

INTRODUCED DISTRIBUTION
Introduced successfully in the Marianas; probably introduced successfully in Sumatra (?) and the Philippines (may be native?); probably introduced but now possibly extinct in Borneo. Introduced unsuccessfully in New Zealand.

GENERAL HABITS
Status: abundant and common. *Habitat:* forest edges, open country with trees, villages, fields and cultivation. *Movements and Gregariousness:* no information. *Foods:* seeds. *Breeding:* Apr-Aug (eastern Java). *Nest:* platform of sticks and twigs, in a tree, bush or shrub. *Eggs:* 2. (Note: habits little recorded, despite being common.)
Goodwin, 1970, pp.139-140.

NOTES ON INTRODUCTIONS
Marianas. The race *S.b. dusumieri* has been introduced to the Marianas (Peters, 1937; Delacour and Mayr, 1946) where they were abundant and partial to rice fields, grasslands and open country (Mayr, 1945) in the southern part of the island (Stophlet, 1946). They still occur on the islands of Saipan, Rota and Guam, but are apparently now uncommon on all three islands (Ralph and Sakai, 1979).

Borneo. There appears to be some doubt about the existence of the Javan Turtledove in Borneo. According to Smythies (1960) it is present as an introduced species, but Gore (1968) says that it was probably a local resident. Goodwin (1970) concedes it may have been introduced, but adds that it may now be extinct there anyway.

Javan Turtledove

Gore has indicated that the only recent record is of two birds on Si-Amil Island off Semporna, in 1962.

Sumatra. The Javan Turtledove has probably been introduced in Sumatra (Smythies, 1960; Delacour, 1947; Goodwin, 1970), but there appear to be no details of any introductions.

Philippines. Goodwin (1970) reports that the Javan Turtledove may have been originally introduced to the Philippines; however, it is generally listed as a native species there.

New Zealand. In 1867 the Otago Acclimatisation Society introduced five Java Doves (Thomson, 1922), presumably of this species. These were kept for some time, then liberated by Mr F. Jones on Green Island, but apparently disappeared soon after.

Both the Nelson and Wellington societies introduced further birds in 1875, but there are no records of them after this date. The Javan Turtledove did not become established in New Zealand.

DAMAGE
None known.

SPOTTED TURTLEDOVE
(Spotted Dove, Indian Turtle Dove, Chinese Spotted Dove, Lace-necked Dove)
Streptopelia chinensis (Scopoli)

DISTINGUISHING CHARACTERISTICS
27-34 cm (10.8-13.6 in). 116-205 g (4.09-7.23 oz)
Upper parts generally grey-brown; wings and back brown; upper wing-coverts with central dark stripe and lighter edges (in some race pattern very conspicuous); black patch on nape, spotted white; skin around eye purplish; chin whitish; throat and breast purplish pink; bill black.
Goodwin, 1970, pp.141-142.
Reader's Digest, 1977, pl. p.232.

GENERAL DISTRIBUTION
Southern Asia: from north-eastern China, Taiwan, Hainan, west to Pakistan and India, and south to Sri Lanka, Burma, Malay Peninsula, Sumatra, Java, Lesser Sunda Islands, Borneo and Palawan.

INTRODUCED DISTRIBUTION
Introduced successfully in eastern Indonesia (Sulawesi, Moluccas and small islands in the Flores Sea), Fijian Group (Viti Levu), New Britain (Rabaul), New Caledonia, New Zealand (Auckland), the Hawaiian Islands, Australia, USA (southern California) and Mauritius.

GENERAL HABITS
Status: very common. *Habitat:* open forest and secondary growth, wooded and cultivated country, parks, rivers and residential and urban areas. *Gregariousness:* solitary or small parties, may congregate in numbers at a food source. *Movements:* mainly sedentary. *Foods:* seeds, grain, green shoots and food scraps. *Breeding:* variable, probably throughout the year (Mar-Nov USA; Feb-Oct Hawaii). *Nest:* rough platform of sticks, in a bush or on buildings. *Eggs:* 2.
Goodwin, 1970, pp.142-143.
Etchécopar and Hüe, 1978, pp.434-435.

NOTES ON INTRODUCTIONS
Indonesian Islands. The race *S.c. tigrina* (Delacour, 1957) has been introduced on some eastern Indonesian Islands (Ripley, 1961) including Sulawesi, Moluccas (Peters, 1937; Delacour and

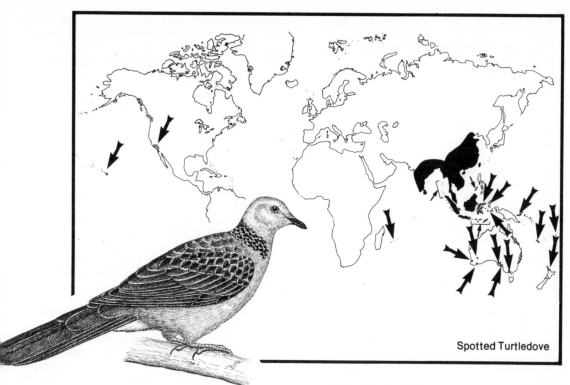

Spotted Turtledove

Mayr, 1946; Goodwin, 1970) and small isles in the Flores Sea (A.O.U., 1957). Stresemann (1936) records that the species was established on the northern peninsula, in central Sulawesi, and the southern peninsula. Meyer (1879) says that they were introduced here from Java in about 1835.

Fiji. The race *S.c. tigrina* has been introduced on Viti Levu (Mayr, 1945; Gorman, 1975) where it is still established.

Parham (1954) records that they were introduced from Australia and were present throughout the main islands in the 1950s. Turbet (1941) reports that they originally escaped from captivity to become established there. Besides Viti Levu they also occur on Nukulau Island and are well established coastally on Taveuni (Blackburn, 1971). They are confined to the towns, villages and cultivated areas and do not occur in the native forests (Holyoak, 1979).

New Britain. The race *S.c. tigrina* has also been introduced to New Britain where it is present around Rabaul (Mayr, 1945).

New Caledonia. S.c. tigrina was introduced from South-east Asia in 1939 and at present is found in many villages and cultivated areas (Delacour, 1966). According to Delacour they have been decimated by shooting in Noumea.

New Zealand. In recent years the Spotted Turtledove *S.c. tigrina* has established itself in the city and suburbs of Auckland (Oliver, 1955). The species is a favourite cage bird in New Zealand and presumedly escaped from captivity to become established.

Wodzicki (1965) reports that they were introduced early in the nineteenth century and are now locally abundant in the North Island. They are reported to be breeding in the suburbs of Auckland from Albany on the North Shore, south to Papakura (Falla *et al,* 1966).

Hawaiian Islands. Introductions of the race *S.c. chinensis,* prior to 1900, established the Spotted Turtledove in the Hawaiian Islands.

The species was well established in the 1940s (Munro, 1960); they reached Niihau from Kauai in about 1930 (Fisher, 1951) and are now widespread on all of the main islands in urban and open rural areas (Peterson, 1961; Hawaiian Audubon Society, 1975). According to Walker (1967) they are now open to hunting in the Hawaiian Islands.

In 1961, eight birds from a Californian game farm were released at the Puu Waawaa Ranch on Hawaii (Lewin, 1971). The reason for this introduction in an area where from all accounts the species is well established is not known.

USA. The Spotted Turtledove was introduced in the Hollywood area of Los Angeles, California, about 1917 (Reuther, 1951) or 1918 (Storer, 1934) or even earlier (McLean, 1958). Cooke and Knappen (1941) say that the first birds were found in 1917 and that later in the same year they were found to be common in the North Hollywood area. Presumably those first established came from the escape of caged birds.

In 1921, they had become firmly established over a considerable part of the city of Los Angeles, and by 1933 had extended their range to such outlying towns as Pasadena and Alhambra, and west and south to Santa Monica and Inglewood (Reuther, 1951). In 1941 they became established as far south as Redlands in Riverside County and in 1946 reached Bakersfield. Reuther was of the opinion that some of this range extension may possibly have been due to further introductions.

In the 1960s the species had spread outwards from Los Angeles to Santa Maria, Bakersfield, and east to Lancaster and Pear Blossom, and south-east to Palm Springs and south to San Diego (McLean). They are still slowly spreading although they still occupy only a limited area of southern California (Gottschalk, 1967).

The race introduced in California was *S.c. chinensis* (A.O.U., 1957).

Australia. Spotted Turtledoves were liberated in the Adelaide Botanical Gardens in 1881 (twenty birds), and many birds escaped or were set free from the zoo and elsewhere during a severe storm in 1931 (Boehm, 1961). Boehm says that they quickly became established about Adelaide and in less than twenty years had reached Clare in the north and Victor Harbour in the south. They were first observed on Kangaroo Island in March 1953 (Condon, 1962) and on Eyre Peninsula in 1966 (Condon, 1968).

The species appears to have been an early introduction into Victoria, possibly some time in the 1860s? Those releases recorded include some in 1870, 1872 and in 1874 (sixteen birds) near Melbourne (Ryan, 1906; Frith, 1973). By the 1950s they were established over an area within 160 km (100 miles) of Melbourne (Tarr, 1950). They were also introduced in New South Wales and were common in coastal areas and especially the Sydney area (Tarr).

In 1960, McGill (1960) reported that in New South Wales they were abundant in most coastal settled areas, but were only occasionally seen west of the Great Dividing Range. They appeared in the Lismore district of north-eastern New South Wales in 1935 (Frith, 1952) and the population was virtually continuous north to Brisbane and south to Kempsey by 1964 (Frith and McKean, 1975).

Spotted Turtledoves were released from Gordonvale, Queensland in about the mid 1940s, soon became numerous in the area and were rapidly spreading (White, 1946). White records that they were seen at Innisfail and Cairns in 1945. They were recorded from the Atherton Shire in 1968 (Bravery, 1970). Probably the first introductions of this species in Queensland occurred in the Brisbane area in 1912 (Laver, 1974) and they are reported to have been well established in the Botanical Gardens and at the University in 1913 (Jenkins, 1977). They are now common in some cities on the east coast of Queensland.

In Western Australia, Spotted Turtledoves were released from the Zoological Gardens, South Perth, from 1898 onwards (Serventy and Whittell, 1951). Although they had become established in the Perth Metropolitan area prior to 1912 they were still being despatched to country centres in the 1920s (Long, 1972). After the mid 1930s they steadily increased their range (Sedgwick, 1957) and were reported from a number of country centres in the south-west of Western Australia. They reached Rottnest Island in 1937 (Storr, 1965).

The Spotted Turtledove is now well established in mainly coastal areas from northern Queensland to South Australia and in the south-west of Western Australia. Although hybrid stocks of *chinensis* and *tigrina* are common over most of Australia (Frith and McKean, 1975) there is evidence that *chinensis* has been introduced in Perth, Adelaide, Melbourne, Sydney and Brisbane in the past, but there are probably no pure stocks of this race in any mainland State. There is pure *tigrina* stock at Innisfail, Queensland and they have probably been introduced in all mainland States at different times and probably to Tasmania (Launceston and Hobart districts) where there seems to be an admixture with some liberated stocks of the nominate race (Condon, 1975).

Mauritius. The Spotted Turtledove was probably introduced to Mauritius from India or southern China, perhaps as early as 1781, and certainly not later than the beginning of the nineteenth century (Rountree *et al*, 1952). Staub (1976) records that they were introduced from Bengal by Cossigny de Palma in 1781.

Meinertzhagen (1912) indicates that the species was common on Mauritius in 1912 and that a single bird had been described as early as 1834. They were common there in the 1950s (Rountree *et al*; Benedict, 1957) and abundant everywhere in the 1970s (Staub, 1976).

The race introduced to Mauritius is possibly *S.c. tigrina* (Condon, 1975) or *S.c. suratensis* (Rountree *et al*; Staub.).

DAMAGE

In Australia the Spotted Turtledove has been accused of being a pest. In Western Australia it frequents city and suburban backyards, eating fowl food, and has been accused of spreading the stickfast flea (*Echidnophaga gallinaceae*) which it sometimes carries (Serventy and Whittell, 1951). They are considered to be a pest about Adelaide, South Australia (Condon, 1962), and in other areas of the eastern part of Australia are said to be destructive in gardens (Cayley, 1953). They damage pine seedlings in nurseries by nipping off the tops of the trees soon after germination, appreciably reducing the stock (Maclean, 1960), and are often accused of ruining seedling vegetable crops.

In the Fijian Islands the species is reported to destroy rice (Parham, 1954; Blackburn, 1971). Mercer (1966) reports that it is the most destructive of the introduced species on these islands and consumes large quantities of rice.

There appear to be few records of the species causing damage in its native range. Cheng (1963) says that in China they feed mainly on the ground, but may become harmful to some extent by scratching up some planted seeds.

SENEGAL TURTLEDOVE
(Laughing Dove, Palm Dove, Town Dove, Little Brown Dove)
Streptopelia senegalensis (Linnaeus)

DISTINGUISHING CHARACTERISTICS

21.5-28 cm (8.6-11.2 in). 64-134 g (2.26-4.73 oz)

Upper parts brown, toned lilac; underparts lilac-brown, chest darker; black patches broadly tipped brown on undersides of neck; belly and under tail white; blue-grey patch on wings; tail tipped white; bill dark brown.

Goodwin, 1970, pp.143-144.

Reader's Digest, 1977, pl. p.233.

GENERAL DISTRIBUTION

Africa — Southern Asia: from São Tomé Island, southern Africa, Israel, Jordan and Asia Minor, Arabia, Turkestan, Iran and Afghanistan to Pakistan, India, extreme north-west China and the Andaman Islands; also Socotra Island.

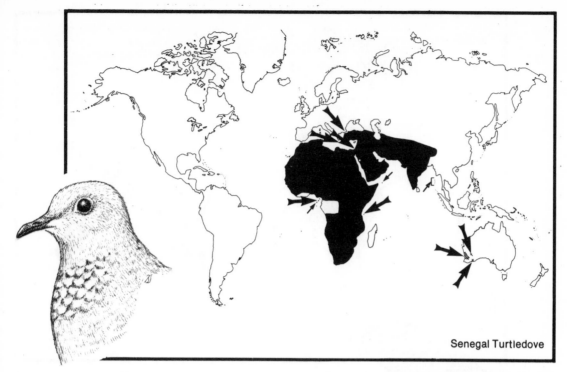

Senegal Turtledove

INTRODUCED DISTRIBUTION
Introduced successfully, locally in Israel, Jordan, Syria, Lebanon, Turkey, Malta and in southern Algeria; probably introduced or colonised Mafia Island (East Africa) and Principé (Gulf of Guinea); introduced successfully in Western Australia.

GENERAL HABITS
Status: very common; frequently kept as a pet in Africa and southern Asia. *Habitat:* woodlands, towns, villages, parks, gardens and cultivated areas. *Gregariousness:* pairs and small flocks. *Movements:* sedentary. *Foods:* small seeds and grain. *Breeding:* variable, almost throughout the year. *Nest:* scanty platform of twigs and sticks, sometimes lined, in a tree, shrub or bungalow. *Eggs:* 2-3.
Goodwin, 1970, p.144.
Centre for Overseas Pest Research, 1975, Rep. 1972-74, pp.1-13.

NOTES ON INTRODUCTIONS
Israel, Jordan, Syria, Lebanon, Turkey and Malta. Goodwin (1967) reports that Senegal Turtledoves have been introduced locally to these countries.
Southern Algeria. Vaurie (1961) records that according to Heim de Balzac (1926) the Senegal Turtledove is very common at El Golea in southern Algeria where it was introduced.
Mafia Island. The Senegal Turtledove may have been introduced to this island (Mackworth-Praed and Grant, 1957).
Principé Island. Snow (1950) reports that a race of the Senegal Turtledove *(S.c. thomé)* from Sâo Tomé was introduced by man to Principé in about 1905. They are now common there especially around human habitation, but also occur in plantations a long way from buildings.
Australia. The race *S.s. senegalensis* (Condon, 1975) was introduced from the South Perth Zoological Gardens, Western Australia, from 1898 on (Serventy

and Whittell, 1951). They have spread rapidly since the 1930s (Sedgwick, 1957-59), reached Rottnest Island about 1930 and Garden Island, and are found in many country centres in the south-west of Western Australia. They range from Geraldton, Merredin and Beacon to the Kalgoorlie and Esperance districts (Serventy, 1948; Serventy and Whittell, 1967; Condon, 1975) and have recently reached both Cue and Mt Magnet east of Geraldton (Davies, pers. comm., 1979).

Elsewhere in Australia Senegal Turtledoves have been recorded in New South Wales (?) and from Toowoomba in Queensland (Tarr, 1950), but have not become permanently established there.

DAMAGE
In Africa the Senegal Turtledove eats small seeds and corn and other crops when available (Mackworth-Praed and Grant, 1957-63) and is unprotected in Rhodesia (Goode, 1962). They cause considerable damage to grain crops in Botswana (Irving and Beesley, 1976).

PEACEFUL DOVE
(Barred Ground Dove, Barred Dove, Zebra Dove)
Geopelia striata (Linnaeus)

DISTINGUISHING CHARACTERISTICS
17-23 cm (6.8-9.2 in). 43-65 g (1.52-2.29 oz)
Upper parts grey-brown; barred black on neck, back and wings; underparts greyish white, barred across crop; skin around eye grey-blue; outer tail-feathers black, tipped white; bill bluish grey or grey-brown. (Races vary somewhat.)
Goodwin, 1970, p.198.
Reader's Digest, 1977, pl. p.235.

GENERAL DISTRIBUTION
South-east Asia–Australia: from Burma (southern Tenasserim), southern Thailand, Malaysia, Pinang Island, Singapore, Sumatra, Java and the Lesser

223

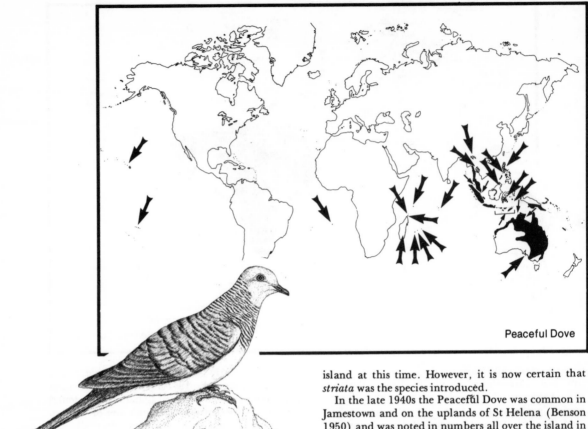

Peaceful Dove

Sunda Islands to Lombok, Timor, Tanimbar and Kai Islands, to southern New Guinea and northern and eastern Australia.

INTRODUCED DISTRIBUTION

Introduced successfully on St Helena, Malagasy, Mauritius, Seychelles, Réunion, Isles Glorieuses, Rodrigues, Chagos Archipelago, Tahiti, the Hawaiian Islands and in central and northern Thailand, Borneo and the Philippines; probably introduced, successfully on Cosmoledos and Farquhar; believed introduced, successfully, in Sulawesi and on Amboina.

GENERAL HABITS

Status: common; often kept in captivity in Malaysia and Thailand and probably elsewhere. *Habitat:* dry forest and arid scrubland, open country, cities, villages, gardens, farms and cultivated areas. *Gregariousness:* solitary, pairs or parties; sometimes small flocks of 25 or more at a food source. *Movements:* sedentary and nomadic. *Foods:* seeds, grain, insects and small invertebrates, also humans' food scraps. *Breeding:* variable, all year some areas (Java) but mainly Aug-Jan (Australia); mainly Nov-Mar in Seychelles; probably all year with up to 5 broods in Hawaii. *Nest:* rough platform of sticks or twigs, in a tree or bush near the ground. *Eggs:* 2. Goodwin, 1970, p.199.

NOTES ON INTRODUCTIONS

St Helena. The race *G.s. striata* was introduced on St Helena (Peters, 1937) probably prior to 1870 from New South Wales, Australia (Melliss, 1870). Melliss describes '*G. tranquilla*' as abundant all over the island at this time. However, it is now certain that *striata* was the species introduced.

In the late 1940s the Peaceful Dove was common in Jamestown and on the uplands of St Helena (Benson 1950) and was noted in numbers all over the island in 1952-53 (Haydock, 1954).

Malagasy. The nominate race of the Peaceful Dove has been introduced and established on the island of Malagasy (Peters, 1937; Yealland, 1958). Rand (1936) (quoting Grandidier, 1879, *Hist. Nat. Madagas., Oiseaux* p.470) indicates that they became common at one time, but have now apparently disappeared. More recently Staub (1976) indicates that the species is common on Malagasy. Perhaps there have been further, more recent introductions on the island.

Mauritius. The Peaceful Dove was probably introduced from the Malay Peninsula (Rountree *et al,* 1952) c.1750 (Meinertzhagen, 1912) and is now generally common on Mauritius (Staub, 1976). According to both Benedict (1957) and Staub they reached Mauritius in 1781, when introduced by Cossigny de Palma.

The presence of Peaceful Doves on Round Island, off Mauritius was reported as early as 1860 (Newton, 1861) and later confirmed in 1948 (Vinson, 1950) when the island was visited. Meinertzhagen says that the species was released on both Round and Flat Island, but became abundant only on the latter, dying out on the other island.

Seychelles. The nominate race of the Peaceful Dove has also been reported to have been introduced to the Seychelles (Yealland, 1958). Newton (1867) records that they were introduced from Mauritius and in 1867 occupied all the lower parts of the island. Penny (1974) reports that they were introduced from India via Mauritius, probably by early Indian traders. The species is now common there especially in populated areas (Gaymer *et al,* 1969).

Cosmoledo. The Peaceful Dove is common on this island where it was probably introduced (Penny, 1974).

Farquhar (Providence Bank). The Peaceful Dove is present but rather scarce on this island where it was also introduced (Penny, 1974). Watson *et al* (1963) record that it is common around settlement there.

Réunion. Presumedly, the Peaceful Dove has been introduced on Réunion as it was introduced from there to the Isles Glorieuses in 1969 (see Benson *et al,* 1975). Watson *et al* (1963) record that it was introduced to Réunion and is abundant there.

Isles Glorieuses. Penny informed Benson *et al* (1975) that the Peaceful Dove was introduced to these islands by a meteorologist, H. Desramais, in 1969. They still occurred there in small numbers in 1970-71.

Rodrigues. The Peaceful Dove was introduced to Rodrigues and is now very common on that island and including some small offshore islands (Gill, 1967). According to Staub (1976) they were introduced to Rodrigues in 1764.

Chagos Archipelago. Introduced in 1960 from the Seychelles by R. Mein, an employee on the island (Loustau-Lalanne, 1962) the Peaceful Dove appears to have become established there. Hutson (1975) says that locals report that sixteen birds were brought to Diego Garcia about nine years earlier. These were initially held in captivity, four died, and the remaining twelve were released. As Loustau-Lalanne found them in 1960 this date of introduction would appear suspect and this fact is supported by Hutson. Loustau-Lalanne reports that he observed some fourteen birds at Pointe Este in 1960. Some were collected in 1965 and in 1967 on the island (Bourne, 1971) and Hutson records that in 1971 they had successfully spread from Pointe Este around the island, but as yet were not common anywhere.

Thailand. A few Peaceful Doves were taken to northern Thailand from Java, by H. H. the late Chao Kaeo Nawarat na Chiang Mai, and set free east of the town of Mae Khao where they became established locally (Deignan, 1945). Lekagul and Cronin (1974) indicate that they have been introduced to central and northern Thailand within the past sixty years.

Deignan (1963) reports that the species is well established on the northern plateau and the central plains (Bangkok) in Thailand. They still appear to be well established in both these regions.

Borneo. Smythies (1960) says that the few Peaceful Doves noted in Borneo are the descendants of birds released by the natives in the past. Odd birds are apparently found in southern Borneo.

Two pairs of Peaceful Doves were introduced to Tanjong Aru, Kota Kinabalu in northern Borneo (now East Malaysia) in 1965 and the species is now established there (Gore, 1968).

Sulawesi and Amboina. The presence of Peaceful Doves, *G.s. striata,* on these islands is believed to be due to introductions (Peters, 1937). Stresemann (1936) records that on Sulawesi the species is established on the southern peninsula and the southern part of central Sulawesi.

Philippines. According to du Pont (1971) the Peaceful Dove has been introduced on Lubang, Luzon, Mindoro and Verde from Borneo. Whitehead (1899) suggests that the species may have been introduced as it is a favourite cage bird in the region. He indicates that between 1893 and 1896 the species had only been recorded on Samar and Luzon.

Tahiti. Evidently the Peaceful Dove was introduced to Tahiti by E. Guild in about 1938, but apparently did not survive there (Guild, 1938). Holyoak (1974) reports that they were introduced to Tahiti in about 1950, by M. Robinson, and originally liberated in the district of Paea. He found them in small numbers in 1972 in the districts of Papara, Punaauia and in the suburbs east of Papeete, and indicates that they are extending their range on the southern and western coasts of Tahiti. They appear to be confined to the neighbourhood of the coasts where they are probably common. Thibault and Rives (1975) report that the species is established from Arue to Papeari.

Hawaiian Islands. There appears to have been some confusion about the small dove species which were imported in 1922 to the Hawaiian Islands. *G.s. striata* appears to have been introduced at this date and was probably common on some of the islands in 1935-37. Some had recently been taken to Hawaii at this time (Munro, 1960). Specimens were collected on Lanai in 1936 and were identified as being of this race.

According to Munro the race *G.s. tranquilla* was also introduced from Australia in 1922. Some were sent to Lanai with other dove species. Munro indicates that this was the only race which became established there and was numerous in 1926, but had disappeared by 1929. He also indicates that the race *G.s. placida* may have been the race which flourished on Lanai for some six years.

According to Schwartz and Schwartz (1950) the Peaceful Dove occupied all of the suitable habitats on the islands prior to 1950, except on Hawaii where they arrived in 1935. They record that densities of 309 birds per square kilometre are common in the Hawaiian Islands.

Walker (1967) reports that *G.s. striata* from Malaysia is now well established and open to hunting in the Hawaiian Islands. The species is established on all the main islands in the group (Oahu, Hawaii and Kauai at least) (Peterson, 1961; Hawaiian Audubon Society, 1975).

Further birds (some eighteen) were released on the Puu Waawaa Ranch, Hawaii in 1961 and 1962 (Lewin, 1971), but the reason for the release of birds in an area where they are already established is not known.

Kangaroo Island. The race *G.s. tranquilla* was introduced to Kangaroo Island in 1937 and again in 1940 (Condon, 1962 and 1968). Three pairs were liberated in September 1937, and five pairs in February 1940 (Anon, 1948).

Several Peaceful Doves were seen by Cleland (1942), but there have been no subsequent records of them on the island (Abbott, 1974).

DAMAGE

In the Hawaiian Islands the Peaceful Dove feeds exclusively on seeds of plants and grasses and there is little competition for food between it and the introduced Spotted Turtledove (Schwartz and Schwartz, 1951). It has not become a pest there.

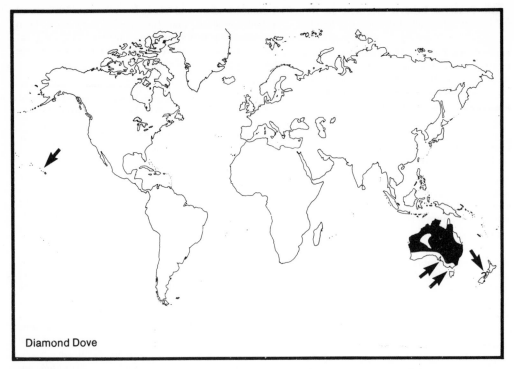

Diamond Dove

DIAMOND DOVE
Geopelia cuneata (Latham)

DISTINGUISHING CHARACTERISTICS
18-21.5 cm (7.2-8.6 in). 28-42 g (.99-1.48 oz)
Upper parts dark grey, with white spots on shoulders;
back and wings brownish; naked skin around eye red;
head, throat and chest blue-grey; abdomen white;
tail grey; bill brown-black.
Goodwin, 1970, pp.195-196.
Reader's Digest, 1977, pl. p.237.

GENERAL DISTRIBUTION
Australia generally, except the wetter coastal districts
of eastern Queensland, southern and south-eastern
Australia.

INTRODUCED DISTRIBUTION
Introduced unsuccessfully in New Zealand, the
Hawaiian Islands, and to Kangaroo Island and (?)
King Island, Australia.

GENERAL HABITS
Status: common. *Habitat:* dry forest, woodlands,
arid scrub, orchards, gardens and streets.
Gregariousness: pairs or small flocks, and larger
flocks at watering places. *Movements:* sedentary and
partly nomadic, occasional irruptions to south of
range. *Breeding:* most months of year, mainly Sept-
Jan. *Nest:* frail platform of twigs, in a low bush, tree,
or on the ground. *Eggs:* 2.
Goodwin, 1970, pp.196-198.

NOTES ON INTRODUCTIONS
New Zealand. Diamond Doves were imported to New
Zealand in 1868, but it is not known whether they
were released in the wild (Thomson, 1922).
Hawaiian Islands. Several importations of Diamond
Doves were made from Australia to the Hawaiian
Islands. Some were probably included in a
consignment to Maui and Lanai in 1922 (Munro,
1960). According to Walker (1967) they were

introduced from an unknown source in 1928, but
failed to become established there.

Kangaroo Island. Diamond Doves were introduced to
Kangaroo Island in 1937 (Condon, 1962). Two pairs
were liberated in September of that year (Anon.,
1948), but there have been no subsequent records of
the species (Abbott, 1974) on the island.

King Island. McGarvie and Templeton (1974)
observed a single bird at Loorana, and suggest that it
was possibly an aviary escapee but could not confirm
this.

DAMAGE
None known.

BAR-SHOULDERED DOVE
Geopelia humeralis (Temminck)

DISTINGUISHING CHARACTERISTICS
27-31 cm (10.8-12.4 in). 114 g (4 oz)
Head and upper breast blue-grey, hindneck and
upper back brown; upper parts barred black; bare
skin around eye blue-grey; belly white, lower breast
pinkish white; tail chestnut with outer feathers tipped
white; bill blue-grey.
Goodwin, 1970, p.200.
Reader's Digest, 1977, pl. p.236.

GENERAL DISTRIBUTION
*Southern New Guinea and northern and eastern
Australia:* Melville, Groote, Dampier Archipelago,
Lewis, Barrow, Lowendal, Monte Bello and North
Sandy and other islands including those in the Coral
Sea.

INTRODUCED DISTRIBUTION
Introduced unsuccessfully in the Hawaiian Islands
and to Kangaroo Island, Australia.

GENERAL HABITS
Status: very common. *Habitat:* mangroves and

226

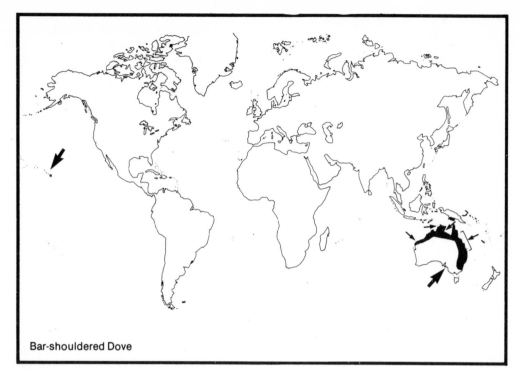

Bar-shouldered Dove

wooded areas near water. *Gregariousness:* solitary or scattered flocks, but larger numbers gather at food sources. *Movements:* sedentary. *Foods:* seeds, fruits and berries. *Breeding:* most months of the year, mainly Aug-Mar. *Nest:* roughly made platform of twigs, lined with roots, in a tree or shrub. *Eggs:* 2. Goodwin, 1970, p.200.

NOTES ON INTRODUCTIONS
Hawaiian Islands. According to Walker (1967) Bar-shouldered Doves were introduced to the Hawaiian Islands, but failed to become established there.

Kangaroo Island. Two pairs of Bar-shouldered Doves were liberated on Kangaroo Island in February 1940 (Anon, 1948), but there have been no subsequent records of them (Abbott, 1974). Evidently the species failed to become established on the island.

DAMAGE
None known.

INCA DOVE
Scardafella inca (Lesson)
DISTINGUISHING CHARACTERISTICS
18-25 cm (7.2-10 in). 45-50 g (1.59-1.76 oz)
Upper parts brownish grey; forehead, crown, face and neck pinkish grey to brownish pink; throat whitish; breast pale vinaceous, abdomen white, each feather tipped dusky giving a scaly appearance; under tail-coverts white; tail squarish, greyish brown, outer feathers black; bill black.
Peterson, 1961, p.154 and pl.23.
Goodwin, 1970, pp.230-231.

GENERAL DISTRIBUTION
Southern USA and northern Central America: from southern Arizona, southern New Mexico, western and southern Texas south to north-western Costa Rica. Spread considerably in Arizona and New Mexico since European colonisation.

INTRODUCED DISTRIBUTION
Introduced in southern Florida, USA (?).

GENERAL HABITS
Status: very common. *Habitat:* open country with scrub cover, scrub desert, cultivated areas and farms, gardens, parks, towns and chicken pens. *Gregariousness:* pairs or small loose flocks, numbers congregate at feeding areas. *Movements:* sedentary (?). *Foods:* seeds and grain. *Breeding:* Mar-Nov (Guatemala), Oct-July (Mexico) and throughout the year (Salvador) in some areas; up to 5 broods per

Inca Dove

227

year. *Nest:* saucer of twigs and straw, in a low bush, tree or shed. *Eggs:* 2.

Goodwin, 1970, pp.231-232.

NOTES ON INTRODUCTIONS

USA. Inca Doves bred at Key West in 1966 and may be established in the southern Florida area (Owre, 1973). They appear to be extending their range naturally northwards into the United States and this spread may be assisted by escapees and released birds.

DAMAGE

None known.

COMMON GROUND DOVE

(Ground Dove, Passerine Dove, Scaly-breasted Ground Dove)

Columbina passerina (Linnaeus)

DISTINGUISHING CHARACTERISTICS

15-18 cm (6-7.2 in). 29-42 g (1.02-1.48 oz)

Upper parts greyish or olive-brown; forehead, sides of neck, breast and abdomen pinkish vinous, feather edges dusky giving a scaled appearance on the neck; crown and nape pale grey; wings with conspicuous black spots; tail-feathers basally grey then black, outer ones tipped white; bill red, orange or yellowish, black tipped. *Female:* lacks pinkish vinous tones.

Gilliard, 1958, pl.78, p.136.

Goodwin, 1970, pp.216-217.

GENERAL DISTRIBUTION

Southern USA to northern South America: from South Carolina, south-eastern Texas, south through Central America to Venezuela, Ecuador, and northern Brazil; also in the West Indies, Trinidad, Margarita Island and Aruba.

INTRODUCED DISTRIBUTION

Introduced (?) successfully in Bermuda.

GENERAL HABITS

Status: locally common, abundant some areas. *Habitat:* forest edges, open woodland, savannah, watercourses, mangroves, cultivated areas and farmlands, villages and roadsides. *Gregariousness:* solitary, pairs, or flocks up to 40. *Movements:* sedentary and partly nomadic. *Foods:* seeds and humans' food scraps (e.g. bread), berries, and insects. *Breeding:* variable, prolonged, probably throughout the year if food is available; 2-3 broods per year. *Nest:* flimsy saucer of plant fibres, grass and twigs in a shrub, vine, cactus, and sometimes on the ground in a shallow depression. *Eggs:* 1-2, occasionally 3.

Goodwin, 1970, p.217.

Meyer de Schauensee and Phelps, 1978, p.95.

NOTES ON INTRODUCTIONS

Bermuda. The Common Ground Dove may have been introduced to Bermuda (Bourne, 1957, quoting Verrill, 1901-02) where the race *C.p. bahamenensis* is now common.

DAMAGE

None known.

NAMAQUA DOVE

(Cape Dove, Masked Dove, Harlequin Dove)

Oena capensis (Linnaeus)

DISTINGUISHING CHARACTERISTICS

21-25 cm (8.4-10 in). 31-48 g (1.09-1.69 oz)

Forehead, in front of eyes and throat to chest black; crown, sides of neck and wing shoulders grey; violet-blue spots on wings; mantle brown; blackish bands across rump; breast to belly white; bill purple, with orange tip. *Female:* lacks black forehead, throat and chest.

Goodwin, 1970, pp.171-172 and pl.2, no.1, opp. p.12.

GENERAL DISTRIBUTION

Africa, south of the Sahara, except parts of western Africa; also Malagasy and south-western Arabia.

INTRODUCED DISTRIBUTION

Introduced unsuccessfully in New Zealand and Australia.

GENERAL HABITS

Status: very common; commonly kept cage bird. *Habitat:* dry open country with scrub, open wooded areas, cultivated areas, towns and villages. *Gregariousness:* singly, pairs or family parties (sometimes large). *Movements:* sedentary, but with some local movements. *Foods:* small weed seeds. *Breeding:* most of the year in Africa. *Nest:* small frail platform of grass stems, rootlets and tendrils in a low bush or sometimes on the ground. *Eggs:* 2.

Goodwin, 1970, p.172.

NOTES ON INTRODUCTIONS

New Zealand. The Canterbury Acclimatisation Society introduced Namaqua Doves to the island of Kawau in the early 1860s. They are supposed to have become numerous there, but according to Thomson (1922) there are no further records of them.

Australia. Namaqua Doves were found on odd occasions in the Metropolitan area of Perth, Western Australia in the 1960s. These were apparently only escapees from aviaries and the species has not become established in the wild.

DAMAGE

The Namaqua Dove was unprotected in Rhodesia (Goode, 1962) but little appears to be recorded on the damage it does to agriculture.

Common Ground Dove

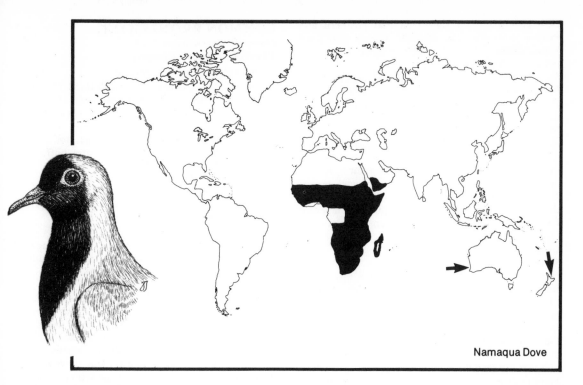

Namaqua Dove

EMERALD DOVE
(Green-winged Dove or Pigeon)
Chalcophaps indica (Linnaeus)

DISTINGUISHING CHARACTERISTICS
23-28 cm (9.2-11.2 in)
Generally red-brown with purple wash on neck, mantle and breast, and iridescent bronze-green wings; white patch on elbow of wing; rump dark brown-black, with two grey bars; tail dark brown, sides greyish and with a subterminal band and white

tip; bill red, tinged blue at base. *Female:* lacks vinaceous tints.
Goodwin, 1970, pp.176-177.
Reader's Digest, 1977, pl. p.238.

GENERAL DISTRIBUTION
Southern Asia to Australia: from northern India, Assam, east to southern China, Taiwan and Hainan, south to Sri Lanka, Andaman Islands, Nicobar Islands, Greater and Lesser Sunda Islands, Philippines, south-eastern New Guinea and islands,

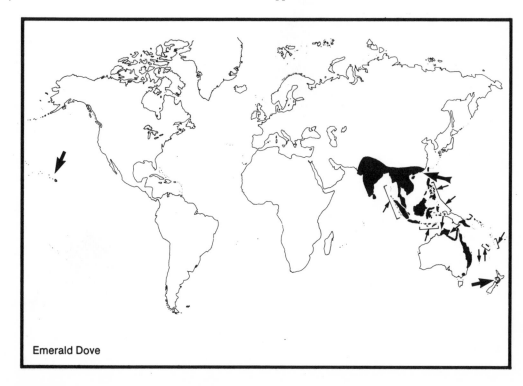

Emerald Dove

New Hebrides, New Caledonia and northern and eastern Australia; also Melville, Groote and Lord Howe Islands.

INTRODUCED DISTRIBUTION
Successfully colonised the island of Hong Kong. Introduced unsuccessfully to the Hawaiian Islands. Possibly introduced, unsuccessfully, to New Zealand.

GENERAL HABITS
Status: common. *Habitat:* forest, thick woodland and lantana scrubs along creeks. *Gregariousness:* solitary, pairs or small parties. *Movements:* unknown, possibly somewhat nomadic. *Foods:* berries, fruits, seeds, grain and perhaps insects. *Breeding:* mainly Aug-Feb (Australia), but possibly throughout the year in some areas; Jan-May in South-East Asia. *Nest:* substantial platform of sticks and twigs, in a bush or tree. *Eggs:* 2.

Goodwin, 1970, p.177.

NOTES ON INTRODUCTIONS
Hawaiian Islands. Emerald Doves were introduced from Singapore to the island of Oahu in 1924 (Munro, 1960), but are not known to be established there (Walker, 1967).

Hong Kong. According to Webster (1975) the Emerald Dove has been introduced to Hong Kong by man and is established and breeding there. Small numbers are seen throughout the year in Tai Po Kau Forestry Reserve, and others have been either seen or trapped in several areas of the New Territories.

New Zealand. Emerald Doves, probably this species, were imported to New Zealand in 1867, but are not known to have been released there (Thomson, 1922).

DAMAGE
None known.

COMMON BRONZEWING
(Forest Bronzewing)
Phaps chalcoptera (Latham)

DISTINGUISHING CHARACTERISTICS
28-34.9 cm (11.2-14 in). 293-400 g (10.33-14.11 oz) Upper parts brown, buff barred all over; white stripe below eye; underparts lilac-mauve; forehead cream; chin white; black bar from bill to eye; spots and patches of bronze and green on wings; bill brown-black. *Female:* forehead grey; breast grey-buff.

Goodwin, 1970, pp.180-181.

Reader's Digest, 1977, pl. p.240.

GENERAL DISTRIBUTION
Australia: Tasmania and Australia generally, except Cape York Peninsula, Queensland.

INTRODUCED DISTRIBUTION
Introduced, probably successfully, to Kangaroo Island, South Australia. Introduced unsuccessfully in New Zealand and the Hawaiian Islands.

GENERAL HABITS
Status: common. *Habitat:* savannah woodland, heavily timbered country and scrub. *Gregariousness:* solitary, pairs, but sometimes form small flocks and occasionally flocks up to 70 birds. *Movements:* sedentary and partly nomadic. *Foods:* berries, seeds, cultivated grains and native fruits. *Breeding:* throughout the year; at least sometimes double-brooded (Western Australia). *Nest:* rough platform of sticks, in a bush, tree, or on the ground. *Eggs:* 2.

Goodwin, 1970, pp.181-182.

NOTES ON INTRODUCTIONS
New Zealand. The Common Bronzewing was introduced a number of times to New Zealand between 1864 and 1884, but failed to become established anywhere there (Thomson, 1922).

Thomson details the introductions to New Zealand: in 1864 the Canterbury Acclimatisation Society liberated two birds in the Society Gardens.

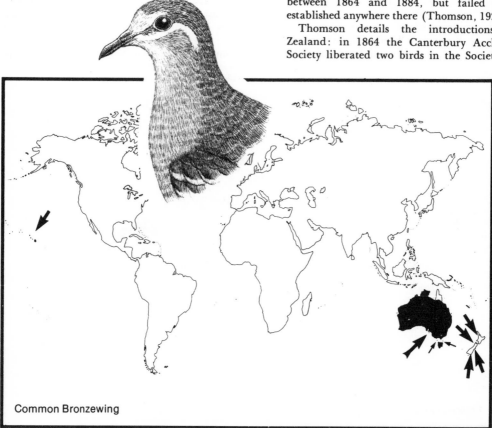

Common Bronzewing

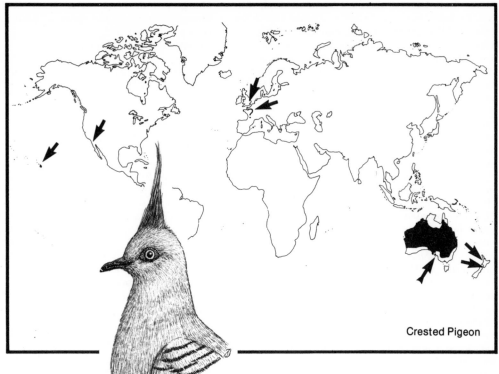

Crested Pigeon

Four more were liberated in 1867 in the same area, and in 1884, twenty were liberated of which there is no further record. Also in 1867, the Otago society liberated six birds in the Dunedin Gardens and the Nelson society also liberated 'a few' birds. The Auckland society liberated six birds at Kaipara in 1867, and more in 1869, but there are no further records of these birds.

In 1882 it was reported that the Common Bronzewings released by the Canterbury society had become established and were doing well. They were reported in 1883 to have been sighted some considerable distance from the Murrumbidgee Mountains where they were liberated, but this sighting was the last record of the species in New Zealand.

Hawaiian Islands. Some Common Bronzewings were apparently brought from Australia to the island of Oahu in 1922, but they did not survive (Munro, 1960) and thus the species did not become established in the Hawaiian Islands (Walker, 1967).

Kangaroo Island. Mainland Australian birds of the race *P.c. chalcoptera* were liberated on Kangaroo Island in September 1937, presumedly because they were becoming rare in South Australia (Condon, 1962 and 1975).

DAMAGE
None known.

CRESTED PIGEON
(Topknot Pigeon)
Ocyphaps lophotes (Temminck and Laugier)

DISTINGUISHING CHARACTERISTICS
30-35 cm (12-14 in). 185-228 g (6.52-8.04 oz)
Upper parts bluish grey; erect black crest; underparts soft grey-blue; wings brownish, with metallic bronze area, and barred; black near bend of wing and white secondaries; bare skin around eye red; tail purple-brown, white tipped; bill black, dark grey at base.
Goodwin, 1970, pp.185-186.
Reader's Digest, 1977, pl. p.242.

GENERAL DISTRIBUTION
Australia: generally, except some coastal and heavy rainfall areas.

INTRODUCED DISTRIBUTION
Introduced, possibly successfully, on Kangaroo Island (South Australia) and in the Hawaiian Islands. Introduced successfully, but later died out in Europe (?) and the USA. Introduced unsuccessfully in New Zealand.

GENERAL HABITS
Status: very common. *Habitat:* woodlands and open country near water. *Gregariousness:* solitary at breeding, but form flocks when feeding and in the non-breeding season. *Movements:* sedentary and partly nomadic. *Foods:* seeds. *Breeding:* most months of the year, but mainly spring and summer. *Nest:* flimsy platform of sticks, in a bush or tree. *Eggs:* 2.
Goodwin, 1970, pp.186-187.

NOTES ON INTRODUCTIONS
Europe. Crested Pigeons are reported to have been released at Woburn in England and also in France. They are said to have established themselves at liberty, locally, some years ago in both areas (in Aust. Avic. Mag., 1965). Apparently they have not persisted as there are no further records of them.

New Zealand. Twelve Crested Pigeons were reported to have been released by the Wellington Acclimatisation Society in 1876-77 (Thomson, 1922). Thomson records that the Canterbury society imported six birds in 1883 (no further records) and that the Auckland society introduced ten in 1887, five of which were actually liberated.

231

The Crested Pigeon did not become established in New Zealand.

USA. Phillips (1928) records that Crested Pigeons appear to have escaped and established themselves in a small way at Berkeley, California, in trees and shrubbery near the Claremont Hotel on the edge of the town. They became established prior to 1925 and were not increasing in numbers if they still existed there in about 1940 (Cook and Knappen, 1941).

Hawaiian Islands. Introduced from Australia to the islands of Oahu, Molokai and Lanai (Munro, 1960) in 1922, the Crested Pigeon failed to become established on any of these islands (Walker, 1967).

More recently Lewin (1971) indicates that they may be established on the Puu Waawaa Ranch, Hawaii, where eight birds from a Californian game farm were released in 1964. They had extended their range by some seven kilometres (four and a half miles) by 1967.

Kangaroo Island. The race *O.l. lophotes* was introduced at Flinders Chase in September 1937 (Condon, 1962). Some twelve birds were introduced and released at this time and a further pair in February 1940 (Anon, 1948).

The Crested Pigeon has rarely been reported from the island, but some were observed in 1966 (Condon, 1968) and it now seems that it is established there in small numbers.

DAMAGE
None known.

PARTRIDGE PIGEON
Petrophassa smithii (Jardine and Selby)

DISTINGUISHING CHARACTERISTICS
25-28 cm (10-11.2 in)

Upper parts brown; throat white; orbital skin bright red or yellow; variable black and white lines surround orbital skin; upper breast with conspicuous patch of blue-grey with black bars; lower breast pinkish brown; belly, flanks and under tail white; bill black. Goodwin, 1970, p.192.

Reader's Digest, 1977, pl. p.244.

GENERAL DISTRIBUTION
Northern Australia: Melville Island and from the Kimberleys in Western Australia to, and doubtfully in, north-western Queensland.

INTRODUCED DISTRIBUTION
Introduced unsuccessfully to the Hawaiian Islands and possibly to New Zealand.

GENERAL HABITS
Status: common. *Habitat:* open country and woodlands. *Gregariousness:* pairs or small flocks 5-20 and up to 50, and occasionally 200-300 birds. *Movements:* sedentary. *Foods:* seeds of grasses and herbaceous plants. *Breeding:* most months of the year, mainly Aug-Jan, but variable. *Nest:* shallow depression, lined with grass, on the ground usually near a tuft of grass or bush. *Eggs:* 2. Goodwin, 1970, p.192.

NOTES ON INTRODUCTIONS
Hawaiian Islands. The Partridge Pigeon was introduced from Australia in 1922, and possibly released on Maui and Lanai (Munro, 1960), but failed to become established on either island (Walker, 1967).

New Zealand. Partridge Pigeons were imported into New Zealand in 1866, but it is not known if any of them were liberated (Thomson, 1922).

DAMAGE
None known.

SPINIFEX PIGEON
Petrophassa plumifera (Gould)

DISTINGUISHING CHARACTERISTICS
19-23 cm (7.6-9.2 in). 86-114 g (3.03-4.02 oz)

Upper parts rusty coloured, with heavy black barring

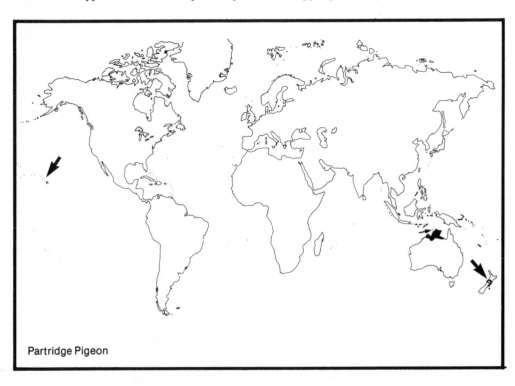

Partridge Pigeon

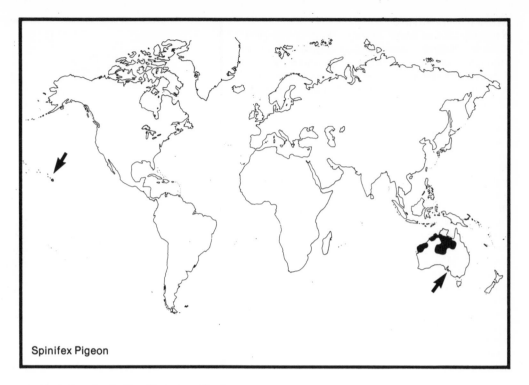

Spinifex Pigeon

on wings and sides of neck; forehead grey; a black line borders the red patch around eye; throat white and black; a bronze area on wings; bill black or brown. Races vary, some having a white breast and others rusty.

Goodwin, 1970, pp.187-188.

Reader's Digest, 1977, pl. p.245.

GENERAL DISTRIBUTION

Australia: northern, north-western and central Australia.

INTRODUCED DISTRIBUTION

Introduced unsuccessfully in the Hawaiian Islands and to Kangaroo Island, Australia.

GENERAL HABITS

Status: common. *Habitat:* spinifex grasslands. *Gregariousness:* small groups up to 15, sometimes much larger groups. *Movements:* sedentary. *Foods:* seeds. *Breeding:* throughout year, mainly Sept-Nov. *Nest:* scrape on the ground lined with pieces of grass. *Eggs:* 2.

Goodwin, 1970, pp.188-189.

NOTES ON INTRODUCTIONS

Hawaiian Islands. Spinifex Pigeons were taken from Australia to Maui and Lanai in 1922, but failed to become established there (Munro, 1960; Walker, 1967).

Kangaroo Island. The race *P.p. leucogaster* was introduced to Kangaroo Island in 1940 (Condon, 1962) when one pair were liberated there (Anon, 1948). However, there have been no further records of the species on the island (Condon, 1968; Abbott, 1974).

DAMAGE

None known.

WHITE-TIPPED DOVE
(White-fronted Dove, Blue Ground Dove)
Leptotila verreauxi Bonaparte

DISTINGUISHING CHARACTERISTICS

25-33 cm (10-13.2 in). 96-168 g (3.39-5.93 oz)

Upper parts olive-brown; forehead white; head vinaceous, hindneck with metallic green; face, breast and sides of neck pale greyish pink; orbital skin white, light blue or greenish blue; throat and abdomen nearly white; central tail-feathers grey-brown; outer feathers dusky, tipped white; bill black.

Allen, 1962, pl.33, p.72.

Goodwin, 1970, pp.235-236.

White-tipped Dove

233

GENERAL DISTRIBUTION

Southern USA to South America: from Texas (Rio Grande Valley), north-western Mexico, south through Central America to southern Brazil, Uruguay, Paraguay, northern Argentina and Bolivia; also Surinam, Aruba, Curaçao, Bonaire, Trinidad, Tobago and Trés Marias Islands.

INTRODUCED DISTRIBUTION

Introduced unsuccessfully in the Hawaiian Islands.

GENERAL HABITS

Status: fairly common. *Habitat:* dry arid regions, forest and woodland clearings, river thickets and cultivated regions. *Gregariousness:* solitary, pairs or small groups, and flocks up to 50 at watering places. *Movements:* sedentary. *Foods:* seeds, berries and insects. *Breeding:* all of the year. *Nest:* frail platform of twigs, in a low tree or bush. *Eggs:* 2.

Skutch, *Wilson Bulletin* vol.76, 1964, pp.211-247.

Goodwin, 1970, pp.236-237.

Meyer de Schauensee and Phelps, 1978, p.97.

NOTES ON INTRODUCTIONS

Hawaiian Islands. The White-tipped Dove was introduced from San Francisco to Maui in 1933 (Munro, 1960), but failed to become established there (Walker, 1967).

DAMAGE

None known.

White-bellied Dove

WHITE-BELLIED DOVE
(Caribbean Dove, Jamaican Dove, Whitebelly)
Leptotila jamaicensis (Linnaeus)

DISTINGUISHING CHARACTERISTICS

27.5-33 cm (11-13.2 in). 162 g (5.71 oz)

Forehead white, head bluish grey; back and sides of neck iridescent green, purple and bronze; chin, throat and underparts largely white; orbital skin dull purple; remainder of upper parts brown; tail grey, central feathers brown and outer feathers with black and a white tip; bill black, grey at base.

Goodwin, 1970, p.242.

Peterson and Chalif, 1973, p.71, pl.11.

GENERAL DISTRIBUTION

West Indies and Central America: Jamaica, Grand Cayman and St Andrew in the West Indies; the northern Yucatan Peninsula and adjacent islands of Cozumel, Mugeres and Holbox, and the Bay Islands, Honduras.

INTRODUCED DISTRIBUTION

Introduced, probably successfully (?) to New Providence, West Indies.

GENERAL HABITS

Status: uncommon (?). *Habitat:* humid forest, lowlands and semi-arid areas. *Gregariousness:* singly or pairs. *Movements:* sedentary. *Foods:* seeds and fallen fruits. *Breeding:* no information. *Nest:* usual pigeon's nest, in a shrub, occasionally on the ground. *Eggs:* 2.

Goodwin, 1970, pp.242-243.

NOTES ON INTRODUCTIONS

New Providence. The White-bellied Dove is listed by Bond (1960) as having been introduced to this island. Brudenell-Bruce (1975) says that the species has been introduced from Jamaica as part of a programme to re-stock the island with birds following the hurricanes

of the late 1920s. At present they are an uncommon resident of New Providence.

DAMAGE

None known.

RUDDY QUAIL-DOVE
(Ruddy Ground Dove, Rufous Quail-Dove)
Geotrygon montana (Linnaeus)

DISTINGUISHING CHARACTERISTICS

20-30 cm (8-12 in). 78-152 g (2.75-5.36 oz)

Upper parts rufous or purplish brown; iridescent on nape, back, sides of neck, mantle and rump; underparts vinaceous buff or pinkish brown, shading to buff on the belly, flanks and under tail-coverts; buffy streak below eye; dark purplish chestnut facial stripes outlining cheeks; a small pale buff patch on sides of breast; orbital skin purplish red; bill red or purplish red, brownish at tip. Female: olive-brown above, paler below.

Goodwin, 1970, p.259.

Meyer de Schauensee and Phelps, 1978, p.97 and pl.7, no.15.

GENERAL DISTRIBUTION

Central and South America and the West Indies: from Mexico south to Peru, northern Paraguay, Bolivia, north-eastern Argentina and southern Brazil; in the Greater Antilles (Cuba and Jamaica) east to Vieques Island and on Guadeloupe, Dominica, Martinique, St Lucia, St Vincent and Grenada in the Lesser Antilles; also Trinidad.

INTRODUCED DISTRIBUTION

Introduced unsuccessfully in the Hawaiian Islands.

GENERAL HABITS

Status: common locally; considerably reduced in numbers. *Habitat:* humid forest, coffee and cacao and other plantations, woodlands and secondary growth. *Gregariousness:* singly or in pairs. *Movements:* little known; some altitudinal

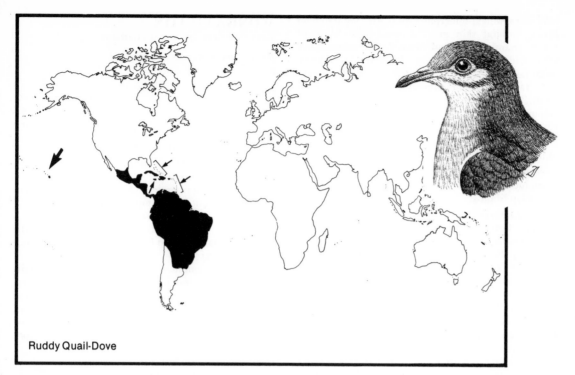

Ruddy Quail-Dove

movements to lower levels in winter. *Foods:* seeds, fruits, slugs and other invertebrates. *Breeding:* Mar-Aug (Costa Rica); Feb-July (Trinidad). *Nest:* extremely flimsy, platform of sticks, lined with green leaves, in undergrowth or occasionally on the ground. *Eggs:* 2.

Goodwin, 1970, p.260.

Meyer de Schauensee and Phelps, 1978, p.97.

NOTES ON INTRODUCTIONS

Hawaiian Islands. Introduced from San Francisco to Maui in 1933, the Ruddy Quail-Dove was recorded there in 1936 (Munro, 1960), but failed to remain established on the island (Walker, 1967).

DAMAGE

None known.

BLEEDING-HEART PIGEON
(Luzon Bleeding-heart)
Gallicolumba luzonica (Scopoli)

DISTINGUISHING CHARACTERISTICS

30 cm (12 in). 250-300 g (8.82-10.58 oz)

Upper parts blue-grey with dark red-brown or black

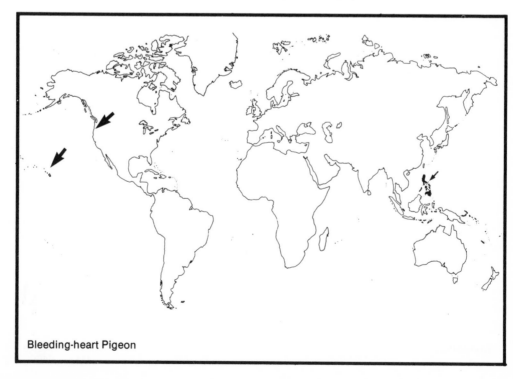

Bleeding-heart Pigeon

bars across wings; underparts white with red patch on breast; orbital skin grey; crown, nape, sides of breast, mantle, back and rump darker greyish, but with iridescent fringes to feathers; primaries, secondaries and central tail-feathers dark brown, outer tail-feathers blue-grey with a black subterminal band; bill blackish, grey at base. Races vary as to colour and size of breast patch.
Goodwin, 1970, pp.265-266.

GENERAL DISTRIBUTION
Philippine Islands.

INTRODUCED DISTRIBUTION
Introduced unsuccessfully to the USA and the Hawaiian Islands.

GENERAL HABITS
Status: fairly common (?). *Habitat:* forests. *Gregariousness:* no information. *Movements:* sedentary. *Foods:* seeds, berries and probably insects and other invertebrates. *Breeding:* not known. *Nest:* typical pigeon nest, probably low down in bushes, vines or trees. *Eggs:* 2.
Goodwin, 1970, p.266.

NOTES ON INTRODUCTIONS
USA. According to Phillips (1928) some Bleeding-heart Pigeons together with several other Oriental birds were said to have been released (*Game Breeder* 25:148, 1924) in about 1924 on an island near Friday Harbour, Washington by a retired lumberjack named T. Moran. There are no further records of them so evidently the species failed to become established (Gottschalk, 1967).
Hawaiian Islands. Although some were introduced from the Philippines to Kauai in 1922 and later to other islands (Bryan, 1958) the Bleeding-heart Pigeon is not known to be established in the Hawaiian Islands (Walker, 1967; Berger, 1972).

DAMAGE
None known.

WONGA PIGEON
Leucosarcia melanoleuca (Latham)

DISTINGUISHING CHARACTERISTICS
36-43 cm (14.4-17.2 in)
Upper parts grey; forehead, face and chin white; a black line from bill to eye; breast bluish grey, lower breast and sides white; abdomen spotted black and white; wings dark brown; orbital skin red; bill and cere pinkish red, bill tipped black.
Goodwin, 1970, p.201.
Reader's Digest, 1977, pl. p.248.

GENERAL DISTRIBUTION
Australia: coastal eastern Australia, from eastern Victoria to about Rockhampton, Queensland.

INTRODUCED DISTRIBUTION
Introduced unsuccessfully in New Zealand, the Hawaiian Islands and to Kangaroo Island, Australia.

GENERAL HABITS
Status: fairly common. *Habitat:* rain forest, heavily timbered ridges and gullies. *Gregariousness:* solitary, but at times in small parties and larger groups at food sources. *Movements:* sedentary. *Foods:* seeds, fruits, berries and insects. *Breeding:* throughout the year, mainly Oct-Jan. *Nest:* rough, flat structure of twigs, in a tree. *Eggs:* 2.
Goodwin, 1970, pp.201-202.

NOTES ON INTRODUCTIONS
New Zealand. Wonga Pigeons were imported to New Zealand a number of times between 1864 and 1876.

The first liberation was probably by the Otago Acclimatisation Society in 1869 (Thomson 1922). Thomson reports that the Canterbury society imported two pairs in 1864, four pairs in 1871 and seven birds in 1883, but that there are no records of any of them being liberated. The Nelson society imported some in 1867 and the Auckland society imported two pairs in 1868 and a further two pairs in 1870, but there are no further records of them.

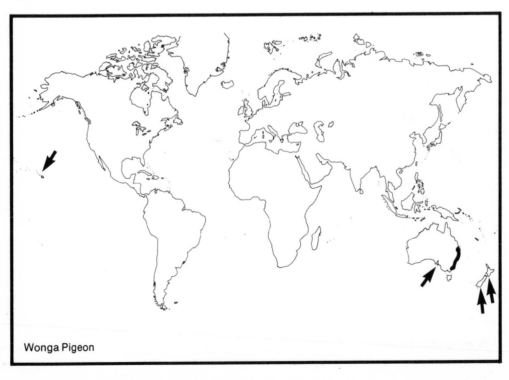

Wonga Pigeon

Twelve birds were liberated by the Otago society in 1869 and twelve in 1875. Twenty-two were also liberated in 1876 by the Wellington society.

The Wonga Pigeon did not become established in New Zealand.

Hawaiian Islands. The Wonga Pigeon was introduced from Australia to both Maui and Lanai in 1922 (Munro, 1960). Munro says that they apparently soon disappeared on Lanai.

Wonga Pigeons failed to become established in the Hawaiian Islands (Walker, 1967).

Kangaroo Island. Two pairs of Wonga Pigeons were introduced to Kangaroo Island in 1946 (Anon., 1948), but there have been no subsequent records of the species there (Abbott, 1974).

DAMAGE
None known.

BLUE-HEADED QUAIL DOVE
(Blue-headed Ground Dove)
Starnoenas cyanocephala (Linnaeus)

DISTINGUISHING CHARACTERISTICS
30-33 cm (12-13.2 in)
Generally brown, with bright blue crown; bib blue and black, white-bordered; black stripe through eye, and white stripe below; breast below bib pinkish purple, shading to buffy brown on belly; wings and tail brown, outer feathers slaty grey, greyish at tip; bill red.
Allen, 1962, pl.34, p.97.
Goodwin, 1970, p.261.

GENERAL DISTRIBUTION
Cuba and (?) Isle of Pines.

INTRODUCED DISTRIBUTION
Introduced unsuccessfully in Jamaica and the Hawaiian Islands.

GENERAL HABITS
Status: now less widespread and extremely rare.

Blue-headed Quail Dove

Habitat: lowland forest undergrowth. *Gregariousness:* no information; habits little recorded. *Movements:* no information; (?) *Foods:* seeds, berries and snails. *Breeding:* no information. *Nest:* usual pigeon nest in shrubbery on or near the ground. *Eggs:* 1-2.
Goodwin, 1970, pp.261-262.

NOTES ON INTRODUCTIONS
Jamaica. The Blue-headed Quail Dove has often been introduced to Jamaica in the past, but apparently has never become established there (Peters, 1937). Lack (1976) records that Gosse (in 1847) said that they were often imported as a cage bird to the island, but had also been reported there in the wild by some eighteenth century naturalists.

According to Goodwin (1967) the species was presumedly introduced, but is now extinct there, so possibly was established or resident there at some period.

Hawaiian Islands. The Blue-headed Quail Dove was introduced to these islands in 1928, but failed to become established there (Munro, 1960; Walker, 1967).

DAMAGE
None known.

NICOBAR PIGEON
(White-tailed Pigeon)
Caloenas nicobarica Linnaeus

DISTINGUISHING CHARACTERISTICS
30-36 cm (12-14.4 in). 460-600 g (1-1.3 lb)
Generally black with a blue, green and copper sheen; long sickle-shaped neck hackles; primaries and secondaries blue, glossed green and purple; tail white; bill and knob at base of bill black. Female: more brownish above; tail tipped darker and is longer.
Goodwin, 1970, pp.262-263.
Lekagul and Cronin, 1974, p.92 and pl.44, p.93.

GENERAL DISTRIBUTION
Indo-Australasian region from the Nicobars to the Solomons: Nicobar Islands, Andaman Islands, islands off Malaya, peninsular Thailand, Kampuchea, south Vietnam, Con Son Island, Sundas to the offshore islands of New Guinea, the Bismarck Archipelago, Palau Archipelago and Solomon Islands. In New Guinea migrates from offshore islands to feed on fruits on the mainland.

INTRODUCED DISTRIBUTION
Introduced unsuccessfully in the Hawaiian Islands.

GENERAL HABITS
Status: possibly not common. *Habitat:* offshore and oceanic islands. *Gregariousness:* solitary, pairs or small flocks. *Movements:* sedentary and partly nomadic or migratory. *Foods:* fruits, seeds, grain and some invertebrates. *Breeding:* colonial, sometimes in thousands. *Nest:* usual pigeon nest, in a tree or bush, only on islands. *Eggs:* 1.
Goodwin, 1970, p.263.

NOTES ON INTRODUCTIONS
Hawaiian Islands. The Nicobar Pigeon was introduced to the islands of Maui in 1922 and Kauai in 1928, from Australia (although it does not occur naturally there), but failed to become established on

237

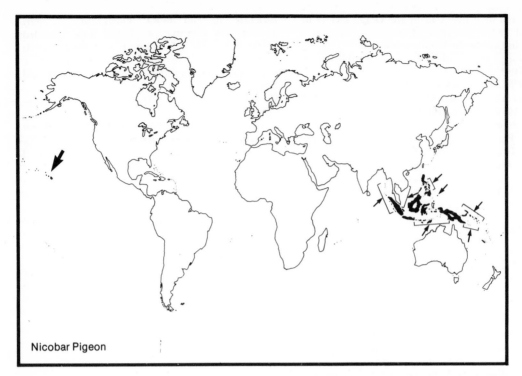

Nicobar Pigeon

either island (Munro, 1960; Walker, 1967).

DAMAGE·
None known.

ORDER: PSITTACIFORMES

Family: *Psittacidae* Cockatoos and Parrots

339 species in 80 genera; about 48 species introduced, probably about 20 established

Although about twenty species of the *Psittacidae* appear to be fairly well established it is possible that some others may be. For many species insufficient information was available. A number of them may be in the process of establishing themselves at present. Six species have definitely failed to become established and at least one (Galah) has extended its range or colonised new territory.

Generally speaking, members of the *Psittacidae* have not been overly successful as introduced species. Most of the successful ones have occurred in areas near or similar to their native haunts. However, in recent years at least two exceptions have come to light. The Monk Parakeet and Rose-ringed Parakeet have become established, the former in North America and the latter in Great Britain, in areas some distance from and different to their native ranges. Both species have largely become established as a result of aviary escapes and indiscriminate deliberate releases. They show great pest potential in their new environments as both are destroyers of agricultural crops.

The Budgerygah, that universal cage bird, which has for many years escaped into the wild in most countries of the world, has now found a new home in the exotic environment of Florida in the United States, and on Tresco, Scilly Islands off the south coast of England. Its future at Tresco may be in some doubt, but in Florida it appears to be well established. An uncertain introduction, not included in the subsequent text, of the Blue and Yellow Macaw to Jamaica in the West Indies, is perhaps worthy of some mention. Lack (1976) says that reports of what were possibly, or probably, the Blue and Yellow Macaw *Ara ararauna* by Sloane (1725), Broune (1789), Gosse (1847) and March (1863-64), would seem to indicate that this species was formerly wild or feral on Jamaica in the past.

KAKAPO

Strigops habroptilus Gray

DISTINGUISHING CHARACTERISTICS
50-64 cm (20-25.6 in). 1.6-2.5 kg (3.5-5.5 lb)
Upper parts bright green, irregularly barred and streaked brown and yellow; underparts greenish yellow, similarly streaked; wings and tail green with brown and yellow barring; a yellow stripe from lores to above eyes; forehead and facial disc yellowish brown; bill yellowish white, brown at base of upper mandible.
Forshaw, 1973, p.269, pl. p.271.

GENERAL DISTRIBUTION
New Zealand: formerly in mountain ranges of the North, South and Stewart islands. Now found only in Fiordland, South Island (only known population confined to Cleddan watershed, Fiordland).

INTRODUCED DISTRIBUTION
Introduced unsuccessfully (?) to several islands off the coast of New Zealand.

GENERAL HABITS
Status: during the first half of this century has declined rapidly, now very rare. *Habitat:* forest and adjoining areas, i.e. meadows, mudflats, etc. *Gregariousness:* solitary. *Movements:* sedentary. *Foods:* fruits, berries, nuts, seeds, green shoots, leaf buds, fern fronds, moss, fungi and probably insects and their larvae. *Breeding:* Jan-Feb. *Nest:* in a

INTRODUCTIONS OF THE PSITTACIDAE

Species	Date introduced	Region	Manner introduced	Reason
(a) Successful Introductions				
Kuhl's Lory	prior 1798	Washington and Fanning Islands, Pacific Ocean	escapees ?	captive birds ?
Sulphur-crested Cockatoo	about 1920 on	New Zealand	escapees and/or colonisation	cage bird
	prior 1951	Palau Archipelago	?	?
	prior 1956	Western Australia	deliberate or escapee	cage bird
Galah	early 1900s on	Australia	range extension	
Brown-throated Conure	prior 1860	St Thomas, Virgin Islands	unknown	?
Monk Parakeet	1968	USA	deliberate and escapees ?	cage bird
	before 1973	Puerto Rico	?	?
Green-rumped Parrotlet	about 1918	Jamaica	deliberate ?	?
Canary-winged Parakeet	after 1964	Peru	escapees	cage bird
	?	Puerto Rico	?	?
	1960	USA	deliberate or escapees ?	cage bird
Hispaniolan Amazon	1960s	Puerto Rico	deliberate ?	?
Brown Parrot	prior 1946	South Africa	escapees	cage bird ?
Rose-ringed Parakeet	about 1886	Mauritius	accidental release	cage bird
	1936 ?	Zanzibar Island	escapees	cage bird
	1903-13	Hong Kong and Macao	?	?
	1855, 1930s, about 1969	Great Britain	deliberate and escapees	cage bird
Moustached Parakeet	prior 1960 ?	Borneo	?	?
Red-shining Parrot	?	Eua, Tonga Islands	?	?
	prior 1945	Viti Levu, Fiji	?	?
Madagascar Lovebird	1906	Seychelles	?	?
Fischer's Lovebird	about 1928	Tanzania	mass release ?	?
	prior 1969	Kenya	escapees ?	?
Masked Lovebird	about 1928	Tanzania	mass release	cage bird ?
	prior 1969	Kenya	escapees ?	cage bird
Crimson Rosella	?	Norfolk Island	?	?
	1910 and ?	New Zealand	deliberate and escapees	?
Eastern Rosella	1910 and ?	New Zealand	deliberate and escapees	?
	prior 1969 ?	South Australia	escapees	?
Yellow-fronted Parakeet	1970	Stephens Island, N.Z.	re-introduction	preservation
Budgerygah	1960s	USA	deliberate	?
(b) Possibly successful introductions				
Blue-streaked Lory	before 1905-06 ?	Kai Islands and Damar, Indonesia	?	?
Rainbow Lorikeet	early 1960s?	Western Australia	escapee	cage bird
Kuhl's Lory	1957	Christmas Island, Pacific Ocean	deliberate	?
Tahitian Lory	prior 1899	Aitutaki, Cook Islands	escapee ?	?
Musk Lorikeet	about 1975	Western Australia	escapee ?	cage bird
Sulphur-crested Cockatoo	?	Ceramlaut and Goramlaut, Indonesia	?	?
Lesser Sulphur-crested Cockatoo	before 1973 ?	Singapore	escapee ?	cage bird
	before 1975 ?	Hong Kong	escapee	cage bird
Salmon-crested Cockatoo	?	Amboina, Moluccas	?	?

continued

INTRODUCTIONS OF THE PSITTACIDAE

Species	Date introduced	Region	Manner introduced	Reason
Goffin's Cockatoo	?	Tual, Kai Islands, Indonesia	?	?
Long-billed Corella	1950s	South Australia	deliberate	preservation
	1968-70	King Island, Aust.	escapees ?	cage bird
Orange-fronted Conure	1960s or early 70s	USA	escapees?	cage bird
Black-hooded Parakeet	1968-69 and 1975	USA	deliberate and escapee	cage bird
	early 1970s	Hawaiian Islands	escapee	cage bird
White-eared Conure	prior 1971	Brazil	deliberate	?
Green-rumped Parrotlet	early 20th century	Barbados	deliberate	?
	1954-55	Curaçao, West Indies	?	?
	1966	Tobago, West Indies	escapee	cage bird
Orange-chinned Parakeet	1960s	USA	escapee	cage bird
White-fronted Amazon	early 1970s	USA	escapee ?	cage bird
Green-cheeked Amazon	early 1970s	USA	escapee ?	cage bird
	early 1970s	Hawaiian Islands	escapee	cage bird
Yellow-crowned Amazon	1962	USA	deliberate and/or escapee	cage bird
	recent	Trinidad	re-introduced (escapees)	cage bird
Eclectus Parrot	?	Palau Archipelago	escapee	captive bird
		Goram, Indonesia	?	?
Great-billed Parrot	prior 1934 ?	Balut Island, Indonesia	?	?
Alexandrine Parakeet	?	India	feral	captive bird
Rose-ringed Parakeet	prior 1912?	Egypt	escapee	cage bird
	?	Oman	?	?
	prior 1962	Aden, Yemen	escapee ?	?
	?	Kuwait	?	?
	prior 1938	Iraq	escapee ?	?
	?	Iran	?	?
	?	Afghanistan	?	?
	prior 1969	Kenya	escapee ?	cage bird
	prior 1964	USA	escapee	cage bird
Moustached Parakeet	?	Pinang Island, Malaysia	?	?
Madagascar Lovebird	?	Rodrigues Island	?	?
	?	Réunion	?	?
	?	Archipel des Comores	?	?
Nyasa Lovebird	prior 1957	Zambia	?	?
Red-backed Parrot	about 1956	Queensland, Australia	escapee ?	?

(c) Unsuccessful introductions

Species	Date introduced	Region	Manner introduced	Reason
Kakapo	1894-1900, 1903, 1912 and recent ?	Islands off New Zealand	deliberate	preservation
Tahitian Lory	about 1938-40	Tahiti	re-introduction	preservation
Gang Gang Cockatoo	1940-47	Kangaroo Island, Australia	?	?
Sulphur-crested Cockatoo	prior 1940s and recently	Hawaiian Islands	deliberate and escapee	?
	prior 1956	Singapore	escapee	cage bird
Pink Cockatoo	about 1926	Fiji	escapee ?	?
Salmon-crested Cockatoo	about 1972	Hawaiian Islands	escapee	cage bird
Galah	prior 1940s and recently	Hawaiian Islands	deliberate ? and escapee	?
Long-billed Corella	1929	Chagos Archipelago	escapee	?

INTRODUCTIONS OF THE PSITTACIDAE

Species	Date introduced	Region	Manner introduced	Reason
Cockatiel	occasional	USA	escapee	cage bird
	1871	New Zealand	not known if released	cage bird ?
Scarlet Macaw	prior 1940s and recently	Hawaiian Islands	deliberate ? and escapee	cage bird
Brown-throated Conure	1960s	USA	escapee ?	cage bird
Monk Parakeet	1936 and recently	Great Britain and Holland	escapee	cage bird
	1970s	Hawaiian Islands	escapee	cage bird
Green-rumped Parrotlet	?	Martinique, Lesser Antilles	?	?
Orange-chinned Parakeet	prior 1940s and recently	Hawaiian Islands	deliberate ? and escapee	cage bird
Red-lored Amazon	1968	USA	escapee ?	cage bird
Yellow-crowned Amazon	1969-70 ?	Hawaiian Islands	escapee ?	cage bird
Orange-winged Amazon	late 1960s	USA	escapee	cage bird
Vasa Parrot	?	Réunion	?	?
Eclectus Parrot	1972	Hawaiian Islands	escapee	cage bird
Blue-naped Parrot	?	Island off Borneo	?	?
Rose-ringed Parakeet	1951 and earlier ?	Singapore	escapee ?	cage bird
	1909	Cape Verde Islands	?	?
	occasional	Hawaiian Islands	escapee	cage bird
	before 1867	Andaman Islands	deliberate	?
Moustached Parakeet	1943	Singapore	escapee	cage bird
Plum-headed Parakeet	early 1970s	USA	escapee ?	cage bird
Red Shining Parrot	?	Tongatabu, Tonga Islands	?	?
	prior 1945	Ovalau, Fiji	?	?
Madagascar Lovebird	prior 1812 ?	Mauritius	?	?
	prior 1913 ?	Zanzibar and Mafia Islands, Africa	?	?
	late 1880s	South Africa	deliberate ?	?
Peach-faced Lovebird	mid-1960s	Western Australia	escapee ?	cage bird
	since 1965 ?	Hawaiian Islands	escapee	cage bird
Masked Lovebird	occasional	USA	escapee	cage bird
Nyasa Lovebird	prior 1965	South West Africa	escapee	?
Crimson Rosella	prior 1969	Lord Howe Island	?	?
Pale-headed Rosella	1877	Hawaiian Islands	deliberate	?
Budgerygah	1871 and occasional	New Zealand	deliberate and escapee	cage bird
	occasional	Japan	escapee	cage bird
	occasional	South America	deliberate and escapee	cage bird
	1975 ?	Hong Kong	escapee	cage bird
	about 1969	Tresco, Scilly Isles, England	deliberate	aesthetic ?
	1960s	Natal, South Africa	deliberate and escapee	cage bird
	1960s	Hawaiian Islands	escapee	cage bird

burrow, in a crevice between rocks, or under tree roots. *Eggs:* 1-4.

Forshaw, 1973, p.270.

NOTES ON INTRODUCTIONS

New Zealand. Between 1894 and 1900 Richard Henry transferred nearly 400 Kakapos from Fiordland to several islands in Dusky Sound in an attempt to safeguard the species from introduced stoats (Gooders, 1969). The project apparently failed because stoats swam to the islands. In 1903 some four birds were liberated on Little Barrier Island, but were not seen again (Williams, 1956). Some were also liberated on Kapiti in 1912 and some may have been seen there as late as 1936. In the South Island some have been recently (?) released in the Resolution Island area and on Stewart Island.

DAMAGE

None known.

Kakapo

BLUE-STREAKED LORY

Eos reticulata (Müller)

DISTINGUISHING CHARACTERISTICS
31 cm (12.4 in)
General colour bright red; a purple-blue band from eyes to mantle; mantle streaked with violet-blue; back and rump streaked blue; primaries, secondaries and greater wing-coverts tipped black; tail, black above, reddish below; bill coral.
Forshaw, 1973, p.50 and pl. p.49.

Blue-streaked Lory

GENERAL DISTRIBUTION
Tanimbar Islands, Indonesia.

INTRODUCED DISTRIBUTION
Possibly introduced successfully to the Kai Islands and Damar Island, Indonesia.

GENERAL HABITS
No details known. *Status:* common (?). *Eggs:* 2 (in captivity).

NOTES ON INTRODUCTIONS
Kai Islands and Damar. According to Peters (1937) the Blue-streaked Lory has been introduced to both the Kai Islands and Damar. Salvadori (1905-06) says that they appear to have been introduced to both Toeal (Tual), Little Kai and Damar in the Banda Sea. No other details of the introductions could be found.

DAMAGE
None known.

RAINBOW LORIKEET
(Red-Collared Lorikeet)

Trichoglossus haematodus (Linnaeus)

DISTINGUISHING CHARACTERISTICS
30-32.5 cm (12-13 in). 70-80 g (2.46-2.82 oz)
Throat and foreneck blackish; breast bright yellowish orange; an extensive greenish black patch on abdomen; thigh and under tail-coverts marked with yellow; nuchal collar yellowish orange, bordered dark blue; reddish markings towards upper mantle; bill coral.
Forshaw, 1969, p.60 and pl. p.24.

GENERAL DISTRIBUTION
Australia, New Guinea and Indonesia to New Caledonia: in northern Australia from the Kimberleys east to the Gulf of Carpentaria; also Melville, Croker, Elcho and Groote islands, and in eastern Australia from Cape York to South Australia and Tasmania; Lesser Sunda Islands, New Guinea and adjacent islands, and from the Bismarck Archipelago to the Solomons, New Hebrides and New Caledonia.

INTRODUCED DISTRIBUTION
Introduced successfully in Perth, Western Australia.

GENERAL HABITS
Status: common; fairly common aviary bird. *Habitat:* forest and woodlands. *Gregariousness:* pairs, small flocks or large flocks up to 100 birds. *Movements:* nomadic. *Foods:* pollen, nectar, fruits, berries, seeds, leaf buds and insects and their larvae.

Rainbow Lorikeet, *Trichoglossus haematodus rubritorquis*

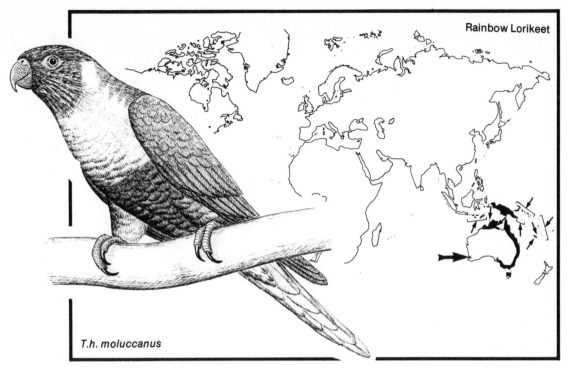

T.h. moluccanus

Breeding: variable, mainly Sept-Jan. *Nest:* hole in a tree, unlined. *Eggs:* 2.

Forshaw, 1969, pp.22-25.

NOTES ON INTRODUCTIONS

Western Australia. A small colony of up to nine birds has existed for some years in the Kings Park — University of Western Australia, area of Perth. Their origin appears to be unknown, but some reports have indicated they may have escaped from a captive colony kept in or near the University of Western Australia.

Some were present there between 1975-77 and they may have been there since the early 1960s. Some were noted at Safety Bay (38 km [24 miles] south of Perth) in February 1978 (Smith, 1978) and a recent report indicates that there may now be as many as fifty birds in the Hollywood area.

The race introduced in Western Australia appears to be that from Queensland, *T.h. moluccanus,* and this appears to have given credence to a theory that the birds arrived unaided.

DAMAGE

The Rainbow Lorikeet causes damage to sorghum in northern Queensland by attacking crops at the 'soft dough stage' (Lavery and Blackman, 1970). According to Lavery and Blackman the damage is small and does not justify any control other than by mechanical frightening of the birds. They are not recorded to have caused any damage in Western Australia, but it is thought that if they become numerous they may cause agricultural damage and compete with native parrot species.

KUHL'S LORY
Vini kuhlii (Vigors)

DISTINGUISHING CHARACTERISTICS
19 cm (7.6 in)
Upper parts green; lower parts scarlet; yellowish on back and rump; crown streaked with paler green; occiput dark blue; thighs purple; under tail and under wings greenish; some scarlet on upper tail, grey below; bill orange.

Forshaw, 1973, p.80 and pl. p.81.

GENERAL DISTRIBUTION
Rimatara, Tabuai Islands.

INTRODUCED DISTRIBUTION
Introduced successfully on Washington, Fanning and probably on Christmas Island in the Line Islands (Pacific Ocean).

Kuhl's Lory

GENERAL HABITS

Few details recorded of habits. *Habitat:* rain forest in vicinity of coconut groves. *Gregariousness:* in pairs or small groups. *Movements:* no information, probably sedentary. *Foods:* pollen and nectar from coconut flowers. *Breeding:* Jan-Mar. *Nest:* in a hollow in a coconut palm or rotting coconut. *Eggs:* 2 (in captivity).

Forshaw, 1973, pp.80, 82; 1978, p.84.

NOTES ON INTRODUCTIONS

Washington and Fanning Islands. Kuhl's Lory has been introduced to both Washington and Fanning Islands (Peters, 1937). Forshaw (1973) indicates that on both islands they were released or escaped from the natives to become established prior to 1798. Bachus (1967) says that the species is now common on both islands.

Christmas Island. According to Gallagher (1960) six Kuhl's Lories were taken from Washington Island in December 1957 and released in London Village. Two were observed in July 1958 and three in early 1959, so possibly the species is still established there.

DAMAGE

None known.

TAHITIAN LORY

Vini peruviana (Müller)

DISTINGUISHING CHARACTERISTICS

18 cm (7.2 in)

Generally mauve-blue; crown streaked paler; ear-coverts, throat and upper breast white; bill orange.

Forshaw, 1973, p.82 and pl. p.81.

GENERAL DISTRIBUTION

Cook Islands, Society Islands and westernmost Tuamotu Islands.

INTRODUCED DISTRIBUTION

Possibly introduced, successfully, to Aitutaki, Cook Islands. Re-introduced unsuccessfully to Tahiti, Society Islands.

GENERAL HABITS

Little information. *Status:* probably rare and possibly in danger of extinction. *Habitat:* forest and coconut thickets. *Gregariousness:* pairs or groups of three or more. *Movements:* no information. *Foods:* flowers of coconuts and other trees and bushes. *Breeding:* Dec-Jan or May-July (?). *Nest:* possibly of plants and twigs in hollows in trees or palms (?); one account indicates nest is placed in a coconut palm and not a hollow. *Eggs:* 2.

Forshaw, 1978, pp.86-87.

Tahitian Lory, *Vini peruviana*

Tahitian Lory

NOTES ON INTRODUCTIONS

Tahiti. Forshaw (1973) says that this species' disappearance from Tahiti is not well documented, but that in about 1940 attempts were made to re-introduce it there. Guild (1938) indicated he released some birds, but says that they disappeared after liberation and were not seen again. Holyoak (1974) indicates that the species does not now occur on Tahiti.

Cook Islands. Amadon (1942) suggests that the Tahitian Lory may have been introduced to Aitutaki, because in 1899 it was the only bird found there and was a common pet of the local natives. Townsend and Wetmore (1919) report its presence on Aitutaki and Cook, where Holyoak (1974) suggests it may have been introduced by the early Polynesians.

DAMAGE

None known.

MUSK LORIKEET

(Musky Lorikeet, Green Keet)

Glossopsitta concinna (Shaw)

DISTINGUISHING CHARACTERISTICS

19.8-22.2 cm (7.9-8.9 in)

Generally bright green, more yellowish on underparts; forehead, lores and band from eyes across ear-coverts to neck bright red; crown blue; nape and mantle bronze, tinted green; wings and tail green; tail margined orange-red; bill black with coral tip. Female: less extensive blue on crown.

Forshaw, 1969, p.35 and pl.34.

GENERAL DISTRIBUTION

Australia including Tasmania: eastern and south-eastern Australia from central Queensland to south-eastern South Australia, Kangaroo Island and Tasmania.

INTRODUCED DISTRIBUTION

Introduced, probably unsuccessfully to Perth, Western Australia.

Musk Lorikeet

Gang Gang Cockatoo

GENERAL HABITS
Status: common. *Habitat:* timbered country, watercourses, parks and gardens. *Gregariousness:* flocks, often with other lorikeets. *Movements:* seasonally nomadic. *Foods:* nectar, native and cultivated fruits, berries, seeds, insects and larvae. *Breeding:* Aug-Jan. *Nest:* hollow limb or hole in a tree. *Eggs:* 2.
Forshaw, 1969, pp.35-36.

NOTES ON INTRODUCTIONS
Western Australia. The Musk Lorikeet was first noted at Alfred Cove, a suburb of Perth in September 1975 and was later found to be breeding there (Corfe, 1977). As many as eight birds were said to be present at any one time. Some doubt exists as to the origin of these birds — some people subscribing to the theory that they arrived unaided from the south-east of Australia, while others say that they may have been escapees from aviaries. I tend towards the latter theory as their discovery came not long after the authorities in Western Australia banned the species from import to that State because of their likely damage if they became established there. It was a popular misconception at the time that banned species held in aviculture would be destroyed by the authorities.

DAMAGE
None known.

GANG GANG COCKATOO
Calocephalon fimbriatum (Grant)

DISTINGUISHING CHARACTERISTICS
30-33 cm (12-13.2 in)
Generally grey with red head and crest; abdomen barred with orange-yellow; bill greyish. Female: head grey; crest and abdomen barred with orange.
Forshaw, 1969, p.73 and pl. p.72.

GENERAL DISTRIBUTION
South-eastern Australia: from eastern New South

Wales to the extreme south-east of South Australia, King Island and northern Tasmania.

INTRODUCED DISTRIBUTION
Introduced unsuccessfully to Kangaroo Island, Australia.

GENERAL HABITS
Status: common (in small range). *Habitat:* mountain forests and wooded valleys. *Gregariousness:* pairs or family parties in breeding season; at other times flocks. *Movements:* nomadic. *Foods:* seeds, berries, nuts, fruits, insects and their larvae. *Breeding:* Oct-Jan. *Nest:* hole in a trunk or dead branch of a tree, lined with a layer of wood chips and wood dust. *Eggs:* 2.
Forshaw, 1969, pp.73-75.

NOTES ON INTRODUCTIONS
Kangaroo Island. An unsuccessful attempt was made to introduce the Gang Gang to Kangaroo Island off the south coast of South Australia in January 1947 (Condon, 1962). Forshaw (1973) lists the species as still established there.

Anon (1948) records that four pairs were introduced in February 1940 and they remained present there up until 1948. There appear to be no subsequent records for their presence on Kangaroo Island (Abbott, 1974).

DAMAGE
None known.

SULPHUR-CRESTED COCKATOO
Cacatua galerita (Latham)

DISTINGUISHING CHARACTERISTICS
46-50 cm (18.4-20 in)
Generally white with yellow crest; ear-coverts pale yellow; under wings and tail yellow; periopthalmic ring naked and white; bill dark grey.
Forshaw, 1969, p.85 and pl. p.84.

GENERAL DISTRIBUTION
New Guinea–Australia: New Guinea and offshore

245

islands, Aru Islands, northern and eastern Australia from the Kimberleys, Western Australia east to Cape York and south to Tasmania.

INTRODUCED DISTRIBUTION

Introduced (or colonised) successfully in New Zealand; introduced successfully in Western Australia; probably introduced successfully in the Palau Archipelago and on Goramlaut and Ceramlaut in Indonesia. Occasional escapees in the Hawaiian Islands and Singapore.

GENERAL HABITS

Status: common; widely kept cage bird. *Habitat:* forest, woodlands, savannah and cultivated areas. *Gregariousness:* pairs or family parties in breeding season, at other times flocks sometimes in hundreds. *Movements:* sedentary, but with some local seasonal movements. *Foods:* seeds, grain, fruits, berries, nuts, flowers, leaf buds, roots, and insects and their larvae. *Breeding:* variable; Aug-Jan in south, May-Sept in north. *Nest:* in cliffs, haystacks, hollow limbs, or a hole in tree. *Eggs:* 2-3.

Forshaw, 1969, pp.85-87.

NOTES ON INTRODUCTIONS

New Zealand. The Sulphur-crested Cockatoo seems to have appeared in New Zealand in about 1920 (Wodzicki, 1965). Thomson (1922) said that they were frequently reported to be seen on the Waitakerei Ranges, where they appeared to be established in 1922. Some were also reported from about Nelson at this time.

Oliver (1930 and 1955) mentions that they were frequently imported from Australia from the 1920s, escaped from captivity and became established in a few localities near Auckland. He reports other colonies at Wellsford, Hunua Hills, Glen Murray, Fordell, Turakina Valley, Hunterville, and at Waikato and Wainuiomata.

Falla *et al* (1966) indicate that although the birds seen in New Zealand are said to have originated from escapees from aviaries, circumstantial evidence suggests that at least some may be self-introduced.

The subspecies found in New Zealand is *C.g. galerita* (Forshaw, 1973) and it is now well established in two localities: limestone country between lower Waikato and Raglan; and watersheds of the Turakina and Rangitikei near the west coast of the North Island (Falla *et al*) where they are locally common (Wodzicki).

Palau Archipelago. Few details. Forshaw (1973) indicates that the Sulphur-crested Cockatoo was introduced on Palau, and Ripley (1951) says that they are spreading and breeding there. According to Ripley the race introduced is *C.g. triton*.

Indonesia. Forshaw (1973) records that the subspecies *C.g. triton* has been introduced to both Ceramlaut and Goramlaut, but there appear to be no details of the introduction.

Western Australia. The Sulphur-crested Cockatoo has become established in Western Australia as a result of escapees or deliberate releases. The earliest record of birds is from Mandurah, south of Perth, in 1935. A pair were observed at Kalamunda in 1956 and three birds in 1963, others were observed at West Swan, 1964 (several); Coolup, 1972 (fifteen to sixteen); Pinjarra, 1972 (twenty-four); Byford, 1972-73 (eleven); Guildford, 1975 (eighteen to twenty-three); Pinjarra-Coolup, 1975 (sixteen to twenty); Mundijong, 1975 (ten to twelve); Peel Inlet, 1975 (twenty-eight); Bullsbrook, 1976; Carrabungup, 1976 (fourteen); and Pinjarra, 1976 (twenty-five to thirty-five).

The species may now be established in an area from Coolup to the Perth metropolitan area and north to Bullsbrook. They may reach as far south as Harvey. They are known to breed at both Pinjarra and Guildford where a flock of approximately one hundred at the former place and sixty at the latter were noted in 1979.

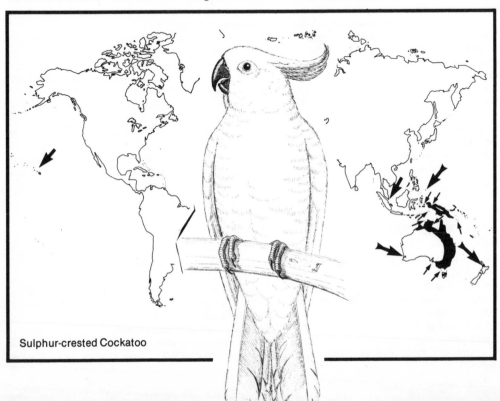

Sulphur-crested Cockatoo

246

The race established appears to be that from north-eastern Queensland, *C.g. galerita*.

Hawaiian Islands. The Sulphur-crested Cockatoo is recorded by Munro (1960) to have been introduced from Australia to the Hawaiian Islands, but apparently failed to become established. More recently, some have escaped from captivity on Oahu, but they are not known to be established there (Berger, 1972).

Singapore. Madoc (1956) says that Sulphur-crested Cockatoos escape from cages in Singapore and are occasionally found as feral birds. Rowley (in Forshaw, 1973) has sighted Lesser Sulphur-crested Cockatoos in the Botanic Gardens there so it may be that this is the species sighted in Singapore.

DAMAGE

The Sulphur-crested Cockatoo is a pest in cereal growing districts in eastern and northern Australia. They are known to raid ripening crops, damage haystacks, dig up newly sown cereals and attack bagged and stored grain.

In New Zealand they have been reported to have caused damage to haystacks by pulling them apart to get at the grain heads (Oliver, 1930-55).

LESSER SULPHUR-CRESTED COCKATOO

Cacatua sulphurea (Gmelin)

DISTINGUISHING CHARACTERISTICS

33 cm (13.2 in)

Generally white with yellow crest; ear-coverts and undersides of flight and tail-feathers yellow; periopthalmic ring naked and creamy white; bill grey-black.

Forshaw, 1973, p.122 and pl. p.121.

GENERAL DISTRIBUTION

Indonesia: Sulawesi, Sunda Islands and islands in the Flores Sea and Java Sea.

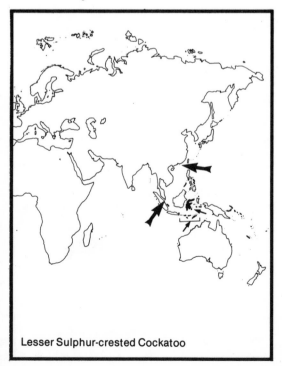

Lesser Sulphur-crested Cockatoo

INTRODUCED DISTRIBUTION

Introduced successfully to Singapore and Hong Kong.

GENERAL HABITS

Status: common in most areas. *Habitat:* open woodland, cultivated fields and forest edges. *Gregariousness:* pairs or small flocks, but larger flocks congregate to feed. *Movements:* no information. *Foods:* seeds, nuts, berries, fruits and probably blossom. *Breeding:* Sept-Oct (?). *Nest:* hollow in tree. *Eggs:* 2-3 (in captivity).

Forshaw, 1973, p.123.

NOTES ON INTRODUCTIONS

Singapore. Rowley (in Forshaw, 1973) reports small parties of Lesser Sulphur-crested Cockatoos in the Singapore Botanic Gardens where they appear to be established.

Hong Kong. The Lesser Sulphur-crested Cockatoo has been introduced and established in Hong Kong, but it is not known whether they have yet bred in the wild. Webster (1975) records that up to thirty birds live in Happy Valley and the University. In 1975 (Vinney, 1976) they were recorded from Victoria Barracks (thirteen birds), Happy Valley (twenty-one), Hong Kong University (twenty-one), Stonecutters Island (six) and were strongly suspected of breeding in the latter area.

Webster says that most feral birds are of the race *citrinocristata* (from Sulawesi), but that there may also be another race present.

DAMAGE

In Indonesia Lesser Sulphur-crested Cockatoos are apparently troublesome birds because they destroy young fruits of *Ceiba* and *Gossampinus* and will attack coconuts, even peeling the mature nuts (Forshaw, 1973).

SALMON-CRESTED COCKATOO

(Moluccan Cockatoo)

Cacatua moluccensis (Gmelin)

DISTINGUISHING CHARACTERISTICS

52 cm (20.8 in)

Generally salmon-pink; underside of crest and flight feathers deep salmon-pink; periopthalmic ring naked, white tinted blue; bill grey-black.

Forshaw, 1973, p.127 and pl. p.128.

GENERAL DISTRIBUTION

Indonesia: Seram, Saparua and Haruku in the southern Moluccas.

INTRODUCED DISTRIBUTION

Possibly introduced to Amboina in the southern Moluccas. Probably an occasional escapee in the Hawaiian Islands.

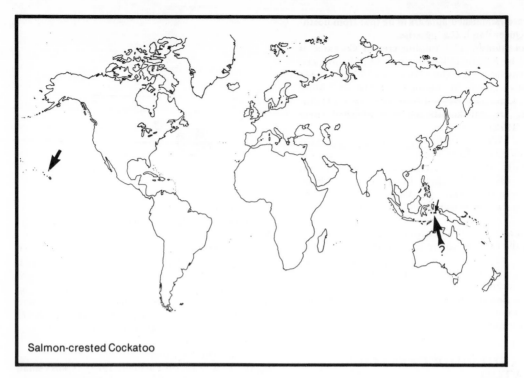

Salmon-crested Cockatoo

GENERAL HABITS

Status: apparently a popular bird in captivity, but little is known about the species in the wild. *Habitat:* woodland (?). *Gregariousness:* pairs, but little information. *Foods:* seeds, nuts, fruits, berries and possibly insects and their larvae. *Breeding:* May (Seram). *Nest:* hollow in a tree. *Eggs:* 2-3 (?).
Forshaw, 1973, p.127.

NOTES ON INTRODUCTIONS

Amboina (southern Moluccas). No details of the introduction appear to be known.
Hawaiian Islands. Berger (1976) adds the Salmon-crested Cockatoo to his list of birds known to have escaped in these islands, but not known to be established. One is reported (Pyle, 1977) to have been seen in the wild in 1972, but there are no subsequent records.

DAMAGE

The Salmon-crested Cockatoo is considered to be a pest in coconut plantations in the southern Moluccas where they attack young coconuts, chewing through the outer layers to get at the 'milk' and soft pulp (Forshaw, 1973).

PINK COCKATOO
(Major Mitchell's Cockatoo, Leadbeater's Cockatoo)
Cacatua leadbeateri (Vigors)

DISTINGUISHING CHARACTERISTICS

33.5-36.3 cm (13.4-14.5 in)
Generally salmon-pink; crown white suffused with salmon-pink; crest scarlet with central band of yellow and tipped white; lower abdomen, under tail-coverts, upper parts and tail white; bill horn coloured.
Forshaw, 1969, p.89.

GENERAL DISTRIBUTION

Australia: the arid and semi-arid interior except the north-east region.

INTRODUCED DISTRIBUTION

Introduced unsuccessfully in Fiji.

GENERAL HABITS

Status: uncommon. *Habitat:* sparsely timbered areas, Acacia scrublands, sandy ridges, mallee, and trees bordering watercourses. *Gregariousness:* pairs, small groups, and rarely large flocks. *Movements:* sedentary and nomadic. *Foods:* seeds, nuts, fruits, berries and roots. *Breeding:* Aug-Dec. *Nest:* hollow limb or hole in a tree. *Eggs:* 2-4.
Forshaw, 1969, pp.89-93.

NOTES ON INTRODUCTIONS

Fiji. Pink Cockatoos were liberated or escaped and

Pink Cockatoo

lived for some time about the public park and Government House at Suva in about 1926 (Wood and Wetmore, 1926). There is no further mention of the species in these islands.

DAMAGE
None known.

GOFFIN'S COCKATOO
Cacatua goffini (Finsch)

DISTINGUISHING CHARACTERISTICS
32 cm (12.8 in)
Generally white; ear-coverts, undersides of flight feathers and tail-feathers tinted pale yellow; periopthalmic ring white; bill grey-white.
Forshaw, 1973, p.129 and pl. p.131.

GENERAL DISTRIBUTION
Indonesia: Tanimbar Islands

INTRODUCED DISTRIBUTION
Possibly introduced successfully on Tual in the Kai Islands, Indonesia.

GENERAL HABITS
Not known, but probably similar to Little Corella (*C. sanguinea*) (Forshaw, 1973). *Eggs:* 3 (in captivity).

NOTES ON INTRODUCTIONS
Tual. Forshaw (1973) mentions that Goffin's Cockatoo has been introduced to Tual in the Kai Islands, but gives no other details.

DAMAGE
None known.

GALAH
(**Rose-breasted Cockatoo, Roseate Cockatoo**)
Cacatua roseicapilla (Vieillot)

DISTINGUISHING CHARACTERISTICS
32-37 cm (12.8-14.8 in). 284-454 g (10.02-16.01 oz)
Underparts rose-pink; upper parts pale grey; crest whitish with pink suffusion; bill whitish.
Forshaw, 1969, p.77, pl. p.79.

Goffin's Cockatoo

GENERAL DISTRIBUTION
Australia generally.

INTRODUCED DISTRIBUTION
Colonised areas south of range in Australia, in some instances probably with the help of escaped and released birds. Unsuccessfully introduced and escaped in the Hawaiian Islands.

GENERAL HABITS
Status: common; familiar pet and cage bird in Australia and elsewhere. *Habitat:* savannah woodland, open grassland, cultivation and urban

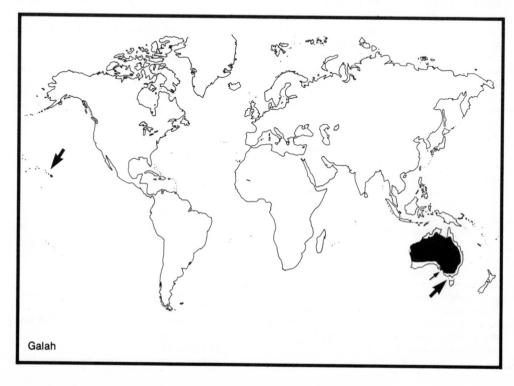

Galah

districts. *Gregariousness*: generally small parties or flocks, but larger flocks of 200-300 common. *Movements*: mainly sedentary, with some nomadic movements. *Foods*: seeds, grain, roots, green shoots, leaf buds, insects and their larvae, and bark. *Breeding*: variable, mainly June-Jan. *Nest*: hollow in limb or trunk of tree. *Eggs*: 2-5, usually 3.

Forshaw, 1969, pp.78-82.

NOTES ON INTRODUCTIONS

Australia. The Galah has been extending its range southwards in both South and Western Australia in recent years. At least in Western Australia the extension of range appears to be assisted by the escape and release of caged birds, especially in the metropolitan area of Perth.

Galahs have been reaching Kangaroo Island off the coast of South Australia since about 1913 and have increased in numbers there since 1930 (Abbott, 1974). Large flocks were seen in 1948 (Cleland, 1948), they were common there in 1960 (Wheeler, 1960) and some 200 birds were reported in 1966 (Swanson, 1968, in Abbott).

King Island. McGarvie and Templeton (1974) record that a single Galah, possibly an aviary escapee, was observed on King Island in September 1971.

Hawaiian Islands. Galahs were possibly introduced to the Hawaiian Islands as Munro (1960) lists them amongst species imported for this reason. More recently some have escaped on Oahu but they have failed to become permanently established (Berger, 1972).

DAMAGE

In Australia the Galah attacks ripening grain crops and sometimes eats sprouting shoots of wheat. They formerly attacked bagged grain in paddocks, but bulk handling of grain has removed the source of bags stored in this manner.

LONG-BILLED CORELLA
Cacatua tenuirostris (Kuhl)

DISTINGUISHING CHARACTERISTICS

35-46 cm (14-18 in). 738 g (1-6 lb)

Generally white with forehead to eyes and bases of feathers of head and breast orange-scarlet; short crest on head; under wings and under side of tail yellow; eye patch naked, and bluish; bill whitish.

Forshaw, 1969, p.95, pl. p.94.

GENERAL DISTRIBUTION

Australia: in southern coastal Western Australia and south-eastern South Australia, western Victoria and adjacent New South Wales.

INTRODUCED DISTRIBUTION

Introduced successfully in a small area of South Australia outside present breeding range; doubtfully established from escapees on King Island, Bass Strait. Accidentally escaped near Chagos Group, but did not survive.

GENERAL HABITS

Status: common in parts of eastern Australia, elsewhere uncommon. *Habitat:* open woodlands, grasslands, cultivated farmlands and watercourses. *Gregariousness:* small flocks and occasionally large flocks of several hundred. *Movements:* nomadic ?). *Foods:* seeds, bulbs and grain. *Breeding:* Aug-Nov. *Nest:* hole in a tree. *Eggs:* 2-3, 4.

250   Forshaw, 1969, pp.96-97.

Long-billed Corella

NOTES ON INTRODUCTIONS

South Australia. The race *C.t. tenuirostris* was introduced in small numbers at Buckland Park, Port Gawler, north of Adelaide in the 1950s (Condon, 1975) and where they appear to be still established.

King Island. Two birds, probably released from an aviary, were seen at Reekara, King Island on several occasions between 1968-70 (McGarvie and Templeton, 1974).

Chagos Archipelago. Two Long-billed Corellas escaped from a ship in about 1929 and flew towards the Chagos Group, some 145 km (90 miles) away (Elkington, 1929), but evidently did not survive as there appear to be no further records of them.

DAMAGE

The Long-billed Corella digs up newly sown cereal crops and eats ripening corn cobs (Forshaw, 1969). In Western Australia the species was formerly troublesome in wheat crops (Serventy and Whittell, 1962) and although it is still accused of digging up newly sown grains the species is not numerous enough now to cause any problems.

COCKATIEL
(Weero, Quarrion, Cockatoo-Parrot)
Nymphicus hollandicus (Kerr)

DISTINGUISHING CHARACTERISTICS

28-32 cm (11-13 in). 85.2-113.6 g (3-4 oz)

Generally grey; forehead, crest and cheek patches yellow; ear-coverts orange; tail dark grey; bill dark grey.

Forshaw, 1969, p.107 and pl. p.106.

GENERAL DISTRIBUTION

Australia generally, mainly in the interior.

INTRODUCED DISTRIBUTION

Introduced unsuccessfully in the USA and possibly in New Zealand.

GENERAL HABITS

Status: common; common aviary bird. *Habitat:*

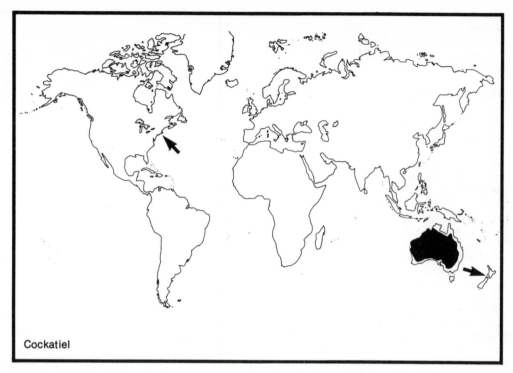

Cockatiel

open woodlands and savannah. *Gregariousness:* pairs or small flocks up to 10, but occasionally larger flocks. *Movements:* nomadic, perhaps migratory in southern parts of range. *Foods:* seeds, grain, fruit and berries. *Breeding:* variable, Aug-Dec. *Nest:* hollow limb or hole in tree, with wood dust bed. *Eggs:* 4-7.
Forshaw, 1969, pp.107-109.

NOTES ON INTRODUCTIONS
USA. Cockatiels are commonly kept in captivity in the United States. In New York they have been occasionally recorded in the wild (Bull, 1973), but have not as yet become permanently established anywhere.
New Zealand. Cockatiels were imported into New Zealand in 1871, but it is not known if they were liberated at this time (Thomson, 1922).

DAMAGE
Cockatiels will raid standing crops, particularly sorghum (Forshaw, 1973), but are generally not a pest in most parts of their range.

SCARLET MACAW
Ara macao (Linnaeus)

DISTINGUISHING CHARACTERISTICS
35-97 cm (34-39 in). Females 900 g (2 lb)
Generally scarlet; upper and under tail-coverts, tail tip, outer primaries and secondaries blue; greater and median coverts yellow; under wing and tail red; bare facial area white, lined with red; bill grey-black.
Forshaw, 1973, p.364 and pl. p.367.

GENERAL DISTRIBUTION
Central and South America: from eastern Mexico to Venezuela, Colombia, north-eastern Brazil, Bolivia and south-eastern Peru; also Trinidad (two sight records).

INTRODUCED DISTRIBUTION
Introduced unsuccessfully in the Hawaiian Islands.

GENERAL HABITS
Status: probably uncommon; common cage bird in the Americas. *Habitat:* open woodland, watercourses, savannah and lowland forest. *Gregariousness:* pairs, parties, or small flocks of up to 30 birds, and formerly larger flocks of up to 200 birds (?). *Foods:* seeds, nuts, fruits, berries and other vegetable material. *Breeding:* Dec-Apr. *Nest:* hollow in a tree. *Eggs:* no information.
Forshaw, 1973, pp.364-365.

NOTES ON INTRODUCTIONS
Hawaiian Islands. Scarlet Macaws were imported to the Hawaiian Islands but there are no details of their

Scarlet Macaw

release (Munro, 1960). In recent years some have escaped from captivity on Oahu, but they are not known to be established there (Berger, 1972).

DAMAGE
None known.

BROWN-THROATED CONURE
(Brown-throated Parakeet)
Aratinga pertinax (Linnaeus)

DISTINGUISHING CHARACTERISTICS
23-26 cm (9-10.4 in). 63-102 g (2.22-3.59 oz)
Generally green, paler on underparts; forehead, lores and sides of head variably orange-yellow to brownish; throat and breast olive-brown; bill brownish.
Forshaw, 1973, pp.399-403 and pl. p.401.

GENERAL DISTRIBUTION
Central and South America: from western Panama, through Venezuela to Guyane; also small islands (Dutch West Indies) in the Caribbean Sea.

INTRODUCED DISTRIBUTION
Introduced successfully to St Thomas (Virgin Islands), and possibly in the USA.

GENERAL HABITS
Status: common. *Habitat:* open forest, woods and scrubland, savannah, semi-deserts, cultivation and frequently towns, villages and fruit plantations. *Gregariousness:* pairs, small flocks of 4-20 birds, but large flocks sometimes at food supplies. *Movements:* seasonal movements in some areas. *Foods:* seeds, fruits, nuts, blossom, insects and their larvae. *Breeding:* Nov-Jan and at other times. *Nest:* hollows in trees, walls bordering roads or in arboreal termite nests. *Eggs:* 4-7, 9.
Forshaw, 1973, pp.403-404.

NOTES ON INTRODUCTIONS
St Thomas. According to Peters (1937) and Bond (1960) the Brown-throated Conure was undoubtedly introduced to St Thomas. Bond records that they came from Curaçao and Peters lists the race established as *A.p. pertinax.* Salvadori (1905-06) indicates that as early as 1892 Graf von Berlepsch expressed the opinion that the species had been introduced to St Thomas.

Forshaw (1973) reports that there is no knowledge of when and how the species was introduced, but that it must have been well over a century ago as specimens were obtained there as early as 1860.

The species was, apparently, common on the island but was almost wiped out during hurricanes in 1926 and 1928 (Nicholls, 1943, in Forshaw). Leopold (1963, in Forshaw) says that they have extended their

Brown-throated Conure

range to most parts of St Thomas and that the population is estimated to be about 400 birds.
USA. The Brown-throated Conure may be in the process of becoming established in the United States. Owre (1973) reports that they have possibly bred in the wild at Key West, Florida and that there are increasing reports of them being present in the Miami area of southern Florida.

DAMAGE
In the West Indies the Brown-throated Conure descends at times to feed on seasonable fruits (Bond, 1960). Dugand (1947, in Forshaw 1973) reports that serious damage is done to maize crops in northern Colombia.

In the Netherlands Antilles flocks of 100 have been observed in fruit plantations and in farmlands where they raid ripening millet crops (Forshaw).

ORANGE-FRONTED CONURE
(Orange-fronted Parakeet)
Aratinga canicularis (Linnaeus)

DISTINGUISHING CHARACTERISTICS
23-24 cm (9-9.6 in)
Generally green with orange frontal band; forecrown dull blue; throat and breast pale olive; abdomen and under tail greenish yellow; primaries blue near tips; periopthalmic ring dull orange-yellow; bill horn.
Forshaw, 1973, pp.396-397 and pl. p.405.

GENERAL DISTRIBUTION
Central America: western Central America from Sinaloa, Mexico, south to western Costa Rica.

INTRODUCED DISTRIBUTION
Possibly established successfully in Florida, USA.

GENERAL HABITS
Status: common. *Habitat:* arid scrubland, deciduous forests and plantations. *Gregariousness:* pairs, small flocks and larger flocks in non-breeding season of up to 200 birds. *Movements:* somewhat nomadic. *Foods:*

Brown-throated Conure, *Aratinga pertinax*

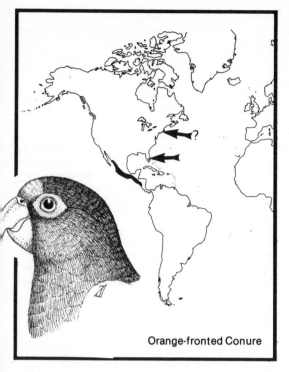

Orange-fronted Conure

Black-hooded Parakeet

fruits, seeds, nuts, berries, blossom and possibly insects and their larvae. *Breeding:* Jan-May (?). *Nest:* entirely in arboreal termite nests. *Eggs:* 1, 3-5. Forshaw, 1973, pp.398-399.

NOTES ON INTRODUCTIONS

USA. In recent years Orange-fronted Conures have been reported, and are thought to be possibly breeding, throughout the Miami area, southern Florida, from northward along the Atlantic Coastal Ridge (Owre, 1973). They are also found as an occasional escapee in the New York area (Bull, 1973).

Although not apparently well established in the Miami area the Orange-fronted Conure shows some potential in this regard. They continue to be reported from areas in the south-eastern United States. A pair were observed at Santa Ana in the south Texas region in November 1975 (Webster, 1976) and some were still present in Dade County, southern Florida in 1976 and 1977 (Heilbrun, 1976 and 1977).

DAMAGE

None known.

BLACK-HOODED PARAKEET

(Nanday Conure, Nenday)
Nandayus nenday (Vieillot)

DISTINGUISHING CHARACTERISTICS

30 cm (12 in)

Generally green, paler on underparts and rump; head black; throat and upper breast bluish; thighs red; outer webs of flight feathers blue; tail olive-green above, grey below; bill black. Forshaw, 1973, p.407 and pl. p.408.

GENERAL DISTRIBUTION

South America: south-eastern Bolivia, Brazil, Paraguay and northern Argentina.

INTRODUCED DISTRIBUTION

Possibly introduced, successfully in the USA and unsuccessfully in the Hawaiian Islands.

GENERAL HABITS

Status: common. *Habitat:* open palm forests, palm groves and savannah. *Gregariousness:* small flocks of from 10-12 birds, but occasionally in very large flocks. *Movements:* sedentary and nomadic (?). *Foods:* seeds, nuts, fruits, berries and probably vegetable matter. *Breeding:* little known, Nov; once per year and perhaps three times in two years. *Nest:* hollow in tree, or fence post. *Eggs:* 3-4. Forshaw, 1973, pp.407, 409.

NOTES ON INTRODUCTIONS

USA. The Black-hooded Parakeet appears to have become established from releases or escapes in a small area of California and possibly New Jersey in 1968-69. According to Hardy (1973) they are established in a small area of Loma Linda, San Bernardino County in California, from releases in 1968 and possibly subsequent escapes. The colony has increased to six birds and it is thought that they have bred at least once in the wild there.

Fisk and Crabtree (1974) observed four birds in the Loma Linda residential area in 1972. They say that the colony originated from birds which escaped in

Black-hooded Parakeet, *Nandayus nenday*

253

1969. The population has subsequently declined and presently seems stable at two to five birds (Shelgren *et al*, 1975). Three birds escaped from a roadside zoo near Moss Landing, Monterey County in 1975, and these still exist there. In Los Angeles County they have been observed in Pasadena (eight to ten birds), West Los Angeles (four to six) and Palos Verdes Peninsula (two) in recent years.

Bull (1973) indicates that the species has escaped into parts of northern New Jersey and has been reported to have at least attempted to breed there. Flocks of between twenty and 200 have been observed in the vicinity of Detroit, Michigan, and Windsor, Ontario (Bull, 1974).

Hawaiian Islands. The Black-hooded Parakeet is possibly established on Oahu, but its present status is not well known (Hawaiian Audubon Society, 1975). Three birds were observed in 1973 and one in 1974, but they have not been recorded again since that date (Pyle, 1977).

DAMAGE

Unger (in Forshaw, 1973) claims that the Black-hooded Parakeet has benefited from crop growing in Paraguay, where it has become abundant, and causes damage to sunflower and maize crops.

WHITE-EARED CONURE
(Maroon-faced Parakeet)
Pyrrhura leucotis (Kuhl)

DISTINGUISHING CHARACTERISTICS
20-23 cm (8-9.2 in)
Generally green, crown and nape brown; forecrown bluish; frontal band and facial region maroon; ear-coverts brownish white; throat and lower cheeks dull bluish; sides of neck and upper breast barred buff and brown; brownish red patches on abdomen, lower back and tail; tail brownish red, duller below; bill greyish brown.

White-eared Conure

254

Forshaw, 1973, p.428, and pl. p.433.
Meyer de Schauensee and Phelps, 1978, p.101 and pl.9, no.7.

GENERAL DISTRIBUTION
South America: northern Venezuela and eastern Brazil.

INTRODUCED DISTRIBUTION
Introduced successfully in Rio de Janeiro, Brazil.

GENERAL HABITS
Status: probably uncommon. *Habitat:* forest. *Gregariousness:* flocks of 15-29 birds. *Movements:* no information. *Foods:* seeds, fruits, nuts, berries and possibly insects and their larvae. *Breeding:* little known. *Nest:* hollow in a limb or trunk of tree (?). *Eggs:* 5-9 (in captivity).
Forshaw, 1973, pp.430-431.

NOTES ON INTRODUCTIONS
Brazil. Forshaw (1973) found the race *P.l. leucotis* to be quite common in the Rio de Janeiro Botanic Gardens in 1971. According to him they are now well established there, where confiscated birds were released by fauna authorities.

DAMAGE
None known.

MONK PARAKEET
(Quaker Parakeet, Grey-headed Parakeet)
Myiopsitta monachus (Boddaert)

DISTINGUISHING CHARACTERISTICS
29 cm (11.6 in)
Forehead, cheeks and throat greyish; breast grey, but variably barred by dark edges to feathers; olive-yellow band on upper abdomen; lower abdomen and vent area bright yellowish green, lower back and rump duller; wings dull green with outer primaries and secondaries blue; nape and hindneck bright green; tail green above, with central blue line and pale below with grey-blue bases; bill brownish, sometimes with rose tinge.
Forshaw, 1973, pp.445-446 and pl. p.447.

GENERAL DISTRIBUTION
South America: central Bolivia and southern Brazil south to central Argentina. (Note: introduced distribution given on range map was at height of spread and now considerably reduced and probably only occurs in few areas.)

INTRODUCED DISTRIBUTION
Introduced successfully in Puerto Rico and the USA (probably still established some areas, but now exterminated in others). Introduced, apparently successfully in England, but colony later retrapped.

GENERAL HABITS
Status: abundant and common; widely kept in aviaries. *Habitat:* open forest, savannah woodland, acacia scrubland, palm groves, farmlands, orchards and watercourses; particularly common in the vicinity of human habitation. *Gregariousness:* highly gregarious, loose flocks 10-15 common, often large flocks with up to 100 or more birds. *Movements:* mainly sedentary, but travel long distances to feed. *Foods:* seed, grain, fruits, berries, nuts, leaf buds, blossom, insects and their larvae. *Breeding:* Oct-Dec; communal; up to 6 clutches per season are possible. *Nest:* enormous, bulky structures of woven twigs, up to 20 compartments, but often single nests, in a tree or other structure. Where introduced in the USA have

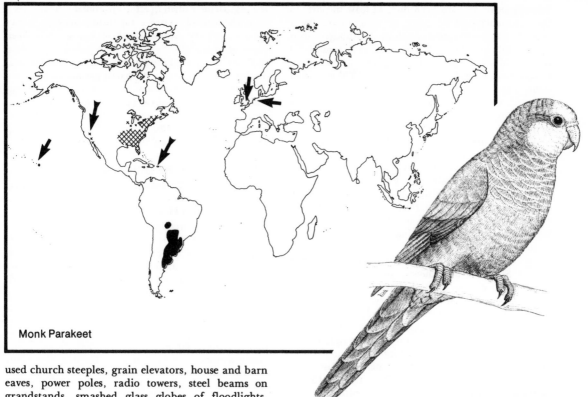

Monk Parakeet

used church steeples, grain elevators, house and barn eaves, power poles, radio towers, steel beams on grandstands, smashed glass globes of floodlights, metal cranes and clothes hoists as nesting sites. *Eggs:* 4-8.

Forshaw, 1973, pp.446-448.

NOTES ON INTRODUCTIONS

Puerto Rico. Fourteen Monk Parakeets have been observed near San Juan, Puerto Rico, where the species is apparently established as a resident (Forshaw, 1973). Neidermyer records some thirty-six to forty birds there in the late summer of 1974 (Neidermyer and Hickey, 1977).

USA. The Monk Parakeet appears to be becoming well established in the United States, although more recently observations of them appear to have become considerably less frequent. A report in 1974 suggested that the species had been found in 50 per cent of the continental United States.

Escapes and releases of Monk Parakeets appear to date back to at least 1967 (Neidermyer and Hickey, 1977). Bull (1973) says that they have been breeding in the Miami area of Florida since 1969 and are now found over a wide area of that State.

By 1972 they were established in New York, southern New England and the Middle Atlantic States (Freeland, 1973). Bump (1971, in Briggs and Hough, 1973) reported them at Watertown, Waterloo, Owega, Binghampton, New York and in Seaford, Virginia. Rockwell (in Briggs and Hough) recorded them at Bradford County, Pennsylvania, and Bull from south-eastern New York and adjacent portions of Connecticut and New Jersey.

Davis (1974) says that they were found in San Diego and Orange Counties and had been sighted in Los Angeles and Sacramento Counties, California. Some fifteen birds were found in San Diego near the San Diego Zoo in 1972, but all but two were recaptured six months later. They had been intentionally released from the San Diego Zoo. In Orange County there were perhaps two to three different flocks, one at Anaheim near Disneyland (eleven birds), one in the city of Orange (nine) and one at Santa Ana (nine). The Anaheim population appears to have bred successfully. Since 1972 some forty-three Monk Parakeets have been found feral in California. From May 1974 to June 1977 at least seventeen birds have been shot by county personnel (Keffer, pers. comm., 1977).

The widespread nature of reports of Monk Parakeets is shown from the following records. In 1973 they were found at Huron, Ohio and at Plymouth, Indiana (Kleen, 1974), and were breeding at Dallas, Texas (Williams, 1974). Hardy (1973) reported them breeding in the San Fernando Valley, California in the same year. According to Ryan (1972) they were at Texas, California, a year earlier. Anon (1974) says that they were established in the wild from Alabama and Texas to Wisconsin and Maine by 1974. Prior to 1974 a feral population in Northwood, North Dakota is reported to have bred successfully (Keffer *et al,* 1974) and in 1972-73 a large flock bred at Asheville in North Carolina (Simpson, 1974) where escapees occurred from pet-bird owners as early as the 1960s.

During the 76th and 77th Audubon Christmas Bird Counts (Heilbrun, 1976 and 1977) they appeared less widespread but were reported from New York (Brooklyn and Lower Hudson), Illinois (Lisle Arboretum), Texas (Dallas) and Florida (Fort Lauderdale, Dade County, Tampa and West Palm Beach). More recently they are known to be present at Norman, Oklahoma (Williams, 1977). The recent less widespread nature of the reports in the United

255

States appears to have been due, at least in part, to the commencement of 'retrieval' programmes by a number of conservation agencies. Although press reports indicated by 1973 that there were some 4000 to 5000 Monk Parakeets in the wild, the 'retrieval' programmes have shown that between 1970 and 1975 there were only 367 birds (confirmed sightings) reported (Neidermyer and Hickey). Some 163 of these birds were successfully 'retrieved' during the period.

Although nesting of Monk Parakeets had been reported as far west as Columbus (Ohio), Owosso (Michigan), Norman (Oklahoma), Omaha (Nebraska) and in California by 1972, the only major increases in population were recorded in New York and northern New Jersey (Neidermyer and Hickey, 1977). Since the initiation of the 'retrieval' scheme the Monk Parakeet population has declined in the United States.

The origin of Monk Parakeets established in the United States is not known, but both deliberate releases and escapes of birds have certainly assisted their rapid initial spread. Bull records that some came from broken crates at Kennedy Airport, and some from intentional releases and escapes from pet shops, aviaries and private homes. Large numbers of Monk Parakeets were imported into the United States at least from 1968 onwards and numerous escapes and releases were inevitable. Bull (1975) cites that 13 000 of them entered the country as cage birds in 1968 alone. David (1974) reports that some 34 627 were imported during the years 1968-70, however, Banks (1977) records that in the five-year period 1968-72, 64 225 Monk Parakeets entered the United States.

Hawaiian Islands. Monk Parakeets have been observed in the wild in the Hawaiian Islands, but are not known to be established there (Berger, 1976).

Great Britain. Monk Parakeets have been successfully kept at liberty in Whipsnade Park, Bedfordshire, some time before 1958 but had to be retrapped because of the damage they caused to orchards in the surrounding area (Yealland, 1958). Lever (1977) says that thirty-one birds were released at Whipsnade in October 1936, where they remained at freedom for a number of years as they have also done from time to time at Woburn. More recently parrots noted at Alfreton, south of Chesterfield, Derbyshire, may have been Monk Parakeets. Elsewhere in Europe they are reported to have bred in the wild in the city parks of Amsterdam, Holland (Bull, 1973).

DAMAGE

In South America large flocks of Monk Parakeets descend on ripening cereal crops, particularly maize and sorghum and frequently cause widespread damage (Forshaw, 1973). They will also raid citrus orchards. Davis records that they raid such crops as corn, sorghum, sunflower, millet and other grain fields, and attack such fruit as pears, grapes, apples and peaches. Crop losses in South America range from 2% - 15% with some as high as 45% annually.

In one province alone in South America between 1958 and 1960 bounties were paid on 427 206 pairs of feet of Monk Parakeets. Fire, shooting, netting and poisons have not been effective in the destruction of the species (Godoy, 1963). Mott (1973) records that the Uruguayan Government has nests sprayed with

the insecticide endrin in efforts to control the species.

In the United States competition between native species and the Monk Parakeet has already been reported from New York and New Jersey. According to Davis, they have been observed killing blue jays and a robin. No commercial crop damage appears to have been reported as yet, but Davis estimates that they will cost the agricultural industry over two million dollars if they become well established in California. Shields (1974) records the Monk Parakeet damaging the crowns of native willows in New Jersey.

GREEN-RUMPED PARROTLET
(Blue-winged Parrotlet, Passerine Parrotlet, Guiana Parrotlet)
Forpus passerinus (Linnaeus)

DISTINGUISHING CHARACTERISTICS

12-14 cm (4.8-5.6 in). 20-28 g (.71-1 oz)

Generally yellowish green, paler and brighter on forehead, cheeks, underparts, lower back and rump; grey tinge on nape and hindneck; wings green with blue bars; lower back pale blue; tail green, paler below; bill pale pinkish. *Female:* similar but without blue markings; forehead more yellow.

Forshaw, 1973, pp.456-457, pl. p.459.

GENERAL DISTRIBUTION

South America: from Trinidad, Guyana, Surinam, Guyane and Venezuela to northern Colombia and northern Brazil.

INTRODUCED DISTRIBUTION

Introduced successfully to Jamaica and Barbados (rare); possibly introduced successfully on Curaçao and Tobago (?). Introduced unsuccessfully to Martinique.

GENERAL HABITS

Status: fairly common. *Habitat:* dry semi-arid regions, savannah, farmland, scrubland, woodland, cultivated fields, gardens and parklands. *Gregariousness:* pairs when breeding, flocks of 5-30 and up to 50 recorded at other times. *Movements:* no information. *Foods:* seeds, berries, fruits, leaf buds and probably blossom. *Breeding:* Feb-Aug. *Nest:* hollow limb or hole in tree, or aboreal termites' nest. *Eggs:* 2-7.

Forshaw, 1973, pp.457-458.

NOTES ON INTRODUCTIONS

Jamaica. Green-rumped Parrotlets were introduced to Jamaica near Old Harbour in about 1918. They

Green-rumped Parrotlet, *Forpus passerinus*

Green-rumped Parrotlet

GENERAL DISTRIBUTION
South America: from Guyane, northern Brazil, south-eastern Colombia and eastern Ecuador, south to northern Argentina, Paraguay and south-eastern Brazil.

INTRODUCED DISTRIBUTION
Introduced successfully in central Peru, Puerto Rico (West Indies) and the USA.

GENERAL HABITS
Status: common. *Habitat:* forest, woodland and farmlands. *Gregariousness:* flocks of 8-10 to 50 and sometimes hundreds; large flocks of up to 1000 birds also known. *Movements:* no information. *Foods:* seeds, fruits, berries, blossom and vegetable matter. *Breeding:* Jan-July. *Nest:* hollow limb, hole in tree or arboreal termites' nest. *Eggs:* 4-6.
Forshaw, 1973, pp.466-468.

NOTES ON INTRODUCTIONS
Peru. Koepcke (1970, in Forshaw, 1973) says that the race *B.v. versicolorus* has been introduced to the Lima area of central Peru. A small population originating from escaped birds became established in the Lima district where birds are regularly offered for sale in the markets (Forshaw, 1973). Plenge (1977, pers. comm.) says that they now thrive around Lima, and possibly some areas of the adjacent countryside, where they were noted some time after 1964. Flocks of up to ten birds have been seen there.

Puerto Rico. Forshaw (1973) records that hundreds of Canary-winged Parakeets have been sighted on Puerto Rico. The species is apparently well established there.

USA. The Canary-winged Parakeet appears to be well established in both California and Florida and possibly on Long Island, New York.

In California it is largely confined to the Palos Verdes Peninsula and vicinity where it was first found in about 1971 (Hardy, 1973). At this time, Hardy

have steadily increased in numbers and range and were widespread in open country in the lowlands on the south side of the island in about the late 1950s (Bond, 1960).

They are still widespread on Jamaica and are at times seen in the natural forests on the island (Lack, 1976).

Barbados. Green-rumped Parrotlets were introduced to Barbados during the early part of the present century, but are now rare and decreasing in numbers (Bond, 1960).

Martinique. Introductions of Green-rumped Parrotlets to Martinique have apparently been unsuccessful (Bond, 1960).

Curaçao. According to Voous (1957, in Forshaw, 1973) the Green-rumped Parrotlet was reported on Curaçao in 1954-55. It is possibly established there, but details are lacking.

Tobago. Ffrench and Ffrench (1966) point out that a pair of Green-rumped Parrotlets found breeding on Tobago were undoubtedly introduced from Trinidad as cage birds. More recently Ffrench (1973) says that a few specimens have been introduced on the island. It is possible that the species may become established there.

DAMAGE
None known.

CANARY-WINGED PARAKEET
(White-winged Parakeet, Bee Bee Parrot)
Brotogeris versicolorus (Müller)

DISTINGUISHING CHARACTERISTICS
22-23 cm (8.8-9.2 in)
Generally dull green, darker on back; periopthalmic ring bluish grey; yellow patch on wings; tail green above, greenish blue below; bill brownish with yellow tinge.
Forshaw, 1973, p.466, pl. p.475.

Canary-winged Parakeet

Canary-winged Parakeet, *Brotogeris versicolorus*

indicates that a flock of thirty birds inhabited Point Fermin on the coast in San Pedro, a flock inhabited Averill Park, and another small flock of up to twelve birds had been reported from Riverside County in 1971. The latter colony is thought to have been extirpated through unknown causes, but the species has recently been confirmed breeding at Point Fermin. There were still twenty-nine of them on the Palos Verdes Peninsula during the 77th Christmas Bird Count (Heilbrun, 1977).

In 1973, a pair of these parrots was observed at San Mateo and in 1974 another at Bakersfield, Kern County. Two birds have been frequently seen in the city of Riverside and three were observed in the Hollywood Hills area in 1973 and 1974. A large number of birds were breeding in the San Pedro – Palos Verdes Peninsula area in 1975 (Shelgren *et al*, 1975) and one bird was shot at Cucamonger in April 1976 (Keffer, pers. comm., 1977). Keffer says that at present two feral populations exist; one at San Francisco (fifteen birds), and the Los Angeles (Palos Verdes — eight birds) population.

Free-flying birds were noted in South Miami, Florida in the late 1960s (Owre, 1973). A flock of fifty were sighted in 1969 (Ogden, 1969, in Owre). Since then they have been reported from Upper Matecumb Key and from the western side of the Everglades (Stevenson, 1971, in Owre); at Lauderdale in 1970 (George, 1971, in Owre), and in flocks of forty to fifty in 1973 (Timmer, in Owre); at Coconut Grove in 1972, where a roost contained nearly 700 birds (Owre); at Sarasota in 1975 (Edscorn, 1976) and at Bradenton, Fort Lauderdale and in Dade County (Heilbrun, 1976). In 1977 a single bird was observed at Port Charlotte in southwest Florida (Stevenson, 1977).

The species was breeding in the Miami area, where up to fifteen nests have been found in the one area (Owre), and appears to be establishing itself in the Florida region. Gore and Doubilet (1976) say that it is the most abundant parrot in the Florida area and flocks of hundreds are all over the Miami area. On the 77th Christmas Bird Count the species was still fairly

widespread in some areas of Florida. They were recorded at Fort Lauderdale, Naples, Tampa and some 394 birds from Dade County (Heilbrun, 1977).

Elsewhere in the United States flocks of up to fifty birds have been reported from eastern Long Island and once from eastern Connecticut on the east coast of America. Bull (1973) says that they have survived at least one winter so appear to be fairly well established in this area.

Their origin in America does not appear to be known. Hardy says that the species is commonly kept in pet shops in the areas where it is established in California. Many of them were imported into the country between 1968 and 1970, Clapp and Banks (1973, in Owre) say some 124 000 in this period, which indicates that they became established probably from escapees or birds deliberately released by private individuals.

DAMAGE

Canary-winged Parakeets have been reported, in the USA, to have destroyed mangoes and other fruits in suburban Miami (Owre, 1973). In 1973 a bird imported into the United States was found to be positive for Newcastle Disease (Hardy, 1973).

ORANGE-CHINNED PARAKEET
(Tovi Parakeet)
Brotogeris jugularis (Müller)

DISTINGUISHING CHARACTERISTICS

15-19 cm (6-7.6 in)

Generally green, but crown, lower back and rump tinged with blue; chin orange; wings with large olive-brown shoulder patch and blue tip; tail blue-green; bill horn.

Forshaw, 1973, p.469, pl. p.471.

GENERAL DISTRIBUTION

Central and South America: from southern Mexico south to northern and western Venezuela and northern Colombia.

INTRODUCED DISTRIBUTION

Introduced, probably unsuccessfully, in the USA and the Hawaiian Islands.

GENERAL HABITS

Status: common. *Habitat:* open forest, open woods, lowlands, farmlands and towns. *Gregariousness:* pairs, family parties and flocks of 10-30 or 50 in the non-breeding season. *Movements:* no information. *Foods:* fruits, nectar, blossoms, seeds and vegetable matter. *Breeding:* Jan-May. *Nest:* holes in trees and arboreal termites' nests. *Eggs:* 4 (in captivity).

Forshaw, 1973, pp.469-472.

Orange-chinned Parakeet, *Brotogeris jugularis*

Orange-chinned Parakeet

were reported to be still present in Dade County (Heilbrun, 1976 and 1977).

Hawaiian Islands. Orange-chinned Parakeets were possibly introduced to the Hawaiian Islands as they were mentioned as having been imported to the islands (Munro, 1960). There are no details of any releases and the species is not now established there. They are known to have escaped from captivity on the island of Oahu on some occasions (Berger, 1972).

DAMAGE
In northern Colombia, Orange-chinned Parakeets cause much damage to cultivated fruits (Darlington, 1931, in Forshaw, 1973).

HISPANIOLAN AMAZON
Amazona ventralis (Müller)

DISTINGUISHING CHARACTERISTICS
28 cm (11.2 in)

Generally green with feathers of upper parts edged black; forehead white; crown and upper cheeks dull blue; ear-coverts black; rose-red spot on chin; variable maroon patch on lower abdomen; wings edged blue; tail green, yellow tipped and basally marked with red; bill horn.

Forshaw, 1973, p.516, pl. p.519.

GENERAL DISTRIBUTION
West Indies: Hispaniola and some offshore islands.

INTRODUCED DISTRIBUTION
Introduced successfully to Puerto Rico.

GENERAL HABITS
Status: locally abundant; popular cage bird. *Habitat:* forest and woodlands. *Gregariousness:* pairs, trios and small flocks, larger flocks at roosts. *Movements:* sedentary, but local movements probably governed by food. *Foods:* fruits, seeds, berries, nuts and probably blossom. *Breeding:* variable, April onwards. *Nest:* hole in a tree. *Eggs:* 2-3, rarely 4.

NOTES ON INTRODUCTIONS
USA. The Orange-chinned Parakeet is occasionally reported as an escapee in the New York area (Bull, 1973) and a group of seven birds was found in Dade County, Florida in 1970 (Owre, 1973). Owre indicates that there is increasing evidence of numbers of Orange-chinned Parakeets around Miami in southern Florida.

The species may yet become permanently established in the USA as recently (late 1976), some

Hispaniolan Amazon

Forshaw, 1973, pp.516-517.

Forshaw, 1973, pp.516-517.

NOTES ON INTRODUCTIONS

Puerto Rico. Hispaniolan Amazons have been introduced to Puerto Rico where they are well established and breeding. According to Forshaw (1973) the introduction was unintentional, birds captured in the Dominican Republic were taken by boat to Puerto Rico for sale in the pet trade. Authorities would not allow their import and they could not be returned because of possible legal action in the Dominican Republic. They were released outside the port of Mayaguez and many reached land.

DAMAGE

Dod (in Forshaw, 1973) says that they eat bananas and plantains and will attack some cultivated crops such as maize and pigeon peas or guandules.

WHITE-FRONTED AMAZON
(White-fronted Parrot)
Amazona albifrons (Sparrman)

DISTINGUISHING CHARACTERISTICS

23-26 cm (9.2-10.4 in)

Generally green, feathers of upper parts edged with black; lores and around eyes red; forehead white; crown blue; red patch on wing edge; wing tips and bar on wings forming an inverted blue V mark; tail green, tipped yellow, and red near base; bill yellowish. Female: similar but lacks red wing patch.

Forshaw, 1973, pp.517-518, pl. p.523.

GENERAL DISTRIBUTION

Central America: from western and southern Mexico to western Costa Rica.

INTRODUCED DISTRIBUTION

Introduced in Florida, USA but doubtfully established there.

GENERAL HABITS

Status: common. *Habitat:* forest and secondary growth, woodland, cacti, watercourses, savannah,

White-fronted Amazon

pinelands and open country. *Gregariousness:* pairs or small flocks up to 20, roosts up to 1000 birds. *Movements:* some seasonal movements. *Foods:* fruits, nuts, seeds, berries, blossom and probably leaf buds. *Breeding:* Nov (?)-Apr, but little known. *Eggs:* no information.

Forshaw, 1973, pp.518-520.

NOTES ON INTRODUCTIONS

USA. According to Owre (1973) the White-fronted Amazon was present in the Miami area of Florida in the early 1970s and may have been breeding there. However, there appear to be no further records of them.

DAMAGE

Forshaw (1973) says that White-fronted Amazons can be troublesome in crop growing districts, feeding on the ripening grain.

GREEN-CHEEKED AMAZON
(Red-crowned Parrot)
Amazona viridigenalis (Cassin)

DISTINGUISHING CHARACTERISTICS

30-33 cm (12-13.2 in)

Generally green, paler and yellower on underparts; feathers of upper parts edged black; crown crimson; violet-blue band above eyes and down neck; cheeks and ear-coverts bright green; red patch on wing edge; tail green, tipped yellow-green; bill yellowish horn.

Forshaw, 1973, pp.526, 528, pl. p.531.

GENERAL DISTRIBUTION

Mexico: north-eastern Mexico from Nuevo Leon and Tamaulipas south to northern Veracruz.

INTRODUCED DISTRIBUTION

Introduced successfully in the USA (Florida ?) and probably in the Hawaiian Islands (Oahu ?).

GENERAL HABITS

Status: common. *Habitat:* deciduous forest, woodlands, dry pine-oak ridges and streamsides. *Gregariousness:* large flocks of 20-100 birds. *Movements:* no information. *Foods:* fruits, seeds, nuts, berries, buds and flowers. *Breeding:* Apr-(?). *Nest:* hole in a tree. *Eggs:* 2.

Forshaw, 1973, p.528.

NOTES ON INTRODUCTIONS

USA. The Green-cheeked Amazon is possibly established in south-eastern Florida and doubtfully established in California and south Texas in the United States.

Owre (1973) says that they are the most abundant of the exotic parrots feral in south-eastern Florida. They have been reported from the Florida Keys and were common throughout metropolitan Miami and Fort Lauderdale. Owre found a flock of thirty-two birds on the University of Miami Campus where they were nesting. In 1975-76 they were still present at Fort Lauderdale, Dade County and at West Palm Beach (Heilbrun, 1976 and 1977) and in 1976, four birds were noted near Lantana, south of West Palm Beach (Edscorn, 1977).

Some were seen in the Rio Grande Delta region of south Texas and also at Madero (Webster, 1974). In 1976 a flock of six birds had been present in Brownsville for over one year, but as yet there was no evidence of breeding (Webster, 1977).

According to Hardy (1973) Green-cheeked

Amazons are rare and very local in California. Two adults were found in north Pasadena, near Orange Grove Boulevard in 1963, however, there is no evidence of them breeding in the area and those seen were probably escapees as the species is common in pet shops in the area.

Hawaiian Islands. Green-cheeked Amazons may be established on the island of Oahu, but their present status is poorly known (Hawaiian Audubon Society, 1975). Heilbrun (1976) reports them as present there in 1975, and Pyle (1976 and 77) indicates that from one to nine birds have been seen in the years since 1971.

DAMAGE

The Green-cheeked Amazon can be a troublesome pest in cornfields in Mexico (Forshaw, 1973).

RED-LORED AMAZON
(Yellow-cheeked Parrot, Red-lored Parrot)
Amazona autumnalis (Linnaeus)

DISTINGUISHING CHARACTERISTICS

31-35 cm (12.4-14 in)

Generally green, feathers on upper parts edged dusky black; forehead and lores red; crown scaled blue; ear-coverts and upper cheeks yellow; wings tipped blue, and with red patch on edge; bill grey, upper mandible with yellowish horn.

Forshaw, 1973, pp.529-530, pl. p.533.

GENERAL DISTRIBUTION

Central and South America: from eastern Mexico, south to western Ecuador, and in the Amazon Basin, Brazil.

INTRODUCED DISTRIBUTION

Introduced possibly successfully in California, USA.

GENERAL HABITS

Status: common. *Habitat:* forest, woodland, plantations, clearings, pine ridges and pine savannah. *Gregariousness:* pairs or flocks of 6-100. *Movements:* no information. *Foods:* fruits, seeds, nuts, berries, buds and blossom. *Breeding:* Feb-June (?). *Nest:* hollow in trunk of tree. *Eggs:* 2 (?).

Forshaw, 1973, pp.530, 532.

NOTES ON INTRODUCTIONS

USA. A small colony of Red-lored Amazons appears to be established in California, but it seems doubtful that they will continue to survive.

Hardy (1973) indicates that they are known from observations in down town San Bernardino, California since about 1968. Fisk and Crabtree (1974) noted two birds in the residential area of Loma Linda, San Bernardino, but add that they were probably feral birds which had escaped or been released, although they are not a common aviary bird.

DAMAGE

Russell (1964, in Forshaw, 1973) reports that in British Honduras they often raid ripening citrus and mango fruits.

YELLOW-CROWNED AMAZON
(Yellow-naped Parrot, Yellow-headed Parrot)
Amazona ochrocephala (Gmelin)

DISTINGUISHING CHARACTERISTICS

30-38 cm (12-15.2 in). Females 406-451 g (14.32-15.91 oz)

Generally green, paler and yellower on underparts; head and neck yellow, variably marked with green; ear-coverts and cheeks emerald-green, or yellow in 261 some subspecies; wings with red patch and violet-blue tip, bend of wing red; tail green, tipped yellowish green and with some red near base; bill dark grey, orange on sides of upper mandible.

Forshaw, 1973, p.542, pls. pp.543, 547.

GENERAL DISTRIBUTION

Central and South America: central Mexico south to the Amazon Basin, Brazil and to eastern Peru; also Trinidad (now rare) and the Trés Marias Islands.

INTRODUCED DISTRIBUTION

Introduced, possibly successfully, in the USA and on Trinidad (?). Introduced unsuccessfully in the Hawaiian Islands.

GENERAL HABITS

Status: common, but becoming rare in many localities through clearing and trapping; popular cage bird. *Habitat:* forest, thorn forest, open woodland, savannah, pine ridges, arid areas, plantations, watercourses, cornfields and suburban areas. *Gregariousness:* pairs or small flocks to about 20 birds, and occasionally flocks up to 300. *Movements:* no information. *Foods:* fruits, seeds, nuts, berries, blossom and probably leaf buds. *Breeding:* Jan-May. *Nest:* hollow in a tree or termites' nest. *Eggs:* 3-4 (?).

Forshaw, 1973, pp.545-546, 548.

NOTES ON INTRODUCTIONS

USA. The Yellow-crowned Amazon appears to be established in at least a small area of California and possibly in New York. They have been observed over a wide area of Los Angeles in California. According to Hardy (1973) a flock of from two to twenty birds has, since about 1962, inhabited Orange Grove Boulevard, Pasadena. Four were noted in 1972 and a flock of thirty in Alhambra in 1970. He records that they have been reported from north Pasadena, Alhambra, Westwood, west Los Angeles, Lomita and San Bernardino. Other observations have come from

Yellow-crowned Amazon,
Amazona ochrocephala auropalliata

Brentwood, Glendale, Altadena, Glendora, Ontario and Pomona. More recently three birds were observed at Loma Linda, San Bernardino in 1973 (Fisk and Crabtree, 1974) and two in the Los Angeles area in 1975 (Heilbrun, 1976).

Those birds seen are undoubtedly accidental escapees or intentional releases, but breeding in the wild is likely as immature birds have been observed.

Elsewhere in the United States occasional escapees are found in the wild. In New York (Bull, 1973) some have survived at least one winter. In 1973 some were recorded in the Rio Grande Delta region of south Texas (Webster, 1974) and a flock of eleven birds was noted at Southmost Palms in 1976 (Webster, 1977).

Hawaiian Islands. Birds of the race *A.o. auropalliata* were reported from around the base of Diamond Head, Oahu, in 1969 and 1970, but the species is not known to be established there (Berger, 1972).

Trinidad. Escaped cage birds occur on Trinidad where the wild species is now rare (Ffrench, 1973).

DAMAGE

Land (1970) says that Yellow-crowned Amazons commonly feed in cornfields in their native range.

ORANGE-WINGED AMAZON
(Orange-winged Parrot)
Amazona amazonica (Linnaeus)

DISTINGUISHING CHARACTERISTICS

31-33 cm (12.4-13.2 in). 298-469 g (10.51-16.54 oz) Generally green, upper feathers edged dusky black; crown and cheeks behind beak yellow; violet-blue above eyes, remainder of cheeks bright green; wings violet-blue tipped, and with an orange patch; tail green, tipped yellow-green, barred with darker green and tinged with orange-red; bill horn.

Forshaw, 1973, p.548, pl. p.551.

GENERAL DISTRIBUTION

South America: northern South America from Colombia, Venezuela, Guyana, Surinam and Guyane south to eastern Peru and southern Brazil; also on Trinidad and Tobago.

INTRODUCED DISTRIBUTION

Introduced unsuccessfully in the USA.

GENERAL HABITS

Status: common; favourite cage bird. *Habitat:* forests, timbered sand ridges, mangroves, and open country with scattered trees. *Gregariousness:* pairs or small flocks up to 50, but congregate in large flocks of up to 600 birds to roost. *Movements:* no information. *Foods:* fruits, seeds, nuts, berries, blossom and leaf buds. *Breeding:* Jan-June. *Nest:* hollow in a tree or palm. *Eggs:* 2-4, 5.

Forshaw, 1973, pp.549-550.

Yellow-crowned Amazon

Orange-winged Amazon

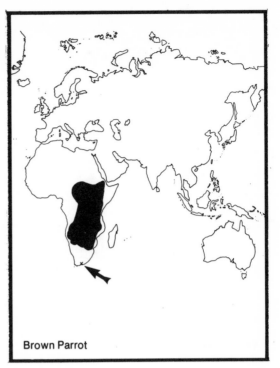

Brown Parrot

USA. Orange-winged Amazons have been noted wild on several occasions in the Miami area of Florida (Owre, 1973). There do not appear to have been any further records of this species for some years and it is doubtful that they became established there.

DAMAGE
Poonai (1969, in Forshaw, 1973) points out that in Guyana the Orange-winged Amazon attacks cultivated fruits particularly oranges and mangoes. Also, in some districts where they occur they are troublesome at times in cacao plantations by eating the beans (Ffrench, 1973).

BROWN PARROT
(Meyer's Parrot)
Poicephalus meyeri (Cretzschmar)

DISTINGUISHING CHARACTERISTICS
21 cm (8.4 in)
Generally sooty brown; yellow band on crown (variable); rump and underparts bluish green; bend of wing and thighs yellow; bill dark grey.
Forshaw, 1973, pp.296, 298, pl. p.297.

Brown Parrot, *Poicephalus meyeri*

GENERAL DISTRIBUTION
Central and eastern Africa: from southern Sudan, western Ethiopia and north-eastern Cameroon south to southern Angola, northern South West Africa and Lesotho.

INTRODUCED DISTRIBUTION
Introduced successfully in Cape Province, South Africa.

GENERAL HABITS
Status: common. *Habitat:* savannah, watercourses, secondary growth near cultivation and acacia scrubland. *Gregariousness:* pairs or small flocks, but large numbers congregate at food sources. *Movements:* sedentary, but local movements in some areas. *Foods:* seeds, nuts, berries, fruits and sometimes grain. *Breeding:* June-Dec. *Nest:* hole in tree. *Eggs:* 2-4.
Forshaw, 1973, pp.298-299.

NOTES ON INTRODUCTIONS
South Africa. Roberts (1946) records that the Brown Parrot has probably been introduced to Cape Province. Clancey (1965, in Forshaw, 1973) says that this isolated population in the eastern Cape Province probably originated from aviary escapees.

The race established is *P.m. transvaalensis* (Mackworth-Praed and Grant, 1957-74).

DAMAGE
Forshaw (1973) indicates that Brown Parrots sometimes attack grain crops, and White (1945, in Forshaw) reports that large flocks raid maize crops in December and January in Zambia.

VASA PARROT
Coracopsis vasa (Shaw)

DISTINGUISHING CHARACTERISTICS
50 cm (20 in)
Generally brownish black, somewhat greyish on the underparts; under tail grey; faint darker band across tail; bill pale horn.

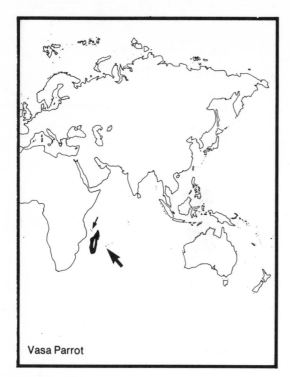

Vasa Parrot

Forshaw, 1973, p.282, pl. p.285.

GENERAL DISTRIBUTION
Malagasy and the Archipel des Comores.

INTRODUCED DISTRIBUTION
Introduced unsuccessfully to Réunion.

GENERAL HABITS
Status: common. *Habitat:* forest, savannah and open country. *Gregariousness:* small parties, but may congregate to feed or roost in flocks of hundreds. *Movements:* no information. *Foods:* fruits, nuts, berries and seeds. *Breeding:* Oct-Dec, not well

known. *Nest:* hollow in a limb, or hole in a tree. *Eggs:* 3 (?).

Forshaw, 1973, pp.282-283.

NOTES ON INTRODUCTIONS
Réunion. The Vasa Parrot has been introduced to Réunion, but there are no reports of its continued presence there so the introduction was probably unsuccessful (Forshaw, 1973).

DAMAGE
Rand (1936) reports that in Malagasy they are a pest in cornfields, attacking standing crops.

ECLECTUS PARROT
Eclectus roratus (Müller)

DISTINGUISHING CHARACTERISTICS
33-35 cm (13.2-14 in)
Generally green with sides of body red; upper tail green, lower black; upper mandible coral, tipped yellow, lower black. Female: generally red, darker on back and wings; lower breast, abdomen and upper mantle dull purple; bend of wing mauve-blue; tail tipped above and below with orange-yellow, lower dusky orange; bill black.

Forshaw, 1973, pp.194, 196, pls. pp.195, 197.

GENERAL DISTRIBUTION
Indonesia to the Solomons: Moluccas, Lesser Sunda, Tanimbar, Aru and Kai Islands (Indonesia), New Guinea and offshore islands, Cape York Peninsula (Australia), Admiralty Islands, the Bismarck Archipelago east to the Solomon Islands.

INTRODUCED DISTRIBUTION
Introduced, probably successfully in the Palau Archipelago and on the Goram Islands, Indonesia. Introduced unsuccessfully in the Hawaiian Islands.

GENERAL HABITS
Status: common. *Habitat:* rainforest, lowlands and savannah. *Gregariousness:* pairs or small parties, but larger flocks congregate at food sources. *Movements:*

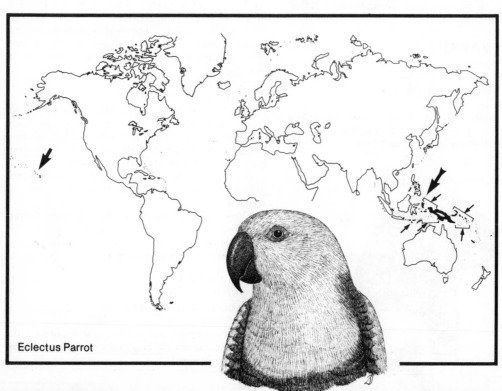

Eclectus Parrot

sedentary. *Foods:* fruits, nuts, seeds, berries, leaf buds, blossom and nectar. *Breeding:* June-Jan; communal (?). *Nest:* hole in the trunk of a tree. *Eggs:* 2.

Forshaw, 1973, pp.198-199.

NOTES ON INTRODUCTIONS

Palau Archipelago. It appears that stray captive Eclectus Parrots have become established on Aulupsechel Island in the Palau Group (Ripley, 1951). Ripley noted one bird on Aulupsechel Island and a flock of ten on another island. Forshaw (1973) records that the race introduced is probably *E.r. polychloros.*

Goram. Forshaw (1973) mentions that the race *E.r. polychloros* has been introduced on the Goram Islands but gives no other details.

Hawaiian Islands. Berger (1972) adds the Eclectus Parrot to his list of escapees in Hawaii, and Pyle (1977) indicates that a single bird was found there in 1972. There are no subsequent records for the species in these islands.

DAMAGE

Eclectus Parrots are reported to be very destructive to fruit crops in native gardens on the Solomon Islands.

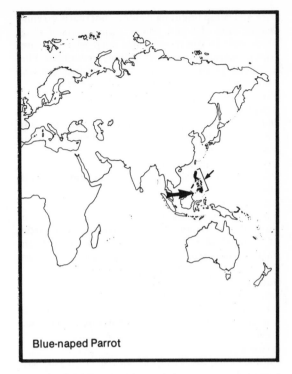

Blue-naped Parrot

BLUE-NAPED PARROT
Tanygnathus lucionensis (Linnaeus)

DISTINGUISHING CHARACTERISTICS

31 cm (12.4 in)

Generally green, brighter on head and rump; a blue patch behind crown on neck; bend of wing black, median coverts black margined with orange-yellow, other wing feathers with blue; tail green above, dusky yellow below; bill red, paler at tip.

Forshaw, 1973, p.190, pl. p.189.

GENERAL DISTRIBUTION

Philippine Islands and small islands in the Celebes Sea.

INTRODUCED DISTRIBUTION

Possibly introduced, successfully on some islands off the Borneo coast and has been recorded on the Borneo mainland (stray captive ?).

GENERAL HABITS

Status: common; popular cage bird. *Habitat:* forest, open country and cultivated fields. *Gregariousness:* flocks of 10-20 birds fairly common. *Movements:* no information. *Foods:* seeds, berries, fruits and nuts. *Breeding:* June, but detail lacking. *Nest:* hole in a tree. *Eggs:* no information.

Forshaw, 1973, pp.190-191.

NOTES ON INTRODUCTIONS

Borneo. According to Hachisuka (1934) an escaped captive Blue-naped Parrot has been collected in eastern Borneo. There are however, no further records of the species in that region.

Small islands off the Borneo coast. Gore (1968) reports that Blue-naped parrots are residents on both Mantanani Island and the Si-amil Islands where they may have been introduced. There were some thirty to 100 birds there in 1962. Kloss (1930, in Forshaw, 1973) suggests that they may have been introduced to islands off the coast of Borneo by sailing craft from the Sula Archipelago. However, according to Thomson (1966, in Forshaw) they are naturally established residents.

DAMAGE

The Blue-naped Parrot is a grain eater and can be troublesome in corn growing areas (Forshaw, 1973).

GREAT-BILLED PARROT
Tanygnathus megalorynchos (Boddaert)

DISTINGUISHING CHARACTERISTICS

41 cm (16.4 in)

Head, upper mantle and upper tail-coverts bright green; lower mantle dull green, tipped pale blue;

Great-billed Parrot

back and rump bright pale blue; underparts greenish yellow; sides of breast yellow; upper parts of wings black, median coverts margined deep yellow, greater coverts margined greenish yellow, remainder blue margined green; tail green above tipped greenish yellow, below dusky yellow; bill red, with paler tip.
Forshaw, 1973, pp.187-188, pl. p.187.

GENERAL DISTRIBUTION
Indonesia: the western Papuan, Tanimbar and Lesser Sunda Islands, Moluccas and islands north and south of Sulawesi.

INTRODUCED DISTRIBUTION
Possibly introduced, successfully on Balut Island, Indonesia.

GENERAL HABITS
Status: fairly common. *Habitat:* coastal areas of small islands. *Gregariousness:* singly or small parties of up to 20 or more. *Movements:* no information. *Foods:* fruits and nuts. *Breeding:* not known, Dec (?). *Nest:* hollow in a tree. *Eggs:* no information.
Forshaw, 1973, pp.188, 190.

NOTES ON INTRODUCTIONS
Balut Island. The race *T.m. megalorynchos* has possibly been introduced to this island (Hachisuka, 1934).

DAMAGE
Forshaw (quoting Toxopeus, in Siebers, 1930) says that the Great-billed Parrot attacks corn crops.

ALEXANDRINE PARAKEET
(Large Parakeet, Great-billed Parakeet)
Psittacula eupatria (Linnaeus)

DISTINGUISHING CHARACTERISTICS
51-58 cm (20.4-23.2 in). 220-225 g (7.76-7.94 oz)
Generally green; cheeks with greyish blue, a faint black stripe from cere to eye, and a broad black stripe across the lower cheek patch; wide rose-pink collar on hindneck; dark purple-red patch on wing shoulder;

Alexandrine Parakeet

tail tipped yellow, under tail yellowish; bill red. Female: duller, no black stripe on rose-pink collar.
Forshaw, 1973, pp.324, 326, pl. p.325.

GENERAL DISTRIBUTION
Southern Asia: from Sri Lanka, eastern Afghanistan and western Pakistan to Indochina and the Andaman Islands.

INTRODUCED DISTRIBUTION
Became feral, or wandering parties in Karachi, Pakistan, Bombay and Calcutta, India.

GENERAL HABITS
Status: common; a favourite pet bird in India and Thailand. *Habitat:* jungle, forest, mangroves, wooded country, cultivated farmland, parks, gardens, plantations, villages and urban areas. *Gregariousness:* parties or small flocks, but flock in large numbers to roost. *Movements:* mainly sedentary, but with some nomadic movements and fluctuations in population. *Foods:* seeds, nuts, berries, fruits, blossom, grain, leaf buds and nectar. *Breeding:* Nov-Apr. *Nest:* hole in tree or rarely a crevice in a chimney, wall or even under the roof of a building. *Eggs:* 2-4.
Forshaw, 1973, p.326.

NOTES ON INTRODUCTIONS
India and Pakistan. Populations of Alexandrine Parakeets around such major cities as Karachi, Bombay and Calcutta could have originated from aviary escapees (Forshaw, 1973), although Eates (1937) suggests that wandering parties could reach Karachi.

DAMAGE
Along with other species Alexandrine Parakeets cause considerable damage to orchard fruit and ripening crops (Ali, 1962) and appear to be wholly harmful to man's interests in India (Abdulali, pers. comm.). Forshaw records that they raid such crops as maize, wheat and rice, and cause considerable damage in orchards where their wasteful feeding habits result in the destruction of much more fruit than is actually eaten.

ROSE-RINGED PARAKEET
(African or Indian Ring-necked Parakeet)
Psittacula krameri (Scopoli)

DISTINGUISHING CHARACTERISTICS
40-41 cm (16-16.4 in). 116-139 g (4.09-4.9 oz)
Generally pale green; chin black and continuing black across lower cheeks; rose-pink collar on hindneck, nape with some blue; tail darker green with central feathers bluish, tipped yellow-green; bill, upper mandible dark red, black towards tip, lower black with red markings near base. Female: no black stripe on chin or cheeks and no rose-pink collar; line from cere to eye less prominent.
Forshaw, 1973, pp.327-328, pl. p.329.

GENERAL DISTRIBUTION
Africa and southern Asia: central and north-eastern Africa from Guinea and Sénégal east to western Uganda, Sudan and north-western Somali Republic. In southern Asia from Afghanistan, Pakistan to India, Nepal, central Burma and Sri Lanka.

INTRODUCED DISTRIBUTION
Introduced successfully in Mauritius, Zanzibar Island and England; possibly or probably introduced, successfully in Oman, Peoples Democratic Republic

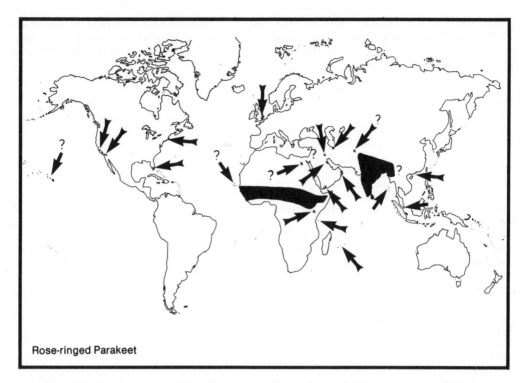

Rose-ringed Parakeet

of Yemen, Hong Kong and Macau, Kenya (? extension in range) and the USA; successfully introduced but now extirpated in Egypt (?) and Singapore. Introduced unsuccessfully to the Cape Verde Islands (?), the Hawaiian and the Andaman Islands.

Note: Forshaw (1973) indicates that unconfirmed reports of this species' presence have come from south-eastern China, Indochina and Lebanon. He suggests that they may have been introduced to such areas as Iraq, Iran, Kuwait and Afghanistan, but that further investigation is needed. Indeed, their presence in so many areas in that region suggests a former much larger distribution joining the African and Asian populations.

GENERAL HABITS

Status: common and abundant; extremely common cage bird. *Habitat:* secondary jungle, wooded country, cultivated farmlands, plantations and the vicinity of habitation. *Gregariousness:* small parties or flocks, but may congregate in huge flocks of hundreds or even thousands at food sources. *Movements:* sedentary, but local movements associated with the ripening of crops. *Foods:* grain, seeds, berries, fruit, blossom and nectar. *Breeding:* varies, Aug-Nov (Africa); Dec-May (India). *Nest:* hollow limb, or hole in a tree. *Eggs:* 2-6, usually 3-4 (Mauritius 4).

Forshaw, 1973, pp.328, 330.

NOTES ON INTRODUCTIONS

Mauritius. The race *P.k. borealis* has been introduced and established on Mauritius. Rountree *et al* (1952) and Staub (1976) claim that they were accidentally released from an aviary in about 1886 in Grand Port where they multiplied rapidly. They indicate that the species is confined to the coastal plains in the south and south-east and the Alma-Quartier Militair and Pamplemousses areas.

Zanzibar. The race *P.k. borealis* was introduced to

Zanzibar from India at an unknown date (Mackworth-Praed and Grant, 1957-74). Pakenham (1939, 43 and 45) records them there in 1936, 1937, 1940 and in 1945. He says that as they are universal cage birds in India, without doubt the present birds on Zanzibar were thus imported and thereafter achieved their liberty. According to Mackworth-Praed and Grant the species is extending its range on the island year by year.

Egypt. It seems likely that the Rose-ringed Parakeet became established in Egypt as a result of the escape of cage birds. Flower (1933) indicates that they were common there long before 1912, although Meinertzhagen (1930) records that they were introduced in the Egyptian Delta at that date. Hachisuka (1924) records that they were common and increasing at El Giza and had been introduced 'not very long ago'. They became numerous in the environs of Cairo about 1915 and in the years 1916 to 1919 some 127 birds were killed in the Giza Zoological Gardens (Flower). In 1930, Meinertzhagen records that they are thoroughly established at El Giza, in isolated areas around Cairo, and are occasionally seen up the Nile to Helwan and at the Delta Barrage. He reports that the nature and source of the introductions are unknown.

Vaurie (1965, in Forshaw, 1973) indicates that the race introduced was *P.k. borealis.* Etchécopar and Hüe (1967, in Forshaw) point out that although they were introduced in the Giza district of Lower Egypt they may no longer survive there.

Oman. Forshaw (1973) reports that this species has been found near Al Khābūrah, Batah and at Suwaik, where they were presumably introduced. Vaurie claims that *P.k. borealis* has been introduced in this country but de Schauensee and Ripley (1953, in Forshaw) ascribe the Oman birds to *P.k. manillensis.*

Peoples Democratic Republic of Yemen. Ennion

(1962) says that Rose-ringed Parakeets are often seen in Tawahi, The Crescent (Aden shopping centre), Crater, Ma'alla and Shaykh Uthman. He estimated that there were at least twenty-two pairs present there in about 1962.

Kuwait. Other than Forshaw's (1973) remark that Rose-ringed Parakeets are present near Ahmadi, there appear no details of any introduction.

Iraq. Marchant (1963, in Forshaw, 1973) observed Rose-ringed Parakeets at Karradah Sharqiyah in 1959 and says that the species was fairly often recorded in the Baghdād area between 1938 and 1952. They have also been observed at Al Kut.

According to Forshaw the paucity of records suggests the decline of a local colony probably originating from escapees.

Iran. Forshaw (1973) reports that Rose-ringed Parakeets have been observed in city gardens in Tehran and at Bandar Abbas on the Persian Gulf.

Hong Kong and Macau. Populations of *P.k. borealis* on Hong Kong and Macau appear to be of uncertain origin. Forshaw (1973) says that it is possible that they arrived without aid, but he suggests (as claimed by Herklots, 1940) that they were introduced some time between 1903 and 1913. Vaughn and Jones (1913) found them commonly and regularly breeding in Hong Kong. Webster (1975) says that they were first reported there in 1903 and are now fairly common and widespread, but mainly on the north side of Hong Kong and the Mong Tseng Peninsula. Recently flocks of thirty were noted in the Homantin/Kowloon Tong area.

Singapore. Rose-ringed Parakeets are reported to have been introduced to Singapore Island. Medway and Wells (1976) say that the species was introduced as a cage bird and that escapees have bred on the island. Eggs were found in January 1951, but a feral population is not known to have persisted.

Cape Verde Islands. A Rose-ringed Parakeet was collected on the island of São Tiago in 1909, but there are no further records of the species there (Forshaw, 1973).

Afghanistan. Niethammer and Niethammer (1967, in Forshaw, 1973) report that they saw Rose-ringed Parakeets at Jalalabad, but point out that the species could occur there naturally. Puget (1970, in Forshaw) has recorded several flocks of twelve to fifteen birds at Kabul and Jalalabad. Only further information can determine whether these birds were actually introduced.

Kenya. Cunningham-van Someren (1969) sighted Rose-ringed Parakeets in the Nairobi National Park in 1969 and suggests that they are more than likely escaped birds or the progeny of escaped birds imported from India. They are apparently breeding there. Forshaw (1973) indicates that the race *P.k. krameri* which is established there, may represent an eastern extension of their range.

Hawaiian Islands. According to Munro (1960) Rose-ringed Parakeets which have escaped from captivity are noted from time to time in the Hawaiian Islands, but they do not appear to have become established permanently. However, more recently they have been sighted on Oahu where they may be established, but their present status is not well known (Hawaiian Audubon Society, 1975). Pyle (1977) indicates that small numbers were noted between 1972 and 1975 but that none have been recorded since the latter date.

USA A small group of Rose-ringed Parakeets were established and breeding in the Highland Park community of Los Angeles, California prior to 1964 (possibly established there as early as 1956), but they have now disappeared (Hardy, 1964). They have been reported in the wild from the vicinity of New York where escaped birds have been sighted on numerous occasions (Bull, 1973). A small colony lived around the Bronx Zoo for a few years (Bull, 1974). In Florida there is evidence to suggest that they have been in north Dade County for at least ten years (Owre, 1973). Owre says that the race there is probably *P.k. manillensis* and that immatures have been sighted so that they are possibly breeding there. At least thirty-seven birds were present in Dade County on the 77th Christmas Bird Count (Heilbrun, 1977). In 1974, two separate populations of Ring-necked Parakeets bred successfully in California (Shelgren *et al*, 1975). A pair nested at the Pomona Cemetery, Los Angeles County and another at Vasona Park, Los Gatos in Santa Clara County. The population living in the Vasona Park area may be as high as fifteen to twenty birds. Another pair are reported to have bred at Solvang in Santa Barbara County in 1973, but this has not been confirmed.

Whether the species will remain established in the United States only time will tell. The only more recent records appear to have been of a small flock of up to six in the Bronx-Weschester area of New York in 1975-76 (Heilbrun, 1976 and 1977) and of two birds which were shot at Cucamonga, California, in April 1976 (Keffer, pers. comm. 1977). A flock of up to sixteen birds may be present in this latter area. Also in 1976, a flock of seven birds was present in St Augustine (north-eastern Florida) where they have been present for at least a year (Edscorn, 1977).

Great Britain. Rose-ringed Parakeets have now become permanently established in a few areas in England and appear to be spreading. They have been an extremely popular cage bird there for many years and Lever (1977) indicates that they have frequently escaped from captivity probably since about 1855. In the 1930s a number of birds apparently frequented the gardens around Epping Forest and remained present there for a few years.

Rose-ringed Parakeet, *Psittacula krameri*

Feral birds have been in the Northfleet area of Kent since 1969, have been reported from the Bromley-Croydon area on the Kent-Surrey border and have been present in the Woodford Green area in south-western Essex since 1971 (Anon, 1974; Hudson, 1974). England (1974) reports that they are established in two areas of Essex, Kent and in two widely separate areas of Surrey.

The species has now survived through several winters and has been reported by Hudson to have bred in 1971 at Croydon and also at Esher in Surrey. Lever (1976, pers. comm.) says that they first bred in the Southfleet area west of Rochester in Kent in 1969. Since then they have spread into other parts of Kent and into neighbouring counties of Essex, Surrey and East Sussex; odd individuals have been seen further afield in West Sussex, Berkshire and Buckinghamshire.

Areas where they have been noted since 1970 include: Esher and Claygate, Surrey in 1970; Woodford Green and Highams Park, Essex in 1971; Old Windsor, Berkshire and Wraysburg, Buckinghamshire in 1972; Bexley area, Kent in 1973; Cuckmere Valley, East Sussex and Chichester Harbour, West Sussex in 1974; Hollingbury Park, Brighton and Herstmonceux, East Sussex in 1975, and have been recorded breeding at Croydon (1971), between Esher and Claygate, Surrey in 1971 and again in 1973-74, Gravesend, Northdown Park and Langley Park (1975), at Thundersley, Essex and at Stockport in Manchester where they have been present since 1974-75 (Lever, 1977).

They are now considered to be well established in a crescent-shaped area extending from south-west through south, south-east and east surrounding the suburbs of London. Within this area family parties of twenty birds or more are not uncommon sights (Lever, 1976, pers. comm.).

The establishment of the Rose-ringed Parakeet in England appears to have been brought about by both escapees and deliberate introductions. England (1974) suggests that although escapees may have added to the numbers, deliberate liberation has almost certainly been the main cause of their establishment. Lever (1977) also indicates that many are kept by aviculturists as free flying homing colonies in England.

Andaman Islands. Colonel R. C. Tyler obtained several pairs of Rose-ringed Parakeets from Calcutta and released them at Port Blair in the time of the convict settlement there (Beavan, 1867). Most were apparently recaptured by the convicts, but some were said to have flown off into the jungle. There are no further records of these parakeets in the Andamans.

DAMAGE

In India, Rose-ringed Parakeets are serious pests causing enormous losses to ripening grain crops and orchard fruits, generally destroying much more than they actually eat (Ali and Futehally, 1967).

At rail sidings it is common to see them clinging to sacks of grain, which they bite into and help themselves to the grain (Ali, 1962). In northern areas of India they frequent cultivation, subsist on fruit and grain and do considerable damage in orchards and market gardens and also to standing food crops.

Sekhon (1966) reports an average loss of 20.6% to a maize crop and 30% damage to guava fruits in the Punjab. Ramzan and Toor (1973) studied the damage caused to maize in this area and say that losses vary between 10.1% and 16.5%. They say that on the basis of their study, the species causes considerable losses to maize crops and warrants some form of control.

Both Sekhon (1966) and Simwat and Sidhu (1973) record damage to a number of crops in the Punjab, all of which are economically important, and all of which were major food sources of the Rose-ringed Parakeet. These included maize, sorghum, pearl-miller, sesame, wheat, Indian mustard, groundnuts, mango, guava, fig, grapes, peach, jambolana, sunflower, barley, gram, sarson and pomegranates.

Little damage due to these parrots appears to have been reported from Africa, although they are recorded (Cunningham — van Someren, 1969) as doing considerable damage to sorghum fields in the Sennar area, Blue Nile.

Where introduced in Mauritius they are now reported to be a destructive pest (Benedict, 1957).

MOUSTACHED PARAKEET
(Princess of Wales' Parakeet, Queen Alexandra's Parakeet)
Psittacula alexandri (Linnaeus)

DISTINGUISHING CHARACTERISTICS
31.7-38 cm (12.6-15.2 in). 133-168 g (4.69-5.93 oz)
Upper parts green, head grey-violet; chin, lower cheeks and line from forehead to eyes black; throat, breast and upper abdomen salmon-pink; lower abdomen and vent green with some blue; tail bluish green; bill coral. Female: breast duller salmon-pink; bill black.
Forshaw, 1973, pp.339-340, pl. p.345.

GENERAL DISTRIBUTION
Southern Asia: from northern India and Nepal to

Moustached Parakeet

Moustached Parakeet, *Psittacula alexandri*

Burma, northern Thailand, southern China; also Java, Bali, islands off Sumatra, Hainan and the Andaman Islands.

INTRODUCED DISTRIBUTION
Introduced successfully in southern Borneo and (?) Pinang Island. Introduced unsuccessfully in Singapore.

GENERAL HABITS
Status: very common. *Habitat:* secondary jungle, forest, woodlands near cultivation, and mangroves. *Gregariousness:* flocks of 10-15 common, occasionally large concentrations at a food source. *Movements:* sedentary, but with local irregular movements often coinciding with the ripening of crops. *Foods:* seeds, nuts, fruits, berries, nectar blossom and leaf buds. *Breeding:* Dec-Apr. *Nest:* hollow in a limb, or hole in a tree. *Eggs:* 3-4.
Forshaw, 1973, p.342.

NOTES ON INTRODUCTIONS
Borneo. Moustached Parakeets were introduced to southern Borneo probably from Java (Smythies, 1960). They have apparently spread little since their introduction.

According to Forshaw (1973) the race introduced was *P.a. alexandri.*

Pinang Island. The Moustached· Parakeet has apparently been introduced to Pinang Island (King *et al,* 1975), but no details are known.
Singapore Island. Gibson-Hill (1949) reports that Moustached Parakeets were seen on several occasions on Changi Promontory in August 1943. He suggests that they were escaped cage birds. Medway and Wells (1976) report that escapees are seen intermittently on Singapore Island where they have laid eggs, but do not become permanently established.

DAMAGE
Moustached Parakeets can cause serious damage to rice crops (Forshaw, 1973). They do not appear to have caused any concern in Borneo as yet.

PLUM-HEADED PARAKEET
(Blossom-headed Parakeet, Rose-headed Parakeet)
Psittacula cyanocephala (Linnaeus)

DISTINGUISHING CHARACTERISTICS
30-36 cm (12-14.4 in). 56-71.5 g (1.98-2.52 oz)
Mainly green, brighter and more yellow on mantle and underparts; head deep red, tinged bluish purple in parts; chin, lower cheeks and narrow collar black; wide bluish green band on neck; wings dark green with bluish appearance near shoulders and dark red patch on coverts; tail blue, tipped white; bill, upper mandible orange-yellow, lower blackish brown. Female: head dull bluish grey, no black markings and replaced by variable yellow collar, no red wing patch; bill, upper mandible yellow, lower greyish.
Forshaw, 1973, pp. 334, 346 and 347, pl. p.337.

GENERAL DISTRIBUTION
Southern Asia: Sri Lanka, India to west Pakistan and Nepal east to Bhutan and West Bengal, southern China, Thailand, Kampuchea, Vietnam, central and southern Annam and southern and central Laos.

INTRODUCED DISTRIBUTION
Introduced unsuccessfully in the USA.

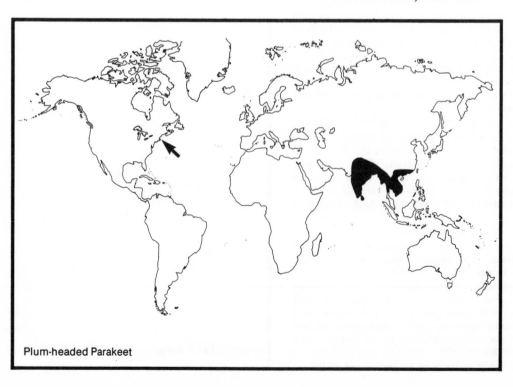

Plum-headed Parakeet

Status: fairly common. *Habitat:* wooded hills and plains, forest near cultivation, secondary growth and open areas. *Gregariousness:* family parties or small flocks, occasionally in large flocks of several hundred. *Movements:* sedentary, but with local movements governed by food supply. *Foods:* fruits, nuts, blossom, seeds, grain and leaf buds. *Breeding:* Dec-May; may breed twice a year in some areas; sometimes colonial. *Nest:* hollow in a limb or hole in a tree, occasionally crevices in buildings. *Eggs:* 4-6, 8. Forshaw, 1973, p.334.

NOTES ON INTRODUCTIONS

USA. Plum-headed Parakeets have been reported in small numbers in the wild in New York (Bull, 1973). There appear to be no more recent records from the United States and the species has more than likely failed to become permanently established.

DAMAGE

According to Forshaw (1973) the Plum-headed Parakeet can be a serious pest in orchards and rice fields in its native range.

RED SHINING PARROT
(Red-breasted Musk-Parrot)
Prosopeia tabuensis (Gmelin)

DISTINGUISHING CHARACTERISTICS

45 cm (18 in)

Head and underparts red or reddish black; collar of dark blue across upper mantle; wings, back and rump bright green; wing feathers mauve-blue towards ends; tail green above with some blue, below grey-black; bill grey-black.

Forshaw, 1973, p.202, pl. p.204.

GENERAL DISTRIBUTION

Fijian Islands.

INTRODUCED DISTRIBUTION

Introduced successfully to Tongatabu (extinct) .and Eua, Tonga Islands and to Viti Levu (scarce) and Ovalau, Fiji.

GENERAL HABITS

Status: fairly common. *Habitat:* rain forest, mangroves and villages. *Gregariousness:* singly, pairs, or associate in small parties. *Movements:* no information. *Foods:* fruits, berries, seeds and probably insect larvae. *Breeding:* Aug (?). *Nest:* hollow in a tree. *Eggs:* 3 (?).

Forshaw, 1973, pp.202-203.

NOTES ON INTRODUCTIONS

Tonga. According to Peters (1937) and Mayr (1945) it is believed that *P.t. tabuensis* has been introduced to the small islets of Tongatabu and Eua. Forshaw (1973) says that they are apparently no longer present on Tongatabu but still occur on Eua.

Fiji. Mayr (1945) indicates that *P.t. splendens* has been introduced on Viti Levu and Ovalau in the Fijian Islands. Forshaw (1973) records that the species is very scarce on Viti Levu, and Holyoak (1979) indicates that small populations occurred near some villages in 1973.

DAMAGE

Forshaw (1973) says that early observers have indicated that large flocks of Red Shining Parrots have done considerable damage to maize and other crops in Fiji. However, there appear to be no recent records of any damage.

GREY-HEADED LOVEBIRD
(Madagascar Lovebird)
Agapornis cana (Gmelin)

DISTINGUISHING CHARACTERISTICS

14 cm (5.6 in). 28-31 g (1-1.1 oz)

Generally green, brighter on rump and yellowish on underparts; head, neck and breast light grey; tail green, barred black near tip and with some yellow

Red Shining Parrot

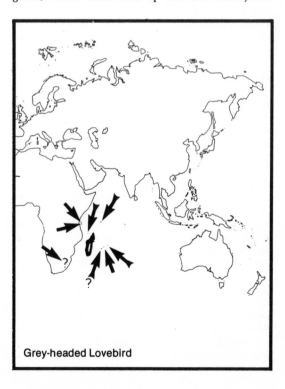

Grey-headed Lovebird

Grey-headed Lovebird, *Agapornis cana*
(male in front, female behind)

spots; bill pale grey. Female: head, neck and breast green.

Forshaw, 1973, pp.301-302, pl. p.305.

GENERAL DISTRIBUTION
Malagasy.

INTRODUCED DISTRIBUTION
Introduced successfully to (?) Rodrigues (rare), (?) Réunion (rare), the (?) Archipel des Comores and the Seychelles; introduced successfully but now died out on Mauritius, Zanzibar and Mafia islands. Possibly introduced, unsuccessfully to Natal, South Africa.

GENERAL HABITS
Status: fairly common. *Habitat:* woodland, scrub, open country on coastal plains and cultivation. *Gregariousness:* small groups of 5-20, but larger flocks of 50-80 have been noted. *Movements:* sedentary. *Foods:* mainly grass seeds, but also grain. *Breeding:* Nov-Apr (?). *Nest:* hollow in a tree to which they carry material such as bark, leaves and stems. *Eggs:* 3-4, 6 (in captivity).

Forshaw, 1973, p.302.

NOTES ON INTRODUCTIONS
Mauritius. The race *A.c. cana* (Peters, 1937) was possibly introduced to Mauritius by the French prior to 1812 (Meinertzhagen, 1912) or by the early Dutch settlers as a cage bird from Madagascar (Staub, 1976). Staub indicates that they were described on Mauritius by Tafforet in 1725. Meinertzhagen indicates that they became plentiful there, but were scarce by 1912. Rountree *et al* (1952) and Staub say that they were probably decimated by the cyclone of April 1892, but this seems unlikely if Meinertzhagen is correct. Both Gill (1967) and Benedict (1957) report that they are no longer present on the island.

Mackworth-Praed and Grant (1952-73) have listed the species as a resident on Mauritius.

Rodrigues. According to Benson (1960) the Grey-headed Lovebird must have been introduced to Rodrigues. Watson *et al* (1963) record that they have been introduced and are fairly common there, but Gill (1967) reports that they are only present in small numbers and Staub (1976) says that they have been considerably reduced in numbers and are now rare, because of the hunting pressure on them.

Réunion. Apparently Madagascar Lovebirds have also been introduced to Réunion, but few details of any introductions are known. Watson *et al* (1963) record that they are constantly re-introduced and

occur there in flocks of up to thirty, but Gill (1967) reports that they are only present in small numbers and Staub (1976) that they are now rare on the island.

Archipel des Comores. The race *A.c. cana* has probably been introduced (Peters, 1937; Benson, 1960) to these islands, although Mackworth-Praed and Grant (1952-73) list them as a resident species. Benson found them present on Anjouan and Mayotte, where they were fairly common around cultivation and open country, and says that more recently they have been found on Grand Comore and Moheli.

Zanzibar and Mafia Islands. Peters (1937) records that the race *A.c. cana* has been introduced to both Mafia and Zanzibar. The species was present in a wild state on both islands up until about 1913, but had disappeared by 1930 (Mackworth-Praed and Grant, 1952-73). The birds introduced may have come from the Comores (Ellis, 1975).

Seychelles. Gaymer *et al* (1969) point out that the Grey-headed Lovebird was introduced to the island of Mahé in 1906 and was once common there.

In the 1930s they were common all over Mahé with huge flocks in Gordon Square, but suffered an abrupt decline in numbers for unknown reasons, and now occur mainly at Port Launay, Anse La Mouche and Anse Boileau in West Mahé (Penny, 1974). Penny says that they also occur on Silouette where they were also introduced.

South Africa. Clancey (1964, in Forshaw, 1973) reports that there was possibly an unsuccessful attempt to introduce *A.c. cana* to Natal in the late 1880s.

DAMAGE
Although Grey-headed Lovebirds feed mainly on fallen rice they are also accused of raiding standing rice crops (Elliott, 1970) in Malagasy. According to Rand (1936) they raid rice which has been spread out to dry around villages. Staub (1976) records that they have been severely reduced in numbers on Rodrigues because of their maize-eating habits.

PEACH-FACED LOVEBIRD
(Rosy-faced Lovebird)
Agapornis roseicollis (Vieillot)

DISTINGUISHING CHARACTERISTICS
15 cm (6 in). 55-56 g (1.94-1.98 oz)
Generally green, more yellowish on underparts; forehead and behind eyes red; lores, cheeks, throat and upper breast rose-pink; rump blue; tail green above, bluish below, barred black at tip; bill horn, tinged green.

Forshaw, 1973, pp.306-307, pl. p.309.

GENERAL DISTRIBUTION
South-western Africa: from southern Angola south to northern Cape Province and inland to Lesotho.

INTRODUCED DISTRIBUTION
Introduced unsuccessfully in Western Australia and to the Hawaiian Islands.

GENERAL HABITS
Status: common. *Habitat:* dry wooded savannah and open country near water, palm groves and mountain country. *Gregariousness:* highly gregarious, in small flocks usually, but flocks of hundreds may congregate at a food source such as maize. *Movements:* no information. *Foods:* seeds, berries, fruits and grain.

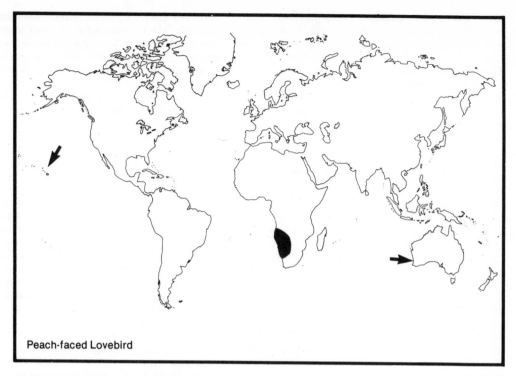

Peach-faced Lovebird

Breeding: Feb-Mar; colonial. *Nest:* in crevices in cliffs or buildings, or in old weavers' nests. *Eggs:* 3-4 (in captivity).
Forshaw, 1973, p.307.

NOTES ON INTRODUCTIONS
Western Australia. Peach-faced Lovebirds are reported (unconfirmed) to have maintained a small colony in the metropolitan area of Perth, around the mid-1960s. They have now disappeared and those seen are generally aviary escapees. A single bird, probably an escapee, was captured at Kelmscott in May 1977.
Hawaiian Islands. The Peach-faced Lovebird has apparently been recorded in the wild on Oahu in the Hawaiian Islands, but is not known to be established there (Berger, 1976).

DAMAGE
Peach-faced Lovebirds are said to do considerable damage to crops when these are planted near their haunts (Roberts, 1940). According to Mackworth-Praed and Grant (1962) they are pests in some grain growing areas of south-western Africa.

FISCHER'S LOVEBIRD
Agapornis fischeri Reichenow

DISTINGUISHING CHARACTERISTICS
15 cm (6 in). 48-53 g (1.69-1.87 oz)
Generally green, more yellowish on underparts; forehead, cheeks and throat orange-red; head olive-green; upper breast and neck collar yellow; tail green with yellow markings and basal black bar on tip; bill red.
Forshaw, 1973, pp.307-308, pl. p.309.

GENERAL DISTRIBUTION
Northern Tanzania, East Africa.

INTRODUCED DISTRIBUTION
Introduced successfully in the Tanga area, Tanzania and in southern Kenya, East Africa.

GENERAL HABITS
Status: common. *Habitat:* grasslands with scattered Acacia, and cultivated country with baobabs. *Gregariousness:* small flocks, but in crop growing areas large flocks of more than 100 may congregate to feed on grain. *Movements:* no information. *Foods:*

Fischer's Lovebird

273

seeds and grains. *Breeding:* May-July; colonial. *Nest:* hole in a tree or cavity in a building, to which nest materials are carried. *Eggs:* up to 5-6 (in captivity).

Forshaw, 1973, p.308.

NOTES ON INTRODUCTIONS

Tanzania. Fischer's Lovebird has been introduced to the Tanga area where they have been breeding in a wild state since about 1928 (Mackworth-Praed and Grant, 1957).

It is possible that many have escaped in a number of areas of Africa. Moreau (1948) mentions that some escaped from a Mr A. C. Robbie of Muholola Farm, a few kilometres south of Saranda, but they did not apparently become established there.

Kenya. Possibly, Fischer's Lovebirds occur naturally in southern Kenya though most reports indicate that they have originated from aviary escapees (Forshaw, 1973). They are however, established in the area and are breeding there, particularly around Lake Naivasha (Cunningham-van Someren, 1969).

Fischer's Lovebirds appear to have been released or escaped at Mombasa where flocks of thirty to forty of them were reported to be present in 1974 (Barlass, 1975). At this time they were said to be hybridising with Masked Lovebirds which were also probably introduced in the area.

DAMAGE

According to Elliott (1970) Fischer's Lovebirds have taken a liking to cultivated millet and have become regarded as pests. Forshaw (1973) says that they attack both millet and maize crops in Africa.

MASKED LOVEBIRD
(Yellow-collared Lovebird)
Agapornis personata Reichenow

DISTINGUISHING CHARACTERISTICS
14.5 cm (5.8 in). 48-56 g (1.69-1.98 oz)

Generally green; forehead, lores, crown and cheeks brownish black, remainder of head dusky olive; throat reddish orange; upper breast and neck collar yellow; upper tail-coverts blue; tail green marked with orange-yellow and basal black bar on tip; bill red.

Forshaw, 1973, p.308 and pl. p.309.

GENERAL DISTRIBUTION
North-eastern Tanzania.

INTRODUCED DISTRIBUTION
Introduced successfully in Dar-es-Salaam, Tanzania, and in Nairobi, Kenya. Introduced unsuccessfully in the USA (escapees).

GENERAL HABITS
Status: common (?). *Habitat:* wooded grasslands dominated by Acacias. *Gregariousness:* small flocks, but occasionally larger ones, and may congregate in thousands when grain is ripe. *Movements:* no information. *Foods:* grass and other seeds, and grain. *Breeding:* Mar-Aug; colonial. *Nest:* bulky, domed-shaped nest of twigs and bark strips in a hole in a tree, especially baobabs, or in crevices in buildings, and swifts' nests. *Eggs:* up to 7-8

Forshaw, 1973, p.308.

NOTES ON INTRODUCTIONS

Tanzania. Masked Lovebirds were introduced to Dar-es-Salaam in about 1928 (Mackworth-Praed and Grant, 1957) when a mass release of trapped birds occurred (Elliott, 1970). It appears that they are still established there.

Kenya. According to Cunningham-van Someren (1969) Masked Lovebirds have recently been introduced and are now breeding in the residential areas of Nairobi. Some twenty of them were reported from Mombasa in 1972 (Ellis, 1975), six in 1974 (Barlass, 1975) and the species appears to be established in the Nyoli Beach area where it hybridises with the introduced Fischer's Lovebird. They are

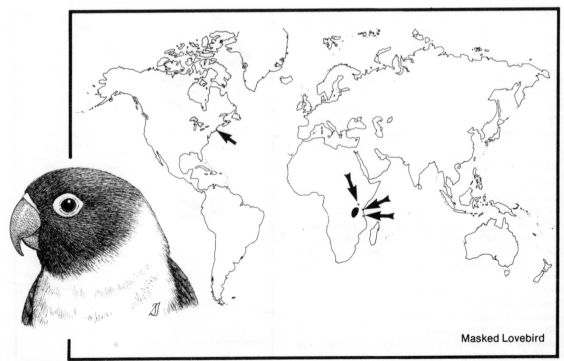

Masked Lovebird

thought to have been released or to have escaped from captivity to become established.

USA. Masked Lovebirds are occasionally reported in the wild in city parks in the New York area (Bull, 1973), but have not become permanently established there.

DAMAGE

The Masked Lovebird has, as has Fischer's Lovebird, taken a liking to cultivated millet and thus is regarded as a pest in Africa (Elliott, 1970).

NYASA LOVEBIRD
(Nyassa Lovebird)
Agapornis lilianae Shelley

DISTINGUISHING CHARACTERISTICS

13.5 cm (5.4 in). 38-43 g (1.34-1.52 oz)

Generally green, more yellowish on underparts and rump; forehead and throat orange-red becoming pinkish on crown, lores, cheeks and upper breast; tail green marked with yellow-orange and with basal bar; bill red.

Forshaw, 1973, p.310, pl. p.309.

GENERAL DISTRIBUTION

East Africa: southern Tanzania, north-western Moçambique, south through Malawi and eastern Zambia to northern Rhodesia.

INTRODUCED DISTRIBUTION

Possibly introduced successfully to Lundazi in Zambia and in South-West Africa (escapees?).

GENERAL HABITS

Status: common (?). *Habitat:* woodlands and cultivated farmlands. *Gregariousness:* flocks of 20-100 or more. *Movements:* considerable local movements. *Foods:* seeds, grain, berries, fruits and leaf buds. *Breeding:* poorly documented in wild; where introduced Jan-Feb (Lundazi). *Nest:* not well known in wild; under the eaves of houses; carry material to the nest (in captivity build a bulky domed

nest of stalks and strips of bark in a nest box). *Eggs:* 3 (?).

Forshaw, 1973, p.310.

NOTES ON INTRODUCTIONS

Zambia. According to Benson and White (1957, in Forshaw, 1973) Nyasa Lovebirds have been introduced to Lundazi. No details are known.

South-West Africa (Namibia). Records of Nyasa Lovebirds from South-West Africa are thought to be of aviary escapees (Clancey, 1965, in Forshaw, 1973).

DAMAGE

Nyasa Lovebirds are sometimes troublesome in crop growing areas, being particularly fond of ripening grain especially millet (Forshaw, 1973).

CRIMSON ROSELLA
(Crimson Parrot, Pennant's Parakeet)
Platycercus elegans (Gmelin)

DISTINGUISHING CHARACTERISTICS

33-36 cm (13.2-14.4 in)

Generally bright crimson with blue cheek patches; nape, back and wing feathers black margined crimson; bend of wing and outer webs of flight feathers blue; tail blue, tipped white; bill greyish white. (Some variation of colour in different races.)

Forshaw, 1969, pp.181, 183, pl. p.182.

GENERAL DISTRIBUTION

Eastern Australia: from the Atherton Tableland to south-eastern South Australia.

INTRODUCED DISTRIBUTION

Introduced successfully to Norfolk Island and to New Zealand. Introduced unsuccessfully to Lord Howe Island.

GENERAL HABITS

Status: very common. *Habitat:* forest, woodland, cultivated areas and suburbs. *Gregariousness:* small flocks or family parties. *Movements:* sedentary, but some local movements. *Foods:* seeds, fruits, blossom,

Nyasa Lovebird

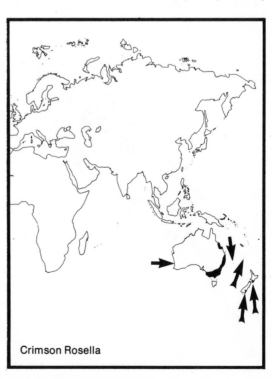

Crimson Rosella

insects and their larvae. *Breeding:* Aug-Feb. *Nest:* hollow in a limb or a hole in a tree. *Eggs:* 5-8.
Forshaw, 1969, pp.183-184.

NOTES ON INTRODUCTIONS

Norfolk Island. The Crimson Rosella *P.e. elegans* is well established and common on Norfolk Island (Forshaw, 1973). Smithers and Disney (1969) found them common there when they visited the island in the late 1960s.

Lord Howe Island. The Crimson Rosella was introduced to this island, but failed to become established there (Forshaw, 1969).

New Zealand. In New Zealand the Crimson Rosella has been reported from the Dunedin district of the South Island and from about Wellington on the North Island, but has never been common there (Hamel, 1970). Presumably, they were introduced off Otago Heads in 1910 when a shipment of these and Eastern Rosellas were released (Oliver, 1930).

A small population still survives in the hills near Dunedin and is said to include hybrids between the Eastern and Crimson species (Falla *et al,* 1966). Falla *et al* say that feral Crimson Rosellas were breeding near Wellington in 1964.

Western Australia. Crimson Rosellas were either deliberately released or escaped from captivity near Perth in about the mid-1960s. A pair were sighted at Darlington in 1966-67 and one at Kelmscott in 1975. A single bird is reported to have been seen in January 1980.

DAMAGE

Some damage is done by Crimson Rosellas to orchards in the apple and pear growing districts of southern New South Wales (Forshaw, 1969).

Where introduced on Norfolk Island, Smithers and Disney (1969) say that they are almost certainly competing for nesting sites with the native Green Parrot, *Cyanoramphus novaezelandiae,* and are probably responsible for the decline of this species there.

276   Crimson Rosella, *Platycercus elegans*

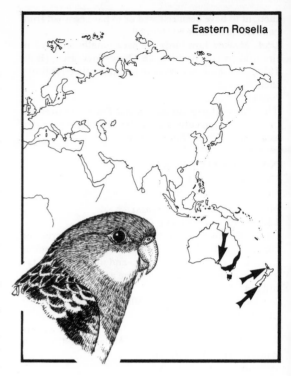

Eastern Rosella

EASTERN ROSELLA
(White-cheeked Rosella)
Platycercus eximius (Shaw)

DISTINGUISHING CHARACTERISTICS

28-30 cm (11.2-12 in)

Head, neck and chest red; cheek patches white; lower breast yellow; abdomen and rump pale green; vent and under tail-coverts red; feathers of back and wings black, margined with greenish yellow; outer webs of flight feathers blue, inner black; tail green and blue, tipped white; bill greyish white. Female: red on head, breast, vent and under tail-coverts duller; white stripe under wing.
Forshaw, 1969, pp.191, 193, pl. p.192.

GENERAL DISTRIBUTION

Eastern Australia including Tasmania: from south-eastern Queensland to south-eastern South Australia and Tasmania.

INTRODUCED DISTRIBUTION

Introduced successfully in New Zealand and near Adelaide, South Australia.

GENERAL HABITS

Status: very common. *Habitat:* lightly timbered country, parks, gardens and cultivated lands. *Gregariousness:* pairs or groups, but in winter congregate in flocks to 100. *Movements:* sedentary. *Foods:* seeds, grain, insects and their larvae, fruits and blossom. *Breeding:* Sept-Jan or earlier; solitary. *Nest:* hollow in a limb, or hole in a tree with bed of chipped wood. *Eggs:* 4-5, 9.
Forshaw, 1969, pp.193-195.

NOTES ON INTRODUCTIONS

New Zealand. Frequently imported by bird dealers before the 1920s, Eastern Rosellas evidently escaped or were liberated by private individuals (Thomson, 1922). Oliver (1930) records that in 1910 a small shipment of both Eastern and Crimson Rosellas were released off Otago Heads when they were refused entry to New Zealand. Oliver also indicates that some escaped in the Auckland district and became established there in the Waitakerei Range.

Falla *et al* (1966) indicate that Eastern Rosellas are well established near Auckland (Manukau Harbour and Whangaroa; rare south of Auckland but extending range northwards) in the North Island and a small population is established near Dunedin in the South Island. Hamel (1970) reports that they are still established in both these regions. Forshaw (1973) says that the race introduced is probably *P.e. eximius.*

South Australia. A population of Eastern Rosellas in the Mt Lofty Ranges near Adelaide is generally thought to have originated from aviary escapees (Forshaw, 1969).

DAMAGE

Where introduced in the Otago area Eastern Rosellas were reported to have caused some damage to fruit before the 1930s (Oliver, 1930-55). More recently Rostrom (1969) says that they also cause damage to citrus crops.

In eastern Australia — Queensland, New South Wales and Tasmania they cause some damage to fruits (Forshaw, 1969).

PALE-HEADED ROSELLA
(Mealy Rosella, Blue Rosella)
Platycercus adscitus (Latham)

DISTINGUISHING CHARACTERISTICS
30 cm (12 in)

Head whitish with yellow tinges; cheek patches blue below, white above; lower breast and abdomen blue, upper breast yellow; feathers of back and wings black margined yellowish, outer webs of flight feathers blue; rump yellowish; vent and under tail-coverts red; tail green and blue, tipped white; bill horn.
Forshaw, 1969, p.197, pl. p.196.

GENERAL DISTRIBUTION
North-eastern Australia: from Cape York Peninsula to northern New South Wales.

INTRODUCED DISTRIBUTION
Introduced successfully (?), but died out in the Hawaiian Islands.

GENERAL HABITS
Status: common. *Habitat:* timbered country, forest clearings and cultivation. *Gregariousness:* singly or small flocks. *Movements:* sedentary. *Foods:* seeds, berries, blossom, nectar, nuts and insects and their larvae. *Breeding:* Sept-June. *Nest:* hollow in a tree. *Eggs:* 3-5.
Forshaw, 1969, pp.199-200.

NOTES ON INTRODUCTIONS
Hawaiian Islands. A pair of Pale-headed Rosellas were reported to have been released in the Hawaiian Islands (on Maui) by a Captain Makee in 1877 (Munro, 1960). Munro reports that they may have been established and become fairly numerous around 1895. Some were noted in Olinda Forest in 1928, but the species must have died out as they are not now established there.

DAMAGE
When present in large numbers Pale-headed Rosellas may become a pest in orchards and amongst maize crops (Forshaw, 1973).

RED-RUMPED PARROT
(Red-backed Parrot)
Psephotus haematonotus (Gould)

DISTINGUISHING CHARACTERISTICS
25-27 cm (10-10.8 in)

Generally green, duller and more bluish on back and wings; abdomen yellow; vent and under tail-coverts white; rump red; yellow patch on wings and outer webs of flight feathers blue; tail green and blue, tipped white; bill black. Female: head and upper

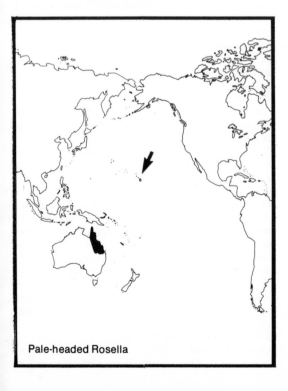

Pale-headed Rosella

Red-rumped Parrot

parts olive-green; neck and breast dull yellowish olive; bill grey.

Forshaw, 1969, p.211, pl. p.210.

GENERAL DISTRIBUTION

Eastern Australia: from southern Queensland to eastern South Australia.

INTRODUCED DISTRIBUTION

Introduced or extended range successfully (?) in Brisbane, Queensland (Australia).

GENERAL HABITS

Status: common. *Habitat:* timbered grassland, open plains, forest clearings and cultivated farmlands. *Gregariousness:* pairs or small parties of 10-20, sometimes larger flocks. *Movements:* largely sedentary, some irregular movements. *Foods:* grass seeds, seeds of herbaceous plants and other green vegetable material. *Breeding:* Aug-Dec, but variable in some areas. *Nest:* hollow in a limb or a hole in a tree. *Eggs:* 4-7, usually 5.

Forshaw, 1969, pp.213-215.

NOTES ON INTRODUCTIONS

Queensland. A colony may exist in the Brisbane area of Queensland. They may have originated from an extension of their range from the west, but perhaps have come from escapees from aviaries.

Red-rumped Parrots have been observed there since 1956 and were observed in 1963, 1964 and in 1969 (Jack and Fien, 1970).

DAMAGE

None known.

YELLOW-FRONTED PARAKEET
(Yellow-fronted Kakariki)

Cyanoramphus auriceps (Kuhl)

DISTINGUISHING CHARACTERISTICS

20-26 cm (8-10.4 in)

Generally green, yellowish on underparts; crimson frontal band, extending to eyes; crimson patch on

Yellow-fronted Parakeet

each side of rump; outer webs of flight feathers violet-blue; bill pale bluish grey, tip darker.

Forshaw, 1973, p.248, pl. p.247.

GENERAL DISTRIBUTION

New Zealand and outlying islands: occurs on islands of Three Kings, Hen, Big, Stewart and surrounding islands, Solander, Auckland and the Chathams (Little Mangare); in the North Island along the central mountain chain and in the South Island in mountains from Nelson to Fiordland. Formerly more widespread.

INTRODUCED DISTRIBUTION

Re-introduced successfully to Stephens Island (Cook Strait), New Zealand.

GENERAL HABITS

Status: range and numbers reduced, but locally common and may be increasing. *Habitat:* low forest and scrub. *Gregariousness:* pairs and small parties. *Movements:* sedentary (?). *Foods:* seeds, fruits, berries and vegetable matter. *Breeding:* prolonged, most of the year, but probably mainly Oct-Dec. *Nest:* hollow in a tree or stump, and in rock crevices on islands. *Eggs:* 5-9.

Forshaw, 1973, pp.248, 250.

NOTES ON INTRODUCTIONS

Stephens Island. The race *C.a. auriceps* was re-introduced to Stephens Island in 1970 (Atkinson and Bell, 1973) and apparently has become established there.

DAMAGE

None known.

BUDGERYGAH

Melopsittacus undulatus (Shaw)

DISTINGUISHING CHARACTERISTICS

18 cm (7.2 in)

Generally green, upper parts barred black and yellow; forehead, face and throat yellow; some feathers of cheeks tipped violet-blue; a series of black spots across throat; cere pale blue; tail blue and green; bill olive-grey. *Female:* cere brownish in breeding season.

Forshaw, 1969, p.279, pl. p.278.

GENERAL DISTRIBUTION

Australia generally, except the coastal areas.

INTRODUCED DISTRIBUTION

Introduced successfully in the USA (Florida) and in England (Scilly Isles), but have now failed in the latter area. Introduced unsuccessfully in South Africa (Natal), the Hawaiian Islands, Japan, Hong Kong, South America (Brazil and Colombia) and New Zealand.

GENERAL HABITS

Status: very common; universal cage bird. *Habitat:* timbered watercourses, timbered grasslands, dry scrublands and open plains. *Gregariousness:* form extremely large flocks at times; numbers in any area fluctuate enormously. *Movements:* nomadic. *Foods:* seeds of grasses and other plants. *Breeding:* variable, Aug-Jan in south and June-Sept in north, but nest following good rains; may have 2-3 broods per season. *Nest:* hollow in a tree, stump or fence post. *Eggs:* 4-6, 8.

Forshaw, 1969, pp.279, 281-282.

NOTES ON INTRODUCTIONS

USA. Budgerygahs frequently escape in many areas of

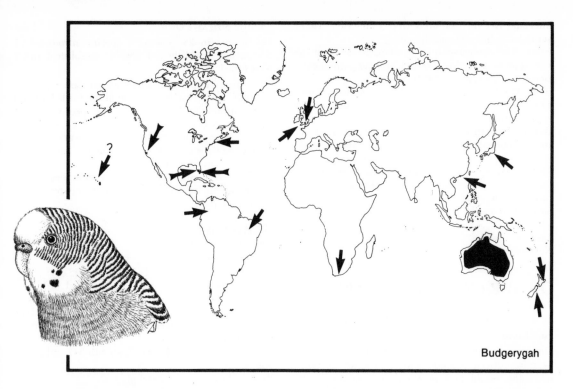

Budgerygah

the United States including California, New York and Florida. Cooke and Knappen (1941) record that free living birds were reported from both Florida and California before 1940. They have become established in the Florida region (Hardy, 1973) where they are widespread in the south of that area (Owre, 1973). According to Owre they were deliberately released and were being fostered at St Petersburg on the west coast. The original release here may have been as early as 1951-52 (Edscorn, 1977).

In 1975-76 they appeared to be well established (Heilbrun, 1976 and 1977) from New Port Richey to Englewood on the west coast and at Cocoa and Dade County on the east coast. A few were observed as far north as Cedar Key, 153 km (95 miles) north of St Petersburg (Edscorn, 1976). As many as 3000 birds were present at St Petersburg. In 1976 some were noted at Port Charlotte and Punta Gorda, about 100 km (62 miles) south of St Petersburg (Edscorn, 1977), and in 1977 a colony was said to be established in Jacksonville in north-eastern Florida (Kale, 1977).

Although Budgerygahs are frequently found in the wild in both New York and California (Bull, 1973; Hardy, 1973) they rarely survive for any length of time. Hardy reports that a colony existed for several years in Lower Topangar Canyon near Malibu Beach, California, but it is not known whether they still exist there. More recently a bird was noted in the residential area of Loma Linda, San Bernardino County (Fisk and Crabtree, 1974).

South Africa. According to the Department of Agriculture and Technical Services in South Africa (pers. comm.) attempts were being made in the early 1960s to introduce and establish the Budgerygah in that country.

Winterbottom (1966) reports that escapes are frequent, and says that recent information indicates the species may be established near Durban. However, the reports need further confirmation.

Great Britain. Many attempts have been made to establish the Budgerygah in Great Britain but without success (Koch, 1956). Temporary colonies have been established locally in a few areas: Margaretting in Essex, Windsor Great Park in Berkshire and in parts of the New Forest at Hampshire. More recently they have bred at Wiggington, Hertfordshire in 1971-72, near Downham Market, Norfolk where thirty birds were released in 1970-71 and at Fenstanton, Huntingdonshire where twelve to fifteen birds were noted in 1974 (Lever, 1977).

In 1971 birds which had been kept as a free-flying flock on Tresco in the Scilly Isles (off the south coast of England) since 1969, were allowed complete freedom. By 1975, the population had built up to an estimated 100 birds and they had been seen on a number of the small neighbouring isles. In 1976 only about a dozen pairs nested there and the colony was thought to be slowly diminishing.

Those on Scilly died out in the winter of 1976-77 as have those breeding in some English counties between 1968 and 1972 (British Trust for Ornithology Records Committee Report, *Ibis,* 120:411).

Hawaiian Islands. Munro (1960) says that Budgerygahs are common as escapees in these islands, but they have never become established there. In more recent years, however, escapees or deliberate releases may have become established on the island of Oahu. Their present status there is, however, poorly known (Hawaiian Audubon Society, 1975). Some were observed (four) at Diamond Head in 1970 (Berger, 1972) and some were also noted in 1973 (Pyle, 1977).

New Zealand. In this country Budgerygahs were liberated at an early date in the Canterbury area. In 1871 between two and four birds were liberated by the

279

Auckland Acclimatisation Society (Thomson, 1922) but failed to become established.

Japan. The Budgerygah is occasionally found in the wild as an escapee, but does not become permanently established (Kaburaki, 1934).

Hong Kong. Budgerygahs are quite commonly seen flying in the wild in Hong Kong, usually single birds or pairs. Some were noted at Kai Tak, Happy Valley and elsewhere in 1975 (Webster, 1975). They are not known to breed in the wild and are probably escapees or birds which have been deliberately released.

South America. Apparently the Budgerygah has escaped or been released in a number of areas, at various times, in at least Brazil and Colombia, but so far has failed to become established in the wild (Sick, 1968).

DAMAGE

None known.

ORDER: STRIGIFORMES

Family: *Tytonidae* Barn Owls

11 species in 2 genera: 2 species introduced, 2 established

Only two species of the *Tytonidae* appear to have been introduced and both have had some success in becoming established in their new environments. Introductions appear to have been mainly for the control of rats and mice on islands, a reason which may appeal to many, but which has no biological basis. Already in the Seychelles the introduced Barn Owl threatens to become a pest by preying on the rare Fairy Tern population.

Family: *Strigidae* Owls

134 species in 23 genera: 4 species introduced, 1 successfully established, 1 possibly established and 2 have failed

The most important introduction amongst the *Strigidae* has probably been that of the Little Owl into Great Britain and New Zealand. The species has been successful in both places, but there have been many arguments as to their true worth. It appears that they have done little damage of an economic nature or to native birds in either area.

Efforts to re-establish the Eagle Owl in Sweden are commendable but little has been documented on the success achieved.

BARN OWL

Tyto alba (Scopoli)

DISTINGUISHING CHARACTERISTICS

30-40 cm (12-16 in). 256-267 g (9.03-9.42 oz)

Upper parts greyish or yellowish, mottled with grey and white; underparts white; prominent heart-shaped facial disc, outlined with buff and dark brown; tail grey, barred buff or brown; bill ivory or yellowish white.

Witherby *et al*, 1938-41, vol.2, pp.343-347 and pl.60, opp. p.330.

Burton, 1973, pp.42-52 and pl. p.45.

GENERAL DISTRIBUTION

Almost worldwide: Europe, Africa, Malagasy, Arabia, India, Burma, Sri Lanka, central and northern Thailand, north and south Vietnam, Java, Lesser Sunda Islands, south-eastern New Guinea and some Melanesian islands, Australia, including

INTRODUCTIONS OF TYTONIDAE AND STRIGIDAE

Species	Date introduced	Region	Manner introduced	Reason
(a) Successful introductions				
Barn Owl	1951-52	Seychelles (Mahé)	deliberate	rat control
	1931	Bermuda	colonisation	—
	1910	Tasmania, Australia	colonisation	—
	about 1937 ?	St Helena	deliberate	?
	1958-63	Hawaiian Islands	deliberate	?
Masked Owl	between 1922 and 1930	Lord Howe Island	deliberate	rat control
Little Owl	1843-1908	England	deliberate	
	1906-10	New Zealand	deliberate	small bird nuisance
(b) Possibly successful introductions				
Eagle Owl	about 1964	Sweden	deliberate	re-establishment
(c) Unsuccessful introductions				
Barn Owl	1949	Isle Platt, Seychelles	deliberate	rat control
	1899	New Zealand	deliberate	?
	between 1922 and 1930	Lord Howe Island	deliberate	rat control
Spotted Owl	1866	New Zealand	deliberate	?
	between 1922 and 1930	Lord Howe Island	deliberate	rat control
Tawny Owl	1873	New Zealand	deliberate	?

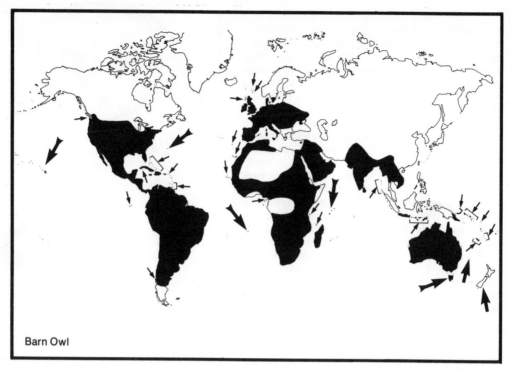

Barn Owl

Tasmania, the United States, Central and South America and the West Indies.

INTRODUCED DISTRIBUTION

Introduced successfully in the Seychelles, St Helena and the Hawaiian Islands (?). Colonised Bermuda and Tasmania. Introduced unsuccessfully in New Zealand and to Lord Howe Island.

GENERAL HABITS

Status: common. *Habitat:* wooded open regions, arid rocky regions, cultivation, villages and towns. *Gregariousness:* solitary or pairs. *Movements:* sedentary and migratory. *Foods:* small animals including mice, shrews, rats, moles, insects and small birds. *Breeding:* most of year, but varies in different regions; often 2 clutches per year. *Nest:* dry hollows in trees, buildings, cliffs, etc. *Eggs:* 2-6, 11.

Burton, 1973, pp.42-52.
Reader's Digest, 1977, p.304.

NOTES ON INTRODUCTIONS

Seychelles. The Barn Owl *T.a. affinis* was introduced successfuly to the island of Mahé in 1951 and 1952 and is now rapidly spreading there (Blackman, 1965).

Initially some were introduced without success to

Barn Owl, *Tyto alba*

the Ile Platte, from East Africa in 1949, as an experiment to see if they could control rats (Penny, 1974). The Department of Agriculture then introduced them in 1951-52 to Mahé where they became established, but did nothing towards the control of the rats. A bounty of thirty rupees has now been placed on the head of the owl in the Seychelles to assist in its control.

Bermuda. The Barn Owl was first recorded on Bermuda in 1931 and now is a fairly common species there (Wingate, 1973). It is thought to have colonised the island from America or the West Indies.

Tasmania. Condon (1975) suggests that the Barn Owl may have colonised Tasmania in the present century. He reports that they were first found there in 1910, and are still present there, but rare.

New Zealand. In 1899 the Otago Acclimatisation Society imported seven birds from London and liberated them at West Taieri (Thomson, 1922). Thomson indicates that these birds were not recorded after 1900, however, the Barn Owl is a straggler to New Zealand and there is sub-fossil evidence (Condon, 1975) that the species may have occurred there naturally in the past.

Falla *et al* (1966) record that specimens of the Australian race *(delicatula)* have been found at Westland in 1947, Haast in 1955 and at Runanga in 1960, but that there is no evidence that they have bred there.

St Helena. A species of Owl (?) was introduced from South Africa to St Helena, and bred there in 1937 (Benson, 1950), but there are few definite details. It has been assumed, with little evidence, that the species introduced was the Barn Owl. From descriptions, Haydock (1954) judged that *T. alba affinis* may be present, but that at least some others may have been an *Otus* species. He ascertained that at least a few owls were imported by the island's first Agricultural Officer.

281

Lord Howe Island. The races *T.a. delicatula* and *T.a. pratincola* (?) from Australia were introduced to this island for the control of rats, but failed to become established (Recher and Clark, 1974). The introductions occurred between 1922 and 1930 when 100 owls of three species were released. A single bird was sighted in 1936, but none have been seen since this date (McKean and Hindwood, 1965).

Hawaiian Islands. The Barn Owl has been introduced to the Hawaiian Islands, but its present status there is uncertain (Peterson, 1961). The race *T.a. pratincola* from North America was released on Hawaii in April, June and October of 1958. Some fifteen birds were imported from California by the State Department of Agriculture and released at Kukuihaele, Hawaii, in 1958, in the hope that they would prey on rats in sugar cane fields. From April 1959 to June 1963, seventy-one more owls were imported and released in the same area of Hawaii, and at Kilohana, Mana, the Kekaha Sugar Co. lands on Kauai, Hauula, Oahu, and on the Molokai Ranch at west Molokai (Berger, 1972). Tomich (1962) found that those released on Hawaii were spreading well towards both Hilo and Kohala.

On Kauai, Au and Swedberg (1966) report that there were releases of eighteen at Kilohana from June 1959 to June 1965 (two had also been released in the Waimea Valley in November 1961, four at Mana in May 1963 and four at Kekaha in June 1963). Of twenty-eight birds released in 1959-63, some twenty-seven had been found dead, sick or injured by June 1965. However, some thirty-five sightings of live birds on the island indicated that they were established and breeding there.

Some Barn Owls were recorded on Hawaii during the Christmas Bird Counts from 1974 to 1976 (Pyle, 1976 and 77).

DAMAGE
Introduced in the Seychelles to control rats the Barn Owl has been found to be lacking in this respect and now threatens the almost-extinct Fairy Tern population on Mahé (Penny, 1974).

MASKED OWL
Tyto novaehollandiae (Stephens)

DISTINGUISHING CHARACTERISTICS
35-46 cm (14-18.4 in). 800-900 g (1.7-1.9 lb)
Upper parts blackish brown, freckled with white; underparts white to pale buff; black spots on breast and flanks; facial disc white to chestnut, with blackish brown edge, rufous around eyes; bill white. *Female:* considerably larger than male.
Burton, 1973, pp.56-57.
Reader's Digest, 1977, p.306 and pl. p.306.

GENERAL DISTRIBUTION
Australia (except the most arid parts), southern New Guinea, Manus Island, Tanimbar Islands and Buru.

INTRODUCED DISTRIBUTION
Introduced successfully (?) on Lord Howe Island.

GENERAL HABITS
Status: uncommon. *Habitat:* forest, woodland, and treeless country with caves. *Gregariousness:* solitary or pairs. *Movements:* sedentary. *Foods:* small animals, insects including grasshoppers. *Breeding:* June-Oct (? not well known). *Nest:* hollow in a tree, or cave. *Eggs:* 2-3.

Masked Owl

Burton, 1973, pp.56-57.
Reader's Digest, 1977, p.306.

NOTES ON INTRODUCTIONS
Lord Howe Island. The Tasmanian race of the Masked Owl *T.n. castanops* was introduced on Lord Howe Island and still apparently occurs there (Recher and Clark, 1974). McKean and Hindwood (1965) have reported that owls of three species were introduced to the island between 1922 and 1930. Some were heard and one sighted in 1963.

The species had no discernible effect on the rat population, the destruction of which precipitated the introduction.

DAMAGE
None known.

EAGLE OWL
Bubo bubo (Linnaeus)

DISTINGUISHING CHARACTERISTICS
46-70 cm (18.4-28 in). Up to 4 kg (9 lb)
Generally rich brown, heavily streaked with black on the flanks and breast; narrow bars on belly and under tail-coverts; upper parts more mottled and less streaked; prominent ear-tufts. *Female:* larger.
Witherby *et al,* 1938-41, vol.2, pp.312-315 and pl.55, opp. p.292.
Burton, 1973, pp.72-77 and pls 72, 73 and 74-5.

GENERAL DISTRIBUTION
Eurasia – North Africa: most of Europe, except parts of western and northern Europe, to eastern Asia (except South-east Asia), India, the Middle East and North Africa.

INTRODUCED DISTRIBUTION
Re-introduced probably successfully in parts of southern Sweden.

GENERAL HABITS
Status: considerably reduced in numbers and range in Europe as a breeding bird. *Habitat:* forests, steep

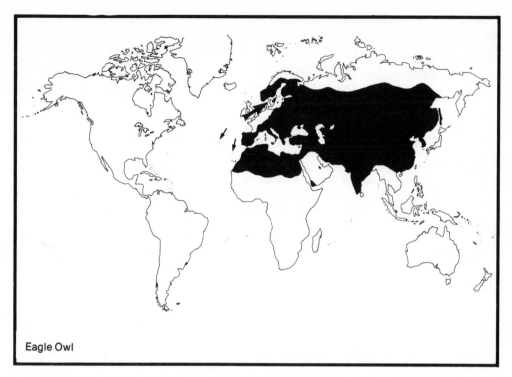

Eagle Owl

rock and ravine regions, mountain cliffs in sandy and stony deserts, and ruins; avoids cultivated areas except perhaps in southern Asia. *Gregariousness:* singly or pairs. *Movements:* sedentary. *Foods:* most animals including mice, rats, squirrels and other small mammals, grouse, ducks, partridges, gulls and other birds, snakes, lizards, frogs, toads, fish and beetles. *Breeding:* Mar-June (Europe), Feb-Mar (China). *Nest:* in cavities in cliffs, pyramids, trees, on rocky ledges and in nests built by crows and other birds of prey. *Eggs:* 2-4, 6.

Witherby *et al,* vol.2, 1938-41, pp.312-315.

Burton, 1973, pp.72-77.

NOTES ON INTRODUCTIONS

Sweden. The European Eagle Owl *B.b. bubo* has been re-established in some Swedish forests using birds bred in captivity (Wayre, 1966).

Twelve Eagle Owls were released in mountain ranges at Kilsbergen in the province of Närke in about 1964 (Curry-Lindahl, 1964).

DAMAGE

None known.

SPOTTED OWL
(Boobook Owl)
Ninox novaeseelandiae (Gmelin)

DISTINGUISHING CHARACTERISTICS

30-35 cm (12-14 in). 227-340 g (8-12 oz)

Underparts buff with pale to dark brown streaks and mottling; upper parts pale to dark brown, with white spots on wings and back; facial disc paler brown with dark patch behind eye; bill blue-grey.

Burton, 1973, pp.149-152 and pl. p.148.

Reader's Digest, 1977, p.303 and pl. p.303.

GENERAL DISTRIBUTION

Timor and surrounding islands, Tanimbar and Kai Islands, southern New Guinea, Australia, including

Tasmania, Lord Howe and Norfolk Islands, and all the islands off New Zealand.

INTRODUCED DISTRIBUTION

Introduced unsuccessfully to New Zealand and Lord Howe Island.

GENERAL HABITS

Status: common. *Habitat:* forest to desert. *Gregariousness·* solitary or pairs. *Movements:* sedentary (some Tasmanian birds move to mainland in winter). *Foods:* small animals and insects.

Spotted Owl

283

Breeding: Sept-Nov. *Nest:* hole or hollow in a tree. *Eggs:* 2-3, 4.

Burton, 1973, pp.149-152.

Reader's Digest, 1977, p.303.

NOTES ON INTRODUCTIONS

New Zealand. In 1866 the Otago Acclimatisation Society introduced two Australian owls (probably ? *N.n. boobook*) and liberated them at Waikouaiti, but they were not seen again after their release (Thomson, 1922).

Lord Howe Island. Birds from the Australian mainland *N.n. boobook* were introduced to Lord Howe Island for the control of rats, but failed to become established (Recher and Clark, 1974). McKean and Hindwood (1965) record that they were introduced between 1922 and 1930.

DAMAGE

None known.

LITTLE OWL
(Brown Owl)
Athene noctua (Scopoli)

DISTINGUISHING CHARACTERISTICS

19-23 cm (7.6-9.2 in)

Upper parts dark brown, each feather spotted white and edged buff, crown streaked; facial disc white; chin, line under facial disc and patch on lower throat white; underparts whitish, heavily streaked dark brown; sides of neck and band across throat mottled dark brown and buff; breast, sides and flanks dark brown and white; belly and under tail-coverts white; tail dark brown barred brownish buff; wings dark brown with some white or buff spots; bill greenish yellow.

Witherby *et al,* vol.2, 1938-41, pp.322-327 and pl.58, opp. p.316.

Burton, 1973, pp.164-166 and pl. p.165.

GENERAL DISTRIBUTION

Eurasia-North Africa: from western Europe and North Africa east to southern Manchuria, north Korea and northern and western China. Winter visitor to south Korea.

INTRODUCED DISTRIBUTION

Introduced successfully to England and New Zealand.

GENERAL HABITS

Status: common. *Habitat:* open forest and woodland, steppe, rocky semi-desert, cultivated areas with trees, and parks. *Gregariousness:* pairs, or small family groups after breeding. *Movements:* sedentary. *Foods:* small rodents and other small animals, large insects including beetles, and frogs and small birds. *Breeding:* Apr-May (Great Britain and China); Apr-Sept (elsewhere). *Nest:* hollow in a tree, hole in stony ground, walls, ruins and burrows. *Eggs:* 2, 4-6, 9.

Witherby *et al,* vol.2, 1938-41, p.322-327.

Burton, 1973, pp.164-166.

NOTES ON INTRODUCTIONS

England. The race *A.n. vidalii* was introduced to England from 1843 onwards and certainly at various times since 1870.

The first attempt appears to have been that by C. Waterton in 1843, when five were released, but failed to become established (Hudson, 1921; Koch, 1956; Lever, 1977). More were introduced by E. G. B. Mead-Waldo in 1874, at Edenbridge, Kent and from

this time until 1880 some forty birds were released. Introductions at Knapp Castle, south-east Kent, and by the Earl of Kimberley near Wymondham, Norfolk in 1876 appeared to fail. Large numbers were apparently introduced (about forty birds) by Lord Lilford in 1888, near Oundle, Northamptonshire and he indicated that several similar experiments were attempted in Herts, Sussex, Norfolk and Yorkshire. Lord Lilford released many more owls up until about 1893 when they were well established in Northamptonshire. In about 1890 Lord Rothschild liberated some at Tring Park, Hertfordshire. In the same year and up to some fifteen years later W. H. St Quinton liberated them near Malton, Yorkshire. Both these introductions appear to have been failures. Introductions at East Grinstead, Sussex in 1900 and 1901, appeared more successful and were followed by others in Essex in 1905 and 1908 and in Yorkshire in 1905 (Witherby *et al,* 1938; Fitter, 1959; Sharrock, 1976; Lever, 1977).

The Little Owl was found to be breeding in the wild in Kent in 1879 where it was already spreading. They reached Dartford, Kent in the 1870s, Swanscombe near Gravesend by 1883 and the outskirts of London in 1897. In the east they reached Shorne about 1893 and Cuxton by 1894. They spread north-west into Surrey (breeding 1907) and crossed the border into Sussex in 1903. In the south-east they reached Cranbrook by 1903, Bilsington by 1906 and Bexley by 1907 (Lever, 1977).

From the early introductions in Northamptonshire they spread into Suffolk and Norfolk by 1901, Huntingdonshire where they bred in 1907, Cambridgeshire in the same year, the Derby-Leicestershire border in 1906, southern Shropshire in 1899 and Shrewsbury in 1908 (Lever).

According to Lever (1977) the Little Owls range in England increased markedly from about 1907. They were breeding at Glamorganshire, Wales by 1916 and were on the Isle of Wight in 1918. By about 1925 or the early 1930s they had extended over most of England and parts of Wales as far north as mid-Lancashire and Yorkshire. In the 1950s they were spreading into the south of Scotland.

The Little Owl now breeds throughout England, Wales and in Scotland locally as far north as Dumfries, Kirkcudbrightshire and Berkshire.

New Zealand. The Little Owl was introduced and liberated by the Otago Acclimatisation Society in several localities between 1906 and 1910 (Thomson, 1922). The introduction may have been prompted by the damage caused by small introduced passerines in orchards (Oliver, 1955).

In 1906 some twenty-eight birds were imported from Germany. Fourteen were liberated at Ashley Downs, Waiwera and fourteen at Alexandra. In 1907, thirty-nine were liberated at Alexandra and in 1908 some eighty were released in various localities. Seventy-two were imported in 1910, fourteen were released by the society and the remaining birds were sold to farmers.

Other liberations include a pair released at Rotorua in about 1908 and possibly some that were released at North Canterbury in 1910.

By 1909 the Little Owl had become well established in the Otago area as Thomson reports that several

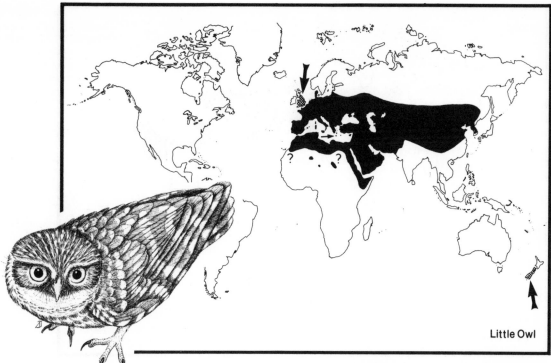

Little Owl

farmers were claiming that they were a boon in their orchards. By 1915 they had reached Invercargill and by 1920 were firmly established in the southern portion of the South Island and were common about Dunedin.

Oliver (1955) reports that Little Owls were abundant from mid-Canterbury to Foveaux Strait, had extended into North Canterbury and had been recorded from some localities in Nelson and Marlborough and on Stewart Island.

The Little Owl is now widespread and common in the South Island of New Zealand (Wodzicki, 1965), from Southland (Puysegur Point) to Marlborough (east of the main range) and more recently in Westland where they are probably increasing (Falla *et al*, 1966). Falla *et al* also report that some have been (recently ?) transferred to the North Island where their present status is uncertain. The race of the Little Owl established in New Zealand is not known with certainty (Kinsky, 1973).

DAMAGE

Few birds appear to have been so violently attacked as to their worth than has the Little Owl in England. The British Trust for Ornithology undertook investigations in 1936-37 (Hibbert-Ware, 1937) on the owl's feeding habits and declared it was a beneficial bird as few instances of depredations on either game or poultry could be confirmed. However, there seems no doubt that this species does prey on poultry and other birds at times, but the damage incurred is probably small (Lancum, 1961; Daglish, 1948).

The Little Owl was introduced to New Zealand to combat the small bird nuisance in orchards and in this respect it initially appeared to have some effect. However, Oliver (1955) later reports on the value of the species to agriculture by consuming harmful insects, and its effects on native birds. He stated that the effects on the latter are contradictory, but that the Little Owl is probably one of the worst introductions to that country. The species has certainly not had much effect on the small bird population and it is doubtful if it has played much of a part in the extinction of native species of birds.

TAWNY OWL
(Tawny Wood Owl)
Strix aluco (Linnaeus)

DISTINGUISHING CHARACTERISTICS

35-46 cm (14-18.4 in). 410-800 g (.9-1.8 lb)

Upper parts reddish brown, marked and spotted dark brown, black and grey; underparts reddish white with transverse brown bars and dusky streaks; white spots on scapulars and wing-coverts; facial disc pale greyish to brown; primaries and tail barred alternately reddish brown; bill greyish yellow.

Witherby *et al,* vol.2, 1938-41, pp.338-342 and pl.60, opp. p.330.

Burton, 1973, pp.132-135 and pl. p.133.

GENERAL DISTRIBUTION

Eurasia-North Africa: from southern Scandinavia, Great Britain, western Europe, North Africa and Iran, east to western Siberia, Korea, China and Taiwan.

INTRODUCED DISTRIBUTION

Introduced unsuccessfully in New Zealand.

GENERAL HABITS

Status: fairly common. *Habitat:* forest, open parklands and woodlands. *Gregariousness:* solitary or pairs. *Movements:* sedentary. *Foods:* small mammals and birds including mice, rats, moles, rabbits, squirrels, also large insects, snails, earthworms, frogs, crabs and fish. *Breeding:* Mar-Apr (Great Britain and China). *Nest:* hollow in a tree, or in ruins, chimneys and burrows. *Eggs:* 1, 2-4, 6.

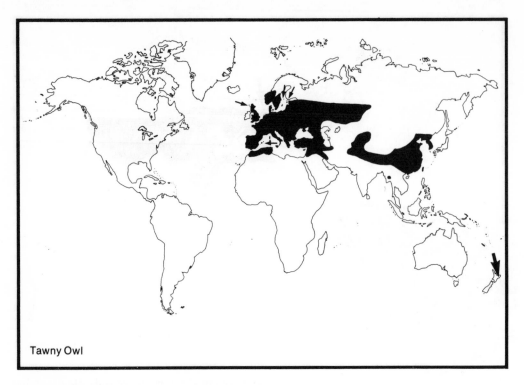

Tawny Owl

Witherby *et al*, vol.2, 1938-41, pp.338-342.
Burton, 1973, pp.132-135.

NOTES ON INTRODUCTIONS
New Zealand. In 1873 a pair of Tawny Owls from England were imported to Napier and released in that province. They disappeared and were not seen again (Thomson, 1922).

DAMAGE
None known.

ORDER: APODIFORMES

Family: *Apodidae* Swifts

76 species in 8 genera; 1 introduced, probably unsuccessfully
The Edible-nest Swiftlet has been introduced to the Hawaiian Islands fairly recently, but may now have died out there.

Family: *Trochilidae* Hummingbirds

331 species in 123 genera; possibly (?) 1 or more species introduced, unsuccessfully
One or more species of hummingbirds have been liberated in a number of areas of South America, including Brazil, Peru, Ecuador and Venezuela, apparently without success.

Apodidae

EDIBLE-NEST SWIFTLET
Collocalia inexpectata Hume

DISTINGUISHING CHARACTERISTICS
12-14 cm (4.8-5.6 in)
Upper parts blackish brown; rump ranges from whitish to dark; tail notched or slightly forked; underparts brown marked grey.

GENERAL DISTRIBUTION
South-East Asia and islands: the Andaman and Nicobar Islands, Sundas, Palawan, southern Philippines, southern Burma, Tenasserim, Malaysia, central and peninsular Thailand, Con Son Island, central and southern Annam, Tonkin and the Marianas. (Note: difficulties with classification and identification have made it necessary to outline only the approximate boundaries of this species' distribution on the range map.)

INTRODUCED DISTRIBUTION
Introduced successfully to the Hawaiian Islands (probably now failed ?).

GENERAL HABITS
Status: common. *Habitat:* off-shore islands, coastal

INTRODUCTIONS OF APODIDAE AND TROCHILIDAE

Species	Date introduced	Region	Manner introduced	Reason
(a) Probably unsuccessful introductions				
Edible-nest Swiftlet	1962 and 1965	Hawaiian Islands	deliberate	?
Hummingbird spp.	about 1967 ?	Brazil	deliberate	re-colonisation
	after 1956	Peru	deliberate	"
	after 1956	Ecuador	deliberate	"
	after 1956	Venezuela	deliberate	"

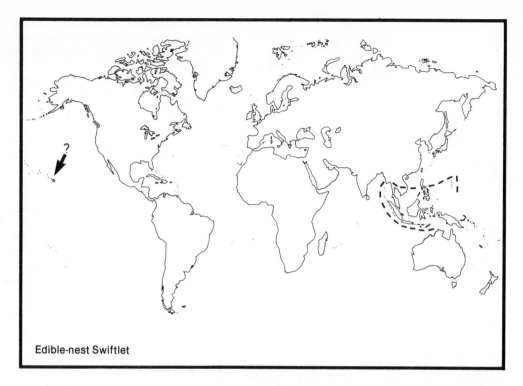

Edible-nest Swiftlet

shores, secondary growth, towns and open scrub. *Gregariousness:* pairs and flocks up to 50. *Movements:* sedentary and partly migratory (some areas). *Foods:* insects. *Breeding:* no information; in large colonies. *Nest:* made entirely of hardened saliva (edible), in marine caves and buildings. *Eggs:* no information.

NOTES ON INTRODUCTIONS

Hawaiian Islands. Between 125 and 175 (not counted) birds of the race *C.i. bartshi* from Guam were released in the Niu Valley, Oahu, in May 1962 by D. Woodside of the State Division of Fish and Game. The birds were collected in Guam and flown to Hawaii where they were liberated en masse. The project was sponsored and paid for by the Hui Manu Organisation in Honolulu (Bowles, 1962).

Woodside also released approximately 200 of them at Waimea Falls on Oahu in January 1965.

None were sighted or reported until November 1969 when W. Donaghho (1970) observed six in North Halawa Valley, and later some twenty-five birds were found in the same area.

At later dates the species has not been found (Berger, 1972), however, they may still be established on Oahu, but their present status is not well known (Hawaiian Audubon Society, 1975).

Trochilidae

NOTES ON INTRODUCTIONS

South America. According to Sick (1968) several Brazilian State Offices have been furnished with hundreds of hummingbirds in the past and which were settled in the wild in the Volieren area. Such 're-colonisations' have also been attempted in Peru, Ecuador and Venezuela sometime after 1956, but apparently the birds just flew off and were not sighted again.

ORDER: CORACIFORMES

Family: *Alcedinidae* Kingfishers

88 species in 14 genera; 1 introduced successfully
The Kookaburra has been introduced successfully in Western Australia, some small islands off the south-eastern coast and to the North Island of New Zealand. Although often said to be a nuisance where introduced its role as a pest appears doubtful.

KOOKABURRA
(Laughing Kookaburra, Jackass)
Dacelo novaeguineae (Hermann) (= *D. gigas*)

DISTINGUISHING CHARACTERISTICS
38-46 cm (15.2 -18.4 in). 255-397 g (9.1-14 oz)
Head whitish, crown dark streaked; a dark line through eye; back dark brown; wings brown with blue mottling on shoulders; underparts whitish; tail barred brown and black, tipped white; bill large, black above and whitish below.
Reader's Digest, 1977, p.319 and pls. pp.318 and 319.

GENERAL DISTRIBUTION
Australia: eastern Australia from Cape York Peninsula, Queensland, south and west to southern Eyre Peninsula, South Australia.

INTRODUCED DISTRIBUTION
Introduced successfully in south-west Western Australia, Kangaroo Island, Flinders Island, Tasmania and New Zealand. Introduced unsuccessfully in Fiji.

GENERAL HABITS
Status: very common. *Habitat:* forest, woodlands, parklands and towns. *Gregariousness:* solitary and family groups. *Movements:* sedentary. *Food:* insects and small animals. *Breeding:* Sept-Jan, occasionally to May. *Nest:* hollow in a tree, termite nest, bank or building. *Eggs:* 1, 2-4.

Kookaburra, *Dacelo novaeguineae*

Parry, 1970.

Parry, *Emu,* vol.73, 1973, pp.81 100.

NOTES ON INTRODUCTIONS

Western Australia. The Kookaburra was introduced from Victoria by the Director of the Zoological Gardens, South Perth, from about 1897 onwards (Serventy and Whittell, 1951). Between 1897 and 1912 hundreds were imported and apparently released in a number of areas of the State (Long, 1972). Earlier independent introductions may have occurred as birds were reported in the Mullewa area in 1896 (Jenkins, 1959).

The species was established in many areas before 1912 and was becoming fairly numerous between the Darling Range and the ocean by the 1920s. They are now established in the south-west forested country north to Jurien Bay and south to the Albany district and Bald Island (Serventy and Whittell, 1967). Serventy and Whittell report that they do not occur as a permanent inhabitant beyond Moora, Bolgart and the Great Southern Railway; however, odd birds penetrate further inland to such places as Kellerberrin, Nangeenan, Dangin, Kweda, Lake Grace, Lake King, Holt Rock, Gnowangerup and Borden. They may now be a permanent resident at Dangin and Kweda. More recently some have been sighted as far east as Ravensthorpe and are a permanent resident of Dudinin (east of Wickepin).

Serventy and Whittell suggest that the species was independently introduced to the Mingenew and Irwin districts and they have been seen as far south as Arramel — 32 km (20 miles) south of Dongarra — Stockyard Gully and Cockleshell Gully.

Kangaroo Island. The Kookaburra was introduced to Kangaroo Island in January 1926 when two pairs were liberated (Anon, 1948). Some were subsequently recorded in 1935 (Lashmar, 1935), 1960 (Wheeler, 1960), 1967 (Condon, 1968), in January 1969 (Basten, 1971, in Abbott, 1974) and the species is probably still established there.

Flinders Island. The Kookaburra has been introduced on Flinders Island (Condon, 1975).

Tasmania. According to Pollard (1967) the Kookaburra was introduced to Tasmania in 1905. Unsuccessful attempts were made by W. McGowan in 1902, but a few years later successful releases were made at Waterhouse Island off the north-east coast and in several areas on the mainland (Jenkins, 1977). Ridpath and Moreau (1965) indicate that the liberation occurred in northern Tasmania and that the species has spread to the east and southern parts of the island.

Kookaburra

INTRODUCTIONS OF ALCEDINIDAE

Species	Date introduced	Region	Manner introduced	Reason
(a) Successful introductions				
Kookaburra	before 1897 ? and 1897-1912	Western Australia	deliberate	?
	1926	Kangaroo Island, Australia	deliberate	?
	1905	Tasmania, Australia	deliberate	?
	?	Flinders Island, Australia	?	?
	1866-80	New Zealand	deliberate	?
(b) Unsuccessful introductions				
Kookaburra	before 1926 ?	Fiji	deliberate ?	?

Fiji. Blackburn (1971) records that the Kookaburra was introduced to Fiji sometime prior to 1926, but failed to become permanently established.

New Zealand. The Kookaburra was first imported to New Zealand in 1864, but there are no records of the two pairs being liberated. From 1866 to 1880 numerous releases occurred (Thomson, 1922). The Otago Acclimatisation Society released four birds in 1866 and two in 1869 near Silverstream, but they later disappeared. The Nelson society imported some in 1867, but there are no further records of these birds. The Auckland society also imported some in 1868. The Wellington society liberated fourteen in 1876 and one in 1879 and of these one was seen in 1885, but this appears to be the last record, although some were reported on the coast near Auckland in 1916.

Thomson records that Sir George Grey introduced a number of Kookaburras to Kawau Island in the early 1860s, but they were reported to have soon died out. Oliver (1930) however, says that all the introductions in New Zealand failed except for those on Kawau. He indicates that from here they crossed to the mainland and were common on the coast opposite that island in the late 1920s.

In 1955, the Kookaburra was established in the North Auckland area from Whangarei to the Waitakerei Ranges and on Kawau Island (Oliver, 1955). More recently, Falla *et al* (1966) say that there is a small but fairly stable population surviving along the western shore of Hauraki Gulf. Here, they occur among the creeks and islands between Cape Rodney and Whangaparoa Peninsula and occasionally reach some offshore islands.

DAMAGE

In Western Australia the Kookaburra has been accused of killing small native birds and attacking young poultry (Glauert, 1956). Elsewhere in Australia they are valued because they feed on snakes and other nuisance animals. Generally, however, it can be said that the Kookaburra causes little damage to other birds and the part that it may have played in the decrease in small bird populations is probably negligible although not well studied.

In New Zealand the species is not widely enough established to have caused much comment.

ORDER: PASSERIFORMES

Family: *Tyrannidae* Tyrant-flycatchers

374 species in 119 genera; 1 species introduced successfully

The Great Kiskadee has been introduced from Trinidad to Bermuda where it has become well established. The story of its introduction illustrates the futility and dangers of liberating a species for biological control of other animals without appropriate study.

GREAT KISKADEE
(Kiskadee Flycatcher, Derby Flycatcher)
Pitangus sulphuratus (Linnaeus)

DISTINGUISHING CHARACTERISTICS

21.6-26 cm (8.64-10.4 in). 52-68 g (1.83-2.4 oz)
Crown and sides of head black; band through and behind eye to neck black; white line above eye across head and with a black line above this; large concealed yellow crest; throat white; back brown; wings and tail brown or cinnamon-rufous; central tail-feathers black, outer edges rufous; underparts bright yellow; bill black.
Allen, 1962, pp.149-150, 233-234 and pl.71, p.161.
Meyer de Schauensee and Phelps, 1978, p.254 and pl.28.

GENERAL DISTRIBUTION

North and South America: southern Texas to north-western Panama, Venezuela, Guyana south through Brazil to eastern Ecuador, Peru, Bolivia, Paraguay, Uruguay, and northern Argentina south to Buenos Aires and west to La Pampa and Mendoza; also Trinidad.

INTRODUCED DISTRIBUTION

Introduced successfully to Bermuda.

GENERAL HABITS

Status: very common. *Habitat:* open woodland, scrub, thickets, streamsides, groves, plantations, parks and towns. *Gregariousness:* solitary or pairs. *Movements:* sedentary. *Foods:* fruits, berries, insects, small fish, lizards, mice, birds' eggs and young. *Breeding:* throughout the year (Surinam and Trinidad); Mar-July (Bermuda); often 2-3 broods per season. *Nest:* bulky, football-shaped, domed structure of grass, leaves and ferns, with side entrance, in a tree, palm or bush. *Eggs:* 2-5.
Allen, 1962, pp.149-150, 233 and 234.
Ffrench, 1973, p.318-320.
Meyer de Schauensee and Phelps, 1978, p.254.

INTRODUCTIONS OF TYRANNIDAE

Species	Date introduced	Region	Manner introduced	Reason
(a) Successful introduction				
Great Kiskadee	1957	Bermuda	deliberate	lizard control

Great Kiskadee

and general feeder was unfortunately overlooked. Food analysis later showed that the lizard only comprised about 10% of the kiskadee diet and it has had little, if any, influence on their numbers. The species is also known to eat soft fruits and to rob other birds' nests of their eggs and young. Wingate says that there is little doubt that the kiskadee was a major cause of the decline of catbirds, cardinals and white-eyed vireos on the island during the 1960s.

Family: *Menuridae* Lyrebirds

2 species in 1 genus; 1 species introduced successfully
The Superb Lyrebird was introduced into two areas of Tasmania between 1934 and 1949 from Victoria, Australia. The species has remained established in both areas, but has not spread nor increased greatly in numbers.

SUPERB LYREBIRD
Menura novaehollandiae Latham
DISTINGUISHING CHARACTERISTICS
Males 80-97 cm (32-38.8 in); tail 55 cm (22 in). Females 45-50 cm (18-20 in)
Upper parts dark grey-brown, darker on face and crown, paler on rump; facial skin bluish black; underparts pale grey-brown, rufous on throat and neck; tail, central feathers filamentous, blackish above, and outer feathers lyre-shaped, blackish brown above and white below with rufous notches; bill black. *Female:* smaller and with dark brown, graduated tail.
Reader's Digest, 1977, p.332 and pls. p.332 and 333.

NOTES ON INTRODUCTIONS
Bermuda. Wingate (1973) reports that this species was introduced by the Department of Agriculture, from Trinidad in 1957, to eat Anolis lizards which were preventing the establishment of predatory beetles (ladybirds) brought in to control scale insect infestations. The scale insect, itself an introduced species, has since about 1945 almost caused the extinction of the endemic 'cedar' or juniper which is apparently an important element in the original vegetation of the island (Crowell and Crowell, 1976).

The Great Kiskadee was introduced from the Port of Spain area, Trinidad, the first shipment arriving in April 1957 (Wingate, pers. comm., 1976). By mid-summer a total of 200 birds had been released from the vicinity of the Aquarium and the Botanical Gardens. They rapidly dispersed throughout the island, at first favouring mangrove swamps, sheltered valleys with watercourses and areas with shade trees. The increase in numbers of the bird was however so rapid that by 1964 they were common in all habitats.

The Great Kiskadee is now the third most abundant, and certainly the most conspicuous resident bird on Bermuda, with populations as high as eight to ten pairs per hectare (Wingate).

DAMAGE
According to Wingate the Great Kiskadee was known to eat the Anolis lizard and it was hoped that it would effect a reduction in the high population living on the island. The fact that it was an extremely adaptable

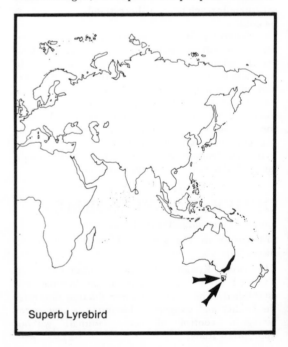

Superb Lyrebird

INTRODUCTIONS OF MENURIDAE

Species	Date introduced	Region	Manner introduced	Reason
(a) Successful introduction Superb Lyrebird	1934-41 or 1949	Tasmania, Australia	deliberate	?

Superb Lyrebird,
Menura novaehollandiae

GENERAL DISTRIBUTION

Australia: south-eastern Australia from Melbourne, Victoria to south-eastern Queensland.

INTRODUCED DISTRIBUTION

Introduced successfully in Tasmania.

GENERAL HABITS

Status: fairly common. *Habitat:* mountain forests particularly ferny gullies and open timber country amongst granite outcrops. *Gregariousness:* solitary, but often in groups of 4-5 birds outside breeding season. *Movements:* sedentary. *Foods:* grubs, worms and insects. *Breeding:* May-Sept. *Nest:* platform of sticks and moss, sometimes surrounded by leaves and bark, untidily domed with grass and fibres, and lined with feathers; on the ground under a log, stone, or in a thick vine. *Eggs:* 1.

Reilly, *Emu,* vol.70, 1970, pp.73-78.

Smith, in *Proc. Inter. Orn. Congr. Canberra* 1976, pp.125-136.

NOTES ON INTRODUCTIONS

Tasmania. From introductions commencing in 1934 the Superb Lyrebird has been established in Tasmania. According to Sharland (1944) some thirteen birds were released in the National Park of Tasmania between 1934 and 1941. Pollard (1967)

reports that eleven males and eleven females were taken from Victoria and released in suitable areas between 1934 and 1949. Wall and Wheeler (1966) indicate that twenty-two birds were transferred from Victoria to Tasmania and that one of these died in captivity and twenty-one were released. Six were released at Hastings in the far south of Tasmania in 1945 and all the others in Mt Field National Park. They record that the birds were first released in 1934 a short distance east of a point between the Five Mile post on the road between the Park entrance and Lake Dobson.

The Superb Lyrebird was well established in both localities in Tasmania in 1943-44 (Sharland), was reported to be spreading somewhat in the early 1960s (Ridpath and Moreau, 1965), but has generally remained established in the small areas of Tasmania (Wall and Wheeler; Slater, 1974) in which it was released.

DAMAGE

None known.

Family: *Xenicidae* New Zealand Wrens

4 species in 3 genera; 1 species introduced

Before disappearing from Stewart Island (south of New Zealand) following the introduction of the rat *(R. rattus)* in 1962, six Stead's Bush Wrens *(Xenicus longipes variabilis)* were transferred to nearby Kaimohu Island. In 1967 and again in 1972, two birds were noted, but in 1977 none could be found and it appears as though this subfamily is now extinct (Mills and Williams, 1979).

Family: *Alaudidae* Larks

66 species in 15 genera; 3 species introduced, 1 successfully

The Skylark has become successfully established in a number of countries, the only notable failure being in the United States. However, they have now colonised the San Juan Islands, Washington and will probably reach the United States mainland eventually from the colony established on Vancouver Island, Canada.

INTRODUCTIONS OF ALAUDIDAE

Species	Date introduced	Region	Manner introduced	Reason
(a) Successful introductions				
Skylark	1864-79	New Zealand	deliberate	aesthetic ?
	1854-81	Australia	deliberate	aesthetic ?
	1862-99	Tasmania, Australia	deliberate	?
	1865, 1870	Hawaiian Islands	deliberate	?
	1903, 1908-10 ?, 1913, 1919	British Columbia Mainland and Vancouver Island, Canada	deliberate	?
(b) Unsuccessful introductions				
Mongolian Lark	1898, 1904, 1914	Hawaiian Islands	deliberate	?
Wood Lark	1852, 1889	USA	deliberate	aesthetic ?
Skylark	1872	New Zealand	not known if released	cage bird ?
	1857	Australia	not known if released	cage bird ?
	1851-96	USA	deliberate	aesthetic ?

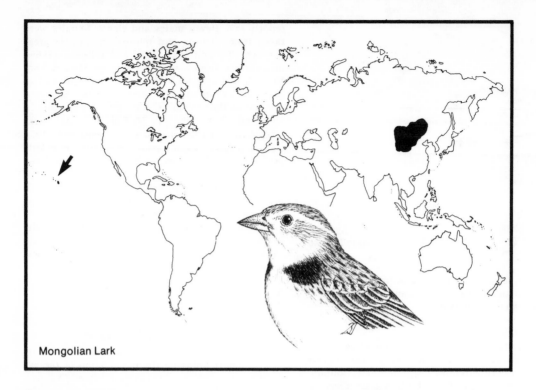

Mongolian Lark

MONGOLIAN LARK
Melanocorypha mongolica (Pallas)

DISTINGUISHING CHARACTERISTICS

19.2-20.6 cm (7.68-8.24 in) . 24-60 g (.85-2.12 oz)
Upper parts brown streaked black; crown, centre of
forehead and neck chestnut, with a lighter patch in
the centre of the crown; lores and eyebrow stripe
white; buff band around nape; wings chestnut, with
white edges; broad black patch on either side of
upper breast and joined at centre of breast; breast
tinged buff; flanks streaked pale chestnut; remainder
of underparts white; tail chestnut, outermost feathers
white; bill yellowish with red-brown mark on upper
mandible and sides of lower mandible.
Dement'ev and Gladkov, vol.5, 1954, transl., 1970,
pp.683-685 and pl. p.685.
Cheng, 1963, pp.501-503.

GENERAL DISTRIBUTION

Eastern Asia: eastern Siberia and northern China
from Dauria, Mongolia and western Manchuria. In
winter south to northern China, Mongolia and south-
western Transbaykalia.

INTRODUCED DISTRIBUTION

Introduced unsuccessfully in the Hawaiian Islands.

GENERAL HABITS

Status: common; favourite cage bird in China.
Habitat: plains and grassy areas in river valleys,
generally near water and avoids barren steppe.
Gregariousness: flocks of several thousand on
migration. *Movements:* sedentary and migratory.
Foods: seeds and insects. *Breeding:* May-June or
July; 2 broods per season. *Nest:* depression on the
ground, sometimes in a tussock of grass. *Eggs:* no
information.
Dement'ev and Gladkov, vol.5, 1954, transl., 1970,
pp.683-685.
Cheng, 1963, pp.501-503.

NOTES ON INTRODUCTIONS

Hawaiian Islands. Munro (1960) reports that the
Mongolian Lark was introduced to Kauai by Mrs D.
Isenberg and is well established there. According to
Bryan (1958) they were introduced to Kauai in 1898,
1904 and in 1914. Peterson (1961) lists the species as
being of uncertain status.
   The Mongolian Lark is not now known to be
established on Kauai (Berger, 1972).

DAMAGE

None known.

WOOD LARK
Lullula arborea (Linnaeus)

DISTINGUISHING CHARACTERISTICS

14.2-17.5 cm (5.68-7 in)
Generally brown, with blackish brown streaks, except
on the belly; creamy white eye-stripe, extending back
around the nape; bushy crest; tail white tipped; bill
brown.
Witherby *et al*, vol.1, 1938-41, pp.176-180, and
pl.18, opp. p.162 and pl.20, opp. p.188.
Dement'ev and Gladkov, vol.5, 1954, transl., 1970,
pp.640-646.

GENERAL DISTRIBUTION

Eurasia – North Africa: from southern England,
southern Sweden and central USSR south to the
Mediterranean region, including north-west Africa,
Turkey, northern Iran and extreme southern USSR.
In winter south to the Mediterranean region, North
Africa and western and central Europe.

INTRODUCED DISTRIBUTION

Introduced, unsuccessfully in the USA and possibly to
Australia and New Zealand.

GENERAL HABITS

Status: fairly common. *Habitat:* forest edges
bordering heathlands, grasslands with scattered trees,
alpine meadows, olive groves, orchards and open

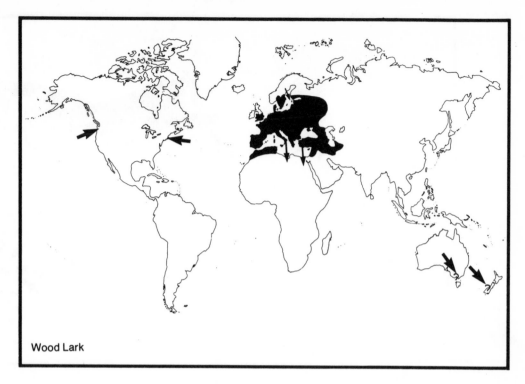

Wood Lark

woods. *Gregariousness:* solitary, pairs or family parties, flocks of 5-10 in winter and at other times larger flocks. *Movements:* sedentary or migratory. *Foods:* insects, small invertebrates and seeds. *Breeding:* Mar-Aug; 2-3 clutches per year. *Nest:* compact, of grass and moss, lined with fine grass and hair, on the ground amongst grass or heather. *Eggs:* 3-5.

Witherby *et al*, vol.1, 1938-41, pp.176-180.
Voous, 1960, pp.186-187.

NOTES ON INTRODUCTIONS

USA. Towards the end of 1852 the Trustees of the Green-Wood Cemetery, on Long Island, New York, purchased a number of British birds including twenty-four Wood Larks which were released in the cemetery (Cleaveland, 1865, in Murphy, 1945). They were reported to have all disappeared and the species to have failed to become established. According to the records of the 'Portland Song Bird Club', ten pairs of Wood Larks were released near Portland, Oregon in the spring of 1889 (Phillips, 1928), but these also failed to become established.

New Zealand. Wood Larks were imported into New Zealand in 1872, but it is not known if they were liberated there (Thomson, 1922).

Australia. Wood Larks were also imported to Victoria in 1857 and possibly at some later dates (Balmford, 1978), but there is no record of any birds being liberated.

DAMAGE

None known.

SKYLARK
(Sky-Lark, Common Skylark, English Skylark)
Alauda arvensis Linnaeus

DISTINGUISHING CHARACTERISTICS

15-20.5 cm (6-8.2 in). 30-43.5 g (1.06-1.53 oz)
Upper parts brown, streaked black; small erectile crest on head; ear-coverts brown, buff line from behind eye to neck; wings and tail brown, outer feathers of tail white; underparts buff or greyish streaked brown or blackish; bill, upper mandible dark brown, lower paler.

Witherby *et al,* vol.1, 1938-41, pp.180-194 and pl.19, opp. p.180 and pl.20, opp. p.188.
Reader's Digest, 1977, p.337 and pl. p.337.

GENERAL DISTRIBUTION

Eurasia – North Africa: from the British Isles across central Asia to the Kurile Islands and Japan. The northern limits in Asia appear uncertain, but in the south reaches northern Iran, north-eastern Afghanistan, China and northern Mongolia. (As a result of the extension of cultivation this species has increased in numbers and markedly expanded its range in western Siberia on the southern border of the Taiga (Voous, 1960).) Winters in southern parts of breeding range and southwards as far as Pakistan, north-western India and Burma.

INTRODUCED DISTRIBUTION

Introduced successfully in New Zealand and on some outlying islands, south-eastern Australia, Tasmania, Kangaroo Island, Lord Howe Island, Hawaiian Islands and Canada (Vancouver Island). Introduced unsuccessfully to the USA (Long Island).

GENERAL HABITS

Status: very common; frequently kept in captivity in Japan. *Habitat:* cultivated areas, grasslands, heathlands and marshes. *Gregariousness:* pairs, and flocks of several hundred on migration. *Movements:* mainly migratory (sedentary as yet in Australia). *Foods:* seeds, green shoots and sprouting plants, insects and other invertebrates, including beetles and weevils, spiders, centipedes, snails and worms. *Breeding:* Apr-July; Oct-Jan (New Zealand) Sept-Jan (Australia); 1-5 broods per season, maximum of 3 successful; 2-3 broods (New Zealand). *Nest:*

293

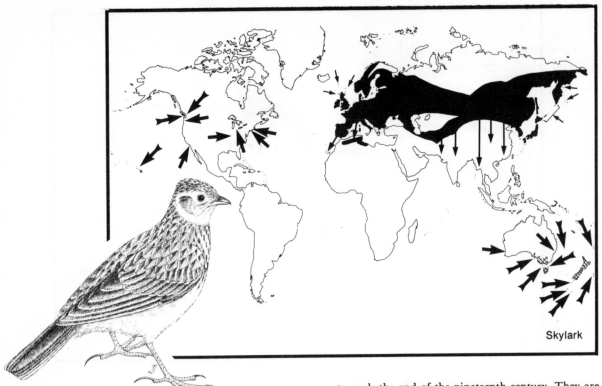

Skylark

usually of dried grass lined with finer material in a scrape or existing depression, on the ground amongst grass or on arable land among crops. *Eggs:* 2-5, 7; 3-7 (New Zealand); 2-4 (Hawaii) 3-5 (Australia).

Witherby *et al*, vol.1, 1938-41, pp.180-184.

Hardman, *Ann. appl. Biol.* vol.76, 1974, pp.337-341.

NOTES ON INTRODUCTIONS

New Zealand. Skylarks were introduced in New Zealand a number of times, and in many areas, from 1864 to 1879 (Thomson, 1922). They were first imported by the Nelson Acclimatisation Society in 1864 when twenty birds arrived. The Otago society liberated four birds in 1867, thirty-five in 1868 and a further sixty-one in 1869. Also at about this time, many were imported and liberated by dealers and private persons.

The Canterbury society introduced Skylarks in 1867 (thirteen birds) and in 1871 (eighteen). The Auckland society received ten birds in 1867 and another fifty-three in 1868. The Wellington society introduced fifty-two in 1874 and a further fifty-six in 1875. Seventy birds were liberated on Stewart Island, off the south coast in 1879.

Thomson records that by 1873 Skylarks were considered to be established in the Auckland area, had disappeared on Stewart Island by 1916, and elsewhere were rapidly increasing in numbers and spreading. They were apparently throughout most of the cultivated areas of New Zealand by the 1920s.

The Skylark is now widespread and common in both the North and South Islands of New Zealand and on Stewart Island (Wodzicki, 1965; Falla *et al,* 1966).

According to Oliver (1955) Skylarks were introduced to the Chatham Islands by L. W. Hood towards the end of the nineteenth century. They are now established on Raoul, the Chatham and Auckland Islands (Wodzicki), also reach the Kermadecs and Campbell Island and breed on both the Auckland and Chatham Islands (Williams). They appear to have first reached the Kermadecs in about 1946 (Williams, 1953).

Australia. From introductions in 1862 in South Australia (Condon, 1962) and in 1863 in Victoria (Harman, 1963) the Skylark is said to have become firmly established in Australia. However, in Victoria records of the species date back to at least 1854 and some were reported in and near Melbourne in 1855, 1857 and 1858 (Balmford, 1978). Seven birds were liberated on the Barrabool Hills, near Geelong in about 1850 or 1854 and many were imported, some of which were probably released, between this date and 1863. Hardy (1928) quoting Wilson (*Trans. Phil. Inst., Vic.,* 1857) indicates that the seven birds were released in 1850 but Balmford reports that it was probably in 1854.

In South Australia, Condon reports that Skylarks were first imported in July 1862. Some eighteen birds were liberated in parklands about Adelaide and at Enfield in 1879. Twenty-two pairs were set free at Dry Creek (north of Adelaide) at about the same time, and a further nine pairs at Enfield. Subsequently 147 were liberated at various places near Adelaide and thirty-six at Kapunda in 1881. By the 1950s they were well established but confined to the Adelaide Plains (Tarr, 1950).

Further introductions of Skylarks occurred near Melbourne, Victoria in 1863, 1867, (eighty birds), 1870 (thirty), 1872, in 1874 (100) (Ryan, 1906), and probably in 1866 (thirty-two) also.

However, it appears that they may have been established in Victoria by private persons before the releases by the Royal Zoological and Acclimatisation

Society of Victoria from 1863 onwards. The species was reported to be fairly widespread in Victoria by the 1950s (Tarr).

Skylarks were also apparently introduced near Sydney, New South Wales in 1866 (Jenkins, 1977), in 1870-72 (Ryan, 1906) and in the 1880s (Jenkins). By the 1950s they were common in the coastal districts and as far west as the central areas of that State (Tarr). The species was also liberated in Western Australia some time prior to 1912 (Long, 1972) and in Queensland in 1869 (Jenkins), but failed to become established in these States.

The Skylark is now established throughout the grasslands of the coastal areas of southern and south-eastern Australia (Cayley, 1953; McGill, 1960; Frith, 1973) and were reported to occur on King and Flinders Islands, Bass Strait before 1950 (Tarr).

Littler (1902) indicates that the Skylark was probably liberated in Tasmania in 1862 or 1872, certainly some were liberated in about 1887 to 1892. The Northern Tasmanian Acclimatisation Society imported thirty-six birds from New Zealand and liberated them in surrounding districts in 1899. They were reported to be plentiful at Risdon and Glenorchy, near Hobart in about 1902. By the 1950s they are recorded from many of the cultivated areas, especially in the south of that State (Tarr).

The species was noted on Lord Howe Island by McKean and Hindwood (1965) in 1963.

Hawaiian Islands. Skylarks were introduced to these islands from England in 1865 and from New Zealand in 1870 (Berger, 1972; Hawaiian Audubon Society, 1975). The first introductions appear to have occurred on the island of Oahu, where they were said (Henshaw, 1904) to be such a success that some were released on the windward side of Hawaii. The species was apparently common on Molokai in 1907 (Bryan, 1958). Some were introduced to Niihau before 1920 by F. Sinclair who later took some to Kauai for release there (Fisher, 1951). They were present on Lanai in 1925 (Munro, 1960) and were found to be on Lehua in 1936 (Caum, 1936). Munro records that their range in the Hawaiian Islands was greatly disturbed by the advent of pineapple growing.

In the late 1950s Skylarks were established on Hawaii, Oahu and Lanai (A.O.U., 1957), shortly after (Peterson, 1961) were established widely on Niihau, Maui, Hawaii, locally on Oahu, Molokai and Lanai, and were scarce on Kauai. More recently the Hawaiian Audubon Society (1975) says they are most common on Hawaii and Maui and especially on the grassy slopes of Haleakala, Mauna Kea and Mauna Loa, but are found on all the main islands.

It appears that the race established in the Hawaiian Islands is *A.a. arvensis* (A.O.U., 1957) although *A.a. japonica* was introduced in 1934, but apparently was not successful (Munro).

Canada. The race *A.a. arvensis* has been established on the Saanich Peninsula, southern Vancouver Island, British Columbia. Some may or may not have been released by Chinese immigrants in the Fraser River Delta at an early date (Scheffer, 1935). In 1903, 100 pairs of Skylarks were released near Victoria by the Natural History Society of British Columbia with financial assistance of the Provincial Government and private persons. In 1913, forty-nine

more were liberated in the same areas (Scheffer, 1935; Sprot, 1937; Carl and Guiguet, 1972). These were released by the society at Rither's Farm (thirty-four birds), at Lansdowne Road (nine) and at Cadboro Bay (six) (Sprot, 1937). Further birds are reported to have been released, at about the same time, on the lower mainland of British Columbia, at the mouth of the Fraser River (Brooks and Swarth, 1925, in Carl and Guiguet). According to Sprot (1937) about ninety-eight pairs were shipped directly to the mainland in 1903. These were made up into small 'parcels' and some forwarded to Duncan, North Saanich, Colwood and Cedar Hill. Some were released in fields, adjoining the Jubilee Hospital and some at Beacon Hill, of which a few survived, but those released at Duncan, Colwood, North Saanich and Beacon Hill soon disappeared.

Mr G. H. Wallace is said to have imported a number of Skylarks and other British birds in 1908 or 1910 which were released on the Saanich Peninsula, but apparently none of these survived. A Mrs E. A. Morton is said to have released five Skylarks at Oak Bay in 1919 (Carl and Guiguet). By 1935 however, the species was established in isolated groups north as far as North and South Saanich, 22 kilometres (13.75 miles) north of Victoria and some were found at Sidney in 1936 (Sprot, 1937).

Stirling and Edwards (1962) examined the range of the Skylark on Vancouver Island in the early 1960s and reported that they inhabited a small area of less than 8100 hectares (20 000 acres) in a low snowfall area. In 1962 the population was estimated at about 1000 birds. Cold winters with persistent snow apparently reduced the population and brief snow periods tended to concentrate the birds. It was thought at this time that the growth of the city of Victoria would restrict the habitat available to the Skylark and reduce the total population.

Carl and Guiguet indicate that this latter statement has been proven correct and that the species is restricted to a small population around the University of Victoria campus, the Rithet Estate, around the airport, along the east side of the McHugh Valley and at other points on the Saanich Peninsula and in the vicinity of Duncan.

Cooke and Knappen (1941) also record that there was an early introduction of Skylarks to Montreal, Quebec, but that this release was unsuccessful in becoming established.

USA. A colony of Skylarks became established in Brooklyn, New York in 1880 (Wetmore, 1964) when probably seventy-four birds were liberated (Philips, 1928). Breeding birds were observed as early as 1887 near Flatbush (Gilliard, 1958).

Towards the end of 1852 the Trustees of the Green-Wood Cemetery on Long Island (New York) purchased a number of British birds including forty-eight Skylarks (Cleaveland, 1865, in Murphy, 1945) which were released but apparently disappeared. The later introduction (in 1880) apparently became established as it is reported (A.O.U., 1957) that those established on Long Island disappeared in about 1913.

Skylarks were also introduced in other parts of the United States in early times. According to Jewett and Gabrielson (1929), Pfluger (1896, *Oreg. Nat.* 3: 32-

154) reported that fifty pairs were released in East Portland, Milwaukee, Molalla and at Waldo Hills some time prior to 1896 (1889-92 ?). Pfluger apparently indicated that these birds had 'increased wonderfully' and had been established there for some years.

Phillips (1928) records a number of early introductions in the United States including: some that were released from a shipment to Wilmington, Delaware in 1853 and some from this same shipment that may have been released in Washington, D.C. Near Cincinnati an attempt was made to introduce some in 1851, but all those released vanished; another attempt in this area may have been made in the 1870s. About 200 birds were liberated in Santa Cruz County, California in 1908, and seventy-five pairs were released near San Jose in about 1896, but all eventually vanished. In 1871 or 1874, fifty pairs were released at Brooklyn, New York and these appeared to become established there.

Other introductions in early times include those at Massachusetts (Cambridge), New Jersey (Bergen and Passaic Counties), Michigan (Detroit) and Missouri (Centreville and St Louis), but all were unsuccessful (Cooke and Knappen, 1941).

According to Gottschalk (1967) the Skylark has been liberated in many places in the United States, but has always failed to become permanently established.

In 1960 a Skylark was observed on the San Juan Islands, Washington (Bruce, 1961), which is some twenty-six kilometres (41 miles) from the colony established on the Saanich Peninsula, Canada. The species was found to be breeding there (twelve pairs, some breeding) on the south coast in 1970 (Wahl and Wilson, 1971) and in 1972 Weisbrod and Stevens (1974) observed twenty-seven males displaying and a total of sixty-three individual birds. The Skylark is now a permanent resident of the island, will possibly colonise other islands from there and may eventually reach the mainland.

DAMAGE
In the USSR the Skylark damages grain shoots at certain times of the year, but is generally considered a useful species (Falkenstein, pers. comm., 1963). They cause damage to spring sown cereals, root and vegetable crops in Great Britain. According to Hardman (1974) they are a sporadic pest doing serious damage to seedlings only when there is a shortage of natural food. He says that damage has been recorded to such garden crops as peas, lettuce, cauliflowers and cabbages.

The damage by Skylarks does not seem to have been important during the first half of this century, but their population in Britain is increasing due to the destruction of trees and hedges, and more damage can be expected in the future.

Since the introduction of modern methods of sugar beet cultivation, such as space drilling, there have been numerous complaints in England of Skylarks causing damage to beet seed and seedlings such as lettuce (Edgar, 1974). With modern mechanisation of planting beet seed in pelleted form there are fewer seeds available for the birds. They are thus able to reduce the yield in patches over wide areas which total some thousands of hectares annually (Dunning, 1974).

Skylarks have not ever been numerous enough in Canada to have caused any damage. Much the same situation appears to pertain in Australia where there appear to be few records of damage. In New Zealand they are reported to be troublesome on farms and in gardens, damaging seedling wheat, turnips and cabbage, pulling out the young plants as they appear above the ground (Oliver, 1955). Here, in the past at least, it has been rated as the most destructive pest after the House Sparrow.

In China the species eats both beans and corn, but most grain and seeds are picked up from the ground and the Skylark is considered to be more beneficial than injurious (Cheng, 1963).

Family: *Hirundinidae* Swallows, martins
70 species in 20 genera; none known to have been introduced
A successful colonist, the Welcome Swallow *Hirundo nigrans* was first recorded in New Zealand in 1946 and was noted breeding there in 1957-58. It is now widely established in the North Island and in some areas of the South Island (Wodzicki, 1965; Williams, 1973).

Family: *Pycnonotidae* Bulbuls
120 species in 15 genera; 4 species introduced, at least 2 successfully
The Red-whiskered Bulbul, a favourite cage bird in South-east Asia, has become fairly widely established as an escapee from captivity. Similarly, the Red-vented Bulbul has now become established on a number of Pacific Ocean islands where it appears to be spreading fairly rapidly.

Although the bulbuls do not appear to be considered great pests in southern Asia they show much potential in this regard. It can be expected that they will become nuisances if not pests of great magnitude wherever fruit is grown.

RED-WHISKERED BULBUL
(Red-eared Bulbul)
Pycnonotus jocosus (Linnaeus)
DISTINGUISHING CHARACTERISTICS
17.3-22 cm (6.92-8.8 in). 23-42 g (.81-1.48 oz)
Upper parts brown, with crested blackish crown; a red patch behind eye; cheeks and throat white; a broken blackish or dark brown band from breast around sides of neck; underparts greyish white; under tail-coverts red; tail brown, tipped white; bill black.
Ali and Ripley, vol.5, 1968-74.
Reader's Digest, 1977, p.350 and pl. p.350.
GENERAL DISTRIBUTION
South-eastern Asia: from India, Nepal and Bangladesh; east to the Vietnam region and south China; also on the islands of Hong Kong, the Andamans and Naochow (absent from the southern Malay Peninsula).
INTRODUCED DISTRIBUTION
Introduced successfully in the southern Malay Peninsula, Singapore, Nicobar Islands, Mauritius, Réunion, Australia, USA and the Hawaiian Islands; probably introduced successfully in Sumatra and Java.

GENERAL HABITS

Status: very common; commonly kept as a cage bird in South-east Asia and elsewhere. *Habitat:* forest edges, secondary growth, woodland, cultivation, parklands, gardens and villages. *Gregariousness:* pairs or loose flocks, often form flocks 20-30 in winter; roost communally. *Movements:* sedentary. *Foods:* fruits, berries, seeds, flower parts and nectar, insects (flies etc.), caterpillars, ants and seedlings. *Breeding:* variable, Jan-Aug; Feb-July (USA); Aug-Mar (Australia); 2-3 broods per season. *Nest:* cup-shaped, of fine twigs, rootlets, grass and other material, in a tree, thatch walls or roofs of huts. *Eggs:* 2-4.

Cheng, 1963, pp.562-565.

Ali and Ripley, vol.5, 1968-74.

NOTES ON INTRODUCTIONS

Malaysia and Singapore. In Malaysia the Red-whiskered Bulbul occurs naturally down the Malay Peninsula to about Pinang where it is fairly common (Madoc, 1956). They occasionally reach Perak and on the east coast are extremely numerous in Kota Bharu, but are less plentiful in southern Kelantan (Gibson-Hill, 1949).

The species is a favourite cage bird of the Malays and escaped birds may have become established in more southerly areas. Populations in the environs of Kuala Trenggannu town, Ipoh, Kuala Lumpur and on the islands of Singapore and Penang are thought to be feral, originally derived from escapees (Medway and Wells, 1976).

They are resident on the outskirts of Kuala Lumpur and were first recorded to be breeding in Kedah in 1946 (Gibson-Hill). Medway and Wells (1963 and 1964) indicate that this population was beginning to spread in 1962-63. The race established in more southerly areas appears to be *P.j. pattani.*

The race *P.j. pattani* has also been introduced to Singapore where it is also a favourite cage bird. Thousands are still to be seen caged ready for sale in the bird markets around the city.

Gibson-Hill records that they appeared to become established in Singapore in about 1924, but that there have been few post-Occupation records and no recent reports of them breeding there. However, as Medway and Wells have indicated, feral birds may still apparently exist there.

Sumatra and Java. The Red-whiskered Bulbul reaches both Sumatra and Java where it may have been introduced as it is a popular cage bird there. Little appears to have been documented. *P. aurigaster* which is sometimes given subspecific status under *P. cafer* appears to have been introduced to Sumatra.

Nicobar Islands. The race *P.j. whistleri* has been introduced and established in these islands (Peters, 1960; Ripley, 1961). Abdulali (1967) says that they were introduced from Port Blair in the Andamans and are now common at Trinkut and Camorta, and possibly at Nancowry, but probably do not occur elsewhere in the Nicobars.

Mauritius. The race *P.j. emeria* has been introduced and established on Mauritius (Leach, 1958; Peters, 1960). Rountree *et al* (1952) record that they were introduced as cage birds from India in about 1892,

INTRODUCTIONS OF PYCNONOTIDAE

Species	Date introduced	Region	Manner introduced	Reason
(a) Successful introductions				
Red-whiskered Bulbul	1940s on	southern Malay Peninsula	escapees/colonisation	cage bird
	1924 on	Singapore	escapees	cage bird
	?	Nicobar Islands	?	?
	about 1892	Mauritius	escapee	cage bird
	1880	Australia	deliberate and escapees	?
	about 1960	USA	escapee	cage bird
	about 1965	Hawaiian Islands	escapee	cage bird
Red-vented Bulbul	about 1903	Fiji	escapee	cage bird
	1912 ? or 1943	Samoa	deliberate	?
	1928-29	Tonga	deliberate or escapee	insect control ?
	about 1965	Hawaiian Islands	deliberate release	cage bird
(b) Probably successful introductions				
Red-whiskered Bulbul	?	Sumatra and Java ?	?	cage bird
	1972	Réunion	deliberate	?
Sooty-headed Bulbul	before mid-1930s	Sumatra	?	?
	before 1936	Sulawesi ?	?	?
(c) Unsuccessful or probably unsuccessful introductions				
Red-vented Bulbul	1917 ?	Australia ?	?	?
	1952	New Zealand	escapee	shipborne
Sooty-headed Bulbul	1923	Singapore	escapee	cage bird
Black Bulbul	before 1953 ?	Chagos Archipelago	deliberate ?	?

Red-whiskered Bulbul

accidentally became liberated, and are now abundant throughout the island.

Meinertzhagen (1912) reports that they were introduced by G. Reynard, increased rapidly and were widely distributed by 1911. However, Staub (1976) says that they arrived on board the sailing vessel *C.J.S.* just before 1892. The Captain apparently presented a caged pair to a Mauritian and these escaped in the cyclone in 1892. The Red-whiskered Bulbul is still abundant on Mauritius.

Réunion. According to Staub (1976), the Mauritius newspaper *Cerneen* of 27 December 1972, contained an article referring to the Red-whiskered Bulbul which had recently been introduced by tourists from Mauritius. It is therefore possible that the species is now established on this island.

Australia. The Red-whiskered Bulbul appears to have been first introduced by the Zoological and Acclimatisation Society in 1880 in New South Wales (Tarr, 1950). Some were reported at Homebush in 1902 and they appear to have been well established around Sydney in 1919-20. They are recorded nesting at Hunters Hill in 1919 and 1920 and were said to be at Wahroonga in about 1921 (Wolstenholme, 1921). MacPherson (1921) observed them at Double Bay in 1917 where they continued to increase in numbers until 1924. There were flocks of up to 100 birds in Sydney suburbs in 1933 (Chaffer, 1933).

Red-whiskered Bulbuls have turned up in Melbourne and Geelong in Victoria, but it does not appear to be known when they were liberated. In 1915-16 some were reported from Ashfield, and a pair

were observed in Melbourne (Tarr, 1950) in 1948.

The few records from around Adelaide, South Australia are said to refer to aviary escapees (Tarr, 1950, Condon, 1962). Those at large in both Victoria and New South Wales have also been reported to have been derived from escaped or liberated birds, certainly the latter escaped from an aviary in Sydney (McGill, 1948; Thomson, 1964).

In the 1950s and 1960s Red-whiskered Bulbuls were reported to be common around Sydney, spreading to outlying areas up to ninety-six kilometres (60 miles) away, and were fairly well established in Melbourne (McGill 1960; Cayley, 1953). The species is still common around Adelaide, Sydney and Melbourne and appears to be slowly spreading.

USA. In California the Red-whiskered Bulbul is fairly widely held in captivity and frequently escapes. From 1968 when they were first detected until 1972, the Department of Agriculture, Los Angeles had destroyed some forty-seven birds in the wild in that city. However, despite their efforts a small population had established itself in the Los Angeles County Arboretum and in the Huntingdon Gardens, where they were apparently breeding (Hardy, 1973). Some birds probably still exist there. By 1977, the total of birds shot had risen to eighty-four bulbuls and definite proof of them breeding in the area had been found (Keffer, pers. comm., 1977) A single bird was recorded from as far away as the Pasadena-San Gabriel Valley in 1975 (Heilbrun, 1976).

The Red-whiskered Bulbul is also well established and breeding in south-eastern Florida (Owre, 1973). Owre reports that they became established in a restricted area of Dade County in about 1960, when some birds escaped from a bird farm. Carleton and Owre (1975) hypothesize that somewhere between five and ten breeding pairs founded the present population of some 250 birds which are established in

298

an area of some eight square kilometres (3 square miles). Present indications are that the species is slowly spreading in this region of Florida, where according to Banks and Laybourne (1968), the race established is *P.j. emeria*.

Hawaiian Islands. The Red-whiskered Bulbul became established on the island of Oahu from the unauthorised release of cage birds in about 1965 or some time before this date (Hawaiian Audubon Society, 1975). In 1965, two birds were reported in the Lower Makiki Heights; by the fall of 1967, twenty-four were counted in this area; four were observed on the Pacific Heights late in 1967 and seven were seen there in December 1968; a pair nested twice in Lower Makiki Heights in the summer of 1971 (Berger, 1972).

The Hawaiian Audubon Society says that Red-whiskered Bulbuls have been observed at Makiki, Kaimuki and in the Punchbowl areas and appear to be extending their range on Oahu. More recently Heilbrun (1976) records that five were noted on the Christmas Bird Count in 1975.

DAMAGE

Throughout their native range Red-whiskered Bulbuls do not appear to be great pests. This may in part be due to lack of documentation. They are reported to do a certain amount of damage in fruit and vegetable gardens in India and Thailand (Ali, 1953-62; Deignan, 1945) and are probably pests throughout most of their range. Baker (1922 and 1924) records damage to fruits such as raspberries *(Rubus albescens)*, oranges, plums and the fruits of *Arbutus*. According to Cheng (1963) they do at times damage cultivated fruits in southern China, but destroy many insects and are considered both good and harmful. Ali and Ripley (1968-74) report that they frequently do damage to ripening fruit in orchards and are a minor scourge in kitchen gardens and to flower beds and seedlings in India.

As an introduced species they are regarded as exhibiting much potential as pests, particularly in fruit growing areas. Where introduced in Mauritius they became a nuisance to fruit growers (Meinertzhagen, 1912), and in Australia have already caused sufficient damage for them to be mentioned as pests. As early as 1924 (MacPherson, 1924) there were references to their onslaughts on peas, figs and strawberries. Later, Chaffer (1933) indicates that they had become a pest to orchards because of their liking for soft fruits.

In America, studies by Carleton and Owre (1975) show that the Red-whiskered Bulbul has not caused any damage to citrus or other large fruits of commercial importance. However, they are not present in large numbers nor have they yet spread very far. Gore and Doubilet (1976) say that they eat mangoes and compete with mockingbirds for berries in Florida.

RED-VENTED BULBUL
Pycnonotus cafer (Linnaeus)

DISTINGUISHING CHARACTERISTICS

20-22 cm (8-8.8 in). 26-45 g (.92-1.59 oz)

Upper parts variably smoke brown to black, each feather darker in the centre, giving a scaled appearance; partially crested black head; throat black; underparts greyish white, breast dark and faintly scaled; under tail-coverts red; tail brown, white tipped; bill black.

MacDonald and Loke, 1962, pl. p.99.

Ali and Ripley, vol.5, 1968-74.

GENERAL DISTRIBUTION

Southern and south-eastern Asia: from Pakistan, east through India and Sri Lanka to the Vietnam region.

INTRODUCED DISTRIBUTION

Introduced successfully in the Fijian Islands, Samoan

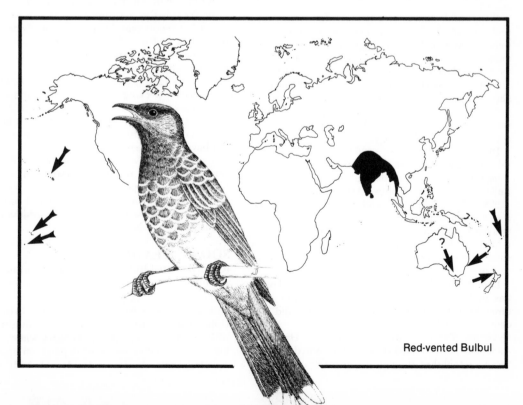

Red-vented Bulbul

Islands, Tonga and the Hawaiian Islands. Introduced unsuccesfully to Australia and New Zealand (extirpated).

GENERAL HABITS

Status: very common. *Habitat:* secondary growth and scrub, cultivation, parks and gardens. *Gregariousness:* pairs, or small flocks in non-breeding season. *Movements:* sedentary. *Foods:* fruits, berries, insects, flower nectar, seeds and buds. *Breeding:* variable, mainly Feb-Oct, Nov; Nov-Jan (Fiji); up to 3 broods per season. *Nest:* cup-shaped of rootlets and sometimes cobwebs, in a bush or tree. *Eggs:* 2-4, 5. (2-4 Fiji).

Ali and Ripley, vol.5, 1968-74.

NOTES ON INTRODUCTIONS

Fiji. The Red-vented Bulbul was introduced to Fiji in about 1903 (Parham, 1954) from India as a cage bird (Mercer, 1966) with Indian immigrants (Watling, 1978). They became established on Viti Levu, were common there in the 1940s (Mayr, 1945) and were particularly common in Suva in the 1970s (Gorman, 1975).

The species has remained restricted to Viti Levu, but has reached some of the smaller adjacent islands of Ovalau, Wakaya, Beqa, Taveuni, Wairiki and Waiyevo. They are abundant in agricultural and suburban habitats and are commonly observed in clearings and secondary growth in forests (Watling).

The race introduced in Fiji is *P.c. bengalensis* (Peters, 1960).

Samoan Islands. Dhondt (1977) indicates that the Red-vented Bulbul probably reached Upolu, in Western Samoa, in the early 1950s (Keith, 1957) and has since spread to other islands in the group including Tutuila and Savai'i. However, the species may have been introduced in Western Samoa by U.S. marines in 1943, although there is an unconfirmed report that they first appeared there of their own accord in 1912 (Watling, 1978).

Clapp and Sibley (1966) say that they were probably introduced to Tutuila some time after 1957, were uncommon in Pago Pago in 1963, but were numerous and several were seen south of the town in 1965. Small numbers were observed by Dhondt (1976) in the Salelolonga and Asau areas of Savai'i in about the mid-1970s.

On the islands of Tutuila and Upolu the Red-vented Bulbul is common only in residential and agricultural areas (Watling).

Dhondt quotes Ashmole (1963) in saying that the subspecies present in Samoa is *bengalensis.*

Tonga. Dhondt (1976) indicated that the Red-vented Bulbul had reached Tonga. According to Watling (1978) the introduction and spread here can be traced from a pair which were either released or escaped on Niuafo'ou in 1928-29: in the 1940s they were brought to Tongatāpu by Prince Tungi to control unwanted insects, and from there they spread to 'Eau.

Dhondt noted that the subspecies present in Tonga was probably *bengalensis* and found it abundant throughout the island of Tongatāpu but did not observe any on Vava'u.

Hawaiian Islands. According to the Hawaiian Audubon Society (1975) the Red-vented Bulbul became established through the unauthorised release of cage birds in about 1965. They are now most common on the windward side of Oahu, in residential areas, but have also been observed regularly in the Manoa Valley and in the Moanulua Gardens. Berger (1975) indicated that the species was well established but confined to the island of Oahu. Heilbrun (1976) indicates that they are well established and reports a count of some 212 birds during the 1975 Christmas Bird Count on Oahu. Prior to this, six were seen at Waipahu in 1966, and by June 1967 they had been reported at Fort Shafter, in Kailua and at Bellows Air Force Station at Waimanalo: subsequently five were observed at Waimanalo in September 1970 (Berger, 1972).

Australia. Red-vented Bulbuls are rarely seen in the vicinity of Melbourne, Victoria (Slater, 1974). Le Souef (1918) reports them in Sydney and Melbourne in 1917, and to be breeding there. Whether a population still exists in Melbourne does not appear to be documented.

New Zealand. Red-vented Bulbuls were known to be present in the suburbs of Auckland from October 1952 (Oliver, 1955; Turbott, 1956). Oliver records that the species bred at Stanley Bay and Remuera in 1954. The species became established in New Zealand despite efforts by the Department of Agriculture to exterminate them. The origin of those which became established was unknown, but they were presumed to have been brought in by ship.

Falla *et al* (1966) say that the race *P.c. bengalensis* escaped or was released from a ship in Auckland Harbour and although they became established for a period, none appear to have now survived the efforts to destroy them.

DAMAGE

In India Red-vented Bulbuls do a certain amount of damage to fruits and vegetables (Ali, 1944-62). The damage according to Ali is offset by their consumption of injurious insects. They do not appear to be regarded as a significant pest. Ali and Ripley (1968-74) report that the species is locally destructive in gardens to fruits, flowers and peas, but is also a good pollinating agent. They too record that they feed on many injurious insects.

Fitzwater (1967) describes how he watched birds of this species pecking away at merchandise on a shopkeeper's table in India. The shopkeeper raised his hand to frighten them away only when their bickering got so noisy as to interfere with the conversation he was having with his neighbour.

Where they have been introduced in Fiji, Red-vented Bulbuls are reported to destroy fruits, flowers, beans, tomatoes, peas (Parham, 1954) and to be harmful to ripe fruit (Turbet, 1941) such as bananas and other soft fruits and to spread the seeds of noxious weeds (Mercer, 1966).

SOOTY-HEADED BULBUL
(Golden-vented Bulbul, White-eared Bulbul)
Pycnonotus aurigaster (Vieillot)

DISTINGUISHING CHARACTERISTICS

18.5-22.5 cm (7.4-9 in). 40-50 g (1.41-1.76 oz)
Upper parts brown; head blackish; hindneck grey with brown streaks; ear-coverts dusky white; narrow blackish line under eye; whitish patch on upper tail-coverts; chest, breast and sides, of body greyish

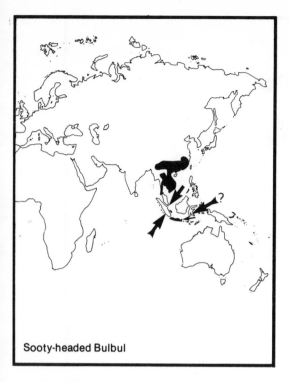

Sooty-headed Bulbul

brown; abdomen dusky white; under tail-coverts yellow to red; tail brown tipped white; bill black.
Cheng, 1963, pp.569-570 and pl.22, no.80.

GENERAL DISTRIBUTION
Southern Asia: southern China, Hong Kong, southern and eastern Burma, Thailand, Indochina Peninsula, Java and Bangka.

INTRODUCED DISTRIBUTION
Introduced, probably successfully in Sumatra, and perhaps Sulawesi. Introduced successfully, but has now died out in Singapore.

GENERAL HABITS
Status: common; cage bird in southern China. *Habitat:* secondary growth, open forest, scrub, gardens, parks and roadsides. *Gregariousness:* generally small groups 3-5 birds, other habits similar to *P. cafer* of which it may be a subspecies. *Movements:* sedentary (?) *Foods:* insects, fruits and nuts. *Breeding:* most months except Oct-Nov; 2 broods per year (China). *Nest:* neatly woven, cup-shaped of twigs and leaves, and lined with fibres, fine grass and straw, in a tree. *Eggs:* 2, 3-4, 6.
Cheng, 1963, pp.570-572.

NOTES ON INTRODUCTIONS
Sumatra. According to Peters (1960) the race *P.a. aurigaster* has been introduced and established in Sumatra. It appears to be still established there as its presence is recorded there by King *et al* (1975).

In the mid-1930s the species inhabited Medan in north-eastern Sumatra and according to Kuroda (1933-36), Dammerman and Kloss (1931, *Treubia* 13 (3-4): 344) believed the species to have been introduced into Sumatra.
Singapore. The race *P.a. aurigaster* has been introduced to Singapore (Peters, 1960) where a few pairs had established themselves before the second World War (Gibson-Hill, 1949).

Medway and Wells (1976) indicate that cage

escapees derived from birds imported from Java persisted in suburban districts of Singapore from 1923 until at least 1950, but that there are no recent records of them.
Sulawesi. Stresemann (1936) recorded that this species had been introduced to Sulawesi and was established on the southern peninsula there. There appear to be no more recent records of the species in that country.

DAMAGE
In southern China, Cheng (1963) reports that 'their diet includes some economically important plants so that their benefit-harm relationship is half and half with respect to agriculture and forestry'.

BLACK BULBUL
(Mauritius Bulbul, Réunion Bulbul, Olivaceous Bulbul)
Hypsipetes borbonicus (Forster)

DISTINGUISHING CHARACTERISTICS
24 cm (9.6 in)
Crown, face and semi-crest black; upper parts black with a brownish tinge; chin greyish, remainder of underparts whitish; tail black; bill orange to bright yellow (Note: the Mauritian bird is said to have yellow-brown eyes and the Réunion bird to have a conspicuous white iris.)
Staub, 1976, pp.27-28 and pl. opp. p.30.

GENERAL DISTRIBUTION
Mauritius and Réunion.

INTRODUCED DISTRIBUTION
Introduced unsuccessfully to Diego Garcia in the Chagos Archipelago.

GENERAL HABITS
Status: fairly common but declining on Mauritius, becoming rare on Réunion. *Habitat:* forest, secondary growth and occasionally gardens. *Gregariousness:* groups or small parties. *Movements:*

Black Bulbul

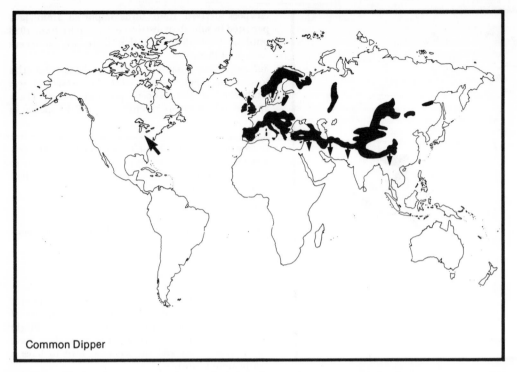

Common Dipper

sedentary, but tends to move to lower elevations in winter. *Foods:* insects, fruits and seeds. *Breeding:* Oct-Dec. *Nest:* roundish bundle of straw and roots, lined with finer material. *Eggs:* 2.

Staub, 1976, pp.27-28.

NOTES ON INTRODUCTIONS

Diego Garcia. Hutson (1975) says that according to the local people the Black Bulbul was introduced to Diego Garcia from Mauritius. He indicates that the introduction has not been recorded previously and it is certainly not mentioned by either Watson *et al* (1963) or Bourne (1971).

Hutson records that the species is said to have become common on the island in about 1953, but suddenly died out soon after and was not re-introduced. Bourne and others indicate that the Myna *(A. tristis)* probably reached Diego Garcia from other islands in the group in 1953 or soon after and it is suggested that the unexplained disappearance of the Black Bulbul coincides with the introduction of this species.

As the introduction occurred with Mauritian birds the subspecies would have been *H.b. olivaceus.*

Family: *Cinclidae* Dippers

5 species in 1 genus; 1 species introduced unsuccessfully

The Common Dipper was an early unsuccessful introduction into the United States. This country already has a native species *(C. mexicanus)* which

does not occur in the eastern part of the country where the introduction was attempted.

COMMON DIPPER
(Black-bellied Dipper, Dipper)
Cinclus cinclus (Linnaeus)

DISTINGUISHING CHARACTERISTICS
16.5-17.8 cm (6.6-7.12 in)

Head and neck chocolate-brown; remainder of upper parts slate-grey; margins of feathers are black giving a scaly appearance; short line over eye whitish; chin, throat and upper breast white; lower breast and central belly chestnut-brown, lower part of belly black-brown; flanks slate-grey marked dark brown; wings black-brown, narrowly tipped brownish white; tail slate-grey with a brown tinge; bill black.

Witherby *et al,* vol.2, 1938-41, pp.220-226 and pl.51, opp. p.220.

GENERAL DISTRIBUTION

Eurasia: Great Britain and Ireland, Norway, Sweden and Finland; southern Europe, and central and south-central Asia.

INTRODUCED DISTRIBUTION
Introduced unsuccessfully to the USA.

GENERAL HABITS

Status: fairly common. *Habitat:* streams and rivulets in hilly and mountainous regions. *Gregariousness:* solitary and pairs. *Movements:* mainly sedentary; may seek lower elevations in winter. *Foods:* aquatic insects and their larvae, small crustaceans, worms,

INTRODUCTIONS OF CINCLIDAE

Species	Date introduced	Region	Manner introduced	Reason
(a) Unsuccessful introduction				
Common Dipper	1872-73	USA	deliberate	aesthetic?

snails, bivalves, fish fry and tadpoles. *Breeding*: Feb-June. *Nest*: large dome-shaped structure of moss, leaves, twigs, etc. in holes or fissures in river banks, amongst roots or under bridges and waterfalls. *Eggs*: 3, 4-6, 7.

Witherby *et al*, vol.2, 1938-41, pp.220-226.

Voous, 1960, p.196.

NOTES ON INTRODUCTIONS

USA. Dippers, probably the common European species, are recorded as having been set free during the Cincinnati acclimatisation experiments of 1872-73 (Phillips, 1928). The species failed to become established in the United States.

Family: *Mimidae* Mockingbirds

31 species in 13 genera; 2 species introduced, 1 successfully

Although introduced deliberately in a number of areas the Northern Mockingbird has had little success except in the Hawaiian Islands. It has however, successfully colonised a number of areas including southern Canada and part of the West Indies.

The Tropical Mockingbird has had some success, probably as a colonist, although some occurrences may have been due to deliberate introduction.

NORTHERN MOCKINGBIRD
(Common Mockingbird)
Mimus polyglottos (Linnaeus)

DISTINGUISHING CHARACTERISTICS

22-28 cm (8.8-11.2 in). 47-50.8 g (1.66-1.79 oz) Upper parts brownish grey, blackish on wings and tail; conspicuous white patch forming two wing bars; underparts white or greyish white; outermost tail-feathers mainly white; bill blackish.

Roberts, 1934, pl.58.

Godfrey, 1966, p.292 and pl.50, no.1, opp. p.237.

GENERAL DISTRIBUTION

North America and West Indies: from north-central California and central New Jersey south to southern

Northern Mockingbird,
Mimus polyglottos

Mexico, the Bahamas and the Greater Antilles east to the Virgin Islands; occurs casually further north in the USA and to southern Canada.

INTRODUCED DISTRIBUTION

Introduced successfully to the Hawaiian Islands, Bermuda (died out), and Barbados (extirpated). Introduced unsuccessfully to St Helena, Tahiti and the northern USA. Successfully colonised southern Canada and some eastern Virgin Islands.

GENERAL HABITS

Status: common. *Habitat:* forest edges, open wooded country, mangroves, gardens, parklands, towns, farmlands, roadsides, mesquite and brush. *Gregariousness:* pairs, or sometimes large flocks in winter. *Movements:* partially migratory and nomadic. *Foods:* insects, grubs, pollen, fruits, berries and seeds. *Breeding:* Mar-Aug; 2-3 broods per season (4 successful recorded). *Nest:* bulky cup of twigs,

INTRODUCTIONS OF MIMIDAE

Species	Date introduced	Region	Manner introduced	Reason
(a) Successful introductions				
Northern Mockingbird	recent ?	southern Canada	colonisation	?
	1928, 1931-33	Hawaiian Islands	deliberate	?
	early 19th century	eastern Virgin Islands	colonisation	?
Tropical Mockingbird	late 18th century	Caucatal, Colombia	deliberate ?	?
	about 1932	Panama	?	?
	about 1930s	Trinidad and Tobago	colonisation ?	?
(b) Unsuccessful introductions				
Northern Mockingbird	1892, 1895	Oregon, USA	deliberate	?
	1893	Bermuda	deliberate	?
	?	Barbados	?	?
	1853	St Helena	deliberate ?	?
	about 1938	Tahiti	deliberate	?
Tropical Mockingbird	?	Barbados and Nevis	?	?

Northern Mockingbird

moss, bark strips, grass and leaves, lined with grass and rootlets, in a bush or tree. *Eggs:* 3, 4-5, 7; 4-6 Hawaii.

Laskey, *Auk* vol.79, 1962, pp.596-606.
Godfrey, 1966, p.292.
Reilly, 1968, pp.343-344.

NOTES ON INTRODUCTIONS
Virgin Islands. The Northern Mockingbird appears to have spread its range eastwards in these islands at least in the early part of this century. According to Robertson (1962) they were first noted on St Thomas in 1916 and have extended their range eastwards to Anegada. They apparently reached the island of St John by about 1927.

USA. In the spring of 1892 the Society for the Introduction of Useful Song-Birds into Oregon set free three pairs of Mockingbirds at Milwaukee, Oregon (Jewett and Gabrielson, 1929). These birds apparently bred the following year. According to Jewett and Gabrielson (quoting Anon, 1895, *Oreg. Nat.* 2:23) a further introduction occurred in about January 1895, when nearly forty pairs were liberated from an aviary in the city. Some may also have been introduced in San Francisco with birds ordered from Louisiana in 1891 (Phillips, 1928).

Canada. According to Godfrey (1966) the Northern Mockingbird has recently spread slowly northward into Canada. They are now a local but permanent resident in a number of areas in southern Canada.

Hawaiian Islands. The Northern Mockingbird was introduced from North America to the Hawaiian Islands in 1928 and became established there on the island of Oahu (Munro, 1960). They were released by the Hui Manu on Oahu in 1931 and 1932, and in 1933 on both Oahu and Maui (Berger, 1972). Munro reports that they were seen on both Maui and Hawaii in 1936.

By the 1960s they were established on Maui and locally on Oahu, Molokai, Lanai and Hawaii (Peterson, 1961) and have now apparently spread to all the main islands and have been observed in the north-west chain on Nihoa, Necker and Tern Islands (Hawaiian Audubon Society, 1975).

Berger indicates that they reached Tern Island, French Frigate Shoal in about October 1960, and Necker Island in about 1966. Although the species may have been released on Kauai (Richardson and Bowles, 1964) Berger indicates that they probably spread there from Oahu. They were locally common on the south coast of Kauai in 1960 and were spreading rapidly. Udvardy (1961) has reported that they were widespread on Maui after introduction there in 1933. Dunmire (1961) recorded the apparent colonisation from Maui to Hawaii in 1959.

Bermuda. The race *M.p. polyglottos* (Peters, 1960) was introduced to Bermuda in 1893 (Bourne, 1957). They became established on the island and were successful there for a period of about twenty years (to about 1914) when they declined in numbers and finally vanished.

According to Bourne, the Northern Mockingbird may have died out on Bermuda because it failed to form a stable equilibrium with the environment. It exhausted the food supply after only a short period of establishment.

Barbados. The race *M.p. orpheus* was introduced to this island successfully, but has now been extirpated (Peters, 1960).

St Helena. American mockingbirds (probably *M. polyglottos ?*) are reported to have been introduced on St Helena, apparently became established, but later died out (Benson, 1950). It is mentioned by Melliss (1870) that 'South American mockingbirds' were introduced to St Helena in 1853.

Tahiti. The Northern Mockingbird was liberated on Tahiti in about 1938, but was not seen again after release (Guild, 1938).

DAMAGE
None known.

TROPICAL MOCKINGBIRD
(Southern Mockingbird)
Mimus gilvus (Vieillot)

DISTINGUISHING CHARACTERISTICS
23-26 cm (9.2-10.4 in). 43-67 g (1.52-2.36 oz)
Head, neck and crown pale grey, with dark shafts to feathers of upper head; dusky stripe through eye; superciliary stripe whitish; lores brownish; wings and tail dark brownish black; wing-coverts and remiges margined white; throat whitish, becoming greyish brown on breast and greyish white on abdomen; tail black, conspicuously white tipped; bill black.

Bond, 1971, pp.166-167 and pl. p.224.

Tropical Mockingbird, *Mimus gilvus*

Tropical Mockingbird

Barbados and Nevis. The race *M.g. antillarum* was successfully introduced to these islands, but has now been extirpated (Peters, 1960).

Colombia. In the second half of the previous century *M.g. tolimensis* from Magdalena was taken to Caucatal where the species is now well established (Sick, 1968).

Panama. According to Meyer de Schauensee (1970) the Tropical Mockingbird has been introduced into Panama where Ridgely (1976) indicates that they were first reported in 1932. The species is now common in the Canal Zone and has spread as far east as Tocumen and Portobello and as far west as Chorrera and Boca del Rio.

Trinidad and Tobago. According to Ffrench (1976) the Tropical Mockingbird is apparently a recent arrival in these islands. In 1931 they were restricted to St Augustine, but by 1956 were common at Piarco, Port of Spain and oil company residential areas of southern Trinidad. They are now found in the Northern Range, on the east coast as far as Toco, at Caroni, Orapouche, Cumuto, and on Bocas Island, west to Chacachacare. Tropical Mockingbirds are now a common resident of both these islands.

DAMAGE
None known.

Meyer de Schauensee and Phelps, 1978, p.295 and pl.32.

GENERAL DISTRIBUTION
Central and South America: southern Mexico south to Panama, the Lesser Antilles, Tobago, Trinidad, Aruba, Curaçao and other small Caribbean Sea islands; western and central Colombia east through Venezuela to Guyane and northern and eastern Brazil.

INTRODUCED DISTRIBUTION
Successfully introduced in Caucatal in Colombia, and colonised Trinidad and Tobago; also introduced in Panama. Successfully introduced to Barbados and Nevis but now extirpated.

GENERAL HABITS
Status: fairly common. *Habitat:* woodland, open settled country, field edges, swampy areas, semi-arid areas, towns, parks, roadsides and gardens. *Gregariousness:* pairs or family groups. *Movements:* no information. *Foods:* insects, fruits (including mango and paw paw), berries, spiders and wasps. *Breeding:* all year, but probably from Feb-July mainly; 2 or more broods per year. *Nest:* open, cup-shaped of twigs, with a lining of rootlets or soft material, in a bush or tree. *Eggs:* 2-4.

Bond, 1971, pp.166-167.
Ffrench, 1973, pp.354-355.
Ridgely, 1976, p.272.

Family: *Prunellidae* Accentors
12 species in 1 genus; 1 species successfully introduced

HEDGESPARROW
(Dunnock, Accentor)
Prunella modularis (Linnaeus)

DISTINGUISHING CHARACTERISTICS
13-15 cm (5.2-6 in). 19 g (.67 oz)
Generally brownish, streaked blackish; breast, throat and head grey; belly whitish; wings and back brown, streaked black; tail brown; bill blackish.
Witherby *et al,* vol.2, 1938-41, pp.208-213 and pl.50, opp. p.198.

GENERAL DISTRIBUTION
Eurasia: British Isles, all Europe (except the entire southern coastal fringe), central western Asia, Turkey, northern Iran and southern USSR. Winters to central and western Europe, the Mediterranean and Tunisia (has considerably extended its breeding range in Scandinavia in the present century (Voous, 1960)).

INTRODUCED DISTRIBUTION
Introduced successfully to New Zealand and outlying islands. Introduced unsuccessfully to the USA.

GENERAL HABITS
Status: very common. *Habitat:* forest, forest edges, woodland, parks, gardens, farmland, and locally in

INTRODUCTIONS OF PRUNELLIDAE

Species	Date introduced	Region	Manner introduced	Reason
(a) Successful introductions				
Hedgesparrow	1859 ?, 1867-82	New Zealand	deliberate	aesthetic ?
(b) Unsuccessful introductions				
Hedgesparrow	1872-74	USA	deliberate	aesthetic ?

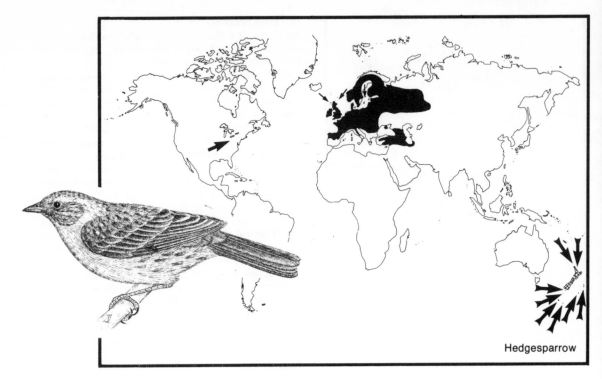

Hedgesparrow

large towns. *Gregariousness:* solitary or small groups. *Movements:* sedentary and migratory. *Foods:* insects, spiders, larvae, and small grass and weed seeds. *Breeding:* Mar-July; Aug-Jan (New Zealand); 2-3 broods per season. *Nest:* deep cup-shaped nest of twigs, moss, etc. and lined with hair, wool or feathers, in a tree or shrub. *Eggs:* 4-6; 2-5 (New Zealand).

Witherby *et al,* 1938-41, vol. 2, pp.208-213.

Voous, 1960, p.197.

NOTES ON INTRODUCTIONS

New Zealand. Three hundred Hedgesparrows were supposed to have been sent to New Zealand in 1859, but this cannot now be verified (Thomson, 1922). Thomson recounts the following introductions for New Zealand:

The Auckland Acclimatisation Society introduced Hedgesparrows in 1867 (one bird), 1868 (two), 1872 (seven), 1874 (nineteen) and in 1875 (eighteen). The Otago society liberated eighteen in 1868 and a further eighty birds in 1871. The Canterbury society liberated nine in 1868 and forty-one in 1871. A number were brought to Christchurch in 1875, some of which were liberated in the city gardens. In 1867 some were liberated by W. Shrimpton at Hawke's Bay. The Wellington society introduced four birds in 1880, twenty-six in 1881 and twenty more in 1882. Both Thomson and Oliver (1930) record that in the 1920s the Hedgesparrow was widely distributed though not abundant throughout New Zealand.

The Hedgesparrow is now widespread throughout both the North and South Islands where it is a common and abundant species (Wodzicki, 1965; Falla *et al,* 1966). They have reached most off-shore islands and extend to the sub-Antarctic as far as Campbell Island.

They have been recorded on the islands of Three Kings, Little Barrier, Hen, Kapiti, Solander, Codfish, Stewart, Campbell, Raoul, the Chathams, Antipodes, Snares and Auckland Islands and apparently breed on at least Campbell, the Antipodes and the Chatham Islands (Oliver, 1955; Williams, 1973). Williams (1953) reports that they arrived on Campbell Island probably prior to 1907 and were recorded on the Snares in 1948.

USA. The Cincinnati society is said to have released the Hedgesparrow between 1872 and 1874 (Phillips, 1928) apparently without success.

DAMAGE

In Europe the Hedgesparrow is not recorded as causing any agricultural damage. It is generally regarded as beneficial in New Zealand and there have been no complaints of any damage.

Families: *Turdidae, Sylviidae, Maluridae, Muscicapidae, Rhipiduridae* and *Timaliidae* Old World flycatchers, warblers and babblers, and thrushes

(Note: Storer in Farner and King (1971) treats the above families as the *Muscicapidae.* Because there is much argument as to a satisfactory arrangement and between the boundaries of each, they are here left as families, but treated together in the table of introductions.)

About 1250 species in numerous genera; 26 introduced, 7 successfully, a further 5 possibly successfully established

Apart from the Cocos-Keeling Islands where the Island Thrush is established all the successes with this assemblage of birds have been in the Pacific area, around Australia, New Zealand and the Hawaiian Islands. The Blackbird and Song Thrush are well known European species and the remaining successful species have come from southern Asia. The former two species are considered pests in New Zealand and to a lesser degree in Australia where they are possibly still spreading.

INTRODUCTIONS OF MUSCICAPIDAE ASSEMBLAGE (TURDIDAE, SYLVIIDAE, MALURIDAE, MUSCICAPIDAE, RHIPIDURIDAE & TIMALLIIDAE)

Species	Date introduced	Region	Manner introduced	Reason
(a) Successful introductions				
White-rumped Shama	1931, 1940	Kauai and Oahu, Hawaiian Islands	deliberate	?
Blackbird	1860-82	Australia	deliberate	?
	1862-75	New Zealand	deliberate	?
Island Thrush	1885-1900	Cocos-Keeling Islands	deliberate	?
Song Thrush	1859-80	Australia	deliberate	?
	1862-78	New Zealand	deliberate	?
Bush Warbler	1929-41	Hawaiian Islands	deliberate	insect control
Melodius Laughingthrush	about 1900	Hawaiian Islands	escapee	cage bird
Red-billed Leiothrix	1918, 1928-29	Hawaiian Islands	deliberate and escapee ?	cage bird ?
(b) Possibly successful introductions				
Magpie Robin	1922, 1932, 1950	Hawaiian Islands	deliberate	?
White-throated Laughingthrush	1919, 1950	Hawaiian Islands	deliberate	?
White-crested Laughingthrush	about 1969	Hawaiian Islands	escapee ?	?
Greater Necklaced Laughing-thrush	1919 ?, about 1970	Hawaiian Islands	deliberate or escapee ?	?
White-browed Laughingthrush	early 1970s	Hong Kong	colonisation or escapee	cage bird
Red-billed Leiothrix	mid-1960s	Colombia	deliberate	?
	various times	Hong Kong	colonisation or escapee	cage bird
(c) Unsuccessful introductions				
European Robin	1857-70	Australia	deliberate	aesthetic ?
	1862-1900	New Zealand	deliberate	?
	1908-10	Canada	deliberate	?
	1852-92	USA	deliberate	?
Japanese Robin	1929-31	Hawaiian Islands	deliberate	?
Temminck's Robin	1931-32	Hawaiian Islands	deliberate	?
Nightingale	1857	Australia	deliberate	aesthetic ?
	1870-97	USA	deliberate	aesthetic ?
	1871-79	New Zealand	not known if liberated	—
	about 1900	South Africa	deliberate	aesthetic ?
Seychelles Magpie Robin	before 1895	Alphonse Island, Amirantes	?	?
Western Bluebird	1938	Tahiti	deliberate	?
Hermit Thrush	1860s or 1870s	Australia	deliberate	?
Blackbird	about 1900	South Africa	deliberate	?
	about 1852	St Helena	deliberate	?
	1852, 1893, 1889	USA	deliberate	?
	prior 1926	Fiji	deliberate	?
Song Thrush	about 1902	South Africa	deliberate	?
	1852, 1889-92	USA	deliberate	?
	about 1900 ?	St Helena	deliberate	?
American Robin	1910 and before 1956 ?	Great Britain	deliberate ?	?
Red-legged Thrush	?	Grand Cayman	escapees ?	?
Whitethroat	1868, 1874	New Zealand	deliberate	?
Blackcap	1872	New Zealand	not known if released	?
	1900-07	USA	not known if released	?
Superb Blue Wren	1923	New Zealand	deliberate	aesthetic ?
Blue Flycatcher	1929	Hawaiian Islands	deliberate	?
Narcissus Flycatcher	just before 1939	Hawaiian Islands	deliberate?	?
Willie Wagtail	1922	Hawaiian Islands	deliberate	insect control
Black-throated Laughing-thrush	1931	Hawaiian Islands	deliberate	?

continued

INTRODUCTIONS OF MUSCICAPIDAE ASSEMBLAGE (TURDIDAE, SYLVIIDAE, MALURIDAE, MUSCICAPIDAE, RHIPIDURIDAE & TIMALLIIDAE)

Species	Date introduced	Region	Manner introduced	Reason
Melodious Laughingthrush	1941	USA	deliberate	?
Red-billed Leiothrix	before 1912 ?	Western Australia	deliberate ?	?
	1898	France	deliberate	?
	before 1956 ?	England	escapee ?	cage bird
	before 1928 ?	USA	escapee ?	cage bird

The Laughingthrushes are not well enough established in the Hawaiian Islands to have become pests but may become a nuisance if they become more numerous. Other than the six species mentioned in the text, a seventh, the Grey-sided Laughingthrush *(G. caerulatus)* may also have been introduced in the Hawaiian Islands. Birds seen in the 1940s and 1950s and a pair in February 1978 on Oahu have been identified as of this species (vide Taylor and Collins, 1979).

The Madagascar Grass Warbler *(Cisticola cherina)* may have been introduced deliberately to the islands of Cosmoledo and Astove, but more than likely colonised these islands from about 1940. They are now abundant there.

In New Zealand the Chatham Island Robin *(Petroica traversi)* has been transplanted from Little Mangere Island to Mangere Island where it was reported to be breeding in the spring of 1977. This species had declined in numbers until only seven birds remained in 1975. By 1977 the population had been transferred to Mangere Island where despite a successful breeding it has remained at a total of seven birds (Mills and Williams, 1979).

Turdidae

EUROPEAN ROBIN
(Robin, Robin Redbreast, Redbreast)
Erithacus rubecula (Linnaeus)

DISTINGUISHING CHARACTERISTICS
13-14 cm (5.2-5.6 in)
Upper parts olive-brown; forehead and breast red, edged with grey; abdomen white; bill blackish.
Witherby *et al*, vol.2, 1938-41, pp.199-204 and pl.50, opp. p.198.

GENERAL DISTRIBUTION
Eurasia-North Africa: from the British Isles, southern Scandinavia and central western Asia south to northern Iran, southern USSR, Turkey, extreme north-western Africa, Açores, Madeira and the Canary Islands. Winters to western and southern Europe, North Africa, southern Iran and Pakistan.

INTRODUCED DISTRIBUTION
Introduced unsuccessfully to (?) Australia, New Zealand, Canada and the USA.

GENERAL HABITS
Status: common. *Habitat:* forest, forest edges, woodlands, gardens and parks. *Gregariousness:*

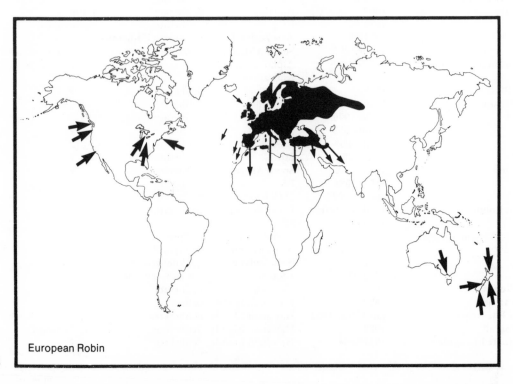

European Robin

pairs. *Movements:* sedentary and migratory. *Foods:* insects (beetles and caterpillars), spiders, earthworms, snails, berries and fruits. *Breeding:* Mar-June (Europe); 2-3 broods per season. *Nest:* bulky structure made of dry grass, leaves and moss, lined with fine grass and feathers, in holes on or in the ground, amongst tree roots, in banks, ditches or walls. *Eggs:* 5-7.

Witherby *et al,* vol.2, 1938-41, pp.199-204.

Voous, 1960, p.220.

NOTES ON INTRODUCTIONS

Australia. The European Robin was probably introduced by the Royal Zoological and Acclimatisation Society of Victoria in the 1860s or 1870s (McCance, 1962). Some were released in 1863 (sixteen birds), 1866 (fourteen) and in 1870 (seventeen) in areas in and near Melbourne (Jenkins, 1977). They may have been imported as early as 1857 (Balmford, 1978), but there is no record of any release at this date. The species failed to become established in Australia.

New Zealand. A single bird was imported to New Zealand in 1862. From 1868 to 1872 the Auckland Acclimatisation Society introduced nine birds. In 1879 the Canterbury society introduced and liberated a number in the society grounds. The Wellington society liberated ten birds in 1883. The Otago society liberated forty birds in 1885, twenty in 1886, and in 1899 a further two were liberated on the Otago Peninsula and this was followed by the release of a single bird in 1900.

Thomson (1922) records that despite these introductions the species failed to become established in New Zealand.

Canada. In 1908-10, Mr G. H. Wallace released a number of British species of birds at various points on the Saanich Peninsula of British Columbia (Carl and Guiguet, 1972). The European Robin appears to have been among the birds released, all of which were unsuccessful.

USA. Near the end of 1852 the Trustees of the Green-Wood Cemetery (Long Island, New York) purchased a number of British birds including twenty-four robins (presumed this sp.) which were freed within the cemetery (Cleaveland, 1865, in Murphy, 1945). They were reported to have all disappeared and the experiment to have been a failure.

European Robins were introduced into Oregon in 1889 and 1892 when five pairs were released by an acclimatisation society (Pfluger, 1896, *Oreg. Nat.* 3: 32-154 in Jewett and Gabrielson, 1929). This introduction apparently failed to become established. Phillips (1928) records that some were also unsuccessfully released in Cincinnati, Ohio (*J. Cincin. Soc. Nat. Hist.* 4: 342, 1881), in California and near Detroit, Michigan.

DAMAGE

None known.

JAPANESE ROBIN
(Komadori)
Erithacus akahige (Temminck)

DISTINGUISHING CHARACTERISTICS

14-15 cm (5.6-6 in)

Upper parts rich rufous-brown; throat, forehead and upper breast orange; lower breast and flanks grey, mottled blackish; narrow breast band black; belly and under tail-coverts white; tail chestnut. Female: lacks black breast band; lower breast and flanks tinged brown.

Yamashina, 1961, p.117 and pl. p.117.

Kobayashi, 1961, pl.17, fig.125, opp. p.38.

GENERAL DISTRIBUTION

Asia: eastern Asia from Japan and adjacent islands and the Ryūkyū Islands. Vagrant to Korea. Winters

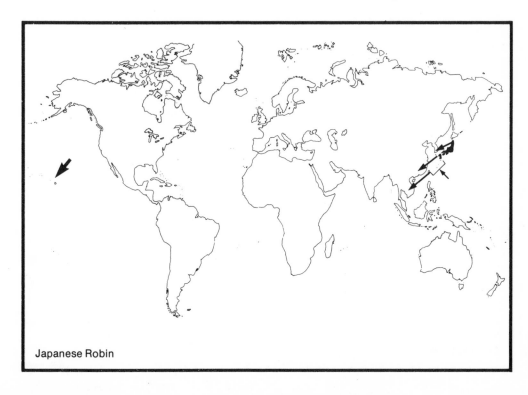

Japanese Robin

south to south-eastern China, Taiwan, and south-eastern Thailand (rarely).

INTRODUCED DISTRIBUTION
Introduced unsuccessfully in the Hawaiian Islands.

GENERAL HABITS
Status: fairly common. *Habitat:* dense damp woodlands and forest undergrowth, often near streams. *Gregariousness and Movements:* no information. *Foods:* insects and other small invertebrates. *Breeding:* no information. *Nest:* on the ground. *Eggs:* no information.
Yamashina, 1961, p.117.

NOTES ON INTRODUCTIONS
Hawaiian Islands. The race *L.a. akahige* was introduced to the island of Oahu in 1929, 1930 and in 1931 (Caum, 1933). Munro (1960) indicates that the species became established on Oahu, but Berger (1972) says that it is not now known to be established anywhere in the Hawaiian Islands.

DAMAGE
None known.

TEMMINCK'S ROBIN
(Akahinga, Korean Robin, Ryūkyū Robin)
Erithacus komadori (Temminck)

DISTINGUISHING CHARACTERISTICS
15 cm (6 in)
Similar to Japanese Robin but with a black throat and breast.
Kobayashi, 1961, pl.17, fig.126, opp. p.38.

GENERAL DISTRIBUTION
Ryūkyū Islands.

INTRODUCED DISTRIBUTION
Introduced unsuccessfully in the Hawaiian Islands.

GENERAL HABITS
Little information. *Habitat:* similar to *E. akahige*. *Movements:* sedentary. *Foods:* insects and other invertebrates.

NOTES ON INTRODUCTIONS
Hawaiian Islands. The race *E.k. komadori* was introduced to the island of Oahu in 1931 and 1932 from Japan (Bryan, 1958; Munro, 1960). Both Munro (1960) and Berger (1972) indicate that the species is not known to be established anywhere in the Hawaiian Islands.

DAMAGE
None known.

NIGHTINGALE
Luscinia megarhynchos Brehm

DISTINGUISHING CHARACTERISTICS
15.8-16.5 cm (6.32-6.6 in)
Generally brown with paler underparts; orbital ring brownish white; chin and centre of throat dull white; sides of throat, upper breast and flanks pale brown; remainder of breast and belly dull white; wings brown; upper tail-coverts and tail chestnut-brown; bill dark brown.
Witherby *et al,* vol.2, 1938-41, pp.187-191 and pl.49, opp. p.182.

GENERAL DISTRIBUTION
Eurasia-Africa: north-western Africa, Portugal and southern England east to central Asia (extreme north-western China). Winters south to central Africa (northern Tanzania).

INTRODUCED DISTRIBUTION
Introduced unsuccessfully to Australia, the USA, South Africa and possibly in New Zealand.

GENERAL HABITS
Status: fairly common. *Habitat:* woods and thickets, forest, swampy areas, gardens and parks. *Gregariousness:* solitary. *Movements:* migratory. *Foods:* insects, grubs, worms, snails, berries and fruits. *Breeding:* May-June (England). *Nest:* loose construction of dead leaves and grass, lined with finer

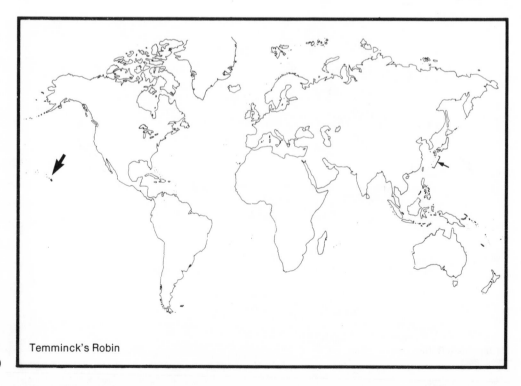

Temminck's Robin

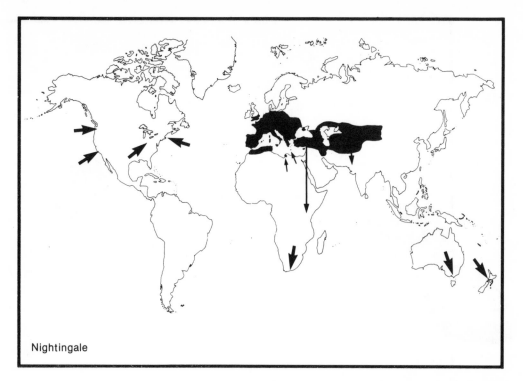

Nightingale

material on or near the ground at the base of a bush.
Eggs: 3, 4-6, 7.
Witherby *et al,* vol.2, 1938-41, pp.187-191.
Voous, 1960, p.219.

NOTES ON INTRODUCTIONS

Australia. Hardy (1928) who quotes Wilson (*Trans. Phil. Inst.,* Vic., 1857) reports that it was arranged with a person in England in 1857 to purchase six Nightingales at eight to ten dollars each. These were imported, but apparently, cats killed one bird and injured another while they were being kept in captivity. The remaining four birds were released some days later from the Botanical Gardens, Melbourne. Two of these birds could not fly and were recaptured and the other two were both seen and heard in the gardens in the following spring. The species also appears to have been imported in 1857 and 1858 (Balmford 1978), but there are no other indications that any more were liberated.

The introductions evidently failed as the Nightingale did not become established in Australia.

USA. Phillips (1928) records that it is certain that Nightingales were liberated during the experiments in acclimatisation in Cincinnati (about 1881), New York (about 1870s), California (1891-1902) and Portland, Oregon (about 1897). He indicates that 100 birds were probably sent to California from England in 1887. Twenty-one pairs were sent to Portland in 1907, but half of these died en route and the remainder perished in an aviary. Between 1901 and 1913 more than 1000 Nightingales were imported into the USA and it is therefore possible that others were released.

New Zealand. Nightingales were imported into New Zealand in 1871, 1875 and 1879, but it is not known if any of them were liberated (Thomson, 1922). Hardy (1928) refers to the recent introduction of four Nightingales to New Zealand.

South Africa. At the end of the last century Rhodes is reported to have introduced Nightingales in the vicinity of Cape Town, South Africa (Winterbottom, 1966).

DAMAGE

None known.

MAGPIE ROBIN
(Dhyal Thrush, Dyal Bird)
Copsychus saularis (Linnaeus)

DISTINGUISHING CHARACTERISTICS
18.6-23 cm (7.44-9.2 in). 36-41 g (1.27-1.45 oz)
Generally black and white; head, neck, breast and mantle blue-black; underparts white; wings black with white patch; tail, central feathers black and outer ones white; bill black. Female: slaty-grey where black in male.
Cheng, 1963, p.684 and pl.47, no.87.
Ali and Ripley, 1968-74.

GENERAL DISTRIBUTION
Asia: from Pakistan, India, Sri Lanka, Bangladesh and Burma, east to southern China, the Vietnam and Malaysian regions to the Philippine Islands; also Hainan and the Andaman Islands.

INTRODUCED DISTRIBUTION
Introduced, possibly successfully in the Hawaiian Islands (status uncertain).

GENERAL HABITS
Status: very common; often caged in China. *Habitat:* towns, villages, gardens, plantations, secondary growth, cultivated areas, open country and mangroves. *Gregariousness:* singly, pairs, or family groups. *Movements:* sedentary. *Foods:* insects, nectar, snails, earthworms, fruits and seeds occasionally. *Breeding:* Nov-Aug; 2 broods per season (Malaysia). *Nest:* usually a pad, but occasionally a bulky shapeless mass of grass, leaves, rootlets and hairs, lined with grass and roots, in a hole

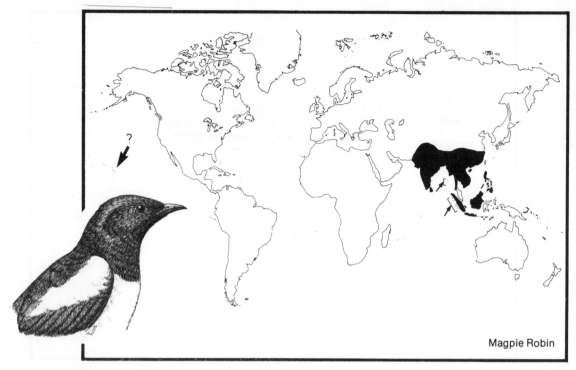

Magpie Robin

in a wall, bank, tree trunk or bough, or under house eaves. *Eggs:* 3-6.

Cheng, 1963, pp.685-686.

Ali and Ripley, 1968-74.

NOTES ON INTRODUCTIONS

Hawaiian Islands. A single pair, of the race *C.s. prosthopellus* imported from Hong Kong, was introduced to Kauai in the Hawaiian Islands by Mrs D. Isenberg in 1922, and an unknown number by the Hui Manu in 1932 (Caum, 1933). Bryan (1958) records that this race was also introduced to Oahu in 1950.

In the late 1950s or early 1960s the Magpie Robin may have been established on Oahu where it was reported to still occur in the upper Manoa and the Tantalus areas (Peterson, 1961). A single bird was noted on Kauai in 1967 and sightings of the species are reported from time to time on Oahu, but its distribution and present status are poorly known (Berger, 1972; Hawaiian Audubon Society, 1975).

DAMAGE

According to Cheng (1963) the Magpie Robin causes no damage in China.

WHITE-RUMPED SHAMA
(Shama Thrush, Magpie Robin, Common Shama)
Copsychus malabaricus (Scopoli)

DISTINGUISHING CHARACTERISTICS

19.5-28 cm (7.8-11.2 in)

Head, throat, upper breast and upper parts blue-black; underparts orange-rufous, or chestnut; rump white; flight feathers black; tail, graduated, black and white; bill black. Female: slaty-brown or grey where male black; belly and under tail-coverts rufous-buff; tail shorter.

Ali and Ripley, 1968-74.

King *et al*, 1965, pl.51, no.880, opp. p.336.

GENERAL DISTRIBUTION

Asia: from India, Bangladesh, Sri Lanka and the Andaman Islands, east to south-western China, Indochina, Malaysia, Borneo, the Greater Sunda Islands and Hainan.

INTRODUCED DISTRIBUTION

Introduced successfully in the Hawaiian Islands.

GENERAL HABITS

Status: very common; favourite cage bird in India. *Habitat:* forest undergrowth and secondary growth, low thickets and overgrown gardens. *Gregariousness:* singly or pairs. *Movements:* sedentary. *Foods:* mainly insects and their larvae, but also worms, caterpillars and fruits. *Breeding:* Mar-Aug. *Nest:* rough, shallow cup or pad of rootlets, grass, bamboo leaves, etc., in natural hollows in trees, or in tangled base of a bamboo clump and occasionally in eaves of houses. *Eggs:* 3-4, 5; 2-5 (Hawaiian Islands).

Ali and Ripley, 1968-74.

NOTES ON INTRODUCTIONS

Hawaiian Islands. The White-rumped Shama was introduced on the island of Kauai in 1931 and appeared to become established there (Munro, 1960). According to Harpham (1953) the Hui Manu imported some in 1940 and released them in the Nuuanu Valley and on the Makiki Heights of Oahu. On Oahu, some were noted at Pauoa Flats in 1948, the upper Manoa Valley in 1949 and at Tantalus in 1950 (Berger, 1972). In 1960 the species was still resident locally on the island of Kauai (Richardson and Bowles, 1964).

The White-rumped Shama now appears to be well established on both Kauai and Oahu in suitable localities (Berger, 1972; Heilbrun, 1972) and is fairly common in the upper valleys and ridges of the Koolau Range (Hawaiian Audubon Society, 1975). Ali and Ripley (1968-74) record that the race introduced is *indicus*.

DAMAGE

None known.

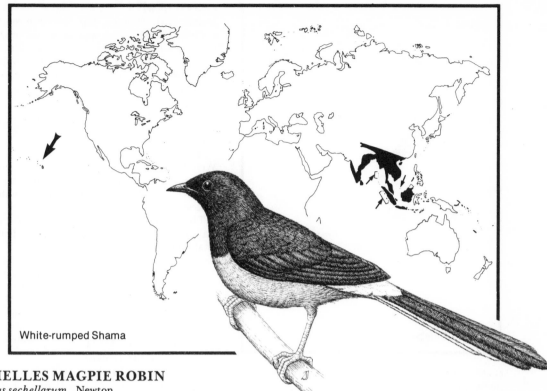

White-rumped Shama

SEYCHELLES MAGPIE ROBIN
Copsychus sechellarum Newton

DISTINGUISHING CHARACTERISTICS
25 cm (10 in)
Entirely black with a blue sheen except for a white patch on the upper wing.
Penny, 1974, p.90 and pl.6, no.4, opp. p.97.

GENERAL DISTRIBUTION
Seychelles: formerly on many islands, now occurs only on Frigate Island.

Seychelles Magpie Robin

INTRODUCED DISTRIBUTION
Introduced successfully to Alphonse Island, Amirantes, but has now died out.

GENERAL HABITS
Status: rare; estimated that only 30-40 birds now remain on Frigate Island. *Habitat:* woodlands and villages. *Gregariousness:* family groups. *Movements:* sedentary. *Foods:* insects, spiders, lizards, termites, millipedes, food scraps and vegetable material. *Breeding:* Nov-Mar; possibly two broods per season. *Nest:* untidy bundle of coconut fibres and vegetation, with neat cup, generally in the bowl-shaped bases of fronds of a coconut palm. *Eggs:* 2.
Penny, 1974, pp.90-91.

NOTES ON INTRODUCTIONS
Alphonse Island. According to Gaymer *et al* (1969) the Seychelles Magpie Robin was introduced to Alphonse but has since died out. Abbott (in Ridgway, 1895) reported that the introduction was successful in 1895. They were reported to be present there in 1940 and were said to be flourishing (Vesey-Fitzgerald, 1940), but were not seen by Loustau-Lalanne (1962) on his visit. Penny (1974) failed to find any in 1965 and indicates that none have been seen there in the past six years.

DAMAGE
None known.

WESTERN BLUEBIRD
Siala mexicana Swainson

DISTINGUISHING CHARACTERISTICS
16-17.5 cm (6.4-7 in). 27-32 g (.95-1.13 oz)
Head, throat, wings and tail blue; breast and back rusty red (in some birds back partially or wholly blue); lower belly and vent whitish; bill black. Female: duller; throat whitish; breast rusty red.

Western Bluebird

Godfrey, 1966, p.302 and pl.52, no.4, opp. p.253.
Reilly, 1968, p.357.

GENERAL DISTRIBUTION

North America: from southern British Columbia and western Montana, to southern California, south-eastern Arizona, New Mexico, western Texas, and to central Mexico. In winter from Puget Sound (British Columbia), southern Utah and south-western Colorado south.

INTRODUCED DISTRIBUTION

Introduced unsuccessfully in Tahiti.

GENERAL HABITS

Status: fairly common. *Habitat:* open conifer forest, scattered trees, farms, and in winter open terrain, brush and desert. *Gregariousness:* small flocks of 2-6 pairs, larger flocks to 50 on migration. *Movements:* migratory. *Foods:* caterpillars, moths, grasshoppers, beetles, other insects and fruits. *Breeding:* Apr-Sept. *Nest:* hole in a tree. *Eggs:* 3, 4-6, 8.

Godfrey, 1966, p.302.
Reilly, 1968, p.357.

NOTES ON INTRODUCTIONS

Tahiti. Guild (1940) reports he obtained some ten Western Bluebirds in the United States and brought them to Tahiti in August 1938. He liberated them in October of that year and some nested there successfully in February 1939.

There appear no further records of the species in Tahiti so evidently they failed to become permanently established there.

DAMAGE

The Western Bluebird is known to feed on grapes in vineyards in California (Boudreau, 1972), but the specific damage and whether this species alone causes economic loss does not appear to be documented.

HERMIT THRUSH
Hylocichla guttata (Pallas)

DISTINGUISHING CHARACTERISTICS

15-19 cm (6-7.6 in). 29.5-32 g (1.04-1.13 oz)

Upper parts brown, more rufous-brown on rump and tail; eye-ring whitish; sides of throat streaked with blackish brown; sides of flanks pale brownish grey; anterior underparts with dusky spots; throat and chest buffy becoming white on abdomen; bill blackish, light brown at base of lower mandible.

Roberts, 1960, pl.60.

Godfrey, 1966, pp.297-298 and pl.51, no.3, opp. p.252.

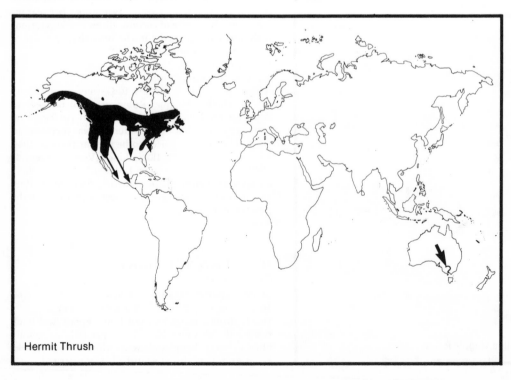

Hermit Thrush

GENERAL DISTRIBUTION

North America: from central Alaska and Canada south to southern California, northern Baja California, south-eastern Arizona, southern New Mexico and western Texas. Winters from the southern United States to Guatemala.

INTRODUCED DISTRIBUTION

Probably introduced, unsuccessfully, in Australia.

GENERAL HABITS

Status: fairly common. *Habitat:* forest, woodlands, thickets and parks. *Gregariousness:* fairly solitary, except when migrating. *Movements:* migratory. *Foods:* insects including beetles and caterpillars, also fruits, berries, worms and seeds. *Breeding:* May-Aug. *Nest:* cup-shaped of moss, grass and rootlets, in a tree or on the ground. *Eggs:* 3-4, 6.

Godfrey, 1966, pp.297-298.

Reilly, 1968, pp. 351-352.

NOTES ON INTRODUCTIONS

Australia. Virginian Nightingales (=Hermit Thrush ?) are reported to have been introduced in Victoria in the 1860s or 70s by the Zoological and Acclimatisation Society (McCance, 1962), but apparently without success.

DAMAGE

None known.

BLACKBIRD
(Common Blackbird)
Turdus merula Linnaeus

DISTINGUISHING CHARACTERISTICS

24-28 cm (9.6-11.2 in). 72.2-109.2 g (2.55-3.85 oz) Generally all black with a metallic sheen; eye-ring yellow; entire plumage white spotted (few spots in non-breeding season); bill yellow (brown in non-breeding). Female: brown, darker on wings and tail; underparts mottled brown; bill brown. (Note: races in southern Asia differ from nominate: to plain grey-brown; black cap; eye-ring orange-yellow; bill orange-yellow.)

Witherby *et al,* vol.2, 1938-41, pp.134-141 and pl.44, opp. p.130.

Reader's Digest, 1977, p.352, pls. p.352.

GENERAL DISTRIBUTION

Eurasia-North Africa: Açores, Canary Islands, and in North Africa in Morocco, Algeria and Tunisia; Europe (except northern Scandinavia, northern Finland and northern USSR) and Asia Minor east to India, Sri Lanka, northern Burma and central-south China. Winters south to North Africa, Tonkin, northern Amman and north-eastern and central Laos.

INTRODUCED DISTRIBUTION

Introduced successfully in Australia, Tasmania and New Zealand, and from where they colonised many offshore islands including Lord Howe Island and Norfolk Island; successfully colonised many areas in Europe. Introduced unsuccessfully to South Africa, St Helena, USA and Fiji.

GENERAL HABITS

Status: very common and abundant. *Habitat:* forest, woodland, streamsides, parks, gardens, cultivated areas, orchards, palm oases and cities. *Gregariousness:* singly or loose flocks, but nominate race can occur sometimes in very large flocks. *Movements:* sedentary and migratory. *Foods:* earthworms, snails, spiders, millipedes, caterpillars, fly larvae and other insects, fruits, berries, seeds and grain. *Breeding:* Mar-July (Great Britain); May-Aug (India); Sept-Jan (Australia); Sept-Dec (New Zealand); two or more broods per year. *Nest:* neat cup-shaped of twigs and grass, reinforced with earth, stems, roots, etc., in a tree, bush, building or on the ground. *Eggs:* 2-5, 9; 1, 2-5 (New Zealand); 3-5 (Australia).

Snow, 1958.

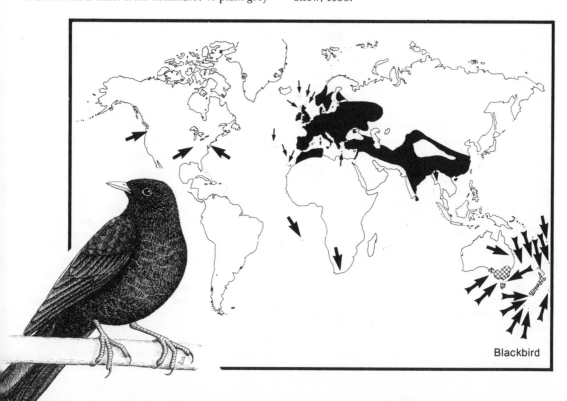

Blackbird

Stein, *Beitr. Vogelk.* vol.20, 1974, pp.467-477.

NOTES ON INTRODUCTIONS

Europe. According to Snow (1958) the Blackbird was once a shy bird of wooded country (around 1804), but by the end of the eighteenth century had become as thoroughly a garden bird as it is now. In parts of Europe the colonisation of gardens is even more recent and the process is probably not yet complete. The earliest beginnings are unrecorded.

Snow reports that in northern France, the low countries, and central and southern Germany the regular colonisation of town gardens started between 100 and 150 years ago and has steadily spread. The Elbe was reached in about 1875, Denmark in about 1890, Mecklenburg in about 1900, Norway in the early 1910s and southern Finland in the early 1920s. In southern France and Italy there is evidence to suggest that the Blackbird has been a garden bird in parts for considerably longer than in northern Europe. In south-eastern Europe it is still a bird of the wooded mountains. It is not known when the species became a garden bird in North Africa.

In Great Britain the Blackbird has now bred on the Shetlands for about seventy years and colonised all but four of the inhabited islands, probably assisted by man (Venables and Venables, 1952).

Australia. Blackbirds were introduced to Australia possibly a number of times in the 1860s and 1870s. Snow (1958) placed the date at about 1868, but Ryan (1906) says that they were released in Melbourne in 1864 (six birds), 1866 (seventeen) and in 1872 (twenty-two). They may also have been released near Sydney at the latter date. A number of Blackbirds in a number of shipments were imported by private individuals in 1857, 1858, 1859 and in 1860, some were reported to have been liberated certainly before December 1860 and the species was probably well established around Melbourne before 1862 (Balmford, 1978).

Some Blackbirds were brought to South Australia in about 1863 and later (Condon, 1962). Liberations occurred at Mt Lofty, Adelaide, Beaumont and Torrens Park by the South Australian Acclimatisation Society in 1879 (four), 1881 and in 1882 (at least forty-five) and the species quickly became established in that State.

Coleman (1939) indicates that some forty-five Blackbirds were liberated (in Victoria ?) between 1864 and 1872. Although some were also released at Sydney, New South Wales in 1872, these possibly failed (?), and the present population is thought to have been derived from an aviary release in 1940 (Frith 1973). Some may have been released in Queensland in about 1869 (Jenkins, 1977), but they apparently failed to become established.

In 1926 the Blackbird was reported to be established at Albury on the southern border of New South Wales and in the Sydney Botanical Gardens (Chisholm, 1926). They were numerous and widespread in Victoria, and in South Australia on the Adelaide Plains and Mt Lofty districts, Victor Harbour, Coorong and Mt Gambier north to Oodnadatta by the 1950s (Tarr, 1950). The first record of the species on Kangaroo Island appears to have been in 1947 (Cooper, 1947). They appeared at Deniliquin, New South Wales in 1954 and were one of the commonest birds there in 1959, and reached Doveton in 1957 and were fairly common there also by 1959 (Hobbs, 1961).

Hobbs records that Blackbirds were to be found along the Murray River wherever there were citrus orchards. He found them at Baroonga, Tocumwal, Mathoura, Tooleybuc, Goodnight and in all the New South Wales parts of the Sunraysia district.

The Blackbird first appeared in the Canberra district in about 1949 and is now widespread there (Frith). They reached Flinders Island in Bass Strait some time before 1950 (Tarr). In 1965 they were recorded at Lane Cove and North Ryde in Sydney, New South Wales (Lane, 1964).

In Tasmania the Blackbird appears to have first bred there some time just prior to 1919 (Dove, 1919). They reached Port Davey in about 1937-38 and were well established along the coast (Recherche, Bound Bay, Spain Bay, Point Eric, Cox's Bight and Moth Creek) before the 1960s (Green and Mollison, 1961) and reached the Bicheno district prior to 1965 (Thomas, 1965). The Blackbird is now widespread in Tasmania.

New Zealand. The Nelson Acclimatisation Society introduced twenty-six birds into New Zealand in 1862. The Otago society liberated two birds in 1865, six in 1867, thirty-nine in 1868, twenty-one in 1869 and seventy in 1871. The Canterbury society liberated forty-six in 1867, 152 in 1868, sixty-two in 1871 and many more in 1875. The Auckland society liberated eight in 1865, thirty in 1867, 132 in 1868 and a large consignment in 1869 (Thomson, 1922).

In ten years the Otago releases had become well established and so numerous that the birds were causing fruit damage. By the 1920s they were considered to be common in many parts of the country (Thomson, 1922) and by the 1950s were throughout both the North and South Islands (Oliver, 1955).

The Blackbird is now widespread and abundant in New Zealand (Wodzicki, 1965; Falla *et al,* 1966) and has reached most of the offshore and outlying islands from the Kermadecs to Campbell Island (Falla *et al*).

Blackbirds were liberated on Stewart Island in 1879 (Thomson, 1922) and have been present there since this date (Oliver, 1955). According to Thomson they found their own way to the Chatham Islands and were reported from the Auckland Islands in 1907. Williams (1953) says that they reached Campbell, Chatham and the Auckland Islands in about 1900, were on the Kermadecs in 1910 and the Snares in 1907.

By 1955 they had been reported on the Kermadecs, Three Kings, Poor Knights, Hen, Little Barrier, Mayor, Karewa, Kapiti, Stewart, Solander, Chathams, Snares, Auckland and Campbell islands (Oliver, 1955). To most of these islands they had spread unassisted (Snow, 1958).

More recently Wodzicki (1965) records the Blackbird on Raoul Island and Williams (1973) says that they have bred on Three Kings, Kermadecs, Chathams, Campbell, Auckland and the Snares. Blackbirds were self introduced, probably from New Zealand, to Lord Howe Island and are now established but sparsely distributed there (McKean and Hindwood, 1965). Some were noted in

1953, again in 1955 and they appeared to be distributed throughout by about 1959. Williams (1953) indicates that they were very likely introduced to Norfolk Island by man in about 1939. Smithers and Disney (1969) found them common there in the late 1960s.

South Africa. A number of bird species, including the Blackbird, were introduced to South Africa by Rhodes at the end of the last century, but failed to become established there (*Agric. and Tech. Serv.,* 1962, pers. comm.; Winterbottom, 1966).

St Helena. Benson (1950) refers to the introduction of numerous English songbirds, including Blackbirds which were introduced to St Helena (probably in the early part of this century ?) but which appeared to have died out. An import of birds in 1852, including Blackbirds, is mentioned by Melliss (1870).

USA. Towards the end of 1852, twelve Blackbirds were amongst a consignment of British birds which were released at Green-Wood Cemetery, Long Island, New York (Cleaveland, 1865, in Murphy, 1945). Cleaveland apparently claimed that the species disappeared soon afterwards and did not become established.

A further introduction occurred in North America when sixteen pairs were released at Portland, Oregon in May 1889 (Storer, 1923; McNeil, 1971) and more were probably liberated in 1892 (Phillips 1928). Two single birds, thought to have possibly been from these releases, were collected one at Oakland, California in December 1891 and another in New York in 1880. McNeil records a single bird at Quebec in 1970-71, but indicated that he did not think it had been introduced there either accidentally or deliberately.

Phillips records that fifteen Gray Song Thrushes (*Arcenthornis = Turdus iliacus*) were also liberated in New York City in 1893. Apparently both *merula* and *iliacus* were commonly imported and kept as cage birds in the United States before the first World War. A third species, *viscivorus* was also imported but was not a common cage bird. The Redwing *T. musicus* was also said to have been released in Cincinnati, Ohio between 1872 and 1874.

It seems more than likely therefore, that the names of the various thrushes could have become confused and probably all those mentioned were liberated as thrushes at some time in the United States.

Fiji. According to Wood and Wetmore (1926) English Blackbirds were liberated at Kanathea, Fiji some time just prior to 1926, but failed to become established there.

DAMAGE

Within its native range the Blackbird causes some damage to fruits. Wright and Brough (1964) say that there is no assessment of the economic importance of the Blackbird to particular fruits, but that they will attack strawberries, raspberries, gooseberries and blackcurrants. Murton (1968) indicates that they damage soft fruits and Brough (1967) states that they are often responsible for losses in cherry orchards, but do not occur in large numbers and the damage is generally negligible. Wright (1959) suggests that they are a more important nuisance in gardens than in orchards where other species such as starlings are more damaging.

In Australia, the Blackbird is said to be generally admired for its song (Cayley, 1968), but to growers of fruit, especially in Tasmania, it is regarded as a serious pest. They feed on many kinds of fruit but are most destructive to cherries. Where introduced in New Zealand they were causing damage to fruits some ten to twelve years later (Thomson, 1922). Here, they are accused of damaging cherries severely and pears, plums, apricots, boysenberries, grapes, strawberries and apples moderately, as well as other fruits slightly (Dawson and Bull, 1969).

On Norfolk Island Smithers and Disney (1969) say the Blackbird is probably competing with the Island Thrush *(T. poliocephalus).*

ISLAND THRUSH
(Grey-headed Blackbird)
Turdus poliocephalus (Latham)

DISTINGUISHING CHARACTERISTICS
22-25 cm (8.8-10 in). 44-52.5 g (1.55-1.85 oz)
Generally brownish black or greyish; throat and upper breast paler and browner or grey; feathers of underparts edged brown; eye-ring yellow; bill yellow.
Mayr, 1945, pp.118, 136, 166, 190, 207 and 251.

GENERAL DISTRIBUTION
Islands from Sumatra and Taiwan to Samoa: Indonesia, Sabah, Sulawesi, southern Moluccas, the Philippines, Taiwan, New Guinea, Bismarck Archipelago, Solomons, Santa Cruz, Loyalty Islands, New Hebrides, New Caledonia, Lord Howe Island, Norfolk Island and east to Fiji and Samoa.

INTRODUCED DISTRIBUTION
Introduced successfully in the Cocos-Keeling Islands, Indian Ocean.

GENERAL HABITS
Status: common locally. *Habitat:* islands in forest, forest edges and clearings. *Gregariousness:* singly, or pairs. *Movements:* sedentary. *Foods:* fruits, seeds, insects and vegetable material. *Breeding:* Oct-Mar

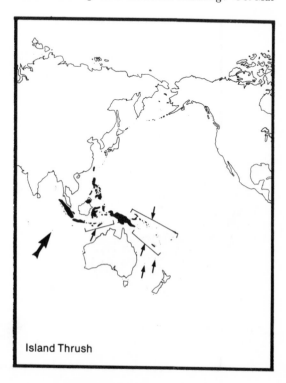

Island Thrush

(Christmas Island); Dec-May (Cocos-Keeling).
Nest: on rocky ledges and in trees. *Eggs:* 1 (?).

NOTES ON INTRODUCTIONS

Cocos-Keeling Islands. The Island Thrush was introduced and established in the Cocos-Keeling Islands between 1885 and 1900, and by the 1940s was plentiful on three of the larger islands (Atlas, Luar and Penjang) in the main atoll (Gibson-Hill, 1949). According to Gibson-Hill the species was brought from Christmas Island and placed on Pulo Luar, but now occurs on the other two islands. He records that *T. javanicus erythropleurus* was established on the Cocos-Keeling Islands, but Van Tets and Van Tets (1967) say that *T. poliocephalus* was the species introduced.

DAMAGE

None known.

SONG THRUSH

Turdus philomelos Brehm

DISTINGUISHING CHARACTERISTICS

22-24 cm (8.8-9.6 in) . 81 g (2.86 oz)

Upper parts brown; underparts buffy white, heavily spotted blackish on breast and flanks; abdomen white; bill black. Female: more heavily spotted on underparts.

Witherby *et al,* vol.2, 1938-41, pp.115-121 and pl.43, opp. p.118.

Reader's Digest, 1977, p.353 and pl. p.353.

GENERAL DISTRIBUTION

Eurasia: British Isles, Europe except the southern coastal fringe and northern Scandinavia, and east to south-western, central and central-western Asia. In winter south to the Canary Islands, Arabia, Iran and south-western Asia.

INTRODUCED DISTRIBUTION

Introduced successfully to Australia and New Zealand and colonised many nearby islands, including Lord Howe Island and Norfolk Island. Introduced unsuccessfully to South Africa, (?) St Helena and the USA.

GENERAL HABITS

Status: common. *Habitat:* forest edges and clearings, woodland, open moorland, coastal acacia, parks and gardens. *Gregariousness:* pairs or small flocks. *Movements:* sedentary and migratory. *Foods:* worms, snails, slugs, grubs, caterpillars, beetles and other insects, berries and fruits. *Breeding:* Feb-Aug; Sept-Jan (Australia); June-Jan (New Zealand); 2-3 broods per year. *Nest:* cup-shaped of twigs, grass stems, leaves, and rounded into a saucer the inside of which is cemented with mud; in a tree, or crevice, or rarely on the ground. *Eggs:* 4-6; 4-5 (Australia); 2, 3-5, 6 (New Zealand).

Witherby *et al,* vol.2, 1938-41, pp.115-121.

Stein, *Beitr. Vogelk.* vol. 20, 1974, pp.467-477.

NOTES ON INTRODUCTIONS

Australia. The Song Thrush was released in Australia at Sydney, Brisbane, Canberra, Melbourne and probably in Adelaide. Liberation of some at Sydney in 1872 did not result in them becoming established (Ryan, 1906; McGill, 1960) and there may have been introductions in New South Wales around 1900-05 but the birds apparently died out (Tarr, 1950). Releases at Canberra succeeded temporarily as the species bred there but later disappeared (McGill; Chisholm, 1950).

At Melbourne in Victoria early releases were successful and the species has become firmly established in parks and gardens of the metropolitan area. They had extended to Sherbrooke Forest, Macedon, Geelong, Belgrave and Ararat (?) (Tarr, 1950) by the 1950s.

The first birds to arrive in Australia appear to have been some in 1856 but the exact fate of these is not known. Certainly, there were several imports to

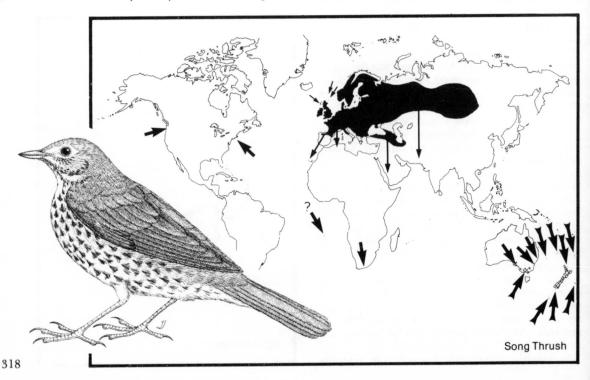

Song Thrush

Melbourne in 1857, 1858 and in 1860 (Balmford, 1978). Balmford records that some were reported to be breeding in the Botanical Gardens in 1860 where forty-eight in 1859 and thirty-seven in 1860 may have been released. In the time of the Acclimatisation Society of Victoria some were liberated on Phillip Island (four birds), in the Botanical Gardens (eighteen), at Royal Park (six) in 1866 and at Gembrook (twelve) in 1880 (Jenkins, 1977).

Some were imported to Brisbane, Queensland from England in 1869 and these were presumably released although their subsequent fate is not known. Birds from New Zealand were released at Canberra in 1935 but this introduction was unsuccessful. Some were also released about Adelaide in South Australia in 1879-80, but these were also unsuccessful in establishing themselves.

The Song Thrush remains established in the vicinity of Melbourne and suburbs, but appears to be slowly spreading outwards from these areas.

New Zealand. Song Thrushes were first introduced and liberated in New Zealand by the Nelson Acclimatisation Society in 1862, but failed to become established. Subsequently, introductions were made by the Otago society, two birds in 1865, four in 1867, forty-nine in 1868, forty-eight in 1869 and forty-two in 1871. The Canterbury society also liberated thirty-six in 1867, twenty-four in 1868, and more in 1871 and 1875. Other liberations were made by the Canterbury society, thirty in 1867 and ninety-five in 1868, and by the Wellington society which released eight in 1878 (Thomson, 1922).

Thomson records that the Otago releases were well established by 1869 and that the Song Thrush was becoming numerous and causing fruit damage by 1881. Those released in the Auckland area also quickly established themselves, but in the Canterbury area it took them some twenty years to become thoroughly established. By the 1930s the Song Thrush was reported to be established throughout New Zealand except in the dense forest country (Oliver, 1930).

The Song Thrush is now a widespread and abundant species in both the North and South Islands (Wodzicki, 1965; Falla *et al,* 1966) and is present on most offshore islands north to the Kermadecs and south to Campbell Island (Falla *et al*).

Offshore and outlying islands of Australia and New Zealand. The Song Thrush has been recorded from the islands of Poor Knights, Hen, Little Barrier, Three Kings, Kapiti, D'Urville, Raoul, Stewart, Codfish, Chathams, Antipodes, Campbell, Snares, Auckland, Macquarie and the Kermadecs (Oliver, 1955, Wodzicki, 1965). They apparently breed on at least Three Kings, Kermadecs, Chathams, Campbell, Auckland and the Snares (Williams, 1973). Williams (1953) indicates that the species reached the Kermadecs before 1910, the Snares around 1900, and the Chathams in about 1922. He says that they probably reached Lord Howe Island from New Zealand in about 1929, and were self introduced to Norfolk Island in about 1913.

On Lord Howe Island some Song Thrushes were noted to be present in 1955-56 and there were about fifty birds there in 1959. They were present and breeding there in the early 1960s (McKean and Hindwood, 1965). On Norfolk Island they were present and breeding in the early 1960s (McKean and Hindwood) and were said to be common there in 1969 (Smithers and Disney, 1969).

St Helena. Thrushes (possibly including this species ?) were included amongst English songbirds introduced to this island (probably in the early part of this century), but which all died out (Benson, 1950).

South Africa. The Song Thrush was introduced by Rhodes to the Cape in the late nineteenth century (Agriculture and Technical Service, 1962 pers. comm.) or shortly before 1902 from Europe (Mackworth-Praed and Grant, 1955-62). Mackworth-Praed and Grant say that the Song Thrush became fairly common at Newlands, Cape Peninsula in about 1936, but that there have been no records of its occurrence there since 1947 and it is probably now extinct. However, Winterbottom (1966) says that they were fairly common in the vicinity of Capetown in 1963, but that there have been no recent reports.

USA. Near the end of 1852 the Trustees of the Green-Wood Cemetery (Long Island, New York) purchased a number of British birds and freed them in the cemetery (Cleaveland, 1865, in Murphy, 1945). Included amongst those released were twelve thrushes (possibly *T. philomelos ?*) which apparently disappeared soon after the release.

According to Jewett and Gabrielson (1929), Pfluger (1896, *Oreg. Nat.* 3:32-154) reports that Song Thrushes *(Arceuthornis iliacus = Turdus iliacus)* were introduced to Oregon when thirty-five pairs were released in 1889 and 1892. Pfluger apparently recorded that since their introduction they had increased remarkably well. The species is not now established in the United States.

DAMAGE

In Europe there appears to be no assessment of the economic importance of the Song Thrush (Wright and Brough, 1964) to particular fruits, but they will attack strawberries, raspberries, gooseberries and blackcurrants in Great Britain. In some situations they are responsible with other species for damage in cherry orchards (Brough, 1967). In Holland they damage soft fruits, apples and pears, in Germany grapes and other fruit (Seubert, 1964), and when the species is present in large numbers in Italy they are said to harm fruits (Ministry Agriculture and Forests 1962, pers. comm.).

In New Zealand the Song Thrush is accused of damaging a number of fruits (Dawson and Bull, 1969) and appears to be one of the more important pests in orchards. They have only a restricted range in Australia and are probably not yet numerous enough to have caused much damage. They do, however, appear to be slowly spreading and may become a more important pest of fruit crops in time to come.

AMERICAN ROBIN
Turdus migratorius Linnaeus

DISTINGUISHING CHARACTERISTICS
22-27 cm (8.8-10.8 in). 62.2-87 g (2.19-3.07 oz)
Head, nape and tail blackish; back dark grey, becoming blackish on the wings; throat white, streaked sooty; breast and sides of flanks, brick red; 319

American Robin

lower abdomen and under tail-coverts white; small white area around eyes; outer tail-feathers tipped white; bill yellow with black tip. Female: head greyer and many feathers edged white.

Roberts, 1960, pl.59.

Godfrey, 1966, pp.294-296 and pl.52, no.5, opp. p.253.

GENERAL DISTRIBUTION

North America: from Alaska to Canada and to the southern United States. In winter south to the southern USA coast, southern Mexico and Guatemala.

INTRODUCED DISTRIBUTION

Introduced unsuccessfully in Great Britain.

GENERAL HABITS

Status: very common. *Habitat:* woodlands and edges, open forest, farmlands, gardens, towns, lawns and orchards. *Gregariousness:* usually small flocks, but large flocks during migration. *Movements:* migratory. *Foods:* beetles, grasshoppers and other insects and their larvae, berries, worms and fruits. *Breeding:* May-July; often colonial; 2-3 broods per season. *Nest:* substantial bowl structure of twigs, stems and grass, with base and wall lined with mud and grass, usually in a tree, occasionally on the ground. *Eggs:* 1, 3-5, 6.

Godfrey, 1966, pp.294-296.

Reilly, 1968, pp.349-350.

Knupp *et al, Auk* vol.94, 1977, pp.80-85.

NOTES ON INTRODUCTIONS

Great Britain. According to Koch (1956) there have been many attempts to introduce the American Robin to Great Britain, but all have been unsuccessful. In 1910 an attempt was made to introduce them near Guildford and several birds, presumedly escapees, were shot before 1938 (Witherby *et al,* 1938).

DAMAGE

In North America this robin, when abundant, can sometimes become injurious to fruit crops (Neff,

1949). In California the species is known to feed on grapes (Boudreau, 1972). Generally, however, attacks by this species appear to be local and of an irregular nature (Neff, 1937).

RED-LEGGED THRUSH
(Blue Thrasher)
Mimocichla plumbea (Linnaeus)

DISTINGUISHING CHARACTERISTICS

25-28 cm (10-11.2 in)

Variable species (especially the underparts), but predominantly slate-grey; chin and throat variously black and white; eye-ring red; chest greyish; abdomen whitish, but may be ochraceous; variable black mark from eye to bill; tail black, with white tips to outer feathers; under tail-coverts white; bill reddish (more or less).

Allen, 1962, pp.157-158, 236 and pl.79, p.170.

Bond, 1971, p.174 and pl. p.145.

GENERAL DISTRIBUTION

West Indies: northern Bahamas (Grand Bahama, Abaco, Andros, New Providence, Eleuthera, and Cat Island), Cuba, Isle of Pines, Swan Islands (formerly), Cayman Brac, Hispaniola, Gonave, Tortue, Puerto Rico and Dominica.

INTRODUCED DISTRIBUTION

Probably introduced, unsuccessfully to Grand Cayman (Cayman Islands), West Indies.

GENERAL HABITS

Status: common. *Habitat:* forest, wooded plantations and gardens. *Gregariousness:* no information. *Movement:* sedentary. *Foods and Breeding:* no information. *Nest:* bulky cup in a bush or tree. *Eggs:* 3-5.

Allen, 1962, pp.157-158, 236.

Bond, 1971, p.174.

NOTES ON INTRODUCTIONS

Grand Cayman. The Red-legged Thrush does not

Red-legged Thrush

occur naturally on Grand Cayman, but has been brought over from a neighbouring island (probably Cayman Brac ?) at least once, and single birds have been known to escape there (Blake, 1977, pers. comm.).

DAMAGE
None known.

Sylviidae

BUSH WARBLER
(Japanese or Chinese Bush Warbler)
Cettia diphone (Kittlitz)

DISTINGUISHING CHARACTERISTICS
12-17.5 cm (4.8-7 in)
Generally brownish with rounded tail. Upper parts olive-brown or rufous-brown, deeper on forehead and crown; whitish or buff line above and below eye; faint black-brown streak through eye; underparts dull grey-white or buffy; flanks brownish; bill, upper mandible brown or slate, lower paler and tending to be greyish pink. *Female:* noticeably smaller.
Yamashina, 1961, p.99 and pl. p.99.
Kobayashi, 1961, pl.13, fig.98, opp. p.30.

GENERAL DISTRIBUTION
Eastern Asia: from Sakhalin to south-eastern China, Japan, Ryūkyū Islands and Bonin. Winters to southern China, Philippines, Taiwan, Hainan, Vietnam and Assam, India.

INTRODUCED DISTRIBUTION
Introduced successfully in the Hawaiian Islands.

GENERAL HABITS
Status: common. *Habitat:* forest, woodland, thickets and brush, gardens and cultivated land. *Gregariousness:* solitary or pairs. *Movements:* migratory. *Foods:* insects, spiders, fruits and nectar. *Breeding:* May-June (Chinkiang). *Nest:* domed with side entrance, of grass, leaves, etc., lined with fine grass and feathers, in a bush near the ground. *Eggs:* 4-5 (China); 4-6 (Hawaii).

NOTES ON INTRODUCTIONS
Hawaiian Islands. The Bush Warbler was released on Oahu by the Board of Agriculture and Forestry in 1929 and by the Hui Manu and others at later dates (Caum, 1933; Munro, 1960). Some were noted on Oahu in 1935. Some were released by the Honolulu Mejiro Club and the Hui Manu several times between 6 January 1931 and 26 December 1941 (Berger, 1977). Berger says that some were released in the Nu'u-anu Valley and 'in bushes of gardens of the F. J. Lowrey residence, Old Pali Road'.

The Bush Warbler is reported to be established in forest undergrowth in the Koolau and Waianee Mountains on Oahu (Peterson, 1961; Berger, 1972; Hawaiian Audubon Society, 1975). Some were recorded there on the Christmas Bird Count of 1975 (Heilbrun, 1976). Although they have been established there for some time, until recently their nesting had not been described. Since the 1960s they have become more common and in 1979 were found for the first time on the island of Molokai (Pyle, 1979).

The introduction of the Bush Warbler in the Hawaiian Islands was presumably made because of the ability of the species to feed on insects (Caum, 1933).

DAMAGE
None known.

WHITETHROAT
(Common Whitethroat, White-throated Warbler)
Sylvia communis Latham

DISTINGUISHING CHARACTERISTICS
14 cm (5.6 in). 9.9-20 g (.35-.71 oz)
Upper parts reddish brown; head grey, tinged brown; wings dusky with coverts edged red;

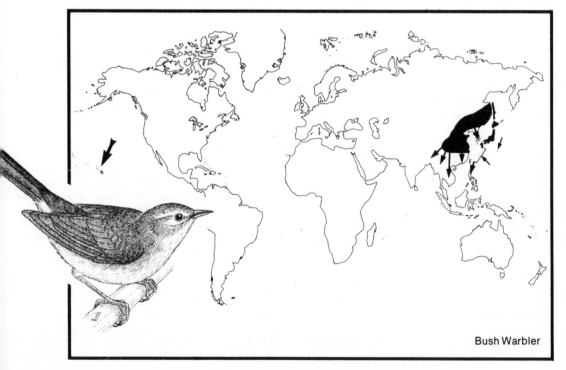

Bush Warbler

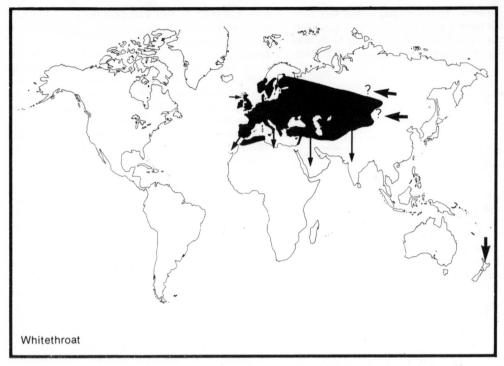

Whitethroat

underparts white, faintly tinged rose; tail dark brown, white tipped; bill greyish horn-brown. *Female:* lacks rose tint on breast.

Witherby *et al,* vol.2, 1938-41, pp.83-86 and pl.39, opp. p.76.

GENERAL DISTRIBUTION

Eurasia-North Africa: Europe except northern Scandinavia, north-west Africa, and in Asia to Mongolia. In winter to tropical Africa, Arabia, Baluchistan and north-western India.

INTRODUCED DISTRIBUTION

Colonised some areas of western Siberia. Introduced unsuccessfully to New Zealand.

GENERAL HABITS

Status: common. *Habitat:* forest edges adjoining bogs and grassland, bush steppe, hedgerows, roadsides, railways, and near cultivation. *Gregariousness:* pairs, small family groups, flocks on migration. *Movements:* migratory. *Foods:* insects, berries and fruits. *Breeding:* May-July (Great Britain); often 2 clutches per year. *Nest:* untidy flimsy saucer of twigs, grass stems and hair with a deep cup lined with wool and fine grass, under a low bush near the ground. *Eggs:* 4-6 (Great Britain).

Witherby *et al*, vol.2, 1938-41, pp.83-86.

Voous, 1960, p.226.

NOTES ON INTRODUCTIONS

Central Asia. The Whitethroat has extended its breeding range into Siberia during this century (Voous, 1960).

New Zealand. In 1868 the Auckland Acclimatisation Society introduced two birds, but these were not seen again after their liberation. Another attempt was made by this society to import the species in 1874, but it ended in failure when they all died on the way to New Zealand (Thomson, 1922).

DAMAGE

The Whitethroat is fond of fruits and visits gardens to feed on currants and raspberries (Hudson, 1921).

This appears to be the only record of the species causing agricultural damage.

BLACKCAP
(Blackcap Warbler)
Sylvia atricapilla (Linnaeus)

DISTINGUISHING CHARACTERISTICS

13.9-14.6 cm (5.56-5.84 in)

Upper parts, wings and tail ash-grey, tinged olive; cap black; throat and breast ash-grey; lower breast and central belly white; bill slaty black to brownish black. *Female:* cap red-brown.

Witherby *et al,* vol.2, 1938-41, pp.79-82 and pl.38, opp. p.66.

GENERAL DISTRIBUTION

Eurasia: Great Britain, southern Norway, Finland, USSR and south to the Black Sea and Mediterranean; also western Siberia, Madeira and the Canary Islands. Winters south to the Mediterranean and Malawi in Africa.

INTRODUCED DISTRIBUTION

Introduced unsuccessfully in the USA and possibly in New Zealand.

GENERAL HABITS

Status: common. *Habitat:* woodlands, gardens, riverine forest and parks. *Gregariousness:* solitary, and parties on migration. *Movements:* migratory and sedentary. *Foods:* insects (including flies and larvae), berries and fruits. *Breeding:* Apr-June. *Nest:* cup-shaped of dry grass, rootlets and hair, in a creeper, bush or tree. *Eggs:* 3, 4-5, 6.

Witherby *et al,* vol.2, 1938-41, pp.79-82.

Stein, *Beitr. Vogelk.* vol.20, 1974, pp.467-477.

NOTES ON INTRODUCTIONS

USA. Phillips (1928) considered that the Blackcap was probably the subject of small or accidental experiments in acclimatisation in the United States. The Portland Song Bird Club imported twenty pairs in 1907 and perhaps others in 1900. Another

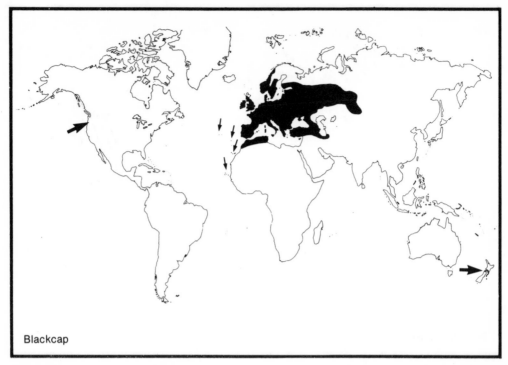

Blackcap

shipment of eighty-four birds was imported to the United States in 1902. No releases are documented.

New Zealand. Blackcap Warblers were imported into New Zealand in 1872, but it is not known if any were liberated there (Thomson, 1922).

DAMAGE

None known.

Maluridae

SUPERB BLUE WREN

Malurus cyaneus (Latham)

DISTINGUISHING CHARACTERISTICS

12-13 cm (4.8-5.2 in)

Crown, ear-coverts, mantle and tail blue; remaining upper parts black; wings brown; throat and breast black with a purple sheen; abdomen white; bill black. *Female:* face brown; upper parts grey-brown; underparts dull white; tail blue; bill brown. Male in non-breeding similar to female.

Rowley, *Emu,* vol.64, 1965, pp.255-258 and pl.12.

Reader's Digest, 1977, p.408 and pl. p.408.

GENERAL DISTRIBUTION

Australia: eastern Australia from southern Queensland to Victoria, Kangaroo Island and Tasmania.

INTRODUCED DISTRIBUTION

Introduced unsuccessfully in New Zealand.

GENERAL HABITS

Status: fairly common. *Habitat:* woodland, savannah, parks and gardens. *Gregariousness:* family groups. *Movements:* sedentary. *Foods:* insects. *Breeding:* July-Feb, and sometimes other months. *Nest:* dome-shaped with side entrance, of grass, rootlets and bark fibre bound with cobwebs and lined with grass, hair, wool or feathers, in a tussock or bush. *Eggs:* 3-4.

Rowley, *Emu,* vol.64, 1965, pp.251-297.

Reader's Digest, 1977, p.408.

NOTES ON INTRODUCTIONS

New Zealand. Four male and eight female Superb

Blue Wrens were introduced to New Zealand in 1923 and released at Rangitaiki, Rotorna Hill, Mokoia Island (Lake Rotorua) and at Mt Tongariro (Westerskov, 1953).

Westerskov reports that the introduction was initiated by the Tourist and Health Resorts Department in 1918 and the twelve birds arrived on the *S.S. Ulimaroa* in Auckland in 1923. They were not sighted again after release.

DAMAGE

None known.

Superb Blue Wren

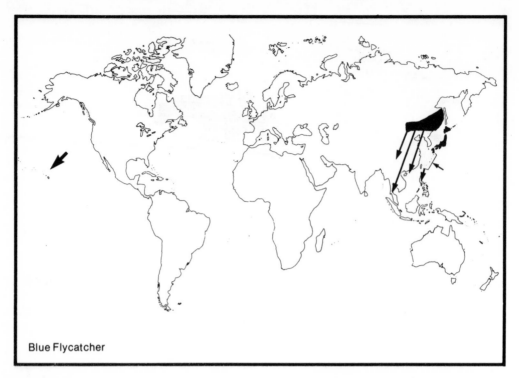

Blue Flycatcher

Muscicapidae

BLUE FLYCATCHER
(Japanese Blue Flycatcher, Blue Nitalva)
Muscicapa cyanomelana (Temminck)

DISTINGUISHING CHARACTERISTICS
14-16.2 cm (5.6-6.48 in)
Upper parts cobalt blue, bordered with black on sides of head and upper breast; underparts white; bill black. *Female:* upper parts olive-brown, with some blue on crown; underparts white, washed brown on throat and breast.
La Touche, 1925-34, 2 vols.
Yamashina, 1961, p.96 and pl. p.96.

GENERAL DISTRIBUTION
Eastern Asia: from Manchuria and northern China to Japan. Winters to Hainan, South-east Asia, Malaysia and Borneo (rare).

INTRODUCED DISTRIBUTION
Introduced unsuccessfully in the Hawaiian Islands.

GENERAL HABITS
Status: common. *Habitat:* forest, woodlands, towns, parklands, orchards and gardens. *Gregariousness:* no information. *Movements:* migratory. *Foods:* insects and berries. *Breeding:* no information. *Nest:* in a hole in a tree. *Eggs:* no information.

NOTES ON INTRODUCTIONS
Hawaiian Islands. The Blue Flycatcher was introduced from Japan to Oahu in 1929, but apparently did not become established on the island (Munro, 1960). Peterson (1961) recorded that its status there was uncertain in about 1960. Some were reported to have been sighted in 1943 and again in 1950 (Bryan, 1958), but the species does not now seem to be established in the Hawaiian Islands (Berger, 1972).

DAMAGE
None known.

NARCISSUS FLYCATCHER
Ficedula narcissina (Temminck)

DISTINGUISHING CHARACTERISTICS
11-13 cm (4.4-5.2 in)
Generally black (some races olive-green) with brilliant yellow rump, throat, and upper breast; eye-stripe white or yellow; wing bar and belly white (belly yellowish in some races); under tail and under wing-coverts white; bill black. *Female:* upper parts olive-green; lores buff-white; underparts whitish washed olive; upper tail-coverts reddish.
Yamashina, 1961, p.95 and pl. p.95.
Kobayashi, 1961, pl.12, fig.93, opp. p.27.

GENERAL DISTRIBUTION
Eastern Asia: the east Asian mainland from Sakhalin to the Ryūkyū Islands. Winters in south-east Asia to Borneo, south-eastern China, Hainan, Taiwan and the Philippines.

INTRODUCED DISTRIBUTION
Introduced unsuccessfully in the Hawaiian Islands.

GENERAL HABITS
Status: common. *Habitat:* forest, woodland, gardens and mangroves. *Gregariousness:* small flocks. *Movements:* migratory. *Foods:* insects and their larvae, and including caterpillars, moths, beetles, flies and spiders. *Breeding:* Apr-June. *Nest:* cup-shaped of moss, leaves and roots in a tree hole. *Eggs:* 3-8, usually 5.
Gooders, vol.7, 1969, p.2247.

NOTES ON INTRODUCTIONS
Hawaiian Islands. The Narcissus Flycatcher was imported, probably just prior to the second World War and possibly released on one of the islands (Munro, 1960). If liberated the species certainly did not become established in the Hawaiian Islands.

DAMAGE
None known.

324

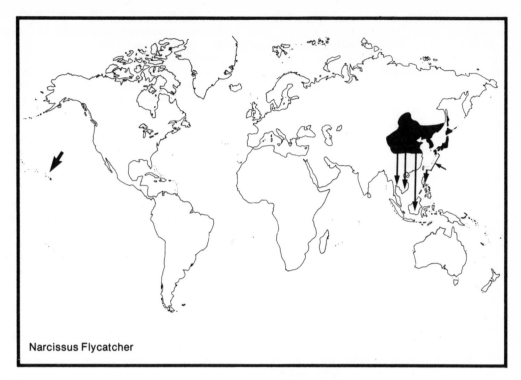

Narcissus Flycatcher

Rhipiduridae

WILLIE WAGTAIL
Rhipidura leucophrys (Latham)

DISTINGUISHING CHARACTERISTICS
20 cm (8 in)
Upper parts glossy black; throat black; conspicuous white eyebrow stripe; occasionally white flecks on throat and foreneck; abdomen white; bill black. (Northern birds smaller than southern birds.)

Reader's Digest, 1977, p.393, pl. p.393.

GENERAL DISTRIBUTION
Indonesia-Australia: Australia, Kangaroo Island, southern New Guinea and islands, Solomon Islands, Moluccas and Lesser Sunda Islands.

INTRODUCED DISTRIBUTION
Introduced unsuccessfully in the Hawaiian Islands.

GENERAL HABITS
Status: very common. *Habitat:* most habitats from the edge of rain forest to the edges of desert, also

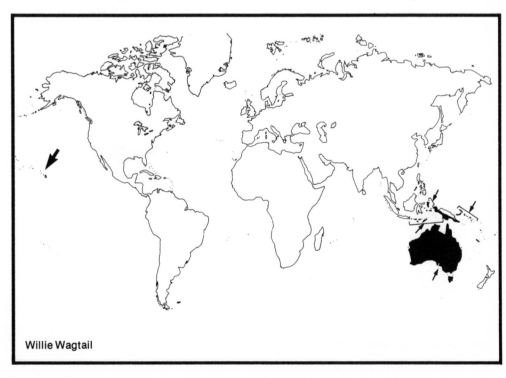

Willie Wagtail

parklands and cultivated areas. *Gregariousness:* solitary or pairs. *Movements:* sedentary (and nomadic). *Foods:* insects, spiders and worms. *Breeding:* June-Feb; may have several clutches in one season. *Nest:* cup-shaped of bark strips and grass, tightly woven with cobwebs in a bush, tree, and occasionally a building or other structure. *Eggs:* 3-4. *Reader's Digest,* 1977, p.393.

NOTES ON INTRODUCTIONS

Hawaiian Islands. The Willie Wagtail was introduced to the Hawaiian Islands in about 1922 (Berger, 1972) from Australia for the purpose of combating flies on livestock (Munro, 1960). Munro says that the species did not become established. They may however, have persisted there for some time as there is a record of one seen on Koko Head, Oahu in 1937.

DAMAGE

None known.

Timaliidae

WHITE-THROATED LAUGHING-THRUSH

(Collared Thrush, Brown Thrush)

Garrulax albogularis (Gould)

DISTINGUISHING CHARACTERISTICS

27-31 cm (10.8-12.4 in). 78-114 g (2.75-4.02 oz)
Upper parts and breast pectoral band olive-brown; forehead tawny; lores and eye rim black; throat, cheeks and breast white; belly and under tail-coverts rufous-orange; tail olive-brown, white tipped on outer four pairs of feathers; wings brown, edged olive-brown and with outer edge grey; bill black.
Ali and Ripley, 1968-74, vol.6, pl.71 and vol.7, pp. 4-6.

GENERAL DISTRIBUTION

Southern Asia: north-western Himalayas, Bhutan, south-eastern Tibet, east to Yunnan, Tonkin and Szechwan in western China, and Taiwan.

INTRODUCED DISTRIBUTION

Possibly introduced, successfully in the Hawaiian Islands (status uncertain).

GENERAL HABITS

Status: common. *Habitat:* evergreen forest and gardens. *Gregariousness:* small noisy flocks of 6-12 birds and sometimes larger flocks in winter of 30 to 100 birds. *Movements:* sedentary. *Foods:* insects, berries and seeds. *Breeding:* Mar-July. *Nest:* loose, cup-shaped of grass, leaves, roots and tendrils, bound with stems, sometimes lined with moss and ferns, in a bush or tree. *Eggs:* 2, 3-4.
Ali and Ripley, vol.7, 1968-74, pp.4-6.

NOTES ON INTRODUCTIONS

Hawaiian Islands. Until recently it was thought that the White-throated Laughingthrush had been introduced to these islands and may have been still established there. However, Zeillemaker (1976) indicates that it may have been the Greater Necklaced Laughingthrush *(G. pectoralis)* and not the white-throated species *(albogularis)* which was introduced to Kauai in 1919.

Caum (1933) records that the white-throated birds were introduced from San Francisco to Kauai in 1919 and became established there. Bryan (1958) says that they were released on Oahu in about 1950.

Peterson (1961) reports that they were still occasionally seen on Kauai, but that their status there is uncertain. They were apparently an uncommon resident in a few lowland areas of Kauai in the 1960s (Richardson and Bowles, 1964) and some were noted near Lihue in 1959 (Berger, 1972).

WHITE-CRESTED LAUGHING-THRUSH

Garrulax leucolophus (Hardwicke)

DISTINGUISHING CHARACTERISTICS

28-30 cm (11.2-12 in). 119-129 g (4.2-4.55 oz)

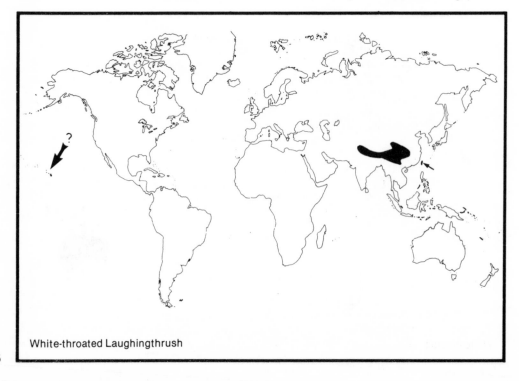

White-throated Laughingthrush

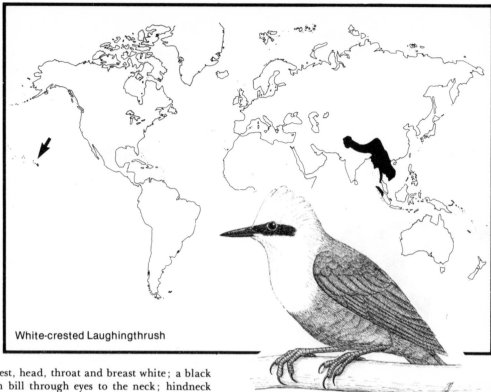

White-crested Laughingthrush

Erectile crest, head, throat and breast white; a black mask from bill through eyes to the neck; hindneck grey; mantle chestnut grading to olive-brown on the remaining underparts; tail blackish; throat, sides of neck and breast whitish, bordered by a rufous band; belly olive-brown; flanks and under tail-coverts chestnut to rufous olive-brown; bill black.
Ali and Ripley, 1968-74, vol.6, pl.72, and vol.7, pp.14-16.
Avon *et al*, 1974, pl. p.113.

GENERAL DISTRIBUTION
Southern Asia: north-western Himalayas east to south-western China and south through the Indochinese subregion; also western Sumatra.

INTRODUCED DISTRIBUTION
Introduced, possibly successfully in the Hawaiian Islands (status uncertain).

GENERAL HABITS
Status: very common. *Habitat:* thickets and undergrowth in forest, secondary growth, bamboo jungle, and scrub country bordering cultivation. *Gregariousness:* small flocks 6-12, and occasionally larger flocks up to 40 often in association with other thrushes. *Movements:* sedentary. *Foods:* insects, berries, seeds, small reptiles and nectar. *Breeding:* Mar-Sept (India); possibly two broods per year. *Nest:* loose, untidy, shallow cup of grass, leaves, moss and tendrils lined with roots and fibres, in a tree or bush. *Eggs:* 2, 3-5, 6.
Ali and Ripley, vol.7, 1968-74, pp.14-16.

NOTES ON INTRODUCTIONS
Hawaiian Islands. A pair of White-crested Laughingthrushes were reported to be breeding on the slopes of Diamond Head, Oahu during 1969 (Berger, 1972). Like many other species found at this time they were probably escapees from captivity.

DAMAGE
None known.

GREATER NECKLACED LAUGHINGTHRUSH
(Black-gorgeted Laughing Thrush)
Garrulax pectoralis (Gould)

DISTINGUISHING CHARACTERISTICS
29-34 cm (11.6-13.6 in). 135-156 g (4.76-5.5 oz)
Mainly olive-brown with rufous nuchal collar; broad black moustachial stripe from bill and separating ear-coverts from throat; eye-stripe black; loral area usually whitish; ear-coverts vary from whitish, black and white streaked, to entirely black; outer wing edge white; throat buff, bordered by white along necklace; centre of belly white; flanks orange-brown; tail black, white tipped; bill, upper mandible blackish brown, lower brown but basal part grey and with a white tip.
La Touche, 1925-34, 2 vols.
Ali and Ripley, 1968-74, vol.6, pl.72, and vol.7, pp.8-10.

GENERAL DISTRIBUTION
Southern Asia: Nepal east to southern China and Hainan, and south to Burma, western Thailand, northern Laos and Tonkin.

INTRODUCED DISTRIBUTION
Introduced, probably successfully in the Hawaiian Islands (status uncertain).

GENERAL HABITS
Status: common. *Habitat:* undergrowth of forest and secondary growth. *Gregariousness:* parties and flocks of 10-25 birds often with other thrushes. *Movements:* sedentary. *Foods:* insects. *Breeding:* Mar-Aug (India). *Nest:* broad, shallow, bulky saucer of leaves, bamboo, grass, roots, etc. lined with finer roots of ferns, in a bush, bamboo thicket or tree. *Eggs:* 3-5, 7.
Ali and Ripley, vol.7, 1968-74, pp.8-10.

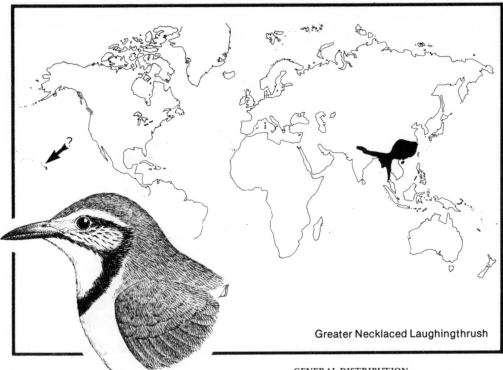

Greater Necklaced Laughingthrush

NOTES ON INTRODUCTIONS
Hawaiian Islands. Berger (1972) says that either the Greater Necklaced Laughingthrush or the Lesser Necklaced Laughingthrush *G. monileger* which are indistinguishable in the field, has been introduced in the Hawaiian Islands. He saw two birds of one of these species near Kapaa, Kauai in July 1970. Zeillemaker (1976), as previously indicated, suggests that the Greater species rather than the White-throated Laughingthrush may have been the one introduced to Kauai in 1919.

The Hawaiian Audubon Society (1975) reports that the species may still be established on Kauai, but that their present status is poorly known. Heilbrun (1976) indicates that they may still be established near Lihue, Kauai, as nineteen were noted there on the Christmas Bird Count of 1975. He says that they have been established for several years, at least since 1972.

DAMAGE
None known.

BLACK-THROATED LAUGHING-THRUSH
(Peko Thrush, Chestnut-backed Laughing Thrush)
Garrulax chinensis (Scopoli)

DISTINGUISHING CHARACTERISTICS
23-29 cm (9.2-11.6 in)
Face and throat black; ear-coverts white, black or brown; crown and nape slate grey; collar rufous-chestnut; remainder of upper parts dark greyish olive to dark olive-brown; outer edge of wing grey; chin and throat black; remainder of underparts grey with olive-brown flanks and under tail-coverts; tail broadly tipped black; bill black.
La Touche, 1925-34, 2 vols.

Ali and Ripley 1968-74, vol.6, pl.71, and vol.7, p.17.

GENERAL DISTRIBUTION
Southern Asia: southern China, Hainan, Burma, Thailand, Vietnam, Laos and Hong Kong.
INTRODUCED DISTRIBUTION
Introduced unsuccessfully in the Hawaiian Islands.
GENERAL HABITS
Status: common; favourite cage bird in eastern China. *Habitat:* forest undergrowth, secondary growth, woodland, bamboo thickets and gardens. *Gregariousness:* small parties, sometimes with other thrushes. *Movements:* sedentary. *Foods:* insects, and probably berries and seeds. *Breeding:* Mar-July. *Nest:* neat compact cup of bracken and inner layer of leaves and grass lined with moss, rootlets and fibre, in a bush. *Eggs:* 2-3.
La Touche, 1925-34, 2 vols.
Ali and Ripley, vol.7, 1968-74, p.17.
NOTES ON INTRODUCTIONS
Hawaiian Islands. Introduced from California to Kauai in 1931 the Black-throated Laughingthrush was said to be established and increasing there in

Black-throated Laughingthrush, *Garrulax chinensis*

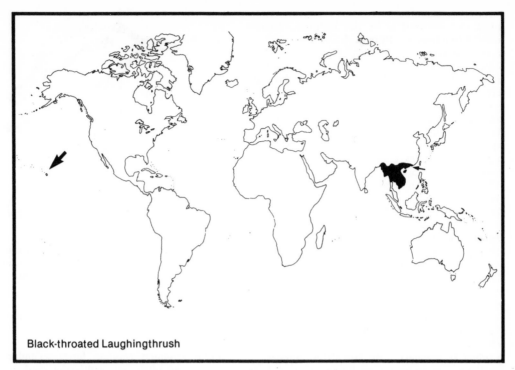

Black-throated Laughingthrush

about the 1940s (Munro, 1960). However, the species is not now known to be established anywhere in the Hawaiian Islands (Berger, 1972).

DAMAGE
None known.

MELODIOUS LAUGHINGTHRUSH
(Hwa-Mei, Chinese Thrush)
Garrulax canorus (Linnaeus)

DISTINGUISHING CHARACTERISTICS
19.7-25 cm (7.88-10 in). 53.8-85 g (1.9-3 oz)

Forecrown tawny, grading to olive-brown on the upper parts; eye-ring and streak behind eye white; crown and nape with blackish streaks; underparts tawny with ash grey centre of belly, and narrow streaks on throat and upper breast; tail faintly barred blackish; bill yellowish or brownish yellow.
La Touche, 1925-34, 2 vols.
Cheng, 1963, p.724 and pl.49, no.97.

GENERAL DISTRIBUTION
Southern Asia: southern China, Hainan, Taiwan, Hong Kong and central Laos.

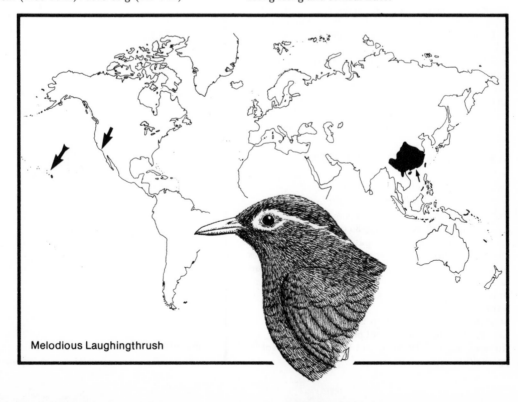

Melodious Laughingthrush

Introduced successfully in the Hawaiian Islands. Introduced unsuccessfully in the USA.

GENERAL HABITS
Status: common; popular cage bird in China. *Habitat:* forest undergrowth, brush, thickets and scrub. *Gregariousness:* solitary, parties or small groups. *Movements:* sedentary. *Foods:* insects (including eggs and larvae), seeds, fruits and vegetable material; possibly omnivorous. *Breeding:* Apr-July (China); May-July (Hawaii). *Nest:* large cup-shaped of leaves, grass and twigs, lined with pine needles, or fine material, near the ground, in a bush or tree and sometimes in a stump. *Eggs:* 3-4, 5; 3-4 (Hawaii).
Cheng, 1963, pp.724-728.

NOTES ON INTRODUCTIONS
Hawaiian Islands. It is thought that the Melodious Laughingthrush escaped from captivity in the fire of 1900, at which time it was a favourite cage bird of the Chinese population in the Hawaiian Islands (Caum, 1933). Later, birds were imported and released on Molokai, Maui and Hawaii, and birds from Oahu were shipped to Kauai in 1918 (Berger, 1972).

According to Munro (1960) the species became well distributed and common, but in some areas was declining in numbers in the late 1940s. However, in the 1960s it was common on Kauai, local on Oahu and Hawaii and scarce on Molokai and Maui (Peterson, 1961; Richardson and Bowles, 1964).

The Hawaiian Audubon Society (1975) reports that the species is now on all the main islands except Lanai, and is common on Kauai. However, its distribution does not appear to be generally well known. Some were observed on Oahu, Kauai and Hawaii on the Christmas Bird Counts of 1975.

USA. Some Melodious Laughingthrushes were introduced at Woodside, California in 1941, but at this time were not known to be permanently established (Isenberg and Williams, 1946, *Avic. Mag.* 53 (2): 48-50, in A.O.U., 1957). There appear to be no further records for the species in California.

DAMAGE
In China the Melodious Laughingthrush is said to eat cultivated plants such as pea seedlings and they are therefore disliked by some people. Cheng (1963) says that this habit has not been confirmed by examinations of stomach contents and the species causes no damage and eats many injurious insects.

WHITE-BROWED LAUGHING-THRUSH
(White-cheeked Laughingthrush)
Garrulax sannio Swinhoe

DISTINGUISHING CHARACTERISTICS
20.7-25 cm (8.28-10 in). 53.8-85 g (1.9-3 oz)
Lores, eyebrow and cheek patch white or buffish; crown chestnut-brown; throat, upper breast and sides of head brown; upper parts brown; lower breast and belly buffy brown, paler in centre; tail rufescent brown; under tail-coverts cinnamon; bill blackish or brownish.
Smythies, 1953, pl.2, fig.6, p.20.
Cheng, 1963, pp.728-729 and pl.49, no.98.
Ali and Ripley, 1968-74, vol.6, pl.72 and vol.7, pp.39-40.

White-browed Laughingthrush, *Garrulax sannio*

GENERAL DISTRIBUTION
Southern Asia: from south-eastern Assam, India, north-eastern and central Burma, northern Laos, northern Vietnam, south-western and southern China, and Hainan.

INTRODUCED DISTRIBUTION
Possibly introduced, successfully to the island of Hong Kong.

GENERAL HABITS
Status: common. *Habitat:* forest, secondary growth, scrub, and often near cultivation and in gardens. *Gregariousness:* solitary, pairs or small parties and groups of up to 20 birds. *Movements:* sedentary (?). *Foods:* insects, seeds and fruits. *Breeding:* Mar-Aug; Mar-June (India). *Nest:* massive, cup-shaped of grass, fern, roots and bamboo leaves, bound with weeds and tendrils and lined with fern roots, etc., in a bush or tree. *Eggs:* 3-4, 5.
Cheng, 1963, pp.729-730.
Ali and Ripley, vol.7, 1968-74, pp.39-40.

NOTES ON INTRODUCTIONS
Hong Kong. King *et al* (1975) list the White-browed

White-browed Laughingthrush

Laughingthrush as a vagrant to Hong Kong. Webster (1975) indicates that they may have been introduced by man and are probably established and breeding there. In the last four years they have been recorded regularly from two areas on Hong Kong island. Webster says that although their origin may have been from wild stock, they are more than likely escapees from captivity.

DAMAGE
None known.

RED-BILLED LEIOTHRIX
(Pekin Robin, Pekin Nightingale, Hill Robin)
Leiothrix lutea (Scopoli)

DISTINGUISHING CHARACTERISTICS
12-15.5 cm (4.8-6.2 in). 20-25 g (.71-.88 oz)
Generally olive-green, or greyish olive; throat yellow, shading to orange on breast; whitish or buff patch around eye; wings black with yellow and crimson edges (lacking in some races) and a small orange or red patch; upper parts generally olive-grey; underparts pale yellow, with olive-grey sides and flanks; upper tail-coverts olive, with pale narrow terminal bar; under tail-coverts pale yellow; tail forked, black above and olive below and black tipped; bill bright orange-red or scarlet, black at base of mandibles. Female: generally paler; lacks red patch on wings.
Cheng, 1963, pp.733-734 and pl.27, no.100.
Ali and Ripley, vol.7, 1968-74, pp.67-69 and pl.76, fig.11, opp. p.64.

GENERAL DISTRIBUTION
Southern Asia: from the north-western Himalayas east to Assam, north-eastern and western Burma, and to west, central and southern China.

INTRODUCED DISTRIBUTION
Introduced successfully in the Hawaiian Islands and possibly to Hong Kong (escapees ?). Introduced unsuccessfully to Australia, Tahiti, France, England, and Colombia in South America (status ?).

GENERAL HABITS
Status: common; popular cage bird in native range and elsewhere. *Habitat:* forest, secondary growth, low growth and scrub areas, towns, and often near cultivation. *Gregariousness:* pairs in breeding season and at other times small flocks of up to 6 (in Hawaii occasionally large flocks of 100 birds have been recorded). *Movements:* sedentary. *Foods:* insects, berries, fruits, seeds and flowers. *Breeding:* Apr-Oct; Mar-Aug (Hawaii). *Nest:* cup-shaped of grass, bamboo leaves, moss, etc. lined with fine roots, grass and tendrils, in a bush, bamboo or low tree. *Eggs:* 3-4, 5; 2-4 (Hawaii).
Cheng, 1963, pp.734-736.
Ali and Ripley, vol.7, 1968-74, pp.67-69.

NOTES ON INTRODUCTIONS
Hawaiian Islands. According to Caum (1933), the Red-billed Leiothrix was first imported to the Hawaiian Islands from San Francisco for liberation on Kauai in 1918; birds from the same source were released on Oahu in 1928. Also, in 1928 and 1929 birds imported from the Orient were released on five islands: Oahu, Molokai, Maui, Hawaii and Kauai.

Fisher and Baldwin (1947) say that the Red-billed Leiothrix was imported as early as 1911 as a cage bird, and suggest that some of these probably escaped and became established prior to 1918. In 1947 they record that the species was increasing its range on all the islands. However, in more recent years they have suffered a decline in numbers beginning about 1968, but no accurate census has been made.

The Hawaiian Audubon Society (1975) reports that they are declining in the lower elevations of both Oahu and Hawaii, but are still present on all the main islands. Berger (1972) says that they were least

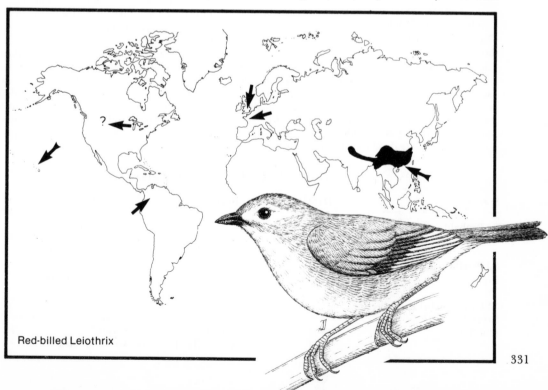

Red-billed Leiothrix

common on Kauai where first intentionally introduced.

Ali and Ripley (1968-73) have recorded that the race introduced to the Hawaiian Islands is *L.l. calipyga.*

Western Australia. The Red-billed Leiothrix was probably liberated in Western Australia some time before 1912, but failed to become established (Long, 1972).

Colombia. The Red-billed Leiothrix has recently been released in Colombia (Sick, 1968), but any success there does not appear to be documented. More than likely they have failed to become established.

France. In 1898 some thirteen Red-billed Leiothrixes were released on a thirty-four hectare (eighty-four acre) property, possibly by M. Thiebaux, near Meaux, France (Etchécopar, 1955). They were sighted once after being released, but there are no further records of them and they evidently failed to become established.

England. Escaped or liberated birds including the Red-billed Leiothrix have often survived in the wild in England for long periods and have been recorded to breed there (Goodwin, 1956). However, they have not become permanently established in that country.

Hong Kong. Webster (1975) reports that Red-billed Leiothrixes are fairly frequently recorded from many localities in Hong Kong. It is so common a cage bird there that it may never be possible to prove the occurrence of wild birds.

In 1975 some were noted at Victoria Peak and in the Tai Po Kau Forestry Reserve (Viney, 1976).

USA. The Red-billed Leiothrix has been known to live for periods in the wild, at least prior to 1928, but has not become permanently established in the United States (Phillips, 1928).

DAMAGE
None known.

Family: *Paridae* Titmice

47 species in 4 genera; 3 species introduced, possibly 2 successfully

The Varied Tit is probably still established in the Hawaiian Islands from liberations dating back to 1890, and the Great Tit may possibly have become permanently established in the Alma-Ata region of the USSR following introductions in 1960-61. The Blue Tit failed to become established in Canada and if released in New Zealand met the same fate.

GREAT TIT
Parus major Linnaeus

DISTINGUISHING CHARACTERISTICS
11.2-15 cm (4.48-6 in). 10.5-21.2 g (.36-.75 oz)
Head, throat and a band down the centre of breast black; cheeks and spot on nape white; back olive-green or greyish with green tinge; abdomen yellowish; wings have steel-blue coverts and a white bar; tail blackish with outer feathers white; bill blackish.
Witherby *et al*, vol.1, 1938-41, pp.245-250 and pl.28, opp. p.254.

GENERAL DISTRIBUTION
Eurasia: Scandinavia, British Isles, Portugal and western North Africa east to the Okhotsk coast, Sakhalin and Japan, and south to northern Thailand, Indochina (except Cochin China), Malay Peninsula, Sunda Islands, Sri Lanka, southern USSR, Iran and Turkey.

INTRODUCED DISTRIBUTION
Transplanted, possibly successfully in the USSR. Introduced unsuccessfully to the USA.

GENERAL HABITS
Status: common. *Habitat:* open woodlands, mangroves, bamboo groves, open forest, cultivated regions and gardens. *Gregariousness:* small parties and flocks. *Movements:* mainly sedentary, but also migratory. *Foods:* seeds, buds, fruits, beechmast, insects and their larvae, and sometimes carrion. *Breeding:* Apr-June (Great Britain); 2 broods per season. *Nest:* loosely built of grass, moss, hair or wool, with a deep cup lined with feathers, in holes in trees, walls, fences, gates and buildings. *Eggs:* 5-7, 16.
Witherby *et al,* vol.1, 1938-41, pp.245-250.
Barnes, 1975.

NOTES ON INTRODUCTIONS
USSR. The Great Tit was introduced in 1960-61 to the Alma-Ata region where it does not occur naturally (Yanushevich, 1966). Yanushevich records that it became locally established there but little is known of its present status.

USA. Great Tits were liberated with other species at Cincinnati, Ohio between 1872 and 1874, but failed to become established (Phillips, 1928). Phillips records that the species was recommended by apple growers for introduction in a number of States as a possible enemy of codlin moth, but that the Bureau of Biological Survey discouraged the attempts because of its injury to fruit in England.

INTRODUCTIONS OF PARIDAE

Species	Date introduced	Region	Manner introduced	Reason
(a) Probably successful introductions				
Varied Tit	1890-1931	Hawaiian Islands	deliberate	?
(b) Possibly successful introductions				
Great Tit	1960-61	Alma-Ata, USSR	deliberate transplant	?
(c) Unsuccessful Introductions				
Great Tit	1872-74	USA	deliberate	insect control ?
Blue Tit	1908-10	Canada	deliberate	?
	1874	New Zealand	not known if released	?

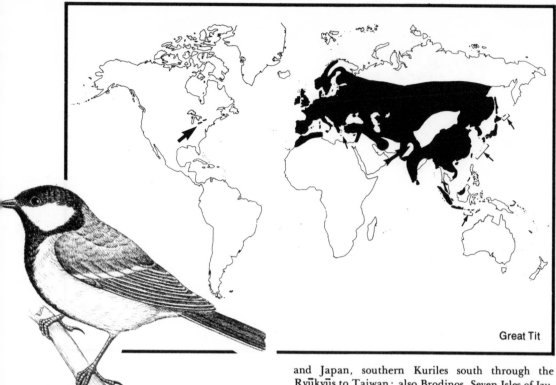

Great Tit

The Great Tit occasionally damages fruit tree buds (Seubert, 1964), but the amount of damage is probably small and not of much economic significance.

VARIED TIT
(Japanese Tit, Yamagara)
Parus varius Temminck and Schlegel

DISTINGUISHING CHARACTERISTICS

12-14 cm (4.8-5.6 in). 15.9-18.2 g (.56-.64 oz)
Head creamy white with a broad black band across forehead from eye to sides of nape; upper parts grey, some chestnut on the shoulders; throat and upper chest black; underparts creamy white; flanks chestnut; back, wings and tail bluish grey; bill black. Dement'ev and Gladkov, 1954, transl., 1970, vol.5, pp.891-893.
Kobayashi, 1961, pl.10, fig.71, opp. p.21.

GENERAL DISTRIBUTION

Eastern Asia: from south-eastern Manchuria, Korea

Varied Tit, *Parus varius*

and Japan, southern Kuriles south through the Ryūkyūs to Taiwan; also Brodinos, Seven Isles of Izu, Cheju Do, Tsushima and Ullung Do.

INTRODUCED DISTRIBUTION

Introduced, probably successfully in the Hawaiian Islands.

GENERAL HABITS

Status: very common. *Habitat:* deciduous and open mixed forests and woodlands, gardens and parks in cities. *Gregariousness:* small flocks. *Movements:* sedentary. *Foods:* insects and small nuts. *Breeding:* Apr-May. *Nest:* in tree cavities and rock crevices, similar to Great Tit. *Eggs:* 5-6, 8.
Dement'ev and Gladkov, vol.5, 1954, pp.891-893.
Higuchi, *Tori* vol.25, 1976, pp.11-20.

NOTES ON INTRODUCTIONS

Hawaiian Islands. The Varied Tit became well established in the Hawaiian Islands from introductions at various times from Japan between 1890 and 1928 (Munro, 1960). The first birds were released on Kauai in 1890, others from Germany and Japan in 1905 and 1907. Some from Japan were liberated on Oahu, Maui and Hawaii in 1928 and 1929, and the Hui Manu brought more to Oahu in 1930 and 1931 (Caum, 1933). According to Berger (1972) they did not survive on either Maui or Hawaii.

In the late 1950s they were reported to be established very locally on Kauai and locally on some trails on Oahu in forest country (Peterson, 1961). Berger indicated that they are established in the Koolan Mountains of Oahu, and Caum and Ord (1967) report their presence in the Kokee area of Kauai. More recently the Hawaiian Audubon Society (1975) says that they may still be established in these areas, but that their status is not well known.

The race introduced to the Hawaiian Islands is *P.v. varius.*

DAMAGE

According to Munro (1960), in the Hawaiian Islands   333

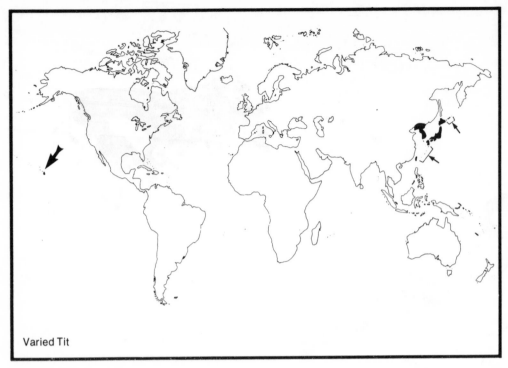

Varied Tit

the Varied Tit has taken the place of some of the vanished species in destroying forest insect pests. It is one of the few species which have penetrated the forest areas rather than man-made environments.

BLUE TIT
Parus caeruleus Linnaeus

DISTINGUISHING CHARACTERISTICS
11.5 cm (4.6 in). 11-14 g (.39-.49 oz)
Cobalt blue cap; white stripe over eye, black stripe through eye; face patch white with blue border; back yellowish green; wings brown; underparts sulphur-yellow with dark streaks extending down from bib; tail blue; bill black.

Witherby *et al,* vol.1, 1938-41, pp.250-254 and pl.28, opp. p.254.
Dement'ev and Gladkov, 1954, transl., 1970, vol.5, pp.886-891.

GENERAL DISTRIBUTION
Europe-North Africa: from the British Isles, southern Scandinavia, Ural Mountains (USSR), south to Iran, Turkey, North Africa and the Canary Islands.

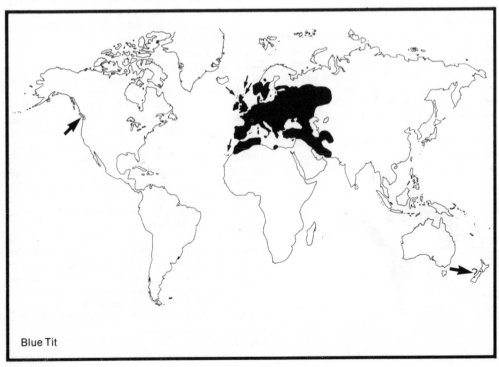

Blue Tit

INTRODUCED DISTRIBUTION

Introduced, unsuccessfully in Canada and possibly in New Zealand.

GENERAL HABITS

Status: very common. *Habitat:* open forest, woodland, farmlands, parkland, gardens, orchards, palm groves, olive groves and other cultivated areas. *Gregariousness:* small flocks. *Movements:* sedentary, but with irruptive movements associated with food supply. *Foods:* insects including caterpillars, moths, and their larvae, also spiders, buds, seeds and other vegetable material. *Breeding:* Apr-June (Great Britain); 1-2 broods per season. *Nest:* of grass, hair and moss felted together, the cup lined with hair, feathers and fur, in a hole in a tree, wall or bank. *Eggs:* 7-8, 12 or more (18 recorded).

Barnes, 1975.

Källander, *Vår Fågelv.* vol.35, 1976, pp.1-7.

NOTES ON INTRODUCTIONS

Canada. In 1908-10 a number of species of British birds were released by G. H. Wallace at various points on the Saanich Peninsula, British Columbia and the Blue Tit is mentioned as one of the birds released (Carl and Guiguet, 1972). There appear no further records of the species in Canada.

New Zealand. Blue Tits were imported into New Zealand in 1874, but it is not known whether any were liberated there (Thomson, 1922).

DAMAGE

The Blue Tit sometimes eats fruit tree buds (Seubert, 1964), but rarely attacks the fruit itself (Wright and Brough, 1964).

Family: *Nectariniidae* Sunbirds

116 species in 5 genera; possibly 1 or 2 species introduced? unsuccessfully

Some sunbirds may have been released in the Hawaiian Islands just before 1939, but the species and any releases do not appear to have been documented.

Family: *Zosteropidae* White-eyes

82 species in 11 genera; 3 species introduced, all successfully

As a result of colonisation and introductions silvereyes and white-eyes now inhabit New Zealand, Norfolk Island, Tahiti, the Hawaiian Islands and the Cocos-Keeling Islands. Because of the damage caused to various soft fruits a number of species have some notoriety in this respect.

GREY-BACKED SILVEREYE
(Silvereye, White-eye, Western Silvereye)
Zosterops lateralis (Latham)

DISTINGUISHING CHARACTERISTICS

11-13 cm (4.4-5.2 in). 8.5-10 g (.3-.35 oz)

Upper parts generally yellow-green and underparts greyish. Crown and face olive-green; ring around eyes white; lores blackish; back dark grey; rump and upper tail-coverts green; throat lemon yellow; abdomen pale grey, shading to brownish on flanks; shoulder greenish yellow; wings and tail blackish; bill dark brown, pale at base. (Races vary widely in colour.)

Reader's Digest, 1977, p.523 and pl. p.523.

GENERAL DISTRIBUTION

Australia and Pacific islands: coastal and adjacent areas of southern, eastern (north to Gulf of Carpentaria) and south-western (Point Cloates to Kalgoorlie and Eucla) Australia, and Tasmania, New Caledonia, New Hebrides, Capricorn and Bunker groups, and islands east to Fiji.

INTRODUCED DISTRIBUTION

Successfully colonised New Zealand and Norfolk Island; introduced successfully in Tahiti. Introduced unsuccessfully to Lord Howe Island.

GENERAL HABITS

Status: very common. *Habitat:* coastal heath to forest undergrowth, but mainly coastal and adjacent areas. *Gregariousness:* small flocks, but sometimes large flocks in the non-breeding season. *Movements:* sedentary, nomadic and partly migratory. *Foods:* fruits, seeds, nectar and insects and their larvae. *Breeding:* Aug-Feb; frequently 2-3 broods per season. *Nest:* cup-shaped of grass, etc., bound with cobwebs, generally suspended from branches of a tree or bush. *Eggs:* 2-3, 4.

Reader's Digest, 1977, p.523.

NOTES ON INTRODUCTIONS

New Zealand. The Silvereye probably reached New Zealand before 1850 at which time it was found to be breeding there. Falla *et al* (1966) say that in June 1856 large flocks appeared on the Wellington coast at Waikanae. Some appeared at Nelson also in 1856, Otago in 1860, Wanganui in 1863, Auckland in 1865 and the Bay of Islands in 1867. However, earlier scattered records in Otago and Southland date back to 1832.

The species is now widespread and common in both the North and South Islands, on Stewart Island and

INTRODUCTIONS OF ZOSTEROPIDAE

Species	Date introduced	Region	Manner introduced	Reason
(a) Successful introductions				
Grey-backed Silvereye	before 1850	New Zealand	colonisation	—
	about 1904	Norfolk Island	colonisation	—
	1938	Tahiti	deliberate	?
Japanese White-eye	1929 and later ?	Hawaiian Islands	deliberate	?
Christmas Island White-eye	1885-1900	Cocos-Keeling Islands	deliberate ?	?
(b) Unsuccessful introductions				
Grey-backed Silvereye	? and 1924, 1931, 1936	Lord Howe Island	colonisation and deliberate	—

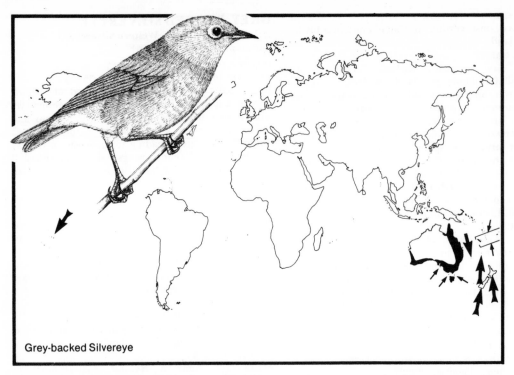

Grey-backed Silvereye

other outlying islands of New Zealand (Wodzicki, 1965; Falla *et al*, 1966). It appears as though they colonised New Zealand from Tasmania or Australia.

Norfolk Island. The Grey-backed Silvereye was first recorded on Norfolk in 1904 (North, 1904) and is now a very common species there (Smithers and Disney, 1969). They appear to have colonised this island from Australia or New Zealand.

Lord Howe Island. McKean and Hindwood (1965) have indicated that *tephropleura* is the dominant, though perhaps not the only, *Zosterops* now existing on Lord Howe Island. However, no birds resembling the other indigenous Silvereye *Z. strenua* or *Z. lateralis* (introduced in 1924), or the so-called 'small-billed silvereyes' (introduced from Norfolk Island in 1931 or 1936) have been noted in recent years, nor does there appear any trace of hybridisation in recent specimens of *tephropleura*.

According to Diamond and Marshall (1976) work by Mees has shown that racial characters of the Lord Howe population have been independently derived from eastern Australia.

Tahiti. Holyoak (1974) suggests that the Silvereye introduction to Tahiti was recent, because neither the Whitney Expedition (in 1920-21) or Curtiss (1938) found them there. Guild (1938) indicates that birds from Tasmania were released by him on Tahiti in 1938, but had not nested at the time of publication of his paper. Other than Guild's record, Holyoak reports that King (1958) appears to have been the first to record the presence of a *Zosterop* species in Tahiti, and Bruner (1972) who identified them as *Z. lateralis*. Perhaps Guild's introduction was successful ?

In 1972, Holyoak found the Silvereye common and widespread on Tahiti, Moorea, in the greater part of Raiatea and less frequently on Bora Bora. He confirmed that the birds were of the nominate race and reports that they may also be present on the islands of Hauhine, Tupai and Maupiti. Many

Silvereyes were released accidentally (?) on the island of Tetiaroa in 1973 (Thibault, 1976), but apparently did not become established there.

DAMAGE

The Grey-backed Silvereye causes damage to soft fruits and grapes in Australia, but is also useful in consuming a number of grubs and aphids. The damage caused by this species is currently being studied in Australia.

JAPANESE WHITE-EYE

Zosterops japonicus Temminck and Schlegel

DISTINGUISHING CHARACTERISTICS

10-12 cm (4-4.8 in)

Upper parts grass green; wings and tail brownish washed green; chin, throat and under tail-coverts bright yellow to greenish yellow; abdomen white or ashy, washed buff on flanks; eye-ring white; bill black.

Yamashina, 1961, p.85 and pl. p.85.

Cheng, 1963, pp.805-806 and pl.52, no.113.

GENERAL DISTRIBUTION

East Asia: eastern and southern China, Hong Kong, Japan, Korea, Taiwan and the Philippines. In winter migrates south to northern Thailand, Burma, Tenasserim, Annam, Tonkin and Laos.

INTRODUCED DISTRIBUTION

Introduced successfully in the Hawaiian Islands.

GENERAL HABITS

Status: very common; often a cage bird in China. *Habitat:* forest, woodland, and cultivated areas. *Gregariousness:* pairs, small flocks, and larger flocks in the non-breeding season. *Movements:* sedentary and migratory (sedentary in Hawaiian Islands). *Foods:* insects, berries, fruit and nectar. *Breeding:* Apr-July; Feb-Nov (Hawaii). *Nest:* neatly woven, cup-shaped of fibres, grass, moss and bark, in a tree or bush. *Eggs:* 2-4, 3-4 (Hawaii).

Cheng, 1963, pp.806-808.

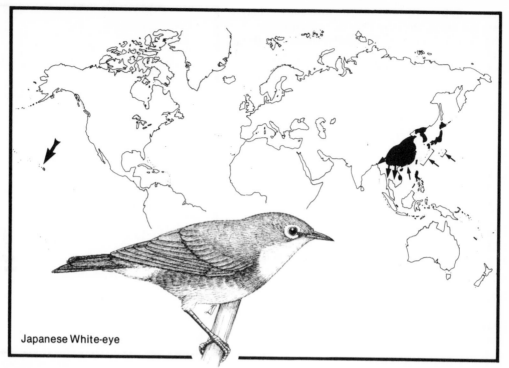

Japanese White-eye

Hawaiian Islands. The Japanese White-eye was introduced to Oahu in 1929 from Japan by the Territorial Board of Agriculture and Forestry (Caum, 1933; Munro, 1960). There were several later importations made by the Hui Manu, the Hawaiian Board of Agriculture, and by private individuals. They were introduced to the island of Hawaii in 1937 (Hawaiian Audubon Society, 1975). According to Keffer *et al* (1976) it is known that some avicultural breeders were instrumental in the initial releases of the species into the Hawaiian Islands in 1928.

Whatever the original date of the first introduction, the Japanese White-eye is said to have rapidly increased in numbers and soon spread to other islands in the group (Fisher, 1951; Gilliard, 1958; Munro, 1960). They were known to be established on Oahu in 1933 (Caum) and were possibly on Kauai. With perhaps the exception of Hawaii their spread to the other islands appears to have been unaided directly by man.

Since the late 1950s (Peterson, 1961) the species has been established on all the main islands of the group (Berger, 1972; Hawaiian Audubon Society, 1975).

DAMAGE

In the Hawaiian Islands the Japanese White-eye is not considered a pest of the extensively grown pineapples, but is a pest to the fruits grown by the small farmer and backyard gardener (Keffer *et al,* 1976). In China the species does not appear to be regarded as a pest (Cheng, 1963).

CHRISTMAS ISLAND WHITE-EYE

Zosterops natalis (Lister)

DISTINGUISHING CHARACTERISTICS

11.7-13.1 cm (4.68-5.24 in)

Forehead yellowish, duller on remainder of head; upper parts and ear-coverts french grey; faintly yellowish on under tail-coverts; underparts washed with fawn; bill black or dark brown, base of lower mandible grey.

GENERAL DISTRIBUTION

Christmas Island, Indian Ocean.

INTRODUCED DISTRIBUTION

Introduced successfully in the Cocos-Keeling Islands.

GENERAL HABITS

Status: fairly common. *Habitat:* no information. *Gregariousness:* small flocks. *Movements:* sedentary.

Christmas Island White-eye

Foods: fruits, seeds and insects. *Breeding:* mainly Sept-Jan but at any time (March ? on Cocos). *Nest and Eggs:* no information, probably similar to other *Zosterops.*

NOTES ON INTRODUCTIONS

Cocos-Keeling Islands. Christmas Island White-eyes were introduced on Pulo Luar between 1885 and 1900. At least until the late 1940s they were confined to that island where they were plentiful. According to the Van-Tets (1967) the species occurred only on Christmas Island until they were introduced on Pulo Luar. They are probably still established there.

DAMAGE

None known.

Family: *Meliphagidae* Honeyeaters

172 species in 39 genera; 1 species introduced, possibly successfully

The Noisy Miner may have been introduced and established on the Olu Malau Islands in the Solomon Islands but there appear to be few details. The species certainly failed to become established after introduction to New Zealand.

Bell Miners *(Manorina melanophrys)* were imported into New Zealand in 1874, but it is not known if any were released in the wild there.

Noisy Miner

NOISY MINER
(Black-headed Miner, Soldier-bird)
Manorina melanocephala (Latham)

DISTINGUISHING CHARACTERISTICS

25-28 cm (10-11.2 in)

Upper parts grey-brown, whitish bars on nape, upper back and sides of neck; crown and face black, forehead and lores white; bare skin behind eye yellow; underparts pale grey, lightly barred brown on breast and paler on abdomen; wings and tail blackish or brownish feathers edged greenish yellow; bill yellow. (Some geographic variation in size and colour.)

Reader's Digest, 1977, p.471 and pl. p.471.

GENERAL DISTRIBUTION

Australia: eastern and south-eastern Australia from about north-central Queensland to south-eastern South Australia and Tasmania.

INTRODUCED DISTRIBUTION

Possibly introduced, probably successfully to the Olu Malau Islands, Solomon Islands. Introduced unsuccessfully to New Zealand.

GENERAL HABITS

Status: common. *Habitat:* woodlands, parks and gardens. *Gregariousness:* in groups and colonies. *Movements:* sedentary. *Foods:* insects, small invertebrates, nectar and fruit. *Breeding:* mainly

June-Dec, but in some areas all months of the year; communal. *Nest:* cup-shaped of bark, twigs, rootlets and grass lined with feathers, wool, etc., bound with spiders' web, in a tree. *Eggs:* 1, 2-4, 5.

Reader's Digest, 1977, p.471.

Dow, *Emu* vol.78, pt.4, 1978, pp.207-222.

NOTES ON INTRODUCTIONS

Solomon Islands. The Noisy Miner has been introduced and established on the Olu Malau Islands in the Solomon Group (Ffrench, 1957; Galbraith and Galbraith, 1962).

New Zealand. Some Noisy Miners were introduced to Canterbury and Nelson from Victoria, Australia before 1871. The Wellington Acclimatisation Society liberated them in 1874 (184 birds), 1876 (eight), 1877 (twelve) and in 1878 (twenty). A colony was seen for a while at Taita. In 1879 the Canterbury society purchased 200 pairs which were liberated in various localities, but the species did not become established anywhere in New Zealand (Thomson, 1922).

DAMAGE

The Noisy Miner is said to occasionally attack fruit in orchards and grapes in vineyards in parts of Australia, but the extent of such damage does not appear to have been recorded.

INTRODUCTIONS OF MELIPHAGIDAE

Species	Date introduced	Region	Manner introduced	Reason
(a) Probably successful introductions				
Noisy Miner	before 1957 ?	Olu Malau Islands, Solomon Group ?	?	?
(b) Unsuccessful Introductions				
Noisy Miner	1874-79	New Zealand	deliberate	?

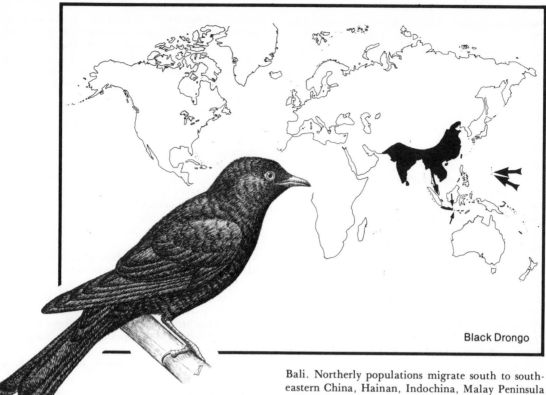

Black Drongo

Family: *Dicruridae* Drongos

20 species in 2 genera; 1 species introduced successfully

The Black Drongo has been introduced to Rota and Guam Islands in the southern Marianas, where it is well established and abundant on both islands.

BLACK DRONGO
(King Crow)
Dicrurus macrocercus Vieillot

DISTINGUISHING CHARACTERISTICS
22.5-31 cm (11-12.4 in). 38-59 g (1.34-2.08 oz)
Generally black with a bluish gloss; eye red; usually a white spot on nape; prominent rictal bristles; tail deeply forked; bill black.
MacDonald and Loke, 1962, pl. p.95.
Ali and Ripley, vol.5, 1968-74, pp.114, 117, 118 and pl.61, fig.4, opp. p.192.

GENERAL DISTRIBUTION
Southern Asia: from south-eastern Iran, south-eastern Afghanistan, east to the Himalayas, northern Burma, China and southern Manchuria; south to Taiwan, Hainan, Indochina, Sri Lanka, Java and Bali. Northerly populations migrate south to south-eastern China, Hainan, Indochina, Malay Peninsula and southern Burma.

INTRODUCED DISTRIBUTION
Introduced successfully to Guam Island and Rota Island, southern Marianas.

GENERAL HABITS
Status: common. *Habitat:* open country, marshes, roadsides, cultivated areas, cities and towns. *Gregariousness:* solitary, pairs, or feeding groups. *Movements:* sedentary and (northerly birds) migratory. *Foods:* insects and nectar. *Breeding:* mainly Feb-Aug. *Nest:* flimsy, shallow saucer of fine twigs, roots and fibres, swathed in cobwebs, in a tree. *Eggs:* 2, 3-4, 5, but variable.
Cheng, 1963, pp.592-594.
Ali and Ripley, vol.5, 1968-74, pp.115-119.

NOTES ON INTRODUCTIONS
Marianas: The race *D.m. harterti* was introduced to Rota in the southern Marianas from Taiwan (Ripley, 1961; Peters, 1962) by the Japanese in 1935 (Baker, 1951). The species is now common and abundant on both Rota and Guam (Ralph and Sakai, 1979), having appeared to have spread unaided to the latter island.

DAMAGE
The Black Drongo has been accused because of its quarrelsome nature of being responsible for the decline of some small passerines in the Marianas, but as yet there appears little direct evidence.

INTRODUCTIONS OF DICRURIDAE

Species	Date introduced	Region	Manner introduced	Reason
(a) Successful introduction				
Black Drongo	1935	Marianas	deliberate	?

Family: *Callaeidae*: Wattle birds

3 species in 3 genera; 1 species introduced successfully
The establishment of two races of the Saddleback on small islands off New Zealand is a notable achievement in the conservation of this species whose survival is threatened. In 1974 it was estimated that only about 1200 of these birds remained.

Efforts to establish the species were to be continued and they may now be established on many more islands than are listed here.

SADDLEBACK

Creadion carunculatus (Gmelin)

DISTINGUISHING CHARACTERISTICS
25 cm (10 in)
Glossy black, with bluish iridescence on head and breast, wing quills dark brown with glossy black outer webs; bright chestnut saddle, composed of back, scapulars, wing-coverts, rump and upper tail-coverts; under tail-coverts chestnut; wattles orange; bill black.
Oliver, 1955, pp.512-516.

GENERAL DISTRIBUTION
New Zealand: North Island (Raukumara Ranges), Hen Island and islets off Stewart Island. Formerly in North and South Islands, Great Barrier, Little Barrier, Kapiti, Stephen, Curvier and Stewart Islands.

INTRODUCED DISTRIBUTION
Introduced successfully to the Chicken Islands, some island groups in the outer Hauraki Gulf, Wairarapa in the North Island, small islands south-west and north-east of Stewart Island, and possibly on Chetwode Island (Cook Strait). Introduced unsuccessfully to Little Barrier Island and Kapiti.

GENERAL HABITS
Status: much reduced in range and numbers, but well established where surviving. *Habitat:* forest. *Gregariousness:* pairs or family parties. *Movements:* sedentary. *Foods:* insects or other invertebrates, fruits, berries and occasionally nectar. *Breeding:* Oct-Jan. *Nest:* shallow, open, loosely built of rootlets, twigs and leaves lined with fern-scales, fibres and grass, in a hollow or on a ledge. *Eggs:* 2-3.
Oliver, 1955, pp.512-516.
Williams, 1976, pp.161-170.

NOTES ON INTRODUCTIONS
New Zealand. Endemic to Hen Island, off Stewart Island, the Saddleback has been introduced to islands in Hauraki Gulf (North Island) and to Chetwode Island in Cook Strait (Williams, 1973). Atkinson and Bell (1973) say that the North Island Saddleback *P.c. rufusater* has been re-established on Curvier Island as it survived only on Hen Island prior to its transfer to other islands.

There have been two attempts to establish birds

INTRODUCTIONS OF CALLAEIDAE

Species	Date introduced	Island	Manner introduced	Reason
(a) Successful introductions				
Saddleback (North Island race)	1964	Middle Chicken, N.Z.		
	1966	Red Mercury (Hauraki Gulf), N.Z.		
	1968	Curvier, N.Z.		
	1968	Fanal, N.Z.		
	1971	Big Chicken, N.Z.		
Saddleback (South Island race)	1964	Big, N.Z.		
	1964	Kaimohu (south-west of Stewart Island), N.Z.		
	1969	Betsy, N.Z.		
	1974	Putauhina, N.Z.	All introductions deliberate in order to preserve the species	
	1976, 1978	Kundy, N.Z.		
	1972	Womans (north-east of Stewart Island), N.Z.		
	1972	North		
	1964-68	Wairarapa district, North Island, N.Z.		
(b) Unsuccessful introductions				
Saddleback	1950	Big Chicken, N.Z.		
	1925	Little Barrier Island, N.Z.		
	1925	Kapiti, N.Z.		
	1965 and 1970	Inner Chetwode, Cook Strait, N.Z.		

Saddleback

from Hen Island on the Chicken Islands. In July 1950, six birds were released at South Cove, on Big Chicken, by officers of the Department of Internal Affairs (Skegg, 1964). Two or more birds were reported from the island in 1953, but there are no subsequent records of any. In January 1964, twenty-three birds were transferred again from Hen Island to Middle Chicken and these were surviving and breeding on the island in 1965 (Merton, 1965).

In October 1925, four pairs were released on Little Barrier Island but were not sighted again; also in the same year four males and five females were released on Kapiti Island, where they survived for some years, but were not reported after 1931 (Merton, 1965).

Since 1964, 127 wild birds of the northern race have been transferred to five islands in four island groups in the outer Hauraki Gulf and eight birds to Mt Bruce Native Bird Reserve in the Wairarapa district (Merton, 1975). Each has resulted in the establishment of viable populations and no further transfers are deemed necessary. The following islands received birds: Middle Chicken twenty-three in 1964, Red Mercury twenty-nine in 1966, Curvier twenty-nine in 1968, Fanal twenty-five in 1968 and Big Chicken twenty-one in 1971. In addition the islands of Whatapuke, Marotiri and Kawhihi received birds and also now have viable populations (Mills and Williams, 1979).

The South Island race *P.c. carunculatus* which was known only from three small islands off the tip of Stewart Island, has now been released on eight small islands and has become established on seven of these. On islands south-west of Stewart Island, Big Island received twenty-one birds in 1964, Kaimohu fifteen in 1964, Betsy sixteen in 1969, Putauhina about twenty-three birds in 1974 and Kundy twenty-three in 1976 and twenty-six in 1978. On islands north-east of Stewart Island, Womans received twenty birds in 1972 and North nineteen in 1972. In Cook Strait the island

of Chetwode received releases of thirty birds in 1965 and seventeen in 1970.

Merton indicates that it is too early to evaluate the most recent transfers (in March 1974), but two attempts on Inner Chetwode have failed. Unlike the northern race which has a total population of almost 1000 the southern race numbers only about 200 birds. It is intended to continue to crop birds every two years and to propagate them on still further islands until they are well established in at least three island groups within their former range.

More recently Williams (1976) reports that the number of islands on which Saddleback populations occur has been increased by the New Zealand Wildlife Service from four to twelve. He indicates that the transfers were made all the more necessary by the accidental introduction in 1963 of ship rats to the three southern islands in the Saddleback's range and their subsequent extinction there.

DAMAGE
None known.

Family: *Grallinidae* Australian Magpie Lark

4 species in 3 genera; 1 species introduced unsuccessfully

Although introduced in New Zealand, the Hawaiian Islands and in Fiji, the Australian Magpie Lark failed to become established anywhere.

AUSTRALIAN MAGPIE LARK
(Mudlark, Peewee)
Grallina cyanoleuca (Latham)

DISTINGUISHING CHARACTERISTICS
25-30 cm (10-12 in). 128 g (4.51 oz)
Upper parts black with broad white patch in wing; rump, lower half and tail tip white; head, throat and upper breast black; with eyebrows; a small spot below eyes and cheeks white; lower breast and

341

INTRODUCTIONS OF GRALLINIDAE

Species	Date introduced	Region	Manner introduced	Reason
(a) Unsuccessful introductions				
Magpie Lark	prior 1922 ?	New Zealand	deliberate	insect control ?
	1920s	Hawaiian Islands	deliberate	control of liverfluke
	prior 1926	Fiji	escapee	cage bird ?

abdomen white; bill white. Female: forehead and throat white; no eyebrows; bill white.
Reader's Digest, 1977, p.566 and pl. p.566.

GENERAL DISTRIBUTION
Throughout Australia (but rare in Tasmania), southern New Guinea, Timor and Lord Howe Island.

INTRODUCED DISTRIBUTION
Introduced unsuccessfully to New Zealand, the Hawaiian Islands and (?) Fiji.

GENERAL HABITS
Status: very common. *Habitat:* open timber, open paddocks, parks, but usually near water. *Gregariousness:* solitary, pairs, and also in loose feeding flocks of up to 300 birds (in winter). *Movements:* sedentary and nomadic. *Foods:* insects, seeds, pond snails and food scraps. *Breeding:* variable throughout the year, but mainly July-Jan. *Nest:* bowl-shaped structure of mud and grass with soft lining of fur, grass and feathers; attached to the bough of tree, or other structure. *Eggs:* 3-5.
Robinson, 1947, *Emu* vol.46, pp.265-281, 382-391; vol.47, pp.11-28, 147-153.
Reader's Digest, 1977, p.566.

NOTES ON INTRODUCTIONS
New Zealand. The New Zealand Department of Agriculture introduced a number of Magpie Larks from Sydney to the west coast of the North Island, but they apparently did not succeed as there is no further record of them (Thomson, 1922).

Hawaiian Islands. The Magpie Lark was introduced from Australia to Oahu and Hawaii in the 1920s as a possible check to liverfluke (host is a pond snail upon which it was hoped the bird would feed), but they apparently failed to become established (Munro, 1960). Berger (1972) indicates that they were introduced to both Oahu and Hawaii in 1922 and 1929.

Fiji. Wood and Wetmore (1926) record that the Magpie Lark has undoubtedly been observed as a cage bird escapee on Fiji, but has probably been unsuccessful in becoming established as there are no recent records of any.

Family: *Cracticidae* Bellmagpies, piping-crows.

10 species in 3 genera; 2 species introduced, 1 successfully

The Australian Magpie has become well established in New Zealand, on Kangaroo Island in South Australia, and on Taveuni in Fiji. It may also be established on Gaudalcanal in the Solomons.

In New Zealand there are claims that the species has been a nuisance in the past to native bird species, but this seems doubtful. It has been described on Taveuni, Fiji, as an undesirable alien.

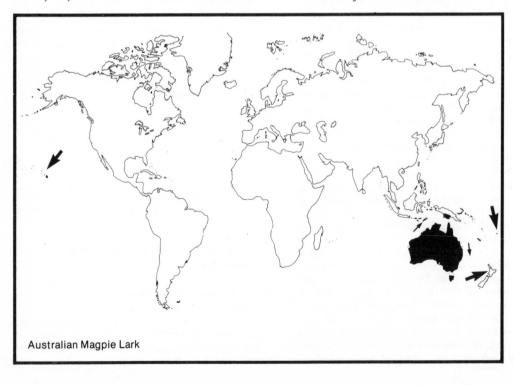

Australian Magpie Lark

Species	Date introduced	Region	Manner introduced	Reason
(a) Successful introductions				
Australian Magpie	1864-74	New Zealand	deliberate	?
	about 1859 ?	Kangaroo Island, Australia	deliberate	?
	before 1941 ?	Taveuni, Fiji Group	?	?
(b) Possibly successful introductions				
Australian Magpie	before 1948 ?	Guadalcanal, Solomon Islands	?	?
(c) Unsuccessful introductions				
Australian Magpie	various times	Rottnest Island, Australia	?	?
	1905	Sri Lanka	deliberate	?
Grey Currawong	before 1926 ?	Viti Levu, Fiji	deliberate	?

AUSTRALIAN MAGPIE
(White-backed Magpie, Black-backed Magpie, Western Magpie)
Gymnorhina tibicen (Latham)

DISTINGUISHING CHARACTERISTICS
36-44 cm (14.4-17.6 in). 284-341 g (10-12 oz)
Mainly black with a broad white collar; broad white band from shoulder to inner wing; rump and tail white; tail with black tip and shafts; vent white; bill bluish white; black tip *(tibicen)*. Back white, but variable amounts of black *(hypoleuca)*; white shafts of tail-feathers *(dorsalis)*. Female: similar or nape dusky *(tibicen)*, back greyish *(hypoleuca)* or black *(dorsalis)*.
Reader's Digest, 1977, p.575 and pl. p.575.

GENERAL DISTRIBUTION
Australia, Tasmania and southern New Guinea.

INTRODUCED DISTRIBUTION
Introduced successfully in New Zealand and probably to the Solomon Islands (Guadalcanal), Fiji (Taveuni), King Island, Flinders Island and to Kangaroo Island, South Australia. Introduced unsuccessfully to Sri Lanka and probably to Rottnest Island, Western Australia.

GENERAL HABITS
Status: very common. *Habitat:* open timber, pasture, parks and gardens. *Gregariousness:* loosely gregarious in family groups of 2-24 birds. *Movements:* sedentary. *Foods:* omnivorous; mainly insects, seeds, grasshoppers, etc. *Breeding:* July-Mar, but mainly Aug-Oct; polygamous. *Nest:* bowl-

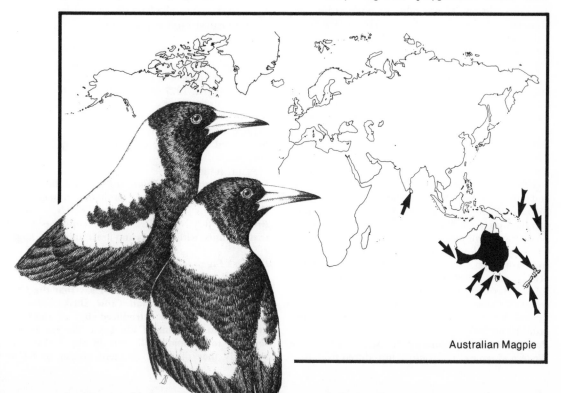

Australian Magpie

shaped structure of twigs, sticks, wire and fibres, lined with grass, wool or hair, in a tree. *Eggs*: 1, 3-5, 6; (2-5 New Zealand).

Reader's Digest, 1977, p.575.

NOTES ON INTRODUCTIONS

New Zealand. Two races, the White-backed Magpie *G.t. hypoleuca* and the Black-backed Magpie *G.t. tibicen* were introduced to New Zealand between 1864 and 1874. Wodzicki (1965) indicates that both races are now restricted in range, but common, in both the North and South Islands.

Between 1864 and 1867 the Canterbury Acclimatisation Society liberated forty-four magpies, some eighteen from Tasmania and the remainder from Victoria. From 1865 to 1869 the Otago society introduced some eighty-one birds. The Auckland society introduced ten in 1867 and a single bird in 1870. E. Dowling obtained a large number of magpies from Tasmania and liberated them at Glenmark in 1870 and a further twenty-four were liberated in 1871. These were reported to have become established and were soon common from south of Waitaki to the Horse Ranges. In 1874 the Wellington society introduced 260 magpies. Sir George Grey is said to have introduced them to Kawau Island at an early date (prior 1867) and these are reported to have become established and spread to the mainland (Thomson, 1922).

In the late 1920s Oliver (1930) reported that the Otago introductions had disappeared but that the magpie was spreading southwards from Canterbury. By the 1945-50 period (Oliver, 1955; McCaskill, 1945) White-backed Magpies were established in the Hokianga district to the Hunua Hills from Taranaki, Lake Taupo and the Waiapu River south to Cook Strait in the North Island. On the eastern side of the South Island they were established from Kaikoura to the Otago Peninsula. The Black-backed Magpie was established at Karaka near Auckland, Wangaehu — Turakina district, Hunterville, Raumati, Clive and Hastings to Waipukurau, Dannevirke to Woodville, Pahiatua, Wairarapa, Waiau (Marlborough) and the Cheviot-Kaikoura district, but was nowhere common.

According to Falla *et al* (1966) the Black-backed Magpie *(tibicen)* was formerly known only from North Canterbury where it spread to Marlborough. It was first recognised in the North Island near Hastings in 1946 and is now known to be widely distributed in Hawke's Bay and some other districts to the South. The White-backed Magpie *(hypoleuca)* is widely but unevenly distributed in the North and South Islands (on the eastern side of the Alps), is still spreading, and wanders to some offshore islands.

Solomon Islands. Cain and Galbraith (1957) report that the Australian Magpie *G.t. tibicen* introduced to Guadalcanal will probably not survive. They noted a bird between Honiara and Tenaru in 1955 or 1956 and record that specimens were collected by Beecher (1945) and Baker (1948) (Cain and Galbraith, 1956). However, Galbraith and Galbraith (1962) report that they saw specimens in grasslands near the Tenaru River, where they say the species is still probably not well established.

Rottnest Island. According to Storr (1965) the Western Magpie *G.t. dorsalis* is introduced from time to time to Rottnest Island, off the coast of Western Australia. Storr reports them building nests there in 1958.

King Island, Flinders Island and Kangaroo Island. Morgan (1929) says that a Mr M. E. Burgess states that the magpie was introduced on Kangaroo Island by Mr Calman around 1850. Campbell (1906) noted them to be common there. Abbott (1974) points out that they are not native to other islands in Bass Strait, so possibly could have been introduced to Kangaroo Island.

Sri Lanka. In 1905 Mr H. Campbell obtained nine Black-backed Magpies *G.t. tibicen* from Australia for introduction at Nuwara, Eliya, Sri Lanka (Campbell, 1906). From his account it can be presumed that they were released there. There do not appear to be any further records of these birds.

Fiji. Turbet (1941) reports that the Australian Magpie is established on the island of Taveuni and in the Lau Islands. There appear to be few other records of the species in the Fiji group. Blackburn (1971) records that this undesirable introduction has become established widely in the lowlands along the north-western side of the island of Taveuni.

DAMAGE

In New Zealand there were some early claims that magpies kill other birds, including some of the small native species. It seems doubtful, however, that they have played a part in the extinction of any species and are probably largely beneficial consuming many insects, some of which are harmful.

Occasionally, some birds attack people, particularly children, but generally these birds have been provoked and are only defending their nests.

GREY CURRAWONG
(Bell Magpie, Squeaker)
Strepera versicolor (Latham)

DISTINGUISHING CHARACTERISTICS

50 cm (20 in)

Plumage variable from brown-grey to brown-black; under tail-coverts and tip of tail white (lacking in some races); base of tail white; bill black.

Reader's Digest, 1977, p.577 and pl. p.577.

GENERAL DISTRIBUTION

Australia: the southern half of Australia.

INTRODUCED DISTRIBUTION

Introduced successfully to Viti Levu, Fiji, but died out.

GENERAL HABITS

Status: common. *Habitat:* forest, woodland and mallee. *Movements:* probably sedentary. *Gregariousness:* singly or pairs. *Foods:* insects. *Breeding:* July-Nov. *Nest:* bulky, cup-shaped and shallow, lined with rootlets and grass, in a tree. *Eggs:* 2-3.

Reader's Digest, 1977, p.577.

NOTES ON INTRODUCTIONS

Fiji. Wood and Wetmore (1926) say that the Grey Currawong (= Australian Crow Shrike, *Strepera melanoptera* ?) was introduced by an unknown naturalist to the island of Viti Levu. The species was reported to be doing well there in about 1926, but evidently they died out as there appear to be no

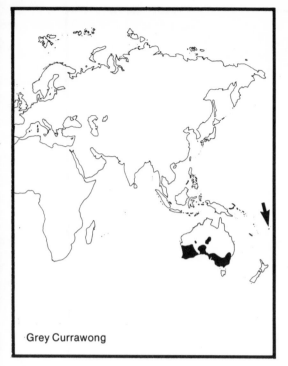

Grey Currawong

Southern Irian Jaya, south-east Papua, New Guinea and the Aru Islands.

INTRODUCED DISTRIBUTION
Introduced successfully to Little Tobago, West Indies.

GENERAL HABITS
Status: fairly common. *Habitat:* forest treetops. *Gregariousness:* small flocks. *Movements:* sedentary. *Foods:* fruits and probably insects. *Breeding:* no information. *Nest:* basin shaped of vines, lined with plant fibres, in a tree. *Eggs:* 2.

NOTES ON INTRODUCTIONS
Little Tobago. Sir William Ingham purchased the island of Little Tobago (18.2 hectares [45 acres]) to serve as a sanctuary for the Greater Bird of Paradise which was feared in 1909 to be in danger of becoming extinct (Herklots, 1961). Plumes were the rage of European fashion in the late 1800s and thousands of Greater Birds of Paradise were being slaughtered annually (Gilliard, 1958) for the adornment of ladies' hats in London, Paris and New York (Herklots).

Sir William equipped an expedition to the Aru Islands off New Guinea which brought back, it was

further records of them in the Fijian Islands.
DAMAGE
None known.

Family: *Paradisaeidae* Birds of Paradise

40 species in 20 genera; 1 species introduced successfully

The Greater Bird of Paradise has been established on the island of Little Tobago in the West Indies since about 1909. The population there has fluctuated somewhat over the years and was severely reduced by a hurricane in 1963. The population is now believed to be very small and possibly in some danger of extinction.

GREATER BIRD OF PARADISE

Paradisaea apoda Linnaeus

DISTINGUISHING CHARACTERISTICS
45-77 cm (18-30.8 in) (without tail wires)
Back, wings and tail maroon-brown; crown and hindneck pale yellow; forehead and chin black with green reflections; throat and foreneck iridescent green; upper breast deep purplish brown; lower breast and abdomen maroon-brown; ornamental tufts on each side of upper breast pale yellow tinged maroon at tips; central tail-feathers modified 'wires'; bill grey-blue. Female: maroon-brown, darker on head and neck, paler on breast and abdomen.

Greater Bird of Paradise,
Paradisaea apoda

INTRODUCTIONS OF PARADISAEIDAE

Species	Date introduced	Region	Manner introduced	Reason
(a) Successful introductions				
Greater Bird of Paradise	about 1909	Little Tobago, West Indies	deliberate	preservation

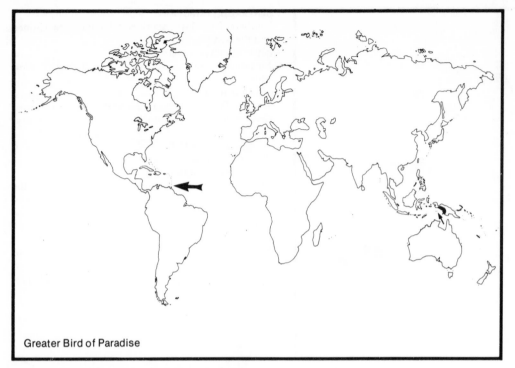
Greater Bird of Paradise

reported, forty-seven or forty-eight immature birds which were subsequently released on Little Tobago. After Sir William's death the island was presented to the British Government by his sons, on the condition that it should be a bird sanctuary in perpetuity with a warden in charge of the Birds of Paradise (Herklots).

According to both Herklots and Gilliard the total population consisted of as few as one dozen or at the most three dozen birds in the late 1950s and early 1960s. Gilliard indicates that this is possibly the maximum population this island can support. He reports that over the years occasional birds hop the channel to Tobago but do not become established there. After half a century of isolation on Little Tobago the birds are still identical in habits and colour to the Aru Island birds. The race introduced is *P.a. apoda* (Peters, 1962).

Ffrench (1973) indicates that studies of the bird were made on the island in 1965-66 and that the population has been reduced to a maximum of seven birds.

DAMAGE
None known.

Family: *Corvidae* Crows, jays, magpies

104 species in 26 genera; 7 species introduced, 3 successfully and 3 possibly successfully

The Common Magpie, House Crow and Rook have all been introduced and established successfully. The House Crow has been widely introduced, particularly in Africa. The Red-billed Blue Magpie may yet become permanently established in the Hawaiian Islands.

The family as a whole could not be considered desirable introductions in any country. Most appear to have some nuisance value at least to agricultural crops and many could have profound effects on small bird populations.

RED-BILLED BLUE MAGPIE
(Blue Magpie or Jay, Blue-pie, Occipital Blue-pie)
Urocissa erythrorhyncha (Boddaert)

DISTINGUISHING CHARACTERISTICS
46.5-70 cm (18.6-28 in). 149-232 g (5.26-8.18 oz)
Head and throat, black; upper parts bluish grey; abdomen and belly white, tinged blue on breast and flanks; back blue; white to blue patch on back of head; nape black; wings blue with white tips; tail blue, with a black subterminal band and white terminal patch; bill red or orange (southerly birds bright, north-easterly birds duller and greyer).
Smythies, 1953, pl.1, fig.4, opp. p.4.
Goodwin, 1977, pp.193-194.

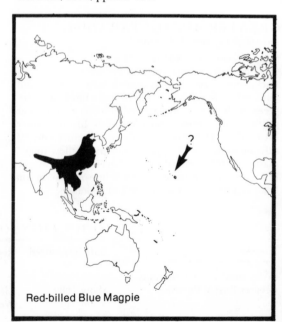
Red-billed Blue Magpie

GENERAL DISTRIBUTION
India and South-east Asia: Himalayas (Punjab to Sikkim), northern China, south to northern Burma, Laos, Vietnam, Kampuchea, the island of Hainan, and Thailand (except peninsular Thailand).

INTRODUCED DISTRIBUTION
Introduced, possibly successfully in the Hawaiian Islands.

GENERAL HABITS
Status: very common. *Habitat:* forest and secondary growth, wooded country, plains, cultivated areas, and gardens. *Gregariousness:* pairs or small groups of 5-6 birds. *Movements:* sedentary; some altitudinal movements. *Foods:* fruits, insects and other invertebrates (including worms, spiders and snails), small mammals and reptiles, eggs, young birds and nectar. *Breeding:* Mar-Sept; probably double

Red-billed Blue Magpie, *Urocissa erythrorhyncha*

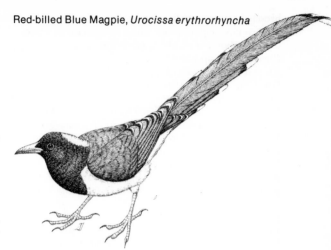

INTRODUCTIONS OF CORVIDAE

Species	Date introduced	Region	Manner introduced	Reason
(a) Successful introductions				
Common Magpie	1598	Kyūshū, Japan	?	?
House Crow	1898-1900 or 1919	Malaysia	deliberate	insect control
	about 1948	Singapore	escapee ? or ship borne ?	?
	before 1960 ?	Kenya	?	
	1972	Natal, South Africa	deliberate or escapee ?	?
	1893-95	Zanzibar Island	deliberate	cleaning up offal
	after 1893-95	Pemba Island	?	?
	about 1846 ? and later	Peoples Democratic Republic of Yemen	deliberate	?
	about 1958	French Territory of Afars and Issas	colonisation from Sudan	?
	1940s ?	Sudan	deliberate ?	?
Rook	1862-73	New Zealand	deliberate	insect control
New Caledonian Crow	before 1966	Mare, New Caledonia	?	?
(b) Possibly successful introductions				
Red-billed Blue Magpie	1965-66	Hawaiian Islands	escapee	cage bird
Jackdaw	ancient ?	Tunis city, Tunisia	escapee	captive bird
		Constantine, Algeria	escapee	captive bird
House Crow	?	south-west Thailand	?	?
	before 1924 ?	Muscat, Oman	?	?
	1910 and 1950 and later	Mauritius	deliberate ? and ship borne ?	?
	?	Laccadive Islands	?	?
(c) Unsuccessful introductions				
Jackdaw	1867-72	New Zealand	deliberate	?
House Crow	before 1867 ?	Andaman Islands	deliberate	sanitary reasons
	1926 on	Australia	ship borne	
Large-billed Crow	about 1874	Nicobar Islands	deliberate	?
Pied Crow	before 1760	Mauritius	deliberate	rat and mice control
Common Crow	1876	Bermuda	deliberate	?

brooded. *Nest:* shallow structure of twigs with a shallow inner cup of roots, fibres or tendrils, in a tree, bamboo clump or shrub. *Eggs:* 3-5, 6.

Cheng, 1963, pp.626-631.

Ali and Ripley, 1968-74, pp.209-212.

Goodwin, 1977, pp.194-195.

NOTES ON INTRODUCTIONS

Hawaiian Islands. Some five Red-billed Blue Magpies were sold by a Honolulu pet shop to an aviculturist in 1965. These escaped in 1965 or early 1966 when a dog broke through the wire of the cage. By mid-1970, they had become established and several adults and immatures were collected in the Kahana Valley, about sixteen kilometres (10 miles) from the release site (Berger, 1972).

DAMAGE

Berger (1972) suggests that the Red-billed Blue Magpie could become a serious pest in the Hawaiian Islands by eating fruit, if it becomes well established. In China they cause some damage to crops, steal birds' eggs and young birds, but only on a small scale and are not considered to be very damaging (Cheng, 1963).

COMMON MAGPIE
(Black-billed Magpie, European Magpie, American Magpie, Magpie)
Pica pica (Linnaeus)

DISTINGUISHING CHARACTERISTICS

40-55 cm (16-22 in). 178-275 g (6.28-9.7 oz)

Head, throat, neck and back black; scapulars and underparts white; wings black, with a blue and green sheen; back has a green and purple sheen; long graduated tail 22.5-30 cm (8-12 in); bill black.

Roberts, 1960, pl.55.

Goodwin, 1977, pp.173-175.

GENERAL DISTRIBUTION

Eurasia, North Africa and North America: from the British Isles, Scandinavia, Portugal and North Africa (central Morocco, northern Algeria and Tunisia) east across Europe and Asia to north-eastern Siberia and south to southern China, Taiwan, Hainan, Vietnam, western China, Pakistan, north-western India, northern Iraq, Iran and Afghanistan; an isolated population on the Arabian Peninsula. In North America from coastal southern Alaska and as far east as Manitoba, Canada, and south in the western United States and as far east as Minnesota and Kansas.

INTRODUCED DISTRIBUTION

Successfully introduced on Kyūshū Island, Japan.

GENERAL HABITS

Status: common. *Habitat:* wooded regions, thorn scrub and semi-desert, sagebrush, river thickets, prairie brush, coastal country (Alaska), cultivated areas, grasslands, gardens and often in villages and towns. *Gregariousness:* pairs, often in small parties of 8-12 and up to 30 birds, and larger flocks at roosts. *Movements:* mainly sedentary, but in USA wanders far east in winter. *Foods:* small animals and birds, grubs, worms, snails, slugs and other insects, seeds, grain, carrion and other birds' eggs. *Breeding:* Mar-May (India and Great Britain); usually solitary but sometimes a tendency for scattered colonies. *Nest:* bulky, domed structure with side entrance, often made of thorny branches, sticks, roots and mud, in a tree or shrub. *Eggs:* 3, 5-9, 13.

Holyoak, *Bird Study* vol.21, 1974, pp.117-128.

Goodwin, 1977, pp.175-181.

NOTES ON INTRODUCTIONS

Japan. The race *P.p. sericea* is said to have been introduced (Peters, 1962) from China (Kaburaki, 1934) or Korea (Voous, 1960; Yamashina, 1961) in 1598 (Voous; Peters).

In about 1960 the species was restricted to the north-west of Kyūshū Island where it was locally

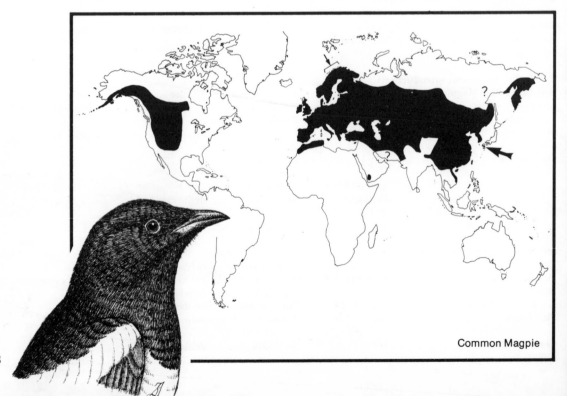

Common Magpie

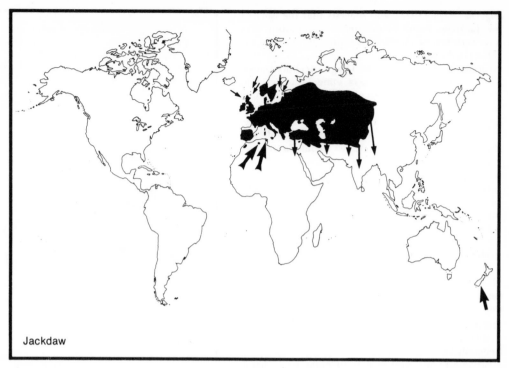

Jackdaw

common, especially around Saga City (Yamashina, 1961). More recently, the Orinithological Society of Japan (1974) indicates that it is still a resident in the area, locally common in Fukuoka, Saga, Nagasaki and Kumanmoto.

DAMAGE

In south-eastern USSR it was concluded by Golow and Osmolovskaja (1955) that the Common Magpie was beneficial to agriculture and forestry and gave some benefit because of the use of its nests by other birds. They record that the only damage it does is to cucurbitaceous crops. According to Falkenstein (pers. comm., 1962) however, they do cause damage to crops, mainly maize in the USSR.

In England they are accused of taking the eggs and young of wild birds and sometimes those of chickens (Lancum, 1961). In China they are sometimes harmful to beans and corn (Liang and Liu, 1959) but eat many injurious insects and are not generally considered harmful (Cheng, 1963).

In Japan, Kaburaki (1934) indicates that they do damage in fields, but he does not specify to which crops. The species is however protected in that country.

JACKDAW
Corvus monedula Linnaeus

DISTINGUISHING CHARACTERISTICS

32-35 cm (12.8-14 in). 162-265 g (5.71-9.35 oz)
Crown and upper parts black with a violet sheen; back of head and nape grey; underparts dull black (in east Asia race *dauricus* has nape, sides of throat and belly white).
Witherby *et al,* vol.1, 1938-41, pp.22-25 and pl.3, opp. p.22.
Goodwin, 1977, pp.74-75.

GENERAL DISTRIBUTION

Eurasia and North Africa: from southern Scandinavia, British Isles and the Iberian Peninsula, east to northern USSR and to about the Chinese and Mongolian borders, south to Afghanistan, northern Iran and Iraq, Turkey and the Mediterranean; isolated populations in northern Morocco and Algeria. In winter south to the southern parts of breeding range and Sinkiang, north-western India, southern Afghanistan, Iraq, Iran, and the Near East (occasionally Egypt).

INTRODUCED DISTRIBUTION

Extended breeding range in northern Europe. Isolated populations in Tunisia (Tunis) and Algeria (Constantine) probably due to introductions. Introduced unsuccessfully to New Zealand.

GENERAL HABITS

Status: common. *Habitat:* open wooded regions, grassland, arable areas, villages and towns. *Gregariousness:* flocks, often large in winter. *Movements:* sedentary and migratory. *Foods:* omnivorous; worms, grubs, insects, grass shoots, acorns, beechmast, carrion, birds' eggs, young mice, birds, grain and fruit. *Breeding:* Apr-May (Great Britain); colonial, often in tens or hundreds. *Nest:* wide structure of sticks, grass and leaves and other material, in a tree, holes or crevices in cliffs, rabbit burrows, river banks, buildings and chimneys. *Eggs:* 3-7.

Goodwin, 1977, pp.75-78.

NOTES ON INTRODUCTIONS

Europe. The Jackdaw has been increasing its breeding range northwards in Finland and Scandinavia. According to Voous (1960), this may be due to increased temperatures, but more likely as a result of extensions in cultivation into northern forest regions. The Jackdaw also appears to be increasing in numbers in cultivated regions in the present century.
Tunisia. The ancient colony of Jackdaws in the city of Tunis was probably founded by escaped captive birds (Payn, 1948).

349

Algeria. Payn (1948) also suggests that the isolated few Jackdaws found in the city of Constantine may have been founded by escaped captive birds as was the colony in the city of Tunis.

New Zealand. In 1867 the Otago Acclimatisation Society were reported to have some Jackdaws, but there are no further records of them. The Canterbury society received one bird in 1868 and in 1872 it was reported that three remained about the society gardens after liberation. A report in 1916 indicates that there were then no Jackdaws about Canterbury (Thomson, 1922).

DAMAGE

Jackdaws sometimes cause damage in orchards and plantations in England (Taylor and Ridpath, 1956) and in the Netherlands to newly sown crops of grain and vegetables (Seubert, 1964). In China they consume large quantities of sown seeds and ripening grains causing serious damage (Cheng, 1963).

HOUSE CROW
(Indian Crow, Ceylon Crow, Colombo Crow)
Corvus splendens Vieillot

DISTINGUISHING CHARACTERISTICS

42-44 cm (16.8-17.6 in). 252-362 g (8.89-12.77 oz)
Generally black, glossed with green, blue and purple; a variable in size whitish grey to milky white band around the neck, breast and upper back (often restricted to nape area); bill black.
Ali and Ripley, vol.5, 1968-74, pp.243-247, and pl.62, fig.2, opp. p.208.
Goodwin, 1977, p.99.
Reader's Digest, 1977, p.581, and pl. p.581.

GENERAL DISTRIBUTION

Southern Asia: from southern coastal Iran, Pakistan, India, Nepal, Bhutan and Assam, east to northern Thailand and southern China, and south to south-western Thailand (rare), southern Burma (Mergui, and Gulf of Siam), Sri Lanka and the Laccadive and Maldive Islands.

INTRODUCED DISTRIBUTION

Introduced successfully in Malaysia and Singapore, Kenya (Mombasa), Zanzibar Island, Peoples Democratic Republic of Yemen (Aden), French Territory of Afars and Issas (Djibouti), Sudan (Port Sudan) and South Africa (Natal); probably introduced successfully in south-west Thailand, Pemba Island (East Africa), Oman (Muscat), Mauritius, and the (?) Laccadive Islands. Introduced unsuccessfully in the Andaman Islands and Australia.

GENERAL HABITS

Status: very common and abundant. *Habitat:* plains, mangroves, villages, towns and cities. *Gregariousness:* small flocks and larger numbers congregate at food sources; communal roosts numbering up to thousands. *Movements:* sedentary. *Foods:* omnivorous; insects, termites, locusts, grain, nectar, fruit, offal, carrion, eggs, young birds, and will pilfer anything edible. *Breeding:* Mar-Sept and Oct-Dec (India); Sept-Jan (Zanzibar); Apr-June (Malaysia); occasionally several breed in one tree. *Nest:* untidy platform of twigs (occasionally wire), with a cup-like depression, lined with fibres etc., in a tree. *Eggs:* 3-5, 6 (Malaysia 3-4).
Ali and Ripley, vol.5, 1968-74, pp.243-247.
Goodwin, 1977, pp.99-101.

350

House Crow

NOTES ON INTRODUCTIONS

Malaysia and Singapore. The race *C.s. protegatus* has been introduced to Klang, Selangor, from Sri Lanka (Delacour, 1947; Gibson-Hill, 1949). The deliberate introduction was made at the end of the last century (Medway and Wells, 1976, give the date as January 1903), or possibly around 1919, to combat a plague of caterpillars threatening coffee plantations (Gibson-Hill; Madoc, 1956). Ward (1968) indicates that there has been a breeding colony there since 1898.

According to Gibson-Hill and Madoc the House Crow has remained established at Klang, but has only spread slowly, probably reaching Port Swettenham in the mid-1950s. Small numbers appeared at Pinang in 1953 and 1954 and remained there for several months (Ward). In 1963 they appeared to be spreading further in Selangor as some had been sighted to the north of Kapar and southern Sembilan (Medway and Wells, 1964).

A small colony became established in the dock area of Singapore in 1948 and over the past twenty years have increased in numbers and now some 200-400 birds roost outside dock gate number three, at Tanjong Pagar (Ward, 1968). Gibson-Hill (1952) suggests that they were derived from escaped birds or birds released from captivity during the Japanese Occupation, but Ward says that the species is a great wanderer and possibly arrived from Klang or even from Burma. Medway and Wells (1976) consider that populations at Prai (Province Wellesley) and George Town (Pinang) and possibly part of the Klang population may have arrived by ship.

More recently, a colony of House Crows has now become established at Pinang, some 483 kilometres (300 miles) south of their natural breeding range (Ward), and at Prai where they were well established in 1967 (Medway and Wells, 1976). Single birds were sighted at Cape Rachado in March 1969, and at Batu Berendam, Malacca in February 1972.

Thailand. The presence of the race *C.s. insolens* in south-western Thailand may be due to introductions (Peters, 1962); however, Lekagul and Cronin (1974) list them as a rare resident and make no mention of any introductions.

East Africa. The House Crow has been introduced to Mombasa, Kenya, and occurs up to six kilometres (3.7 miles) from the town (Mackworth-Praed and Grant, 1960).

South Africa. Some five or six House Crows were noted at South Pier, Durban, Natal in September-October 1972 (Sinclair, 1974). The same number were observed near Old Fort, Durban in November of the same year (Clancey, 1974). Clancey records that they were still there some two months later and he suggests that they had been deliberately or accidentally liberated from captivity.

Zanzibar and Pemba Islands. The House Crow was introduced in the early 1900s to Zanzibar (Mackworth-Praed and Grant, 1960) and also to Pemba Island (Williams, 1962, pers. comm.) at some later date. According to Pakenham (1943, 45 and 59) they have been established in Zanzibar from Bombay, India since about 1893-95. Vaughan (1930) says that they were introduced by Dr Charlesworth and Sir Gerald Portal for the purpose of cleaning up offal around the town. They are still plentiful in the town and have extended their range to become established in some distant villages.

Peoples Democratic Republic of Yemen. Barnes (1893) appears to have been the first to take much interest in strange 'crows' at Aden; he noted them there in 1866 and again in 1892 and describes what are possibly House Crows as the species *culminatus.* Barnes was given to believe that *splendens* was imported some twenty years before his 1866 record by an officer of the Bombay Infantry.

Yerbury (1886) also noted strange 'crows' in Aden when he observed three of them just prior to 1886. He believed them to have been imported to Aden. Meinertzhagen (1924) records that a single House Crow found in December 1921 may have been an escapee or even a straggler.

Browne (1950) found House Crows fairly well established there in about 1950 and in parties of up to thirty birds. Sage (1959) reported seeing a dozen birds in Aden Town at Steamer Point and others elsewhere in the town.

The House Crow is now a common resident throughout the Aden area and at Shaykh Uthman (Ennion, 1962).

French Territory of Afars Issas. The House Crow probably spread to Djibouti from Port Sudan, some 241 kilometres (150 miles) north-east (Clarke, 1967). Clarke records that several were found in the town in May, 1958.

Sudan. Meinertzhagen (1949) records having seen a colony of forty House Crows in the public gardens in Port Sudan in the late 1940s. Cave and MacDonald (1955) say that the species was introduced from India and report that in the 1950s there was a fairly large colony breeding amongst the girders of the big bridge near the harbour, and that the species was commonly seen in the public gardens.

The House Crow is now common in Port Sudan (Clarke, 1967).

Oman. The race *C.s. zugmayeri* appears to have been introduced and established in Muscat (Peters, 1962) although Ripley (1961) reports that its status there is uncertain. Meinertzhagen (1924) indicates that the species occurred occasionally in Muscat, at least in the early 1920s.

Mauritius. Rountree *et al* (1952) report that the House Crow has probably been introduced on many occasions to Mauritius from India and Sri Lanka. They indicate that some thirty to forty years ago a number of black crows congregated around the meat market in Port Louis. Meinertzhagen (1912) says that some House Crows were introduced to Port Louis from India in about 1910, but did not seem to thrive there.

More recently a pair of 'black crows' accompanied the S.S. *Ikauna* from Colombo to Mauritius in November 1950. Until 1951, a single 'black crow' was seen regularly at the slaughter house, Roche Bois. In 1957, Benedict indicated that although House Crows had been introduced to Mauritius they were now extinct there. However, Staub (1976) indicates that there are about 100 of them, mainly around the slaughter houses, but also in the Jardin de la Compagnie and Jardin de la Plaine Verte at Port Louis. He reports that they have been seen as far north as Grand Baie and as far south as Mahebourg.

Andaman Islands. Beavan (1867) records that Colonel R. C. Tyler introduced the House Crow at Port Blair in the time of the convict settlement there for sanitary reasons. The species did not however, thrive there. Ali and Ripley (1968-1974) record the date of introduction as in about 1860.

Laccadive Islands. Ali and Ripley (1968-1974) report that the House Crow may have been introduced to these islands.

Australia. Although the House Crow is not infrequently transported on ships to some Australian ports, they do not appear to have gained a permanent foothold in either Western Australia or Victoria, where they have often been recorded.

In Victoria three birds flew ashore from the merchant vessel *Tavince* from Colombo, at Geelong

House Crow, *Corvus splendens*

in May 1959 (Gibson, 1961). A single bird was sighted south-west of Melbourne in March 1963 (Smith, 1967).

A considerable number of House Crows have arrived in Western Australia since 1926 (Jenkins, 1959; Robinson, 1950; Ruddiman, 1952; Long, 1967 and 1972). From 1926 to 1950 some fifteen or so birds were recorded to reach Western Australia and from 1950 to 1967 they arrived regularly, accompanying ships from southern Asia and the authorities destroyed at least thirty birds (Long, 1972).

DAMAGE

Although the status of the House Crow is regarded as neutral in India, it does raid crops such as wheat and maize, and causes severe damage to fruit in orchards (Ali, 1944 and 1953). They are a useful scavenger and probably eat many injurious insects, but also attack small birds and eat their eggs. According to Fitzwater (1967) they fly in and out of houses without restraint and pilfer anything edible.

Where introduced in Africa they have increased in numbers and range sufficiently to have become a nuisance and are expected to spread even further (Mackworth-Praed and Grant, 1957-63). They compete with local native species and destroy their nests and eggs (Williams 1962, pers. comm.). On Zanzibar in an endeavour to exterminate the pest the government annually destroys large numbers of them, at a high cost, but with very little effect on their numbers (Pakenham, 1959).

NEW CALEDONIAN CROW
Corvus moneduloides Lesson

DISTINGUISHING CHARACTERISTICS

40-42 cm (15-16.54 in)

All black, glossed purple and dark blue; throat feathers have a hairy texture; bill black.

New Caledonian Crow

Goodwin, 1977, p.112.

GENERAL DISTRIBUTION

New Caledonia and the Loyalty Islands.

INTRODUCED DISTRIBUTION

Introduced successfully to the island of Mare, New Caledonia.

GENERAL HABITS

Status: fairly common. *Habitat:* forest and plantations. *Movements:* sedentary. *Gregariousness:* singly, pairs or small flocks; not in large groups. *Foods:* insects and fruit, nuts, small birds, eggs, snails, etc. (omnivorous). *Breeding:* Sept-Nov. *Nest:* platform of sticks in a tree. *Eggs:* 2.

Delacour, 1966.

Goodwin, 1977, pp.113-114.

NOTES ON INTRODUCTIONS

Mare (Loyalty Islands). The New Caledonian Crow has been introduced to the island of Mare where it did not previously occur (Delacour, 1966). The introduction occurred at least before 1945 as it is recorded by Mayr (1945).

DAMAGE

According to Delacour (1966) the introduction to Mare was disastrous to other birds, as the species is a dangerous pillager of nests and causes considerable losses particularly to pigeons. It destroys birds plus their young and eggs, and will take the eggs and chicks of domestic poultry. Delacour says that the species is not destroyed on New Caledonia because it is an endemic bird.

ROOK
Corvus frugilegus Linnaeus

DISTINGUISHING CHARACTERISTICS

30.5-49.6 cm (12.2-19.8 in). 340-500 g (12-17.64 oz)

All black with purple and violet sheen; base of bill and nostrils covered with white scurf; bill black.

Witherby *et al,* vol.1, 1938-41, pp.17-22, and pl.1, opp. p.6.

Goodwin, 1977, pp.80-81.

GENERAL DISTRIBUTION

Eurasia: from eastern coastal Finland, southern Scandinavia and the British Isles, east to the eastern coast of Siberia, and south to central China, southern USSR, northern Iran, north-eastern Iraq and Turkey, Bulgaria, Yugoslavia, Germany and northern France. Winters in southern parts of breeding range and south to north-western Africa, Egypt, Arabia, southern Iran, north-western India, south-eastern China, South Korea and Japan.

INTRODUCED DISTRIBUTION

Introduced successfully in New Zealand.

GENERAL HABITS

Status: common. *Habitat:* forest margins, wooded steppe, riverine forest, meadows, parkland and cultivated regions. *Gregariousness:* small flocks, large flocks in winter (100-2000 birds known). *Movements:* sedentary and migratory. *Foods:* worms, grubs, insects and their larvae, germinating seed, fruits, eggs and rarely the young of other birds. *Breeding:* Mar-Apr; Sept-Oct (New Zealand); colonial, often tens or hundreds together (nearly 7000 in one area in Aberdeenshire). *Nest:* large construction, up to 61 cm (24.5 in) or more in diameter, of twigs, branches, sticks, sometimes solidified earth and often constructed on previous

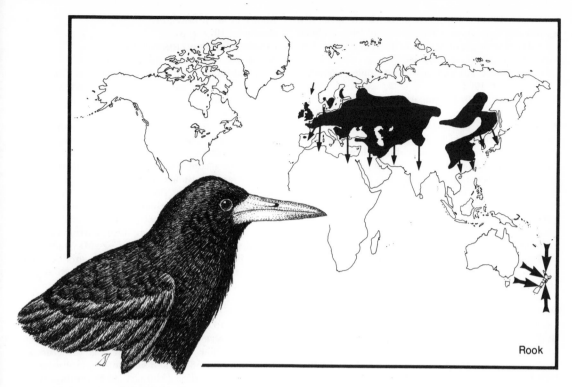

Rook

season's nest, lined with grass, wool, hair, etc. in a tree. *Eggs:* 2-7, 2-5 (New Zealand).

Goodwin, 1977, pp.81-87.

NOTES ON INTRODUCTIONS

New Zealand. Rooks were liberated in New Zealand between 1862 and 1873 (Thomson, 1922) and are still locally common there in both the North and South Islands (Wodzicki, 1965). They are reported to have been originally introduced to the Hawke's Bay area to destroy insect pests (Bull and Porter, 1975).

Three Rooks were introduced to Nelson in 1862 but disappeared after a few years. Also in 1862, some were introduced at Canterbury but were reported to have been killed by cats. In 1869 the Auckland Acclimatisation Society introduced two, and in 1870, sixty-four more. Birds from this latter introduction were last reported in 1874 when they were apparently not doing well. The Canterbury society liberated five birds at Christchurch in 1871 and a further thirty-five in 1873. These were reported to be well established in 1890 and fairly common there by about 1916 (Thomson, 1922).

According to Bull and Porter (1975) Rooks were introduced to Hawke's Bay at least twice during the early 1870s. Some were possibly liberated in 1872 and in 1873 near Big Bush (near Mangateretere some 4.8 km [3 miles] north-east of Hastings). In October 1874, a consignment of seventy-two Rooks arrived at Napier in the vessel *Queen Bee* for the Hawke's Bay Acclimatisation Society, and were presumably released although this cannot be confirmed. Of the North Island introductions only those at Napier appear to have been successful, thus Hawke's Bay has probably provided the Rooks that later established colonies elsewhere in the North Island.

In the late 1950s there were five isolated Rook populations in New Zealand (Bull, 1957). They were well established in two North Island districts (Hawke's Bay and southern Wairarapa) and in three South Island ones (Christchurch, Banks Peninsula and Peel Forest). Bull records that only one of these colonies could be traced to the early liberations, however there were reasons for believing that at least some of the remaining ones resulted from liberations rather than natural spread.

The Rook has spread only slowly in New Zealand and even after eighty years was still limited to the areas mentioned above (Bull and Porter). In the Hawke's Bay area, however, the breeding population doubled in the period 1965-69 when control measures were relaxed and crop acreages increased. Rooks in Hawke's Bay have taken ninety-six years to spread from Napier to Woodville, a distance of only 129 kilometres (80 miles). They have generally spread at the rate of 1.3-3.1 km (.8-2 miles) per annum southwards and somewhat slower in the north. In the North Island they are now well established over the Hawke's Bay area and rookeries have been established in a number of localities in the Auckland and Wellington areas.

Following the initial liberations at Christchurch in the South Island in 1871 and 1873 the Rook population slowly increased until there were 1000 birds present in about 1925 (Stead, 1927, in Coleman, 1971). Between 1926 and 1956 the population built up to some 10 000 birds (Bull, 1957). Coleman (1971) reported that this population was reduced by extensive poisoning between 1956 and 1967 until only about 700 were left. They still exist at West Melton, Sunnyside, Banks Peninsula and at Geraldine.

The Rook has also been recorded on the Chatham Islands (Williams, 1973).

DAMAGE

As early as 1509 in England, an Act of Parliament was passed placing a price on the head of the Rook

(Collinge, 1920). The species has been generally regarded by farmers as a nuisance, and frequently as a serious pest to grain crops. In England and other parts of Europe they dig up newly sown maize seeds, damage cereal crops and pears and apples (Wright, 1962; Seubert, 1964).

In the late 1960s investigations into the damage caused by Rooks began in Scotland. Dunnet and Patterson (1968) indicate that although these birds are generally regarded as a pest, no clear assessment of their economic status had been made. Investigations showed that the greatest losses occurred in spring sown cereals, especially oats (Feare, 1974). Losses were high in early or late sown crops and attacks on potatoes did not significantly affect the yield.

In New Zealand where the Rook is established as an introduced species it is regarded as a pest. As early as 1917 they were reported to be causing damage to walnuts and there had been complaints of the species attacking lambs and pulling up seedling wheat (Thomson, 1922). Later reports indicate that they have caused serious damage to crops, especially maize, oats, pumpkins and potatoes (Oliver, 1955). Bull and Porter (1975) say that farmers have been shooting and poisoning Rooks since 1915. In 1971 large-scale poison trials were commenced by the Pest Destruction Board in Hawke's Bay, using DRC-1339. By July 1973, some 16 000 Rooks had been killed.

COMMON CROW
(American Crow)
Corvus brachyrhynchos Brehm

DISTINGUISHING CHARACTERISTICS
41.9-53.3 cm (16.5-21 in)
Entirely black, with a violet or greenish blue gloss, more conspicuous on back, wings and tail; bill black.
Roberts, 1960, pl.55.

Common Crow

Reilly, 1968, pp.313-314.
Goodwin, 1977, p.87.
GENERAL DISTRIBUTION
North America: southern Canada south to northern Baja California, central Arizona, central Texas, Gulf of Mexico and southern Florida. Winters from southern Canada southwards to Sonora, Mexico.
INTRODUCED DISTRIBUTION
Introduced unsuccessfully (?) to Bermuda, but is now present as a successful colonist (?).
GENERAL HABITS
Status: very common. *Habitat:* agricultural areas, open country, woods and forest. *Gregariousness:* small flocks, larger flocks in winter. *Movements:* sedentary, but northerly populations partly migratory. *Foods:* insects, invertebrates, reptiles, small mammals, eggs, young birds, carrion, wild and cultivated fruits and nuts. *Breeding:* May-June; Mar-June (Bermuda); singly, occasionally small colonies. *Nest:* of sticks, lined with soft material such as grass, moss, leaves and bark, in a tree, shrub or on a pole. *Eggs:* 3, 4-6.
Reilly, 1968, pp.313-314.
Goodwin, 1977, pp.88-90.
NOTES ON INTRODUCTIONS
Bermuda. The Common Crow was introduced to Bermuda in 1876 and became established and abundant for a time (Phillips, 1928). Phillips reports that a specimen was collected there (*Auk* 32:229, 1915) in 1912.

Wingate (1973) makes no mention of any introduction of this species to Bermuda. It now occurs there as a resident, breeding from March to June.
DAMAGE
According to Godfrey (1966) the Common Crow is destructive to crops particularly corn, often takes the eggs and young of birds, and is generally thought to be more harmful than beneficial. The species is unprotected on Bermuda because of the damage it does to agricultural crops (Wingate). In the United States, with jays and magpies it causes damage to nut crops such as almonds, walnuts and pistachios (Clark, 1977).

LARGE-BILLED CROW
(Jungle Crow)
Corvus macrorhynchos Wagler

DISTINGUISHING CHARACTERISTICS
40.5-53 cm (16.2-21.2 in). 320-650 g (11.29-22.93 oz)
Entirely black, glossed with blue and violet; massive black bill.
Smythies, 1960, pl.44, no.10, opp. p.511.
Ali and Ripley, vol.5, 1968-74, pp.252-258 and pl.62, fig.1, opp. p.208.
Goodwin, 1977, pp.101-102.
GENERAL DISTRIBUTION
Eastern and Southern Asia: Sakhalin, Japan, Kurile Islands, Ryūkyū Islands, Manchuria, Korea, China, Taiwan and Hainan, west to southern Tadzhikistan, southern Transcaspia, Afghanistan, eastern Iran and India, and south to Sri Lanka, Burma, Andaman Islands, Malay Peninsula, southern Indochina, Greater and Lesser Sunda Islands to Timor and Wetar, and the Philippines.

Large-billed Crow

Goodwin, 1977, p.132.

GENERAL DISTRIBUTION

Africa and islands south of latitude 20° north, Fernando Póo, Senegal to Somali Republic and South Africa (lacking in most desert areas); also on Aldabra, the Archipel des Comores and Malagasy. Breeding distribution not well established (Hall and Moreau, 1970).

INTRODUCED DISTRIBUTION

Introduced unsuccessfully in Mauritius.

GENERAL HABITS

Status: abundant and widespread. *Habitat:* towns, villages, open country, desert edges and woodland. *Gregariousness:* occasionally flocks of 100s; roost communally in flocks up to 1000. *Movements:* erratic migratory movements. *Foods:* omnivorous; including small animals, reptiles, fruit, grain, seeds, insects, garbage, offal, corn and palm-nuts. *Breeding:* varies, most of the year, except perhaps February. *Nest:* bulky structure of sticks, lined with rags and other soft material, in a tree, on rocks or occasionally telegraph poles. *Eggs:* 1, 3-6, 7.

Goodwin, 1977, pp.132-134.

NOTES ON INTRODUCTIONS

Mauritius. Meinertzhagen (1912) records that Pied Crows were introduced to Mauritius on at least three occasions from either Malagasy or Africa, but did not succeed in becoming established. They were apparently introduced to control rats and mice.

Rountree *et al* (1952) say that they were released prior to 1760 and on several subsequent occasions from Malagasy. Staub (1976) records that Bernardin de Saint Pierre reported that only three males remained at the time of his visit in 1760. The Pied Crow does not now occur on Mauritius.

DAMAGE

The Pied Crow is probably a useful species in most situations, although it will take the eggs and young of

INTRODUCED DISTRIBUTION

Introduced unsuccessfully on Camorta Island, Nicobar Islands.

GENERAL HABITS

Status: fairly common. *Habitat:* open country, wooded areas, coastal areas, towns and villages. *Gregariousness:* singly, pairs, and small flocks up to several dozen; communal roosts. *Movements:* sedentary, but nomadic locally in some areas. *Foods:* omnivorous including carrion, eggs of birds and their young, insects, fruits, etc. *Breeding:* Jan-June (Malaya), Nov-June (India-Burma). *Nest:* large structure of sticks, with a shallow cup lined with grass, hair and other soft material, in a tree. *Eggs:* 3-4, 5.

Ali and Ripley, vol.5, 1968-74, pp.252-258.
Goodwin, 1977, pp.102-103.

NOTES ON INTRODUCTIONS

Nicobar Islands. A few Jungle Crows were taken from Port Blair in the Andaman Islands and released on Camorta in the central Nicobars in about 1874 (Hume, 1874). According to Abdulali (1967) there is no evidence for their survival there.

DAMAGE

According to Ali (1953) and Ali and Ripley (1968-74) the Jungle Crow can become a great nuisance. It is destructive in fruit gardens, occasionally takes young poultry and can be destructive to other birds by eating their eggs and young. In southern USSR they sometimes become a nuisance at deer breeding establishments (Bogachev, 1961).

PIED CROW

Corvus albus Müller

DISTINGUISHING CHARACTERISTICS

45-52 cm (18-20.8 in)

Generally a black and white bird; broad collar across the base of hindneck, and chest to upper belly white; remainder glossy blue-black; bill black.

Pied Crow

other birds. In western Africa they have been reported to do much damage to ground-nut cultivation, and in eastern Africa to maize crops (Mackworth-Praed and Grant, 1973). On Malagasy they are often destructive to corn (Rand, 1936). It is probably just as well that they did not become established in Mauritius, where they were found to raid poultry and were said to have been exterminated for this reason.

Family: *Sturnidae* Starlings, mynas

111 species in 26 genera; 9 species introduced; 6 successfully

Starlings and Mynas have had a high degree of success as introduced species. Both the Starling and Common Myna have been widely introduced throughout the world, the Myna particularly, has become established in many areas as an escapee from captivity. Their ability to colonise new areas is amply illustrated in the following text and they will undoubtedly reach many other areas in the Pacific and South America.

Both the Starling and Common Myna have become pests of agriculture where they have been introduced. Many of the species in the family associate with man and gather in immense flocks and exhibit much pest potential as introduced species to crops and native birds.

A single Rothschild's Starling, *Leucopsar rothschildi* seen on Oahu (Hawaiian Islands) in April and December 1977 has been assumed to be an aviary escapee or a deliberate release by a tourist. The species is endemic to Bali where it is now rare.

WHITE-HEADED MYNA
(Andaman Myna)
Sturnus erythropygius (Blyth)

DISTINGUISHING CHARACTERISTICS
20 cm (8 in)
Head, neck and breast white, becoming light grey on abdomen; back pale grey; rump white; wings black with a green gloss on edges; tail black, outer feathers with white tips; bill yellow.

GENERAL DISTRIBUTION
The Andaman Islands, and Car Nicobar and Katchal Island, in the Nicobar Islands.

INTRODUCED DISTRIBUTION
Introduced unsuccessfully to Camorta Island, Nicobar Islands.

GENERAL HABITS
Little information. *Habits:* said to be similar to those of Common Starling. *Foods:* insects, fruits and seeds.

NOTES ON INTRODUCTIONS
Camorta Island. The White-headed Myna *S.a. adamanensis* from the Andamans, was introduced to the island of Camorta in the central Nicobars (Richmond, 1903). Abdulali (1967) failed to find any there and says that there is no evidence that they survived for any length of time.

DAMAGE
None known.

ROSE-COLOURED STARLING
(Rosy Pastor, Rose-coloured Pastor)
Sturnus roseus (Linnaeus)

DISTINGUISHING CHARACTERISTICS
20-23 cm (8-9.2 in). 53-80 g (1.87-2.82 oz)
Generally rose-pink, with head, neck, upper breast, wings and tail black; mantle, back, rump, lower breast, flanks and belly rose-pink; pointed crest on crown (not often erected) and nape black; wings, upper and under tail-coverts and tail glossed bluish purple and green, bill pinkish orange with base of lower mandible black (brownish in winter). *Female:* browner head, shorter crest, duller wings, and tail less pink.

Witherby *et al,* vol.1, 1938-41, pp.45-47 and pl.4, opp. p.36.

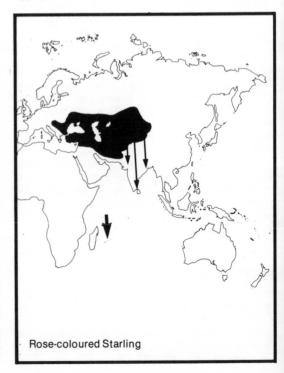

White-headed Myna

Rose-coloured Starling

INTRODUCTIONS OF STURNIDAE

Species	Date introduced	Region	Manner introduced	Reason
(a) Successful introductions				
Starling	20th century	western and northern Europe	colonisation	—
	1935-41	Iceland	colonisation	—
	1890-91	USA	deliberate	aesthetic
	1914 on	Canada	colonisation from USA	—
	1952	Alaska	colonisation from Canada	—
	1953	Mexico	colonisation from USA	—
	mid-1950s	Bermuda	colonisation from North America	—
	1903-04	Jamaica, West Indies	deliberate	?
	1898-99	South Africa	deliberate	?
	1862-83	New Zealand	deliberate	?
	late 19th century	Chatham Islands	deliberate	?
	1907	Campbell Island	colonisation from New Zealand	—
	before 1910	Kermadec Island	colonisation from New Zealand	—
	1948	The Snares	colonisation from New Zealand	—
	1952	Antipodes	colonisation from New Zealand	—
	about 1930	Macquarie Island, Australia	colonisation from New Zealand	—
	1913	Norfolk Island	colonisation from New Zealand and/or Australia	—
	1924	Lord Howe Island	colonisation from New Zealand and/or Australia	—
	1857, 1863-81	Australia	deliberate	?
	1860	Tasmania, Australia	deliberate	?
	1920s or about 1948 ?	Oni-i-Lau, Fijian Islands	colonisation from Kermadecs ?	—
Common Myna	?	Indochina	range extension and/ or introductions	—
	about 1900	Malaysia	range extension and/ or introductions	—
	1936	Singapore	range extension and/ or introductions	—
	early 20th century	northern Thailand	range extension and/ or introductions	—
	?	southern Vietnam	range extension and/ or introductions ?	—
	?	southern China	range extension and/ or introductions ?	—
	1952	Hong Kong	escapee or deliberate ?	cage bird
	1862-72 and later	Australia	deliberate	insect control
	1870-76	New Zealand	deliberate	?
	1888 or 1900	South Africa	deliberate	?
	1830 or later	Seychelles	escapee or deliberate	cage bird ?
	1755-59	Réunion	deliberate	insect control
	prior 1795	Rodrigues Island	deliberate ?	insect control ?
	1759 or later	Mauritius	deliberate	insect control

continued

INTRODUCTIONS OF STURNIDAE

Species	Date introduced	Region	Manner introduced	Reason
	early 18th century and 1875	Malagasy	deliberate	insect control
	about 1960 ?	Nossi-Be, Malagasy	deliberate	insect control
	about 1906-07 prior 1905 and	Archipel des Comores Chagos	deliberate ? escapees ? and	? cage bird ?
	1954-55	Archipelago	deliberate	
	1885	St Helena	deliberate	?
	?	Ascension Island	?	?
	?	Solomon Islands	?	?
	1920s	Cook Islands	deliberate	insect control
	1876 or 1890-1900	Fijian Islands	deliberate	insect control
	?	New Caledonia	?	?
	1908-15	Society Islands	deliberate	insect control
	1865	Hawaiian Islands	deliberate	insect control
Jungle Myna	prior 1925 or 1940-45 ?	Singapore	escapees ?	cage bird
	1890-1900	Fiji	deliberate	insect control
	1972	Samoa	?	?
Crested Myna	prior 1920	Pinang Island, Malaysia	?	?
	1894 or 1897	Canada	accidental or deliberate	ship borne or cage bird?
	1849-52	Luzon, Philippines	deliberate	insect control
Hill Myna	1960-61	Hawaiian Islands	escapee	cage bird
	early 1970s ?	Florida, USA	escapee ?	cage bird

(b) Probably successful introductions

Species	Date introduced	Region	Manner introduced	Reason
Starling	?	New Hebrides	?	?
	?	Tonga	?	?
Common Myna	before 1867	Andaman Islands	?	?
	?	Laccadive and Maldive Islands	?	
	prior 1903	Nicobar Islands	?	?
	late 1950s	Tasmania, Australia	colonisation from Mainland ?	
	?	New Hebrides	?	?
Jungle Myna	?	Sumatra	?	?
Crested Myna	?	Japan	?	?

(c) Unsuccessful introductions

Species	Date introduced	Region	Manner introduced	Reason
White-headed Myna	prior 1903 ?	Camorta Island, Nicobar Group	deliberate ?	?
Rose-coloured Starling	1892	Mauritius	deliberate	?
Starling	1954	Ulan-Ude, USSR	deliberate	insect control ?
	1949	Venezuela	accidental	ship borne
	1875, 1889, 1892	Canada	deliberate	?
	1872-73	USA	deliberate	?
	recent ?	Cuba	deliberate ?	?
Black-collared Starling	1969	Hawaiian Islands	escapee ?	cage bird ?
Common Myna	about 1900	Tasmania, Australia	deliberate	?
	1930, 1949	California, USA	escapees ?	?
	before 1956 ?	England	escapees	cage bird
	before 1867	Andaman Islands	?	?
Hill Myna	1829	St Helena	?	?
	?	Chagos Archipelago	?	?

Species	Date introduced	Region	Manner introduced	Reason
	1975 ?	Hong Kong	escapees	cage bird
	1923	Christmas Island, Indian Ocean	deliberate ?	?
Jungle Myna	before 1867	Andaman Islands	deliberate	?
	about 1904	Christmas Island, Indian Ocean		?

Ali and Ripley, vol.5, 1968-74, pp.163-166 and pl.60, fig.9, opp. p.160.

GENERAL DISTRIBUTION

Eurasia: from eastern Europe (Hungary), west across southern USSR to southern Siberia (Kirghiz Steppes), and south to Turkey, Near and Middle East, Iran and Afghanistan. In winter migrates south to southern Iran, Pakistan, India and Sri Lanka. (The species also has a widespread, erratic, occurrence outside the normal range and reaches western Europe, Ireland, the Faeroes, North Africa, the Andaman Islands and Sinkiang, China.)

INTRODUCED DISTRIBUTION

Introduced unsuccessfully in Mauritius.

GENERAL HABITS

Status: abundant. *Habitat:* grass steppe, open country with rocky hills, cultivation and croplands. *Gregariousness:* small flocks of about a dozen and large flocks of hundreds or even thousands. *Movements:* migratory (often irruptive and erratic). *Foods:* berries, fruits, grain, nectar, small lizards, locusts, grasshoppers and other insects and their larvae. *Breeding:* May-June (but ill-defined); colonial (small or huge crowded colonies). *Nest:* pile of straw, twigs, roots and grass, lined with fine material such as wool and feathers, in cavities and holes in grass steppe, walls, rock piles, under bridges and occasionally on bare ground. *Eggs:* 3, 5-6, 9.

Witherby *et al*, vol.1, 1938-41, pp.45-47.

Cheng, 1963, pp.601-605.

Ali and Ripley, vol.5, 1968-74, pp.163-166.

NOTES ON INTRODUCTIONS

Mauritius. Meinertzhagen (1912) records that the Rose-coloured Starling was introduced to Mauritius from India in 1892 by G. Regnard. However, those released died out immediately and the species did not become established on the island.

DAMAGE

In India the Rose-coloured Starling causes considerable damage to ripening grain crops, but is valued as a destroyer of locusts and scale (Ali, 1962). In Asia Minor they were considered as 'holy birds' in May because they destroyed locusts, but as 'devil's birds' in July because they ate ripening grapes (Voous, 1960). According to Cheng (1963) they are somewhat harmful to grape, mulberry and other plants producing berries.

STARLING
(Common Starling, European Starling)
Sturnus vulgaris (Linnaeus)

DISTINGUISHING CHARACTERISTICS

18.7-22 cm (7.48-8.8 in). 55-96 g (1.94-3.39 oz)

Glossy black with a purple and green sheen; wings and tail blackish, edged buff; in the breeding season numerous buffy spots on upper parts and whitish ones on underparts; bill, in breeding season, yellow with base of lower mandible grey, in non-breeding season dusky.

Witherby *et al*, vol.1, 1938-41, pp.39-44 and pl.4, opp. p.36.

Reader's Digest, 1977, p.546 and pl. p.546.

GENERAL DISTRIBUTION

Eurasia: from the British Isles, France and Scandinavia, east in Asia to Lake Baykal. Winters south to northern Africa, the Middle East, Arabia, Iraq, southern Iran, north-west India and north-eastern China.

INTRODUCED DISTRIBUTION

Extended breeding range in Europe. Introduced successfully in the USA, Jamaica, South Africa, Australia, New Zealand and the Chatham Islands (?); colonised Iceland, Bahamas, Bermuda, Canada, Alaska, Mexico, many of the small islands off Australia and New Zealand and probably the Fijian Group (Oni-i-Lau, etc.); possibly introduced successfully in the New Hebrides and on Tonga. Introduced unsuccessfully in Cuba, Venezuela and in the USSR (Ulan-Ude).

GENERAL HABITS

Status: very common and increasing in numbers. *Habitat:* wooded regions, open country, cultivated areas, grassland, gardens, orchards, parks, villages, towns and cities. *Gregariousness:* small to large flocks, migrating flocks may contain 100 000 to 200 000 birds and roosting flocks are known to contain millions. *Movements:* sedentary and migratory (probably sedentary in Australia). *Foods:* seeds, grains, fruits, roots, insects and their larvae including beetles and moths, and earthworms, slugs, snails, etc. *Breeding:* Apr-June; Aug-Jan and at other times (Australia); 2-3 broods per season but generally 1. *Nest:* mass of straw and rubbish, lined with grass, feathers, wool or moss, in caves, rocks, buildings, shrubs or trees. *Eggs:* 2, 3-7, 8; 4-8 (Australia); 2-6 (New Zealand).

Witherby *et al*, vol.1, 1938-41, pp.39-44.

Voous, 1960, p.405.

Cheng, 1963, pp.605-609.

NOTES ON INTRODUCTIONS

Europe. In the course of the present century the Starling has extended its breeding range, possibly due to the increase in agricultural lands and amelioration of climate, in western and northern Europe and greatly increased in numbers (Voous, 1960). In Great Britain they have extended into parts of Scotland,

Ireland, western Wales, Devon and Cornwall, during the last 150 years, where previously they were not known to breed (*Min. Agric. F. and Food,* 1962). Similarly, they have spread northwards in Scandinavia during this century and have been recorded breeding north as far as Spitzbergen. In the USSR no Starlings occur in the Ulan-Ude region, but in 1954 some fifty-eight were imported and released. They were present there between 1955 and 1957 and bred in 1955, but disappeared thereafter (Prokog'ev, 1960).

Iceland. According to Voous (1960) the Starling was breeding in Iceland in 1935, but settled only as a permanent resident after about 1941.

North America. The Starling first became established in North America when they were introduced in Central Park, New York in 1890 and 1891 (Kessel, 1953; Wing, 1956; Howard, 1959; Ballard, 1964). In March 1890, some sixty (eighty according to Wood, 1924) were released in Central Park by a group who planned to introduce all the birds mentioned by Shakespeare (Wetmore, 1964). This was followed by a second introduction of a flock (Silverstein and Silverstein, 1974) of forty birds (Wood, 1924; Wetmore, 1964) in 1891. Both of these releases appear to have been extremely successful. Earlier attempts at the introduction of Starlings in New York in 1872-73 had failed (Anderson, 1934), as did an attempt in Portland, Oregon in about 1890 (Ballard, 1964). Jewett and Gabrielson (1929) record that thirty-five pairs were released by the acclimatisation society in 1889 and 1892 near the City Park in Portland, Oregon. This colony may have been successful for a short period.

From 1891 on the Starling spread rapidly in the United States. They appeared at Connecticut and New Jersey in 1904, reached Pennsylvania in 1908 (Tousey and Griscom, 1937) and crossed the Allegheny Mountains in 1916 (Roberts, 1960). They reached Alabama in 1918 (Imhof, 1962) and were recorded in Kentucky in 1919, Louisiana in 1921, Ohio in 1924, Illinois and South Carolina in 1925, Texas in 1926, Oklahoma in 1929, northern Mississippi in 1930, South Dakota in 1933, Colorado and Nevada in 1938, New Mexico, Montana and Utah in 1939, Idaho in 1941, California in 1942, Oregon and Washington in 1943 and Arizona in 1946 (Howard; Ballard and others). By 1938 they had extended their range to the 103rd parallel and were breeding as far west as the Mississippi and probably in eastern Texas (Dickerson, 1938). The first appearance of Starlings in an area was generally by flocks of winter stragglers. Establishment lagged behind their first appearance as a breeding bird by about five years (Wing, 1943), although, in some areas such as Montana it was as little as four years (Mills, 1943) and in others such as Oregon as long as seven (Quaintance, 1951). Wing estimated that by 1940 they occupied an area of slightly more than seven million square kilometres (2 702 000 square miles) in North America.

In Canada attempts were made to establish Starlings in Quebec in 1875, 1889 and in 1892, but all apparently failed (Anderson). According to Godfrey (1966) they were recorded at Niagara Falls, Ontario in 1914 and at Halifax, Nova Scotia in 1915.

The spread in Canada can be traced from records given by Godfrey and others: they were recorded at Betchouane, Quebec in 1917, Toronto, Ontario in 1922, Grand Manam, New Brunswick in 1924, Tignish, Prince Edward Island in 1930 or 31, Camrose, Alberta in 1934, Tregarva, Saskatchewan in 1937, Tomkins, Newfoundland in 1943 and at Williams Lake, British Columbia in 1945-46. They were first recorded breeding in British Columbia in 1948, and by 1953 were breeding throughout the southern interior, were sparsely distributed on the coast on Vancouver Island, and had reached the Queen Charlotte Islands (Carl and Guiguet, 1972). Some indication of the speed with which the species colonised new areas in Canada can be gained from Tucks' (1958) account. Following the first record in Newfoundland in 1943 the species was breeding in an area of some 5200 square kilometres (2000 square miles) by 1956.

To the north the Starling reached Juneau, Alaska in 1952 (Howard, 1959) and was observed breeding at St Petersburg in 1963 (Stewart, 1964). In the south they were penetrating into the north-eastern corner of Mexico (Kessel, 1953). Coffey (1959) indicates that they may have penetrated the north-eastern corner of Mexico as early as 1935. Some were sighted at Anaxhuac, east of Nuevo Laredo in December 1938, and ten birds were found at Santa Lucia between Laredo and Monterrey in December 1939. In 1946, 500 of them were observed at Nuevo Laredo, and in 1948 some were seen at Linares, Nuevo Léon. Peterson and Chalif (1973) indicate that they have reached Guanajuanto, northern Veracruz and Yucatan in Mexico and are still spreading southwards. In 1974, four starlings were found on the Chukchi coast at Kotzebue, and single birds at Cordova and Homer in Alaska. As early as 1962 some three starlings had been reported from Fort Yukon, north of the Arctic Circle in Alaska (Yocum, 1963) and in 1969 a bird was observed at Inuvik (near the Beaufort Sea) in the North West Territory of Canada (Sealy, 1969). They nested at Fairbanks in 1978 (Gibson, 1978).

The Starling is now spread from southern Alaska across southern Canada and south to southern Mexico. From the more recent reports it may already range even further.

The race introduced in North America is *S.v. vulgaris* (Peters, 1962).

Bermuda. The Starling colonised Bermuda from North America in the mid-1950s (Wingate, 1973). Wingate says that they have increased explosively there through the early 1960s and are now second in abundance to the introduced House Sparrow.

Bahamas. The Starling is found in Nassau on New Providence, but is still only an uncommon winter visitor in the northern Bahamas (Brudenell-Bruce, 1975). They were first recorded there in 1956 and by 1962-63 more than 100 birds were present.

West Indies. The Starling was introduced to Annotto Bay, Jamaica in 1903-04, and is now well established there (Bond, 1960). Taylor (1953) says that they were not established around Annotto Bay in the 1940s, but at the Parish of St Ann about 40-43 km (24.8-26 miles) further inland where flocks of 200-300 were seen in 1947. He records that Bond found

Starling

them 24 km (15 miles) west near Brownstown in 1949 and some were seen at Castleton Botanical Gardens 42 km (26 miles) away in 1951 and at Ocho Rios on the north coast 16 km (10 miles) away in 1952.

They have been recorded from other areas in the West Indies including Grand Bahama, New Providence, Eleuthera and from Gibar in Cuba.

Blake (pers. comm., 1977) indicates that they may have been deliberately introduced to Cuba, but apparently were not successful there. He feels that the lack of success of the Starling in the West Indies region is probably due to the tropical climate. However, according to Lack (1976) they have spread rapidly on Jamaica in recent years and are now widespread in wooded cultivation and lowland areas, with some at midlevels, but are not found in natural habitats. Jamaica has been less cleared of natural forest than some islands and I would think that this factor rather than the climate has prevented a more rapid spread of the Starling on the island.

Venezuela. Five Starlings flew ashore from a ship (from Falmouth, England) passing Venezuela near Lago de Maracaibo, in November 1949 (Scott, 1950). These birds disappeared and were not seen again (Sick, 1968). Sick suggests that the Starling has a great future, particularly in southern South America, if it becomes established there.

South Africa. The race *S.v. vulgaris* (Peters, 1962) was introduced to South Africa in about 1898, at Cape Peninsula (Mackworth-Praed and Grant, 1963). Winterbottom and Liversidge (1954) record that the initial introduction of eighteen birds by Cecil Rhodes in 1899 was at Groote Schuur, Rondebosch,

near Cape Town. According to the Agriculture and Technical Service (pers. comm., 1962) they have also been introduced at both Durban and East London.

The Starling reached Wynburg in 1905, Robben Island in 1907 and Stellenbosch in 1910. They were at Worcester and Elgin in 1922 and reached Riversdale by 1930. In 1940 they reached the Great Brac River and by 1944-45 were at Knysna and Hermanus (Winterbottom and Liversidge, 1954). By 1953 they occupied an area stretching from Kleinvlei in the north to Plettenberg Bay in the east.

The spread from Cape Town was fairly rapid, the species colonising the Cape Flats reaching George (Winterbottom, 1966) in 1948 (Liversidge, 1962). In the 1950s they invaded the Karoo and became abundant at Majesfontein (Winterbottom, 1957). Liversidge reports that they reached Port Elizabeth in 1954, Uitenhage in 1956, Grahamstown in 1958 and King Williams Town and Addo in 1961. According to him the Starling in Africa has spread by 'long jumps', the controlling factor appearing to be the presence of European-type dwellings.

The Department of Agriculture and Technical Services indicates that the Starling was throughout the Cape Province by 1962. However, Winterbottom says that King Williams Town appeared to be the eastern limit of the species at this time. Quickelberge (1972) records that they reached East London in 1966, Gonubie in 1969, Kei Mouth in about 1970, and Keisammahoek and Seymour north-west of King Williams Town in 1969 and 1970 respectively.

New Zealand. The first Starlings were introduced to New Zealand in 1862 by the Nelson Acclimatisation

361

Society. The first birds liberated were probably some in 1867. From 1862 to 1883 large numbers (at least 653 birds) were imported and released by the Nelson, Otago, Canterbury, Auckland and Wellington acclimatisation societies. Private individuals probably released many more (Thomson, 1922).

By the 1920s the Starling was abundant in most parts of the country. They are now widespread and abundant in both the North and the South Islands (Wodzicki, 1965) and have reached many of the offshore and outlying islands as far as Campbell Island and Macquarie Island (Falla *et al*, 1966).

Within thirty to forty years of their introduction to New Zealand, Starlings began appearing on offshore islands (Williams, 1953). They were taken to the Chatham Islands by L. W. Hood before 1900 (Oliver, 1955). Oliver reports them in the 1950s on Three Kings, Kermadecs, Mokohinau, Hen, Little Barrier, Great Barrier, Poor Knights, Mayor, Kapiti, Karewa, Chatham, Stewart, Snares, Auckland, Campbell and Macquarie Islands. They arrived on Campbell Island in about 1907, the Kermadecs before 1910, Lord Howe Island in 1924, the Snares in 1948 and the Antipodes in 1952 (Williams). They colonised Macquarie Island in about 1930 (Williams; Thomson, 1964) and are now found on this island, Campbell, Snares and Auckland (Wodzicki, 1965). Williams (1973) reports that they breed on Three Kings, Kermadecs, Chathams, Antipodes, Campbell, Auckland and Macquarie Islands, but apparently have not as yet bred on the Snares.

The Starling is now also a resident on Lord Howe Island (McKean and Hindwood, 1965) and is abundant on Norfolk Island (Smithers and Disney, 1969) where they probably arrived about 1913 (Williams, 1953).

Australia. Some Starlings were imported by private individuals to Melbourne, Victoria in 1856, 1857 and in 1858 (Balmford, 1978) and it is possible that some were released at these dates. Ryan (1906) records that they were liberated by the acclimatisation society in 1863 (thirty-six birds), 1864 (six), 1866 (fifteen) and in 1871 (twenty). Jenkins indicates that they were released on Phillip Island in 1860 (six) and in 1866 (six), and that as many as 120 were released in the Melbourne metropolitan area in 1865. It is certainly indicated (see Balmford, 1978) that the Starling may have been established in Victoria by 1862.

In 1869-70 Starlings were introduced at Brisbane, Queensland (Lavery, 1974), although there appears some doubt as to whether they were actually released (Frith 1973), and it is possible that they colonised Queensland from the south.

They were introduced in South Australia by the acclimatisation society at Black Hills and Torrens Park near Adelaide in 1881 (eighty-nine birds) and later (Condon, 1962). They spread rapidly and were firmly established on Eyre Peninsula in 1900 and were present on Kangaroo Island (Cooper, 1947) before 1910.

In both Victoria and New South Wales (some introduced in 1880) the spread of Starlings was rapid. They were throughout the settled parts of the latter State by 1926 (Chisholm, 1926) and invaded Stanthorpe, Queensland from there in 1919 (Lavery, 1974). Tarr (1950) reports that they were throughout most of Victoria by 1950, and in Queensland were common around Brisbane and along the coastline up to Marlborough; in South Australia were probably not north of Augusta and were on Eyre Peninsula and Kangaroo Island.

In Tasmania Starlings were liberated in about 1860 when D. L. Crowther released seventy-five birds from New Zealand at Hobart. Littler (1902) says that they reached Sorrel in 1899 and in 1902 were plentiful in Hobart and the surrounding areas, but had not spread much beyond Sandy Bay, some six kilometres (3.7 miles) from Hobart; north of this they had reached Bridgewater and inland for about thirty-two kilometres (20 miles). By 1950 they were common in most of the cultivated areas of Tasmania (Tarr, 1950).

The Starling is now spread over much of south-eastern Australia from south-eastern Queensland to Eyre Peninsula, Tasmania and King and Flinders Islands. In South Australia its range extends west to the Western Australian border. They appear to be still spreading in most areas in Australia.

The first record of Starlings in Western Australia was at Gingin in 1936 when a single bird was shot (Jenkins, 1959; Long, 1965). Another bird may have been found at Albany in about 1917 (Whittell, 1950). In 1970 a single bird was shot a few kilometres from Esperance (Long, 1972) and this initiated an extensive search in the area during which, two small colonies were found well established and breeding in an area some sixty-four kilometres (40 miles) east of Esperance. Both of these colonies were extirpated by Agriculture Protection Board officers. In 1976 however, the Starling began invading Western Australia from South Australia and at present attempts are being made to prevent their establishment beyond the Western Australia – South Australia border. Unlike the colonisation of North America where the first Starlings noted in a new area were winter visitors the western expansion into Western Australia has so far been mainly by birds seeking breeding sites.

Peters (1962) records that the race introduced into Australia is *S. v. vulgaris*.

New Hebrides. Starlings were reported from the New Hebrides by Cain and Galbraith (1957), but their present status and details of their introduction were not found.

Fijian Group. The Starling was found to be well established on the island of Ono-i-lau an isolated island in the Fijian Group some 368 km (229 miles) south-east of Suva in the early 1950s (Hill, 1952). Hill records that the native peoples say that they arrived in about 1922 and he suggests that they may have come from the Kermadecs, 1224 km (770 miles) south, which contain the closest Starling population to that island.

Carrick and Walker (1953) examined the Starling population on Ono-i-lau and report that some natives say the species was not there prior to 1948, but others that it may have arrived in the 1920s. In 1953 they were well spread on the island (possibly numbering some 1000 adults) and were also on the Tuvana Islands, Vatoa (129 km [80 miles] north-north-east of Ono-i-lau) and Doi Islands. Some hundreds of Starlings were reported from Vatoa (Manson-Bahr,

1953). Control of the species, to prevent its establishment on other islands, was also advocated at this date.

The Starling is still established on southern Lau, Vatoa, Ono and some of the smaller clusters (Mercer, 1966).

Tonga. Dhondt (1976) records the presence of the Starling on Tonga where he states that they were often seen feeding on the lawns in Nuku'alofa and a group of several hundred were seen at the airport.

DAMAGE

Although there appear to be few assessments of the economic importance of Starlings in Europe they are reported to cause extensive damage to ripening fruits, particularly soft fruits and cherries. More recently Tahon (1972) and Seubert (1964) have reviewed their damage. Serious damage appears to be caused to cherries, grapes and olives particularly.

In the German Federal Republic Starlings cause serious damage to cherry orchards and in vineyards. In Luxembourg, France and Switzerland they are especially harmful to ripening grapes in autumn. In Belgium and the Netherlands they are considered to be a pest to cherry growers.

Tahon records flocks of 200 000 Starlings and estimates that 400 tonnes (406 tons) of cherries (more than 20% of the crop) are eaten each year by between one and two million Starlings in 300 square kilometres (116 square miles) of growing area. Bernard (1963) indicates that in Alsace and Germany Starlings cause great damage in cherry orchards and vineyards, but are a useful species in their breeding season when they feed on insects, molluscs and worms. In China where the species is a migrant Cheng (1963) records that they gather in orchards after fruits or in paddy fields to eat the grain, but eat many injurious insects and are helpful to agriculture locally.

In North America millions of dollars annually are spent in efforts to control the ever increasing number of Starlings. From 1962 to 1967 the University of California conducted much research into the biology and control of the species. In 1966, about twenty-five years after arriving in California, one roost was found to contain some five million Starlings. A programme to control them in some Solamo County cattle feed lots began in 1964. Nine million Starlings were killed over the next three years, but some 5000 still remained alive at the end of the campaign.

The harmful effects of Starlings have been well documented in North America by Howard (1959) and Shuyler (1963). It includes the damaging effect on native fauna, damage caused to buildings by defacement, the damage to crops and stock feed and the species' role as a disease carrier. In this latter respect they appear to be involved in the transmission of histoplasmosis — a fungus disease of the lungs — which is prevalent amongst people engaged in agriculture in America. Godfrey (1966) says that they are responsible for the decline of the Red-headed Woodpecker and Blue-bird in Canada.

In Australia, Thomas (1957) reviewed the damage caused by Starlings here and overseas. He suggested that there was not sufficient evidence available to judge the status of the species. However, in more recent years the damage caused by the Starling leaves little doubt that it is a pest in Australia.

Frith (1973) records that in horticultural districts the Starling is a major pest of soft fruits. In the Mildura district it has been estimated that 143 tonnes (145 tons) of grapes valued at twenty thousand dollars were destroyed in 1954 (Thomas). Morris (1969) reports that they were responsible for the wastage of eleven tonnes (10.8 tons) of feed per annum in a poultry cage house in Victoria, and Douglas (1972) states that they have contributed to the decline of native species, particularly parrots in that State.

The reputation of the Starling is no better in New Zealand. Here, they are accused of usurping the nest of other birds and damaging such fruits as plums and peaches. Dawson and Bull (1969) say, based on the results of their survey of farmers, that the Starling appears to be one of the more important fruit destroyers. They record damage to strawberries, grapes, cherries, pears, plums and peaches.

BLACK-COLLARED STARLING
Sturnus nigricollis (Paykull)

DISTINGUISHING CHARACTERISTICS
22.5-29.6 cm (9-11.84 in). 122-210 g (4.3-7.41 oz)
Head and throat white; a black neck collar, broader on chest; upper parts dark brown; white spots on wings; rump, under tail and tail tip white; underparts white shading to brown on flanks; orbital skin yellow; bill black.
Smythies, 1953, pl.10, fig.6, p.212.
Cheng, 1963, pp.611-612 and pl.45, no.75.

GENERAL DISTRIBUTION
South-eastern Asia: southern China, Burma, south throughout the Indochinese region to the base of the Malay Peninsula.

INTRODUCED DISTRIBUTION
Introduced unsuccessfully in the Hawaiian Islands.

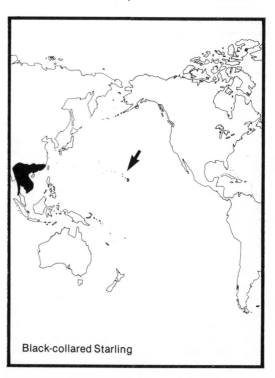

Black-collared Starling

GENERAL HABITS

Status: very common. *Habitat:* open country, scrub, paddy fields, cultivation, villages and gardens. *Gregariousness:* pairs, and large flocks at roosts. *Movements:* sedentary. *Foods:* insects, including grasshoppers and crickets. *Breeding:* Mar-Aug (China and Burma); 2-3 broods per year; partly colonial (several to a tree in Burma). *Nest:* huge untidy domed nest of grass, leaves and other material, in a tree. *Eggs:* 3-5 (China and Burma).

Smythies, 1953, pp.216-217.

Cheng, 1963, pp.612-614.

NOTES ON INTRODUCTIONS

Hawaiian Islands. A single bird was collected by State Fish and Game Department personnel in Kaneohe, on Oahu in April 1969 (Berger, 1972). No further reports of the species appear to have been recorded in the Hawaiian Islands and the bird collected was probably an aviary escapee.

DAMAGE

None known.

COMMON MYNA
(House Myna, Indian Myna [often spelled Mynah])
Acridotheres tristis (Linnaeus)

DISTINGUISHING CHARACTERISTICS

21-25 cm (8.4 - 10 in). 82-138 g (2.89-4.87 oz)
Generally dark brown; throat, upper breast, head and tail blackish; tail black tipped white; abdomen whitish; bare skin around eye yellow; large white patch on wings; under tail-coverts white; bill bright yellow.

Ali and Ripley, vol.5, 1968-74, pp.177, 180 and pl.59, fig.4, opp. p.128.

Reader's Digest, 1977, p.547 and pl. p.547.

GENERAL DISTRIBUTION

Southern and south-eastern Asia: from Afghanistan, Russian Turkestan, India and Sri Lanka, east to south-western China and Indochina: also the Andaman Islands.

INTRODUCED DISTRIBUTION

Extended range and/or introduced successfully in Malaysia, Singapore, northern Thailand, Indochina generally, Hong Kong and possibly in parts of southern China; successfully introduced in Australia, New Zealand, South Africa, St Helena, Seychelles, Réunion, Rodrigues, Mauritius, Comores, Malagasy, Chagos Archipelago, Ascension, Solomons, New Caledonia, Fiji, Society, Cook and Hawaiian Islands; probably successfully introduced in the Nicobar, Laccadive and Maldive Islands, and the New Hebrides. Introduced unsuccessfully in the Andaman Islands (died out), the USA and England. Possibly introduced and established in Samoa (probably error as bird established appears to be the Jungle Myna).

GENERAL HABITS

Status: very common. *Habitat:* forest edges, open country near human habitation, agricultural land, gardens, orchards, towns, cities and villages. *Gregariousness:* pairs, parties or small flocks; roost communally often in large flocks. *Movements:* sedentary. *Foods:* omnivorous; fruits, grains, seeds, berries, insects including grasshoppers, earthworms, flower nectar, etc. *Breeding:* mainly Feb-Sept; Sept-Mar (Australia); Feb-Aug (Hawaii); Nov-Dec (Malagasy); Oct-Apr (New Zealand); usually 1 but often 2 or even 3 broods per season (Hawaii 1-3); communal. *Nest:* collection of twigs, leaves, roots, paper and rags, etc., in a tree hole, wall, building or palm. *Eggs;* 3-6; 3-6 (New Zealand and Australia); 2-3 (Seychelles); 2-5 (Hawaii); 3-4 (Malagasy); 3-4 (Fiji).

Ali and Ripley, vol.5, 1968-74, vol.5, pp.177-181.

NOTES ON INTRODUCTIONS

Vietnam, Malaysia and Singapore. As a result of extensions of range and/or introductions the race *A.t. tristis* has spread through this region (Peters, 1962).

The expansion of range was first noted on the Malay Peninsula at the beginning of the present century (Chasen, 1939; Gibson-Hill, 1949; Madoc, 1956; Medway and Wells, 1976). The first record of the species in the northern limits of the peninsula was at Pakchan Estuary in 1919. Madoc considered that they were scarcely known in the north of Malaya in the early 1930s. In 1929 they were at Phatthalung and at Province Wellesley in 1931. By 1932 they were common in Taiping (in Perak) and reached Kuala Lumpur in 1933. The first record of them in Singapore was in 1936 and they were certainly resident and breeding there in the 1940s. Chasen thought that the Singapore population may have been derived from escaped birds, a suggestion with which Gibson-Hill did not agree. He considered that they arrived as a result of spread from the north. In 1948 the Myna was present at Kuala Trengganu, was still generally scarce and local in the north-eastern part of the Malay Peninsula in 1952, but by 1957 was widespread at Trengganu.

The Common Myna is now common in Singapore (Ward, 1968) and is abundant throughout the Malay Peninsula in suitable habitat (Medway and Wells).

Thailand. The Common Myna appeared in northern Thailand, whether through human agency or as an immigrant, not earlier and possibly much later, than the beginning of the twentieth century.

They were apparently unknown around the beginning of the century, but by 1914 were rather abundant, especially around villages in the northern parts of the country. By 1937 they were widespread but not beyond the sight of human habitation.

Lekagul and Cronin (1974) indicate that they inhabit open country but are still primarily around human habitation; they quickly establish themselves wherever man goes. They were rare around Bangkok and the central plains in the 1920s but are now abundant there.

Other mainland areas. Wildash (1968) indicates that they occur locally throughout South Vietnam, so probably have either spread there from areas in Indochina or have escaped or been introduced at some time. Little appears to be known of them in southern China, but it is possible that they have also colonised this area from further west in southern Asia.

Hong Kong. King *et al* (1975) record that the Common Myna has been introduced to Hong Kong. Webster (1975) reports that they were first seen there in January 1952. Small numbers are now established and breeding in the Mong Tseng Peninsula and there are several records from other parts of the colony.

Andaman and Nicobar Islands. Ali and Ripley (1968-74) and King *et al* (1975) report that the Common Myna has been introduced to both these

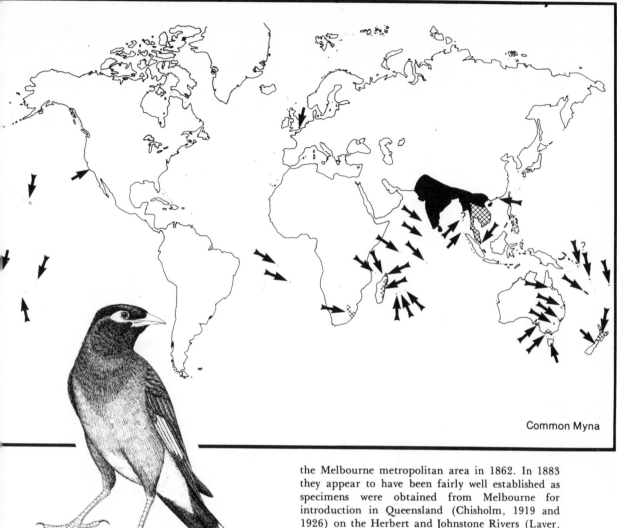

Common Myna

groups of islands. They were found to be numerous at Nancowry Harbour in the Nicobars, where they were said to have been introduced (Richmond, 1903), but were not found by Abdulali (1967) who concluded that they had died out there. Beavan (1867) records that they were introduced at Port Blair in the Andamans by Colonel R. C. Tyler in the time of the convict settlement there. He indicates that the species had bred there prior to 1867. On the other hand, Wood (1924) says that they were introduced to Ross Island in the Andamans in about 1880 and seem to breed there all the year.

Laccadive and Maldive Islands. Ali and Ripley (1968-74) record that the Myna has probably been introduced to both these groups where they are established and common.

Australia. Several introductions of the Common Myna are recorded in Australia in the period between 1862 and 1872. Some forty-two birds were introduced at Melbourne, Victoria in 1863 and other introductions occurred in 1864 (forty birds), 1866 (?) and in 1872 (seventy) (Ryan, 1906). Jenkins (1977) records that more than 100 were liberated in

the Melbourne metropolitan area in 1862. In 1883 they appear to have been fairly well established as specimens were obtained from Melbourne for introduction in Queensland (Chisholm, 1919 and 1926) on the Herbert and Johnstone Rivers (Laver, 1974). They were reported to be common around Sydney in 1896 (Chisholm, 1926) and some were recorded at Ryde in about 1884 (Hone, 1978).

The reasons for the original liberations do not appear to be known, but it is certain that they were taken to Queensland to combat insect pests (Chisholm, 1950) particularly plague locusts (Chisholm, 1919) and cane beetles (Hone).

Common Mynas were introduced to Tasmania in about 1900, or shortly afterwards (Sharland, 1958), but failed to thrive and were not reported until after 1914 when they reached the island from the mainland.

In 1957 Mynas were reported in some suburbs near Adelaide, South Australia (Blair, Athol and Enfield) and are now spreading there (Condon, 1962), although there appear to be few recent records.

By 1950 the Myna was reported to be common in the Melbourne metropolitan area and extending to some outer areas; they were common around Sydney Harbour in New South Wales; in Queensland they were found at Mackay, Mossman and throughout the cane growing areas (Tarr, 1950).

In New South Wales they were recorded at Lane Cove and North Ryde in 1950 and by 1964 were firmly established there (Lane, 1964). They were recorded in the Thirroul area in 1960 and have since been found breeding in the Wollongong area (Sefton

365

and Devitt, 1962). They are now well established in the Sydney-Wollongong area, are still spreading and have been observed as far west as Marulan and Marrangaroo and north to Tweed Heads (Hone, 1978). Hone suggests that the species was probably introduced in New South Wales during the same period (1863-72) that it was introduced in Victoria.

In Queensland they are common in Townsville in urban areas (Lavery and Hopkins, 1963), throughout the cane growing areas and at Cairns (White, 1946). According to Walker (1952) they were first released at Cairns in 1918 by a Mr B. Robinson, who also took eight to Toowoomba in the Darling Downs. Walker records that they were thought to have been introduced in the Biddeston area by the Hon. A. J. Thynne, and nested there in 1921-22. They were recorded in the Atherton shire in 1931 and are now everywhere except in the heavy rainforest areas (Bravery, 1970).

The Common Myna is now well established in cities and towns of south-eastern Victoria, in Sydney, and in northern Queensland from Townsville to Cairns. Some appeared in south-eastern Queensland in 1945, and since 1960 birds occasionally turn up in north-eastern New South Wales (Frith, 1973). In the late 1960s (Anon. 1969) it was found that the bird had been deliberately released into the Australian Capital Territory where it is now breeding.

New Zealand. Common Mynas were first introduced by private individuals and acclimatisation societies in the 1870s in New Zealand (Thomson, 1922). In 1870, a Mr F. Banks introduced eighteen birds from Melbourne, Australia, and Mr T. Brown imported some to Dunedin in the early 1870s. In 1910 a few were reported from about the town of Christchurch. In 1877 they were apparently plentiful at Nelson, but subsequently disappeared as did most of the other early introductions. Although they were widely introduced in the South Island, most had disappeared before 1890 (Cunningham, 1948; Falla *et al,* 1966).

In 1875 and 1876 the Wellington Acclimatisation Society introduced some seventy birds. Progeny from these were common around Tuparoa in 1912, around Taranaki in 1916, and in the late 1920s about Wellington and up the coast to Wanganui and throughout Taranaki and Wairarapa (Thomson).

The Common Myna appears to have spread only slowly in the North Island. Cunningham (1948) records that in 1947 they were confined to five towns in the Wairarapa district, were numerous in parts of Hawke's Bay but in the Manawatu district were not numerous south of Wanganui. The population appeared to be expanding from Waikato to Auckland. By 1953 they ranged from Auckland to Wanganui (Oliver, 1955) and were reported in the 1960s to be widespread and abundant in the northern half of this island (Wodzicki, 1965). Falla *et al* say they are common north of Wanganui and in southern Hawke's Bay, are increasing on Volcanic Plateau where they first became established in the middle 1940s, and are still spreading northwards where they reached the Bay of Islands in about 1960. Two birds were seen at Nelson in the South Island in 1956.

The race introduced in New Zealand is recorded as *A.t. tristis* (Peters, 1962).

South Africa. The Common Myna *A.t. tristis* (Peters,

1962) was introduced at Durban, Natal in 1888 or 1900 from India (Roberts, 1946; Mackworth-Praed and Grant, 1963). There is a popular story of a Mr Leon St Guillaune, releasing three pairs of Mynas from Mauritius, from the top of a double-decker horse-drawn tram in 1888 (Calder, 1953; Burton, 1969). Another story indicates that bird dealers allowed several pairs to escape at Durban in about 1900 (Calder, 1953).

The Myna is now found in Natal and Johannesburg, Transvaal (Mackworth-Praed and Grant). According to Winterbottom (1966) they have spread throughout Natal and reached Johannesburg (at Bramley) in about 1938, but that their distribution on the Witwatersrand remains patchy. They were reported to be at the Melrose Bird Sanctuary in 1946, and were established at Zoo Lake by 1947, but did not reach the southern suburbs until about 1960. They appeared at Kimberley in 1964 when the nearest colonies were in the southern Transvaal and north-eastern Orange Free State (Bigalke, 1964).

St Helena. The Common Myna was introduced to St Helena in 1885 and became established there (Gosse, 1938; Benson, 1950). There are apparently three specimens of the species from St Helena in the American Museum of Natural History. Benson indicates that the present birds seem more like *G. religiosa* to him, however specimens obtained by Haydock (1954) have been definitely identified as *A. tristis.* Haydock found the species to be the most numerous and prolific land bird on St Helena and offshore islands.

Seychelles. The race *A.t. tristis* (Benson, 1960) has been introduced to Mahé in the Seychelles (Benson; Ripley, 1961) and is now abundant and widespread there on all the larger islands (Crook, 1961; Gaymer *et al,* 1969). Gaymer *et al* suggest that the species was introduced in the Seychelles in about 1830. Penny (1974) suggests that they were introduced in the late eighteenth century, soon after the first colonisation by Mahé de Labourdonnais, who arranged for birds to be sent from Mauritius where they had already been introduced from India to control locusts. There are no locusts on the Seychelles so the species was more than likely introduced there as a cage bird. Newton (1867) found them to be the most common bird on Mahé when he visited there in about 1867.

Réunion. The Common Myna, race *A.t. tristis* has been introduced to Réunion (Benson, 1960) where it is now common (Watson *et al,* 1963).

They were introduced there in 1755 (Decary, 1962) or 1759 (Staub, 1976) by the then Governor General, Desforges-Boucher and the Manager Poivre, for the purpose of destroying locusts which were regarded as an important pest in Malagasy at this time.

Rodrigues. The race *A.t. tristis* (Benson, 1960) has been introduced to this island where it was common and abundant (Gill, 1967) in the late 1950s and 1960s. Staub (1976) indicates that they were introduced there before 1795 as they are mentioned as having achieved success as an insect controller at that time.

Mauritius. The race *A.t. tristis* (Benson, 1960; Milon *et al,* 1973) has been introduced from India, probably to control locusts and became well established on Mauritius (Penny, 1974).

They were introduced in about 1760 (Rountree *et al*, 1952; Benedict, 1957), probably in 1767 (Staub, 1976) from the Coromandel Coast for locust control, and are now the most conspicuous bird on the island. Staub reports that an earlier introduction in 1759 by Desforges-Boucher, Governor General of Mauritius and Réunion, was successful but that the birds were destroyed because of their depredations on the cereal crops of the early Dutch and French settlers. Meinertzhagen (1912) records that they were introduced by La Bourdonnais and in the early 1900s became one of the commonest birds. They were protected at this time because of the numbers of insects they eat.

Malagasy. Decary (1962) indicates that it took two introductions to establish the Common Myna in Malagasy. The first of these was early in the eighteenth century, and later in 1875 further birds were introduced by the Consul Alfred Grandidier. The race introduced appears to have been *A.t. tristis* (Van Someren, 1947; Benson, 1960).

Decary, quoting Maillard (1863) says that they were at first considered to be the 'saviour of agriculture', but finally it was admitted that they did little to control insects and it was found that they also fed on fruits. He indicates that the species was common at Tamatave and Point Larree in 1885.

Grandidier mentions how common the species had become in 1879 around Tamatave, following the introduction in 1875 (Milon *et al*, 1973). By 1930, Rand (1936) indicates that they were common from Tamatave to Brickville and that they had been noted at Fénérive and at Maroantsetra.

In 1948 they had advanced towards Tananarive and as far as Mouneyres and Rogez. In 1952 they were conspicuous at Mananjary, Manakara, Vohipeno and Vatomandry and a colony was observed at Maroantsetra in 1953. They are now common at Farafangana and further towards Ihosy (Milon *et al*).

Both Rand and Milon *et al* suggest that the extensions in range in Malagasy have been helped by the residents, who like this familiar bird and often keep it caged and transport it from place to place. The latter reports that the species has been introduced into other parts of Malagasy to control insects. Thus, several pairs have been introduced to Ambanja on the coast of Sambirano in 1957-58, and more recently on the island of Nossi Be off the northwest coast. Some were seen in 1969 at Amboasary and at Berenty, on baobabs in the plantations of sisal.

Archipel des Comores. Common Mynas of the race *A.t. tristis* have been introduced and established in the Comores (Benson, 1960). Benson records them on Grande Comore, Mohéli, Anjouan and Mayotte where they are common.

The first records of the species on the Comores appears to have been in 1906-07 when specimens were collected on Anjouan. At this time they appear to have been absent from Grande Comore and Mayotte. They are recorded again on the Comores by Voeltzkow in 1914 and 1917 (in Benson, 1960), who stated that they had previously been released on Anjouan by a French planter named Regoin.

Chagos Archipelago. According to Loustau-Lalanne (1962) the Common Myna has been introduced to this archipelago. Hutson (1975) indicates that locals say that they were introduced in the mid-1950s. They say that fifteen birds were brought from Mahé in the Seychelles in 1953, but died before reaching the island. A second consignment of twelve birds from Agalega in 1954 or 1955 were apparently released.

They were common on Egmont in 1905 (Bourne, 1971) where they escaped from captivity (Loustau-Lalanne) and reached Diego Garcia in about 1953. Some were noted on Diego Garcia in 1960 and by 1964 it was one of the commonest birds there. In 1967 flocks of forty to sixty birds were common and the species has remained common on the island to the mid-1970s (Hutson).

Ascension Island. The Common Myna has been introduced and established on Ascension Island (Stonehouse, 1962). Stonehouse says that they numbered some 400 birds when he visited the island.

Solomon Islands. The race *A.t. tristis* has been introduced (Galbraith and Galbraith, 1962) to the Solomons and appears to be well established (Cain and Galbraith, 1956 and 1957) on the Russell Islands, Guadalcanal and on the Olu Malau Islands (Galbraith and Galbraith). French (1957) records them breeding on the Olu Malau Islands.

New Caledonia. the Common Myna has been introduced into New Caledonia, where it is commonly found in gardens, villages and cultivated areas (Delacour, 1966).

New Hebrides. Mayr (1945) reports that the Common Myna has possibly been introduced to some of the islands in this group.

Fiji. The Common Myna was probably introduced to Fiji between 1890 and 1900 (Parham, 1954), although it could have been considerably earlier in about 1876 (Wood and Wetmore, 1926), to control insect pests of sugar cane.

Wood and Wetmore have suggested that dissemination of the species was assisted by the fact that the East Indian population carried them about as pets in cages from which they frequently escaped or were released. They were common there in the 1920s but many were killed on Viti Levu (Lyon-Field, 1938) in the hurricane of 1931. However, they were common again in the early 1950s (Parham).

Stoner (1923) found them on the island of Makaluva some 6 km (3.7 miles) from Suva in about 1923 and Blackburn (1971) later indicates that they occurred in the coastal villages of the island of Taveuni in the early 1970s.

The Common Myna is now found on the four main islands in the group (Mercer, 1966) and on many of the smaller islands (Watling, 1978). According to Gorman (1975) they were common in Suva in the mid-1970s. Watling reports that in Fiji they live in close association with man and that the largest concentrations occur in urban and suburban areas.

Society Islands. The Common Myna was introduced to Tahiti between 1908 and 1915 (Holyoak, 1974) to destroy wasps (Bruner, 1972). The Whitney Expedition (in 1920-21) found them common on Tahiti and Moorea, but absent from the other islands.

In 1972 Holyoak found them to be common on Tahiti, Moorea and Raiatea, probably present on Huahine, but absent from Bora Bora. He was in some doubt as to their presence on the other islands. At this time they were common in the villages and towns, on all the cultivated country, in the valleys, and in the mountains up to one thousand metres.

Samoan Islands. According to Dhondt (1976) the Common Myna has recently arrived on the island of Upolu where it can be seen occasionally in small flocks. He indicates that they have been present there at least since 1972 and on his visit he observed several small groups in the Apia area.

In 1978, Watling (1978) could find no trace of Common Mynas, however in several localities he observed Jungle Mynas *(A. fuscus).* Watling is familiar with both species on Fiji and it seems that it is the Jungle species which is now establised on Upolu.

Cook Islands. The Common Myna was introduced from New Zealand to Rarotonga in the 1920s in the hope of controlling agricultural insect pests (Syme, 1975).

The species is now established throughout the cultivated parts, valleys and also on tidal flats and airfields of the island of Rarotonga (Turbott, 1977).

Hawaiian Islands. In 1865 Dr W. Hillebrandt introduced the Common Myna to the Hawaiian Islands to help keep down various insect pests such as army worms which were damaging pastures on some islands (Caum, 1933; Munro, 1960). The species was self introduced to Niihau in the 1870s (Fisher, 1951).

According to Caum the Myna was abundant in Honolulu by 1879, and McGregor (1902) records that it was the most conspicuous bird in about 1902. They are now established abundantly on all the main islands in the chain and are widespread in towns and agricultural lands (Peterson, 1961; Berger, 1972). Frings and Frings (1965) estimated that there were roosting populations of more than 4000 birds in two trees in Honolulu.

USA. In 1949 the Common Myna was said to be established and breeding in the Los Angeles area of California, but there appear to be no recent records of them there.

Prior to this report two birds had been found breeding there in July 1930 (Willett, 1930) and one of these was shot (Miller, 1930). Miller indicates that some six birds were collected in the Los Angeles area at this time.

England. According to Goodwin (1956) numerous cage birds escape or are released in the wild in England. A Common Myna was a resident in London for about four years some time prior to 1956.

DAMAGE
In southern Asia Common Mynas are not generally considered to be pests. They are to a large extent commensals of man and are frequently abundant around towns where they roost communally. They feed on fruits, berries and insects, but do not appear to affect cultivated fruits much. According to Sengupta (1968) and Ali and Ripley (1968-74) the species is a friend of the farmer doing immense good by eating many insect pests, but Ali and Ripley also state that they often cause damage to orchard fruit and standing cereal crops. Because of their fruit-eating habits the species is regarded by many as being a potential pest in areas where they have been introduced.

In Australia, in Queensland particularly, the Myna

has already been accused of becoming a pest to fruit, especially figs (Walker, 1952). In some areas it nests in the walls and ceilings of buildings thus becoming a nuisance (White, 1946).

In the Hawaiian Islands, bird malaria has been detected in this species and they are also subject to extensive parasitic infection. Bird mites *(Ornithonyssus bursa)* often become annoying when they invade houses and offices from their nests (Berger, 1972). Phillips (1928) records that the Common Myna had become a pest in the Hawaiian Islands prior to 1928.

More recently in the Hawaiian Islands it is indicated that the Common Myna may be a significant predator on the eggs of the Wedge-tailed Shearwater *(Puffinus pacificus).* Byrd (1979) found that on Kilauea Point, Kauai about 23% of the eggs laid by this species in his study area were destroyed by Mynas. He recommended that an annual control programme be instigated against the Common Myna.

On St Helena they are reported to cause considerable damage to fruit orchards (Gooders, 1969) and in Tahiti to eat cultivated fruits (Holyoak, 1974). They frequent the markets and streets of Papeete, Tahiti and steal food from the tables of some of the hotels. Holyoak says that the inhabitants once ate the bird, but that this habit has now disappeared. He says that it appears that they have an evil influence on the indigenous bird species because of the competition for food and because they are also a carrier of avian malaria. In Fiji as early as the 1920s (Stoner, 1923) they were said to have done little towards the control of insects and had lost many friends because of their habit of nesting in chimneys and on the roofs of houses.

JUNGLE MYNA
(Buffalo Myna)
Acridotheres fuscus (Wagler)

DISTINGUISHING CHARACTERISTICS
23-24 cm (9.2-9.6 in). 72-98 g (2.54-3.46 oz)
Upper parts dark greyish brown; head black, with short black crest; throat and breast dark grey, shading to white on under tail-coverts; wings dark brown with white patch; bill yellow-orange, with deep blue base; tail black with white tip.
(Note: *A.f. javanicus* is considered by some to be a separate species.)
Robinson and Chasen, 1927-39, vol.1, p.282 and pl.25 (lower); vol.4, p.364.
Ali and Ripley, vol.5, 1968-74, pp.183-187 and pls.59, fig.10, opp. p.128 and 58, fig.3, opp. p.80.

GENERAL DISTRIBUTION
Southern and South-east Asia: from northern India, Nepal, Assam, north-eastern Burma and southern China, south to the Malay Peninsula and Indochina; also Java and the southern peninsula of Sulawesi.

INTRODUCED DISTRIBUTION
Introduced successfully in Singapore, the Fijian Islands and Western Samoa; probably introduced successfully to Sumatra, and possibly successfully to the Andaman Islands. Introduced unsuccessfully to Christmas Island, Indian Ocean (disappeared!).

GENERAL HABITS
Status: fairly common. *Habitat:* forest edges, open country, grasslands, cultivation, paddy fields, cities

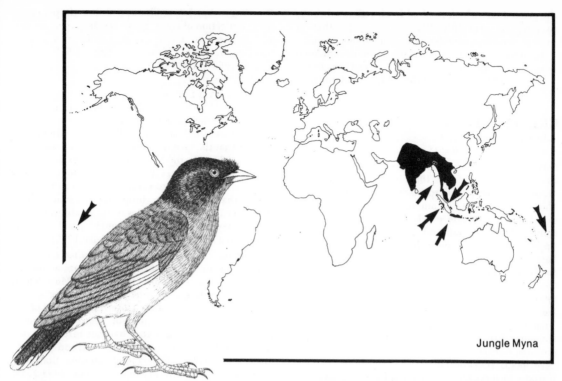

Jungle Myna

and gardens. *Gregariousness:* pairs or small parties, and flocks of 10-30 or more birds. *Movements:* sedentary, but locally migratory (?) in some areas. *Foods:* insects including grasshoppers; also wild figs, lantana and other fruits and berries, and flower nectar. *Breeding:* Feb-July; May (Singapore); 2 successive broods; colonial. *Nest:* collection of twigs, roots, grass and rubbish, stuffed in a tree hole. *Eggs:* 3, 4-6.

Robinson and Chasen, 1927-39, vol.1, p.282; vol.4, p.364.

Ali and Ripley, 1968-74, vol.5, pp.183-187.

NOTES ON INTRODUCTIONS

Singapore. A few pairs of the Jungle Myna established themselves on Singapore Island during the second World War, and during recent years have become plentiful and common on some parts of the island (Gibson-Hill, 1949 and 1950). Chasen (1925) indicates that they may have been introduced there before 1925 and it may well be that the colony dates from this period. Gibson-Hill (1952) says that the race *A.f. javanicus* presumedly established itself on the island from the escape of caged birds. They are still well established and common there (Ward, 1968), and Medway and Wells (1976) report that they have extended their range into and around Johore Bahru and to Pinang Island.

Sumatra. The Jungle Myna, *A.f. javanicus* has been introduced to Sumatra probably from Java (Delacour, 1947; Ripley, 1961) but no details of the introduction could be found.

Christmas Island. The race *A.f. javanicus* has been introduced to Christmas Island, Indian Ocean (Ripley, 1961). Chasen (1933) indicates that the species was introduced in about 1904, but thereafter disappeared.

Andaman Islands. Beavan (1867) records that Colonel R. C. Tyler introduced the Jungle Myna from Burma to Port Blair in the time of the convict settlement there. They were apparently thriving in the area in 1867 and some had been seen on Ross Island.

Fiji. Most of the early references to Mynas in the Fijian Islands allude to the Bank Myna *(A. ginginianus)*, however it now seems certain that these references referred to the Jungle Myna.

The introduction is said to have been made to Fiji between 1890 and 1900 (Parham, 1954) for the purpose of combating army worms (Mercer, 1966). Lyon-Field (1938) says that it is thought that the birds came from Burma, but that there is no proof of this. He reports that at this time there were many attempts to catch and transport large numbers of them to Vanua Levu and other islands, apparently with little success.

The Jungle Myna is now common on Viti Levu and also on Nukulau Island (Blackburn, 1971).

Samoa. In January 1978 the Jungle Myna was found established on Upolu in Western Samoa (Watling, 1978). Previously the Common Myna had been reported from Upola (Dhondt 1976) but this now seems to have arisen through error. The Jungle Myna is not common on Upolu but found in small flocks in the suburbs and environs of Apia (Watling, 1978).

DAMAGE

The introduced race of the Jungle Myna *(A.f. javanicus)* may be replacing the Malay Peninsula race *(A.f. torquatus)* in Singapore (Gibson-Hill, 1952) where they are probably inter-breeding (Ward, 1968).

In Fiji, Turbet (1941) says that they are of undoubted benefit to agriculturists and Parham (1954) records that they cause no damage. However, according to a recent study by Watling (1975), both *fuscus* and *A. tristis* are involved in causing damage in Fiji. He reports a serious case involving attacks on ground nuts when the plumules are emerging from the ground and which resulted in an estimated thirty to forty per cent loss. Watling concludes that at present damage is rare, but potentially more serious.

In India, the Jungle Myna is not a well documented pest, but Ali and Ripley (1968-74) record that in the South India hills they do considerable local damage to the fruits in orchards.

CRESTED MYNA
(Chinese Crested Myna)
Acridotheres cristatellus (Linnaeus)

DISTINGUISHING CHARACTERISTICS
22.5-26.3 cm (9-10.5 in). 108-140 g (3.81-4.94 oz)
Mainly blackish; underparts washed grey; wings black; base of primaries and outer secondaries white, forming a large white patch; low blackish crest on front of forehead; tail and under tail-coverts black, tipped white; bill pale yellowish, rose-coloured at base.
La Touche, 1925-34, 2 vols.
Cheng, 1963, pp.614-615 and pl.45, no.76.

GENERAL DISTRIBUTION
South-east Asia: from Bangladesh, Burma and Thailand, east to central and southern China, Hainan, Taiwan and south to Indochina and southern Burma.

INTRODUCED DISTRIBUTION
Introduced successfully in Malaysia (Pinang Island), the Philippines (Manila), and Canada (British Columbia). Introduced, probably unsuccessfully in Japan.

GENERAL HABITS
Status: fairly common; favourite pet and cage bird in China. *Habitat:* plains, cultivated areas, fields, villages, gardens and orchards. *Gregariousness:* small flocks, often of 8, but up to 20 birds. *Movements:* sedentary. *Foods:* insects, worms, slugs, snails, mussels, fruits, nuts, grains, roots and leaves.

Breeding: Apr-July (China); 2 broods per year.
Nest: collection of trash, grass, weeds, paper, rootlets and feathers, in a tree cavity, crevice in a wall or building, or in other birds' nests. *Eggs:* 4-6, 7.
Cheng, 1963, pp.615-617.
Reilly, 1968, p.377.

NOTES ON INTRODUCTIONS
Malaysia. The Crested Myna has been a permanent resident in the vicinity of George Town, Pinang Island since 1920 (Gibson-Hill, 1949). Gibson-Hill records that the race *A.c. brevipennis* was present and common there in the late 1940s, but was apparently formerly more numerous. According to him, they have not spread far into rural districts and there is no doubt that the Pinang birds are descended from introduced stock. The species is still established there where they frequent open country, parklands and suburban gardens (Medway and Wells, 1976).

Philippines. The race *A.c. cristatellus* has been introduced and established around Manila, on the island of Luzon (Delacour and Mayr, 1946; Peters, 1962). According to Whitehead (1899) the species was imported by one of the Governors General of the Philippines for the purpose of destroying locusts. Between 1893 and 1896 they had not spread beyond the neighbourhood of Manila. Wood (1924) mentions that McGregor (1920, quoting Blair and Robertson, 1907, *The Philippine Islands 1493-1898,* p.127) records that at least three attempts were made by the Spanish Government between 1849 and 1852 to introduce and establish 'le Martin' in Manila. In 1924 it had still not spread far from the towns around that city.

Japan. The Crested Myna has been introduced and established in Japan (A.O.U., 1957). There appear to be no other records of the species in this country.

Canada and USA. The Crested Myna is believed to have arrived on coastal British Columbia around the

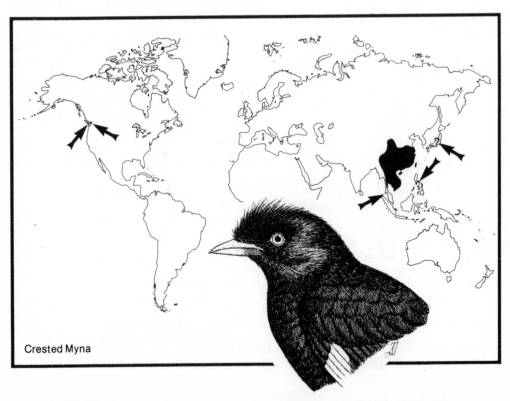

Crested Myna

turn of the century, probably introduced by Oriental immigrants living in Vancouver, or to have accidentally arrived aboard ships (Carl and Guiguet, 1972). Wood (1924) indicates that the first definite report of them was in 1897 when two pairs were found in the city of Vancouver, but says that they were certainly known as early as 1894.

In 1904 the species was reported to be scarce, but between this date and 1920 the population increased rapidly, until they were common during the 1930s (Carl and Guiguet). It was estimated in 1924 that there were some 6000-7000 birds in Vancouver alone (Wood) and by 1927 the total population was estimated to be approximately 20 000 birds (Mackay and Hughes, 1963). By 1960 the population had declined to an estimated 2000-3000 birds which were confined to the immediate vicinity of Greater Vancouver, with the exception of Nanaimo on Vancouver Island (Mackay and Hughes). At present they may have declined still further and are largely confined within the city, but are seen in rural areas around Vancouver and New Westminster (Carl and Guiguet).

Records of Crested Mynas have come from Victoria, Courtenay, Union Bay, Vancouver Island (Carl and Guiguet), Lulu Island, the western parts of the Fraser Delta (Godfrey, 1966) and from Washington and western Oregon in the USA (A.O.U., 1957).

Jewett *et al* (1953) record that the Crested Myna was formerly a rare permanent resident of northwestern Washington in the United States. Kelly (1927) states that they were reported at Bellingham. Twelve birds were noted at Lake Washington in August 1929 and six were seen at Juanita Bay, near Seattle in August 1933 (Jewett *et al*).

The race introduced in Canada appears to be *A.c. cristatellus* (A.O.U.).

DAMAGE

Anderson (1934) reports that the Crested Myna damages cherries, blackberries and apples in Canada. However, the species would now appear to be present only in small numbers and it seems doubtful that it causes much damage.

In the United States it is a prohibited import because it is said to become extremely destructive to fruits and to horticultural crops. Ball (1960) lists several undesirable characteristics for the species. He says that they compete with native species in Canada and indicates that they cause a great deal of agricultural damage within their native range.

La Touche (1925-34) reports that they probably cause some damage to vegetables and fruit in gardens, but are not a devourer of field crops in eastern China. Cheng (1963) says that they are more useful than harmful in China.

HILL MYNA
(Indian Grackle, Grackle)
Gracula religiosa (Linnaeus)

DISTINGUISHING CHARACTERISTICS
25-40 cm (10-16 in). 173-246 g (6.1-8.68 oz)
Glossy jet black; white patch on wings; patches of

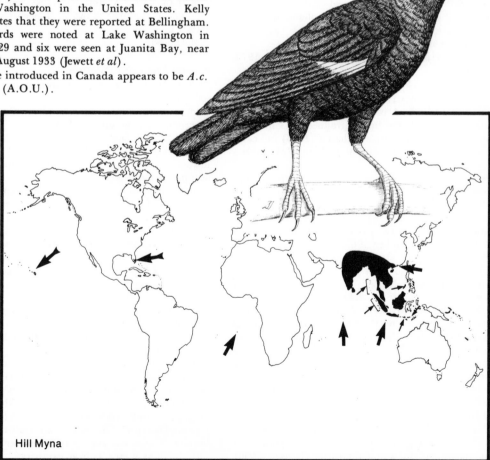

Hill Myna

naked skin and wattles on head, bright yellow; bill orange to red, often with a yellow tip.

Cheng, 1963, pp.618-619 and pl.24, no.87.

Ali and Ripley, vol.5, 1968-74, pp.191-197 and pls.59, fig.5, opp. p.128, and 58, fig.1, opp. p.80.

Avon et al, 1974, pl. p.83.

GENERAL DISTRIBUTION

Southern and South-east Asia: from the Himalayas and northern India, Nepal and Burma east to the extreme south of China, Hainan, and south to Indochina, Malay Peninsula, Sumatra and west Mentawai Islands, Borneo, the Sunda Islands, Palawan, and the Andaman and Nicobar Islands.

INTRODUCED DISTRIBUTION

Introduced, successfully in the Hawaiian Islands and USA; introduced, unsuccessfully on Christmas Island (Indian Ocean). May have been introduced, certainly unsuccessfully on St Helena, the Chagos Archipelago and Hong Kong (escapees?).

GENERAL HABITS

Status: very common; a favourite cage bird in South-east Asia. *Habitat:* hill forest, forest edges, secondary growth, wooded country, field borders and plantations. *Gregariousness:* pairs, small noisy flocks of up to twelve birds after breeding season, occasionally larger flocks; roost communally. *Movements:* sedentary. *Foods:* fruits, berries, insect larvae, ants and termites, and nectar, seeds and other vegetable material; also lizards. *Breeding:* Dec-Oct; Dec-Apr (Malaya); Mar-May (China); 1-2 broods per year (China). *Nest:* collection of grass, leaves and feathers, occasionally lined with twigs, palm fibres and green leaves, stuffed in hollows in trees or buildings. *Eggs:* 2, 3-4.

Cheng, 1963, pp.619-620.

Bertram, *Anim. Behav. Monogr.* vol.3, pt.2, 1970, pp.81-192.

Ali and Ripley, 1968-74, vol.5, pp.191-197.

NOTES ON INTRODUCTIONS

Christmas Island. According to Peters (1962) the race *G.r. religiosa* has been introduced to Christmas Island in the Indian Ocean. Chasen (1933) indicates that the species was introduced in about 1923, but has now disappeared.

Hawaiian Islands. Donaghho (1966) reports that three Hill Mynas escaped from a pet shop in Hawaii in 1960, and five more in 1961. These soon became established in the Upper Manoa Valley. Some twelve birds were noted at the Lyon Arboretum, University of Hawaii in November 1965, one was seen in the Woodlawn area of Manoa Valley in October 1966, and they have also been reported from the State Forestry Division Nursery in Makiki Valley, in Kahana Valley and at the Mokuleia County Park.

No further Hill Mynas were seen from 1969 on until four were observed on the Christmas Bird Count in 1976 (Pyle, 1977). Berger (1972) suggests that they may be established on Oahu, but little appears to be known of them on that island. They may be established on both Kauai and Oahu, but their present status is poorly known (Hawaiian Audubon Society, 1975).

St Helena. It appears as though the Hill Myna may have been introduced on St Helena in 1829 (Melliss, 1870). It was reported to be common in Jamestown and the uplands for a time thereafter (Benson, 1950)

at least until 1870 (Melliss). However, Benson records that there is some confusion as to whether this species or the Common Myna was introduced. The Hill Myna, if introduced, has evidently failed to become permanently established.

Chagos Archipelago. Either the Hill Myna or Common Myna was introduced to this archipelago. Loustau-Lalanne (1962) does not resolve the problem and says that what are probably escaped birds were established on Egmont Atoll. However, it does appear as though the bird established there may be the Common Myna.

USA. The Hill Myna is established locally from Palm Beach County southwards through Dade County in south-east Florida, and breeds there (Owre, 1973). Owre records that they are a popular cage bird stocked by most pet shops throughout the area.

Some Hill Mynas were still present in the Florida area in 1975, as two were reported at West Palm Beach on the Christmas Bird Count in that year (Heilbrun, 1976). According to Gore and Doubilet (1976) the species competes with woodpeckers for nesting cavities in Florida.

Hong Kong. Occasional escapees are found on the island of Hong Kong (King et al, 1975) but the Hill Myna does not appear to have become established permanently there. Webster (1975) records that they are frequently seen at Pokfulam, on the Peak, in some parts of the New Territories in recent years and may well become established before long. Viney (1976) reports that during 1975, one or two were noted at She Shan, one at Victoria Barracks, one at Ho Man Tin, one at Fanling and two on Stonecutters Island.

DAMAGE

None known.

Family: *Passeridae:* Sparrows

37 species in 7 genera; 4 species introduced, 3 successfully

(Note: as this family is generally included in the *Ploceidae* only the sub-family Passerinae [see Peters, 1962] have been included in the *Passeridae* here.)

The success of the House Sparrow as a colonist and an introduced species is well known. It probably now occupies two-thirds or more of the earth's surface and is still spreading in many areas. The species is the most successfully introduced bird and as early as 1899 was termed the 'avian rat'.

Although much has been written about the House Sparrow's economic importance little seems to be done to prevent further expansion of its range.

The Tree Sparrow has not had the success enjoyed by its contemporary, but attempts have not been made to establish them as widely.

The Spanish Sparrow has had success as a colonist or introduction on some Atlantic Ocean islands. Its potential as an invader and as a pest would appear to rival that of the House Sparrow.

The Pegu House Sparrow *(P. flaveolus)* of south-eastern Asia began to colonise the Malay Peninsula from the north probably in the 1930s and 1940s. Ward (1968) indicated that they should soon reach Singapore thus completing colonisation of that region. This species has not been included in the text because it does not appear to have been assisted by introductions or escapes from captivity.

INTRODUCTIONS OF PASSERIDAE

Species	Date introduced	Region	Manner introduced	Reason
(a) Successful introductions				
House Sparrow	late 19th and 20th century	northern Europe and Siberia	colonisation	expansion of agriculture
	1850-81	USA	deliberate	aesthetic and insect control
	about 1930s	Mexico	colonisation from USA	—
	1864 and later	Canada	deliberate and colonisation from USA	—
	about 1974	Guatemala	colonisation from Mexico	—
	1872 or 1873	Argentina	deliberate	insect control
	about 1920	Paraguay	colonisation from Argentina	—
	about 1900	Uruguay	deliberate ?	?
	1905 or 1906 and 1910	Brazil	deliberate	insect control
	1904 and 1915	Chile	deliberate	?
	about 1951	Peru	deliberate ? or colonisation from Chile	—
	1928	Easter Island	deliberate ?	?
	1919	Falkland Islands	ship borne from Uruguay	—
	?	Cuba, Jamaica and St Thomas, West Indies	deliberate ?	?
	1870s	Bermuda	deliberate or colonisation from USA	—
	1871 and ? later	Hawaiian Islands	deliberate	?
	1863-72	Australia	deliberate	aesthetic
	1863-73	Tasmania, Australia	deliberate	—
	about 1939	Norfolk Island	colonisation from Australia or New Zealand	—
	1859-71	New Zealand	deliberate	insect control
	about 1880 or 1910	Chatham Islands	colonisation from New Zealand	—
	about 1907	Campbell Island	colonisation from New Zealand	—
	about 1948	The Snares	colonisation from New Zealand	—
	before 1955	Auckland Island, New Zealand	colonisation from New Zealand	—
	before 1928	New Caledonia	deliberate ?	?
	1890-97 and later	South Africa	deliberate	?
	about 1961	South West Africa	colonisation from South Africa	—
	about 1956	Botswana	colonisation from South Africa	—
	about mid-1950s	Rhodesia	deliberate and colonisation from South Africa	—
	about 1965	Zambia	colonisation from Rhodesia	—
	1955	Moçambique	deliberate and colonisation from South Africa	—

continued

Species	Date introduced	Region	Manner introduced	Reason
	?	Somali Republic	deliberate ?	?
	?	Northern Sudan	?	?
	before 1929 ?	Zanzibar Island	?	?
	about 1879	Archipel des Comores	deliberate ?	?
	?	Amirante Islands	ship borne ?	?
	about 1965	Seychelles	?	?
	about 1859-67	Mauritius	deliberate	?
	?	Réunion	?	?
	?	Rodriguez Island	?	?
	about 1905 ?	Chagos Archipelago	?	?
	about 1960	Açores	deliberate	aesthetic ?
	before 1924 ?	Cape Verde Islands	?	?
Spanish Sparrow	mid-19th century	Canary Islands	colonisation ?	—
	about 1865	Cape Verde Islands	deliberate or colonisation ?	—
	about 1935	Madeira	colonisation ?	—
Tree Sparrow	before 1893-96	Philippines	deliberate	?
	?	Lombok and Ambon, Indonesia ?	?	?
	before 1936 ?	Southern Sulawesi	?	?
	about 1728	Pescadores (Peng-hu)	deliberate	?
	1863-81	Australia	deliberate	?
	1870	USA	deliberate	?
	?	Sardegna	colonisation from Europe	—
	about 1964	Borneo	ship borne	?

(b) Probably successful introductions

Species	Date introduced	Region	Manner introduced	Reason
House Sparrow	before 1957 ?	New Hebrides	?	?
	about 1955	Kenya	?	?
Tree Sparrow	early ?	Singapore	colonisation ?	

(c) Unsuccessful introductions

Species	Date introduced	Region	Manner introduced	Reason
House Sparrow	before 1957 ?	Philippines	?	?
	about 1880	Greenland	deliberate	?
	1870s	Bahamas	deliberate	?
	1976	Papua New Guinea	?	?
	early 20th century ?	St Helena	deliberate	?
	before 1975 ?	South Georgia Island	deliberate	?
Tree Sparrow	1868, 1871	New Zealand	deliberate	?
	19th century ?	Bermuda	deliberate ?	?
Scaly-fronted Weaver	about 1929	St Helena	deliberate	?

HOUSE SPARROW
(English Sparrow, European Sparrow)
Passer domesticus (Linnaeus)
DISTINGUISHING CHARACTERISTICS
14.3-15.5 cm (5.72-6.2 in). 25-37 g (.88-1.3 oz)
Crown, nape and lower back dark grey; lores black; nape through eye brown; white stripe over eye; back brown streaked black; wings brown with a single white bar on middle coverts; throat and breast black; cheeks and sides of neck white; belly whitish or greyish; tail dull brown; bill black. Female: generally lacks as much black on throat; upper parts dusky brown; bill brown.

Witherby *et al*, vol.1, 1938-41, pp.156-160, and pl.17, opp. p.154.
Reader's Digest, p.526 and pl. p.526.

GENERAL DISTRIBUTION
Eurasia and North Africa: from the British Isles, all mainland Europe, and across central Siberia to western Amurland, and south to southern Morocco, Algeria, Tunisia, Egypt, Sudan, Arabia, Iran, India, Sri Lanka and southern Burma.

INTRODUCED DISTRIBUTION

Extended breeding range in Eurasia. Introduced successfully in the USA, Canada, Argentina, Uruguay, Brazil, Chile, Peru, Ecuador, Easter Island, Falkland Islands, Cuba, Hawaiian Islands, Australia, New Zealand, New Caledonia, South Africa, Moçambique, Somali Republic, northern Sudan, Zanzibar, Amirantes, Mauritius, Réunion, Rodrigues, Chagos Archipelago, Açores and Cape Verde Islands (São Vincente) ; colonised successfully from nearby countries, Mexico, Guatemala, Paraguay, Bermuda (?), Norfolk Island and many outlying Australian and New Zealand islands, South West Africa, Botswana, Rhodesia, Zambia and southern Moçambique; probably introduced, successfully in the Archipel des Comores and Seychelles, and possibly introduced successfully in the New Hebrides and in Kenya. Introduced unsuccessfully in Jamaica (died out ?), Bahamas (extirpated), St Helena (died out), Greenland, Western Australia (extirpated), the Philippines, Papua New Guinea (?) and on South Georgia Island.

GENERAL HABITS

Status: extremely common and abundant. *Habitat:* open forest, wooded country, grasslands, cultivated areas, parks, gardens, cities, towns and everywhere there is human settlement. *Gregariousness:* small to enormous flocks. *Movements:* mainly sedentary, but also partially migratory. *Foods:* seeds, grain, flower and leaf buds, plant shoots, fruits, berries, insects including caterpillars, nymphs, grubs, moths, and spiders and food scraps. *Breeding:* all year; 2-3 or more broods per year; Feb-Dec, 3-6 broods per year (India) ; Sept-Jan, 5 or more broods per year (New Zealand) ; all year (Hawaiian Islands) ; spring and summer and at other times (Australia). *Nest:* large, untidy, spherical nest of grass, wool, feathers, etc., stuffed in a tree hole, haystack, ceiling, wall, building, etc; when in a tree usually domed with side entrance. *Eggs:* 2-7; 3-6 (Australia) ; 5-7 (New Zealand) ; 4-7 (Hawaiian Islands).

Summers-Smith, 1963.
Kendeigh and Pinowski, 1973.
Pinowski and Kendeigh, 1977.

NOTES ON INTRODUCTIONS

Eurasia. The House Sparrow has been introduced by man in many places in northern Europe and Siberia (Voous, 1960). The spread northwards up the Norwegian coast reached the Arctic Circle in the 1870s and was almost certainly assisted by ships (Lund, 1956). Shortly after 1930 the Sparrow reached the Faeroe Islands.

In the course of the present century they have rapidly increased in numbers in Siberia, simultaneously with the expansion of agricultural land, and at the same time have extended their range considerably (Southern 1945; Voous, 1960). They travelled up the Ob' River on grain boats and established themselves on the Yamal Peninsula; they reached Alexandrovsk in 1919, following horses and their food, and were found established in Murmansk on the Kola Peninsula in 1923 (Grote, 1933). The eastward spread across Asiatic USSR was largely due to the increase in agriculture and the following of horses. Southern indicates that the eastern limit of the sparrow in 1910 was Irkutsk in the Lake Baykal

region, but by 1932 they were found most of the way to the mouth of the Amur River (to Nikolaievsk). In the 1840s the species also spread southwards with Russian colonisation into the Kazakh area. Voous suggests that the House Sparrow was perhaps originally a bird of the arid regions of south-western Asia.

Greenland. House Sparrows of the race *P.d. domesticus* were introduced to Irigut, Frederikshåb district in about 1880. However, they succumbed after a few years (Salomonsen, 1950).

North America. The first recorded introduction of Sparrows occurred in North America in 1850 when eight pairs were released in Brooklyn, New York, USA to control cankerworms (Wetmore, 1964). Robbins (1973) says that the birds arrived in 1850, but were held in cages and not released until the early spring of 1851. The introduction was made by the directors of the Brooklyn Institute (Roberts, 1960), but the Sparrow failed to become established. About 100 birds were brought out from Europe in 1852 of which fifty were released on arrival at the Narrows and the remaining birds were kept caged and released in 1853 at the Green-Wood Cemetery in Brooklyn, New York (Robbins). The latter introduction is said to have been the first successful release of the House Sparrow in the United States (Silverstein and Silverstein, 1974). Some were also released in Portland, Maine in 1854 and 1858 and a little later at various places including Boston, New York, Philadelphia and in Quebec, Canada (Phillips, 1928).

These initial introductions were followed by numerous others and also by much transplanting of the species from one place to another. Roberts reports that they were introduced in about one hundred cities in the United States and Canada. Most of the early introductions were made for aesthetic reasons or to control insects (Anderson, 1934). Robbins records that it was partly because European immigrants longed for familiar birds and partly because they were thought to be useful in controlling insects. He says that the most often quoted insect pest is the dropworm, larvae of the snow-white linden moth *(Ennomos subsignarius).*

From the original successful introduction the House Sparrow spread quickly. In the first five years they had spread to a radius of 40 km (25 miles), this had reached 80 km (50 miles) after ten years and up to 161 km (100 miles) or more after fifteen years (Robbins, 1973).

One of the largest introductions of House Sparrows occurred in 1869 when 1000 birds from Europe were released in Philadelphia by the civic authorities there (Carl and Guiguet, 1972). Between 1850 and 1881 some 1600 House Sparrows were introduced directly from England, and most were released in the eastern United States. During the same period however, stock from established populations was transferred to many parts of the United States and eastern Canada (Carl and Guiguet). Liberations were made at Maine in 1854 and 1858, Rhode Island in 1858 (Neff, 1937) Boston, Massachusetts in 1858, 1868 and 1869 (Robbins, 1973), Kentucky in 1865-70 (Mengel, 1965), San Francisco in 1871 or 72 (Bryant, 1916), and at Salt Lake City in 1877 (Neff). Records of the establishment of sparrows from 1864 on include:

Quebec, Canada in 1864; Galveston, Texas and New Haven, Connecticut in 1867; Cleveland, Ohio and Philadelphia, Pennsylvania in 1869; Alabama in 1880. They probably invaded British Columbia, Canada shortly after 1886 and were well established in California, northern Utah and Kentucky at this date or shortly after.

Following its introduction the House Sparrow spread faster in America than did the Starling (Wing, 1956) but as Roberts has indicated, it probably had much more help. Eastbrook (1907) records that by 1875 it had spread practically all over the whole area east of the Mississippi. By 1886 it occupied nearly two million five hundred and ninety thousand square kilometres (one million square miles) of territory. In the subsequent year alone it was said to have occupied another one and a quarter million square kilometres (482,525 square miles), and by 1905 practically the whole of the USA was covered (Barrows, 1889; Skinner, 1905) although there were probably still many areas it had not yet colonised. Wing (1943) whose estimate is probably more reliable indicates that the spread was more rapid in the southern and south-central States than in the north. He records that the spread was fastest in the twenty-six to thirty years after its introduction and that by 1940 it occupied an area of nine and a half million square kilometres (3 667 950 square miles).

In the 1930s House Sparrows were recorded as far south as San Luis Potosi and Guadalajara in Mexico (Heilfurth, 1931), and as far north in Canada as the limits of cultivation and along the railroads (Weaver, 1939). By 1950 they had reached Tuxtla Gutierrez in the Chiapas in southern Mexico (Alvarez del Toro, 1950). The House Sparrow is now established from central and north-eastern British Columbia, south-western Mackenzie, north-western and central Saskatchewan, northern Manitoba, northern Ontario, south-western Quebec, Anticosti Island and northern Newfoundland, south to central Baja California and southern Mexico.

Recent work has shown that the House Sparrow population in North America does not differ morphologically from those of the original stock in England and Germany (Selander and Johnston, 1967).

House Sparrow, *Passer domesticus*
(male on left, female on right)

Central America. Land (1970) has indicated that although the House Sparrow had reached the Chiapas in southern Mexico it had not yet invaded Guatemala. However, Peterson and Chalif (1973) report that they had reached Chichicastenango-Alden at least by 1973. Some eight birds were reported at Lake Atitlan, Cerro de Oro (central-southern Guatemala) in late 1974, this population had built up to thirty birds by late 1975 (Heilbrun, 1976) and fifty were recorded there in late 1976 (Heilbrun, 1977).

South America. In 1872 or 1873, E. Bieckert liberated twenty cages of House Sparrows in Buenos Aires, Argentina for the purpose of destroying a psychid moth *Oiketicus kirbyi* (Wetmore and Swales, 1926; Hinton and Dunn, 1967). Although several other importations may have been made, Sparrows first attracted attention in the 1890s and by 1898 were said to be spread over a radius of some '50 leagues' from Buenos Aires. Gibson (1918) observed them in that city in 1890 and records that they had reached Cape San Antonia province in 1916-17.

In 1920 they were reported to be throughout the settled provinces of Argentina and were extending their range rapidly. They had reached Risistencia and Chaco where they were reported to have arrived as early as 1909. In 1926 they were plentiful at Las Palmas, Chaco where they are said to have arrived before 1917. Also at this time they had been recorded as far as Santa Fé and at Concepcion, Corrientes (Wetmore and Swales).

The House Sparrow was noted at Asunción, Paraguay in 1920. Although it was rumoured that it had been brought from Buenos Aires, it is thought to have invaded Paraguay of its own accord.

By 1936 they were common at Lavalle, Buenos Aires and at Cape San Antonia in Argentina. To the south they were common in Bahia Blanca and extended along the railroad as far west as Zapala, Neuquen at the base of the Andes. They were noted at Rio Negro, Puesto Horno, Maquinchao and Huanuluan in 1920-21, and were also at Aimaicha, Tucuman by 1926. Olrog (1959) records that they were throughout Argentina in 1959.

Sparrows in Uruguay are supposed to have come from an importation made at Colonia in about 1900. They were reported as common throughout that country in 1913. Wetmore and Swales record that they were noted at St Vincente, Lazcano, Corrales and Rio Negro in 1926.

In 1919 the House Sparrow was reported to be established in south-eastern Brazil, in Rio de Janeiro and Rio Grande do Sol. Sick (1957) says that they were first introduced to Rio de Janeiro in 1905 and are now found in all the towns in southern Brazil and far into central Brazil. Smith (1973) gives the date of introduction as 1906 and says that they were introduced to combat the mosquito problem in Rio de Janeiro. He adds that Sparrows were taken to the south of Brazil by the Mayor of Bagé in 1910, and rapidly colonised this region.

Sparrows were found at Belém near the mouth of the Amazon in 1928 (Müller, 1967). They may have been blown there, but more than likely they arrived by ship (Sick, 1968). They were however, exterminated. In more recent years the House Sparrow seems to have spread rapidly in Brazil. They

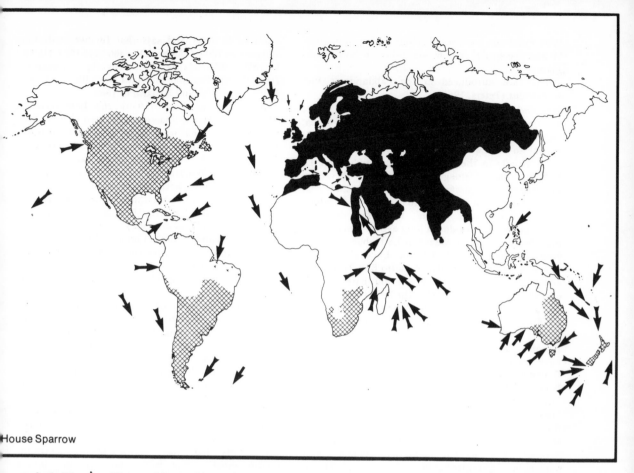

House Sparrow

reached Rio das Mortes, Matto Grosso in 1954, Brasilia (Distrito Federal) in 1959, Teófilo Otoni, Minas Geraise in 1965 and were at Côrrego Bley in Espirito Santo in 1959. Their spread further north has probably been aided by the development of highways in central Brazil after 1957. In 1964-65 they were noted at Imperatriz, Maranhão, at Uruçui and Floriano and also at Rio Parnaiba, Piani. In 1963 a pair were reported from Goiás, east of Brasilia, and they were noticed in Recifé, Pernambuco, probably having arrived by ship. Smith (1973) however, says that they were deliberately released at Recifé to feed on noxious park insects. They were noted at Fortaleza, Ceará on the north-eastern coast in 1968 (Sick, 1968).

Sparrows had spread some 800 km (500 miles) from Brasilia to Imperatriz along the Belém-Brasilia Highway in the space of about six years (Müller, 1967). In 1971, a flourishing colony was observed at Maraba on the Tocantins River in the State of Para, where locals remember a breeding pair as early as 1964. The species is now well situated for potential colonisation along the Transamazon Highway (Smith, 1973).

House Sparrows were introduced to Chile in 1904 by A. Cousino, and again in about 1915 by a Frenchman at Los Andes and Rio Blanco, Aconcagua (Johnson, 1965). Johnson has indicated that they spread rapidly in Chile and in the 1960s occurred from Arica to Tierra del Fuego. By 1951 they were sufficiently widespread in Chile to have invaded southern Peru. They had spread as far north as Callao (Sick, 1968) in that country by 1953 or earlier. Leck

(1973) refers to them as having been introduced in the parks of Lima, Peru in 1951 and says that they have become common and now outnumber the Rufous-collared Sparrow (Zonotrichia capensis).

Since 1969 they have apparently been present in Ecuador (Ortiz Crespo, 1977), but whether this is the result of independent introductions or spread from Peru is not determined. The race introduced in South America appears to have been P.d. domesticus.

Easter Island. The House Sparrow was introduced from Chile to Easter Island in 1928 and has now overrun the island of Pascua (Johnson, Millie and Moffett, 1970; Sick, 1968).

Falkland Islands. Although it has been stated that the House Sparrow arrived in the Falklands in 1936, it did in fact arrive as early as 1919 (Hamilton, 1944). Several (about twenty according to Wood, 1975) arrived as stowaways on four whaling ships from Montevideo, Uruguay in 1919 (Wetmore and Swales, 1926; Bennett, 1926). Hamilton records that there were probably other arrivals at later dates and from the same area.

The House Sparrow was well naturalised in the Falklands by the 1940s, but occurred mainly in the town of Stanley. Some had spread to some farms, up to 48 km (30 miles) away, but did not appear to be well established there (Hamilton). By 1960 they were common in Stanley and had spread westwards to Fitzroy (22.5 km [14 miles]), Darwin (96.6 km [60.38 miles]) and to the north-west had reached Teal Inlet some 48 km (30 miles) away (Cawkell and Hamilton, 1961). In October 1959, three pairs arrived at Carcass Island and remained there; nearby 377

West Point also has a small colony dating from 1958-59 and the species is now established in both places (Wood, 1975).

The race introduced in the Falklands is *P.d. domesticus* (Peters, 1962).

West Indies. The race *P.d. domesticus* (Peters, 1962) has been introduced in the West Indies to Cuba, Jamaica and St Thomas (Bond, 1960), but there appear to be few details. Bond indicates that they occur chiefly in the large towns in Cuba (e.g. La Habana and Camagüey) although they are widespread. On Jamaica they occur in and near Annotto Bay, and on St Thomas occur in Charlotte Amalie. Blake (pers. comm., 1977) says that they were apparently introduced long ago to Jamaica and that they are fairly abundant in La Habana, but not noticeably so elsewhere in Cuba. Lack (1976) says that they were introduced at Annotto Bay, Jamaica in about 1903, spread a short way but have recently declined in numbers, and that the last record of them appears to have been in 1966 (Agar, 1966, *Goose Bd. Cl Broadsh.* 7:22). He failed to find any on his visit in 1971.

Bahamas. Bond (1960) reports that House Sparrows have been introduced to New Providence in the Bahamas, but that they have been extirpated there. Brudenell-Bruce (1975) indicates that this unsuccessful introduction occurred in the 1870s at Nassau. He reports that there are other records of the presence of the species, but that these are probably of strays brought over by boat from Florida, USA.

Bermuda. The race *P.d. domesticus* (Peters, 1962) was either self-introduced (Bourne, 1957) or deliberately liberated (Wingate, 1973) on Bermuda in the 1870s from the American continent (Bourne). The species was apparently abundant everywhere on the island in the mid-1950s and was still so some fifteen years later.

Hawaiian Islands. Some nine House Sparrows were imported from New Zealand and released in Honolulu in 1871, but it is not known if there were any further introductions (Caum, 1933). They were reported to be numerous in Honolulu in 1879 (Caum) and in 1902, but were not noted elsewhere (McGregor, 1902).

The race *P.d. domesticus* (Peters, 1962) is now well established on all the main islands, with perhaps the exception of Niihau (Peterson, 1961), although, it appears more recently that it is also established on that island (Hawaiian Audubon Society, 1975).

Berger (1972) records that the House Sparrow has not had the spectacular success in Hawaii that it has had on the North American continent. It is most common in metropolitan areas and is only found in rural areas around human habitation.

Australia. In 1862, sixty Sparrows were sent to Australia from England in the ship *Suffolk,* but none reached shore as they all died on the voyage (Le Souef, 1958). Le Souef records that in January 1863, nineteen sparrows arrived safely in Victoria, in the *Princess Royal* and a month later 130 small birds, mostly sparrows and chaffinches arrived in the *Relief.* Thirty or forty of these birds were apparently given to a Colonel Champ of Pentridge Stockade, who released them in October 1863. Ryan (1906) records that 120 were released in the Melbourne Botanical Gardens in 1863 and says that further birds were released in 1864 (125 birds), 1866 (?), 1867 (?) and in 1872 (100). Hardy (1928) reports that sparrows from China, England and Java were liberated at St Kilda, Pentridge and Ballarat in 1864.

According to Tarr (1950) the first recorded liberation of House Sparrows appeared to have been in September 1863, when eighty birds were liberated by G. Sprigg. Some were sent to J. O'Shannasy at Boroondara in 1864 and others were released successfully at Ballarat when some six were liberated in 1864. Sparrows were also apparently liberated in South Australia in about 1863 and were recorded at Magill, near Adelaide in 1868, at Mt Gambier as early as 1874 (Condon, 1962), and were present on Kangaroo Island by 1893 (Cooper, 1947).

They were also introduced in Queensland soon after the Victorian introductions in the 1860s. Some were liberated at Brisbane in 1869-70 (Lavery, 1974).

In 1865 two boys found a House Sparrow's nest in a street tree in Warrnambool and were fined five pounds for destroying the eggs (Pescott, 1943). Fourteen birds were released at Ararat in October 1867, and the Victoria Acclimatisation Society announced that House Sparrows had been distributed to Beechworth, Benalla, Kyneton, Ballarat, Castlemaine, Daylesford, Warrnambool, Geelong, St Arnaud, Heathcote, Somerton, Winchelsea, Meredith, Gisborne, Ararat, Portland, Maryborough and the Murray (Tarr, 1950). From all these areas the society had had indications of successful establishment. Some were also sent to Hobart Tasmania (Le Souef) probably from Victoria between 1863 and 1873 in mistake for Tree Sparrows (Littler, 1902).

People were complaining about the release of Sparrows in 1868, as the birds had taken to eating fruit in Collins Street, Melbourne. In 1875 a request to introduce them to Champion Island in Torres Strait was refused (Le Souef). By 1906 Ryan reported that the House Sparrow was well spread in Victoria, southern New South Wales, in South Australia and Tasmania.

About twenty years after their liberation in 1863, the South Australian Government had paid bonuses for 37 875 Sparrow heads at sixpence a dozen and for 209 793 Sparrow eggs at two shillings and sixpence a hundred, in a futile attempt to exterminate them (Condon, 1962).

By the 1950s the House Sparrow was plentiful throughout New South Wales and many areas of Victoria; they were as far north as Rockhampton in Queensland and Marree in South Australia, and as far west as Tarcoola, also in South Australia. They were plentiful in the settled parts of Tasmania and on King and Flinders Islands (Tarr).

The House Sparrow is now established over most of eastern and southern Australia from northern Queensland to western South Australia, Kangaroo Island, Flinders and King Islands in Bass Strait, and the settled parts of Tasmania. They were well established and breeding on Kangaroo Island in 1960 (Wheeler, 1960) and had reached Moth Creek in the south of Tasmania (Green and Mollison, 1961). In Queensland they were first recorded in Atherton in

October 1965 and have now spread to Tolga and Kairi, and are breeding there (Bravery, 1970). More recently they are known to have invaded the Northern Territory across the border from Queensland.

The first record of House Sparrows in Western Australia was in 1897 when five birds were shot near central Perth (Long, 1972). It is thought that these birds probably arrived accidentally by boat as many more have done since that date. They have been recorded to arrive in 1927, 1930, 1946, in 1963-64 and many times in recent years. Most were destroyed by the authorities soon after their arrival.

In about 1914 House Sparrows crossed the border between Western Australia and South Australia at Eucla and reached as far west as Mundrabilla — 58 km (36 miles) west of the South Australian border — in 1918, but died out the following year.

Norfolk Island. According to Williams (1953) the House Sparrow colonised Norfolk in about 1939. It is now abundant in urban areas, around homesteads, and in paddocks on the island (Smithers and Disney, 1969).

New Zealand. Hargreaves (1943) reports that a Mr Brodie had 300 sparrows taken to New Zealand in the vessel *Swordfish* in August 1859 and apparently liberated them. They were reported to be doing well in September of that year, and also to be doing an immense service in devouring caterpillars.

In 1862 the Wanganui Acclimatisation Society introduced some House Sparrows, and in 1865 the Auckland society landed two birds. In 1864 the Nelson society landed one bird alive from a shipment of them (Thomson, 1922). The first birds liberated in the 1860s appear to have been those released in 1867 (forty birds) by the Canterbury society (Thomson, 1922; Oliver, 1930). The Auckland society liberated forty-seven birds in 1867. The Nelson society imported six in 1871 and liberated them at Stoke where they soon increased in numbers. In 1868-69 the Otago society liberated twenty-three Sparrows (Thomson).

The House Sparrow increased in numbers in all the settled parts of New Zealand where it had been introduced. By 1907 it was considered to be a serious pest. In the 1930s they were well distributed in both the North and South Islands.

The race introduced to New Zealand is *P.d. domesticus* (Peters, 1962) and it is now widespread and abundant throughout New Zealand (Wodzicki, 1965; Falla *et al,* 1966) and has reached many of the offshore and outlying islands.

Williams (1953) indicates that they were established on the Chatham Islands in 1910, probably reached Campbell Island around 1907, and the Snares about 1948. By 1930 they had reached the islands of Poor Knights, Little Barrier, Great Barrier, Kapiti and Stewart (Oliver 1930). Oliver (1955) says that they found their own way to the Chathams in about 1880 and by 1955 were on the additional islands of Three Kings, Mokohinau, Mayor, Karewa, Codfish, Snares and Auckland Island. In 1956 Wodzicki (1956) records that they had become established recently on White Island, Bay of Plenty. Williams (1973) records that they breed on the Chathams, Campbell, Auckland and Snares, but not apparently on Three Kings.

New Hebrides. Cain and Galbraith (1957) report the presence of the House Sparrow in the New Hebrides.

New Caledonia. Thomson (1964) reports that the House Sparrow has been introduced to New Caledonia. Apparently Leach (1928) found them there as early as 1928. Delacour (1966) records that they are now extremely common there in towns and villages.

Papua New Guinea. In 1976, four House Sparrows were observed in the grounds of the Central Veterinary Laboratory, Kila Kila, a suburb of Port Moresby (Ashford, 1978). The birds were last seen there in January 1977 and so appear to have been unsuccessful in becoming permanently established.

Philippines. The House Sparrow has apparently been unsuccessfully introduced to Manila, Luzon (A.O.U., 1957), but no details of any releases could be found.

Africa. In South Africa some doubt appears to surround the exact date of what appears to have been a number of releases of sparrows. Summers-Smith (1963) indicates that the race *P.d. indicus* was released at Durban in about 1890 and *P.d. domesticus* in East London at about the same time. Mackworth-Praed and Grant (1963) state that *indicus* was first liberated in 1893 and again in 1897, and that *domesticus* from Surrey, England was liberated at Durban, Natal in 1914. Winterbottom (1966) says that an introduction by Rhodes at Cape Town in 1902 was 'frustrated'. Harwin and Irwin (1966) quote him as stating that the East London releases were in 1907, but to later state the date as in 1927. Harwin and Irwin observe that Courtenay-Latimer gave the date of release there as late as 1930. They say that Clancey more correctly suggests that in all probability the Durban introductions arose from the release of birds by Indians at the end of the nineteenth century, and were of the opinion that the East London population resulted from the release of cage birds imported from Durban. They suggest, however, that the latter assumption is unlikely because of the presence of *domesticus* there.

By the 1950s the House Sparrow had reached Fort Beaufort, King Williamstown, East London, the Butterworth area and in Natal was at Nylstroom, Pretoria, Johannesburg and the Bethlehem areas and southern Zululand (Mackworth-Praed and Grant, 1955-63; Cave, 1955). Harwin and Irwin say that after reaching Bethlehem in 1949 the House Sparrow population in South Africa underwent an explosion. This resulted in the species spreading some 1600 km (994 miles) in three different directions — south-west to Cape Peninsula, north-west to Great Namaqualand and north to Zambia. They record that the Sparrow took some fifty years to colonise Natal and then in the space of some three or four years colonised the whole of Orange Free State and the southern and central Transvaal. By 1959 they had reached Springfontein, Bloemfontein and Kroonstad in Orange Free State (Markus, 1960). In 1952 they were recorded at Nylstroom and the following year had reached Northam, some 113 km (70 miles) to the west. They were observed at Waterval Boven in 1953, at Mankiana in Swaziland in 1954 (Long, 1959), at Skukuza in Kruger National Park in 1957 (Wetmore, 1957), at Letaba in 1959 (van Bruggen, 1960), at Shingwedsi in north-eastern Transvaal in 1961 and were present as far north as Mafeking in 1956 or earlier (Cole, 1958). They are recorded from Port Nolloth in 1962 and from Olifantshoek and Kuruman in the northern Cape also in 1962 (Clancey, 1963) and at Cape Town by 1964. In South West Africa (Namibia) the first record of the House Sparrow appears to have been at Grunan in 1961 (Udys, 1962). By 1968 they had reached Swakopmund, Gobabeb, Etemba and Gobabis, and by May 1969 were at Heliordor near Otavi and still spreading northwards (Winterbottom, 1971).

In Botswana the House Sparrow was established at Lobatse by 1956, at Pitsani in 1958, Ramah since 1956 or earlier, Gaberone by 1960, and was present at Molepolole, Palapye and Mahalapye in 1958. To the north they were reported from Francistown in 1958 (Vernon, 1962) and also to be on the Botswana side of the Tuli Circle in 1963 (Harwin and Irwin). Harwin and Irwin report that as the species was also present across the Rhodesian border at Plumtree in 1960 or before, the spread indicates a westerly dispersal from adjacent Transvaal. The Sparrow had also been recorded at such remote desert stations as Lothlekane in 1964 and at Rakops on the Botletle River in the same year. Harwin and Irwin say that the date of the first appearance of the Sparrow in Rhodesia may never be known. It was certainly being kept in captivity by aviculturists in the mid-1950s, but there is little evidence to show that artificial releases played any part in its spread. A few birds were apparently imported from Britain and released, but do not seem to have had any effect upon the population. Winterbottom says that the northward spread was assisted by an introduction at Salisbury, but gives no other details. According to Harwin and Irwin they were at Bulawayo in 1956 or earlier, and some were released in Salisbury in 1957 but were still confined to the release point in 1962.

The following dates give some indication of the spread of the House Sparrow in Rhodesia. They were at Gwelo in 1959, Plumtree in 1960, Essexvale, Nyamandhlovu, Somabula, Que Que and Karoi in 1961, Gwanda, Lupane, Dett, Wankie, Bannockburn, Gutu, Selukwe, Beatrice and Marandellas in 1962, Bembesi, Filabusi, Triangle, Sinoia, Banket, Mtoroshanga, Rusape and at Umtali in 1963, Belingwe, West Nicholson, Gatooma, Enkeldoorn, Shabani, Sipolilo, Inyanga, Forbes, Odzi, Chipinga and Hippo Valley in 1965. At this time, Harwin and Irwin concluded that they were throughout Rhodesia, but possibly patchily distributed in some localities.

There appear to be no records of the House Sparrow in Zambia until 1965, when a permanent foothold was gained at Livingston and they appeared at Kalomo and Lusaka. Harwin and Irwin suggest that they colonised Zambia from Rhodesia.

The race *P.d. domesticus* was introduced to Lourenço Marques, Moçambique from Portugal in 1955 (da Rosa Pinto, 1959). Harwin and Irwin record that the status of the House Sparrow within Moçambique is poorly known. They suggest that the birds invading Sul do Save in southern Moçambique are of the race *indicus* which probably reached there from Swaziland at about the same time the nominate race was being introduced at Lourenço Marques.

House Sparrows were reported to have reached the Rhodesian border at Malvernia in 1960 and it now appears that they have colonised at least southern Moçambique.

In other parts of Africa the race *P.d. niloticus* (?) has been introduced to Berbera, Somali Republic (Mackworth-Praed and Grant, 1960; Peters, 1962). The race *P.d. bactrianus* (Peters) and/or *P.d. indicus* (Mackworth-Praed and Grant) and possibly other races have been introduced in the northern Sudan, where they are now a common resident from Wadi Halfa to about Renk. They have been seen in the Kosti area of Khartoum (Khatim, pers. comm., 1962). The House Sparrow may also have been introduced to Mombasa on the Kenya coast (A.O.U., 1957; Mackworth-Praed and Grant, 1955-73), but details are lacking. They appear to be fairly well established in most of these areas.

Zanzibar Island. The race *P.d. indicus* appears to have been introduced on this island (Peters, 1962). In 1929 it was confined to the town of Zanzibar (Vaughan, 1930), but had spread throughout the island by the mid-1940s (Pakenham, 1943-45).

Archipel des Comores. According to Benson (1960) *P.d. arboreus* was recorded in the Comores in 1879. The exact identity of the race on Grande Comore presents some confusion. Besides *arboreus,* Mackworth-Praed and Grant (1963) list the race as *indicus* and Peters (1962) claims that both *indicus* and *rufidorsalis* have been introduced there. Watson *et al* (1963) record that *arboreus* is common on Grande Comore, around human settlement on Mohéli, and on the isles of Pamanzi near Mayotte.

Amirante Islands. Gaymer *et al* (1969) report that House Sparrows are common on Alphonse and D'Arros islands in the Amirantes. Penny (1974) says that they were presumedly introduced there from Africa, probably by accident in a shipload of rice. He records that they breed freely on Desroches, Resource, St Joseph, D'Arros, Alphonse and probably other islands in the group.

Seychelles. The House Sparrow has recently been reported from Port Victoria in the Seychelles by Gaymer *et al* (1969), who suggest that the race seen may be *arboreus* as occurs in the Comores. Penny (1974) observed a flock of twenty birds behind the Post Office in Port Victoria in 1965 and suggests that this appears to be the first record of House Sparrows in the Seychelles.

Mauritius. The race *P.d. indicus* has been successfully established on Mauritius (Mackworth-Praed and Grant, 1963; Peters, 1962). Rountree *et al* (1952) say that they were introduced in about 1859-67 from India, and are widespread and common there. More recently, Benedict (1957) and Staub (1976) indicate that they are still an abundant and common species there.

An early story of how the House Sparrow reached the island, commonly quoted in the early 1900s, is related by Meinertzhagen (1912): a British soldier is said to have brought a pair of sparrows out from home to Mauritius and it was his wish that they be liberated when he died. The story now seems unlikely particularly as the race reported established is *indicus.*

Réunion. The race *P.d. indicus* has been successfully

established on Réunion (Peters, 1962). Both Watson *et al* (1963) and Staub (1976) record that the species is common there.

Rodrigues. The race *P.d. indicus* has been established successfully on the island of Rodrigues (Mackworth-Praed and Grant, 1963; Peters, 1962), where it is now common and has reached most of the offshore islands (Gill, 1967).

Chagos Archipelago. Bourne (1971) reports that the House Sparrow was recorded on Peros Banhos and Salomon in this archipelago in 1905, and that the Percy Sladen Trust Expedition were informed that they had been introduced there from Mauritius. Loustau-Lalanne (1962) records that they are still common on these islands, but do not occur on Diego Garcia.

St Helena. Benson (1950) refers to twenty-six 'London sparrows' which were introduced to St Helena in the early part of this century, but which died out and did not establish themselves.

Açores. House Sparrows were introduced to Terciera by soldiers from the continent in about 1960 (Bannerman and Bannerman, 1966). They are now breeding there and slowly spreading.

Cape Verde Islands. Bannerman and Bannerman (1968) say that details of the introduction of House Sparrows to these islands is unknown, but it was presumedly prior to 1924. Bourne (1966) collected specimens of them there in 1924 and suspected that they had been brought to the islands by cargo vessels from Europe. They were apparently common in the centre of the town of Mindelo, São Vincente in 1965 and appear to occur only on that island.

South Georgia. The House Sparrow was apparently introduced to South Georgia island where it failed to become established (Watson, 1975).

DAMAGE

Before the 1960s the largest single effort at determining the status of Sparrows as pests appears to have been that by Southern (1945). He reviewed most of the data on the economic importance of House Sparrows throughout the world until that time. He concluded that it seems probable that the Sparrow does harm in arable areas, and possibly also in other agricultural land and town premises, when these are adjacent to arable land and/or when the birds reach a certain density.

It is generally conceded in Europe that the House Sparrow can cause serious damage to wheat and other cereals at harvest time. They will eat garden vegetables as they appear above the soil in spring time, dig up newly sown seeds, eat currants, gooseberries, fruit buds and block drain and water pipes with nesting materials. They are often linked with the Bullfinch with regard to bud damage of fruit trees. However, in many areas of Europe they are said to do much good by the control of insect pests in cultivated areas.

As an introduced species the House Sparrow appears to be less liked. Much has been written about its economic importance in America. Here, it appears that they became a pest about twenty years after their introduction. They have been reported to cause damage to grain, sorghum and fruit crops, and are pests in canteens, food depots and stores. They block gutters and drain pipes with their nest materials, thus causing damage to buildings. They displace at least some indigenous insectivorous birds, distribute poultry cestodes and nematodes, and are general nuisances by causing contamination with their droppings.

Much the same situation pertains in Australia where the first voice was raised against them in about 1868. At this time, they were apparently attacking fruit in Collins Street, Melbourne. They are occasional pests to wheat crops, cause damage to garden produce and fruits, and also cause minor damage such as the defacement of buildings and by blocking downpipes. In Queensland and Victoria they sometimes become an economic problem by consuming food in cage poultry sheds.

In New Zealand the House Sparrow is accused of being a pest to both fruit and grain. A survey conducted by Dawson and Bull (1966) revealed that such fruit as strawberries, grapes, apples, raspberries, cherries, pears, plums and peaches were affected. The buds of such fruit trees as peaches, apples and nectarines were also destroyed by them, but most damage was caused to grapes and peach tree buds. Dawson (1970) attempted to estimate the grain loss due to House Sparrows in New Zealand and reported that it averaged about 5%, but was as high as 20% in a few crops in the areas he examined.

In other parts of the world where they have been introduced, the reputation of the House Sparrow is no better. They are accused of being a pest wherever they have become established.

Frequently raised is the fact that House Sparrows displace indigenous species. In North America they have been accused of displacing the Cliff Swallows *Petrochelidon albifrons* (Stoner, 1939; Buss, 1942) and *P. pyrrhonota* (Samuel, 1969). Buss showed in Wisconsin that with the destruction of House Sparrows the Cliff Swallows increased from 1000 to 2000 birds in some thirty-eight years. Also in North America, it has been claimed that numbers of the Purple Finch *(Carpodacus purpureus)* declined as the House Sparrow spread across that country (Wetmore, 1964). In South America House Sparrows are reported to be competitors of the Saffron Finch *(Sicalis flaveola),* the Rufous-collared Sparrow *(Zonotrichia capensis)* (Escalante, pers. comm., 1976) and the Hornero *(Furnarius leucopus)* (Burger, 1976).

The House Sparrow has also been implicated in the spread of a disease affecting man. In Brazil, Smith (1973) says that they may assist in the spread of Chagas' Disease, an infection which is sometimes fatal to man. Sparrows in São Paulo State were found to be carrying the first instar nymphs of *Triatoma sordida* (a known vector of Chagas) in their feathers. These nymphs can easily be picked up from around nests and carried from house to house.

In 1965 great interest was revived in the damage caused by sparrows and other granivorous species in Europe and other countries by the Institute of Ecology of the Polish Academy of Science. Under the auspices of the International Biological Programme experts from many countries contributed to investigations on the importance of granivorous birds in the flow of energy through the ecosystem of man (see Kendeigh and Pinowski, 1973). The final results of these investigations (see Pinowski and Kendeigh, 1977) have given economic ornithologists a valuable reference for years to come. The wholesale poisoning of such species as sparrows and starlings is questioned. It is suggested that in examining their relative importance that both economic and aesthetic values be included and that both quantitative and abstract parameters be considered when determining the nature of the impact of such species. It is not denied that they do cause damage, but it is suggested that the cost-benefit of control programmes should be examined more thoroughly and not restricted to the perhaps small region where such damage may be occurring.

Probably, the role of the House Sparrow will continue to be debated for many years to come. It is, however, an unwelcome guest when in large numbers and undoubtedly cannot be considered a truly beneficial introduction anywhere.

SPANISH SPARROW
Passer hispaniolensis (Temminck)

DISTINGUISHING CHARACTERISTICS
15 cm (6 in). 18-33 g (.63-1.16 oz)
Crown, neck and wing shoulders brown; mantle black, with buff streaks, rump grey and black; white stripe over eye; black stripe through eye; sides of face and neck white; a broad white wing bar; chin to chest black; sides of flanks streaked black and white; centre of breast to under tail whitish; bill brown, yellowish below and at base. *Female:* indistinguishable from female House Sparrow.
Ali and Ripley, vol.10, 1968-74, pp.68-69 and pl.107, fig.11, opp. p.128.

GENERAL DISTRIBUTION
Southern Europe and North Africa to southern USSR: from southern Spain, Sardegna, Corse, Sicilia, Italy, Greece and Turkey, east to the Chinese border in southern USSR; in North Africa from northern Morocco and Algiers, Tunisia, extreme north-eastern Libya and parts of the Middle East. In winter to North Africa (north of the Sahara), and south to the Sudan, northern Arabia, parts of south-western Asia and north-western India.

INTRODUCED DISTRIBUTION
Introduced to or colonised successfully the Canary Islands, Cape Verde Islands and Madeira.

GENERAL HABITS
Status: common locally in some areas; appear to be extending their range in North Africa. *Habitat:* thorn scrubs, low shrub and thickets bordering water courses, plantations, olive groves and towns. *Gregariousness:* small to large foraging flocks, and enormous flocks at roosts. *Movements:* mainly migratory, but hybrid *(domesticus* x *hispaniolensis)* populations sedentary. *Foods:* grain, seeds and insects. *Breeding:* Apr-June (Tunisia), Feb-Apr (Canary Islands); colonial; 1-2 clutches per year. *Nest:* globular structure, with side entrance, in a tree, bush, building and occasionally a rock crevice. *Eggs:* 4-5.
Voous, 1960, p.262.
Gavrilov, *J. Bombay nat. Hist. Soc.* vol.60, 1963, pp.301-317.
Ali and Ripley, vol.10, 1968-74, pp.68-69.

NOTES ON INTRODUCTIONS
Canary Islands. Lack and Southern (1949) say that the Spanish Sparrow arrived in the Canary Islands only in the middle of the nineteenth century, and it is argued that its passage there was assisted by man, although there is no evidence for this. Bannerman (1963) records that they have increased their range in the Canaries since the 1850s. He says that they were formerly found only on Fuerteventura and Lanzarote (c. 1820-30), spread to Gran Canaria prior to 1856, and arrived on Tenerife between 1871 and 1887

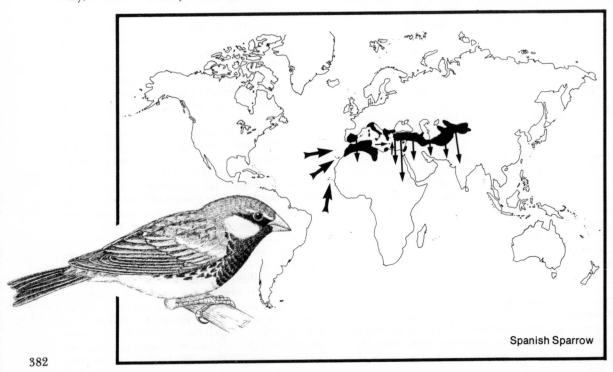

Spanish Sparrow

(probably about 1880) where they were probably introduced deliberately. Meade-Waldo (1893) reported that they had failed to become established, but in 1905 von Thanner found them common at Santa Cruz. In more recent years they have spread to both La Palma and Gomera (Cullen, 1949) and now occur on Gran Canaria, Tenerife, La Palma, Gomera, Fuerteventura and Lanzarote in the group.

Cape Verde Islands. The Spanish Sparrow was possibly introduced to the Cape Verdes in about 1865, as Keulemans (1866) found them on São Nicolau and São Tiago at this date. Exactly how the species arrived on the islands is not known. In 1898 (Barboza du Bocage) they were found to be on Brava and they apparently had reached Fogo, Boa Vista (Fea, 1898-99) and also Maio (Alexander, 1898).

The species apparently died out on Brava before 1951, but has now colonised all the inhabited islands (Bourne, 1955) including São Nicolau, Boa Vista, São Tiago and Fogo (Bannerman, 1953). Bourne (1966) found them abundant on São Vincente in 1951 and says that they were still abundant around Mindelo in 1964.

Madeira. Spanish Sparrows have been self-introduced to Madeira (Bannerman, 1965). They were unknown there prior to 1935, but in this year following continuous easterly winds, were found at various places on the island. They are now well established in Funchal and have spread in both directions along the coast, but appear to be increasing only slowly in numbers.

DAMAGE

In North Africa, where it is possibly extending its range, the Spanish Sparrow has in the past damaged grain crops in Dongola. There have been no recent large-scale emigrations of the species into the Sudan and hence little crop damage (Khatim, pers. comm. 1962). Prior to 1930, at least, the species was most destructive to grain and young green crops in areas of Upper Egypt (Meinertzhagen, 1930).

With the House Sparrow it causes the most damage of any birds to grain crops in the USSR (Falkenstein, pers. comm. 1962). Gavrilov (1961) says that they are a serious pest of grain crops in southern Kazakhstan, and large-scale poisoning and nest destruction are resorted to in an effort to control them. In the late 1950s or early 1960s some 1.8 million were destroyed near Frunze, southern USSR (Abdulali, pers. comm., 1962).

In the Canary Islands the Spanish Sparrow has flourished in the vicinity of houses and has ousted the indigenous Rock Sparrow *(Petronia petronia)* from some areas. On some of the islands it is eaten for food and this is said to compensate for its depredations on crops there (Bannerman, 1953 and 63). In the Cape Verde Islands it threatens to oust the indigenous Rufous-backed Sparrow *(Passer iagoensis)* (Voous, 1960).

TREE SPARROW

Passer montanus (Linnaeus)

DISTINGUISHING CHARACTERISTICS

11.6-15 cm (4.64-6 in). 17-27 g (.6-.95 oz)
Crown and back of head chestnut; lores, line beneath eye to above ear-coverts, chin and throat black; ear-coverts white, with black patch; neck almost surrounded by white collar; upper parts brown, streaked black; underparts whitish or ashy; rump, upper tail-coverts and tail buffish brown; wing with two white bars; bill brown or greyish.

Witherby *et al,* vol.1, 1938-41, pp.160-163 and pl.17, opp. p.154.

Cheng, 1963, pp.810-812 and pl.29, no.112.

GENERAL DISTRIBUTION

Eurasia: from the British Isles, Scandinavia, northern USSR, north-central Siberia, Sakhalin, southern Kuriles and Japan, south to the Iberian Peninsula, Sicilia, Greece, northern Turkey, northern Iran, Afghanistan, northern India, Burma, Malay Peninsula, Indochina, Greater Sundas, southern China, Hainan, Taiwan, and the Ryūkyū Islands.

INTRODUCED DISTRIBUTION

Introduced successfuly in the Philippines (Luzon and Cebu), Marianas (Saipan, Rota, Guam), Lesser Sunda Islands (Ambon and Lombok), southern Sulawesi, Pescadores (Penghu), Australia, central USA, and East Malaysia (south-western Sabah); possibly introduced, successfully in Singapore. Successfully colonised (?) Sardegna. Introduced unsuccessfully in New Zealand and Bermuda.

GENERAL HABITS

Status: very common in eastern Asia, less common in Europe. *Habitat:* wooded regions, open fields, grasslands, parks, gardens, orchards, villages and towns. *Gregariousness:* small flocks, and autumn flocks of several thousand. *Movements:* mainly sedentary, but large dispersal flights in central and northern Europe. *Foods:* seeds, rice and other grains, and insects. *Breeding:* Dec-June; (Sept-Jan Australia); often colonial; 2-3 clutches per year. *Nest:* untidy domed nest of plant stems, grass and feathers, in a tree hole, haystack, woodpile or crevices and holes in buildings. *Eggs:* 2, 4-6, 8. 4-6 (Australia).

Cheng, 1963, pp.812-816.
Kendeigh and Pinowski, 1973.
Pinowski and Kendeigh, 1977.

NOTES ON INTRODUCTIONS

Philippines. The race *P.m. saturatus* has been introduced to Manila on the island of Luzon, from Japan or Taiwan; the race *P.m. malaccensis* has been introduced to Cebu City on the island of Cebu, from the Malay Peninsula (Parkes, 1959; du Pont, 1971). Du Pont also records that the latter race has been reported from the island of Negros.

Both races are apparently well established in the cities where they were introduced. Whitehead (1899) indicates that he thought that they had been introduced by the Chinese: he records the Tree Sparrow's presence in both Manila and Cebu between 1893 and 1896. Delacour and Mayr (1946) found them common around Manila and other inhabited parts of Luzon, and on Cebu.

Marianas. The Tree Sparrow appears to be present in the Marianas as an introduced species. They are now common on Saipan and Rota and uncommon on Guam (Ralph and Sakai, 1979).

Lesser Sunda Islands. Tree Sparrows of the race *P.m. malaccensis* have been introduced on Lombok and also to Ambon (Peters, 1962) where they are apparently established.

Sulawesi. The race *P. m. malaccensis* has also been

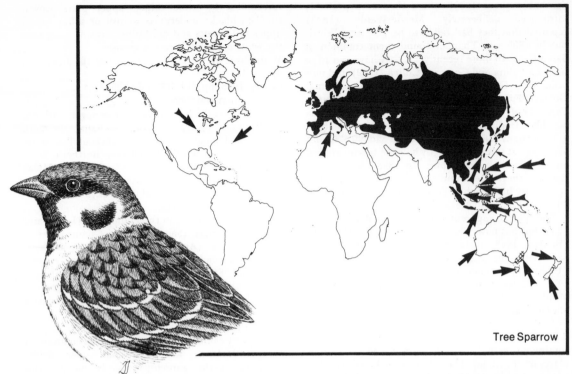

Tree Sparrow

introduced to southern Sulawesi (Peters, 1962) where it is established. Stresemann (1936) indicates that they were confined to the southern peninsula in the 1930s.

Pescadores (Penghu, Taiwan Hai Sai). P.m. dilutus has been introduced to the Pescadores in the Taiwan Hai-Sai between China and Taiwan (Peters, 1962). Hachisuka and Udagawa (1951) say that according to Horikawa (1936) a Chinese named Rosuirin in about 1728, liberated Sparrows from the Chinese mainland. They say that this appears true for Pescadores but not for Taiwan where the birds differ from those in southern China.

Australia. It is probable that Tree Sparrows were inadvertently introduced into Victoria during the time that House Sparrows were being released. The first release of them may have been that by Colonel Champ of Pentridge who in 1863 liberated 'Chinese Sparrows' (Le Souef, 1958). Certainly between 1863 and 1881 a number of birds of Chinese origin were introduced (Sage, 1956). Ryan (1906) records that Chinese Sparrows were introduced into Victoria in 1863 (forty-five birds) and in 1864 (twenty), but that these gradually disappeared. They were also introduced to Tasmania but apparently died out (Tarr, 1950).

According to Sage the Tree Sparrow is more numerous around Melbourne than anywhere else, but in 1956 was recorded some 640 km (400 miles) east of there. At this time they were reported to be spreading along the Melbourne to Sydney railway. During 1954-59 they established themselves at Tocumwal and Moama (Hobbs, 1961), and one was recorded in Sydney in 1949 (McGill, 1960). In some northern Victorian towns such as Cobran and Shepparton they were said to rival the House Sparrow in numbers (Hobbs).

The Tree Sparrow is now established in south-eastern Australia from Melbourne to Sydney. They were first recorded in Western Australia when two were shot in September 1966. These came from a boat from South-east Asia and landed at Geraldton (Long, 1972). Since this date another was shot in Palmyra, a Perth suburb, in December 1970, but the species has not been successful in gaining a permanent foothold in Western Australia.

Keve (1976) examined a small sample of Australian Tree Sparrows and is of the opinion that the Australian race is a mixture including *P.m. saturatus, catellatus* and *montanus.*

USA. Imported from Germany in 1870, twenty (or twelve pairs) Tree Sparrows were liberated at Lafayette Park, in St Louis, Missouri (Phillips, 1928; Wetmore, 1964). Barlow (1973) says that they were released in Lafayette Park by C. Daenzer in April of that year. According to Musselman (1950) they flourished near Shaws' Garden in St Louis until about 1877 when the House Sparrow arrived and displaced them somewhat. At this time the colony broke into several isolated groups which drifted slightly eastwards and southwards. A flock of ninety birds was reported from Horseshoe Lake, Illinois in 1938-39 (Cooke and Knappen, 1941). In 1946 some nested at Hannibal, Missouri and in 1947 at Hull, Illinois, 16 km (10 miles) east of Hannibal. Eight pairs were noted at Mauvaiterre, south-east of Jacksonville, Illinois in about 1953 (Musselman, 1953).

In 1957 the species was established in central-eastern Missouri (Charles County) and western Illinois (Jacksonville, Springfield, Calhoun and St Clair counties) (A.O.U. 1957). Occasionally birds appear in other areas as they have done since early times. Mengel (1965) indicates that Pindar in 1889 records them appearing in Fulton County, Kentucky, where they arrived by steamboat from St Louis.

However, Wetmore records that until the early 1960s they had barely spread beyond the city limits and were still confined to St Louis and adjacent areas of Missouri and Illinois. Barlow reports that since 1964 they appear to have been spreading slowly north and have established colonies as far north as Virginia in Cass County and that there may now be some 25 000 or more birds distributed over 22 000 km (13 670 miles) of range. The race introduced in the USA is *P.m. montanus* (Peters, 1962).

Sardegna. In Sardegna the Tree Sparrow seems to have been introduced by man (Voous, 1960).

East Malaysia. Gore (1968) reports that the Tree Sparrow is a recent accidental arrival in Sabah. He gives some details of a small colony discovered at the docks at Sandakan in September 1964. Some three to four birds apparently arrived by boat from Hong Kong in early 1964 and have settled and bred there. Progeny from these birds are now spreading through Sandakan, and in 1966 another small flock was discovered on Labuan Island, off the coast of south-western Sabah.

Singapore. Robinson and Chasen (1927) suggest that the Tree Sparrow was one of the first birds introduced to Singapore by the early immigrants in the beginning of the nineteenth century. However, Ward (1968) says that there is no proof that they were not associated with some of the smaller villages existing in Malaya and Singapore prior to modern settlement.

New Zealand. In 1868 the Otago Acclimatisation Society liberated two Tree Sparrows, and the Auckland society three. The Auckland society liberated nine more birds in 1871, but they all disappeared (Thomson, 1922). Thus the Tree Sparrow failed to become established in New Zealand.

Bermuda. The Tree Sparrow was introduced to Bermuda in the nineteenth century (Bourne, 1957), but apparently had little success and there are no recent records of them there (A.O.U., 1957). The race introduced to Bermuda was *P.m. montanus* (Peters, 1962).

DAMAGE

The Tree Sparrow is more numerous in eastern and south-eastern Asia than the House Sparrow. It appears to occupy a position similar to that species in Western Europe. In Japan, at times, flocks of several thousand will feed on ripening rice and their depredations are sometimes serious indeed (Yamashina, 1961). Although much damage is caused in barley fields in Tibet, the local people seem quite unconcerned and make no effort to control the species (Ludlow, 1950).

Large-scale control programmes, involving a large percentage of the human population, have been reported (in press) to have been carried out in China. Liang and Liu (1959) report that in Hunan the Tree Sparrow is certainly harmful, living almost entirely on rice and some grass seeds. In farming areas of southern China where crop cultivation is extensive the damage is apparently very serious. Cheng (1963) reports that they cause damage when the grain is drying, being threshed, fed to domestic animals and stored in open grain bins; in warehouses they not only eat the grain but spoil much with their manure; in fruit orchards they cause damage to grapes, pears and peaches and in vegetable gardens to young seedlings and the leaves of the vegetables; they often damage houses by nesting in them.

In Europe the Tree Sparrow is probably only involved, in most instances, in minor or local damage and is often quoted as being a useful species destroying many harmful insects. As an introduced species it has not built up into such numbers as the House Sparrow and consequently is not regarded with the same contempt. It has probably been most successful in Australia, but only time will indicate whether it will become as much of a nuisance there as its contemporary.

SCALY-FRONTED WEAVER
(Scaly-feathered Finch)
Sporopipes squamifrons (Smith)

DISTINGUISHING CHARACTERISTICS

10-11.2 cm (4-4.48 in)

Scaly black and white pattern on forehead, similarly on wing-coverts and secondaries; upper parts, ear-coverts and the remainder of head ashy grey; moustachial streak and patch in front of eye black; wing-coverts, inner secondaries and tail black, with white edges; remainder of flight feathers dusky; underparts ash or whitish; bill pink or rose-pink.

Mackworth-Praed and Grant, ser.2, vol.2, 1952-73, p.561 and pl.65.

GENERAL DISTRIBUTION

Southern Africa: southern Angola and South West Africa, east to Zambia and Rhodesia, and south to northern and eastern Cape Province.

INTRODUCED DISTRIBUTION

Introduced unsuccessfully on St Helena.

GENERAL HABITS

Status: common. *Habitat:* dry thorn country and villages. *Gregariousness:* small flocks or parties in the non-breeding season; roost communally.

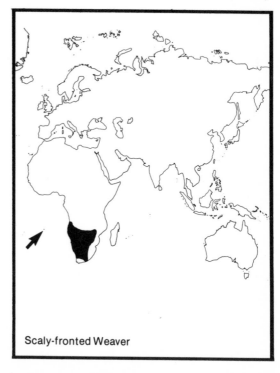

Scaly-fronted Weaver

Movements: sedentary (?). *Foods:* grass and weed seeds. *Breeding:* all year, but mainly Sept-Dec; more or less colonial; often 2 broods at least. *Nest:* untidy oval of grass with entrance at end, lined with feathers and down, in a bush; also uses other weavers' nests. *Eggs:* 3-5, 6.

Mackworth-Praed and Grant, ser.2, vol.2, 1952-73, pp.561-562.

NOTES ON INTRODUCTIONS

St Helena. Some Scaly-fronted Weavers were imported from South Africa and released on St Helena by an agricultural officer, H. Bruins-Lich, in about 1929, but failed to become established (Haydock, 1954).

DAMAGE

None known.

Family: *Ploceidae* Weavers

96 species in 11 genera; 16 species introduced, at least 5 and possibly another 3 successfully

The Spotted-backed Weaver is firmly established in the West Indian region where it has become a pest. The Madagascar Weaver has been widely introduced on small islands in the Indian Ocean and to St Helena in the Atlantic Ocean. It is a notorious pest of rice crops in its native Malagasy and has become so on St Helena. The Red Bishop and White-winged Widowbird in Australia and the Pin-tailed Whydah in Hawaii have not as yet become widespread, but will probably become pests should they increase in numbers substantially.

CAPE WEAVER

Ploceus capensis (Linnaeus)

DISTINGUISHING CHARACTERISTICS

17.5 cm (7 in) . 31.9-51.5 g (1.13-1.82 oz)

Head yellow with a chestnut wash (eastern birds) and

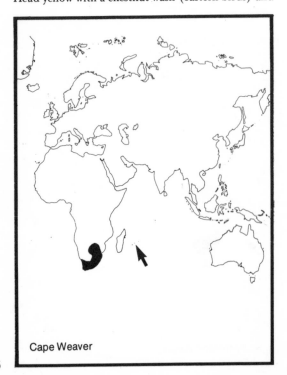

Cape Weaver

olive on ear-coverts and throat (western birds); underparts yellow; nape, mantle, scapulars, wing-coverts, rump and upper tail-coverts green, back streaked darker; flight feathers black with yellow edges; bill black. Female and male in non-breeding: upper parts grey-green; underparts pale yellow; lacks yellow on head, bill horn.

Mackworth-Praed and Grant, ser.2, vol.2, 1963, p.563 and pls. 66, 69.

GENERAL DISTRIBUTION

South Africa: the Cape Province, Natal, Zululand, Orange Free State and eastern Transvaal.

INTRODUCED DISTRIBUTION

Probably introduced, unsuccessfully in Mauritius.

GENERAL HABITS

Status: fairly common. *Habitat:* open country with trees and bushes. *Gregariousness:* flocks in winter. *Movements:* sedentary. *Foods:* flowers and soft parts of plants, nectar, seeds and insects. *Breeding:* May-Jan; colonial; polygamous. *Nest:* kidney-shaped, entrance below, made of coarse grass or reeds; male builds 2-3 nests. *Eggs:* 2-4, 5.

Mackworth-Praed and Grant, ser. 2, Vol. 2, 1963, pp.563-564.

NOTES ON INTRODUCTIONS

Mauritius. The Cape Weaver may have been introduced to Mauritius from Natal in 1892. Meinertzhagen (1912) recounts that it was introduced by Monsignor Meyer and was common near Flacqu in 1910, but had not spread from there.

The Cape Weaver is not mentioned subsequently in Mauritius and could possibly have been mistaken for the more commonly introduced *P. cucullatus.*

MASKED WEAVER

(Southern Masked Weaver, Vitelline Masked Weaver)

Ploceus velatus Vieillot

DISTINGUISHING CHARACTERISTICS

13.7-15 cm (5.48-6 in) . 17.8-33 g (.63-1.16 oz)

Back green and slightly streaked; mantle yellow-green streaked dusky; top of head saffron; around eye, sides of face, ear-coverts and throat black; nape and underparts yellow; bill black. (Some variation in colour, pattern and size between races: one race suffused with chestnut, but in some the black mask does not extend below the chin, and the throat and crown are suffused with chestnut.) In non-breeding season: head, sides of face and mantle olive-yellow; underparts paler yellow; belly white; bill horn. *Female:* upper parts yellow-green; mantle streaked dusky; underparts bright yellow; bill horn. In non-breeding season female similar to male in non-breeding, but more olive.

Mackworth-Praed and Grant, 1952-73, ser.1, vol.2, pp.899-901 and pls. 85, 88, 87 and 89; ser.2, vol.2, pp.569-570 and pls.66, 69; ser.3, vol.2, pp.621-623 and pls. 81, 84.

GENERAL DISTRIBUTION

Africa south of the Sahara: Sénégal to Nigeria, the Sudan, Ethiopia, Somali, Kenya and Uganda, southern Angola, southern Zaire, southern Tanzania and Moçambique south to Cape Province, South Africa.

INTRODUCED DISTRIBUTION

Introduced unsuccessfully on St Helena.

INTRODUCTIONS OF PLOCEIDAE

Species	Date introduced	Region	Manner introduced	Reason
(a) Successful introductions				
Spotted-backed Weaver	about 1783 ?	Hispaniola, West Indies	escapee	cage bird
	about 1930 ?	Puerto Rico	?	?
	?	Réunion	deliberate	?
	about 1886	Mauritius	?	?
Madagascar Weaver	?	Amirante Islands	escapee ?	?
	about 1860 or earlier, and later	Seychelles	deliberate	?
	prior 1884	Chagos Archipelago	?	?
	about 1850 ?	Archipel des Comores?	colonisation or deliberate	?
	18th century or earlier ?	Mauritius	?	?
	?	Réunion	deliberate ?	?
	after 1865	Rodriguez Island ?	deliberate ?	?
	18th century or later ? (before 1870)	St Helena	escapee	cage bird ?
Red Bishop	about 1926	Australia	escapee	cage bird
White-winged Widow-bird	about 1931	Australia	deliberate or escapee ?	cage bird ?
Pin-tailed Whydah	since 1965	Hawaiian Islands	deliberate or escapee	cage bird
(b) Probably successful introductions				
Spotted-backed Weaver	?	Sâo Tomé ?	colonisation ?	?
Black-headed Weaver	between 1909-28	Sâo Tomé	?	?
Madagascar Weaver	?	Assumption Island ?	?	?
	?	Aldabra Island ?	?	?
	?	Isles Glorieuses	colonisation ?	?
	?	Cargados Garajos ?	?	?
Yellow-crowned Bishop	since 1965	Hawaiian Islands (Oahu)	deliberate or escapee	cage bird
Red Bishop	since 1965	Hawaiian Islands (Oahu)	deliberate or escapee	cage bird
(c) Failed or probably failed				
Cape Weaver	1892	Mauritius	deliberate	?
Spotted-backed Weaver	prior 1924	Cape Verde Islands	?	?
Golden Weaver	before 1879	Cocos-Keeling Islands	?	?
Baya Weaver	since 1965	Hawaiian Islands	deliberate or escapee	cage bird ?
	1970	Hong Kong	escapee	cage bird
Seychelles Weaver	1965	D'Arros Island, Amirantes	deliberate	conservation ?
Red Bishop	about 1940	Tahiti	deliberate	aesthetic ?
	1929	St Helena	deliberate	?
Village Combassou	since 1965	Hawaiian Islands	deliberate or escapee	cage bird ?
Pin-tailed Whydah	about 1903 or earlier	Archipel des Comores	?	?
	?	Puerto Rico	deliberate ?	?
Masked Weaver	1929	St Helena	deliberate	?
White-winged Widow-bird	1929	St Helena	deliberate	?
Long-tailed Widow-bird	1929	St Helena	deliberate	?
Shaft-tailed Whydah	1929	St Helena	deliberate	?
Paradise Whydah	1929	St Helena	deliberate	?

Masked Weaver

GENERAL HABITS
Status: common and abundant. *Habitat:* open woodland, Acacia country, thick bush, low-lying country and along streams. *Gregariousness:* small flocks. *Movements:* no information. *Foods:* seeds, flowers, fruit and insects. *Breeding:* all year but varies in different areas; polygamous; somewhat colonial. *Nest:* heart- or pear-shaped of grass with a short entrance tunnel from below, suspended in branches. *Eggs:* 2-4.

Mackworth-Praed and Grant, 1952-73, ser.1, vol.2, pp.899-901; ser.2, vol.2, pp.569-570; ser.3, vol.2, pp.621-623.

NOTES ON INTRODUCTIONS
St Helena. Imported to St Helena and released in 1929 by an agricultural officer, H. Bruins-Lich, the Masked Weaver was unsuccessful in establishing itself (Haydock, 1954).

DAMAGE
The Masked Weaver is commonly found on grain crops in Africa and in some localities is a pest to these crops (Mackworth-Praed and Grant, 1963). They are also reported to attack cultivated fruits.

SPOTTED-BACKED WEAVER
(Village Weaver, Black-headed Weaver, V-marked Weaver)
Ploceus cucullatus (Müller)

DISTINGUISHING CHARACTERISTICS
16-17.5 cm (6.4-7 in)
Head and neck black, variably forming an apex in front of lower neck; mantle and scapulars mottled black and yellow; rump and upper tail-coverts yellow; flight feathers and wing-coverts black, edged yellow; chest and sides chestnut; remainder of underparts yellow; tail dusky green; bill black. Male non-breeding: head and neck dark green; mantle, scapulars and rump earth brown; underparts, chin to chest yellow; remainder white; bill horn. Female: similar to male in non-breeding, but paler green; bill dark brown.

Mackworth-Praed and Grant, 1952-73, ser.1, vol.2, pp.889-891 and pls. 85, 88; ser.2, vol.2, pp.565-567 and pls. 66, 69; ser.3, vol.2, pp.613-617 and pls. 81, 84.

GENERAL DISTRIBUTION
Southern Africa: from Sénégal east to Ethiopia and south to southern Angola, northern Botswana, Rhodesia and eastern coastal South Africa; also Fernando Póo and Mafia Island.

INTRODUCED DISTRIBUTION
Introduced successfully in Puerto Rico, Haiti, and the Dominican Republic in the West Indies, probably successfully to Mauritius and Réunion in the Mascarene Islands; introduced or colonised successfully São Tomé in the Gulf of Guinea and introduced unsuccessfully in the Cape Verde Islands.

GENERAL HABITS
Status: very common. *Habitat:* swampy country, open grassland, villages, and usually near water. *Gregariousness:* small groups, and large flocks often of several hundred. *Movements:* sedentary. *Foods:* insects, seeds, grains, flower nectar and pollen. *Breeding:* mainly Sept-May, all year some areas; in crowded often large colonies; polygamous. *Nest:* large kidney-shaped grass structure, opening below with or without spout, lined with fine grass and other soft material; often builds more than one nest. *Eggs:* 1-3.

Colias and Colias, *Auk,* vol.84, 1967, pp.396-411.
Colias and Colias, *Ostrich* suppl. no.9, 1971, pp.41-52.
Mackworth-Praed and Grant, 1952-73, ser.1, vol.2, pp.889-891; ser.2, vol.2, pp.565-567; ser.3, vol.2, pp.613-617.

NOTES ON INTRODUCTIONS
West Indies. The Spotted-backed Weaver was probably introduced from West Africa when the slave ships were plying between this region and the West Indies (Wetmore and Swales, 1931). Fitzwater (1971) claims that they were present in Hispaniola in 1783 when there was a colony established near Tron Caiman, Haiti. Wetmore and Swales have recorded that they were not noted there until about 1917 and were well established in 1920, but suggest that they were probably introduced during the French colonisation, more than likely as escapees from aviaries. They were apparently resident locally in both Puerto Rico and Haiti in about 1930. Several birds were noted near Port de 'Estere, Thomazeau between Port-au-Prince and L'Arcahaie, and a nesting colony north of Trouin in Haiti in the early 1930s (Wetmore and Lincoln, 1933). Dod (pers. comm., 1977) says that a group were found established at Cul-de-Sac, Haiti in 1927.

During the 1960s the Spotted-backed Weaver population in Haiti and the Dominican Republic underwent an explosion and built up to such numbers that it became a serious pest to rice crops (Fitzwater). In the Dominican Republic, where the species is known as Madam Saga or Sara, they are now found in large flocks of hundreds, and although they are shot and poisoned they are still as abundant as ever in all parts of the lowland country where there is water (Dod).

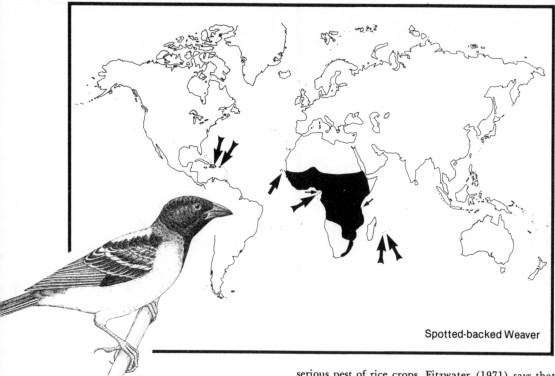

Spotted-backed Weaver

According to Bond (1960) the race introduced into the West Indies is *P.c. cucullatus*.

Mauritius. Peters (1962) records that the race *P.c. spilonotus* has been introduced and established on this island. Rountree *et al* (1952) report that they were introduced in about 1886 from South Africa. According to Staub (1976) they were released in the north of the island near Cap Malheureux, for no apparent reason. Benedict (1957) records that they were steadily increasing in numbers there in the 1950s and threaten to become a pest.

Réunion. Peters (1962) records that the race *P.c. spilonotus* has been introduced to this island. Staub (1976) reports that a Mr Beylier introduced them to Réunion. Watson *et al* (1963) say that the species was common there in the 1960s, and Staub reports that they still inhabit the lowlands on the island.

São Tomé. Peters (1962) records that the race *P.c. cucullatus* has probably been introduced to this island.

Cape Verde Islands. The Spotted-backed Weaver (race *P.c. cucullatus*) was introduced to Praia, São Tiago in the Cape Verdes prior to 1924, but has now probably died out there (Bannerman and Bannerman, 1968).

DAMAGE

The active, quarrelsome Spotted-backed Weaver is locally abundant in parts of East Africa. In northern Uganda they cause some damage to crops (Mackworth-Praed and Grant, 1963) and in Nigeria they are reported to do some damage to Palm Trees *Elais guinensis* (Good, pers. comm. 1962). In parts of East Africa at least they were an unprotected species (Goode, pers. comm., 1962).

In Haiti and the Dominican Republic since their population explosion in the 1960s they have become a serious pest of rice crops. Fitzwater (1971) says that they cause up to 20% of the rice crop to be lost. According to Dod (pers. comm., 1977) they strip leaves from trees for their nests, often killing the tree. Flocks are so large that rice plantations are destroyed in a very short time and although they are shot, and in recent years have been poisoned, they are still an abundant species in that country.

BLACK-HEADED WEAVER
Ploceus melanocephalus (Linnaeus)

DISTINGUISHING CHARACTERISTICS

15 cm (6 in)

Forehead to nape, sides of face, ear-coverts, chin, throat and upper chest black; hindneck, sides of neck, chest, lower rump, upper tail-coverts and remainder of underparts yellow; mantle and scapulars olive-yellow; flight feathers and wing-coverts blackish with yellow edges; tail olive-green; bill black. In non-breeding black replaced by olive-green; mantle, scapulars and rump earth brown, streaked dusky, except rump; underparts buff; bill horn. *Female:* similar to male in non-breeding plumage.

Mackworth-Praed and Grant, 1952-73, ser.2, vol.2, pp.570-571 and pls. 66, 69; ser.3, vol.2, pp.623-624 and pls. 81, 84.

GENERAL DISTRIBUTION

Central Africa: from Guinea, east to Nigeria and Cameroon; southern Central African Republic and down the Congo River; eastern Congo and Zaire to north-western Zambia. An apparently isolated population in Ethiopa.

INTRODUCED DISTRIBUTION

Possibly introduced successfully to São Tomé in the Gulf of Guinea, Africa.

GENERAL HABITS

Status: common. *Habitat:* grassy riverbanks and 389

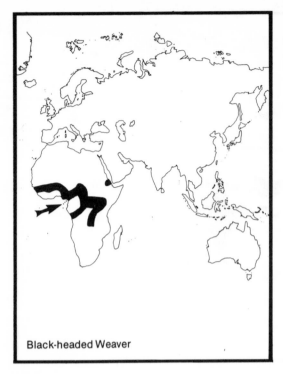

Black-headed Weaver

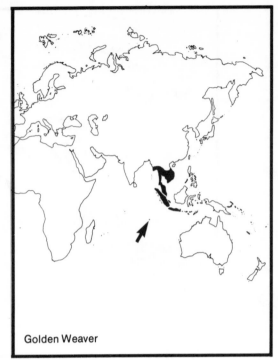

Golden Weaver

papyrus swamps. *Gregariousness:* large colonies. *Movements:* sedentary, but somewhat nomadic at times. *Foods:* grass seeds and some insects. *Breeding:* most months of year; usually a few pairs together, but also large nesting colonies. *Nest:* of grass lined with fine grass, without spout, in a tussock or papyrus. *Eggs:* 2.

Mackworth-Praed and Grant, 1952-73, ser.2, vol.2, pp.570-571; ser.3, vol.2, pp.623-624.

NOTES ON INTRODUCTIONS
São Tomé. Snow (1950) reports that a *Sitagra* sp. was introduced to the island of São Tomé between 1909 and 1928 and is now fairly common there. Peters (1962) records that the race *P.m. capitalis* has perhaps been introduced to São Tomé.

DAMAGE
None known.

GOLDEN WEAVER
Ploceus hypoxanthus (Sparrman)

DISTINGUISHING CHARACTERISTICS
14.5-15 cm (5.8-6 in)
Head and underparts golden yellow with a black mask and throat; back and wings blotched with chestnut-brown; rump and upper tail-coverts yellow; tail brown; bill brownish black. Non-breeding male and female: lack black facial mask and golden yellow; female whitish on lower belly and under tail-coverts; lacks yellow rump; bill brownish.

Kuroda, 1933-36, 2 vols.
King *et al*, 1975, pl.64, no.1146, opp. p.433.

GENERAL DISTRIBUTION
South-eastern Asia: from southern Burma, central Thailand through Indochina and Kampuchea; also Sumatra and Java.

INTRODUCED DISTRIBUTION
Introduced unsuccessfully to the Cocos-Keeling Islands, Indian Ocean.

GENERAL HABITS
Status: locally common some areas, but generally not common. *Habitat:* near water in secondary growth, open grassy regions, reed beds and cultivation. *Gregariousness:* small groups throughout the year. *Movements:* somewhat nomadic (?). *Foods:* seeds, grains and insects (?). *Breeding:* May-Nov (Burma). *Nest:* ragged appearance with entrance at side or bottom ? and lacks spout. *Eggs:* no information.

NOTES ON INTRODUCTIONS
Cocos-Keeling Islands. The race *P. h. hypoxanthus* was probably introduced to the Cocos-Keeling Islands before 1879, as they were recorded there at this time (Gibson-Hill, 1949). Gibson-Hill reports that there were none there in 1909 and that conditions were not favourable in his opinion for the species to become established there.

DAMAGE
None known.

BAYA WEAVER
(**Baya, Common Weaver-bird**)
Ploceus philippinus (Linnaeus)

DISTINGUISHING CHARACTERISTICS
13.5-15 cm (5.4-6 in). 18-32 g (.63-1.13 oz)
Upper plumage brownish black; feathers margined yellow; rump and remainder tawny; crown yellow, with a blackish brown facial mask; underparts yellow and unstreaked; bill dark horny brown, yellowish at base. Female and male in winter: dull tawny, often indistinct streaks on breast; bill yellowish horn.

Cheng, 1963, pp.820-821 and pl.30, no.114.
Ali and Ripley, vol.10, 1968-74, pp.88-93, and pl.108, fig.5, opp. p.144 and pl.105, fig.1, opp. p.80.

GENERAL DISTRIBUTION
Southern Asia: Pakistan, India (except south-west coastal strip), Nepal to Bangladesh and east to south-west China, and south to Sri Lanka, Burma, Malay

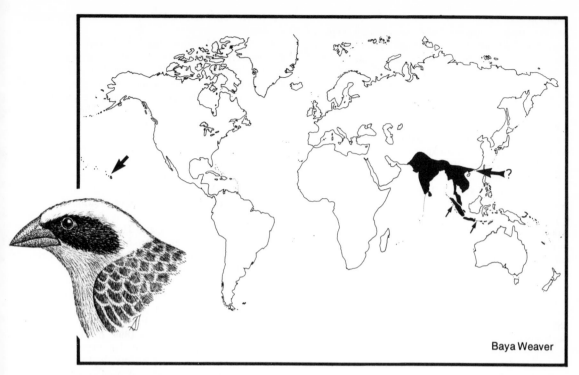

Baya Weaver

Peninsula, Thailand, Cochinchina, south Vietnam, Sumatra, Nias, Java and Bali.

INTRODUCED DISTRIBUTION
Introduced unsuccessfully in the Hawaiian Islands and to Hong Kong (escapees ?).

GENERAL HABITS
Status: very common. *Habitat:* forest edges, secondary growth, brushland, grassland, ricefields, cultivation and gardens. *Gregariousness:* often in flocks of from 10 to 40 birds and up to 200 in non-breeding season; communal roosts. *Movements:* sedentary, or locally nomadic governed by availability of foods. *Foods:* seeds, grain, insects and their larvae and spiders. *Breeding:* Apr-Nov (India) Dec-June (Malaysia) Mar-Aug (China); colonial; 2-3 broods per year. *Nest:* globular hanging structure, woven from grass strips, interior cemented with mud; builds several nests. *Eggs:* 2-4, 5.

Ali and Ripley, vol.10, 1968-74, pp.88-93.

Mathew, *J. Bombay nat. Hist. Soc.,* vol.73, no.2, 1976, pp.249-260.

NOTES ON INTRODUCTIONS
Hawaiian Islands. The Baya Weaver has been intentionally or accidentally released or escaped since 1965 on Oahu (Berger, 1972), but is not known to be established there.

Hong Kong. Flocks of Baya Weavers have been seen on Hong Kong Island, and near Ping Shan on a number of occasions, mainly in 1970 (Webster, 1975). Many appear to be escapees from aviaries, but the species is not known to breed there in the wild.

DAMAGE
Ali (1961) says that the Baya Weaver occasionally damages rice crops in India but generally obtains most of its grain from the ground. However, Ali and Ripley (1968-74) say that they raid ripening crops of gowar, maize, rice and other cereals often causing considerable damage. Recent studies in Andhra Pradesh found that although they attacked various crops, the damage was not serious, but nor did they do significant service to the standing crop (Mathew, 1976).

According to the California Department of Agriculture, they do cause extensive damage to grain in parts of their native range, sufficient for them to be banned from importation into that State in the United States.

Cheng (1963) records that they eat rice at various growing stages and cause damage in Hsi-shuang Pan-na province of Yunnan, China.

MADAGASCAR WEAVER
(Red Fody, Madagascar Fody or Cardinal)
Foudia madagascariensis (Linnaeus)

DISTINGUISHING CHARACTERISTICS
12-13 cm (4.8-5.2 in). 13.5-18.3 g (.48-.65 oz)
Generally vivid orange-red or red in breeding plumage, with some black streaks on the back; wings dark brown with white wing bar on coverts; upper wing-coverts with some red; mantle dark brown; narrow dark brown to blackish diamond shaped streak from base of bill to behind eye; tail brown; bill black. Female, and male in non-breeding: brown or yellowish brown, with streaked back; bill of female yellowish.

Milon *et al,* 1973, p.246 and pl.18, figs. 4 and 5.

GENERAL DISTRIBUTION
Malagasy.

INTRODUCED DISTRIBUTION
Introduced successfully on the Amirantes, Seychelles, Chagos Archipelago, Mauritius, Réunion, Rodrigues and St Helena; introduced or colonised successfully the Archipel des Comores and Isles Glorieuses; may have been introduced or colonised Assumption, Aldabra and Cargados Garajos, but details lacking.

391

GENERAL HABITS

Status: very common; fairly commonly kept in captivity. *Habitat:* forest clearings, open savannah, plantations, cultivated areas, villages, gardens and parks. *Gregariousness:* small compact flocks of 2 or 3 to 50 birds, and in winter extensive flocks of hundreds. *Movements:* sedentary. *Foods:* insects, seeds and grain. *Breeding:* Sept-May; Nov-Mar (Seychelles); somewhat colonial. *Nest:* flimsy, loosely twined and woven structure of needles, palm and grass strips, lined with kapok, with tubular down-curved entrance, in a tree, bush or palm. *Eggs:* 2-4 (3-4 in Mascarenes).

Crook, *Ibis* vol.103a, no.1, 1961, pp.517-518.

Milon *et al,* 1973, p.246.

NOTES ON INTRODUCTIONS

Amirantes. The Madagascar Weaver has been introduced from the Seychelles to most of the cultivated Amirante Islands, possibly in some instances by accident. It now flourishes there on most of the islands except Alphonse (Penny, 1974).

Seychelles. The Madagascar Weaver was first recorded on the island of Mahé in small numbers in 1867 (Newton, 1867), having been introduced probably in about 1860 (Gaymer *et al,* 1969). Penny (1974) also reports that they appear to have been introduced in about 1860, or even earlier. He cites a story attached to their introduction: 'two neighbours were in dispute over the ownership of a plot of land upon which one of them was growing rice. One of them, for revenge on his rival, sent to Mauritius for the weavers which were known to be a pest in the ricefields, and released them into his neighbour's territory'.

Crook (1961) says that they were apparently deliberately liberated there (Mahé?) in 1879, to Des Roches in 1882 and to Praslin in 1902. He records that they reached other islands in the group in later years; Cousin in the late 1950s and were observed on Cousine for the first time in 1958. They were well established on Frigate Island by 1939, but the actual date of arrival does not appear to be known.

At present the Madagascar Weaver is common and widespread on all the larger islands (Gaymer *et al*).

Chagos Archipelago. Perhaps or presumedly the Madagascar Weaver has been introduced to Diego Garcia (Saunders, 1886; Peters, 1962). Saunders reports that they were present there, but rare in 1886. Loustau-Lalanne (1962) and Hutson (1975) do not mention them as an introduced species in the Archipelago, but report that they occur on all three atolls and are especially well established on Diego, but scarce on Peros Banhos and on Salomon.

Bourne (1971) reports that the Madagascar Weaver was recorded on Diego Garcia by Finsch (1887) in 1884, at which time they were common; some were collected there in 1899, but the species is not mentioned by the Percy Sladen Trust Expedition in 1905. They were found on the Ile du Coin, Peros Banhos in 1957 (Bourne) and occur on Ile Grande Barbe in small numbers (Hutson, 1975).

Archipel des Comores. Benson (1960) reports that the Madagascar Weaver is only a recent arrival in the Comores, possibly unaided by man, as there is no evidence of it being kept there extensively as a caged bird. According to him, it may be presumed that it has been established there for less than a century.

The first definite record of the species on the island of Mayotte appears to be in 1888 (Milne-Edwards and Oustalet, 1888, in Benson), however, Crook (1961) says that it has been recorded there in other areas

Madagascar Weaver

since the middle of the nineteenth century. He cites the collection of specimens from Mohéli in 1864 and in 1879, and says that they probably reached Anjouan and Grande Comore after 1906-07.

The Madagascar Weaver now occurs on all the islands in the group.

Mauritius. The Madagascar Weaver has evidently been established in Mauritius since the eighteenth century (Newton, 1959; Crook, 1961) and may have been introduced prior to that date (Benedict, 1957). Rountree *et al* (1952) agree that it was introduced some time during the eighteenth century from Malagasy. They report that the species is now widespread and common on the island.

Réunion. Peters (1962) records that the Madagascar Weaver has been introduced and established on this island. Watson *et al* (1963) report that they are common there and Staub (1976) says that they are the most common introduced bird occurring in natural forest on the island.

Isles Glorieuses. According to Benson *et al* (1975) the Madagascar Weaver probably colonised the Isles Glorieuses, presumedly without man's help.

St Helena. A favourite cage bird on St Helena since the eighteenth century, the Madagascar Weaver is said to have become established as a result of the release or escape of birds from captivity (Crook, 1961). Ball (1960) reports that their establishment there may have been fairly recent, however Melliss (1870) records that they were common there in 1870 or shortly before. In 1952-53, Haydock (1954) found them to be quite numerous both in the coastal area and highlands of the island.

Assumption, Aldabra, Cargados and Rodrigues. The Madagascar Weaver is believed to have been introduced and to have become established on these islands but details for many appear to be lacking. Watson *et al* (1963) record that they have been introduced on Rodrigues where they breed in October and November. Staub (1976) says that Moreau (1960, *J. Orn., Lpz.* 101 [1-2] : 29-49) indicated that they were introduced some time after 1865 on Rodrigues.

DAMAGE

In Malagasy, flocks of Madagascar Weavers are so numerous and destructive when rice is ripening or ripened, that the Malagach construct huts on stilts in which a child sits all day scaring them away (van Someren, 1947; Rand, 1936; Milon *et al*, 1973). According to Ball (1960) these weavers form large flocks after the breeding season which then feed on the rice crops.

Where the Madagascar Weaver has been introduced on St Helena they have multiplied to such an extent that they have become a nuisance to the farmers there. In the Seychelles it was suspected that their establishment was assisting the extinction of the endemic Toq Toq *F. sechellarum* on at least some of the island. Crook's study (1961) showed however, that each species occupies its own ecological niche, although this differs from that occupied by them originally, and there appears to be no interaction. The presence of the introduced form has not altered the status of the endemic species. Newton (1959) also found that on Mauritius they are not competing with the native *F. rubra*.

Seychelles Weaver

SEYCHELLES WEAVER
(Toq Toq, Seychelles Fody)
Foudia sechellarum Newton

DISTINGUISHING CHARACTERISTICS

13-13.5 cm (5.2-5.4 in)

Generally dark brown; crown and bib golden (male in breeding) or dull greenish yellow (non-breeding); back streaked darker brown; bill black (breeding). Female: lacks golden forehead and throat; paler below.

Penny, 1974, p.117 and pl.8, no.3, opp. p.113.

GENERAL DISTRIBUTION

Seychelles: now surviving only on Frigate, Cousin and Cousine Islands.

INTRODUCED DISTRIBUTION

Introduced probably unsuccessfully in the Amirante Islands (D'Arros).

GENERAL HABITS

Status: uncommon and possibly declining. *Habitat:* open forest, mangroves, casuarina with clearings, and cultivation. *Gregariousness:* family parties. *Movements:* sedentary. *Foods:* insects, fruits, seeds, copra and eggs of sea birds. *Breeding:* all year, peak in Sept-Oct. *Nest:* large untidy spherical structure, in a low bush or occasionally palms, etc. *Eggs:* 2-3.

Crook, *Ibis* vol.103a, no.1, 1961, pp.517-548.

Penny, 1974, pp.117-119.

NOTES ON INTRODUCTIONS

Amirante Islands. Five birds were sent to D'Arros Island in August 1965 in an attempt to establish the Seychelles Weaver there (Gaymer *et al*, 1969). They were apparently introduced by the Bristol Seychelles Expedition (Penny, 1974).

Gaymer *et al*, report that they were still present on the island at the end of September 1965, but Penny says that they have not been seen since 1968 when they were still surviving there. Their present status is uncertain.

DAMAGE

None known.

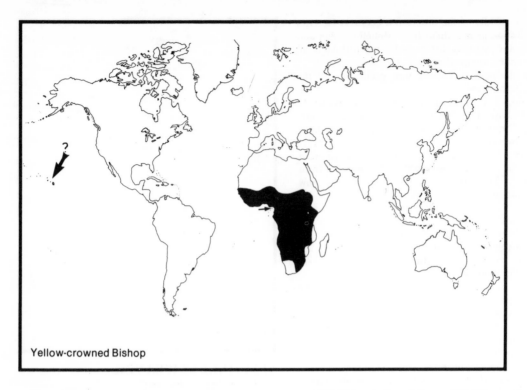

Yellow-crowned Bishop

YELLOW-CROWNED BISHOP
(Golden Bishop, Yellow Weaver, Napoleon Weaver)
Euplectes afra (Gmelin)

DISTINGUISHING CHARACTERISTICS
11.2-12.7 cm (4.48-5.08 in)
Forehead to nape, lower mantle, rump, upper and lower tail-coverts bright yellow; sides of mantle, band across hindneck, scapulars, flight feathers, wing-coverts, face, ear-coverts, tail and from chin to belly black (yellow breast band in race *afra*); bill black. Female, and male in non-breeding: streaked black and buff above (broader in male); buff stripe over eye; underparts buff, streaked brown on sides of chest, flanks, chin, throat, lower belly and under tail-coverts; bill brown.
Mackworth-Praed and Grant, 1952-73, ser.1, vol.2, pp.957-960 and pl.90; ser.2, vol.2, pp.605-606 and pls. 68, 70; ser.3, vol.2, pp.670-671 and pls. 85, 87.
Avon, *et al,* 1974, pl. p.19.

GENERAL DISTRIBUTION
Africa: Fernando Póo, Sénégal to the Sudan, western Ethiopia and the Congo, and south to Angola, western Kenya, eastern Tanzania, eastern Cape Province, Transvaal and Orange Free State.

INTRODUCED DISTRIBUTION
Introduced in the Hawaiian Islands (status uncertain).

GENERAL HABITS
Status: widespread, but locally common. *Habitat:* swampy grassland. *Gregariousness:* in winter forms flocks with other weavers. *Movements:* sedentary and somewhat nomadic ? *Foods:* grass seeds and insects. *Breeding:* all year (varies); polygamous. *Nest:* neat, compact, of grass lined with fine grass, porched over entrance at side of top, in low vegetation, such as grass or reeds. *Eggs:* 3-4, 5.

394   Mackworth-Praed and Grant, 1952-73, ser.1, vol.2,

pp.957-960; ser.2, vol.2, pp.605-606; ser.3, vol.2, pp.670-671.

NOTES ON INTRODUCTIONS
Hawaiian Islands. The Yellow-crowned Bishop was intentionally or accidentally, released or escaped, since 1965 on the island of Oahu (Berger, 1972). The Hawaiian Audubon Society (1975) reports that it may still be established there, but that its present status is not well known.
The species has been observed on Oahu during the Christmas Bird Counts of 1966 and from 1969 to 1972 in small numbers, but there are no subsequent records until a single bird was observed in 1976 (Pyle, 1976 and 1977).
Berger records that the race *E.a. afra,* and known as the Napolean Weaver, is the one that has been found on Oahu.

DAMAGE
None known.

RED BISHOP
(Grenadier Weaver, Durra Bird)
Euplectes orix (Linnaeus)

DISTINGUISHING CHARACTERISTICS
11-13.7 cm (4.4-5.48 in). 16.9-32 g (.6-1.13 oz)
Top of head, sides of face, ear-coverts and breast to belly black; remainder red, orange-red or occasionally orange-yellow; wings and tail dusky; bill black. Female, and male in non-breeding: broadly streaked above with brownish buff and black; superciliary stripe buff; underparts buffish, belly paler; chest and flanks streaked dark brown; bill pale brown.
Mackworth-Praed and Grant, 1952-73, ser.1, vol.2, pp.949-951 and pls. 87, 90; ser.2, vol.2, pp.600-601 and pls.68, 70; ser.3, vol.2, pp.666-667 and pls.85, 87.

GENERAL DISTRIBUTION

Africa: from Sénégal east to Ethiopia and the Sudan, and south through Kenya, Uganda, Tanzania west to eastern and southern Zaire and to Angola, and south through the remainder of southern Africa.

INTRODUCED DISTRIBUTION

Introduced successfully in South Australia and possibly to the Hawaiian Islands (status uncertain). Introduced unsuccessfully in Tahiti and to St Helena.

GENERAL HABITS

Status: very common. *Habitat:* brush and grassland along rivers and swampy country. *Gregariousness:* small groups, and in the non-breeding season joins large flocks of mixed species of up to 300 birds. *Movements:* sedentary and locally migratory or nomadic. *Foods:* seeds, grains, and probably insects. *Breeding:* most of year, mainly May-Oct and Dec-May; in loose scattered colonies; double brooded; polygamous. *Nest:* grass or reed, oval structure, entrance at top of side, in reeds, tall grass or palm fronds. *Eggs:* 2-5, 7; 3-4 (Australia).

Skead, *Ostrich* vol.27, no.3, 1956, pp.112-126.

Mackworth-Praed and Grant, 1952-73, ser.1, vol.2, pp.949-951; ser.2, vol.2, pp.600-601; ser.3, vol.2, pp.666-667.

NOTES ON INTRODUCTIONS

Australia. The Red Bishop was first reported in a wild state in South Australia in 1926 (Condon, 1962), and again in 1932 (Condon, 1948). In 1933 a colony of fifteen to twenty birds was found established near Woods Point, some 40 km (25 miles) south of Adelaide (Morgan, 1933). They were present there in 1936, 1941 and in 1947 (Condon, 1948) when they were still maintaining their numbers, but not apparently spreading (Lendon, 1948).

Other reports of Red Bishops from Hope Valley in 1932, McLaren Flat in 1933, Murray Bridge, Noarlunga in 1936, Finnis (near Alexandrina) in 1936 and Berri in 1941, have not been repeated (Condon) and are possibly escapees from aviaries. Some birds were also observed at Kuringai and near Turramurra, Sydney, in New South Wales in 1944, but the species has not become established there (Tarr, 1950). The Red Bishop is probably still established in the Murray Bridge area of South Australia.

Tahiti. Guild (1940) reports that almost fifty 'orange weavers' were present in the wild in 1940. They were presumedly one of his many introductions on the island. There appear to be no subsequent records of the species on Tahiti.

Hawaiian Islands. The Red Bishop was intentionally, or accidentally released or escaped since 1965, on the island of Oahu (Berger, 1972). Some were observed on the Christmas Bird Counts in 1966 and from 1969-73 in small numbers, and a single bird in 1976 (Pyle, 1976 and 1977). Berger records that the birds seen are of the race *E.o. franciscana.*

St Helena. Imported from South Africa the Red Bishop was released by H. Bruins-Lich in about 1929, but did not become permanently established on St Helena (Haydock, 1954).

DAMAGE

The Red Bishop is somewhat of a pest in South Africa, gathering into large flocks and in company with other weavers, raids ripening grain crops (Mackworth-Praed and Grant, 1963; Brown, pers. comm., 1962; Agric. Tech. Serv. pers. comm., 1962).

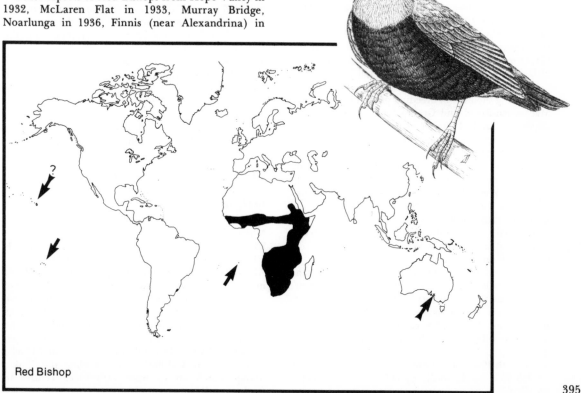

Red Bishop

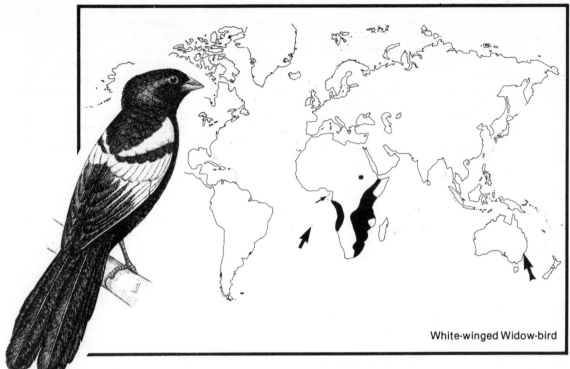

White-winged Widow-bird

WHITE-WINGED WIDOW-BIRD
Euplectes albonotatus (Cassin)

DISTINGUISHING CHARACTERISTICS
15-18.7 cm (6-7.48 in)
Head, neck, scapulars, mantle, rump, upper tail-coverts, flight feathers, tail and underparts black; tail elongated; bases of flight feathers and greater part of primary and secondary coverts white; wing shoulder yellow, but varies to cinnamon-brown; bill bluish grey. Female: upper parts streaked brown and black; underparts buff with pale brown streaks; sides of face and chin washed yellowish; bill brown. Male in non-breeding: similar to female but has wings and yellow wing shoulder of breeding plumage.
Mackworth-Praed and Grant, 1952-73, ser.1, vol.2, pp.965-966 and pl.90; ser.2, vol.2, pp.609-611 and pls.68, 70; ser.3, vol.2, pp.674-675 and pls.85, 87.

GENERAL DISTRIBUTION
Africa: from the Sudan (isolated population ?) and Ethiopia south to eastern Cape Province, South Africa. In West Africa in western Gabon and Angola: also on São Tomé Island in the Gulf of Guinea.

INTRODUCED DISTRIBUTION
Introduced successfully in Australia (NSW). Introduced unsuccessfully to St Helena.

GENERAL HABITS
Status: locally common. *Habitat:* grasslands and moist places in dry acacia savannahs. *Gregariousness:* flocks, sometimes fairly large. *Movements:* sedentary. *Foods:* grass and other seeds. *Breeding:* Dec-May; polygamous. *Nest:* spherical woven structure, with porch over side entrance, lined with fine grass, in tall grass. *Eggs:* 2-3.
Mackworth-Praed and Grant, 1952-73, ser.1, vol.2, pp.965-966; ser.2, vol.2, pp.609-611; ser.3, vol.2, pp.674-675.

NOTES ON INTRODUCTIONS
Australia. The White-winged Widow-bird was liberated in New South Wales in about 1931 (McGill, 1960). Tarr (1950) reports that they are supposed to have escaped from the wrecked vessel *Malabar*. Odd birds were apparently observed breeding in rank vegetation near the Hawkesbury River, New South Wales for several years.
Lane (1975) says that apparently a few birds were recorded up until 1953: in 1967 about fifty were seen and some were noted again in 1968. The species is probably still established around Windsor on the Hawkesbury River.
St Helena. Imported from South Africa, the White-winged Widow-bird was released by H. Bruins-Lich in about 1929, but did not become established on St Helena (Haydock, 1954).

DAMAGE
According to Brown (pers. comm., 1962) this species is a pest of small grain within its native range.

LONG-TAILED WIDOW-BIRD
(Sakabula, Giant Whydah)
Euplectes progne (Boddaert)

DISTINGUISHING CHARACTERISTICS
Males 47.5-58.7 cm (19-23.5 in) (summer), 19.4-23.7 cm (7.76-9.5 in) (winter); tail 31-49 cm (12.4-19.6 in) (summer), 8-14 cm (3.2-5.6 in) (winter).
Almost wholly black with orange-red wing shoulder; median wing-coverts white; tail long, central pair of feathers elongated; lighter edges to wings; bill bluish white. In non-breeding season shoulder patch orange and buff; underparts streaked buff or light brown; tail short. Female: 14.3-17.5 cm (5.72-7 in). Upper parts broadly streaked with buff or tawny and black; underparts streaked buff on breast, chest and flanks; orange patch on shoulder with black centres to feathers; bill horn.

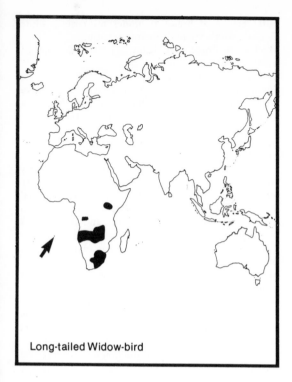

Long-tailed Widow-bird

Mackworth-Praed and Grant, 1952-73, ser.1, vol.2, p.971 and pl.90; ser.2, vol.2, p.614 and pls.68 and 70.

GENERAL DISTRIBUTION
Southern and eastern Africa: western and central Kenya, southern Zaire, Angola, Zambia and eastern South Africa.

INTRODUCED DISTRIBUTION
Introduced unsuccessfully to St Helena.

GENERAL HABITS
Status: locally common. *Habitat:* open grasslands and swampy grassy areas. *Gregariousness:* small groups of 1 or 2 males and a number of females: large flocks in non-breeding season which roost communally. *Movements:* no information. *Foods:* seeds and insects including termites. *Breeding:* Oct-July, but depends on rains; male polygamous and generally has 6-10 females. *Nest:* large domed structure of grass lined with seed heads, with side entrance, in a tussock. *Eggs:* 2-3, 4.

Mackworth-Praed and Grant, 1952-73, ser.1, vol.2, pp.971-972; ser.2, vol.2, pp.614-615.

NOTES ON INTRODUCTIONS
St Helena. The Long-tailed Widow-bird was imported from South Africa and released on St Helena in about 1929 by agriculture officer, H. Bruins-Lich, but was unsuccessful in becoming established there (Haydock, 1954).

DAMAGE
None known.

Viduinae

VILLAGE COMBASSOU
(Senegal Combassou, Green Indigo-bird, Black-winged Combassou)
Vidua chalybeata (Müller)

DISTINGUISHING CHARACTERISTICS
11.2-11.4 cm (4.48-4.56 in)
Wholly steel-blue, often with a greenish or violet or blue sheen; wing and tail-feathers black; axillaries white; bill pinkish white, but varies from white to red to coral. Female and male in non-breeding season: pale buff-brown, with darker centres to feathers; crown brown with broad pale central streak; throat and belly whitish; remainder of underparts buffish brown.

Mackworth-Praed and Grant, 1952-73, ser.1, vol.2, pp.1040-1041 and pl.94; ser.2, vol.2, pp.663-664 and pl.74; ser.3, vol.2, p.739.

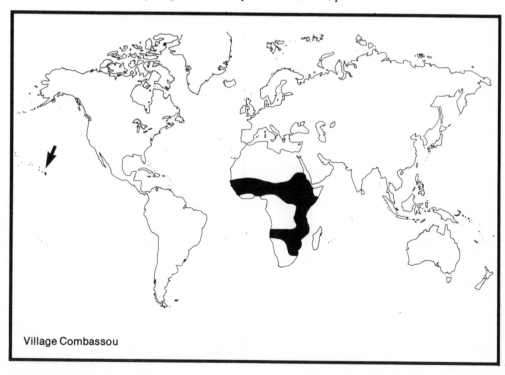

Village Combassou

GENERAL DISTRIBUTION

Africa south of the Sahara: from Sénégal, Gambia, Sierra Leone and Mali east to the Sudan, Ethiopia, eastern Zaire, and south to Transvaal, Zululand, Moçambique, Tanzania and south-west Angola.

INTRODUCED DISTRIBUTION

Introduced unsuccessfully in the Hawaiian Islands.

GENERAL HABITS

Status: common. *Habitat:* waste ground in open bush, and towns. *Gregariousness:* small flocks. *Movements:* sedentary and nomadic ? *Foods:* seeds. *Breeding:* Mar-June; parasitic. *Nest:* parasitises *Lagnosticta* spp. *Eggs:* probably 4-5.

Mackworth-Praed and Grant, 1952-73, ser.1, vol.2, p.1041; ser.2, vol.2, p.664.

NOTES ON INTRODUCTIONS

Hawaiian Islands. The Village Combassou was intentionally or accidentally released, or escaped since 1965 on Oahu, but is not known to be established there (Berger, 1972). One bird was observed in 1969 (Pyle, 1976) but there appear to be no subsequent records.

DAMAGE

None known.

SHAFT-TAILED WHYDAH
(Shaft-tailed Widow-bird)
Vidua regia (Linnaeus)

DISTINGUISHING CHARACTERISTICS

Males 30-56 cm (12-22.4 in). Females 11-15 cm (4.4-6 in)

Mainly black; collar on hindneck, cheeks, ear-coverts and underparts tawny; under wing white; tail with central feathers elongated and with white tips; bill reddish orange. In non-breeding plumage: upper parts and wings buff and tawny with black centres to feathers; lacks long tail-feathers; stripe over eye, sides of face, ear-coverts, chin and chest to flanks buff; centre of breast to under tail-coverts white. Female: similar to male in non-breeding.

Mackworth-Praed and Grant, ser.2, vol.2, 1952-73, p.669 and pl.74.

GENERAL DISTRIBUTION

South Africa: southern Angola and South West Africa east to northern South Africa, Rhodesia, south-western Zambia and southern Moçambique.

INTRODUCED DISTRIBUTION

Introduced unsuccessfully to St Helena.

GENERAL HABITS

Status: fairly common. *Habitat:* dry-thorn country. *Gregariousness:* small parties. *Movements:* sedentary, but some seasonal movement. *Foods:* seeds and possibly insects. *Breeding:* Nov-June, but depends on host species; parasitic and polygamous. *Nest:* parasitises weavers of the genera *Estrilda* and *Uraeginthus.* *Eggs:* probably one egg in any one nest, but 1-3 in a nest known.

Mackworth-Praed and Grant, ser.2, vol.2, 1952-73, p.669.

NOTES ON INTRODUCTIONS

St Helena. The Shaft-tailed Whydah was imported from South Africa by an agricultural officer, H. Bruins-Lich, and released there in about 1929 (Haydock, 1954). The introduction was unsuccessful.

DAMAGE

None known.

PARADISE WHYDAH
(Paradise Widow-bird)
Vidua paradisaea (Linnaeus)

DISTINGUISHING CHARACTERISTICS

Males 32-40 cm (12.8-16 in) (tail 22-30 cm [8.8-12 in]). 17.5-21.3 g (.62-.75 oz)

Mainly black with broad yellow collar around neck; chest chestnut; breast to belly buff; retrices tapered to tip; bill black. In non-breeding plumage: creamy

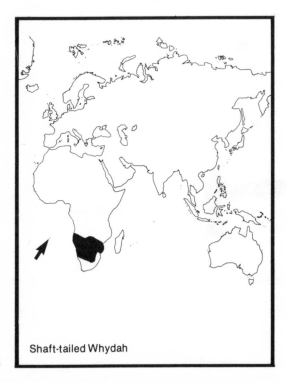

Shaft-tailed Whydah

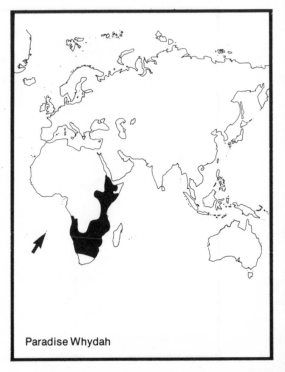

Paradise Whydah

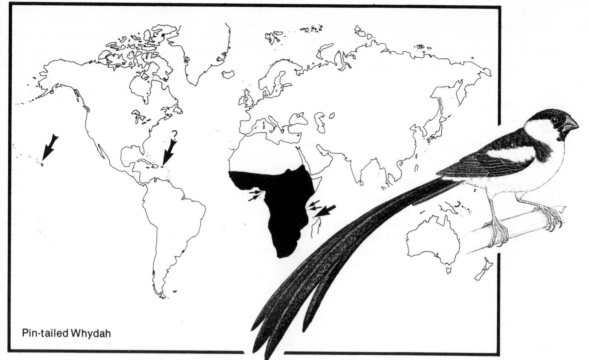

Pin-tailed Whydah

streak from forehead to occiput and streaked black; sides of face and throat creamy white; mantle and scapulars tawny streaked black; tail lacks long central and broad feathers. Female: 15 cm (6 in); similar to male in non-breeding, but duller and chest and flanks buffish brown.

Mackworth-Praed and Grant, 1952-73, ser.1, vol.2, pp.1049-1050 and pl.94; ser.2, vol.2, pp.670-671 and pl.74.

GENERAL DISTRIBUTION
Southern and eastern Africa: Ethiopia and eastern Sudan south to Angola and northern South Africa.

INTRODUCED DISTRIBUTION
Introduced unsuccessfully to St Helena.

GENERAL HABITS
Status: common. *Habitat:* thorn country and open savannah with trees. *Gregariousness:* small flocks and larger flocks to 100 birds in non-breeding season. *Movements:* some seasonal movements ? *Foods:* grass and other seeds, and insects. *Breeding:* all year, but dependent on host species; parasitic; polygamous. *Nest:* parasitises *Pytilia* spp. and some other weavers. *Eggs:* 1-4 in host nest known, but may be more than 1 bird involved.

Mackworth-Praed and Grant, 1952-73, ser.1, vol.2, pp.1049-1050; ser.2, vol.2, pp.670-671.

NOTES ON INTRODUCTIONS
St Helena. Imported similarly to *V. regia* but also failed to become established.

DAMAGE
None known.

PIN-TAILED WHYDAH
Vidua macroura (Pallas)

DISTINGUISHING CHARACTERISTICS
Males 27-37.5 cm (10.8-15 in). Tail up to 26 cm (10.4 in)
Head, mantle, wings, chin and tail black; sides of face, ear-coverts, underside of chin, and patch on wings white; white collar on hindneck; rump and upper tail-coverts white, with black streaks; bill red to orange-coral. Male in non-breeding: streaked black and tawny; lacks long ventral tail feathers. Female: 12.5 cm (5 in); similar to male in non-breeding; bill in breeding, upper dark brown and lower greenish pink to dusky; bill in non-breeding, red or pale red.

Mackworth-Praed and Grant, 1952-73, ser.1, vol.2, pp.1046-1047 and pl.94; ser.2, vol.2, pp.667-668 and pl.74; ser.3, vol.2, pp.741-742 and pl.91.
Avon *et al,* 1974, pl. p.23.

GENERAL DISTRIBUTION
Africa and islands: in Africa from Sénégal east to Ethiopia and south to Cape Province, South Africa; also Fernando Póo, São Tomé, Zanzibar and Mafia Islands.

INTRODUCED DISTRIBUTION
Introduced, probably successfully in the Hawaiian Islands and possibly to Puerto Rico (?). Introduced (?) unsuccessfully to Mayotte in the Archipel des Comores.

GENERAL HABITS
Status: common. *Habitat:* cultivated country, farmlands, open bushy areas and semi-marshes. *Gregariousness:* small groups of 6-7 birds and in non-breeding season flocks to 100 or more. *Movements:* sedentary (?) *Foods:* grass and other small seeds, and possibly insects. *Breeding:* mainly Sept-July, but any time; parasitic and polygamous. *Nest:* in other waxbill (Estrildine) nests. *Eggs:* 1 usually, but may be up to 4 (?).

Mackworth-Praed and Grant, 1952-73, ser.1, vol.2, pp.1046-1047; ser.2, vol.2, pp.667-668; ser.3, vol.2, pp.741-742.

NOTES ON INTRODUCTIONS
Archipel des Comores. The Pin-tailed Whydah has been introduced to the island of Mayotte, but has now become extinct there (Benson, 1960). Benson records

that Milne-Edwards and Oustalet reported them there in 1888 and also that three were collected on Mayotte in 1903. Some ten specimens were collected when the islands were visited in 1906-07, but none have been recorded there again. More recently, the species is often listed as a resident there.

Hawaiian Islands. According to Heilbrun (1976) Pin-tailed Whydahs have been recorded on Oahu in the Kapiolani Park-Diamond Head area in seven out of the last ten Christmas Bird Counts. Berger (1972) suggests that they were intentionally or accidentally released or escaped since 1965.

In 1975, the Hawaiian Audubon Society said that they appeared to be established locally in the Kapiolani Park and Na Laau Arboretum areas. Pyle (1976 and 1977) has recorded that they have been observed in small numbers in the Hawaiian Islands on every Christmas Bird Count since 1966.

Puerto Rico. Blake (1975) indicates that the species was introduced to Puerto Rico but gives no details.

DAMAGE

None known.

Family: *Estrildidae* Waxbills, mannikins, grassfinches

126 species in 28 genera; 35 species introduced, 13 successfully and a further 6 probably successfully

Commonly kept in aviaries, waxbills, mannikins and finches of this family seem prone to escape and establishment in new environments. The Java Sparrow, once found on Sumatra, Java and Bali alone, is now widely established in south-eastern Asia as an escapee. In the Hawaiian Islands, mainly in the mid-1960s, ten species escaped or were accidentally or intentionally released as a result of avicultural pursuits. At least four of these appear to be well established, another four are sighted regularly and may be established there.

Many of the species in this family show some pest potential for agricultural crops, especially the mannikins of the genera *Lonchura*. Such species as the Spice Finch, which has some notoriety as a destroyer of grain crops, may become a pest of crops in Australia where already it has been found to be an able competitor of the indigenous finches.

INTRODUCTIONS OF ESTRILDIDAE

Species	Date introduced	Region	Manner introduced	Reason
(a) Successful introductions				
Red-cheeked Cordon-bleu	since 1965	Hawaiian Islands	deliberate or escapee ?	cage bird
Lavender Waxbill	since 1965	Hawaiian Islands	deliberate or escapee ?	cage bird
Orange-cheeked Waxbill	prior 1874	Puerto Rico, West Indies	deliberate ?	?
	prior 1965	USA	deliberate or escapee	cage bird
	prior 1965	Hawaiian Islands	deliberate or escapee	cage bird
Common Waxbill	18th century ?	Mauritius	?	?
	prior 1870	St Helena	deliberate ?	?
	19th century ?	Ascension Island	?	?
	about 1764	Rodrigues Island	?	?
	early settlers	Amirante Islands ?	?	?
	1786	Seychelles	released or escaped ?	cage bird
	18th century ?	Réunion	deliberate ? or escapee	cage bird
	1865	Cape Verde Islands	escapee	ship borne cage birds
	between 1908-15 and 1938	Tahiti	deliberate	aesthetic ?
	before 1945 ?	New Caledonia	?	?
	about 1848 or prior 1870	Brazil	escapee ?	cage bird
Black-rumped Waxbill	about 1964	Portugal	escapee ?	cage bird
	since 1965	Hawaiian Islands	deliberate or escapee ?	cage bird
Red Avadavat	1900-10	Hawaiian Islands	escapee	cage bird
	prior 1906	Fiji	escapee ?	cage bird
	before 1946 ?	Philippines (Luzon)	escapee ?	cage bird
Red-browed Waxbill	about 1958	Western Australia	deliberate or escapee?	cage bird
	1899 and 1938	Tahiti	deliberate ?	cage bird ?
Zebra Finch	prior 1962	Nauru Island	deliberate ?	?
Bronze Mannikin	French colonisation	Puerto Rico (West Indies)	escapee ?	cage bird

INTRODUCTIONS OF ESTRILDIDAE

Species	Date introduced	Region	Manner introduced	Reason
	prior 1876	Archipel des Comores	colonisation	?
	about 1929	Fernando Póo (Gulf of Guinea)	colonisation	?
Spice Finch	about 1930	Australia	escapee	cage bird
	prior 1949 ?	Palau Archipelago	?	?
	after 1927 ?	Singapore (?)	escapee ?	cage bird ?
	?	Réunion	?	?
	1865	Hawaiian Islands	deliberate	?
	about 1800	Mauritius	?	?
Black-headed Mannikin	?	Halmahera Island, Moluccas	?	?
	about 1959	Hawaiian Islands	deliberate or escapee	cage bird
Chestnut-breasted Finch	about 1899, and 1938	Society Islands	deliberate ?	aesthetic ?
	?	New Caledonia	?	?
Java Sparrow	?	Indochina	deliberate or escapee	?
	prior 1860 ?	southern China	deliberate and escapee	cage bird
	since 1860 or earlier ?	Hong Kong	deliberate and escapee	cage bird
	prior 1925 ?	South Vietnam	deliberate and escapee	cage bird
	prior 1930s	Burma	escapee	cage bird
	prior 1910 ?	Malay Peninsula	escapee	cage bird
	1849 or earlier ?	Singapore	escapee	cage bird
	prior 1938 and later	Thailand	escapee ?	cage bird
	before 1870 and recent ?	Sri Lanka	escapee	cage bird
	prior 1860	Borneo and eastern Malaysia	escapee	cage bird
	about 1913 ?	Sulawesi	?	?
	prior 1936	Moluccas, Indonesia	?	?
	prior 1938	Philippines	escapee ?	cage bird
	about 1917	Christmas Island, Indian Ocean	?	?
	before 1828	Cocos-Keeling Islands	?	?
	about 1857	Zanzibar Island, Tanzania	deliberate	?
	about 1964	Hawaiian Islands	escapee	cage bird
	about 1930	Fiji	escapee	cage bird
	about 1960 or earlier	Florida, USA	escapee ?	cage bird
	before 1870	St Helena	escapee ?	cage bird

(b) Probably successful introductions

Species	Date introduced	Region	Manner introduced	Reason
Cordon-bleu	between 1900 and 1950	São Tomé, Gulf of Guinea	colonisation or introduction ?	?
	recent ?	Principé (Gulf of Guinea)	?	?
	1934 and 1936	Zanzibar Island	escapee ?	cage bird ?
	since 1965	Hawaiian Islands	deliberate or escapee ?	cage bird
Blue-capped Cordon-bleu	since 1965	Hawaiian Islands	deliberate or escapee ?	cage bird
Common Waxbill	?	Puerto Rico	?	?
	about 1903	Archipel des Comores	?	?

continued

Species	Date introduced	Region	Manner introduced	Reason
	?	São Tomé, Gulf of Guinea	?	?
Red Avadavat	?	Sumatra	?	?
	prior 1940	Japan	escapee	cage bird
	about 1953 ?	Hong Kong	deliberate or escapee ?	cage bird
	about 1905 and later	Egypt ?	escapee ?	cage bird ?
Green Avadavat ?	prior 1961?	Lahore, Pakistan	escapee	cage bird
Red-browed Waxbill	prior 1945 ?	New Caledonia	?	?
Banded Finch	prior 1965 ?	northern Queensland, Australia	escapee ? or range extension ?	
Common Silverbill	1960s ?	Hawaiian Islands	escapee	cage bird
	early 1970s ?	Puerto Rico	?	?
Magpie Mannikin	about 1936 ?	Zanzibar Island, and Tanzania	?	?
Javan Mannikin	1923 on	Singapore	escapees ?	cage bird ?
Black-headed Mannikin	prior 1951	Palau Archipelago	deliberate release	cage bird
	about 1929	Australia	escapee ?	cage bird
Java Sparrow	?	Lesser Sunda Islands	?	?
	?	Tanzania	?	?
	?	Pemba Island	?	?
	?	Puerto Rico	?	?

(c) Probably unsuccessful introductions

Species	Date introduced	Region	Manner introduced	Reason
Red-billed Firefinch	since 1965	Oahu, Hawaiian Islands	deliberate or escapee ?	cage bird
Common Waxbill	?	Principé	?	?
	prior 1945 ?	Fiji	?	?
Red Avadavat	since 1880	Singapore	deliberate or escapee	cage bird
Black-headed Mannikin	prior 1934 ?	Japan	escapee ?	cage bird
Java Sparrow	?	Seychelles	?	?
	prior 'Restoration' and since	Japan	escapee and deliberate	cage bird
	prior 1936 and since	Taiwan	escapee or deliberate	cage bird

(d) Unsuccessful introductions

Species	Date introduced	Region	Manner introduced	Reason
Green-winged Pytilia	about 1929	St Helena	deliberate	?
Red-billed Firefinch	1938	Tahiti	deliberate	aesthetic ?
Cordon-bleu	1938	Tahiti	deliberate	aesthetic ?
	about 1929	St Helena	deliberate	?
Red-cheeked Cordon-bleu	prior 1924	Cape Verde Islands	?	?
	1938	Tahiti	deliberate	aesthetic ?
Violet-eared Waxbill	about 1929	St Helena	deliberate	?
Orange-cheeked Waxbill	1938	Tahiti	deliberate	aesthetic ?
Yellow-bellied Waxbill	about 1929	St Helena	deliberate	?
Common Waxbill	?	Malagasy	?	?
Black-rumped Waxbill	1938	Tahiti	deliberate	aesthetic ?
Black-cheeked Waxbill	about 1929	St Helena	deliberate	?
Red Avadavat	1935	northern Thailand	escapee ?	?
	prior 1892	Mauritius	?	?
	1884 and 1904	Archipel des Comores	?	?
	prior 1867	Andaman Islands	deliberate	?
	1938	Tahiti	deliberate	aesthetic ?
	about 1874	Sri Lanka	escapee	cage bird

Species	Date introduced	Region	Manner introduced	Reason
Orange-breasted Waxbill	1938	Tahiti	deliberate	aesthetic ?
	about 1929	St Helena	deliberate	?
Red-browed Waxbill	?	Fiji	?	?
	?	New Caledonia ?	not known if released	?
	?	New Zealand	?	?
Diamond Firetail	1866, 1874, and later	New Zealand	deliberate	?
	prior 1926 and 1938	Tahiti	deliberate	aesthetic ?
	about 1920s	Fiji	?	?
	since 1965	Hawaiian Islands	escapee ?	cage bird ?
Star Finch	1938	Tahiti	deliberate	aesthetic ?
Zebra Finch	before 1885, and since	New Zealand	deliberate ? and escapee	cage bird
	1938	Tahiti	deliberate	aesthetic ?
	1937	Kangaroo Island, Australia	deliberate	?
Banded Finch	1938	Tahiti	deliberate	aesthetic ?
Long-tailed Finch	1938	Tahiti	deliberate	aesthetic ?
Pin-tailed Parrotfinch	1938	Tahiti	deliberate	aesthetic ?
Blue-faced Parrotfinch	1938	Tahiti	deliberate	aesthetic ?
Red-throated Parrotfinch	1938	Tahiti	deliberate	aesthetic ?
Red-headed Parrotfinch	1938	Tahiti	deliberate	aesthetic ?
Gouldian Finch	1938-40	Tahiti	deliberate	aesthetic ?
Plum-headed Finch	1938	Tahiti	deliberate	aesthetic ?
Bronze Mannikin	1938	Tahiti	deliberate	aesthetic ?
Magpie Mannikin	1938	Tahiti	deliberate	aesthetic ?
Spice Finch	1868	New Zealand (?)	not known if liberated	?
	1906	Seychelles	?	?
	1938	Tahiti	deliberate	aesthetic ?
Black-headed Mannikin	1938	Tahiti	deliberate	aesthetic ?
Sharp-tailed Mannikin	?	Réunion	?	?
Chestnut-breasted Finch	prior 1864, 1867 and 1871	New Zealand	deliberate	?
Java Sparrow	about 1927 and various times since	India	escapees ?	cage bird ?
	about 1750	Mauritius	escapee ?	cage bird
	about 1903	Archipel des Comores	?	?
	1865 and about 1900	Hawaiian Islands	deliberate ?	cage bird
	1862 and 1867	New Zealand ?	not known if liberated	cage bird
	1856 ?, 1863	Australia	deliberate	?

GREEN-WINGED PYTILIA
(Melba Finch, Melba Waxbill)
Pytilia melba (Linnaeus)

DISTINGUISHING CHARACTERISTICS
12.5-13.7 cm (5-5.5 in) . 12.1-18.4 g (.43-.65 oz)
Forehead, malar stripe, chin and throat red, remainder of head grey; red of throat merges to yellow or buff on breast and lower abdomen; abdomen barred or spotted white and black or white and olive-green; back and wings olive-green; upper tail-coverts, central tail-feathers and tail edges crimson; bill red. (Barring varies as does the colour of the breast and face.) Female: lacks red on head; chin and throat often barred.
Mackworth-Praed and Grant, 1952-73, ser.1, vol.2, pp.1007-1009 and pl.92; ser.2, vol.2, pp.642-643 and pl.72; ser.3, vol.2, pp.710 711 and pl.89.

GENERAL DISTRIBUTION
Africa south of the Sahara: Sénégal and northern Nigeria to the Sudan, Ethiopia and Somali Republic, and south to eastern Zaire, Zambia, Moçambique and northern South Africa; also Angola and northern South West Africa.

INTRODUCED DISTRIBUTION
Introduced unsuccessfully to St Helena.

GENERAL HABITS
Status: fairly common; commonly kept aviary bird. *Habitat:* bush and scrub in open country, generally near water. *Gregariousness:* singly, pairs or family parties. *Movements:* sedentary. *Foods:* grass and

Green-winged Pytilia

from South Africa and released by H. Bruins-Lich in about 1929, but the introduction was unsuccessful (Haydock, 1954).

DAMÂGE
None known.

RED-BILLED FIREFINCH
(African Firefinch)
Lagonosticta senegala (Linnaeus)

DISTINGUISHING CHARACTERISTICS
8.8-10.1 cm (3.52-4.04 in). 6.4-8.7 g (.23-31 oz)
Generally cerise-red; mantle and rump pale brownish, washed cerise-red; belly and under tail-coverts pale brown; a few white spots on sides of chest; flight feathers brown; tail black, edged red; bill pinkish red, culmen ridge black. Female: lores cerise-red; upper parts brown; sides of face with red wash.
Mackworth-Praed and Grant, 1952-73, ser.1, vol.2, pp.1012-1015 and pl.93; ser.2, vol.2, pp.646-648 and pl.72; ser.3, vol.2, pp.715-717 and pl.90.

GENERAL DISTRIBUTION
Central and southern Africa: Gambia and Sierra Leone east to the Sudan, Ethiopia and central Somali Republic, and south to Nigeria, northern Zaire, Uganda, and south through Kenya, Tanzania, and west to northern Angola, and south to Cape Province in South Africa.

INTRODUCED DISTRIBUTION
Introduced unsuccessfully in Tahiti and the Hawaiian Islands (?)

GENERAL HABITS
Status: common; often kept in captivity. *Habitat:* coastal savannah, grasslands, towns and villages. *Gregariousness:* pairs, parties or small flocks. *Movements:* sedentary. *Foods:* grass seeds and some insects. *Breeding:* any time of year. *Nest:* loose ball of grass, rags or other material with entrance hole at

other seeds, insects including termites. *Breeding:* all year, but varies in different areas; Nov-Aug (Transvaal). *Nest:* rough oval of grass, with rough porch and side entrance, lined with feathers and plant down, in a low bush. *Eggs:* 3, 4-5, 7.
Mackworth-Praed and Grant, 1952-73, ser.1, vol.2, pp.1007-1009; ser.2, vol.2, pp.642-643; ser.3, vol.2, pp.710-711.
Skead, *Ostrich* Suppl. no.11, 1975, pp.1-55.

NOTES ON INTRODUCTIONS
St Helena. The Green-winged Pytilia was imported

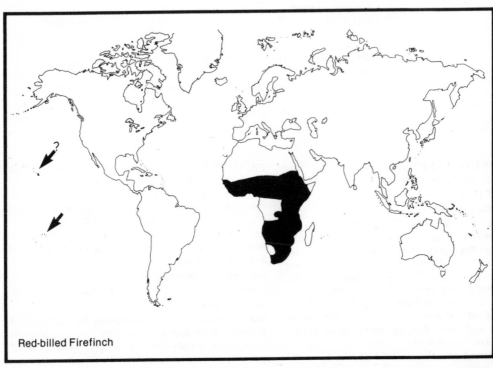

Red-billed Firefinch

side of top, often porched, and lined with feathers, in thatch, wall or bush. *Eggs:* 3-6.

Mackworth-Praed and Grant, 1952-73, ser.1, vol.2, pp.1012-1015; ser.2, vol.2, pp.646-648; ser.3, vol.2, pp.715-717.

NOTES ON INTRODUCTIONS

Tahiti. Red-billed Firefinches were released on Tahiti in 1938 and were reported to have nested and reared young there (Guild, 1938). The species does not appear to be mentioned from the island again and presumably failed to become established.

Hawaiian Islands. The Red-billed Firefinch was intentionally or accidentally released or escaped, since 1965 on Oahu (Berger, 1972) and has been observed every year in small numbers up until 1970, but not since that time (Pyle, 1976). The Hawaiian Audubon Society (1975) reports that they may still be established there, but their present status is poorly known.

DAMAGE

None known.

CORDON-BLEU
(Blue Waxbill, Blue-breasted Waxbill, Cordon-bleu Waxbill)
Uraeginthus angolensis (Linnaeus)

DISTINGUISHING CHARACTERISTICS

11.2-12.5 cm (4.5-5 in). 8.1-13 g (.29-.46 oz)
Upper parts earth brown; rump, upper tail-coverts and tail blue; around eye, sides of face, ear-coverts, chin to chest, and flanks blue; centre of breast to under tail-coverts buff-brown; bill mauve, with a black tip and cutting edges. Female: bill blue-grey.

Mackworth-Praed and Grant, 1952-73, ser.1, vol.2, pp.1033-1034 and pl.93; ser.2, vol.2, pp.659-661 and pl.73; ser.3, vol.2, pp.735-736 and pl.91.

GENERAL DISTRIBUTION

Southern Africa: from Angola, southern Congo, southern Zaire and southern Tanzania, south to eastern Cape Province.

INTRODUCED DISTRIBUTION

Introduced, probably successfully on Zanzibar and in the Hawaiian Islands; introduced or colonised successfully the islands of São Tomé and Principé in the Gulf of Guinea. Introduced unsuccessfully to Tahiti and St Helena.

GENERAL HABITS

Status: common; frequently kept cage bird. *Habitat:* cultivated areas, grasslands and villages. *Gregariousness:* pairs, small parties or flocks to 40 or more. *Movements:* sedentary. *Foods:* small seeds and insects (termites). *Breeding:* Nov-Aug. *Nest:* spherical or oval, with side entrance, of grass and lined with fine grass and feathers, in a bush, tree, hut or occasionally on telegraph poles. *Eggs:* 3, 4-6.

Mackworth-Praed and Grant, 1952-73, ser.1, vol.2, pp.1033-1034; ser.2, vol.2, pp.659-661; ser.3, vol.2, pp.735-736.

Skead, *Ostrich* Suppl. no.11, 1975, pp.1-55.

NOTES ON INTRODUCTIONS

Zanzibar Island. The race *U.a. niassensis* has been introduced to Zanzibar Island (Peters, 1968). Pakenham (1939) records that some were shot in the town of Zanzibar in 1934 and that the species was noted there in 1936. Both he and Mackworth-Praed and Grant (1955-60) indicate that the birds seen may have escaped from captivity. Their present status on Zanzibar is not known.

São Tomé and Principé (Gulf of Guinea). Peters (1968) records that the race *U.a. angolensis* has been introduced on São Tomé. Snow (1950) places the date of introduction as some time between 1900 and 1950, but it is possible that the species is a recent coloniser from mainland Africa. According to Snow, the Cordon-bleu is also a recent introduction to the island of Principé.

Hawaiian Islands. The Cordon-bleu was intentionally

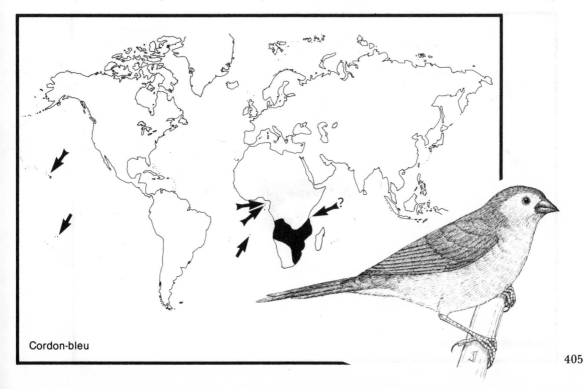

Cordon-bleu

or accidentally released or escaped, since 1965 on the island of Oahu (Berger, 1972), where it appears to have become established in the Na Laau Arboretum area (Hawaiian Audubon Society, 1975). Heilbrun (1976) says that they have been in the Kapiolani-Diamond Head area for possibly seven to ten years. The Hawaiian Audubon Society reports that they may also be established at Hualalai on the island of Hawaii.

There appears to be some doubt as to which species of Cordon-bleu has been noted in the Hawaiian Islands, but according to Berger he has seen all three *Uraeginthus* species.

Tahiti. The Cordon-bleu was released by E. Guild on Tahiti in about 1938, but was not seen again after its liberation (Guild, 1938).

St Helena. Imported from South Africa, the Cordon-bleu was released by H. Bruins-Lich in about 1929 on St Helena, but failed to become established (Haydock, 1954).

DAMAGE

None known.

RED-CHEEKED CORDON-BLEU
(Cordon-bleu)
Uraeginthus bengalus (Linnaeus)

DISTINGUISHING CHARACTERISTICS

11.4-12.7 cm (4.6-5.08 in). 9.8-12 g (.35-.42 oz)

Only differs from the preceding species in that the male has red ear-coverts and the bill tends to be pinkish with a black tip. (It is often considered only a subspecies of *angolensis*).

Mackworth-Praed and Grant, 1952-73, ser.1, vol.2, pp.1034-1037 and pl.93; ser.2, vol.2, p.661; ser.3, vol.2, pp.736-738 and pl.91.

GENERAL DISTRIBUTION

Central Africa: from Senegal and Guinea, east to the Sudan and Ethiopia, and south to Kenya, Tanzania, Zambia, eastern Angola and southern Zaire.

INTRODUCED DISTRIBUTION

Introduced successfully in the Hawaiian Islands. Introduced unsuccessfully in the Cape Verde Islands (died out) and to Tahiti.

GENERAL HABITS

Status: common; frequently kept in captivity. *Habitat:* savannah woodland, grassland, cultivated areas and villages. *Gregariousness:* pairs or small parties. *Movements:* sedentary (?). *Foods:* seeds and insects. *Breeding:* all year, except perhaps July. *Nest:* spherical or oval-shaped, of grass, lined with fine grass and feathers, entrance hole low down on side, in a bush or tree. *Eggs:* 3, 4-5, 6.

Mackworth-Praed and Grant, 1952-73, ser.1, vol.2, pp.1034-1037; ser.2, vol.2, p.661; ser.3, vol.2, pp.736-738.

NOTES ON INTRODUCTIONS

Cape Verde Islands. Bannerman and Bannerman (1968) record that the Red-cheeked Cordon-bleu (race *bengalus*) was introduced to São Vincente prior to 1924, as specimens were obtained there at this time. It no longer occurs on the island.

Tahiti. Red-cheeked Cordon-bleus were released by E. Guild on Tahiti in 1938 (Guild, 1938). At this time he reported that they had nested there and reared young soon after their introduction. They no longer occur on Tahiti so evidently did not remain established for long.

Hawaiian Islands. According to Berger (1972) the Red-cheeked Cordon-bleu was also intentionally or accidentally released or escaped, on the island of Oahu since about 1965. Some have been observed (small numbers) on the Christmas Bird Counts in every year up until and including 1976 (Pyle, 1976 and 1977). The Hawaiian Audubon Society reports that the species appears to be established, but that its present status is poorly known. In late 1976 or early

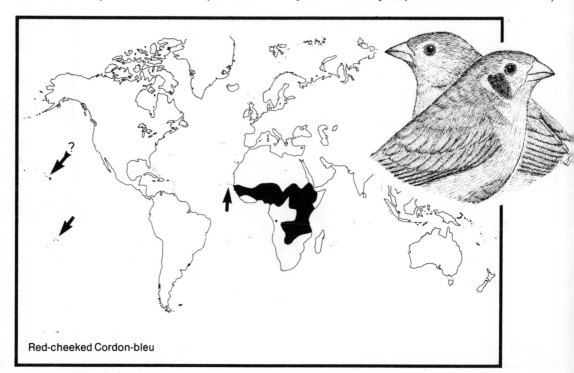

Red-cheeked Cordon-bleu

1977 the population was estimated at thirty to fifty birds in the Diamond Head area (Ralph and Pyle, 1977).

DAMAGE
None known.

BLUE-CAPPED CORDON-BLEU
Uraeginthus cyanocephalus (Richmond)

DISTINGUISHING CHARACTERISTICS
11.4-12.7 cm (4.56-5.08 in)
Forehead to nape blue, uniform with sides of face and underparts; bill red, deep pink or beetroot, and tipped black. Similar to Cordon-bleu except for above. Female: blue on top of head confined to forehead, or absent.
Mackworth-Praed and Grant, ser.1, vol.2, 1952-73, p.1037 and pl.93.

GENERAL DISTRIBUTION
Eastern Africa: from northern Kenya, southern Somali Republic, and adjacent Ethiopia, south through eastern Kenya to Dodoma and Kilosa in Tanzania.

INTRODUCED DISTRIBUTION
Introduced, possibly successfully in the Hawaiian Islands (Oahu ?).

GENERAL HABITS
Status: locally common; common cage bird. *Habitat:* dry country. *Gregariousness:* pairs or small parties. *Movements:* sedentary. *Foods:* grass seeds and termites. *Breeding:* Nov-Jan, also recorded in June (?). *Nest:* oval or barrel-shaped, of grass with entrance hole low on side. *Eggs:* 4-6, at least.
Mackworth-Praed and Grant, ser.1, vol.2, 1952-73, p.1037.

NOTES ON INTRODUCTIONS
Hawaiian Islands. The Blue-capped Cordon-bleu was intentionally or accidentally released or escaped on Oahu since 1965 (Berger, 1972). Some were observed in 1969 and 1970 and again in 1975 (Pyle, 1976;

Heilbrun, 1976), and the species may be established, although those seen may only have been escapees (Heilbrun). Its present status is, however, poorly known (Hawaiian Audubon Society, 1975).

DAMAGE
None known.

VIOLET-EARED WAXBILL
(Grenadier Waxbill)
Uraeginthus granatina (Linnaeus)

DISTINGUISHING CHARACTERISTICS
12.5-14 cm (5-5.6 in). 9-13.9 g (.32-.49 oz)
Generally rich chestnut except for a bright blue forehead and upper tail-coverts; cheeks violet; chin, throat, centre of belly and long graduated tail black; bill crimson or purple-pink. Female: duller; back mouse brown and with a chestnut wash on head; forehead, upper tail-coverts and sides of face paler; underparts buff; wings earth brown.
Mackworth-Praed and Grant, ser.2, vol.2, 1952-73, pp.662-663 and pl.73.

GENERAL DISTRIBUTION
Southern Africa: southern Angola, south-western Africa, western Rhodesia, south-western Zambia to southern Moçambique and northern Cape Province.

INTRODUCED DISTRIBUTION
Introduced unsuccessfully to St Helena.

GENERAL HABITS
Status: fairly common. *Habitat:* thorn country and arid steppe. *Gregariousness:* pairs or small parties often with other species. *Movements:* sedentary. *Foods:* seeds and insects. *Breeding:* Jan-June. *Nest:* loose spherical structure with a side entrance, lined with feathers, in a thorn bush. *Eggs:* 3-4, 5.
Mackworth-Praed and Grant, ser.2, vol.2, 1952-73, pp.662-663.
Skead, *Ostrich* Suppl. no.11, 1975, pp.1-55.

NOTES ON INTRODUCTIONS
St Helena. Violet-eared Waxbills were imported from

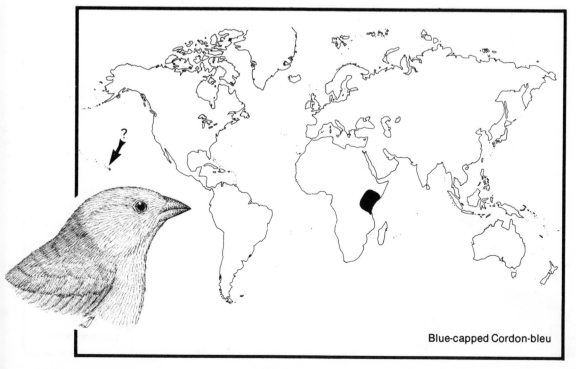

Blue-capped Cordon-bleu

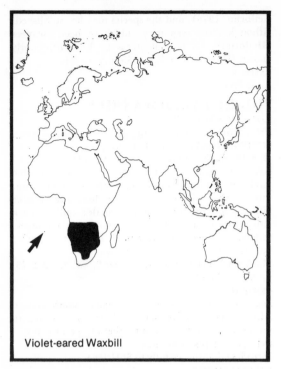

Violet-eared Waxbill

Generally dusky grey, with paler underparts; lores, eye-stripe and chin black; lower rump and upper tail-coverts red; lower belly and under tail-coverts blackish; tail black; bill blue-grey.

Mackworth-Praed and Grant, 1952-73, ser.1, vol.2, pp.1027-1028; ser.2, vol.2, pp.655-656 and pl.73; ser.3, vol.2, pp.729 and pl.90.

GENERAL DISTRIBUTION

Southern Africa: from Gabon, south to western Angola, and east through the southern Congo, northern Zambia to Tanzania and Moçambique: also from southern Rhodesia and Moçambique, south to Natal and Zululand.

INTRODUCED DISTRIBUTION

Introduced successfully in the Hawaiian Islands (Oahu).

GENERAL HABITS

Status: uncommon; fairly common in captivity. *Habitat:* open spaces in forest with thick bush. *Gregariousness:* singly or in pairs. *Movements:* sedentary (?). *Foods:* small grass seeds. *Breeding:* Oct-Mar; double brooded. *Nest:* large, retort-shaped nest of fine grass with short tubular entrance sloping downwards, lined with seed heads, in a shrub, bamboo or small tree. *Eggs:* 4-6.

Mackworth-Praed and Grant, 1952-73, ser.1, vol.2, pp.1027-1028; ser.2, vol.2, pp.655-656; ser.3, vol.2, p.729.

NOTES ON INTRODUCTIONS

Hawaiian Islands. There appears to have been some doubt as to whether *E. perreini* or *E. caerulescens* (a similar species but having red under tail-coverts) has become established on Oahu. Those reports with sufficient descriptive detail indicate that the species has black under tail-coverts and is therefore *perreini*.

Berger (1972) reports that they were intentionally or accidentally released or escaped, on the island since 1965. They have been recorded in the Kapiolani Park — Diamond Head area on every Christmas Bird

South Africa and released by agriculture officer, H. Bruins-Lich in about 1929, but failed to become established on St Helena (Haydock, 1954).

DAMAGE

None known.

LAVENDER WAXBILL
(Lavender Firefinch, Grey Waxbill)
Estrilda perreini (Vieillot)

DISTINGUISHING CHARACTERISTICS
11.2 cm (4.48 in)

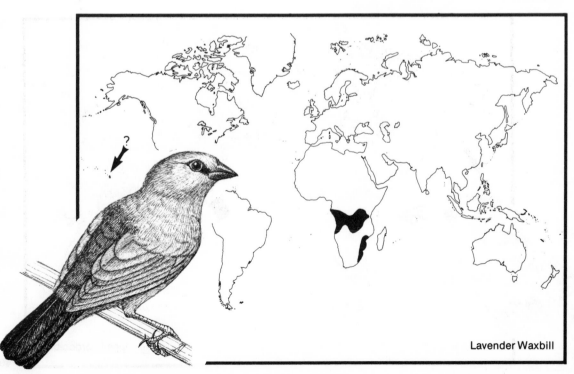

Lavender Waxbill

Count, from 1966 to 1976 (Pyle, 1976 and 1977; Heilbrun, 1976), and appear to be well established although they have not yet been recorded to breed there. In late 1976 or early 1977 the population was estimated to be thirty to fifty birds (Ralph and Pyle, 1977).

More recently Ashman and Pyle (1979) found *E. caerulescens* (?) established in a small area near the Puu Waawaa Ranch on the island of Hawaii in 1978. They also indicate that this is the species established on Oahu.

DAMAGE

None known.

YELLOW-BELLIED WAXBILL
(Swee Waxbill)
Estrilda melanotis (Temminck)

DISTINGUISHING CHARACTERISTICS

8.7-10 cm (3.5-4 in)

Sides of face and chin black, remainder of head grey; back olive-green, faintly and narrowly barred; rump and upper tail-coverts orange-scarlet or crimson; breast pale grey merging to pale buff or yellow on abdomen and under tail-coverts; wings green with indistinct barring; short square tail black; upper mandible black, lower red. Female: lacks black on face.

Mackworth-Praed and Grant, 1952-73, ser.1, vol.2, pp.1018-1019 and pl.93; ser.2, vol.2, pp.649-651 and pl.73; ser.3, vol.2, pp.721-722 and pl.91.

GENERAL DISTRIBUTION

Eastern and southern Africa: Ethiopia and southern Sudan to eastern Zaire, Uganda, Tanzania, Zambia, Malawi, Rhodesia, southern Moçambique and eastern Cape Province; also southern and central-western Angola.

INTRODUCED DISTRIBUTION

Introduced unsuccessfully to St Helena.

Yellow-bellied Waxbill

GENERAL HABITS

Status: common. *Habitat:* grassy highland clearings and thickets, coastal bush, streamsides and gardens. *Gregariousness:* pairs or small parties. *Movements:* no information. *Foods:* grass seeds and insects. *Breeding:* all year. *Nest:* long ovoid grass nest, lined with feathers and seed down, insecurely attached to a shrub or tree. *Eggs:* 3-5 (up to 10 known, but possibly due to more than one bird).

Mackworth-Praed and Grant, 1952-73, ser.1, vol.2, pp.1018-1019; ser.2, vol.2, pp.649-657; ser.3, vol.2, pp.721-722.

NOTES ON INTRODUCTIONS

St Helena. Imported from South Africa, the Yellow-bellied Waxbill was released on St Helena in about 1929 by an agricultural officer, H. Bruins-Lich, but failed to become established (Haydock, 1954).

ORANGE-CHEEKED WAXBILL
Estrilda melpoda (Vieillot)

DISTINGUISHING CHARACTERISTICS

8.8-10.6 cm (3.5-4.2 in). 6.9 g (.24 oz)

Forehead to nape grey; hindneck, mantle, scapulars, wing-coverts and upper rump earth brown; lower rump and upper tail-coverts crimson; lores, around eye, sides of face and ear-coverts orange, or scarlet-orange; chin and throat whitish; flight feathers dusky, with brown edges; underparts pale grey, with buffish yellow; tail blackish; bill pale red.

Mackworth-Praed and Grant, 1952-73, ser.2, vol.2, p.654 and pl.73; ser.3, vol.2, pp.726-727 and pl.90.

GENERAL DISTRIBUTION

Central West Africa: from Sénégal, east to the Central African Republic, and south to the Congo, western Zaire and northern Angola.

INTRODUCED DISTRIBUTION

Introduced successfully to Puerto Rico, the USA (southern California) and the Hawaiian Islands (Oahu). Introduced unsuccessfully in Tahiti.

GENERAL HABITS

Status: very common; frequently kept aviary bird. *Habitat:* forest clearings, grasslands and cultivation. *Gregariousness:* small flocks. *Movements:* sedentary. *Foods:* grass seeds. *Breeding:* most of the year. *Nest:* oval or bottle-shaped of grass, with short tubular entrance, in grass or a bush near ground. *Eggs:* 5-6.

Mackworth-Praed and Grant, 1952-73, ser.2, vol.2, p.654; ser.3, vol.2, pp.726-727.

NOTES ON INTRODUCTIONS

West Indies. The race *E.m. melpoda* has been introduced and established on Puerto Rico (Bond, 1960; Peters, 1968) and now occurs over much of the south-west part of the island (Bond, 1971). According to Biaggi (1963) they were introduced from western Africa some time before 1874.

They were first recorded there at this date when they were established on the coastal plain from Anasco to Mayagüez and Cabo Rojo (Wetmore, 1927). Wetmore records that at this time (mid-1920s ?) they occurred in the same area except for an extension in range to Yauco.

USA. The Orange-cheeked Waxbill was noted to have become established in southern California at Averill Park, San Pedro in 1965 (Hardy, 1973). Hardy reports that flocks of between fifteen and twenty birds have been consistently observed in the area and that

409

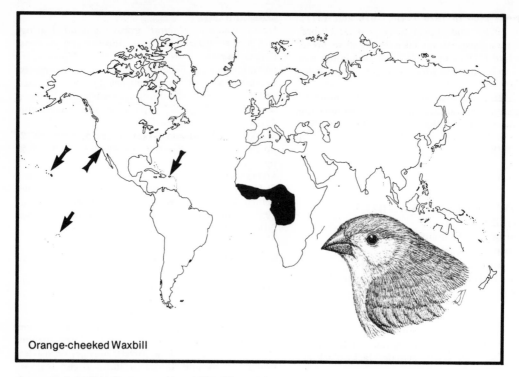

Orange-cheeked Waxbill

they were breeding there as early as 1968. The species was still present in the area in 1972.

Hawaiian Islands. Eight Orange-cheeked Waxbills were seen on the Na Laau Trail in the Diamond Head area of Oahu in 1965, and later in the same year some thirty were counted; six were seen in 1966 and more than twenty in each of the following three years during the Christmas Bird Counts (Berger, 1972).

The species has now been sighted on every Christmas Bird Count from 1966 to 1976 and appears to be increasing slowly in numbers (Pyle, 1976 and 1977).

Tahiti. Orange-cheeked Waxbills were reported to have been released in Tahiti by E. Guild in 1938 (Guild, 1938). He reported that they had nested and reared young soon after their liberation. The species does not now occur on Tahiti so evidently was unsuccessful in becoming permanently established.

DAMAGE
None known.

COMMON WAXBILL
(Waxbill, St Helena Waxbill, Astrild)
Estrilda astrild (Linnaeus)

DISTINGUISHING CHARACTERISTICS
10-12.5 cm (4-5 in)
Forehead to nape grey-brown; upper parts pale brown, closely and narrowly barred dusky; lores and streak through eye to ear-coverts crimson-red; sides of face, chin and throat white, washed variably with pinkish; remainder of underparts barred dusky white and pale brown; centre of breast and belly pale crimson-red; lower belly and under tail-coverts black; bill red.
Mackworth-Praed and Grant, 1952-1973, ser.1, vol.2, pp.1019-1021 and pl.93, ser.2, vol.2, pp.651-653 and pl.73; ser.3, vol.2, pp.722-724 and pl.90.

GENERAL DISTRIBUTION
Southern Africa: Sierra Leone and Liberia, Cameroon, southern Central African Republic, southern Sudan, Ethiopia and south to the Republic of South Africa.

INTRODUCED DISTRIBUTION
Introduced successfully on St Helena, Mauritius, Ascension Island, Rodrigues, Amirantes, Seychelles, Réunion, Cape Verde Islands, São Tomé, New Caledonia, Tahiti, and to Brazil in South America; introduced probably successfully on Puerto Rico. Introduced successfully, but not now present on Malagasy (extinct), Archipel des Comores (died out ?), Principé (extinct) and (?) Fiji (died out ?).

GENERAL HABITS
Status: very common; frequently kept cage bird. *Habitat:* woodlands, grasslands, marshy country, cultivated areas, gardens and villages. *Gregariousness:* usually small flocks to twenty or thirty birds, but occasionally very large flocks in non-breeding season. *Movements:* sedentary (?). *Foods:* grass and weed seeds, and insects. *Breeding:* most of the year; Oct-Mar (Seychelles). *Nest:* large, pear-shaped grass nest, lined with feathers and down; frequently with spare chamber and straight tunnel entrance; in a grass tuft or low cover (on St Helena in holes in caves and cliffs). *Eggs:* 4, 5-6, 8.
Mackworth-Praed and Grant, 1952-73, ser.1, vol.2, pp.1019-1021; ser.2, vol.2, pp.651-653; ser.3, vol.2, pp.722-724.

NOTES ON INTRODUCTIONS
St Helena. Either the race *E.a. astrild* (Peters, 1968) or *E.a. jagoensis* (Bourne, 1955) has been introduced successfully on St Helena. Melliss (1870) found the species to be common and abundant there in about 1870.

Haydock (1954) collected specimens in 1952-53 and compared them with a number of African sub-

410

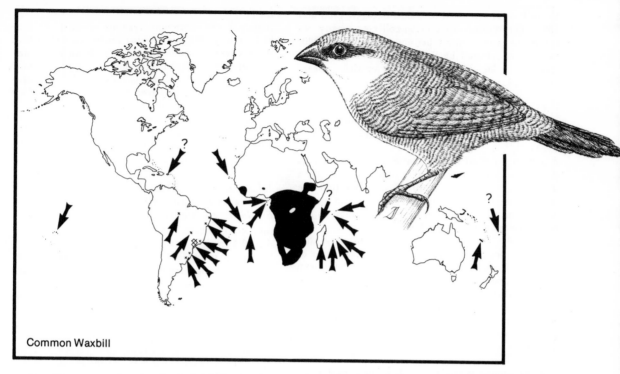

Common Waxbill

species. He suggests that the race is *astrild* and not an indigenous one, *sanctae-helenae,* and was probably imported originally from Africa at some unknown early date.

Mauritius. The Common Waxbill (*E.a. astrild*) was successfully introduced to Mauritius (Meinertzhagen, 1912) as a cage bird in the eighteenth century. They escaped from captivity to become established and are gradually becoming more abundant and widespread there (Rountree *et al,* 1952; Benedict, 1957; Staub, 1976).

Malagasy. The race *E.a. astrild* has been introduced to Malagasy but is now extinct there (Peters, 1968).

Archipel des Comores. Common Waxbills were found in the Comores in 1903 (Reichenow, 1908 in Benson, 1960), but have not been recorded again and presumably died out (Benson, 1960). Peters (1968) reports that the species is now extinct there although Gaymer *et al* (1969) say that it has been successful.

Ascension Island. Stonehouse (1962) reports that the Common Waxbill was introduced to Ascension some time in the last century. He found on his visit to the island that there were some 300-400 birds still present there.

Rodrigues. The race *E.a. astrild* has been introduced and established on Rodrigues (Gill, 1967; Peters, 1968) and is now common over most of the island. According to Staub (1976) they were introduced from Mauritius around 1764.

Amirante Islands. The race *E.a. astrild* has also been successfully introduced to the Amirantes (Peters, 1968). According to Penny (1974) they are still found on the island of Alphonse, and were once recorded on Desroches, where they were presumably introduced by the early settlers from Africa.

Seychelles. Common Waxbills may have been introduced to the Seychelles as long ago as 1786

(Gaymer *et al,* 1969) as a cage bird from Africa by the earliest of settlers (Penny, 1974). They are now common on the plateau of La Digue and near the west coast of the island of Mahé.

Réunion. The race *E.a. astrild* has been successfully introduced to Réunion (Peters, 1968). Watson *et al* (1963) record that the species is common there breeding in December and January. Staub (1976) indicates that they were an early introduction, originally as a cage bird.

Cape Verde Islands. Common Waxbills escaped in 1865 on São Vincente when a French bird-dealer from Goree was shipping some to Europe. The steamer on which the birds were housed was wrecked and hundreds of them escaped (Bannerman, 1949).

In 1967 the species was plentiful on the islands of São Tiago and Brava, and had recently arrived on Fogo, but had been exterminated some time earlier on São Vincente; the species was also found on Santo Antão in 1924 but was not present there in 1966 (Bannerman and Bannerman, 1968).

The race established in the Cape Verde Islands appears to be that from Angola, *E.a. jagoensis.*

São Tomé and Principe (Gulf of Guinea). According to Bourne (1955) the race *E.a. jagoensis* has been introduced to both São Tomé and Principé. Peters (1968) records that they are probably now extinct on Principé.

New Caledonia. The Common Waxbill has been introduced to New Caledonia (Mayr, 1945). At present they occur there in large numbers in gardens and cultivated areas (Delacour, 1966).

Fiji. Either the Common Waxbill or the Red-eared Waxbill *(Aegintha temporalis)* has been introduced and established on the island of Viti Levu (Mayr, 1945). There do not now appear to be any records, except the above, of either species on the island.

Tahiti. Holyoak (1974) reports that the Common 411

Waxbill was introduced to Tahiti between 1908 and 1915. The Whitney Expedition collected twenty-two specimens there in November and December of 1920. Some were released by E. Guild in 1938 and were reported to be breeding shortly after their release (Guild, 1938).

The species is now common in the coastal zones, but rare in the interior of both Tahiti and the island of Moorea, where they had not previously been recorded (Holyoak, 1972; Thibault and Rives, 1975).

Brazil. Sick (1966) reports that *E. astrild* and not as previously thought *E. troglodytes,* has been introduced successfully in Brazil. He says that the species came to that country prior to 1870 and that its distribution there has been provoked by man as has the House Sparrow (*Passer domesticus*).

Mitchell (1957), quoting Santos (1948), says that they were possibly brought to Brazil in the days of Emperor Dom Pedro I, in which case they have been established for well over one hundred years. Mitchell indicates that the species has never spread far and at this time was established in the Botanical Gardens in Rio de Janeiro. Sick (1968) reports that they were imported to South America in the period up until 1889 when slave ships were plying between there and Africa.

The Common Waxbill has only become established in the vicinity of towns and in this respect was in Vitória, Espirito Santo, some time after 1940, Salvador, Bahia, at least since 1964, Recife, Pernambuco, in 1967, and also possibly in Meceio, Algoas; escaped birds became established in Manaus in 1967 and in Belo Horizonte, Minas Geraise in 1968 (Sick, 1968).

Puerto Rico. Blake (1975) indicates that the species has been introduced to Puerto Rico, but does not mention whether it is at present established there.

Although the Common Waxbill appears to cause little, if any, damage in Africa it has caused at least some concern where introduced. Bannerman and Bannerman (1968) say that they are a pest to tomato crops in the Cape Verde Islands. In the Seychelles they apparently caused great harm to the crops of the early settlers, but now the species is not very numerous owing to fewer seed crops being grown and the drainage of grasslands for plantations (Penny, 1974). The species feeds on rice in Tahiti (Holyoak, 1974), but there is no record of them destroying crops.

BLACK-RUMPED WAXBILL
(Red-eared Waxbill, Grey Waxbill)
Estrilda troglodytes (Lichtenstein)

DISTINGUISHING CHARACTERISTICS
8.8-10.2 cm (3.5-4 in). 6.9 g (.24 oz)
Upper parts greyish tawny, with indistinct, close, narrow barring; crimson streak from lores through eye to top of ear-coverts; underparts buffish, with pink wash and barring; small crimson patch in centre of lower belly; flanks greyish tawny and barred; under tail-coverts whitish; upper tail-coverts black; tail black, with white edging; bill red.
Mackworth-Praed and Grant, 1952-73, ser.1, vol.2, pp.1021-1022; ser.3, vol.2, p.725 and pl.90.

GENERAL DISTRIBUTION
From Senegal to central Sudan and north-western Ethiopia, and south to north-western Uganda and northern Zaire.

INTRODUCED DISTRIBUTION
Introduced successfully in Portugal and the Hawaiian Islands. Introduced unsuccessfully in Tahiti.

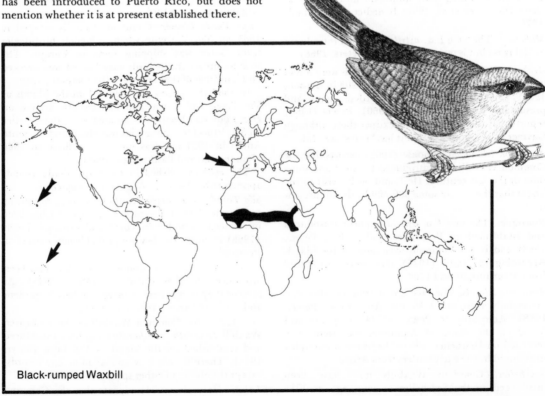

Black-rumped Waxbill

Formerly thought to have been introduced successfully in Brazil, but species present there now identified as *E. astrild*.

GENERAL HABITS

Status: fairly common locally. *Habitat:* swampy areas, banks of streams and dry bush country in the arid zone. *Gregariousness:* usually small, but occasionally large flocks. *Movements:* sedentary (?). *Foods:* seeds and insects. *Breeding:* June-Nov. *Nest:* oval or pear-shaped of grass, with porch on one side, on the ground or in a tuft of grass. *Eggs:* 3-6, or more.

Mackworth-Praed and Grant, 1952-73, ser.1, vol.2, pp.1021-1022; ser.3, vol.2, p.725.

NOTES ON INTRODUCTIONS

Portugal. The Black-rumped Waxbill has been imported into Portugal from Africa as a cage bird for many years. Fairly recently it was reported to be established in the wild there (Vincente, 1969). Vincente reports that a possible explanation for its presence is that a few escaped from a private aviary near Lagoa de Obidos (some 100 km [62 miles] north of Lisbon) and have since increased to some 1000 birds. One hundred were seen in August 1964 at Obidos and they were breeding there in 1965-66.

Several hundred birds were observed between Obidos and Vau in 1967, some 200 were sighted at the Obidos railway station in the same year, and some were sighted at Galeota south of there. They were observed at Ponta da Erva in November 1967, and at the end of 1968 at Pintens, some 70 km and 60 km (44 and 37.5 miles) respectively, south of the Obidos region.

Hawaiian Islands. Like many other species of small finch, the Black-rumped Waxbill was intentionally or accidentally released or escaped, since 1965 on the island of Oahu (Berger, 1972). They now appear to be established in the Kapiolani Park — Diamond Head area where they have been observed on every Christmas Bird Count from 1966 to 1976 (Hawaiian Audubon Society, 1975; Pyle, 1976 and 1977). Pyle says that their numbers appear to be slowly increasing.

Tahiti. Black-rumped Waxbills were released on Tahiti by E. Guild (1938) in 1938 and were reported to have nested and reared young there. Guild (1940) later reports that they were still established, but there appear to have been no records of them in more recent years. Evidently the species was unsuccessful there.

DAMAGE

None known.

BLACK-CHEEKED WAXBILL

Estrilda erythronotos (Vieillot)

DISTINGUISHING CHARACTERISTICS

12-13 cm (4.8-5.2 in)

Mainly grey with vinous pink suffusion on upper parts and breast; rump, flanks and lower breast deep crimson; sides of face, chin, lower abdomen and tail black; upper parts narrowly and indistinctly barred dusky; wings barred black and white or greyish white; bill black or blue-grey. (One race is paler and pinker and one lacks black on abdomen and has little or none on the chin.) Female: flanks paler red and birds less vinous.

Black-cheeked Waxbill

Mackworth-Praed and Grant, 1952-73, ser.1, vol.2, pp.1031-1032; ser.2, vol.2, pp.657-658 and pl.73.

GENERAL DISTRIBUTION

Southern and north-eastern Africa: Ethiopia and southern Somali Republic to Kenya, Uganda and northern Tanzania; south-western Angola and northern South West Africa to northern Cape Province.

INTRODUCED DISTRIBUTION

Introduced unsuccessfully to St Helena.

GENERAL HABITS

Status: common. *Habitat:* acacia scrubs and rocky country. *Gregariousness:* pairs or small parties of up to 15 birds. *Movements:* no information. *Foods:* grass seeds, green vegetable material and insects. *Breeding:* Jan-Apr. *Nest:* large, untidy, rounded grass nest, lined with finer grass, porched with entrance tube at the side and facing downwards, in a tree. *Eggs:* 3, 4-6.

Mackworth-Praed and Grant, 1952-73, ser.1, vol.2, pp.1031-1032; ser.2, vol.2, pp.657-658.

NOTES ON INTRODUCTIONS

St Helena. The Black-cheeked Waxbill was imported from South Africa by an agricultural officer, H. Bruins-Lich, and released in about 1929 (Haydock, 1954). However, the species did not become established on St Helena.

DAMAGE

None known.

RED AVADAVAT

(Strawberry Finch, Red Waxbill, Scarlet Amandava, Amadavat, Red Munia)

Amandava amandava (Linnaeus)

DISTINGUISHING CHARACTERISTICS

9.3-10 cm (3.7-4 in)

Generally brownish red, stippled with white spots; upper tail-coverts and breast crimson; lower belly blackish, dark brown or orange-yellow; flanks spotted   413

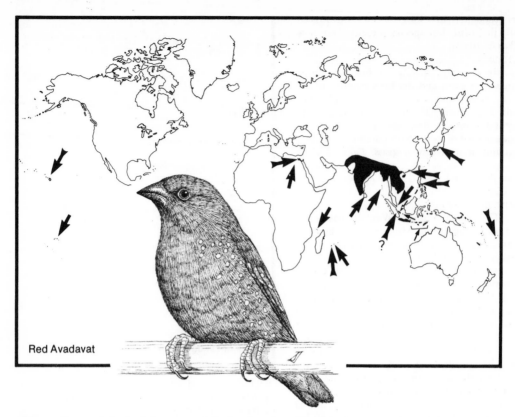

Red Avadavat

white; tail rounded, dark brown and finely tipped white; bill red, dusky at base of culmen. Female and male in non-breeding: upper parts brownish; underparts buffy brown, lighter on belly and throat.
Ali and Ripley, vol.10, 1968-74, pp.101-103 and pl.105, fig.7, opp. p.80.
Avon *et al,* 1974, pl. opp. p.46.

GENERAL DISTRIBUTION
Southern and south-eastern Asia: western Pakistan, India and southern Nepal, east to southern China (Yunnan) and Hainan, and south to Indochina, Java, Bali, Lombok, Flores, Sumba and Timor.

INTRODUCED DISTRIBUTION
Introduced successfully in Sumatra (?), Philippines (Luzon), Japan, Réunion (now rare), Hawaiian Islands (Oahu), Fiji and in Egypt; introduced successfully or vagrant in Hong Kong. Introduced successfully but not now present in Singapore (died out ?), Mauritius (extirpated ?), Archipel des Comores (died out ?) and in Sri Lanka (died out ?).

Introduced unsuccessfully in the Andaman Islands and on Tahiti.

GENERAL HABITS
Status: fairly common; popular and frequently kept cage bird. *Habitat:* wet grasslands, reeds, secondary growth, scrub, gardens, villages and cultivation (especially rice fields). *Gregariousness:* pairs and small flocks to 30 birds and often with other mannikins; occasionally very large flocks. *Movements:* sedentary, but somewhat erratic movements probably dependent on food. *Foods:* seeds, grain and insects. *Breeding:* June-Dec and at other times, mostly after rains. *Nest:* small, untidy, globular structure of grass, lined with fine grass and feathers, in a bush, tussock or bracken. *Eggs:* 4-7, 10.
414   Ali and Ripley, vol.10, 1968-74, pp.101-103.

NOTES ON INTRODUCTIONS
Singapore. The race *A.a. punicea* (Peters, 1968) has been introduced on Singapore Island (Delacour, 1947; Gibson-Hill, 1949). Gibson-Hill records that Hume (1880) said that the species was plentiful there in a wild state in 1880. They were still numerous in 1924, but there appear to be few later records.

Gibson-Hill suggested in 1949 that the Red Avadavat was no longer breeding on the island in a feral state, although it was still being imported in large numbers as a cage bird. The few records of them after the second World War are probably of escapees or those deliberately released at intervals.
Thailand. A specimen of the race *A.a. amandava* was caught in northern Thailand in 1935, presumably a feral bird, however, the species occurs naturally in most of Thailand (Lekagul and Cronin, 1974).
Sumatra. The race *A.a. punicea* (Peters, 1968) has been introduced to Sumatra (Delacour, 1947; Ali and Ripley, 1968-1974).
Philippines. According to du Pont (1971) the Red Avadavat is established around Manila on the island of Luzon, from South-east Asia. Delacour and Mayr (1946) record that it became established as a result of escapees from cages.
Hong Kong. The present status of the Red Avadavat in Hong Kong is uncertain. Webster (1975) reports that they are regularly observed in parties of up to thirty-five birds on the Mai Po Marshes, at Long Valley and occasionally elsewhere, and probably breed in the wild there. Those seen may be birds which have escaped or been released as the species is a popular cage bird, but it is also possible that they reached Hong Kong as a vagrant from the Chinese mainland. Some were noted at Mai Po as early as 1953 (Dove and Goodhart, 1955).

Japan. Kaburaki (1940) records that the Red Avadavat has been introduced and established in Japan. There appear to be few recent records, but the species is said to still breed in Honshu and southwards as an escapee from captivity (Ornithological Society of Japan, 1974).

Mauritius. Apparently the Red Avadavat was imported in early times to Mauritius, became established there, but was wiped out in the cyclone of 1892 (Benedict, 1957; Rountree *et al,* 1952) or shortly after in 1896 (Staub, 1976). A colony was reported to be flourishing in part of the west coast savannah in about 1951, but the report could not be verified (Rountree).

Réunion. Staub (1976) records that the Red Avadavat was also introduced to Réunion at an early date and is now rare there.

Archipel des Comores. The Red Avadavat has been recorded, and specimens were collected in 1884 and 1904, but the species is not now a resident on the Comores (Benson, 1960). Milne-Edwards and Oustalet (1888, in Benson) reported a specimen collected, which cannot now be traced, from Mayotte in 1884; Reichenow (1908, in Benson) collected five birds on Mohéli in 1904.

Andaman Islands. Beavan (1867) records that Colonel R. C. Tyler released some twenty-five Red Avadavats at Port Blair in the Andamans in the time of the convict settlement there. These birds were not seen again after their release.

Sri Lanka. Legge (1874) mentions that the Red Avadavat has escaped and become established at Colombo where cages of them had been imported from Bengal, India. There appears to be no further mention of the species in Sri Lanka.

Hawaiian Islands. Red Avadavats probably came to Hawaii some time between 1900 and 1910, as many were imported as cage birds during this period, and it was supposed that some escaped (Caum, 1933). They were established for many years about Pearl Harbour on Oahu (Peterson, 1961).

Some were observed on the Christmas Bird Counts in 1966, but few have been seen since then (Pyle, 1976). The species may still be established in grassy areas on the Waipio Peninsula (Hawaiian Audubon Society, 1975). More recently, some have been recorded again on Oahu, but well away from the peninsula area.

Fiji. The Red Avadavat has become established on the island of Viti Levu (Parham, 1954; Gorman, 1975), having possibly escaped from aviaries (Turbet, 1941) some time prior to about 1906 (Wood and Wetmore, 1926). According to Wood and Wetmore they were introduced by the Hon Mr Remenchneider in the suburbs of Suva (deliberately ?). The species is restricted to the larger islands of Viti Levu and Vanua Levu where it is present in small numbers (Mercer, 1966; Holyoak, 1979).

Tahiti. Red Avadavats were released on Tahiti in 1938 by E. Guild and were reported by him to have nested and reared young soon after their release (Guild, 1938).

The species does not now occur on the island, so was apparently unsuccessful.

Egypt. Safriel (1975) records the reoccurrence of Red Avadavats four kilometres (3 miles) south-west of Isma'iliya, on the western bank of the Suez Canal in Egypt. This location is well west of the species' present range and their presence there may be due to escaped birds.

According to Meinertzhagen (1930) the species was introduced in Egypt and prior to about 1924 they were common near El Giza, Inshas, Bilbeis and at the Delta Barrage, but thereafter disappeared. He notes that some were recorded at Faiyum (by Hachisuka, 1924) and that the first appearance of the species in the Delta region was in 1905. No further birds appear to have been seen after 1924, except for some at Luxor in 1928 by Meinertzhagen, until the recent reoccurrence in 1975. Nicoll reportedly informed Hachisuka (1924) that the species had been resident, since 1914, within a radius of thirty-two kilometres (20 miles) of Cairo. The species was breeding at El Giza, Delta Barrage and at Inshas in the early 1920s (Raw *et al,* 1921).

DAMAGE

Mercer (1966) reports that the Red Avadavat has been recorded as a pest of immature rice in the Fijian Islands.

GREEN AVADAVAT
(Green Munia)
Amandava formosa (Latham)

DISTINGUISHING CHARACTERISTICS
10-10.2 cm (4-4.1 in)

Upper parts olive-green; underparts yellowish, but breast, centre of belly and under tail-coverts brighter; flanks barred with blackish brown (or olive-brown) and white; tail, rounded, black; bill scarlet. Female: browner upper parts; duller and paler underparts.

Ali and Ripley, vol.10, 1968-1974, pp.103-104 and pl.107, fig.8, opp. p.128.

Avon *et al,* 1974, pl. p.45.

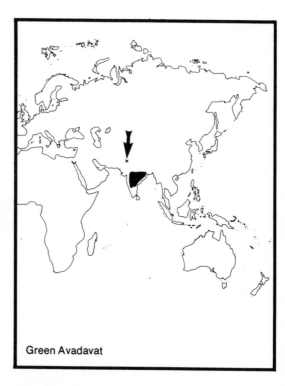

Green Avadavat

Central India: from northern Gujarat and southern Rajasthan, east through Madhya Pradesh and southern Uttar Pradesh to Bihar, Orissa and West Bengal.

INTRODUCED DISTRIBUTION

Probably introduced successfully in Lahore, Pakistan.

GENERAL HABITS

Status: local and uncommon. *Habitat:* open deciduous forest, stony scrub jungle, grassland with bush and sugar cane fields. *Gregariousness:* flocks of 30-50 in non-breeding season. *Movements:* sedentary. *Foods:* grass seeds. *Breeding:* recorded in Oct-Jan and May and July; colonial. *Nest:* large globular structure of coarse grass, lined with fine grass, with lateral entrance hole and short tunnel, attached to sugar cane. *Eggs:* 5-6.

Ali and Ripley, vol.10, 1968-74, pp.103-104.

NOTES ON INTRODUCTIONS

Pakistan. A colony of escaped Green Avadavats is established in Lahore (Ripley, 1961).

DAMAGE

None known.

ORANGE-BREASTED WAXBILL
(Zebra Waxbill)

Amandava subflava (Vieillot)

DISTINGUISHING CHARACTERISTICS

8.7-10 cm (3.5-4 in)

Upper parts and wings brown; crimson stripe from lores to behind eye; upper tail-coverts crimson; ear-coverts olive-green; underparts, chin to belly yellow; under tail-coverts orange; flanks olive-green, barred olive and pale yellow; tail blackish; bill red. Female: lacks stripe over eye.

Mackworth-Praed and Grant, 1952-73, ser.1, vol.2, pp.1023-1024 and pl.93; ser.2, vol.2, pp.658-659 and pl.73; ser.3, vol.2, pp.732-733 and pl.91.

GENERAL DISTRIBUTION

Central and southern Africa: Sénégal to Sierra Leone, and east to the Sudan and northern Ethiopia, south to north-western Angola, Zambia and eastern Cape Province: also Pemba, Zanzibar and Mafia Island.

INTRODUCED DISTRIBUTION

Introduced unsuccessfully in Tahiti and St Helena.

GENERAL HABITS

Status: common; frequently kept in captivity. *Habitat:* grasslands, marshes and cultivation. *Gregariousness:* small flocks. *Movements:* sedentary. *Foods:* grass seeds, other small seeds and insects. *Breeding:* most of the year, but varies throughout range. *Nest:* barrel-shaped of grass, lined with feathers, in tall grass; also uses other weaver birds' nests. *Eggs:* 3, 4-5, 6.

Mackworth-Praed and Grant, 1952-73, ser.1, vol.2, pp.1023-1024; ser.2, vol.2, pp.658-659; ser.3, vol.2, pp.732-733.

NOTES ON INTRODUCTIONS

Tahiti. Orange-breasted Waxbills were reported to have been released by E. Guild on Tahiti in 1938. He records that they had nested and reared young soon after their release there (Guild, 1938). The species does not now occur on Tahiti and thus failed to become permanently established.

St Helena. Orange-breasted Waxbills were imported from South Africa and released by H. Bruins-Lich on St Helena in about 1929, but they failed to become established (Haydock, 1954).

DAMAGE

None known.

RED-BROWED WAXBILL
(Sydney Waxbill, Red-browed Firetail)

Aegintha temporalis (Latham)

DISTINGUISHING CHARACTERISTICS

11.2-12 cm (4.5-5 in)

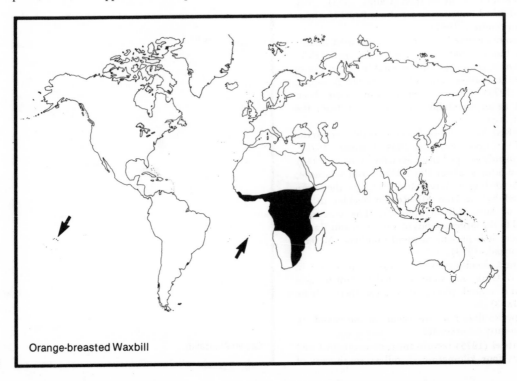

Orange-breasted Waxbill

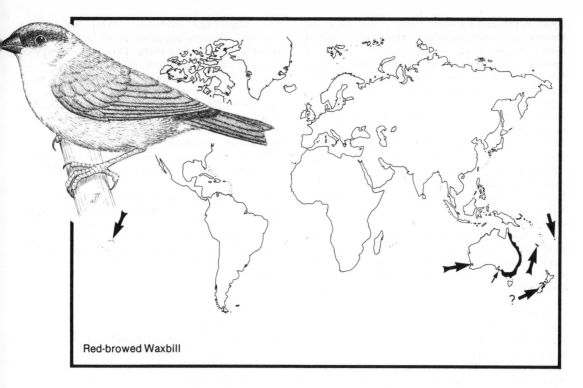

Red-browed Waxbill

Upper parts yellowish olive, a yellowish patch on side of neck; head grey; eyebrow stripe, throat and breast pale grey, tinged brown; rump and upper tail-coverts crimson; underparts greyish; tail dusky brown or grey; bill red, with black above and below. Female: eyebrow stripe usually longer and more tapered.

Immelmann, 1965, pp.66-67 and pl.4, nos. 1 and 2, opp. p.74.

Reader's Digest, 1977, p.528 and pl. p.528. (Note: in first issue plates transposed and this species appears on p.530.)

GENERAL DISTRIBUTION

Eastern and southern Australia: northern Queensland, south to the Mt Lofty Ranges, South Australia, and Kangaroo Island.

INTRODUCED DISTRIBUTION

Introduced successfully in Western Australia and on Tahiti. Introduced unsuccessfully, if released in New Zealand, Fiji and New Caledonia.

GENERAL HABITS

Status: common, often kept in captivity. *Habitat:* mangroves, forest and nearby open country, parks and gardens. *Gregariousness:* loose flocks of 10 or more, smaller groups in breeding season. *Movements:* sedentary and possibly somewhat nomadic. *Foods:* seeds and insects. *Breeding:* mainly Sept-Apr. *Nest:* domed grass structure occasionally with pieces of bark or leaves, with side entrance tunnel, in a bush. *Eggs:* 4-6, 8.

Immelmann, 1965, pp.67-73.

Reader's Digest, 1977, p.528.

NOTES ON INTRODUCTIONS

Western Australia. The Red-browed Waxbill was found to be well established in orchard clearings in the Darling Range, east of Perth in 1958 (Dell, 1965). They occupied a small area there for some years but are now reported to be relatively scarce.

New Caledonia. The Red-browed Waxbill has been introduced in New Caledonia and is common in grasslands there (Mayr, 1945). There is no information on the species' recent status, but Delacour (1966) makes no mention of them.

Fiji. The Red-browed Waxbill or the Common Waxbill *(E. astrild)* may have been introduced to Fiji. The species does not appear to be present anywhere in the group at present.

Tahiti. The Red-browed Waxbill *(A.t. temporalis)* has been introduced to Tahiti in the Society Islands (Keast, 1958) where they probably became established at the end of the nineteenth century (Holyoak, 1974; Thibault and Rives, 1975).

Townsend and Wetmore (1919) record that a specimen was collected on Tahiti in 1899. The Whitney Expedition obtained twenty-eight specimens on Tahiti and three on Moorea in 1920-21. Some were liberated there by E. Guild in 1938 and he reported that they had nested and reared young soon after their release (Guild, 1938).

In 1972, Holyoak found them to be abundant on Tahiti, but failed to find any on Moorea. On Tahiti they inhabit the valleys up to six kilometres (4 miles) into the interior and are seen in small groups of up to fifteen, often in company with *L. castaneothorax.*

New Zealand. Red-browed Waxbills were imported into New Zealand in 1867 and 1871, but there appear to be no records of any releases into the wild (Thomson, 1922).

DAMAGE

None known.

DIAMOND FIRETAIL
(Spotted-sided Finch)
Emblema guttata (Shaw)

DISTINGUISHING CHARACTERISTICS

11-12 cm (4.4-5 cm)

Upper parts and wings pale buff-brown; rump and   417

upper tail-coverts crimson; head, crown, face and hindneck grey, with black lores; throat white; breast black; flanks black, spotted white; centre of abdomen white; tail black; bill red, blue at base. Female: lores brown; breast band usually narrower.

Immelmann, 1965, pp.31-32 and pl.1, no.1, opp. p.34.

Reader's Digest, 1977, p.529 and lower pl. p.529.

GENERAL DISTRIBUTION
Eastern and south-eastern Australia: Dawson River, Queensland, south to Eyre Peninsula, South Australia and to Kangaroo Island.

INTRODUCED DISTRIBUTION
Introduced unsuccessfully in New Zealand, Tahiti, Fiji and the Hawaiian Islands.

GENERAL HABITS
Status: fairly common. *Habitat:* savannah woodland and mallee. *Gregariousness:* small groups or flocks in non-breeding season. *Movements:* sedentary. *Foods:* seeds and insects. *Breeding:* Aug-Jan and perhaps later. *Nest:* domed, spherical structure usually made of fresh vegetation, with two entrances, one tunnelled, in a tree or bush. *Eggs:* 4, 5-6, 7.

Immelmann, 1965, pp.32-39.

Reader's Digest, 1977, p.529.

NOTES ON INTRODUCTIONS
New Zealand. The Canterbury Acclimatisation Society introduced a number of Diamond Firetails in 1864. Flocks were reported (at Canterbury) in 1866, but there are no further records of them. Twelve birds were introduced by the Wellington Society in 1874, but there are no further records of these birds. There may also have been some releases by the Nelson society, but details of their efforts are lacking. Sir George Grey liberated about one hundred birds on Kawau Island but the species failed to survive there (Thomson, 1922). The Diamond Firetail was unsuccessful in the wild in New Zealand.

Fiji. Wood and Wetmore (1926) record that Diamond Firetails appeared to be quite common about Suva in the mid-1920s. There appear to be no further reports of them in the Fijian group.

Tahiti. Holyoak (1974) records that Diamond Firetails were introduced to Tahiti at an unknown date, but did not acclimatise and disappeared. Some were liberated by E. Guild in 1938 and these were reported by him to be established, but not to have bred in the wild (Guild, 1938).

No specimens have apparently been obtained on the island and the species evidently failed to become established.

Hawaiian Islands. Diamond Firetails have been intentionally or accidentally released or escaped, since 1965 on the island of Oahu (Berger, 1972). There appear to be no further records of the species from the island, so it has probably failed to become permanently established.

DAMAGE
None known.

STAR FINCH
(Red-tailed Finch, Rufous-tailed Finch)
Neochmia ruficauda (Gould)

DISTINGUISHING CHARACTERISTICS
10-12 cm (4-4.8 in)
Generally olive-brown, browner on the wings; front of head, ear-coverts, chin and upper throat crimson; lower throat, foreneck and sides light olive-grey; centre of breast and abdomen yellowish white; upper tail-coverts carmine; white spots on lower face and sides; bill scarlet. Female: lores and feathers above and below eye and chin dull crimson.

Immelmann, 1965, p.57, 59 and pl.3, nos.1-4, opp. p.58.

Reader's Digest, 1977, p.532 and pl. p.532.

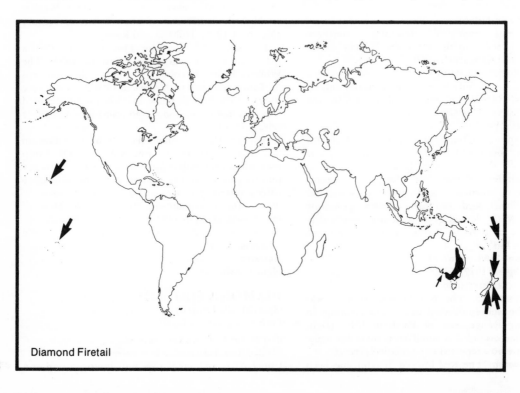

Diamond Firetail

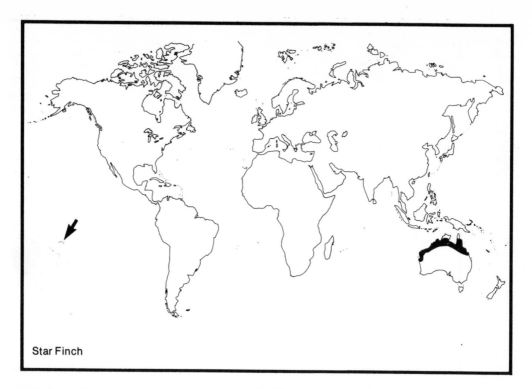

Star Finch

GENERAL DISTRIBUTION
Northern Australia: from about Rockhampton, Queensland, to the Ashburton River, Western Australia. Formerly occurred in central northern New South Wales and in southern Queensland.

INTRODUCED DISTRIBUTION
Introduced unsuccessfully to Tahiti.

GENERAL HABITS
Status: fairly common, often kept in captivity. *Habitat:* rank grass and rushes around swamps and rivers. *Gregariousness:* small groups of 10-20, and large flocks of up to 200 birds outside breeding season. *Movements:* sedentary. *Foods:* grass seeds, and insects (flies, termites, moths) when breeding. *Breeding:* Dec-Aug. *Nest:* rounded shape, of grass, lined with feathers, without entrance tunnel. *Eggs:* 3-6.
Immelmann, 1965, pp.59-65.
Reader's Digest, 1977, p.532.

NOTES ON INTRODUCTIONS
Tahiti. Guild (1938) says that he released Star Finches on Tahiti in about 1938. There appear to be no further records of the species there and so they evidently failed to become established.

DAMAGE
None known.

ZEBRA FINCH
(Chestnut-eared Finch)
Poephila guttata (Vieillot)

DISTINGUISHING CHARACTERISTICS
9-10 cm (3.6-4 in)
Greyish brown, with rump and upper tail-coverts barred black and white; head grey; ear patch chestnut; face white, bordered with black streaks; throat and breast grey, finely barred black; flanks chestnut, spotted white; bill red. Female: lacks chestnut ear patch and much barring; plain buff-white below.
Immelmann, 1965, pp.136-137 and pl.6, nos.1 and 2, opp. p.130.
Reader's Digest, 1977, p.534 and pl. p.534.

GENERAL DISTRIBUTION
Australia and Lesser Sunda Islands: throughout Australia except portions of the south-western and south-eastern coasts. Indonesian islands of Lombok, Sumbawa, Flores, Alor, Sumba, Savu, Samau, Timor, Wetar, Letti, Kisar, Sermatta, Luang and Moa Islands.

INTRODUCED DISTRIBUTION
Introduced successfully on Nauru (Pacific Ocean). Introduced unsuccessfully in New Zealand, Tahiti and on Kangaroo Island.

GENERAL HABITS
Status: very common; universal cage bird. *Habitat:* woodland and open arid country. *Gregariousness:* in breeding season flocks of 5-25 pairs, in non-breeding season flocks of 50-100 or more. *Movements:* sedentary and nomadic. *Foods:* seeds and insects. *Breeding:* variable, after rain, sometimes continuous. *Nest:* domed structure, roughly made of twigs and grass and lined with feathers or wool, sometimes with entrance tunnel, in a tree or bush. *Eggs:* 4-6.
Immelmann, 1965, pp.137-150.
Reader's Digest, 1977, p.534.

NOTES ON INTRODUCTIONS
Nauru. Four Zebra Finches *(P.g. castonotis)* were apparently introduced to Nauru from Australia some time prior to 1962 (Pearson, 1962). Pearson found six birds in grassland in the centre of the island in 1962 and says that the species is probably breeding there.
New Zealand. Zebra Finches were imported into New Zealand before 1885, but it is not known if they were deliberately released (Thomson, 1922). They 419

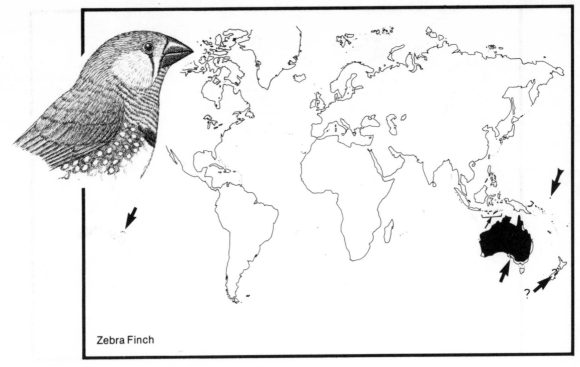

Zebra Finch

probably escape from time to time, but have never become permanently established in that country.

Tahiti. Zebra Finches were released on Tahiti by E. Guild in 1938 and were reported by him to have nested and reared young soon after their liberation (Guild, 1938). They are not now found on Tahiti so evidently failed to become permanently established.

Kangaroo Island. Zebra Finches were introduced on Flinders Chase in September 1937 (Condon, 1962), when twelve birds (Anon, 1948) of the race *P.g. castonotis* were liberated. According to Abbott

(1974) there have been no subsequent records for the species on this island.

DAMAGE

None known.

BANDED FINCH
(Double-bar Finch, Bicheno)
Poephila bichenovii (Vigors and Horsfield)

DISTINGUISHING CHARACTERISTICS
10-11 cm (4-4.4 in)
Generally upper parts pale brown, with fine dark-

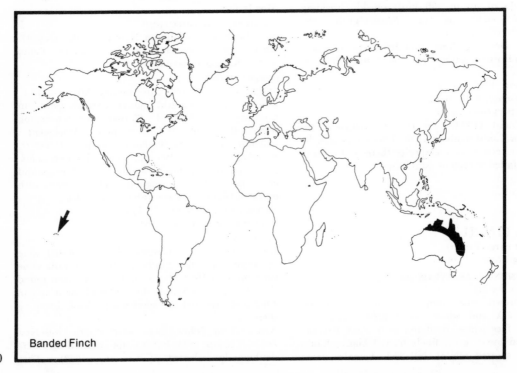

Banded Finch

brown barring; lores, above eyes, cheeks, ear-coverts, chin and throat white, bordered with a narrow black line; neck and chest white, with a narrow black band across chest; upper wings brown, lower wings brownish black with white spots; rump black or white; under tail-coverts black; tail brown or brownish black; bill bluish grey. (Under tail-coverts black in eastern race, white in western race.)
Immelmann, 1965, pp.127-129 and pl.7, nos.3-5, opp. p.130.
Reader's Digest, 1977, p.538 and (upper) pl. p.538.

GENERAL DISTRIBUTION
Northern Australia: from central-western New South Wales to Broome, Western Australia.

INTRODUCED DISTRIBUTION
Extended range in northern Queensland, Australia. Introduced unsuccessfully in Tahiti.

GENERAL HABITS
Status: common; often kept in captivity. *Habitat:* open woodlands and grasslands near rivers, dry plains, margins of canefields, gardens and parks. *Gregariousness:* loose flocks of 4-20 birds, larger flocks in dry years. *Movements:* sedentary. *Foods:* seeds of grass and herbaceous plants. *Breeding:* mainly Dec-Mar, but also in other months. *Nest:* round-shaped of grass lined with soft grass or plant wool, with or without entrance tunnel. *Eggs:* 4-5.
Immelmann, 1965, pp.129, 131-135.
Reader's Digest, 1977, p.538.

NOTES ON INTRODUCTIONS
Australia. According to Immelmann (1965) the Banded Finch has recently become established in many districts (mainly coastal) where it was previously unknown in northern Queensland.
Tahiti. Introduced to this island by E. Guild in 1938, the Banded Finch was reported by him to be established, but not to have bred there in the wild (Guild, 1938).

This species was also apparently unsuccessful in remaining permanently established on Tahiti.

DAMAGE
None known.

LONG-TAILED FINCH
(Long-tailed Grass Finch, Hecks' Finch, Blackheart)
Poephila acuticauda (Gould)

DISTINGUISHING CHARACTERISTICS
15-17.1 cm (6-6.8 in)
Crown and nape grey; mantle pinkish fawn; back and wings brown; upper and under tail-coverts and lower abdomen white; lores, band on tail, chin, throat, upper chest and patch on either flank black; bill (varies with races) yellow or orange.
Immelmann, 1965, pp.109-110 and pl.6, no.5, opp. p.114.
Reader's Digest, 1977, p.537 and pl. p.537.

GENERAL DISTRIBUTION
Northern Australia: from Derby, Western Australia to the Leichhardt River, Queensland.

INTRODUCED DISTRIBUTION
Introduced unsuccessfully to Tahiti.

GENERAL HABITS
Status: fairly common; often kept in captivity. *Habitat:* savannah woodland, open forest, particularly bordering watercourses. *Gregariousness:* pairs or groups of 20-30 birds, and occasionally loose flocks of many thousands. *Movements:* sedentary. *Foods:* grass seeds and flying insects (termites, ants, flies). *Breeding:* Jan-May, but earlier or later. *Nest:* of grass lined with plant wool and feathers and with long entrance tunnel. *Eggs:* 4, 5-6, 9.
Immelmann, 1965, pp.110-113, 115-121.
Reader's Digest, 1977, p.537.

NOTES ON INTRODUCTIONS
Tahiti. E. Guild released Long-tailed Finches on

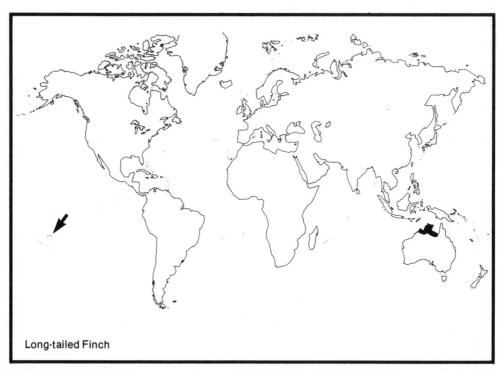

Long-tailed Finch

Tahiti in about 1938 (Guild, 1938), but they failed to become established there.

DAMAGE

None known.

PIN-TAILED PARROTFINCH
(Pin-tailed Nonpareil)

Erythrura prasina (Sparrman)

DISTINGUISHING CHARACTERISTICS

11.2-15 cm (4.5-6 in)

Upper parts green; throat and sides of head blue; lores black; wing-coverts and tertiaries green; underparts tawny buff, with red or gold patch on upper belly; rump, upper tail-coverts and tail red; tail with long pointed central feathers; bill black. Female: sides of head green; throat greyish green; tail yellowish brown, central feathers not elongated.

Robinson and Chasen, 1927-39, vol.2, p.270 and vol.4, p.374.

Kuroda, 1933-36, 2 vols.

King *et al*, 1975, pl.64, no.1148, opp. p.433.

GENERAL DISTRIBUTION

South-east Asia: Greater Sunda Islands (Java and Sumatra), Borneo, Malaysia, peninsular Thailand and northern and central Laos. Also found in north-eastern and north-western Thailand and reaches Tenasserim (migrant ?). Breeding range generally not well defined.

INTRODUCED DISTRIBUTION

Introduced unsuccessfully to Tahiti.

GENERAL HABITS

Status: common some areas, rare in others (i.e. Malaysia). *Habitat:* forest, scrub, bamboo and rice-fields. *Gregariousness:* large flocks of 20-40 birds. *Movements:* not well known, nomadic or migratory ? *Foods:* seeds and grain. *Breeding:* little information, probably Mar-Nov. *Nest:* little information, probably similar to other *Erythrura* (in captivity:

spherical of fibres and grass in a bush or hollow). *Eggs:* 3-6 (in captivity from 2-7).

NOTES ON INTRODUCTIONS

Tahiti. The Long-tailed Parrotfinch was released on Tahiti by E. Guild in 1938, but the birds were not seen again (Guild, 1938).

DAMAGE

According to Medway and Wells (1976) this species is a sporadic pest of paddy fields in Sumatra.

BLUE-FACED PARROTFINCH
(Blue-faced Finch, Tri-coloured Parrot Finch)

Erythrura trichroa (Kittlitz)

DISTINGUISHING CHARACTERISTICS

11.4-13 cm (4.6-5.2 in)

Upper parts dark grass-green; face and forehead blue; rump and upper tail-coverts dull scarlet; underparts pale grass-green; flight feathers black edged green; tail black, edged dull scarlet; bill black.

Immelmann, 1965, p.75 and pl.4, no.4, opp. p.74.

Reader's Digest, 1977, p.544 and pl. p.544.

GENERAL DISTRIBUTION

Indonesia to islands of the south-western Pacific and on Cape York, Australia. South-central Sulawesi, northern Moluccas (Ternate, Halmahera, Batjan), southern Moluccas (Seram, Buru), New Guinea, Goodenough Island, Tagula, Kakar, Maram, Sudest, Dampier, Vulcan, Caroline, New Britain, New Ireland, Loyalty, Solomons and New Hebrides; coastal north-eastern Queensland south to Cairns and the Atherton Tablelands.

INTRODUCED DISTRIBUTION

Introduced unsuccessfully to Tahiti.

GENERAL HABITS

Status: fairly common; often kept in captivity. *Habitat:* edges of mangroves, grasslands and clearings bordering rain forest. *Gregariousness:*

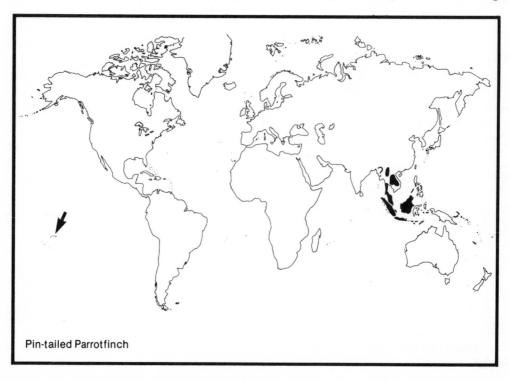

Pin-tailed Parrotfinch

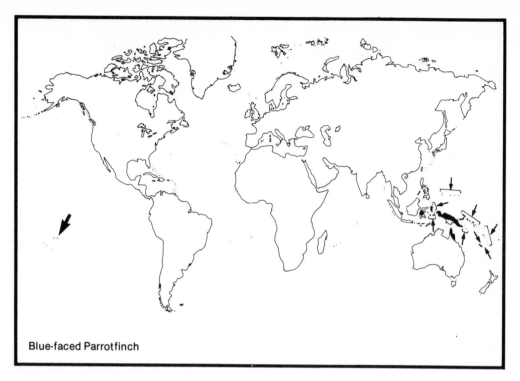

Blue-faced Parrotfinch

solitary, pairs and small feeding flocks of 20-30 birds. *Movements:* probably sedentary, *Foods:* seeds. *Breeding:* little known (Nov-Mar Australia). *Nest:* pear-shaped, domed, loose structure of moss and fibres, in a tree or bush. *Eggs:* 3-6.

Immelmann, 1965, pp.74-79.

Reader's Digest, 1977, p.544.

NOTES ON INTRODUCTIONS

Tahiti. The Blue-faced Parrotfinch was released on Tahiti in 1938 by E. Guild who initially (Guild, 1938) reported that it had disappeared, but later (1940) records that it had bred there. It is not now known to be established on the island.

DAMAGE

None known.

RED-THROATED PARROTFINCH
(Red-throated Finch, Red-faced Parrot-Finch)
Erythrura psittacea (Gmelin)

DISTINGUISHING CHARACTERISTICS

10.7-12 cm (4.3-4.8 in)

Head and upper breast bright red; rump red; central tail-feathers elongated; remainder bright green; bill blackish, base of lower mandible brown.

Australian Aviculture, vol.31, no.12, pl. between pp.178-179.

Mayr, 1945, pp.105 and 175.

Delacour, 1966.

GENERAL DISTRIBUTION

New Caledonia.

INTRODUCED DISTRIBUTION

Introduced unsuccessfully to Tahiti.

GENERAL HABITS

Status: fairly common. *Habitat:* secondary forest and open grassland. *Gregariousness:* pairs and small flocks. *Movements:* sedentary. *Foods:* seeds and (?) insects. *Breeding:* Aug-Nov. *Nest:* large domed

structure, in a hole, crevice in rocks, or huts of natives. *Eggs:* 7-8.

Mayr, 1945, pp.105 and 175.

NOTES ON INTRODUCTIONS

Tahiti. The Red-throated Parrotfinch was released by E. Guild on Tahiti in 1938, was reported to have bred in the wild (Guild, 1938 and 1940), but apparently was unsuccessful as it does not now occur there.

DAMAGE

None known.

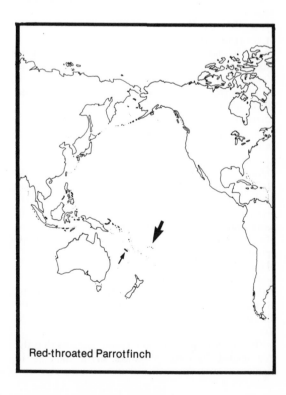

Red-throated Parrotfinch

423

Red-headed Parrotfinch

RED-HEADED PARROTFINCH
(Royal Parrot Finch, Peale's Parrot-finch)
Erythrura cyaneovirens (Peale)

DISTINGUISHING CHARACTERISTICS
10 cm (4 in)
Variable species, from generally green with deep blue on throat and upper breast to generally blue with greenish blue on lower back, flight feathers and belly; head red; tail short and scarlet; bill brownish.
Australian Aviculture, vol.31, no.12, pl. between pp.178-179.
Mayr, 1945, pp.123, 147, 199-200.

GENERAL DISTRIBUTION
Pacific Ocean Islands: Savai'i and Upolu, Samoan Islands; Kandavu, Viti Levu and adjacent islands, Vanua Levu and Taveuni, Fiji Islands; northern New Hebrides (Mai, Epi, Tongoa, Lopevi, Tauuma) and Banks Islands (Gaua); Efate Island, New Hebrides; Aneityum Island and southern New Hebrides.

INTRODUCED DISTRIBUTION
Introduced unsuccessfully to Tahiti.

GENERAL HABITS
Status: common; fairly often kept in captivity.
Habitat: forest and coastal areas. *Gregariousness:* singly, pairs or small flocks (rare ?). *Movements:* sedentary (?). *Foods:* seeds, fruits, flowers, buds, fig seeds and also insects. *Breeding:* no information.
Nest: globular, oblong structure of grass and fibres, entrance near top, in a tree. *Eggs:* 3-4.
Mayr, 1945, pp.123, 147 and 199-200.

NOTES ON INTRODUCTIONS
Tahiti. The race *E.c. regia* was released on Tahiti by E. Guild in 1938, but was not seen again after liberation (Guild, 1938).

DAMAGE
In the Fijian Islands, Mercer (1966) records that the Red-headed Parrotfinch causes slight damage to immature rice crops.

GOULDIAN FINCH
Chloebia gouldiae (Gould)

DISTINGUISHING CHARACTERISTICS
12.5-14 cm (5-5.6 in)
Upper parts generally green; lores, cheeks, ear-coverts and forehead black, red or yellow, and bordered with a line of black widening to patch on throat and followed by a band of blue; foreneck and chest purple, margined with band of yellowish orange; breast, sides and abdomen rich yellow; lower abdomen and under tail-coverts white; wing tips

Gouldian Finch

brown edged green; rump and upper tail-coverts blue, tail black; bill greyish white, often pinkish at tip.

Immelmann, 1965, pp.80-81, 82, and pl.5, nos.1-5, opp. p.82.

Reader's Digest, 1977, p.543 and pls. p.543.

GENERAL DISTRIBUTION

Northern Australia: from Derby, Western Australia to about Charters Towers in Queensland.

INTRODUCED DISTRIBUTION

Introduced unsuccessfully to Tahiti.

GENERAL HABITS

Status: fairly common; commonly kept aviary bird. *Habitat:* open grassy plains with trees and mangroves. *Gregariousness:* flocks, of several hundred in non-breeding season. *Movements:* sedentary and nomadic (regular south movement in wet season). *Foods:* grass seeds, and insects (termites, ants) in the breeding season. *Breeding:* Jan-Apr; often several pairs together; 2-3 broods per season. *Nest:* poor grass nest, without tunnel but sometimes roofed, in a tree hole or termite mound, occasionally in a tree. *Eggs:* 4-8.

Immelmann, 1965, pp.83-94.

Reader's Digest, 1977, p.543.

NOTES ON INTRODUCTIONS

Tahiti. Guild (1938) reported that he had released Gouldian Finches on Tahiti. He later (1940) says that he liberated some 700 of them and was preparing to release a further 100 birds. The species does not now occur on Tahiti.

DAMAGE

None known.

PLUM-HEADED FINCH
(Cherry Finch)
Aidemosyne modesta (Gould)

DISTINGUISHING CHARACTERISTICS

10.2-11.5 cm (4.1-4.6 in)

Upper parts olive-brown; forehead, chin and top of head claret-red, chin darker; lores black; ear-coverts white, barred brown; cheeks white; wings dark olive-brown, tipped white; rump and upper tail-coverts subterminally barred white; underparts white, barred brown; tail black, outer feathers with white spots at tip; bill black, with blue at base. Female: lacks claret-red on chin.

Immelmann, 1965, p.151 and pl.4, no.3, opp. p.74.

Reader's Digest, 1977, p.538 and (lower) pl. p.538.

GENERAL DISTRIBUTION

Eastern Australia: from Mogoa River and Port Denison, Queensland to southern and central-western New South Wales.

INTRODUCED DISTRIBUTION

Introduced unsuccessfully on Tahiti.

GENERAL HABITS

Status: uncommon to rare; not common in captivity. *Habitat:* grasslands, reeds along river margins and wooded savannah. *Gregariousness:* pairs or small flocks, occasionally large flocks up to 300 birds. *Movements:* sedentary and nomadic. *Foods:* grass seeds, and insects in the breeding season. *Breeding:* mainly Sep-Jan. *Nest:* laterally depressed structure of woven grass sometimes lined with feathers, without entrance tunnel, in a tussock or low bush. *Eggs:* 4-7.

Immelmann, 1965, pp.152-157.

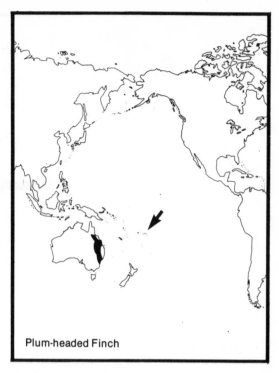

Plum-headed Finch

Reader's Digest, 1977, p.538.

NOTES ON INTRODUCTIONS

Tahiti. Plum-headed Finches were released by E. Guild on Tahiti in 1938, but were not seen again after their liberation (Guild, 1938).

DAMAGE

None known.

COMMON SILVERBILL
(White-throated Munia or Mannikin, Warbling Silverbill)
Lonchura malabarica (Linnaeus)

DISTINGUISHING CHARACTERISTICS

10-12 cm (4-4.8 in). 10-14 g (.35-.49 oz)

Upper parts pale sandy brown; underparts creamy white; rump blackish; wings and tail dark brown; faint barring on back and spotted on head *(cantans),* more pronounced in some races *(orientalis);* upper tail-coverts white, with no barring *(malabarica);* tail and upper tail-coverts bronzy black *(cantans);* bill blue-grey.

Common Silverbill, *Lonchura malabarica*
(front bird, *L. malabarica malabarica,* back bird *L. malabarica cantans)*

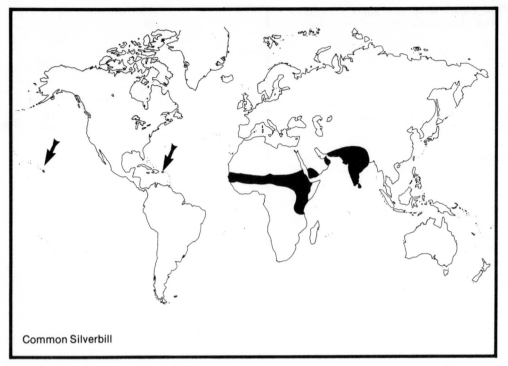

Common Silverbill

Mackworth-Praed and Grant, 1952-73, ser.1, vol.2, pp.979-981; ser.3, vol.2, pp.683-684 and pl.86 (Note: African sub spp. only).

Ali and Ripley, vol.10, 1968-74, pp.105-107, and pl. 107, fig.8, opp. p.128.

GENERAL DISTRIBUTION

North Africa and southern Asia: in Africa from Sénégal to the Sudan and Ethiopia and south to Tanzania; in Asia in western Arabia, Oman, southern Iran, Afghanistan, Pakistan and northern India (Himalayas) south to Sri Lanka.

INTRODUCED DISTRIBUTION

Introduced successfully, probably in the Hawaiian Islands and to Puerto Rico.

GENERAL HABITS

Status: common; often kept in captivity. *Habitat:* acacia steppe, grasslands, dry open country, sparse scrub and bush country and also villages. *Gregariousness:* parties or flocks of 10-12, sometimes considerably larger flocks to 60 birds; roost as family parties of 5-6 in old nests. *Movements:* sedentary, some altitudinal migration in some parts of India. *Foods:* grass and weed seeds, grain, ants and other small insects. *Breeding:* variable, all year (mainly Sep-May in Africa and Jan-Mar in central India but varies in different areas); may have 2 or more broods per season. *Nest:* large globular structure of coarse grass lined with softer grass, vertical side entrance, sometimes porched, in a tree or long grass; often nests in other weavers' nests. *Eggs:* 4-6, 8 (India), 5-6, 12 (Africa).

Mackworth-Praed and Grant, 1952-73, ser.1, vol.2, pp.979-981; ser.3, vol.2, pp.683-684.

Ali and Ripley, vol.10, 1968-74, pp.105-107.

NOTES ON INTRODUCTIONS

Hawaiian Islands. The race *L.m. cantans* appears to be well established on the island of Hawaii (Hawaiian Audubon Society, 1975) and has been confirmed to breed there (Berger, 1975).

Puerto Rico. Continued reports of the presence of the Common Silverbill at Cabo Rojo, Puerto Rico has been received in the last few years. Heilbrun (1977) lists the species as seen there on the 77th Christmas Bird Count in late 1976. Blake (1975) indicates that it has been introduced but gives no other details.

DAMAGE

None known.

BRONZE MANNIKIN
(Bronze-winged Mannikin)
Lonchura cucullata (Swainson)

DISTINGUISHING CHARACTERISTICS

8.7-10 cm (3.5-4 in). 7.9-12.2 g (.28-.43 oz)

Top of head, sides of face and wing shoulder brown, with glossy green wash; chin and upper chest glossy bronze black; hindneck, mantle and wings brown or ash-coloured; lower rump and upper tail-coverts barred ashy and black; remainder of underparts white; flanks and under tail-coverts barred blackish; tail black; bill black and blue-grey.

Mackworth-Praed and Grant, 1952-73, ser.1, vol.2, pp.975-976; ser.2, vol.2, pp.615-616 and pl.71; ser.3, vol.2, pp.680-681 and pl.86.

GENERAL DISTRIBUTION

Central and southern Africa: from Sénégal east to western Ethiopia, and south to about central Angola, Zambia, north-eastern Botswana and the eastern portion of the Republic of South Africa. Also Zanzibar and Mafia Islands, and São Tomé and (?) Principé in the Gulf of Guinea.

INTRODUCED DISTRIBUTION

Introduced successfully on Puerto Rico in the West Indies. Successfully colonised the Archipel des Comores and Fernando Póo in the Gulf of Guinea. Introduced unsuccessfully to Tahiti.

GENERAL HABITS

Status: common and abundant; fairly commonly

Bronze Mannikin

found in captivity. *Habitat:* wooded savannah, brushland, forest edges, open country, cultivated areas and villages. *Gregariousness:* flocks of 8-10 and up to 20 birds, but often larger flocks; roost communally. *Movements:* sedentary. *Foods:* grass seeds, rice, millet, nectar and insects (termites). *Breeding:* most of the year and several broods raised (breeds May-Aug and has 2 broods in Puerto Rico). *Nest:* large untidy structure of grass lined with feathers, with a tunnel entrance, in a bush or the thatch of huts. *Eggs:* 1, 4-6, 8.

Mackworth-Praed and Grant, 1952-73, ser.1, vol.2, pp.975-976; ser.2, vol.2, pp.615-616; ser.3, vol.2, pp.680-681.

Woodall, *Ostrich* vol.46, 1975, no.1, pp.55-86.

NOTES ON INTRODUCTIONS

Puerto Rico. The race *L.c. cucullata* (Peters, 1968) has been introduced and established in Puerto Rico (Bond, 1960), where they are particularly common in San Juan (Bond, 1971).

The Bronze Mannikin was probably introduced to the West Indies when slave ships were plying between these islands and Africa. The species was so well established by the 1930s that it was thought that their introduction dates back to the French colonisation when they probably escaped from aviaries (Wetmore, 1927; Wetmore and Swales, 1931). The manner of their establishment may never be definitely known, but certainly specimens were obtained in early times. According to Wetmore, Robert Swift obtained a specimen there in 1864-65 which is now in the United States National Museum, and another in 1866. They were locally common there in 1903 (Bowdish, 1903) and further specimens were collected in 1920. In about 1927 they were a common resident of the coastal plains and especially common near Cabo Rojo where flocks of several hundred were noted (Wetmore).

Archipel des Comores. Benson (1960) records that the race *L.c. scutata* may be a recent colonist from Africa to the Comores. He says that the species is not a popular cage bird and it is unlikely to have been introduced there. Bronze Mannikins were reported to be common on Anjouan in 1876 and some were collected there and on Mayotte in 1884 and 1886. The species is now common on Grande Comore, Moheli, Anjouan and Mayotte.

Fernando Póo. The Bronze Mannikin was first recorded on this island in 1929 and is now fairly common there (Fry, 1961). It is possibly a recent colonist, but may have been deliberately introduced there.

Tahiti. Bronze Mannikins were released on Tahiti by E. Guild in 1938, but were not sighted again after their liberation (Guild, 1938).

DAMAGE

According to Woodall (1975) the Bronze Mannikin has been known to cause damage in gardens by pecking the leaves of lettuce, but is not considered an important destroyer of the plants in Africa.

MAGPIE MANNIKIN
Lonchura fringilloides (Lafresnaye)

DISTINGUISHING CHARACTERISTICS
11.4-13 cm (4.6-5.2 in). 17.6-19.7 g (.62-.7 oz)
Generally glossy blue-black; mantle brown, with black centres to feathers and some white shaft stripes; wings dusky; abdomen white; lower belly and under tail-coverts washed with buff; flanks have black and brown markings; bill blackish, lower mandible grey.

Mackworth-Praed and Grant, 1952-73, ser.1, vol.2, pp.978-979; ser.2, vol.2, pp.618-619 and pl.71; ser.3, vol.2, p.683 and pl.86.

Avon *et al,* 1974, pl. opp. p.62.

GENERAL DISTRIBUTION
Central and southern Africa: from Guinea east to southern Sudan and East Africa, south to Gabon,

427

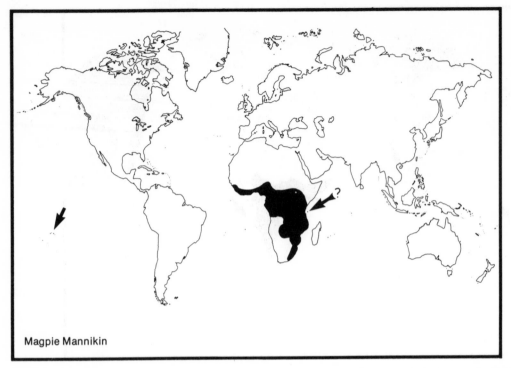

Magpie Mannikin

Congo, Zaire, eastern Angola, northern Botswana and coastal eastern South Africa.

INTRODUCED DISTRIBUTION
Possibly introduced successfully on Zanzibar Island. Introduced unsuccessfully to Tahiti.

GENERAL HABITS
Status: common locally; not common in captivity. *Habitat:* cultivated areas and gardens. *Gregariousness:* usually flocks of about a dozen. *Movements:* sedentary and nomadic (?). *Foods:* grass seeds, millet and wild rice. *Breeding:* throughout the year. *Nest:* untidy grass nest with leaves and stems plastered on, and lined with fine grass and reeds, in a tree. *Eggs:* 4, but up to 6.
Mackworth-Praed and Grant, 1952-73, ser.1, vol.2, pp.978-979; ser.2, vol.2, pp.618-619, ser.3, vol.2, p.683.

NOTES ON INTRODUCTIONS
Zanzibar Island. The Magpie Mannikin was reported in the wild in Zanzibar in 1936 (Pakenham, 1939) and is now extremely local there (Peters, 1968).
Mackworth-Praed and Grant (1963) list the species as a resident on the island and make no mention of any introduction.
Tahiti. Magpie Mannikins were liberated on Tahiti by E. Guild in 1938 and were reported by him to have nested and reared young (Guild, 1938). They do not now occur on the island so evidently failed to become permanently established.

DAMAGE
None known.

SPICE FINCH
(Nutmeg Mannikin, Scaly-breasted Munia, Spotted Munia)
Lonchura punctulata (Linnaeus)

DISTINGUISHING CHARACTERISTICS
10-11.9 cm (4-4.8 in). 11.5-15.5 g (.41-.55 oz)

Upper parts cinnamon-brown; rump brown but often golden yellow; head and throat chestnut-brown; breast and flanks marbled black and white or brown and white; centre of abdomen white; edges of tail-feathers golden yellow; bill black.
Ali and Ripley, 1968-74, vol.10, pp.113-116 and pl.105, fig.6, opp. p.80.
Reader's Digest, 1977, pl. p.542.

GENERAL DISTRIBUTION
Southern and South-east Asia: from India, Assam, Bangladesh and Sri Lanka, east to southern China (Yunnan), Hainan, Taiwan, Indochina and also Java, Sumatra, the Lesser Sunda Islands, Sulawesi and the Philippines.

INTRODUCED DISTRIBUTION
Introduced successfully in Australia, the Hawaiian Islands, Yap Island and the Palau Archipelago, Singapore, Mauritius and Réunion (now rare). Introduced unsuccessfully in the Seychelles, Tahiti and probably in New Zealand.

GENERAL HABITS
Status: common; favourite cage bird in its native range and elsewhere. *Habitat:* secondary growth, open and timbered grassland, cultivated areas, ricefields, gardens and villages. *Gregariousness:* small parties or loose flocks, and occasionally flocks up to 200 birds in non-breeding season; roost communally. *Movements:* sedentary and nomadic. *Foods:* seeds, rice, berries and insects. *Breeding:* all year but mainly during monsoons (Feb-Aug in Malaysia and Mar-July China), (Australia all year); colonial; 2-3 broods per year. *Nest:* domed, globular structure of grass and bark strips, with short entrance tunnel, in a bush or tree. *Eggs:* 4, 5-7, 10 (Hawaii 3-4; Australia 4-7).
Immelmann, 1965, pp.158-166.
Ali and Ripley, vol.10, 1968-74, pp.113-116.

NOTES ON INTRODUCTIONS
Australia. The Spice Finch *L.p. topela* (Peters, 1968)

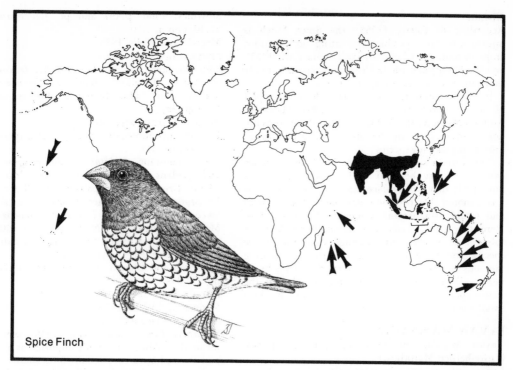

Spice Finch

was first noted in Brisbane, Queensland, in about 1937. Lavery (1974) indicates that the species probably escaped there in about 1930. They failed to gain much attention until the 1950s.

Spice Finches were noted in Townsville in 1951 (Bell, 1961; Lavery and Hopkins, 1963) after liberation in 1950 (Lavery) and at Innisfail in 1955, Esk in 1955-56 and Mackay in 1959-60 (Bell). Some were reported from 193 km (120 miles) north of Cairns at Cooktown in 1961 and some were observed at Airlie and Noosaville in the same year (Wheeler, 1962). They were first recorded at the Atherton Railway Station in June 1964 and are now well established and breeding there (Bravery, 1970).

The Spice Finch was also introduced into New South Wales (McGill, 1960), also becoming established in that State as a result of escapes from aviaries. Although they were increasing their range and numbers there in the 1960s they had not spread far beyond the County of Cumberland boundaries (McGill, 1960).

In Queensland, Immelmann (1960) reported that they were one of the commonest birds in northern Queensland towns and were to be found in the sugar cane fields and cultivated areas. More recently (Lavery, 1974) they are abundant in the Brisbane river basin and in north-east Queensland. Slater (1974) describes their present range as around Sydney and coastal Queensland from Brisbane to Cooktown.

New Zealand. Spice Finches were imported into New Zealand in 1868, but it is not known whether they were actually released in the wild (Thomson, 1922).

Hawaiian Islands. The Spice Finch *L.p. topela* (Peters, 1968) was introduced to Hawaii by Dr W. Hillebrand in 1865 (Munro, 1960; Berger, 1972) from South-east Asia (Hawaiian Audubon Society, 1975). They were common on Maui around 1902 (McGregor, 1902).

The species is now established and widespread in open grassy areas on all the main islands in the group.

Yap Island and the Palau Archipelago. Ripley (1951) reports a flock of Spice Finches on the island of Koror in the Palaus. Peters (1968) records that the race *L.p. cabanisi* has presumably been introduced there. Marshall (1949) found them breeding in the grasslands on Babelthuap Island and suggested that they had recently been introduced to that island. The species is now rare on this island, but is apparently still common on Yap Island (Ralph and Sakai, 1979) where it has also been introduced.

Singapore Island. Ward (1968) says that the Spice Finch is an abundant garden bird in Singapore and has probably increased in numbers in recent years. He states that the species is not mentioned by Robinson (1927), is a popular cage bird in the area, and that it has probably been introduced there.

Mauritius. The Spice Finch is reported to have been introduced from Java in about 1800 and to have been well established on Mauritius in the early 1900s (Meinertzhagen 1912). Benedict (1957) says that the species was becoming abundant there in the 1950s, and Staub (1976) records them as fairly abundant in the 1970s. The race recorded there is *L.p. topela* (Peters, 1968).

Réunion. Peters (1968) records that the Spice Finch *L.p. topela* has been introduced to Réunion. Watson *et al* (1963) say that the species is becoming rare there and Staub (1976) that it is now very rare.

Seychelles. Gaymer *et al* (1969) report that Nicoll found a Spice Finch on Mahé in the Seychelles in 1906, but say that there have been no further records since that time. Penny (1974) makes no mention of the species on these islands.

Tahiti. Spice Finches were released by E. Guild on Tahiti in 1938, but the species was not seen again after liberation (Guild, 1938).

429

According to Cheng (1963) the Spice Finch is injurious to farm produce by eating unripe grain crops in southern China. In both India (Ali, 1953) and the Philippines (de la Cruz, pers. comm., 1962) they cause damage to crops, principally rice.

In the Hawaiian Islands they were formerly a pest of rice and sorghum crops (Caum, 1933; Hawaiian Audubon Society, 1975), but now that these crops are not extensively grown the bird is described as an 'interesting wayside species'.

The introduction of the Spice Finch in Australia can in no way be seen to be advantageous, as potentially they will replace many of the indigenous forms should they become numerous and widespread and would also become a menace to some crops. Here, they have already shown themselves to be more tolerant of human surroundings than the native species and to have a greater variety of feeding methods as compared with these species. They breed nearly all the year with large clutches whereas the native species breed but twice a year and produce smaller clutches (Immelmann, 1960).

JAVAN MANNIKIN
(Javan Munia, 'White-bellied Munia', Javan White-bellied Mannikin)
Lonchura leucogastroides (Horsfield and Moore)

DISTINGUISHING CHARACTERISTICS
10-12 cm (4-4.8 in)
Generally dark brown; face black; breast dark and sharply distinguished from white belly; sides and flanks white; tail brown; bill dark grey (similar in appearance to White-bellied Mannikin *L. leucogastra* and is often only given sub-specific rank; differs in having underparts paler brown; tail brown without yellow tinge and sides and flanks white instead of blackish brown).
Kuroda, 1933-36, 2 vols.

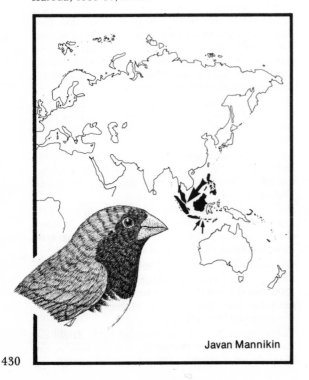

Javan Mannikin

Smythies, 1960, p.497 and pl. *(leucogastra)* 42, no.10, opp. p.489.
Medway and Wells, 1976.

GENERAL DISTRIBUTION
Sumatra, Java, Bali and Lombok. (*L. leucogastra* in peninsular Thailand, southern Tenasserim and Malaya, and also Sumatra, Borneo and the Philippines).

INTRODUCED DISTRIBUTION
Possibly introduced, successfully on Singapore Island.

GENERAL HABITS
Status: common. *Habitat:* secondary growth, scrub and gardens (*leucogastra* in forest clearings and edges). *Gregariousness:* pairs and small groups up to 10. *Movements:* sedentary. *Foods:* seeds. *Breeding: leucogastra* Mar-May (Malaysia) *leucogastroides* May-Oct (Singapore). *Nest:* spherical with lateral entrance, of grass stems, flower heads or palm leaves, in a small tree. *Eggs:* no information.
Robinson and Chasen, 1927-39 vol.2, p.272; vol.4, pp.372-374.
Kuroda, 1933-36, 2 vols.
Medway and Wells, 1976.

NOTES ON INTRODUCTIONS
Singapore Island. Gibson-Hill (1949) says that the Javan Mannikin is commonly imported as a cage bird and escaped birds occasionally form small colonies in various parts of Singapore, but that they have some difficulty in maintaining their populations for any length of time. They have been recorded to breed there in 1923, 1944 and in 1945.

Ward (1968) reports that the species is an occasional visitor to Singapore and that it cannot be determined whether the birds originated from imported cage birds or spread there naturally from Malaya.

DAMAGE
L. leucogastra regularly causes considerable damage to rice fields in Borneo (Berwick, pers. comm. 1962).

BLACK-HEADED MANNIKIN
(Black-headed Munia, Tri-coloured Munia, Chestnut Munia, Chestnut-breasted Munia)
Lonchura malacca (Linnaeus)

DISTINGUISHING CHARACTERISTICS
10-12 cm (4-4.8 in). 10-15 g (.35-.53 oz)
Upper parts brown; rump reddish brown; head, neck and breast black; underparts brown, with a black or white patch in centre of abdomen; vent, thighs and under tail-coverts black; abdomen white; upper tail-coverts and tail yellow to orange-red; bill silver-grey or slaty blue.
Ali and Ripley, vol.10, 1968-74, pp.116-119 and pls.105, Fig.3, opp. p.80 and 108, Fig.6, opp. p.144.
Reader's Digest, 1977, pl. (lower) p.541.

GENERAL DISTRIBUTION
Southern and South-east Asia: central and northern India, Bangladesh, Burma to south-western China, Taiwan and Hainan and south to Indochina, the Philippines, Borneo, Sulawesi and Indonesia (Greater Sundas).

INTRODUCED DISTRIBUTION
Introduced successfully in the Moluccas (Halmahera Island), on the Palau Archipelago, Guam Island and in the Hawaiian Islands; probably introduced

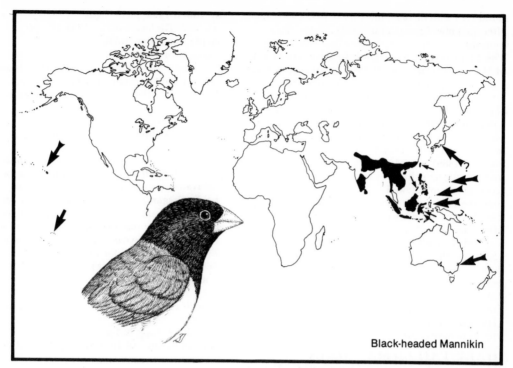

Black-headed Mannikin

successfully in Australia and Japan (?). Introduced unsuccessfully in Tahiti.

GENERAL HABITS

Status: common; commonly found in captivity. *Habitat:* secondary growth, grasslands, swampy areas, cultivated areas, rice fields and villages. *Gregariousness:* small parties or flocks, and sometimes large flocks of 100 or more often in company with other species; large social roosts. *Movements:* sedentary, with some local movements depending on monsoons. *Foods:* grass and weed seeds, and grain (rice). *Breeding:* all year, chiefly after rains; Dec-Oct (Malaysia) May-Nov (India); solitary or in groups (two or more broods in Hawaii). *Nest:* ball of coarse grass lined with finer grass, lateral entrance hole at end of short spout, in a low bush, tree or grass tussock. *Eggs:* 4, 5-7, 8 (Hawaii 3-4).

Ali and Ripley, vol.10, 1968-74, pp.116-119.

NOTES ON INTRODUCTIONS

Moluccas. Ripley (1961) and King *et al* (1975) record that the Black-headed Mannikin has been introduced to Halmahera Island in the Moluccas. Peters (1968) records that the race *L.m. jagori* is a resident on the island.

Palau Archipelago. Ripley (1951) found *L.m. ferruginosa* breeding on Babelthuap and Koro in the Palaus and suggests that they are possibly a hybrid population as could be expected from released cage birds. The species is still common on the former island (Ralph and Sakai, 1979).

Guam Island (Marianas). The race *L.m. ferruginosa* has also been introduced on Guam where it is now abundant (Ralph and Sakai, 1979).

Australia. Black-headed Mannikins *L.m. atricapilla* were found to be breeding in the wild at Centennial Park near Sydney in 1929, and at Dee Why Swamps in 1948 (Tarr, 1950). They were observed at Long Neck Swamps in 1937 and some were trapped there at this

time. McGill (1960) suggested that these birds originated from aviary escapees.

The species may still be established in these areas, was reported present in 1960, but is confined to rank, swampy areas near Sydney.

Hawaiian Islands. Udvardy (1960) first reported the Black-headed Mannikin as a breeding bird in Hawaii in 1959. The present population may be the result of unauthorised releases of cage birds first imported from South-east Asia between 1936 and 1941 (Hawaiian Audubon Society, 1975).

Berger (1972) found the race known as the Tricoloured Mannikin *L.m. malacca* near the Waikiki Aquarium on several occasions in May 1970, but also records that the race *atricapilla* has been found on Oahu. Some Black-headed Mannikins frequented the thickets and open grassy areas of West Loch, where Ord (1963) estimated that between 400 and 500 were present.

The species now appears to be established, primarily in the grassy lowlands of the Waipio Peninsula on Oahu (Hawaiian Audubon Society), but is at present spreading and has been recorded up to twenty-four kilometres (15 miles) inland and at Laie (Ralph and Pyle, 1977). It has recently been recorded on the island of Kauai where in 1977 it appeared to be well established (Pratt, 1977).

Japan. Kaburaki (1934) records that the Black-headed Mannikin is established in Japan, but with a restricted distribution. He reports (1940) that they were still present there in about 1940 or shortly before this date.

There appear to be few further records of them, but it is possible that *L.m. atricapilla* occurs as an escapee from captivity and may breed in the wild although records are uncertain (Ornithological Society of Japan, 1974).

Tahiti. Black-headed Mannikins were released by E. 431

Guild on Tahiti in 1938, but they were not seen again after their liberation (Guild, 1938).

DAMAGE

The Black-headed Mannikin is so abundant in parts of Malaysia that it is a pest to rice growers (Delacour, 1947). They frequent the grain fields sometimes in large flocks to feed on the ripening grain in June (Smythies, 1953).

Smythies (1960) says that they are the worst pest of padi fields in Borneo, and are one of the six pests listed in the Iban prayer. As early as the 1880s, Sharpe (1889) records them as a pest in rice fields and also suggests that they may have been introduced to Borneo from Sulawesi.

In the Philippines they are so abundant that they have become a nuisance to the country's rice growers (Delacour and Mayr, 1946), relishing the 'milky stage' of the ripening rice. De la Cruz (pers. comm., 1962) says that there is no record of the extent of the damage, but on Luzon it is serious at least in some areas.

Where introduced in the Hawaiian Islands, they are considered a threat to agricultural crops (Hawaiian Audubon Society, 1975), but do not appear to have caused any damage as yet.

SHARP-TAILED MANNIKIN
(White-rumped Munia, Sharp-tailed Munia, Striated Mannikin, Bengalese [domestic form])
Lonchura striata (Linnaeus)

DISTINGUISHING CHARACTERISTICS

9.9-12 cm (4-4.8 in). 9.5-13 g (.34-.46 oz)

Generally black or dark brown and white; abdomen and rump white; dark parts of plumage have narrow whitish streaks; breast has narrow buffy scales and belly indistinct dark brown streaks; tail, wedge-shaped, black or dark brown; bill bluish or black. Domestic form may be variegated with black, brown and white in many combinations.

Sharp-tailed Mannikin

Smythies, 1953, pl.11, fig.5, p.228.
Ali and Ripley, vol.10, 1968-74, pp.107-110 and pl.105, fig.5, opp. p.80.

GENERAL DISTRIBUTION

Southern and South-east Asia: from India, Nepal and Sri Lanka, east to southern China, Taiwan and Hainan: also the Nicobar and Andaman Islands and Sumatra.

INTRODUCED DISTRIBUTION

Introduced unsuccessfully to Réunion.

GENERAL HABITS

Status: very common; domesticated form a universal cage bird. *Habitat:* forest clearings, woodlands, open cultivated country, grasslands, gardens and rice fields. *Gregariousness:* small parties 6-15 birds, flocks up to 50, and sometimes larger flocks; roost communally in small groups. *Movements:* sedentary. *Foods:* grass seeds, grain (rice) and insects. *Breeding:* mainly June-Sep but nearly all the year; Feb-Nov (eastern China); several broods per year; somewhat colonial. *Nest:* large untidy, globular, grass nest with lateral entrance hole, sometimes a tunnel, in a low bush, bamboo, or long grass. *Eggs:* 3, 5-6, 8.

Cheng, 1963, pp.823-826.
Ali and Ripley, vol.10, 1968-74, pp.107-110.

NOTES ON INTRODUCTIONS

Réunion. The Sharp-tailed Mannikin has, I believe, been introduced to Réunion (Isle de Bourbon) from Pondicherry in India. The attempt was apparently unsuccessful, but I am unable to locate any references to it.

DAMAGE

The Sharp-tailed Mannikin, for a substantial part of the year in China, gathers in flocks to feed on crops thus causing considerable damage (Cheng, 1963). In India also, the species occasionally occurs in flocks of considerable size which cause local damage to cereal crops (Ali and Ripley, 1968-74).

CHESTNUT-BREASTED FINCH
Lonchura castaneothorax (Gould)

DISTINGUISHING CHARACTERISTICS

10-12 cm (4-4.8 in)

Upper parts cinnamon-brown; rump orange-yellow; crown and nape mottled grey-brown; face and throat black; pale streaks on cheeks; breast chestnut, with a black bar on lower breast; abdomen white, with black barred flanks; under tail-coverts black; bill blue-grey.

Immelmann, 1965, pp.167-168 and pl.8, no.3, opp. p.178.
Reader's Digest, 1977, p.540 and pl. p.540.

GENERAL DISTRIBUTION

New Guinea, northern and eastern Australia: from Derby, Western Australia, to the Gulf of Carpentaria, Northern Territory, and in eastern Australia from Cape York, northern Queensland to Sydney, New South Wales: also Melville Island and New Guinea.

INTRODUCED DISTRIBUTION

Introduced successfully to the Society Islands and on New Caledonia. Escapees may be established in south-western Australia. Introduced unsuccessfully to New Zealand.

GENERAL HABITS

Status: common; often kept in captivity. *Habitat:*

grasslands, reedy swamps, rivers and mangroves. *Gregariousness:* flocks up to several hundred. *Movements:* sedentary and nomadic. *Foods:* seeds and insects. *Breeding:* mainly Jan-Apr, but in all months; after rain in some areas; colonial. *Nest:* domed, spherical grass structure, side opening, in grass, reeds, etc. *Eggs:* 4, 5-6.

Immelmann, 1965, pp.169-174.
Reader's Digest, 1977, p.540.

NOTES ON INTRODUCTIONS

Society Islands. Chestnut-breasted Finches *L.c. castaneothorax* have been introduced in the Society Islands (Peters, 1968). According to Holyoak (1974) they were introduced to Tahiti at the end of the nineteenth century. Townsend and Wetmore (1919) say that the specimens were collected on Tahiti and Bora Bora in 1899. The Whitney Expedition (1920-21) collected some thirty-four specimens on Tahiti and sixteen on Moorea. Some were released on Tahiti in 1938 and were reported to have nested and reared young soon after their liberation (Guild, 1938).

Many individuals were apparently introduced (accidentally ?) in April 1973 on the island of Tetiaroa, but they did not become established there (Thibault, 1976).

In 1972, Holyoak found Chestnut-breasted Finches abundant on Tahiti, Moorea, Raiatea, Tahaa, Bora Bora and Huahine, and felt that they were probably also on Maupiti. He records that they inhabit the coastal borders to the interior valleys, but do not occur in the mountainous forests above seven hundred metres. (2300 feet). They are often seen in groups of 50-100, often accompanying *E. temporalis.*

Western Australia. Between 1973 and 1977 Chestnut-breasted Finches were sighted in small flocks in Osborne Park, a suburb of Perth (Kolichis, 1978).

They have not been recorded to breed there and are presumably escapees from local aviaries. The species occurs naturally in the northern areas of Western Australia.

New Zealand. Up until 1864 some six Chestnut-breasted Finches were imported and released somewhere in New Zealand, but details appear to be lacking. In 1867 the Auckland Acclimatisation Society liberated twenty-five birds and in 1871 another two, but these disappeared and were not seen again. Earlier the Canterbury Society obtained twelve birds from Sydney, but there are no further records of these birds (Thomson, 1922).

New Caledonia. According to Delacour (1966) the Chestnut-breasted Finch has been acclimatised in New Caledonia from northern Australia. It is now commonly found in gardens and cultivated areas where it feeds on seeds on the ground.

DAMAGE

In Australia, the Chestnut-breasted Finch is known to regularly attack crops of barley near the coast in New South Wales, but the extent of such damage does not appear to have been documented. The species may become a pest in New Caledonia and the Society Islands, where it appears to be abundant, but no damage has yet been reported.

JAVA SPARROW
(Rice or Paddy Bird, Javan Finch)
Padda oryzivora (Linnaeus)

DISTINGUISHING CHARACTERISTICS
14.5-16 cm (5.8-6.4 in)

Head, chin, upper throat, band behind ear-coverts, upper tail-coverts and tail black; sides of face to ear-coverts and under tail-coverts white; remainder grey; belly and lower flanks vinous; bill pink. A pure-white form occurs occasionally in nature and particularly in aviculture.

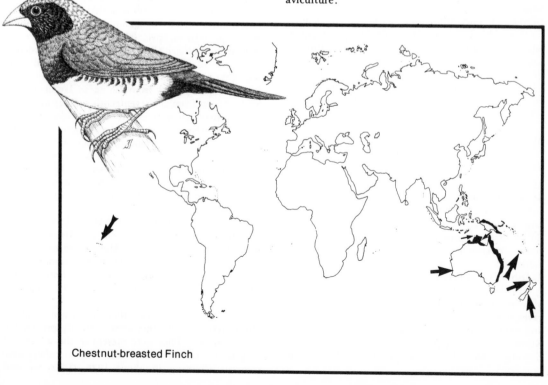

Chestnut-breasted Finch

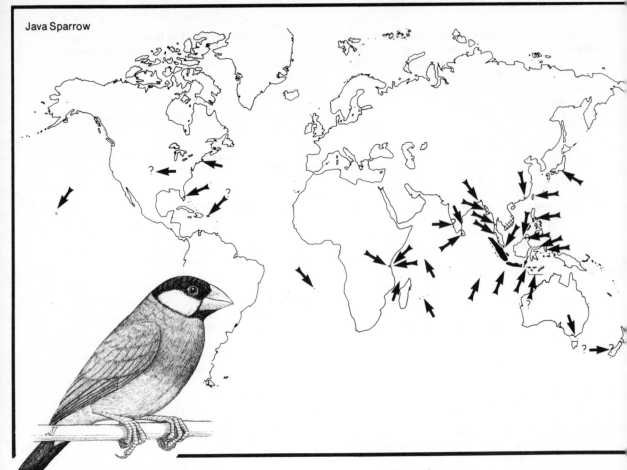

Kuroda, vol.1, 1933, pp.66-68.
Avon *et al*, 1974, pl. p.28.

GENERAL DISTRIBUTION
Java, Bali and Sumatra.

INTRODUCED DISTRIBUTION
Introduced successfully in parts of Indochina, southern China, Burma, Malay Peninsula, Singapore Island, Pinang Island, Thailand, Sri Lanka, Borneo, Lesser Sunda Islands, Sulawesi, Moluccas, Philippines, Christmas Islands, Cocos-Keeling Islands, Tanzania, Zanzibar and Pemba Islands, Hawaiian Islands, Fiji, Japan, Taiwan (?), St Helena, USA (Florida) and Puerto Rico (?).

Introduced successfully, but later died out on Mauritius, Archipel des Comores and in India. Introduced unsuccessfully in the Seychelles, Australia and possibly New Zealand.

GENERAL HABITS
Status: very common; common aviary bird. *Habitat*: ricefields, villages, cities, mangroves and scrub. Now largely in association with man. *Gregariousness*: flocks, often of considerable size; immense flocks at roosts. *Movements*: sedentary. *Foods*: corn, seeds, cultivated grains and some insects. *Breeding*: Zanzibar, Christmas Island and Cocos-Keeling May-Aug; colonial. *Nest*: bell-shaped or rounded, domed, of woven grass, entrance hole at side, placed under eaves and roofs of buildings or in bushy trees, thickets and walls. *Eggs*: 4-5, 8 (up to 5 in Malaya).
Kuroda, vol.1, 1933, pp.66-68.
Kuroda, *Tori* vol.9, no.45, 1937, pp.478-484 (in Japanese).

NOTES ON INTRODUCTIONS
Indochina and southern China. According to Riley (1938) the Java Sparrow was originally wild only on Java, Bali and Sumatra, but is now found in both Indochina and southern China as an introduced species. McClure (1974) says that they have been widely introduced in the region, both deliberately and as a cage bird escapee. The species is a successful resident in southern China, but has been recorded as far north as Shanghai. They were recorded from Shanghai in 1891 and in the Swatow area in 1892. Birds were imported from China to Japan as cage birds at least from the seventeenth century on so it is possible that they were established in China at a very early date (Kuroda, 1937). La Touche (1925-34) indicates that they occurred sparsely in south-east China and records them along the Kiangsu coast and in Fukien and Kwangtung provinces. He observed some at Swatow and mentions that others have seen them in Hong Kong. Swinhoe (1860) records them at Amoy in southern China in 1860.

They have been introduced to Hong Kong (King *et al*, 1975) where they have been recorded as early as the 1860s (Swinhoe, 1861). More recently, they are reported there almost annually in small numbers, but a flock of about 150 was noted near Sek Kong in 1967 (Webster, 1975). They are still a common cage bird in the area.

Wildash (1968) reports that they are throughout south Vietnam where they were originally imported in large numbers. They were present in the suburbs of Saigon (Ho Chi Min City) and large numbers were seen at Nhatrang in about 1925 (Delacour and

Jabouille, 1927). Specimens were also obtained from Phanrang at about the same time (Delacour and Jabouille, 1931).

Burma. Smythies (1953) indicates that the Java Sparrow was established in Arakan and Tenasserim in the 1950s. He records that Hopwood (1912, *J. Bomb. nat. Hist. Soc.*, 21: 1196) reported that they were thoroughly established in Arakan in 1912 and that Blyth (in Oats, E. W. and Blandford, W. T., 1889-98, *Faun. Brit. Ind.*, Tayl. and Franc.: Lond., Vol.2, ed.1, p.182) found them to be feral in Tenasserim in the late 1800s. Kuroda (1933-36) records them from Tenasserim in the mid-1930s.

More recently, King *et al* (1975) report that they are now well established residents in both western Burma and Tenasserim.

Malay Peninsula, Singapore and Pinang Island. Java Sparrows were probably introduced to the Malay Peninsula at Kuala Lumpur before 1910 and to Singapore in 1922 (Glenister, 1951; Delacour, 1947; Madoc, 1956; Gibson-Hill, 1949). However, Ward (1968) indicates that Oxley (1849), Ridley (1898) and Bucknill and Chasen (1927) reported them from Singapore at very early dates. Kelham (1881) records them there in 1879. Ward says that the species was probably abundant there from 1850 to 1950, but has now become rare owing to changes in habitat.

Kuroda (1933-36) and Riley (1938) record them in the Malay States in the late 1930s. They occurred in fairly early times in both George Town, Pinang Island and in Alor State, and were present in Ipoh and sporadically so in the Dindings before 1941 (Gibson-Hill, 1949).

In both Singapore and Kuala Lumpur the Java Sparrow has largely kept to the town areas, mixing freely with the Tree Sparrow. It flourished in these areas prior to the war, but seemed to exist chiefly on fallen grain and cooked rice placed out for chickens. During the Japanese occupation numbers decreased because little rice was available. However, in the late 1940s (Delacour, 1947) they were considered to be common throughout Malaysia around fields and villages, but to owe their existence (Madoc, 1956) largely to the escape of caged birds.

More recently, McClure (1974) says that the Java Sparrow, although a widely introduced species, has only been successful locally in Malaya. However, Medway and Wells (1976) say feral populations are reported in the Kangar district (Perlis), Alor district (Kedah), Pinang, Ipoh (Perak), Kuala Lumpur (Selangor), Seremban (Negri Sembilan), Malacca and on Singapore. They report that colonies in the central and southern Malayan States are strictly associated with human settlement; numbers fluctuate and are probably sustained by periodic fresh introductions. Only in Kedah and Perlis do they breed in open country and frequent truly open areas.

Thailand. The Java Sparrow has been introduced to Thailand in the central plains (Riley, 1938) around Bangkok, from Malaysia, (Deignan, 1963) and still occurs there (King *et al*, 1975). Lekagul and Cronin (1974) say that they were introduced into the Bangkok area during the past thirty-five years and are now established in the wild around that city.

Several have been found nesting under the eaves of the terminal building at Don Muang Airport.

India. The Java Sparrow has been introduced into parts of India at various times. According to Kuroda (1937), Robinson describes their nesting behaviour as seen by him at Madras around 1927. Wait (1931) also mentions that a colony appears to be established near Madras and Law (1932) reports that a colony was established in Calcutta in 1931. Although Ripley (1961) says that there are no records of permanent establishment, Ali and Ripley (1968-74) intimate that the species may still be established in some areas although it is uncommon and has not spread much.

Sri Lanka. Henry (1955) reports that Java Sparrows escape from captivity and are found in Colombo and other parts of the island. They have been known from Sri Lanka for many years, but do not appear to spread or increase much in numbers, although they breed freely in the wild. Phillips (1966) reports that the colony established at Colombo before 1870 is still surviving and the species is apparently (King *et al*, 1975) still established on the island.

Borneo and eastern Malaysia. Java Sparrows are feral in a number of localities in Borneo, probably the first introduction or escape occurring some time prior to 1860 (Smythies, 1960). According to Sharpe (1889) they were imported to Labuan Island by the Governor, the Hon Hugh Low. At this time he reported that they were abundant to common there and were causing great damage to the natives' rice fields, but had not as yet reached the mainland.

At one time it was feared that they would breed and spread throughout the region, but fortunately they have only been able to sustain themselves in a few localities (Smythies). They still occur in the Labuan and Tuaran districts of eastern Malaysia (Berwick, pers. comm., 1962), but are nowhere common except on Labuan Island.

Gore (1968) says that the species has recently been reported from Kotu Kinabalu and Tuaran.

Lesser Sunda Islands. King *et al* (1975) record that Java Sparrows have been introduced and established on the Lesser Sunda Islands, but gives no other details except to indicate that the species is still established there. As early as 1933 at least, Kuroda (1933-36) reported them from the island of Lombok.

Sulawesi. Kuroda (1937) indicates that Stresemann reported Java Sparrows from Sulawesi in 1913. They were certainly present in the period 1933 to 1937 (Kuroda, 1933-36; Stresemann, 1936) and Stresemann says that at this time they were established on the southern peninsula and the eastern part of the northern peninsula.

There appear to be no recent reports of their status, but King *et al* (1975) record the introduction and indicate that the species is still established in Sulawesi.

Moluccas. King *et al* (1975) record that the Java Sparrow has been introduced and established in the Moluccas and indicate that it still occurs there.

Philippines. Kuroda (1933-36) and Riley (1938) reported in the 1930s that Java Sparrows were then found in the Philippines. They became naturalised around Manila on the island of Luzon and in many other parts of the Philippines (Delacour, 1946; Delacour and Mayr, 1946) and are now recorded on many islands there (du Pont, 1971).

Christmas Island. Introduced on Christmas Island (Gibson-Hill, 1947), the Java Sparrow was fairly common near settlement on the north coast in the 1940s (Watson *et al,* 1963) and was present in large numbers (flocks up to fifty) near settlement there (van Tets and van Tets, 1967) in the mid-1960s. According to Watson *et al* and the van Tets they were introduced to the island about fifty years before. Chasen (1933) records that they were first introduced in about 1923, but says that the population obviously receives 'frequent additions'.

Cocos-Keeling Islands. Java Sparrows were probably introduced to the Cocos-Keeling Islands before 1828 (Holman, 1846, 'Journey around the World' p.382, in Gibson-Hill, 1949). Gibson-Hill says that they were common there in 1909 (see Wood-Jones, 1909) and in 1941 were plentiful on Pulo Tikus and in small numbers on Pulo Luar and Pulo Selma. He mentions that they occur only on the three inhabited islands and probably obtain some food (rice ?) placed out for poultry.

East Africa. (Tanzania, Zanzibar and Pemba). Riley (1938) indicates that the Java Sparrow was in East Africa in the late 1930s. Vaughan (1930) found them common in the town area of Zanzibar, in about 1929; and indicates that particulars of their introduction are unknown. However, he later (in 1932) states that Richard Burton in 'Zanzibar: City, Island, and Coast' says that the Java Sparrow was introduced by Captain Ward, the captain of a Salem ship, in about 1857. They have remained established on Zanzibar (Pakenham, 1936-1945) at least since 1929 and possibly from 1857, probably reached Pemba Island fairly recently, and were on the mainland in Tanzania at least before 1957 and more than likely since the 1930s.

The species appears to be well established on Zanzibar Island where it is spreading slowly (Mackworth-Praed and Grant, 1957-60), and has become sufficiently well established on Pemba Island to become a nuisance to rice crops there (Williams, pers. comm., 1962).

Mauritius. The Java Sparrow was introduced from Malaya in about 1750, as a cage bird, escaped and became established and a pest, but was last seen there in 1892 (Rountree *et al,* 1952; Benedict, 1957). Both Decary (1962) and Meinertzhagen, (1912) (probably quoting Le Gentil, 1781) say that by 1765 the species had increased in numbers on the island to an incredible extent, flocks of 200 and 300 settling on fields of oats and corn and destroying much of them. Decary says that they would have destroyed the crops completely, but for the resourcefulness of the farmers in frightening them away.

In 1771 a toll was levied on their heads, and in 1804 it was suggested that sparrow hawks be introduced to assist in killing some of them (Meinertzhagen). Meinertzhagen suggested in 1912 that the Java Sparrow no longer existed on the island because their food supply had disappeared, however, Decary indicates that many may have been destroyed during early measures of systematic destruction. Rountree *et al* say that they may have been decimated by the cyclone of 1892 as no birds have been seen since that time.

Seychelles. The Java Sparrow was introduced to the Seychelles (Mackworth-Praed and Grant, 1957-60), but apparently without success.

Archipel des Comores. According to Benson (1960) the Java Sparrow was recorded on the island of Mayotte in 1903 (by Reichenow, 1908), but apparently was not found there when the islands were visited in 1906-07. The species evidently died out there.

St Helena. The Java Sparrow became established on the island of St Helena possibly in the 1860s. They were reported to be present in the late 1930s (Riley, 1938) and are still established there (Mackworth-Praed and Grant, 1960).

Melliss (1870) described them as fairly abundant and says that it is not many years since they were introduced. They were apparently first imported to St Helena as a cage bird.

Haydock (1954) indicates that Moreau (in 1931) found them to be a common species on St Helena. However, during his fourteen-week stay in 1952-53 he saw only ten birds and says that the species is likely to be decreasing in numbers with the reduction in the amount of seed crops grown on the island.

Hawaiian Islands. Caum (1933) says that Java Sparrows may have been introduced to Hawaii by Dr W. Hillebrand in about 1865, and some may have been imported in about 1900. At this time, however, the species did not survive (Phillips, 1928; Berger, 1972).

A single bird was noted in the grounds of the Bishop Museum, Honolulu, in July 1964 and two were seen at Fort Shafter in August 1965 (Berger). Throp (1969) reported that some had bred and raised young on Diamond Head, Oahu, in late 1968 or early 1969.

Java Sparrows have now been seen on every Christmas Bird Count since 1969 and their numbers appear to be increasing: 231 were counted in 1976 (Pyle, 1976-77). The Hawaiian Audubon Society (1975) reports that the species is established on Oahu from escaped cage birds and is expanding its range from Kapiolani Park to Manoa, Makiki and Kalihi.

Fiji. The Java Sparrow escaped from captivity (Turbet, 1941) and has now become established throughout most of the larger islands in the Fijian group (Parham, 1954).

Mercer (1966) places the date of introduction at about 1930 and records that they are now found on the two main islands, occasionally in flocks of seventy to eighty birds.

The species appears to be common in the lowlands and about Suva on Viti Levu (Gorman, 1975; Holyoak, 1979).

Australia. Java Sparrows are reported to have been released by the Acclimatisation Society of Victoria in the Melbourne Botanical Gardens and at Royal Park in 1863, when thirty-five birds at the former and 200 birds at the latter place were liberated (Ryan, 1906).

More than likely there were earlier releases as some were recorded, presumably 'free flying', in the Gardens in 1856 (Balmford, 1978). Further birds (twenty) were also probably released at Ballarat in about 1863.

Undoubtedly, as with such a favourite cage bird, the species has escaped from time to time in Australia, but has not become established anywhere, either from the early releases or subsequent escapes.

New Zealand. In 1862 and 1867 Java Sparrows were imported to New Zealand, but it is not known whether they were actually released into the wild (Thomson, 1922).

Japan. According to Kaburaki (1934 and 1940) the Java Sparrow was introduced to Japan prior to the Restoration, and is now widespread there.

Kuroda (1937) says that they are described in 'Wakun Sho' (Dictionary of the Japanese language) published in the eighteenth century and 'Honho Shokkan' (Handbook of Japanese Foods) published in the seventeenth century. The former book records that they have recently come from abroad. In the era of the Tokugawa shogunate (seventeenth century) they were apparently bred in garden aviaries after importation from China. Prior to 1937, at least, large numbers were imported by bird keepers and many escaped from captivity.

In 1913 a colony of thirty to forty birds was established at Haneda, Tokyo (Kuroda, 1913) and in 1937 some were noted in farmlands at Minami Miyagi-cho, Adachi-Ku, Tokyo (Uchida, 1937). Before 1937 many had apparently escaped from crates at Yokohama after arrival from Shanghai. Kuroda (1937) reports that in many areas colonies maintain themselves for some time but eventually disappear. There appear to be few recent records of the species in Japan, but they still breed in Honshu and southwards as an escapee from captivity (Ornithological Society of Japan, 1974).

Taiwan. Kuroda (1937) records that the Java Sparrow is a most common cage bird on Taiwan and often is found in the wild in the suburbs of Tainan, Kaohsiung and Taipei. The Taiwanese apparently also had (have ?) the custom of 'Hojo' (setting birds free at mass for the dead) and the birds found in the wild are probably the results of such ceremonies (Horikawa, 1936).

USA. The Java Sparrow has been introduced successfully into Miami in south-eastern Florida (Owre, 1973). Owre reports that they are breeding there and at least fifty to 100 have been observed at one roost. They have been a favourite cage bird in the area for many years and were seen in the wild at Coral Gables as early as 1960. They are now spread over an area of several square kilometres and breed in both residential and downtown areas.

More recently, in 1975, Java Sparrows were recorded in Dade County (Heilbrun, 1976), so evidently the species remains well established in south-eastern Florida.

Phillips (1928) reports that the Bureau of Biological Survey allows the importation of these common cage birds with the understanding that they are not to be liberated. Restrictions such as these did not prevent the species becoming established in more recent times.

Early introductions of Java Sparrows in the USA include a liberation in Central Park, New York, by J. Jones in 1878 and possibly there were many others which were released or escaped in many places as many birds were imported before 1928 (Phillips).

Puerto Rico. Blake (1975) indicates that the Java Sparrow has been introduced in Puerto Rico, but gives no other details.

DAMAGE

According to Boosey (1958) the Java Sparrow is a much dreaded perennial curse in the rice fields of South-east Asia, descending in hordes to devour the ripening grain. There appears, however, little documentary evidence of damage in their native range.

Where the Java Sparrow has been introduced in eastern Malaysia they have been causing damage, particularly on Labuan Island, since the late 1800s. Berwick (pers. comm., 1962) says that they can cause serious damage to padi, but have fierce competition from the indigenous munia species.

On Pemba Island in East Africa they cause some damage to rice crops (Williams, pers. comm., 1962).

Family: *Fringillidae* Cardueline Finches

122 species in 20 genera; 21 species introduced, 9 successfully (2 more possibly successful)

The most successful introductions of Cardueline Finches have been in the Australia-New Zealand area, with no less than four species now well established there. Both the Chaffinch and Redpoll have become pests of fruit in New Zealand and the remainder show some potential in this regard.

In other areas of the world, the House Finch has become a pest in the Hawaiian Islands and the Cape Canary and Yellow-fronted Canary in the Mascarenes.

Many members of the family appear to feed on fruits and buds and do attack or are capable of attacking cultivated varieties. Such species as the Bullfinch are notorious pests.

INTRODUCTIONS OF FRINGILLIDAE

Species	Date introduced	Region	Manner introduced	Reason
(a) Successful introductions				
Chaffinch	1862-77	New Zealand and islands	deliberate	?
	1898 or about 1900	South Africa	deliberate	aesthetic
Canary	1910	Midway Island, Hawaiian Group	deliberate	?
	?	Açores	colonisation or introduction	?
Cape Canary	about 1900 ?	Réunion	?	?
Yellow-fronted Canary	mid-18th century	Mauritius	?	aesthetic
	?	Réunion	?	?

437

continued

INTRODUCTIONS OF FRINGILLIDAE

Species	Date introduced	Region	Manner introduced	Reason
	1764	Rodrigues Island	deliberate	?
	since 1965	Hawaiian Islands	deliberate or escapee ?	cage bird
Yellow Canary	?	Ascension Island	?	?
	before 1870 or 1929 ?	St Helena	deliberate ?	?
Greenfinch	1863, 1872	Australia	deliberate	?
	about 1939	Norfolk Island	colonisation from Australia or New Zealand	—
	1862-68	New Zealand and islands	deliberate	?
	about 1890	Açores	?	?
	about 1929	Uruguay	escapee ?	?
Goldfinch	about 1890	Açores	colonisation or introduction	?
	1863-79	Australia	deliberate	?
	1862-83	New Zealand and islands	deliberate	?
	fairly recent ?	Uruguay	?	?
	before 1875, 1885 and 1893	Bermuda	deliberate and escapee ?	aesthetic and cage bird
Common Redpoll	1862-75	New Zealand and islands	deliberate	?
House Finch	about 1940	eastern USA	deliberate and/or escapee ?	avoiding prosecution
	before 1870	Hawaiian Islands	?	?

(b) Possibly or probably successful introductions

Species	Date introduced	Region	Manner introduced	Reason
White-rumped Seedeater	since 1965	Hawaiian Islands	deliberate or escapee	cage bird
Yellow-fronted Canary	?	São Tomé and Annobon (?)	?	?
Lesser Goldfinch	?	Cuba	?	?
	?	Panama	escapee ?	?
Goldfinch	before 1964	Cape Verde Islands	deliberate	?
	occasionally ?	Argentina (Buenos Aires)	escapee ?	cage bird ?

(c) Unsuccessful introductions

Species	Date introduced	Region	Manner introduced	Reason
Chaffinch	1863-72	Australia	deliberate	?
	1878, 1889-1907	USA	deliberate (and escapee ?)	?
Bramble Finch	1868-77	New Zealand	deliberate	?
	1879-80	Australia	deliberate	?
Canary	frequently ?	USA	escapee	cage bird
	1872 and later	Australia	deliberate and escapee	cage bird
	frequently ?	New Zealand	deliberate and escapee	cage bird
	?	Bermuda	deliberate ?	?
	frequently	England	escapee	cage bird
	16th century	Italy	escapee	shipwreck
Cape Canary	before 1812	Mauritius	deliberate ?	?
	1938	Tahiti (?)	deliberate	?
	about 1924	St Helena	?	?
Yellow-rumped Seedeater	1929	St Helena	deliberate	?
Yellow-fronted Canary	1929	St Helena	deliberate	?
	before 1884 ?	Amirante Islands	?	?
Greenfinch	?	St Helena	deliberate ?	?
	1889-92	USA	deliberate	?

INTRODUCTIONS OF FRINGILLIDAE

Species	Date introduced	Region	Manner introduced	Reason
Siskin	1876, 1879	New Zealand	deliberate and escapee ?	?
	1864, 1872	Australia	deliberate	?
	1889	USA	deliberate	?
American Goldfinch	mid-19th century	Bermuda	?	?
	1938	Tahiti	deliberate	?
Goldfinch	1846, 1872-1900	USA	deliberate	?
	1877 ?, 1908-10	Canada	deliberate and escapee ?	?
	about 1899-1902	South Africa	escapee ?	?
Twite	1862	New Zealand	deliberate	?
Linnet	1862-75	New Zealand	deliberate	?
	1860s ?	Australia (?)	deliberate	?
	1908-10	Canada	deliberate	?
	1889-92	USA	deliberate	?
Parrot Crossbill	1889	USA	deliberate	?
Bullfinch	1870, 1875	New Zealand	deliberate	?
	1860s ?, 1879-80	Australia (?)	deliberate ?	?
	1870s, 1889-92	USA	deliberate	?
Hawfinch	1860s ?	Australia (?)	deliberate ?	?

CHAFFINCH
Fringilla coelebs (Linnaeus)

DISTINGUISHING CHARACTERISTICS
15-17 cm (6-6.8 in). 19-31 g (.67-1.19 oz)
Upper parts brown, shading to olive on the rump; head, behind eye and crown slate-blue; breast pink; wings brownish black with two white wing bars; tail blackish with outer feathers white; underparts pinkish brown; bill blackish (whitish in spring). Female: olive-brown.
Witherby *et al*, vol.1, 1938-41, pp.102-104 and pl.11, opp. p.92.
Newton, 1972, pl.1 no.1, opp. p.32.

GENERAL DISTRIBUTION
Eurasia-North Africa: Açores, Madeira and Canary Islands, and from the British Isles and Scandinavia across Europe to central Asia. In winter south to the Mediterranean countries including North Africa, Iraq and the Middle East.

INTRODUCED DISTRIBUTION
Extended range northwards and eastwards in Eurasia. Introduced successfully in New Zealand and outlying islands and to South Africa (Cape Province). Introduced unsuccessfully in Australia and the USA.

GENERAL HABITS
Status: very common. *Habitat:* forest and wooded regions, cultivated areas including parks, gardens, orchards and olive groves. *Gregariousness:* large flocks in winter (sexes often segregated). *Movements:* sedentary and migratory. *Foods:* seeds of grass, weeds and trees, and grain, beech mast, small fruits, leaf buds, green plant material and insects including caterpillars, aphids, weevils and beetles; also snails, worms and spiders. *Breeding:* Apr-June (New Zealand Sep-Jan); usually 2 clutches per season. *Nest:* neat round nest of moss, lichens, wool, feathers and hair, well woven with lichens and spiders' web, in a bush or tree. *Eggs:* 1, 4-6, 8; 2, 4-6 (New Zealand).

Voous, 1960, p.398.
Newton, 1972.

NOTES ON INTRODUCTIONS
Asia. Since about 1930 the Chaffinch has been extending its range northwards and has in the course of this century extended its breeding range a considerable distance into western Siberia (Voous, 1960).

New Zealand. The Chaffinch was fairly widely introduced into New Zealand between 1862 and 1877. The Nelson Acclimatisation Society introduced twenty-three birds between 1802 and 1864, but there are no further records of them. The Auckland society liberated several birds in 1864, 1867 (forty-five birds), 1868 (sixty-eight) and a considerable number in 1869. The Canterbury society liberated some in 1867 (eleven), 1868 (five) and in 1871 (?), and three years later they were considered to be thoroughly established there. Later, in 1874 and 1877 the Otago society liberated more Chaffinches: in 1874 (seventy), 1876 (three) in 1877 (two) and more in subsequent years (Thomson, 1922).

According to Thomson many more were released by private individuals and dealers at most of the principal centres of that time.

In the 1920s the Chaffinch was said to be throughout both islands of New Zealand and to be very abundant in parts, especially from Taupo northwards (Thomson). The species is now widespread and abundant in both the North and South Islands (Wodzicki, 1965) and has penetrated the bush as has no other introduced finch (Falla *et al*, 1966) in New Zealand. It is now one of the commonest finches and breeds as far south as Campbell Island.

Outlying islands of New Zealand. In 1879 an attempt was made to establish the Chaffinch on Stewart Island when seventy birds were liberated there (Thomson, 1922). Although Thomson mentions that by 1916

439

Chaffinch

none had been seen for years, Oliver (1930) reports that they were present there at least by 1930.

The Chaffinch had reached the islands of Mayor and Kapiti, also before the 1930s (Oliver) and were later reported from Three Kings, Mokohinau, Little Barrier, Codfish, Snares, Auckland and Campbell Islands (Oliver, 1955). Williams (1953) records that they had reached the Snares before 1948, and Wodzicki (1965) that they had reached Macquarie Island. Williams (1973) reports that they have now bred on Three Kings, the Chathams, Antipodes, Campbell and Auckland Islands, but have not been recorded to have done so on the Kermadecs or Snares.

South Africa. The Chaffinch was introduced from England in about 1900 and became established in the Cape Peninsula (Mackworth-Praed and Grant, 1955-63; Roberts, 1946). The introduction is thought to have been made by C. J. Rhodes in 1898, when a large number of English songbirds were released (Sec. Ag. Tech. Serv., pers. comm., 1962).

The race introduced, *F.c. gengleri,* appears to be still surviving in the area where it was originally established (Wattel, 1971): gardens and woodlands of Cape Peninsula from Sea Point to Tokai and Hout Bay (Winterbottom, 1966). Two birds were observed at Kenton-on-Sea in the south-east Cape in January 1961, but it is not known how they arrived there (Skead, 1961) or whether the species became permanently established there.

Australia. The Chaffinch was introduced and liberated by the Acclimatisation Society of Victoria in the 1860s, but failed to become established. Releases were made near Melbourne in 1863 (forty birds), 1864 (220) and in 1872 (235). Some were imported to Melbourne as early as 1856 (Balmford, 1978), but there appears to be no record of any releases prior to 1863. Three birds were also liberated by the South Australian Acclimatisation Society in about 1879-80 (Jenkins, 1977) but the species did not become established in that State.

There appear to be no further records of the Chaffinch in Australia except for probably a few escapees at different times.

USA. A single male Chaffinch lived in Central Park, New York, for about three years prior to 1905 (Hix, 1905). Jewett and Gabrielson (1929) record that Pfluger (1896, *Oreg. Nat.* 3: 32-154) reported that forty pairs had been introduced by the 'Society' in Oregon in 1889. These birds apparently failed to become established there. Phillips (1928) reports that the species was introduced to Central Park, New York, by J. Jones in 1878, that at least thirty or forty pairs were released in New York City for several seasons prior to 1893 and that a further twenty pairs in 1907 and twenty more at a later date may have been liberated in Oregon. He also indicates that some were released in the San Francisco region of California as a single bird was shot at Monterey in 1905 and one was sighted in Berkeley in 1908.

DAMAGE

In Great Britain the Chaffinch occasionally causes damage to horticultural crops. As an introduced species its reputation as a pest is not great. In South Africa it has not increased in numbers or spread sufficiently to have ever become a nuisance; however, in New Zealand they became so abundant prior to the 1920s that some councils in grain growing areas paid bonuses for their destruction (Thomson, 1922).

More recently in New Zealand, Dawson and Bull (1969) report that they damage the buds of apricots, peaches, apples and nectarines, but were not considered by them to be one of the more important pests.

BRAMBLE FINCH
(Brambling)
Fringilla montifringilla Linnaeus

DISTINGUISHING CHARACTERISTICS

14.3-15 cm (5.7-6 in). 22-33 g (.78-1.16 oz)
Head and back brown or blackish; shoulder patch, throat and belly orange-buff; belly whitish; wing bar white, axillaries lemon-yellow; rump white; upper tail-coverts black, fringed brown; bill black (yellow or greyish in winter). Female: paler; buff breast; brown head with dark stripes.
Witherby *et al,* vol.1, 1938-41, pp.107-110 and pl.13, opp. p.114.
Newton, 1972, pl.1, no.1, opp. p.32.

GENERAL DISTRIBUTION

Eurasia-North Africa: from Scandinavia east through Siberia to Kamchatka and south to southern Norway and central USSR. In winter south to the British Isles, the Mediterranean, North Africa, Near East, Iran, Turkestan, north-west India, China, Taiwan and Japan.

INTRODUCED DISTRIBUTION

Introduced unsuccessfully to New Zealand and Australia.

GENERAL HABITS

Status: common. *Habitat:* taiga, woods, riversides, open forest, fields and cultivation. *Gregariousness:* large flocks in winter. *Movements:* migratory. *Foods:* small invertebrates including caterpillars, aphids, flies and other insects, also berries, beech mast, seeds of grasses, weeds and trees, and cereal grain and buds. *Breeding:* Feb-Aug; 1-2 broods per season (?).

Nest: small, compact, of moss and grass, interwoven with feathers and spider's web and lined with feathers and hair, in a tree. *Eggs:* 3, 6-7, 9.
Voous, 1960, p.261.
Newton, 1972.

NOTES ON INTRODUCTIONS

New Zealand. Bramble Finches were liberated a number of times in New Zealand from 1868 to 1877. In 1868, two were liberated by the Canterbury Acclimatisation Society. A further six birds were liberated by this same society in 1871. Some three birds in 1874 and one in 1877 were liberated by the Wellington society (Thomson, 1922).

Thomson records that some birds were reported in 1885, but there appear to be no further records of the species in New Zealand.

Australia. Bramble Finches (seventy-eight) were apparently liberated in South Australia by the acclimatisation society in about 1879-80 (Jenkins, 1977), but failed to become established.

DAMAGE

None known.

CANARY
Serinus canarius (Linnaeus)

DISTINGUISHING CHARACTERISTICS

12.7-14 cm (5-5.6 in). 16-17 g (.56-.6 oz).
(Nominate wild race) Forehead and cheeks golden yellow; head and nape greenish yellow with blackish brown streaks; lores dusky yellow; sides grey, streaked black; belly and under tail-coverts white; mantle and back ashy brown, broadly streaked blackish brown; rump olive-yellow; wings and tail black, margined whitish; bill pale horn. Female: more grey-brown and duller yellow.
Bannerman, 1963, vol.1, p.284; vol.2, pl.8, opp. p.95.

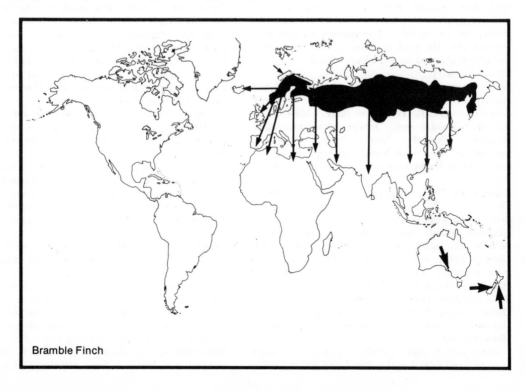

Bramble Finch

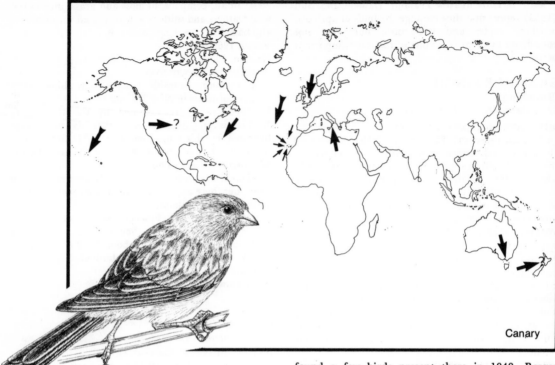

Canary

GENERAL DISTRIBUTION

Canary Islands and Madeira: on the western Canary Islands including Gran Canaria, Tenerife, Palma, Gomera and Hierro (?); also on Madeira.

INTRODUCED DISTRIBUTION

Introduced successfully in the Hawaiian Islands (Sand Island); introduced or colonised, successfully the Açores. Introduced unsuccessfully in Australia, USA, New Zealand, Bermuda, England, Italy (?) and probably other areas. Bred in captivity throughout the world and frequently escapes or is released into the wild in many places, but rarely becomes established for any length of time.

GENERAL HABITS

Status: common; universal cage bird. *Habitat:* cultivated areas, pastures and orchards. *Gregariousness:* flocks, often large. *Movements:* sedentary. *Foods:* seeds, tender leaves and buds. *Breeding:* Feb-July. *Nest:* flimsy cup-shaped structure of twigs, well lined with vegetable down, hair, wool, or feathers, in a shrub or small tree. *Eggs:* 3-5.

Bannerman, 1963, vol.1, pp.284-288; vol.2, pp.95-97.

NOTES ON INTRODUCTIONS

Hawaiian Islands. Escaped domestic canaries have become established on many of the main islands (Berger, 1972). A pair were taken to Midway Island from Honolulu in March 1909; these and ten offspring were released in July 1910, began nesting in December and about sixty bred in this first season (Bryan, 1912). Munro (1960) records that Mr D. Morrison introduced them to Sand Island in the Midway group.

Fisher and Baldwin (1945) counted some thirty birds on Sand Island in May 1945, and Bailey (1956) found a few birds present there in 1949. Berger reports that they apparently still exist there, but says that there has been no recent census of numbers. The Hawaiian Audubon Society (1975) records that the species is well established and breeding on the island.

USA. Domestic Canaries frequently escape in the USA but do not appear to become established anywhere (Anderson, 1934). The situation would appear to have changed little in the United States since the 1930s.

Australia. A deliberate attempt to establish the Canary in Australia was made by the Victorian Acclimatisation Society, between 1861 and 1872, when some eighteen were released near Melbourne. Jenkins (1977) gives the date of release as 1859 and Ryan (1906) as 1872; Balmford (1978) indicates that it was between 1862 and 1869, but records that they were imported as early as 1856. However, all the early introductions were unsuccessful.

The species frequently escapes from aviaries or is deliberately released into the wild in Australia, but has been unable to persist for any length of time as a wild bird.

New Zealand. According to Thomson (1922) there were no serious early attempts to introduce the Canary into New Zealand, but it is known that several private attempts have been made to establish them. The species however has failed to become established there.

Bermuda. The Canary was introduced on Bermuda (Peters, 1968) where it survived only temporarily (Wingate, 1973).

Açores. Bannerman and Bannerman (1966) say that the Canary either spread or was introduced to the Açores where it is now plentiful on all the islands.

Italy. Canaries were introduced on the Isle of Elba when a ship carrying breeding cages full of them foundered off the coast of that island; the birds escaped and became feral on the island in the sixteenth century (Zeuner, 1963). There appear to be no further records of these birds.

England. The Canary apparently escapes from captivity frequently in England and sometimes survives for long periods at liberty (Goodwin, 1956) but has not become permanently established anywhere.

DAMAGE

Domesticated as a pet the Canary probably has no economic value other than to breeders themselves.

Bannerman and Bannerman (1966) say that the wild form sometimes becomes a nuisance when in large numbers in cultivated areas in the Açores. They do not, however, mention in what way they are pests.

CAPE CANARY
(Yellow-crowned Canary)
Serinus canicollis (Swainson)

DISTINGUISHING CHARACTERISTICS

12.5-14 cm (5-5.6 in)

Forehead to nape, sides of face, chin and breast, golden green; abdomen yellow; ear-coverts, hindneck and sides of neck, grey; mantle, scapulars, wing-coverts and rump yellowish green, streaked dusky except on the rump; flight feathers and tail black, edged green; bill dusky, tipped paler. Female: chin and chest greyish and more streaked above.

Mackworth-Praed and Grant, ser.2, vol.2, 1963, p.685 and pl.75.

GENERAL DISTRIBUTION

South Africa: from eastern and southern Rhodesia, eastern Transvaal, Zululand and Natal to southern Cape Province.

INTRODUCED DISTRIBUTION

Introduced successfully on Réunion. Introduced unsuccessfully to Mauritius, Tahiti and (?) St Helena.

GENERAL HABITS

Status: common. *Habitat:* forest, woodland, gardens and orchards. *Gregariousness:* usually small flocks, sometimes large flocks at roosts in non-breeding season. *Movements:* sedentary. *Foods:* seeds of plants and shrubs. *Breeding:* July-Feb. *Nest:* neat, cup-shaped of grass and tendrils, lined with seed down and soft material, in a bush or tree. *Eggs:* 3-4, 5.

Mackworth-Praed and Grant, ser.2, vol.2, 1963, pp.685-686.

NOTES ON INTRODUCTIONS

Mauritius. The race *S.c. canicollis* has been introduced to Mauritius (Peters, 1968). Meinertzhagen (1912) records that the introduction was made before 1812 and Rountree *et al* (1952) and Staub (1976) report that they were introduced from Cape Province, South Africa.

The species apparently flourished there for some years until many were wiped out in the cyclone of 1892 (Benedict, 1957; Decary, 1962). The last specimen was seen on the island in 1913.

Réunion. The race *canicollis* was also introduced and established on Réunion during the eighteenth century (Staub, 1976; Peters, 1968) and was plentiful there in the early 1900s (Meinertzhagen, 1912). Watson *et al* (1963) record that the species is common there, breeding in December. Staub (1976) says that they are confined to scrub and cultivated patches between 600 m and 2000 m on the island.

Tahiti. Guild (1938) mentions the introduction of 'Cape Canaries' on Tahiti in about 1938. He does not specifically identify the species that was liberated. It may possibly have been *canicollis,* but I suggest that it could equally have been *S. mozambicus,* which in some avicultural circles of that period was known as Cape Canary. The latter species was most certainly the more common aviary bird. Neither bird now occurs in Tahiti.

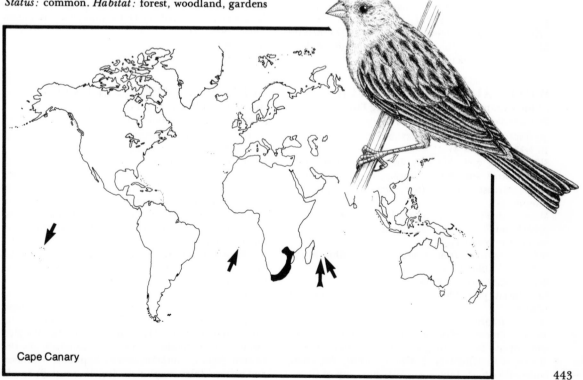

Cape Canary

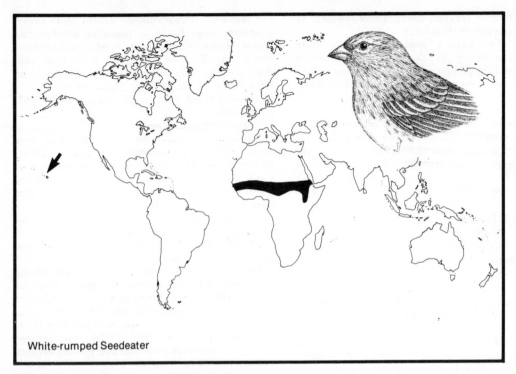

White-rumped Seedeater

St Helena. Haydock (1954) indicates that Huckle (in 1924) mentions the presence of Cape Canaries on St Helena. If introduced the species did not become permanently established on the island.

DAMAGE

Decary (1962) indicates that the Cape Canary introduced in the Mascarenes destroys to some extent, grains, fruits and vegetables. Little appears to be documented on the pest status of the species in Africa, but Williams (pers. comm., 1962) says that in his opinion they would be a dangerous introduction in grain growing areas. Staub (1976) records that they proved a threat to cereal crops whilst established on Mauritius and that they were extensively hunted there prior to their extinction.

WHITE-RUMPED SEEDEATER
(White-rumped Serin, Grey Singing Finch)
Serinus leucopygius (Sundevall)

DISTINGUISHING CHARACTERISTICS

10.1-13.5 cm (4-5.4)

Sides of face and chin ashy grey; upper parts ashy grey, spotted and streaked dusky; throat and rump white; breast greyish (sometimes streaky); bill brown.

Mackworth-Praed and Grant, 1952-73, ser.1, vol.2, p.1073; ser.3, vol.2, pp.756-757 and pl.92.

GENERAL DISTRIBUTION

Northern Africa: from Sénégal and Gambia to the Sudan and Ethiopia.

INTRODUCED DISTRIBUTION

Introduced, probably unsuccessfully in the Hawaiian Islands.

GENERAL HABITS

Status: common. *Habitat:* cultivated lands, gardens and open bush. *Gregariousness:* small flocks. *Movements:* sedentary ? *Foods:* seeds, including millet. *Breeding:* July-Nov. *Nest:* neat cup of fibres,

plant stems and hair, lined with feathers and down. *Eggs:* 3-4.

Mackworth-Praed and Grant, 1952-73, ser.1, vol.2, p.1073; ser.3, vol.2, pp.756-757.

NOTES ON INTRODUCTIONS

Hawaiian Islands. Intentionally or accidentally released or escaped, since 1965 on Oahu (Berger, 1972), the White-rumped Seedeater frequents the Kapiolani Park area (Hawaiian Audubon Society, 1975) of that island. Some were observed on the Christmas Bird Counts from 1966 to 1971, but they have not been noted on Oahu since the latter date (Pyle, 1976-77).

DAMAGE

None known.

YELLOW-RUMPED SEEDEATER
(Black-throated Canary, Peach Canary)
Serinus atrogularis (Smith)

DISTINGUISHING CHARACTERISTICS

11-12 cm (4.4-4.8). 8-14 g (.28-.49 oz)

Upper parts brown, back streaky grey or blackish; underparts pale dusky brown; rump yellow; above eye white; throat and chin black; variable amounts of white on front and sides of neck; wing-coverts and secondaries blackish; wings and short tail feathers with narrow yellowish edges; bill dark brownish, lower mandible paler.

Mackworth-Praed and Grant, 1952-73, ser.1, vol.2, pp.1074-1076; ser.2, vol.2, pp.691-693 and pl.75; ser.3, vol.2, pp.757-758 and pl.92.

GENERAL DISTRIBUTION

Southern and eastern Africa, and south-western Arabia: from Arabia (Hejaz south to Yemen and Aden and east to Hadhramaut in the Peoples Democratic Republic of Yemen), Ethiopia, south-eastern Sudan, southern Somali Republic, southern and eastern Zaire, south-west Angola, south to South

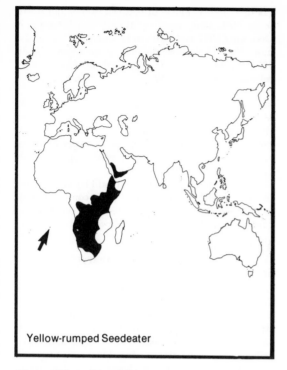

Yellow-rumped Seedeater

West Africa (Namibia), northern South Africa, Tanzania, Zambia and Rhodesia.

INTRODUCED DISTRIBUTION
Introduced unsuccessfully to St Helena.

GENERAL HABITS
Status: common. *Habitat:* bush or woodland, generally near water and cultivation. *Gregariousness:* pairs or small parties. *Movements:* some local movements, not well known. *Foods:* grass seeds, flowers and termites. *Breeding:* all the year, varies in different areas. *Nest:* small cup of rootlets and grass stems, lined with plant down and bound with cobwebs. *Eggs:* 3-4, 5.

Mackworth-Praed and Grant, 1952-73, ser.1, vol.2, pp.1074-1076; ser.2, vol.2, pp.691-693; ser.3, vol.2, pp.757-758.

NOTES ON INTRODUCTIONS
St Helena. The Yellow-rumped Seedeater was imported from South Africa and released on St Helena by an agricultural officer, H. Bruins-Lich in 1929, but failed to become established (Haydock, 1954).

DAMAGE
None known.

YELLOW-FRONTED CANARY
(Yellow-bellied Canary, Green Singing Finch)
Serinus mozambicus (Müller)

DISTINGUISHING CHARACTERISTICS
10-11.4 cm (4-4.6 in). 10.7-12.6 g (.38-.44 oz)
Variable species with upper parts greyish green and heavily streaked, to yellow-green and lightly streaked; forehead, streak over eye and lower rump yellow; crown variably greyish; upper tail-coverts green; cheeks yellow; a black moustachial stripe; underparts dull green, streaked dusky; tail and wings dusky, edged yellowish green, and tail white tipped; bill, upper mandible brown, lower white.

Mackworth-Praed and Grant, 1952-73, ser.1, vol.2, pp.1061-1063 and pl.95; ser.2, vol.2, pp.678-679 and pl.75; ser.3, vol.2, pp.749-751 and pl.92.
Avon *et al,* 1974, pl. p.56.

GENERAL DISTRIBUTION
Africa: Africa south of the Sahara, except South West Africa, western South Africa, parts of eastern Ethiopia and Somali Republic, and much of southern Zaire and the Congo; also present on Mafia Island.

INTRODUCED DISTRIBUTION
Introduced successfully to Mauritius, Réunion, Rodrigues and the Hawaiian Islands; probably

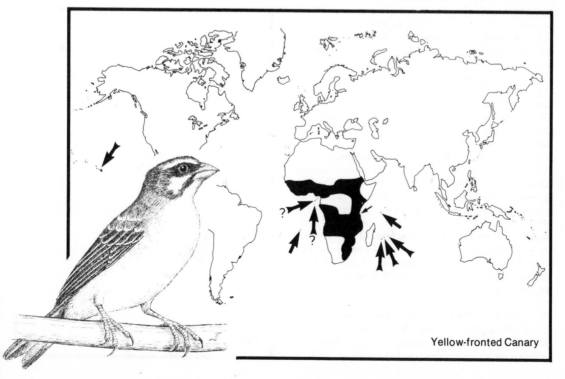

Yellow-fronted Canary

445

introduced to some isles in the Gulf of Guinea (São Tomé and Annobon [?]). Introduced successfully to the Amirante Islands but has since died out. Introduced unsuccessfully to St Helena.

GENERAL HABITS

Status: common and abundant; frequently kept as a cage bird. *Habitat:* savannah, cultivated areas and gardens. *Gregariousness:* small parties, or flocks of 6-12 in the non-breeding season. *Movements:* sedentary. *Foods:* grass and weed seeds, buds and blossom. *Breeding:* most of the year. *Nest:* shallow, compact cup of grass, stems, etc. bound with cobwebs and lined with rootlets, in a tree or shrub. *Eggs:* 3-4, 6.

Mackworth-Praed and Grant, 1952-73, ser.1, vol.2, pp.1061-1063; ser.2, vol.2, pp.678-679; ser.3, vol.2, pp.749-751.

NOTES ON INTRODUCTIONS

Mauritius. Rountree *et al* (1952) say that the Yellow-fronted Canary was introduced to Mauritius, probably from the Moçambique coast, in about the middle of the eighteenth century. Meinertzhagen (1912) records that they were imported by the French who introduced them partly as an experiment and partly as a present to the ladies of that time.

The Yellow-fronted Canary *S.m. mozambicus* was plentiful on Mauritius in the wild in 1912, was still common in the late 1950s, and is still well established and breeding there (Staub, 1976).

Réunion. The race *S.m. mozambicus* has been introduced and established on Réunion (Mackworth-Praed and Grant, 1955-63; Peters, 1968) where it is common and breeds in December (Watson *et al,* 1963).

Rodrigues. The race *S.m. mozambicus* has been introduced to Rodrigues (Peters, 1968). Staub (1976) quoting Vinson (1965, *Proc. Roy. Soc. Arts Sci. Mau.* 2: 263-277) says that they were brought to the island around 1764. He indicates that the species is still well established there.

Amirante Islands. According to Penny (1974) the Yellow-fronted Canary must have been introduced to the Amirantes very early in the island's history. Some were collected on Des Roches in 1884 and in 1892, but it has become rare since that time and now may have died out. The race introduced was *mozambicus* (Peters, 1968).

Gulf of Guinea Isles. The race *S.m. tando* has probably been introduced to both São Tomé and Annobon (Peters, 1968).

St Helena. Imported from South Africa and released by H. Bruins-Lich in about 1929, the Yellow-fronted Canary failed to become permanently established on St Helena (Haydock, 1954). Haydock indicates that Sclater mentions that the species was present there in 1930.

Hawaiian Islands. The Yellow-fronted Canary has been intentionally or accidentally released or escaped since about 1965 on the island of Oahu (Berger, 1972). Berger (1977) later says that they were first reported there in 1964.

The species has now been observed on every Christmas Bird Count on Oahu from 1966 to 1977 (Pyle, 1976-78), in the Kapiolani Park area (Hawaiian Audubon Society, 1975), and was recorded as nesting there in 1974 and in 1976-77

(Berger, 1977). Flocks of between twenty and thirty-seven birds were noted on Mauna Kea, Hawaii, in December 1977 and again in February 1978 and have more than likely bred on that island (Van Ripper, 1978). The species is suspected of having been released from the Puu Waawaa Ranch on Hawaii.

DAMAGE

Meinertzhagen (1912) relates how the natives on Mauritius had to stay in the fields all day to frighten these birds away from their crops. Decary (1962) points out that they are a great destroyer of cereal crops and will become an even greater menace if more crops are grown in the Mascarenes.

The species was (and probably still is) unprotected in southern Rhodesia (Goode, pers. comm., 1962). Mackworth-Praed and Grant (1957-73) say that they cause damage to both fruit and flower buds in Africa.

YELLOW CANARY
(Yellow Seed-eater, Swainson's Canary)
Serinus flaviventris (Swainson)

DISTINGUISHING CHARACTERISTICS

12.5-13.7 cm (5-5.5 in)

Top of head, mantle and scapulars moss green, streaked darker; rump plain moss green; forehead, stripe over eye, moustachial stripe and underparts yellow; ear-coverts green; wings black, edged green; bill dark horn, stripe on lower mandible green. Female: top of head, mantle and scapulars streaked black and brown; stripe over eye buff-white.

Mackworth-Praed and Grant, ser.2, vol.2, 1952-73, pp.680-681 and pl.75.

GENERAL DISTRIBUTION

South Africa: from South West Africa (Namibia) to Cape Province, south-western Transvaal, Orange Free State, Botswana and Lesotho.

INTRODUCED DISTRIBUTION

Introduced successfully on Ascension Island and to St Helena.

Yellow Canary

Status: common; frequently kept cage bird. *Habitat:* scrub and open bush country near water. *Gregariousness:* small flocks in non-breeding season. *Movements:* sedentary. *Foods:* seeds and termites. *Breeding:* July-Mar. *Nest:* open cup of stems and rootlets, lined with seed-down and soft material, in a shrub or bush. *Eggs:* 3-4, 5.

Mackworth-Praed and Grant, ser.2, vol.2, 1952-73, pp.680-681.

NOTES ON INTRODUCTIONS

Ascension Island. The Yellow Canary has been introduced and established on Ascension Island. There were at least 100-200 birds present there in the early 1960s (Stonehouse, 1962).

St Helena. The race *S.f. flaviventris* has been introduced (Peters, 1968) and established on the island of St Helena. Melliss (1870) records that the 'canary' *'Crithagra butyracea'* is most abundant on St Helena and may have been referring to this species. More recently, however, Haydock (1954) says that the race *S.f. marshalli* was imported from South Africa and released by H. Bruins-Lich in about 1929.

Haydock indicates that *butyracea* (by Melliss, 1875) *mozambicus* (by Sclater, 1950) and *canicollis* (by Huckle, 1924) have all been mentioned for the island, but that he collected five specimens of *flaviventris* during his stay and doubts the presence of any other species.

DAMAGE

None known.

GREENFINCH
(European Greenfinch, Green Linnet)
Carduelis chloris (Linnaeus)

DISTINGUISHING CHARACTERISTICS
14.3-15.2 cm (5.7-6.1 in). 26-36 g (.85-1.27 oz)
Mainly dull olive-green; breast and rump greenish yellow; wing bars lemon yellow; sides of tail yellow; bill whitish. Female: duller and browner, and with less yellow.

Witherby *et al,* vol.1, 1938-41, pp.54-57 and pl. opp. p.54.

Newton, 1972, pp.31-34 and pl.3, no.3, opp. p.48.

Reader's Digest, 1977, pl. p.525.

GENERAL DISTRIBUTION

Eurasia — North Africa: from the British Isles, Açores, Morocco and Algiers to central western Asia, and southern Asia east of the Aral Sea. In winter to southern Europe, Sinai Peninsula, Egypt, Iraq, southwestern Iran and northern Afghanistan.

INTRODUCED DISTRIBUTION

Successfully colonised parts of the British Isles. Introduced successfully in Australia, New Zealand and outlying islands, Uruguay and the Açores (?). Introduced unsuccessfully on St Helena (died out) and in the USA.

GENERAL HABITS

Status: very common. *Habitat:* forest edges, groves, cultivated areas, parks, gardens, orchards and grasslands. *Gregariousness:* family groups and flocks, large flocks at times. *Movements:* sedentary and migratory. *Foods:* seeds of grasses, weeds and trees, and grain, berries, flower and leaf buds, green plant

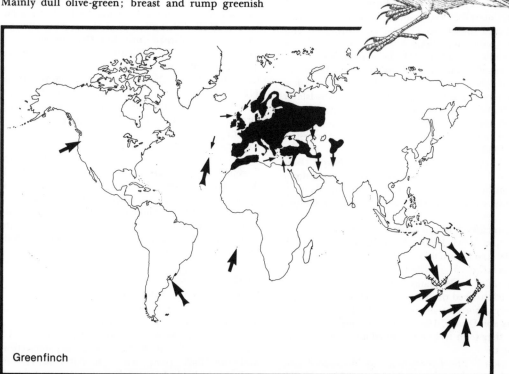

Greenfinch

material and insects including caterpillars, aphids and beetle larvae. *Breeding:* Apr-Aug; Oct-Jan (Australia); Sep-Jan (New Zealand); loose colonies; 2 and occasionally 3 broods per season (double brooded in New Zealand). *Nest:* loose structure of grass, twigs and moss, lined with hair, feathers, etc., in a bush or hedge. *Eggs:* 4-6 (New Zealand and Australia 4-6).

Voous, 1960, pp.255-256.
Newton, 1972.

NOTES ON INTRODUCTIONS

British Isles. The Greenfinch has recently colonised some areas in which it was formerly absent, i.e. the Inner Hebrides, Isles of Scilly, and parts of Mayo and Donegal in Ireland (Parslow, 1968).

Australia. The first releases of the Greenfinch in Australia were probably in Victoria where they were known in the central districts from about the 1860s (Chisholm, 1919). There were probably several releases near Melbourne; in 1863 (fifty birds), 1864 (forty) and in 1872 (twenty) (Ryan, 1906) although there may only have been one, at Royal Park, of twenty birds in 1863 (Jenkins, 1977; Balmford, 1978). They were also probably released in New South Wales as they are reported to have been thriving in the vicinity of Sydney in about 1896 (Chisholm, 1926). Liberation of Greenfinches occurred in South Australia in 1879 (seven pairs) or earlier, and subsequently there were many more up until 1900 (Condon, 1962).

In New South Wales, Greenfinches were in Albury and Bathurst and other areas around 1910 (Chisholm, 1919). However, they were still not common in the 1950s (Tarr, 1950) and were restricted mainly to the Sydney area, but had extended as far west as Bathurst and Orange by the 1960s (McGill, 1960). They were common about Melbourne in Victoria and had been recorded before 1950 at Coleraine, Daylesford, Geelong, Caramut, Ballarat and Inglewood (Tarr). In South Australia they were common about Adelaide, the Mt Lofty Ranges and south to Victor Harbour (Condon).

The Greenfinch was first recorded in the Marrawah district of Tasmania in 1945 (Sharland, 1958). A few birds were recorded at Stanley and on Robbins Island before 1950 (Tarr) and they were seen at Port Davey in November 1951. Sharland says that they spread along the north-west coast and reached Launceston prior to 1958.

A few birds were recorded on Flinders Island (Bass Strait) in 1948 (Tarr) and the species is regularly present in flocks of over 100 birds on King Island in April-May each year (McGarvie and Templeton, 1974).

The Greenfinch is now spread over much of south-eastern New South Wales, Victoria, southern South Australia and Tasmania. The race introduced in Australia is *C.c. chloris* (Peters, 1968).

Norfolk Island. Williams (1953) says that the Greenfinch arrived on Norfolk Island in about 1939. They were reported there in 1965 (Wakelin, 1968, in Smithers and Disney, 1969) and Smithers and Disney say that they seem to be established and are probably breeding there.

New Zealand. The Greenfinch was introduced and liberated a number of times between 1862 and 1868 in New Zealand. In 1862 the Nelson Acclimatisation Society introduced five birds, but there are no further records of them. The Auckland society liberated several birds in 1865, eighteen in 1867 and thirty-three in 1868, and the Otago Society liberated eight in 1868 (Thomson, 1922).

By the 1920s the Greenfinch was reported to be abundant in all the settled parts of the country (Thomson).

According to Wodzicki (1965) from introductions between 1862 and 1880 the species has become widespread and common on both the North and South Islands of New Zealand. Thomson records that they reached the Chatham Islands prior to 1920, and in the 1930s (Oliver, 1930) they were apparently on Kapiti Island. Oliver (1955) later records them from the islands of Little Barrier, Stewart, Auckland and Campbell. Williams (1973) reports that they have been recorded breeding on the Chathams and Campbell Island, but not on the Kermadecs, Auckland, or on the Snares.

Açores. Bannerman and Bannerman (1966) say that the Greenfinch was introduced to the Açores in about 1890 and is now uncommon there on the islands of São Miguel and Terceira. Marler and Boatman (1951) reported that they were apparently only established in small numbers on the island of Pico in about 1950. The race introduced is reported (Peters, 1968) to be *C.c. aurantiventris.*

St Helena. A reference is given by Benson (1950) to the introduction of five 'green linnets' (possibly Greenfinches ?) to St Helena, but which did not become well established and appear to have died out there.

Uruguay. Escalante (pers. comm., 1976) informs me that Cuello and Gerzenstein (1962) record that the Greenfinch has been nesting in the wild in Uruguay since 1929. Sick (1968) says that they have been established there for approximately forty years and have a small distribution near the south coast, but have not yet spread into Rio Grande do Sul in southern Brazil. He indicates that the species was particularly numerous in 1966.

USA. Jewett and Gabrielson (1929) quote Pfluger (1896, *Oreg. Nat.* 3: 32-154) as reporting that fifteen pairs of Greenfinches were introduced into Oregon in 1889 and 1892. They apparently failed to become established there.

DAMAGE

There appears to be little evidence as yet that the Greenfinch has caused any harm to crops in Australia. In New Zealand, however, they were apparently causing damage to both fruit and grain crops by the 1920s (Thomson, 1922). Damage by the species to such fruits as apricots, cherries, peaches and plums has been recorded recently (Dawson and Bull, 1969).

SISKIN
(European Siskin, Pine Siskin)
Carduelis spinus (Linnaeus)

DISTINGUISHING CHARACTERISTICS

11.1-12.3 cm (4.44-4.92 in). 10.5-19 g (.37-.67 oz)
Upper parts yellowish green, underparts paler; crown and chin black; rump, wing bar, outer tail-feathers and stripe behind eye yellow; abdomen whitish,

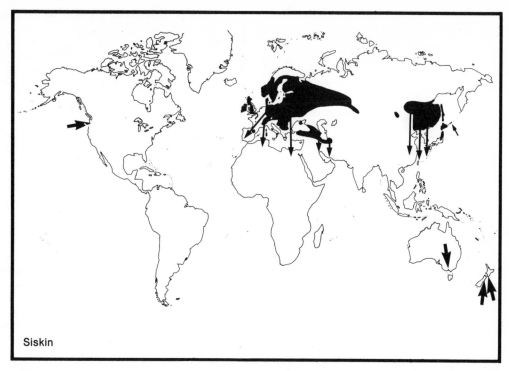

Siskin

streaked blackish brown; Female: lacks black cap and chin; underparts heavily streaked.

Witherby *et al,* vol.1, 1938-41, pp.61-63 and pl.7, opp. p.60.

Newton, 1972, pp.39-43 and pl.3, no.2, opp. p.48.

GENERAL DISTRIBUTION

Europe and Asia: from Ireland and Scotland, southern Scandinavia and central Europe, east to central Asia. In east Asia from Sakhalin to northern Japan and North Korea. In winter south to England, the Iberian Peninsula, Mediterranean area, North Africa, Near East, south-eastern China, South Korea, southern Japan and islands to Taiwan. Irruptive movements reach North Africa and Iran; mass migrations in east Asia, where it is an irregular winter migrant south of breeding range.

INTRODUCED DISTRIBUTION

Colonised parts of England and Ireland. Introduced unsuccessfully in New Zealand, Australia and the USA.

GENERAL HABITS

Status: fairly common. *Habitat:* coniferous forest, woodlands, parklands and gardens. *Gregariousness:* generally in large flocks to 100 birds, huge flocks at times. *Movements:* migratory and nomadic, irruptive at times. *Foods:* conifer and weed seeds, buds, insects including caterpillars and aphids. *Breeding:* Apr-June; usually 1 clutch but often 2. *Nest:* flat saucer-shaped of twigs, grass, moss, etc. and lined with hair, wool or feathers, in a conifer (fir). *Eggs:* 3-5, 6.

Voous, 1960, p.256.

Newton, 1972.

NOTES ON INTRODUCTIONS

England and Ireland. It appears likely that the Siskin was formerly restricted to Scotland until about the mid-nineteenth century. Since then it has colonised Ireland and much of England. Early records of the species in these areas were dismissed as escaped birds, but it seems now that they may have been the beginnings of a colonisation which is probably still continuing.

New Zealand. Two Pine Siskins were introduced by the Wellington Acclimatisation Society in 1876, and the Canterbury society liberated several birds in 1879 (Thomson, 1922). Thomson says that the species became established in Hagley Park in Christchurch, Canterbury. He reports that although some were occasionally seen in later years they were probably aviary escapees. Stidolph (1933) records that the Pine Siskin had a restricted distribution in New Zealand in the 1930s. The species, however, failed to remain established in New Zealand.

Australia. 'Siskin finches' are mentioned as having been introduced to Australia in the 1860s. In Victoria, forty birds may have been liberated in 1864 and a further twenty in 1872, but these were not recorded again after release.

Some twenty are reported to have been released at Royal Park in 1866 (Jenkins, 1977), but these apparently failed to become established.

USA. Jewett and Gabrielson (1929) quote Pfluger (1896, *Oreg. Nat.* 3: 32-154) as reporting that forty pairs were introduced into Oregon by the Acclimatisation Society in 1889. The species apparently failed to become established there.

DAMAGE

According to Cheng (1963) the Siskin eats the seeds of pine and *Cryptomeria japonica* thus causing some damage to forestry in China.

AMERICAN GOLDFINCH
(Goldfinch)

Carduelis tristis (Linnaeus)

DISTINGUISHING CHARACTERISTICS

11.2-13.7 cm (4.5-5.5 in). 10.2-14.5 g (.36-.51 oz)

Generally canary yellow; crown, forehead, space in front of eyes, most of wings and tail black; tail- 449

American Goldfinch

coverts, middle wing-coverts and the edges of some flight feathers white; bill orange-yellow, darker at tip. Female: upper parts brownish olive, tinged yellowish; lacks black cap; underparts greenish yellow; bill yellow.

Godfrey, 1966, pp.376-377 and pl.64, no.1, opp. p.317.

Reilly, 1968, pp.470-471.

GENERAL DISTRIBUTION

North America: from southern Canada, south-western Newfoundland, south to north-western Baja California, southern Colorado, north-eastern Texas, northern Louisiana, central Alabama and South Carolina. Winters south to Mexico, Gulf Coast and southern Florida.

INTRODUCED DISTRIBUTION

Introduced unsuccessfully to Bermuda and Tahiti.

GENERAL HABITS

Status: common. *Habitat:* weedy field edges, fields and cultivated areas including orchards. *Gregariousness:* small flocks and large flocks of hundreds. *Movements:* migratory, but somewhat irregular and erratic. *Foods:* seeds of conifers, grass and weeds; also insects. *Breeding:* June-Sep; 2 broods per season. *Nest:* cup-like of shredded bark, stems and grass, lined with thistle-down and other material, in a tree or shrub. *Eggs:* 2, 4-6, 7.

Godfrey, 1966, pp.376-377.

Reilly, 1968, pp.470-471.

Middleton, *Condor* vol.80, no.4, 1978, pp.401-406.

NOTES ON INTRODUCTIONS

Bermuda. The American Goldfinch was introduced to Bermuda sometime in the nineteenth century, but not very successfully (Bourne, 1957).

The species does not seem to have gained mention by Peters (1968) or Wingate (1973) so evidently failed to become established there.

Tahiti. American Goldfinches were liberated on

Tahiti in about 1938, but were not seen again after their release (Guild, 1938).

DAMAGE

The American Goldfinch and the Lesser Goldfinch are known to sometimes cause damage by removing the buds of fruit trees and to be nuisances in commercial flower and vegetable seed production areas (Neff, 1937; Clark, 1977). Also in the United States they occasionally peck at the seeds from the surface of strawberries causing the fruit to decay where these are removed and making them unfit for marketing.

LESSER GOLDFINCH
(Green-backed Goldfinch, Dark-backed Goldfinch)
Carduelis psaltria (Say)

DISTINGUISHING CHARACTERISTICS

10-12 cm (4-4.8 in)

Upper parts generally glossy black, but varies amongst races to a black crown and the remainder dull greenish olive; underparts light yellow; wings black, with speculum and tertials margined white; tail black, outer feathers white; bill flesh coloured. *Female:* upper parts olive greenish; underparts dull yellow; two pale white wing bars.

Wetmore, 1964, p.344 and pl. p.344.

Reilly, 1968, pp.471-472.

Meyer de Schauensee and Phelps, 1978, p.268 and pl.40.

GENERAL DISTRIBUTION

North and South America: from western Oregon, northern Nevada and Utah, northern Colorado, central Texas, south through Central America to north-western Peru, Colombia, northern Venezuela and western Ecuador.

INTRODUCED DISTRIBUTION

Introduced successfully in Cuba in the West Indies and to Panama (escapees ?).

GENERAL HABITS

Status: fairly common. *Habitat:* open country, pasture lands and shrubbery, gardens and wooded streams. *Gregariousness:* pairs or small flocks of 4-6, otherwise mixed flocks with other species; flocks at food sources reach 200-300 birds. *Movements:* sedentary, and migratory in north. *Foods:* seeds, buds, leaves, fruits and some insects. *Breeding:* Mar-Oct. *Nest:* woven cup-shaped, of fine grass, fibres and down, in a tree, bush or tangled vegetation. *Eggs:* 3, 4-5, 6.

Coutlee, *Condor* vol.70, 1968, pp.228-242; pp.378-384.

Reilly, 1968, pp.471-472.

Lesser Goldfinch, *Carduelis psaltria*

Lesser Goldfinch

NOTES ON INTRODUCTIONS

Cuba. The Lesser Goldfinch has been introduced into western Cuba (in Habana and Bauza) (A.O.U., 1957), probably from the Yucatan and is now found established only in Habana Province (Bond, 1960). No information was available on its present status there.

Panama. Although the Lesser Goldfinch occurs naturally in Panama, Ridgely (1976) is of the opinion that most individuals in the Canal Zone area are probably escaped cage birds.

DAMAGE

See American Goldfinch. No information on damage where introduced.

EUROPEAN GOLDFINCH
(Goldfinch)
Carduelis carduelis (Linnaeus)

DISTINGUISHING CHARACTERISTICS

12-13 cm (4.8-5.2 in). 13-22 g (.46-.76 oz)

Face and forehead red; cheeks white; black line from bill to eyes; sides of neck white; back of head black, forming a half collar on the back of the neck; wings black, with a yellow patch; back and flanks chestnut; belly and rump whitish; bill whitish (black tipped in winter).

Witherby *et al*, vol.1, 1938-41, pp.58-61 and pl.5, opp. p.48.

Newton, 1972, pp.35-39 and pl.3, no.1, opp. p.48.

GENERAL DISTRIBUTION

Eurasia-North Africa: from the British Isles, southern Sweden, east to north-central USSR and central Siberia, south to the Açores, Madeira, Canary Islands, and east to Morocco, Algiers, central Tunisia, Egypt, Israel, Jordan, Iran, Afghanistan, Baluchistan, south-central Siberia and central Outer Mongolia.

INTRODUCED DISTRIBUTION

Introduced successfully to or colonised the Açores.

Introduced successfully in the Cape Verde Islands, Australia and New Zealand and offshore islands, Uruguay, Argentina (escapees ?) and Bermuda. Introduced successfully but now died out in the USA. Introduced unsuccessfully in Canada and South Africa.

GENERAL HABITS

Status: fairly common; frequently kept cage bird. *Habitat:* forest edges, wooded country, cultivated area with trees, waste areas, orchards, tree-lined streets, gardens and parks. *Gregariousness:* small flocks or groups in breeding season, large flocks 500-1000 in non-breeding season. *Movements:* sedentary, and migratory or nomadic. *Foods:* tree, grass and weed seeds; green plant material, and insects including caterpillars, aphids and beetle larvae. *Breeding:* Apr-Sep; Sep-Mar (Australia); loose colonies; in some areas may have 2-3 broods per season (double brooded in New Zealand). *Nest:* neat, small and cup-shaped of grass, fine roots, moss, etc., lined with lichens, wool and thistledown, in a bush or tree. *Eggs:* 3-7 (New Zealand 2-7; Australia 3-7).

Voous, 1960, p.256.

Newton, 1972.

NOTES ON INTRODUCTIONS

Açores. The Goldfinch was apparently unknown in the Açores in 1865, but was present there in 1903. The species was probably introduced in about 1890 by man (Bannerman and Bannerman, 1966) from Madeira (Bannerman, 1965).

Bannerman says that they are rare on São Jorge, Faial, São Miguel and on Terciera. Marler and Boatman (1951) reported them from Pico where they were said to be present in small numbers.

Cape Verde Islands. Goldfinches were deliberately introduced, by persons unknown, to Porto Praia where they settled in the suburb of Fazenda. They were breeding there in 1964 (Bannerman and Bannerman, 1968) and are probably still established.

Australia. The first liberations of Goldfinches in Australia appear to have been near Melbourne, Victoria where in 1863 some twenty birds and in 1864, thirty-four birds were released (Ryan, 1906) by the Victorian Acclimatisation Society. Jenkins (1977) records that twelve were liberated by the Society at 'Kerang, etc.' in 1863. However some were imported to Melbourne as early as 1857 and 1858 (Balmford, 1978) and it seems likely that they may have been released before 1863. An earlier consignment to South Australia arrived in 1862, but it is not known whether these birds were released. Some were liberated in and near Adelaide in 1879 (forty-three or more) and in 1881 (110) (Condon, 1962). There appear to be no records of early introductions in New South Wales, but they were present there in the wild before 1886 (Chisholm, 1926), as some were shot near Ashfield at about this time. Some also appear to have been released in this State in 1880 in a number of areas (Jenkins, 1977).

In the early 1900s the Goldfinch was plentiful around Melbourne and Geelong (Le Souef, 1903), between Winchester and Colac in 1904 (Brown, 1950), and they were noted in the mallee area of Victoria at Pine Plains in 1906 (McLennan, 1906). They had reached Castlemaine by 1913 (Wilson, 451

1928) and were recorded at Carraragarmungee between Wangaratta and Beechworth (Cheyney, 1915) and in Genoa in east Gippsland in 1915 (Chisholm, 1915). In 1928 they were some forty-eight to sixty-four kilometres (30-40 miles) north of Bendigo and it seems likely that they were established in all suitable areas of Victoria by the 1930s (Middleton, 1965).

Following the early report of their occurrence at Ashfield in New South Wales Goldfinches had reached Goulburn by 1913 (Le Souef, 1913). They were abundant in the Capital Territory at Duntroon and Tuggranong (Barret, 1922), and at Boree south of Armidale in 1922 (Norton, 1922). In the 1920s they were reported from Tumbarumba (Chisholm, 1924), Sofala (Bourke, 1957), Bega (Edwards, 1925), Armidale, and had been for some years around Tamworth (Wright, 1925) and Glen Innes (Lawrance, 1926). Odd birds were recorded from Gilgandra in 1939 and they were reported as numerous in towns along the western railway as far as Dubbo (Bourke, 1957). Tarr (1950) reported that they were throughout New South Wales in 1950.

In South Australia Goldfinches were reported from Mt Remarkable in 1923 (White, 1923) and were found to be throughout the Mt Lofty Ranges, Adelaide Plains, southern York Peninsula, and north to Clare and east to the Victorian border in the 1950s (Tarr). They have been present on Kangaroo Island since 1910-20 (Cooper, 1947).

It is thought that the Goldfinch probably spread into Queensland from northern New South Wales. They were reported at Stanthorpe in 1919 (Chisholm, 1919) and from Stradbroke Island where they were thought to have been escapees from aviaries (Chisholm, 1925). Some were recorded present in the Hamilton area, near Brisbane in 1932 (Jack, 1952). In the 1950s they were restricted to the Darling Downs and a few coastal areas near Brisbane (Tarr, 1950).

Goldfinches were liberated in Perth, Western Australia sometime prior to 1912. Some were recorded from Graylands, a Perth suburb, in 1927 and in 1930 (Long, 1972). Free-living birds were found in the Supreme Court Gardens, central Perth in 1933 (Jenkins, 1959). The species spread slowly in Western Australia and by 1967 was widely distributed in the metropolitan area and surrounds west of the Darling Scarp (Long, 1972).

European Goldfinch,
Carduelis carduelis

Since the late 1960s the species has suffered a decline in numbers in the Perth area and is now rarely observed. They were established at Albany, 381 km (237 miles) south of Perth in 1955 (Jenkins, 1959) and were still established there in the 1960s, but do not appear to have been recorded since then.

Several Goldfinches arrived in Hobart, Tasmania, aboard the ship *Wansted* in 1827 (Lawson, 1949). Littler (1902) said that they had been established in Tasmania for about twenty years (1882 ?). He reports that they were numerous around Hobart, Derwent Valley, New Norfolk, Glenora and Macquarie Plains, and on the north-western coast near Latrobe and Davenport. They were present at Latrobe in large numbers in 1909 (Fletcher, 1909). Chisholm (1926) saw large flocks of 200 birds in the north of Tasmania in 1926. By the 1950s they were common throughout the cultivated areas of Tasmania (Tarr, 1950).

The Goldfinch now occurs over much of south-eastern Australia, Tasmania, King Island and Flinders Island and on Kangaroo Island.

Smithers and Disney (1969) record seeing the species near the Melanesian Mission on Norfolk Island. They say that young birds were observed so the species is probably breeding there.

New Zealand. From 1862 to 1883 a number of introductions and liberations of Goldfinches occurred in New Zealand. In 1862 the Nelson Acclimatisation Society liberated 118 birds. The Auckland society liberated eleven in 1867 and forty-four in 1871, the Canterbury society ninety-five in 1871 and more in 1875. Between 1877 and 1883 the Wellington society liberated some 177 Goldfinches (Thomson, 1922).

According to Thomson the species established itself quickly in New Zealand and by the 1920s was extremely abundant around most areas of settlement in that country. They are now widespread and abundant in both the North and South Islands (Wodzicki, 1965) and have colonised outlying islands from the Kermadecs south to Campbell Island (Falla *et al,* 1966).

Before 1920 they had been found on Auckland Island and on the Chathams (Thomson). Oliver (1930 and 1955) reported them on Kapiti, Stewart, Snares, Kermadecs, Campbell, Antipodes, Three Kings, Mokohinau and Little Barrier Islands. Williams (1953) records them again on the Snares and Wodzicki (1965) from Raoul Island.

In 1956 a specimen was collected from Macquarie Island which is some 885 km (550 miles) south of New Zealand (Keith and Hinds, 1958). They appear to have been recorded on the Antipodes, Campbell, Snares and Auckland as early as about 1900 and from the Kermadecs and Chathams from about 1910.

Williams (1973) says that they have bred on the Chathams, Antipodes, Campbell, Auckland and Snares, but have not on some of the other islands such as Three Kings, Kermadecs and Macquarie.

Uruguay. The Goldfinch occurs in Uruguay, but only in the provinces of Montevideo and Canelones (Cuello and Gerzenstein, 1962, in Sick, 1968). Sick reports that the species is evidently the last successful bird naturalisation in South America, hence it is probably a fairly recent introduction. Escalante (pers. comm., 1976) says that the species is still breeding there.

Argentina. Sick (1968) indicates that the Goldfinch

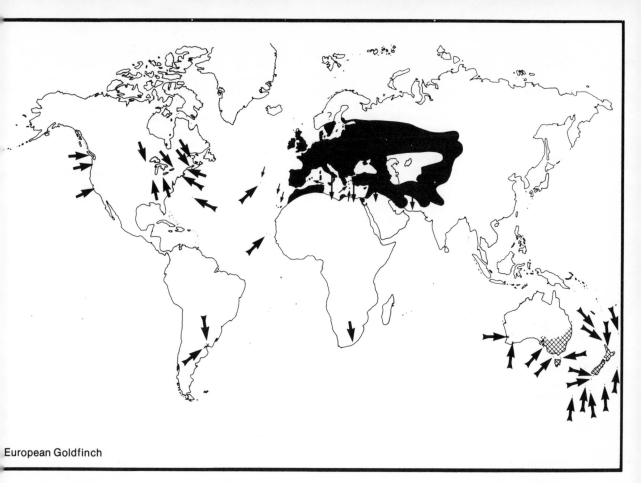

European Goldfinch

occurs occasionally in the port of Buenos Aires, Argentina, probably as a result of escaped caged birds.

Bermuda. Goldfinches were introduced into Bermuda in the 1870s (Bourne, 1957) at least before 1875 (A.O.U., 1957). However, according to Wingate (1973) the main introduction to the island is supposed to have taken place in about 1885, although the species was a common cage bird there prior to that date. Austin (1968) records that *C.c. parva* became established on Bermuda when they escaped from a ship in 1893, but that the stock now there was brought from the Açores by the many early residents who emigrated to Bermuda.

Apparently the Goldfinch became remarkably abundant following its introduction on Bermuda and by 1914 was the second most common bird there. Thereafter numbers declined and in 1920 they were considered as common as the native bluebird. In 1940 they were one of the more scarce species, ranking about fifth in abundance. They are, however, still a common resident on the island (Wingate, 1973).

There appears to be some doubt as to the race which has been introduced, either *C.c. parva* from Madeira (Austin, 1963) or *C.c. britannica* from Great Britain (A.O.U., 1957).

USA. The earliest record of Goldfinch liberations in the USA appears to have been in Brooklyn, New York in 1846 and these birds appeared to have become established. Further birds were unsuccessfully set free by the Cincinnati Acclimatisation Society from 1872 to 1874. Also between these dates a considerable number were released by the Society for the Acclimatisation of Foreign Birds at Mount Auburn Cemetery, in Cambridge, Massachusetts and these birds flourished until about 1900. During the 1880s and 1890s Goldfinches were continually reported in Massachusetts and as far north as Toronto, Ontario in Canada where four were noted in 1887. In about 1891 some Goldfinches were released near San Francisco, but these also failed to become established (Phillips, 1928).

The Goldfinch was also introduced in various other areas of the USA in the nineteenth century (Wetmore, 1964; Austin, 1968) including Portland, Oregon in 1890; St Louis, Missouri in 1870; Cincinnati, Ohio in 1870; Hoboken, New Jersey in 1878; Boston, Massachusetts in 1899; and older records of temporary or casual occurrence are scattered from Oregon and California to Wisconsin, Missouri and Massachusetts (A.O.U. 1957). Jewett and Gabrielson (1929) quote Pfluger (1896, *Oreg. Nat.* 3:32-154) as recording that the species became plentiful throughout Oregon following the introduction of forty pairs by the 'Society' from 1889 to 1892. Phillips also records that at least twenty and probably forty more pairs were released here in 1907 and later, but not even a temporary success was achieved on the Pacific coast.

Towards the end of 1852 the Trustees of the Green-Wood Cemetery (Long Island, New York) purchased a number of British birds including forty-eight Goldfinches (Cleaveland, 1865, in Murphy, 1945). These were released in the cemetery, but were said to have all disappeared soon after their release. In the 1890s, however, the Goldfinch was a common resident

453

of Central Park, New York, and was present there from 1915 to 1936 (Nichols, 1936).

According to Adney (1886) they appeared in Central Park in 1879 having crossed the Hudson River from Hoboken, New Jersey (where released in 1878). He found them breeding there in 1886. They are reported to have been seen on Long Island in 1889, 1891 and in 1900 (Mills, 1937). A few were said to be present in Central Park in New York in about 1905 (Hix, 1905). A single bird was noted at Riverside Park, Milwaukee, Wisconsin in 1935 (Jung, 1936) and another at Hanover, New Hampshire in 1937 (Mills, 1937).

They were present at Buffalo in 1929 (Shadle, 1930) and at Ithaca in New York in 1940 (Montagna, 1940). Besides these areas some were also reported from Manchester in Massachusetts and from Larkspur and Elk Valley in California in the period 1935-40 (Cooke and Knappen, 1941).

The Goldfinch was established on Long Island in the communities of Garden City, Freeport and Massapequa until the building boom in the mid-1950s removed their natural habitat (Wetmore, 1965). Those seen since are believed to be escapees from aviaries and the species was thought to have possibly disappeared from the USA (Gottschalk, 1967). However, odd birds continue to be recorded in the 1970s. Further birds were apparently released on Long Island, New York in 1976 (Paxton et al, 1978).

The race which became established in the USA was C.c. britannica (A.O.U., 1957).

Canada. A Goldfinch was collected at Toronto, Ontario in 1887, and a recent sight record in New Brunswick may represent strays from Long Island, USA, but the possibility that they were escaped cage birds cannot be excluded (Godfrey, 1966).

In 1908 or 1910 a number of British birds were released by G. H. Wallace at various points on the Saanich Peninsula, Vancouver Island, B.C. The Goldfinch was included amongst the species which were released at this time (Carl and Guiguet, 1972), and which apparently failed to become established.

South Africa. Winterbottom (1956) while examining 'Ornithological and other Oddities' (F. Finns, 1907) found reference to the Goldfinch in South Africa. A soldier returning from the South African war, 1899-1902, had caught two birds on the hills of Heidelberg, Transvaal. Winterbottom suspects that they were escapees, but it appears as though the species may have been established there at least temporarily.

DAMAGE

Examination of the foods and food habits of the Goldfinch in Australia indicate that the species is unlikely to be a pest of economic importance. However, evidence from New Zealand suggests that this species can become a nuisance in some circumstances. Oliver (1955) records that they occasionally eat grain and also the seeds from strawberries. The attacks upon strawberries are not widespread, but may become economically important if they increase.

In Great Britain the species is not recognised as a pest, but has been implicated in the past in damaging fruit tree buds (Taylor and Ridpath, 1956). Apparently in earlier times (around 1698) considerable damage was caused to gooseberry buds

and there have been some isolated recent recurrences of this type of damage (Wright and Brough, 1964).

COMMON REDPOLL
(Redpoll)
Acanthis flammea (Linnaeus)

DISTINGUISHING CHARACTERISTICS

10.6-15 cm (4.24-6 in). 10-19 g (.35-.67 oz)

Upper parts grey-brown; forehead red or crimson; chin black; two white wing bars; rump often greyish white; breast and rump washed pinkish; wings and tail greyish brown; cheeks often pinkish; remainder of underparts white; bill pale yellowish. Female: lacks pinkish on breast and rump.

Witherby et al, vol.1, 1938-41, pp.66-72, and pl.8, opp. p.64 and pl.9, opp. p.68.

Godfrey, 1966, pp.374-375 and pl.64, no.4, opp. p.317.

Newton, 1972, pp.51-56 and pl.2, no.1, opp. p.33.

GENERAL DISTRIBUTION

Northern Eurasia, Iceland, Greenland and northern North America: in Eurasia from the British Isles to Scandinavia and east to Kamchatka; in North America from Alaska, east across northern Canada; also southern coastal Greenland and in Iceland. Winters south to Eurasia, irregularly to Korea, central Asia and southern Europe; in North America south to northern California, Colorado, Kansas, Ohio, West Virginia and South Carolina.

INTRODUCED DISTRIBUTION

Introduced successfully in New Zealand and has colonised many offshore and outlying islands from that country.

GENERAL HABITS

Status: fairly common. Habitat: coniferous forest, woodland, swampy thickets, river banks, pine plantations and gardens. Gregariousness: small to large flocks of 200-300 birds and sometimes larger flocks in the non-breeding season. Movements: sedentary and irregularly migratory or nomadic. Foods: seeds, buds, fruit, insects including caterpillars, aphids and beetle larvae; also green plant material. Breeding: Apr-Aug (Europe); Sept-Jan (New Zealand); often in loose colonies; generally one, but often 2 clutches (double brooded in New Zealand). Nest: saucer-shaped of twigs, grass, moss and lichens, and lined with hair, feathers and wool, in a low tree, bush, or rock cleft. Eggs: 4-7 (New Zealand 4-6).

Voous, 1960, pp.256-257.

Godfrey, 1966, pp.374-375.

Newton, 1972.

NOTES ON INTRODUCTIONS

New Zealand. Redpolls were introduced into New Zealand between 1862 and 1875. The Nelson Acclimatisation Society imported two birds in 1862, and the Otago Society introduced ten in 1868 and seventy-one in 1871. The Canterbury society liberated fourteen birds in 1868 and a further 120 in 1871. In 1871 the Auckland society introduced one bird, but liberated some 209 of them in various districts south of Auckland in 1872. A Mr R. Bills imported Redpolls and liberated them in the Christchurch Gardens in 1875. The Wellington society also introduced two birds in the same year (Thomson, 1922).

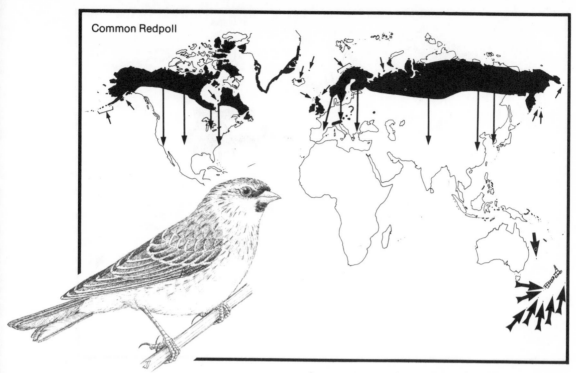

Common Redpoll

Thomson records that the Redpoll was well established about towns and in the settled districts on both islands of New Zealand by the 1920s. The species is now widespread and abundant there (Wodzicki, 1965).

Two races, *cabaret* and *flammea* were apparently introduced into New Zealand, but the bulk of the present population now appears to be of the *cabaret* type (Falla *et al*, 1966).

Outside the North and South Islands, the Redpoll had reached Kapiti, Stewart and Campbell Islands by the 1930s (Oliver, 1930). Oliver later (1955) reports them from the islands of Three Kings, Chathams, Snares and Auckland Island and says that they had reached Macquarie Island as a straggler. They were recorded on this latter island as early as 1912 and probably reached Campbell Island and the Snares in about 1907 (Williams, 1953). Williams (1973) says that the Redpoll breeds on the Chathams, Antipodes, Campbell, Auckland, Snares, and probably on Macquarie Island. They are not known to breed on the Three Kings or the Kermadecs. The Redpoll arrived on Lord Howe Island in about 1913 (Williams, 1953) from New Zealand, but there appear to be few recent records of them on that island.

DAMAGE

In New Zealand the Common Redpoll was reported to be a useful bird, attacking turnip green-fly and similar insects (Oliver, 1955). According to Hawkins (1962) and Bull (1962) it was regarded as one of the few introductions that did not interfere with man's activities in some way. However, in central Otago in more recent years, they have been making increasingly heavy attacks on blossoms and young fruits in orchards. The damage is said to have been severe to apricots, but several kinds of fruit have been attacked. Control measures have been implemented in some areas and some 2500 birds were destroyed in nine orchards in one attempt to lessen the damage.

TWITE
Acanthis flavirostris (Linnaeus)

DISTINGUISHING CHARACTERISTICS
13-13.7 cm (5.2-5.48 in). 14-21 g (.49-.74 oz)
Generally buff, streaked with blackish and brown on upper parts and paler on underparts; throat orange-buff; tail and primaries dark brown; rump rose-pink in summer, paler in winter; bill light yellow (greyish in breeding season).
Witherby *et al*, vol.1, 1938-41, pp.74-78 and pl.7, opp. p.60.
Newton, 1972, pp.49-51 and pl.2, no.3, opp. p.32.

GENERAL DISTRIBUTION
Parts of northern Europe and south-central Asia: in Europe from the northern parts of the British Isles and Norway, and in Asia from the Black Sea, eastern Turkey and the Caspian Sea to the northern Himalayas, Tibet, western China and Mongolia. Winters in Europe slightly south of breeding range and in Asia to Pakistan and north-western India.

INTRODUCED DISTRIBUTION
Introduced unsuccessfully in New Zealand.

GENERAL HABITS
Status: fairly common. *Habitat:* rocky ground with bushes, sea coasts, heathlands, moors, stony grassland, alpine meadows, barren steppe and pasture. *Gregariousness:* small or large flocks. *Movements:* sedentary, but with irregular dispersal movements. *Foods:* seeds. *Breeding:* Apr-Aug; usually in small colonies. *Nest:* small, twigs and rootlets interwoven with moss, grass, lichens or wool, the cup lined with soft material, on the ground in heather, or in a bush. *Eggs:* 3, 4-6.
Voous, 1960, p.256.
Newton, 1972.

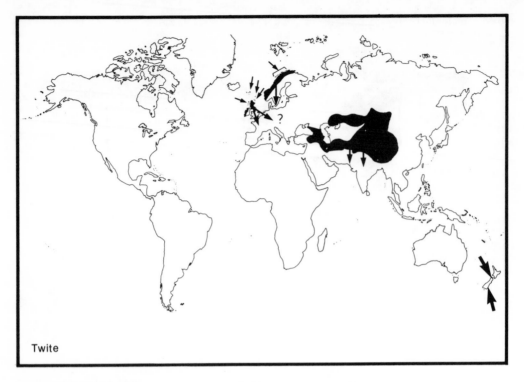

Twite

NOTES ON INTRODUCTIONS

New Zealand. In 1862 the Nelson Acclimatisation Society imported two Twites, but there appear to be no records of what happened to them. The Otago society liberated thirty-eight birds in the Dunedin Botanical Gardens, but these were not sighted again (Thomson, 1922). The species failed to become established in New Zealand.

DAMAGE

None known.

LINNET

Acanthis cannabina (Linnaeus)

DISTINGUISHING CHARACTERISTICS

13-14.3 cm (5.2-5.72 in). 16.5-24 g (.58-.85 oz)

Upper parts fawn, shading to almost white; head greyish brown, mottled or streaked with darker brown; crown and breast crimson (in summer) or pinkish; back chestnut-brown (in winter); wing-coverts brown; tail black; flight feathers and tail have white edges; flanks rufous-brown; bill horn

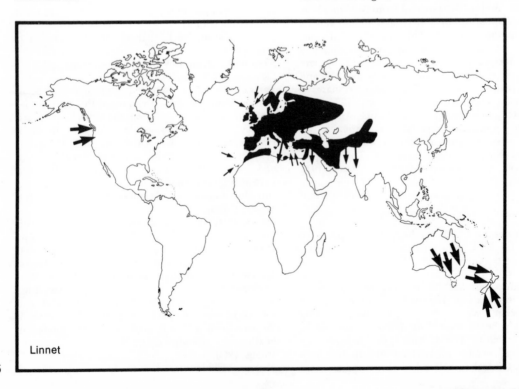

Linnet

456

(winter) or grey. Female: lacks crimson and is darker streaked.

Witherby *et al*, vol.1, 1938-41, pp.78-81 and pl.7, opp. p.60.

Newton, 1972, pp.43-49 and pl.2, no.4, opp. p.33.

GENERAL DISTRIBUTION
Eurasia-North Africa: from the British Isles, Madeira and Canary Islands, southern Scandinavia, east to Iran and south-central Asia. In winter to Baluchistan, north-western India, Afghanistan, southern Iran, Iraq and the Mediterranean region.

INTRODUCED DISTRIBUTION
Introduced unsuccessfully in New Zealand, Australia, Canada and the USA.

GENERAL HABITS
Status: common. *Habitat:* forest edges, wooded areas, open heathland and cultivated areas such as orchards and vineyards. *Gregariousness:* small flocks of 4-5 birds, and large flocks in winter. *Movements:* sedentary and migratory. *Foods:* insects including caterpillars, aphids, beetle larvae and moths, also spiders, grass and weed seeds, short grass and other green plant material. *Breeding:* Apr-Aug; frequently in small colonies; usually 2 but up to 3 clutches per year. *Nest:* twigs and rootlets bound together with grass, hair, wool and down, in a bush close to the ground. *Eggs:* 4-6.

Voous, 1960, p.256.

Newton, 1972.

NOTES ON INTRODUCTIONS
New Zealand. A number of introductions of the Linnet occurred in New Zealand between 1862 and 1875, when fifty of these birds were released by the Nelson, Otago and Canterbury Acclimatisation Societies. Although the species was reported to be established in Auckland Province in 1880 (perhaps confusion with the Greenfinch?) they did not become established and disappeared soon after being liberated (Thomson, 1922).

Australia. Some seven or eight 'brown linnets' are reported to have been liberated not far from Alfredton, Victoria, in the 1860s (Pollard, 1967). Jenkins (1977) records that nineteen were liberated by the Acclimatisation Society of Victoria in 1865. Some were imported into Victoria in 1856, 1857 and in 1858 (Balmford, 1978) but there are no records of any liberations at these early dates. Jenkins indicates that some were liberated in South Australia in about 1879-80 and some in New South Wales in a number of areas in 1880. The species did not become established in Australia.

Canada. In 1908 and 1910 a number of British birds were released by G. H. Wallace at various points on the Saanich Peninsula, Vancouver Island, British Columbia. The Linnet is also mentioned as being amongst those released (Carl and Guiguet, 1972), but apparently failed to become established there.

USA. According to Jewett and Gabrielson (1927), Pfluger (1896, *Oreg. Nat* 3:32-154) reports that thirty-five pairs of Linnets were introduced into Oregon in 1889 and 1892 by the 'Society'. The species apparently failed to become established there.

DAMAGE
None known.

HOUSE FINCH
(Linnet)
Carpodacus mexicanus (Müller)

DISTINGUISHING CHARACTERISTICS
12.5-14.4 cm (5-5.76 in)
Forehead, stripe over eye and rump red or rose-pink; remainder of upper parts brownish grey, streaked darker brown, often washed reddish; wings and tail dusky, pale edged; two pale wing bars; throat and upper breast reddish; lower breast, abdomen, sides, flanks and under tail-coverts whitish, streaked grey-brown; bill dark. Female: lacks red, which is replaced with brown on upper parts and with whitish striped grey-brown on throat and upper breast.

Godfrey, 1966, pp.371-372 and pl.65, no.6, opp. p.332.

Reilly, 1968, p.465.

GENERAL DISTRIBUTION
North America: from southern British Columbia, central western and southern Idaho, Wyoming and western Nebraska, south to southern Baja California, Guerrero and central Oaxaca in southern Mexico.

INTRODUCED DISTRIBUTION
Introduced successfully in the eastern USA and the Hawaiian Islands.

GENERAL HABITS
Status: common; often kept in captivity in America. *Habitat:* open woodland, coastal scrub, farmland, orchards, towns, canyons and desert. *Gregariousness:* small flocks of 5-6 birds, larger flocks and occasionally immense flocks outside breeding season. *Movements:* sedentary, but some altitudinal movements. *Foods:* seeds, soft fruits, berries and insects. *Breeding:* Mar-Aug; Feb-Aug (Hawaii); 2 or more broods per year. *Nest:* cup-shaped of grass, twigs, rootlets, and wool in a tree cavity, in buildings, other birds' nests, and in trees and vines. *Eggs:* 2, 3-5, 6.

Godfrey, 1966, pp.371-372.

Reilly, 1968, p.465.

NOTES ON INTRODUCTIONS
USA. In the eastern United States the House Finch (race *C.m: frontalis*) became established following the release of caged birds (Gilliard, 1958; Pyle, 1963) on Long Island, New York in about 1940, when dealers were prohibited from selling the species (Elliot and Arbib, 1953). When shipments from

House Finch, *Carpodacus mexicanus*

House Finch

species probably escaped from captivity to become established. They were abundant on the island of Maui in about 1902 (McGregor, 1902). They are now common in urban and rural areas on all the main islands in the group (Berger, 1972; Hawaiian Audubon Society, 1975).

DAMAGE

In the United States the House Finch damages fruit crops by consuming the ripening fruit and also by eating the buds. They cause damage to apricots, cherries, peaches, pears, nectarines, plums, avocados, grapes, apples, figs, strawberries, blackberries and raspberries. They also cause minor damage to maize, lettuce, broccoli, flax, tomato and other crops.

Palmer (1972) states that the House Finch and Starling represent two of the principal bird pests causing crop damage in California. Annually they cost agriculturists an estimated one and a half million dollars in losses. The House Finch alone affects more than twenty different crops.

In the Hawaiian Islands, the species has become somewhat of a pest to ripening fruit, buds and vegetables.

The House Finch is still spreading in the eastern United States and will undoubtedly in time be found to be a nuisance to crops in these areas.

California were stopped by the Fisheries and Wildlife Service many dealers may have released their birds to avoid prosecution, although the evidence for this is only circumstantial. Elliot and Arbib record that the species was first found breeding on Long Island in 1943, although a single bird was noted as early as 1941, and by 1951 the population was estimated to be some 280 birds.

By about 1956 they were well established and breeding in southern Nassau and south-western Suffolk Counties; breeding was also recorded in Greenwich township, Fairfield County and south-western Connecticut (A.O.U., 1957). Pyle reports that they nested in New Jersey in 1959 and in Pennsylvania at Columbia in 1962. They reached North Carolina in February 1963 (Potter, 1964) and nested in north-western Kansas for the first time in about 1977 (Lohoefener, 1977).

Peters (1968) recorded that the species had spread to New Jersey and north to Massachusetts and south to South Carolina by 1968. Nests have now been found as far west as Cleveland, Ohio and as far north as Brunswick, Maine (Gee, 1977). More recently they have reached Ontario and Quebec in southern Canada, and Birmingham, Alabama (David and Gosselin, 1978; Goodwin, 1978). Individuals have been reported from more distant areas.

In the western United States the species appears to have recently undergone a northerly range expansion across Washington and into some of the southern valleys of British Columbia, Canada. More recently they have reached western Montana where they are well on the way to becoming an established resident (Hand, 1970).

Hawaiian Islands. The race *C.m. frontalis* has become established in the Hawaiian Islands from birds imported from California prior to 1870. According to Caum (1933) and Munro (1960) the

PARROT CROSSBILL
Loxia pytyopsittacus Borkhausen

DISTINGUISHING CHARACTERISTICS
16.5-17.7 cm (6.6-7.1 in)
Similar to Crossbill *(L. curvirostra)*. Generally red or orange-red; wings and tail black or blackish brown; bill with mandibles crossed. Female: generally yellowish green.
Witherby *et al,* vol.1, 1938-41, pp.99-100.
Newton, 1972, pp.80-81 and pl.4, no.3, opp. p.49.

GENERAL DISTRIBUTION
Northern Europe: northern Norway east to the Kola Peninsula and south to the southern end of the Baltic Sea, Estonia, and east to Smolensk in the western USSR. An irregular migrant to Western Europe, England and western Siberia.

INTRODUCED DISTRIBUTION
Introduced unsuccessfully to the USA.

GENERAL HABITS
Status: fairly common. *Habitat:* coniferous forests. *Gregariousness:* small flocks. *Movements:* sedentary and nomadic within range; irruptive, irregular movements in years of food shortage. *Foods:* pine seeds, catkins and berries. *Breeding:* Dec-June, but variable. *Nest:* untidy nest of branches and twigs, lined with grass, hair and feathers, in a pine. *Eggs:* 3-4, 5.
Voous, 1960, pp.258, 260.
Newton, 1972.

NOTES ON INTRODUCTIONS
USA. According to Jewett and Gabrielson (1929) who quote Pfluger (1896, *Oreg. Nat.* 3: 32-154), twenty pairs of Parrot Crossbills were introduced into Oregon by the acclimatisation society in 1889. There appear to be no further records of these birds.

DAMAGE
None known.

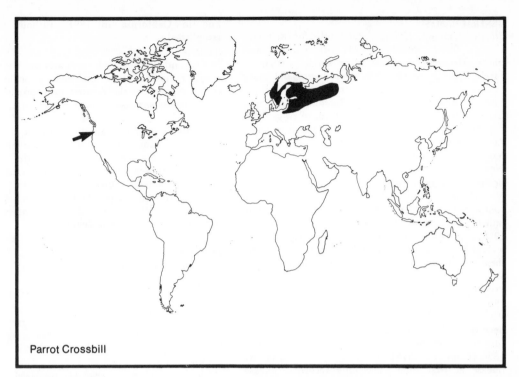

Parrot Crossbill

BULLFINCH
Pyrrhula pyrrhula (Linnaeus)

DISTINGUISHING CHARACTERISTICS
13.7-15 cm (5.5-6 in). 21-34 g (.74-1.2 oz)
Cap and chin black; back slate or blue-grey; rump white; wings black, with a white wing bar; chest and abdomen rose-red; tail black; bill black. Female: pinkish brown underparts and yellowish brown upper parts.
Witherby *et al*, vol.1, 1938-41, pp.84-88 and pl.10, opp. p.84.

Newton, 1972, pp.64-68 and pl.1, no.4, opp. p.32.

GENERAL DISTRIBUTION
Eurasia: from the British Isles, southern Scandinavia and northern Spain, east across northern and central Asia to Kamchatka, Sakhalin and northern Japan. In Europe more or less sedentary, but in eastern Asia winters south to southern China, southern Japan and Korea.

INTRODUCED DISTRIBUTION
Introduced unsuccessfully in New Zealand, Australia and the USA.

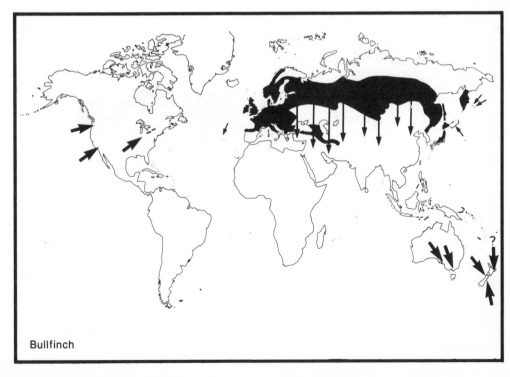

Bullfinch

GENERAL HABITS

Status: common. *Habitat:* coniferous forest, taiga, riverine forest, woodland, orchards, gardens and parks. *Gregariousness:* pairs or small parties, or rarely flocks up to 100 birds. *Movements:* sedentary and migratory. *Foods:* weed, grass and tree seeds; buds, berries, fruits and insects. *Breeding:* Apr-Sept; 2-3 broods per season. *Nest:* platform of twigs, with cup of fine roots, lined with hair, in a tree or bush. *Eggs:* 3, 4-6.

Voous, 1960, p.258.

Newton, 1972.

NOTES ON INTRODUCTIONS

New Zealand. The Bullfinch was liberated near Nelson before 1870 and in Canterbury in 1875, but failed to become established in New Zealand (Oliver, 1930). According to Oliver they were reported from several North Island localities, just prior to 1930, but these were thought to have been escaped cage birds. Williams (1953) recorded that the species was extremely rare or extinct in New Zealand in the 1950s.

Australia. It is believed that Bullfinches may have been released in Australia in about the 1860s or some time soon after. Some were imported into Victoria in 1856 (Balmford, 1978) but there is no record of any release at that time. The only recorded release appears to have been that in South Australia where fourteen were liberated at Mt Lofty in about 1879-80 (Jenkins, 1977). They certainly have not become established anywhere in Australia.

USA. Jewett and Gabrielson (1929) quote Pfluger (1896, *Oreg. Nat.* 3: 32-154) as reporting that twenty pairs of Bullfinches were introduced into Oregon by the acclimatisation society in 1889 and 1892. The species apparently failed to become established there. Phillips (1928) also records that they were released at Cincinnati, Ohio in the 1870s,

and in California in 1891, without becoming established.

DAMAGE

In England the Bullfinch consumes the buds of fruit trees, removing them on such a scale that it constitutes one of the greatest problems with which the fruit industry has to contend (Thearle, 1968). It is not uncommon for whole orchards of trees that normally produce several tonnes of fruit to be almost denuded of buds and to yield only a few kilograms of fruit (Newton, 1966). Certain varieties are more severely attacked than others, preferences differ locally and annually, but dessert varieties suffer most (Wright and Summers, 1960). It is therefore most fortunate that the species did not become established in either Australia or New Zealand.

HAWFINCH

Coccothraustes coccothraustes (Linnaeus)

DISTINGUISHING CHARACTERISTICS

16.2-10.3 cm (6.5-4.12 in). 41-63 g (1.45-2.22 oz)

Generally reddish or pinkish brown; head chestnut; bib and from beak to eyes black; nape greyish; back brown; wings blue-black, with a white wing bar; tail black, with a white tip; bill blue-black in spring, brownish in winter.

Witherby *et al* vol.1, 1938-41, pp.51-54 and pl.5, opp. p.48.

Newton, 1972, pp.61-64 and pl.1, no.3, opp. p.32.

GENERAL DISTRIBUTION

Eurasia-North Africa: from England and northern Morocco, east across central Asia to northern Japan, and as far south as northern Baluchistan, Pakistan. Winters in the Mediterranean countries and south to north-west India, north-eastern China, southern Korea and Japan.

INTRODUCED DISTRIBUTION

Possibly introduced, unsuccessfully in Australia.

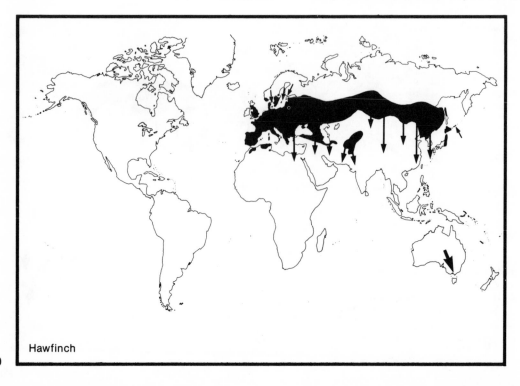

Hawfinch

460

GENERAL HABITS

Status: fairly common. *Habitat:* forest, woodlands, orchards, gardens and parks. *Gregariousness:* solitary, small flocks of up to a dozen and at times large flocks of several hundred. *Movements:* sedentary and migratory. *Foods:* berries, seeds, fruit stones, insects including caterpillars, and buds and shoots. *Breeding:* Apr-Aug; in colonies of 3-6 and up to 20 pairs; up to 3 broods per season. *Nest:* small untidy structure of twigs, roots and fibres, lined with fine material such as hair, in a bush or tree. *Eggs:* 3, 4-5, 7.

Voous, 1960, p.255.

Newton, 1972.

NOTES ON INTRODUCTIONS

Australia. Chinese Hawfinches may have been introduced into Victoria, probably in the 1860s (McCance, 1962), but the species failed to become established.

DAMAGE

The Hawfinch is capable of causing minor or local damage to fruit and horticultural crops in Great Britain and China and would not have been a welcome addition to the Australian avifauna.

Family: *Drepanididae* Hawaiian Honeycreepers

21 species in 12 genera; 1 species introduced successfully

The Laysan Canary has been established on Southeast Island on Pearl and Hermes Reef and on Tern Island in French Frigate Shoal in the Hawaiian Islands. The reasons for the introductions are not documented, but they were probably to extend the present range for conservation reasons, although they appear to be fairly common on Laysan and Nihoa islands.

LAYSAN CANARY

(Telespiza, Laysan Finch, Nihoa Finch)
Loxioides cantans (Wilson)

DISTINGUISHING CHARACTERISTICS

13.7-16.2 cm (5.5-6.5 in). 22g (.78 oz)
Generally yellow, with head, throat and breast brighter; abdomen whitish; tail and wings brownish streaked yellowish green; back greenish yellow, streaked black; lower back and under tail-coverts greyish, sometimes tinged yellow; primaries black

Laysan Canary

with large yellow areas; bill light brown to bluish grey. Female: brownish; streaked and spotted black on the head and breast.

Berger, 1972, pp.150, 155-161 and pl.47, p.154.

GENERAL DISTRIBUTION

Laysan and Nihoa Islands in the Hawaiian Islands.

INTRODUCED DISTRIBUTION

Introduced successfully to Pearl and Hermes Reef (Southeast Island) and French Frigate Shoal (Tern and East Islands) in the Hawaiian Archipelago. Introduced successfully, but has died out on Midway Island.

GENERAL HABITS

Status: fairly common. *Habitat:* in grassy and shrubby areas in all the plant associations of Laysan Island. *Gregariousness:* no informaton. *Movements:* sedentary. *Foods:* insects, seeds, fruits, flower buds and tender shoots; also birds' eggs and carrion. *Breeding:* Feb-June. *Nest:* low cup of woven grass, on

INTRODUCTIONS OF DREPANIDIDAE

Species	Date introduced	Region	Manner introduced	Reason
(a) Successful introductions				
Laysan Canary (race *cantans*)	1967	Southeast Island, Hawaiian Islands	deliberate	conservation ?
(race *ultima*)	1967	Tern Island, Hawaiian Islands	deliberate	conservation ?
(b) Unsuccessful introductions				
Laysan Canary (race *cantans*)	1891, 1905 ?	Midway Island, Hawaiian Islands	deliberate	?
	1905 ?	Oahu, Hawaiian Islands	deliberate	?
(race *ultima*)	1967	East Island, Hawaiian Islands	deliberate	conservation ?

the ground amongst grass, rocks or in bushes. *Eggs:* 2, 3-4.

Berger, 1972, pp.150, 155-161.

NOTES ON INTRODUCTIONS

Midway Island. Munro (1960) reports that two Laysan Canaries were introduced prior to or in about 1891 to Midway by the sons of Captain Walker. Some were also introduced in about 1905 (Bryan, 1912) and later in the same year to Eastern Island, where they were established at least until 1908.

Large numbers of Laysan Canaries were taken to both Honolulu (on Oahu) and Midway Island. The Honolulu birds all died but those on Midway became established. The species appears to have remained established there until it disappeared in about 1944 (Peterson, 1961). The bird introduced was the Laysan race *L.c. cantans* (Peters, 1962).

Pearl and Hermes Reef. Personnel of the United States Bureau of Sport, Fisheries and Wildlife released 108 Laysan canaries *(L.c. cantans)* on Southeast Island in March, 1967. This population had increased to about 350 birds by 1970 (Berger, 1972), continued to thrive and increase and reached 500 by 1974 (Hawaiian Audubon Society, 1977).

French Frigate Shoal. Personnel from the United States Bureau of Sport, Fisheries and Wildlife transplanted forty-two Nihoa Finches *(L.c. ultima)* to French Frigate Shoal also in March 1967. Of these, thirty-two were released on Tern Island and ten on East Island. Those on East Island disappeared and only six birds remained on Tern Island in 1970 (Berger, 1972) and these were still there in 1974 (Hawaiian Audubon Society, 1977).

DAMAGE

None known.

Family: *Emberizidae* Tangers, buntings, New World sparrows, cardinals, grosbeaks, plush-capped finch

554 species in 133 genera; 34 species introduced, 11 successfully (possibly or probably another 3 species successfully)

Many members of this family are popular cage birds. Of the 11 species established, probably five have escaped from captivity or have been released as a result of cage bird activities (i.e. aircraft breakdown en route).

The Yellowhammer in New Zealand and Common Cardinal in the Hawaiian Islands are not popular as introduced species because of the damage they cause to crops. The introduction of the grassquits in the West Indies area may be deleterious in time. They can be expected to compete with the similar species present on some islands.

INTRODUCTIONS OF EMBERIZIDAE

Species	Date introduced	Region	Manner introduced	Reason
(a) Successful introductions				
Yellowhammer	1862-71	New Zealand	deliberate	?
Cirl Bunting	1871 and 1879-80	New Zealand	deliberate	?
Common Diuca-finch	1928	Easter Island	deliberate ?	?
Saffron Finch	early 19th century, before 1847	Jamaica	escapee ?	cage bird
	about 1951	Panama	escapee	cage bird
	about 1967	Hawaiian Islands	escapee	cage bird
Yellow Grass-finch	about 1900	Barbados	?	?
	after 1900 ?	Martinique	colonisation from Barbados	—
	after 1900 ?	St Lucia	colonisation from Barbados	—
	after 1900 ?	Guadeloupe	colonisation from Barbados	—
	prior 1973 ?	St Vincent	colonisation from Barbados ?	—
Cuban Grassquit	1963	New Providence	deliberate release en route cage birds	aircraft breakdown
Yellow-faced Grassquit	1963	New Providence	deliberate release en route cage birds	aircraft breakdown
Red-crested Cardinal	1928	Oahu, Hawaiian Islands	deliberate	?
Yellow-billed Cardinal	1930 or recent ?	Hawaiian Islands	escapee ?	?
Common Cardinal	since 1900	Southern Canada	colonisation	—
	since early 19th century	Northern USA	colonisation	—
	1929-31	Hawaiian Islands	deliberate	?
	early ?	Bermuda	deliberate ?	?
Blue-grey Tanager	about 1961	Florida, USA	escapee	cage bird

Species	Date introduced	Region	Manner introduced	Reason
(b) Possibly or probably successful introductions				
Cuban Grassquit	?	Isle of Pines, Cuba	?	?
Puerto Rican Bullfinch	recent ?	St John, Virgin Islands	colonisation or ship borne ?	—
Lesser Antillean Bullfinch	1971	St John, Virgin Islands	colonisation or ship borne ?	—
Red-crested Cardinal	about 1965	Florida, USA	escapee ?	cage bird ?
	about 1957	Natal, South Africa	escapee	cage bird
Blue-grey Tanager	before 1977	Lima, Peru	escapee	cage bird
Red-legged Honeycreeper	?	Cuba ?	?	?
(c) Unsuccessful introductions				
Yellowhammer	1863 and 1864	Australia	deliberate	?
	1872-74	USA	deliberate	?
Ortolan Bunting	1885	New Zealand	deliberate	?
	1863	Australia	deliberate	?
Reed Bunting	1871	New Zealand	deliberate	?
Rufous-collared Sparrow	about 1951	Falkland Islands	ship borne	—
White-collared Seedeater	?	Cuba	?	?
Yellow-faced Grassquit	about 1974	Hawaiian Islands	escapee ?	cage bird ?
Green Cardinal	about 1965	Hawaiian Islands	escapee ?	cage bird ?
Red-headed Cardinal	1931 and about 1965	Hawaiian Islands	deliberate or escapee ?	cage bird
Red-capped Cardinal	since 1965	Hawaiian Islands	deliberate or escapee ?	cage bird
Common Cardinal	about 1952 ?	Tahiti	?	?
Indigo Bunting	1934	Hawaiian Islands	deliberate	?
Painted Bunting	? 1930s	Hawaiian Islands	deliberate	?
? Mexican or Butterfly Bunting	about 1938	Hawaiian Islands	deliberate	?
Orange-breasted Bunting	1941 and 1947	Hawaiian Islands	deliberate	?
White-lined Tanager	1938	Tahiti	deliberate	?
Summer Tanager	1868	New Zealand	deliberate	?
Olive Tanager	about 1964	Tahiti	deliberate ?	?
Silver-beaked Tanager	1938	Tahiti	deliberate	?
Scarlet Tanager	1938	Tahiti	deliberate	?
Scarlet-rumped Tanager	1940	Tahiti	deliberate	?
Blue-grey Tanager	about 1940	Tahiti	deliberate	?
Blue-hooded Euphonia	1910	Vieques Island, Puerto Rico	deliberate and escapee	re-introduction
Golden Tanager	1938	Tahiti	deliberate	?
Masked Tanager	1938	Tahiti	deliberate	?
Red-legged Honeycreeper	1938	Tahiti	deliberate	?

YELLOWHAMMER
(Yellow Bunting)
Emberiza citrinella Linnaeus

DISTINGUISHING CHARACTERISTICS
15-17 cm (6-6.8 in)
Head, neck, breast and underparts yellow, streaked dusky; upper parts red-brown, spotted dusky; flanks streaked red-brown; rump and upper tail-coverts chestnut and greyish tipped; tail brown-black; bill dark bluish horn, lower mandible paler. Female: spotted dull reddish brown; black moustachial line.
Witherby *et al*, vol.1, 1938-41, pp.113-116, and pl.12, opp. p.112 and pl.13, opp. p.114.
Gilliard, 1958, p.366, pl.214.
GENERAL DISTRIBUTION
Eurasia: from the British Isles, Europe except the southern fringe and parts of northern Scandinavia, to eastern Siberia and Sakhalin. Eastern populations winter south to Iran, Pakistan, north-west India, China, Korea and Japan. (Note: on the range map *E. leucocephalus* has been included in the distribution shown; the two interbreed extensively and are not separated here for this reason.)
INTRODUCED DISTRIBUTION
Introduced successfully in New Zealand. Introduced unsuccessfully in Australia and the USA.
GENERAL HABITS
Status: common. *Habitat:* forest edges, open woods, pine plantations, hedgerows, wasteland, cultivated areas and gardens. *Gregariousness:* small flocks, occasionally large flocks. *Movements:* sedentary and migratory. *Foods:* seeds, corn, grass shoots, wild fruits, insects, centipedes, spiders and worms. *Breeding:* Apr-Aug and rarely Sept; Oct-Feb (New Zealand); often 2-3 clutches per year (usually double

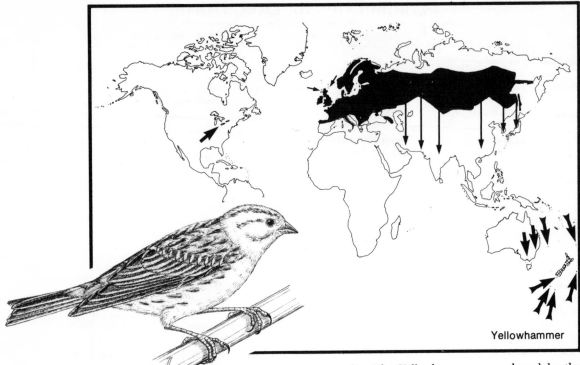

Yellowhammer

brooded in New Zealand). *Nest:* neat bulky structure of grass, stalks, roots and moss, lined with hair or fine plants, on the ground in grass or in a bush. *Eggs:* 1, 3-6 (1, 3-5 New Zealand).

Witherby *et al,* vol.1, 1938-41, pp.113-116.

Voous, 1960, p.236.

NOTES ON INTRODUCTIONS

New Zealand. The Yellowhammer was introduced to various places in New Zealand a number of times between 1862 and 1871 (Thomson, 1922). The Nelson Acclimatisation Society introduced three birds in 1862, but there are no further records of them. The Auckland Society introduced more than 345 birds between 1865 and 1871, at least 312 of them in 1871. The Otago society introduced eight in 1868 and thirty-one in 1871.

Thomson records that the species spread rapidly in New Zealand. By the 1920s they had apparently reached most areas of that country. They are now widespread and common in both the North and South Islands in open country (Wodzicki, 1965; Falla *et al,* 1966) and have been found on a number of off-shore and outlying islands.

Thirty-two birds were liberated on Stewart Island in 1879, but the species had disappeared from there prior to 1922 (Thomson). They were recorded on the Chatham Islands in 1910 and reached the Kermadecs in about 1946 (Williams, 1953). They have been recorded on the islands of Stewart, Raoul, Chathams, Three Kings, Mokohinau, Little Barrier, Kapiti, Codfish, Auckland and Campbell (Wodzicki, 1965; Oliver, 1955). Williams (1973) indicates that they have bred on the Kermadecs and Chatham Islands only. Williams (1953) records that they reached Lord Howe Island between New Zealand and Australia in about 1949.

Australia. The Yellowhammer was released by the Victorian Acclimatisation Society at Royal Park near Melbourne in 1863 (fifteen birds) and 1864 (fifteen), but they failed to become established (Frith, 1973). Some may have been liberated in a number of areas in New South Wales in 1880 (Jenkins, 1977) but these also failed to become established.

USA. The Cincinnati Acclimatisation Society is said to have released Yellowhammers between 1872 and 1874 (Phillips, 1928). They evidently failed to become established.

DAMAGE

In Great Britain, Lancum (1961) says that the Yellowhammer can destroy crops, but on the whole is a beneficial species. However, whilst examining the undesirable characteristics of wild birds, Ball (1960) found that the species occasionally gathers into large flocks and invades grainlands causing considerable losses. The species was banned from importation into the USA for this reason.

Before the 1920s Yellowhammers were destroyed as a noxious pest in grain growing districts of New Zealand. Oliver (1955) says that the species is one of the most harmful introductions to that country, because it feeds on grain and newly sown grass seed.

ORTOLAN BUNTING
(Ortolan)

Emberiza hortulana Linnaeus

DISTINGUISHING CHARACTERISTICS

15-17.7 cm (6-7.08 in). 17-26.3 g (.6-.93 oz)

Head and upper breast greyish olive; throat pale yellow; olive moustachial stripe; upper parts reddish chestnut; mantle pale chestnut-brown, streaked black; rump and upper tail-coverts yellowish, streaked darker; wings dark brown, edged brown and greyish; two buff wing bars; tail black-brown, with white on outer feathers; orbital skin yellow; bill brownish red.

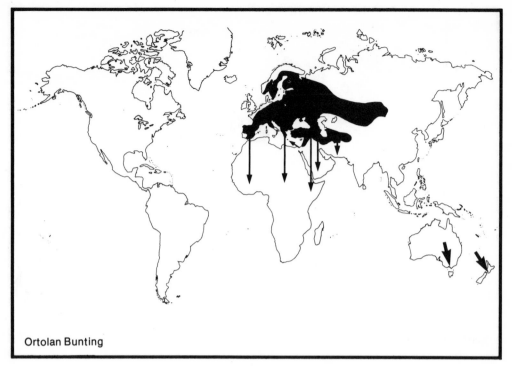

Ortolan Bunting

Witherby *et al,* vol.1, 1938-41, pp.129-131, and pl.12, opp. p.112 and pl.15, opp. p.128.

GENERAL DISTRIBUTION
Eurasia: Europe except the coastal fringe from France to Denmark, and northern and western Scandinavia, northern Iran, Afghanistan and east to Mongolia. In winter south to western Africa, Somali Republic, Arabia and southern Iran.

INTRODUCED DISTRIBUTION
Introduced unsuccessfully to New Zealand and Australia.

GENERAL HABITS
Status: common. *Habitat:* arid regions, grasslands, bush steppe and cultivated areas with trees. *Gregariousness:* small flocks. *Movements:* migratory. *Foods:* insects and their larvae (grasshoppers, beetles, etc.), seeds and snails. *Breeding:* May-July; 2 broods per year. *Nest:* slight hollow of grass, roots, leaves, and lined with finer material, on the ground under vegetation. *Eggs:* 2-6.
Witherby *et al,* vol.1, 1938-41, pp.129-131.
Voous, 1960, p.254.
Conrads, *Vogelwelt,* vol.98, 1977, pp.81-105.

NOTES ON INTRODUCTIONS
New Zealand. In 1885 the Wellington Acclimatisation Society imported three pairs of Ortolan Buntings which were released near Otaki in New Zealand. In the following year a small flock was reported present there, but they were not seen again (Thomson, 1922).
Australia. The Ortolan Bunting was introduced in Australia, near Melbourne, when some sixteen birds were liberated by the Victoria Acclimatisation Society in 1863 (Ryan, 1906; McCance, 1962; Frith, 1973). Ryan records that they died out soon after their release.
DAMAGE
None known.

CIRL BUNTING
Emberiza cirlus Linnaeus

DISTINGUISHING CHARACTERISTICS
15-17 cm (6-6.8 in)
Crown olive-green, streaked black; chin, throat, neck and band from bill through eye black; band above and below eye yellow; breast olive-grey, chestnut on sides; belly dull yellow; back brownish red, spotted dusky; tail black-brown, outer feathers whitish; bill bluish horn. Female: lacks black and yellow on head, and brown parts much striated.
Witherby *et al,* vol.1, 1938-41, pp.126-129, and pl.12, opp. p.112 and pl.13, opp. p.114.

GENERAL DISTRIBUTION
Europe-North Africa: from southern England and southern European mainland to Transcaucasia, some Mediterranean islands, and the northern coastal parts of Morocco, Algeria and Tunisia.

INTRODUCED DISTRIBUTION
Introduced successfully in New Zealand.

GENERAL HABITS
Status: uncommon. *Habitat:* open woods, fields,

Cirl Bunting, *Emberiza cirlus*

465

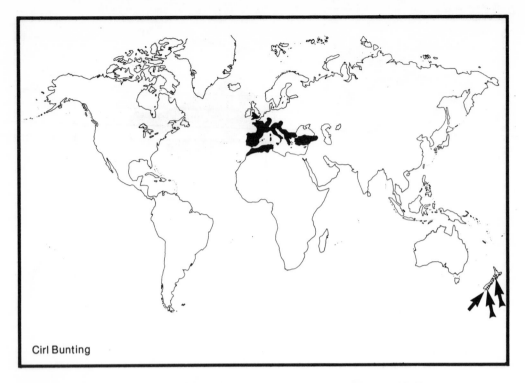

Cirl Bunting

hedgerows, orchards, plantations and cultivated areas generally. *Gregariousness:* small flocks. *Movements:* sedentary (New Zealand nomadic in winter). *Foods:* insects and seeds. *Breeding:* May-Aug; 2 clutches per year (usually double brooded in New Zealand). *Nest:* bulky structure of grass, moss and hair, in a bush or occasionally on the ground. *Eggs:* 3, 4-6 (3-5 New Zealand).

Witherby *et al,* vol.1, 1938-41, pp.126-129.
Voous, 1960 p.236.
Groh, *Mitt. Pollichia,* vol.63, 1975, pp.72-139.

NOTES ON INTRODUCTIONS
New Zealand. The race *E.c. cirlus* from Europe has become established in New Zealand. The Otago Acclimatisation Society liberated seven birds in 1871 (Thomson, 1922) and four birds were liberated at Wellington in 1880 (Oliver, 1930). Some eighteen birds were also liberated on Stewart Island in 1879, but the species apparently failed to become established on that island.

According to Thomson the introductions at Otago became established. In 1916 they occurred in Taranaki and in flocks along the coast at Hawera. By 1933 they had a small restricted distribution in New Zealand (Stidolph, 1933). In 1955, Oliver records that they were at Tauranga, Hawke's Bay, Manawatu, Wairarapa, Hutt Valley, Wellington, Canterbury, Otago and on Resolution Island.

The Cirl Bunting has not become as widespread in New Zealand as have some of the many other introduced birds. Falla *et al* (1966) say that they are rather rare except in a few favoured localities. They have recently been reported from the southern portion of the North Island, and widely in the South Island, east of the Alps from Marlborough to Otago.

DAMAGE
None known.

REED BUNTING
Emberiza schoeniclus (Linnaeus)
DISTINGUISHING CHARACTERISTICS
14-16 cm (5.6-6.4 in)
Head, chin and throat black; nape, sides of neck and line extending to bill white; upper parts variegated with reddish brown and dusky; underparts white, streaked dusky on flanks and spotted on lower breast; tail, central feathers brown, remainder black, outer pair white; bill dark brown. Female: head light brown, with dusky and brown spots; white neck less distinct; underparts reddish white, with dusky spots.
Witherby *et al,* vol.1, 1938-41, pp.140-143 and pl.16, opp. p.140.

GENERAL DISTRIBUTION
Eurasia: British Isles and the European mainland except for the south-east coastal fringes, east to Kamchatka, southern Sakhalin and northern Japan. In winter to southern parts of breeding range, south to North Africa, Pakistan, northern India and Korea (rarely).

INTRODUCED DISTRIBUTION
Introduced unsuccessfully in New Zealand.

GENERAL HABITS
Status: fairly common. *Habitat:* margins of streams, marshes, rivers and lakes. *Gregariousness:* small flocks with other finches. *Movements:* sedentary and migratory. *Foods:* seeds of marsh plants and grasses, small snails and other aquatic animals, insects and their larvae. *Breeding:* Apr-Aug; 2-3 clutches per year. *Nest:* untidy structure of grass, leaves, stems of aquatic plants, with the cup lined with fine grass, roots and hair, in a bush, rushes or on the ground. *Eggs:* 3-6, 7.
Witherby *et al,* vol.1, 1938-41, pp.140-143.
Voous, 1960, p.255.

NOTES ON INTRODUCTIONS
New Zealand. The Otago Acclimatisation Society

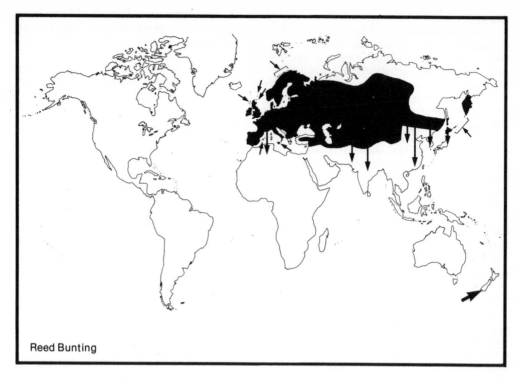

Reed Bunting

liberated four Reed Buntings in 1871, but there are no further records of the species (Thomson, 1922) and they did not become established in New Zealand.

DAMAGE
None known.

RUFOUS-COLLARED SPARROW
(Song Sparrow, American Song Sparrow)
Zonotrichia capensis (Müller)

DISTINGUISHING CHARACTERISTICS
13-15 cm (5.2-6 in). 19.1-23 g (.57-.81 oz)
Crown with grey central stripe, bordered black; face dusky; throat white; orange-rufous to chestnut collar on hindneck and sides of breast; black patch on each side of chest; back and wings brown striated with buff and brown; underparts pale brown to greyish white; tail dark brown, pale edged; bill brown.
Allen, 1962, pp.205-206, 242 and pl.98, p.204.
Johnson, vol.2, 1967, pp.389-394 and pl. p.365.

GENERAL DISTRIBUTION
Central and South America: south-eastern Mexico to Colombia, coastal Peru, Venezuela, Guyana, Surinam, Guyane and south to Tierra del Fuego; also Hispaniola, Curaçao and Aruba.

INTRODUCED DISTRIBUTION
Introduced unsuccessfully to the Falkland Islands.

GENERAL HABITS
Status: very common. *Habitat:* forest edges, brushy fields, villages, cities, pastures, parks, orchards, gardens, roadsides and open pinelands. *Gregariousness:* flocks. *Movements:* sedentary, and altitudinally or latitudinally migratory; southern populations tend to move northwards in winter. *Foods:* insects and seeds. *Breeding:* Sept-Feb (Chile); Aug-Sept (Guatemala); or continuous (Colombia); 2-3 broods per year. *Nest:* cup-shaped of grass and lined with other plant material, on or near the ground. *Eggs:* 2, 3-4, 5.

Johnson, vol.2, 1967, pp.389-394.
Frith and Calaby, 1976, pp.309-382.

NOTES ON INTRODUCTIONS
Falkland Islands. Cawkell and Hamilton (1961) record that three Rufous-collared Sparrows were reported at West Point Island in 1951, and that at least one bird arrived by boat and flew ashore at Stanley. Wood (1975) reports that they are often seen in the Falklands and may eventually colonise them from the mainland.

Rufous-collared Sparrow

467

DAMAGE

In Chile the Rufous-collared Sparrow causes damage to crops for a short period each year when these are newly sown. Johnson (1965) says that this may be partly true, but any such damage is far outweighed by the grubs and insects destroyed by these birds. However, it is thought that the establishment of the species in the Falklands would not be without detriment to both agriculture and native birds.

In North America *Zonotrichia* species are accused of destroying seedlings, disbudding and attacking blossoms of fruit trees, and causing damage to alfalfa fields. They cause losses in garden and commercial crops including lettuce, sugar beet, broccoli and beans (Koehler, 1963).

COMMON DIUCA-FINCH
(Diuca Finch)
Diuca diuca (Molina)

DISTINGUISHING CHARACTERISTICS
15.5-18 cm (6.2-7.2 in)
Upper parts and wing-coverts slate grey; remiges black, edged slate grey; eyebrow, throat, lower breast and abdomen white; upper breast and lower neck slate grey; under tail-coverts edged cinnamon; tail dusky, outermost feathers mostly white; bill black. Female: slate grey, tinged with brownish grey.
Johnson, vol.2, 1967, pp.365-367; pl. p.365.

GENERAL DISTRIBUTION
South America: south-eastern Brazil, Uruguay, Argentina and central Chile. Southern breeding birds migrate north to northern Argentina and Brazil.

Common Diuca-finch

INTRODUCED DISTRIBUTION
Introduced successfully to Easter Island, Pacific Ocean.

GENERAL HABITS
Status: very common. *Habitat:* forest, bushy hillsides, cultivated fields, villages, gardens, sand dunes and arid gravelly hills. *Gregariousness:* no information. *Movements:* sedentary, and southern breeders migratory to north. *Foods:* insects, seeds and fruits. *Breeding:* Sept-Feb; 2-3 broods per season. *Nest:* open cup-shaped of grasses and roots, lined with wool or soft vegetation, in a bush or tree. *Eggs:* 2-4.
Johnson, vol.2, 1967, pp.365-367.

NOTES ON INTRODUCTIONS
Easter Island. The Common Diuca-finch was introduced to Easter Island in 1928. The species is still established and holding its own on the island (Johnson, Millie and Moffett, 1970).

DAMAGE
None known.

SAFFRON FINCH
(Wild Canary)
Sicalis flaveola (Linnaeus)

DISTINGUISHING CHARACTERISTICS
13-15 cm (5.2-6 in). 20-24 g (.71-.85 oz)
Upper parts greenish yellow; forehead orange; sides of head and underparts bright yellow; back grey, with dusky streaks; wings and tail dark greyish; bill, upper mandible brownish or greyish, lower yellowish. Female: upper parts streaked dusky brown; underparts buffy white, streaked dusky on sides and breast.
Allen, 1962, pp.186-187, 241 and pl.95, pp.202-203.
Ridgely, 1976, p.336 and pl.31.
Meyer de Schauensee and Phelps, 1978, p.364 and pl.40.

GENERAL DISTRIBUTION
South America: northern Argentina, Uruguay, southern Bolivia, Venezuela, Colombia, Guyana, Guyane, south-western Ecuador, north-western Peru and southern and eastern Brazil; also Trinidad and Surinam (rare).

INTRODUCED DISTRIBUTION
Introduced successfully in Jamaica, Panama, the Hawaiian Islands and probably to Tobago.

GENERAL HABITS
Status: very common. *Habitat:* open country, fields, gardens, grassland, towns and river valleys. *Gregariousness:* pairs or family parties, but often in feeding and roosting flocks sometimes up to 50 birds outside breeding season. *Movements:* nomadic. *Foods:* weed, grass and tree seeds and probably insects. *Breeding:* July-Nov (Venezuela); all year (Jamaica); June-Jan (Trinidad). *Nest:* cup-shaped of rootlets and grass within a tree cavity, at the base of palm fronds, or under the eaves of houses; often in old orioles' nests. *Eggs:* 2, 3-4.
Allen, 1962, pp.186-187, 241.
Bond, 1971, pp.228-229.
Ffrench, 1973, pp.436-437.

NOTES ON INTRODUCTIONS
Jamaica. The Saffron Finch has been introduced successfully in Jamaica (Bond, 1960; Allen, 1962; Meyer de Schauensee, 1970). Allen records that they

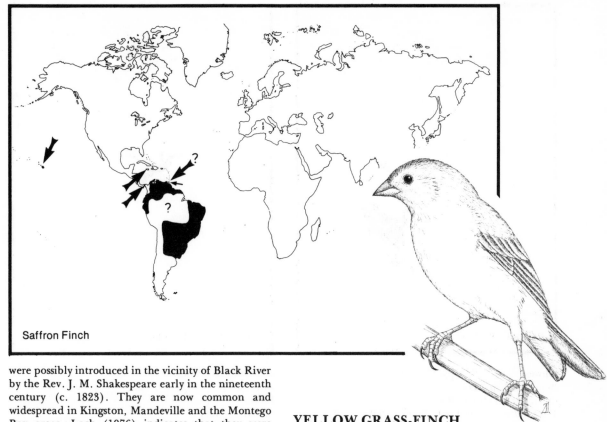

Saffron Finch

were possibly introduced in the vicinity of Black River by the Rev. J. M. Shakespeare early in the nineteenth century (c. 1823). They are now common and widespread in Kingston, Mandeville and the Montego Bay areas. Lack (1976) indicates that they were introduced well before 1847 and are now widespread in lowland cultivation, but not in the natural woodlands.

The species is a favourite cage bird in Jamaica, Venezuela and probably elsewhere in South America, and the probability exists that it escaped from captivity to become established.

Panama. The Saffron Finch has been introduced to and probably successfully established in central Panama (Peters, 1970; Meyer de Schauensee, 1970). Some were present in the Atlantic area (near Gatun ?) during the 77th Christmas Bird Count (Heilbrun, 1977).

According to Scholes (1954) a pair were noted at Gatun in July 1951 and the species was present there until 1953 to his knowledge. At this time he suggested that the Saffron Finch may have become established as a result of escaped cage birds.

The species is now locally common in residential and park-like areas of the Caribbean coast of the Canal Zone from Gatun Dam to Gatun and Coco Solo and occasionally wanders elsewhere.

Tobago. A few birds were introduced at Charlotteville on Tobago in 1958 (Ffrench, 1973).

Hawaiian Islands. The Saffron Finch has been recorded on the Christmas Bird Counts from 1967 to 1972, and again in the period 1974 to 1976 (Pyle, 1976-77) and appears to be established in the Hawaiian Islands. The Hawaiian Audubon Society (1975) says that they frequent Kapiolani Park on the island of Oahu, and the area from Kona to Kamuela on Hawaii, as escaped cage birds.

DAMAGE

None known.

YELLOW GRASS-FINCH
(Grass Sparrow, Grassland Yellow-finch)
Sicalis luteola (Sparrman)

DISTINGUISHING CHARACTERISTICS

10-14 cm (4-5.6 in)

Upper parts and face olive-green, streaked dusky; lores, orbital area and underparts yellow; (greyish pectoral band in southern populations); rump and upper tail-coverts yellowish green; wings and tail dark brown or greyish. Female: browner; throat, breast and flanks light greyish brown; belly yellow.

Johnson, vol.2, 1967, pp.357-358 and pl. p.356.

Ridgely, 1976, p.336 and pl.31.

Meyer de Schauensee and Phelps, 1978, p.364 and pl.40.

GENERAL DISTRIBUTION

Central and South America: southern Mexico, central southern Guatemala, Costa Rica, Panama, Venezuela, south to Paraguay, Uruguay, southern Argentina and southern Chile.

INTRODUCED DISTRIBUTION

Introduced successfully on Barbados, from whence it colonised the Grenadines, Guadeloupe, St Lucia, Martinique and St Vincent in the West Indies.

GENERAL HABITS

Status: common. *Habitat:* open fields, grasslands, pasture, alfalfa, cliffs and borders of marshes, and occasionally open woods. *Gregariousness:* pairs or small flocks, sometimes large flocks of 50 to several hundred in winter. *Movements:* sedentary, and southern populations may migrate northwards. *Foods:* seeds and insects. *Breeding:* Sept-Jan (Chile and Argentina). *Nest:* cup-shaped of grass roots and moss, lined with hair and other soft material, on the ground or in tuft of grass. *Eggs:* 3, 4-5.

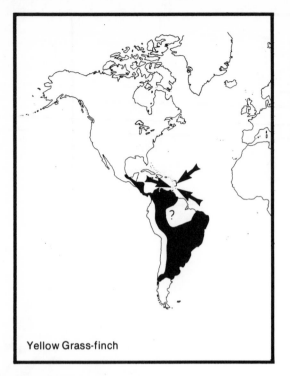

Yellow Grass-finch

White-collared Seedeater

Johnson, vol.2, 1967, pp.357-358.
Bond, 1971, p.229.
NOTES ON INTRODUCTIONS
West Indies. According to Bond (1960 and 1971) the Yellow Grass-finch was introduced to and became established on Barbados in about 1900 and from there spread to other islands in the Lesser Antilles. These include the islands of Martinique, St Lucia, the Grenadines and Guadeloupe. Lack *et al* (1973) report that E. Kirby informed them that the Yellow Grass-finch arrived on St Vincent recently from Barbados following a hurricane in the area. They saw several birds near the Arnos Vale airfield. The species is now established and breeding there (Lack, 1976). The race introduced into the area appears to be *S.l. luteola* (Peters, 1970).
DAMAGE
None known.

WHITE-COLLARED SEEDEATER
Sporophila torqueola (Bonaparte)
DISTINGUISHING CHARACTERISTICS
9-11.2 cm (3.6-4.48 in)
Upper parts largely black; rump white; two white wing bars and patch at base of primaries white; underparts whitish, extending over sides of neck to form an incomplete collar; black band across breast; bill black or greyish. (Races vary from cinnamon to whitish below and may be black or pale throated.) Female: upper parts buffy brown; underparts whitish, washed buff; wing bars pale.
Wetmore, 1964, p.338 and pl. p.338.
Reilly, 1968, p.465.
Ridgely, 1976, p.333.
GENERAL DISTRIBUTION
Central America: extreme southern North America and Central America, from southern Texas south to Panama.

INTRODUCED DISTRIBUTION
Introduced, probably unsuccessfully in Cuba, West Indies.
GENERAL HABITS
Status: very common. *Habitat:* forest edges, brush and fields, roadsides and often near human habitation. *Gregariousness:* flocks, loose flocks of 100 or more in non-breeding season. *Movements:* sedentary. *Foods:* mainly seeds and possibly some insects. *Breeding:* Mar-Oct. *Nest:* compact open cup of cobwebs, hair and fibres, in a bush. *Eggs:* 4-5 (Texas) ; 2-3 (Honduras and Nicaragua).
Reilly, 1968, p.465.
Gooders, vol.8, 1969, pp.2410-2412.
NOTES ON INTRODUCTIONS
Cuba. According to Bond (1960 and 1971) the White-collared Seedeater was introduced to Cuba, where it thrived for several years in Marianao, near Havana, but there appear to be no recent reports of its presence.
DAMAGE
None known.

CUBAN GRASSQUIT
(Cuban Finch, Melodious Grassquit)
Tiaris canora (Gmelin)
DISTINGUISHING CHARACTERISTICS
8.75-11.25 cm (3.5-4.5 in)
Upper parts yellow-green; crown grey; face and throat black; ruff of yellow feathers on each side of neck and extending to above the eye; abdomen pale and whitish; bill greyish. Female: ruff less well developed; black of face replaced mostly by chestnut.
Bond, 1971, p.235.
GENERAL DISTRIBUTION
Cuba and (?) Isle of Pines.
INTRODUCED DISTRIBUTION
Possibly introduced to the Isle of Pines and

Cuban Grassquit

Yellow-faced Grassquit

introduced successfully to New Providence in the West Indies.

GENERAL HABITS

Status: common; often kept in captivity. *Habitat:* woodlands, pine woods and field borders of grassland. *Gregariousness:* small flocks. *Movements:* sedentary. *Foods:* seeds and insects. *Breeding:* no information. *Nest:* globular grass nest, with side entrance tunnel, low in a bush or tree. *Eggs:* 2-3.
Bond, 1971, p.235.

NOTES ON INTRODUCTIONS

West Indies. The Cuban Grassquit was introduced to New Providence in 1963 (Bond, 1971) and may still be established there. Peters (1970) also suggests that the species may have been introduced to the Isle of Pines off Cuba.

An aircraft carrying a consignment of 600 Cuban Grassquits from Cuba to a European zoo made an emergency landing at Nassau, New Providence in March 1963 (Brudenell-Bruce, 1975). Some 200 of these birds died as a result of the delay in Nassau and most of the remainder were released. It has been estimated that about 300 were Cuban Finches, but Indigo Buntings, Yellow-faced Grassquits and others were also released. By 1966 it was reported that Cuban Grassquits were fairly common in Nassau and in eastern New Providence.

DAMAGE

None known.

YELLOW-FACED GRASSQUIT
(Yellow-faced Grass Bird, Olive Finch)
Tiaris olivacea (Linnaeus)

DISTINGUISHING CHARACTERISTICS
9-11 cm (3.6-4.4 in). 9 g (.32 oz)
Upper parts greyish green; stripe above eye, lower eyelid, chin and upper throat orange-yellow; forecrown, cheeks, sides of neck and chest black;

remainder of underparts greyish olive; bill blackish. Female: lacks black on underparts; head markings faintly yellow; breast dusky.
Gooders, vol.8, 1969, pp.2409-2410 and pl. p.2409.
Ridgely, 1976, p.332 and pl.31.
Meyer de Schauensee and Phelps, 1978, p.360 and pl.40.

GENERAL DISTRIBUTION

Central and South America and West Indies: the Greater Antilles (West Indies) including the Cayman Islands, east to Vieques and Culebra; eastern Mexico south to western Colombia and north-western and western Venezuela.

INTRODUCED DISTRIBUTION

Introduced, probably successfully on New Providence in the West Indies, and probably unsuccessfully in the Hawaiian Islands.

Yellow-faced Grassquit, *Tiaris olivacea*

Status: very common to fairly common; often kept in captivity. *Habitat:* forest edges and clearings, fields, roadsides, gardens, grasslands, marshes and thickets in open country. *Gregariousness:* solitary or in flocks and small parties up to 15 or 20 birds. *Movements:* no information. *Foods:* seeds, and probably small fruits. *Breeding:* mainly May, but almost any month; probably more than 1 brood per year. *Nest:* globular, roofed structure of fine grass with a side entrance, on or near the ground. *Eggs:* 2-3.

Gooders, vol.8, 1969, pp.2409-2410.

Bond, 1971, p.233.

NOTES ON INTRODUCTIONS

New Providence. The Yellow-faced Grassquit was introduced to New Providence in 1963 (Bond, 1971). In 1966 it was reported to have become established in at least two localities (Brudenell-Bruce, 1975) and may still occur there.

Hawaiian Islands. The Yellow-faced Grassquit is possibly established on the island of Oahu, but its present status is not well known (Hawaiian Audubon Society, 1975). They were noted there for the first time in about 1974, probably originating from escaped cage birds. There appear to have been no subsequent records of their presence.

DAMAGE

Although the Yellow-faced Grassquit does not appear to do any damage, as a native or where introduced, in New Providence it has been said (Brudenell-Bruce, 1975) that it may in time affect the local population of Black-faced Grassquits *(Tiaris bicolor).*

PUERTO RICAN BULLFINCH

Loxigilla portoricensis (Daudin)

DISTINGUISHING CHARACTERISTICS

16.2-20 cm (6.48-8 in)

Mainly black; crown, chin, throat, foreneck, upper chest and under tail-coverts rufous.

Bond, 1971, p.231.

GENERAL DISTRIBUTION

Puerto Rico (and formerly St Kitts).

INTRODUCED DISTRIBUTION

Probably introduced to the island of St John in the Virgin Islands, West Indies (present status unknown).

GENERAL HABITS

Status: common. *Habitat:* rain forest, woodland, plantations, arid wasteland and mangroves. *Gregariousness:* pairs and small flocks. *Movements:* sedentary. *Foods:* insects and seeds. *Breeding:* mainly Feb-June, but irregular. *Nest:* bulky cup-shaped or globular structure of leaves, grass and stems, lined with grass and rootlets, with side entrance, in a bush or tree. *Eggs:* 3.

Bond, 1971, p.231.

NOTES ON INTRODUCTIONS

St John. The Puerto Rican Bullfinch is said by Blake (1975) to have been transplanted to St John. Bond (1971) makes no mention of the introduction so it must have been fairly recent.

DAMAGE

According to Wetmore (1927) it is claimed that the Puerto Rican Bullfinch causes damage to the coffee crop by stripping the berries.

LESSER ANTILLEAN BULLFINCH

Loxigilla noctis (Linnaeus)

DISTINGUISHING CHARACTERISTICS

13.7-15 cm (5.48-6 in)

Inconspicuous spot above lores; chin and throat rufous; under tail-coverts black, partly rufous or entirely rufous; remainder black. Female: upper parts dark olive-grey; some brown on wings; under

Puerto Rican Bullfinch

Lesser Antillean Bullfinch

parts greyish; under tail-coverts tawny.
Bond, 1971, p. 232.

GENERAL DISTRIBUTION
Lesser Antilles, apart from the Grenadines.

INTRODUCED DISTRIBUTION
Introduced or colonised successfully St John in the Virgin Islands, West Indies.

GENERAL HABITS
Status: common. *Habitat:* shrubbery, cactus woodland, forest undergrowth, and gardens. *Gregariousness:* pairs and small flocks. *Movements:* sedentary. *Foods:* seeds, and fruits of cactus and other plants. *Breeding:* Jan-Feb (?). *Nest:* globular structure of grass, twigs, vines and lined with plant fibres, with side entrance, in a bush, tree or cactus. *Eggs:* 2-3.
Bond, 1971, p.232.
Raffaele and Roby, *Wilson Bull.* vol.89, no.2, 1977, pp.338-342.

NOTES ON INTRODUCTIONS
St John. Raffaele and Roby (1977) say that the first birds were found on St John in the Virgin Islands in April 1971. In January and February 1972, there were perhaps about 100 birds there.

How the species arrived in the Virgin Islands is not definitely known. Raffaele and Roby indicate that they were taken there as a cage bird, but may equally have arrived by cruise ship. Several factors support the theory of natural colonisation of the islands. The race *ridgwayi* has the closest distribution to the Virgin Islands and it has now been found on both Norman and Peter Islands which are both in the path of such a colonisation. Also, the pattern of distribution at present found on St John appears to favour a natural expansion rather than a human-induced one.

DAMAGE
None known.

GREEN CARDINAL
(Yellow Cardinal, Black-crested Cardinal)
Gubernatrix cristata (Vieillot)

DISTINGUISHING CHARACTERISTICS
19-20 cm (7.6-8 in)
Upper parts olive-green, streaked black; lower cheeks, throat, eyebrow and moustachial streaks yellow; head yellow with a black crest, crown and bib; underparts greenish yellow; wings dark brown; tail yellow, with two central feathers black; bill greyish horn. Female: dull grey-green; dull white where male yellow.
Avon *et al*, 1974, pl. p.79.

GENERAL DISTRIBUTION
South America: from extreme south-eastern Brazil (Rio Grande do Sul), Uruguay to eastern and north-eastern Argentina south to Rio Negro.

INTRODUCED DISTRIBUTION
Introduced, probably unsuccessfully in the Hawaiian Islands.

GENERAL HABITS
Status: common; commonly kept as cage bird in South America. *Habitat:* shrubbery and wooded country. *Gregariousness and Movements:* no information. *Foods:* insects, seeds (?), fruits and buds. *Breeding:* no information. *Nest:* cup-shaped of grass, lined with feathers and hair in a bush (in captivity). *Eggs:* 3-4 (in captivity).

Green Cardinal

NOTES ON INTRODUCTIONS
Hawaiian Islands. The Green Cardinal was reported on Diamond Head, Oahu in 1965 and at Puu Waawaa, Hawaii in 1966 (Berger, 1972), but there appear to be no subsequent records of its presence. The birds noted were undoubtedly aviary escapees.

DAMAGE
None known.

RED-CRESTED CARDINAL
(Brazilian Cardinal)
Paroaria coronata (Miller)

DISTINGUISHING CHARACTERISTICS
17.5-19 cm (7-7.6 in)
Head, crest, face and throat bright red; behind crest, sides of neck and underparts white; remainder of upper parts blue-grey to blackish; wings and tail-feathers blackish with grey edges; bill pale brown with dark upper edge.
Reilly, 1968, pp.453-454.
Gooders, vol.8, 1969, pp.2488-2489 and pl. p.2488.

GENERAL DISTRIBUTION
South America: extreme south-eastern Brazil, Uruguay, Paraguay, eastern Bolivia and northern Argentina.

INTRODUCED DISTRIBUTION
Introduced, successfully in the Hawaiian Islands and possibly successfully in South Africa and the USA (Florida).

GENERAL HABITS
Status: fairly common (?). *Habitat:* thickets and bush, towns, wet scrub and shrubbery. *Gregariousness:* small flocks, but often found in large flocks. *Movements:* sedentary. *Foods:* seeds, insects, fruits and berries. *Breeding:* Oct-Nov (Argentina); may have more than 1 brood per year (Hawaiian Islands). *Nest:* open cup-shaped of vegetable material, in a tree or bush. *Eggs:* 2-4.

473

Reilly, 1968, pp.453-454.

Gooders, vol.8, 1969, pp.2488-2489.

NOTES ON INTRODUCTIONS

USA. Owre (1973) records that the Red-crested Cardinal was first noted at the Crandon Zoo in south-eastern Florida in 1965. There have been scattered reports of the species there since then and in 1973 they were reported from Fort Lauderdale. Owre says that they may be breeding in both Dade and Broward Counties.

Hawaiian Islands. Red-crested Cardinals from South America were introduced to the island of Oahu in 1928 by Mr W. McInerny, and Mrs D. R. Isenberg imported some to Kauai (Munro, 1960). Caum (1933) records that releases were made on Oahu during the three years following 1928. According to Peterson (1961) the species was widespread on Oahu and local on Kauai and Maui in about 1960.

Red-crested Cardinals are now found in the residential and lowland areas of all the larger main islands, although they are still uncommon on Oahu (Hawaiian Audubon Society, 1975). Heilbrun (1976) indicates that there have been recent extensions in range in the southern part of that island.

The species may not be as widespread as indicated above because Richardson and Bowles (1964) found none on Kauai in 1960. Some were noted on Molokai (by Pekelo in 1967) and although they were listed as scarce on Maui by Ord (1967) none were seen by Berger (1972) on subsequent trips to that island.

South Africa. Winterbottom (1966) records that Red-crested Cardinals (presumed this species ?) escaped and bred at Hermanus in 1957, and appear to have now become established in a small area near Durban in Natal.

DAMAGE

None known.

RED-HEADED CARDINAL
(Pope Cardinal, Red-cowled Cardinal, Dominican Cardinal)

Paroaria dominicana (Linnaeus)

DISTINGUISHING CHARACTERISTICS

17.5-18.7 cm (7-7.48 in)

Head, face, throat and upper breast glossy scarlet; top of head peaked but not crested; upper back black, spotted white; lower back grey; wings and tail black; wings have white edged secondaries; bill, upper mandible blackish, lower paler.

Avon *et al*, 1974, pl. p.77.

GENERAL DISTRIBUTION

South America: north-eastern Brazil from southern Maranhão to Ceará and south to northern Minas Gerais.

INTRODUCED DISTRIBUTION

Introduced unsuccessfully in the Hawaiian Islands.

GENERAL HABITS

Status: common; favourite cage bird in Brazil. *Habitat:* open wooded areas and near cultivated areas. *Gregariousness and Movements:* no information. *Foods:* insects and their larvae, and seeds. *Breeding:* no information. *Nest:* open cup-shaped, in a thicket. *Eggs:* 3-4.

NOTES ON INTRODUCTIONS

Hawaiian Islands. Munro (1960) indicates that Red-headed Cardinals were introduced to Oahu by the Hui Manu in 1931, but they did not find conditions suitable and failed to become established. More recently, the Red-headed Cardinal has been intentionally or accidentally released or has escaped from captivity on the island of Oahu (Berger 1972).

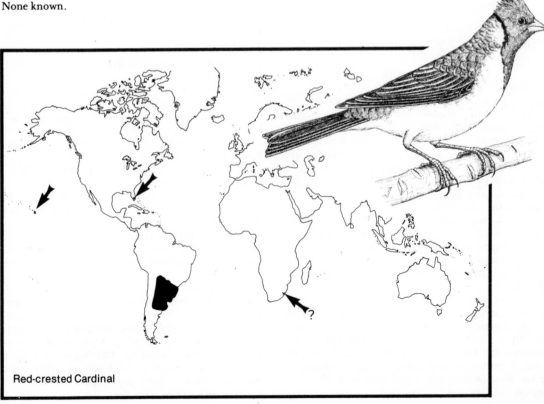

Red-crested Cardinal

Red-headed Cardinal

Red-capped Cardinal

Berger reports that they have been occasionally noted on the island since 1965.

DAMAGE

None known.

RED-CAPPED CARDINAL
(Black-eared Cardinal, Black-faced Cardinal)
Paroaria gularis (Linnaeus)

DISTINGUISHING CHARACTERISTICS

16.2-17.5 cm (6.48-7 in)

Head and upper throat dark red; lower throat, bib and small streak around eye black; back, wings and tail black, with a blue gloss; underparts white; bill black, with a light yellowish patch at the base of the lower mandible.

Meyer de Schauensee, 1964, p.388 and pl.20, opp. p.384.

Meyer de Schauensee and Phelps, 1978, p.356 and pl.39.

GENERAL DISTRIBUTION

South America: Venezuela to eastern Colombia and south to Guyane, Brazil (Amazonia), eastern Ecuador, north-eastern Peru and eastern and north-eastern Bolivia; also on Trinidad (rare).

INTRODUCED DISTRIBUTION

Introduced, probably unsuccessfully in the Hawaiian Islands (?).

GENERAL HABITS

Status: fairly common. *Habitat:* forest edges and clearings, open woodland, plantations, mangrove swamps, campos, lakes, cultivated areas and margins of rivers and streams. *Gregariousness:* pairs or small groups. *Movements:* sedentary (?). *Foods:* seeds, fruits, green vegetation, insects and other invertebrates. *Breeding:* Sept (Trinidad). *Nest:* open cup-shaped, solidly constructed of vegetable material, in a thicket. *Eggs:* 2-4.

Ffrench, 1973, p.422.

Meyer de Schauensee and Phelps, 1978, p.356.

NOTES ON INTRODUCTIONS

Hawaiian Islands. The Red-capped Cardinal has been intentionally or accidentally released or escaped, since 1965 on the island of Oahu (Berger, 1972). There appear to be no more recent records.

DAMAGE

None known.

YELLOW-BILLED CARDINAL
Paroaria capitata (d'Orbigny and Lafresnaye)

DISTINGUISHING CHARACTERISTICS

16.2-17.5 cm (6.48-7 in)

Head, face and chin bright red; no crest; black inverted triangle on throat; narrow black strip on nape; almost or complete white nuchal collar; back and tail black; underparts from nape white; bill yellow-orange or brownish pink.

GENERAL DISTRIBUTION

South America: from southern Brazil, Paraguay and south-eastern Bolivia to northern Argentina.

INTRODUCED DISTRIBUTION

Introduced successfully in the Hawaiian Islands.

GENERAL HABITS

Status: no recent information. *Habitat:* shrubbery in humid areas (coastal thickets in Hawaiian Islands).

Yellow-billed Cardinal, *Paroaria capitata*

475

Yellow-billed Cardinal

Gregariousness: pairs and small flocks. *Movements:* no information. *Foods:* insects and spiders. *Breeding:* no information. *Nest:* cup-shaped of twigs, grass and other soft material. *Eggs:* no information.

NOTES ON INTRODUCTIONS
Hawaiian Islands. The Yellow-billed Cardinal appears to have been first recorded in Hawaii in 1973, although there is some evidence to assume that it may have been there since about 1930 (Collins, 1976). The species now inhabits the coastal thickets on the North Kona coast of Hawaii and small flocks of up to twelve birds were seen there in about 1975.

DAMAGE
None known.

COMMON CARDINAL
(Cardinal, Red Cardinal, Red Bird, Virginian Cardinal)
Cardinalis cardinalis (Linnaeus)

DISTINGUISHING CHARACTERISTICS
16-23 cm (6.4-9.2 in). 35-50.3 g (1.23-1.77 oz)
Generally bright red, with a pointed crest; forepart of face and upper throat black; back mixed with grey; bill reddish. Female: brownish grey upper parts and buffy brown underparts; crest and flight feathers red.
Roberts, 1934, Rev. 1960, pl.79.
Godfrey, 1966, pp.363-364 and pl.63, no.1, opp. p.316.
Reilly, 1968, pp.452-453.

GENERAL DISTRIBUTION
North and Central America: southern Ontario, south-eastern South Dakota, east to Connecticut, and south to the Gulf of Mexico and southern Florida; from south-eastern California, central Arizona, southern New Mexico and northern Texas, south to southern Mexico, Belize and Guatemala (Petén).

INTRODUCED DISTRIBUTION
Extended range into north-eastern parts of the USA and southern Canada (colonisation). Introduced successfully in south-western California, the Hawaiian Islands and Bermuda. Introduced probably successfully but has now died out on Tahiti. Probably introduced, unsuccessfully in Australia.

GENERAL HABITS
Status: very common; often kept in captivity. *Habitat:* woodland, shrub and river thickets, parks, gardens and towns. *Gregariousness:* pairs or family parties, and flocks of 5-20 and up to 50 occasionally in winter. *Movements:* migratory and sedentary. *Foods:* berries, fruits, seeds, insects, and other vegetable material. *Breeding:* Mar-Sept; all year (Hawaiian Islands); 3-4 broods per year. *Nest:* loosely constructed open cup of twigs, bark, stems, rootlets and grass, lined with grass, rootlets or hair, in a shrub or small tree. *Eggs:* 2-5, 6.
Godfrey, 1966, pp.363-364.
Reilly, 1968, pp.452-453.

NOTES ON INTRODUCTIONS
Canada. The Common Cardinal has extended its breeding range northwards into Canada in the past half of this century (Godfrey, 1966). Godfrey says that they first nested in Canada at Point Pelee, Ontario in 1901. At present the species breeds in southern Ontario and occasionally in southern Manitoba. They wander considerably further north and have been recorded at Lake Nipissing, Ottawa, and in Nova Scotia, Quebec and southern Saskatchewan.

USA. A mixture of races of the Common Cardinal have been established in south-western California in the San Gabriel River bottom from El Monte south to Whittier (A.O.U., 1957). According to Hardy (1973) they have been repeatedly introduced there since 1880. Certainly they have been recorded in California since that date (Miller, 1928). Miller records that Belding (*Land Birds of the Pacific District,* 1890, p.175) reports the introduction near Galt, Sacramento County of six birds from Missouri, which subsequently remained there for several years. He felt that the birds found in the San Gabriel River bottom had become established from the liberation or escape of caged birds. The population in 1972, in this area of California, numbered about twenty pairs established within an area of almost eighty hectares (197 acres). Observations of individuals are annually made elsewhere in the Los Angeles basin, but are probably escaped birds or stragglers from the established colony.

The Common Cardinal has been spreading northwards in the United States apparently unaided (Austin, 1968). They were first recorded in Michigan in 1837, by 1919 were a fairly common resident, and have been throughout that State since about 1930 (Burns, 1958). According to Krause and Froiland (1956) they have extended their range since 1904 in South Dakota and by 1956 occupied approximately one quarter of that State. The species has also spread north in Wisconsin and other areas since 1900 (Young, 1946).

According to Austin the northern advance of the Cardinal was most rapid and extensive in the Mississippi Valley during the 1890s and from 1900 to

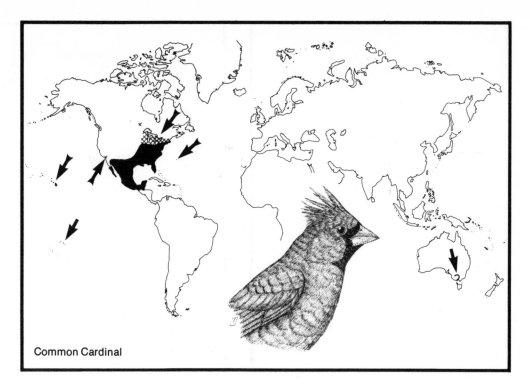

Common Cardinal

1940. Much of the advance occurred in the winter periods.

Hawaiian Islands. A mixture of races of the Common Cardinal have been introduced into the Hawaiian Islands (A.O.U., 1957). They have been introduced to these islands since 1929 from the eastern United States and were well established on Kauai, Oahu and Hawaii by the 1940s (Munro, 1960). Caum (1933) records that they were released several times on Oahu, on Kauai and at Hilo, Hawaii, between 1929 and 1931. Fisher (1951) reports that they were introduced to Kauai in about 1931 and spread from there to Niihau where they were numerous in about 1950.

The Common Cardinal is now established in residential and lowland areas on probably all the larger main islands (Peterson, 1961; Berger, 1972; Hawaiian Audubon Society, 1975).

Bermuda. Common Cardinals were introduced to Bermuda from Virginia, USA early in the colonial history of the island (Wingate, 1973). Wingate says that the species was formerly abundant, but has been replaced by the House Sparrow in the built-up areas. Numbers have been diminished from about the 1950s in rural areas by the loss of the cedar forests, the introduction of the Kiskadee and Starling, and by the increased urbanisation which has occurred on the island. Bourne (1957) reported that the species was still common in woods and parklands at this time.

Australia. 'Virginian cardinals' were probably released in Victoria in the 1860s or 1870s, but failed to become established there.

Tahiti. The Common Cardinal is not mentioned by Curtiss (1938), nor were any observed by the Whitney Expedition (in 1920-21) to Tahiti, but the species was without doubt introduced some time later (Holyoak, 1974). Bruner (1972) reports that they existed in the districts of Punaauia, Paea, and Tautira in Tahiti, and were formerly common almost everywhere on the island. He indicates that they were introduced in about 1952.

The species has now evidently failed on Tahiti as Holyoak (1972) failed to find them in any of the areas mentioned.

DAMAGE

Although the Common Cardinal does not appear to be a great pest in the United States, in the Hawaiian Islands it has become a nuisance because of the damage it causes to fruit.

INDIGO BUNTING
(Indigo Bird)
Passerina cyanea (Linnaeus)

DISTINGUISHING CHARACTERISTICS

11-13 cm (4.4-5.2 in). 11.9-15.5 g (.42-.55 oz)

Generally blue, darker and more purplish on the head; wings and tail black, edged blue; bill, upper mandible black, lower blue-grey. Male in non-breeding plumage resembles female but always has blue on tail. Female: upper parts olive-brown; underparts buffy whitish, breast and sides streaked brown.

Roberts, 1960, pl.80.

Godfrey, 1966, pp.366-367 and pl.63, no.3, opp. p.316.

Reilly, 1968, pp.459-460.

GENERAL DISTRIBUTION

North America: eastern North America from south-eastern Canada, eastern USA, to the Gulf coast and northern Florida. Winters south, mainly from central Mexico, Cuba and the Bahamas to central Panama.

INTRODUCED DISTRIBUTION

Introduced unsuccessfully in the Hawaiian Islands.

GENERAL HABITS

Status: common. *Habitat:* secondary growth, fields, brush, woodland edges, streams and lakesides. *Gregariousness:* parties, or large loose flocks in non-

Indigo Bunting

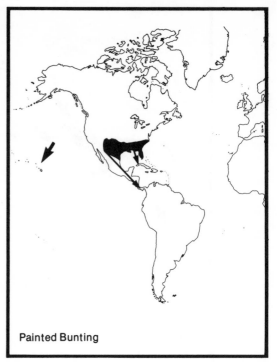

Painted Bunting

breeding season. *Movements:* migratory. *Foods:* seeds, insects and their larvae (including caterpillars, weevils, bugs, grasshoppers and beetles), berries and other fruits. *Breeding:* Mar-Aug; possibly double brooded. *Nest:* cup-shaped of woven twigs, grass, bark and sometimes leaves, lined with grass or hair, in a thicket or shrub. *Eggs:* 2, 3-4, 6.

Godfrey, 1966, pp.366-367.

Reilly, 1968, pp.459-460.

NOTES ON INTRODUCTIONS

Hawaiian Islands. The Indigo Bunting was imported to the Hawaiian Islands from San Francisco in 1934, but is not known to have become established (Bryan, 1958; Munro, 1960).

DAMAGE

None known.

PAINTED BUNTING
(Non-Pariel Bunting, Butterfly Finch)
Passerina ciris (Linnaeus)

DISTINGUISHING CHARACTERISTICS

12-14 cm (4.8-5.6 in)

Top and sides of head deep purplish blue; back green; mantle yellowish green; rump purplish red; upper tail-coverts red; underparts bright red; wings green and purplish; bill, upper mandible black, lower blue-grey. Female: upper parts dull green; underparts olive-yellow, fading to yellow on mid-abdomen.

Wetmore, 1964, p.334 and pl. p.334.

Reilly, 1968, pp.460-461 and pl. p.458.

GENERAL DISTRIBUTION

North America: from southern and south-eastern USA to northern Mexico. Winters to Florida, Mexico and to central Panama and Cuba.

INTRODUCED DISTRIBUTION

Introduced unsuccessfully in the Hawaiian Islands.

GENERAL HABITS

Status: fairly common. *Habitat:* woodlands, roadsides, brush and riversides. *Gregariousness:* no information. *Movements:* sedentary and migratory. *Foods:* insects and seeds. *Breeding:* May-July; 2 broods per year. *Nest:* woven cup of grass, stems and leaves, lined with hair and fibres, in a bush or low tree. *Eggs:* 3-5.

Wetmore, 1964, p.334.

Reilly, 1968, pp.460-461.

NOTES ON INTRODUCTIONS

Hawaiian Islands. The Painted Bunting was introduced into the Hawaiian Islands (Munro, 1960) but failed to become established.

Another species, the Mexican or Butterfly Bunting (?) was also imported, just prior to 1939, and also failed to establish itself.

DAMAGE

None known.

ORANGE-BREASTED BUNTING
(Leclanchers Nonpariel Bunting, Rainbow Bunting)
Passerina leclancheri Lafresnaye

DISTINGUISHING CHARACTERISTICS

12-14 cm (4.8-5.6 in)

Crown green; breast orange; upper parts azure blue; underparts yellow; wings and tail greenish tinged blue. Female: upper parts grey-green; wings and tail tinged blue; underparts yellowish, pale on throat and belly.

Avon *et al,* 1974, pl. p.67.

Peterson and Chalif, 1973, pp.240-241 and pl.45.

GENERAL DISTRIBUTION

Mexico: south-western Mexico from Jalisco south to the western Chiapas.

INTRODUCED DISTRIBUTION

Introduced unsuccessfully into the Hawaiian Islands.

Orange-breasted Bunting

White-lined Tanager

GENERAL HABITS

Status: fairly common. *Habitat:* woodlands, shrub, brush and abandoned fields. *Gregariousness and Movements:* no information. *Foods:* seeds and insects. *Breeding:* no information. *Nest:* open cup-shaped, near ground. *Eggs:* no information.

NOTES ON INTRODUCTIONS

Hawaiian Islands. The Orange-breasted Bunting was introduced to the island of Oahu in 1941 and 1947, and was reported to be breeding in the Manoa Valley in 1950 (Bryan, 1958). According to Peterson (1961) the status of the species was uncertain in 1960, but Berger (1972) says that they apparently did not become permanently established.

DAMAGE

None known.

WHITE-LINED TANAGER
(Black Tanager, White-shouldered Tanager)
Tachyphonus rufus (Boddaert)

DISTINGUISHING CHARACTERISTICS

16-20 cm (6.4-8 in). 31-47.5 g (1.09-1.66 oz)

Generally blue-black; upper wing-coverts and under wing-coverts white; bill black, with grey-white markings at base of mandibles. Female: bright rufous-brown, paler below.

Ffrench, 1973, pp.417-418 and pl.26.
Ridgely, 1976, p.324 and pl.29.
Meyer de Schauensee and Phelps, 1978, p.346 and pl.37.

GENERAL DISTRIBUTION

Central and South America: eastern Costa Rica, western Panama, Venezuela, Guyana, Surinam, Guyane, Brazil, Ecuador, Peru, Bolivia, northern Argentina, Paraguay and Colombia; also Trinidad and Tobago.

INTRODUCED DISTRIBUTION

Introduced unsuccessfully in Tahiti.

GENERAL HABITS

Status: common. *Habitat:* forest edges, open woodland, shrub, gardens and roadsides. *Gregariousness:* pairs, or family parties in non-breeding season. *Movements:* sedentary. *Foods:* fruits, berries, nectar, ants and other insects. *Breeding:* Feb-Aug (all year in Surinam). *Nest:* bulky, open cup of grass and leaves, lined with fine plant material, in a low tree or shrub. *Eggs:* 2-3.

Gooders, vol.8, 1969, pp.2522-2523.
Snow and Snow, *Auk,* vol.88, 1971, pp.291-322.
Ffrench, 1973, pp.417-418.

NOTES ON INTRODUCTIONS

Tahiti. White-lined Tanagers were liberated by E. Guild on Tahiti in 1938, and reported by him to be breeding soon after their release (Guild, 1938). There appear to be no subsequent records for the species on the island so it evidently failed to become permanently established.

DAMAGE

Feeds on some commercially grown fruits (Ffrench, 1973), but not recorded to cause any damage.

SUMMER TANAGER
(Scarlet Tanager)
Piranga rubra (Linnaeus)

DISTINGUISHING CHARACTERISTICS

16.5-19.3 cm (6.6-7.72 in)

Generally rose-red or dull crimson, wings darker; flight feathers brownish edged dull red; bill pale yellowish. In transitional plumage blotched rosy red. Female and male in non-breeding season: upper parts olive; underparts yellow; no wing bars.

Godfrey, 1966, p.363 and pl.61, no.2, opp. p.300.
Reilly, 1968, p.451.
Gooders, vol.8, 1969, pp.2515-2516 and pl. p.2516.

GENERAL DISTRIBUTION

North America: central and southern USA to central   479

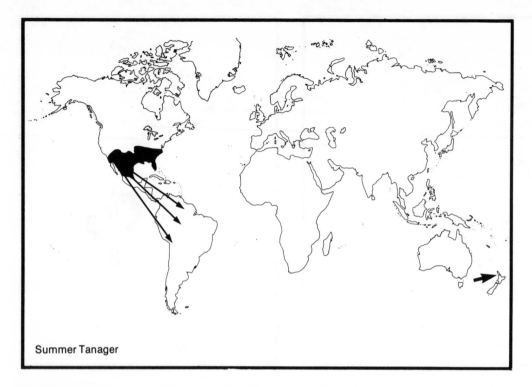

Summer Tanager

Mexico. Winters from central Mexico south to Brazil (western Amazonia), Bolivia, south-eastern Peru, Colombia, Venezuela, Guyana and eastern and western Ecuador; also Trinidad (uncommon).

INTRODUCED DISTRIBUTION
Introduced unsuccessfully in New Zealand.

GENERAL HABITS
Status: fairly common locally. *Habitat:* open woods and woodland. *Gregariousness:* solitary or pairs, flocks on migration. *Movements:* migratory. *Foods:* fruits, berries, insects and their larvae, and other invertebrates (including bees, wasps, beetles, spiders, ants and flies). *Breeding:* May-June. *Nest:* shallow cup of plant stems and lichens, lined with fine grass, in a tree. *Eggs:* 3-4, 5.

Reilly, 1968, p.451.
Gooders, vol.8, 1969, pp.2515-2516.

NOTES ON INTRODUCTIONS
New Zealand. In 1868 the Auckland Acclimatisation Society introduced two Summer Tanagers. They were apparently present in the Auckland Gardens in 1869, but subsequently disappeared and the species failed to become permanently established (Thomson, 1922).

DAMAGE
None known.

OLIVE TANAGER
(Scarlet Tanager)
Piranga olivacea (Gmelin)

DISTINGUISHING CHARACTERISTICS
15.7-18.7 cm (6.28-7.48 in). 27.5-29.5 g (.97-1.04 oz)

Generally scarlet with black wings and tail; bill buffy yellow with dusky tip. Female: upper parts, wings and tail olive (or yellow-green); lower parts greenish yellow. Male in winter like female but wings and tail black; abdomen and under tail-coverts bright yellow. Transitional plumage splotched with red.

Godfrey, 1966, pp.362-363 and pl.61, no.3, opp. p.300.
Reilly, 1968, pp.449-450.
Gooders, vol.8, 1969, pp.2517-2519 and pl. p.2518.

GENERAL DISTRIBUTION
North and South America: from south-eastern Canada (south-eastern Manitoba east to New Brunswick) to the eastern USA (Oklahoma and northern Georgia). Winters south to Colombia, Bolivia and western Amazonia (Brazil).

Olive Tanager

Probably introduced, unsuccessfully in Tahiti.

GENERAL HABITS

Status: common. *Habitat:* forest and open wood-land, parks and suburban woods. *Gregariousness:* flocks on migration. *Movements:* migratory. *Foods:* insects, berries and seeds. *Breeding:* May-July. *Nest:* flimsy structure of twigs and rootlets, lined with grass, in a tree. *Eggs:* 3-5.

Reilly, 1968, pp.449-450.

Gooders, vol.8, 1969, pp.2517-2519.

NOTES ON INTRODUCTIONS

Tahiti. The Olive Tanager was apparently introduced to Tahiti during the 1960s (Holyoak, 1974). Holyoak says that he can find no other records of the species on the island, nor could he find any of the birds themselves other than the report that one was seen on the western coast of Tahiti in 1965.

DAMAGE

None known.

SILVER-BEAKED TANAGER
(Maroon Tanager)
Ramphocelus carbo (Pallas)

DISTINGUISHING CHARACTERISTICS

16-18 cm (6.4-7.2 in). 23-37.5 g (.81-1.32 oz)

Entire plumage blackish maroon-crimson to blackish, darker above; throat and breast deep crimson; wings and tail brownish black; bill black with base of lower mandible silvery. Female: upper parts brownish red, clearer red on rump and upper tail-coverts; underparts dark carmine-red or brownish red (blackish in some races); bill black.

Allen, 1962, pp.185, 240-241 and pl.93, p.200.

Meyer de Schauensee and Phelps, 1978, pp.344-345 and pl.37.

GENERAL DISTRIBUTION

South America: Venezuela, Guyana, Surinam, Guyane, Ecuador, Peru, Brazil, Paraguay, Bolivia, Colombia and Trinidad.

INTRODUCED DISTRIBUTION

Introduced unsuccessfully in Tahiti.

GENERAL HABITS

Status: common. *Habitat:* forest edges, open woodland, bushland, plantations, cultivated areas and towns. *Gregariousness:* solitary, pairs or small loose flocks of 6-8 birds. *Movements:* sedentary. *Foods:* insects (including caterpillars and flies), fruits, berries and nectar. *Breeding:* all year; several broods per year. *Nest:* open cup of grass and leaves, lined with roots and other fine material, in a grass tuft, tree or shrub. *Eggs:* 1-3.

Allen, 1962, pp.185, 240-241.

Snow and Snow, *Auk,* vol.88, 1971, pp.291-322.

Ffrench, 1973, pp.413-414.

NOTES ON INTRODUCTIONS

Tahiti. Guild (1938) released Silver-beaked Tanagers on Tahiti in 1938. He reported that they were returning daily to feed, but had not yet nested in the wild there. There are no subsequent records of the species on the island.

DAMAGE

None known.

SCARLET TANAGER
Ramphocelus bresilius (Linnaeus)

DISTINGUISHING CHARACTERISTICS

18-19 cm (7.2-7.6 in)

Generally blood red, with wings, tail and thighs black; patch behind bill yellow; base of mandible silvery. Female: head and neck dull brown, back red-brown; rump and underparts dull crimson; wings and tail brownish black.

GENERAL DISTRIBUTION

South America: eastern Brazil from Paraiba south to eastern São Paulo and Santa Catarina.

Silver-beaked Tanager

Scarlet Tanager

INTRODUCED DISTRIBUTION
Introduced unsuccessfully in Tahiti.

GENERAL HABITS
Status: common. *Habitat:* forest edges, open woodland, scrubby growth, parks and gardens. *Gregariousness:* flocks in winter of 7-8 or more birds. *Movements:* sedentary. *Foods:* insects and fruits (?). *Breeding and Nest:* no information. *Eggs:* 2-3.

NOTES ON INTRODUCTIONS
Tahiti. Guild (1938) reports that he released Scarlet Tanagers with other species in 1938, and that soon after their liberation they were returning daily to be fed. There are no subsequent records for the species which evidently failed to become established on the island.

DAMAGE
None known.

CRIMSON-BACKED TANAGER
Ramphocelus dimidiatus Lafresnaye

DISTINGUISHING CHARACTERISTICS
14-18 cm (5.6-7.2 in)
Similar to *R. carbo* but has a darker crimson throat and upper breast and extensive black on centre of breast. Lower back, rump, upper tail-coverts and most of underparts crimson; crimson (or maroon-crimson) less vivid on head, upper back and chest; central abdomen blackish; wings, thighs and tail blackish brown; bill bluish or silvery. Female: duller; blackish areas in male brownish; throat and upper chest maroon-brown; lower back, rump, upper tail-coverts and underparts crimson-brown.
Meyer de Schauensee, 1964, p.366-367.
Ridgely, 1976, p.320 and pl.28.
Meyer de Schauensee and Phelps, 1978, p.344 and pl.37.

GENERAL DISTRIBUTION
Central and northern South America: Panama, Isla de Coiba, Archipelago de Perlas, northern and western Colombia, and north-western Venezuela.

INTRODUCED DISTRIBUTION
Introduced successfully in Tahiti.

GENERAL HABITS
Status: fairly common. *Habitat:* forest edges, open forest, brushlands, open woods, plantations and cultivated areas. *Gregariousness:* solitary, pairs or loose flocks of 3-6 birds. *Movements:* sedentary ? *Foods:* insects, berries and fruits. *Breeding:* probably all the year. *Nest:* large open cup nest in a thicket or bush. *Eggs:* 2.
Ridgely, 1976, p.320.
Meyer de Schauensee and Phelps, 1978, p.344.

NOTES ON INTRODUCTIONS
Tahiti. E. Guild reports that he liberated Crimson-backed Tanagers on Tahiti before 1940 (Guild, 1940). He indicated at this time that the species was breeding in the wild there soon after their release.

The Crimson-backed Tanager now occurs in small numbers in gardens of Punaauia, Paea and Taravao districts (Thibault and Rives, 1975). Evidently the species became established from Guild's introductions as there appear to be no other records of any releases.

DAMAGE
None known.

BLUE-GREY TANAGER
(Blue Tanager, Silver-blue Tanager)
Thraupis episcopus (Linnaeus) *(= T. virens)*

DISTINGUISHING CHARACTERISTICS
14-17.5 cm (5.6-7 in). 30-45 g (1.06-1.59 oz)
Mainly pale greyish blue, darker blue on back, wings and tail; shoulders purplish blue, violet or white (some white shouldered races have white wing bars); bill dark grey. Female: slightly tinged greenish.
Allen, 1962, pp.182-184, 240 and pl.91, pp.198-199.
Ridgely, 1976, p.319 and pl.28.

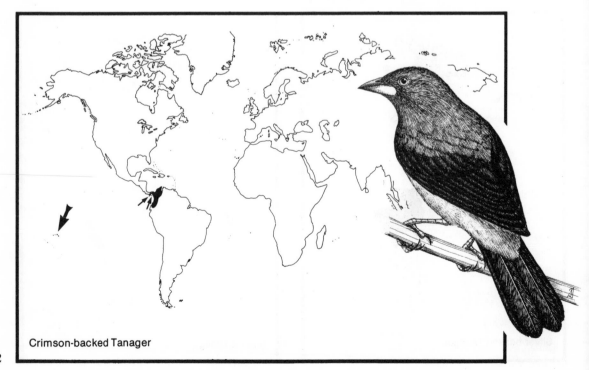

Crimson-backed Tanager

Blue-grey Tanager,
Thraupis episcopus

Meyer de Schauensee and Phelps, 1978, pp.342-343 and pl.37.

GENERAL DISTRIBUTION
Central and South America: southern Mexico south through Central America to Venezuela, Guyana, Surinam, Guyane, Brazil, Ecuador, north-western Peru and northern Bolivia; also Trinidad, Tobago and the Archipelago de Perlas.

INTRODUCED DISTRIBUTION
Introduced successfully in the USA (Florida) and probably in Peru (Lima). Introduced unsuccessfully in Tahiti.

GENERAL HABITS
Status: very common. *Habitat:* forest edges, woodland borders, brush, field edges, semi-open areas, plantations, parks, towns and cultivated areas. *Gregariousness:* pairs and loose flocks. *Movements:* sedentary. *Foods:* fruit, spiders, insects (caterpillars and their larvae), berries and nectar. *Breeding:* throughout the year (Surinam and Trinidad); 2 or more broods per year. *Nest:* deep open cup of plant material, moss and fibres, lined with roots and leaves, in a tree. *Eggs:* 1-3, 4.
Allen, 1962, pp.182-184, 240.

Snow and Snow, *Auk,* vol.88, 1971, pp.291-322.
Ffrench, 1973, pp.409-411.

NOTES ON INTRODUCTIONS
USA. The Blue-grey Tanager is established about Miami, Florida, as a result of birds escaping from aviaries (Gottschalk, 1967). They were recorded to be nesting in the Hollywood area in 1961-62 and were first noted there in about 1960 (Owre, 1973). A number were seen in the south Miami area in 1972.

Blue-grey Tanagers were still present in Dade County, Florida, in December 1975 (Heilbrun, 1976) so the species appears to have become permanently established in that area.
Peru. A few Blue-grey Tanagers are to be found around Lima where the species does not occur naturally. According to Plenge (pers. comm., 1977) they probably escaped from cages of birds brought in from Iquitos in the north.
Tahiti. Guild (1940) reported that he released Blue-grey Tanagers in about 1940 on Tahiti and that they had bred there in the wild. There are no subsequent records of the species on Tahiti.

DAMAGE
Ffrench (1976) mentions that on Trinidad Blue-grey Tanagers are known to feed on a number of commercially grown fruits or vegetables. They do not appear however, to cause any damage.

BLUE-HOODED EUPHONIA
(Mistletoe Bird)
Euphonia musica (Gmelin)

DISTINGUISHING CHARACTERISTICS
9.9-13.3 cm (3.96-5.32 in)
Crown and nape blue, with a reddish (or yellow) spot on forehead; upper parts and throat deep ultramarine (violet-blue); rump and underparts golden yellow (or yellow or varying to tawny yellow); bill black or greyish. (Note: Lesser Antillean males

Blue-grey Tanager

Blue-hooded Euphonia

tend to resemble the female.) Female: upper parts mainly olive or green; forehead rufous-chestnut (or yellow or yellowish); crown and nape blue; underparts yellowish olive.

Bond, 1971, pp.209-210 and pl. p.193.

Norgaard-Olesen, vol.1, 1973, pp.33-40.

Meyer de Schauensee and Phelps, 1978, p.338 and pl.36.

GENERAL DISTRIBUTION

Central and South America and the West Indies: north-western Mexico to southern Colombia, southern Ecuador, Venezuela, Surinam, Guyane, eastern Peru, eastern Bolivia, Paraguay, Brazil, Uruguay and northern Argentina; also Trinidad, Hispaniola, Gonave, Puerto Rico, and the Lesser Antilles (Saba, St Bartholomew, Barbuda, Antigua, Montserrat, Guadeloupe, Dominica, Martinique, St Lucia, St Vincent, Bequia and Grenada).

INTRODUCED DISTRIBUTION

Re-introduced unsuccessfully to Vieques Island, West Indies.

GENERAL HABITS

Status: fairly common. *Habitat:* open forest, woodland, open secondary growth, particularly areas with mistletoe, plantations and suburban areas. *Gregariousness:* often in pairs, and small flocks. *Movements:* possibly migratory. *Foods:* berries and fruits, especially the berries of mistletoe. *Breeding:* Mar-Apr (El Salvador); July (Trinidad). *Nest:* globular, of dried grass and moss, lined with fine fibres, with a side entrance, in a vine, palm or tree. *Eggs:* 2-4.

Bond, 1971, pp.209-210.

Ffrench, 1973, p.403.

NOTES ON INTRODUCTIONS

Vieques Island. An attempt was made to re-introduce the race *E.m. sclateri* to Vieques (just east of Puerto Rico) in 1910 by Mr Reed, a Presbyterian minister (Wetmore, 1916). Wetmore says that some forty birds were purchased in Ponce (Puerto Rico) and of these, twelve accidentally escaped on the playa at Port Mulas as the birds were being brought ashore and the others were kept in cages, but over some months escaped a few at a time. The birds apparently remained in the area for some time as three months later a flock of twelve were seen, but by 1916 had certainly all disappeared.

DAMAGE

None known.

GOLDEN TANAGER
(Black-eared Golden Tanager)
Tangara arthus Lesson

DISTINGUISHING CHARACTERISTICS

12.7-15 cm (5.08-6 in)

Generally golden yellow, mantle streaked black; lores, ear-coverts, wings and tail black; wing-coverts edged greenish gold to orange-yellow; underparts golden yellow (darker in some races and breast, sides and under tail-coverts chestnut); bill black.

Gilliard, 1958, p.358 and pl.198.

Meyer de Schauensee and Phelps, 1978, p.334 and pl.35.

GENERAL DISTRIBUTION

South America: Venezuela, Ecuador, Peru, Bolivia and Colombia.

Golden Tanager

INTRODUCED DISTRIBUTION

Introduced unsuccessfully in Tahiti.

GENERAL HABITS

Status: common. *Habitat:* forest and secondary growth. *Gregariousness:* solitary or in flocks up to 30 birds. *Movements:* no information. *Foods:* fruits, berries and insects. *Breeding, nest and eggs:* no information.

Meyer de Schauensee and Phelps, 1978, p.334.

NOTES ON INTRODUCTIONS

Tahiti. The race *T.a. aurulenta* was released by E. Guild (1938) on Tahiti. The species was reported by him to be returning to feed each day, but had not nested in the wild. There are no subsequent records for the Golden Tanager in Tahiti.

DAMAGE

None known.

MASKED TANAGER
(Mrs Wilson's Tanger, Golden Masked Tanager)
Tangara nigrocincta (Bonaparte)

DISTINGUISHING CHARACTERISTICS

11.8-14 cm (4.72-5.6 in)

Head mainly coppery golden buff (purplish blue bordered silvery blue in some races); upper back and breast band black; lower back, upper tail-coverts and rump turquoise or cornflower blue; abdomen white; sides purplish blue; facial mask and wings black edged blue; wings and tail black; bill black.

Norgaard-Olesen, vol.1, 1973, pp.136-141 and fig.3, pl.2.

Meyer de Schauensee and Phelps, 1978, p.335 and pl.35.

GENERAL DISTRIBUTION

Central and South America: from southern Mexico south to north-western Ecuador, southern Venezuela, Guyana, Peru, western Brazil, northern Bolivia and Colombia east of the Andes.

Masked Tanager

Red-legged Honeycreeper

INTRODUCED DISTRIBUTION
Introduced unsuccessfully in Tahiti.

GENERAL HABITS
Status: fairly common. *Habitat:* forest edges and clearings, plantations, open woodland and cultivated areas. *Gregariousness:* pairs or small flocks. *Movements:* no information. *Foods:* berries and other fruits, and possibly insects. *Breeding:* Apr-Nov. *Nest:* open cup-shaped in a tree or in a hole (?) in a tree. *Eggs:* 2.

Meyer de Schauensee and Phelps, 1978, p.335.

NOTES ON INTRODUCTIONS
Tahiti. Guild (1938) indicates that he released Masked Tanagers (probably *T.n. larvata*) on Tahiti and says that they were returning daily to feed, but had not as yet nested there. He later (1940) records that they were still present and breeding. There are no subsequent records of the Masked Tanager on Tahiti.

DAMAGE
None known.

RED-LEGGED HONEYCREEPER
(Yellow-winged Sugar-bird, Blue Honeycreeper)
Cyanerpes cyaneus (Linnaeus)

DISTINGUISHING CHARACTERISTICS
10-14 cm (4-5.6 in). 11.8-16 g (.42-.56 oz)
Forehead, mantle, wings, tail and under tail-coverts black; crown bright turquoise-blue; sides of head, nape, line around crown patch, lower back, scapulars, upper tail-coverts and undersurface purple-blue; bill curved, black. Female: upper parts grass green; throat and eyebrow stripe yellowish white; breast and sides dull grass-green; breast streaked yellowish; wings and tail dusky.

Bond, 1971, p.208 and pl. p.176.

Avon *et al,* 1974, pl. p.91.

Meyer de Schauensee and Phelps, 1978, p.331 and pl.34.

GENERAL DISTRIBUTION
Central and South America: from south-eastern Mexico to western Ecuador, northern Venezuela, Guyana, Surinam, Guyane, south to Bolivia and south-eastern Brazil; also Trinidad, Tobago and (?) Cuba.

INTRODUCED DISTRIBUTION
Probably introduced, successfully in Cuba in the West Indies. Introduced unsuccessfully in Tahiti.

GENERAL HABITS
Status: common. *Habitat:* forest edges, secondary growth, coastal areas, plantations, parks, towns and villages. *Gregariousness:* often in small loose flocks outside breeding season. *Movements:* nomadic, and possibly altitudinally migratory. *Foods:* spiders, insects, fruits, berries and nectar. *Breeding:* Mar-July. *Nest:* small flimsy cup of fibres, rootlets, grass or moss, lined with fibres and fastened with cobweb, in a tree. *Eggs:* 2.

Gooders, vol.8, 1969, pp.2529-2530.

Ffrench, 1973, pp.398-399.

NOTES ON INTRODUCTIONS
Cuba. According to Meyer de Schauensee (1964) the Red-legged Honeycreeper has probably been introduced to Cuba where it now occurs.

Tahiti. E. Guild (1938) records that he liberated Red-legged Honeycreepers in Tahiti in 1938. He later (1940) reports that they had bred in the wild there. There are no subsequent records for the species on Tahiti.

DAMAGE
None known.

Family: *Icteridae* Troupials, New World blackbirds

92 species in 25 genera; 9 species introduced, 6 successfully

Probably the most significant introduction in this family is that of the Shiny Cowbird. From the records available it appears that escapees were responsible for its establishment in Chile. However, they are a successful colonist and now occur in most of the Lesser Antilles and the Dominican Republic. The species is parasitic and is said to be affecting other blackbird and oriole populations on some islands.

Others of the family which have probably escaped or have escaped to become established include the Spotted-breasted Oriole in the United States (Florida) and the Common Troupial in Puerto Rico. This latter species also occurs from time to time as an escapee on a number of West Indian islands, but does not remain permanently established.

The Red-breasted Blackbird has colonised south-western Costa Rica recently, the Western Meadowlark has been successfully introduced into the Hawaiian Islands and the Carib Grackle has been introduced to Barbuda and Antigua.

INTRODUCTIONS OF ICTERIDAE

Species	Date introduced	Region	Manner introduced	Reason
(a) Successful introductions				
Spotted-breasted Oriole	about 1949	USA	escapee	cage bird ?
Common Troupial	?	Jamaica	?	?
	before 1878 ?	Puerto Rico ?	deliberate or escapee (perhaps native)	cage bird
	?	St Thomas, Virgin Islands	?	?
	1927-29	Itamaraca Island, Venezuela	deliberate or colonisation ?	?
Red-breasted Blackbird	about 1976	South-western Costa Rica	colonisation ?	?
Western Meadowlark	1931 and 1934	Hawaiian Islands	deliberate	?
Carib Grackle	1912-14	Barbuda, Lesser Antilles	?	?
	1912-14 ?	Antigua	?	?
Shiny Cowbird	about 1877 and later	Chile	deliberate or escapee ?	?
	1860s	Vieques Island, Puerto Rico		
	about 1899	The Grenadines	colonisation	—
	1901	Grenada	colonisation	—
	1916	Barbados	colonisation	—
	1924	St Vincent	colonisation	—
	1931	St Lucia	colonisation	—
	1934	St Croix	colonisation	—
	1948	Martinique, Lesser Antilles	colonisation	—
	1959	Marie-Galente, West Indies	colonisation	—
	1959	Antigua	colonisation	—
	1955	Puerto Rico	colonisation	—
	1971	Isla Mona	colonisation	—
	about 1972	Dominican Republic	colonisation	—
(b) Unsuccessful introductions				
Moriche Oriole	various times	Trinidad	escapee (or rare visitor) ?	cage bird ?
Common Troupial	?	St John, Virgin Islands	escapee ?	cage bird ?
	?	Antigua	escapee ?	cage bird ?
	?	Dominica, Lesser Antilles	escapee ?	cage bird ?
	?	Grenada, Lesser Antilles	escapee ?	cage bird ?
	1932 and 1964-66	Trinidad	escapee	cage bird
Yellow-hooded Blackbird	before 1975 ?	Peru	deliberate or escapee	cage bird ?
Red-breasted Blackbird	1885	Easter Islands	deliberate ?	?
Red-breasted Meadowlark	1931	Hawaiian Islands	deliberate	?
Carib Grackle	1912-14	St Kitts, Lesser Antilles ?	?	?

Not mentioned in the following text, the Red-winged Blackbird was imported into New Zealand in 1869, but it is not known if any were actually liberated in the wild. Also, the Moriche Oriole *(Icterus chrysocephalus)* is a rare resident on Trinidad where some of those noted may be escaped cage birds.

SPOTTED-BREASTED ORIOLE
(Spot-breasted Oriole)
Icterus pectoralis (Wagler)

DISTINGUISHING CHARACTERISTICS
20-24 cm (8-9.6 in)
Head orange; front of head, throat, mid-back and tail black; remainder mainly yellow-orange; breast spotted black on sides; wings black, base of primaries white, secondaries edged white; bill black with lower half of lower mandible blue-grey.
Reilly, 1968, p.441.
Peterson and Chalif, 1973, pp.223-224 and pl.41.

GENERAL DISTRIBUTION
Central America: from southern Mexico, southern Guatemala, El Salvador and Honduras to northern Nicaragua and north-western Costa Rica.

INTRODUCED DISTRIBUTION
Introduced successfully in southern Florida, USA.

GENERAL HABITS
Status: fairly common. *Habitat:* plantations, brush and scrublands, agricultural lands and villages. *Gregariousness:* no information. *Movements:* sedentary ? *Foods:* insects and fruit. *Breeding:* Sept (USA); 2 broods per year. *Nest:* flimsy woven cup or pendant structure of plant fibres, in a tree. *Eggs:* 3-5. Skutch, 1954, pp.274-275.
Reilly, 1968, p.441.

NOTES ON INTRODUCTIONS
USA. The Spotted-breasted Oriole was first found breeding in the United States by C. M. Brookfield and O. Griswold, along the Miami River in September 1949 (Gilliard, 1958). Gilliard records that they were probably introduced accidentally as cage bird escapees, and by 1956 had spread over an area of some forty-two kilometres (26 miles) in diameter.

The race *I.p. pectoralis* is now established in Palm Beach, Broward and Dade Counties of south-eastern Florida (Peters, 1968). It became established in about 1949 in suburban Miami where it was sold regularly as a cage bird. By 1961 they had reached Hypoloxo Islands, Broward County, in 1962 reached West Palm Beach, in 1968 they were some sixty-four

Spotted-breasted Oriole

Spotted-breasted Oriole, *Icterus pectoralis*

kilometres (40 miles) south of Miami, and are now appearing somewhat north of the Tropical Zone of Florida (Owre, 1973). Forty-seven birds were noted at Palm Beach in October 1975 (Edscorn, 1976) and some have been reported from as far south as Stuart (Heilbrun, 1976).

DAMAGE
None known.

COMMON TROUPIAL
(Troupial, Common Hangnest)
Icterus icterus (Linnaeus)

DISTINGUISHING CHARACTERISTICS
22.5-27.5 cm (9-11 in)
Generally black and orange, with much white on wings; black bib extending to upper breast, a broad orange-yellow band across hindneck (back all orange in some races); bare skin around eye blue; rump and upper tail-coverts orange-yellow; wings and tail black, shoulders yellow; underparts orange or yellow-orange; bill black, base blue-grey.
Allen, 1962, pp.178, 239 and pl.87, p.195.
Bond, 1971, p.220 and pl. p.224.
Meyer de Schauensee and Phelps, 1978, pp.312-313 and pl.38.

GENERAL DISTRIBUTION
South America and West Indies: from northern and eastern Colombia, Venezuela, west to eastern Peru, Ecuador, northern Bolivia and south to eastern Bolivia and south-western Brazil; also Aruba, Curaçao and Margarita Island.

INTRODUCED DISTRIBUTION
Introduced successfully in Jamaica (now extinct), Puerto Rico and St Thomas in the West Indies, and possibly to the island of Itamaracá, Venezuela (colonisation ?); also in (?) Trinidad, St John, Antigua, Dominica and Grenada where they are probably only escapees from aviaries.

Common Troupial

Status: common. *Habitat:* forest, secondary growth, semi-arid woodlands, mangrove swamps, pastures and watercourses. *Gregariousness:* solitary or pairs. *Movements:* sedentary, but move somewhat locally. *Foods:* fruits, berries, spiders, roaches, termites, bugs, caterpillars and maggots. *Breeding:* no information. *Nest:* loosely woven, deep purse-shaped pendant structure of plant material such as bark, leaves, wool and moss, with a side entrance, in a tree. *Eggs:* no information.

Allen, 1962, pp.178, 239.

Bond, 1971, p.220.

Meyer de Schauensee and Phelps, 1978, pp.312-313.

NOTES ON INTRODUCTIONS

West Indies. The race *I.i. icterus* (Herklots, 1961) has been introduced and established on Jamaica, Puerto Rico and St Thomas (including Water Island), probably from Curaçao (Bond, 1960; Herklots, 1961; Allen, 1962; Meyer de Schauensee, 1970). Both Bond and Allen record that the species has been reported from other islands including St John, Antigua, Dominica and Grenada (escaped cage birds?).

Peters (1968) records that the race *I.i. ridgwayi* is established on Puerto Rico and St Thomas and not *icterus* as Herklots suggests. Bowdish (1903) found it a popular cage bird there in the early 1900s which was said to occur in the wild in some localities. He apparently saw none and makes no mention of any introduction.

Allen says that on Puerto Rico the Common Troupial is an uncommon local resident, possibly introduced many years ago, although it may be a native to the island. Blake (pers. comm., 1977) informs me that it is still a common cage bird, hence may have become established from escapees. He indicates that they are probably scarce wherever they have been introduced in the West Indies. Wetmore (1927) records that Gundlach found them established and breeding on Puerto Rico in about 1878 at Quebradillas. Lack (1976) reports that they were at one time partly naturalised on Jamaica, but are now extinct on that island.

Venezuela. According to Sick (1968) the presence of *I.i. jamacaii* on the island of Itamaracá, Pernambuco is accepted by most as an unnatural occurrence. Whether it was introduced or colonised the island from Venezuela does not appear to be known for certain, but it arrived there between 1927 and 1929.

Trinidad. A number of Common Troupials were seen on Trinidad in suburban areas between 1964 and 1966. Ffrench (1976) says that those seen were probably escapees as the species is a popular cage bird on the island. Some individuals were also seen in 1932, but these may have been visitors from the mainland.

DAMAGE

None known.

YELLOW-HOODED BLACKBIRD
(Yellow-headed Marshbird)
Agelaius icterocephalus (Linnaeus)

DISTINGUISHING CHARACTERISTICS

16.5-21 cm (6.6-8.4 in). 24-40 g (.85-1.41 oz)

Head, neck and upper breast bright yellow; eyebrow and throat dull yellow; lores black; remainder glossy black; bill black. Female: olive; back, wings and tail brown; back streaked dusky; underparts greyish brown (but vary in intensity of colour), shaded with olive-yellow.

Ffrench, 1973, pp.377-378 and portr.6, foll. p.144.

Meyer de Schauensee and Phelps, 1978, pp.311-312 and pl.38.

GENERAL DISTRIBUTION

South America: northern and eastern Colombia,

Yellow-hooded Blackbird

Red-breasted Blackbird

north-eastern Venezuela, Guyana, Surinam, Guyane, and northern Brazil, west to north-eastern Peru; also Trinidad.

INTRODUCED DISTRIBUTION

Introduced around Lima, Peru, but may now have died out.

GENERAL HABITS

Status: common. *Habitat:* brushland, grassy swamps, rice fields and bushy river banks. *Gregariousness:* in flocks, especially at the roost or nest. *Movements:* no information, probably sedentary. *Foods:* insects; also seeds especially rice. *Breeding:* May-Nov (Trinidad); colonial. *Nest:* deep cup of reeds or grasses in reeds or grass near shore or in shallow water, occasionally in trees or mangroves. *Eggs:* 3-4.

Ffrench, 1978, pp.377-378.

NOTES ON INTRODUCTIONS

Peru. Caged Yellow-hooded Blackbirds were brought in from Iquitos or Pucallpa and probably escaped or were released in Lima where they became established in a marsh (Laguna de Villa) south of that city (Plenge, pers. comm., 1977). Plenge says that the population has not exceeded fifty individuals in the past. He has been unable to sight the birds since 1975 and they have now probably died out.

DAMAGE

None known.

RED-BREASTED BLACKBIRD
(White-browed Blackbird, Red-breasted Marshbird)

Leistes militaris (Linnaeus)

DISTINGUISHING CHARACTERISTICS

17.5-19 cm (7-7.6 in). 38.5-51 g (1.36-1.8 oz)
Mainly black; throat, breast, upper belly and inner wing-coverts crimson; remainder black, with feathers broadly edged sandy brown (non-breeding season).

Female: crown dark brown; central streak and eyebrow buff; upper parts streaked sandy brown and blackish; underparts buff, stained crimson on breast and streaked dusky at sides.

Gooders, vol.8, 1969, pp.2592 and pl. p.2592.
Ridgely, 1976, p.312 and pl.26.
Meyer de Schauensee and Phelps, 1978, p.314 and pl.38.

GENERAL DISTRIBUTION

South America: the Pacific slope of Panama, northern and eastern Colombia, Venezuela to Brazil, eastern Peru and Bolivia, south to Paraguay, Uruguay and northern Argentina; also Trinidad.

INTRODUCED DISTRIBUTION

Recently extended range into south-western Costa Rica. Introduced successfully on the Easter Islands, Pacific Ocean, but has now died out.

GENERAL HABITS

Status: common. *Habitat:* forest, secondary growth, grassy plains, marshes, swamps and ricefields. *Gregariousness:* loose flocks, or several birds together in the one area. *Movements:* sedentary ? *Foods:* seeds, insects and rice. *Breeding:* Mar-Dec (Trinidad); Jan-Nov (Surinam); males polygamous (?). *Nest:* deep open cup of grass, lined with finer grass, on the ground in swamp vegetation. *Eggs:* 2-4.

Gooders, vol.8, 1969, p.2592.
Ffrench, 1973, pp.381-382.
Meyer de Schauensee and Phelps, 1978, p.314.

NOTES ON INTRODUCTIONS

Easter Islands. The Red-breasted Blackbird was introduced to the Easter Islands in 1885, became established there, but was last seen in 1942 (Johnson, Millie and Moffett, 1970).

Costa Rica. There has apparently been some recent extension of range northwards for the Red-breasted Blackbird in Central America. Ridgely (1976) mentions that the species is now present in south-western Costa Rica to which it has only recently spread.

DAMAGE
None known.

RED-BREASTED MEADOWLARK
(Greater Red-breasted Meadowlark, Long-tailed Meadowlark, Military Starling)
Pezites militaris (Linnaeus)
(= *Sturnella loyca vide* Short, 1968, *Am. Mus. Nov.* no.2349.)

DISTINGUISHING CHARACTERISTICS
20-28.7 cm (8-11.48 in)
Upper parts brownish grey with black markings; throat, mid-neck, breast and upper abdomen scarlet; line in front of eye red and line behind eye white; bend of wing red; flanks blackish with grey edges; cheeks and sides of neck blackish; bill horn. Female: line in front of eye and throat white; upper breast greyish speckled black; lower breast and abdomen rose-tinted.
Johnson, vol.2, 1967, pp.336-338 and pl. p.336.

GENERAL DISTRIBUTION
South America: from Ecuador, north-eastern Peru, south-eastern Brazil, Uruguay and north-eastern Argentina to Tierra del Fuego and the Falkland Islands.

INTRODUCED DISTRIBUTION
Introduced unsuccessfully in the Hawaiian Islands.

GENERAL HABITS
Status: fairly common. *Habitat:* pastures,

Red-breasted Meadowlark

grasslands, farmlands, plantations, irrigated fields and damp meadows. *Gregariousness:* loose flocks in winter. *Movements:* some populations tend to move north in winter. *Foods:* seeds, bulbs, insects and their larvae and small crustaceans. *Breeding:* Sept-Jan; occasionally 2 broods per season. *Nest:* semi-domed grass nest, interwoven with grass and stems and lined with grass, on the ground. *Eggs:* 3-4.
Johnson, vol.2, 1967, pp.336-338.

NOTES ON INTRODUCTIONS
Hawaiian Islands. The Red-breasted Meadowlark was introduced from Washington to the island of Kauai in 1931 (Munro, 1960). Munro records that some birds were seen there in 1936. The species is not now established in the Hawaiian Islands (Munro, 1960; Berger, 1972).

DAMAGE
In the Falkland Islands, the Red-breasted Meadowlark tends to gather in flocks in winter and have been accused, in recent years, of scratching to potatoes near the surface and pecking at them (Cawkell and Hamilton, 1961).

WESTERN MEADOWLARK
Sturnella neglecta Audubon

DISTINGUISHING CHARACTERISTICS
20-25 cm (8-10 in). 99-112 g (3.49-3.95 oz)
Crown stripe buff, bordered by a blackish stripe; pale stripe over eye from bill yellowish, remainder of sides of head greyish white except for black line extending back from eye; sides, flanks and under tail-coverts buffy white spotted black; back brown, streaked with black, buff and white; abdomen, breast and throat bright yellow, with a black V on breast; wings barred with black and brown, and bend of wing yellow; outer tail-feathers white, remainder brownish grey barred black.
Roberts, 1960, pl.73.
Godfrey, 1966, pp.353-354 and pl.61, no.8, opp. p.300.
Reilly, 1968, p.437.

GENERAL DISTRIBUTION
North America: from central British Columbia east to central Saskatchewan, southern Manitoba and Ontario, south to southern California, north-western Baja California, south-central Texas and central Mexico. Winters in breeding range, except northern parts, south to southern Baja California, southern Mexico, Louisiana and Mississippi.

INTRODUCED DISTRIBUTION
Introduced successfully in the Hawaiian Islands. Possibly introduced, unsuccessfully to New Zealand.

GENERAL HABITS
Status: common. *Habitat:* open fields, meadows, plains and prairies. *Gregariousness:* flocks. *Movements:* partially migratory. *Foods:* mainly insects including grasshoppers, beetles, crickets and caterpillars; also seeds and grains. *Breeding:* Apr-Aug; polygamous; 2 broods per season. *Nest:* a scrape on the ground in grass, partly domed and cup-shaped, of grass lined with finer material. *Eggs:* 3-7 (Hawaii).
Godfrey, 1966, pp.353-354.
Reilly, 1968, p.437.

NOTES ON INTRODUCTIONS
Hawaiian Islands. The Western Meadowlark was

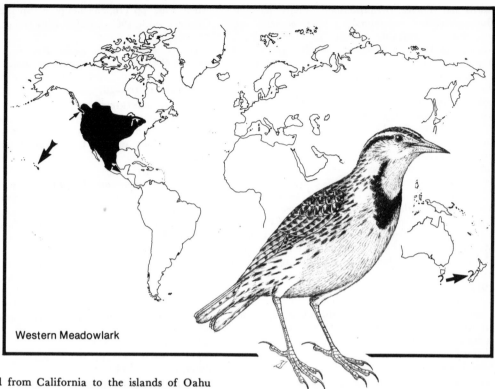

Western Meadowlark

introduced from California to the islands of Oahu and Kauai in 1931, to Niihau in 1934, and also to Maui at about the same time (Munro, 1960). Munro records that they became established only on Kauai although a single bird was reported from Molokai in 1936.

Although they appear to be still well established on Kauai and fairly common, they are highly localised and occur mainly in fields near Lihue, Kokaha, Kapaa, Kilauea and Hanalei (Peterson, 1961; Berger, 1972; Hawaiian Audubon Society, 1975; Heilbrun, 1976).

New Zealand. Western Meadowlarks were imported into New Zealand in 1869, but it is not known if any were liberated there (Thomson, 1922).

DAMAGE
None known.

CARIB GRACKLE
(Lesser Antilean Grackle)
Quiscalus lugubris Swainson

DISTINGUISHING CHARACTERISTICS
20-27.5 cm (8-11 in). 49-78 g (1.73-2.75 oz)
Generally shiny purple-black; wings and fan-shaped tail greenish black or bluish green; bill, decurved, black. Female: uniformly brownish black (or greyish above and lighter below).
Allen, 1962, pp.174-175, 238 and pl.84, p.191.
Meyer de Schauensee and Phelps, 1978, p.311 and pl.18.

GENERAL DISTRIBUTION
South America and West Indies: in South America from northern Venezuela, Guyana, Surinam and Guyane to eastern Colombia and extreme north-eastern Brazil; on the West Indies and Caribbean islands of Monserrat, Guadeloupe, Marie-Galente, Dominica, Martinique, St Lucia, St Vincent, Grenada, Grenadines, Barbados, Trinidad, Los Testigos, Los Hermanos, Margarita and Los Frailes Islands (Venezuela).

INTRODUCED DISTRIBUTION
Introduced successfully on Barbuda, Antigua, (?) St Kitts and St Martin in the West Indies. Possibly introduced, successfully on Tobago.

GENERAL HABITS
Status: fairly common. *Habitat:* open country, coastal marshes, mangroves, ricefields, gardens,

Carib Grackle

491

towns and villages. *Gregariousness:* singly, pairs or flocks; roost communally. *Movements:* no information, probably sedentary. *Foods:* fruit, insects, spiders, earthworms, lizards, grain and human's food scraps. *Breeding:* May-Feb (Trinidad), Apr-Aug (Surinam); often in colonies (up to 10 nests). *Nest:* deep, cup-shaped of grass, coarse plants and mud, lined with fine grass, in a bush, tree or palm. *Eggs:* 2, 3-5.

Allen, 1962, pp.174-175, 238.

Bond, 1971, pp.215-216.

Ffrench, 1973, pp.375-377.

NOTES ON INTRODUCTIONS

West Indies. Peters (1968) records that the race *Q.i. fortirostris* was successfully introduced, between 1912 and 1914 on Barbuda, Antigua, and possibly to St Kitts, probably from Barbados. Blake (1975) also mentions that the species has been introduced on St Martin but gives no other details. The species may also have been introduced to Tobago from Trinidad in about 1905, where it is now common (Ffrench, 1973).

Holland and Williams (1978) indicate that Danforth (1934, *Auk,* p.41) recorded Carib Grackles on Antigua in 1934 and that the species is now a common resident of the island.

DAMAGE

None known.

SHINY COWBIRD

(Argentine Thrush, Glossy Cowbird, Common Cowbird)

Molothrus bonariensis (Gmelin)

DISTINGUISHING CHARACTERISTICS

17.5-22 cm (7-8.8 in). 28-41.5 g (.99-1.46 oz)

All black, with a metallic bluish sheen; wings and tail glossed green; bill black. Female: greyish brown, paler on the underparts; wings and tail brown.

Allen, 1962, pp.176, 238 and pl.85, pp.192-193.

Gooders, vol.8, 1969, pp.2600-2601 and pl. p.2601.

GENERAL DISTRIBUTION

South America: from eastern Panama, Colombia, western Peru, northern Venezuela, south to eastern Bolivia, Paraguay and northern Argentina; also Trinidad and Tobago.

INTRODUCED DISTRIBUTION

Introduced successfully in Chile; colonised and/or introduced to many islands in the Lesser Antilles and in Puerto Rico and the Dominican Republic, West Indies.

GENERAL HABITS

Status: very common. *Habitat:* forest, secondary growth, open fields, pasture and cultivated areas, suburban areas, riverbeds and swampy areas. *Gregariousness:* pairs and flocks 20-40, large flocks at the end of summer; roost in flocks which may number hundreds. *Movements:* migratory or partially migratory. *Foods:* seeds, grains and insects. *Breeding:* May-Jan; polygamous; parasitic. *Nest:* uses other birds' nests. *Eggs:* 3 or more, probably 4-5 per season, usually 1 in each of several nests; often several females lay in same nest and up to 14 eggs recorded.

Allen, 1962, pp.176, 238.

Gooders, vol.8, 1969, pp.2600-2601.

Bond, 1971, pp.214-215.

NOTES ON INTRODUCTIONS

Chile. The race *M.b. bonariensis* has been introduced and established in Chile (Peters, 1968). It is not definitely known how the species arrived, but it may have been the results of colonisation from Argentina or as Hellmayr (1932) suggests, from escaped or liberated caged birds. Friedman (1929) doubts that the species would have crossed the Andes without aid.

Johnson (1967) says that they are now very common and are established from Atacama (Copiapó

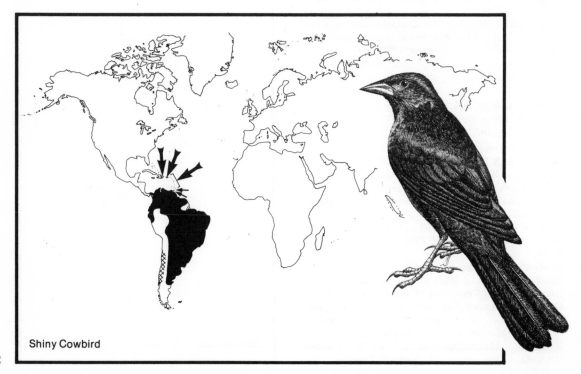

Shiny Cowbird

Valley) in the north to Aysen in the south. Hellmayr records that few were noted in Chile prior to 1877, when they were rarely found. However, by 1910-12 considerable flocks were observed near Machalí.

Friedman says that between 1906 and 1914 large numbers were imported to Chile as cage birds.

West Indies. The Shiny Cowbird has been extending its range in the West Indies probably since the 1860s when it was first recorded on Vieques Island, ten kilometres (6 miles) west of Puerto Rico by Newton. Further birds were found on Carriacou in the Grenadines in 1899 (Post and Wiley 1976 and 1977).

According to Post and Wiley it seems that the species has spread to other islands from these centres, as there are no birds between Antigua and St Croix, a distance of some 300 kilometres (186 miles). They contend that the expansion of the race *M. b. minimus,* has been aided by man in the area as it is a favourite cage bird. In the Lesser Antilles following the finding of birds in the Grenadines, the Shiny Cowbird is recorded from Grenada in 1901, Barbados in 1916, St Vincent in 1924, St Lucia in 1931, Martinique in 1948 and Marie-Galente and Antigua in 1959. However, none were noted on Antigua between 1972 and 1977 by Holland and Williams (1978). Following the collecting of the specimen on Vieques in 1860 no further birds appear to have been seen until some were noted on St Croix in 1934. Further birds are recorded from St John and Cabeza de San Juan, Puerto Rico, in 1955 (Robertson, 1962), in western Puerto Rico in 1965 and 1969, and on Isla Mona in 1971.

Dod (pers. comm., 1977) reports that they reached the Dominican Republic in 1972, although she says that they were so well established at this time that it is more than likely that they had been there for some considerable period. They are now well established on the east and northern coasts as well as around the capital, Santo Domingo, and are still spreading. In Puerto Rico they now outnumber the indigenous Yellow-shouldered Blackbird *(Agelaius xanthomus).*

DAMAGE

Colonisation of Puerto Rico by the Shiny Cowbird is said to have been a crucial factor in the decline of the Yellow-shouldered Blackbird *(A. xanthomus).* It is parasitised by the Cowbird which has increased and spread phenomenally (Post and Wiley, 1976). A recent study (Post and Wiley, 1977) of reproduction over one breeding season and survival data collected over a three-year period indicates that the blackbird may not be maintaining itself on Puerto Rico, due in part to Cowbird brood parasitism.

In the Dominican Republic it is thought to parasitise the Black-crowned Oriole *(Icterus dominicanus),* but few observations have yet been made (Dod, pers. comm., 1977).

BIBLIOGRAPHY

Abbott, I. (1974), 'The Avifauna of Kangaroo Island and Causes of its Impoverishment,' *Emu* 74 (3) :124-34.

Abbott, W. L. (1894), 'Notes on the Natural History of Aldabra, Assumption and Glorioso Islands, Indian Ocean,' *Proc. U.S. natn. Mus.* 16 :759-64.

Abdulali, H. (1967), 'Birds of the Nicobar Islands, with Notes on Some Andaman Birds,' *J. Bombay nat. Hist. Soc.* 64 (2) :139-90.

Adney, E. T. (1886), 'Naturalization of the European Goldfinch in New York City and Vicinity,' *Auk* 3 (3) :409-10.

Ainslie, D. (1907), The Little Owl in Bedfordshire, *Zoologist* : 353.

Alcorn, J. R. and Richardson, F. (1951), 'The Chukar Partridge in Nevada,' *J. Wildl. Mgmt.* 15 :265-75.

Aldrich, J. W. (1947), 'The Hungarian and Chukar Partridges in America,' *U.S. Dep. Interior Wildl. Serv., Wildl. Leafl.* (292) :1-10.

Alexander, B. (1898), 'An Ornithological Expedition to the Cape Verde Islands,' *Ibis* (7 Ser.) 4 (13) :74-118.

— (1898), 'Further Notes on the Ornithology of the Cape Verde Islands,' *Ibis* (7 Ser.) 4 (14) :277-85.

Alexander, W. B. (1958), 'The Spread of the Sparrow,' *Emu* 58 :335.

Alford, C. E. (1928), 'Field Notes on the Birds of Vancouver Island,' *Ibis* 4 (12 Ser.) (2) :181.

Ali, S. (1944), *The Book of Indian Birds,* 3rd Edn, Natural History Society, Bombay.

— (1953), *The Birds of Travancore and Cochin,* Oxford University Press, London.

— (1962), *The Birds of Sikkim,* Oxford University Press, London.

Ali, S. and Futehally, L. (1967), *Common Birds,* National Book Trust, New Delhi.

Ali, S. and Ripley, S. D. (1968-1974), *Handbook of the Birds of India and Pakistan,* Vols 1-10, Oxford University Press, Bombay and London.

Aliev, F. F. and Khanmamedov, A. I. (1963), 'The Results and Prospectus of Acclimatising Birds in the Transcaucasus', *Akad. Nauk. Kirgiz.*

—— (1966), 'Results of Prospectus of the Acclimatization of Birds in Transcaucasia,' in A. I. Yanushevich (ed) *Acclimatization of Animals in the USSR,* Proc. Conf. Acclim. Anims. USSR held Frunze, May 10-15, 1963, Israel Programme for Scientific Translations, Jerusalem, pp.33-34.

Allan, P. S. (1939), 'Starlings in New Mexico,' *Auk,* 56 :477-78.

Allard, H. A. (1940), 'The Starlings Family Life and Behaviour,' *J. Wash. Acad. Sci.* 30 :34-36.

Allen, A. A. (1946), 'Management Program Controls Starlings,' *N.Y. St. Exp. Stn., Farm. Res.* 12 (4) :1-2.

Allen, D. L. (1954), *Our Wildlife Legacy,* Funk and Wagnall, New York.

— (1956), *Pheasants in North America,* Stackpole, Pennsylvania and Wildlife Management Institute, Washington.

— (1962), *Pheasants Afield: The Pheasant in North America — History, Habits and Future,* 1953, Stackpole, Pennsylvania; 1962, Collier, New York.

Allen, G. M. (1962), *Birds and Their Attributes,* 1st Print., 1926; Repr. 1962. Dover Publications, New York.

Allen, R. P. (1956), Flamingoes: Their Life History and Survival. *Nat. Aud. Soc. New York, Res. Rep.* (5) :1-285.

— (1962), *Birds of the Carribean,* Thames and Hudson, London.

Almquist, R. (1972), 'Kanadágasen i Norrbotten,' *Svensk jakt* 110 :78-81.

Alvarez del Toro, M. (1950), 'English Sparrow in the Chiapas', *Condor* 52 :166.

Amadon, D. (1942), 'Birds Collected During the Whitney South Sea Expedition: Notes on some Non-Passerine Genera,' *Am. Mus. Novit.* (1176) :1-21.

American Ornithologists Union Committee (1957), *Checklist of the Birds of North America,* 5th Edn, American Ornithologists Union, Baltimore.

Ammann, G. A. (1951), 'Results of Sharptailed Grouse Plantings in Michigan', *13th Midwest Wildl. Conf. Minneapolis, Dec. 12-14, 1951,* 1-6.

Ammann, G. A. and Palmer, W. L. (1958), 'Ruffed Grouse Introductions on Michigan Islands,' *J. Wildl. Mgmt.* 22 (3) :322-25.

Anderson, R. M. (1934), 'Effects of the Introduction of Exotic Animal Forms,' in *Proc. 5 Pac. Sci. Congr., Vic and Vanc., B.C., 1933:* University Toronto Press, pp.769-78.

Anderson, T. R. (1977), 'Population Studies of European Sparrows in North America,' *Occ. Pap. Mus. nat. Hist., Univ. Kansas* (70).

Anderson, W. (1968), 'Experimental Release of Pheasants in Warbash County, Illinois,' *Trans. Ill. St. Acad. Sci.* 61 (4) :367-75.

Anderson, W. L. (1964), 'Survival and Reproduction of Pheasants Released in Illinois,' *J. Wildl. Mgmt.* 28 (2) :254-64.

—— (1969), 'Condition Parameters and Organ Measurements of Pheasants from Good, Fair and Poor Range in Illinois,' *J. Wildl. Mgmt.* 33 (4) :979-87.

Anderson, W. L. and Stewart, P. L. (1969), 'Relationship Between Inorganic Ions and the Distribution of Pheasants in Illinois,' *J. Wildl. Mgmt.* 33 (2) :254-70.

André, F. (1969), 'Försöksjakt pa Kanadagäss,' *Jaktsignalen* 26 (4) :18-19.

Andreev, A. V. (1975), 'Winter Life and Feeding of *Lagopus mutus* in North-eastern USSR,' *Zoologicheskii zhurnal* (Russian with English Summary) 54 :727-33.

Andrew, J. (1890), 'Remarks on a Recent Proposal to Introduce Ostriches into Tasmania,' *Proc. R. Soc., Tas.* :176-84.

Andrle, R. F. and Axtell, H. H. (1961), 'Cattle Egrets in Mexico,' *Wilson Bull.* 73 :280.

Anon. (1890), 'Chinese Pheasants in America,' *Forest and Stream* 35 :28.

— (1898), 'General Notes,' *Prod. Gaz. and Settl. Rec., West Aust.* 5 (1) :17.

— (1898), 'Destructive Birds: Prohibition of Starlings,' *Prod. Gaz. and Settl. Rec., West Aust.* 5 (1) :28.

— (1933), 'Tick and Blowfly Problems — Suggested Use of the Cattle Egret Bird (*Bubulcus cormandus),' J. Coun. Scient. ind. Res. Aust.* 6 (3) :213.

— (1936), 'Chukar Partridge — New Success in State,' *Calif. Conserv.* 1 (11) :10-11.

— (1942), 'Should We Introduce Exotic Game Birds?,' *Wild. Conserv.* 6 (7) :3, 15.

— (1944), 'The Chukar Partridge in Wisconsin,' *Passenger Pigeon* 6 (2) :41-42.

— (1946), 'White Swans,' *N.Z. Bird Notes* 2 (1) :16.

— (1946), 'Breeding Habits of Starlings,' *N.Z. Bird Notes* 2 (1) :8-10.

— (1947), 'Introduced Upland Game Birds in North Dakota,' *N. Dak. Outdoors* 9 (7) :11-12.

— (1947), 'How have the Turkey's Fared,' *Wyo. Wild.* 11 (10) :4-12, 39.

— (1948), 'Flinders Chase. Kangaroo Island,' *S. Aust. Orn.* 18 :76-77.

— (1956), 'Senor Red Legs: Latest Utah Emigrant,' *Utah Fish Game Bull.* 12 (2) :2-3.

— (1956), 'New Partridges Non-competitive,' *Tex. Game Fish* 14 (7) :23.

— (1956), 'The Reeves Pheasant in Ohio,' *Ohio Div. Wildl. Game Surv. News* 3 (1) :1-4.

— (1958), 'California Introduces the Barbary Partridge,' *Mod. Game Breeding* 28 (5) :9-10.

— (1958), 'Birds of Central Pennsylvania,' *Pa. Univ. St. Coll. Agric. Bull.* (632) , June.

— (1959), 'The Pheasant in Connecticut: Asset or Liability?', *Conn. Wildl. Conserv. Bull.* 5 (1) :1, 5-7.

— (1959), 'Fazany v Podmoskov'e' (Pheasants in the Moscow Vicinity),' *Okhota Okhotn. Khoz.* 6 :56 (In Russian).

— (1962), 'Notes on Introductions and Escapees,' *Camb. Bird Club* (35) :1-48.

— (1963), 'Parakeet City — A Tourist Attraction,' *Fla. Nat.* 36 :18.

— (1964), 'Sorghum in Queensland,' *Qd. agric. J.* 90 :5-18.

— (1964), 'Federal Aid in Fish and Wildlife Restoration,' *Ann. Rep. on D-J and P-R Progs. for Yr. ending 30th June, 1963.* Wildl. Mgmt. Inst. Sport Fish Inst., Washington, D.C. 1-80.

—— (1965), 'Crested Bronze-winged Dove in Europe,' *Aust. Avicult.* 1965.

— (1969), 'Indian Mynas in Canberra,' *Çanb. Bird Notes* 5 :3-4.

— (1977), 'A New Bird,' (R.A.O.U., Melb.), *Atlas Newsl.* (4) :4.

Anonymous (1962), 'The Foreign Game Introduction Program,' *Mod. Game Breeding* 32 (5) :12-13.

— (1963), 'Data on the Acclimatisation and Hybridisation of Wild Ungulates and Birds,' *Gossel' Khozizdat; Kiev* :1-135. (In Russian).

— (1967), 'Man versus Bird,' *Annals* :5-6, Feb, 1967.

— (1974), 'Parakeets Run Wild in S.E. England,' *New Scientist* :119, July, 1974.

— (1975), 'Cage Birds in Great Britain,' in *Proc. 12th int. Un. Game Biol.*

Arinkina, T. and Kolesnikov, I. (1927), 'Dalneyshi nablyudeniya nad biologii vorodya i nad prinosimin im vredom' (Further Observations on Biology of Sparrows and the Damage they Incur), *Byull. Sredne-aziatskago Gosudar stvenago Universiteta* 16 :255-72 (in Russian).

Armour, C. J. (1963), 'The Use of Repellents for Preventing Mammal and Bird Damage to Trees and Seed: A Revision,' *For. Abstr.* 24 (4) :27-38.

Armstrong, J. S. (1932), *Handlist to the Birds of Samoa,* Bale and Sons, Danielsson, London.

Arthofer, R. (1974), 'Occurrence of Damage and Control of *Sturnus vulgaris* in the Grapevine Industry of Burgenland, Austria,' *Pflanzenschutz Berichte* (44) (1-4) :35-61.

Ashby, E. (1919), 'Introduction of Birds,' *Emu* 19 (1) :1-73.

Ashford, R. W. (1978), 'First Record of the House Sparrow for Papua New Guinea,' *Emu* 78 (1) :36.

Ashman, P. and Pyle, P. (1979), 'First Records of Lavender Fire-Finch on Hawaii,' *Elepaio* 40 (1) :12.

Ashmole, M. J. (1963), *Guide to the Birds of Samoa,* Pacif. Sci. Info. Centre, Bernice P. Bishop Mus., Honolulu, Hawaii :1-22.

Association of Applied Biology (1974), 'Bird Damage to Crops and the Background to Control,' *Ann. appl. Biol.* 76 :325-66.

Astle, N. L. (1940), 'Starlings Injure Cattle,' *Vet. Med.* 36 :235.

Atkinson, I. A. E. and Bell, B. D. (1973), 'Offshore and Outlying Islands,' in *Natural History of New Zealand: An Ecological Survey* 15 :372-92, Reed, Wellington.

Atkinson, L. L. (1958), 'European Starlings,' *Calif. Dep. Agric. Bull.* 47 :208.

Au, S. and Swedberg, G. (1966), 'A Progress

Report on the Introduction of the Barn Owl *(Tyto alba pratincola)* to the Island of Kauai,' *Elepaio* 26 : 58-60.

Austin, O. L. (1963), 'On the American Status of *Tiaris canora* and *Carduelis carduelis,'* *Auk* 80 (1) : 73-74.

—— (1968), (Ed) 'A. C. Bents Life Histories of North American Cardinals, Grosbeaks, Buntings, Towhees, Finches, Sparrow and Allies,' *Smithson, Inst., U.S. natn. Mus. Bull.* (237), Pts. 1-3.

Australian Fauna Authority (1963), *Proceedings of the Australian Fauna Authorities Conference, Hobart, 3-7 Sept., 1962,* Animals and Birds Protection Board, Hobart.

Avetisyan, O. R. (1964), 'Harmfulness of Sparrows in Armenia,' *Izv. Akad. Nauk. Armyan S.S.R. Biol. Nauk.* 17 (12) : 55-64 (In Russian).

Avon, D. and Tilford, T. (1974), *Birds of Britain and Europe in Colour,* Blandford Press, London.

Bach, R. N. (1946), 'The Status of the Pheasant and Hungarian Partridge in North Dakota,' *N. Dak. Outdoors* 9 (4) : 3-4.

Bachus, G. J. (1967), 'Changes in the Avifauna of Fanning Island, Central Pacific Between 1924 and 1963,' *Condor* 69 : 207-09.

Bade, A. (1935), 'Mr Chukar — Now a Naturalized Californian,' *Game Breeder and Sportsman* 39 (5) : 118, 143.

—— (1937), 'The Chukar Partridge in California,' *Calif. Fish Game* 23 (3) : 233-36.

—— (1937), 'The Chukar Partridge in California,' *Trans. N. Am. Wildl. Conf.* 2 : 485-89.

Bailey, A. M. (1942), 'A Starling Roost in the Chicago Area,' *Wilson Bull.* 44 : 40-41.

—— (1956), 'Birds of the Midway and Laysan Islands,' *Denver Mus. Pict.* (12).

Bailey, W. and Rinell, K. T. (1967), 'Management of the Eastern Turkey in the Northern Hardwoods,' in O. H. Hewitt (ed) *The Wild Turkey and its Management,* Wildlife Society, Washington, D.C., 261-302.

Baker, E. C. S. (1922), *The Fauna of British India, including Ceylon and Burma,* vol.1, 2nd Edn, Taylor and Francis, London.

Baker, H. G. and Stebbins, G. L. (1965), 'The Genetics of Colonizing Species,' *Proc. 1st Int. Un. Biol. Sci., Symp. on Gen. Biol,* Academic Press, New York.

Baker, R. H. (1951), 'The Avifauna of Micronesia, its Origin, Evolution and Distribution,' *Univ. Kansas Publ. Mus. nat. Hist.* 3 : 1-359.

Baldwin, P. H. (1945), 'Fate of the Laysan Rail,' *Audubon Mag.* 47 : 343-48.

—— (1945), 'The Hawaiian Goose, Its Distribution and Reduction in Numbers,' *Condor* 47 : 27-37.

Baldwin, W. P. (1947), 'Trapping Wild Turkeys in South Carolina,' *J. Wildl. Mgmt.* 11 : 24-36.

Balham, R. W. (1952), 'Grey and Mallard Ducks in the Manawatu District, New Zealand,' *Emu* 52 : 163-91.

Ball, K. E. (1950), 'Breeding Behaviour of Ring-Necked Pheasants on Pellee Island, Ontario,' *Can. Fld.-Nat.* 64 (6) : 201-207.

Ball, S. C. (1933), 'Jungle Fowls from Pacific Islands,' *Bernice P. Bishop Mus. Bull.* (108).

Ball, W. S. (1960), 'Distribution and Undesirable Characteristics of Certain Wild Birds and Animals Barred from Importation or Restricted in Importation into the State of California,' *Bull. Dep. Agric., Calif.* 49 (3) : 177-85.

Ballard, J. (1964), 'Starlings: They Can be Controlled,' *Am. Fruit Grower* 84 (2) 22-23, 38.

Balmford, R. (1978), 'Early Introductions of Birds to Victoria,' *Aust. Bird Watcher* : 237-48.

Banks, R. C. (1977), 'Wildlife Importations into the United States, 1900-1972,' *U.S. Dep. Interior Fish Wildl. Serv., Spec. Sci. Rep.-Wildl.* (200) : 1-18.

Banks, R. C. and Laybourne, R. C. (1968), 'The Red-whiskered Bulbul in Florida,' *Auk* 85 : 141.

Bannerman, D. A. (1949), *The Birds of Tropical West Africa,* Vol.7. Oliver and Boyd, London.

—— (1953), *The Birds of West Equatorial Africa,* Oliver and Boyd, London.

—— (1963), *Birds of the Atlantic Islands: 1, History of the Birds of the Canary Islands and Salvages,* Oliver and Boyd, London.

—— (1963), *The Birds of the British Isles. vol. 12,* Oliver and Boyd, Edinburgh.

—— (1965), *Birds of the Atlantic Islands: 2. History of the Birds of Madeira, the Desertas and Porto Santo Islands,* Oliver and Boyd, London.

Bannerman, D. A. and Bannerman, W. M. (1966), *Birds of the Atlantic Islands: 3. History of the Birds of the Azores,* Oliver and Boyd, London.

—— (1968), *Birds of the Atlantic Islands: 4. History of the Birds of the Cape Verde Islands.* Oliver and Boyd, London.

—— (1971), *Handbook of the Birds of Cyprus and Migrants of the Middle East,* Oliver and Boyd, Edinburgh.

Baptista, L. F. (1976), 'Autumnal Breeding in Chinese Spotted Doves,' *Wilson Bull.* 88 (1) : 158.

Barboza du Bocage, J. V. (1898), 'Aves do Archipelago de Cabo-verde,' *J. Sci. Math.* (5) : 140-150.

Barbush, R. J. (1961), *The Ring-necked Pheasant in Northeast Idaho.* M. S. Thesis, Ohio State University; 1-83.

Barlass, J. C. (1975), Correspondence: Introduced Lovebirds in Mombasa, *Avicult. Mag.* 81 (1) : 55-56.

—— (1975), Correspondence: Lovebirds in East Africa, *Avicult. Mag.* 81 (4) : 235-36.

Barlow, J. C. (1973), 'Status of the North American Population of the European Tree Sparrow,' in S. C. Kendeigh (Ed) 'Symp. on House Sparrow and Eur. Tree Sparrow in N. Am, *Orn. Monogr.* (14) : 10-23.

Barlow, M. (1972), 'The Establishment, Dispersal and Distribution of the Spur-winged Plover in New Zealand,' *Notornis* 19 (3) : 201-11.

Barlow, M. L., Muller, P. M., and Sutton, R. R. (1972), 'Breeding Data on the Spur-winged Plover in Southland, New Zealand,' *Notornis* 19 (3) : 212-49.

Barnes, H. E. (1893), 'On the Birds of Aden,' *Ibis* 5 : 57-83.

Barnes, I. R. (1955), 'Cattle Egrets Colonize a New World,' *Atl. Nat.* 10 (5) : 238-47.

Barnes, J. A. G. (1975), *Titmice of the British Isles,* David and Charles, Newton Abbot.

Barnett, D. C. (1953), 'Chukar Partridge Introductions in Washington,' *Proc. 32 a. Conf. west Ass. St. Game Fish Commnrs., Jne. 15-17, 1952* : 154-61.

Barrau, J. and Devambez, L. (1957), 'Some Unexpected Results of Introductions in New Caledonia,' *La Terre et la Vie* 104 (4) : 324-34.

Barret, C. (1922), 'Birds Around a Homestead,' *Emu* 21 (4) : 257-61.

Barrett, C. L. (1926), 'Introduction of British Birds,' *Victorian Nat.* 43 (6) : 190-91.

Barrett-Hamilton, G. E. H. (1899), 'The Introduction of the Black Grouse and Some Other Birds into Ireland,' *Ir. Nat.* 1899 : 37-43.

Barros-Valenzuela, R. (1964), 'Varias Aves Cuya Aclimatacion Convendria Al Paris,' (Several Birds whose Acclimatization in Chile should be Convenient), *Acad. Chilena Cienc. Nat.* 49 (27) : 109-12 (in Spanish).

Barrows, W. B. (1889), 'The English Sparrow *(Passer domesticus)* in North America, Especially in its Relations to Agriculture,'

U.S. Dep. Agric. Div. Econ. Orn. Mammal. Bull. (1) : 1-606.

Bartholomew, J. (1929), 'Capercaillie in West Stirling,' *Scott. Nat.* : 61.

Baskett, T. S. (1947), 'Nesting and Production of the Ring-necked Pheasant in North Central Iowa,' *Ecol. Monogr.* 17 (1) : 1-30.

Basten, M. (1971), No Title, *S. Aust. Orn.* 25 : 229.

Baumgardner, I. C. (1962), 'The Story of the Ring-necked Pheasant — that Oriental Bombshell,' *Pa. Game News* 33 (6) : 25-28.

Baumgartner, F. M. (1944), 'Dispersal and Survival of Game Farm Bobwhite Quail in North-central Oklahoma,' *J. Wildl. Mgmt.* 8 : 112-18.

Baumgartner, M. (1942), 'Some Notes on the Starling *(Sturnus vulgaris),'* *Indiana Audubon Yr. Bk.* 20 : 10-14.

Bayliss-Smith, T. P. (1973), 'A Recent Immigrant to Ontong Java Atoll, Solomon Islands,' *Bull. Brit. Orn. Club* 93 : 52-53.

Beavan, R. C. (1867), 'The Avifauna of the Andaman Islands,' *Ibis* 3 (11) : 314-34.

Beer, J. R. (1961), 'Winter Feeding Patterns in the House Sparrow,' *Auk* 78 : 63-71.

Behle, W. H. (1954), 'Changing Status of the Starling in Utah,' *Condor* 56 : 49-50.

Beidleman, R. G. (1949), 'Starling and Rusty Blackbird Records for Boulder County, Colorado,' *Condor* 51 (2) : 97.

Belcher, W. J. (1929), 'Fragmentary Notes on Bird Life in the Fijis,' *Condor* 31 : 19-20.

Belhnap, J. (1952), 'The Hungarian Partridge in New York State,' *Kingbird* 2 (4) : 80-82.

Bell, H. L. (1961), 'The Introduced Spice Finch in North-eastern Queensland,' *Emu* 61 (2) : 94-96.

Bell, S. C. (1945), 'The European Starling in Gaspé,' *Auk* 62 : 79-97.

Bendell, J. F. (1957), 'Dispharynx nasuta in Hungarian Partridge in Ontario,' *J. Wildl. Mgmt.* 21 (2) : 238.

Benedict, B. (1957), 'The Immigrant Birds of Mauritius,' *Avicult. Mag.* 63 : 155-57.

Benedict, H. S. (1936), 'Observations on the European Starling: Proc. of the Wilson Ornith. Club,' *Wilson Bull.* 48 : 56-67.

Bennett, A. G. (1926), 'A List of the Birds of the Falkland Islands and Dependencies,' *Ibis* 2 (12th Ser.) (2) : 306-32.

Bennett, H. S. and Eddy, G. (1949), 'European Starling in King County, Washington,' *Murrelet* 30 : 18.

Benson, C. W. (1950), 'A Contribution to the Ornithology of St Helena and Other Notes from a Sea Voyage,' *Ibis* 92 : 75.

—— (1960), 'The Birds of the Comoro Islands: Results British Ornithological Union Centennial Expedition — 1958,' *Ibis* 103b : 5-106.

—— (1970), 'An Introduction of *Streptopelia picturata* into the Amirantes,' *Atoll Res. Bull.* 136 : 195-96.

Benson, C. W., Beamish, H. H., Jouanin, C., Salvin, J. and Watson, G. E. (1975), 'The Birds of the Isles Glorieuses,' *Atoll Res. Bull.* (176) : 1-30.

Benson, C. W. and White, C. M. N. (1957), *Checklist of the Birds of Northern Rhodesia,* Government Printer, Lusaka.

Benson, D. (1969), 'Releasing Hand-Reared Redheads to Establish Breeding Colonies in New York,' *Trans. N. East. Sect. Wildl. Soc., 25th N. East. Fish Widl. Conf., 9-12 Feb., 1969* : 91-110.

Benson, D. and Robeson, S. B. (1960), 'Winter Feeding of Pheasants,' *N.Y. St. Conserv.* 14 (4) : 28-29.

Benson, S. V. (1952), *The Observers Book of Birds,* F. Warne, London.

Berger, A. J. (1972), 'Hawaiian Birds 1972,' *Wilson Bull.* 84 (2) : 212-22.

—— (1972), *Hawaiian Birdlife,* University Press, Honolulu, Hawaii.

—— (1975), 'The Japanese Bush Warbler on Oahu,' *Elepaio* 36 : 19-21.

—— (1975), 'Red-whiskered and Red-vented

Bulbuls on Oahu,' *Elepaio* 36 (2) :16-19.

—— (1976), 'Names for Hawaii's Introduced Birds,' *Elepaio* 36 (12) :143-46.

—— (1977), 'Nesting of the Yellow-fronted Canary on Oahu,' *Elepaio* 37 (11) :128.

—— (1977), 'Nesting of the Bush Warbler,' *Elepaio* 37 (12) :148.

—— (1977), 'Rothchilds' Starling in Wai-Kiki,' *Elepaio* 37 (12) :149.

Berger, J. A. (1975), 'The Warbling Silverbill, a New Nesting Bird in Hawaii,' *Pacif. Sci.* 29:51-54.

Bergerud, A. T. (1963), 'Newfoundland Wildlife Management and Annual Report, 1962-3,' 68-126. *Newfoundland: Annual Report Department Mines, Agriculture and Resources for Year Ending 31st March, 1963.*

Bergerud, A. T. and Hemus, H. D. (1975), 'An Experimental Study of the Behaviour of Blue Grouse *(Dendragapus obscurus).* 1. Differences Between the Founders from Three Populations,' *Can. J. Zool.* 53 (9) :1229-37.

Bergman, G. (1956), 'Merihanhikannan Palauttamisesta Istutusten Avulla' (On the Introduction of Grey lag Goose), *Suomen Riista* 10:121-28 (in Finnish).

Bernard, J. (1963), 'Les Etourneaux, ménace serieuse pour le vignoble alsacien' (Starlings serious menace for Alsation Vineyards), *Phytoma* 145 :20-22 (in French).

Bernstein, H. A. (1861), 'Uber Nester und Eier javanischer Vogel,' *J.F.O.,* 1861.

Bertram, B. (1970), 'The Vocal Behaviour of the Indian Hill Mynah, *Gracula religiosa,*' *Anim. Behav. Monogr.* 3 (2) :81-192.

Besser, J. F. (1962), 'Research on Agricultural Bird Damage Control Problems in the Western United States,' *Natn. Bird Contr. Sem., Bowling Green, Ohio, Jly. 11-12, 1962.*

Besser, J. F., De Grazio, J. W. and Guarino, J. L. (1968), 'Cost of Wintering Starlings and Red-winged Blackbirds at Feedlots,' *J. Wildl. Mgmt.* 32 (1) :179-80.

Beveridge, A. E. (1964), 'Dispersal and Destruction of Seed in Central North Island Podocarp Forests,' *Proc. N.Z. Ecol. Soc.* 11:48-55.

Biaggi, V. (1963), 'The First Record for Puerto Rico of the Nests of the Scarlet-cheeked Weaver Finch,' *Wilson Bull.* 75 (1) :91.

Bierman, D. R. (1943), 'A Survey of Starling Nesting Sites,' *Passenger Pigeon* 5 (4) :95.

—— (1944), 'A Starling Nesting Study,' *Passenger Pigeon* 6 (2) :46-48.

Bigalke, R. C. (1964), 'Indian Mynas *(Acridotheres tristis)* in Kimberley,' *Ostrich* 35 (1) :60.

Birkan, M. G. (1971), 'Success Factor as Regards Releases of Farm Raised Grey Partridges, *Perdix perdix* L. and Red-legged Partridges, *Alectoris rufa* L.,' *Trans. 10th Congr. int. Un. Game Biol.* :356-58.

Bizeau, E. (1963), 'Chukar Partridge in Idaho,' *Idaho Wildl. Rev.* 15 (1) :3-4.

Bjor, K. (1959), 'Damage to Spruce Plants by Capercaillie Feeding,' *Norsk. Skogbr.* 55:339-40.

Blackburn, A. (1971), 'Some Notes on Fijian Birds,' *Notornis* 18 (3) :147-74.

Blackburn, B. (1932), 'The Starling,' *Victorian Nat.* 49 (6) :156.

Blackford, J. L. (1955), 'Nesting of the European Starling in Western Montana,' *Condor* 57:122-23.

Blackman, R. (1965), 'Bristol University Seychelles Expedition, 7,' *Biol. Contr. Anims.* 8 :72-74.

Blair, F. D. (1942), 'The Chukar Partridge in Minnesota,' *Conserv. Volunt.* 4 (21) :16-20.

Blake C. H. (1961), 'Notes on the History of the Cattle Egret in the New World,' *Chat* 25 :24-27.

—— (1975), 'Introductions, Transplants and Invaders,' *Am. Birds* 29 (5) :923-926.

Blake, E. R. (1939), 'African Cattle Egret

Taken in British Guiana,' *Auk* 56 :470-71.

—— (1977), *Manual of Neotropical Birds,* Vol. 1. University Chicago Press, Chicago and London.

Blaker, D. (1971), 'Range Expansion of the Cattle Egret,' *Ostrich* 10th Suppl. (9) :27-30.

Blank, T. H. (1970), 'Reeve's Pheasant,' *Game Conserv. a.Rev., 1969-70* :81-82.

Blathwayt, F. L. (1902), 'The Little Owl in Lincolnshire,' *Zoologist,* 1902:112.

—— (1904), 'The Little Owl in Lincolnshire,' *Zoologist,* 1904 :74.

Blignaut, J. (1958), 'European Starling, *Sturnus vulgaris,* at Uniondale,' *Ostrich* 29 (1) :49.

Blurton-Jones, N. G. (1956), 'Census of Breeding Canada Geese, 1953,' *Bird Study* 3:153-70.

Blus, L. J., Joanen, T., Belisle, A. A. and Prouty, R. M. (1975), 'The Brown Pelican and Certain Environmental Pollutants in Louisiana, *Bull. Env. Contam. Toxicol.* 13:646-55.

Boardman, G. A. (1889), 'An English Starling in Maine,' *Forest and Stream* 33:85.

Boback, A. W. (1952), *Das Auerhuhn, Die neue Brehm Bucherei,* Leipzig.

Boehm, E. F. (1961), 'Indian Turtledove Extends Range in South Australia,' *Emu* 61:55.

Bogachev, A. S. (1961), 'The Large-billed Crow, *Corvus levaillanti mandshurikus* But.' *Byull. Moskov. Obs. Isp. Prir. Otdel. Biol.* 66 (1) :132-33 (In Russian).

Bohl, W. H. (1957), 'Chukars in New Mexico, 1931-57,' *N. Mex. Dep. Game Fish Bull.* (6) :1-69.

—— (1957), 'A Study of the Introduction, Release and Survival of Asiatic Game Birds,' *N. Mex. Dep. Game Fish.* Job Completion Report Project W-58-R-5. (4) :1-84.

—— (1964), 'A Study of the Japanese Green and the Korean Ring-necked Pheasant,' *U.S. Fish. Wildl. Serv. Spec. Rep. Wildl.* (83) :1-65.

—— (1968), 'Results of Foreign Game Introductions,' *Trans. 33rd N. Am. Wildl. Nat. Resour. Conf.* :389-98.

Bohl, W. H. and Bump, G. (1970), 'Summary of Foreign Game Bird Liberations 1960-68 and Propagation 1966-68,' *U.S. Fish. Wildl. Serv. Sci. Rep. — Wildl.* (130) :1-61.

Bolen, E. G. (1971), 'Some Views on Exotic Waterfowl,' *Wilson Bull.* 83 (4) :430-34.

Bolle, C. (1856) 'Die Vogelwelt auf den Inseln des grünen Vorgebirges, *J.F.O.* :17-31.

Bonar, H. N. (1907), Capercaillie in Midlothian. *Ann. Scot. Nat. Hist.* :51-52.

—— (1910), 'Capercaillie in East Lothian,' *Ann. Scot. Nat. Hist.* :120.

Bond, J. (1960), *Birds of the West Indies,* Collins, London.

—— (1971), *Sixteenth Supplement to the Checklist of the Birds of the West Indies (1956),* Academy of Natural Science, Philadelphia.

Bond, R. M. (1957), 'The Cattle Egret in Jamaica, British West Indies,' *Condor* 59 :269.

Boosey, E. J. (1958), *Foreign Bird Keeping,* Cage Birds, London.

Booth, E. S. (1948), 'Starlings in Washington State,' *Condor* 50 :165.

Borden and Hochbaum (1966), in *Trans. 31st N. Am. Wildl. Nat. Res. Conf.* :79-88.

Borell, A. E. (1940) 'Starlings Arrive in the Rio Grande Valley of New Mexico,' *Condor* 42 (1) :86.

Borset, E. and Krafft, A. (1973), 'Black Grouse and Capercaillie Brood Habits in Norwegian Forests,' *Oikos* 24 :1-7.

Bortoli, L. (1972), 'Sparrows in Tunisia,' in S. C. Kendeigh and J. Pinowski (Eds) *Productivity, Population, Dynamics and Systematics of Granivorous Birds,* Proc. Gen. Meet. Work. Group Graniv. Birds, I. B. P. Pt. Sect., Hague, Holland, Sep. 6-8,

1970:249-61, P. W. N. Polish Sci. Publ., Warszawa.

Bossenmaier, E. F. (1957), 'The Status of the Chukar Partridge in Wyoming,' *Proc. 37th a. Conf. west. Assn. St. Game Fish Commnrs:* :234-38.

Boudreau, G. W. (1972), 'Factors Related to Bird Depredations in Vineyards,' *Am. J. Enol. Viticult.* 23 (2) :50-53.

Bourke, P. A. (1957), 'Introduced Birds of New South Wales,' *Emu* 57:263-64.

Bourne, W. R. P. (1955), 'The Birds of the Cape Verde Islands,' *Ibis* 97:508-56.

—— (1957), 'The Breeding Birds of Bermuda,' *Ibis* 99 :94.

—— (1966), 'Further Notes on the Birds of Cape Verde Islands,' *Ibis* 108:425-29.

—— (1971), 'The Birds of the Chagos Group, Indian Ocean,' *Atoll Res. Bull.* (149) :175-207.

Bowdish, B. S. (1903), 'Birds of Porto Rico,' *Auk* 20 :10-23.

Bowles, J. (1962), 'The Guam Edible Nest Swiftlet,' *Elepaio* 23 :14-15.

Boyd, A. W. (1917), 'Birds of the Suez Canal Zone and Sinai Peninsula,' *Ibis* (10th Ser.) 5 :547.

Boyd, E. M. (1951), 'A Survey of Parasitism in the Starling *(Sturnus vulgaris* L.) in North America,' *J. Parasit.* 37 (1) :58-84.

Brackbill, H. (1952), 'Starlings, *Sturnus vulgaris,* catching insects on the Wing,' *Auk* 69:88-89.

Bradshaw, C. J. (1901), 'A Little Owl at Henley,' *Zoologist,* 1901 :476.

Bravery, J. A. (1970), 'Birds of the Atherton Shire, Queensland,' *Emu* 70 (2) :49-63.

Bray, R. P. (1970), 'Measuring the Mortality of Released Pheasants,' *VIIIth int. Congr. Game Biol.* :366-68.

Bready, M. B. (1929), *The European Starling on his Western Way,* Knickerbocker Press, New York.

Breckenridge, W. J. (1941), 'The Starling, A Universal Alien,' *Conserv. Volunt.* 3 (15) :10-13.

Breese, P. L. (1959), 'Information on Cattle Egret, a Bird New to Hawaii,' *Elepaio* 20 :33-34.

Breiding, G. H. (1943), 'Starlings Nesting in Colorado,' *Wilson Bull.* 55 :247.

Briggs, J. N. and Haugh, J. R. (1973), 'Habitat Selection in Birds with Consideration of the Potential Establishment of the Parakeet *(Myiopsitta monachus)* in North America,' *Kingbird* 23 (1) :1-9.

British Ornithological Union (1974), 'Records Committee (B.O.U.) Eighth Report,' *Ibis* 116 (4) :579.

Brocklebank, E. W. (1926), 'European Starlings at Casselman, Ontario,' *Can. Fld.-Nat.* 40 (6) :142.

Bronson, W. S. (1948), *Starlings,* Harcourt, Brace and Co, New York.

Brookfield, C. M. and Griswold, O. (1956), 'An Exotic New Oriole Settles in Florida,' *Natn. geogr. Mag.* 109 :261-64.

Brough, T. (1967), 'The Starling Menace,' *The Grower,* 1967, 17th July.

Brovkina, E. T. (1957), 'Data on the Diet and Forest Economic Importance of Thrushes in the Moscow Oblast,' in *Proc. 3rd Baltic Orn. Conf. — 1957* (in Russian).

Brown, A. G. (1950), 'The Birds of Turkeith, Victoria,' *Emu* 50 (2) :105-13.

Brown, C. P. (1954), 'Distribution of the Hungarian Partridge in New York,' *N.Y. Fish Game J.* 1 (2) :119-29.

—— (1959), 'The Ring-necked Pheasant in New York,' *N.Y. Dep. Conserv.* :30 (from *W.R.* 104:53.)

Brown, C. P. and Robeson, S. B. (1959), 'The Ring-necked Pheasant in New York,' *N.Y. Dep. Conserv.* 1-39.

Brown, P and Amadon, D. (1968), *Eagles, Hawks and Falcons of the World,* 2 Vols. Country Life, London.

Brown, R. (1868), 'Synopsis of the Birds of Vancouver Island,' *Ibis* 4 (16) :414-27.

Browne, P. W. P. (1950), 'Notes on the Birds Observed in South Arabia,' *Ibis* 92:52-65.

Bruce, J. A. (1961), 'First Record of the European Skylark on San Juan Islands, Washington,' *Condor* 63 (5):418.

Brudenell-Bruce, P. G. C. (1975), *Birds of New Providence and the Bahama Islands*, Collins, London.

Bruner, P. L. (1972), 'A Field Guide to Birds of French-Polynesia: Tahiti,' *Pacif. Sci. Info. Centre, Bernice P. Bishop Mus. Bull.* (93).

Bruning, D. F. (1974), 'Social Structure and Reproductive Behaviour of the Greater Rhea, *Living Bird* 13:251-94.

Bryan, E. H. (1958), *Checklist and Summary of Hawaiian Birds*, Books about Hawaii, Honolulu, Hawaii.

Bryan, E. H. and Greenway, J. C. (1944), 'A Contribution to the Ornithology of the Hawaiian Islands,' *Bull. Mus. comp. Zool. Harv.* 96 (2):79-142.

Bryan, W. A. (1912), 'The Introduction and Acclimatization of the Yellow Canary on Midway Island,' *Auk.* 29:339-40.

— (1908), 'Some Birds of Molokai,' *Occ. Pap. Bernice P. Bishop Mus.* 4:133-76.

Bryant, H. C. (1916), 'The European House Sparrow and Its Control in California,' *Calif. Fish Game Commn. Teachers Bull.* (7) June, 1916.

Buchanan, J. (1944), 'Control The Starlings,' *Ontario Dep. Agric. Ext. Circ.* (67).

Buckman, C. A. (1967), 'The Rugged Ring-necked Pheasant of Minnesota,' *Minn. Dep. Conserv. Div. Game Fish*: 1-23.

Bucknill, J. S. and Chasen, F. N. (1927), *Birds of Singapore Island*, Government Printer, Singapore.

Buikstra, C. A. (1968), 'The Re-Establishment of the Wild Turkey in Payne County, Oklahoma,' M.S. Thesis., Oklahoma State University.

Bull, J. (1971), 'Monk Parakeets in the New York City Region,' *Linnean Newsl.* 25 (1):2pp.

— (1973), 'Exotic Birds in the New York City Area,' *Wilson Bull.* 85 (4):501-05.

— (1975), 'Introduction to the United States of the Monk Parakeet — A Species with Pest Potential,' *12th Bull. int. Counc. Bird Preserv.* 12:98.

Bull, J. and Ricciuti, E. R. (1974), 'Polly Want an Apple?,' *Audubon*, 1974:48-54.

Bull, P. C. (1946), 'Notes on the Breeding Cycle of the Thrush and Blackbird in New Zealand,' *Emu* 46:198-208.

— (1957), 'Distribution and Abundance of the Rook (*Corvus frugilegus* L.) in New Zealand,' *Notornis* 7 (5):137-61.

— (1959), 'Birds of the Hutt Valley,' *Proc. N.Z. Ecol. Soc.* (6):52-58.

— (1966), 'When our Feathered Friends the Birds Become Problems,' *Service, N.Z.,* Winter, 1966:13-15.

— (1973), 'The Starling: Friend or Foe?,' *N.Z. agric. J.* 127:55-59.

— (1966), 'Introduced Birds,' *Notornis* 13:122-23.

Bull, P. C. and Porter, R. E. R. (1975), 'Distribution and Numbers of the Rook (*Corvus frugilegus* L.) in the North Island of New Zealand,' *N.Z. J. Zool* :2 (1):63-92.

Buller, W. L. (1872-73), *History of the Birds of New Zealand*, Voorst, London.

Bullough, W. S. (1942), 'The Starling (*Sturnus vulgaris* L.) and Foot-and-Mouth Disease,' *Proc. R. Soc. (Ser. B. Biol. Sci.)* 131 (862):1-12.

— (1945), 'British Continental Races of the Starling, *Sturnus vulgaris* L., in Canada,' *Nature* 155:756-57.

Bump, G. (1941), 'The Introduction and Transplantation of Game Birds and Mammals into the State of New York,' *Trans. N. Am. Wildl. Conf.* 5:409-20.

— (1951), 'Game Introductions — When, Where and How,' *Trans. N. Am. Wildl. Conf.* 16:316-26.

— (1957), 'Foreign Game Introductions into the Southeast,' *Proc. 11th a. Conf. S. East. Ass. Game Fish Commn.* :17-20.

— (1958), 'New Birds for Old,' *Colo. Outdoors* 7 (2):17-20.

— (1958), 'Red-legged Partridges of Spain,' *U.S. Fish. Wildl. Serv. Sci. Rep.* (39):1-38.

— (1963), 'History and Analysis of Tetraonid Introductions into North America,' *J. Wildl. Mgmt.* 27 (4):855.

— (1968), 'Foreign Game Investigation: A Federal-State Co-operative Program,' *U.S. Dep. Interior Fish Wildl. Serv. Res. Publ.* (49):1-14.

— (1968), 'Exotics and The Role of the State-Federal Foreign Game Investigation Program,' in Symp. *Introduction Exotic Animals: Ecological and Socioeconomic Considerations,* C. Kleberg Res. Prog. in Wildl. Ecol., Coll. Agric., Texas, A. and M. Univ., Texas. :5-8.

— (1971), 'The South American Monk, Quaker, or Grey-headed Parakeet,' *U.S. Fish Wildl. Serv., Bur. Sport Fish Wildl., Wildl. Leafl.* (496):4pp.

Bump, G. and Bohl, W. H. (1964), 'Summary of Foreign Game Bird Propagation and Liberations 1960-63,' *U.S. Fish Wildl. Serv. Spec. Sci. Rep.* (80):1-48.

Bump, G. and Bump, J. W. (1964), 'A Study and Review of the Black Francolin and Gray Francolin,' *U.S. Fish Wildl. Serv. Spec. Rep.* (81), Apr., 1964.

Bump, G. R. W., Darrow, R. W., Edminster, F. C. and Crissey, W. F. ((1947), *The Ruffed Grouse: Life History, Propagation, Management,* N.Y. St. Conserv. Dep., New York.

Burger, G. V. (1954), The Status of Introduced Wild Turkeys in California. *Calif. Fish Game* 40 (2):123-45.

— (1954), 'Wild Turkeys in Central Coastal California,' *Condor* 56 (4):198-206.

— (1964), 'Survival of Ring-necked Pheasants Released on a Wisconsin Shooting Preserve,' *J. Wild. Mgmt.* 28 (4):711-21.

Burger, J. (1976), 'House Sparrows Usurp Hornero Nests in Argentina,' *Wilson Bull.* 88 (2):357-58.

Burget, M. (1948), 'Wild Turkeys are Coming Back,' *Colo. Conserv. Comments* 10 (5):11-12, 21.

Burns, R. D. (1958), 'A History of the Entry of the Cardinal into Michigan,' *Jack-Pine Warbler* 36 (1):19-21.

Burris, O. E. (1965), 'Game Transplants in Alaska,' in *Proc. 45 a. Conf. west. Ass. St. Game Fish Commnrs. Anchorage, Alaska, July 7-8, 1965* :93-104.

Burton, M. and Burton, R. (1969), *The International Wildlife Encyclopedia,* B.P.C. Publ. Ltd, Great Britain.

Burton, J. A. (1973), *Owls of the World,* Dutton and Co, New York.

Buss, I. O. (1942), 'A Managed Cliff Swallow Colony in Southern Wisconsin,' *Wilson Bull.* 54:153-61.

Buxton, P. A. (1907), 'The Spread of the Little Owl in Hertfordshire,' *Zoologist,* 1907:430.

Buyckx, E. J. (1972), 'Meeting Discussion: Sparrows in Tunisia,' in S. C. Kendeigh and J. Pinowski (eds) *Prod., Pop. Dyn. and Syst. Graniv. Bds.,* 252, P.W.N. — Polish Sci. Publs, Warszawa.

Byrd, G. V. (1979), 'Common Myna Predation of Wedge-tailed Shearwater Eggs,' *Elepaio* 39 (7):69-70.

Cahn, A. R. (1938), 'Climatographic Analysis of the Problem of Introducing Three Exotic Game Birds into the Tennessee Valley and Vicinity,' *Trans. N. Am. Wildl. Conf.* 3:807-17.

Cain, A. J. and Galbraith, I. C. J. (1956), 'Field Notes on Birds of the Eastern Solomon Islands,' *Ibis* 98 (2):262-95.

— (1957), 'Birds of the Solomon Islands,' *Ibis* 99:128.

Calder, D. (1953), 'Distribution of the Indian Mynah,' *Bokmakerie* 5 (1):4-6.

California Department Food and Agriculture and California Department Fish and Game (1975), *Laws and Regulations Governing the Importation, Transportation and Possession of Live Wild Animals into the State of California,* Office of State Printer, California.

Calman, W. T., *et al* (1931) 'Discussion on the Introduction of Alien Species,' *Proc. Lin. Soc., London,* 142nd Sess. :6, 11, 17.

Campbell, A. G. (1906), 'Report on the Birds of Kangaroo Island: A Comparison with Mainland Forms,' *Emu* 5:139-45.

Campbell, H. (1906), 'Introduction of Australian Magpies to Ceylon,' *Emu* 5:231-32.

Campbell, H. (1956), 'Pheasants in New Mexico,' *N. Mex. Wildl.* 1 (4):5.

— (1972), 'Population Studies of the Lesser Prairie Chicken in New Mexico,' *J. Wildl. Mgmt.* 36:689-99.

Campbell, J. M. (1906), 'Capercaillies in Ayrshire,' *Ann. Scot. nat. Hist.* :186.

Campbell, P. O. (1972), 'The Feeding Ecology and Breeding Biology of the Goldfinch (*Carduelis carduelis* L., 1758) at Havelock North, New Zealand,' M.Sc. Thesis, Massey University, New Zealand.

Campbell, W. S. (1943), 'The English Sparrow in Australia,' *Victorian Nat.* 60:9-11.

Cant, G. (1962), 'The House Finch in New York State,' *Kingbird* 12:68-72.

Carié, P. (1910), 'Notes sur L'acclimatation du Bulbul (*Otocompsa jocosa* L.),' *Bull. Soc. natn. Acclim. Fr.* :462-64.

— (1916), 'L'Acclimatation à L'île Maurice. Mammifères et Oiseaux,' *Bull. Soc. natn. Acclim. Fr.* :1-62.

Carl, G. C. (1952), 'Alien Animals on Vancouver Island,' *Victoria Nat.* 9 (1):7-10.

Carl, G. C. and Guiguet, C. J. (1972), *Alien Animals in British Columbia,* 1st Edn 1957, Rev. 1972, Brit. Col. Prov. Mus. Dep. Recr. Cons. Hndbk (14):1-103.

Carleton, A. R. and Owre, O. T. (1975), 'The Red-whiskered Bulbul in Florida, 1960-61,' *Auk* 92:40-57.

Carlson, C. E. (1941), 'The Hungarian Partridge in Minnesota,' *Conserv. Volunt.* 2 (7):41-44.

Carnevale Mijno, P. (1965), 'Repopulation of Hunting Lands in Italy with Artificially Bred Pheasants,' *Trans. 6th Congr. int. Un. Game Biol., 7-12 Oct., 1963* :49-54.

Carrick, R. and Walker, C. (1953), 'Report on the European Starling, *Sturnus vulgaris,* at Oni-i-Lau,' *Trans. Proc. Fiji Soc. (1951-54)* 5:51-58.

Carroll, A. L. K., (1963), 'Food Habits of the North Island Weka,' *Notornis* 10 (6):289-300.

— (1970), The White-faced Heron in New Zealand,' *Notornis* 17 (1):3-24.

Caughley, G. (1962), 'Habitat Occupation of Birds in a New Zealand High Country Drainage During the Breeding Season,' *Emu* 62 (2):129-39.

Caum, E. L. (1933), 'The Exotic Birds of Hawaii,' *Occ. Pap. Bernice P. Bishop Mus.* 10 (9):1-55.

— (1936), 'Notes on the Fauna and Flora of Lehua and Kaula Islands,' *Occ. Pap. Bernice P. Bishop Mus.* 21:2-17.

Cave, F. O. and MacDonald, J. D. (1955), *Birds of the Sudan,* Oliver and Boyd, Edinburgh.

Cawkell, E. M. and Hamilton, J. E. (1961), 'The Birds of the Falkland Islands,' *Ibis* 103a (1).

Cayley, N. W. (1931-65) *What Bird is That,* 1931, 3rd Edn. 1959, Repr. 1965. Angus & Robertson, Sydney.

Centre for Overseas Pest Research (1975), 'The Problem of Damage to Sorghum by

Doves in Botswana: Report for 1972-1974,' C. for O.P.R. :1-13.

Chaffer, N. (1933), 'The Bulbul', Emu 33 (2) :136-37.

Chalbreck, R. H., Dupuie, H. H. and Belsom, D. J. (1975), Establishment of a Resident Breeding Flock of Canada Geese in Louisiana, Proc. a. Conf. SE Assoc. Game Fish Comm. 28:442-55.

Chalmers, C. E. (1972), 'Cattle Egret in the Gippsland Area,' Emu 72 (4) :136-37.

Chambers, G. D. (1965), 'Summary of Foreign Game Bird Propagation; 1964 and Liberations 1960-64,' Missouri Conserv. Comm. :1-42.

Chapman, F. B. (n.d.), 'Wild Turkey, Ruffed Grouse and Snoeshoe Hare Restoration in Ohio,' Ohio Dep. nat. Resour. Final Rep., Federal Aid Project W-80-D-1 :1-10.

Chapman, F. M. (1925), 'The European Starling as an American Citizen,' Nat. Hist. (N.Y.) 25:480-85.

Chasen, F. N. (1924), 'On the Occurrence of Certain Alien Birds in Singapore,' J. Malay. Brch. R. Asiat. Soc. 2 (1) :68-70.

— (1925), 'Further Remarks on the Birds of Singapore Island,' Singapore Nat. 5:71-73.

— (1933), 'Notes on the Birds of Christmas Island, Indian Ocean,' Bull. Raffles Mus. (8) :55-87.

Cheney, G. M. (1915), 'Birds of the Wangaratta District, Victoria,' Emu 14 (4) :199-213.

Cheng, T. (ed) (1963), Chung-Kuo Ching-Chi Tung-wu Chich-Niao Lei (China's Economic Fauna: Birds), Science Publication Society, Peiping.

— (1976), Distributional List of Chinese Birds, Rev. Edn, Science Publication Society, Peiping.

Cherry, T. (1968), 'Let's not Release Game Farm Wild "Turkeys", Wildl. N. Carolina 32 (2) :22-23.

Chisholm, A. H. (1915), 'The Mallacoota Excursion,' Emu 14 (3) :126-34.

— (1919), 'Introduced Birds of Queensland,' Emu 19:61.

— (1925), 'Spread of the Goldfinch,' Emu 25 (2) :93.

— (1950), 'Birds Introduced to Australia,' Emu 50:97.

Chisholm, E. C. (1924), 'The Avifauna Around Tumbarumba, NSW, Emu 24 (2) :102-06.

— (1926), 'Birds Introduced into New South Wales,' Emu 25:219.

Christensen, G. C. (1954), 'The Chukar Partridge in Nevada,' Nev. Fish Game Comm. Biol. Bull. (1) :1-77.

— (1958), 'The Effects of Drought and Hunting on the Chukar Partridge,' Trans. 23rd N. Am. Wildl. Conf. :329-41.

— (1961), 'Preliminary Results from Nevada's Participation in the Foreign Game Introductions Project,' Proc. 41st a. Conf. west. Ass. St. Game Fish Commnrs. :130-35.

— (1962), 'Indian Sandgrouse, Pterocles exustus hindustan, Captured in the Thar Desert for Introduction to America,' Nev. Fish Game Commn. (In W.R. 26 (4) :399).

— (1963), 'Sandgrouse Released in Nevada Found in Mexico,' Condor 65 (1) :67-68.

— (1963), 'Exotic Game Bird Introductions into Nevada,' Nev. Fish Game Commn. Biol. Bull. (3).

— (1965), 'Nevada's Himalayan Snow Partridge Program,' Proc. 45th a. Conf. west. Ass. St. Game Fish Commnrs., Anchorage, Alaska, Jly. 7-8, 1965 :73-75.

— (1967), 'The Status of Nevada's Exotic Bird Program,' Proc. a. Conf. west. Ass. St. Game Fish Commnrs., Honolulu, Hawaii, Jly. 16-20, 1967 :84-93.

— (1970), 'The Chukar Partridge. Its Introduction, Life History and Management,' Nev. Dep. Fish Game Biol. Bull. (4) :1-82.

Christensen, R. (1963), 'A Short History of "John Ringneck",' S. Dak. Conserv. Dig. 30 (5) :12-14.

Christisen, D. M. (1951), 'History and Status of the Ring-necked Pheasant in Missouri,' Missouri Conserv. Comm. :1-66.

Christy, C. (1897), 'Field Notes on the Birds of San Domingo,' Ibis 3 (11) :317-42.

Civil Aviation Authority (1973), 'Bird Strikes to United Kingdom Aircraft 1966-71,' London: C.A.A. Airworth. Note (106).

Clancey, P. A. (1963), 'The House Sparrow on the Atlantic Seaboard of the Cape,' Ostrich 34 (3) :168.

— (1964), The Birds of Natal and Zululand, Oliver and Boyd, Edinburgh.

— (1965), 'A Catalogue of the South African Sub Region, Part 11: Families Glareolidae — Pittidae,' Durban Mus. Novit. 7:305-86.

— (1974), 'The Indian House Crow in Natal,' Ostrich 45 (1) :31-32.

Clapp, R. C. and Sibley, F. C. (1966), 'Notes on the Birds of Tutuila, American Samoa,' Notornis 13:157-64.

Clapp, R. B. and Banks, R. C. (1973), 'Birds Imported into the United States in 1971,' Bur. Sport. Fish Wildl., Spec. Sci. Rep. — Wildl. (170).

Clark, D. O. (1977), 'An Overview of Depredating Bird Damage Control in California,' in Proc. 7th Bird Contr. Sem., Bowl. Green State Univ., Bowling Green, Ohio :21-27.

Clarke, G. (1967), 'Bird Notes from Aden Colony,' Ibis 109 (4) :516-20.

Clegg, W. E. (1941), 'Birds of the "L'Ile de la Camargue et la Petite Camargue",' Suppl. Ibis 5 (14th Ser.) (4) :556-609.

Cleland, J. (1942), 'Birds Seen on Kangaroo Island by Members of the Ralph Tate Society,' S. Aust. Orn. 16:19-21, 31-33.

Cleland, J. B. (1910), 'The Australian Fauna and Flora and Exotic Invasions,' J. Nat. Hist. Sci. Soc., West Aust. 3 (1) :12-18.

— (1948), No Title. S. Aust. Orn. 19:9.

Clough, L. K. (1923), 'Hungarian Partridge and Pheasant in Eastern Washington,' Murrelet 5:5-7.

Coffey, B. B. (1959), 'The Starling in Eastern Mexico,' Condor 61 (4) :299.

Cole, D. T. (1958), 'House Sparrows in Mafeking, C. P.,' Ostrich 29 (2) :87.

— (1962), 'House Sparrows in Northern Cape and Bechuanaland,' Ostrich 33:54-55.

Colebatch, H. (1929), The Story of 100 Years: Western Australia 1829-1929. Chapt. 30. Government Printer, Perth.

Coleman, E. (1939), 'Notes on the Increase of the Blackbird,' Emu 38 (5) :515-21.

Coleman, J. D. (1971), 'The Distribution, Numbers and Food of the Rook, Corvus frugilegus L., in Canterbury, New Zealand,' N.Z. J. Sci. 14 (3) :494-506.

— (1972), 'The Breeding Biology of the Rook, Corvus frugilegus L., in Canterbury, New Zealand,' Notornis 19 (2) :118-39.

Coleman, S. (1949), 'The Chukar Partridge in Nevada,' Proc. a. Conf. west. Ass. St. Game Fish Commnrs. 29 :135-38.

Collias, N. E. and Collias, E. C. (1967), 'Quantitative Analysis of the Breeding Behaviour of the African Weaver Birds,' Auk 84 :396-411.

— (1971), 'Comparative Behaviour of the West African and South African Subspecies of Ploceus cucullatus,' Ostrich Suppl. (9) :41-52.

Collier, C. (1904), 'Birds of the Island of Raasay,' Ibis 4:506.

Collinge, W. E. (1919), 'The Plague of Starlings,' Nat. Rev. (434) :252-57.

— (1920-21), 'The Starling — Is it Injurious to Agriculture,' Agriculture 27:1114-21.

— (1920-21), 'The Rook — Its Relation to the Farmer, Fruit Grower and Forrester,' Agriculture 27:868-75.

Collins, M. S. (1976), 'South American Cardinal Populations on the Big Island,' Elepaio 37 (1) :1-2.

Colson, R. B. (1968), 'New Pheasant Introductions/A Progress Report,' Conservationist 23 (2) :2-4.

Colthred, J. B. (1966), 'The Domestic Fowl in Ancient Egypt,' Ibis 108:217-23.

Conder, P. J. (1948), 'The Breeding Biology of the Continental Goldfinch, Carduelis carduelis carduelis,' Ibis 90 (4) :493-525.

Condon, D. (1968), No Title, S. Aust. Orn. 25:36.

Condon, H. T. (1948), 'Birds Introduced onto Kangaroo Island,' S. Aust. Orn. 18:78.

— (1948), 'The Introduced Grenadier Weaver or Red Bishop Bird,' S. Aust. Orn. 19 (1) :1.

— (1962-68), 'A Handlist of the Birds of South Australia,' S. Aust. Orn. 23 (6-8) 1962, 2nd Edit. Rev., 1968. Adelaide: South Australian Ornithological Association.

— (1975), Checklist of the Birds of Australia. 1. Non-passerines, R.A.O.U., Melbourne.

Conrads, K. (1977), 'Ergebnisse einer mittelfristigen Bestandsaufnahme (1964-76) de Ortolans (Emberiza hortulana) auf einer Probefläche der Senne (Ostmunsterland),' Vogelwelt 98:81-105.

Cooke, M. T. (1925), 'Spread of the European Starling in North America,' U.S. Dep. Agric. Circ. (336) :1-7.

— (1928), 'Spread of the European Starling in North America (to 1928)' US. Dep. Agric. Circ. (40) :1-10.

Cooke, M. T. and Knappen, P. (1941), 'Some Birds Naturalized in North America,' Trans. N. Am. Wildl. Conf. 5:176-83.

Cookingham, R. A. and Ripley, T. H. (1964), 'Vital Characteristics of an Insular Bobwhite Population,' J. Wildl. Mgmt. 28 (4) :855-57.

Cooper, H. M. (1947), 'Some Notes on Kangaroo Island Birds,' S. Aust. Orn. 18:48.

Cooper, J. A. (1978), 'The History and Breeding Biology of the Canada Geese of Marshy Point, Manitoba,' Wildl. Monogr. (61) :1-87.

Corbeau, L. (1951), 'That Honey the Hun,' N. Dak. Outdoors 14 (4) :4-6.

Corfe, B. (1977), 'Musk Lorikeets at Alfred Cove,' West. Aust. Nat. 13 (8) :209.

Cottam, C. (1929), 'Status of the Ring-necked Pheasant in Utah,' Condor 31:117-23.

— (1943), 'Is the Starling Population Decreasing in the North-eastern U.S.?,' Auk 60:439-40.

— (1941), 'European Starlings in Nevada,' Condor 43:293-94.

— (1944), 'Starlings Feeding on the Backs of Cattle,' Migrant 15:24-25.

— (1956), 'The Problem of Wildlife Introductions — Its Successes and Failures,' 46th Conv. int. Ass. Game Fish Conserv. Commnrs. :94-111.

Cottam, C. and Saylor, L. W. (1940), 'The Chukar and Hungarian Partridges in America,' U.S. Dept. Interior Biol. Surv. Wildl. leaflet (BS-159) :1-6.

Cottam, C., Sooter, C. A. and Griffiths, R. E. (1942), 'The European Starling in New Mexico,' Condor 44 (4) :182.

Cottam, C. and Stanford, J. A. (1959), 'Coturnix Quail in America,' 48th Conv. int. Ass. Game Fish Conserv. Commnrs. :111-19.

Coues, E. (1879), 'On the Present Status of Passer domesticus in America with Special Reference to Western States and Territories,' Bull. U.S. Geol. Surv. :175-93.

Coues, W. P. (1890), 'Passer domesticus in Cape Breton,' Auk 7 (2) :212.

Councilman, J. J. (1974), 'Breeding Biology of the Indian Mynah in City and Aviary,' Notornis 21:318-33.

Courtenay-Latimer, M. (1942), 'English Hedge-Sparrow Introduced into South Africa at East London,' Ostrich 13:181.

Coutlee, E. L. (1968), 'Comparative

Behaviour of Lesser and Lawrence's Goldfinches,' *Condor* 70:228-42.

— (1968), 'Maintenance Behaviour of the Lesser and Lawrence's Goldfinches,' *Condor* 70:378-84.

Cowan, I. Mc. (1943) 'Economic Status of the Pheasant on the Cultivated Lands of the Okanagan Valley, British Columbia,' *Br. Columbia Game Comm. Rep. 1942* :49-62.

Cowan, T. A. and Blyton, E. (1936), *Birds of Wayside and Woodland,* 1st Edn, F. Warne, London.

Cowardin, L. M. (1961), 'The Wild Turkey in Massachusetts — An Experiment in Restoration,' M.S. Thesis, Univ. Mass. :1-174.

Craft, B. R. (1966), 'An Ecological Study of the Black Francolin in the Gum Cove Area of Southwestern Louisiana,' M.S. Thesis, La. State Univ. :1-97.

Craib, C. L. (1971), 'Breeding of the European Starling at Grahamstown,' *Ostrich* 42 (2):145-46.

Cramp, S. and Simmons, K. E. L. (1977), *Handbook of the Birds of Europe, the Middle East and North Africa: The Birds of the Western Palearctic,* Vol.1, Oxford University Press, London.

Cronan, J. M. (1964), 'Pheasant Depredations on Potatoes,' *J. Wildl. Mgmt.* 28 (1):165-66.

Crook, J. H. (1961), 'The Fodies (Ploceinae) of the Seychelle Islands,' *Ibis* 103a (1):517-48.

Crosby, G. T. (1972), 'Spread of the Cattle Egret in the Western Hemisphere,' *Bird Banding* 43:205-12.

Crossner, K. A. (1977), 'Natural Selection and Clutch Size in the European Starling,' *Ecology* 58 (4):885-92.

Crowe, D. W. (1965), 'The House Sparrow, *Passer domesticus* L., at Plettenberg Bay,' *Ostrich* 36 (2):99.

Crowell, K. L. and Crowell, M. R. (1976), 'Bermuda's Abundant, Beleaguered Birds,' *Nat. Hist.* 85 (8):48-56.

Crump, W. I. (1950), 'Turkeys on the Move,' *Wyo. Wildl.* 14 (10):10-13.

Crump, W. I. and Sanderson, H. B. (1950), 'Wild Turkey Trapping and Transplanting,' *Wyo. Wildl.* 5 (4):4-11, 36-37.

C.S.I.R.O. (1933), 'Blow Fly Problems — Suggested Use of the Cattle Egret (*Bubulcus coromandus*),' *C.S.I.R.O. Melbourne* 6 (3):213.

Cuello, J. and Gerzenstein, E. (1962), 'Las Aves del Uruguay,' *Com. Zool. Mus. Hist Nat., Montevideo* 6 (93):1-91.

Cullen, J. M., Guiton, P. E., Horridge, G. A. and Peirson, J. (1952), 'Birds of Palma and Gomera,' *Ibis* :68-84.

Cunningham, J. M. (1948), 'Distribution of Myna in New Zealand,' *Notornis* (N.Z. Bird Notes) 3:57-64.

— (1951), 'Position of the Mynah in 1950,' *Notornis* 4 (4):66-67.

— (1954), 'Further Notes on the Distribution of the Myna,' *Notornis* 5 (7):210.

Cunningham, R. L. (1965), 'Predation on Birds by the Cattle Egret,' *Auk* 82:502-03.

Cunningham-van Someren, G. R. (1948), '*Agapornis swinderniana*,' *Notornis* 90:603-04.

— (1969), 'Escapes of *Psittacula Krameri* and *Agapornis* Spp. Breeding in Kenya,' *Bull. Br. Orn. Club* 89:137-39.

Curry-Lindahl, K. (1964), 'The Reintroduction of Eagle Owls in Sweden,' *Norfolk Wildl. Park a. Rep., 1964* :31-33.

Curtiss, A. (1938), *A Short Zoology of Tahiti,* Guide Press Co, New York.

Cutten, F. E. A. (1966), 'Clutch Size and Egg Dimensions of the Black Swan, *Cygnus atratus,* at Lake Ellesmere, Canterbury, New Zealand,' *Emu* 65 (3):223-25.

Daglish, E. F. (1948), *Birds of the British Isles,* Dent and Sons, London.

Dale, F. H. (1941), ' "Judgement Suspended" on Hungarian Partridge Projects in Michigan,' *Mich. Conserv.* 10 (10):6-7.

— (1942), 'Influence of Rainfall and Soil on Hungarian Partridges and Pheasants in South-eastern Michigan,' *J. Wildl. Mgmt.* 6 (1):17-18.

— (1943), 'History and Status of the Hungarian Partridge in Michigan,' *J. Wildl. Mgmt.* 7 (4):368-77.

Dalke, P. D. (1935), 'Economic Status of the Pheasant and the Relation of Farming Practices in Southern Michigan Thereto,' *Am. Wildl.* 24 (6):86, 94.

Dalrymple, B. W. (1950), 'Operation Snow Grouse,' *Sports Afield* 123 (1):28-29, 65-68.

Dambach, C. A. and Leedy, D. L. (1948), 'Ohio Studies with Repellent Materials with Notes on Damage to Corn by Pheasants and Other Wildlife,' *J. Wildl. Mgmt.* 12 (4):392-98.

— (1949), 'Prevention of Crop Damage by Pheasants,' *Trans. N. Am. Wildl. Conf., 1948,* 14:592-603.

Daniels, T. S. (1954), 'House Sparrows in Eastern Cape,' *Ostrich* 25 (1):37-38.

Danforth, S. T. (1929), 'Notes on the Birds of Hispaniola,' *Auk* 46:358.

Da Rosa Pinto, A. A. (1959), 'Alguns novos Records de Aves para Sul do Save e Moçambique, incluindo o di genera novo para a sub-regiao de Africa do Sul, com a desciçao de Nova Subespecies,' *Bol. de Soc. Estudos da Prov. de Moçambique* 118:15-25.

David, N. and Gosselin, M. (1978), 'The Spring Migration March 1-May 31, 1978: Quebec Region,' *Am. Birds* 32 (5):981-83.

Davidson, J. (1907), 'Capercaillies in Moray,' *Ann. Scot. nat. Hist.* :52.

Davies, S. J. J. F. (1968), 'Aspects of the Study of Emus in Semi-Arid and Arid Western Australia,' *Proc. ecol. Soc. Aust.* 3:160-66.

Davis, D. E. (1950), 'The Growth of Starling, *Sturnus vulgaris,* Population,' *Auk* 67:460-65.

— (1955), 'Population Changes and Roosting Time of Starlings in Maryland,' *Ecology* 36:423-30.

— (1958), 'Relation of "Clutch Size" to Number of Ova Ovulated by Starlings,' *Auk* 75 (1):60-65.

— (1959), 'The Sex and Age Structure of Roosting Starlings,' *Ecology* 40:136-39.

— (1960), 'Comments on the Migration of Starlings in the Eastern U.S.,' *Bird Banding* 31 (4):216-19.

Davis, L. R. (1974), 'The Monk Parakeet: A Potential Threat to Agriculture,' in *Proc. 6th Vert. Pest Contr. Conf., March 5-7, Anaheim, Calif.* 253-56.

Dawson, D. G. (1970), 'Estimation of Grain Loss due to Sparrows (*Passer domesticus*) in New Zealand,' *N.Z. J. agric. Res.* (3):681-88.

Dawson, D. G. and Bull, P. C. (1969), 'A Questionnaire Survey of Bird Damage to Fruit,' *N.Z. J. agric. Res.* 13 (2):362-71.

— (1969), 'Results of a Questionnaire on Bird Damage in Orchards,' *Orchardist N.Z.* 42 (3):38-44.

Day A. M. (1949), 'A New Look at Exotics,' *Field and Stream* 54 (1):54-55, 145-47.

— (1949), 'Introduction of Exotic Species,' *Conv. int. Ass. Game Fish. Conserv. Commnrs.* 38:138-44.

Dear, E. (1951), 'Rooks in Fielding District,' *Notornis* 4:69.

Dearborn, N. (1912), 'The English Sparrow as a Pest,' *U.S. Dept. Agric., Farmers Bull.* (493).

Decary, R. (1962), 'Sur des introductions imprudentes d'animaux aux Mascareignes et à Madagascar (Unwise Introductions of Animals into the Mascareignes and Madagascar),' *Bull. Mus. natn. Hist. nat. Paris* (2nd Ser.) 34 (5):404-07.

Deignan, H. G. (1945), 'The Birds of Northern Thailand,' *U.S. nat. Hist. Mus.,*

Smithson. Inst., Washington, Bull. (186).

— (1963), 'Checklist of the Birds of Thailand,' *U.S. nat. Hist. Mus., Smithson. Inst., Washington, Bull.* (226).

Delacour, J. (1943), 'A Revision of the Subfamily Estrildinae of the Family Ploceidae,' *Zoologica N.Y.* 28 (2):69-86.

— (1947), *Birds of Malaysia,* MacMillan, New York.

— (1954-64), *Waterfowl of the World,* 4 Vols, *Country Life,* London.

— (1959), *Wild Pigeons and Doves,* All Pets Books, Wisconsin, USA.

— (1965), *The Pheasants of the World,* 1951, 4th Impr. 1965, *Country Life,* London.

— (1966), *Guide des oiseaux de la Nouvelle — Calédonie et de ses Dependances* Delachaux et Niestlé, Neuchâtel (Switzerland).

Delacour, J. and Amadon, D. (1973), *Curassows and Related Birds,* American Museum Natural History, New York.

Delacour, J. and Jabouille, P. (1927), 'Recherches Ornithologiques dans les Provinces du Tranninh (Laos) de Thua-Thien et de Kontoum (Annam),' *Archiv. Hist. nat. Soc. natn. Acclim. Fr.* (3):1-216.

— (1931), *Les Oiseaux de l'Indochine Française,* 4 Vols, Exposition Coloniale Internationale, Paris.

Delacour, J. and Mayr, E. (1946), *Birds of the Philippines,* MacMillan, New York.

Dell, J. (1965), 'The Red-browed Finch, *Aegintha temporalis,* in Western Australia,' *W. Aust. Nat.* 9 (7):160-69.

Dement'ev, G. P. and Gladkov, N. A. (eds) (1954), *Birds of the Soviet Union* (Ptitsy Sovietskogo Soiuza) Transl. IPST., 1970 (Moscow).

Denham, R. (1959), 'Cattle Egret (*Bubulcus ibis*) on Cozumel Island, Quintana Roo, Mexico,' *Auk* 76 (3):359.

Dennis, J. V. (1955), 'A Fall Study of the Food Habits of the Common Starling (*Sturnus vulgaris*) in Northern Virginia,' *Raven* 26 (4):51-54.

Dennis, R. (1964), 'Capture of Moulting Canada Geese on the Beauly Firth,' *Wildl. Trust a. Rep.* 15:71-74.

Denny, H. (1844), 'Bobwhite Quail in Norfolk,' *Ann. Mag. nat. Hist.* 13:405-06.

Department of Fish and Game (1950), *California's Fish and Game Program: Report to the Wildlife Conservation Board,* Dep. Fish Game, Sacramento, California.

— (1961), *46th Biennial Report,* Dep. Fish Game, Sacramento, California.

Department Lands and Natural Resources (1976), 'Nene Restoration Project, 1st July 1972-30th June 1975. State Department Lands National Resources,' in *Elepaio* 36 (9):104-08.

Department of Agriculture, N.S.W. (1918), 'The Food of Australian Birds,' *Dep. Agric. N.S.W. Sci. Bull.* (15).

Despeissis, A. J. (1906), 'The Starling Scare,' *J.. agric. West Aust.* 13 (3):238-40.

Dexter, J. S. (1922), 'The European Gray Partridge in Saskatchewan,' *Auk* 39:253-54.

Dhondt, A. A. (1976), 'Bird Notes from the Kingdom of Tonga,' *Notornis* 23:4-7.

— (1976), 'Bird Observations in Western Samoa,' *Notornis* 23:29-43.

— (1977), 'Breeding and Postnuptial Molt of the Red-vented Bulbul in Western Samoa,' *Condor* 79 (2):257-60.

Diamond, J. M. and Marshall, A. G. (1976), 'Origin of the New Hebridean Avifauna,' *Emu* 76 (4):187-200.

Dickerman, R. W. (1964), 'Cattle Egrets Nesting in Mexico,' *Wilson Bull.* 76:290.

Dickerson, L. M. (1938), 'The Western Frontier of the European Starling in the United States as of February, 1937,' *Condor* 40:118-23.

Dilks, P. J. (1974), Diet of Feral Pigeons (*Columba livia*) in Hawkes' Bay, New Zealand. *N.Z. J. agric. Res.* 18:87-90.

Dill, H. H. and Lee, F. B. (1970), 'Home Grown Honkers,' *U.S. Dept. Interior Fish Wildl. Serv., Washington* : 154 pp.

Doerr, P. D. *et al* (1974), 'Characteristics of Winter Feeding Aggregations of Ruffed Grouse in Alberta,' *J. Wildl. Mgmt.* 38:601-15.

Donaghho, W. (1966), 'Indian Hill Mynah in Hawaii,' *Elepaio* 26:110-11.

—— (1970), 'Observation of the Edible Nest Swiftlet on Oahu,' *Elepaio* 30:64-65.

Donohoe, R. W. (1963), 'Wild Turkey Restocking, 1956-61,' *Game Res. Ohio* 2:235-37.

—— (1965), 'Wild Turkey Restocking, 1956-63,' *Game Res. Ohio* 3:62-64.

Dorian, H. (1965), 'The Economic Value of the Chukar Partridge to Nevada,' *Proc. a. Conf. west. Ass. St. Fish Game Commnrs., Anchorage, Alaska, Jly. 7-8, 1965* :55-56.

Dorward, D. F. (1957), 'The Night-Heron Colony in the Edinburgh Zoo,' *Scott. Nat.* 69:32-36.

Doty, H. A. and Kruse, A. D. (1972), 'Techniques for Establishing Local Breeding Populations of Wood Ducks,' *J. Wildl. Mgmt.* 36:428-35.

Doughty, R. (1978), 'The English Sparrow in the American Landscape: A Paradox in Nineteenth Century Wildlife Conservation,' *Univ. Oxford Sch. Geogr. Res. Pap.* (19):1-36.

Douglas, G. W. (1964), 'Review of Technical Progress in Vermin Control in Victoria 1960-64,' in *Aust. Verm. Conf., 1964, Canberra, A.C.T.* :22-26.

—— (1972), 'Ecological Problems Caused by Introduced Animals and Plants,' *Victoria Res.* 14 (4):1-6.

Douglas, M. E. (1970), 'Rook on the Waiuku Peninsula,' *Notornis* 17 (4):300-02.

Dourdine, A. D. (1975), 'Acclimatization of the Rock Partridge *(Alectoris graeca)* in Crimea and in Transcarpathia,' *Trans. 10th Congr. int. Un. Game Biol.* :361.

Dove, H. S. (1919), 'The Blackbird in Tasmania,' *Emu* 19 (1):70.

Dove, R. S. and Goodhart, H. J. (1955), 'Field Observations from the Colony of Hong Kong,' *Ibis* 97 (2):311-40.

Dow, D. (1978), 'Breeding Biology and Development of the Young of *M. melanocephala,* A Communal Breeding Honeyeater,' *Emu* 78 (4):207-22.

Dresser, H. E. (1902), *Manual of Palaearctic Birds,* London :290.

Drummond, J. (1906), 'Introduced Birds,' *Trans N.Z. Inst.* 39:227-52.

—— (1907), 'Dates on which Introduced Birds have been Liberated or have Appeared in the Different Districts of New Zealand,' *Trans. Proc. N.Z. Inst.* 39 (45):503-08.

Drury, W. H., Morgan, A. H. and Stackpole, R. (1953), 'Occurrence of an African Cattle Egret *(Ardeola ibis ibis)* in Massachusetts,' *Auk* 70:364-65.

Due, L. A. and Ruhr, C. E. (1957), 'The Coturnix Quail in Tennessee,' *Migrant* 28 (4):48-53.

Dugand, A. (1955), 'Nuevas observaciones de *Bubulcus ibis* ibis en Colombia,' *Caldasia* 7 (31):81-86.

—— (1956), *'Bubulcus ibis* in the Cauca Valley, Colombia,' *Auk* 73:559-60.

Du Mont, P. A. (1945), 'The Invasion of the Starling into Iowa,' *Iowa Bird Life* 14 (2):30-33.

Dunmire, W. W. (1961), *Birds of the National Parks in Hawaii,* Hawaii Natural History Association, Honolulu.

Dunnet, G. M. and Patterson, I. J. (1968), 'The Rook Problem in North-East Scotland,' in R. K. Murton and E. N. Wright (eds) *Problem of Birds as Pests,* Academic Press, London, 119-39.

Dunning, R. A. (1974), 'Bird Damage to Sugar Beet,' *Ann. appl. Biol.* 76:325-35.

du Pont, J. E. (1971), *Philippine Birds,* Delaware Mus. nat. Hist., Monogr. Ser. (2).

—— (1972), 'Notes from Western Samoa, Including the Description of a New Parrot-Finch *(Erythrura),'* *Wilson Bull.* 84 (4):375-76.

—— (1976), *South Pacific Birds,* a Monogr. Ser. (3). Delaware Mus. nat. Hist.

Eastbrook, A. H. (1907), 'The Present Status of the English Sparrow Problem in America,' *Auk* 24:129-34.

Eastman, M. (1969), *Life of the Emu,* Angus & Robertson, Sydney.

Eates, K. R. (1937), 'The Distribution of the Large Indian Paraquet *(P. eupatria nipalensis* (Hodg.)) in Sind,' *J. Bombay nat. Hist. Soc.* 39:414-18.

Eaton, W. F. (1924), 'Decrease of the English Sparrow in Eastern Massachusetts,' *Auk* 41:604-06.

Eddinger, R. C. (1967), 'A Study of the Breeding Behaviour of the Mynah *(Acridotheres tristis* L.),' *Elepaio* 28 (1):1-5, 11-15.

Edgar, W. H. (1974), 'Observations on Skylark Damage to Sugar Beet and Lettuce Seedlings in East Anglia,' in Proc. Assoc. Appl. Biol. *Ann. appl. Biol.* 76:335-37.

Edminster, F. C. (1937), 'The Reeves Pheasant in New York,' *Trans. N. Am. Wildl. Conf.* 2:490-93.

Edscorn, J. B. (1976), 'Fall Migration, Aug. 1-Nov. 30, 1975: Florida Region,' *Am. Birds* 30 (1):54-58.

—— (1977), 'The Autumn Migration, Aug. 1-Nov. 30, 1976: Florida Region,' *Am. Birds* 31 (2):166-69.

Edwards, H. V. (1925), 'Birds of a New South Wales Garden,' *Emu* 24 (4):282-86.

Edwards, M. H. (1965), 'Cattle Egret in Guerrero, Mexico,' *Condor* 67:191.

Einarsen, A. S. (1942), 'Specific Results from Ring-necked Pheasant Studies in the Pacific Northwest,' *Trans. N. Am. Wildl. Conf.* 7:130-38.

—— (1945), 'Some Factors Affecting Ring-necked Pheasant Density,' *Murrelet* 26:2-9.

Eisenmann, E. (1955), 'Cattle Egret, Marbled Godwit, Surfbird and Brown-chested Martin in Panama,' *Auk* 72:426-28.

Eisner, E. (1957), 'The Bengalese Finch,' *Avicult. Mag.* 63:101-08.

Elkington, J. S. C. (1929), 'A Bird Diary from Sydney to Antwerp,' *Emu* 29:268-75.

Elkins, W. A. and Nelson, U. C. (1957), 'Wildlife Introductions and Transplants in Alaska,' *Sci. in Alaska, 1954* :29-30.

Elliott, H. (1970), 'Birds of the World: Lovebirds,' *Birds World* 4 (9):1236-39.

Elliott, H. N. (1964), 'Starlings in the Pacific North West,' in *Proc. 2nd Vert. Pest Contr. Conf., Mar. 4-5, 1964, Anaheim, California* :29-39.

Elliot, J. J. and Arbid, R. S. (1953), 'Origin and Status of the House Finch in the Eastern United States,' *Auk* 70:31-37.

Ellis, B. A. (1944), 'The White-faced Heron,' *N.Z. Bird Notes* 1 (1):109-110.

Ellis, J. A. and Anderson, W. L. (1963), 'Attempts to Establish Pheasants in Southern Illinois,' *J. Wildl. Mgmt.* 27 (2):225-39.

Ellis, M. (1975), Correspondence: 'Birds Introduced into East Africa,' *Avicult. Mag.* 81 (2):115-16.

Ellison, A. (1907), 'Little Owls Breeding in Hertfordshire,' *Zoologist,* 1907:430.

Ellison, L. N. (1973), 'Seasonal Social Organization and Movements of Spruce Grouse,' *Condor* 75 (4):375-85.

—— (1976), 'Winter Food Selection of Alaskan Spruce Grouse,' *J. Wildl. Mgmt.* 40 (2):205-13.

Ellwood, J. (1971), 'Goose Conservation,' *Wildlife Association Great Britain and Ireland Report and Yearbook, 1970-71* :59-60.

Elton, C. S. (1958), *The Ecology of Invasions by Animals and Plants,* Methuen, London.

Emmerez de Charmoy, A. (1941), 'Le Boul-Boul *(Otocompsa jocosa peguensis),'* *La Rev. Agric. de L'île Maurice* 20:154-58.

England, M. D. (1970), 'Escapes,' *Avicult. Mag.* 76:150-52.

—— (1974), 'A Further Review of the Problem of Escapes,' *Brit. Birds* 67 (5):177-97.

—— (1974), 'Feral Populations of Parakeets,' *Brit. Birds* 74 (7):393-94.

Ennion, H. E. (1962), 'Notes on Birds Seen in Aden and the Western Aden Protectorate,' *Ibis* 104 (4):560-62.

Ennis, T. (1965), 'The Arrival and Spread of the Collared Dove *(Streptopelia decaocto)* in Northern Ireland,' *Ir. Nat. J.* 15:63-67.

Etchécopar, R. D. (1955), 'L'Acclimatation des Oiseaux en France au Cours des 100 Dernieres Annees,' *La Terre et la Vie* 102 (1):42-53.

Etchécopar, R. D. and Hüe, F. (1978), *Les Oiseaux de Chine de Mongolie et de Corée: non passereaux,* Les Editions du pacific, Tahiti.

Every, B. (1962), 'House Sparrows on Bird Island, Algoa Bay,' *Ostrich* 43 (2):131-32.

Fabricius, E. (1970), 'A Survey of the Canada Goose *(Branta canadensis)* in Sweden,' *Zool. Revy.* 32:19-25.

Falla, R. A. (1942), 'White Herons in the Okarito District,' *N.Z. Orn. Soc. Bull.* 2:68.

—— (1947), 'Destruction of Rooks *(Corvus frugilegus),'* *N.Z. Bird Notes* 2:70.

Falla, R. A., Sibson, R. B. and Turbott, E. G. (1966), *A Field Guide to the Birds of New Zealand,* Collins, London.

Farley, F. L. (1935), 'The European Starling *(Sturnus vulgaris)* in Alberta,' *Can. Fld.-Nat.* 49:119.

Faruqi, S. A., Bump, G., Nanda, P. C. and Christensen, G. C. (1960), 'A Study of the Seasonal Foods of the Black Francolin *(Francolinus francolinus* (L.)), the Grey Francolin *(Francolinus pondicerianus* (Gmelin)) and the Common Sandgrouse *(Pterocles exustus* (Temm.)) in India and Pakistan,' *J. Bombay nat. Hist. Soc.* 57 (2):1-8.

Fea, L. (1898-99), 'Dalle Isole del Cabo-Verde,' Letters: *Boll. Soc. geogr. Ital.* (Ser. 2) 11:358-68, 537-52, 12: 7-26, 163-74, 302-12.

Feare, C. J. (1974), 'Ecological Studies of the Rook *(Corvus frugilegus)* in North-East Scotland,' *J. appl. Ecol.* 11 (3):897-914.

Feilden, H. W. (1889), 'On the Birds of Barbados,' *Ibis* (6th Ser.) 1 (4):477-503.

Ferguson, A. D. (1913), 'Introductions of Foreign Game Birds into the Southern San Joaquin and Tributary Section,' *Calif. Div. Fish Game, Game Bull.* 1:35-40.

Ferrel, C. M. (1949), 'Starling in the Sacramento Valley, California,' *Condor* 51:150.

Ferrel, C. M., Twining, H. and Herkenham, N. B. (1949), 'Food Habits of the Ring-necked Pheasant *(Phasianus colchicus)* in the Sacramento Valley, California,' *Calif. Fish Game* 35 (1):51-69.

Ffrench, R. (1973-76), *A Guide to the Birds of Trinidad and Tobago,* Wynnewood, Pennsylvania, 1973, Harwood Books, Pennsylvania, 1976.

Ffrench, R. P. and Ffrench, M. (1966), 'Recent Records of Birds in Trinidad and Tobago,' *Wilson Bull.* 78:5-11.

Fieldsa, J. (1977), 'Coot and Moorhen,' *Av-media Biol. Monogr., Copenhagen,* 56 pp.

Finley, W. L. (1907), 'English Sparrow Notes,' *Condor* 9:108-09.

Finsch, O. (1887), 'Ein Besuch auf Diego Garcia im Indischen Ozean,' *Deutsche geographische Blatter Bremen,* 1887:30-42.

Fish and Game Commission (1963), 'Nevada Exotic Game Bird Introductions Fruitful so far, Hold Promise for Future,' *Nev. Wildl.* 3 (7):1-5.

Fisher, H. I. (1948), 'The Question of Avian Introductions in Hawaii,' *Pacif. Sci.* 2:59-64.

—— (1951), 'The Avifauna of Niihau Island,
501

Hawaiian Archipelago,' *Condor* 53 (1) : 31-42.

Fisher, H. I. and Baldwin, P. H. (1945), 'A Recent Trip to Midway Islands, Pacific Ocean,' *Elepaio* 6 : 11-13.

—— (1947), 'Notes on the Red-billed Leiothrix in Hawaii,' *Pacif. Sci.* 1 : 45-51.

Fisher, J. (1953), 'The Collared Turtle Dove in Europe,' *Brit. Birds* 46 (5) : 153-81.

Fisher, W. R. (1907), *Dr Schlich's Manual of Forestry*, 4, Forest Protection, London, 2nd Ed.

Fisk, E. J. (1968), 'White-winged Doves Breeding in Florida,' *Fla. Nat.* 41 : 126.

Fisk, L. H. and Crabtree, D. M. (1974), 'Black-hooded Parakeet: New Feral Breeding Species in California,' *Am. Birds* 28 (1) : 11-13.

Fitter, R. S. R. (1950), 'Man's Additions to the British Fauna,' *Discovery, Norwich* 11 : 58-62.

—— (1959), *The Ark in our Midst*, Collins, London.

—— (1964), Naturalized Birds, in A. L. Thomson (ed) *A New Dictionary of Birds*, Nelson, London : 505-07.

—— (1967), 'Animal Introductions and Their Ecological Effects in Europe,' in *Proc. 10 Tech. Meet. I.U.C.N., 1966, Part III Changes due to Introd. Birds,* I.U.C.N. Publ., Morges, Switzerland (9) : 177-80.

Fitzwater, W. D. (1967), 'Hindu P.C.O's have Problems American P.C.O's haven't thought of,' *Pest Control* 10 (35) : 70-78.

—— (1971), 'The Weaver Finch of Hispaniola,' *Pest Control* 39 (10) : 19.

Flatt, C. A. (1921), 'The Breeding and Rearing of Turkeys,' *Agriculture* 27 : 1128.

Fletcher, J. A. (1909), 'Stray Feathers: Cleveland (Tasmania) Notes,' *Emu* 9 (2) : 95.

Fletcher, J. J. (1923), 'Linnean Society of New South Wales, Meeting of 26th July, 1922' (Notes on Bulbul), *Proc. Linn. Soc., N.S.W.* 47 (5) 15-25.

Flower, S. S. (1930), 'European Starling in North America,' *Ibis* 6 (2) : 373-74.

—— (1933), 'Notes on Some Birds in Egypt,' *Ibis* (Ser. 13) 3 : 34-46.

Fog, M. (1972), 'Kanadisk gås i Europa,' *Jagt og fiskeri* 43 (4) : 6-7.

Forbes, J. E. and Brown, L. P. (1974), 'The New York Monk Parakeet Retrieval Program,' *Trans. N-East. Fish Wildl. Conf., Feb., 25, 28, 1974* : 1-8.

Forbush, E. H. (1920), 'The Starling,' *Mass. St. Dep. Agric. Circ.* 45 : 1-23.

Forshaw, J. (1969), *Australian Parrots,* Lansdowne, Melbourne.

—— (1973), *Parrots of the World,* Lansdowne, Melbourne.

Frank, H. (1970), 'Über die Einburgerung von Wildputen' (On the Introduction of the Wild Turkey), *8th Int. Congr. Game Biol.* : 382-86 (in German).

Frazier, F. P. (1964), 'New Records of Cattle Egret in Peru,' *Auk* 81 : 553-54.

Freeland, D. B. (1973), 'Some Food Preferences and Aggressive Behaviour by Monk Parakeets,' *Wilson Bull.* 85 (3) : 332-34.

French, W. (1957), 'Birds of the Solomon Islands,' *Ibis* 99 : 126.

Friedman, H. (1929), *The Cowbirds: A Study in the Biology of Social Parasitism,* Charles Thomas, Springfield, Illinois.

Frings, C. and Frings, S. (1965), 'Random Jottings about Mynahs,' *Elepaio* 26 : 48-49.

Frith, H. J. (1952), 'Notes on the Pigeons of the Richmond River, N.S.W.,' *Emu* 52 : 89-99.

—— (1955), 'Reconnaisance of Bird Depredations in the N.W. of Australia,' *C.S.I.R.O. Melbourne,* Rep., May, 1955.

—— (1957), 'Clutch Size in the Goldfinch,' *Emu* 57 (4) : 287-88.

—— (1962), *The Mallee Fowl,* Angus & Robertson, Sydney.

—— (1967), *Waterfowl in Australia,* Angus & Robertson, Sydney.

—— (1973), *Wildlife Conservation,* Angus & Robertson, Sydney.

Frith, H. J., Brown, B. K. and Morris, A. K. (1977), 'Food Habits of the Stubble Quail, *Coturnix pectoralis,* in South-eastern Australia,' *C.S.I.R.O. Melbourne, Div. Wildl. Res., Tech. Paper* (32) : 1-70.

Frith, H. J. and Calaby, J. (eds) (1976), 'The Biology of Crowned Sparrows,' in *Proc. 16th Orn. Congr., Canberra.* Symposium (5) : 309-82.

Frith, H. J. and McKean, J. L. (1975), 'Races of the Introduced Spotted Turtledove, *Streptopelia chinensis* (Scopoli), in Australia,' *Aust. J. Zool.* 23 : 295-306.

Froggatt, W. W. (1912), 'The Starling: A Study in Agricultural Zoology,' *Agric. Gaz., N.S.W.* 23 (7) : 610-16.

Fry, C. H. (1961), 'Notes on the Birds of Annobon and Other Islands in the Gulf of Guinea,' *Ibis* 103a (1) : 267-76.

Fuller, W. A. (1955), 'First Record of the Starling in the North-west Territories,' *Can. Fld.-Nat.* 69 (1) : 27.

Furguson, M. S. (1936), 'Notes on the Relation of the European Starling to Other Species of Birds,' *Auk* 53 : 87-88.

Furniss, O. C. (1944), 'The European Starling in Central Saskatchewan,' *Auk* 61 : 469-70.

Gabrielson, I. N. and Lincoln, F. C. (1959), *The Birds of Alaska,* Stackpole, Pennsylvania.

Gabrielson, I. N. *et al,* (1956), 'Trumpeter Swan,' *Auk* 73 : 119-23.

Gabrielson, N. and Kalmback, E. R. (1921), 'Economic Value of the Starling in the United States,' *U.S. Dep. Agric., Bull.* (868).

Gadow, H. and Gardiner, J. S. (1907), 'The Percy Sladon Trust Expedition to the Indian Ocean. Aves, with some Notes on the Distribution of Land-birds of the Seychelles,' *Trans. Linn. Soc., London, Zool.* 11, 12 : 103-10.

Galbraith, I. C. J., and Galbraith, E. H. (1962), 'Land Birds of Guadalcanal and the San Cristoval Group, Eastern Solomon Islands,' *Bull. Brit. Mus. nat. Hist. Zool. Ser.* 9 (1).

Galbreath, D. S. and Moreland, R. (1953), 'The Chukar Partridge in Washington,' *Wash. St. Game Dep. Biol. Bull.* (11) : 1-54.

Gallagher, M. D. (1960), 'Bird Notes from Christmas Island, Pacific Ocean,' *Ibis* 102 (4) : 489-502.

Game Bird Committee (1961), 'Western States Exotic Game Bird Committee: Annual Report,' *Western States Exotic Game Bird Committee, Annual Report, May 1, 1960 — Apr. 30, 1961* (8).

Gaselee, J. (1963), 'The Precious Ne-Ne,' *Animals* 1 (5) : 15-18.

Gavrilov, E. I. (1961), 'On Methods of Controlling Passing Flocks of Sparrows' (In Russian), *Tr. Nauch-Issled Inst. Zash. Rast. Kazak., Acad. Sel'sk. Nauk.* 6 : 297-306 (In *W.R.* 113 : 55).

—— (1962), 'Biologiya is panskogo vorob'ya (*Passer hispaniolensis* Temm) i mery bor'bry s nim v Kazakhstane.' (Biology of *P. hispaniolensis* and Control Measures in Kazakhstan), *Tr. Nauch-Issled Inst. Zash. Rast. Kazak. SSR.* 7 : 459-528.

—— (1963), 'The Biology of the Eastern Spanish Sparrow, *P.h. transcaspicus,* in Kazak,' *J. Bombay nat. Hist. Soc.* 60 : 301-17.

Gaymer, R., Blackman, R. A. A., Dawson, P. G., Penny, M. and Penny, C. M. (1969), 'Endemic Birds of Seychelles,' *Ibis* 111 (2) : 157-76.

Gebhardt, E. (1944), '*Passer d. domesticus* in Sudamerika,' *Orn. Monatsb.* 52 : 95-98.

—— (1954), 'Die gegenwärte Verbreitung von Haussperling, Star und Buchfink in

Südafrika,' *J. fur Orn.* 95 : 58-60.

—— (1959), 'Europäische Vögel in überseeischen Ländern,' *Bonn. zool. Beitr.* 10 (3/4) : 310-42.

Gee, J. P. (1977), 'The Changing Seasons. *Am. Birds* 31 (5) : 966-71.

Geroudet, P. (1977), 'The Reintroduction of the Bearded Vulture in the Alps,' *World Conf. Birds Prey* 1 : 392-97 (In French).

Gerstell, R. (1938), 'An Analysis of the Reported Returns Obtained from Release of 30 000 Artificially Propagated Ring-necked Pheasants and Bobwhite Quail,' *Trans. N. Am. Wildl. Conf.* 3 : 724-29.

—— (1940), 'The Hungarian and Chukar Partridges — Their Status in Pennsylvania,' *Pa. Game News* 11 (13) : 3, 32.

—— (1941), 'The Hungarian and Chukar Partridges in Pennsylvania,' *Trans. N. Am. Wildl. Conf.* 5 : 405-09.

George, J. L. and Wingard, R. G. (1967), 'Birds, Lands and People,' *Pa St. Univ. Coll. Agric. nat. Resour. Ser./Spec. Circ.* (84) : 1-32.

George, W. (1971), 'Canary-winged Parakeets,' *Fla. Nat.* 44 : 25.

Gibson, D. D. (1978), 'The Spring Migration March 1-May 31, 1978: Alaska Region,' *Am. Birds* 32 (5) : 1043-45.

Gibson, E. (1918), 'Further Ornithological Notes from the Neighbourhood of Cape San Antonio, Province of Buenos Aires. Part 1. Passeres,' *Ibis* 6 (10th Ser.) : 363-415.

Gibson, J. D. (1961), 'Colombo Crows in Australia,' *Emu* 61 (3) : 244-45.

Gibson-Hill, C. A. (1947), 'Field Notes on the Birds of Christmas Island, Indian Ocean,' *Bull. Raffles Mus.* 18 : 87-165.

—— (1949), 'The Birds of the Cocos-Keeling Islands (Indian Ocean),' *Ibis* 91 : 221-43.

—— (1949), 'Annotated Checklist of the Birds of Malaya,' *Bull. Raffles Mus.* 20 : 1-299.

—— (1949), 'A Checklist of the Birds of Singapore Island,' *Bull. Raffles Mus.* 21 : 132-83.

—— (1952), 'Notes on the Alien Birds Recorded from Singapore Island,' *Bull. Raffles Mus.* 21 : 132-83.

Gigstead, G. (1937), 'Habits of the Wisconsin Pheasant,' *Wilson Bull.* 44 (1) : 28-34.

Gill, E. L. (1952), 'The European Starling at the Cape,' *Ostrich* 23 : 129-30.

Gill, F. B. (1967), 'Birds of Rodriguez Island (Indian Ocean),' *Ibis* 109 (3) : 383-90.

Gillespie, J. H., Kessel, B. and Fabricant, J. (1950), 'The Isolation of Newcastle Disease Virus from a Starling,' *Cornell Vet.* 40 (1) : 93-94.

Gilliard, E. T. (1958), 'Feathered Dancers of Little Tobago,' *Nat. geogr. Mag.* 114 (3) : 428-440.

—— (1958), *Living Birds of the World,* Hamish & Hamilton, London.

Gilpin, D. D. (1959), 'Recent Results of Wild Turkey Restocking Efforts in West Virginia,' *Proc. 1st natn. Wild Turkey Symp., Memphis.* : 87-96.

Giltz, M. (1960), 'The Nature and Extent of Bird Depredations on Crops,' *Trans. N. Am. Wildl. Conf.* 25 : 96-99.

Ginn, W. E. (1961), 'Ring-necked Pheasant Becomes Naturalized,' *Outdoor Indiana* 14 (4) : 16-17.

—— (1962), 'The Ring-necked Pheasant in Indiana: History, Research and Management,' *Indiana Dep. Conserv., P-R Bull.* (6) : 1-107.

Gladstone, H. S. (1906), 'Capercaillie in Ayrshire,' *Ann. Scot. nat. Hist.,* 1906 : 116.

—— (1921), 'The Last of the Indigenous Scottish Capercaillie,' *Scot. Nat.,* 1921 : 169-77.

—— (1923), 'Blackgame Damaging Young Larch,' *Scot. Nat.,* 1923 : 54.

—— (1923), 'Introduction of the Ring-necked Pheasant to Great Britain,' *Brit. Birds* 17 (2) : 36-37.

Glass, R. S. and Woodell, S. R. J. (1957),

'Random Occurrences of the Cattle Egret,' *Chat* 21 (3) : 66-67.

Glauert, L. (1956), Problems of Conservation, (c) Introductions of Exotics, in 'Fauna Conserv. in W. Aust', *West Aust Fisheries and Fauna Bull.* (1).

Glazener, W. C. (1947), 'New Homes for Turkeys,' *Tex. Game Fish* 5 (6) : 9-10, 20.

— (1950), 'Wildlife Transplants for 1948-49,' *Wyo. Wildl.* 15 (7) : 25-28.

— (1963), 'Wild Turkey Restoration Progress in Texas,' *Tex. Game Fish* 21 (1) : 8-10, 27.

— (1963), 'An Example of Wild Turkey Restoration,' *Tex. Game Fish* 21 (1) : 22-24, 27.

— (1967), 'Management of the Rio Grande Turkey,' in O. H. Hewitt (ed) *Wild Turkey and Its Management*, Chapt. 15 : 453-92. Wildlife Society, Washington, D.C.

Glenister, A. G. (1951), *The Birds of the Malay Peninsula, Singapore and Penang*, Repr 1974, Oxford University Press, London and Kuala Lumpur.

Glover, F. A. (1953), 'Record of the Starling in Humbolt Co., California,' *Condor* 55 (4) : 219.

Goddard, M. T. (1955), 'Notes on the Breeding of the Cattle Egret in North-eastern New South Wales,' *Emu* 55 (4) : 275-77.

Godfrey, W. E. (1949), 'European Starling Reaches the Pacific Coast,' *Can. Fld.-Nat.* 63 : 165.

— (1966), 'The Birds of Canada,' *Natn. Mus. Can., Bull.* 203, Biol. Ser. (73). 1966, Repr. 1974, Information Canada, Ottawa.

Godoy, J. C. (1963), 'Fauna Silvestre,' *Cons. Fed. de Inversiones, Buenos Aires, Argentina.* : 220-25.

Golow, B. A. and Osmolovskaja, U. I. (1955), 'The Biology and Economic Status of the Magpie in the Natural and Artificial Forested Areas of South East European USSR, *Inst. Geografii* 66 : 257-73 (In Russian). Rev. in *Ibis* : 99.

Gompertz, T. (1957), 'Some Observations on the Feral Pigeon in London,' *Bird Study* 4 : 2-13.

Goodall, J. D., Johnson, A. W. and Philippi, R. A. (1951-57), *Las Aves de Chile*, Platt Establecimientos Gráficos; Buenos Aires, 2 Vols. and Suppls.

Gooders, J. (ed) (1969), *Birds of the World*, 10 vols, I.P.C. Magazines, London.

Goodrich, A. L. (1940), 'Starling Attacks upon Warble-Infested Cattle in the Great Plains Area,' *J. Kans. ent. Soc.* 13 : 33-40.

Goodrum, P. (1949), 'Status of the Bobwhite in the United States,' *Trans. N. Am. Wildl. Conf.* 14 : 359-67.

Goodwin, C. E. (1978), 'The Spring Migration March 1-May 31, 1978: Ontario Region,' *Am. Birds* 32 (5) : 997-1001.

Goodwin, D. (1956), 'The Problems of Birds Escaping from Captivity,' *Brit. Birds* 49 (9) : 339-49.

— (1970), *Pigeons and Doves of the World*, Trustees Brit. Mus. (Nat. Hist.), London.

— (1977), *Crows of the World*, British Mus. (Nat. Hist.), London.

Gordon, S. (1915), *Hill Birds of Scotland*, ??London.

Gore, M. E. J. (1968), 'Checklist of the Birds of Sabah, Borneo,' *Ibis* 110 (2) : 165-96.

Gore, M. E. J. and Won, P. (1971), *The Birds of Korea*, Taewon Publ. Co. Seoul, Korea and Charles E. Tuttle Co., Tokyo.

Gore, R. and Doubilet, D. (1976), 'Florida, Noah's Ark for Exotic Newcomers,' *Nat. geogr. Mag.* 50 (4) : 538-58

Gorman, M. L. (1972), 'The Origin of the Avifauna of Urban and Suburban Suva, Fiji,' *Fiji agric. J.* 34 : 35-38.

— (1975), 'Habitats of the Land Birds of Viti Levu, Fiji Islands,' *Ibis* 117 (2) : 152-61.

Gosse, P. (1938), *St Helena, 1502-1938*.

Gottschalk, J. S. (1966), 'Our Experiences with Exotics,' *Va. Wildl.* 27 : 14-15, 18-21.

— (1967), 'The Introduction of Exotic Animals into the United States,' in *Proc. 10. Tech. Meet. I.U.C.N., 1966, Part III Changes Due to Introd. Spp.,* I.U.C.N. Publ. Morges, Switzerland, New Ser. (9) 124-40.

Gould, E. W. (no date), 'A Study of the Pheasant in New Hampshire During the Spring and Early Summer,' *N. H. Fish Game Dep.* : 1-10.

Graham, S. A. and Hesterberg, G. (1948), 'The Influence of Climate on the Ring-necked Pheasant,' *J. Wildl. Mgmt.* 12 (1) : 9-14.

Grant, J. (1949), 'The European Starling in the Canadian Rockies,' *Can. Fld.-Nat.* 63 : 117.

Grant, W. and Cubby, J. (1973), 'The Capercaillie Reintroduction Experiment at Grizedale,' *Wildlife Association Great Britain and Ireland, Report and Yearbook 1972-3.* : 96-99.

Grasby, W. C. (1906), 'Beware of the Starling,' *West Aust. (Newspaper)* col. 2., 22 Feb, 1906.

Grater, R. K. (1942), 'Starlings in Southern Utah,' *Condor* 44 (1) : 41.

Gray, R. (1882), 'The Introduction of Reeve's Pheasant into Scottish Game Preserves,' *Proc. Roy. Soc., Edinburgh* 7 : 239.

Greely, F., Labisky, R. F. and Mann, S. H. (1962), 'Distribution and Abundance of Pheasants in Illinois,' *Ill. nat. Hist. Surv. Biol. Notes* 47 : 1-16.

Green, W. E. and Hendrickson, G. O. (1938), 'The European Partridge in North-Central Iowa,' *Iowa Bird Life* 8 (2) : 18-22.

Green, R. H. and Mollison, B. C. (1961), 'Birds of Port Davey and south Coast of Tasmania,' *Emu* 61 : 223-36.

Greene, R. and Ellis, R. (1971), 'Merriam's Turkey,' in F. W. Howell and T. W. Mussehl (eds) *Game, Mgmt. in Montana*, Chapt. 20 : 167-73. Montana Fish and Game Department, Helena, Montana.

Greenhalgh, C. M. (1954), 'Some Possible Factors in Chukar Introductions into Utah,' *Proc. 33rd a. Conf. west. Ass. St. Game Fish Commnrs. Jne. 1-3, 1953:* 147-49.

— (1957), 'Seesee Partridges,' *Proc. 37th a. Conf. west. Ass. St. Game Fish Commnrs.* : 277-79.

Greenhalgh, C. M. and Nielson, L. R. (1953), 'Chukar Introductions into Utah,' *Proc. 32nd a. Conf. west. Ass. St. Game Fish Commnrs.* : 165-67.

Grekor, V. S. (1962), '*Streptopelia decaocto* in Odessa,' *Ornitol.* 4 : 328-33 (in Russian).

Grinnell, J. (1906), 'Foolish Introductions of Foreign Birds,' *Condor* 8 : 58-59.

— (1925), 'Risks Incurred in the Introduction of Alien Game Birds,' *Science* 61 : 621-23.

— (1929), 'Ringed Turtle Dove at Large in Los Angeles,' *Condor* 31 : 130-31.

— (1930), 'McAtee on Naturalizing Birds,' *Condor* 32 : 133-34.

— (1936), 'Further Note on the Status of the Skylark on Vancouver Island,' *Condor* 38 : 122.

Griscom, L. (1932), 'The Distribution of Bird Life in Guatemala,' *Bull. Am. Mus. nat. Hist.* 64 : 1-439.

Grittner, I. (1941), 'Zugverhältnisse des europaischen Stieglitzes, *Carduelis carduelis* (L.)' (Migration and Habits of European Goldfinch), *Der Vogelzug, Berlin* 12 (2/3) : 56-73.

Groh, G. (1975), 'Biologie *Emberiza cirlus* in der Pfalz,' *Mitt. Pollichia* 63 : 72-139.

Grote, H. (1933), 'Uber die Ausdehnung des Brutgebietes von *Passer domesticus* nach Norden,' *Beitr. Fortpfl Biol. Vogel* 9 : 15-16.

Groves, F. W. (1956), 'Report of the Committee on the Introduction of Exotic Animals,' *46th Conv. int. Ass. Game Fish Conserv. Commnrs.* : 77-85.

Grzmek, B. (1972), *Animal Encyclopaedia*,

Birds, part. 1, vol.7, Van Nostr. Reinh., London.

Guiguet, C. J. (1952), 'European Starling,' *Victoria Nat.* 9 (2) : 22.

— (1952), 'Another Record of Crested Mynah on Vancouver Island,' *Victoria Nat.* 9 (5) : 52-53.

— (1952), 'The European Starling on Vancouver Island,' *Can. Fld.-Nat.* 66 (1) : 37.

— (1961), 'The Birds of British Columbia : (4) Upland Game Birds,' *Br. Columbia Prov. Mus., Dep. Recr. Conserv., Victoria.* Hndbk. Ser. (10).

Guild, E. (1938), 'Tahitian Aviculture: Acclimatisation of Foreign Birds,' *Avicult. Mag.* 3 : 8-11.

— (1940), 'Western Bluebirds in Tahiti,' *Avicult. Mag.* 5 (5) : 284-85.

Guiler, E. R. (1974), 'The Conservation of the Cape Barren Goose,' *Biol. Conserv.* 6 (4) : 252-57.

Gullion, G. W. (1949), 'Starlings on Point Reyes Peninsula, Marin County, California,' *Condor* 51 : 273.

— (1951), 'Birds of the Southern Willamette Valley, Oregon,' *Condor* 53 (3) : 129-49.

— (1956), 'The Current Status of the Starling in Nevada,' *Condor* 58 : 446.

— (1965), 'A Critique Concerning Foreign Game Bird Introductions,' *Wilson Bull.* 77 (4) : 409-14.

Gullion, G. W. and Christensen, G. C. (1957), 'A Review of the Distribution of Gallinaceous Game Birds in Nevada,' *Condor* 59 : 128-38.

Gunther, R. T. (1917), 'Note on the Acclimatisation of the Black Swan,' *Ibis* 5 (10th Ser.) (2) : 241-44.

Guppy, P. L. (1931), 'Colonization of *P. apoda* on Little Tobago,' *Avicult. Mag.* 9 (4) : 5-8.

Gurney, J. H., Russell, C. and Coues, E. (1885), *The House Sparrow,* Gurney and Jackson, London.

Gurr, L. (1951), 'Age Groups and Sex Ratio of the California Quail in Central Otago in the 1948-49-50 Shooting Season,' *Notornis* 4 (6) : 144-45.

— (1953), 'A Recent Attempt to Introduce Virginian Quail into New Zealand,' *Notornis* 5 (5) : 164.

— (1954), 'A Study of the Blackbird, *Turdus merula*, in New Zealand,' *Ibis* 96 : 225-61.

Guthrie, D. (1903), 'Canada Geese in the Outer Hebrides,' *Ann. Scot. nat. Hist.* : 119.

Gwynn, A. M. (1953), 'Some Additions to the Macquarie Island List of Birds,' *Emu* 53 : 150-52.

Hachisuka, M. U. (1924), 'Notes on Some Birds from Egypt,' *Ibis* 6 (11th Ser.) (14) : 771-73.

— (1934), *The Birds of the Philippine Islands, with Notes on the Mammal Fauna*, Part III. Witherby, London.

Hachisuka, M. and Udagawa, T. (1951), 'Contribution to the Ornithology of Formosa,' *Q. J. Taiwan Mus.* 4 (1-2) : 1-180.

Haftorn, S. (1966), 'Våre Fugler,' *Oslo (Mortensen)* : 247 pp.

Hagenstein, W. (1950), 'European Starling (*Sturnus vulgaris*) at Medina, King County, Washington,' *Murrelet* 31 : 11.

Halla, B. F. (1966), 'The Mute Swan in Rhode Island,' a paper presented at *N-East. Wildl. Conf., Boston, Massachusetts.*

Halloran, A. F. and Howard, J. A. (1956), 'Aransas Refuge Wildlife Introductions,' *J. Wildl. Mgmt.* 20 (4) : 460-61.

Hamel, J. (1970), 'Hybridization of Eastern and Crimson Rosellas in Otago,' *Notornis* 17 (2) : 126-29.

Hamilton, J. E. (1944), 'House Sparrows in the Falkland Islands,' *Ibis* 86 : 553-54.

Hamilton, W. J. (1949), 'Effect of Snow Cover on Feeding Habits of Starling in New York,' *Auk* 66 : 367-68.

503

Hammerton, J. (1898), 'English Starling at Mortlake, Victoria,' *Wombat* 3 (4) :75.

Hand, R. L. (1970), 'House Finches *(Carpodacus mexicanus)* in Montana,' *Condor* 72 :115-16.

Hankla, D. J. (1968), 'Summary of Canada Goose Transplant Programme on Nine National Wildlife Refuges in the South-east, 1953-65,' in R. L. Hine and C. Schoenfeld (eds) *Canada Goose Management* , Dembar Educational Research Service Inc., Madison, Wisconsin.

Handley, C. O. (1935), 'The Survival of Liberated Bobwhite Quail,' *Trans. Am. Game Conf.* 21 :377-80.

—— (1938), 'Recent Progress in Wild Turkey Propagation in Virginia,' *Trans. N. Am. Wildl. Conf.* 3 :847-51.

Hanson, C. (1960), 'Easter Vacation Trip to Maui and Hawaii,' *Elepaio* 20 :87-88.

Hanson, C. L. (1963), 'Exotic Game Bird Introduction Program in Ohio: A Preliminary Evaluation,' *Game Res. Ohio* 2 :205-14.

Hanson, H. G. (1946), 'Pheasant in Oklahoma,' *Okla. Game Fish News* 2 (9) :8-9.

Hanus, V. (1957), 'Release of Young Artificially-Raised Pheasants and Their Degree of Survival,' *7th Int. Congr. Game Biol.* :393-95 (In Russian).

Hanzak, J. (1974), *The Pictorial Encyclopedia of Birds*, Paul Hamlyn, Sydney, London, New York.

Hardman, J. A. (1974), 'Biology of the Skylark,' in Proc. Ass. Appl. Biol., *Ann. appl. Biol.* 76 :337-41.

Hardy, A. D. (1928), 'Skylarks and Nightingales in Australia,' *Emu* 27 :300-01.

Hardy, E. (1938), 'Movements of House Sparrows inside Liverpool,' *Field*, 9th Jne., 1938.

Hardy, F. C. (1959), 'Results of Stocking Wild-Trapped and Game Farm Turkeys in Kentucky,' *Proc. 1st Natn. Wild Turkey Symp.*, Memphis :61-65.

Hardy, J. W. (1964), 'Ringed Parakeets Nesting in Los Angeles, California,' *Condor* 66 :445-47.

—— (1965), 'Various Techniques of Evaluating Exotic Game Bird Releases,' *Proc. 17th a. Conf. S-East. Ass. Game Fish Comm.*, 1963 :108-11.

—— (1973), 'Feral Exotic Birds in Southern California,' *Wilson Bull.* 85 (4) :506-12.

Hargreaves, A. (1943), 'Introduction of Sparrows,' *Victorian Nat.* 60 :96.

Harman, I. (1963), 'Skylark "Centenary",' *Aust. Avicult.* :72.

—— (1963), 'A Dandy Among British Finches: Goldfinch,' *Aust. Avicult.* :113.

—— (1963), 'A Sturdy Britisher — The Greenfinch,' *Aust. Avicult.* :122.

Harper, H. A. (1955), 'Band Returns from Game Farm Pheasant Releases in Northern Idaho,' *Proc. 35th a. Conf. west. Ass. St. Game Fish Commnrs.* :236-42.

Harper, H. T. (1963), 'The Red-legged Partridge in California,' *Proc. 43rd a. Conf. west. Ass. St. Game Fish Commnrs.* :193-95.

Harper, H. T., Harry, B. H., and Bailer, W. D. (1958), 'The Chukar Partridge in California,' *Calif. Fish Game* 44 (1) :5-50.

Harpham, P. (1953), 'Tantalus Bird Notes: The Shama Thrush,' *Elepaio* 13 :74-76.

Harris, M. (1974), *A Field Guide to the Birds of the Galapagos*, Collins, London.

Hart, D. (1967), 'Evolving Pheasant Populations,' *Va. Wildl.* 28 (3) :10-11, 19 (*W.R.* 125 :44).

Hart, F. E. (1943), 'Hungarian Partridges in Ohio,' *Ohio Conserv. Bull.* 7 (4) :4-5, 26.

Harting, J. E. (1883), 'The Local Distribution of the Red-legged Partridge,' *Field* 61 :130-31.

Hartman, G. F. (1959), 'Wisconsin Wild Turkey Project,' *Proc. 1st natn. Wildl. Turkey Symp.*, Memphis :22-23.

504 Harvie-Brown, J. A. (1879), *The Capercaillie*

in Scotland, David Douglas, Edinburgh.

—— (1880), 'The Capercaillie in Scotland,' *Scot. Nat.*, 1880 :289-94.

—— (1898), 'Capercaillie in South East Lanarkshire,' *Ann. Scot. nat. Hist.*, 1898 : 118.

Harvie-Brown, J. A. and Buckley, T. E. (1892), *A Vertebrate Fauna of Argyll and The Inner Hebrides*, David Douglas, Edinburgh.

Harvey, N. (1975), 'Chukars are our Newest Game Bird,' *Aust. Outdoors* :14-17. Apr., 1975.

Harwin, R. M. and Irwin, M. P. S. (1966), 'The Spread of the House Sparrow, *Passer domesticus*, in South-Central Africa,' *Arnoldia* 2 (24) :1-17.

Haverschmidt, F. (1947), 'Cattle Egret in Surinam, Dutch Guiana,' *Auk* 64 :143.

—— (1950), 'Occurrence of the Cattle Egret, *Bubulcus ibis ibis*, in Surinam, Dutch Guiana,' *Auk* 67 :380-81.

—— (1951), 'The Cattle Egret, *Bubulcus i. ibis*, in British Guiana,' *Ibis* 93 :310-11.

—— (1953), 'Cattle Egret in South America,' *Audubon Mag.* 55 :202-04.

—— (1958), 'Notes on the Cattle Egret in Surinam,' *Ardea* 45 (3-4) 168-76.

Hawaiian Audubon Society (1975), *Hawaii's Birds*, 3rd Pr. Rev. 1975. Hawaii Audubon Society, Honolulu.

Hawkins, J. E. (1962), 'Controlling Redpolls in Otago Orchards,' *Orchardist, N.Z.* May, 1962.

Haydock, E. L. (1954), 'A Survey of the Birds of St Helena Island,' *Ostrich* 25 :62-75.

Heatwole, H. (1965), 'Some Aspects of the Association of Cattle Egrets with Cattle,' *Anim. Behav.* 13 (1) :78-83.

Heilbrun, L. H. (Ed) (1976), 'The Seventy-sixth Christmas Bird Count,' *Am. Birds* 30 (2) :155-633.

—— (1977), 'The Seventy-seventh Audubon Christmas Bird Count,' *Am. Birds* 31 (4):391-909.

Heilfurth, F. (1931), *Passer domesticus* L. in Mexico,' *J. Orn., Lpz.* 79 :317-19.

Heim de Balsac, H. (1926), 'Contribution à L'ornithologie du Sahara Central et du Sud-Algérien,' *Mem. Soc. Hist. nat. Afr. N.* (1).

Heinzel, H., Fitter, R. S. R. and Parslow, J. L. F. (1976), *The Birds of Britain and Europe*, 3rd Edn, Collins, London.

Hellmayr, C. E. (1932), 'Birds of Chile,' *Fld. Mus. Nat. Hist., Chicago Zool. Ser.* 19 (308).

Helms, R. (1898), 'Useful and Noxious Birds: The House Sparrow *(Passer domesticus),'* *Prod. Gaz. and Settl. Rec., West. Aust.* 5 (3) :178-81.

—— (1898), 'Useful and Noxious Birds: The Starling *(Sturnus vulgaris),'* *Prod. Gaz. and Settl. Rec., West Aust.* 5 (4) :299-302.

Henderson, H. N. (1925), 'The Cardinal in Southern California,' *Condor* 27 :211.

Henry, G. M. (1955), *A Guide to the Birds of Ceylon*, Oxford University Press, London.

Henshaw, H. W. (1904), 'Complete List of the Birds of the Hawaiian Possessions, with Notes on their Habits,' *Thrum's Haw. Almanac and Annual, 1904* :113-45.

Herklots, A. C. (1961), *The Birds of Trinidad and Tobago*, Collins, London.

Hester, F. E. and Dermid, J. (1973), *World of the Wood Duck*, Lippincott, Philadelphia.

Hewitt, J. M. (1960), 'The Cattle Egret in Australia,' *Emu* 60 (2) :99-102.

Hewitt, O. H. (Ed) (1967), *The Wild Turkey and Its Management*, Wildlife Society, Washington, D.C.

Hey, D. (1964), 'The Control of Vertebrate Problem Animals in the Province of the Cape of Good Hope, Republic of South Africa,' in *Proc. 2nd Vert. Pest Contr. Conf., March 4-5, 1964, Anaheim, Calif.*: 57-68.

—— (1967), 'Recent Developments in the Control of Vertebrate Problem Animals in the Province of the Cape of Good Hope,

Republic of South Africa,' in *Proc. 3rd Vert. Pest. Contr. Conf., March 7-8, 9, 1967, San Francisco, Calif.*

—— (1967), 'Recent Developments in the Control of Vertebrate Problem Animals in the Province of the Cape of Good Hope, Republic of South Africa,' in *Proc. 3rd Vert. Pest Contr. Conf., March 7-8, 9, 1967, San Francisco, Calif.*

Hiatt, R. W. (1947), 'The Relationship of Pheasants to Agriculture in the Yellowstone Bighorn River Valleys of Montana,' *Mont. St. Fish Game Commn., Montana* :1-72.

Hibbert-Ware, A. (1937), 'Report of the Little Owl Food Enquiry, 1936-7,' *Brit. Birds* 31 :162-87, 205-29, 249-64.

Hicks, L. E. (1933), 'The First Appearance and Spread of the Breeding Range of the European Starling *(Sturnus vulgaris)* in Ohio,' *Auk* 50 (3) :317-22.

—— (1936), 'Food Habits of the Hungarian Partridge in Ohio,' *Ohio Div. Conserv. Bull.* (104) :1-7.

—— (1936), 'History of the Importation and Naturalization of the Ring-necked Pheasant in the United States,' *Ohio Div. Conserv. Bull.* (106) :1-3.

—— (1938), 'Population Studies of the European Starling in America,' *C. R. gme. Congr. Orn. Int., Rouen* :457-74.

—— (1940), 'The Role of Exotics in Ohio Valley and the Lower Great Lakes Region,' *Ohio Wildl. Res. Station*, Release (133) :1-4.

—— (1941), 'The Role of Exotics in the Ohio Valley,' *Trans. N. Am. Wildl. Conf.* 5 :420-24.

Higuchi, H. (1976), 'Comparative Study of the Breeding of Mainland and Island Subspecies of the Varied Tit,' *Tori* 25 :11-20.

Hill, W. R. (1952), 'The European Starling in Fiji,' *Emu* 52 :218.

Hindwood, K. A. (1948), 'A Communal Roost of the Indian Mynah,' *Emu* 47 (4) :315-17.

—— (1960), 'The Birds of Sydney,' *Aust. Mus. Mag.* 13 (8) :241-45.

Hindwood, K. A. and Cunningham, J. M. (1950) 'Notes on the Birds of Lord Howe Island,' *Emu* 50 :23-25.

Hinton, H. E. and Dunn, A. M. S. (1967), *Mongooses: Their Natural History and Behaviour*, Oliver and Boyd, London.

Hix, G. E. (1905), 'A Year with the Birds in New York City,' *Wilson Bull.* 12 (2) :35.

Hjersman, H. A. (1947), 'A History of the Establishment of the Ring-necked Pheasant in California,' *Calif. Fish Game* 33 (1) :3-11.

Hjersman, H. J. (1948), 'The Californian Valley Quail in New Zealand,' *Calif. Fish Game* 34 (1) :33-36.

Hobbs, D. F. (1955), 'Do Newly Introduced Species Present a Separate Problem,' *Proc. N.Z. ecol. Soc.* (2) :12-14.

Hobbs, J. N. (1961), 'Birds of the South West New South Wales,' *Emu* 61 (1) :54.

Hoffman, E. C. (1930), 'The Spread of the European Starling in America,' *Wilson Bull.* 42 :80.

Holbrook, H. L. and Lewis, J. C. (1967), 'Management of the Eastern Turkey in the Southern Appalachian and Cumberland Plateau Region,' in O. H. Hewitt (ed) *The Wild Turkey and Its Management*, Chapt 12 :343-70, Wildlife Society, Washington, D.C.

Holland, C. S. and Williams, J. M. (1978), 'Observations on the Birds of Antigua,' *Am. Birds* 32 (6) :1095-1105.

Holyoak, D. T. (1974), 'Oiseaux des Isles de la Société,' *Oiseau Revue fr. Orn.* 44 (1) :1-27; 44 (2) :153-81.

—— (1974), 'Ecology, Behaviour and Territory of the Magpie,' *Bird Study* 21 :117-28.

—— (1979), 'Notes on the Birds of Viti Levu and Taveuni, Fiji,' *Emu* 79 (1) :7-18.

Hone, J. (1978), 'Introduction and Spread of

the Common Myna in New South Wales,' *Emu* 78 (4) :227-30.

Hoogerwerf, A. (1971), 'On a Collection of Birds from Vogelkop, near Marokwari, North-Western New Guinea,' *Emu* 71 (1) :1-12.

Hopkins, F. (1940), 'The Wild Turkey Problem in Wisconsin,' *Wis. Conserv. Bull.* 5 (12) :47-48.

Horikawa, Y. (1936), 'On the Animals Imported from Formosa,' *Formosa in Sci.* 4 (2) :68-70.

Howard, W. E. (1959), 'The European Starling in California,' *Calif. Dep. Agric. Bull.* 38 (3) :171-78.

—— (1960), 'Innate and Environmental Dispersal of Individual Vertebrates,' *Am. Midl. Nat.* 63 (1) :152-61.

Howard, W. E., Cummings, M. W. and Zajanc, A. (1961), 'Comments on Bird Problems in California,' *Calif. Vector News* 8 (3) :13-16, 17.

Howell, A. B. (1943), 'Starlings and Woodpeckers,' *Auk* 60 :90-91.

Howells, G. (1963), 'The Status of Red-legged Partridges in Britain,' *Game Res. Ass. a. Rep.* 2:46-51.

Howitt, H. (1925), 'The Starling at Guelph, Ontario,' *Auk* 42:446-47.

Hubbard, J. P. (1966), 'The Cattle Egret on the Pacific Coast of Chiapas, Mexico,' *Wilson Bull.* 78:121.

Huckle, C. H. (1924), 'Birds of Ascension Island and St Helena,' *Ibis* 11 (6) :818-21.

Hudson, G. E. and King, J. R. (1951), 'Nesting of the European Starling in Adams County, Washington,' *Murrelet* 32:24.

Hudson, R. (1965), 'The Spread of the Collared Dove in Britain and Ireland,' *Brit. Birds* 58:105-39.

—— (1972), 'Collared Doves in Britain and Ireland, 1965-70,' *Brit. Birds* 65 :139-55.

—— (1974), 'Feral Parakeets near London,' *Brit. Birds* 67 (9) :33, 174.

—— (1976), 'Ruddy Ducks in Britain,' *Brit. Birds* 69 (4) :132-43.

Hudson, W. H. (1920), *Birds of La Plata*, 2 vols. Dent and Sons, New York.

—— (1921), *British Birds*, Longman, Green, London.

Huey, L. M. (1932), 'Some Light on the Introduction of Gambel Quail on San Clemente Island, California,' *Condor* 34:46.

Hume, A. O. (1874), 'Contributions to the Ornithology of India : The Islands of the Bay of Bengal,' *Stray Feathers* 2 :29-324.

—— (1880), 'The Birds of the Western Half of the Malay Peninsula' (Third Notice), *Stray Feathers* 8:107-32.

Humphrey, P. S., Bridge, D., Reynolds, P. W. and Peterson, R. T. (1970), *Birds of the Isla Grande (Tierra del Fuego)*, Prelim. Smithson. Man, Smithson Institute. : 1-411.

Hung-Shou, P. (1962), 'Animals of Western Szechuan,' *Nature* 196 (4849) :14.

Hunt, C. J. (1926), 'The English Starling at Chicago, Illinois,' *Auk* 43 (2) :239-40.

Hutchins, R. E. (1938), 'Invasion of Northern Mississippi by the Starlings,' *Wilson Bull.* 45 (3) :140-41.

Hutchinson, F. (1900), 'Introduced Birds of Scinde Island,' *E. Cst. Nat.* (5) :28.

Hutson, A. M. (1975), 'Observations on the Birds of Diego Garcia, Chagos Archipelago, with Notes on Other Vertebrates,' *Atoll Res. Bull.* (75) :1-25.

Hutton, F. W. (1869), 'The Introduction of Pheasants into Auckland Province,' *Trans. N.Z. Inst.* 2:80.

Hylton, C. G. (1927), 'Colombo Crows Reach Australia,' *Emu* 27 (1) :44.

Imber, M. J. (1971), 'The Identity of New Zealand's Canada Geese,' *Notornis* 18 (4) :253-61.

Imber, M. J. and Williams, G. R. (1968), 'Mortality Rates of a Canada Goose Population in New Zealand,' *J. Wildl. Mgmt.* 32 (2) :256-66.

Imhof, T. A. (1958), 'Recent Additions to the Avifauna of Alabama,' *Auk* 75 :354-57.

—— (1962), *Alabama Birds*, Dep. Conserv. Game and Fish Div. University Alabama Press, Alabama.

—— (1978), 'The Spring Migration March 1-May 31, 1978 : Central Southern Region,' *Am. Birds* 32 (5) :1017-21.

Immelmann, K. (1960), 'The Spread of Introduced Birds in Northern Queensland,' *Aust. J. Sci.* 23 (4) :130.

—— (1965), *Australian Finches in Bush and Aviary*, Angus & Robertson, Melbourne.

Ingram, C. (1915), 'A Few Notes on *Tetrao urogallus* and its Allies,' *Ibis* 3 (10th Ser.) :128-33.

Ingram, W. (1911), 'Acclimatization of the Greater Bird of Paradise *(P. apoda)* in West Indies,' *Avicult. Mag.* 2 :142-47.

Iredale, T. (1956), *Birds of New Guinea*, 2 vols, Georgian House, Melbourne.

Irving, N. S. and Beesley, J. S. S. (1976), *Bird Pest Research Project, Botswana : Final Report 1972-75*, Ministry of Overseas Development, Govt. Botsw., ODM. Res. Sch. R. 2664.

Ivanauskas, T. and Zubavichus, T. (1955), 'An Attempt to Introduce the Gray Goose in Latvia,' *Biull. Moskov. Obs. Isp. Prir. Biol.* 60 (4) :97-98 (In Russian).

Jack, N. (1952), 'Goldfinches Around Brisbane,' *Emu* 52:222-23.

Jack, N. and Fien, I. (1970), 'The Red-backed Parrot in the Brisbane Area,' *Emu* 70 (1) :34.

Jackson, A. S. (1957), 'Spanish Red-legged and Seesee Partridge Introductions in the Texas Panhandle,' *Proc. 37th a. conf. west. Ass. St. Game Fish Commnrs.* :291-94.

—— (1964), 'A Study of the Introduction, Release and Survival of Certain European and Asiatic Game Birds,' *Trans. 29th N. Am. Wildl. Conf.* :259-69.

Jackson, A. S., De Arment, R. and Bell, J. (1957), 'Release of the Redlegs,' *Tex. Game Fish* 15 (12) :16-17, 26-27.

Jacot-Guillarmod, C. (1960), 'European Starling *Sturnus vulgaris* in Grahamstown,' *Ostrich* 31 (4) :173.

Janson, R., Hartkorn, F. and Greene, R. (1971), 'Ring-necked Pheasant,' in T. W. Mussehl and F. W. Howell (eds), *Game Management in Montana*, Montana Fish and Game Department, Helena, Montana, Chapt. 18 :153-59.

Jeffery, A. (1957), 'Birds of Flinders Chase, Kangaroo Island,' *S. Aust. Orn.* 22 :49-52.

Jenkins, C. F. H. (1929), 'The Starling,' *Emu* 29 (1) :49-51.

—— (1929), 'Java Sparrows in Western Australia,' *Emu* 28 (3) :235.

—— (1959), 'Introduced Birds in Western Australia,' *Emu* 59 (3) :201-07.

—— (1977), *The Noah's Ark Syndrome*, General Printing, Perth, Western Australia.

Jenkins, C. F. H. and Ford, J. (1960), 'The Cattle Egret and Its Symbionts in South-Western Australia,' *Emu* 60 (4) :245-49.

Jenkins, D., Watson, A. and Miller, G. R. (1963), 'Population Studies on Red Grouse, *Lagopus lagopus scoticus* (Lath.) in North-East Scotland,' *J. Anim. Ecol.* 32 (3) :317-76.

Jewett, S. G. (1942), 'The European Starling in California,' *Condor* 44 :79.

—— (1946), 'The Starling Taken in the State of Washington,' *Condor* 48 :143.

—— (1946), 'The Starling in Oregon,' *Condor* 48 :245.

Jewett, S. G. and Gabrielson, I. N. (1929), 'Birds of the Portland Area, Oregon,' Cooper Orn. Club, *Pacif. Cst. Avifauna* (19) :1-54.

Jewett, S. G., Taylor, W. P., Shaw, W. T. and Aldrich, J. W. (1953), *Birds of Washington State*, University Washington Press, Seattle.

Job, H. K. (1923), *Propagation of Wild Birds*, Doubleday, Page Co, New York.

Jobin, L. (1952), 'The European Starling in Central British Columbia,' *Condor* 54:318.

Johns, J. E. and Erickson, C. W. (1970), 'Breeding of Free-Living Trumpeter Swans in Northeastern Washington,' *Condor* 72:377-78.

Johnsgard, P. A. (1973), *Grouse and Quails of North America*, University Nebraska Press, Lincoln, Nebraska.

Johnson, A. W. (1965-67), *The Birds of Chile and Adjacent Regions of Argentina, Bolivia and Peru*, 2 vols, Platt Estab. Graficos, Buenos Aires, S.A.

Johnson, A. W., Millie, W. R. and Moffett, G. (1970), 'Notes on the Birds of Easter Islands,' *Ibis* 112 (4) :532-38.

Johnson, B. D. (1959), 'History of Turkey Restoration in Mississippi and its Effects on Present Management,' *Proc. 1st natn. Wild Turkey Symp., Memphis* :65-69.

Johnson, D. A. (1960), Chukars, 'The Exotic Partridge,' *Naturalist* 11 (2) :29-32.

Johnson, M. (1957), 'The Hun and its Limiting Factors,' *N. Dak. Outdoors* 19 (10) :7-9.

Johnston, R. F. and Selander, R. K. (1964), 'House Sparrows: Rapid Evolution of Races in North America,' *Science* 144 :548-50.

Johnstone, G. W. (1967), 'Blackgame and Capercaillie in Relation to Forestry in Britain,' *For. Suppl.* 40 :68-77.

Jollie, M. (1951), 'A Positive Breeding Record of the Starling in Idaho,' *Murrelet* 32 :13.

Jonas, R. (1966), 'Meriam's Turkey in Southeastern Montana,' *Mont. Fish Game Dep. Tech. Bull.* (3) :1-36.

Jones, F. L. (1950), 'The Starling in Glenn County, California,' *Condor* 52:141.

Jones, V. E. (1946), 'The Starling in Idaho,' *Condor* 48 (3) :142-43.

Jonkel, G. M. (1954), 'A Comparative Study of Survival of Fall and Spring Released Chukar Partridges *(Alectoris graeca chukar)*,' *Western States Chukar Comm., Qu. Rep.* 2 (1) :1-47.

Joubert, H. J. (1945), 'Starlings and Others' (Introductions), *Ostrich* 16 (3) :214-16.

Journal Hawaiian Audubon Society (1977), 'Accounts of Endangered Hawaiian Birds' from Report of the Am. Orn. Un. Commission on Conserv., 1974-75, *Suppl. to Auk* (1975) 92 (4), in *Elepaio* 35 (10) :105-08.

Jung, C. S. (1936), 'The European Goldfinch *(Carduelis carduelis)* in Wisconsin,' *Auk* 53:340-41.

—— (1945), 'A History of the Starling in the United States,' *Passenger Pigeon* 7 (4) :111-16.

Kaburaki, T. (1934), 'Effects of Some Exotic Plants and Animals Upon the Flora and Fauna of Japan,' in *Proc. 5th Pacif. Sci. Congr. Vic and Vanc., B.C., 1933* :801-05, University Toronto Press, Canada.

—— (1940), 'Further Notes on the Effects of Some Exotic Animals upon the Fauna and Flora of Japan,' in *Proc. 6th Pacif. Sci. Congr., Berkeley, Calif.* 4 :229-30.

Kale, H. W. (1977), 'The Spring Migration, April 1-May 31, 1977 : Florida Region,' *Am. Birds* 31 (5) :988-92.

Källander, H. (1976), 'Data on the Breeding Biology of the Blue Tit in Scania,' *Vår. Fågelvårld* 35:1-7 (Swedish with English summary).

Kalmbach, E. R. (1922), 'A Comparison of the Food Habits of British and American Starlings,' *Auk* 39 :189-95.

—— (1930), 'English Sparrow Control,' *U.S. Dep. Agric. Leafl.* (61) :1-8.

—— (1931), 'The European Starling in the United States,' *U.S. Dept. Agric. Farm Bull.* (1571) :1-26.

—— (1932), 'Winter Starling Roosts of Washington,' *Wilson Bull.* 39 (2) :65-75.

—— (1940), 'Economic Status of the English Sparrow in the United States,' *U.S. Dep. Agric. Tech. Bull.* (711).

— (1945), 'Review of Suggestions for Combating Objectionable Roosts of Birds with Special Reference to those of Starlings,' *U.S. Dep. Interior Wildl. Leafl.* (172):1-19.

Kalmbach, E. R. and Gabrielson, I. N. (1921), 'Economic Value of the Starling in the United States,' *U.S. Dep. Agric. Bull.* (868):1-66.

Kashkarov, D. N. (1926), 'Nablyudeniya nad biologii vorodya i nad prinosimim im vredom' (Observations on Biology of Sparrows and on Damage Incurred through them), *Byull. Sredne — Asiatskago gosudar stvenago universiteta* 13:61-80.

Kauffman, H. H. (1962), 'Pennsylvania Wild Turkeys in Germany,' *Pa. Game News* 33 (5):27-29 (In *W.R.* 107:73).

Kay, F. C. L. (1904), 'Capercaillie in Argyll,' *Ann. Scot. nat. Hist.,* 1904:189.

Kays, C. E. (1972), 'Red Junglefowl Introductions in Kentucky: A Final Report,' *Ky. Dep. Fish Wildl. Res., P-R Game Mgmt. Tech. Ser.* (18):1-16.

Kear, J. (1964), 'Wildfowl and Agriculture in Britain,' *Proc. M.A.R. Conf. I.U.C.N. Publ., New Ser.* (3):321-31.

— (1965), 'The Assessment of Goose Damage by Grazing Trials,' *Trans. 6th int. Un. Game Biol.* :333-39.

Kear, J. and Duplaix-Hall, N. (1975), *Flamingos,* Poyser, Berkhamsted.

Keast, A. (1958), 'Infraspecific Variation in the Australian Finches,' *Emu* 58:219-46.

Keeler, J. E. (1963), 'Status of the Red Jungle Fowl in the Southeastern States,' *Proc. 17th a. Conf. S-East. Ass. Game Fish Commnrs.,* 1963:107.

Keffer, M., Davis, L., Clark, D., *et al,* (1974), 'Pest Evaluation — Monk Parakeet, *Myiopsitta monachus,*' *Calif. Dep. Food Agric. Publ.* :1-23.

— (1976), 'An Evaluation of the Pest Potential of the Genus Zosterops (White Eyes) in California,' *Calif. Dep. Food Agric. Spec. Serv. Unit* :1-22.

Keith, A. R. (1957), 'Bird Observations in Fiji and Samoa,' *Elepaio* 18:25-27.

Keith, K. and Hinds, M. P. (1958), 'New and Rare Species of Birds at Macquarie Island During 1956 and 1957,' *C.S.I.R.O. Wildl. Res.* 3 (1):50.

Kelham, H. R. (1881), 'Ornithological Notes made in Strait Settlements and in Western States of the Malay Peninsula,' *Ibis* 5 (2):501-31.

Kelly, W. N. (1927), 'The Japanese Starling in Vancouver, British Columbia,' *Murrelet* 8:14.

Kelso, L. (1932), 'A Note on the Food of the Hungarian Partridge,' *Auk* 49:204-11.

Kendeigh, S. C. and Pinowski, J. (eds) (1972), 'Productivity, Population Dynamics and Systematics of Granivorous Birds,' *Proc. Gen. Meet. Work. Grp. Graniv. Birds, I.B.P., Pt. Sect., Hague, Holland, Sept. 6-8, 1970, P.W.N.* — Polish Scie. Publs., Warszawa.

Kent, C. C. (1927), 'The Indian Mynah in Natal,' *S. Afr. J. nat. Hist.* 6:127-29.

Kessel, B. (1953), 'Distribution and Migration of the European Starling in North America,' *Condor* 55:49-67.

— (1953), 'Second Broods in the European Starling in North America,' *Auk* 70:479-83.

— (1957), 'Breeding Biology of the European Starling (*Sturnus vulgaris*) in North America,' *Am. Midl. Nat.* 58:257-331.

Keulemans, J. G. (1866), 'Opmerkingen over de Vogels van de Kaap-Verdische Eilanden. En van Prins Eiland,' *N.T.D.* 3:368-74.

Keve, A. (1950), 'Further Notes on the Range-increasing and Oecology of the Indian Ring-dove,' *Aquila* 51-54:116-22.

— (1976), 'Some Remarks on the Taxonomic Position of the Tree Sparrow Introduced into Australia,' *Emu* 76 (3):152-53.

Kikkawa, J. and Boles, W. (1976), 'Seabird Island No. 15.: Heron Island, Queensland,' *Aust. Bird Bander* 14 (1):3-6.

Kikkawa, J. and Yamashina, Y. (1966), 'Breeding of Introduced Black Swans in Japan,' *Emu* 66 (4):377-81.

Killpack, M. L. and Crittenden, D. N. (1952), 'Starlings as Winter Residents in the Unita Basin, Utah,' *Condor* 54:338-44.

Kimball, J. W. (1945), 'Pheasant Crop Damage,' *S. Dak. Conserv. Dig.* 12 (5):10.

Kincaid, E. (1962), 'Starlings Between Hawaii and California,' *Condor* 64 (6):512.

King, B. (1959-60), 'Feral North-American Ruddy Ducks in Somerset,' *Wildfowl Trust a. Rep.* :167-68.

King, B. F., Dickinson, E. C. and Woodcock, M. W. (1975), *A Field Guide to the Birds of South-East Asia,* Repr. 1976. Collins, London.

King, J. E. (1958), 'Some Observations on the Birds of Tahiti and the Marquesas Islands,' *Elepaio* 19:14-17.

King, R. T. (1942), 'Is it Wise Policy to Introduce Exotic Game Birds,' *Audubon Mag.* 44 (3):136-45; 44 (4):230-36; 44 (5):306-10.

Kinghorn, J. R. (1931), 'Notes on the Starling,' *Emu* 30 (3):225-26.

— (1933), 'A Report of the Distribution, Migratory Movements and Control of the Starling in Australia,' *Aust. Dep. agric. J.* 36 (10):1154-58.

— (1933), 'The Starling in Australia, Its Distribution and Suggestions for Control,' *Agric. Gaz., N.S.W.* 44:512-15.

Kingsmill, W. (1920), 'Acclimatization,' *J. Proc. R. Soc. West. Aust.* 5:33-38.

Kinsky, F. C. (1973), 'The Subspecific Status of the New Zealand Population of the Little Owl, *Athene noctua* (Scopoli, 1769),' *Notornis* 20:9-13.

Kirk, T. W. (n.d.), 'Notes on the Breeding Habits of the European Sparrow (*Passer domesticus*) in New Zealand,' *N.Z.J. Sci.* 1 (2):9-12.

Kirkpatrick, R. D. (1959), 'Coturnix Investigation: Final Report,' *Indiana Dep. Conserv. Div. Fish Game, Indianapolis P-R Project W-2-R.*

— (1960), 'Movements and Longevity of Japanese Quail Released in Indiana,' *Indiana Audubon Q.* 38 (4):58-59.

— (1965), 'Introduction of the Japanese Quail (*Coturnix coturnix japonica*) in Indiana,' *Proc. Indiana Acad. Sci.* 75:289-92.

Kleen, V. M. (1974), 'The Fall Migration Aug 1-Nov 30, 1973: Middle Western Prairie Regions,' *Am. Birds* 28 (1):28-121.

— (1976), 'Fall Migration Aug 1-Nov 30, 1975: Middle Western Prairie Regions,' *Am. Birds* 30 (1):77-82.

Kleinschnitz, F. C. (1957), 'History of the Introduction of the Spanish Red-legged Partridge in Colorado,' *Proc. 37th a. Conf. west. Ass. St. Game Fish Commnrs.* :280-82.

Klimstra, W. D. and Hankla, D. (1953), 'Preliminary Report on Pheasant Stocking in Southern Illinois,' *Trans. Ill. St. Acad. Sci.* 46:235-39.

Kloss, C. B. (1903), *In the Andamans and Nicobars,* John Murray, London.

Knupp, D. M. (1977), 'Reproductive Biology of the American Robin in Northern Maine,' *Auk* 94:80-85.

Koch, L. (1956), *The Encyclopaedia of British Birds,* Waverley Book Co, London.

Kobayashi, K. (1961), *Birds of Japan in Natural colours,* Hoikusha, Japan.

Koehler, J. W. (1963), 'How to Control Some Offbeat Birds,' *Pest Control* 31 (9):35.

Koehler, W. (1962), 'Wprowadzenie Baizanta do Polski' (Introduction of the Pheasant in Poland), *Chrónmy Przyrode Ojczysta* 18 (3):26-30, 54 (In Polish). (In *W.R.* 110:48.)

Koepcke, H-W. and Koepcke, M. (1964-71), 'Las Aves silvestres de importancia economica del Peru,' *Min. de Agric., Serv. For. y de Caza, Lima, Peru.* (5-18):33-152.

Kolichis, N. (1978), 'Chestnut-breasted Finch, *Lonchura castaneothorax,* at Osborne Park,' *West Aust. Nat.* 14 (2):51.

Korhonen, S. (1972), 'Tuloksia kana-danhanhen istutuskokeilusta Inplanterings — forsok med kanadagås (*Branta canadensis*),' *Suomen Riista* 24:52-56 (In Finnish).

Korschgen, L. J. and Chambers, G. D. (1970), 'Propagation, Stocking and Food Habits of Reeves Pheasants in Missouri,' *J. Wildl. Mgmt.* 34 (2):274-82.

Kovacs, B. (1955), 'Untersuchungsresulate des Kropfinhaltes der Feld-und Haussperlinge, sowie deren wirtschaftliche Bedentung an dem Gebiete der Landwirtschaft der Akademie in Debrecen,' *Debrec. Mezögazdasági Akad. Evkönyve* :63-93.

Kozlik, F. M. (1948), 'Gentle Release Method of Stocking Pheasants,' *Wis. Conserv. Bull.* 13 (5):12-14.

Kozlik, F. M. and McLean, D. D. (1958), *Waterfowl in California,* State Printing Office, Sacramento, California. :1-32.

Krause, H. and Froiland, S. G. (1956), 'Distribution of the Cardinal in South Dakota,' *Wilson Bull.* 68 (2):111-17.

Kuroda, N. (1913), 'A Flock of Java Sparrows Settled Down in Haneda Village,' *Zool. J.* 25:563-66 (In Japanese).

— (1922), 'On the Birds of Tsushima and Iki Islands, Japan,' *Ibis* (4th Ser.) 4 (1):75-104.

— (1933-36), *Birds of the Island of Java,* 2 vols, Private Publications, Tokyo.

— (1937), 'Buncho Ni Tsuite' (Notes on the Java Sparrow), *Tori* 9 (45):478-84 (In Japanese).

Kuzmina, M. A. (1955), 'Ecology and Morphology of *Alectoris Graeca Dzungarica* Sushk. and *Tetraogallus Himalayensis* Sewertzowi Gray,' *Zoologicheskii zhurnal* :34 (1):175-90 (In Russian).

Labisky, R. F. (1961), 'Reports of Attempts to Establish Japanese Quail in Illinois,' *J. Wildl. Mgmt.* 25 (3):290-95.

Labisky, R. F. and Anderson, W. L. (1965), 'Changes in the Distribution and Abundance of Pheasants in Illinois, 1958 "V" 1963,' *Trans. Ill. St. Acad. Sci.* 58 (2):127-35.

Lack, D. (1943), 'The Breeding Birds of Orkney,' *Ibis* 85 (1):1-27.

— (1976), *Island Biology, Illustrated by the Land Birds of Jamaica,* Studies in Ecology 3, University California Press, Berkeley and Los Angeles.

Lack, D., Lack, E., Lack, P., and Lack A. (1973), 'Birds on St Vincent (West Indies,) *Ibis* 115 (1):46-52.

Lack, D. and Southern, H. N. (1949), 'Birds on Tenerife,' *Ibis* 91:607.

Lagenbach, J. R. (1940), 'Crop Damage by Ring-necked Pheasants,' *Pa. Game News* 10 (12):10-11.

Lancan, F. and Mougin, J.-L. (1974), 'Les Oiseaux des Isles Gambier et de quelques Atolls Orientaux de L-archipel des Tuamotu (Ocean Pacifique),' *Oiseau Revue fr. Orn.* 44 (3):191-280.

Lance, A. N. (1974), 'Release of Pen-Reared Red Grouse (*Lagopus l. scoticus*) to Restock Breeding Populations in Ireland,' *11th Int. Congr. Game Biol., 1973* :225-29.

Lancum, H. F. (1961), 'Wild Birds and the Land,' *Min. Agric. Fish Food, London,* Bull. (140), 1948, 9th Impr., 1961.

Land, H. C. (1970), *Birds of Guatemala,* Livingston, Wynnewood, Pennsylvania.

— (1963), 'A Collection of Birds from the Caribbean Lowlands of Guatemala,' *Auk* 75:354-57.

Lane, S. G. (1964), 'First Arrivals at Lane Cove and North Ryde, NSW,' *Emu* 64 (1):47.

— (1975), 'The White-winged Widowbird

near Windsor, NSW,' *Aust. Bird-bander* 13 (3) :61.

Langseth, R. (1965), 'Tyrkerduen har nådd Island,' *Sterna* 6 :311.

Larrison, E. J. (1947), 'Eastern Starling in Snohomish County, Washington,' *Murrelet* 28 :21.

Lashmar, A. F. C. (1935), 'Bird Notes in the Eastern Portion of Kangaroo Island,' *S. Aust. Orn.* 13 :508.

—— (1937), 'Nesting Activities in the Eastern Portion of Kangaroo Island,' *S. Aust. Orn.* 14 :59-64.

Laskey, A. R. (1962), 'Breeding Biology of Mockingbirds,' *Auk* 79 :596-606.

Latham, R. M. (1941), 'History of the Wild Turkey in Pennsylvania,' *Pa. Game News* 12 (9) :6-7.

—— (1956), *Complete Book of the Wild Turkey,* Stackpole, Harrisburg, Pennsylvania.

La Touche, J. D. D. (1925-34) *A Handbook of the Birds of Eastern China,* 2 vols, Taylor and Francis, London.

Lavery, H. J. (1964), 'The Brolga, *Grus rubicundus* (Perry) on Some Coastal Areas in North Queensland: Fluctuations in Populations and Economic Aspects,' *Qd. J. agric. Sci.* 21 :261.

—— (1968), 'Queensland Bird Pest Problems,' in *Aust. Verm. Contr. Conf., 1968 Melbourne, Vic.* :145-57.

—— (1969), 'Collisions Between Aircraft and Birds at Townsville, Queensland,' *Qd. J. agric. Anim. Sci.* 26 (3) :447.

—— (1974), 'Species Introduced by Man,' in *Fauna of Queensland Yearbook, 8-9,* Government Printers, Brisbane.

Lavery, H. J. and Blackman, J. G. (1969), 'Cranes of Australia,' *Qd. agric. J.,* Mar., 1969 :156-62.

—— (1970), 'Sorghum Damage by Lorikeets,' *Qd. agric. J.* 96 :785-87.

Lavery, H. J. and Hopkins, N. (1963), 'Birds of the Townsville District of North Queensland,' *Emu* 63 (3) :242-52.

Law, S. C. (1932), 'Place of the Java Sparrow (*Munia oryzivora* L.) in the Indian Avifauna,' *J. Bombay nat. Hist. Soc.* 35 :683-85.

Lawrence, A. M. (1926), 'Distribution of the Goldfinch,' *Emu* 25 (3) :219.

Lawson, W. (1949), *Blue Gum Clippers and Whale Ships of Tasmania,* Georgian House, Melbourne.

Laycock, G. (1970), *The Alien Animals,* Ballantine Books, New York.

Leach, J. A. (1928), 'Notes made during a Holiday Trip to New Caledonia,' *Emu* 28 :42.

—— (1958), *An Australian Bird Book,* 9th Edn. Rev, Whitcombe & Tombs, Melbourne.

Leach, H. R., Ferrel, C. M. and Clark, E. E. (1953), 'A Study of the Food Habits of the Ring-necked Pheasant on Irrigated Pasture in California,' *Calif. Fish Game* 39 (4) :517-25.

Leck, C. F. (1973), 'A House Sparrow Roost in Lima, Peru,' *Auk* 90 (4) :888.

Leckie, N. (1897), 'Capercaillie in Linlithgowshire,' *Ann. Scot. nat. Hist.* :44.

Lee, J. (1941), 'Starlings in the Lower Rio Grande Valley of New Mexico,' *Condor* 43 (4) :197.

—— (1955), 'Preliminary Observations on the Turkish Chukar in New Mexico,' *Proc. 34th a. Conf. west. Ass. St. Game Fish Commnrs.* :227-230.

—— (1959), 'The Present Status of the Wild Turkey in New Mexico,' *Proc. 1st natn. Wild Turkey Symp., Memphis* :11-18.

Lee, W. H. and Lewis, J. (1959), 'Establishment and Spread of the Wild Turkey in South-western Michigan,' *J. Wildl. Mgmt.* 23 (2) :210-15.

Lees, S. G. (1967), 'The Breeding of the House Sparrow, *Passer domesticus,* in Rhodesia,' *Ostrich* 38 (1) :3-4.

Legge, W. V. (1874), 'On the Distribution of Birds in Southern Ceylon,' *Ibis* 4 (13) :7-33.

Lehmann, F. C. (1959), 'Observations on the Cattle Egret in Colombia,' *Condor* 61 :265-69.

Lehmann, V. W. (1943), 'Pheasants in South Texas,' *Tex. Game Fish* 1 (10) :5, 18.

—— (1948), 'Restocking on King Ranch,' *Trans. N. Am. Wildl. Conf.* 13 :236-39.

Leicester, Earl of (1921), 'Date of the Introduction into England of the Red-legged Partridge,' *Field* 137 :372.

Leicester, M. (1959), 'Clutch Size in the Goldfinch, *Carduelis carduelis,*' *Emu* 59 (4) :295-96.

Lekagul, B. and Cronin, E. W. (1974), *Bird Guide of Thailand,* 2nd Edn Rev, Kuruspa, Bangkok.

Lemke, C. W. (1957), 'The Hungarian Partridge,' *Wis. Conserv. Bull.* 22 (10) :19-22.

Lendon, A. H. (1948), 'A Further Report on the Introduced Grenadier Weaver,' *S. Aust. Orn.* 19 (1) :2.

—— (1952), 'Bulbuls in Melbourne,' *Emu* 52 :67-68.

Leopold, A. (1933), *Game Management,* C. Scribner's Sons, New York.

—— (1937), '1936 Pheasant Nesting Study,' *Wilson Bull.* 44 (2) :91-95.

—— (1940), 'Spread of the Hungarian Partridge in Wisconsin,' *Trans. Wis. Acad. Sci. Arts Lett.* 32 :5-28.

Leopold, A. S. (1944), 'The Nature of Heritable Wildness in Turkeys,' *Condor* 46 (4) :133-97.

—— (1978), *The California Quail,* University California Press, Berkeley, California.

Leopold, A. S. and McCabe, R. A. (1957), 'Natural History of the Montezuma Quail in Mexico,' *Condor* 59 (1) :3-26.

Lepine, M. P. and Sautter, V. (1951), 'Sur L'infection des Pigeons Parisiennes par la Virus de L'Ornithose,' *Bull. Acad. natn. Méd.* 135 :332-38.

Le Souef, A. S. (1913), no title (in Stray Feathers), *Emu* 12 (3) :190.

Le Souef, J. C. (1958), 'The Introduction of Sparrows into Victoria,' *Emu* 58 :264-66.

Le Souef, L. (1912), 'Acclimatisation,' *Handbook of Western Australia* :249-52.

Le Souef, S. J. C. (1922), 'Starlings Roost in the Zoological Gardens,' *Emu* 21 (4) :316.

Le Souef, W. H. D. (1890), 'Acclimatisation in Victoria,' *Rep. 2nd Meet. Aust. Ass. Adv. Sci., Victoria.* :476-82.

—— (1903), 'Goldfinch in Australia and Tasmania,' *Zoologist* 7 (4th Ser.) (191) :743.

—— (1918), 'Red-vented Bulbul,' *Emu* 17 (3) :236.

Leuthold, W. (1977), 'Breeding Biology of the Ostrich in Tsavo East National Park, Kenya,' *Ibis* 119 (4) :541-44.

Lever, C. (1957), 'The Mandarin Duck in Britain,' *Country Life* :829-31.

—— (1977), *The Naturalised Animals of the British Isles,* Hutchinson & Co, London.

Léveque, R. (1964), 'Notes on Ecuadorian Birds,' *Ibis* 106 (1) :52-62.

Levi, H. W. (1952), 'Evaluation of Wildlife Importations,' *Sci. Monthly* 74 (6) :315-22.

—— (1954), *Bibliography on the Introduction of Exotic Animals,* (Rev, 1954). Author, University Wis. Zool. Dep.

Lewin, V. (1965), 'The Introduction and Present Status of the California Quail in the Okanagan Valley of British Columbia,' *Condor* 67 (1) :61-66.

—— (1971), 'Exotic Game Birds of the Puu Waawaa Ranch, Hawaii,' *J. Wildl. Mgmt.* 35 (1) :141-55.

Lewin, V. and Holmes, J. C. (1971), 'Helminths from the Exotic Game Birds of the Puu Waawaa Ranch, Hawaii,' *Pacif. Sci.* 25 :372-81.

Lewis, H. F. (1925), 'The First Labrador Record of the Starling (*Sturnus vulgaris*),' *Auk* 42 :272-73.

—— (1927). 'A Distributional and Economic Study of the European Starling in Ontario,' *Univ. Toronto Studies, Biol. Ser.* (30) :1-57.

—— (1931), 'Notes on the Starling (*Sturnus vulgaris*) in the Northern Parts of its North American Range,' *Auk* 48 :605-06.

—— (1934), 'Some Observations Indicating the North eastward Extension of the Starling,' *Auk* 51 :88-89.

—— (1935), 'Nesting of the Starling (*Sturnus vulgaris vulgaris* L.) in the Labrador Peninsula,' *Auk* 52 :313.

Lewis, H. G. (1932), 'The Occurrence of the European Starling (*Sturnus vulgaris*) in the James Bay Region,' *Auk* 49 :225.

Lewis, J. B. (1961), 'Wild Turkeys in Missouri, 1940-60,' *Trans. N. Am. Wildl. Conf.* 26 :505-13.

—— (1966), 'Hybridization Between Wild and Domestic Turkeys in Missouri,' *J. Wildl. Mgmt.* 30 :431-32.

—— (1967), 'Management of the Eastern Turkey in the Ozarks and Bottomland Hardwoods,' in O. H. Hewitt (ed), *Wild Turkey and its Management,* Wildlife Society, Washington, D.C.; Chapt. 13 :371-407.

—— (1973), *The World of the Wild Turkey,* Lippincott, Philadelphia.

Lewis, J. B., McGowan, J. D. and Baskett, T. S. (1968), 'Evaluating Ruffed Grouse Reintroductions in Missouri,' *J. Wildl. Mgmt.* 32 (1) :17-28.

Leys, H. N. (1964), 'Het Voorkomen van de Turkse Tortel (*Streptopelia decaocto* Friv.) in Nederland' (Occurrence of the Collared Dove in the Netherlands), *Limosa* 37 :232-63. (in *Ibis* 107 (4)).

—— (1967), 'Census of the Collared Turtle Dove in the Netherlands,' *Int. Counc. Bird Preserv. Bull.* 10 :147-54.

Liang, C. H. and Liu, S. L. (1959), 'Preliminary Report of Food Habits of the Common Species of Passerine Birds from Changsha Area, Hunnan,' *Chinese J. Zool.* 2 (4) :212-19.

Lienau, C. H. A. (1947), 'Crested Pigeon, Pallid Cuckoo, Blackbird, Indian Dove, White-plumed Honeyeater,' *S. Aust. Orn.* 18 (5) :47.

Lignon, J. S. (1943), 'Mountain Turkeys in Wyoming,' *Wyo. Wildl.* 8 (10) :1, 14-16.

—— (1946), 'Upland Game Bird Restoration through Trapping and Transplanting,' *N. Mex. Game Fish Comm.* :1-77.

—— (1946), 'History and Management of Merriam's Wild Turkey,' *Univ. N. Mex. Publ. in Biol.* :1-84.

Lindemann, W. (1950), 'Einburgerung der tetraonen,' *Columba* 1 :38 (in German).

—— (1951), 'Einburgerung des Auerwildes,' *Die Pirsch* 7 :242 (in German).

—— (1951), 'Einburgerung des Birkwildes,' *Die Pirsch* 8 :286 (in German).

—— (1953), 'Das Haselwild,' *Der deutsche Jäger* 24 :400 (in German).

—— (1956), 'Transplantation of Game in Europe and Asia,' *J. Wildl. Mgmt.* 20 (1) :68-70.

Lindley-Cohen, L. (1898), 'General Notes,' *Prod. Gaz. and Settl. Rec., West. Aust.* 5 (1) :28; 5 (2) :162; 5 (3) :223-29.

Lindroth, H. and Lingren, L. (1950), 'The Significance for Forestry of Capercaillie Feeding on Pine Needles,' *Suomen Riista* 5 :60-81.

Lindsey, A. A. (1939), 'Food of the Starling in Central New York State,' *Wilson Bull.* 51 (3) :176-82.

Lindzey, J. S. (1967), 'Highlights of Management.' in O. H. Hewitt, (ed) *Wild Turkey and Its Management,* Chapt. 9 :245-59. Wildlife Society, Washington, D.C.

Littler, F. M. (1902), 'European Birds in Tasmania,' *Emu* 1 (3) :121-24.

Liversidge, R. (1962), 'The Spread of the European Starling in the Eastern Cape,' *Ostrich* 33 (3) :13-16.

Lockerbie, C. W. (1939), 'Starlings Arrive in Utah,' *Condor* 41:170.

Loetscher, F. W. (1953), 'Present Increase of English Sparrow in Veracruz, Mexico,' *Auk* 70:370.

Lohoefener, M. (1977), 'Nesting of the Housefinch in Northwestern Kansas,' *Kans. Orn. Soc. Bull.* 28 (1) :9-10.

Long, J. L. (1964), 'The Sparrow,' *J. Agric. West. Aust.* 5 (6) :357-64.

— (1965), 'The Starling,' *J. Agric. West. Aust.* 6 (3) :144-47.

— (1967), 'The Indian Crow,' *J. Agric. West. Aust.* 8 (4) :170-73.

— (1967), 'The European Goldfinch, *Carduelis carduelis*, in the Metropolitan Area of Perth, Western Australia,' *Inst. Agric. Technol., West. Aust.* Thesis, Sept., 1967.

— (1968), 'The Spice Finch, the Red-whiskered Bulbul and the Indian Mynah,' *J. Agric. West. Aust.* 9 (8) :376-79 and 9 (11) :510-11.

— (1969), 'The Java Sparrow,' *J. Agric. West. Aust.* 10 (5) :212-13.

— (1969), 'Introduction of the Red-browed Finch to Western Australia,' *J. Agric. West. Aust.* 10 (12) :2-3.

— (1970), 'The European Goldfinch in Western Australia,' *J. Agric. West. Aust.* 11 (7) :152-54.

— (1971), 'The Feral Pigeon, *Columba livia* Gmelin, in W.A. and Control Experiments with Alpha-chloralose in an Urban Environment,' *Unpublished Dep. Rep., Agric. Protection Board, Perth.*

— (1972), 'Introduced Birds and Mammals in Western Australia,' *Agric. Protection Board, West. Aust. Tech. Ser.* (1) :1-30.

Long, R. C. (1959), 'The European House Sparrow, *Passer domesticus*, in Swaziland,' *Ostrich* 30 :44.

Lord, E. A. R. (1950), 'The Senegal Dove.' *Emu* 49 (4) :295.

Loughrey, A. G. and Stinson, R. H. (1955), 'Feeding Habits of Juvenile Ring-necked Pheasants on Pelee Island, Ontario,' *Can. Fld.-Nat.* 69 (2) :59-65.

Loustau-Lalanne, P. (1962), 'The Birds of the Chagos Archipelago, Indian Ocean,' *Ibis* 104 (1) :67-73.

Lovell, H. B. and Clay, W. M. (1942), 'Nesting of the Starling in Kentucky,' *Ky. Warbler* 18 :29-34.

Loyttyniemi, K. (1968), 'On Eating of Terminal Shoots of Pine Seedlings by the Black Grouse *(Lyrurus tetrix L.)* in a Nursery,' *Silva fenn.* 2 (4) :264-66 (In Finnish).

Lowe, P. R. (1933), 'The Differential Characters in the Tarso-metatarsi of *Gallus* and *Phasianus* as they bear on the Problem of the Introduction of the Pheasant into Europe and the British Isles,' *Ibis* (Ser.13) 3 (2) :332-43.

Ludlow, F. (1950), 'The Birds of Lhasa (Tibet),' *Ibis* 92 :34-45.

Lueps, P. (1975), 'The Red-legged Partridge, *Alectoris rufa*, in Switzerland,' *Naturhist. Mus. Stadt. Bern. Jahrb.* 5 :133-51. (In German).

Lund, H. M-K. (1955), 'Penguins North of the Polar Circle,' *Norsk Hvalfangst-Tidende* 44 (2) :95-100.

— (1963), 'Canadagåsen i Norge,' *Jakt-fiske-friluftsliv* 92 :534-36.

Lund, M. K. (1956), 'Gråspurven *(Passer domesticus* (L.)) : Nord-Norge,' *Dansk Orn. Foren. Tidsskr.* 50 :67-76 (Rev. *Ibis* 99).

Lundquist, A. R. (1934), 'The Starling in Day County, South Dakota,' *Wilson Bull.* 46 :62.

Lustin, V. S. (1964), 'Restoration of the Pheasant in Akchina Hunting Tract,' in Comm. Game Anims. in Uzbek, *Akad. Nauk. Uzbeksk SSR* :76-81 (in Russian).

L'vov, I. A. (1962), 'Akklimatizatsiya faznov na Ukraine' (Acclimatization of Pheasants in Ukraine), *Ptitsevodstvo* 10 :22-24.

Lyon-Field, B. (1938), 'Mynah Birds,' *Fiji agric. J.* 9 (2) :19-22.

MacArthur, R. F. and Klopfer, P. (1958), 'North American Birds Staying on Board Ship During Atlantic Crossing,' *Brit. Birds* 51:358.

MacDonald, D. and Jantzen, R. A. (1967), 'Management of the Merriam's Turkey,' in O. H. Hewitt (ed), *Wild Turkey and its Management,* Wildlife Society, Washington, D.C. Chapt. 16:493-534.

MacDonald, M. and Loke, C. (1962), *Birds in the Sun,* Witherby, London.

MacDonald, J. D. (1973), *Birds of Australia,* Reed, Sydney.

Mace, R. U. (1963), 'Oregon's Experience with the Merriam's Wild Turkey,' *Proc. 43rd a. Conf. west. Ass. Game Fish Commnrs.* 43:196-201.

Mackay, V. M. and Hughes, W. M. (1963), 'Crested Mynah in British Columbia,' *Can. Fld.-Nat.* 77 (3) :154-62.

MacKeith, T. T. (1916), 'The Capercaillie in Renfrewshire,' *Scott. Nat.* :270.

Mackenzie, W. D. (1900), 'Capercaillie in Strathnairn,' *Ann. Scot. nat. Hist.* :51.

Mackworth-Praed, C. W. and Grant, C. H. B. (1952-55), *African Handbook Birds: Birds of Eastern and North-eastern Africa,* Ser.1, Vol.1, 2nd Edn. 1957 and Vol.2, 2nd Edit. 1960, Longmans, London.

— (1962-63), *African Handbook Birds: Birds of the Southern Third of Africa,* Ser.2, 2 vols. Longmans, London.

— (1970-73) *African Handbook Birds: Birds of West Central and Western Africa,* Ser.3, 2 vols, Longmans, London.

Maclean, G. (1976), 'Adaptations of Sandgrouse for Life in Arid Zones,' in H. Frith and J. Calaby (eds), *Proc. Int. Orn. Congr., Canberra* :502-16.

MacLean, G. H. (1960), 'Animal Damage in N.S.W. Forests,' in *Verm. Contr. Conf., Hobart, Tasmania, March, 1960* :29-35.

MacLean, G. L. (1962), 'House Sparrow, *Passer domesticus*, at Van Rhynsdorp,' *Ostrich* 33 (2) :75.

MacMillan, A. T. (1965), 'The Collared Dove in Shetland,' *Scott. Birds* 3 (6) :292-300.

MacMullan, R. A. (1961), 'Ring-necked Pheasant Habitat Management in the United States,' *Trans. 26th. N. Am. Wildl. Conf.* :268-72.

MacPherson, J. (1921), 'The Red-eyed Bulbul,' *Emu* 21 (2) :145-46.

— (1924), 'Further Notes on the Red-eyed Bulbul,' *Emu* 23 (3) :218-19.

Madoc, G. C. (1956), *An Introduction to Malayan Birds,* Rev. Edn, Caxton Press, Kuala Lumpur.

Madson, J. (1962), *The Ring-necked Pheasant,* Conserv. Dep. Olin Math. Chem. Corp.: East Alton, Illinois, 104 pp.

Maguire, P. (1977), 'Canada Goose Cohabiting with Breeding Mute Swans,' *Brit. Birds* 70 (7) :298.

Manson-Bahr, P. E. C. (1953), 'The European Starling in Fiji,' *Ibis* 95 (4) :699-700.

Maples, S. (1907), 'The Little Owl in Hertfordshire,' *Zoologist,* 1907:353.

Marcus, M. B. (1958), 'The House Sparrow in Bechuanaland,' *Ostrich* 29:129.

Marion, W. R. (1976), 'Plain Chachalaca Food Habits in South Texas,' *Auk* 93:376-79.

Markus, M. (1960), 'Some Records of the House Sparrow, *Passer domesticus,* in the Orange Free State and Cape Province,' *Ostrich* 31 (3) :106.

Marler, P. and Boatman, D. J. (1951), 'Observations on the Birds of Pico, Azores,' *Ibis* 93 (1) :90.

Marples, B. J. (1934), 'The Winter Starling Roosts of Great Britain, 1932-33,' *J. Anim. Ecol.* 3 :187-203.

— (1942), 'A Study of the Little Owl in New Zealand,' *Trans. Proc. R. Soc., N.Z.* :237-52.

— (1950), 'Chukor Investigation,' *N.Z. Bird Notes* 3 (8) :197.

Marples, B. J. and Gurr, L. (1953), 'The Chukar in New Zealand,' *Emu* 53 (4) :283-91.

Marsh, R. E. (1965), 'Methods of Controlling Rodents and Birds in Rice Fields,' *Congr. de la Protect. des Cult. Trop., Marseille* :633-37.

Marshall, H. B. (1907), 'Capercaillie in Peeblesshire,' *Ann. Scot. nat. Hist.,* 1907:224.

Marshall, J. T. (1949), 'The Endemic Avifauna of Saipan, Tinian, Guam and Palau,' *Condor* 51:200-21.

Martin, N. and Pyrah, D. (1971), 'Sage Grouse,' in T. W. Mussehl and F. W. Howell (eds) *Game Management in Montana,* Chapt 16:135-41. Montana Fish and Game Department, Helena, Montana.

Mason, C. (1958), 'Return of a Native: The Wild Turkey Digs in to Stay,' *N.Y. St. Conserv.* 13 (2) :32-33.

Masson, V. (1959), 'The Chukar in the Southeast Region,' *Ore. St. Game Commn. Bull.* 14 (6) :3, 6-8.

Matheson, C. (1963), 'The Pheasant in Wales,' *Brit. Birds* 44 (12) :452-56.

Mathew, D. N. (1976), 'Ecology of the Weaver Birds,' *J. Bombay nat. Hist. Soc.* 73 (2) :249-60.

Mathisen, J. E. and Mathisen, A. (1960), 'History and Status of Introduced Game Birds in Nebraska,' *Nebr. Bird Rev.* 28 (2) :19-22.

Maxwell, H. (1905), 'Naturalization of the Golden Pheasant,' *Ann. Scot. nat. Hist.,* 1905 :53-54.

— (1907), 'Capercaillie in the South of Scotland,' *Ann. Scot. nat. Hist.,* 1907:116.

Mayr, E. (1945), *Birds of the South West Pacific,* MacMillan, New York.

— (1965), 'The Nature of Colonization in Birds,' in *Genetics of Colonizing Species,* H. G. Baker and G. L. Stebbins (eds), *Proc. Int. Un. Biol. Sci., Symp. Gen. Biol.,* Academic Press, New York.

McAtee, W. L. (1925), 'Introduction upon Introduction,' *Auk* 42 (1) :160.

— (1929), 'Game Birds Suitable for Naturalization in the United States,' *U.S. Dep. Agric. Circ.* (96) :1-24.

— (1944), 'The European Migratory Quail in North America,' *Auk* 61 :652.

McCabe, R. A. (1947), 'The Homing of Transplanted Wood Ducks,' *Wilson Bull.* 59 (2) :104-09.

McCabe, R. A. and Hawkins, A. S. (1946), 'The Hungarian Partridge in Wisconsin,' *Am. Midl. Nat.* 36 (1) :1-75.

McCance, N. (1962), 'Reckless Acclimatization,' *Aust. Avicult.,* Aug. 1962:105.

McCaskie, R. G. (1965), 'The Cattle Egret Reaches the West Coast of the United States,' *Condor* 67 :89.

McCaskill, L. W. (1945), 'Preliminary Report on the Present Position of the Australian Magpies *(G. hypoleuca* and *G. tibicen)* in New Zealand,' *N.Z. Bird Notes* 1 (8) :86-104.

McClure, H. E. (1974), *Migration and Survival of the Birds of Asia,* SEATO Medic. Res. Lab., Bangkok, Thailand.

McCoy, J. W. (1941), 'Injuries to Texas Cattle Caused by Starlings,' *Vet. Med.* 36 :432-33.

McDiarmid, A. (1960), 'Diseases of Free Living Wild Animals,' *F.A.O., Anim. Health Brch. Monogr.* (1).

McDougall, W. A. (1944), 'An Investigation of the Rat Pest Problem in Queensland Canefields: 1 Economic Aspects,' *Qd. J. agric. Sci.* 1 :32-47.

McGarvie, A. M. and Templeton, M. T. (1974), 'Additions to the Birds of King Island, Bass Strait,' *Emu* 74 (2) :91-96.

McGill, A. R. (1946), 'Nesting Habits of the Goldfinch,' *Emu* 46 (3) :235-36.

508

— (1948), 'The Asiatic Ring Dove as an Escapee,' *Emu* 47 (4) :232-33.

— (1949), 'Australian Status of the Colombo Crow,' *Emu* 49 (2) :83-84.

— (1960), *A Handlist of the Birds of New South Wales*, Fauna Protection Panel, Sydney.

McGregor, R. C. (1902), 'Notes on a Small Collection of Birds from the Island of Maui, Hawaii,' *Condor* 4 :59-62.

McKean, J. L., Evans, O. and Lewis, J. H. (1976), 'Notes on the Birds of Norfolk Island,' *Notornis* 23 (4) :299.

McKean, J. L. and Hindwood, K. A. (1965), 'Additional Notes on the Birds of Lord Howe Island,' *Emu* 64 (2) :79-97.

McKenzie, H. R. (1953), 'Virginia Quail in Wairora, H.B., District,' *Notornis* 5 (4) :123.

McLachlan, G. R. (1955), 'European Starling seen in Port Elizabeth,' *Ostrich* 26 (3) :157.

McLean, D. D. (1958), *Upland Game of California*, Dep. Fish Game, Sacramento, California.

McLennan, C. H. (1906), No Title, in 'Emu Stray Feathers: Mallee (Victoria) Notes, Season, 1906,' *Emu* 6 (3) :131-32.

McMillan, I. I. (1947), 'Establishment of Artificially Propagated Quail,' *Condor* 49 :170.

McNeel, J. (1973), 'The Japanese Versicolor Pheasant,' *Idaho Wildl. Rev.* 26 (1) :12-15.

McNeil, R. (1971), 'European Blackbird (*Turdus merula*) in Quebec,' *Auk* 88 :919-20.

McPherson, J. (1924), 'Further Notes on the Red-eyed Bulbul,' *Emu* 23 (3) :218-19.

Meade-Waldo, E. G. B. (1893), 'List of the Birds Observed in the Canary Islands,' *Ibis* :185-207.

Medway, L. and Wells, D. R. (eds) (1963), 'Bird Report: 1962,' *Malay. Nat. J.* 17 (3) :123-44.

— (eds) (1964), 'Bird Report: 1963,' *Malay Nat. J.* 18 (2-3) :133-67.

— (1976), *The Birds of the Malay Peninsula*, Vol.5 Witherby, London: Penerbit University, Kuala Lumpur, Malaya.

Meinertzhagen, R. (1912), 'On the Birds of Mauritius,' *Ibis* :82-108.

— (1924), 'A Contribution Towards the Birds of Aden Protectorate,' *Ibis* 6 (11 Ser.) (4) :625-42.

— (1930), *Nicoll's Birds of Egypt*, 2 Vols, Hugh Rees, London.

— (1949), 'Notes on Saudi Arabian Birds,' *Ibis* 91 :465.

— (1954), *Birds of Arabia*, Oliver and Boyd, Edinburgh and London.

Meise, W. (1940), 'Zur Systematik der Sperling,' *J. Orn., Lpz.* 84 :631-72.

Melliss, J. C. (1870), 'Notes on the Birds of St Helena,' *Ibis* 6 (21) :97-106.

Mellor, J. W. (1911), 'Mallee-Fowl on Kangaroo Island,' *Emu* 11 :35-37.

— (1912), 'Kangaroo Island Reserve,' *Emu* 12 :39-40.

Ménégaux, A. (1920), 'Enquête sur la disparition du moineau,' *Oiseaux Revue fr. Orn.* 12 :32-36, 52-55, 77-78.

Mengel, R. M. (1965), 'Birds of Kentucky,' *Am. Orn. Un. Monogr.* (3).

Menzel, K. E. (1960), 'Introduction and Investigation of *Coturnix coturnix* Spp. in Nebraska: Final Report,' *Nebr. Game For. Parks Commn., P-R Proj., W-30-R-3* :1-24.

Menzdorf, A. (1975), 'Vorkommen Doppelbruten Huhn, Alectoris,' *Vogelwelt* 96 :135-39.

Menzies, W. S. (1907), 'Capercaillie and Willow Grouse in Moray,' *Ann. Scot. nat. Hist.*, 1907 :116-17.

Mercer, R. (1966), *A Field Guide to Fiji Birds*, Spec. Publ. (1) :1-39, 3rd Impr., 1970, Fiji Mus., Fiji.

Merikallio, E. (1958), *Finnish Birds: Their Distribution and Numbers*, Helsingfors Helsinki.

Merne, O. J. (1970), 'The Status of the Canada Goose in Ireland,' *Ir. Bird Rep.* 17 :12-17.

Merrill, J. C. (1876), 'The European Tree Sparrow in the United States,' *Am. Midl. Nat.* 10 :50-51.

Mettler, B. J. (1977), 'Factors Contributing to the Increase of the Grey Partridge in Minnesota,' *Loon* 49 (4) :205-10.

Merton, D. V. (1965), 'A Brief History of the North Island Saddleback,' *Notornis* 12 (4) :208-11.

— (1965), 'Transfer of Saddlebacks from Hen Island to Middle Chicken Island, January 1964,' *Notornis* 12 (4) :213-22.

— (1975), 'Success in Re-establishing a Threatened Species: The Saddleback — Its Status and Conservation,' *12th Bull. int. Counc. Bird Preserv.* 12 :150-58.

Meyer, A. B. (1879), 'Field Notes on the Birds of Celebes: Part 2,' *Ibis* 3 (10) :125-46.

Meyer de Schauensee, R. (1964), *The Birds of Colombia and Adjacent Areas of South and Central America*, Livingston Publ. Co., Narberth, Pennsylvania.

— (1966-70), *The Species of Birds of South America and their Distribution*, Livingston Publ. Co, Narberth, Pennsylvania.

Meyer de Schauensee, R. and Phelps, W. (1978), *The Birds of Venezuela*, Princeton University Press, New Jersey.

Mezennyj, A. A. (1957), 'The Influence of Capercaillie on the Crown Form of Larch,' *Bot. ž.* 42 :84-85 (in *For. Abstr.* 19 :4449).

Middleton, A. D. and Chitty, H. (1937), 'The Food of Adult Partridges, *Perdix perdix* and *Alectoris rufa*, in Great Britain,' *J. Anim. Ecol.* 6 (2) :322-36.

Middleton, A. L. A. (1965), The Ecology and Reproductive Biology of the European Goldfinch, *Carduelis carduelis*, near Melbourne, Victoria, Ph.D. Thesis, Monash University, Melbourne.

— (1970), 'Foods and Feeding Habits of the European Goldfinch near Melbourne,' *Emu* 70 (1) :12-16.

— (1978), 'Annual Cycle of the American Goldfinch,' *Condor* 80 (4) :401-06.

Mijno, P. C. (1965), 'Population of Hunting Lands in Italy with Artificially Bred Pheasants,' *Trans. 6th Congr. int. Un. Game Biol., 1963* :49-54.

Milbert, J. (1812), 'Voyage pittoresque à L'Ile de France, au Cap de Bonne Espérance et à L'Ile de Ténériffe,' *Paris* 2 :249-60.

Miller, A. H. (1928), 'The Status of the Cardinal in California,' *Condor* 30 :243-45.

— (1951), 'Comparison of the Avifaunas of Santa Cruz and Santa Rosa Islands, California,' *Condor* 53 (3) :117-23.

Miller, L. (1930), 'The Asiatic Mynah in Los Angeles, California,' *Condor* 32 :302.

Mills, D. H. (1937), 'European Goldfinch at Hanover, New Hampshire,' *Auk* 54 :544-45.

Mills, H. B. (1943), 'Starlings Nesting in Montana,' *Condor* 45 :197.

Mills, J. A. and Williams, G. R. (1979), 'The Status of Endangered New Zealand Birds,' in M. Tyler (ed), 'Status of Endangered Australasian Wildlife,' *Proc. Cent. Symp. R. Zool. Soc., S.A., Adelaide, Sept. 1978* :147-68.

Milne-Edwards, A. and Oustalet, E. (1888), 'Etudes sur les mammiferes et les oiseaux des Isles Comores,' *Nouv. Arch. Mus. Paris* 10 :219-97.

Milon, P. (1951), 'Sur la Distribution du Martin à Madagascar,' *Naturaliste malagache* 3 :67.

Milon, P., Petter, J-J. and Randrianasolo, G. (1973), *Faune du Madagascar*, Part 35, Birds, Orstom, Tananarive and CNRS, Paris.

Ministry Agriculture, Fisheries and Food (1962), 'The House Sparrow,' *Min. Agric. Fish. Food Adv. Leafl.* (169).

— (1962), 'The Starling,' *Min. Agric., Fish. Food Adv. Leafl.* (208).

— (1966), 'The Bullfinch,' *Min. Agric., Fish. Food Adv. Leafl.* (234).

Mitchell, A. J. (1907), 'Sparrows,' *Agric. Gaz., N.S.W.* 18 (10) :814-815.

Mitchell, M. H. (1957), *Observations on the Birds of Southeastern Brazil*, University Toronto Press, Canada.

Moeed, A. (1975), 'Food of Skylarks and Pipits, Finches and Feral Pigeons near Christchurch,' *Notornis* 22 (2) :135-42.

— (1975), 'Diets of Nestling Starlings and Mynas at Havelock North, Hawke's Bay,' *Notornis* 22 (4) :291-94.

— (1976), 'Foods of the Common Myna (*Acridotheres tristis*) in Central India and in Hawke's Bay, New Zealand,' *Notornis* 23 :246-49.

Monnie, J. B. (1966), 'Re-introduction of the Trumpeter Swan to its Former Prairie Breeding Range,' *J. Wildl. Mgmt.* 30 (4) :691-96.

Monson, G. (1948), 'The Starling in Arizona,' *Condor* 50 :45.

Montagna, W. (1940), 'European Goldfinch in New York,' *Auk* 57 :575-76.

Montcrieff, P. (1931), 'Certain Introduced Birds of New Zealand,' *Emu* 30 :219.

Moon, G. J. H. (1956), 'White-faced Heron Nesting in New Zealand,' *Notornis* 6 :244.

Moos, L. M. and Graves, D. (1941), 'Forty-First Christmas Bird Census, Billings, Montana,' *Audubon Mag.* 43 (Suppl.) :135.

Moran, R. J. and Palmer, W. L. (1963), Ruffed Grouse Introductions and Population Trends on Michigan Islands,' *J. Wild. Mgmt.* 27 (4) :606-14.

Moreau, R. E. (1944), 'Clutch Size in Introduced Birds,' *Auk* 61 :583-86.

— (1948), 'Aspects of Evolution in the Parrot Genus Agapornis,' *Ibis* 90 :449.

— (1960), 'The Ploceine Weavers of the Indian Ocean Islands,' *J. Orn.* 101 :29-49.

Moreland, R. (1950), 'Success of Chukar Partridge in the State of Washington,' *Trans. N. Am. Wildl. Conf.* 15 :399-409.

Moreton, S. E. (1943), 'Starlings Remove Larvae from Backs of Cattle,' *Migrant* 14 :54-55.

Morgan, A. M. (1929), No Title, *S. Aust. Orn.* 10 :132-33.

— (1933), 'An Addition to the Introduced Avifauna of South Australia,' *S. Aust. Orn.* 12 (1) :31.

Morgan, B. and Morgan, J. (1965), 'Cattle Egrets in Brisbane,' *Emu* 64 (3) :230-32.

Morgan, H. K. (1958), 'House Sparrow, *Passer domesticus*,' *Ostrich* 29 (2) :87.

Morris, J. G. (1969), 'The Control of Feral Pigeons and Sparrows Associated with Intensive Animal Production,' *Aust. J. Sci.* 32 (1) :9-14.

Mosby, H. S. (1940), 'Restoring the Wild Turkey in Virginia,' *Va. Wildl.* 4 (1) :11-15.

— (1942), 'Successful Turkey Restocking is Possible,' *Va. Wildl.* 5 (2) :69-78.

— (1959), 'General Status of the Wild Turkey and Its Management in the United States,' *Proc. 1st natn. Turkey Symp., Memphis* :1-11.

Mosby, H. S. and Handley, C. O. (1943), 'The Wild Turkey in Virginia: Its Status, Life History and Management,' *Va. Commn. Game Inland Fish., Richmond* :1-28.

Mott, D. F. (1973), 'Monk Parakeet Damage to Crops in Uruguay and its Control,' *Proc. 6th Bird Contr. Sem., Bowling Green State University* :79-81.

— (1973), 'An Investigation of Bird Damage Problems in Uruguay,' *U.S. Dep. Interior Bur. Sport Fish. Wildl.* :1-7.

Mourashka, I. P. and Valius, M. I. (1961), 'Natural Re-acclimatisation of the Mute Swan in Lithuania and Neighbouring Territories, *Proc. Baltic Orn. Congr.* 4 :71-80 (In Russian).

Mousley, H. (1923), 'The Starling (*Sturnus*

vulgaris) Breeding at Hatley, Quebec,' *Auk* 40:537.

— (1925), 'Further Notes on the Breeding of the Starling *(Sturnus vulgaris)* at Hatley, Quebec, 1924,' *Auk* 42:273-75.

— (1926), 'Further Notes on the Starling in Canada,' *Auk* 43 (3) :372-73.

Mull, M. E. (1978), 'Expanding Range of Kalij Pheasant on the Big Island,' *Elepaio* 38 (7) :74-75.

Muller, P. (1967), 'Zur Verbreitung von *Passer domesticus* in Brasilien,' *J. Orn.* 108 (4) :497-99.

Mundinger, P. (1976), 'Song Dialects and Colonization in the House Finch, *Carpodacus mexicanus,* on the East Coast,' *Condor* 77 (4) :407-22.

Munro, G. C. (1944), *Birds of Hawaii,* 1st Edn 1944, Rev. Edn 1960, Bridgeway Press, Japan.

Munro, J. A. (1922), 'The "Japanese Starling" in Vancouver, British Columbia,' *Can. Fld.- Nat.* 36:32-33.

— (1947), 'Starling in British Columbia,' *Condor* 49:130.

— (1956), 'Starlings at Vanderhoof, British Columbia,' *Auk* 73:130.

— (1959), *'Birds of Canada's Mountain Parks,* 2nd Edn, National Parks Brch., Ottawa, Canada.

Munro, J. A. and Cowan, I. M. (1947), *A Review of the Bird Fauna of British Columbia,* Sec. publ. (2), Brit. Col. Prov. Mus., B.C., 1-285.

Murphy, D. C. (1936), *Oceanic Birds of South America,* Am. Mus. nat. Hist. 1 and 2, 1936.

Murphy, R. C. (1915), 'Birdlife of Trinidad Islet,' *Auk* 32:332-48.

— (1924), 'The Marine Ornithology of the Cape Verde Islands, with a List of all the Birds of the Archipelago,' *Bull. Am. Mus. nat. Hist.* 50 (Art. 3) :211-78.

— (1924), 'Birds Collected during the Whitney South Sea Expedition 1,' *Am. Mus. Novit.* (115).

— (1945), 'Middle Nineteenth Century Introductions of British Birds to Long Island, New York,' *Auk* 62:306.

Murray, R. E. (1963), 'The Black Francolin,' *Proc. 17th a. Conf. S-East Ass. Game Fish Commn.* :117, 120-21.

Murray, W. J. C. (1963), 'Under Royal Protection,' *Animals* 2 (1) :24-47.

Murton, R. K. (1968), 'Some Predator-Prey Relationships in Bird Damage and Population Control,' in R. K. Murton and E. N. Wright, (eds.) *Symp. Inst. Biol.* (17) *Problems of Birds as Pests,* Academic Press, London :157-69.

Murton, R. K., Isaacson, A. J. and Westwood, N. J. (1965), 'The Relationship Between Wood-pigeons and their Clover Food Supply and the Mechanism of Population Control,' *J. appl. Ecol.* 3 :55-96.

Murton, R. K. and Westwood, N. J. (1963), 'The Food Preferences of Pheasants and Wood-pigeons in Relation to the Selective use of Stupefying Baits,' *6th Congr. int. Un. Game Biol., 7-12 Oct., London.*

Murton, R. K., Westwood, N. J. and Isaacson, A. J. (1964), 'The Feeding Habits of the Wood-pigeon, *Columba palumbus,* Stock Dove, *C. oenas* and Turtledove, *Streptopelia turtur,' Ibis* 106 :174-88.

Murton, R. K. and Wright, E. N. (1968), *The Problem of Birds as Pests,* Academic Press, London.

Mussehl, T. W. and Howell, F. W. (1971), *Game Management in Montana,* Fish Game Department, Helena, Montana.

Musselman, T. E. (1950), 'European Tree Sparrows at Hannibal, Missouri,' *Auk* 67:105.

— (1953), 'European Tree Sparrow Extending Its Range in United States,' *Wilson Bull.* 65 (1) :48.

Musson, C. T. (1904-05), 'The House Sparrow in New South Wales,' *Agric. Gaz., N.S.W.* (in *Emu* 9:159-61).

— (1905), 'The "Sparrow Circular" — Preliminary Observations on Reports Received at Hawkesbury Agricultural College,' *Agric. Gaz., N.S.W.* 16 (4) :378-80.

— (1907), 'The House Sparrow in New South Wales,' *Agric. Gaz., N.S.W.* 18 (6) :535-38. 19 (2) :914-17.

— (1908), 'Title not known, *Agric. Gaz., N.S.W.* :127-35.

Myers, J. E. (1970), 'The Ecology of Wild-Trapped and Transplanted Ring-necked Pheasants near Centre Hall, Pennsylvania,' *Trans. 35th N. Am. Wildl. nat. Resour. Conf.* :216-20.

Myers, J. G. and Atkinson, E. (1924), 'The Relation of Birds to Agriculture in New Zealand: VII The Herons and Ducks,' *N.Z. agric. J.,* Jan. 21, 1924.

Myrberget, S. (1976), 'Merking av Fasan i Norge,' *Sterna* 15:174-76.

Myres, M. T. (1958), 'The European Starling in British Columbia: 1947-57,' *Occ. Pap. Br. Columbia prov. Mus.* (11) :1-60.

Nagel, W. O. (1939), 'A Preliminary Report of Chukar Partridges in Missouri,' *Trans. N. Am. Wildl. Conf.* 4:416-21.

— (1940), 'The Chukar Partridge and Other Introduced Game Birds,' *Proc. Minn. Wildl. Conf., Short Course* 2 :12-13.

— (1945), 'Adaptability of Chukar Partridges to Missouri Conditions,' *J. Wildl. Mgmt.* 9 (3) :207-16.

Nagel, W. O. and Bennitt, R. (1945), 'The Chukar Partridge,' *Missouri Conserv.* 2 (4) :2, 7.

Nazarenko, L. F. and Gurskii, I. G. (1963), 'The Acclimatization of Pheasants in the area Northwest of the Black Sea,' *Ornitologiya* 6:477-78 (In Russian).

Nef, L. (1959), Title Unknown, *Bull. Soc. For. Belg.* 66:1-8.

Neff, J. A. (1937), 'Procedures and Methods in Controlling Birds Injurious to Crops in California,' *U.S. Dep. Agric. Bur. Biol. Surv., and Calif. St. Dep. Agric.* :87-89.

— (1949), 'Protecting Home Gardens and Small Fruits from Attacks by Birds,' *U.S. Dep. Interior, Washington, Wildl. Leaflet* (268) :1-13.

Nefedov, N. I. (1943), 'The Agricultural Importance of the Partridge *(Perdix perdix L.)* on the Lower Volga,' *Zoologicheskii zhurnal* 22:41-43.

Neidermyer, W. J. and Hickey, J. J. (1977), 'The Monk Parakeet in the United States, 1970-75,' *Am. Birds* 31 (3) :273-78.

Nelson, H. K. (1963), 'Restoration of Breeding Canada Goose Flocks in North Central States,' *Trans. N. Am. Wildl. Conf.* 28:133-50.

Nelson, L. K. (1963), 'Introductions of the Blackneck Pheasant Group and Crosses into the Southeastern States,' *Proc. 17th a. Conf. S-East Ass. Game Fish Commn.* :111-19.

— (1964), 'A Ten-year Study of Ring-necked Pheasant Introductions in Kentucky: A Final Report,' *Ky. Dep. Fish Wildl. Res., P-R Game Mgmt. Tech. Serv.* (14) :1-153.

— (1972), 'A Five-Year Study of a Black Francolin Introduction in Kentucky: A Final Report,' *Ky. Dep. Fish Wildl. Res., P-R Game Mgmt. Tech. Serv.* (17) :1-37.

Nevada, Fish and Game Commission (1963), 'Nevada Exotic Game Bird Introductions,' *Nev. Wildl.* 3 (7) :1-5.

Newman, C. C. (1945), 'Turkey Restocking Efforts in Eastern Texas,' *J. Wildl. Mgmt.* 9 (4) :279-89.

Newton, A. and Newton, E. (1859), 'Observations on the Birds of St Croix, West Indies, made between February 20th and August 6th, 1857, and between March 4th and September 28th, 1858,' Part III, *Ibis* 1 (3) :255.

Newton, E. (1861), 'Ornithological Notes from Mauritius. 1. A visit to Round Island,' *Ibis* :180-82.

— (1867), 'On the Land Birds of the Seychelles Archipelago,' *Ibis* 3 (11) :335 60.

— (1888), 'President's Address to the Members of the Society, with a List of Birds of the Mascarene Islands, including the Seychelles,' *Trans. Norf. Nor. nat. Soc.* 4 :537-54.

Newton, I. (1966), 'The Bullfinch Problem,' *Birds* 1 (4) :74-77.

— (1967), 'Attacks on Fruit Buds by Redpolls, *Carduelis flammea,' Ibis* 109 (3) :440-41.

— (1967), 'The Adaptive Radiation and Feeding Ecology of Some British Finches,' *Ibis* 109 (1) :33-98.

— (1972), *Finches,* Collins, London.

Newton, R. (1959), 'Notes on Two Species of Foudia in Mauritius,' *Ibis* 101 (2) :240-43.

Nicholls, E. D. B. (1928), 'The Starling Menace,' *Emu* 27 (4) :293-94.

Nichols, J. T. (1936), 'The European Goldfinch near New York City, 1915-35,' *Auk* 53:429-31.

— (1937), 'Notes on Starling Spread and Migration,' *Auk* 54:209-10.

— (1937), 'North-South "v" Northeast-Southwest Migration of the Starling,' *Auk* 54:542.

Nichols, W. F. (1967), 'Cattle Egrets in Ventura County, California,' *Condor* 69:608.

Niedrach, R. T. (1945), 'Colorado Nesting Records of Starlings,' *Wilson Bull.* 57:261.

Niethammer, G. (1963), *Die Einbürgerung von Saügetiere und Vogeln in Europa* (Introduced Mammals and Birds in Europe), Paul Parey, Hamburg and Berlin.

— (1963), 'Taxonomie europaischer in Neuseeland eingebureter Vogel,' *J. fur Orn.* 112 (2) :202-26.

— (1970), 'Clutch Size of Introduced European Passeriformes in New Zealand,' *Notornis* 17 (3) :214-22.

— (1971), 'Some Problems Connected with the House Sparrow's Colonization of the World,' Proc. 3rd Pan Afr. Orn. Congr. 1969, *Ostrich* Suppl. (8) :445-48.

Nilsson, N. N. (1957), 'Nevada's Experience with Exotic Game Birds,' *Proc. 37th a. Conf. west. Ass. St. Game Fish Commnrs.* :283-85.

Norgaard-Oleson, E. (1973), *Tanagers,* Vol.1. Skibby-Books, Denmark.

Norris, C. S. (1912), 'The True Story of a Starling,' *Oologist* 29 :229-31.

Norris, R. A. (1956), 'Introduction of Exotic Game Birds in Georgia,' *Oriole* 21 (1) :1-6.

Norton, S. P. W. (1922), 'Bird Notes from Boree (New England Plateau), *Emu* 22 (1) :39-44.

Nowak, E. (1965), *Die Türkentaube (Streptopelia decaocto),* Wittenberg, A. Ziemsen Verlag, Lutherstadt.

O'Brien, T. G. and Scanlon, P. F. (1977), 'The Use of Christmas Bird Counts in Monitoring Presence of Free-Ranging Exotic Bird Species,' *Va. J. Sci.* 28 (2) :65.

Ogilvie, M. A. (1969), 'The Status of the Canada Goose in Britain, 1967-69,' *Wildfowl* 20 :79-85.

— (1977), 'The Numbers of Canada Geese in Britain, 1976,' *Wildfowl* 28 :27-34.

O'Gorman, F. (1970), 'The Development of Game in Ireland,' *8th Int. Congr. Game Biol., Helsinki* :387-96.

Ojala, H. and Sjöberg, J. (1968), 'Turkinkyyhky *(Streptopeli decaocto)* pesinyt Naantalissa,' *Ornis fenn.* 45 :139-42.

Oldys, H. (1908), 'Game Protection in 1907,' *U.S. Department Agriculture Year Book, 1907* :594.

— (1910), 'Introduction of the Hungarian Partridge into the United States,' *U.S. Department Agriculture Year Book, 1909* :249-58.

Oliver, W. R. B. (1930), *Birds of New Zealand,* Fine Arts, Wellington, N.Z.

— (1955), *Birds of New Zealand*, Reed, Wellington, N.Z.

Olrog, C. C. (1959), *Las Aves Argentinas*, Univ. Nac. de Tucuman, Inst. Miguel Lillo, Argentina.

Olson, A. C. (1943), 'Starling in Northern Idaho,' *Condor* 45:197.

Ord, W. M. (1963), 'Black-headed Mannikins and Strawberry Finches,' *Elepaio* 23:42.

— (1967), *Hawaii's Birds*, Hawaii Audubon Society, Honolulu.

Ornithological Society, Japan (1974) *Check List of Japanese Birds*, 3 Vols., 5th Edn. Rev. Gakken Co, Tokyo.

Ortiz Crespo, F. I. (1977), 'La Presencia del Gorrion Europeo, *Passer domesticus* L., en el Ecuador,' *Rev. Univ. Catol., Quito* 16:193-97.

Osmolovskaya, V. I. (1969), 'Artificial Settlement of Game Birds as a Means of Maintaining and Increasing Their Abundance,' *Byul. Mosk. Obsh. Isp. Prir. Otd. Biol.* 74 (1):15-24 (in Russian).

Owens, W. S. (1941), 'The Chukar Partridge,' *Wyo. Wildl.* 6 (4):8, 16-17.

Owre, O. T. (1959), 'Cattle Egret in Haiti,' *Auk* 76 (3):359.

— (1973), 'A Consideration of the Exotic Avifauna of Southeastern Florida,' *Wilson Bull.* 85 (4):491-500.

Oxley, T. (1849), 'The Zoology of Singapore,' *J. Indian Arch.* 3:594-97.

Pakenham, R. H. W. (1936), 'Field Notes on the Birds of Zanzibar and Pemba,' *Ibis* (13 Ser.) 4 (2):249-72.

— (1939), 'Birds of Zanzibar and Pemba,' *Ibis* (14 Ser.) 3:522-54.

— (1943), 'Field Notes on Birds of Zanzibar and Pemba Islands,' *Ibis* 85:165-89.

— (1945), 'Field Notes on Birds of Zanzibar and Pemba Islands,' *Ibis* 87:216-23.

— (1959), 'Field Notes on the Birds of Zanzibar and Pemba,' *Ibis* 101 (2):245-47.

Palermo, R. (1968), 'Louisiana Exotic Game Bird Program,' *La. Conserv.* 20 (3 and 4):20-22.

Palmer, C. E. (1965), 'The Capercaillie,' *For. Commn. Leafl.* (37).

Palmer, R. S. (ed) (1976), *Handbook of North American Birds*, 3 Vols, Yale University Press, New Haven and London.

Palmer, T. K. (1972), 'The House Finch and Starling in Relation to California's Agriculture,' in S. C. Kendeigh and J. Pinowski (eds), *Proc. Gen. Meet. Work. Grp. Graniv. Bds., I.B.P., Pt. Sect., Hague, Holland, Sept. 6-8, 1970* :276-90. P.W.N. — Polish Sci. Publs, Warszawa.

Palmer, T. S. (1898-99), 'The Danger of Introducing Noxious Animals and Birds,' *U.S. Dep. Agric. Yr. Bk., 1898* :87-110.

— (1913), 'Introduction of the Ruffed Grouse on Washington Island, Wisconsin,' *Auk* 30:582.

Palmer, T. S. and Oldys, H. (1904), 'Importation of Game Birds and Eggs for Propagation,' *U.S. Dep. Agric. Biol. Surv. Farm. Bull.* (197):1-27.

Paludan, K. (1959), 'Results of Pheasant Markings in Denmark, 1949-55,' *Danish Rev. Game Biol.* 4 (1):1-23.

— (1963), 'Partridge Markings in Denmark,' *Danish Rev. Game Biol.* 4 (1):25-58.

Parham, B. E. V. (1954), 'Birds as Pests in Fiji,' *Fiji agric. J.* 25:9-14.

Parker, R. L. (1968), 'Quarantine and Health Problems Associated with Introductions of Animals,' in Symp. *Introduction Exotic Animals: Ecology and Socioeconomic Considerations*, C. Kleberg Res. Prog. in Wildl. Ecol., Coll. Agric., Texas A. and M. Univ., Texas, Aug.-Sep. 1967 :21-22.

Parkes, K. C. (1959), 'Subspecific Identity of the Introduced Tree Sparrows, *Passer montanus*, in the Philippine Islands,' *Ibis* 101 (2):243-44.

— (1962), 'The Red Jungle Fowl of the Philippines — Native or Introduced,' *Auk* 79 (3):479-81.

Parry, V. A. (1970), *Kookaburras*, Lansdowne, Melbourne.

— (1973), 'The Auxiliary Social System of the Kookaburra and its Effect on Territory and Breeding,' *Emu* 73:81-100.

Parsons, F. E. (1926), 'Some Notes re Kangaroo Island Birds,' *S. Aust. Orn.* 8:240.

Parsons, H. F. (1909), 'Sparrows in Condobolin District,' *Agric. Gaz., N.S.W.* 20 (10):868.

Paxton, R. O., Buckley, P. A. and Cutler, D. A. (1976), 'Release of Peregrine Falcons,' in Fall Migr., Aug. 1-Nov. 30, 1975: Hudson-Delaware Region, *Am. Birds* 30 (1):39-46.

— (1978), The Spring Migration March 1-May 31, 1978, *Am. Birds* 32 (5):983-87.

Payn, W. H. (1948), 'Notes from Tunisia and Eastern Algeria, Feb. 1943 to Apr. 1944,' *Ibis* 90 (1):1-21.

Pearse, I. (1953), 'European Starling on Vancouver Island, B.C.,' *Can. Fld.-Nat.* 67:94.

Pearson, A. J. (1962), 'Field Notes on the Birds of Ocean Island and Nauru During 1961,' *Ibis* 104 (3):421-24.

Pearson, E. W. (1967), 'Birds and Airports,' in *Proc. 3rd Vert. Pest. Contr. Conf., March 6-9, San Francisco, California* :79-86.

Peitzmeier, J. (1957), 'The Extension and Ecology of the Collared Turtle-dove (*Streptopelia decaocto*) in Westfalen,' *J. Orn.* 98 (4):441-44.

Pekić, B. (1958), 'A Contribution to the Knowledge of the Oecology of *Corvus frugilegus*,' *Zashtita Bilja* 46:3-16.

Pennie, I. D. (1950-51), 'The History and Distribution of the Capercaillie in Scotland,' *Scott. Nat.* 62: 65-87, 157-78 and *Scott. Nat.* 63:4-18, 135.

Penny, M. (1974), *The Birds of Seychelles and Outlying Islands*, Collins, London.

Pepper, A. Y. (1970), 'Letter to the Editor, *West. Aust. Avicult. Mag.*, Oct. 1970:19.

Pescott, E. E. (1943), 'The English Sparrow in Australia,' *Victorian Nat.* 60 (3):47.

Peters, D. (1970), 'Indian Mynas in Queanbeyan,' *Canberra Bird Notes* 8:13.

Peters, J. L. (1931-68), *Checklist of Birds of the World*, University Press, Cambridge; Harvard and Mus. Comp. Zool., Hefferman Press, Cambridge and Massachusetts, Vols. 1-10, 14, 15.

Peterson, R. T. (1954), 'A New Immigrant Bird Arrives,' *Nat. geogr. Mag.* 106:281-92.

— (1961), *A Field Guide to Western Birds*, Houghton Mifflin Co., Boston.

Peterson, R. T. and Chalif, E. L. (1973), *A Field Guide to Mexican Birds and Adjacent Central America*, Houghton Mifflin Co, Boston.

Peterson, R. T., Mountfort, G. and Hollom, P. A. D. (1954), *A Field Guide to the Birds of Britain and Europe*, 8th Impr., 1963, Collins, London.

Phelps, W. H. (1944), '*Bubulcus ibis* in Venezuela,' *Auk* 61:656.

Philippi, R. A. (1954), 'Sobre costumbres predatorias del Gorrion comun *Passer d. domesticus* L.,' *Rev. Chilena Hist. Nat.* 54 (10):127-28.

Phillips, J. C. (1915), 'Notes on American and Old World English Sparrows,' *Auk* 32:51-59.

— (1928), 'Wild Birds Introduced and Transplanted into North America,' *U.S. Dep. Agric. Tech. Bull.* 61:1-63.

Phillips, W. W. A. (1966), 'A Revised Checklist of the Birds of Ceylon,' *Natn. Mus. Ceylon, nat. Hist. Ser. (Zool.)*, 1st Print., 1953.

Pierce, D. A. (1961), 'Re-establishment of the Wild Turkey in Massachusetts: Population and Habitat Studies,' *Ms. Thesis, Univ. Mass.* :1-182.

Pierce, R. A. (1956), 'Some Thoughts Concerning the Introduction of Exotic Game Birds,' *Wilson Bull.* 68:80-82.

Pinowski, J. and Kendeigh, S. C. (eds) (1977), *Granivorous Birds in Ecosystems. International Biological Programme 12*, Cambridge University Press, London, New York, Melbourne.

Pirnie, M. D. (1938), 'Restocking of the Canada Goose Successfully in Southern Michigan,' *Trans. N. Am. Wildl. Conf.* 3:624-27.

Pollard, J. (1967), *Birds of Paradox*, Lansdowne, Melbourne.

Pope, P. (1948), 'European Starling at Walla Walla, Washington,' *Murrelet* 29:29.

Popov, B. H. and Low, J. B. (1953), 'Game Fur Animals and Fish Introductions into Utah,' *Utah Dep. Fish Game., Misc. Publ.* (4):1-85.

Porter, R. D. (1955), 'The Hungarian Partridge in Utah,' *J. Wildl. Mgmt.* 19 (1):93-109.

Post, P. W. (1970), 'First Reports of Cattle Egret in Chile and Range Extensions in Peru,' *Auk* 87:361.

Post, W. and Wiley, J. W. (1976), 'The Yellow-shouldered Blackbird — Present and Future,' *Am. Birds* 30 (1):13-20.

— (1977), 'The Shiny Cowbird in the West Indies,' *Condor* 79 (1):119-21.

— (1977), 'Reproductive Interactions of the Shiny Cowbird and Yellow-shouldered Blackbird,' *Condor* 79 (2):176-84.

Potter, E. F. (1964), 'First House Finch Collected in North Carolina,' *Auk* 81:439-40.

Potter, S. D. (1935), 'Some British Birds in New Zealand,' *Avicult. Mag.* 4 (13):62-66.

Powell, J. A. (1967), Management of the Florida Turkey and the Eastern Turkey in Georgia and Alabama, in O. H. Hewitt (ed) *The Wild Turkey and Its Management*, Chapt. 14:409-51, Wildlife Society, Washington, D.C.

Powell, J. A. and Gainey, L. F. (1959), 'The Aerial Drop Method of Releasing Wild Trapped Turkeys for Restocking Purposes,' *Proc. 1st natn. Wild Turkey Symp., Memphis* :55-85.

Power, D. M. and Rising, J. D. (1975), 'The Cattle Egret in Central Baja California, Mexico, *Condor* 77 (3):353.

Power, J. H. (1958), 'House Sparrow in the Northern Cape,' *Ostrich* 29 (2):87.

Pracy, L. T. (1969), 'Weka Liberations in the Palliser Bay Region,' *Notornis* 16 (3):212.

Pratt, D. (1977), 'The Black-headed Munia Discovered on Kauai,' *Elepaio* 38 (2):18.

Pratt, T. (1975), 'The Kalij Pheasant on Hawaii,' *Elepaio* 35:66-67.

Preston, J. R. (1959), 'Turkey Restoration Efforts in the Ozark Region of Arkansas,' *Proc. 1st. natn. Wild Turkey Symp., Memphis* :43-45.

Prévost, J. and Mougin, J-L. (1970), *Guide des Oiseaux et Mammifères des Terres Australes et Antarctiques Françaises*, Guides Natur., Delachaux et Niestlé Edit., Neuchâtel, Switzerland :1-230.

Prokog'ev, M. A. (1960), 'The First Attempt to Acclimatize Starlings in the Buryat Autonomous S.S.R.,' in *Cons. Nat. Landsc., Moskov.* 2:114-18 (in Russian).

Pyle, L. (1979), 'Japanese Bush Warbler and Northern Cardinal on Molokai,' *Elepaio* 40 (2):27.

Pyle, R. L. (1963), 'House Finch Reaches District of Colombia and Virginia,' *Atl. Nat.* 18 (1):32-33.

— (1976), 'Recent Observations of Birds on Oahu, July 1975 to April 1976, and May to July, 1976,' *Elepaio* 37 (1):6-9 and 37 (4):45-47.

— (1976-78), 'The 1975, 1976 and 1977 Christmas Bird Counts,' *Elepaio* 36 (8):91-98, 37 (8):80-87, and 38 (8):85-89.

— (1978), 'Recent Observations of Birds, August to November,' *Elepaio* 38 (9):101-06.

Quaintance, C. W. (1946), 'The Starling Arrives in Oregon,' *Condor* 48:95.

—— (1949), 'Further Records of the Starling in Oregon,' *Condor* 51:271.

—— (1951), 'Pioneer Starling Nesting in Eastern Oregon,' *Condor* 53:50.

Quickelberge, C. D. (1972), 'Status of the European Starling at its Present Approximate Eastern Limits of Spread,' *Ostrich* 43 (3):179-80.

Rabor, D. S. and Rand, A. L. (1958), 'Jungle and Domestic Fowl, *Gallus gallus,* in the Philippines,' *Condor* 60:138-39.

Racey, K. (1950), 'Status of the European Starling in British Columbia,' *Murrelet* 31 (2):30-31.

Radcliffe, F. (1910), 'Starlings in Australia,' *Field* 116:633.

Raffaele, H. A. and Roby, D. (1977), 'The Lesser Antillean Bullfinch in the Virgin Islands,' *Wilson Bull.* 89 (2):338-42.

Rahman, K. A. and Bhalla, H. R. (1941), 'Common Indian Crow *(Corvus splendens)* in Relation to Agriculture,' *Proc. Indian Soc. Congr.* 27:230.

Raikow, R. J. (1968), 'Maintenance Behaviour of the Common Rhea,' *Wilson Bull.* 80:312-19.

—— (1969), 'Sexual and Agnostic Behaviour of the Common Rhea,' *Wilson Bull.* 81 (2):196-206.

Rakhilin, V. K. (1968), 'The Future of Feral Pigeons in Moscow,' *Zhiv. Nas. Moskvy and Podmos., Geogr. Inst. Acad. Sci., U.S.S.R. (Moscow), 1967* :85-86 (in Russian).

Ralph, C. J. and Pyle, R. L. (1977), 'The Winter Season, Dec. 1, 1976-Feb. 28, 1977: Hawaiian Islands Region,' *Am. Birds* 31 (3):376-77.

Ralph, C. J. and Sakai, H. F. (1979), 'Forest Bird and Fruit Bat Populations and Their Conservation in Micronesia: Notes on a Survey,' *Elepaio* 40 (2):20-26.

Ramzan, M. and Toor, H. S. (1973), 'Danger to Maize Crops by Rose-ringed Parakeets, *Psittacula krameri* (Scopoli) in the Punjab,' *J. Bombay nat. Hist. Soc.* 70:201-03.

Rana, B. D. (1975), 'Breeding Biology of the Indian Ring Dove in the Rajasthan Desert,' *Auk* 92:322.

Rand, A. L. (1936), 'The Distribution and Habits of Madagascar Birds, Summary of Field Notes on the Mission Zoologique Franco — Anglo — Americaine a Madagascar,' *Bull. Am. Mus. nat. Hist.* 72:143-499.

Rand, A. L. and Gilliard, E. T. (1967), *Handbook of New Guinea Birds,* Weidenfeld and Nicholson, London.

Ranson, W. H. (1948), 'European Starling Taken in Cowlitz County, Western Washington,' *Murrelet* 29:28.

Raw, W., Sparrow, R. and Jourdain, F. C. R. (1921), 'Field Notes on the Birds of Lower Egypt,' *Ibis* 3 (11th Ser.) (2):238-64.

Rawley, E. V. (1964), 'Utah Upland Game Birds,' *Utah Dep. Fish Game., Publ.* 63-72.

Reader's Digest (1977), *Complete Book of Australian Birds,* Rev. 1977, Readers Digest Service, Sydney.

Recher, H. F. and Clark, S. S. (1974), 'A Biological Survey of Lord Howe Island with Recommendations for the Conservation of the Island's Wildlife,' *Biol. Conserv.* 6 (4):263-73.

Reese, J. G. (1975), 'Productivity and Management of Feral Mute Swans in Chesapeake Bay,' *J. Wildl. Mgmt.* 39 (2):280-86.

Reichenow, A. (1908), 'Vögel von den Inseln Ostafrikas,' in Prof. Dr. A. Voeltzkow, *Reise in Ostafrika 1903-05,* Wiss. Ergeb. 2, Stuttgart.

Reilly, E. M. (1968). *The Audubon Illustrated Handbook of American Birds,* McGraw-Hill, New York.

Reilly, P. (1970), 'Nesting of the Superb Lyrebird in Sherbrooke Forest, Victoria,' *Emu* 70:73-78.

Resadny, C. D. (1965), 'Huns on the Move,' *Wis. Conserv. Bull.* 30 (6):21-23.

Reuther, R. T. (1951), 'The Chinese Spotted Dove at Bakersfield, California,' *Condor* 53:300-01.

Reuterwall, D. F. (1956), 'The Collared Turtle-dove *(Streptopelia decaocto)* Breeding in Varberg,' *Vår. Fågelvärld* 15 (4):262-68.

Rice, D. W. (1956), 'Dynamics of Range Expansion of Cattle Egrets in Florida,' *Auk* 73 (2):259-66.

Richardson, F. and Bowles, J. (1964), 'A Survey of the Birds of Kauai, Hawaii,' *Bull. Bernice P. Bishop Mus.* 227:1-51.

Richmond, C. W. (1903), 'Birds Collected by Dr W. L. Abbott and Mr C. B. Kloss in the Andaman and Nicobar Islands,' *Proc. U.S. natn. Mus.* 25:287-314.

Ridgely, R. S. (1976), *A Guide to the Birds of Panama,* Princeton University Press, New Jersey.

Ridgeway, R. (1894), 'Description of Some New Birds from Aldabra, Assumption and Gloriosa Islands, collected by Dr W. L. Abbott,' *Proc. U.S. natn. Mus.* 17:371-73.

—— (1895), 'On Birds Collected by W. L. Abott on the Seychelles, Amirantes, Glorioso, Assumption, Aldabra and Adjacent Islands, with Notes on Habits by the Collector,' *Proc. U.S. natn. Mus.* 18:509-46.

Ridley, H. N. (1898), 'Birds of the Botanic Garden, Singapore,' *J. Straits Brch. R. Asiat. Soc.* 25:60-67.

Ridpath, M. G. and Moreau, R. E. (1965), 'The Birds of Tasmania: Ecology and Evolution,' *Ibis* 108 (3):348-93.

Riggert, T. L. (1975), 'The Management of the Emu *Dromaius novaehollandiae* in Western Australia,' *Dep. Fish Wildl. West. Aust., Widl. Res. Bull.* (4).

Riley, J. H. (1938), 'Birds of Siam and the Malay Peninsula,' *Smithson Inst. U.S. natn. Mus. Bull.* (172).

Ringleben, H. (1960), 'The Pigeon Nuisance in Cities,' *Disinf. u. Gesundheitswesen* 52:124-28.

Ripley, S. D. (1951), 'Migrants and Introduced Species in the Palau Archipelago,' *Condor* 53 (6):299-300.

—— (1961), *A Synopsis of the Birds of India and Pakistan: Together with Those of Nepal, Sikkim, Bhutan and Ceylon:* Bombay Natural History Society, Madras, India.

—— (1977), *Rails of the World,* D. R. Godine, Massachusetts.

Rippin, A. B. and Boag, D. A. (1974), 'Recruitment to Populations of Male Sharp-tailed Grouse,' *J. Wildl. Mgmt.* 38:616-21.

Ritchie, J. (1929), 'Northward Extension of Capercaillie to Sutherland,' *Scott. Nat.,* 1929:126.

Robbins, C. S. (1973), 'Introduction, Spread and Present Abundance of the House Sparrow in North America,' in Symp. on House Sp. in N. Am, C. S. Kendeigh (ed), *Orn. Monogr.* 14:3-9.

Roberts, A. (1940), *The Birds of South Africa,* Witherby, London.

Roberts, H. A. (1959), 'Aspects of Harvest and Hunting Pressure in Pa's Wild Turkey Range,' *Proc. 1st natn. Wild Turkey Symp., Memphis* :31-35.

Roberts, T. S. (1960), *Bird Portraits in Colour,* 1934, Rev. Edn, 1960, University Minneapolis Press, Minneapolis.

Robertson, W. B. (1958), 'Investigations of Ring-necked Pheasants in Illinois,' *Ill. Dep. Conserv. Tech. Bull.* 1:1-137.

—— (1962), 'Observations on the Birds of St John, Virgin Islands,' *Auk* 79:44-76.

Robertson, D. B. (1976), 'Weka Liberation in Northland,' *Notornis* 23:213-19.

Robinson, A. H. (1947), 'Magpie Larks A Study in Behaviour,' *Emu* 46:265-81, 382-94, 47:11-28, 147-53.

—— (1950), 'Immigration of the Indian Crow to Western Australia,' *West Aust. Nat.* 2 (4):81.

Robinson, H. C. and Chasen, F. N. (1927-39) *Birds of the Malay Peninsula,* Vols. 1-4, Witherby, London.

Robinson, L. H. (1969), 'Introduction of Exotic Game Birds in South Carolina,' *Proc. 23rd a. Conf. S-East. Ass. Game Fish Commn.* :152-59.

Roby, E. F. (1950), 'A Two-year Study of Pheasant Stocking in the Gallatin Valley, Montana,' *J. Wildl. Mgmt.* 15 (3):299-307.

Rockwell, R. B. (1939), 'The Starling in Colorado.' *Wilson Bull.* 51:46.

Rolls, E. C. (1969), *They All Ran Wild,* Angus & Robertson, Melbourne.

Roscoe, D. R., Zeh, J. B., Stone, W. B., Brown, L. P. and Renkavinsky, J. L. (1973), 'Observations on the Monk Parakeet in New York State,' *N.Y. Fish Game J.* 20 (2):170-73.

Rose, B. J. (1958), 'An Evaluation of Two Introductions of Merriam's Wild Turkey into Montana,' *Mont. Wildl.,* 1958:5-8.

Rosene, W. (1969), *The Bobwhite Quail Its Life and Management,* Rutgers University Press, New Brunswick, New Jersey.

Ross, D. M. (1897), 'Capercaillie in the Mid-Deveron District,' *Ann. Scot. nat. Hist.,* 1897:254.

Rostrom, A. (1969), 'Rosella Parrots: NZ's most Beautiful Pests,' *N.Z. agric. J.* 118:40.

Rountree, F. R. G. (1951), 'Some Aspects of Bird-Life in Mauritius,' *Proc. R. Soc. Arts Sci. Maurit.* 1 (2):83-96.

Rountree, F. R. G., Guerin, R., Pelte, S. and Vinson, J. (1952), 'Catalogue of the Birds of Mauritius,' *Bull. Maurit. Inst.* 3 (3):155-217.

Rowan, M. K. (1964), 'House Sparrow *(Passer domesticus)* Reaches the South-western Cape,' *Ostrich* 35 (2):240.

Rowan, W. (1927), 'Details of the Release of the Hungarian Partridge in Central Alberta,' *Can. Fld.-Nat.* 41 (5):98-101.

—— (1936), 'The Partridge Situation in Western Canada,' *Sportsman* 20 (3):43, 63.

—— (1938), 'The Hungarian Partridge on the Canadian Prairies,' *Outdoors Am.* 3 (4):6-7.

—— (1952), 'The Hungarian Partridge *(Perdix perdix)* in Canada,' *Trans. R. Soc. Canada,* Section III, 46:161-62.

Rowley, I. (1965), 'Life History of the Superb Blue Wren *Malurus cyaneus,' Emu* 64:255-58.

Royal Australian Ornithological Union (1963), 'R.A.O.U. Conservation Policy,' *Emu* 63 (3):256.

Royall, W. C. and Neff, J. A. (1961), 'Bird Repellents for Pine Seed in the Mid-Southern States,' *Trans. 26th N. Am. Wildl. nat. Resour. Conf., Mar. 6-8* :234-38.

Ruddiman, J. L. (1952), '*Corvus splendens* in W.A.,' *Emu* 52:138.

Ruhl, H. D. (1941), 'Game Introductions in Michigan,' *Trans. N. Am. Wildl. Conf.,* 5:424-27.

Rusinova, K. I. (1926), 'Pitanie vorobev po anapizu soderzhimogo zheludkov,' *Byull. Sredne-aziatskago gosudar stvenago Universiteta* 13:159-76.

Russell, D. N. (1971), 'Food Habits of the Starling in Eastern Texas,' *Condor* 73:369-72.

Russo, J. P. (1958), 'Kaibab Turkey Transplant,' *Proc. 38th a. Conf. west. Assn. St. Game Fish Commnrs.* :175-78.

Rutgers, R. and Norris, K. A. (1970-77), *Encyclopaedia of Aviculture,* 3 Vols, Blandford Press, London.

Rutherford, R. M. (1949), 'The Chukar Makes Good,' *Outdoors* 17 (3):10-11.

Ryan, C. S. (1906), 'On European and Other Birds Liberated in Victoria: Presidential Address,' *Emu* 5 (3):110-19.

Ryan, R. (1972), 'The Problem of Exotics,' *Am. Birds* 26 (6):934-35.

Safriel, U. N. (1975), 'Re-occurrence of the Red Avadavat, *Amandava amandava* (L.). (Aves: Estrildidae), in Egypt,' *Israel J. Zool.* 24 (1/2):79.

Safronov, M. (1963), 'Experiences in Transplanting Grouse,' *Okhota Okhotn. Khoz.* 4:4-5 (In Russian).

Sage, B. L. (1955), 'The Breeding Season Distribution of the Goldfinch in Hertfordshire,' *Trans. Herts. nat. Hist. Soc.* 24 (4):129-33.

— (1956), 'Remarks on the Racial Status, History and Distribution of the Tree Sparrow, Introduced to Australia,' *Emu* 56:137.

— (1958), 'Hybrid Ducks in New Zealand,' *Bull. Brit. Orn. Club* 78 (6):108-13.

— (1959), 'Some Recent Observations at Aden,' *Ibis* 101 (2):252-53.

Sainio, P. (1966), 'Metsähänhen Istutuskokeilu' (Experimental Introduction of Bean Goose *(Anser fabalis)* in Western Parts of Central Finland), *Suomen Riista* 19:94-99.

Sakane, M. (1960), 'Bambusicola thoracica Sonorivox Increasing in Hyogo,' *Tori* 15:286-89 (in *Auk* 79 (1), 1962).

Salganskii, A. A. and Salganskaya, L. A. (1959), 'Nandu v S.S.S.R.' (Rheas in the USSR), *Priroda* 10:104-05 (in Russian).

Salter, M. T. (1950), 'Introduction of Starlings,' *Victorian Nat.* 67 (3):59.

Salter, R. L. (1953), 'Chukar Partridge Introductions in Idaho,' *Proc. 32nd a. Conf. west. Ass. St. Game Fish Commnrs.*:162-64.

Salomonsen, F. (1950), *The Birds of Greenland*, Pts. 1, 2 and 3, Munksgaard, Copenhagen.

Salvadori, T. (1905-06), 'Notes on Parrots' (Parts 1-5), *Ibis* (8th Ser.) 5:401-29, and (8th Ser.) 6:124-31, 451-65.

Samorodov, A. V. (1956), 'The Usefulness and Harmfulness of the Rook,' *Priroda* 7:96-97 (in Russian).

Samuel, D. E. (1969), 'House Sparrow Occupancy of Cliff Swallow Nests,' *Wilson Bull.* 81 (1):103-04.

Sandeman, P. W. (1965), 'Attempted Re-introduction of White-tailed Eagle to Scotland,' *Scott. Birds* 3:411.

Sandfort, W. (1963), 'We Can Have More Pheasants,' *Colo. Outdoors* 12 (2):1-6.

Sandfort, W. W. (1952), 'Chukar Partridge,' *Colo. Conserv.* 1 (2):15-19.

— (1955), 'Evaluation of Chukar Partridge Range in Colorado,' *Proc. 34th a. Conf. west. Ass. St. Game Fish Commnrs., 1954* :244-50.

Sansom, O. (1951), 'Spur-winged Plover in New Zealand,' *Notornis* 4 (6):138-39.

Sappington, J. N. (1977), 'Breeding Biology of the House Sparrow in Northern Mississippi,' *Wilson Bull.* 89 (2):300-09.

Sarmento, A. A. (1936), 'Aves do Arquipélago da Madeira. Indigeras e de passagem: Birds (1936),' in *Vertebrates da Madeira, 1948* :89-233.

Sauer, E. G. and Sauer, E. M. (1966), 'Behaviour and Ecology of the South African Ostrich,' *Living Bird* 5:45-75.

— (1966), 'Social Behaviour of the South African Ostrich,' *Ostrich* Suppl. (6):183-91.

Saunders, H. (1886), 'Birds of the Island of Diego Garcia, Chagos Group,' *Proc. Zool. Soc., London*:335-37.

Savage, C. (1952), *The Mandarin Duck*, A. and C. Black, London.

Savory, C. J. (1978), 'Food Consumption of the Red Grouse in Relation to Age and Productivity of Heather,' *J. Anim. Ecol.* 47:269-82.

Scheffer, P. M. (1967), 'Exotic Non-Game Bird Introductions — Pro and Con,' in *Proc. 47th a. Conf. west. Ass. St. Game Fish Commnrs., Honolulu, Hawaii, Jly. 16-20, 1967* :113-22.

Scheffer, T. H. (1935), 'The English Skylark on Vancouver Island,' *Condor* 37:256-57.

— (1955), 'Present Status of the Introduced English Skylark on Vancouver Island and of the Chinese Mynah on Vancouver Mainland,' *Murrelet* 36:28-29.

Scheffer, T. H. and Cottam, C. (1935), 'The Crested Mynah or Chinese Starling in the Pacific Northwest,' *U.S. Dep. Agric. Tech. Bull.* (467):1-26.

Schleh, - (1883), 'Der Nutzen und Schaden des Sperlings *(Passer domesticus* Linnaeus) im Haushalt der Natur,' *Landw. Jbr.* 12:337-61.

— (1884), *Landw. Jbr.* 13:789-812.

Schneider, C. O. (1938), 'Notas sobre La aclimatación des algunas aves extrangeras en Chile,' *Act. Soc. Sci., Chile* 63-65:135-38.

Schneider, F. (1957), 'An Introduction of European Gray Partridge of Danish Stock into the Willamette Valley, Oregon,' *Proc. 37 a. Conf. west. Ass. St. Game Fish. Commnrs.* :271-73.

Schodde, R. (1959), 'Indigenous and Introduced Birds Recovered from Flinders Range Region of South Australia,' *S. Aust. Nat.* 34 (1):13-14.

Scholes, K. T. (1954), 'Notes from Panama and the Canal Zone,' *Condor* 56:166-67.

Schorger, A. W. (1942), 'The Wild Turkey in Early Wisconsin,' *Wilson Bull.* 54 (3):173-82.

— (1952), 'Introduction of the Domestic Pigeon,' *Auk* 69 (4):462-63.

— (1958), 'Extirpation of a Flock of Wild Turkeys in Adams County,' *Passenger Pigeon* 20 (4):170-71.

Schorger, N. W. (1947), 'The Introduction of the Pheasant into Wisconsin,' *Passenger Pigeon* 9 (3):101-02.

Schrader, T. A. (1944), 'The Ring-necked Pheasant,' *Conserv. Volunt.* 7 (3):17-22.

Schubert, T. (1973), 'Status of Monk Parakeet Program,' *N.J. Div. Fish Game Shell Fish., Rep. 1973.*

Schwartz, C. W. and Schwartz, E. R. (1949), *A Reconnaisance of the Game Birds of Hawaii*, Board of Commerce Agric. and For., Honolulu, Hawaii.

— (1950), 'The California Quail in Hawaii,' *Auk* 67 (1):1-38.

— (1950), 'Breeding Habits of the Barred Dove in Hawaii with Notes on Weight and Sex Ratio,' *Condor* 52 (6):241-46.

— (1951), 'Food Habits of the Barred Dove in Hawaii,' *Wilson Bull.* 63 (3):149-56.

— (1951), 'An Ecological Reconnaisance of the Pheasants of Hawaii,' *Auk* 68:281-314.

Scott, H. G. (1961), 'Pigeons, Public Health, Importance and Control,' *Pest Control*, Sept., 1961:9.

Scott, K. (1957), 'A First Record of the Cattle Egret in Peru,' *Condor* 59 (2):143.

Scott, P. (1950), 'Transatlantic Voyage of Starlings,' *Brit. Birds* 43:369.

— (1965), *A Coloured Key to the Waterfowl of the World*, 1950, Rev. Edn 1965. Wildfowl Trust, London.

— (1967), Cause and Effect in the Introduction of Exotic Species, in Proc. and Papers 10 Tech. Meet. I.U.C.N. 1966, *Towards a New Relat. of Man and Nat. in Temp. Lands, Part III Changes due to Introd. Spp.* I.U.C.N. Publ., Morges, Switzerland, New Ser. (9):120-23.

— (1972), *The Swans*, Michael Joseph Ltd, London.

Sealy, S. G. (1969), 'Starling at Inuvik,' *Arctic* 22:444 (*Ibis* :114, 1972).

Seaman, G. A. (1955), 'Cattle Egret in the Virgin Islands,' *Wilson Bull.* 67:304-05.

— (1958), 'Nesting of the Cattle Egret in the Virgin Islands,' *Wilson Bull.* 70:93-94.

Secker, H. L. (1951), 'Habits of the Lesser Redpoll in the Wellington Peninsula,' *Notornis* 4:63-66.

Section of Food Habits (1938), 'Two Home-made traps for English Sparrows,' *Div. Wildl. Resour. U.S. Dep. Agric., Bur. Biol.*

Surv., Wildl. Resour. Mgmt. Leafl. (BS-121):1-9.

Sedgwick, E. H. (1957), 'Occurrence of the Goldfinch at Albany,' *West Aust. Nat.* 5 (8):230.

— (1958), 'The Introduced Turtledoves in W.A.,' *West Aust. Nat.* 6:92-10, 112-127.

— (1976), 'Supplementary Notes on Turtledoves, Streptopelia, in Western Australia,' *West Aust. Nat.* 13 (7):175-76.

Sefton, A. R. and Devitt, J. A. (1962), 'Additions to the Birds from the Illawarra District,' *Emu* 62:186.

Seibert, H. C. (1965), 'Food of the Feral Reeves Pheasant,' *Game Res. Ohio* 3:55-61.

Seibert, H. C. and Donohoe, R. W. (1965), 'The History of the Reeves Pheasant Program in Ohio,' *Ohio Game Monogr.* (1):1-20.

Sekhon, S. S. (1966), 'Studies on the Identification, Behaviour and Damage by Sparrows and Parrots in the Punjab,' *M. Sc. Thesis, Punjab Agric. University, Ludhiana.*

Selander, R. K. and Johnston, R. F. (1967), 'Evolution in the House Sparrow. 1. Intra-population Variation in North America,' *Condor* 99 (3):217-58.

Sengupta, S. (1968), 'Studies of the Common Mynah, *Acridotheres tristis tristis* (Linnaeus),' *Proc. zool. Soc., Calcutta* 21:1-27.

Sergeeva, N. A. and Sumina, E. V. (1963), 'Attempts at Acclimatizing *Perdix daurica* and Re-Acclimatizing of *Lagopus lagopus* in the Central Zone,' *Ornitologia* 6:86-95 (in Russian). (In *Ibis* 107 (2), 1965.)

Serventy, D. L. (1928), 'Congress Reports: W.A.,' *Emu* 27 (3):157-58.

— (1935), 'Acclimatisation Activities. A Criticism,' *West Austr.*, Perth, 4th. Sept., 1935.

— (1936), 'Animal Acclimatisation. Need for Continued Vigilance,' *West. Aust.*, Perth, 12th May, 1936.

— (1937), 'The Menace of Acclimatisation,' *Emu* 36 (3):189-96.

— (1948), 'The Birds of the Swan River District, Western Australia,' *Emu* 47 (4):241-86.

Serventy, D. L. and Whittell, H. M. (1951-67) *Handbook of the Birds of Western Australia*, 2nd Edn 1951 to 4th Edn 1967, Paterson Brokensha, Perth.

Serveheen, C. and English, W. (1976), 'Bald Eagle Rehabilitation Techniques in Western Washington,' *Raptor Res.* 10:84-87.

Seubert, J. L. (1964), 'Highlights of Bird Control Research in England, France, Holland, and Germany,' in *Proc. 2nd. Vert. Pest Contr. Conf., March 4-5, 1964, Anaheim, California* :150-59.

Shadle, A. R. (1930), 'The European Goldfinch at Buffalo, New York,' *Auk* 47:566-67.

Shaffer, C. H. (1961), 'Tom Turkey Tests,' *Va. Wildl.* 12 (8):4-5, 12.

Shaffer, C. H. and Gwynn, J. V. (1967), 'Management of the Eastern Turkey in the Oak-Pine Forests of Virginia and the Southeast,' in O. H. Hewitt (ed) *Wild Turkey and its Management*, Wildlife Society, Washington, D.C., Chapt. 11:303-42.

Sharland, M. (1944), 'The Lyrebird in Tasmania,' *Emu* 44:64-71.

— (1958), *Tasmanian Birds*, 1945, 3rd. Edn. Rev. 1958. Angus & Robertson, Sydney.

— (1958), 'Egrets at Ulmarra, N.S.W.,' *Emu* 57 (5):295-301.

Sharpe, R. B. (1889), 'On the Ornithology of Northern Borneo,' Part IV, *Ibis* (6th. Ser.) 1 (4):409-43.

Sharrock, J. T. R. (1972), Correspondence: 'Status of Reeves' Pheasant and Other Feral Species — Request for Information,' *Ibis* 114 (1):110.

— (1976), *The Atlas of Breeding Birds in*

Britain and Ireland, Brit. Trust for Ornithology, London.

Shaw, W. T. (1908), The China or Denny Pheasant in Oregon with Notes on the Native Grouse of the Pacific North West, J. B. Lippincott and Co., Philadelphia and London.

Shelgren, J. H., Thompson, R. A., Palmer, T. K. et al (1975), 'An Evaluation of the Pest Potential of the Ring-necked Parakeet, Nanday conure and the Canary-winged Parakeet in California,' Calif. Dep. Food. Agric. Spec. Serv. Unit : 25 pp.

Shields, T. J. and Neudahl, H. K. (1970), 'Pheasant Release Program of the Minnesota Future Farmers of America 1965-69,' Minn. Dep. Education : 1-22.

Shields, W. M. (1974), 'Use of Native Plants by Monk Parakeets in New Jersey,' Wilson Bull. 86 (2) : 172-73.

Shlapak, G. (1959), 'Fazan na ostrove Biryuchem' (Pheasants on Biryuchiy Island). Okhota Okhotn. Khoz. 3 : 13-14 (in Russian).

Shuyler, H. R. (1963), 'Bird Control in Kansas City,' Pest Control 31 (9) : 9-17.

Sick, H. (1957), 'Von Haussspatzen (Passer domesticus) in Brasilien,' Vogelwelt 78 (1) : 1-18.

— (1959), 'A Invasão da America Latina pelo pardal, Passer domesticus L., com referencia especial ao Brasil,' Boll. Mus. Nac., Rio de Janeiro, Zool. (207) : 1-31 (in Portuguese).

— (1966), 'Sobre a espécia existente de Estrilda (Ploceidae: Aves) o Chamado Bico-de-Lacre, no Brasil,' An. Acad. brasil Ciências 38 (1) : 169-71.

— (1967), 'Introduced Species of Birds in South America,' Int. Biol. Prog. Research Planning Conf., Caracas, 22-24 XI, 1967. Sect.: Anim. Spp. of Expanding Range (Unpublished).

— (1968), 'Über in Südamerika Eingefuehrte Vogelarten,' Bonn. zool. Beitr. 19 (3/4) : 298-306 (in German).

Sickels, A. C. (1959), 'Comparative Results of Stocking Game Farm and Wild Trapped Turkeys in Ohio,' Proc. 1st. natn. Wild Turkey Symp., Memphis : 75-86.

Siebe, C. C. (1964), 'Starlings in California,' in Proc. 2nd. Vert. Pest. Contr. Conf., Anaheim, California, March 4-5, 1964 : 40-42.

Siegfried, W. R. (1970), 'Wildfowl Distribution, Conservation and Research in Southern Africa,' Wildfowl 21 : 89-98.

— (1971), 'Chukar Partridge on Robben Island,' Ostrich 42 (2) : 158.

Sierpinski, Z. (1965), 'Blackcock (Lyrurus tetrix L.) — A Pest of Young Plantations of Pine,' Sylwan 109 (3) : 49-53 (in Polish).

Silverstein, A. and Silverstein, V. (1974), Animal Invaders: The Story of Imported Wildlife, Atheneum, New York.

Simpson, M. B. (1974), 'Monk Parakeets Breeding in Buncombe County, North Carolina,' Wilson Bull. 86 (2) : 171-72.

Simwat, G. S. and Sidhu, A. S. (1973), 'Notes on the Feeding Habits of the Rose-ringed Parakeet, Psittacula krameri (Scopoli),' Indian J. agric. Sci. 43 (6) : 607-09.

— (1974), 'Developmental Period and Feeding Habits of the Bank Mynah, Acridotheres ginginianus (Latham), in Punjab, J. Bombay nat. Hist. Soc. 71 : 305-08.

Sinclair, J. C. (1974), 'Arrival of the House Crow in Natal,' Ostrich 45 (3) : 189.

Skaggs, M. B. (1936), 'The Mute Swan and European Wigeon in Ohio,' Wilson Bull. 43 (2) : 131.

Skead, C. J. (1956), 'Study of the Red Bishop Bird,' Ostrich 27 (3) : 112-26.

— (1961), 'Chaffinch, Fringilla coelebs, at Kenton-on-Sea,' Ostrich 32 (4) : 189. .

— (1962), 'The European Starling, Sturnus vulgaris, at King William's Town,' Ostrich 33 : 1.

— (1966), 'The European Starling in the King William's Town and East London Districts,' Ostrich 37 (4) : 229.

Skead, D. M. (1975), 'Ecological Studies of Four Estrildines in Central Transvaal,' Ostrich Suppl. (11) : 1-55.

Skegg, P. D. (1964), 'Birds of the Hen and Chicken Islands,' Notornis 11 (3) : 159-76.

Skinner, J. O. (1905), 'The House Sparrow (Passer domesticus),' Smithson. Inst. Rep. : 423-28.

Skottesberg, C. J. F. (1920), The Natural History of Juan Fernandez and Easter Island, 3 Vols., Upsala, Sweden.

Skutch, A. F. (1954), 'Life Histories of Central American Birds,' Pacif. Cst. Avifauna (31).

— (1964), 'Life Histories of Central American Pigeons,' Wilson Bull. 76 : 211-47.

— (1968), 'Habits of the Chestnut-winged Chachalaca,' Wilson Bull. 75 (3) : 262.

Slaney, H. B. (1944), 'Starlings Useful,' Emu 44 : 171.

Slater, P. (1970-74), A Field Guide to Australian Birds, 2 vols, Rigby Ltd, Adelaide.

Slemons, R. D., Cooper, R. S. and Orsborn, J. S. (1973), 'Isolation of Type-A Influenza Viruses from Imported Exotic Birds,' Avian Dis. 17 (4) : 746-51.

Slud, P. (1957), 'Cattle Egret in Costa Rica,' Condor 59 (6) : 400.

Smith, C. F. and Aldous, S. E. (1947), Title not known, J. For. 45 : 361-69.

Smith, D. S. (1969), 'An Evaluation of Indian Red Jungle Fowl Releases in Baldwin,' Proc. 23rd a. Conf. S-East. Ass. Game Fish. Commn. : 157-71.

Smith, G. (1976), 'Ecology and Behavioural Comparisons Between Atrichornithidae and Menuridae,' in Proc. 16th. Int. Orn. Congr., Canberra : 125-36.

Smith, J. D. (1952), 'The Hawaiian Goose (Nene) Restoration Program,' J. Wildl. Mgmt. 16 : 1-9.

Smith, J. D. and Woolworth, J. R. (1950), 'A Study of the Pheasant, Californian Quail, and Lace-necked Dove in Hawaii: A Progress Report, Project 5-R-I,' Hawaii Board of Commerce Agric. For., Fish Game Div., Spec. Bull. : 1-58.

Smith, K. D. (1957), 'An Annotated Checklist of the Birds of Eritrea,' Ibis 99 : 1-307.

Smith, L. A. (1978), 'Rainbow Lorikeets at Safety Bay,' West. Aust. Nat. 14 (3) : 75.

Smith, N. J. H. (1973), 'House Sparrows (Passer domesticus) in the Amazon,' Condor 75 (2) : 242-43.

Smith, R. H. (1957), 'An Early Attempt to Introduce Pheasants to North America,' N.Y. Fish Game J. 4 (1) : 119-20.

Smith, T. H. (1967), 'A Sighting of the Colombo Crow (Corvus splendens) in Victoria,' Aust. Bird Watcher 3 (2) : 49-50.

Smith, W. A. (1969), 'Wild Turkey for the Future,' Trans. 15th. a. Meet., Calif. — Nev. Sect. Wildl. Soc. : 22-24.

Smith, W. J. (1958), 'Cattle Egret (Bubulcus ibis) Nesting in Cuba,' Auk 75 (1) : 89.

Smithers, C. N. and de S. Disney, H. J. (1969), 'The Distribution of Terrestrial and Fresh-water Birds on Norfolk Island,' Aust. Zool. 15 (2) : 127-40.

Smyth, T. (1926), 'Is the Starling Migratory,' Auk 43 (3) : 371-72.

Smythies, B. E. (1953), Birds of Burma, Oliver and Boyd, London.

— (1960), The Birds of Borneo, Oliver and Boyd, London.

Snow, D. W. (1950), 'Birds of São Tome and Principé in the Gulf of Guinea,' Ibis 92 (4) : 579-95.

— (1958), A Study of Blackbirds, Allen and Unwin, London.

Snow, B. K. and Snow, D. W. (1971), 'Feeding Ecology of Tanagers and Honey-creepers in Trinidad,' Auk 88 : 291-322.

Soper, M. F. (1972), New Zealand's Birds, Whitcombe & Tombs, Christchurch.

Solyom, V. (1940), 'The Chukar Partridge in Tennessee,' Migrant 11 (1) : 11-12.

Sooter, C. A. (1945), 'Starlings Wintering in Southern Texas,' Condor 47 (5) : 219.

Sooter, C. A. and Goldman, L. C. (1943), 'European Starling Problem in Eastern New Mexico and Adjacent Western Texas,' Condor 45 (4) : 161.

Southern, H. N. (1945), 'The Economic Importance of the House Sparrow: A Review,' Ann. appl. Biol. 32 (1) : 57-67.

Southwood, T. R. E. (1967), 'The Ecology of the Partridge II,' J. Anim. Ecol. 36 : 557-62.

Southwood, T. R. E., Blank, T. H. and Cross, D. J. (1967), 'The Ecology of the Partridge I,' J. Anim Ecol. 36 : 549-56.

Southwood, T. R. E. and Cross, D. J. (1969), 'The Ecology of the Partridge III,' J. Anim. Ecol. 38 : 497-509.

Springett, B. P. and Mathiesson, J. N. (1975), 'Predation on Potato Moth, Phthorimaea operculella (Lepidoptera: Gelechiidae) by the Western Silvereye, Zosterops gouldi (Aves: Zosteropidae),' Aust. J. Zool. 23 : 65-70.

Sprot, G. D. (1937), 'Notes on the Introduced Skylark in the Victoria District of Vancouver Island,' Condor 39 : 24-31.

Sprunt, A. (1953), 'Newcomer from the Old World,' Aubudon Mag. 55 : 178-81.

— (1955), 'The Spread of the Cattle Egret,' Smithson. Inst. a. Rep. 1954 (4198) : 259-76.

— (1956), 'The Cattle Egret in North America,' Audubon Mag. 58 : 174-77.

Sprunt, A. and Zim, H. S. (1961), Game Birds: Guide to North American Species and Their Habits, Golden Press Inc, New York.

Spurr, R. (1963), 'Dovecotes,' Animals 1 (24) : 26.

Stager, K. E. (1947), 'Starlings in Southern California,' Condor 49 : 169.

Stanford, J. A. (1957), 'Coturnix or Japanese Quail Investigations in the United States: A Progress Report: October, 1957,' 11th a. Conf. S-East. Ass. Game Fish Commn. : 1-8.

— (1957), 'A Progress Report of Coturnix Quail Investigations in Missouri,' Trans. 22nd. N. Am. Wildl. Conf. : 316-59.

Start, T. (1978), 'Silver Pheasant in Porongorups National Park: Summary of Occurrence,' File 57/76 Pheasants: A.P.B. Perth, W.A.

Staub, F. (1976), Birds of the Mascarenes and Saint Brandon, Mauritius: Org Normale des Enterpr. L'Tée.

Stead, D. G. (1938), 'Tragedies of Australian Acclimatisation with Special Reference to Recent Proposals,' Aust. Wildl. J. and Preservation Soc., Aust. 2 (2) : 33-72.

Stead, E. F. (1927), 'The Native and Introduced Birds of Canterbury,' in R. Speight, A. Wall and R. M. Laing (eds) Natural History of Canterbury, Simpson and Williams, New Zealand.

Steele-Elliot, J. (1907), 'The Little Owl in Bedfordshire,' Zoologist, 1907 : 384.

Stein, J. (1974), 'Ein Beitrag zur Brutbiologie von Singdrossel, T. philomelos, T. merula und Mönchsgrosmücke S. atricapilla,' Beitr. Vogelk. 20 : 467-77.

Stenhouse, D. (1960), 'The Redpoll in New Zealand,' Agric. Bull., Wellington, N.Z. (366).

— (1962), 'A New Habit of the Redpoll, Carduelis flammea, in New Zealand,' Ibis 104 : 250-52.

— (1962), 'Taxonomic Status of the New Zealand Redpoll, Carduelis flammea : A Reassessment,' Notornis 10 (2) : 61-66.

Stephens, C. H. (1962), 'Coturnix Quail Investigations in Kentucky,' Proc. 16th. a. Conf. S-East. Ass. Game Fish Commn. : 126-13?.

— (1966), 'Reeves' Pheasant Investigation in Kentucky,' Ky. Dep. Fish. Wildl. Resour. Game Mgmt. Tech. Serv. (15) : 1-32.

— (1967), 'Reeves' Pheasant Investigations

in Kentucky,' *Proc. 21st. a. Conf. S-East. Ass. Game Fish Commn.* :222-31.

Stevenson, H. M. (1977), 'The Winter Season, Dec. 1, 1976-Feb. 28, 1977: Florida Region,' *Am. Birds* 31 (3) :322-25.

Stewart, P. A. (1964), 'Bird Notes from Southeast Alaska,' *Condor* 66 (1) :78-79.

Stidolph, R. H. D. (1933), 'Destructive Civilisation in New Zealand,' Part II, *Emu* 33 :93-94.

— (1952), 'White-faced Heron in New Zealand,' *Notornis* 51 :18-19.

— (1974), 'Feral Barbary Doves in Masterton,' *Notornis* 21 :383-84.

Stirling, D. and Edwards, R. Y. (1962), 'Notes on the Skylark on Vancouver Island,' *Can. Fld.-Nat.* 76 (3) :147-52.

Stokes, A. W. (1968), 'An Eight-Year Study of a Northern Utah Pheasant Population,' *J. Wildl. Mgmt.* 32 (4) :867-74.

Stolt, B. O. and Risberg, E. L. (1971), 'The Collared Turtle-dove, *Streptopelia decaocto,* in Uppsala 1959-69; Occurrence and Winter Biology,' *Var Fågelvärld* 30 :194-200 (in Swedish).

Stone, C. P. (1973), 'Bird Damage to Agricultural Crops in the United States — A Current Summary,' *Proc. 6th. Bird Contr. Sem., Bowling Green State University* :264-67.

Stonehouse, B. (1962), 'Ascension Island: British Ornithological Union Centenary Expedition, 1957-59,' *Ibis* 103b (2) :107.

Stoner, D. (1923), 'The Mynah — A Study in Adaptation,' *Auk* 40 :328-30.

— (1939), 'Parasitism of the English Sparrow on the Northern Cliff Swallow,' *Wilson Bull.* 51 (4) :221-22.

Stophlet, J. J. (1946), 'Birds of Guam,' *Auk* 63 :534-59.

Storer, R. W. (1971), 'Classification of Birds,' in D. S. Farner and J. R. King (eds) *Avian Biology,* Academic Press, New York and London, Vol.1, pp.1-18.

Storer, T. I. (1923), 'The English Blackbird in California,' *Condor* 25 :67-68.

— (1931), 'Known and Potential Results of Bird and Animal Introductions, with Special Reference to California,' *Dep. Agric. Calif. Monthly Bull.* (20) :267-73.

— (1934), 'Economic Effects of Introducing Alien Animals to California,' in *Proc. 5th. Pacif. Sci. Congr., 1933.* 1 :779-84.

Storr, G. M. (1965), 'The Avifauna of Rottnest Island, Western Australia: Part III Land Birds, *Emu* 64 (3) :172-80.

Stott, K. (1957), 'A First Record of the Cattle Egret in Peru,' *Condor* 59 :143.

Strabala, L. (1925), 'The Starling at Leetonia, Ohio,' *Auk* 42 :447.

Stresemann, E. (1913), 'Die Vogel von Bali,' *Novit. zool.* 20 (in German).

— (1936), 'A Nominal List of the Birds of Celebes,' *Ibis* (13 Ser.) 4 (2) :356-68.

Stresemann, E. and Nowak, E. (1958), 'Die Ausbreitung der Turkentaube in Asien und Europa,' *J. Orn.* 99 :243-96 (in German).

Studholme, A. T. (1948), 'A Bird in the Hand is Worth Two in the Bush,' *Trans. N. Am. Wildl. Conf.* 13 :207-13.

Suetsugu, H. Y. and Menzel, K. E. (1963), 'Wild Turkey Introductions in Nebraska,' *Trans. 28th. N. Am. Wildl Conf.* :297-307.

Sugden, L. G. (1976), 'Waterfowl Damage to Canadian Grain,' *Occ. Pap. Can. Wildl. Serv., Ottawa.* (24) :1-25.

Sumina, E. B. (1963), 'Some Results of Acclimatization of Chinese Partridge and of Re-Acclimatization of Willow Grouse as shown by Banding,' in Acclim. of Anims. in USSR, *Akad. Nauk Kazakhsk S.S.R.* :175-77 (in Russian).

Summers-Smith, D. (1956), 'Movements of House Sparrows,' *Brit. Birds* 49 (12) :465-88.

Summers-Smith, J. D. (1963), *The House Sparrow,* New Naturalist Series, Collins, London.

— (1964), 'Aviculture,' in A. L. Thomson

(ed) *New Dictionary of Birds,* Nelson, London and New York.

Sutton, J. (1935), 'Acclimatisation in South Australia,' *S. Aust. Orn.* 13 (3) :92-103.

Swanson, N. A. (1968), No Title, *S. Aust. Orn.* 25 :36 and 25 :37.

Swarth, H. S. (1927), 'Valley Quail Imported from Chile,' *Condor* 29 :164.

Swedberg, G. E. (1969), 'Sightings of Wild Koloa on the Island of Hawaii and History of a Past Release,' *Elepaio* 29 :87-88.

Swezey, O. H. (1937), 'Notes on the Food of the California Quail in Hawaii,' *Proc. Hawaii ent. Soc.* 9 (3) :432.

Swift, J. (1974), 'Pintail; A Project Assessing the Release of Hand-Reared Birds,' *Wildlife Association Great Britain and Ireland Report and Yearbook, 1973-74* :55-58.

Swinhoe, R. (1860), 'The Ornithology of Amoy (China),' *Ibis* 2 (1) :45-68.

— (1861), 'Notes on the Ornithology of Hong Kong, Macao and Canton, made during the latter end of Feb, March, Apr and Beginning of May, 1860,' *Ibis* 3 (9) :23-57.

Syme, R. (1975), *Isles of the Frigate Bird,* Michael Joseph, London.

Szickel, F. C. (1966), 'Winter Food Habits of Capercaillie in North-eastern Scotland,' *Brit. Birds* 59 (8) :325-36.

Tahon, J. (1972), 'Request for an I.B.P. Subgroup "*Sturnus vulgaris* L." to Study the Biology of Starlings and to Control the Damage they Cause,' in S. C. Kendeigh and J. Pinowski (Eds) *Prod. Pop. Dyn. and Syst. Graniv. Birds, Proc. Gen. Meet. Work. Grp. Graniv. Bds., I.B.P., Pt. Sect., Hague, Holland, Sept. 6-8, 1970,* P.W.N. Polish Sci. Publs, Warszawa, 291-97.

Taka-Tsukasa, N. and Hachisuka, M. U. (1925), 'A Contribution to Japanese Ornithology,' *Ibis* 12 (1) :898-908.

Tangen, H. I. L. (1974), 'Forsok med canadagås i Norge,' *Fauna* (Oslo) 27 :166-76 (in Norwegian).

Tarr, H. E. (1949), 'Another Introduced Bird Making Headway in Australia,' *Emu* 49 (2) :142-43.

— (1950), 'The Distribution of Foreign Birds in Australia,' *Emu* 49 :189-95.

Taylor, A. and Ridpath, M. G. (1956), 'Bird Damage and the Fruit Grower,' *R.H.S. Fruit Year Book* (9) :73-77.

Taylor, A. L. and Collins, M. S. (1979), 'Rediscovery and Identification of the "Mystery" Garrulax on Oahu,' *Elepaio* 39 (8) :79-81.

Taylor, R. G. (1953), 'Starlings in Jamaica,' *Ibis* 95 (4) :700-01.

Taylor, W. L. (1948), 'The Capercaillie in Scotland,' *J. Anim. Ecol.* 17 :155-57.

Taylor, W. P. (1923), 'Upland Game Birds in the State of Washington, with Discussion on some Principles of Game Importation,' *Murrelet* 4 :3-15.

Teal, J. M. (1965), 'Cattle Egret in Georgia,' *Oriole* 21 :33.

Terry, M. (1963), 'Exotic Pests? We've Got the Lot,' *People* 14 (11) :12-15.

Tavener, P. A. (1927), 'Hungarian Partridge "is" Sharp-tailed Grouse,' *Can. Fld.-Nat.* 41 (7) :147-49.

Thearle, R. J. P. (1968), 'Urban Bird Problems,' in R. K. Murton and E. N. Wright (eds) *The Problem of Birds as Pests,* Academic Press, London :181-97.

Thibault, J.-C. (1976), 'L'avifaune de Tetiaroa (Archipel de la Société, Polynésie française),' *Oiseau Revue fr. Orn.* 46 :29-45.

Thibault, J.-C. and Rives, C. L. (1975), *Birds of Tahiti,* Transl. by D. T. Holyoak, Les Editions du Pacifique, Papeete, Tahiti.

Thistle, A. (1962), 'Observations on Cattle Egret — Oahu, July, 1962,' *Elepaio* 23 :15.

Thomas, C. B. (1977), 'The Mortality of Yorkshire Canada Geese,' *Wildfowl* 28 :35-47.

Thomas, D. G. (1965), 'Birds of the

R.A.O.U., 1964 Field Outing, Bicheno District, Tasmania,' *Emu* 64 (3) :172-80.

Thomas, E. S. (1934), 'A Study of Starlings Banded at Columbus, Ohio,' *Bird Banding* 5 :118-28.

Thomas, H. F. (1957), 'The Starling in the Sunraysia District, Victoria,' *Emu* 57 (1) :31-48; (2) :131-44; (3) :151-160; (4) :269-84.

Thompson, H. V. (1953), 'The Use of Repellents for Preventing Mammal and Bird Damage to Trees and Seeds,' *For. Abstr.* 14 (2) :129-36.

Thompson, H. W. (1960), 'Economic Ornithology,' *Ann. appl. Biol.* 48 (2) :405-08.

Thompson, M. C. (1966), 'Birds from North Borneo,' *Univ. Kans. Publ. nat. Hist.* 17 :377-433.

Thompson, W. L. and Coutlee, E. L. (1963), 'The Biology and Population Structure of Starlings at an Urban Roost,' *Wilson Bull.* 75 (4) :358-72.

Thomson, A. L. (ed) (1964), *A New Dictionary of Birds.* Nelson, London.

Thomson, G. M. (1922), *The Naturalisation of Animals and Plants in New Zealand,* Cambridge University Press, New Zealand.

— (1926), *Wildlife in New Zealand; Part II. Introduced Birds and Fishes,* N.Z. Board Sci. and Art, Manual (5), Government Printer, Wellington.

Throp, J. (1969), 'Java Ricebird,' *Elepaio* 29 :80.

Ticehurst, C. B. (1924), 'The Birds of Sind: Part VII (Conclusions),' *Ibis* (11 Ser.) 6 (3) :459-518.

Tomer, J. S. (1967), 'Cattle Egret Nesting in Northeastern Oklahoma,' *Wilson Bull.* 79 :245.

Tomich, P. Q. (1962), 'Notes on the Barn Owl in Hawaii,' *Elepaio* 23 :16-17.

Tomlinson, D. (1976), 'Surrey's Chinese Duck,' *Country Life* 159 (4115) :1248-49.

Toschi, A. (1962), 'Preliminary Results of the Release of Partridge *(Perdix perdix)* in Italy,' *Trans. 5th. Congr. int. Un. Game Biol., Bologna, 4-10 Sept., 1961* :261-68.

Toso, S. (1977), 'Notes on the Introduction into the Wild by Two Buzzards *(Buteo buteo)* Reared in Captivity,' *World Conf. Birds Prey* 1 :375-78.

Tousey, R. H. and Griscom, L. (1937), 'Notes on Starling Spread and Migration,' *Auk* 54 :209-10.

Townsend, C. W. (1915), 'Notes on the Rock Dove *(Columba domestica),' Auk* 32 :306-16.

— (1926), 'The European Starling in Mississippi and in Florida,' *Auk* 43 :371.

Townsend, C. W. and Wetmore, A. (1919), 'Reports on the Scientific Results of the Expedition to the Tropical Pacific in charge of A. Agassiz on the U.S. Fish Commission Steamer *Albatross,' Bull. Mus. comp. Zool. Harv.* 63 :151-225.

Trautman, C. G. (1952), 'Pheasant Food Habits in South Dakota and their Economic Significance to Agriculture,' *S. Dak. Dep. Game Fish Parks Tech. Bull.* (1) :1-89.

Trenholm, L. (1926), 'The Starling in Tennessee,' *Bird-Lore* 28 (5) :334.

Trimm, W. (1972), 'The Monk Parrot,' *Conservationist* 26 (6) :4-5.

— (1973), 'The Monk Parrots — A Year Later,' *Conservationist* 27 (6) :32-33.

True, G. H. (1937), 'The Chukar Partridge of Asia,' *Calif. Fish Game* 23 (3) :299-331.

Trueblood, R. and Weigand, J. (1971), 'Hungarian Partridge,' in T. W. Mussehl and F. W. Howell (eds) *Game Management in Montana,* Montana Fish and Game Department, Helena, Montana, Chp. 18 :153-59.

Tuck, L. M. (1958), 'The Present Distribution and Population of the Starling in Newfoundland,' *Can. Fld.-Nat.* 72 (3) :139-44.

—— (1968), 'Recent Newfoundland Bird Records,' *Auk* 85:304-11.

Tufts, R. W. (1926), 'Starlings Nest at Toronto,' *Can. Fld.-Nat.* 40:89.

Turbet, C. R. (1941), 'Introduction and Acclimatization of Animals,' *Trans. Proc. Fiji Soc. Sci. Ind., 1938-40* :7-12.

Turbott, E. G. (1956), 'Bulbuls in Auckland,' *Notornis* 6 (7):185-93.

—— (1957), 'Native and Introduced Birds,' in *Science in New Zealand* :97-111. Reed, Wellington.

—— (1961), 'The Interaction of Native and Introduced Birds in New Zealand,' *Proc. N.Z. ecol. Soc.* 8:62-66.

—— (1977), 'Rarotongan Birds with Notes on Land Bird Status,' *Notornis* 24 (3):149-57.

Turbott, E. G., Braithwaite, D. H. and Wilkin, F. W. (1963), 'Cattle Egret: A New Bird for New Zealand,' *Notornis* 10:316.

Turner, J. S., Smithers, C. N. and Hoogland, R. D. (1968), 'The Conservation of Norfolk Island,' *Spec. Publ. Aust. Conserv. Found.* (1):1-41.

Tuttle, H. J. (1959), 'Virginia's Foreign Game Program — A Progress Report,' *Proc. 13th a. Conf. S-East. Ass. Game Fish Commn.* :70-73.

—— (1963), 'Japanese Green and Kalij Pheasants in Virginia,' *Proc. 17th a. Conf. S-East. Ass. Game Fish Commn.* :121-23.

Twomey, A. C. (1936), 'Climatographic Studies of Certain Introduced and Migratory Birds,' *Ecology* 17 (1):122-32.

Uchida, S. (1937), 'Birds in Japan,' :236-37 (in Japanese).

Udagawa, T. (1949), 'The Eastern Ring-Dove may be Extirpated in Japan,' *Tori* 12:267-69.

Udall, S. L. (1963), *Annual Report of the Secretary of the Interior, 1963,* U.S. Government Printer, Washington, D.C.

Udvardy, M. D. F. (1960), 'The Black-headed Mannikin, *Lonchura malacca atricapilla,* a New Breeding Bird on the Hawaiian Islands,' *Elepaio* 21:15-17.

—— (1961), 'The Occurrence of the Mocking Bird on the Island of Maui,' *Elepaio* 21:72.

—— (1966), Review of 'Introduction of Mammals and Birds to Europe,' *J. Wildl. Mgmt.* 30 (1):240-41.

Udys, C. J. (1962), 'The House Sparrow, *Passer domesticus,* at Grunau,' *Ostrich* 33 (4):39.

United States Department of the Interior (1976), 'Conserving Our Fish and Wildlife Heritage,' *U.S. Fish Wildl. Serv., Washington, D.C., Annual Report, 1976.*

University of California (1962-67), 'Progress Reports on Starling Control,' *Univ. Calif. Res. Comm., Div. Agric. Sci.,* Davis, California.

Urner, C. A. (1921), 'Notes on the Starling,' *Auk* 38:459.

Valentine, J. M. (1958), 'The Cattle Egret at Chincoteague, Virginia,' *Raven* 29 (8):68-96.

Valyrus, M. (1959), 'Re-acclimatization of the Grey Goose *Anser anser* L. in the Zhivintas Reserve,' *Okhota Okhotn. Khoz.* 11:26-27 (in Russian).

Van Bruggen, A. C. (1960), 'Notes on Observations on Birds in the Transvaal Southern Rhodesia and Portuguese East Africa,' *Ostrich* 31:30-31.

Van Ripper, C. (1978), 'Discovery of the Yellow-fronted Canary on Mauna Kea, Hawaii,' *Elepaio* 38 (9):99-100.

Van Someren, V. D. (1947), 'Field Notes on Some Madagascar Birds,' *Ibis* 89:235-67.

Van Tets, G. F. and Van Tets, P. A. (1967), 'A Report on the Resident Birds of the Territory of Christmas Island,' *Emu* 66:309-17.

Van Wormer, J. (1968), *World of the Canada Goose,* Lippincott, Philadelphia.

Vaughan, J. H. (1930), 'The Birds of Zanzibar and Pemba,' *Ibis* (12 Ser.) 6 (1):1-47.

—— (1932), 'Additional Notes on the Birds of Zanzibar and Pemba,' *Ibis* (13 Ser.) 2 (2):351-53.

Vaughan, R. E. and Jones, K. H. (1913), 'The Birds of Hong Kong, Macao and the West River or Si Kiang in South East China, with Special Reference to Their Nidification and Seasonal Movements,' *Ibis* :17-76, 163-201, 351-84.

Vaught, R. W. (1964), 'Results of Transplanting Flightless Young Blue-winged Teal,' *J. Wildl. Mgmt.* 28 (2):208-12.

Vaurie, C. (1961), 'Systematic Notes on Palearctic Birds, No. 49 Columbidae: The Genus Streptopelia,' *Am. Mus. Novit.* (2058):1-25.

Venables, L. S. V. and Venables, U. M. (1952), 'The Blackbird in Shetland,' *Ibis* 94:636-52.

Vernon, C. J. (1962), 'Passerinae at Francistown, Bechuanaland Protectorate,' *Ostrich* 33:239-40.

Vertse, A., Zsák, Z. and Kaszab, Z. (1955), 'Food and Agricultural Importance of the Partridge (*Perdix perdix* L.) in Hungary,' *Aquila* 59-62:13-68 (in Hungarian).

Vessey-Fitzgerald, D. (1940), 'On the Birds of Seychelles. 1. The Endemic Land Birds,' *Ibis* 14 (4):480-89.

Vestal, E. H. (1948), 'The Starling Appears at Leevining, Mono County, California,' *Condor* 50:89.

Viehmeyer, G. (1942), 'The Hungarian Partridge and its Range in Northern Nebraska,' *Nebr. Bird Rev.* 10 (2):37-43.

Vincent, D. J. (1971), No Title, *S. Aust. Orn.* 26:17.

Vincente, R. O. (1969), 'A New Introduced Species in Europe: The Red-eared Waxbill,' *Ibis* 111 (4):614.

Viney, C. A. (1976), *The Hong Kong Bird Report, 1975,* Hong Kong Bird Watching Society, Hong Kong.

Vinson, J. (1950), 'L'Ile Ronde et L'Ile aux Serpents,' *Proc. R. Soc. Arts Sci. Maurit.* 1 (1):32-52.

Von Jarchow, B. L. (1943), 'Starlings Frustrate Sparrow Hawks in Nesting Attempt,' *Passenger Pigeon* 5:51.

Von Thanner, R. (1905), 'Notizen aus Tenerife,' *Orn. Fahrb.* 16:211-14.

Voous, K. H. (1960), *Atlas of European Birds,* Nelson and Son, London.

Wace, N. M. and Holdgate, M. W. (1976), 'Man and Nature in the Tristan da Cunha Islands,' *I.U.C.N. Monogr.* (6):1-114.

Wahl, T. R. and Wilson, H. E. (1971), 'Nesting Record of European Skylark in Washington State,' *Condor* 73:254.

Wait, W. E. (1931), *Manual of the Birds of Ceylon,* 2nd Edn, Colombo Museum, Colombo.

Walker, A. (1949), 'The Starling Reaches the Pacific,' *Condor* 51:271.

Walker, A. F. G. (1970), 'The Moult Migration of Yorkshire Canada Geese,' *Wildfowl* 21:99-104.

Walker, E. A. (1949), 'The Status of the Wild Turkey West of the Mississippi River,' *Trans. N. Am. Wildl. Conf.* 14:336-54.

Walker, R. B. (1952), 'Indian Mynah on the Darling Downs,' *Emu* :64-65.

Walker, R. L. (1967), 'Indian Hill Mynah, Cattle Egret, and Red-vented Bulbul,' *Elepaio* 28:23-24.

—— (1967), 'A Brief History of Exotic Game Birds and Mammal Introductions into Hawaii — with a look to the Future,' *Proc. 47th a. Conf. west Ass. St. Game Fish Commrs. Honolulu, Hawaii, Jly. 16-20, 1967* :94-112.

—— (1970), 'Nene Restoration Project Report,' *Elepaio* 31:1-7.

Wall, L. E. and Wheeler, W. R. (1966), 'Lyrebirds in Tasmania,' *Emu* (2):123-31.

Wandell, W. N. (1949), 'Status of the Ring-necked Pheasant in the United States,' *Trans. N. Am. Wildl. Conf.* 14:370-87.

Ward, P. (1968), 'The Origin of the Avifauna of Urban and Suburban Singapore,' *Ibis* 110 (3):239-54.

Ward, P. and Poh, G. E. (1968), 'Seasonal Breeding in an Equatorial Population of the Tree Sparrow, *Passer montanus,' Ibis* 110 (3):359-63.

Warner, R. E. (1968), 'The Role of Introduced Diseases in the Extinction of the Endemic Hawaiian Avifauna,' *Condor* 70:101-20.

Watling, R. J. (1975), 'Observations on the Ecological Separation of Two Introduced Congeneric Mynahs (Acridotheres) in Fiji,' *Notornis* 22:37-53.

—— (1978), 'Observations on the Naturalised Distribution of the Red-vented Bulbul in the Pacific, with Special Reference to the Fiji Islands,' *Notornis* 25:109-17.

—— (1978), 'A Myna Matter,' *Notornis* 25:117.

Watson, G. E. (1966), 'The Chukar Partridge (Aves) (Morphology and Ecology) of St Helena Island, South Atlantic Ocean' *(Alectoris chukar.),' Proc. biol. Soc., Wash.* 79:179-82.

—— (1975), *Birds of the Antarctic and Sub-Antarctic,* Am. geophys. Union, Washington, D.C.

Watson, G. E., Zusi, R. L. and Storer, R. E. (1963), *Preliminary Guide to the Birds of the Indian Ocean,* U.S. natn. Mus. Smithson. Inst., Washington.

Wattel, J. (1971), 'The Subspecies of *Fringilla coelebs* L. Inhabiting the Cape Peninsula,' *Ostrich* 42 (3):229.

Way, R. D. (1961), 'Bird Damage to Fruit Crops,' *Plants and Gardens* 17 (3):51-55.

Wayne, A. T. (1925), 'The Starling on the Coast of South Carolina,' *Auk* 42:271-72.

Wayre, P. (1966), 'The Role of Aviculture in Helping to Save Threatened Species,' *Dep. Fish and Fauna, Perth, Monthly Serv. Bull.* 16 (10):14-17.

—— (1969), *A Guide to the Pheasants of the World, Country Life,* London.

—— (1975), 'Reintroduction of the Cheer Pheasant,' *12th Bull. int. Counc. Bird Preserv.* 12:222-23.

Weatherbee, D. K. and Jacobs, K. F. (1960), 'Migration of the Common Coturnix in North America,' *Proc. N. East. Sect. Wildl. Ass. a. Conf., Providence, R. I., Jan. 10-13, 1960* :1.

Weatherby, H. (1947), Title not known, *Timber of Canada* 7 (9):29.

Weaver, R. L. (1939), 'The Northern Distribution and Status of the English Sparrow in Canada,' *Can. Fld.-Nat.* 53:95-99.

—— (1942), 'Growth and Development of English Sparrows,' *Wilson Bull.* 54:183-91.

—— (1943), 'Reproduction in English Sparrows,' *Auk* 60:62-73.

Webb, L. G. (1969), 'Exotic Game Bird Investigations,' *S. Carolina Wildl. Res. Dep. a. Progressive Rep. Project (W-38-5)* :1-81.

Webb, P. M. (1957), 'The Introduction of the Grey Francolin in Arizona: A Progress Report,' *Proc. 37th a. Conf. west. Ass. St. Game Fish Commnrs.* :274-76.

—— (1960), 'Turkey Trapping and Transplanting in Arizona. *Proc. a. Conf. west. Ass. St. Game Fish Commnrs.* :182-87.

Webster, F. S. (1974), 'South Texas Region,' in 'Fall Migration Aug. 1-Nov. 30, 1973,' *Am. Birds* 28 (1):28-121.

—— (1976), 'Fall Migration Aug. 1-Nov. 30, 1975: South Texas Region,' *Am. Birds* 30 (1):95-97.

—— (1977), 'The Autumn Migration, Aug. 1-Nov. 30, 1976: South Texas Region,' *Am. Birds* 31 (2):197-99.

Webster, M. A. (1975), *An Annotated Checklist of the Birds of Hong Kong,* 1st Edn, 1960, 3rd Edn (Rev.), 1975, Bird Watching Society, Hong Kong.

Weeks, M. F. (1949), 'Bird Population of Exotic Forests, 1940-48,' *N.Z. Bird Notes* 3:83-84.

Weeks, S. E. (1973), 'Behaviour of the Red-winged Tinamou,' *Zoologica N.Y.* 58 (1):13-40.

Weisbrod, A. R. and Stevens, W. F. (1974), 'The Skylark in Washington,' *Auk* 91 (4):832-35.

Weller, M. W. (1969), 'Potential Dangers of Exotic Waterfowl Introductions,' *Wildfowl* 20:55-58.

Wells, G. R. (1953), 'Wyoming Chukar Partridge Transplant Experiences,' *Proc. 32nd. a. Conf. west. Ass. St. Game Fish Commnrs.* :168-70.

Wells, W. H. (1939), 'The Starling in Eastern Kansas,' *Oologist* 56:57-58.

— (1940), 'Starlings Attack Cattle in Kansas and Other Pacific States,' *Oologist* 57:76-77.

Welty, J. C. (1962), *The Life of Birds*, Saunders, Philadelphia and London.

Wellwood, J. M. (1968), *Hawkes' Bay Acclimatisation Society Centenary 1868-1968*; Cliff Press, Hastings, New Zealand.

Wessell, C. W. (1939), 'The Chukar Partridge,' *Pa. Game News* 9 (12):10-11, 31.

West, R. R., Brunton, R. B. and Cunningham, D. J. (1969), 'Repelling Pheasants from Sprouting Corn with a Carbamate Insecticide,' *J. Wildl. Mgmt.* 33 (1):216-19.

Western States Exotic Game Bird Committee (1961), *Annual Report, 8th May 1960-April, 1961*, Western States Exotic Game Bird Committee.

Westerskov, K. (1949), 'The Recent Decline of the Hungarian Partridge,' *Ohio Conserv. Bull.* 13 (3):20-21.

— (1952), 'General Principals of Pheasant Management,' *N.Z. Outdoors* 16 (8-9):8-10, 10-11.

— (1952), 'Wildlife Research and Management in Scandinavia,' *N.Z. Sci. Rev.* 10 (9):136-44.

— (1953), 'Techniques of Pheasant Liberation,' *N.Z. Dep. Internal Affairs Wildl. Publ.* (25):1-28.

— (1953), 'Introduction into New Zealand of Australian Blue Wren in 1923,' *Notornis* 5:106-07.

— (1953), 'Taxonomic Status of the Redpoll in New Zealand,' *Notornis* (6):189-91.

— (1954), 'Spread of the Australian Magpie within the Rotorua Acclimatisation District,' *Notornis* 5 (8):243-48.

— (1955), 'Productivity of New Zealand Pheasant Populations: A Study of the Pheasant, *Phasianus colchicus*, under New Zealand Conditions: Its Reproductive Capacity, Taxonomy, Distribution and Management,' *Ph.D. Thesis, Vict. University Coll., University of N.Z.*

— (1956), 'Productivity of New Zealand Pheasant Populations,' *N.Z. Dep. Internal Affairs Wildl. Publ.* (40a):1-79.

— (1956), 'Pheasant Management and Shooting in New Zealand: 'An Evaluation of Restocking and Shooting, and some Suggestions for Management,' *N.Z. Dep. Internal Affairs Wildl. Publ.* (40c):1-57.

— (1956), 'History and Distribution of the Bobwhite Quail in New Zealand,' *N.Z. Outdoors* 21 (10):12-14, 35-36, and *N.Z. Dep. Internal Affairs Wildl. Publ.* (43):1-8.

— (1956), 'History and Distribution of Hungarian Partridges in Ohio, 1909-48,' *Ohio J. Sci.* 56 (2):65-70.

— (1957), 'Taxonomic Status of the Bobwhite Quail in New Zealand,' *Notornis* 7 (4):95-98.

— (1957), 'The Pheasant in Nelson,' *N.Z. Dep. Internal Affairs Wildl. Publ.* (50):3-12 (From 89th a. Rep. Nelson Acclim. Soc. :15-24).

— (1958), 'The Partridge as a Game Bird,' *N.Z. Dep. Internal Affairs Wildl. Publ.* (51):1-10.

— (1960), 'Danish Partridges in New Zealand: Establishing a New Breeding Stock, 1959,' *N.Z. Dep. Internal Affairs Wildl. Publ.* (70):1-11.

— (1962), 'The Pheasant in New Zealand,' *N.Z. Dep. Internal Affairs Wildl. Publ.* (40), 1955, Repr., 1962:1-35.

— (1963), 'Superior Survival of Black-necked over Ring-necked Pheasants in New Zealand,' *J. Wildl. Mgmt.* 27 (2):239-45.

— (1963), 'Evaluation of Pheasant Liberations in New Zealand Based on a Twelve-year Banding Study,' *N.Z. Dep. Internal Affairs Wildl. Publ.* (17):1-68.

— (1965), 'Winter Ecology of the Partridge (*Perdix perdix*) in the Canadian Prairie,' *Proc. N.Z. ecol. Soc.* 12:23-30.

— (1966), 'Winter Food and Feeding Habits of the Partridge, *Perdix perdix*, in the Canadian Prairie,' *Can. J. Zool.* 44 (2):303-22.

— (1974), 'Probably the First Breeding of the Cattle Egret (*Bubulcus ibis*) in New Zealand,' *Notornis* 21:239-46.

Wetmore, A. (1916), 'The Birds of Vieques Island, Porto Rico,' *Auk* 33:403-19.

— (1926), 'Birds of Argentina, Paraguay, Uruguay and Chile,' *Smithson. Inst. U.S. natn. Mus. Bull.* (133).

— (1927), 'Scientific Survey of Porto Rico and The Virgin Islands,' *N.Y. Acad. Sci.* 9 (3-4).

— (1957), 'An Extension in Range of the House Sparrow, *Passer domesticus*,' *Ostrich* 28:239-40.

— (1963), 'An Early Record of the Cattle Egret in Colombia,' *Auk* 80:547.

— (1964), *Song and Garden Birds of North America*, National Geographic Society, Washington.

Wetmore, A. and Lincoln, F. C. (1933), 'Additional Notes on the Birds of Haiti and the Dominican Republic,' *Smithson. Inst. U.S. natn. Mus. Bull.* 82 (2966):1-68.

Wetmore, A. and Swales, B. H. (1931), 'The Birds of Haiti and The Dominican Republic,' *Smithson. Inst., U.S. natn. Mus. Bull.* (155).

Wheatley, J. J. (1970), 'Status of the Carolina Duck (*Aix sponsa*) in Surrey,' *Surrey Bird Club, Q. Bull.* 55:15.

— (1973), 'Recent Carolina Duck Breeding Records in Surrey,' *Surrey Bird Rep.* 20:64-65.

Wheeler, J. R. (1960), 'R.A.O.U. Campout at Kangaroo Island, South Australia,' *Emu* 60:265-80.

— (1962), 'Observations on the Cattle Egret in Eastern Australia,' *Emu* 62:192-93.

Wheeler, R. J. (1947), 'Wild Turkey Restoration in North Carolina,' *Wildl. in N. Carolina* 11 (3):8, 18.

— (1948), 'The Wild Turkey in Alabama,' *Alabama Dep. Conserv.*, 1948:1-92.

Whistler, H. (1923), *Popular Handbook of Indian Birds*, 2nd Edn 1935, Gurney and Jackson, London.

White, S. A. (1923), 'Birds Observed on and Around Mt Remarkable During R.A.O.U. Visit,' *Emu* 22 (3):216-17.

White, S. A. and Chisholm, A. H. (1926), 'Noxious Birds,' in *Australian Encyclopaedia* 2:219-20.

White, S. R. (1946), 'Notes on the Bird Life of Australia's Heaviest Rainfall Region,' *Emu* 46 (2):122.

Whitehead, J. (1899), 'Field Notes on Birds Collected in the Philippine Islands in 1893-96,' Part 2, *Ibis* 5 (18):210-45; Part 4. *Ibis* 5 (20):485-501.

Whitney, C. (1971), 'Chukar Partridge,' in T. W. Mussehl and F. W. Howell (eds) *Game Management In Montana*, Montana Fish and Game Department, Helena, Montana, Chp. 21:175-79.

Whittell, H. M. (1950), 'The Starling in Western Australia,' *West. Aust. Nat.* 2 (6):137.

Whittell, H. M. and Serventy, D. L. (1948), 'A Systematic List of the Birds of Western Australia,' *Pub. Lib., Mus. and Art Gall., W.A., Spec. Publ.* (1).

Wildash, P. (1968), *Birds of South Vietnam*, Tuttle and Co, Vermont and Tokyo.

Wiley, R. H. (1973), 'Territory and Mating in the Sage Grouse,' *Anim. Behav. Monogr.* (6) Pt.2:87-169.

Willett, G. (1930), 'The Common Mynah Breeding in Los Angeles,' *Condor* 32:301-02.

Willey, C. H. (1968), 'The Ecology, Distribution and Abundance of the Mute Swan (*Cygnus olor*) in Rhode Island,' *Unpubl. M. Sc. Thesis, University of Rhode Island.*

— (1968), 'The Ecological Significance of the Mute Swan in Rhode Island,' *Trans. N. East. Sect. Wildl. Soc., 25th N.East. Fish Wildl. Conf., 14-17 Jan., 1968*:121-34.

Williams, F. (1974), Southern Great Plains Region, in 'Fall Migration Aug. 1-Nov. 30, 1973,' *Am. Birds* 28 (1):28-121.

— (1977), Southern Great Plains Region, in 'Fall Migration Aug. 1-Nov. 30, 1976,' *Am Birds* 31 (2):194-97.

Williams, G. R. (1950), 'Chukar in New Zealand,' *N.Z. Sci. Rev.* 20:2-6.

— (1951), 'Further Notes on the Chukar,' *Notornis* 4 (6):151-57.

— (1952), 'The Californian Quail in New Zealand,' *J. Wildl. Mgmt.* 16 (4):460-83.

— (1953), 'The Dispersal from New Zealand and Australia of Some Introduced European Passerines,' *Ibis* 95:676-92.

— (1955), 'Some Aspects of the Life History and Management of California Quail in New Zealand,' *N.Z. Dep. Internal Affairs Wildl. Publ.* (36):1-31.

— (1956), 'The Kakapo (*Strigops habroptilus* Gray): A Review and Re-Appraisal of a Near Extinct Species,' *Notornis* 7 (2):29-55.

— (1960), 'The Birds of the Pitcairn Islands, Central South Pacific Ocean,' *Ibis* 102 (1):58-70.

— (1962), 'Story of the New Zealand California Quail Populations,' *Ammohouse Bull.* 1 (12):6-8.

— (1963), 'A Four-Year Population Cycle in Californian Quail, *Lophortyx californicus* (Shaw), in the South Island of New Zealand,' *J. Anim. Ecol.* 33 (3):441-59.

— (1967), 'Breeding Biology of California Quail in New Zealand,' *Proc. N.Z. ecol. Soc.* 14:88-99.

— (1968), 'The Cape Barren Goose (*Cereopsis novaehollandiae* Latham) in New Zealand,' *Notornis* 15 (2):66-69.

— (1973), 'Birds,' in *The Natural History of New Zealand: An Ecological Survey*, Reed, Wellington.

— (1976), 'The New Zealand Wattlebirds,' in *Proc. 16th Int. Orn. Congr., Canberra, 1976*:161-70.

Williams, L. (1968), 'Med jägarhaläning (om kanadagås),' *Svensk Jakt* 106:100-01.

Williams, M. (1969), 'Brown Teal Released on Kapiti Island,' *Notornis* 16:61.

— (1971), 'Distribution and Abundance of the Paradise Shelduck (*Tadorna variegata* Gmelin) in New Zealand from the Pre-European times to the Present Day,' *Notornis* 18 (2):71-86.

Wilmore, S. B. (1974), *Swans of the World*, David and Charles, London.

Wilson, A. H. R. (1928), 'Bird Notes from Yarraberb,' *Emu* 28 (2):121-28.

Wilson, C. J. (1924), 'On the Occurrence of a Javanese Bird, *Pycnonotus a. aurigaster* (Viell.) in Singapore,' *Singapore Nat.* 4:86-87.

Wilson, E. O. (1965), 'The Challenge from Related Species,' in Gen. of Colon. Spp., H. G. Baker and G. L. Stebbins (eds), *Proc. 1 Intern. Un. Biol. Sci., Symp. on Gen. Biol.*,

Academic Press, New York and London.

Wilson, H. L. and Lewis, J. (1959), 'Establishment and Spread of the Wild Turkey in Southwestern Michigan,' *J. Wildl. Mgmt.* 23 (2) :210-15.

Wilson, J. E. (1949), 'A History of the Ring-necked Pheasant in Michigan,' *J. For.* 47 (3) :218.

— (1959), 'Status of the Hungarian Partridge in New York,' *Kingbird* 9 (2) :54-57.

Wilson, S. B. (1907), 'Notes on the Birds of Tahiti and the Society Group,' *Ibis* (9 Ser.) 3 :373-77.

Wing, L. (1943), 'Spread of the Starling and English Sparrow,' *Auk* 60 :74-87.

— (1943), 'The Starlings in Eastern Washington,' *Condor* 45 :159.

Wing, L. W. (1956), *Natural History of Birds*, Ronald Press, New York.

Wingate, D. B. (1973), *A Checklist and Guide to the Birds of Bermuda*, Island Press, Bermuda.

Wint, G. B. (1956), 'Stubble Quail, A New Exotic,' *Okla. Game Fish News.* 12 (8) :4.

— (1957), 'Preliminary Report on the Japanese Stubble Quail in Oklahoma,' *Proc. 37th a. Conf. west. Ass. St. Game Fish Commnrs.* :295-301.

Winterbottom, J. M. (1955), 'Distribution of European Starling,' *Ostrich* 26 (1) :46.

— (1955), 'European Starling at Storms River,' *Ostrich* 26 (2) :136.

— (1956), 'Red-eyed Dove in the Western Cape,' *Ostrich* 27 (4) :184.

— (1957), 'European Starling, *Sturnus vulgaris* L., at Calitzdorp and Oudtshoorn,' *Ostrich* 27 (2) :124.

— (1957), 'European Starling at Majesfontein,' *Ostrich* 28 (2) :124-25.

— (1959-61), 'Expansion of the Range of the House Sparrow,' *Cape Dep. Nat. Conserv. Rep.* (16) :92-94.

— (1962), 'The House Sparrow, *Passer domesticus*, at Touws River,' *Ostrich* 33 (2) :75.

— (1965), 'House Sparrow at Kalkrand,' *Ostrich* 36 (2) :91.

— (1966), 'Goldfinches in the Transvaal ?' *Bokmakierie* 8 (1) :19.

— (1966), 'Some Alien Birds in South Africa,' *Bokmakierie* 18 :61-62.

— (1971), 'A Preliminary Checklist of the Birds of South West Africa,' *S.W. Afr. Sci. Soc., Windhoek* :1-268.

Winterbottom, J. M. and Liversidge, R. (1954), 'The European Starling in the South West Cape,' *Ostrich* 25 (2) :89-96.

Witherby, H. F., Jourdain, F. C. R., Ticehurst, N. F. and Tucker, B. W. (1938-41), *The Handbook of British Birds*, 5 Vols. Witherby, London.

Witherby, H. F. and Ticehurst, N. F. (1908), 'Spread of the Little Owl in Britain,' *Brit. Birds* 1 :335-42.

Wodzicki, K. (1950), 'Introduced Mammals of New Zealand,' *N.Z. Dep. Sci. ind. Res. Bull.* (98).

— (1956), 'Breeding of the House Sparrow away from Man in New Zealand,' *Emu* :56 :146-47.

— (1965), 'The Status of Some Exotic Vertebrates in the Ecology of New Zealand,' in Gen. of Colon. Spp., H. G. Baker and A. L. Stebbins (eds), *Proc. 1st int. Un. Biol. Sci., Symp. Gen. Biol.*, Academic Press, New York and London.

Wolfe, L. R. (1961), 'Cattle Egret in Mexico,' *Auk* 78 :640-41.

Wollard, L. L., Sparrowe, R. D. and Chambers, G. D. (1977), 'Evaluation of a Korean Pheasant Introduction in Missouri,' *J. Wildl. Mgmt.* 41 (4) :616-23.

Wolstenholme, H. (1921), 'Letter Regarding the Red-eyed Bulbul,' *Emu* 21 (1) :74.

Wood, C. A. (1924), 'The Starling Family at Home and Abroad,' *Condor* 26 :123-36.

Wood, C. A. and Wetmore, A. (1926), 'A Collection of Birds from the Fiji Islands: Part III Field Observations,' *Ibis* (12 Ser.) 2 (1) :91-136.

Wood, R. W. (1975), *The Birds of the Falkland Islands*, Compton Press, Great Britain.

Woodall, P. F. (1975), 'On the Life History of the Bronze Mannikin,' *Ostrich* 46 (1) :55-86.

Wood-Gush, D. G. M. (1964), 'Domestication,' in A. L. Thomson, (Ed) *A New Dictionary of Birds,* Nelson, London and New York.

Wood-Jones, F. (1909), 'Fauna of the Cocos-Keeling Atoll, Aves,' *Proc. zool. Soc., London.* :137-42.

Wright, C. M. (1925), 'Goldfinches *(Carduelis carduelis)* at Armidale, N.S.W.,' *Emu* 25 (1) :43.

Wright, E. N. (1959), 'Bird Damage to Horticultural Crops,' *J.R. Hortic. Soc.* 34 (9) :426-34.

— (1962), 'Experiments with Anthroquinone and Thiram to Protect Germinating Maize Damage by Birds,' *Ann. Epiphyties.* 13 :27-31.

Wright, E. N. and Brough, T. (1964), 'Bird Damage to Fruit,' *Fruit Present and Future:* 168-80.

Wright, E. N. and Summers, D. D. B. (1960), 'The Biology and Economic Importance of the Bullfinch,' *Ann. appl. Biol.* 48 (2) :415-18.

Wright, P. L. (1943), 'Starling in Western Montana,' *Condor* 45 (3) :119.

Wydoski, R. S. (1964), 'Seasonal Changes in the Colour of Starling Bills,' *Auk* 81 :542-50.

Yaldwyn, J. C. (1952), 'Notes on the Present Status of Samoan Birds,' *Notornis* 5 :28-30.

Yamashina, Y. (1961), *Birds in Japan: A Field Guide*, Tokyo News Service, Japan.

Yanushevich, A. I. (1966), 'Acclimatization of Animals in the USSR,' in *Proc. Conf. Acclim. Anims. U.S.S.R., Frunze, 10-15 May, 1963*, I.P.S.T., Jerusalem.

Yealland, J. (1940), 'The Blue Lories,' *Avicult. Mag.* (5 Ser.) 5 :308-13.

— (1958), *Caged Birds in Colour*, Witherby, London.

— (1964), 'Cage Birds,' in A. L. Thomson (ed) *New Dictionary of Birds*, Nelson, London and New York.

Yeatter, R. E. (1934), 'The Hungarian Partridge in the Great Lakes Region,' *Univ. Mich. School For. Conserv. Bull.* (5) :1-92.

Yerbury, J. W. (1886), 'On the Birds of Aden and Neighbourhood,' *Ibis* (5 Ser.) 4 (13) :11.

Yocum, C. F. (1943), 'The Hungarian Partridge, *Perdix perdix* L., in the Palouse Region, Washington,' *Ecol. Monogr.* 13 :167-201.

— (1963), 'Starlings above the Arctic Circle in Alaska, 1962,' *Auk* 80 :544.

— (1970), 'The Giant Canada Goose in New Zealand,' *Auk* 87 (4) :812-14.

Young, C. E. (1932), 'A Note on the Common Mynah *(A. tristis)* in Province Wellesley,' *Bull. Raffles Mus.* 6 :154.

Young, H. (1946), 'Further Studies on the Cardinal,' *Passenger Pigeon* 8 (4) :104-09.

Young, J. G. (1972), 'Distribution, Status and Movements of Feral Grey Lag Geese in Southwest Scotland,' *Scott. Birds* 7 :170-82.

— (1972), 'Breeding Biology of Feral Greylag Geese in South-West Scotland,' *Wildfowl* 23 :83-87.

Youngworth, W. (1944), 'The Starling in South Dakota, North Dakota and Minnesota,' *Iowa Bird Life* 14 (4) :76.

Yurgenson, P. B. (1964), 'The Result of Artificial Settlement of Wild Birds as a Method of Restoration on Hunting Tracts,' in *Problemy Ornitologii*, L'vov: L'vovskii Univ. 92-95 (in Russian).

Zahl, P. A. (1967), 'New Scarlet Bird in Florida Skies,' *Nat. geogr. Mag.* 132 :874-82.

Zeillemaker, F. (1976), Letter to the Hawaiian Audubon Society, *Elepaio* 36 (9) :113-14.

Zeitz, R. (1920), 'Monthly Conversazione held National Museum 7th April,' *Emu* 19 (4) :334.

Zeuner, F. E. (1963), *A History of Domesticated Animals*, Hutchinson, London.

Zimmerman, D. A. (1967), '*Agapornis fischeri, Lybius guifsobalito* and *Striphrornis erythrothorax* in Kenya,' *Auk* 84 :594-95.

Zwickel, F. and Bendell, J. (1972), 'Black Grouse Habitat and Populations,' in *Proc. 15th int. Orn. Congr., 1970* :150-69.

LIST OF ALTERNATIVE GEOGRAPHIC NAMES

Name used in Text	Alternative name
Açores	Azores
Archipelago de Perlas	Pearl Islands
Archipel des Comores	Comoro Islands
Balearic Islands	Islas Baleares
Belize	British Honduras
Bonin Islands	Ogasawara Gunto
Borneo	Kalimantan
Canary Islands	Islas Canarias
Cape Verde Islands	Arquipelago de Cabo Verde
Caucasus Mountains	Bol'shoy Kavkaz
Cheju Do	Quelpart Island
Ching Hai	Kuku Nor
Corse	Corsica
Crete	Kriti
Faeroes	Faererne
Falkland Islands	Islas Malvinas
French Territory of Afars and Issas	French Somaliland
Guyana	British Guiana
Guyane	French Guiana
Isle de Gonave	Gonave Island
Isle of Pines	Isla de Pinos
Isle de Vieques	Vieques Island
Java	Djawa
Komandorskiye Islands	Commander Islands
Kurile Island	Kurilskiye Ostrova
Malagasy	Madagascar
Moluccas	Maluku
New Hebrides	Vanuata
North Borneo	Eastern Malaysia
Olu Malau Island	Three Sisters Island
Penghu	Pescadore Island
Pinang Island	Penang Island
Rhodesia	Zimbabwe
Rodrigues	Rodriguez
Ryukyu Islands	Ryukyu Retto
Sardegna	Sardinia
Seven Islands of Izu	Izu Shoto
Shetland Islands	Zetland
South West Africa	Namibia
Sulawesi	Celebes

INDEX TO COMMON NAMES

Page numbers in bold indicate main reference

Accentor **305**
accentors 305
Akahinga **310**
Amandava, Scarlet **413**
Amandavat **413**
Amazon, Green-cheeked 240,
    260
    Hispaniolan 239, **259**
    Orange-winged 241, **262**
    Red-lored 241, **261**
    White-fronted 240, **260**
    Yellow-crowned 240, 241,
        261
Astrild **410**
Avadavat, Green 402, **415**
    Red 12, 400, 402, **413**
Avocet, Red-necked **196**

babblers 306
Baya **390**
bellmagpies 342
Bengalese **432**
Bicheno **420**
Bird, Durra **394**
    Dyal **311**
    Indigo **477**
    Mistletoe **483**
    Paddy **433**
    Red 394, **476**
    Rice **433**
Bird of Paradise, Greater 345
birds of paradise 345
birds, perching 12
Bishop, Golden **394**
    Red 386, **387**
    Yellow-crowned 387, **394**
bitterns 68
Blackbird 306, 307, **315**
    Common **315**
    Grey-headed **317**
    Red-breasted 486, **489**
    Red-winged **487**
    White-browed **489**
    Yellow-hooded 486, **488**
    Yellow-shouldered **493**
blackbirds, New World 485
Blackcap 307, **322**
Blackheart **421**
Bleeding-heart, Luzon **235**
Bluebird, Western 307, **313**
Blue-bird **363**
Blue Flycatcher, Japanese **324**
Blue Magpie, Red-billed 346,
    347
Blue-pie **346**
    Occipital **346**
Blue Wren, Superb 307, **323**
Boatbill 68
Bobwhite, Common **120**
    Crested **123**
Brambling **441**
Brant, Black **33**
Brolga 187, **195**

Bronzewing, Common 206,
    207, **230**
    Forest **230**
Brush-Turkey 85, **86**
Budgerygah 238, 239, 240, **278**
Bulbul, Black 297, **301**
    Golden-vented **300**
    Mauritius **301**
    Olivaceous **301**
    Red-eared **296**
    Red-vented 12, 296, 297,
        299
    Red-whiskered 12, **296**, 297
    Reunion **301**
    Sooty-headed 297, **300**
    White-eared **300**
bulbuls 11, 296
Bullfinch 381, 439, **459**
    Lesser Antilean 463, **472**
    Puerto Rican 463, **472**
Bunting, Butterfly **463**
    Cirl 462, **465**
    Indigo 463, **477**
    Leclanchers **478**
    Mexican 463
    Non-pareil **478**
    Nonpariel **478**
    Orange-breasted 463, **478**
    Ortolan 463, **464**
    Painted 463, **478**
    Rainbow **478**
    Reed 463, **466**
    Yellow **463**
buntings 462
Bush-Quail, Jungle 112, **154**
    Red **154**
    Rock **154**
Bush Warbler **321**
    Chinese **321**
    Japanese **321**
Button-quail, Madagascar 187,
    194
    Painted 187, **193**
button-quail 187, 193
Buzzard **77**
    Common 74, **77**
    Steppe **77**

Canary 437, 438, **441**
    Black-throated **444**
    Cape 437, 438, **443**
    Laysan **461**
    Peach **444**
    Swainson's **446**
    Wild 441, **468**
    Yellow 438, **446**
    Yellow-bellied **445**
    Yellow-crowned **443**
    Yellow-fronted 19, 437, 438,
        445
Canvasback **33**
Capercaillie 91, 92, **93**, 96
Caracara, Chimango 74, 75,
    80

Cardinal **476**
    Black-crested **473**
    Black-eared **475**
    Black-faced **475**
    Brazilian **473**
    Common 462, 463, **476**
    Dominican **474**
    Green 463, **473**
    Madagascar **391**
    Pope **474**
    Red **476**
    Red-capped 463, **475**
    Red-cowled **474**
    Red-crested 462, 463, **473**
    Red-headed 463, **474**
    Virginian **476**
    Yellow **473**
Yellow-billed 462, **475**
cardinals 462
Carrion-hawk, Chimango **80**
cassowaries 25
Cassowary, Australian **27**
    Bennett's 25
    Double-wattled **27**
Chachalaca, Chestnut-winged
    81, **84**
    Common **83**
    Eastern **83**
    Grey-headed **84**
    Plain 80, 81, **83**
    Rufous **84**
    Rufous-tailed 80, 81, **84**
    Rufous-vented **84**
chachalacas 80
Chaffinch 437, **439**
Chicken, Greater Prairie 91,
    92, **104**
    Lesser Prairie 92, **105**
    Prairie **104**
    Sage **103**
Chimango **80**
Chukar **126**
    Arabian 110, **134**
    Indian **129**
    Persian **129**
    Turkish 128, 129, 130
Chukor **126**
Cliff Swallows **381**
Cockatiel 241, **250**
Cockatoo, Gang Gang 240, **245**
    Goffin's 240, **249**
    Leadbeater's **248**
    Lesser Sulphur-crested 239,
        247
    Major Mitchell's **248**
    Moluccan **247**
    Pink 240, **248**
    Roseate **249**
    Rose-breasted **249**
    Salmon-crested 239, 240,
        247
    Sulphur-crested **245**
Cockatoo-Parrot **250**
cockatoos 12, 238

Colon, Crested **123**
    Scaly **114**
    Virginian **120**
Combassou, Black-winged **397**
    Senegal **397**
    Village 387, **397**
Companion, Native **195**
condors 74
Conure, Brown-throated 239,
    241, **252**
    Nanday **253**
    Orange-fronted 240, **252**
    White-eared 240, **254**
Coot **187**
    Common **187**
coots 187
Cordon-bleu 401, 402, 405,
    406
    Blue-capped 401, **407**
    Red-cheeked 400, 402, **406**
Corella, Long-billed 240, **250**
Cormorant, Black **31**
    Common **31**
    Great **31**
    Guanay **32**
    Peruvian **32**
    White-breasted **31**
cormorants 30
Cornrake 187, **189**
Cowbird, Common **492**
    Glossy **492**
    Shiny 485, 486, **492**
Crane, Demoiselle 187, **195**
cranes 187
Crossbill, Parrot 439, **458**
Crow, American **354**
    Carrion **75**
    Ceylon **350**
    Colombo **350**
    Common 347, **354**
    House 13, 347, **350**
    Indian **350**
    Jungle **354**
    King **339**
    Large-billed **354**
    New Caledonian 347, **352**
    Pied 347, **355**
crows 346
Crow Shrike, Australian **344**
Curassow, Black 80, **81**
    Crested **80**
    Great 80, 81, **82**
    White-crested **80**
curassows 80
Curlew, Eastern **196**
Currawong, Grey 343, **344**

Dipper, Black-bellied **302**
    Common **302**
dippers 302
Diuca-finch, Common 462, **468**
Dotterel, Black-fronted **196**
Dove, African Collared **216**
    Barbary **216**

Barred 223
Barred Ground 223
Bar-shouldered 207, 226
Blue Ground 233
Blue-headed Ground 237
Blue-headed Quail 207, 237
Cape 228
Caribbean 234
Chinese Spotted 220
Collared 204, 216
Common Ground 206, 228
Diamond 207, 226
Emerald 206, 207, 229
Green-winged 229
Ground 228
Half-collared 219
Harlequin 228
Inca 206, 227
Indian 204
Indian Turtle 220
Jamaican 234
Javanese Collared 219
Java 220
Java Ring 219
Lace-necked 220
Laughing 222
Little Brown 222
Masked 228
Mesquite 213
Mourning 206, 212
Namaqua 207, 228
Palm 222
Passerine 228
Peaceful 204, 206, 207, 223
Philippine Collared 219
Red-collared 215
Red-eyed 205, 219
Ring 216
Rock 204, 208
Ruddy Ground 234
Ruddy Quail 207
Scaly-breasted Ground 228
Spotted 220
Stock 204, 215
Town 222
Turtle 212
White-bellied 206, 234
White-fronted 233
White-tipped 207, 233
White-winged 205, 206, 213
Zebra 223
doves 12, 17, 200, 204
Drongo, Black 339
drongos 339
Duck, American black 33
American Wood 34, 35, 61
Australian Wood 35
Black-bellied Whistling 49
Carolina 61
'East India' 32
'English wild' 32
Grey 57
Hawaiian 56
'Indian' 33
Korean 33
Mandarin 34, 35, 62
Meller's 34, 35, 57
Muscovy 33, 35, 53
North American Wood 61
Paradise 51
Red-billed Whistling 49
Ruddy 34, 66
Tufted 35, 65
White-faced Whistling 35, 50
Wood 49
ducks 12, 32
Dunnock 305

Eagle, Bald 74
Golden 74
Grey Sea 76
White-tailed 74, 76

eagles 74
Egret, Cattle 11, 68, 69
Emu 25, 26
Euphonia, Blue-hooded 463, 483

Falcon, Peregrine 74, 75, 79
falcons 75
Finch, Banded 402, 403, 420
Bicheno 420
Blue-faced 422
Bramble 438, 441
Butterfly 478
Cherry 425
Chestnut-breasted 401, 403, 432
Chestnut-eared 419
Common Diuca 468
Cuban 470
Diuca 468
Double-bar 420
Grassland Yellow- 469
Green Singing 445
Grey Singing 444
Gouldian 403, 424
Heck's 421
House 437, 438, 457
Javan 433
Laysan 461
Long-tailed 403, 421
Long-tailed Grass 421
Melba 403
Nihoa 461
Olive 471
Plum-headed 403, 425
Purple 381
Red-faced Parrot- 423
Red-tailed 418
Red-throated 423
Rufous-tailed 418
Saffron 381, 462, 468
Scaly-feathered 385
Spice 17, 18, 400, 401, 403, 428
Spotted-sided 417
Star 403, 418
Strawberry 413
Tri-coloured Parrot 422
Zebra 400, 403, 419
finches 400
cardueline 437
Firefinch, African 404
Lavender 408
Red-billed 402, 404

Firetail, Diamond 403, 417
Red-browed 416
Flamingo 67
Common 67
Greater 67
flamingos 67
Flycatcher, Blue 307, 324
Derby 289
Japanese Blue 324
Kiskadee 289
Narcissus 307, 324
Old World 306
Fody, Madagascar 391
Red 391
Seychelles 393
Fowl, Common 162
Domestic 162
Green Jungle 110, 165
Grey Jungle 112, 166
Guinea 87
Jungle 16, 162
Red Jungle 108, 109, 110, 112, 162
Francolin, Bare-necked 143
Bare-throated 110, 143
Black 108, 109, 111, 135
Chinese 108, 110, 136
Clapperton's 111, 141

Close-barred 139
Erkel's 108, 110, 141
Gray 138
Grey 19, 108, 110, 111, 138
Heuglin's 111, 140
Indian Black 135
Red-billed 109, 139
Red-necked 142
Red-throated 108, 142
Sharpes 141
Yellow-throated 143
francolins 106

Gadwall 34, 60
Galah 238, 239, 240, 249
Gallinule, Common 187, 191
Hawaiian 192
Purple 187, 192
geese 12, 32, 33
China 33
'Toulouse' 33
Goldfinch 438, 439, 449, 451
American 439, 449
Dark-backed 450
European 451
Green-backed 450
Lesser 438, 450
Goose, Bean 35, 43
Blue 41
Canada 33, 34, 35, 44
Cape Barren 34, 35, 40
Egyptian 34, 35, 52
Falkland Upland 48
Greater Magellan 48
Greater Snow 41
Greylag 34, 35, 42
Hawaiian 20, 34, 47
Lesser Magellan 48
Lesser Snow 41
Magellan 35, 48
Maned 49
Pink-footed 43
Sandwich Island 47
Spur-winged 34, 39
Snow 34, 41
Swan 33
Whitefronted 33
Grackle 371
Carib 486. 491
Indian 371
Lesser Antillean 491
Grass Bird, Yellow-faced 471
grassfinches 400
grassfinch, yellow 462, 469
Grassquit, Cuban 13, 462, 463, 470
Melodious 470
Yellow-faced 13, 462, 463, 471
Grassquits 462
Greenfinch 438, 447
European 447
grosbeaks 462
Ground Dove 228
Blue 233
Blue-headed 237
Common 206, 228
Ruddy 234
Scaly-breasted 228
Grouse, Black 91, 92, 95
Blue 91, 92, 99
Brush 103
Dusky 99
Franklin's 99
Hazel 91, 92, 100
Pinnated 104
Pin-tailed 103
Red 96
Ruffed 91, 92, 101
Sage 91, 92, 103
Sharp-tailed 91, 92, 103
Snow 98

Sooty 99
Spruce 91, 99
White-breasted 103
Willow 91, 92, 96
Guan, Crested 81, 82
Purple 83
Purplish 82
Guanay 30, 31, 32
guans 80
Guineafowl 87
Helmeted 87
Tufted 87
Guinea Fowl 87
Gull, Silver 196, 198
Western 196, 200

Hangnest, Common 487
Harrier, Marsh 74, 75, 77
Swamp 77
Hawfinch 439, 460
Hawk, Swamp 77
hawks 74
Hedgesparrow 305
Hen, Hazel 100
Sage 103
Heron, Black-crowned Night- 68, 69, 72
Buff-backed 68
Night 72
White-faced 68
herons 68
Hirundinidae 296
Hirundo nigrans 296
Hoki 158
honeyeaters 338
Honeycreeper, Blue 485
Red-legged 463, 485
honeycreepers, Hawaiian 461
Honker 44
Hornero 381
hummingbirds 286
Hwa-Mei 329

ibises 68
Ibis, Scarlet 18, 68, 69, 73
White 18, 68, 74
Impeyan 157
Indigo-bird, Green 397

Jackass 287
Jackdaw 347, 349
Jay, Blue 346
jays 346
Junglefowl, Sonnerat's 166
Jungle Fowl, see Fowl 162

Kakapo 238, 240
Kakariki, Yellow-fronted 278
Kaleej 160
Kalij, Nepal 160
Swinhoes 161
White-crested 160
Keet, Green 244
kingfishers 287, 288
Kiskadee, Great 289
kites 74
Kiwi, Brown 28
Little Spotted 28, 29
kiwis 28
Komadori 309
Kookaburra 287
Laughing 287

Landrail 189
Lapwing 196, 197
lapwings, 196
Lark, Australian Magpie 341
Mongolian 291, 292
Wood 291, 292
larks 291
Laughingthrush, Black-throated 307, 328

Greater-necklaced 307, **327**
Grey-sided 308
Lesser Necklaced 328
Melodious 307, 308, **329**
White-browed 307, **330**
White-cheeked **330**
White-crested 307, **326**
White-throated 307, **326**
laughingthrushes 308
Laughing Thrush, Black-
gorgeted **327**
Chestnut-backed 328
Leiothrix, Red-billed 307, 308,
331
Linnet 439, **456**, 457
Green 447
Lorikeet, Rainbow 239, **242**
Red-collared 242
Musk 239, **244**
Musky 244
Lory, Blue-streaked 239, **242**
Kuhl's 239, **243**
Tahitian 239, 240, **244**
Lovebird, Fischer's 239, **273**
Grey-headed 271
Madagascar 239, 240, 241,
271
Masked 239, 241, **274**
Nyasa 240, 241, **275**
Nyassa 275
Peach-faced 241, **272**
Rosy-faced 272
Yellow-collared **274**
Lyrebird, Superb **290**
lyrebirds 290

Macaw, Blue and Yellow 238
Scarlet 241, **251**
Magpie 348
American **348**
Australian 342, **343**
Bell 344
Black-backed 343
Black-billed 348
Blue 346
Common 347, **348**
European 348
Red-billed Blue 346, **347**
Western 343
White-backed **343**
Magpie Lark, Australian 340
Magpie Robin, Seychelles 313
magpies 346
Mallard 18, 33, 34, 35, 54
Common 54
Green-headed 54
Malleefowl 85
Mandarin 62
Mannikin, Black-headed 401,
402, 403, **430**
Bronze 400, 403, **426**
Bronze-winged 426
Javan 402, **430**
Magpie 402, 403, **427**
Nutmeg 428
Sharp-tailed 403, **432**
Striated **432**
White-bellied **430**
White-throated **425**
mannikins 400
Marshbird, Red-breasted 489
Yellow-headed 488
Masked Weaver, Southern **386**
Vitelline **386**
martins 296
Meadowlark, Greater Red-
breasted **490**
Long-tailed 490
Red-breasted 486, **490**
Western 486, **490**
Miner, Bell 338
Black-headed **338**

Noisy **338**
Mockingbird, Common 303
Northern 303
Southern 304
Tropical 303, **304**
mockingbirds 303, 304
Monal, Himalayan 157
Moorhen 191
Gough 187, **192**
Purple 192
Tristan da Cunha 192
moundbuilders 84
Mudlark 341
Munia, Black-headed 430
Chestnut 430
Chestnut-breasted 430
Green 415
Javan 430
Red 413
Scaly-breasted 428
Sharp-tailed **432**
Spotted 428
Tri-coloured 430
White-bellied 430
White-rumped 432
White-throated 425
Musk-Parrot, Red-breasted 271
Myna, Andaman 356
Bank 369
Buffalo 368
Chinese crested 370
Common 11, 17, 356, 357,
358, **364**, 372
Crested 358, **370**
Hill 358, **371**
House 364
Indian 364
Jungle 358, 359, **368**
White-headed **356**, 358
Mynah 364
mynas 11, 12, 356

Nenday 253
Nene 47
Nitalva, Blue 324
Night-heron, Black-crowned
68, 69, 72
Nankeen 69, 72
Nightingale 307, **310**
Pekin 331
Virginian 315
Nonpareil, Pin-tailed 422

Oriole, Black-crowned 493
Moriche 486
Spot-breasted 487
Spotted-breasted 486, **487**
Ortolan 464
Ostrich 25
Owl, Barn **280**
Boobook 283
Brown 284
Eagle 280, **283**
Little 280, **284**
Masked 280, **282**
Spotted 280, **283**
Tawny 280, **285**
Tawny Wood 285
owls 280
Barn 280

Paoui 80
Parakeet, African Ring-necked
266
Alexandrine 240, **266**
Black-hooded 240, **253**
Blossom-headed 270
Brown-throated 252
Canary-winged 12, 239, **257**
Great-billed 266
Grey-headed 254
Indian Ring-necked 266

Large 266
Maroon-faced 254
Monk 238, 239, **254**
Moustached 239, 240, 241,
269
Orange-chinned 240, 241,
258
Orange-fronted 252
Pennant's 275
Plum-headed 241, **270**
Princess of Wales' 269
Quaker 254
Queen Alexandra's 269
Rose-headed 270
Rose-ringed 238, 239, 240,
241, **266**
Tovi 258
White-winged 257
Yellow-fronted 239, **278**
Parrot, Bee Bee 257
Blue-naped 241, **265**
Brown 239, **263**
Crimson 275
Eclectus 240, 241, **264**
Great-billed 240, **265**
Meyer's 263
Orange-winged 262
Red-backed 240, **277**
Red-breasted Musk- 271
Red-crowned 260
Red-lored 261
Red-rumped 277
Red Shining 239, 241, **271**
Vasa 241, **263**
White-fronted 260
Yellow-cheeked 261
Yellow-headed 261
Yellow-naped 261
parrots 12, 17, 238, 363
Parrotlet, Blue-winged 256
Green-rumped 239, 240,
241, **256**
Guiana 256
Passerine 256
Parrotfinch, Blue-faced 403,
422
Peale's 424
Pin-tailed 403, **422**
Red-headed 403, **424**
Red-throated 403, **423**
Royal 424
Parrot-finch, Peales 424
Red-faced 423
Royal 424
Pastor, Rose-coloured 356
Rosy 356
Partridge, Bamboo 108, 112,
156
Barbary 107, 109, 110, 111
Bearded 108, 111, **147**
Black 99, **135**
Brown 138
Ceylon 106
Chinese 106, **147**, 156
Chinese Bamboo 156
Chukar 106, 107, 109, 110,
111, **126**
Chukor 126
Common 144
Crested Green Wood 155
Daurian 147
European 106, 108, 110,
111, **144**
Formosan Hill 112, 155
French 131
Gray 144
Grey 138, **144**
Hey's Sand 125
Hey's Seesee 125
Himalayan Snow 126
Hungarian 144
Indian Hill 126

Jungle 106
Madagascar 108, 111, **148**
Mexican 106
Mongolian 147
Mountain 113
Red-crested Wood 112, **155**
Red-legged 107, 109, 110,
111, **131**
Rock 126
Sand 125
Seesee 110, **125**
Snow 110, **126**
Spruce 99
partridges 11, 106
Paui 80
Peafowl 181
Blue 181
Common 109, 113, **181**
Indian 181
Peewit 197
Peewee 341
Pelican, Brown 30, 31
pelicans 30
Penelope, Purple 82
Penguin, 'golden' 29
King 29, **30**
'spectacled' 29
penguins 29
phalaropes 196
Pheasant, Amherst 109, 113,
179
Brown-eared 112, **158**
Cheer 20, 108, 112, **166**
Chinese Ring-necked 169,
172
Chir 166
Common 167
Copper 113, **177**
Crested Fireback 109, 112,
162
Elliot's 106
English 168
Golden 11, 109, 113, **178**
Green 167, 169, 171, 172,
174
Impejan 112, **157**
Impeyan 157
Iranian black-necked 171
Japanese 171
Kalij 108, 112, **160**
Lady Amherst's **179**
Monal 157
Mongolian **167**, 169, 171,
172, 174
mutant 172
Nepal 160
Prince of Wales 169
Reeve 109, 110, 113, **175**
Reeves' 175
Ring-necked 16, 19, 106,
108, 110, 112, **167**
Silver 11, 109, 112, **158**
Swinhoe 20, 109, 110, **161**
Swinhoe's **161**
pheasants 11, 12, 106
Pigeon, Bleeding-Heart 207,
235
Christmas Island Imperial
204
Common 208
Crested 206, 207, **231**
Domestic 12, 205, 206, **208**
feral 204, 205, 206, 208
Flock 204
Green-winged **229**
Imperial 204
Indian 204
Island Imperial 204, **207**
Nicobar 207, **237**
Partridge 207, **232**
Pink-headed Imperial 204
Solomon Island 204

Spinifex 207, 232
Topknot 231
White-tailed 237
Wonga 207, 236
Wood 211
pigeons 12, 17, 200, 204, 208
Pintail 58
Common 34, 58
Northern 58
piping-crows 342
Plover, Black-bellied 197
Golden 196, 198
Green 197
Grey 196, 197
Masked 196
plovers 196
Pochard 35, 64
Common 64
Red-breasted 33
Red-headed 64
White-backed 64
Ptarmigan 92, 98
Rock 98
Willow 96
Pukeko 39, 192
Pytilia, Green-winged 402, 403

Quail, black-breasted 106
Black-necked 194
Blue 114
Blue-breasted 109, 110, 112, 153
Bobwhite 18, 107, 109, 111, 120, 170
Bob-white 120
Brown 108, 109, 151, 152
California 16, 107, 110, 115
'Californian' 115
Chinese 153
Common 108, 109, 111, 149
Coturnix 149
Crested 107, 123
Desert 119
Egyptian 150
European 149
Gambel's 107, 109, 110, 119
Grey 151
Harlequin 111, 124
Indian 106
Japanese 149
Jungle Bush 112
King 153
Madagascar 150
Mearn's 124
Mexican 114
Migratory 149
Montezuma 124
Mountain 107, 109, 110, 113,
Painted 113, 124, 153, 193
Pectoral 151
Pigmy 153
Scaled 107, 110, 114
Stubble 112 151
Swamp 110, 151, 152
Valley 115
Virginia 120
quails 11, 12, 106
Quail Dove, Blue-headed 207, 234
Ruddy 207
Rufous 234
Quarrion 250

Rail, Land 187
Laysan 187, 190
Laysan Island 190
rails 187
Redbreast 308
Robin 308
Redhead 34, 65
Redpoll 437, 454
Common 438, 454

Redwing 317
Rhea, Common 24
Darwin's 24
Greater 23, 24
Lesser 23, 24
rheas 23
Ring Dove, Java 219
Ringneck, Chinese 167
Robin, American 307, 319
Chatham Island 308
European 307, 308
Hill 331
Japanese 307, 309
Korean 310
magpie 307, 311, 312
Pekin 331
Ryūkyū 310
Seychelles Magpie 307, 313
Temminck's 307, 310
Rook 347, 352
Rosella, Blue 277
Crimson 239, 241, 275
Eastern 239, 276
Mealy 277
Pale-headed 241, 277
White-cheeked 276
Roulroul 155

Saddleback 20, 340
Sakabula 396
Sandgrouse, Black-bellied 202
Chestnut-bellied 203
Common 200, 203
Imperial 200, 202
Indian 203
Large Pintailed 201
Pallas's 200, 201
Pintailed 200, 201
Small Pintailed 203
White-bellied 201
sandgrouse 200
sandpipers 196
Seedeater, White-collared 463, 470
White-rumped 438, 444
Yellow 446
Yellow-rumped 438, 444
seed-eater, Yellow 446
Serin, white-rumped 444
Shama, Common 312
White-rumped 307, 312
Shearwater, Wedge-tailed 368
Shelduck, Paradise 34, 51
Shrike, Australian Crow 344
Silvereye 335
Grey-backed 335
Western 335
silvereyes 335
Silverbill, Common 402, 425
Warbling 425
Siskin 439, 448
European 448
Pine 448
Sky-Lark 293
Skylark 19, 291, 293
Common 293
English 293
Snipe 196
snipe, New Zealand 196
Chatham Island 196
Snowcock, Himalayan 126
Soldier-bird 338
song thrush, 'gray' 317
Sparrow, American Song 467
English 374
European 374
Grass 469
House 11, 13, 17, 18, 19, 372, 373, 374
Java 400, 401, 402, 403, 433
Pegu House 372
Rock 383

Rufous-backed 383
Rufous-collared 381, 463, 467
Song 467
Spanish 372, 374, 382
Tree 372, 374, 383
sparrows 11, 18, 372
New World 462
Spoonbill, Royal 68
spoonbills 68
Spurfowl 142
Squeaker 344
Starling 17, 19, 357, 358, 359
Black-collared 358, 363
Common 359
European 359
Military 490
Rothschild's 356
Rose-coloured 356, 358
starlings 11, 18, 356
stilts 196
Sugar-bird, Yellow-winged 485
sunbirds 335
Swallow, Cliff 381
Welcome 296
swallows 296
Swamphen 192
Swan, Black 34, 38
Mute 33, 34, 36
Trumpeter 33, 34
White 36
swans 32
Swiftlet, Edible-nest 286
swifts 286

Tanager, Black 479
Black-eared 484
Blue 482
Blue-grey 462, 463, 482
Crimson-backed 482
Golden 463, 484
Golden Masked 484
Maroon 481
Masked 463, 484
Mrs Wilson's 484
Olive 463, 480
Scarlet 463, 479, 480, 481
Scarlet-rumped 463
Silver-beaked 463, 481
Silver-blue 482
Summer 463, 479
White-lined 463, 479
White-shouldered 479
tanagers 462
Teal, Blue-winged 35, 57
Brown 33
teal 33
Telespiza 461
Tern, Fairy 72, 280, 282
Thrasher, Blue 320
Thrush, Argentine 492
Brown 326
Chinese 12, 329
Collared 326
Dhyal 311
'gray' song 317
Hermit 307, 314
Island 306, 307, 317
Peko 328
Red-legged 307, 320
Shama 312
Song 306, 307, 318
thrushes 306
Tinamou, Argentine 22
blue 21
brushland 21
canyon 21
Chilean 21
Chilean brushland 21
crested 21
Elegant 23
Elegant crested 23

Great 21
Martineta 23
pale-spotted 21
Red-winged 21, 22
Rufous 21, 22
Rufous-winged 22
spotted 21
tinamous 21
Tit, Blue 332, 334
Great 332
Japanese 333
Varied 332, 333
titmice 332
Toq Toq 393
Tragopan 113 157
Cabot's 157
Satyra 157
Temminck's 157
Tree-Duck, Black-bellied 34, 35, 49
White-faced 50
Troupial 487
Common 486, 487
troupials 485
Turkey 182
Brush- 86
Eastern 185
Merriam's 185
Ocellated 182
Rio Grande 185, 186
Scrub 86
Wild 182
turnstones 196
Turtle Dove, 214
Indian 220
Turtledove, Collared 205, 206, 207, 216
Common 206, 214
European 214
Javan 206, 207, 219
Madagascar 205, 206, 207, 215
Red 206, 207, 215
Red-collared 215
Senegal 17, 204, 206, 222
Spotted 17, 204, 205, 220
Twite 439, 455

Vulture, Bearded 74
Turkey 74, 75
vultures, American 74
Old World 74

Wagtail, Willie 307, 325
Warbler, Blackcap 322
Blackpoll 72
Bush 307, 321
Chinese Bush 321
Japanese Bush 321
Madagascar Grass 308
Myrtle 72
White-throated 321
warblers 306
Waxbill, 410
Black-cheeked 402, 413
Black-rumped 400, 402, 412
Blue 405
Blue-breasted 405
Common 12, 400, 401, 402, 410
Cordon-bleu 405
Grenadier 407
Grey 408, 412
Lavender 400, 408
Melba 403
Orange-cheeked 400, 402, 409
Orange-breasted 403, 416
Red 413
Red-browed 400, 402, 403, 416

Red-eared 411, 412
St Helena 410
Swee 409
Sydney 416
Violet-eared 402, 407
Yellow-bellied 402, 409
Zebra 416

waxbills 400

Weaver, Baya 387, 390
   Black-headed 387, 388, 389
   Cape 386, 387
   Golden 387, 390
   Grenadier 394
   Madagascar 386, 387, 391

Masked 386, 387
Napolean 394
Scaly-fronted 374, 385
Seychelles 387, 393
Southern Masked 386
Spotted-backed 12, 18, 386, 387, 388
Village 388
Vitelline Masked 386
V-marked 388
Yellow 394

Weaver-bird, Common 390

weavers 386

Weero 250

Weka 187, 188
White-eye 335
   Christmas Island 335, 337
   Japanese 335, 336
White-eyes 335
Whitebelly 234
Whitethroat 307, 321
   Common 321

Whydah, Giant 396
   Paradise 387, 398

   Pin-tailed 386, 387, 399
   Shaft-tailed 387, 398

Widow-bird, Long-tailed 387, 396

Paradise 398
   Shaft-tailed 398
   White-winged 386, 387, 396
Wigeon 59
   European 35, 59
woodcocks 196
Woodhen, New Zealand 188
Woodpecker, Red-headed 363
Woodpigeon 207, 211, 215
Wren, Stead's Bush 291
   Superb Blue 307, 323
wrens, New Zealand 291

Yamagara 333
Yellowhammer 462, 463
Yellow-finch, Grassland 469

INDEX TO SCIENTIFIC NAMES

Page numbers in bold indicate main reference

Acanthis cannabina 456
　flammea 454
　flavirostris 455
Accipitridae 74, 76
Acridotheres cristatellus 370
　fuscus 368
　ginginianus 369
　tristis 11, 17, 302, 364
acuta, Anas 58
acuticauda, Poephila 421
adscitus, Platycercus 277
adspersus, Francolinus 139
Aegintha temporalis 416, 433
aegyptiacus, Alopochen 52
aeruginosus, Circus 77
afer, Pternistes 142
afra, Euplectes 394
Agapornis cana 271
　fischeri 273
　lilianae 275
　personata 274
　roseicollis 272
Agelaius icterocephalus 488
　xanthomus 493
Agriocharis ocellata 182
Aidemosyne modesta 425
Aix galericulata 62
　sponsa 61
akahige, Erithacus 309
Alauda arvensis 19, 293
Alaudidae 291
alba, Tyto 280
　Gygis 78
albicilla, Haliaeetus 76
albifrons, Amazona 260
　Anser 32
　Petrochelidon 381
albogularis, Garrulax 326
albonotatus, Euplectes 396
albus, Corvus 355
　Eudocimus 68
Alcedinidae 287, 288
alchata, Pterocles 201
alector, Crax 80
Alectoris barbara 133
　graeca 126
　melanocephalus 134
　rufa 133
Alectura lathami 86
alexandri, Psittacula 269
Alopochen aegyptiacus 52
aluco, Strix 285
amandava, Amandava 12, 413
Amandava amandava 12, 413
　formosa 415
　subflava 416
Amazona albifrons 260
　amazonica 262
　autumnalis 261
　ochrocephala 261
　ventralis 259
　viridigenalis 260
amazonica, Amazona 262
americana, Aythya 65
　Rhea 24

amherstiae, Chrysolophus 179
Ammoperdix griseogularis 125
　heyi 125
Anas acuta 58
　aucklandica 33
　crecca 33
　discors 57
　melleri 57
　obscura 33
　penelope 59
　platyrhynchos 18, 54
Anas, strepera 60
　superciliosa 18, 57
　vallisneria 33
Anatidae 32
angolensis, Uraeginthus 405
Anser albifrons 32
　anser 42
　caerulescens 41
　cygnoides 33
　fabalis 43
anser, Anser 42
Anseriformes 12, 32
Anthropoides virgo 195
apoda, Paradisaea 345
Apodidae 286
Apodiformes 286
apricaria, Pluvialis 198
Aptenodytes patagonica 30
Apterygidae 28
Apteryx australis 28
　oweni 29
Aquila chrysaetos 74
Ara araruana 238
　macao 251
Aratinga canicularis 252
　pertinax 252
arborea, Lullula 292
Arborophila crudigularis 155
Arcenthornis 317, 319
Ardeola ibis 11, 68
　novaehollandiae 68
Ardeidae 68
Ardeiformes 68
argoondah, Perdicula 154
arthus, Tangara 484
arvensis, Alauda 19, 293
asiatica, Perdicula 154
　Zenaida 213, 219
astrild, Estrilda 12, 410
Athene noctua 284
atra, Fulica 191
atratus, Cygnus 38
atricapilla, Sylvia 322
atrogularis, Serinus 444
aucklandica, Anas 33
　Coenocorypha 196
aura, Cathartes 75
araruana, Ara 238
auriceps, Cyanoramphus 278
aurigaster, Pycnonotus 300
australis, Apteryx 28
　Coturnix 152
　Gallirallus 188

autumnalis, Amazona 261
　Dendrocygna 49
Aythya americana 65
　ferina 64
　fuligula 65

Bambusicola thoracica 156
barbara, Alectoris 133
barbata, Perdix 147
barbatus, Gypaetus 74
bengalus, Uraeginthus 406
bennetti, Casuarius 25
bichenovii, Poephila 420
bicinctus, Pterocles 200
bitorquata, Streptopelia 219
bonariensis, Molothrus 492
Bonasa umbellus 101
bonasia, Tetrastes 100
borbonicus, Hypsipetes 301
bougainvillei, Phalacrocorax 32
brachyrhynchos, Corvus 254
Branta canadensis 44
　nigricans 33
　sandvicensis 20, 47
bresilius, Ramphocelus 481
Brotogeris jugularis 258
　versicolorus 257
Bubo bubo 282
bubo, Bubo 282
buccinator, Olor 33
Buteo buteo 77
buteo, Buteo 77
butyracea, Crithagra 447

Cacatua galerita 245
　goffini 249
　leadbeateri 248
　moluccensis 247
　roseicapilla 249
　sulphurea 247
　tenuirostris 250
caerulatus, Garrulax 308
caerulescens, Anser 41
　Estrilda 408, 409
caeruleus, Parus 334
cafer, Pycnonotus 298
Cairina moschata 33, 53
caledonicus, Nycticorax 72
californicus, Lophortyx 115
Callaeidae 340
Callipepla squamata 114
Calocephalon fimbriatum 245
Caloenas nicobarica 237
camelus, Struthio 25
cana, Agapornis 271
canadensis, Branta 44
　Dendragapus 99
canarius, Serinus 441
canicollis, Serinus 443
canicularis, Aratinga 252
cannabina, Acanthis 456
canora, Tiaris 13, 470
canorus, Garrulax 329

cantas, Loxioides 461
capensis, Oena 228
　Ploceus 386
　Zonotrichia 381, 467
capitata, Paroaria 475
carbo, Phalacrocorax 31
　Ramphocelus 481
Cardinalis cardinalis 476
cardinalis, Cardinalis 476
Carduelis carduelis 451
　chloris 447
　psaltria 450
　spinus 448
　tristis 449
carduelis, Carduelis 451
Carpodacus mexicanus 457
　purpureus 381
carunculatus, Creadion 20, 340
castaneothorax, Lonchura
　417, 432
Casuariidae 25
Casuariiformes 25
Casuarius bennetti 25
　casuarius 27
casuarius, Casuarius 27
Cathartes aura 75
Cathartidae 74, 75
Caterus wallichii 20, 166
Centrocercus urophasianus 103
Cereopsis novaehollandiae 40
Cettia diphone 321
Chalcophaps indica 229
chalcoptera, Phaps 230
chalybeata, Vidua 397
Charadriidae 196, 197
Charadriiformes 196
Charadrius melanops 196
Chenonetta jubata 49
cherina, Cisticola 308
chimango, Milvago 80
chinensis, Coturnix 153
　Garrulax 328
　Streptopelia 220
Chloebia gouldiae 424
Chloephaga picta 48
chloris, Carduelis 447
chloropus, Gallinula 191
chrysaetos, Aquila 74
chrysocephalus, Icterus 487
Chrysolophus amherstiae 179
　pictus 11, 178
Ciconiiformes 68
Cinclidae 302
Cinclus cinclus 302
　mexicanus 302
cinclus, Cinclus 302
Circus aeruginosus 77
ciris, Passerina 478
cirlus, Emberiza 465
Cisticola cherina 308
citrinella, Emberiza 463
clappertoni, Francolinus 141
Coccothraustes coccothraustes
　460

coccothraustes, Coccothraustes 460
coelebs, Fringilla 439
Coenocorypha aucklandica 196
colchicus, Phasianus 167
Colinus cristatus 123
    virginianus 18, 120
Collocalia inexpectata 286
Columba livia 208
    oenas 204
    palumbus 211
Columbidae 204, 205
Columbiformes 12, 200
Columbina passerina 228
communis, Sylvia 321
    Turtur 214
concinna, Glossopsitta 244
Copsychus malabaricus 312
    saularis 311
    sechellarum 313
Coraciformes 287
Coracopsis vasa 263
coramandelica, Coturnix 106
coronata, Dendroica 72
    Paroaria 473
Corvidae 346, 347
Corvus albus 355
    brachyrhynchos 354
    frugilegus 352
    macrorhynchus 354
    monedula 349
    moneduloides 352
    splendens 13, 350
Coturnix australis 152
    chinensis 153
    coramandelica 106
    coturnix 149
    novaezelandiae 151
    pectoralis 151
    ypsilophorus 151
coturnix, Coturnix 149
Cracidae 80, 81
Cracticidae 342, 343
cranchii, Pternistes 142
Crax alector 80
    rubra 82
Creadion carunculatus 20, 340
crecca, Anas 33
Crex crex 189
crex, Crex 189
cristata, Gubernatrix 473
cristatellus, Acridotheres 370
cristatus, Colinus 123
    Fuligula 66
    Pavo 181
Crithagra butyracea 447
Crossoptilon mantchuricum 158
crudigularis, Arborophila 155
cucullata, Lonchura 426
cucullata, Ploceus 12, 18, 388
cuneata, Geopelia 226
cupido, Tympanuchus 104
curvirostra, Loxia 458
cyanea, Passerina 477
cyaneovirens, Erythrura 424
Cyanerpes cyaneus 485
cyaneus, Cyanerpes 485
    Malurus 323
cyanocephala, Psittacula 270
    Starnoenas 237
cyanocephalus, Uraeginthus 407
cyanoleuca, Grallina 341
cyanomelana, Muscicapa 324
Cyanoramphus auriceps 278
cygnoides, Anser 33
Cygnus atratus 38
    olor 36
Cyrtonyx monteuzmae 124

Dacelo gigas 287
    novaeguinea 287

dauuricae, Perdix 147
decaocto, Streptopelia 216
Dendragapus canadensis 99
    obscurus 99
Dendrocygna autumnalis 49
    viduata 50
Dendroica coronata 72
    striata 72
Dicruridae 339
Dicrurus macrocercus 339
dimidiatus, Ramphocelus 482
Dinornithiformes 28
diphone, Cettia 321
discors, Anas 57
Diuca diuca 468
diuca, Diuca 468
domesticus, Passer 11, 19, 374
dominicana, Paroaria 474
dominicana, Icterus 493
Drepanididae 461
Dromaiidae 25
Dromaius novaehollandiae 26
Ducula rosacea 204

Eclectus roratus 264
elegans, Eudromia 23
    Platycercus 275
ellioti, Syrmaticus 106
Emberiza cirlus 465
    citrinella 463
    hortulana 464
    schoeniclus 466
Emberizidae 462
Emblema guttata 417
Eos reticulata 242
episcopus, Thraupis 482
Erithacus akahige 309
    komadori 310
    rubecula 308
erkelii, Francolinus 141
erythronotos, Estrilda 413
erythropygius, Sturnus 356
erthyrorhyncha, Urocissa 346
Erythrura cyaneovirens 424
    prasina 422
    psittacea 423
    trichroa 422
Estrilda astrild 12, 410
    caerulescens 408, 409
    erythronotos 413
    melanotis 409
    melpoda 409
    perreini 408
    troglodytes 412
Estrildidae 400
Eudocimus albus 18, 68
    ruber 18, 73
Eudromia elegans 23
Eunetta falcata 33
eupatria, Psittacula 266
Euphonia musica 483
Euplectes afra 394
    albonotatus 396
    orix 394
    progne 396
eximius, Platycercus 276
exustus, Pterocles 203

fabalis, Anser 43
falcata, Eunetta 33
Falco peregrinus 79
    sp. ? 75
Falconidae 75, 79
Falconiformes 74
ferina, Aythya 64
Ficedula narcissina 324
fimbriatum, Calocephalon 245
fischeri, Agapornis 273
flammea, Acanthis 454
flaveola, Sicalis 381, 468
flaveolus, Passer 372
flavirostris, Acanthis 455

flaviventris, Serinus 446
formosa, Amandava 415
Forpus passerinus 256
Foudia madagascariensis 391
    rubra 393
    sechellarum 393
Francolinus adspersus 139
    clappertoni 141
    erkelii 141
    francolinus 135
    icterorhynchus 140
    pintadeanus 136
    pondicerianus 19, 138
francolinus, Francolinus 135
Fringilla coelebs 439
    montifringilla 441
Fringillidae 437
fringilloides, Lonchura 427
frugilegus, Corvus 352
Fulica atra 187
Fuligula cristatus 66
fuligula, Aythya 65
Furnarius leucopsus 381
fuscus, Acridotheres 368

galericulata, Aix 62
galerita, Cacatua 245
Gallicolumba luzonica 235
Galliformes 11, 12, 80
Gallinula chloropus 191
    nesiotis 192
Gallirallus australis 188
gallopavo, Meleagris 183
Gallus gallus 162
    soneratii 166
    varius 165
gallus, Gallus 162
gambelii, Lophortyx 119
gambensis, Plectropterus 39
garrula, Ortalis 84
Garrulax albogularis 326
    caerulatus 308
    canorus 329
    chinensis 328
    leucolophus 326
    monileger 328
    pectoralis 327
    sannio 330
Geopelia cuneata 226
    humeralis 226
    striata 223
    tranquila 224
Geotrygon montana 234
gigas, Dacelo 287
gilvus, Mimus 304
ginginianus, Acridotheres 369
Glossopsitta concinna 244
goffini, Cacatua 249
gouldiae, Chloebia 424
Gracula religiosa 371
gracea, Alectoris 126
Grallina cyanoleuca 341
Grallinidae 341, 342
granatina, Uraeginthus 407
griseogularis, Ammoperdix 125
Gruidae 187, 195
Gruiformes 187
Grus rubicundus 195
Gubernatrix cristtata 473
gularis, Paroaria 475
guttata, Emblema 417
    Hylocichla 314
    Poephila 419
Gygis alba 78
Gymnorhina tibicen 343
Gypaetus barbatus 74

habroptilus, Strigops 238
haematodus, Trichoglossus 242
haematonotus, Psephotus 277
Haliaeetus albicilla 76
    leucocephalus 74

heyi, Ammoperdix 125
himalayensis, Tetraogallus 126
Hirundinidae 296
Hirundo nigrans 296
hispaniolensis, Passer 382
histrionica, Phaps 204
hollandicus, Nymphicus 250
hortulana, Emberiza 464
humeralis, Geopelia 226
Hylocichla guttata 314
hypoxanthus, Ploceus 390
Hypsipetes borbonicus 301

iagoensis, Passer 383
ibis, Ardeola 11, 68
Icteridae 485, 486
icterocephalus, Agelaius 488
icterorhynchus, Francolinus 140
Icterus chrysocephalus 487
    dominicanus 493
    icterus 487
    pectoralis 487
icterus, Icterus 487
ignita, Lophura 162
iliacus, Turdus 317, 319
impejanus, Lophophorus 157
inca, Scardafella 227
indica, Chalcophaps 229
inexpectata, Collocalia 286

jamaicensis, Leptotila 234
    Oxyura 66
japonicus, Zosterops 336
javanicus, Turdus 318
jocosus, Pycnonotus 296
jubata, Chenonetta 49
jugularis, Brotogeris 258

komadori, Erithacus 310
krameri, Psittacula 266
kuhlii, Vini 243

Lagnosticta senegala 404
Lagopus lagopus 96
    mutus 98
    scoticus 96
lagopus, Lagopus 96
Laridae 196, 198
Larus novaehollandiae 198
    occidentalis 200
lateralis, Zosterops 335
lathami, Alectura 86
leadbeateri, Cacatua 248
leclancheri, Passerina 478
Leiothrix lutea 331
Leipoa ocellata 85
Leistes militaris 489
Leptolia jamaicensis 234
    verreauxi 233
leucocephalus, Haliaeetus 74
leucogastra, Lonchura 430
leucogastroides, Lonchura 430
leucolophus, Garrulax 326
leucomelana, Lophura 160
leucophrys, Rhipidura 325
Leucopsar rothschildi 356
leucopus, Furnarius 381
leucopygius, Serinus 444
Leucosarcia melanoleuca 236
leucoscepus, Pternistes 143
leucotis, Pyrrhula 254
lilianae, Agapornis 275
livia, Columba 208
Lonchura castaneothorax 417, 432
    cucullata 426
    fringilloides 427
    leucogastra 430
    leucogastroides 430
    malabarica 425
    malacca 430

punctulata 17, 428
striata 432
longipes, Xenicus 291
Lophophorus impejanus 157
Lophortyx californicus 115
gambelii 119
lophotes, Ocyphaps 231
Lophura ignita 162
leucomelana 160
nycthemera 11, 158
swinhoei 20, 161
Loxia pytyopsittacus 458
curvirostra 458
Loxigilla noctis 472
portoricensis 472
Loxioides cantans 461
loyca, Sturnella 490
lucionensis, Tanygnathus 265
lugubris, Quiscalus 491
Lullala arborea 292
Luscinia megarhynchos 310
lutea, Leiothrix 331
luteola, Sicalis 469
luzonica, Gallicolumba 235

macao, Ara 251
macrocercus, Dicrurus 339
macrorhynchos, Corvus 354
macroura, Vidua 399
Zenaida 212
madagascariensis, Foudia 391
Margaroperdix 148
major, Parus 332
Tinamus 21
malabarica, Lonchura 425
malabaricus, Copsychus 312
malacca, Lonchura 430
Maluridae, 306, 307, 323
Malurus cyaneus 323
Manorina melanocephala 338
melanophrys 338
manthuricum Crossoptilon 158
Margaroperdix
madagascariensis 148
megalorynchos Tanygnathus
265
Megapodiidae 85
megarhynchos, Luscinia 310
melanocephala, Manorina 338
melanocephalus, Alectoris 134
Ploceus 389
Melanocorypha mongolica 292
melanoleuca, Leucosarcia 236
melanophrys, Manorina 338
melanops, Charadrius 196
melanoptera, Strepera 344
melanotis, Estrilda 409
melba, Pytilia 403
Meleagrididae 183
Meleagris gallopavo 183
melagris, Numida 87
Meliphagidae 338
melleri, Anas 57
Melopsittacus undulatus 278
melpoda, Estrilda 409
Menura novaehollandiae 290
Menuridae 290
merula, Turdus 315
mexicana, Siala 313
mexicanus, Carpodacus 457
Cinclus 302
meyeri, Poicephalus 263
migratorius, Turdus 319
miles, Vanellus 196
militaris, Leistes 489
Pezites 490
Milvago chimango 80
Mimidae 303
Mimocichla plumbea 320
Mimus gilvus 304
polyglottos 303
modesta, Aidemosyne 425

modularis, Prunella 305
Molothrus bonariensis 492
moluccensis, Cacatua 247
monachus, Myiopsitta 254
monedula, Corvus 349
moneduloides, Corvus 352
mongolica, Melanocorypha 292
monileger, Garrulax 328
montana, Geotrygon 234
montanus, Passer 383
montezumae, Crytonyx 124
montifringilla, Fringilla 441
moschata, Cairina 33, 53
mozambicus, Serinus 19, 443,
445
Muscicapa cyanomelana 324
Muscicapidae 306, 307, 324
musica, Euphonia 483
musicus, Turdus 317
mutus, Lagopus 98
Myiopsitta monachus 254

Nandayus nenday 253
narcissina, Ficedula 324
natalis, Zosterops 337
Nectariniidae 335
neglecta, Sturnella 490
nenday, Nandayus 253
Neochmia ruficauda 418
nesiotis, Gallinula 192
Netta rufina 33
nicobarica, Caloenas 237
nigrans, Hirundo 296
nigricans, Branta 33
nigricollis, Sturnus 363
Turnix 194
nigrocincta, Tangara 484
Ninox novaehollandiae 283
noctis, Loxigilla 472
noctua, Athene 284
Northoprocta perdicaria 22
novaeguinea, Dacelo 287
novaehollandiae, Ardea 68
Cereopsis 40
Dromaius 26
Larus 198
Menura 290
Recurvirostra 196
Tyto 282
novaeseelandiae, Ninox 283
novaezelandiae, Coturnix 151
Numida meleagris 87
Numididae 87
nycthemera, Lophura 11, 158
Nycticorax caledonicus 72
nycticorax 72
nycticorax, Nycticorax 72
Nymphicus hollandicus 250

obscura, Anas 33
obscurus, Dendragapus 99
ocellata, Agriocharis 182
Leipoa 85
occidentalis, Larus 200
Pelecanus 30
ochrocephala, Amazona 261
Ocyphaps lophotes 231
Oena capensis 228
oenas, Columba 204
olivacea, Piranga 480
Tiaris 13, 471
Olor buccinator 33
olor, Cygnus 36
Oreortyx pictus 113
orientalis, Pterocles 202
Streptopelia 214
orix, Euplectes 394
Oratlis garrula 84
ruficauda 84
vetula 83
oryzivora, Padda 433
Otus sp. 281

oweni, Apteryx 29
Oxyura jamaicensis 66

pacificus, Puffinus 368
Padda oryzivora 433
pallidicinctus, Tympanuchus
105
palmeri, Porzanula 190
palumbus, Columba 211
Paradisaea apoda 345
paradisae, Vidua 398
Paradisaeidae 345
paradoxus, Syrrhaptes 201
Paridae 332
Paroaria capitata 475
coronata 473
dominicana 474
gularis 475
Parus caeruleus 334
major 332
varius 333
Passer domesticus 11, 19, 374
flaveolus 372
hispaniolensis 382
iagoensis 383
montanus 383
Passeridae 372, 373
Passeriformes 289
passerina, Columbina 228
Passerinae 372
Passerina ciris 478
cyanea 477
leclancheri 478
passerinus, Forpus 256
patagonica, Aptenodytes 30
Pauxi 80
Pavo cristatus 181
pectoralis, Coturnix 151
Garrulax 327
Icterus 487
Pedioecetes phasianellus 103
Pelicanidae 30
Pelicaniformes 30
Pelecanus occidentalis 30
Penelope purpurascens 82
penelope, Anas 59
pennata, Pterocnemia 24
perdicaria, Northoprocta 22
Perdicula argoondah 154
asiatica 154
Perdix barbata 147
dauuricae 147
perdix 144, 148
perdix, Perdix 144, 148
peregrinus, Falco 79
perreini, Estrilda 408
personata, Agapornis 274
pertinax, Aratinga 252
peruviana, Vini 78, 244
Petrochelidon albifrons 381
pyrrhonota 381
Petroica traversi 308
Petronia petronia 383
petronia, Petronia 383
Petrophassa plumifera 232
smithii 232
Pezites militaris 490
Phalacrocoracidae 30, 31
Phalacrocorax bougainvillei 32
carbo 31
Phaps chalcoptera 230
histrionica 204
phasianellus, Pedioecetes 103
Phasianidae 106, 183
Phasianus colchicus 167
philippensis, Rallus 187
philippinus, Ploceus 390
philomelos, Turdus 318
Phoenicopteridae 67
Phoenicopteriformes 67
Phoenicopterus ruber 67
Pica pica 348

pica, Pica 348
picta, Chloephaga 48
picturata, Streptopelia 215
pictus, Chrysolophus 11, 178
Oreortyx 113
pintadeanus, Francolinus 136
Pipile 80
Pipile pipile 80
pipile, Pipile 80
Piranga olivacea 480
rubra 479
Pitangus sulphuratus 289
Platalea regia 68
Platycercus adscitus 277
elegans 275
eximius 276
platyrhynchos, Anas 18, 54
Plectropterus gambensis 39
Ploceidae 372, 386, 387
Ploceus capensis 386
cucullatus 12, 18, 388
hypoxanthus 390
melanocephalus 389
philippinus 390
velatus 386
plumbea, Mimocichla 320
plumifera, Petrophassa 232
Pluvialis apricaria 198
squatarola 197
Poephila acuticauda 421
bichenovii 420
guttata 419
Poicephalus meyeri 263
poliocephalus, Turdus 317
polyglottos, Mimus 303
pondicerianus, Francolinus 19,
138
Porphyrio madagascariensis
193
porphyrio 192
porphyrio, Porphyrio 192
portoricensis, Loxigilla 472
Porzanula palmeri 190
prasina, Erythrura 422
progne, Euplectes 396
Prosopeia tabuensis 271
Prunella modularis 305
Prunellidae 305
psaltria, Carduelis 450
Psephotus haematonotus 277
psittacea, Erythrura 423
Psittacidae 238
Psittaciformes 12, 238
Psittacula alexandri 269
cyanocephala 270
eupatria 266
krameri 266
Pternistes afer 142
cranchii 142
leucoscepus 143
Pterocles alchata 201
bicinctus 200
exustus 202
orientalis 202
Pteroclididae 200
Pterocnemia pennata 24
Ptilonopus purpuratus 78
Puffinus pacificus 368
punctulata, Lonchura 17, 428
purpurascens, Penelope 82
purpuratus, Ptilinopus 78
purpureus, Carpodacus 381
Pycnonotidae 296
Pycnonotus aurigaster 300
cafer 299
jocosus 296
pyrrhonota, Petrochelidon 381
Pyrrhula pyrrhula 459
pyrrhula, Pyrrhula 459
Pyrrhura leucotis 254
Ptyilia melba 403
pytyopsittacus, Loxia 458